WHERE *to* SKI AND *Snowboard* 2012

Published in Great Britain by
NortonWood Publishing
The Oaks, Bath Road
Norton St Philip
Bath BA2 7LW
United Kingdom

tel 0844 9911 123
email w16@wtss.co.uk

Editors Chris Gill and Dave Watts
Assistant editors Mandy Crook,
Wendy-Jane King, Chris Allan,
Sheila Reid, Rebecca Miles
Contributors Minty Clinch,
Alan Coulson, Nicky Holford,
James Hooke, Eric Jackson,
Tim Perry, Ian Porter, Adam Ruck,
Helena Wiesner, Fraser Wilkin

Advertising manager
Dave Ashmore

Design by Val Fox
Production by Guide Editors
Contents photos generally
by Snowpix.com / Chris Gill
Production manager
Sarah Carreck
Ad production manager
Ian Stratford
Proofreader Lynda Watson
Printed and bound in Italy
by Lego SpA

10 9 8 7 6 5 4 3 2 1

ISBN-13: 978–0–9558663–3–3

A CIP catalogue entry for this book
is available from the British Library.

Book trade sales are handled by
Portfolio Books Ltd
2nd Floor, Westminster House
Kew Road
Richmond
TW9 2ND

tel 020 8334 1730
fax 020 8334 1609

email sales@portfoliobooks.com

**Individual copies of the book can be
bought (for delivery anywhere in the
world) at a discount price by going to
our website – www.wtss.co.uk**

WHERE *to* SKI
AND *Snowboard* 2012

The Definitive Guide
to the 1,000 Best Winter Sports Resorts in the World

Edited by
Chris Gill
and
Dave Watts

NortonWood

Contents 1

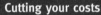

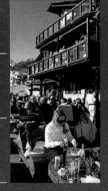

That's the start of it – turn the page for the heart of it ...

CRYSTAL

Great Value No Fuss

SKI Plus Packages

   +

Flights   Transfers   Accommodation   Ski/board hire or carriage   Lift pass

7 nights from £395

Val d'Isère - Kitzbühel - Val Thorens - Arinsal - La Thuile
Les Deux Alpes - Les Arcs - Söll - Cervinia - Avoriaz - Sauze d'Oulx
La Plagne - Kaprun - Soldeu and many more

crystalski.co.uk/wtss
020 8241 5080

Price includes web discount - based on 4 people sharing a bed & breakfast apartment in Poblado Apts, Arinsal, Andorra. Dep. 25 March 2012 for 7nts from London Gatwick. Price subject to availability and change. Under occupancy, room and regional flight supplements may apply. Boots not included. If ski hire is required, bronze skis will be supplied.

Contents 2

Resort chapters

9

About this book

It's simply the best

Dave Watts

Chris Gill

Where to Ski and Snowboard – Britain's only established annual guidebook to ski resorts worldwide – is the very best guide you can buy. Here's why:

- With every new edition we introduce **improvements and innovations**. This year, we've invested a lot of time in extending our Resort Price Index survey, introduced two years back, to cover lift passes, lessons and ski hire, as well as restaurant prices. And we've improved our presentation of smaller resorts that don't get a chapter to themselves – check out the Sella Ronda chapter in Italy, for example.

- By making the most of technology we are able to publish at the right time while going to press very late by conventional book publishing standards – so we can include the late-breaking news that makes the book **up to date for the season ahead**. The earliest editions of this book went to press in June; this year, it's 1 August, only about five weeks ahead of publication day.

- We work hard to make our information **reader-friendly**, with clearly structured text, comparative ratings and no-nonsense verdicts for the main aspects of each resort.

- We don't hesitate to express **critical views**. We learned our craft at Consumers' Association, where Chris became editor of *Holiday Which?* magazine and Dave became editor of *Which?* itself – so a consumerist attitude comes naturally to us.

- Our resort chapters give an **unrivalled level of detail** – including scale plans of each major resort, so that you get a clear idea of size – and all the facts you need.

- The book benefits enormously from the **hundreds of reports** that readers send in on the resorts they visit. Every year, the 100 best reports are rewarded by a free copy of the book. Read page 12 for more about this.

- We use **colour printing** fully – we include not only piste maps for every major resort but also scores of photographs, carefully chosen so that you can see for yourself what the resorts are like.

Our ability to keep on investing in *Where to Ski and Snowboard* is largely due to the support of our advertisers – many of whom have been with us since the first edition in 1994. We are grateful for that support, and hope readers will in turn support our advertisers. It also helps if you tell them that you saw their ads in these pages: we know advertising in the book works, but advertisers can't be reminded too often.

We are absolutely committed to helping you, our readers, to make an informed choice; and we're confident that you'll find this edition the best yet. Enjoy your skiing and riding this season.

Chris Gill and Dave Watts
Norton St Philip, 1 August 2011

Win a free week with Pierre & Vacances

There are too many resorts for us to visit them all every year, and too many hotels, bars and mountain restaurants for us to visit them all. So we are always keen to encourage readers to send in reports on their holiday experiences. Every year, we give 100 copies of the next edition to the writers of the best reports. But now there's an extra incentive: all book winners will automatically be entered for a draw to win a week in a Pierre & Vacances apartment.

The winner will get a week in a studio or one-bedroom apartment in a Pierre & Vacances-owned residence in Avoriaz, in the famously extensive Franco-Swiss Portes du Soleil area. With the exception of the French school holidays, you'll be able to choose your preferred dates (subject to availability). You must confirm your choice of date at least one month before travel.

Your resort reports must be based on resort visits made during the 2011/12 season, and must be received by the end of April 2012. We much prefer to receive reports in digital form. Ideally, we'd like you to use our online form at www.wheretoski.co.uk/resortreport. If you prefer, you can send an email to reports@wtss.co.uk – but please check www.wtss.co.uk first for advice on the kind of information we particularly want, and how it should be structured. And it's vital that you give us the date of your trip, so that we can interpret your report sensibly – plus your postal address (to send your book to if you win).

Or win a free week with Lagrange

A surprising number of ski resort tourist offices are incapable of providing photos of their resort that meet our needs – that is, visually strong images showing interesting aspects of the resort that are also sharp and properly exposed. Which is why, every year, we now use a dozen or more shots provided by readers. We've given modest prizes in the past for the best shots, but a year or two back Lagrange Holidays kindly agreed to up the ante by offering a splendid prize.

There's no luck involved here. The prize will go to whoever submits the pics that best meet our editorial needs, as decided by the editors. The pics must be taken during the 2011/12 season, and sent in by the end of April 2012. As last year, we'll be setting up a special website for the purpose, reachable via our main site at www.wtss.co.uk.

The winner will get a week in an apartment in a Lagrange residence. The details of the range of options will be made clear on our website. With the exception of Christmas/New Year and the period around February half term, you'll be able to choose your preferred dates (subject to availability).

The editorial

The editors have their say

HOW WAS IT FOR YOU?

Last season was certainly a strange one. We were probably lucky, but we enjoyed excellent piste skiing throughout January, February and March in various parts of the Alps, and even some worthwhile off-piste here and there. No, we never needed goggles. Yes, we did ski on quite a bit of artificial snow (including the bit at Mayrhofen shown below). But we hit stones on a piste only a couple of times, in the French Alps in late March. Other people weren't so lucky, and our snow statistics meister Fraser Wilkin has the figures:

The northern Alps endured one of its least snowy winters on record: 2.3m of snowfall in Val d'Isère and 3.4m in Lech is less than half of what they get in an average winter. But this doesn't quite tell the whole story. Most of this snow fell early in the season (when it was also cold) and, at altitude at least, the base was laid for a reasonable season. Things weren't so good lower down, especially in the north-western Alps, where the likes of Morzine and Villars never really got off the ground. Eventually, a brutal spring thaw put paid to any hopes of a late flourish.

Seriously impressive snowmaking was in evidence all along the Zillertal in March, including here at the Ahorn cable car at Mayrhofen ↓

The southern Alps fared better, with 3.8m for Arabba in the Dolomites, 5m for Courmayeur (mid-station) – close to average – and a way-above-average 6m for Isola 2000. Snowiest of all, though, was little-known Limone-Piemonte, south of Turin and close to the Mediterranean, with an impressive 9.7m. Meanwhile, North American resorts had the best overall winter for 36 years. Both Breckenridge in Colorado (13.2m) and Snowbird in Utah (19.8m) broke their all-time records; but this year's top spot belongs to Kirkwood in California with a massive 20.4m.

THE RAIN IN FLAINE FALLS MAINLY ...

While we had Fraser's attention, we put to him an interesting question posed by reader John Rockliff when he reported on his January holiday in Les Carroz, in Flaine's Grand Massif region: 'When we were in Les Carroz it poured with rain up to a point above 2000m. In January 2008 we got exactly the same thing in Châtel, not far away. Have we just been unlucky? Or is rain more likely in this part of the Alps?'

The short answer, John, seems to be: Yes, but also Yes. You could, of course, have visited those resorts without hitting rain, but it seems rain is more likely in these places than in some other regions (and we've had rain in both resorts too). Fraser explains:

Altitude, of course, affects the likelihood of rain, but geographical location is also key. Rain at altitude in winter is almost always associated with warm fronts – advancing boundaries between a warm air mass and a cold air mass. These generally arrive from the west and mostly affect the northern Alps – so the north-western Alps are most at risk. Here, rain has been known to reach 2700m, even in midwinter. If you encounter rain in Morzine, your instructor will pop into a phone box and come out wearing a cape, so that his suit doesn't get soggy. That tells you something about the incidence of rain.

This risk of rain quickly drops as you move south and east. As you go south, you get fewer warm fronts. As you go east, the effect of the fronts is reduced. In the heart of the Alps, in valleys sheltered from the westerly winds, cold air gets trapped in, while advancing warmer air rides over the top. You can get rain over 2000m in Chamonix on one side of Mont Blanc while it is snowing at 1200m in Courmayeur on the other side. If you really want to minimise the risk of rain, pick a high resort deep within the Alps: best of all would be St Moritz, where midwinter rain is virtually unheard of. It has to be said, though, that low-risk-of-rain resorts are also not the snowiest of resorts. The famously snowy resorts of north-west Austria, in the Bregenzerwald and Arlberg regions, can have a rain problem. [I've skied in pouring rain in Lech in midwinter, adds editor Gill.] Further south, as in the French Alps, the risk diminishes.

THE RUSSIANS ARE … WAITING TO WELCOME YOU

If you've been unimpressed by the Russian invasion of some Alpine resorts, here's your chance to get your own back. Crystal is the first operator to add the 2014 Olympics resort of Sochi to its programme. (It is exclusive to Crystal, they say.)

Actually, of course, Sochi (like Albertville) isn't where the events will be happening, and isn't where Crystal will be taking you. There are three resorts. Crystal has a swanky hotel at Gasprom, which sounds rather like going to a resort near Albertville called Electricité de France, and a more modest place at the larger resort of Rosa Khutor, 1km away. The steeper resort of Mountain Carousel is an unspecified distance away and reached by taxis at an unspecified cost. Pistes 'planned' for 2011/12 total 100km across the three hills. 'Huge snowfalls' can be expected. You fly with Turkish Airlines via Istanbul, and the transfer time is only an hour. Prices for eight nights half board (yes, eight) start at £1350.

AT YOUR SERVICE

We were struck this year by one of the paradoxes of Austrian mountain restaurants – that a great many of them do table-service, but most serve you at shared tables and don't take reservations. Obviously those two things more or less go hand in hand, reservations at shared tables being somewhat difficult to administer. But we're not at all keen on parading up and down the terrace looking for signs of imminent departure, so that you can then hang around a likely-looking table for a further five minutes waiting to seat your group. It's only a small step up from self-service – which unaccountably is viewed as acceptable in the world of skiing. People who would not dream of eating in self-service restaurants in Majorca have somehow been persuaded that it is appropriate on the slopes of Les Menuires. We don't get it.

FILLING THOSE ROOMS

Alpine hoteliers are a bit inclined to think that all they have to do is upgrade their spa every decade, and the world will beat a path to their door. We remember driving into Grindelwald in January some years back and walking into hotels with empty car parks and empty dining rooms, asking for their best offer. We were met by blank stares, and a finger pointing at the rack rates. So it's good to see a bit of real enterprise at work.

"Applying lessons learned from other glide sports, the BBR is a completely new ski concept in terms of shape, feel, and versatility. It is simply more fun in more conditions."
- Bertrand Krafft (aka BBR)
  Salomon alpine ski developer and Shaper of the BBR

THE FU

SEE WHAT
SHAPE IS A

SALOMON

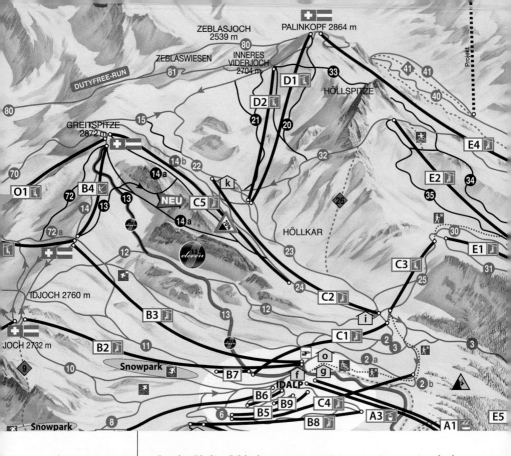

↑ Masterly numbering of runs in Ischgl: note the two instances of run 13 (going to quite different points) and of run 14a; having runs called 14 and 14b in addition to the two versions of 14a isn't brilliant, either

Reader Philip Gibb drew our attention to an impressive deal being offered by a hotel in Mayrhofen, in Austria's Zillertal. Well, actually, it's a hotel near Mayrhofen rather than in it, which is why the hotelier has hit on the cute idea of throwing in with the room not just free toiletries, but … a free car. You get the car at Munich airport (well, near Munich airport) and it costs you 20 euros cleaning charge plus the Austrian motorway vignette, which for a week is another 4.50 euros. 'A great deal,' says Philip. Indeed! See www. gutshof.cc/page/gutshof-car. Reader Brian Gee drew our attention to another Austrian hotel (the Edelweiss in Kitzbühel) that 'supplies bags for you to take food from the breakfast table for lunch' – a far cry from the stern notices we've seen elsewhere.

GIVE BEGINNERS A BREAK

We are very conscious of the fact that we have to look after the beginners among our readers, or the beginners being taken to the mountains by our readers. It's very easy to focus on the stuff that matters to us, and neglect the stuff that matters to them. But we do try. One thing we've tried to do more thoroughly, over recent editions, is nail down what beginners have to spend on lifts. This varies hugely, and can have a serious impact on holiday costs.

The basic divide is between resorts that have nursery slopes at village level and those that don't. Many upmarket French resorts, ironically, have very good free lifts which may be all a slow learner needs for several days; often, there is then a limited pass that will get you skiing longer runs and building confidence without paying for a full pass. Contrast this with places like Ischgl and Soldeu, with no nursery slopes at village level, which expect beginners to fork out close on £200 for a six-day pass – £30 a day, say – regardless of the fact that many of them are going to spend the entire week on a handful of short lifts.

We think resorts like these should have free beginner lifts at mid-mountain and should swallow the cost of the cable car and gondola rides up to those lifts.

AND NOW WE HAVE NAMING OF PISTES
We seem to be talking a lot about Austria this year, but since it is poised to regain top slot on the British market perhaps we can be permitted. We did visit quite a few other Alpine countries last season, honest.

We talked in last year's Editorial about the confusion in Schladming, where two pistes had the same number. We've become more aware of this problem this year; and it seems to be very common in Austria. We came upon examples last season in Lech and in Ischgl. You can see the Ischgl problem illustrated on the left – insane duplication of the same run number on different runs. What *are* they thinking of? Our instructor-guide in Ischgl agreed when we expressed astonishment at the confusion, and said he couldn't understand what the lift company was doing, either. Apart from anything else, he pointed out, when reporting an accident, it makes it practically impossible to pin down the location. We've never encountered this problem outside Austria.

The editorial

17

Interactive resort shortlist builder at **www.wtss.co.uk**

Berner Oberland ✚

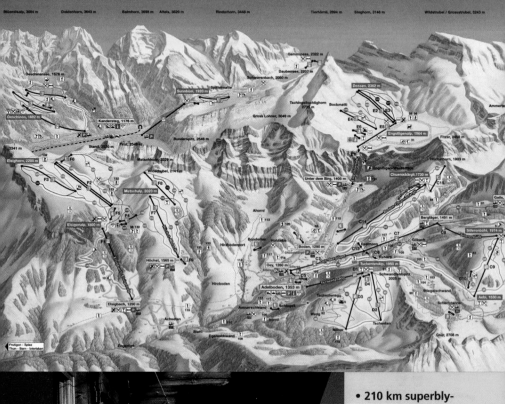

- **210 km superbly-prepared pistes**
- **72 lift facilities**
- **47 ski huts / bars**
- **AUDI FIS Ski World Cup 07. / 08. 01. 2012**
- **Family-friendly**
- **Snow secure from December to April**

Further Information:
Adelboden Tourismus
Dorfstrasse 23
CH-3715 Adelboden
Switzerland

Adelboden
Frutigen

DON'T SKIP THE COUNTRY INTROS

One of the things we invite readers to tell us, when reporting on their holidays, is this: What surprised you about the resort you visited? We got a striking answer this year from someone who has been sending in reports since he bought our first edition in 1994. After toying with Italy, Sweden and Colorado, Andrew Lawson discovered Austria: reports followed on Söll, Zell, Mayrhofen, Königsleiten, Kaltenbach, Gerlos, Bad Gastein, Sölden, Niederau, Kitzbühel, Ellmau. Then, this year, he went to France, to Les Deux-Alpes. Big mistake, it turns out.

Andrew's reply to our question was: 'I was surprised at the lack of après-ski. I've mainly holidayed in Austria and you come to expect pumping music from various bars; here, the only venue with any music was La Pano at the top of the Jandri Express – and the music was hard-core rave, not as enjoyable as cheesy Austria-pop, and it only happened for an hour between 3pm and 4pm. I found that most bizarre.' Quite. The lesson here is: if you are about to try a resort in a different country, read our country introductions and note the differences (it's all explained there).

NEW LIFT, NEW TERRAIN

For next season, Val Thorens is installing its fifth twin-cable jumbo gondola. That in itself is fairly amazing, but what's striking about this particular lift is that it is not replacing an old one; it is opening up a virgin mountainside – actually, two virgin mountainsides, since we understand it will access off-piste beyond the ridge it reaches, as well as pistes beneath the lift. This is quite unusual, these days, and merits a small cheer.

PAT ON THE BACK FOR VAL D'ISÈRE

Reader Tim Perry said of Val d'Isère this year: 'On the very few occasions where there was a queue starting to form, the lift operators ensured lifts were filled efficiently to help clear the queue.' This sort of thing is routinely done in North America but all too rarely in Europe; in recent seasons, we've spotted it in no more than a handful of places. Reader Rachel Williams also said this year: 'I was always impressed by the lift attendants, who were generally very pleasant and courteous, particularly when it came to children – the man who put my five-year-old safely on to the chair to get back down to the village was lovely.' So, to Val's lifties and its training programme: well done, and keep it up.

BLACK MARK FOR BRECKENRIDGE

We've always liked the system used by some US resorts of classifying their steeper intermediate runs as double blue or blue-black. So we were dismayed to find in Breckenridge last season that they had scrapped their blue-black classification and made all those runs blacks. These runs are always groomed, and are great fast cruises. Giving them black status will put off some intermediates who would love them. And those intermediates who try them and like them may believe that other blacks will be similar and get a nasty shock when they find themselves on gnarly, ungroomed slopes. On the other hand, Breck and sister resorts Vail, Beaver Creek and Keystone introduced a good concept – 'Lunch for Less' – where $9.99 (plus tax) buys you something like soup, a sandwich and a soft drink at various mountain restaurants.

PISTE CROWDS AND COLLISIONS

We continue to get reports of overcrowded pistes and reckless skiers causing collisions. This year they came from Sauze d'Oulx, Morzine, Montgenèvre, Hochkönig and many other resorts.

Typical is Dr Garvey who wrote of his stay in Montgenèvre: 'The biggest concerns were the bottom parts of the two home runs on opposite sides of the village – which get busy and carry all sorts of skiers from beginners to expert – and those who go fast and are out of control. We saw several injuries during the week and three people in our hotel were hit. Several of the "accidents" were the result of now-too-common hit-and-run collisions.' Clearly resorts have to do something about this state of affairs – we said last year that we'd come to the view it was time for the introduction of piste police on the mountain to slow down fast and out of control skiers. And a repeat visit to the US last season where piste police are the norm has reinforced our view.

Another reporter, Paul Carter, asks whether resorts know how many people are skiing on any one day. Most resorts now have hi-tech hands-free passes, and many can track skiers around the mountain, knowing which lifts they use, so they must know. But we are aware of only two that claim to limit the number of people on the mountain and stop selling day passes when that number is reached – Lech-Zürs in Austria and Deer Valley in Utah.

INVALUABLE PRICE REPORTING

A key part of our Resort Price Index (see page 29) is the cost of restaurant food and drink. We could not do this without your help and are very grateful to everyone who sent in prices. Altogether we received over 2,000 prices to analyse. Typically, readers send in maybe a dozen prices covering perhaps two restaurants. Some filed just a single price; it all helps. But some filed hundreds. Please keep them coming next season, so we can keep our information up to date and as useful as possible. Go to our website and you'll find information on what we need, and a link to an online system for filing prices.

REPORTS AND PHOTOS MEAN ... PRIZES!

Every year, 100 readers win a free copy of the new edition as a small token of our appreciation of their efforts in sending in really useful, detailed resort reports – a key part of our annual updating process. This year, for the first time, the 100 winners of those books have also gained entry to a prize draw for a week's holiday in a Pierre & Vacances Premium apartment in the French Alps. And the winner of the prize is ... Mr DD Mackenzie.

For the second year, we also have a prize for the best resort photo sent in by a reader for use in the book – in this case, a week in a Lagrange residence. Twelve readers' pics made it into this edition – you'll find their names in the relevant photo credits. And the editors have arrived at the view that the best one is Dee Chilton's shot of the Laguzuoi cable-car and Dolomite landscape in the Cortina chapter – page 418.

Congratulations to both our winners. We'll be repeating these prize competitions next season, so keep the reports and the photos coming in. There's more information about next season's competitions on page 12.

The editorial

Interactive resort shortlist builder at **www.wtss.co.uk**

What's new?

In this chapter we summarise major developments in ski resorts last season and those planned for 2011/12. Most major resort chapters have a 'News' panel near the start; you'll find many more news items in those panels. To keep up to date with resort developments and regular news items, go to our website at www.wtss.co.uk and sign up for our email newsletters.

ANDORRA

GRANDVALIRA OPENS NEW AREA, WITH BIG NEW TERRAIN PARK

A newly developed area – Sunset Park Peretol – has opened between Grau Roig and Soldeu, with a terrain park and beginner slopes served by draglifts.

AUSTRIA

ANOTHER GONDOLA FOR HINTERTUX

For 2011/12 a 10-person gondola is due to replace the double chair from Tuxer Fernerhaus on the glacier.

HOCHKÖNIG UNITED, DIENTEN T-BAR DITCHED FOR SIX-PACK

For 2011/12, in Dienten, a six-pack is due to replace a long T-bar from the valley towards Wastlhöhe, with a new ski route from there to Hochkönigalm. Last season, a gondola from Aberg to Gabühel (above Hinterthal) completed the links from Maria Alm to Mühlbach. And a six-pack replaced the old chair and drag up to Gabühel from Hinterthal.

SIX-PACKS GALORE FOR ISCHGL, GONDOLA UPGRADE PLANNED

For 2011/12 a six-pack is due to replace the Sonnenlift T-bar, on the nursery slopes at Idalp. Work will start in 2011 on a new Pardatschgrat gondola for 2012/13. Last season, a six-pack was built from the Höllenkar valley to Greitspitz, serving its northern slopes. On the Swiss side, a six-pack replaced the Mullerbahn quad from Alp Trida to Alp Bella.

KITZBÜHEL-KIRCHBERG: NEW LIFTS SPEED UP ACCESS

A 10-seat gondola and an eight-seat chair above it have replaced the slow Maierl chairs out of Kirchberg towards Ehrenbachhöhe.

LECH-ZÜRS PLANS HYBRID LIFT

For 2011/12 a chondola (fast hybrid lift of chairs and gondola cabins) will replace the Weibermahd quad above Oberlech.

SIX-PACK FOR MAYRHOFEN / ZILLER VALLEY

A six-pack is due to replace the Katzenmoos double chair on Penken, above Finkenberg, for 2011/12. Last season, a hybrid gondola/chair lift replaced the triple chair just above the Penken gondola. And three eight-seat gondolas opened in the Ziller valley.

SAALBACH-HINTERGLEMM TACKLES WEAKEST LINK

Access to the Hinterglemm slopes from Saalbach will be improved by an eight-seat gondola towards Bernkogel, replacing a famously slow and unreliable chairlift. The drags above are not being replaced until 2012, but there will be a new six-pack going on to Reiterkogel for the coming season. Last season, an eight-seat gondola replaced the T-bar serving the terrain park.

Schladming peaks better connected, more terrain
A covered eight-pack with heated seats has replaced the two top draglifts from Hauser Kaibling to Planai. The Reiteralm area was extended into the Preunegg valley, with an eight-seat gondola and 2km-long red run.

Super-modern gondolas open in Sölden
Two new state-of-the-art gondolas, an eight-seater and a 24-person one above it, have replaced the bottom-to-top gondola on Gaislachkogl.

Stay at St Anton's new Mooserwirt
For 2011/12 the Mooser hotel, adjoining the legendary Mooserwirt bar, is due to open in December 2011, with luxury rooms and 10 suites, spa, pool and restaurant.

Smooth dining for the Stubai valley
At the glacier, the Eisgrat restaurant complex was rebuilt, including a smooth table-service section.

Vorarlberg – Bregenzerwald slopes extended
At Damüls a six-pack was installed, serving 4km or so of new slopes.

Vorarlberg – Montafon: going for gondolas, two of them
For 2011/12 a new gondola is planned from St Gallenkirch to the Hochjoch ski area, effectively linking the Hochjoch and Nova ski areas. Another new gondola is planned above it to the ski area high-point (replacing an old double chair). New slopes are due. Last season, Gargellen gained a six-pack and a new beginner draglift.

FRANCE

One lift replacing two in Arcs 1600
For 2011/12 a six-pack is to replace the slow Mont Blanc chair from Arc 1600 and a drag lift above, up to Les Deux Têtes. Last season, a fixed-grip quad opened at the southern end of Plan-Peisey to improve access to the main lifts. And the terrain park has a new lift.

Avoriaz to open smart new apartments
New 5-star luxury Pierre & Vacances apartments (L'Amara – with spa, pool, saunas etc) are due to open near the top of the resort. An ice rink is planned for the centre.

New hut for Chamonix?
For 2011/12 a new mountain restaurant is planned in the Balme area, above the Charamillon mid-station.

Châtel to upgrade Avoriaz link – at last!
For 2011/12 a fast six-pack is due to replace the Rochassons double from Plaine Dranse to the link with Avoriaz.

Courchevel's original fast quad to be upgraded
A six-pack is due to replace the Plantrey fast quad at Courchevel 1850 for 2011/12.

Les Deux-Alpes to replace old 'devil' gondola
For 2011/12 a six-pack is due to replace the Diable gondola. At last! Last season a fast quad opened from below Toura to the top of the Fée area.

Two old chairs to go in Flaine
For 2011/12 a new six-pack, the Désert Blanc, is due to replace the old Perdrix and Platé chairs in the main bowl.

Les Gets gondola spruced up
The Chavannes gondola was improved with new six-seat cabins.

AVORIAZ
1 8 0 0
2012 - Year of Avoriaz

1. **CAR FREE RESORT**
2. **FRANCE'S LARGEST SKI AREA**
3. **STASH SNOWBOARD PARK**
4. **VILLAGES DES ENFANTS SKI SCHOOL**
5. **MUSIC EVENTS ALL SEASON**

6. **STAY ON THE SLOPES**

Pierre & Vacances has over 1000 ski apartments in 11 different residences perfectly located on the Avoriaz slopes. From budget studios to cosy family apartments to luxury spa residences. The choice is yours...

L'Amara NEW ★★★★★

Les Crozats NEW ★★★★

Apartments from only €98 per person per week

Pierre (&) Vacances

LES MENUIRES DEVELOPS ITS 'BELLES' SIDE

Two smart new apartment complexes will open in Reberty/Les Bruyères for 2011/12.

NEW GONDOLA, NEW PISTE ABOVE MÉRIBEL

For 2011/12 the upper stage of the Saulire gondola from Méribel is due to be replaced by a faster eight-seater meeting the cable car up from Courchevel. A new green run will link the mid-station to the Blanchot piste to create a green run all way to the resort.

NEW FAST QUAD FOR MONTGENÈVRE

For 2011/12 a fast quad is due to replace the Montquitaine double chair from Claviere towards Montgenèvre.

MORZINE SIX-PACK: ACCESS IMPROVED

A new six-pack to the top of Chamossière replaced the triple chair and Blanchots draglift last season.

FAST CHAIR TO UPGRADE LA PLAGNE BOTTLENECK

For 2011/12 a new six-pack is due to replace the slow Verdons Sud chair from the Champagny sector to Les Verdons above Plagne-Centre – at last!

PUY-ST-VINCENT QUADS INSTALLED

Two fixed-grip (slow) quads have replaced the Rocher Noir draglift and the double chair to the ski area high-point of La Pendine.

SERRE-CHEVALIER NEW LIFT A WINNER

A six-pack opened in the Cucumelle valley (starting at Fréjus), hugely improving access from Villeneuve to Le Monêtier.

BEGINNERS GO HIGHER IN LA TANIA

A new beginner area opened at the top of the gondola last season, served by a moving carpet.

NEW LOOK FOR TIGNES VILLAGE, AND NEW GONDOLA

Building work is under way to transform the old village of Les Boisses into the new ski station of Tignes 1800; the first phase is due to open at the end of 2012. Last winter, a new 18-person gondola replaced the old double chair up to the slopes from there.

VAL THORENS TO OFFER NEW LIFT-SERVED TERRAIN

For 2011/12 a new jumbo gondola is planned above the Portette chair, opening up new blue and red runs on the front of the mountain, and off-piste on the back.

FAST QUAD FOR VARS/RISOUL

In Risoul, the slow Razis chair (which accesses the Vars sector) is due to become a fast quad for 2011/12.

ITALY

CERVINIA TINKERS WITH LIFT AND PISTES

Renovation of the Plateau Rosa cable car is due for completion in 2011/12. Last season black run 59 – from the Pancheron chair (Plan Torrette) – was new. In the same area, red run 9 was designated a 'slow ski' zone; red run 24 has a short new black variant.

SINGLE NO MORE IN CORTINA D'AMPEZZO

In the Cinque Torri sector, a new double chairlift is planned from mid-mountain to the top to replace the ancient single-person chair and subsequent rope tow.

MADONNA DI CAMPIGLIO – PINZOLO: MARRIAGE ON TRACK

The long-awaited gondola link between Madonna's Cinque Laghi sector of slopes and Pinzolo, due last season, is now expected for

2011/12. On Grostè the Boch chair is to be replaced by a fast quad, with an additional blue run. Last season Pinzolo opened an eight-person gondola at Tulot (just outside the town) serving new black and red runs. A fixed-grip quad chairlift opened above Marilleva.

MONTEROSA GONDOLA TO BE REPLACED
For 2011/12 at Gressoney, a new gondola is to replace the existing one from Stafal to Gabiet.

SAUZE D'OULX AND SESTRIERE: ANOTHER RESHUFFLE
There are plans to move two high-speed quads (Triplex and Pian della Rocca) on the upper part of Sauze's ski area to make moving around the mountain easier and to replace two existing slow chairs.

SELLA RONDA CHAIRS TO SPEED UP ACCESS
The Bamby quad between San Cassiano and La Villa is to be upgraded to a six-pack, and a new quad is to replace one of the double chairs from Passo Campolongo to Monte Cherz. Last season the Prè Ciablun quad chair opened in the Corvara/San Cassiano area. In La Villa, a quad replaced the Rua triple chair.

NEW QUAD FOR SELVA
A fast quad is due to replace the Sasso Levante triple chair at Passo Sella for 2011/12. Last winter a new funicular replaced the old Rasciesa single-seat chairlift from Ortisei to Rasciesa.

SWITZERLAND

ANDERMATT TRANSFORMATION BEGINS
Work has started on a huge luxury development, with the flagship hotel Chedi and many designer apartments due to open in 2013.

CHAMPÉRY TO IMPROVE AVORIAZ LINK
In Les Crosets, a fast six-pack is due to replace the slow Grand Conche chair towards Avoriaz.

STAY UP THE MOUNTAIN IN CRANS-MONTANA
The Chetzeron mountain restaurant, opened in 2009/10, plans to add smart lodging for December 2011. A fast quad replaced the Cry d'Er/Bella-Lui drag last winter.

QUAD NUMBER FIVE FOR DAVOS-KLOSTERS MOUNTAIN
On Jakobshorn, the mountain's fifth fast chair (a quad) is due to replace the Brämabüel draglift up from Jschalp. Last winter the second stage of the Parsenn funicular was upgraded.

GRINDELWALD GONDOLA CARRIES MORE, SIX-PACK INSTALLED
Capacity on the First gondola was increased by 50% for 2010/11. A six-pack also replaced the Salzegg draglift to Eigergletscher.

LAAX TO DITCH DRAGLIFTS, SIX-PACK TO REPLACE THEM
For 2011/12 a six-pack is due to replace two draglifts above Laax, from Alp Dado to the ridge above Crap Sogn Gion. New blue runs are planned for this area too. Capacity was increased on the gondola out of Flims and on the Laax cable car last season.

SCENIC CABINS FOR ST MORITZ GONDOLA
New panoramic cabins with windows to floor level are planned for the Diavolezza cable car, and it will be closed for fitting them from 26 November 2011 until 11 February 2012.

SIX-PACK TO REPLACE OLD VERBIER CHAIRS
For 2011/12 there are plans for a new fast six-seat chair (Mayentzet) to replace two successive slow chairs from just above the top of the nursery slopes to Les Ruinettes.

Fast chair to replace Villars oldie
A six-pack is due to replace the double chair to Petit Chamossaire for 2011/12.

Zermatt restaurant review
Last season the Blauherd restaurant was rebuilt to be a new smart bar-lounge, with a larger terrace. And the big Sunnegga table-service restaurant became a self-service.

USA – California

Heavenly restaurant opens
A big new mountain restaurant has opened at the top of the Heavenly gondola (California side), with a food court and bar.

Mammoth Mountain: new chair to speed up mountain ride.
For 2011/12 a fast quad is due to replace the three-person slow Chair 5 – good news for bad weather days.

Squaw Valley names and classifies its trails – Yippee!
For 2011/12 all trails are being named and classified for difficulty, and signs are being installed.

USA – Colorado

New quad for Aspen's Buttermilk
For 2011/12 a new high-speed quad is due to replace the existing slow lifts at Tiehack on Buttermilk, cutting ride time by 60%.

New fast lift for Beaver Creek
For 2011/12 a fast quad is to replace the Rose Bowl triple chairlift.

Vail plans new restaurant
A much-needed new table-service restaurant is due to open at Mid-Vail for 2011/12. Last season, the High Noon fast quad replaced a slow chair on the Sun Up and Sun Down back bowls.

USA – Utah

Whole new playground at Canyons
A new fast quad has opened up the resort's ninth peak, Iron Mountain, with 300 acres of varied terrain. Another new quad departs the resort to a point near the top of the Sun Peak lift.

Park City plans chair upgrade, new beginner zone
At Resort Base, a new triple chair is due to replace the Three Kings double, serving the terrain park and super-pipe, as well as a new beginner area (also to have two moving carpets).

USA – Rest of the West

Triple-up at Jackson Hole
A new triple chair, Marmot, is planned from base of the Thunder quad to the top of the Bridger gondola for 2011/12.

Canada – Western Canada

Kicking Horse opens fourth bowl – experts only
Fifteen new black-diamond chutes opened in Super Bowl, accessed by a new trail from the gondola across the head of Bowl Over.

Rip it up on new Revelstoke terrain
For 2011/12 Revelstoke will offer a limited amount of backcountry skiing where you are transported by snowmobile from the end of one run to the start of the next – for experts only. And another 100 acres of slopes are now available from the Ripper Chair.

Cutting your costs

We name the resorts where your pound will go further

by **Chris Gill**

RPI	115
lift pass	£220
ski hire	£130
lessons	£135
food & drink	£170
total	**£655**

RPI	100
lift pass	£200
ski hire	£115
lessons	£120
food & drink	£125
total	**£560**

RPI	85
lift pass	£190
ski hire	£90
lessons	£80
food & drink	£120
total	**£480**

Two years back, in response to the declining power of the pound and resulting high cost of staying in a top ski resort, we introduced our Resort Price Index figures, designed to make it simple to see which major resorts were affordable, and which were not. Last year, we extended it to cover minor as well as major resorts.

Now we're taking a further step: as well as looking at the costs of food and drink, we have looked at lift passes, ski hire and lessons. Our RPI figures are now based on a total of all four costs. But, as you can see from the examples in the margin, we also show the separate costs that feed into the RPI calculation.

The WTSS team has assembled the new elements of the RPI. But the food and drink element, as in earlier years, is based on a huge survey carried out mainly by our faithful readers, who last season recorded over 2,000 prices in the bars and restaurants of the Alps (and a few from further afield). If you find this survey helpful, please contribute to the exercise next season, via our website.

Exchange rate movements affected our RPIs in the last edition, and have done so again this year. As anyone who holidayed in Switzerland in 2010/11 will tell you, the most striking shift is the increase in value of the Swiss franc. The decline in the pound means that, in the four years from 2007 to 2011, costs for British visitors to euro resorts have gone up by 40%; but in Swiss resorts the increase is 85% – that is, the cost of living has almost doubled in that time.

Before we extended our RPI survey, we did a bit of research among readers to see what would be most useful. This is what we ended up including in our 'basket' of items:

- a six-day adult lift pass in high season; there's further explanation in the margin box
- hire for six days of good but not extravagant skis; boots are not included; online prices will be lower
- one private lesson for four hours, split between two people; there's further explanation in the margin box
- six days' modest consumption of food and drink – each day, a cheap pasta or pizza lunch with a quarter-litre of house wine, a small beer, a coke and a large coffee or cappuccino; obviously, many people will spend a lot more than our budget figure.

The margin boxes give more detail or guidance on each element.

FOOD & DRINK

By including four different drinks, we have tried to be fair to countries where one kind of drink may be more expensive than others. Bear in mind that if you're not happy with simple lunches day after day, you may spend much more than our budget figure, especially in resorts where the budget figure itself is quite high (ie top French and most Swiss resorts).

LIFT PASSES

Our lift pass figures are for the pass we reckon you're most likely to buy.

In Europe, where a resort sells a pass covering other linked resorts, we have used that pass price. Where available, in America we have used special passes aimed at the international market (such as the Tri Area Pass, around Park City in Utah).

LESSONS

Our budget figure is half the cost of a four hour private lesson for two people.

Generally, we have taken prices from the main schools. You may pay more at other schools (Brit-run outfits especially) or sometimes less.

Some schools, eg the ESF in France, quote an hourly rate, easily multiplied by four. Where the standard offering is a lesson of 2.5 hours or 3.5 hours or whatever, we scaled the cost up to four hours.

In margin boxes in each resort chapter we present these budget figures, and a total. And at the top of the box, we give the resulting RPI. This index compares the total budget for the resort to the average across all European resorts; 100 represents the average resort. (Given the relatively small number of people going to North America, and the high index figures for all resorts there, we decided a European basis made sense.) As shown in the margin on the previous page, high index figures (115 up) are coloured red, low ones (85 down) green; ones in between are blue. Note than the overall RPI is only part of the picture, though; in particular, the overall figures don't always match the cost of food and drink.

The group of resorts with roughly average RPIs (from 95 to 105) is very largely French, with some of the smarter Austrian resorts and a couple of the very cheapest Swiss resorts. The low-cost group has eastern European countries at the bottom, but then includes a healthy mix of resorts in Austria, France and Italy, with resorts from all three countries figuring in the cheapest four in the Alps. Cheapest in the main Alpine countries is Passo Tonale, in Italy, a great place to learn to ski on good snow. The pricey group is dominated by resorts in North America and Switzerland, with just a couple of French resorts – Méribel and Courchevel – and the most fashionable Austrian resort, Lech. Sharing top slot are Aspen and neighbouring Snowmass, in Colorado, and Swiss St Moritz.

WAYS TO KEEP HOLIDAY COSTS UNDER CONTROL

A good way of avoiding the full impact of high resort restaurant prices is to go on a catered chalet holiday. With chalet holidays you get a filling breakfast and afternoon tea, as well as a substantial dinner, so your lunchtime needs can be minimised. Some tour ops offer 'piste picnic' packed lunches for a small extra charge. Crucially, in a chalet you get wine included with dinner – and you can organise your own aperitifs, or buy beer and mixers in the chalet at modest cost.

It's no coincidence that in these difficult times the demand for chalet holidays is soaring, and that operators are expanding their programmes to meet that demand. Ski Total has 25 new chalets this year, for example, while Inghams' programme has expanded from a modest 20 properties to an impressive 63 chalets and chalet hotels, across the Alps and in Finland.

Chalet holidays are not the only way to keep costs under control. A few tour operators such as Ski 2 offer 'all inclusive deal' options, quoting a price that includes half-board, vouchers for lunch at mountain restaurants, lift pass, and more. Club Med is a well-established operator of big hotels where everything is included (check out its full-page ad in our 'Luxury chalets' chapter). Crystal has introduced all-inclusive deals in half a dozen hotels and ten chalets, including not only packed lunches but unlimited après-ski beer, wine and soft drinks.

And of course there is self-catering. Now that it is so easy to find comfortable apartments with room to prepare meals and a dishwasher to deal with the aftermath – and with attached spas and pools of hotel standard, in many cases – self-catering is very attractive, especially for families.

RPI	Resort	Country	Page
40	Poiana Brasov etc	Romania	671
50	Bansko etc	Bulgaria	668
70	Kranjska Gora etc	Slovenia	672
70	Passo Tonale	Italy	436
75	Alpbach	Austria	112
75	Puy-St-Vincent	France	336
75	Ste-Foy-Tarentaise	France	357
80	Garmisch-Partenkirchen	Germany	398
80	Livigno	Italy	425
80	Monterosa Ski	Italy	432
80	La Rosière	France	341
80	Sauze d'Oulx	Italy	438
80	Vars / Risoul	France	393
85	Arinsal	Andorra	93
85	Ellmau	Austria	118
85	Hintertux / Tux valley	Austria	122
85	Mayrhofen	Austria	153
85	Montgenèvre	France	312
85	Pyrenees	France	338
85	Schladming	Austria	173
85	Sestriere	Italy	458
85	Söll	Austria	182
85	La Thuile	Italy	460

RPI	Resort	Country	Page
85	Bregenzerwald	Austria	208
85	Zugspitz Arena	Austria	212
90	Bad Gastein	Austria	115
90	Cervinia	Italy	409
90	Courmayeur	Italy	420
90	Les Deux-Alpes	France	272
90	Flaine	France	278
90	Les Gets	France	285
90	Hochkönig	Austria	128
90	Saalbach-Hinterglemm	Austria	166
90	Samoëns	France	345
90	Sella Ronda	Italy	443
90	Selva / Val Gardena	Italy	451
90	Serre-Chevalier	France	347
90	Montafon	Austria	204
95	Formigal etc	Spain	661
95	Avoriaz 1800	France	242
95	Châtel	France	257
95	La Grave	France	288
95	Madonna di Campiglio	Italy	429
95	Megève	France	290
95	Meiringen	Switzerland	497
95	Morzine	France	316
95	Obertauern	Austria	163

Cutting your costs

OVER THE PAGE: MORE PRICE COMPARISON TABLES >>>>>

31

Interactive resort shortlist builder at www.wtss.co.uk

SKI HIRE

Our budget figures are for 'performance' skis that a keen intermediate or advanced skier might choose; not a beginner or top end demo ski. We looked at several shops.

If you book in advance online, many shops will offer a serious discount.

EUROZONE

In these tables of budget figures for food and drink and for lift passes we show the lowest and highest figures in Austria, France and Italy, and add in a top Swiss resort for comparison.

EXCHANGE RATES

We converted prices to £££ using tourist rates published in July 2011:
€1.07
SFr1.30
US$1.57
CAN$1.51

SKY HIGH

In these tables we show the lowest and highest RPI figures in Switzerland and North America. Remember that an RPI of 100 is for the European average resort, and that isn't cheap (not least because the average includes Swiss resorts).

THE PICTURE BY COUNTRY

Let's start with the big problem for the British skier who has developed a taste for the best lunches and arguably the best views in the Alps: Swiss prices. Because of the strength of the franc, only three Swiss resorts are outside our high-cost group when you look at the overall RPI. All Swiss resorts are expensive for eating and drinking, with budget figures, even for our very modest 'basket', ranging from £180 to £260 – that is, £30 to over £40 a day. For lift passes, too, many resorts are pricey. For lessons and ski hire, the picture is much more mixed, with lots of resorts in the middle of the range for one or both items. In one of our tables below we look at Switzerland in isolation, to identify relative bargains.

EUROZONE EXTREMES: FOOD/DRINK

Resort	Country	Budget
LOW		
Monterosa Ski	Italy	£95
Livigno	Italy	£100
Passo Tonale	Italy	£100
Schladming	Austria	£100
Garmisch Parten'n	Germany	£105
Hochkönig	Austria	£105
Sauze d'Oulx	Italy	£105
Selva	Italy	£105
Sestriere	Italy	£105
Alpbach	Austria	£115
Bad Gastein	Austria	£115
Ellmau	Austria	£115
Söll	Austria	£115
HIGH		
Ischgl	Austria	£140
Obertauern	Austria	£140
Alpe-d'Huez	France	£145
Les Arcs	France	£145
Avoriaz	France	£145
Flaine	France	£150
La Plagne	France	£150
Samoëns	France	£150
Tignes	France	£150
Chamonix	France	£155
Lech	Austria	£155
Val Thorens	France	£155
Megève	France	£165
Val d'Isère	France	£165
Méribel	France	£170
Courchevel	France	£175
AND A SWISS COMPARISON		
Zermatt	Switzerland	£230

EUROZONE EXTREMES: LIFT PASSES

Resort	Country	Budget
LOW		
Ste-Foy-Tarentaise	France	£100
Puy-St-Vincent	France	£130
Alpbach	Austria	£150
La Rosière	France	£160
La Thuile	Italy	£160
Vars / Risoul	France	£160
Megève	France	£170
Montgenèvre	France	£170
Passo Tonale	Italy	£170
Sauze d'Oulx	Italy	£170
Sestriere	Italy	£170
HIGH		
Les Arcs	France	£210
Madonna di C'glio	Italy	£210
La Plagne	France	£210
Tignes	France	£210
Val d'Isère	France	£210
Cortina d'Ampezzo	Italy	£220
Courchevel	France	£220
Les Menuires	France	£220
Méribel	France	£220
Obergurgl	Austria	£220
Selva / Val Gardena	Italy	£220
Sölden	Austria	£220
St Martin de B'ville	France	£220
La Tania	France	£220
Val Thorens	France	£220
AND A SWISS COMPARISON		
Zermatt	Switzerland	£280

SWISS EXTREMES: OVERALL RPI

Resort	Country	RPI
LOW		
Meiringen	Switzerland	95
Val d'Anniviers	Switzerland	100
Engelberg	Switzerland	110
Andermatt	Switzerland	115
Villars	Switzerland	115
HIGH		
Verbier	Switzerland	135
Zermatt	Switzerland	135
Crans-Montana	Switzerland	135
St Moritz	Switzerland	150

AMERICAN EXTREMES: OVERALL RPI

Resort	Country	RPI
LOW		
Big Sky	USA	115
Big White	Canada	120
Silver Star	Canada	120
Squaw Valley	USA	120
HIGH		
Beaver Creek	USA	140
Deer Valley	USA	140
Whistler	Canada	140
Aspen	USA	150
Snowmass	USA	150

All resorts in North America fall in the pricey group overall, because of expensive lift passes and lessons (the latter particularly in the US). Ski hire costs are generally high, though there are a few resorts that fall outside the pricey bracket. But the picture is completely different when you come to look at your daily food and drink budget. Most places are positively cheap, and even swanky resorts like Aspen and Beaver Creek have budget figures of only £125 – roughly £21 a day, which is less than you will pay in many run-of-the-mill Alpine resorts. So if you don't take lessons or hire skis, and can live with the lift pass prices (as well as the flight prices of course), North America is not going to feel expensive. As with Switzerland, we have assembled a table of North American resorts on the facing page, to identify relative bargains.

Although France doesn't stand out from our overall RPI figures as expensive, out of the three main Alpine destinations it is way the most expensive for food and drink, with lots of resorts coming in with budget figures of £135 or more (£22.50 a day) and some in the pricey bracket, with figures of around £150 (£25 a day) or more – many of the most popular resorts on the UK market have figures around £170 (£28 a day) for very modest consumption.

Both Austria and Italy have more resorts where the costs overall are below average, and have plenty of resorts with below-average food and drink costs. We have put together some food and drink comparisons on the facing page.

The bigger resorts of Andorra are about average, with only Arinsal below. Spain costs less than average, and Slovenia appreciably less. But Bulgaria and Romania retain a firm grip on the real budget end of the market.

Making the most of a quick snow-fix

34

A mini ski-trip to Courchevel last December gave us three excellent days on the slopes, including on our arrival day. Whether you travel independently or part of a package (as we did), short-stay trips are easier to arrange now; the choice of airlines, destination airports and onward transfers is wider than ever. Midweek trips can be even better than weekends: cheaper deals and, in some resorts, quieter slopes.

With just a few days, you'll need to plan your short break carefully; but that's all part of the fun. We sum up the options here, with a few handy tips to help you to maximise your slope time.

WHERE SHALL WE GO?

Resorts closest to your arrival airport may seem the obvious starting point, but travelling a bit further can avoid any weekend crowds. You could also try smaller resorts that you might not normally bother with for a week's holiday.

Geneva is the classic gateway to the western Alps, with Chamonix just over an hour away, and other major French resorts such as Megève, Flaine and Morzine close by. Allow extra time for the Trois Vallées and the Tarentaise resorts. You could also head into Switzerland and visit Villars, Verbier or Crans-Montana. In Italy, Turin is an underused alternative approach to the Aosta Valley, with Courmayeur, Champoluc and La Thuile conveniently reached and Sauze d'Oulx and Montgenèvre even nearer.

Further east, Engelberg and Andermatt are popular options easily accessible from Zürich. Meiringen, or the Montafon (in Austria) offer smaller, quieter alternatives. In Austria, Innsbruck provides a fantastic opportunity to combine a city break with doorstep skiing. There are lots of resorts surrounding the city, and the Stubai Valley with its reliable glacier is nearby too. Similarly Salzburg has lots of resorts within an hour or two.

The Pyrenees offer short break opportunities too: flights into Pau and Lourdes put you close to Cauterets, and even Formigal on the Spanish side. And for a budget break, you could explore Slovenia very cheaply with flights to Ljubljana – the nearest ski area is just 8km from the airport.

WHERE TO STAY?

The range of short-stay accommodation is improving, but can still be limited in some major resorts – places such as Chamonix, Crans-Montana and Morzine, with big summer or conference business,

are easier. From Salzburg or Innsbruck you could take the daily shuttles to different resorts. If you have a rental car, valley towns such as Chur, Sion or Interlaken in Switzerland, Aosta in Italy, Moûtiers or Bourg-St-Maurice in France or Radstadt in Austria are cheaper bases from which you can visit different resorts nearby.

PRICING THE OPTIONS

Costs vary enormously. Tour operators have special deals with hotels and can organise the essentials to save you time. Around 50% of Ski 2's business is short breaks to Champoluc (Italy). Three nights' B&B in a 3-star hotel, private transfers from any of six airports within striking distance (meeting any flight), a three-day lift pass, first-day guiding and lunches costs from £466; you book your own flights. Flexiski offers three- or four-night stays in its own chalet properties in St Anton, Méribel and Courchevel, as well as various hotels. Three nights in the Saint Louis in Courchevel 1850 costs from £460 mid-season. Stanford has similar-length stays in a Megève chalet starting at £295 including transfers but not flights. Skiweekends.com features 17 major resorts and offers overnight coach travel or flight options. A four-night coach package to Brides-les-Bains (for Méribel) costs from £289 per person. Momentum offers flights, car hire or transfers, and three nights' B&B in a 3-star hotel from £398 for Courmayeur. Momentum, STC and Alpine Weekends will tailor-make short breaks for you.

TIPS FOR THE TRIP

Unless booking at short notice, avoid low resorts where snow may be unreliable and high, treeless resorts with slopes that may close in bad weather. Go for early or late flights to get the most slope-time – but note that Sunday evening traffic can be horrendous with locals going home. Book a transfer or rental car in advance; it's often cheaper and saves time on arrival. And choosing a different car hire company from the one your airline promotes can avoid queuing with others from your flight too. Taxis are generally very expensive, and public transport times between airports and resorts are rarely convenient (though Switzerland has good rail links). Rather than taking your own equipment, consider renting: most airlines impose hefty fees for ski/board carriage.

Short breaks

35

Interactive resort shortlist builder at **www.wtss.co.uk**

New gear for 2012

The latest kit means more fun for less effort

Every year, new developments and technology mean that the skis, boots and snowboards on offer get better and better. This year is no exception, with some great leaps forward for every type of equipment. The key innovations for the coming season are designed to improve versatility, ease of use and comfort. The main stories are that Salomon has a revolutionary new ski that is likely to acquire cult status, skis in general are still getting wider, more skis and snowboards are featuring 'rocker' technology, boots are getting comfier with more custom-fit options and ski-walk modes, and clothing is lighter and stretchier.

by **Dave Watts**
snowboard expert:
Mark Harries

↑ The ski test site in Bormio, Italy last March

Salomon's new BBR ski (top) and Enduro LX (bottom) ↓

Last March I went on a week-long test of all the new skis for 2011/12 organised by the Snowsports Industries of Great Britain, a trade body of ski distributors and retailers. There were over 750 pairs available, and I tested skis in all categories from intermediate piste skis through all-mountain to expert freeride.

REVOLUTIONARY NEW SALOMON BBR SKIS

The new Salomon BBR skis were the talk of the test. These have hugely wide shovels of 140mm or more (compared with, say, 120mm for more conventional skis) and pointed tips. The guy who came up with the very successful Salomon X-Scream and Pocket Rocket skis designed them, and the story is that the BBR concept was inspired by the way that a surfboard works, with the tip pushing water out of the way. Salomon refuses to categorise them as any particular type of ski because they are so different from any other skis currently on the market. It claims they are a 'powder ski that carves on-piste' and 'a piste ski that floats in powder'. Marketing hype maybe but I loved them and thought they were great fun, turning remarkably quickly and giving a solid, confidence-building platform, both on- and off-piste. My guess is they will prove hugely popular and you'll see these blue monsters everywhere for the next few seasons. They are available in a 7.9 model (easier to use) and an 8.9 (for faster, more aggressive skiers).

WIDER AND WIDER

There were lots of other excellent skis at the test too, and the trend to wider skis continues. Ten or so years ago Rossignol Vipers were among the best-selling skis and were 68mm underfoot and 111mm at the front. Now the norm is more like

↑ From left: Nordica Spitfire, Fischer Viron 2.2, K2 AMP Aftershock, Völkl RTM, Atomic Crimson Ti, Scott Venture, K2 Superburnin, Rossignol Attraxion

78mm underfoot and 120mm at the widest point. Wider skis are more stable, easier to ski and more versatile – they float a lot more easily through powder and crud as well as still turning easily because of the greater sidecut. Snow+Rock now divides its skis into four main groups based on the width underfoot: On Piste 63mm to 73mm; All Mountain 74mm to 81mm; Freeride 82mm to 102mm; Big Mountain 103mm or more.

The versatility of wider skis is also improved by the spread of 'rocker technology'. Basically, this means that the tips (and often the tails) of the skis are lifted up from the snow, which improves flotation in powder and crud and makes turning easier (on- as well as off-piste) because less of the ski is in contact with the snow so pressure is concentrated in the centre section. Now lots of skis have 'rocker'; K2, for example, has it on virtually its whole range.

Of the piste skis aimed at decent skiers, the Atomic Vario D2 75, Völkl Code PSi, Fischer Progressor 800 and, especially, Nordica Fire Arrow EDT and Blizzard R Power Full Suspension (not surprising considering their £859 price) did well. First-time buyers should take a look at the Völkl Sensor 2, Salomon 24 GT Pro and Rossignol Zenith 72. Snow+Rock is offering a special package aimed at first-time buyers: Fischer Viron 2.2 skis plus bindings, poles, ski bag and a pair of Salomon Mission 4 or Divine 4 boots for just £320, an amazing bargain (it would cost £540 to buy them all separately and the skis and binding alone would normally sell for £340).

All-mountain skis are designed to be skied off- as well as on-piste and for many readers of this book who like to do both, this is the type they should be looking for (it is certainly the type I look for). There is a huge choice of excellent skis available, including the K2 AMP Aftershock, Salomon Enduro XT, Rossignol Experience, Atomic Nomad Blackeye Ti, Völkl RTM, Völkl Grizzly and Scott Reverse. Intermediates looking for their first all-mountain skis could look at the Salomon Enduro LX and Scott Aztec.

With freeride skis (for people who want to spend most of their time off-piste but with some on-piste), top performers include the Fischer Watea 84, Rossignol S3, Scott Venture and Völkl Kendo. In the big mountain category – for people who spend a lot of time in the mountains and want a great ski for powder days – the Atomic Bent Chetler, Völkl Gotama and Rossignol S7 did well at the test.

Kästle skis were not on the test. Snow+Rock has an exclusive deal to be the only Kästle stockist in the UK and I tried them at the Hemel Hempstead indoor snow centre and thought they were great and gave a really smooth ride.

SNOW+ROCK TIP

TOP ON-PISTE SKIS
FOR EXPERTS
Nordica Spitfire XBI CT
FOR EXPERT WOMEN
Völkl Fuego
FOR RED RUN SKIERS
K2 AMP Charger
FOR RED RUN WOMEN
Atomic Cloud D2 73

SNOW+ROCK TIP

TOP FREERIDE SKIS
FOR EXPERTS
Atomic Crimson Ti
FOR EXPERT WOMEN
Völkl Aura
FOR ADVANCED SKIERS
Rossignol Experience 88
FOR ADVANCED WOMEN
Rossignol S3 Women's

New gear for 2012

Interactive resort shortlist builder at www.wtss.co.uk

SKIS ESPECIALLY FOR WOMEN

Nearly every manufacturer now produces a range of skis designed specifically for women (from novice to expert), taking account of their different physical make-up to men. In general, women tend to be lighter and less powerful; so manufacturers give their women's skis a different construction, flex and shape. Favourite on-piste skis included: K2 Superburnin, Völkl Fuego, Dynastar Exclusive Active, Atomic Cloud, Rossignol Attraxion. All-mountain: Völkl Sol and Tierra, Scott Luna, K2 SuperStitious, Rossignol Temptation 78 and Salomon Intense Black. Freeride: Atomic Elysian, Rossignol S3 Women's, Scott Rosa and Völkl Aura and Kenja.

BOOTS CUSTOM FITTED AND MADE FOR HIKING

Salomon introduced its Custom Shell concept three years ago. Now it is available on a much wider range including the Impact and women's Idol ranges. The boot is warmed up in an oven in the shop, you then step in to it, and the plastic outer shell as well as the liner are moulded to the individual shape of your foot.

When it cools down, you have a perfect fit. All in 20 minutes.

Fischer have a new Vacuum Fit boot that uses a new type of plastic 15% lighter than normal which when heated in a special oven becomes very soft and malleable. It can then be moulded, using special equipment and compressed air, to the exact shape of your foot. Fischer says that this heating and moulding can be repeated up to five times if you are not happy when you go skiing.

Tecnica introduced a new Airshell boot last season and this season have extended the concept to nine of their models – you inflate or deflate a bladder contained in the boot to customise the fit. Because the bladder traps air next to the foot there is greater insulation and warmth too.

Last season, Salomon introduced a Quest range of lighter high-performance boots that has been extended for 2011/12 and makes hiking up to find powder and ski touring easier. As well as a more grippy sole than on a normal boot there's a walk mode clip that slackens the cuff of the boot.

SNOWBOARDS STILL ROCKING

As with skis, 'rocker technology' has influenced board design, and most manufacturers now offer a platter of different board profiles, keeping traditional camber in the mix but offering rocker, a hybrid of both, and zero camber. Some companies, such as K2, have completely eliminated camber from their line; this year K2 has developed its new Ollie Bar technology that places a camber-shaped carbon bar within the core of some of its boards to enhance their liveliness. This works to make some of its zero camber and rocker boards perform more like cambered boards in and out of turns, but offers better powder performance and a more forgiving ride.

Brands such as Ride and Capita are working with a more traditional camber profile, using enough to give the board explosive

↑ Capita Totally F'kn Awesome
Rome Agent Rocker
Kjus Detour jacket ↓

pop but also using a subtle rocker in the tip and tail to improve flotation and forgiveness. This can be seen on the Ride Berzerker, for example. Capita's Totally F'kn Awesome and Black Snowboard Of Death use a similar construction but have a unique reverse sidecut section through the middle of the sidecut. This gives the board added bite through a turn, making it grip exceptionally well on-piste. Other companies are also developing new sidecuts, most notably for this season Rome Snowboard's QuickRip sidecut featured on boards such as the Agent Rocker and Headline. This effectively combines two sidecuts that create two mid-board contact points. At slower speeds the mid-section contact points engage, making it agile and playful, benefiting freestyle riding; at higher speeds the full running length sidecut engages to improve edge hold and stability – so it's great at both high and low speeds.

With bindings, riders looking for maximum weight savings should look at Union's Contact Pro and new SL. Other companies have focused on making bindings more customisable. The Rome Targa 'Yes I can't' system includes three interchangeable canted pads for anatomically correct stance widths and different levels of nose and tail power, as well as three flex options on your ankle strap via removable EVA pads. Burton has a new AutoCant dual density foam footbed which automatically settles your boot into a natural position regardless of stance width or angles for improved comfort and reduced fatigue.

STRETCH CLOTHING RULES

With ski clothing a key trend is to lighter clothing that stretches well – with four-way stretch fabrics and stretch material used in seams as well as the main fabric. Claire Collins of Snow+Rock says, 'Gore-Tex is now facing competition from technical textile companies such as Dermizax which specialise in stretch fabrics. Next season its new top-end very elastic fabric will be exclusive to Kjus clothing and has waterproof and breathability ratings that are off the charts. Most shells on the market are Gore-Tex, but Salomon now offers a range of non-Gore outerwear at great prices.'

Men's colours for next season will be less bright, with muted limes, greens, reds and blues being popular. Scandinavian brand Sweet will have a range of jackets and pants that, at first glance, do not seem to match in terms of colours – but the style grows on you. Men's snowboard fashion is going in a different direction; the overwhelming trend is for a return to a streetwear look, with heavier fabrics and a tough weave. The key colour for women is purple – worn with lime or orange for a sporty look or with black for a more sophisticated appearance. Down jackets will also be big this season.

New gear for 2012

Interactive resort shortlist builder at **www.wtss.co.uk**

Smart apartments

Enjoy full independence in comfortable surroundings

by **Dave Watts**

Apartment holidays used to be the budget option for most people – at least on holidays to France. Shoehorn six people into a studio advertised for six and you'd have a cheap but not very comfortable time. Now things have changed, especially in France where lots of plush new apartment blocks have been built in recent years. Most have dishwashers, and many share a pool, sauna, steam room and gym to add to the pampering. Some even have comfortable furniture to relax in, too. Sure, the budget option still exists, but now you can have a comfortable apartment holiday with all the other advantages that it brings (see below). We've looked for smart apartments to recommend throughout the Alps and included them in the resort chapters.

I've been taking my annual ski holiday with my wife and a couple of friends in apartments for around 20 years. That's because we value the freedom an apartment gives you. You don't have to stick to meal times (and meals) dictated by the hotel or chalet staff; you can slob around in whatever clothes you want; you can go out and come back in whenever you choose. And, crucially in our case, you are free to have a big lunch up the mountain without worrying about having to eat a huge meal – which your chalet staff or hotel will have prepared for you – in the evening; if you lack the appetite for a full meal in the evening, you can buy snacks such as oysters, smoked salmon, pâté and local cheeses along with a good bottle of wine or two from the supermarket. If you are hungry, you can go out to a restaurant to eat. Staying in an apartment doesn't mean having to cook big meals – not for us anyway.

When we started this apartment lark, we couldn't find the sort of thing we were looking for in tour operators' brochures – all the apartments were of the cram-'em-in-and-make-it-cheap variety. So we ended up booking independently.

Now, at least in France – the country that used to have the smallest, most sordid apartments – a few tour operators (including those advertising in this chapter) offer some really smart and

PEAK RETREATS

Smart apartments now come more stylishly and comfortably furnished than they used to ↓

Ski (&) Spa

Pierre (&) Vacances
premium

Truly relax in our stylish ski apartments with heated swimming pools and spas. We are found in all the top French resorts including our new L'Amara residence in Avoriaz. There is also a new luxury spa in Arc 1950 and our Flaine residence is the first in France to be awarded 5* status. **Prices start from €180 per person per week.**

visit: **www.pierreetvacances.co.uk** or call: **0870 026 7144**

Aime la Plagne / Arc 1950 / Arc 1800 / Avoriaz / Carroz d'Araches / Chamonix
Couchevel 1850 / Flaine / Les Menuires / Meribel - Mottaret / Tignes

spacious places, mostly with leisure facilities such as pools, saunas and steam rooms. The French smart apartment concept was kick-started by apartments built by or opened in the Montagnettes and MGM names. Now they've been joined by other brands. PV Holidays launched its Pierre & Vacances Premium brand last winter, and it now features 12 residences in the French Alps. Lagrange has 17 Alpine and six Pyrenean residences in its Prestige range.

So why the sudden change? Xavier Schouller of Peak Retreats and Ski Collection says, 'A lot of smart new 4-star residences have been built in the last five years because of tax breaks for people buying them – you get the VAT back if you agree to rent them out for several years and French residents can set costs against income tax too. This is good news for people wanting to rent an apartment for a holiday – we now have over 200 residences on our books.' And the French have recently announced a new classification scheme for residences that includes a 5-star rating and that will come fully into force by July 2012. The criteria for five stars seems to depend more on having staff who speak English, internet access, beds made on arrival and towels provided than on real luxury, though.

Ski Amis is best known as a catered chalet company, but it has moved into apartments in a big way. Instead of offering big residences such as the companies mentioned above do, it offers privately owned apartments and chalets, mainly in the Tarentaise, which includes the Three Valleys, Paradiski and Espace Killy resorts. It will have a staggering 6,000 to 8,000 available this winter from budget to luxury. Christine Van Zadelhoff, a director of Ski Amis, says, 'They will all be on our website, and you can access a selection by putting in either a budget and the number of people or more

PEAK RETREATS

Lots of smart apartments come with leisure facilities such as pools, saunas and steam rooms – but check whether there's a charge for them ↘

specific requirements such as three bedrooms, dishwasher, Wi-Fi, hot tub. You can book many online.'

Sadly, although there are luxurious apartments to be found in the other Alpine countries, few of them are featured by UK tour operators. Exceptions include in Grimentz (see p517 – bookable through Mountain Heaven, who also have French

apartments in La Plagne and La Rosière), Champéry and Laax in Switzerland and Kühtai in Austria (the last three bookable through Erna Low as well as direct).

So what do you need to look for if you're booking what you hope is a smart apartment? Most importantly, you still need to check whether the space is enough to meet your expectations – and whether the number it's advertised for involves anyone sleeping in the living room, bunk beds, on a mezzanine or in a cabin (which can mean an alcove). Also check the number of bathrooms and toilets. If the leisure facilities such as a pool, sauna, steam room and gym are important to you, check whether there is a charge for using these; sadly, there often is. And while most smart apartments come with a modern design, dishwasher and smartish furniture, we're sometimes disappointed by the lack of really comfy sofas and easy chairs – often because sofas double up as beds and are more comfortable to sleep in than sit on – so check that if you can.

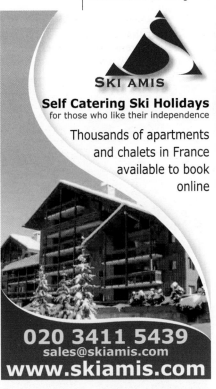

Luxury chalets

The ultimate ski holiday?

by **Chris Gill**

The catered chalet holiday is a uniquely British idea. The deal, in case you're new to it, is that tour operators install their own cooks and housekeepers in chalets that they have rented for the season, then package half-board in these chalets (well, half-board plus teatime cake) with travel from the UK. So you get the privacy and relaxed atmosphere of a temporary home in the mountains, without the hassle of self-catering or the cost of eating out in restaurants every night.

In the beginning, in the 1960s and 70s, the chalet business didn't do luxury. Chalet holidays meant creaky old buildings with spartan furniture and paper-thin walls, and six or more people sharing a bathroom. My, how things have changed. Now you can stay in some very plush places indeed – rivalling top 5-star hotels. More importantly, standards have risen across the board. When we first visited Méribel in 1974, en suite bathrooms were unheard of. They are now the norm. Spacious living rooms with log fires, sun terraces and boot warmers are common. Start looking at the slightly more expensive places, and you find spa facilities such as a sauna, steam room or indoor hot tub; some have an outdoor hot tub (the proper form, really) and/or a swimming pool. And all at prices we ordinary mortals can contemplate paying. It's these chalets that this chapter is about.

Because of the huge number of chalet holidays available, choosing the right one can be difficult. Some very helpful websites have been set up by agents, allowing you to sift out chalets that suit you best; some advertise in this chapter, or elsewhere in the book.

The greatest concentration of smart chalets is found – surprise, surprise – in the British skier's favourite French resort, **Méribel**. Ski Total, with a wide range of properties, has two new chalets this year

SKI TOTAL

Chalet Isba in Méribel is a Total Platinum property, with sauna, outdoor hot tub, billiard room and cinema ↓

that deservedly get the firm's top Platinum rating; hot tubs, of course, and cinema and billiard room in the case of chalet Isba. Alpine Action has seven smart-looking chalets (one new for 2011/12) in various parts of the resort (including Méribel Village, and a couple close to the resort centre), most with saunas, some with hot tubs. Purple Ski has five top-notch and highly individual chalets – in good positions, with lovely interiors and outdoor hot tubs. Ski Olympic took a big step into the luxury market a few years back with the acquisition of the Parc Alpin, formerly run as a boutique hotel – 12 luxurious rooms (all with plasma screen TVs), dinky swimming pool and sauna. Skiworld has two very swish places, especially La Ferme. One of the many chalets new to the Inghams programme is an attractive one with outdoor hot tub. Other companies to consider include Consensio, Meriski and VIP.

Over the hill is **Courchevel**, a resort of parts. Courchevel 1850 is well established as the 'smartest' resort in France, with the highest prices and the swankiest hotels and chalets. Operators such as Supertravel, Kaluma, Consensio and Scott Dunn have some lovely properties here. Ski Total has some chalets bordering on the luxury category, and it's also worth taking a look at Flexiski's chalet hotel Saint Louis, in an excellent position close to the piste.

The big UK chalet centre is Courchevel 1650, where Le Ski's range of properties continues to slide upmarket, with many having sauna or steam room. New this year are five small chalets in a single development, with spacious lounges and a shared swanky spa area with hot tub and wave pool. One of Ski Olympic's flagship Gold Collection chalets is here – chalet Monique, with TVs in the rooms and an outdoor hot tub. Skiworld has some smart-looking chalets here too – the 21-bed Estrella is one of its top places, with outdoor hot tub.

La Tania, not far away on the road towards Méribel, has developed quite a range of comfortable chalet properties. Ski Amis has seven smart-looking places, several with outdoor hot tubs and some offering its Premium service. Le Ski has three neat-looking properties here. Ski Power's chalets include one wood-built property with outdoor hot tub.

In **Les Menuires** there are smart places on offer in the recently developed areas. In Les Bruyères, Ski Amis has several chalets with outdoor hot tubs. And in **St-Martin** the Alpine Club's chalet Abode is a beautifully renovated farmhouse with stylish furnishings.

Val d'Isère is the great rival to Méribel in the French chalet business. The local specialist, YSE, has several very swish places. At the top end of Le Ski's programme are two very attractive places sharing a hot tub – La Bouclia and La Pierre de Compia. Skiworld's ten chalets include one of their top properties, chalet Tolima. Ski Total has lots of smart places, including three very swanky chalets in

Club Med ♈

The **more** exclusive **more** inclusive alternative to a luxury ski chalet

- Return flights, resort transfers
- Spacious ensuite accommodation
- Breakfast, Lunch and Dinner including beer, wine and soft drinks
- Gourmet buffets, mountain chalets and speciality restaurants
- Unlimited bar drinks & snacks
- Many resorts ski from the door
- 5 full days Ski or Snowboard tuition
- 6 day lift pass
- Children's Clubs and lessons from 4 years
- Apres-ski and great entertainment

All Inclusive ski from just £875 per person

23 Resorts including:
- **Espace Killy** - Val d'Isere 4♈ & 5♈, Tignes Val Claret 4♈
- **Paradiski** - La Plagne 2100 4♈, Peisey-Vallandry 4♈, Aime la Plagne 3♈, Arcs Extreme 3♈
- **3 Vallees** - Meribel Aspen Park 4♈, Meribel Antares 4♈, Meribel le Chalet 4♈, Val Thorens 3♈
- **France** - Valmorel 4♈, 5♈ and Luxury Chalet Apartments, Chamonix 4♈, Avoriaz 3♈, Serre Chevalier 3♈, Les Deux Alpes 3♈
- **Italy** - Cervinia 4♈
- **Switzerland** - Villars sur Ollon 4♈, St Moritz Roi-Soleil 4♈, Wengen 3♈
- **Japan** - Sahoro 4♈
- **China** - Yabuli 4♈

Skiline.co.uk

For more information
www.skiline.co.uk/clubmed
020 8313 3999

ABTA
ABTA No.V6608

their Platinum range – one with outdoor hot tub, two with saunas. Flexiski has one of its two chalets here – the stylishly furnished Balias, with sauna. Crystal's range includes two of its Finest properties, with saunas. Other companies to look at include Scott Dunn, Consensio and Le Chardon Mountain Lodges.

In **Tignes** Skiworld's programme includes some chalets with sauna and hot tub, and a swanky chalet hotel with pool and sauna. Ski Total has some very smart places with pool, hot tub and sauna, including two in their Platinum range. Crystal and Ski Olympic have some smart chalets too.

The other great French mega-area, Paradiski, offers lots of chalets in **La Plagne** and growing numbers at **Peisey-Vallandry**, on the Les Arcs side of the cable car link from La Plagne. Few chalets stand out, but Ski Amis has one of its Premium service chalets in each of these resorts.

There are lots of chalets in **La Rosière**, but few notable ones. As well as Mountain Heaven's smart-looking Penthouse, with grand top-floor living space and outdoor hot tub, Ski Olympic has two chalets in a development with its own pool, sauna, steam room and hot tub. Skiworld has five smart mid-sized properties.

Chalets are not common in **Avoriaz**, so it's good to see that Ski Total's handful includes one of its Platinum chalets, with sauna and log fire. Down the hill in **Les Gets**, the Ferme de Montagne is a kind of cross between a small hotel and a chalet – a beautifully renovated farmhouse with eight luxury bedrooms and gourmet

THE CHALET HOLIDAY – A PRIMER

Generally, you can either book a whole chalet (the smallest typically sleep six or eight) or share a larger chalet with others. This works surprisingly well, usually.

In the beginning, the cooking and cleaning was done by your chalet girl – often straight out of college or finishing school, and mainly intent on having a fun season. Chalet girls still exist, but now there are just as many boys, and grown-ups, including couples. It would be an exaggeration to say that service is generally professional, but training standards have certainly improved.

Breakfast is usually a buffet with the option of some cooked items. At teatime, cakes and tea are put out. Often beer and soft drinks are sold at modest prices, on an honesty basis. Dinner is a no-choice affair at a communal table, including wine – unlimited in quantity but often severely limited in quality. In the middle of the week, the staff have a night off, and you're left to your own devices – most people like to dine in a restaurant, but you can buy in a picnic.

Note that chalet hotels, a sub-species, are different in many ways. You may have individual tables, or large ones you share with other parties. There may be a choice of dishes at dinner. There will usually be a conventional bar.

Luxury chalets

Weekly news updates and resort links at www.wtss.co.uk

food. They take short-break as well as week-long bookings.

Further south in **Alpe-d'Huez**, both Ski Total and Inghams have smart places with outdoor hot tub.

In Switzerland, **Verbier** is the chalet capital. Ski Total runs the former Relais & Châteaux 4-star hotel Rosalp as a chalet hotel, not surprisingly now in the new Platinum category. It has also acquired the hotel Montpelier to run as a chalet hotel, with panoramic pool. Other companies to look at include Ski Verbier.

Zermatt, curiously, has not traditionally been a great chalet resort, but Ski Total is setting about putting that right with nine extra chalets this year in a new development sharing a smart spa area. Other companies to consider include Scott Dunn and Supertravel. In nearby **Saas Fee**, Ski Total's chalet hotel Ambassador is right at the foot of the slopes with indoor pool.

In cute little **Grimentz** (covered in our Val d'Anniviers chapter), Mountain Heaven has the very smooth slope-side Cole Ridge, with outdoor hot tub.

In Austria, **St Anton** is chalet central. Ski Total now leads the pack, with a dozen places ranging from six beds to the cool 32-bed Inge, with wellness area. Flexiski has the absolutely central Amalien Haus. Crystal has some good places in Nasserein. Just over the hill in **St Christoph**, Inghams has its flagship chalet hotel – ski-in/ski-out, with a good-sized pool. Ski Total also has two smart chalet hotels (one with an indoor pool) in **Lech**. Other firms to look at in this area include Kaluma and Scott Dunn.

In North America, only Skiworld now has much of a chalet programme, with good places in Winter Park, Breckenridge, Vail and Whistler. Ski Independence has a chalet in Vail, and Crystal has a Finest property in Breckenridge.

SKI TOTAL

Chalet la Rocheure is a Total Platinum property in Val d'Isère, with sauna – it's a converted farmhouse; ski-in location, given decent snow ↓

A home in the snow

Make your dream of a bolt-hole in the snow come true

by **Dave Watts**

Buying a place in a ski resort is an ambition for lots of keen skiers and snowboarders. The last few years have been difficult times for the Alpine property market because of the economic problems. And for UK buyers it has been made even more difficult by the weak pound. But there are some bargains still to be had and who knows what the future of the pound is? Despite restrictions on new building in many parts of the Alps and on foreigners buying property in parts of Switzerland and Austria, there are still plenty of attractive new developments on offer, as well as resale properties.

CONTACTS

Erna Low Property
020 7590 1624
www.ernalowproperty.
co.uk
Investors in Property
020 8905 5511
www.investorsin
property.com

52

INVESTORS IN PROPERTY

The living room of one of the apartments in Veysonnaz in Switzerland on offer by Investors in Property ↓

Simon Malster, managing director of Investors in Property, has been selling property in the Alps for over 20 years. He says, 'Obviously, the market has slowed down compared with a few years ago. But there is still some extremely attractive property available – especially in Switzerland and Austria. These countries have traditionally restricted sales to foreigners and so prices have not been forced up to the inflated levels they reached in some other countries. But now they are opening up sales to foreigners more and more. We have also been searching out properties in the Italian Dolomites, where the scenery is simply stunning.'

Over the last few years, Investors in Property has sold a lot of apartments in Veysonnaz (a small quiet resort in Switzerland with stunning views over the Rhône valley and a ski area linked to Verbier's). It now has more apartments there, starting at just over SF620,000 for two bedrooms in a small development with sauna and hot tub. Investors in Property also has properties in two other resorts linked to Verbier's ski area – apartments right on the piste at La Tzoumaz (from SF433,000 for two bedrooms) and detached chalets in Les Collons with fabulous views (from SF675,000 for three bedrooms). And it has apartments in Wengen with panoramic views over the Lauterbrunnen valley (SF440,000 for one bedroom,

from SF1,050,000 for two bedrooms). Apartments in Engelberg are being developed by the lift company just 200m from the gondola. The resort wants them to be full as much of the year as possible, so two-thirds of them will have an obligation to allow them to be rented out, but owners will be able to use them themselves for up to four weeks a year. Prices run from SF500,000 for two bedrooms.

Investors in Property has been selling an increasing number of properties in Austria too. Until recently, foreigners were banned from buying in most of Austria, but now new rules mean that all the properties mentioned below are available to foreigners as long as they agree to make them available for renting when not using them personally – this also means that you save 20% VAT on the purchase price (the prices given below exclude the VAT). Investors in Property has apartments right on the piste in Sölden just above the Gaislachkogl gondola station and by the new Zentrum Shuttle lift (see p177) – a two bedroom place costs from 390,000 euros. In Kappl (five miles from Ischgl and with its own ski area – foreigners are still not allowed to buy in Ischgl itself) it has two hugely contrasting properties on offer. Ski-in/ski-out apartments are being created in a traditional old 4-star hotel (with lounge, bar, restaurant and wellness facilities); two bedrooms will cost from 345,000 euros. And Residence Ice Cool is being built from scratch in ultra-modern style with huge floor-to-ceiling windows and stunning views and wellness facilities including an indoor-outdoor pool; these have been selling like hot cakes, and just three of the 12 apartments were still available when we went to press – costing from 795,000 euros for three bedrooms. Investors in Property also has apartments on the edge of Bramberg at the foot of the local Wildkogel ski area (with 55km of pistes) and right next to a gondola that opened last season; they are also just three minutes' drive from a gondola into the Kitzbühel ski area and within easy reach of many others such as Gerlos/Zell am Ziller and Kaprun (both around 30 minutes); prices for two bedrooms start at 338,000 euros.

In the beautiful Dolomites region of Italy, Investors in Property has just started selling apartments in Corvara (which is part of the

INVESTORS IN PROPERTY

Apartments in Residence Ice Cool near Ischgl in Austria have been selling like hot cakes ↓

A home in the snow

huge Sella Ronda area); a two-bedroom place 200m from the lifts costs around 2 million euros (yes, you read it right!).

France remains a favourite place for British skiers and boarders to buy property. Joanna Yellowlees-Bound, CEO of Erna Low Property, says: 'We are largely focusing on Arc 1950, which was built in the early to mid-2000s and is a traffic-free, ski-in/ski-out complete mini-resort with attractive buildings, outdoor pools and hot tubs, restaurants, bars, shops and ski school. Some of the original buyers find their circumstances have changed and now need to sell. Current prices are a bargain for purchasers, and UK sellers are still making a profit in £ terms because of the exchange rate change. We now have an office in Arc 1950 and currently have properties ranging from studios to four-bedroom duplexes.' A two-bedroom apartment might cost around 300,000 euros if, like most, there is an arrangement for a few years that you can use it a certain number of weeks a year and it goes in a rental pool the rest of the time.

Erna Low also has some new developments. These include one right by the gondola in Briançon (part of the Serre-Chevalier ski area) where a two-bedroom apartment costs from 159,000 euros with a guaranteed rental return of up to 4.5%, and a very smart-looking 4-star development in Val Thorens (with pool, spa, sauna, steam and a restaurant managed by a two-Michelin-starred chef) with two-bedroom apartments for 277,000 euros.

WHAT TO LOOK FOR WHEN BUYING A HOME IN THE SNOW

First, you need to decide whether you want somewhere just for the skiing or whether you want a place in a resort that is attractive in the summer as well. Many French resorts developed after the 1950s can be deadly dull in summer, whereas others are attractive for summer as well as winter use. Second, if you want the place primarily for skiing and snowboarding, you will want reliable snow. And with global warming likely to continue, that means going for somewhere with access to high, snow-sure slopes and with good snowmaking. Third, if you intend to use the place frequently yourself, you will probably want somewhere within a couple of hours of an easily accessible airport. Fourth, make sure you understand the legal and taxation aspects – buying and running costs, all types of taxes and any resale restrictions. It is highly advisable to get professional advice on these. Fifth, make sure you understand any arrangements that you may be offered for 'sale and leaseback' or 'guaranteed return' from renting it out – these can vary enormously and may enable you to save money on the purchase price in some circumstances. Sixth, if you are intending to rent the property out yourself, don't overestimate the income you will get from it.

Interactive resort shortlist builder at **www.wtss.co.uk**

Some observations on skiing with children in tow

by **Chris Gill**

There has been no repetition this year of the family trip I mentioned in last year's introduction, so perhaps that will be the last of them for the Gill family – until, that is, Val and I become grandparents and get cast in the role of unpaid nanny. That's something I shall be resisting, I can tell you. But I'd bet all potential grandparents say that, until their potential is realised and they go all soppy over their darling offspring's darling offspring. I'd settle for a further decade of baby-free skiing, which right now looks possible. Fingers crossed.

TRANSATLANTIC TEMPTATION RESISTED, THIS YEAR

Last year I relayed a bulletin from a regular reporter of many years' standing, Stuart McWilliam, on a road trip around Canadian resorts with his wife Jill, encumbered by not only their three-year-old son but also a brand-new four-month-old daughter. Well, as someone who never attempted anything vaguely adventurous with his kids, I confess to smiling when I started reading this year's report from Stuart on ... a week in La Plagne with Esprit Ski. What a relief: maybe Val and I weren't such inadequate parents, after all.

It sounds like family McWilliam adapted without too much trouble to a humdrum week in the Alps. 'We enjoyed the Paradiski area,' says Stuart, 'even though at times the runs were much busier than we are used to in Canada.' (You can say that again – take a look at page 325 for evidence.) 'Ski Esprit were excellent from start

to finish. All the staff seemed to be enjoying their work, and the nursery staff genuinely wanted to make your stay as stress free as possible. The chalet hotel Deux Domaines was great for us – you were not worried if your children were running about or a baby was crying as we were all in the same boat. Really good food and service throughout the whole week.' Sounds like it will be an Esprit Ski chalet for the foreseeable future, then.

FAMILY LIFT PASS DEALS

Don't get too excited. This item is not going to give you an instant answer to the question 'Where can my family ski for the minimum cost?' What it might do, though, is alert you to the kind of deals that are on offer for children or for family groups.

In each of our resort chapters we summarise in a margin box the lift pass deals available. We've had a look over the ones in Austria, France and Italy (we reckon not many families will be interested in Switzerland and North America, these days) to see what's on offer.

As you might hope, infants basically ski free. But what is an infant? Typically in France it's under five, but in Austria it's generally under six and Italy under eight. That could make a big difference if your kids are in that age range.

Then there are discounts for older children. The age limits vary, of course, and the discount isn't usually enormous, but there are exceptions. Cervinia gives a generous discount of 40% to the under 13s, for example. Look out for special deals like the one in Alpbach, where, in low season, children up to 15 ski free when accompanied by a fare-paying adult.

If you have older teenagers, look out for special family deals that

give substantial discounts for kids as old as 17 or even up to 20 – there are local passes in the Trois Vallées resorts, for example, that give good savings in that age range.

WHERE TO SKI FAMILY FORUM
If you make much use of website forums, you'll know that activity breeds activity. We've had a forum on our site about family matters for years, but it's been pretty quiet for a year or two. If you're planning your first trip and have questions that more experienced parents might be able to answer, why not drop in and post them, and see if you can stir up some debate?

WHO TO GO WITH?
You can, of course, have family skiing holidays more or less completely unaided. Or you can call on the support of resort nurseries, and childcare facilities associated with resort ski schools. But huge numbers of British families are wedded to the comfortable childcare arrangements offered by British tour operators (of the kind the McWilliams have now plugged into). And if you plan to do that, you have a choice of three main types of supplier.

First, you have small, specialised companies which are well represented by the firms advertising in this chapter. These firms go to a small range of resorts that they know inside out (only one resort, in the cases of Snowbizz and Ski 2), and are basically owner-operated, so you can reasonably expect them to be very responsive to the needs of the individual.

Many, but not all, operate catered chalets. If that doesn't mean much to you, check out our chapter on luxury chalets, on page 44,

The catered chalet holiday is as popular as ever, especially with families. Since en suite bathrooms and comfy sofas became the norm rather than the exception, the attractions of the chalet – more private and less formal than hotels – have increased considerably. Now, more people are discovering the merits of the chalet's bigger cousin, the chalet hotel.

Chalet operators have for years set the pace in childcare. It was a natural extension of hiring British gels as cooks and housekeepers to hire a few as nannies, too; then all the operator had to do was identify a suitable room in a suitable chalet, and bingo – a crèche was born. For British parents reluctant to accept the brutality of French nurseries, the chalet was the obvious solution.

Chalet hotels are a larger version of the same thing, with some additional advantages. Some are purpose-built, but usually they are based on buildings that have operated as proper hotels. As a result, bedrooms typically are more generous than in chalets. Facilities are often better – there is likely to be a bar (with lower-than-usual prices, if you're lucky), and there may be a swimming pool, spa or gym, for example. There may be a menu choice at dinner.

Two of the most long-established firms dominate the family chalet hotel market; Esprit Ski was the original family chalet specialist. Its programme is still dominated by chalets – in total about 50 – but it now also includes five chalet hotels. Mark Warner has always focused on chalet hotels, and has crèches in most of its 12 properties. The editorial Gill family took several successful holidays with these firms in the days when the kids needed even more attention than they do now.

Strikingly, these firms major on top resorts. They both have chalet hotels with childcare in Courchevel 1850, Méribel, Val d'Isère and La Plagne. Esprit's flagship is the super-cool Deux Domaines at Belle-Plagne, which has a decent pool and spa – young children are not allowed in the latter – and a good ski-in/ski-out location on the edge of the village. The other Esprit resorts are Saas-Fee and Alpe-d'Huez. Mark Warner also has family-oriented properties in Tignes, Les Deux-Alpes and St Anton.

Family holidays

59

Interactive resort shortlist builder at www.wtss.co.uk

which includes an explanation of this splendid, uniquely British concept. (Unless your infants are appreciably better behaved than the editorial ones were, you probably won't want to let them loose in anything resembling luxury, of course; but the explanation in that chapter is a general one.)

Then there is Esprit Ski, also a chalet operator, but on a much bigger scale. Esprit Ski claims to be 'No 1 for Family Skiing', and it's not an unreasonable claim, with holidays in 10 French resorts plus an interesting sprinkling across the rest of the Alps. The business started life in much the same way as its smaller rivals, but earlier – 29 years ago, in fact, so about nine years before I first used them. In that time it has grown and grown to the point where it is now a different animal (along with Total and Inghams, part of Hotelplan).

As well as an unmatched range of chalets, Esprit has lots of chalet hotels – hotel buildings operated along chalet lines. If the chalet formula sounds a bit claustrophobic for your taste, the chalet

Austria

Obergurgl	Esprit Ski
Niederau	Crystal
Scheffau	Crystal
St Anton	Esprit Ski

France

Alpe-d'Huez	Esprit Ski, Crystal
Les Arcs etc	Esprit Ski, Ski Amis
Ardent (Avoriaz)	Family Ski
Les Coches (La Plagne)	Family Ski
Courchevel	Esprit Ski, Ski Amis
Flaine	Crystal
Les Gets	Esprit Ski, Ski Famille
Les Menuires	Family Ski, Ski Amis, Ski Famille
Méribel	Esprit Ski, Ski Amis
Morzine	Mountain Heaven
Peisey-Vallandry (Les Arcs)	Esprit Ski, Mountain Heaven
La Plagne etc	Crystal, Esprit Ski, Family Ski, Mountain Heaven, Ski Amis
Puy-St-Vincent	Snowbizz
La Rosière	Esprit Ski, Mountain Heaven
La Tania	Ski Amis
Tignes	Crystal, Esprit Ski, Ski Amis
Val d'Isère	Esprit Ski, Ski Amis
Val Thorens	Ski Amis

Italy

Champoluc (Monterosa)	Ski 2
Claviere	Crystal
Selva	Esprit Ski
Val di Fassa	Crystal

Switzerland

Grimentz	Mountain Heaven
Saas-Fee	Esprit Ski, Family Ski

hotel may be the solution. Read our feature panel. A clear advantage of increased scale is that it supports wider travel options: Esprit flies to Geneva (for France and Switzerland) from the obvious regional airports and Edinburgh, and this year has added Southampton. It has Chambéry flights (for France) from a range of regional airports, again including Southampton and my favourite, Bristol. For Austria and Italy, it's Gatwick and Manchester to Innsbruck.

Your third option is bigger still – the mainstream operators such as Crystal, which operate the same sort of childcare in a selection of the many resorts where they sell holidays.

To save you the work of figuring out who goes to which resorts, we've drawn up a table showing exactly that. The table covers the advertisers in this chapter and Crystal, to give you an idea of your options. Note that some of the smaller operators are less specialised in family holidays than others, and don't have full childcare facilities in every chalet or even every resort.

Of course, there are plenty of other operators offering childcare. Last time we checked, there were over 40 UK firms doing it; there's a list in the families section of our website at www.wtss.co.uk – with links to all their websites.

Family holidays

Interactive resort shortlist builder at **www.wtss.co.uk**

Corporate ski trips

A great way to motivate your staff and clients

by **Dave Watts**

The market for corporate ski trips used to be big. A few seasons ago we had 13 advertisers in this chapter. Now we have one. Obviously, in difficult economic times, companies cut back on expenditure; and corporate hospitality is an easy target. It is still happening, but companies aren't spending as much and there aren't as many 'jollies' where staff and clients just go away to bond and enjoy themselves.

Amin Momen of Momentum Ski, which does a lot of corporate business, says, 'Business dropped in winter 2009 but recovered significantly over the next two years, and 2012 looks like being even better. One thing that is very noticeable is that firms that used to organise a trip purely for bonding purposes are now making them more business-focused, incorporating meetings and forums into the programme. For example, each year Lambert Smith Hampton runs a three-day corporate trip to Courmayeur for around 250 people in the commercial property industry; but now it includes an invitation-only forum that takes place before the ski day (Seb Coe spoke at it last year). And in 2011 we organised a four-day Reproductive Medicine Symposium for 50 to 60 doctors in Crans-Montana, with post-skiing seminars from 5pm to 8pm; in 2012 they are going to Courmayeur. Every year, Ford runs a trip linked to the Geneva Motor Show – it invites motoring journalists to the show and then to test drive cars by driving them to and from the Alps, and maybe try 4x4s out on an ice-driving circuit.'

Mountain Heaven is a company that has catered chalets and self-catering accommodation in four French resorts and in Grimentz in Switzerland. Nick Williams, its MD, says, 'For the last three winters we've pioneered a new concept of great-value corporate trips. A firm of management consultants takes over all our self-catered accommodation in La Plagne Montalbert for its staff. They arrive from all over – the UK, Spain, Germany, Italy, France, USA – and we organise transfers from whatever airport suits them or from Aime railway station. They hold a two-day conference in Montalbert's own conference centre midweek but are free to arrive early or leave late to enjoy time on the slopes – they have the apartments for the whole week. We also deliver breakfast each day and organise lunches and dinners – including a dinner up the mountain.'

Roger Walker of Ski 2 (a company that specialises in Champoluc in the Monterosa area of the Italian Alps) says, 'Our corporate clients tend to be different from those of other companies. Most are very budget conscious, nearly all want to go out over a weekend, and the whole thing is based more on internal team bonding than on entertaining clients. Most don't want us to organise meeting facilities for them either – so we are going against the trend of cutting down on "jollies". But with some of the companies, the staff contribute to the cost – they may pay for the accommodation themselves while the company arranges the flights, picks up the tab for wine with dinner, or pays for lift passes, ski rental and lessons, for example. We'll pick guests up from any of six airports within striking distance – companies like the flexibility we offer.'

This season the 13th annual City Ski Championships will be held in Crans-Montana in Switzerland (from 16 to 18 March 2012) rather than Courmayeur in Italy where they have been held until now. Organiser Amin Momen said, 'It was time for a change and Crans-Montana is a great venue – they have held music festivals and World Championship races and have excellent hotels and first class venues where we can hold parties and prize givings. This year we are running the Momentum Ski Festival the same weekend to attract non-competitors too – there will be five-star entertainment on and off the mountain, including top comedians (Marcus Brigstocke is already confirmed), big name DJs and live bands. There will be up to 500 people out to enjoy it. We have chartered a flight with Snowjet for over 100 people to and from Sion airport (just 45 minutes from the resort), and that was booked up by July. It's looking likely that Damon Hill, Heston Blumenthal, Lawrence Dallaglio and Colin Jackson will be among the celebrities there again. Warren Smith will run both performance and pre-race coaching clinics with his team of instructors.'

The Saturday GS race is the main event. But two other races are held on the Friday: the Accenture parallel slalom and the Zai Ski Radar Trap Challenge (speed skiing). On both days there's a race-side buffet in the Savills Alpine Homes race paddocks. On the Friday evening there's a Cavendish Ware welcome drinks party, and on the Saturday a Valais reception followed by a gala prize presentation dinner and then ... clubbing until dawn. Sunday is free for skiing.

For more details call 020 7371 9111 or visit www.cityskichampionships.com.

Former British downhiller Konrad Bartelski (left) and motor racing ace Damon Hill (right) with current British ski cross champion Emily Sarsfield ↗

MOMENTUM SKI

HOW TO ORGANISE IT AND WHERE TO GO

Organising the whole thing yourself is a real hassle. People based in different areas of the country are likely to want to fly from different airports and at different times of day. And many hotels in the Alps don't want to take bookings for just a few days, or to provide the number of single rooms that you might want. Numbers are likely to change as people drop out for various reasons. Your group is likely to have skiers and boarders of widely differing ability and maybe some complete beginners or non-skiers, so you need to organise ski instructors or guides to teach or lead different groups. You need to organise equipment (and maybe clothing) rental and lift passes. You might want to organise 'jollies' such as dinner up the mountain and a torchlit descent back or a lunchtime BBQ on the piste, or a 'treasure hunt' event for teams on the slopes. And you might need rooms to hold business meetings in.

But that's what you use a tour operator or event organiser for – to deal with all the hassle and organise things on your behalf. And the great thing is that they don't charge you any extra for doing all that – it's part of the business to them.

Because corporate trips tend to be short, you'll want to keep the travel time to the minimum. Transfer times from airports to resorts generally range from one to four hours, and you'll probably want to operate at the lower end of that range if you can. That's why resorts such as Courmayeur and Champoluc in Italy (close to Geneva and Turin airports), Engelberg in Switzerland (close to Zürich), Kitzbühel in Austria (close to Salzburg and Innsbruck) and Garmisch in Germany (close to Munich) are popular. All these resorts have hotels that are happy to offer short break bookings too.

Corporate ski trips

Interactive resort shortlist builder at **www.wtss.co.uk**

Flying to the snow

Flights and transfers for independent travellers

by **Wendy King**

64

ONLINE BOOKING

Most budget airlines expect you to make your booking online, and many charge less if you book such 'extras' as hold baggage and ski carriage online too. The web addresses of the airlines we list are given as links on our own website at www.wtss.co.uk.

THE EXTRAS

Charges on top of the basic flight cost vary between airlines.

In July 2011, we looked at three budget airlines for flights to Geneva for the same week in February 2012. Basic return fares varied from £50 to £110. Extra charges then included:

1 checked-in 20kg bag return ....£20-£50

1 skis/snowboard/ boots return..£50-£80

Check-in fee ...£6-£12

Credit card payment fee £13

These can add over £100 to the original cost, and the priciest of our three flights worked out at £195.

Also, you might be offered priority check-in/boarding for, say, £20 and insurance for, maybe, £12 (which may not cover winter sports adequately – do check). Packing ski boots separately is considered a second bag and costs extra – though most airlines allow boots as well as skis if you pay extra for ski carriage.

There are lots of flights to the Alps and Pyrenees; and you can often avoid the crowds by opting for quieter, queue-free regional airports. But finding your way through the minefield of routes and extra charges is hard work – and the extras can double or triple the basic cost.

So-called budget airlines go to mainstream airports such as Geneva and Milan but also to smaller places, making it easier to get to many resorts in places such as Austria, the Dolomites, the Pyrenees, Slovenia and eastern Europe. You'll find a wide choice of affordable transfers too. National carriers can be competitive, both on cost and destination, so don't ignore them when planning a trip. But note that some winter routes stop operating before the season ends.

THE LEADING GROUP

EasyJet has a big range of flights, many to Geneva, from a broad choice of UK hubs. Other key destination airports include Zürich, Innsbruck, Munich and Salzburg. New for 2011/12 is Luton to Salzburg (twice weekly). From Stansted, Ljubljana is handy for Slovenian resorts and eastern Austria.

Ryanair operates mainly from Stansted, with a few flights from other UK airports. Routes/frequency change regularly, but a wide choice is offered – including Lourdes (for the western and central Pyrenees) and Memmingen (western Germany and Austria).

Jet2.com has flights to Geneva, Salzburg, Chambéry and Toulouse – mainly from northern England, but also from Edinburgh, Glasgow and Belfast. Its dedicated ski website allows you to pre-book extras, such as ski hire.

Flybe has increased its UK departure airports and serves Geneva, Salzburg, Berne, Milan, Chambéry, Pau, Toulouse, Nice and, unusually, Stuttgart (handy for Germany and western Austria).

Bmibaby flies from four UK airports to Geneva and from East Midlands to Chambéry, Toulouse, Munich and Nice. Some of the Manchester routes now operate under **Germanwings**, which offers twice weekly flights to Friedrichshafen (good for Germany, western Austria, eastern Switzerland).

British Airways goes to lots of relevant airports, including Innsbruck, from a variety of UK ones. **Swiss** has lots of flights to Zürich and Geneva, some to Basel.

Snowjet has weekend flights from Gatwick and Stansted to Chambéry, and from Stansted to Sion, Switzerland (Fri, Sat, Sun). The Sion route gives lots of resort choice in the Valais region, halving transfer times to Zermatt (1hr30). We found flights to be sensibly timed, punctual, queue- and stress-free. Free buses to the station are included. Tour operator charter flights are also sometimes sold on a seat-only basis. There are now weekly charters to the Spanish Pyrenees, to Huesca (convenient for Formigal) and, new for 2011/12, to Lleida-Alguaire (shorter transfers to Andorra).

PRICING IT UP ...

Charges and rules for baggage and for equipment carriage vary, so it's important to check the detail. We noted EasyJet charging

Head to the slopes!

Chambery, Geneva & Salzburg

Fly from Belfast, Edinburgh, Glasgow, Leeds, Manchester & Newcastle

fm £29.99
one way inc. taxes

JET2.COM OFFERS YOU THE LOWEST FARES TO THE SLOPES PLUS:

- Great flight times
- 22kg baggage allowance*
- 20kg ski and board carriage*
- A dedicated group booking service
- Visit Jet2.com/ski for all the know on the snow!

BOGOF† ON SKI OR BOARD CARRIAGE ON BOOKINGS THIS SEPTEMBER! QUOTE 'JET2SKI'

Jet2.com®
Low fares to the slopes

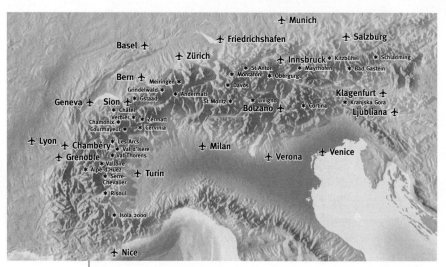

different fees for the first bag, dependent on destination (£18-£22 return). Ryanair permits either a standard 15kg for a first bag, priced at £30 return, or 20kg for £50; but skis/board carriage will set you back from £80 return – which is often higher than the basic air fare. BA effectively charges for skis: one checked-in bag is free up to 23kg; additional bags on European flights cost from £60 return. Swiss and Lufthansa still allow one set of skis and boots free in addition to a 23kg bag. There are other extras that inflate the price too (see margin panel). And with some airlines you can now reserve seats or pre-book a meal on board – all for a fee, of course. Airport costs such as drop-off and trolley fees can also add to the overall spend.

FROM PLANE TO RESORT

Car rental can be cost-effective for a short break or with a group – but, again, watch for hidden extras. Most Swiss and Austrian airports have good public transport links to lots of places. Special rail passes may be cheaper than return tickets (see page 464 for Swiss passes). In Italy, buses run to the Dolomites from Verona and Innsbruck, and to the Aosta valley from Turin. Reaching French resorts is slightly trickier, but private minibus transfers are plentiful. Tour operator Ski Amis offers a public shared minibus service from Geneva and Chambéry to the Three Valleys, La Plagne Montalbert and Peisey-Vallandry. Prices start at £65 per person return. Holiday Taxis (www.holidaytaxis.com) covers over 400 resorts from major airports and some stations. Transfer companies and their relevant links are listed on our website: www.wtss.co.uk.

Travelling by rail

Make tracks to the snow (greener ones)

by **Wendy King** | **Whether you're an enthusiast or not, rail travel has its advantages for travelling to the snow. As well as the leisurely journey aspect, taking the train can avoid overcrowded airports, traffic congestion and high baggage charges to fly. There are efficient high-speed links between London and Paris, and daytime services to French resorts can take as little as 7.5 hours (with Eurostar direct). A wider choice of overnight services now makes destinations beyond France sensibly reachable too. Many ski resorts have their own railway stations, so transfers can be relatively straightforward. Here we sum up the main options.**

The starting point of most European rail trips is likely to be the Eurostar high-speed train from London St Pancras or from Ashford or Ebbsfleet stations in Kent.

DIRECT SERVICES TO THE FRENCH ALPS
The fastest way to France is Eurostar's direct services to the Tarentaise region – such as to Moûtiers (for the Trois Vallées) and to Bourg-St-Maurice (for Les Arcs, La Rosière, Ste-Foy, Tignes and Val d'Isère). Overnight services allow you eight days on the slopes. Daytime services give you the regular six days, the same as flying. Generally allow an hour or so for onward bus transfers, depending on the resort – though Moûtiers to Méribel takes a lot less.

Overnight trains will depart from London every Friday at 7.30pm from 23 December 2011 to 13 April 2012. These will get you into Bourg at 6.40am. Return services will leave Bourg at 10pm on Saturdays, arriving in London at 7.15am. There are no special sleeping arrangements – you doze (or not) in your seat. The daytime service will leave on Saturdays at 10am, getting you to Bourg by 7pm, from 17 December 2011 until 14 April 2012. The return service leaves Bourg at 9.50am and arrives at 4.15pm.

A Standard adult return costs from £149 (non-flexible). For £229 a Standard Premier ticket (non-flexible) gets you a bigger seat pitch and basic meals. There are discounts for the under-25s and over-60s. Semi-flexible fares are available. Seats can also be booked as part of a package holiday.

INDIRECT SERVICES TO THE FRENCH ALPS
The French regular rail network (SNCF) can get you to lots of places, such as Chambéry, Briançon or Grenoble – for onward buses to more southerly resorts. For Chamonix, an overnight train from Paris Austerlitz, via St-Gervais, would put you in resort by 10am next morning; prices from £150 to £200 return. A pre-bookable taxi service to get you between the Paris stations is offered through snowcarbon.co.uk; you ring or email to reserve a place and the driver will meet your train. It costs 30 euros each way for up to eight people; ski carriage is included too. SNCF has saver cards for young and older travellers – the Carte 12-25 entitles you to 25% or 60% discount, depending on times/days and peak periods. These cards cost about £45.

HIGH-SPEED TO SWITZERLAND

The Swiss do rail travel very well, with lots of options. Allow travel times of around 10–12 hours from London. High-speed trains from Paris can get you in resort by evening – assuming a lunchtime departure. Lots of resorts, such as Andermatt, Davos, Engelberg, Grindelwald, Klosters, Meiringen and Zermatt, have convenient local railway stations. It's easy to get to others, such as Saas Fee and Verbier, by a combination of train and post bus. Eurostar has connecting fares to five major Swiss cities, including Geneva, Zürich and Basel; journeys are also bookable from Paris to 18 other Swiss hubs – such as Chur, Sion and Visp. The Lyria des Neiges will run directly three times a week from 11 December 2011 until 1 April 2012. Trains will depart Paris Gare de Lyon at 4pm, stopping at Sion, Aigle and Brig – which give access to lots of resorts.

It might be cheaper to buy a return ticket to the Swiss border and a Swiss Transfer ticket (from £80) for onward travel rather than a straightforward return ticket to your destination resort. This Transfer ticket allows one return journey from the point of entry into Switzerland to any other station in the country, regardless of distance – you will need to buy it in the UK before you travel. For more about train ticket options in Switzerland, see the feature panel on page 464.

AUSTRIA AND GERMANY

The great advantage of rail travel to Austria is that many resorts have their own convenient stations. City Night Line is part of a large network of European rail services, with weekend sleeper trains departing from Paris and Amsterdam. Winter services from Paris Est include trains direct to Innsbruck or Wörgl (Fridays), arriving late morning; or via Munich (Sat, Sun, Mon). Onward connections can get you to resorts such as St Anton, Zell am See, Mayrhofen and the SkiWelt. From Munich it's an easy hop to Garmisch-Partenkirchen. Typical fares start from £200, including Eurostar to Paris. Check out www.citynightline.de for more details.

THE ITALIAN JOB

Most Italian resorts are hard work to reach by train, but there are exceptions. The Dolomites are close to the line through Trento and Bolzano, reachable from Munich (as an onward connection from the City Night Line), from Innsbruck to the north, or from Verona to the south. Resorts of the Val di Susa are easily reached via trains from Paris Gare de Lyon to Turin and Milan. These run twice a day and stop at Bardonecchia and Oulx – a 15-minute bus ride from Sauze d'Oulx and a bit further from Sestriere. A flexi-return fare from Paris starts at £90. Check out www.artesia.eu.

PLANNING AND BOOKING

Rail fares have the advantage of few hidden charges such as baggage fees, weight excesses or extra taxes. But like air fares, the cheapest fares are best secured early. Booking is normally only up to 90 days in advance. Main sites include: Rail Europe (www.raileurope.co.uk), Eurostar (www.eurostar.com), Swiss railways (www.sbb.ch/en) or Austrian railways (www.oebb.at). Some local lines such as Martigny to Le Châble (for Verbier) and Bex up to Villars may have to be organised separately. Detailed general websites include www.seat61.com and www.snowcarbon.co.uk.

Drive to the Alps

And ski where you please

by **Chris Allan**

Because the Channel gets in the way, because many of us take package holidays and because the British Isles are the centre of the low-cost airline business, we're inclined to travel to the Alps by air. The French, the Germans and the Dutch, in contrast, mainly go by car. And for Brits, too, driving has various advantages.

Even for those going on a pretty standard week in the Alps, many people find driving is less hassle than taking charter flights. For families (especially those going self-catering), it simplifies the job of moving half the contents of your house to the Alps. If there are four or five people in your party, the cost can be low. If you fancy something a bit more adventurous than a standard week in one resort, taking a car opens up the exciting possibility of touring around several resorts in one trip, and even making up your plans as you go, so that you go where the snow looks best.

The experience of driving out can be a pleasant one. Cross-Channel ferries are faster and more comfortable than ever, with the possibility of a seriously good lunch on short crossings as an alternative to the quicker shuttle-trains through the tunnel. And the motorway networks in north-eastern France and on the approaches to the Alps have improved immensely in recent years. You can now get to most resorts easily in a day from south-east England, in some cases using motorways virtually all the way from departure to arrival.

Another plus point is that you can easily extend the standard six-day holiday. You can spend a full day on the slopes on the final Saturday (a blissfully quiet day on the slopes of most resorts) and then drive for a few hours before stopping for the night; this means you won't find Sunday's journey too demanding, and you may even have time for a traditional French Sunday lunch before making for the Channel port.

AS YOU LIKE IT

If you fancy visiting several resorts, you can do it in three ways: use one resort as a base and make day trips to others; use a valley town as a base, and make resort visits from there; or go on a tour, moving on every day or two. There are some notable regional lift passes that might form the basis of a trip, in Austria especially. Using one of these means that you don't pay a premium for skiing multiple resorts, and don't even have to waste any time acquiring lift passes each morning. Check out the Ski Amadé pass in our Austria introduction, for example.

AROUND THE ALPS IN SEVEN DAYS

The most rewarding – although the least relaxing – approach to exploring the Alps is to go touring, moving every day or two to a different resort and enjoying the complete freedom of going where you want, when you want. Out of high season there's no need to book accommodation in advance. And a touring holiday doesn't mean you'll be spending more time on the road than on the piste – provided you plan your route carefully. An hour's drive after the

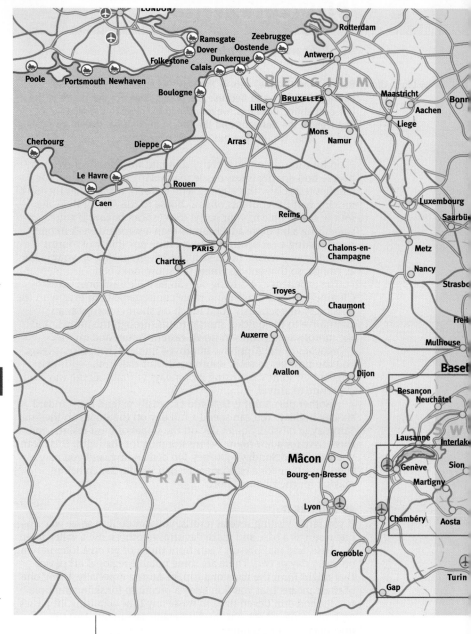

This map should help you plan your route to the Alps, at least in outline. All the main routes from the Channel and all the routes up into the mountains funnel through (or close to) three 'gateways', picked out on the map in larger type – Mâcon in France, Basel in Switzerland and Ulm in Germany.

Decide which gateway suits your destination, and pick a route to it from your planned arrival port at the Channel. Occasionally, using different Channel ports will lead you to use different gateways.

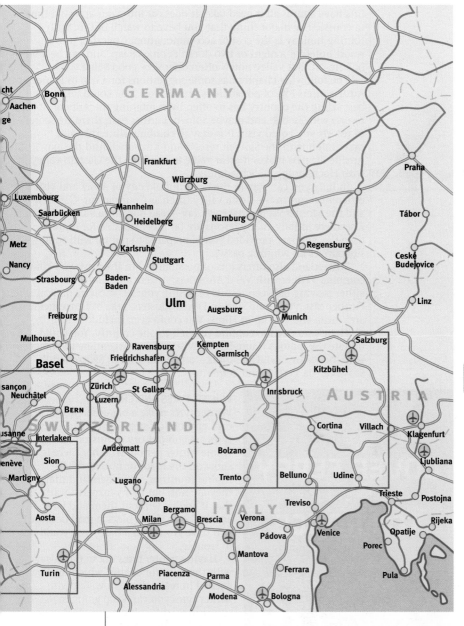

The boxes on the map correspond to the areas covered by the more detailed maps in our introductory chapters on the four main Alpine countries:

Austria page 102
France page 216
Italy page 400
Switzerland page 462

Drive to the Alps

Interactive resort shortlist builder at **www.wtss.co.uk**

lifts have shut is all it need take. It does eat into your après-ski time, of course. The major thing that you have to watch out for with a touring holiday is the cost of accommodation. Checking into a resort hotel for a night or two doesn't come cheap, and can be a bit of a rip-off. But valley hotels often offer very good value.

The following chapter has some suggestions for a trip to France. Austria offers lots of possibilities. In the west, you could take in the best skiing the country has to offer, by combining the Arlberg resorts with Ischgl, and maybe Sölden. Further east, there are scores of resorts you could visit. It is easy to combine Hintertux and Mayrhofen with the SkiWelt resorts and Kitzbühel. And the Ski Amadé lift pass makes it great value to combine the Gastein valley with Hochkönig and Schladming.

In Italy you can stay in the beautiful old city of Aosta and visit a different resort in the Aosta valley (such as Courmayeur, Cervinia and the Monterosa resorts) each day – read our Aosta valley chapter. Elsewhere in Italy, many resorts are far more suitable for tourers than day trippers, provided you're prepared to put up with some slow drives on winding passes.

Switzerland also offers lots of possibilities. In the west, you could combine Verbier with Val d'Anniviers, Anzère and Crans-Montana – either moving between resorts or basing yourself in Sierre or Sion. Further east, you could start in Davos/Klosters, take in Lenzerheide and Arosa and end up in Flims. You could even include St Moritz.

There's no need to confine yourself to one country. You could imitate the famous Haute-Route by starting in Argentière in France – up the valley from Chamonix – and ending up in Switzerland's Saas-Fee, via Verbier and Zermatt.

WINTER TYRES AND CHAINS

Winter tyres make a big difference to a car's grip on ice, snow and slush. These tyres are compulsory in Austria for the whole winter period, whether there is snow on the roads or not. In other Alpine countries, we understand that they are not; but many 'experts' warn that if you go without them and have an accident – or if you block a road because you have ground to a halt – you could be in trouble.

Having winter tyres doesn't do away with the need for chains, which may be needed in really deep snow. But with winter tyres you can keep going in surprisingly difficult conditions if your car also has traction control, to stop the wheels spinning. This usually forms part of the electronic stability systems that are now fitted to many new cars.

Cars hired in Austria and Switzerland should always be equipped with winter tyres. Cars hired elsewhere may not be. Be careful when hiring cars from airports in Germany to drive to Austrian resorts; there are rip-offs in operation.

Drive to the French Alps

To make the most of them

by **Chris Gill**

If you've read the preceding chapter, you'll have gathered that we are pretty keen on driving to the Alps in general. But we're particularly keen on driving to the French Alps. The drive is a relatively short one, whereas many of the transfers to major French resorts from Geneva airport are relatively long. And the route from the Channel is through France rather than Germany, which for Francophiles like us means it's a pleasant prospect rather than a vaguely off-putting one. Especially if you are using a short Channel crossing rather than a ferry to one of the Normandy ports, the drive is pleasantly low-pressure, because you don't have to tangle with Paris.

The French Alps are the number-one destination for British car-borne skiers. The journey time is surprisingly short, at least if you are starting from south-east England. From Calais, for example, you can comfortably cover the 900km/560 miles to Chamonix in about nine hours plus stops – with the exception of the final few miles, the whole journey is on motorways. And except on peak weekends the traffic is relatively light, if you steer clear of Paris.

With some exceptions in the southern Alps, all the resorts of the French Alps are within a day's driving range, provided you cross the Channel early in the day (or overnight). Saturday is still the main changeover day for resorts, and traffic into and out of many can be heavy. This is especially true between Albertville and the Tarentaise resorts (from the Three Valleys to Val d'Isère). Things are nothing like as bad as they were 25 years ago, before road improvements for the 1992 Olympics removed some of the main bottlenecks; but the resorts have expanded further, and the jams are back – on peak-season Saturdays you can encounter serious queues around Moûtiers. There are traffic lights placed well away from the town, to keep the queues and associated pollution away from Moûtiers.

DAY TRIP BASES

As we explained in the previous chapter, a car opens up different kinds of holiday for the adventurous holidaymaker – day tripping from a base resort, for example.

In the southern French Alps, Serre-Chevalier and Montgenèvre are ideal bases for day tripping. They are within easy reach of one another, and Montgenèvre is at one end of the Milky Way lift network, which includes Sauze d'Oulx and Sestriere in Italy – you can drive on to these resorts, or reach them by lift and piste. On the French side of the border, a few miles south, Puy-St-Vincent is an underrated resort that is well worth a visit for a day – as is the Vars/Risoul area, a little further south. The major resorts of Alpe-d'Huez and Les Deux-Alpes are also within range, as is the cult off-piste resort of La Grave. Getting to them involves crossing the high Col du Lautaret, but it's a major route and is kept open pretty reliably.

The Chamonix valley is an ideal destination for day tripping. The Mont Blanc Unlimited lift pass covers all the Chamonix areas, plus Courmayeur in Italy (easily reached through the Mont Blanc tunnel) and Verbier in Switzerland (a bit of a trek, even if the intervening passes are open). Megève and Les Contamines are close

by, and Flaine and its satellites are fairly accessible. You could stay in a valley town such as Cluses, to escape resort prices – but Chamonix itself is not an expensive town.

MOVING ON

A look at the map on the facing page shows that a different approach will pay dividends in the Tarentaise region of France. Practically all the resorts here – from Valmorel to Val d'Isère – are found at the end of long winding roads up from the main valley. From a valley base such as Aime or Bourg-St-Maurice it's easy enough to visit some, but to visit all of them would be pretty hard work. If instead you stayed in a series of different resorts for a day or two each, moving on from one to the next in the early evening, you could have the trip of a lifetime. Compagnie des Alpes, owner of the lift systems in many of the big-name resorts of this area, sells a Holiski pass that gets discounts on day passes at most of them.

GETTING THERE

There are three 'gateways' to the different regions of the French Alps. For the northern Alps – Chamonix valley, Portes du Soleil, Flaine and neighbours – you want to head for Geneva. If coming from Calais or another short-crossing port, you no longer have to tangle with the busy A6 from Paris via Beaune to Mâcon and Lyon. The relatively new A39 autoroute south from Dijon means you can head for Bourg-en-Bresse, well east of Mâcon.

For the central Alps – the mega-resorts of the Tarentaise, from Valmorel to Val d'Isère, and the Maurienne valley – you want to head for Chambéry. For the southern Alps – Alpe-d'Huez, Les Deux-Alpes, Serre-Chevalier – you want to head for Grenoble. And for either of these gateways first head for Mâcon and turn left at Lyon.

If you are taking a short Channel crossing, there are plenty of characterful towns for an overnight stop between the Channel and Dijon – Arras, St-Quentin, Laon, Troyes, Reims.

From the more westerly Channel ports of Le Havre or Caen, your route to Geneva or Mâcon sounds dead simple: take the A13 to Paris then the A6 south. But you have to get through or around Paris in the process. The most direct way around the city is the notorious périphérique – a hectic, multi-lane urban motorway close to the centre, with exits every few hundred yards and traffic that is either worryingly fast-moving or jammed solid. If the périphérique is jammed, getting round it takes ages. The more reliable alternative is to take a series of motorways and dual carriageways through the south-west fringes of Greater Paris. The route is not well signed, so it's a great help to have a competent navigator.

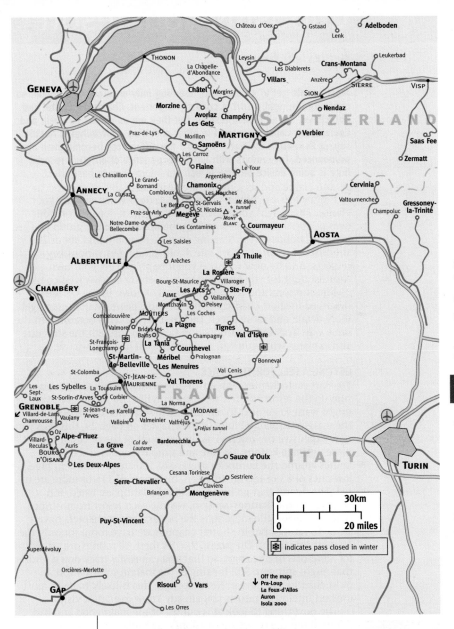

Pick the right gateway – Geneva, Chambéry or Grenoble – and you can hardly go wrong. Generally, there are no mountain passes involved. The exception is the approach to Serre-Chevalier and Montgenèvre, which involves the 2060m Col du Lautaret; the road is a major one and is ploughed frequently, but we felt the need for chains here on one occasion. Crossing the French-Swiss border between Chamonix and Verbier involves two closure-prone passes – the Montets and the Forclaz. When necessary, one-way traffic runs beside the tracks through the rail tunnel beneath the passes.

Choosing your resort

Get it right first time

Most people get to go skiing or boarding only once or twice a year, so choosing the right resort is crucially important. Chamonix, Châtel and Courchevel are all French resorts, but they are as similar as chalk and Camembert. Consider resorts in other countries – Kitzbühel in Austria, say, or Zermatt in Switzerland – and the differences become even more pronounced. For readers with limited experience of different resorts, here is some advice on how to use our information to best effect.

Lots of factors need to be taken into account when making your choice. The weight you attach to each of them depends on your own personal preferences, and on the make-up of the group you are going on holiday with. Starting on page 85 you'll find about 20 shortlists of resorts that we rate as outstanding in various key respects. And by now we hope you'll be able to get your own shortlist built for you by going to our website at www.wtss.co.uk.

Minor resorts and regions not widely known in the UK are described in short chapters of two or three pages. Major resorts get more detail, and more pages. Each resort chapter is organised in the same way. This short introduction takes you through the structure and explains what you will find under each heading we use.

GETTING A FEEL FOR THE PLACE

We start each chapter with a two-line verdict, in which we aim to sum up the resort in a few words. If you like the sound of it, you might want to go next to our unique Resort Price Index (RPI), in the margin. Explained fully in the chapter on page 29, this tells you how expensive the resort is, taking account of the prices of lift passes, private lessons, ski hire and simple lunches and drinks; figures around the European average of 100 are presented in blue, low ones of 85 or less are in green, high ones of 115 or more are in red. The figures that go into the RPI calculation are listed, too.

Then, in the 'Ratings' section, we rate each resort from various points of view – the more stars the better. Longer chapters have a set of 18 ratings, but in shorter chapters we have room for only the 10 most important. On pages 79 to 84 these 10 ratings are set out for all resorts in one chart, so that you can easily track down resorts that might suit you. Still looking at the margin information, in most chapters we have a 'News' section; this is likely to be of most use and interest in resorts you already know from past visits.

The next thing to look at is our list of the main good and bad points about the resort and its slopes, picked out with ➕ and ➖. This is followed by a summary in **bold type**, in which we've aimed to weigh up the pros and cons, coming off the fence and giving our view of who might like the resort. These sections should give you a good idea of whether the resort is likely to suit *you*, and whether it's worth reading our detailed analysis of it.

You'll know by now, for example, whether this is a high, hideous, convenient, purpose-built resort with superb, snow-sure, challenging slopes but absolutely no nightlife; or a pretty, traditional village with gentle wooded slopes, ideal for beginners on the rare occasions when it has some decent snow.

THE RESORT

In this first section of each chapter, we try to sort out the character of the place for you. Later, in the 'Staying there' section, we tell you more about the hotels, restaurants, bars and so on. Resorts vary enormously in some key respects and we have separate sections for each of the following headings. These match our star ratings.

Village charm At the extremes of the range are the handful of really hideous modern apartment-block resorts thrown up in France in the 1960s, and the ancient, captivating mountain villages of which Switzerland has an unfair number. But it isn't simply a question of old versus new. Some purpose-built places can have a much friendlier feel than some long-established resorts with big blocky buildings. Some places are working towns. Some are full of bars, discos and shops; others are peaceful backwaters. Traffic may choke the streets; or the village may be traffic-free.

Convenience This means how easy it is to get around the resort once you are there (not how easy the resort is to get to from the UK). Some places can be remarkably strung out, whereas others are surprisingly compact; our village plans are drawn to a standard scale, to help you gauge this. And of course proximity of lodgings to pistes determines how much walking or bussing you do.

Scenery Mountains are of course generally scenic, but there are differences, from the routinely hilly Colorado to the jaw-droppingly marvellous scenery of the Italian Dolomites and the Swiss Jungfrau region, to name two favourites.

THE MOUNTAINS

Extent of slopes Some mountains and lift networks are vast and complex, while others are much smaller and lacking variety.

Fast lifts Gondolas and fast chairlifts travel at three times the speed of slow chairlifts – cable cars and funicular railways even faster; these lifts offer short ride times, and most also shift queues quickly. We summarise the kinds of lifts you'll spend your time on. On our piste maps, we use a chair symbol to identify only fast chairs; lifts not marked with a symbol are slow chairs or draglifts.

Queues Monster queues are largely a thing of the past, but it still pays to avoid the resorts with the worst queues, especially in high season. Crowding on the pistes is more of a worry in many resorts, and we mention problems of this kind under this heading.

Terrain parks We summarise here the specially prepared fun parks and other terrain features most resorts now arrange for freestylers.

Snow reliability This is a crucial factor for many people, and one that varies enormously. In some resorts you don't have to worry at all about a lack of snow, while others are notorious for treating their paying guests to ice, mud and slush. Whether a resort is likely to have decent snow on its slopes normally depends on the height, the direction most of the slopes face (north good, south bad), its snow record and how much snowmaking it has. But bear in mind that in the Alps high resorts tend to have rocky terrain, where the runs will need more snow than those on the pasture land of lower

Choosing your resort

Interactive resort shortlist builder at **www.wtss.co.uk**

resorts. Many resorts have increased their snowmaking capacity in recent years; in the 'Key facts' section we list the latest amount they claim to have, and comment on it in the snow reliability text.

For experts, intermediates, beginners Most (though not all) resorts have something to offer beginners, but relatively few will keep an expert happy for a week's holiday. As for intermediates, whether a resort will suit you really depends on your standard and inclinations. Places such as Cervinia and Obergurgl are ideal for those who want easy cruising runs, but have little to offer intermediates looking for more challenge. Others, such as Sölden and Val d'Isère, may intimidate the less confident intermediate who doesn't know the area well. Some areas linking several resorts, such as the Trois Vallées and Portes du Soleil, have vast amounts of terrain, so you can cover different ground each day. But some other well-known names, such as Mürren and Courmayeur, and many North American resorts, have surprisingly small areas.

For boarders In earlier editions we had a special panel in longer chapters but now deal with boarders' requirements in the main text, commenting on things like flat areas (bad) and the main types of lifts – gondolas, cable cars and chairs (all good) or draglifts (bad).

For cross-country We don't pretend that this is a guide for avid cross-country skiers. But we do try to help.

Mountain restaurants Here's a subject that divides people clearly into two opposing camps. To some, having a decent lunch in civilised surroundings – either in the sun, contemplating amazing scenery, or in a cosy hut, sheltered from the elements – makes or breaks their holiday. Others regard a prolonged midday stop as a waste of valuable skiing time, as well as valuable spending money. We are firmly in the former camp. We get very disheartened by places with miserable restaurants and miserable food (eg many resorts in America); and there are some resorts that we go to regularly partly because of the cosy huts and excellent cuisine (eg Zermatt).

Schools and guides This is an area where we rely heavily on readers' reports of their own or their friends' experiences.

For families We sum up the merits of the resort, where possible evaluating the childcare arrangements. But, again, to be of real help we need first-hand reports from people whose children have actually used the facilities.

STAYING THERE

Chalets, hotels, apartments Some resorts have few hotels or few chalets. Note that we also have feature chapters on notably good chalets and apartments. If there are interesting options for staying in isolation on the slopes above the resort village, or in valley towns below it, we pick them out at the end of this section.

Eating out The range of restaurants varies widely. Even some big resorts, such as Les Arcs, have little choice because most visitors dine in their apartments. Most US resorts offer lots of choice.

Après-ski Tastes and styles vary enormously. Most resorts have pleasant places in which to have an immediate post-skiing beer or hot chocolate. Some then go dead. Others have noisy bars and discos until the early hours.

Off the slopes This is largely aimed at assessing how suitable a resort is for someone who doesn't intend to use the slopes, such as a non-skiing spouse. But of course it is also of interest to anyone who wants some variety of evening entertainment.

Resort ratings at a glance

ANDORRA | AUSTRIA

	Arinsal	Pas de la Casa	Soldeu		Alpbach	Bad Gastein	Ellmau	
Page	93	95	97		112	115	118	
Extent	*	***	***		*	***	****	
Fast lifts	**	**	**		***	***	****	
Queues	***	***	***		***	***	****	
Snow	****	****	***		**	***	**	
Expert	*	*	*		*	***	*	
Intermediate	**	***	****		**	****	****	
Beginner	****	****	****		****	**	****	
Charm	*	*	*		*****	***	***	
Convenience	***	****	***		**	**	***	
Scenery	***	***	***		***	***	***	

	Hintertux / Tux valley	Hochkönig	Ischgl	Kitzbühel	Lech	Mayrhofen	Obergurgl	
Page	122	128	130	137	145	153	158	
Extent	***	***	****	***	****	***	**	
Fast lifts	**	***	*****	****	****	****	*****	
Queues	***	****	****	***	****	*	*****	
Snow	*****	***	****	**	****	***	*****	
Expert	***	**	****	***	****	**	**	
Intermediate	***	****	****	****	****	***	***	
Beginner	**	***	**	**	****	**	****	
Charm	***	***	***	****	****	***	****	
Convenience	**	**	***	**	***	*	****	
Scenery	***	***	***	***	***	***	***	

	Obertauern	Saalbach-Hinterglemm	Schladming	Sölden	Söll	St Anton	Stubai valley	
Page	163	166	173	177	182	190	200	
Extent	**	***	***	***	****	****	***	
Fast lifts	*****	*****	****	****	****	***	***	
Queues	****	****	****	***	***	***	***	
Snow	****	**	****	*****	**	****	*****	
Expert	***	**	**	***	*	*****	***	
Intermediate	****	****	****	****	****	***	***	
Beginner	****	***	***	***	**	*	**	
Charm	**	****	***	**	***	****	****	
Convenience	****	****	***	**	**	***	**	
Scenery	***	***	***	***	***	***	****	

Want to see the full set?

Major resort chapters in the book have an additional eight ratings shown at the start of the chapter. And you can see the full set of ratings for 200 resorts on our website.

www.wtss.co.uk

Resort ratings at a glance

Weekly news updates and resort links at www.wtss.co.uk

	Alpe-d'Huez	Les Arcs	Avoriaz 1800	Chamonix	Châtel	Courchevel	Les Deux-Alpes	
Page	222	232	242	247	257	262	272	
Extent	****	***	*****	***	*****	*****	***	
Fast lifts	***	***	****	***	**	****	****	
Queues	****	****	***	**	***	****	**	
Snow	****	****	***	****	**	****	****	
Expert	****	*****	***	*****	***	****	****	
Intermediate	****	****	****	**	****	*****	**	
Beginner	*****	***	****	**	***	****	***	
Charm	**	**	**	****	***	**	**	
Convenience	***	****	*****	*	**	****	***	
Scenery	****	***	***	*****	***	***	****	

	Flaine	Les Gets	La Grave	Megève	Les Menuires	Méribel	Mont-Genèvre	
Page	278	285	288	290	297	302	312	
Extent	****	*****	*	*****	*****	*****	**	
Fast lifts	**	**		*	****	*****	**	
Queues	***	***	****	****	****	****	***	
Snow	****	**	***	**	****	***	****	
Expert	****	***	*****	**	****	****	**	
Intermediate	*****	****	*	****	*****	*****	****	
Beginner	*****	****	*	***	***	****	*****	
Charm	*	****	***	****	*	***	***	
Convenience	*****	***	***	**	*****	***	***	
Scenery	****	***	****	*****	***	***	***	

	Morzine	La Plagne	Puy-St-Vincent	La Rosière	Samoëns	Serre-Chevalier	Ste-Foy-Tarentaise	
Page	316	324	336	341	345	347	357	
Extent	*****	****	**	***	****	****	*	
Fast lifts	**	**	**	*	**	**	**	
Queues	***	**	***	****	****	***	*****	
Snow	**	****	***	***	***	***	***	
Expert	***	****	***	**	****	***	****	
Intermediate	****	*****	***	***	*****	****	***	
Beginner	***	****	***	*****	**	****	**	
Charm	***	**	**	***	****	***	***	
Convenience	**	*****	*****	***	*	***	***	
Scenery	***	***	****	****	****	***	***	

Want a shortlist shortcut?

Our website will build a shortlist for you: you specify your priorities, and the system will use
our resort ratings to draw up a shortlist – confined to one area or country, if you like.

www.wtss.co.uk

FRANCE   GERMANY   ITALY

	St-Martin-de-Belleville	La Tania	Tignes	Val d'Isère	Val Thorens	Vars / Risoul		
Page	359	361	365	376	386	393		
Extent	*****	*****	*****	*****	*****	***		
Fast lifts	****	****	***	****	*****	*		
Queues	****	****	****	****	***	****		
Snow	***	***	*****	*****	*****	***		
Expert	****	****	*****	*****	****	**		
Intermediate	*****	*****	*****	*****	*****	****		
Beginner	**	***	**	***	****	****		
Charm	****	***	*	***	**	**		
Convenience	***	****	****	***	*****	****		
Scenery	***	***	***	***	***	***		

	Garmisch-Partenkirchen		Cervinia	Cortina d'Ampezzo	Courmayeur	Livigno	Madonna di Campiglio	
Page	398		409	415	420	425	429	
Extent	*		***	***	**	**	***	
Fast lifts	**		****	***	***	****	***	
Queues	***		****	****	****	****	***	
Snow	***		*****	***	****	****	***	
Expert	****		*	**	***	*	**	
Intermediate	***		****	***	****	***	****	
Beginner	*		*****	*****	*	****	****	
Charm	***		**	****	****	***	***	
Convenience	**		***	*	*	**	***	
Scenery	****		****	*****	****	***	****	

	Monterosa Ski	Passo Tonale	Sauze d'Oulx	Sella Ronda	Selva / Val Gardena	Sestriere	La Thuile	
Page	432	436	438	443	451	458	460	
Extent	***	**	****	*****	*****	****	***	
Fast lifts	*****	****	***	****	****	***	***	
Queues	****	****	***	***	***	***	****	
Snow	****	****	**	****	****	****	****	
Expert	****	*	**	**	***	***	**	
Intermediate	****	***	****	*****	*****	****	****	
Beginner	**	*****	*	****	***	***	****	
Charm	***	**	**	***	***	*	***	
Convenience	***	***	**	***	***	***	***	
Scenery	****	***	***	*****	*****	***	***	

Resort ratings at a glance

81

Interactive resort shortlist builder at www.wtss.co.uk

Want to keep up to date?

Our website has weekly resort news throughout the year, and you can register for our monthly email newsletter – with special holiday offers, as well as resort news highlights.

www.wtss.co.uk

	ADELBODEN	ANDERMATT	CHAMPÉRY	CRANS-MONTANA	DAVOS	ENGELBERG	GRINDELWALD
Page	470	473	475	478	480	487	489
Extent	***	**	*****	***	****	**	***
Fast lifts	***	*	*	****	****	***	***
Queues	***	**	****	***	***	**	**
Snow	***	****	**	**	****	***	**
Expert	**	****	***	**	****	****	**
Intermediate	***	**	****	****	*****	***	****
Beginner	****	*	**	***	**	**	***
Charm	****	****	****	**	**	**	****
Convenience	**	***	*	**	**	*	**
Scenery	****	***	****	****	****	****	*****

	KLOSTERS	LAAX	MEIRINGEN	MÜRREN	SAAS-FEE	ST MORITZ	VAL D'ANNIVIERS
Page	493	495	497	500	504	509	516
Extent	****	****	*	*	**	*****	**
Fast lifts	****	****	****	****	****	****	*
Queues	**	****	****	***	***	***	****
Snow	****	***	**	***	*****	****	****
Expert	****	***	**	***	**	****	****
Intermediate	*****	*****	***	***	****	****	***
Beginner	***	****	***	**	*****	**	***
Charm	****	***	***	*****	*****	**	*****
Convenience	**	***	***	***	**	*	**
Scenery	****	***	****	*****	****	****	****

	VERBIER	VILLARS	WENGEN	ZERMATT
Page	520	531	533	538
Extent	*****	***	***	****
Fast lifts	****	**	***	*****
Queues	***	***	***	***
Snow	***	**	**	****
Expert	*****	**	**	****
Intermediate	***	***	****	****
Beginner	**	****	***	**
Charm	***	***	*****	****
Convenience	**	**	***	**
Scenery	****	***	*****	*****

Want a shortlist shortcut?

Our website will build a shortlist for you: you specify your priorities, and the system will use our resort ratings to draw up a shortlist – confined to one area or country, if you like.

www.wtss.co.uk

| | CALIFORNIA | Mammoth | Squaw | COLORADO | Beaver | Brecken- | |
	Heavenly	Mountain	Valley	Aspen	Creek	ridge	Snowmass
Page	553	558	563	566	573	575	580
Extent	★★★	★★★	★★★	★★★★	★★	★★	★★★★
Fast lifts	★★★★	★★★★	★★★	★★★★	★★★★★	★★★	★★★★★
Queues	★★★★	★★★★	★★★★	★★★★	★★★★★	★★★★	★★★★
Snow	★★★★	★★★★	★★★★	★★★★★	★★★★★	★★★★★	★★★★★
Expert	★★★	★★★★	★★★★	★★★★★	★★★★	★★★★	★★★★★
Intermediate	★★★★	★★★★	★★	★★★★★	★★★★	★★★★	★★★★★
Beginner	★★★★	★★★★	★★★★	★★★★★	★★★★★	★★★★★	★★★★★
Charm	★	★★	★★★	★★★★	★★	★★★	★★
Convenience	★	★★	★★★★	★★	★★★★	★★★	★★★★
Scenery	★★★★	★★★	★★★	★★★	★★★	★★★	★★★★

| | | Winter | UTAH | | | | |
	Vail	Park	Alta	Canyons	Deer Valley	Park City	Snowbird
Page	582	589	594	596	598	600	605
Extent	★★★★	★★★	★★★	★★★	★★	★★★	★★★
Fast lifts	★★★★★	★★★★	★★★★	★★★	★★★★	★★★	★★★★
Queues	★★	★★★★	★★★	★★★★	★★★★	★★★★	★★★
Snow	★★★★★	★★★★★	★★★★★	★★★★	★★★★	★★★★	★★★★★
Expert	★★★★	★★★★	★★★★★	★★★★	★★★	★★★★	★★★★★
Intermediate	★★★★★	★★★★	★★★	★★★★	★★★★	★★★★	★★★
Beginner	★★★	★★★★★	★★★	★★	★★★★	★★★★	★★
Charm	★★★	★★	★★	★★	★★★	★★★	★
Convenience	★★★	★★★	★★★★	★★★★	★★★★	★★	★★★★★
Scenery	★★★	★★★	★★★	★★★	★★★	★★★	★★★

| | REST OF THE WEST | |
	Big Sky	Jackson Hole
Page	608	613
Extent	★★★★	★★★
Fast lifts	★★	★★★
Queues	★★★★★	★★★
Snow	★★★★★	★★★★
Expert	★★★★	★★★★★
Intermediate	★★★★	★★
Beginner	★★★★★	★★★
Charm	★★	★★★
Convenience	★★★★	★★★★
Scenery	★★★	★★★

Resort ratings at a glance

83

Interactive resort shortlist builder at www.wtss.co.uk

Want to see the full set?

Major resort chapters in the book have an additional eight ratings shown at the start of the chapter. And you can see the full set of ratings for 200 resorts on our website.

www.wtss.co.uk

Resort ratings at a glance

	WESTERN CANADA Banff	Big White	Fernie	Kicking Horse	Lake Louise	Revelstoke	Silver Star	
Page	623	630	633	638	640	645	647	
Extent	***	***	***	***	***	***	***	
Fast lifts	****	****	**	***	****	*****	****	
Queues	****	*****	****	****	****	*****	*****	
Snow	****	*****	****	****	***	****	****	
Expert	****	***	*****	****	****	*****	****	
Intermediate	****	****	**	***	****	**	***	
Beginner	***	****	****	***	***	*	****	
Charm	***	**	**	**	***	**	***	
Convenience	*	****	****	****	*	*	*****	
Scenery	****	***	***	***	****	****	***	

	Sun Peaks	Whistler						
Page	649	651						
Extent	***	****						
Fast lifts	**	*****						
Queues	*****	**						
Snow	****	****						
Expert	***	*****						
Intermediate	****	*****						
Beginner	****	***						
Charm	***	***						
Convenience	****	****						
Scenery	***	***						

Weekly news updates and resort links at www.wtss.co.uk

www.wtss.co.uk / www.wheretoskiandsnowboard.com

Our website is designed to complement this book. We like to think it's one of the best in the ski business. On the site you'll find:

- twice-weekly news and updates on all the resorts in this book throughout the season

- full editors' ratings for 200 resorts – three times the number we can fit into the book

- interactive resort shortlist builder – you plug in what you want most from a resort (eg village charm, extensive slopes, convenient lodgings) and up pops a shortlist to suit you

- snow reports and resort weather forecasts

- links to thousands of useful sites such as resorts, tour operators, hotels, ski schools, airlines, transfer companies

- free competitions with great prizes

- special offers from leading tour operators

- blogs from the editors on their travels

- dozens of background feature articles (eg for families)

- forums where you can exchange views, seek advice, give vent to those grumbles

- a resort reporting system, where you can file a report and maybe win next year's edition of the book

- a signup for monthly e-newsletters (essential reading for all keen skiers and boarders)

You know how good the book is. Don't miss the site. Visit today and sign up.

Resort shortlists

To help you spot resorts that will suit you

To streamline the job of spotting the ideal resort for your own holiday, here are lists of the best ten or so resorts for 22 different categories. Some lists embrace European and North American resorts, but many we've confined to Europe, because the US has too many qualifying resorts (eg for beginners) or because the US does things differently, making comparisons invalid (eg for off-piste).

SOMETHING FOR EVERYONE
Resorts with everything from reassuring nursery slopes to real challenges for experts
Alpe-d'Huez, France 222
Les Arcs, France 232
Aspen, Colorado 566
Courchevel, France 262
Flaine, France 278
Mammoth, California 558
Vail, Colorado 582
Val d'Isère, France 376
Whistler, Canada 651
Winter Park, Colorado 589

INTERNATIONAL OVERSIGHTS
Resorts that deserve as much attention as the ones we go back to every year, but don't get it
Alta, Utah 594
Andermatt, Switzerland 473
Bad Gastein, Austria 115
Big Sky, Montana 608
Hochkönig, Austria 128
Laax, Switzerland 495
Monterosa Ski, Italy 432
Sella Ronda, Italy 443
Val d'Anniviers, Switzerland 516
Vars/Risoul, France 393

HIGH-MILEAGE PISTE-BASHING
Extensive intermediate slopes with big lift networks
Alpe-d'Huez, France 222
Davos/Klosters, Switz 480/493
Grand Massif, France 287
Laax, Switzerland 495
Milky Way: Sauze d'Oulx (Italy), Montgenèvre (France) 438/312
Paradiski, France 322
Portes du Soleil, France/Switz 335
Sella Ronda, Italy 443
Selva, Italy 451
SkiWelt/Kitzbühel, Austria 118/137/182
St Moritz, Switz 509
Trois Vallées, France 374
Val d'Isère/Tignes, France 376/365
Whistler, Canada 651

RELIABLE SNOW IN THE ALPS
Alpine resorts where snow is rarely in short supply
Bregenzerwald, Austria 208
Chamonix, France 247
Cervinia, Italy 409
Courchevel, France 262
Hintertux, Austria 122
Lech/Zürs, Austria 145
Obergurgl, Austria 158
Obertauern, Austria 163
Saas-Fee, Switzerland 504
Sölden, Austria 177
Val d'Isère/Tignes, France 376/365
Val Thorens, France 386
Zermatt, Switzerland 538

OFF-PISTE WONDERS
Alpine resorts where, with the right guidance and equipment, you can have the time of your life
Alpe-d'Huez, France 222
Andermatt, Switzerland 473
Chamonix, France 247
Davos/Klosters, Switz 480/493
La Grave, France 288
Lech/Zürs, Austria 145
Monterosa Ski, Italy 432
St Anton, Austria 190
Val d'Isère/Tignes, France 376/365
Verbier, Switzerland 520

DRAMATIC SCENERY
Resorts where the mountains are not just high and snowy, but spectacularly scenic too
Chamonix, France 247
Cortina, Italy 415
Courmayeur, Italy 420
Heavenly, California 553
Jungfrau resorts (Grindelwald, Mürren, Wengen), Switzerland 489/500/533
Lake Louise, Canada 640
Megève, France 290
Sella Ronda, Italy 443
Selva, Italy 451
St Moritz, Switz 509
Zermatt, Switzerland 538

BACK-DOOR RESORTS
Cute little Alpine villages linked to big, bold ski areas, giving you the best of two different worlds
Les Brévières (Tignes), France 365
Champagny (La Plagne), France 324
Leogang (Saalbach), Austria 166
Montchavin (La Plagne), France 324
Peisey (Les Arcs), France 232
Le Pré (Les Arcs), France 232
Samoëns (Flaine), France 345
St-Martin (Three Valleys), France 359
Stuben (St Anton), Austria 190
Vaujany (Alpe-d'Huez), France 222

VILLAGE CHARM
Resorts with traditional character – from mountain villages to mining towns
Champéry, Switzerland 475
Courmayeur, Italy 420
Les Gets, France 285
Lech, Austria 145
Megève, France 290
Mürren, Switzerland 500
Saas-Fee, Switzerland 504
Val d'Anniviers, Switzerland 516
Wengen, Switzerland 533
Zermatt, Switzerland 538

BLACK RUNS
Resorts with steep, mogully, lift-served slopes within the safety of the piste network
Alta/Snowbird, Utah 594/605
Andermatt, Switzerland 473
Argentière/Chamonix, France 247
Aspen, Colorado 566
Beaver Creek, Colorado 573
Courchevel, France 262
Jackson Hole, Wyoming 613
Whistler, Canada 651
Winter Park, Colorado 589
Zermatt, Switzerland 538

POWDER PARADISES
Resorts with the snow, the terrain and (ideally) the lack of crowds that make for powder perfection
Alta/Snowbird, Utah 594/605
Andermatt, Switzerland 473
Big Sky, Montana 608
Big White, Canada 630
Fernie, Canada 633
La Grave, France 288
Jackson Hole, Wyoming 613
Kicking Horse, Canada 638
Monterosa Ski, Italy 432
Revelstoke, Canada 645
Ste-Foy, France 357

CHOPAHOLICS
Resorts where you can have a day riding helicopters or cats
Aspen, Colorado 566
Courmayeur, Italy 420
Fernie, Canada 633
Lech/Zürs, Austria 145
Monterosa Ski, Italy 432
Revelstoke, Canada 645
La Thuile, Italy 460
Verbier, Switzerland 520
Whistler, Canada 651
Zermatt, Switzerland 538

TOP TERRAIN PARKS
Alpine resorts with the best parks and pipes for freestyle thrills
Les Arcs, France 232
Avoriaz, France 242
Cervinia, Italy 409
Davos, Switzerland 480
Les Deux-Alpes, France 272
Ischgl, Austria 130
Laax, Switzerland 485
Lech, Austria 145
Livigno, Italy 425
Mayrhofen, Austria 153
Méribel, France 302
La Plagne, France 324
Saalbach-Hinterglemm, Austria 166
Saas Fee, Switzerland 504
St Moritz, Switzerland 509

WEATHERPROOF SLOPES
Alpine resorts with fairly snow-sure slopes if the sun shines, and trees in case it doesn't
Les Arcs, France 232
Courchevel, France 262
Courmayeur, Italy 420
Laax, Switzerland 495
Schladming, Austria 173
Selva, Italy 451
Serre-Chevalier, France 347
Sestriere, Italy 458
La Thuile, Italy 460

MOTORWAY CRUISING
Long, gentle, super-smooth pistes to bolster the frail confidence of those just off the nursery slope
Les Arcs, France 232
Breckenridge, Colorado 575
Cervinia, Italy 409
Cortina d'Ampezzo, Italy 415
Courchevel, France 262
Megève, France 290
La Plagne, France 324
Snowmass, Colorado 580
La Thuile, Italy 460
Vail, Colorado 582

RESORTS FOR BEGINNERS
European resorts with gentle, snow-sure nursery slopes and easy, longer runs to progress to
Alpe-d'Huez, France 222
Cervinia, Italy 409
Courchevel, France 262
Flaine, France 278
Montgenèvre, France 312
Passo Tonale, Italy 436
La Plagne, France 324
La Rosière, France 341
Saas-Fee, Switzerland 504
Soldeu, Andorra 97

SPECIALLY FOR FAMILIES
Alpine resorts where you can easily find accommodation surrounded by snow, not by traffic and fumes
Les Arcs, France 232
Avoriaz, France 242
Flaine, France 278
Lech, Austria 145
Montchavin (La Plagne), France 324
Mürren, Switzerland 500
Puy-St-Vincent, France 336
La Rosière, France 341
Saas-Fee, Switzerland 504
Ste-Foy, France 357
Vars/Risoul, France 393
Wengen, Switzerland 533

SNOW-SURE BUT SIMPATICO
Alpine resorts with high-rise slopes, but low-rise, traditional-style buildings
Andermatt, Switzerland 473
Arabba (Sella Ronda), Italy 443
Argentière (Chamonix), France 247
Ischgl, Austria 130
Lech/Zürs, Austria 145
Monterosa Ski, Italy 432
Obergurgl, Austria 158
Saas-Fee, Switzerland 504
Val d'Anniviers, Switzerland 516
Zermatt, Switzerland 538

SPECIAL MOUNTAIN RESTAURANTS
Alpine resorts where mountain restaurants can really add an extra dimension to your holiday
Alpe-d'Huez, France 222
Serre-Chevalier, France 347
Cortina d'Ampezzo, Italy 415
Courmayeur, Italy 420
Kitzbühel, Austria 137
Megève, France 290
La Plagne, France 324
Saalbach, Austria 166
Selva, Italy 451
Zermatt, Switzerland 538

MODERN CONVENIENCE
Alpine resorts where there's plenty of slope-side accommodation where you can ski from the door
Les Arcs, France 232
Avoriaz, France 242
Courchevel, France 262
Flaine, France 278
Les Menuires, France 297
Obertauern, Austria 163
La Plagne, France 324
Puy-St-Vincent, France 336
La Tania, France 361
Tignes, France 365
Val Thorens, France 386

LIVELY NIGHTLIFE
European resorts where you'll have no difficulty finding somewhere to boogie
Chamonix, France 247
Ischgl, Austria 130
Kitzbühel, Austria 137
Mayrhofen, Austria 153
Méribel, France 302
Pas de la Casa, Andorra 95
Saalbach, Austria 166
Sauze d'Oulx, Italy 438
Sölden, Austria 177
St Anton, Austria 190
Val d'Isère, France 376
Verbier, Switzerland 520
Zermatt, Switzerland 538

OTHER AMUSEMENTS
Alpine resorts where those not interested in skiing or boarding can still find plenty to do
Bad Gastein, Austria 115
Chamonix, France 247
Cortina d'Ampezzo, Italy 415
Davos, Switzerland 480
Kitzbühel, Austria 137
Megève, France 290
St Moritz, Switzerland 509

AFFORDABLE FUN
Resorts towards the bottom of our RPI league table that have good reasonably extensive slopes
Bad Gastein, Austria 115
Hochkönig, Austria 128
Monterosa Ski, Italy 432
Pyrenees (Baqueira-Beret, Formigal), Spain 661
Pyrenees (La Mongie, St-Lary-Soulan), France 338
Sauze d'Oulx, Italy 438
Schladming, Austria 173
Sella Ronda, Italy 443
SkiWelt (Ellmau, Söll), Austria 118/182

Interactive resort shortlist builder at www.wtss.co.uk

Our resort chapters

How to get the best out of them

FINDING A RESORT

The bulk of the book consists of the chapters listed on the facing page, devoted to individual major resorts, plus minor resorts that share the same lift system. Sometimes we devote a chapter to an area not dominated by one resort, in which case we use the area name (eg Monterosa Ski in Italy, Hochkönig in Austria, Val d'Anniviers in Switzerland).

Chapters are grouped by country: first, the six major European countries (now including Germany); then the US and Canada (where resorts are grouped by states or regions); then minor European countries; and finally Japan. Within each group, resorts are ordered alphabetically. In Austria, the main skiing regions of Vorarlberg, the westernmost 'land', are dealt with under that name.

Short cuts to the resorts that might suit you are provided (on the pages preceding this one) by a table of comparative **star ratings** and a series of **shortlists** of resorts with particular merits.

At the back of the book is an **index** to the resort chapters, combined with a **directory** giving basic information on hundreds of other minor resorts. If the resort you are looking up is covered in a chapter devoted to a bigger resort, the page reference will be to the start of the chapter, not to the exact page on which the minor resort is described.

There's further guidance on using our information in the chapter 'Choosing your resort', on page 76 – designed to be helpful particularly to people with little or no experience of ski resorts, who may not appreciate how big the differences between one resort and another can be.

READING A RESORT CHAPTER

There are various standard items at the start of each resort chapter. In the left margin, **star ratings** summarise our view of the resort, including its suitability for different levels of skill. The more stars, the better. In major resort chapters we give an expanded set of 18 ratings. Then comes our **Resort Price Index** – explained in outline on the facing page and in detail in the feature chapter on page 29.

We give web addresses of the **tourist office** (in North America, the ski lift company) and phone numbers for recommended **hotels**. We give star ratings for hotels – either official ones or ones awarded by major tour operators. The UK tour operators offering **package holidays** in major resorts are listed in the chapter, along with those of minor resorts that are covered in the same chapter.

Our **mountain maps** show the resorts' own classification of runs. On some maps we show black diamonds to mark expert terrain without defined runs. We do not distinguish single diamond terrain from the steeper double diamond.

We include on the map any lifts definitely planned for construction for the coming season.

MAJOR LIFTS

On our piste maps we use the following symbols to identify **fast lifts**. Slow chairlifts do not get a chair symbol.

  fast chairlift

  gondola

  hybrid chondola

  cable car

  railway/funicular

THE WORLD'S BEST WINTER SPORTS RESORTS

To find a minor resort, or if you are not sure which country you should be looking under, consult the index/directory at the back of the book, which lists all resorts alphabetically.

RESORT PRICE INDEX BOXES

Our RPI figures show how prices in each resort compare with the average European resort, taking account of food and drink, lift pass, ski hire and lessons. RPIs around the average figure of 100 are in blue boxes. RPIs of 85 or less get a green box. RPIs of 115 or more get a red box. Our price survey is fully explained, and some of the results are summarised, in our chapter on 'Cutting your costs', on page 29.

RPI	85
RPI	100
RPI	115

89

Our resort chapters

Interactive resort shortlist builder at www.wtss.co.uk

Andorra

Andorra is a tiny, almost entirely mountainous state sandwiched between France and Spain. It has built its prosperity on the twin pillars of tax-haven status and low-cost tourism – particularly winter tourism, and particularly in the UK market. Andorra used to be seen primarily as a cheap and cheerful holiday destination, attracting singles and young couples looking for a good time in the duty-free bars and clubs, as well as learning to ski or snowboard. But the place has changed radically over the last 25 years.

Even in our first edition, published 17 years ago, we noted that rising package prices meant you could get holidays to Italy for less than you paid to go to Andorra (though on-the-spot prices were higher in Italy). We applauded heavy investment in snowmaking, but noted a lack of investment in lifts, which we described as 'antiquated'. So we viewed the place as a bit backward, and dealt with it at the back of the book, along with eastern Europe.

Then, over the next decade, the lift systems and piste-grooming fleets were transformed, making the skiing much more appealing to intermediates as well as beginners. Upmarket hotels were built (though they often resembled Spanish summer package hotels, with self-service buffet meals). Prices continued to rise, but the rises seemed justified by improvements that put the resorts – Soldeu and its neighbours, in particular – in the same league as many Alpine resorts. Eight years ago, we recognised that Andorra had arrived: we moved it from the back of the book into the main sequence of European skiing countries, along with the Alpine big four.

We really had no choice: at that stage, Andorra was the fourth most popular winter sports destination for Brits, and threatened to displace Italy from third place. Industry estimates were that Andorra had an amazing 14% of the UK skiing package market – more than Switzerland, the USA and Canada combined. And practically all these people were going to three resorts – the resorts we cover in the following chapters. Then, the bubble burst. Prices continued to rise, and during the last decade Andorra's market share declined relentlessly.

Now, it seems the decline has bottomed out; the two latest editions of the *Crystal Ski Industry Report* put Andorra's share of the package holiday market at 6% and (for last season) 6.4% (about the same as Switzerland and well under half of Italy's share).

But we'll be amazed if Andorra regains anything like its former popularity: our price survey shows Arinsal to be cheap, but much bigger Soldeu is as expensive as many high-profile Alpine resorts. Frankly, Soldeu is not in the same league as many of those resorts. Strikingly, the lift pass is one of the most expensive in Europe. You can get a pass covering 350 lifts and 1000km of pistes around Kitzbühel for the same sort of money.

So where does this leave Andorra as a holiday destination for skiing Brits? Well, Pas de la Casa is a bit cheaper than Soldeu – and package holidays may be appreciably cheaper there. Arinsal may look a bit of a bargain, but it's not a resort we are very keen on, and there are lots of much better resorts in the Alps that cost the same,

LIFT PASSES

Ski Andorra
The Ski Andorra pass covers all Andorran areas and allows skiing at any single one of them each day: €193 for five non-consecutive days

GRANDVALIRA

← Andorra's main ski area, Grandvalira, shared between Pas de la Casa and Soldeu, has a good mix of wooded and open terrain

NEWS

2010/11: In Arcalis there is a new extended and covered moving carpet in the snow garden. More snowmaking has been added to the newish green run, El Pont. And there are three new rope tows to improve connections in the Basera and Canaleta areas.

Phone numbers
From abroad use the prefix +376

TOURIST OFFICES

Ski Andorra
skiandorra@ski
andorra.ad
www.skiandorra.ad

Arcalis
info@vallnordturisme.
com
www.vallnord.com

or less. Basically, if you are looking at holidays in Andorra, it now makes obvious sense to look at Italy and Austria too.

STAYING DOWN THE VALLEY

Several valley towns can be used as alternative bases to the main resorts. **Encamp** has a powerful 18-seat gondola giving a quick way into the Grandvalira ski area shared by Soldeu and Pas de la Casa. It is relatively cheap, but plagued by its situation on the traffic-choked main road. **La Massana** is a more appealing town, and is linked by gondola to the Pal-Arinsal ski area. It is also fairly convenient for trips to Arcalis (covered by the lift pass). **Ordino** is nearer still to Arcalis, and pleasantly rustic, but it has no direct access to slopes.

The capital, **Andorra la Vella**, is not far down the valley from Encamp and also choked by traffic and fumes. There are plenty of high-quality hotels and restaurants, plus bars and nightclubs and duty-free shopping. The clientele is mainly Spanish. At Escaldes-Engordany, just outside the centre, the splendid Caldea spa has a fantastic array of pools, baths and treatments.

OUTINGS TO ARCALIS

Arcalis is the most remote area of slopes in Andorra, tucked away at the head of a long valley, and most British visitors to Soldeu or Pas de la Casa never bother with it. But for non-beginners it makes a very worthwhile day trip, particularly from Arinsal and Pal. The terrain is varied and scenic, the slopes are usually deserted except at weekends (when locals pour in), and the snow is usually the best around. There is excellent intermediate and beginner terrain, but what marks it out is the expert terrain, including lots of off-piste between the marked runs. 'A real jewel – the boarder in our group was in heaven,' said a reporter. There is no accommodation at the mountain.

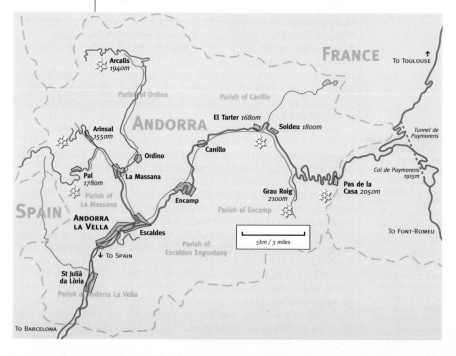

Arinsal

Lively base that suits beginners best, with a cable car link to Pal to keep intermediates amused

TOP 10 RATINGS

Extent	★
Fast lifts	★★
Queues	★★★
Snow	★★★★
Expert	★
Intermediate	★★
Beginner	★★★★
Charm	★
Convenience	★★★
Scenery	★★★

RPI	85
lift pass	£160
ski hire	£115
lessons	£80
food & drink	£125
total	**£480**

NEWS

2011/12: More snowmaking is planned.

2010/11: In Arinsal, the terrain park gained snowmaking. In Pal, a new family fun area opened at La Caubella.

VALLNORD

Pal's slopes, reached by cable car, are attractively wooded and more extensive than Arinsal's ↓

- ➕ Lively bars
- ➕ Ski school geared to British needs
- ➕ Cable car link with Pal and shared Vallnord lift pass with Arcalis
- ➕ Pretty, treelined slopes in Pal

- ➖ Arinsal slopes are bleak and very confined (though this does mean children can't stray far)
- ➖ Long, dour village with no focus
- ➖ Poor bus link to Arcalis

Tour operators are able to tempt British beginners here in large numbers. The Brit-oriented ski school must be the key factor; prices are no longer greatly different from those in more attractive Austrian and Italian resorts.

THE RESORT

Arinsal sits near the head of a steep-sided valley north of Andorra la Vella. Pal has a more open setting in another valley. The two are linked by cable car.

The lower town of La Massana is linked by gondola to Pal's slopes, and makes a better base for competent skiers and riders wanting to spend some time at Arcalis (read the Andorra introduction). The Vallnord lift pass covers all of these areas.

Village charm The resort is a long, narrow village of grey, stone-clad buildings – with some rustic appeal, despite newer development. The atmosphere is friendly and relaxed.

Convenience The main gondola starts from the village centre, and staying close to it is convenient; the alternative is a six-pack 1km from the centre at Cota, with a piste to return. There are free buses running through the village linking the lift bases.

Scenery Shady valleys and nicely wooded slopes dominate. Pic Negre gives a decent viewpoint.

THE MOUNTAINS

The area above Arinsal is an open but narrow, east-facing bowl. Pal has the most densely wooded slopes in Andorra. Most face east; those down to the link with Arinsal face north. The latest piste map has lost its ghastly sepia tint, but remains a poor affair. Signposting is good though.

Slopes Arinsal's slopes consist essentially of a single, long, narrow bowl above the upper gondola station at Comallempla, served by a network of chairs and drags, including a quad and a six-pack. Almost at the top is the cable car link with Pal. Pal's slopes are widely spread around the mountain, with four main lift bases, all reachable by road. The main one, La Caubella, at the opposite extreme from the Arinsal link, is the arrival point of the gondola from La Massana.

Fast lifts Access is by gondola or fast chairlift. Other fast chairs exist, but there are still many slow lifts too.

Queues Reporters note few problems. But downloading on Arinsal's gondola may generate queues at peak times. The cable car link with Pal can be closed by high winds.

Terrain parks Arinsal's big freestyle area is regularly upgraded. It has its own lift, a huge half-pipe, rails and jumps, a boardercross, a beginner zone and a chill-out area.

Snow reliability With most runs above 1950m, the north-easterly orientation and a decent amount of snowmaking, snow is relatively assured. In 2011 the pistes were 'kept in excellent shape', despite the prolonged drought. There are plans to increase snowmaking for 2011/12. Grooming is good.

Experts This isn't a great area for experts, but there is some great tree

KEY FACTS

Resort	1475m
	4,840ft
Slopes	1550-2560m
	5,090-8,400ft
Lifts	31
Pistes	63km
	39 miles
Green	16%
Blue	36%
Red	38%
Black	10%
Snowmaking	40%

UK PACKAGES

Crystal, First Choice,
Inghams, Neilson,
Skitracer, Solo's, STC,
Thomson

Phone numbers
From abroad use the
prefix +376

TOURIST OFFICE

Arinsal and Pal
www.vallnord.com

skiing in Pal. Arcalis has more to offer.
Intermediates Arinsal offers a fair
range of difficulty, but competent
intermediates will want to explore the
much more interesting, varied and
extensive Pal slopes, and perhaps
make a day trip or two to Arcalis.
Beginners Around half the guests here
are beginners. A special pass is
available (15 euros per day), though
we guess most people will book ski/
pass/tuition packs from their tour
operators. The wide, gentle nursery
slopes set apart from the main runs
are 'great, exactly what my beginner
girlfriend needed'. They can get
crowded at peak times, though. There
are long easy runs to progress to, as
well.
Snowboarding It's a fine place to
learn, but over half the lifts are drags
and some of them are vicious. There
are some flat sections in Pal.
Cross-country There isn't any.
Mountain restaurants These are mainly
uninspiring self-service snackeries, and
crowded.
Schools and guides A key factor in the
appeal of the resort; over half the
instructors are native English speakers.
A 2011 reporter was very impressed
with the group lessons: 'The instructor
was excellent and very encouraging.'
He was also impressed by the school's
low prices, though again many people
will book through tour operators.
Private snowboard lessons were also
rated 'good value'.
Families There are themed ski
kindergartens for four- to eight-year-
olds and nurseries for children aged
one to four at both Pal and Arinsal.

STAYING THERE

Hotels The Princesa Parc (736500) is a
big, glossy 4-star place near the
gondola – a 'lovely hotel, with good
rooms and exceptional staff'; swanky
spa (open to non-guests) and a
bowling alley. Rooms in the hotel
Arinsal (838889) are not large, but it is
ideally placed and has a pleasant bar.
The 3-star Crest (738020) is at the
bottom of the run to Cota, handy for
the fast chair up to the slopes;
'spacious apartment, perfectly good
meals'. The Xalet Verdú (737140) is a
smooth little 3-star. The Micolau
(737707) is a characterful stone house
near the centre with a jolly, beamed
restaurant.
Self-catering There is a reasonable
choice of places.
Eating out The Surf disco-pub comes
highly recommended in 2011 for 'the
best steaks ever'. The Sidreria Pub
Herri (formerly Rocky Mountain) also
does steaks and grills. El Cisco is a
Tex-Mex place in a lovely wood and
stone building.
Après-ski Arinsal has plenty of lively
bars and discos. The hotel Arinsal has
good-value pints. The Derby Irish is a
'good place to relax and watch your
ski school video'. Quo Vadis is tipped
for a 'pint and pizza'.
Off the slopes There are helicopter
rides, dog sledding, snowmobiling,
snowshoeing, tobogganing, snow
bikes and ice-diving. But a past
reporter found family entertainment
limited in the evenings. Andorra la
Vella is half an hour away by taxi or
infrequent bus.

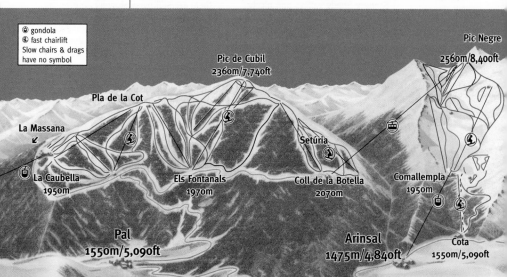

Pas de la Casa

Andorra's liveliest resort – great if you like that kind of thing; we prefer to ski the extensive Grandvalira ski area from a quieter base

TOP 10 RATINGS

Extent	★★★
Fast lifts	★★
Queues	★★★
Snow	★★★★
Expert	★
Intermediate	★★★
Beginner	★★★★
Charm	★
Convenience	★★★★
Scenery	★★★

RPI   105

lift pass	£210
ski hire	£145
lessons	£100
food & drink	£135
total	**£590**

NEWS

2010/11: A newly developed area – Sunset Park Peretol – opened between Grau Roig and Soldeu, with a terrain park and beginner slopes served by draglifts.

GRANDVALIRA

Although there are trees above Pas, practically all the slopes are open to the weather ↓

➕ Grandvalira area including Soldeu rivals major Alpine resorts for size

➕ Some conveniently placed hotels

➕ Andorra's liveliest nightlife

➕ Attractive hotel at Grau Roig

➖ Pas is an eyesore and suffers from traffic (and fumes)

➖ Weekend crowds from France

➖ Exposed, open slopes with few trees for poor-weather days

Pas has the reputation as Andorra's wildest party resort, and we don't doubt it. Having driven through it and skied down to it, we are quite happy to stay over the hill in Soldeu – or, for doorstep access to the Grandvalira slopes, at secluded Grau Roig. So are you, it seems: reports are rarely sighted.

THE RESORT

Pas de la Casa is right on the border between Andorra and France, and owes its development as much to duty-free sales to the French as to skiing. The resort attracts a lot of French and Spanish families, as well as Brits on a budget. The slopes extend over a ridge to the mini-resort of Grau Roig (pronounced 'Rosh') and beyond to Soldeu – all operating under the name Grandvalira. You can drive to central Andorra via a toll tunnel, which avoids the high Port d'Envalira pass.
Village charm The resort is a sizeable collection of dreary concrete-box-style apartment blocks and hotels, a product of the late 1960s and early 1970s. The central area at the base of the slopes is traffic-free, but elsewhere traffic and fumes are intrusive. By contrast, Grau Roig has an isolated hotel in attractively wooded setting.

Convenience Most accommodation is conveniently placed near the lift base and slopes. There are plenty of shops and bars, as well as a sports centre.
Scenery Pas has a bleak position near the top of a high mountain pass, but there are fine views from the ridges.

THE MOUNTAINS

The slopes above Pas are all open, and vulnerable to bad weather. But there is some attractively wooded terrain in the Grau Roig valley.
Slopes The Grandvalira ski area offers almost 200km of pistes – comparable to big-name Alpine resorts such as Kitzbühel and Les Deux-Alpes.

The home slopes, facing north-east, descend from a high, north-south ridge; lifts go up to it at four points. Runs on the far side of the ridge converge on Grau Roig. And a single lift goes on further west to the bowl of Llac del Cubil and the rest of the Grandvalira ski area. On the far side of this bowl is the arrival station of the 6km gondola up from Encamp. In the opposite direction out of Pas, a six-pack serving two runs heads towards another ridge and the French border.
Fast lifts Fast chairs exist, but they are outnumbered by slow ones and drags.
Queues Queues are rarely serious during the week. But at weekends and French school holidays some can develop, especially at Grau Roig.
Terrain parks There's a slope-style area with jumps at Grau Roig, the Isards terrain park and a boardercross at Pas.
Snow reliability The combination of height and lots of snowmaking means good snow reliability and a season that often lasts until late April. But we've found the snow has been better in the Soldeu sector.

KEY FACTS

Resort	2100m
	6,890ft

Grandvalira (Soldeu/
El Tarter/Pas/Grau
Roig)

Slopes	1710-2560m
	5,610-8,400ft
Lifts	65
Pistes	193km
	120 miles
Green	16%
Blue	35%
Red	29%
Black	20%
Snowmaking	43%

UK PACKAGES

Crystal, First Choice,
Independent Ski Links,
Inghams, Lagrange,
Neilson, Skitracer,
Thomson

Phone numbers
From abroad use the
prefix +376

Central reservations
phone number
For all resort
accommodation call
801074

TOURIST OFFICE

www.grandvalira.com

Experts There are few challenges on-piste – the black runs are rarely of serious steepness, and moguls are sparse. But there seem to be plenty of off-piste slopes inviting exploration – above Grau Roig, in particular.

Intermediates The local slopes cater for confident intermediates best, with plenty of top-to-bottom reds on the main ridge; they lack variety – and can be tricky for more timid intermediates, for whom Soldeu perhaps makes a better base.

Beginners There are beginner slopes in Pas and Grau Roig. The Pas area is a short but inconvenient bus ride out of town. Progression to longer runs is easier in the Grau Roig sector.

Snowboarding Boarding is popular with the young crowd the resort attracts. Drags are usually avoidable.

Cross-country There are 13km of loops near Grau Roig.

Mountain restaurants There are routine places on the ridge above Pas and the top of the gondola from Encamp, most serving 'good basic food'. There are better places at Grau Roig. The Rifugi dels Llacs dels Pessons at the head of the bowl is a cosy, beamed table-service place with BBQ specials – 'loved it; ate and drank too much'. The Grau Roig itself does 'lovely food, reasonably priced' – but of course it's a valley restaurant, so doesn't count.

Schools and guides The ski school has a high reputation – good English.

Families There are ski kindergartens at Pas and Grau Roig, and a non-ski one at the latter.

STAYING THERE

There are lots of hotels and apartments.

Hotels Himàlaia-Pas (735 515) is the place we hear most about (which is not saying much): 'good position, nice bar, reasonable food, comfy rooms'; and a pool and sauna. The Grau Roig hotel (755 556) is in a league of its own (as well as a valley of its own); very comfortable and smart, with a spa. 'Lovely food,' says a reporter this year. Beware of hotels catering for the 18-30 crowd.

Apartments The Frontera Blanca are simple, but in pole position at the foot of the slopes.

Eating out It's not a resort for gourmets – but there is a wide enough choice of places to eat. Local tips include Cal Padrí (Catalan food) and KSB (good steakhouse).

Après-ski Après-ski can be very lively, at least at peak holiday times (a March visitor found the resort 'quite quiet'). The most popular watering holes at present are Deja Beer, a quirky pub with tapas and Wi-Fi, Paddy's Irish Pub and the lively Underground. But we really could use more reports from readers.

Off the slopes You can go dog sledding, snowmobiling and snowshoeing; otherwise there's visiting the leisure centre, shopping, or taking a trip to Andorra la Vella for more serious and stylish shopping and the Caldea spa (more about this in the introduction to Andorra).

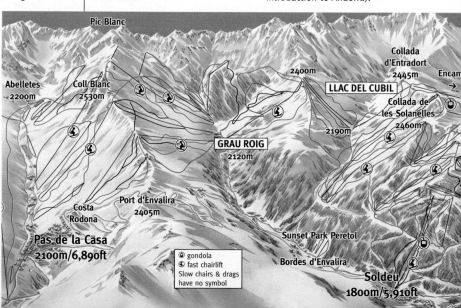

Soldeu

Our favourite place to stay in Andorra: not an attractive village, but centrally placed in the impressive Grandvalira ski area

RATINGS

The mountains

Extent	★★★
Fast lifts	★★
Queues	★★★
Terrain p'ks	★★★★
Snow	★★★
Expert	★
Intermediate	★★★★
Beginner	★★★★
Boarder	★★★★
X-country	★
Restaurants	★★
Schools	★★★★★
Families	★★

The resort

Charm	★
Convenience	★★★
Scenery	★★★
Eating out	★★★
Après-ski	★★★★
Off-slope	★

RPI	110
lift pass	£210
ski hire	£155
lessons	£100
food & drink	£150
total	**£615**

NEWS

2010/11: A newly developed area – Sunset Park Peretol – opened between Grau Roig and Soldeu, with a terrain park and beginner slopes served by draglifts, open until 9pm daily.

GRANDVALIRA

The direct runs back to the lift base, parallel to the lift line, are the steepest runs here, and just about genuine blacks ➜

+ Grandvalira area including Pas de la Casa rivals major Alpine resorts in terms of size

+ Excellent beginner and early intermediate terrain

+ Ski school has excellent British-run section for English-speaking visitors

– Village is spread along a busy through-road, lacking atmosphere

– Slopes can get very crowded

– Very little to interest experts

– Expensive lift pass, and beginners may be charged the full cost

– Not much to do off the slopes

If we were planning a holiday in Andorra, it would be in Soldeu (or the isolated hotel at Grau Roig, up the road – covered in Pas de la Casa). It is best placed to explore the extensive Grandvalira area. But the village is a difficult place to like, and beginners are forced to buy one of Europe's most pricey passes.

THE RESORT

Soldeu is set on a steep hillside facing the ski area across the valley. It is on the busy road that runs down the valley from France to Andorra la Vella and on to Spain; El Tarter, a few miles down the valley, and Canillo, a few miles further, are alternative bases with major lifts. The slopes link with Pas de la Casa – see separate chapter – to form the Grandvalira area. Outings to other resorts in Andorra are possible – Arcalis (read the Andorra intro chapter) in particular is worth the trip, but it's easiest by car. The Ski Andorra lift pass covers all the resorts.

VILLAGE CHARM ★
An urban ribbon
The village is an ever-growing ribbon of modern hotels, apartments and bars, with the occasional shop, with traditional stone cladding and mostly chalet-style roofs. Sounds OK, but it isn't; this is not a place to wander about at tea-time – there is no focus or atmosphere, and traffic on the through-road can be heavy and sometimes fast.

CONVENIENCE ★★★
Over the river
A steep hillside leads down from the village to the river, and the slopes are on the opposite side. A gondola from village level or a six-pack take you to the heart of the slopes at Espiolets, and a wide bridge across the river forms the end of the piste home, with elevators to take you up to street level. There are ski lockers at the bottom or top of the gondola. Along the road down to El Tarter, hotels and apartments are sold by tour operators under the Soldeu banner – so check where your proposed accommodation is if you want to avoid long walks or lots of bus rides. There is a valley bus running every 20 minutes (1.40 euros).

SCENERY ★★★
Unremarkable
Soldeu sits in a long, quite attractively wooded valley, and from the slopes there are wide mountain views, but they don't include much of a dramatic nature.

THE MOUNTAINS

Soldeu's main local slopes are on open mountainsides above the woods; there are runs in the woods back to most of the lift bases, but they can be challenging especially when conditions are not particularly good. Reporters praise signposting, but classification of the runs often overstates difficulty.

EXTENT OF THE SLOPES ★★★☆☆
Pleasantly varied but crowded
The gondola rises over wooded, north-facing slopes to **Espiolets**, a broad shelf that is virtually a mini-resort – the ski school is based here, and there are extensive nursery slopes. From Espiolets, a gentle run to the east takes you to an area of long, easy runs served by a six-pack. Beyond that is an extensive area of more varied slopes that links with the Pas de la Casa area. Going west from Espiolets takes you to the open bowl of **Riba**

Escorxada and the arrival point of the gondola up from El Tarter. From here, another six-pack serves sunny slopes on Tosa dels Espiolets and a fourth goes to the high point of Tossal de la Llosada and the link with **El Forn** above Canillo.

FAST LIFTS ★★☆☆☆
Fine access but ...
Most of Grandvalira's key lifts are high-speed chairs or gondolas, but there are a lot of slow lifts too.

QUEUES ★★★☆☆
Some bottlenecks
The lift system generally copes. There can be morning queues for the gondola but the next-door chair offers a choice. Up the mountain, the chairlifts in both directions out of Grau Roig are the main bottleneck; the quad at Cubil and access to Tosa Espiolets are also 'awful', says a February 2011 visitor. You may find

KEY FACTS

Resort	1800m
	5,910ft

Grandvalira (Soldeu/ El Tarter/Pas/Grau Roig)	
Slopes	1710-2560m
	5,610-8,400ft
Lifts	65
Pistes	193km
	120 miles
Green	16%
Blue	35%
Red	29%
Black	20%
Snowmaking	43%

crowds on some blue slopes (including lots of school classes snaking along) – the reds and blacks are much quieter.

TERRAIN PARKS ★★★★☆
Now there are two
The main park above Riba Escorxada has a good reputation; the shaping crew service it daily and organise frequent events. A park-only day pass is available. Features include a triple line of kickers, huge gap jump, jib and giant airbag. There's a great selection of rails, including a big rainbow rail and wave-box and two wall rides. For beginners there are three small jumps, 5m medium jump and a couple of fun boxes. A half-pipe is built when conditions permit. A draglift serves the park, but a fast quad nearby takes you slightly higher up. The new Sunset Park, above Bordes d'Envalira, opened in 2011 and caters for all levels. It is floodlit in the evenings, with music.

SNOW RELIABILITY ★★★☆☆
Much better than people expect
Despite its name (Soldeu means Sun God) the slopes generally enjoy reliable snow. Most slopes are north-facing, with a good natural snow record and there's extensive snowmaking. Excellent grooming helps maintain good snow.

FOR EXPERTS ★☆☆☆☆
Hope for good snow off-piste
It's a limited area for experts, at least on-piste. The Avet black run down to Soldeu deserves its grading, but most of the other blacks would be no more than reds (or even blues) in many resorts. The blacks on Tosa dels Espiolets are indistinguishable from the neighbouring (and more direct) red and blue, for example. And don't go looking for moguls – the grooming is too thorough. But there is plenty of off-piste potential – notably in the bowl above Riba Escorxada, in the

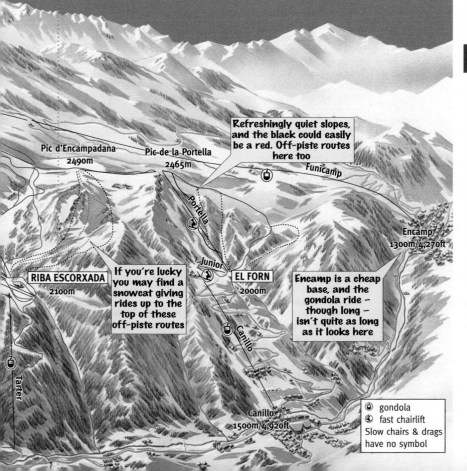

Image labels:

Pic d'Encampadana 2490m

Pic-de-la-Portella 2465m

Refreshingly quiet slopes, and the black could easily be a red. Off-piste routes here too

Funicamp

Portella

Encamp 1300m/4,270ft

Junior

RIBA ESCORXADA 2100m

If you're lucky you may find a snowcat giving rides up to the top of these off-piste routes

EL FORN 2000m

Encamp is a cheap base, and the gondola ride – though long – isn't quite as long as it looks here

Canillo

Tarter

Canillo 1500m/4,920ft

gondola
fast chairlift
Slow chairs & drags have no symbol

Interactive resort shortlist builder at www.wtss.co.uk

In the centre every inch is built on or paved – note the balconies overhanging the pavements – and despite the carefully styled buildings the place lacks charm ➜

GRANDVALIRA

LIFT PASSES

Grandvalira

Prices in €

Age	1-day	6-day
under 12	31	153
12 to 17	38	196
18 to 64	42	221
over 65	19	111

Free under 6, over 70
Beginner pass €26 per day in Canillo, El Tarter, Grau Roig and Pas de la Casa / Portes des Neiges

Notes
Covers all lifts in Soldeu, El Tarter, Canillo, Grau Roig and Pas de la Casa; pedestrian and half-day passes available

Alternative passes
The Ski Andorra pass covers all Andorran areas and allows skiing at any single one of them each day; €193 for five non-consecutive days

Espiolets and Solanelles areas (we've had a great time there in fresh powder), and above El Forn (including off-piste routes, dotted on our map). And the off-piste remains untouched for days because most visitors are beginners and early intermediates. When conditions permit at weekends, a snowcat takes people up to Pic d'Encampadana, from where four off-piste routes descend to Riba Escorxada. There's no definition of what an off-piste route is on the piste map of course (ie whether it is avalanche controlled, marked and patrolled).

FOR INTERMEDIATES ★★★★
Lots to explore
There is plenty to amuse intermediates. The area east of Espiolets is splendid for building confidence, and those already confident will be able to explore the whole mountain. Riba Escorxada is a fine section for mixed-ability groups. The Canillo/El Forn sector has an easy, little-used blue run along the ridge with excellent views all the way to Pal and Arinsal and an easy black in the valley. Many of the blues and reds have short steeper sections, preceded by a 'slow' sign and netting in the middle of the piste to slow you down.

FOR BEGINNERS ★★★★
Good, but not ideal
In some respects this is an excellent place to start, particularly because of the school. But it's not ideal: you have to go up the mountain to the nursery slopes, which is not only inconvenient but also expensive. There is no special

beginner pass here (unlike other base villages in the area). If you buy a ski pack through your tour operator, you may not care, of course. Soldeu's Espiolets nursery area is vast, and there's a smaller area at Riba Escorxada, above El Tarter – both with a moving carpet. They are relatively snow-sure, and there are numerous easy pistes to move on to (though the crowds can be off-putting). The runs to resort level can be quite challenging because of crowds and snow conditions. Near-beginners are often better off riding a lift down.

FOR BOARDERS ★★★★
Pick of the Pyrenees
Soldeu has become the home of snowboarding in the Pyrenees. This is a perfect place for beginners to learn on wide, gentle slopes that are served mainly by chairs, not drags. For the more advanced, Soldeu offers some good off-piste and the best terrain parks in the Pyrenees. Backcountry enthusiasts should also visit Arcalis, which has the steepest terrain and heli-boarding, and Pal, for the tree boarding. Loaded is a snowboard shop run by pro rider Tyler Chorlton.

FOR CROSS-COUNTRY ★
Er, what cross-country?
There are loops not far away at Grau Roig (read the Pas de la Casa chapter), reachable by bus.

MOUNTAIN RESTAURANTS ★★
Not a highlight
A reporter this year sums things up well: lots of places combining 'long queues and terrible food, but dig

SCHOOLS
Soldeu
t 735191

Classes
15hr: €120
Private lessons
From €86 for 2hr for
1 person; €8 extra
per additional person

CHILDCARE
**Nurseries run by ski
school**
Ages 2 to 4; €41 per
day
**Snow gardens run by
ski school**
Ages 3 to 6; five days
€156

Ski school
For ages 6 to 11;
15hr: €111

GETTING THERE
Air Toulouse
170km/110 miles
(2hr45)

Rail L'Hospitalet-Près-
L'Andorre (25km/
16 miles); buses and
taxis to Soldeu

ACTIVITIES
Indoor Thermal spas,
bowling (at Pas),
leisure centre (pools,
hot tub, gym)
Outdoor Helicopter
rides, snowmobiling,
dog sledding, tubing,
snowshoeing,
paragliding

UK PACKAGES
Crystal, Elegant
Resorts, First Choice,
Inghams, Lagrange,
Neilson, Skitracer, STC,
Thomson
El Tarter First Choice,
Neilson

Phone numbers
From abroad use the
prefix +376
**Central reservations
phone number**
Call 801074

TOURIST OFFICE
www.grandvalira.com

deeper and there are some gems'. An earlier reporter enjoyed 'really nice Catalan sausage, roast cod, beef shank, pasta' at various places. The table service section of Pi de Migdia at the top of the El Tarter gondola has a 'relaxed atmosphere and courteous staff'. Not far away the Riba Escorxada restaurant includes a trattoria-pizzeria with a neat little terrace. At Espiolets, the Gall de Bosc (steakhouse) has table service. But the best places are over towards Pas de la Casa – read that chapter.

SCHOOLS AND GUIDES ★★★★★
One of the best for Brits
The school is well set up to deal with the huge numbers of beginner Brits, with a dedicated team of mostly native English-speaking instructors led by an Englishman. Recent reporters include one who was 'unimpressed', but we've also had endorsements: 'could not praise the school enough'; 'by the end of the week our two beginners were skiing parallel on red runs'.

FOR FAMILIES ★★☆☆☆
Unconvincing
Soldeu doesn't strike us as a great place for families, with its busy through-road and remote slopes. Whether skiing or not, children are looked after at the mid-mountain stations. There are nurseries and snow gardens for children aged three to six at various points, and a kids' circuit with themed runs at Riba Escorxada above El Tarter.

STAYING THERE
A wide range of UK tour operators offer packages here, mainly in hotels but with some apartments and chalets.
Hotels Beware hotels sold under the Soldeu name that are actually some way out of town.
★★★★★Sport Hotel Hermitage (870670) At the foot of the slopes; all bedrooms are suites with mountain views. A huge spa is part of the hotel.
★★★★Sport Hotel Village (870550) Right by the Hermitage. Stylish public areas – comfortable chairs and sofas, high ceilings, beams and picture windows.
★★★★Sport (870600) Over the road from the other two Sports. Lively, comfortable bar and disco-bar.
★★★★Piolets Park (871787) Beside the gondola, with a pool and spa. 'Good buffet-style food.'

★★★★Himàlaia (878515) Central, with sauna, steam and hot tub. Impressed a reporter with 'good rooms, excellent food, helpful staff'.
★★★★Euro Esquí (3027 7154) On road to El Tarter but hotel 'provides a minibus and is comfortable with large rooms and good buffet food'.

EATING OUT ★★★☆☆
Some atmospheric places
Most of Soldeu's restaurants are hotel-based. But we've enjoyed meals in two atmospheric old restored buildings: Fat Albert's (steaks, fish, burgers), and Borda del Rector (Andorran cuisine), nearer to El Tarter than Soldeu. Upstairs in Pizzerama is 'a great find' for 'fresh pasta, friendly service'. The Bruxelles hotel does 'delicious food, reasonable prices'.

APRES-SKI ★★★★☆
No shortage of live music
A reporter this year who 'enjoyed the live music at the Villager' but little else is pressing for a cut to 3 stars for this traditionally lively resort, and we are tempted. But others seem to have had a bit more fun – 'great atmosphere' and live music at the Aspen, 'people of all ages until the early hours' at very busy Fat Albert's. New last season was the Harp, an Irish place with live music which we hear was very successful.

OFF THE SLOPES ★☆☆☆☆
Head downhill
Soldeu has lots of sporting activities, including tubing and ballooning, but is otherwise not great in this respect. The Sport Hotel Hermitage (pricey) and Piolets Park (cheaper) both have excellent spas. Down in Canillo is the Palau de Gel – see below. Andorra la Vella has good shopping and the Caldea spa – see Andorra intro.

LINKED RESORT – 1710m
EL TARTER
El Tarter has grown over recent years and is rather sprawling, with no real centre. It is 'dull' at night. But it's otherwise a good base for the area.

LINKED RESORT – 1500m
CANILLO
This acceptably pleasant spot has no runs to valley level, but has the impressive Palau de Gel – an Olympic ice rink plus pool, gym, tennis etc.

Austria

Austria's holiday recipe is quite distinctive. It doesn't suit everybody, but for many holidaymakers nothing else will do; in particular, French resorts will not do.

Austria is the land of cute little valley villages clustered around onion-domed churches – there are no monstrous modern apartment blocks here. It's the land of friendly wooded mountains, reassuring to beginners and timid intermediates in a way that bleak snowfields and craggy peaks will never be. It's the land of friendly, welcoming people who speak good English. And it's the land of jolly, alcohol-fuelled après-ski action – in many resorts starting in mid-afternoon with dancing in mountain restaurants, and going on as long as you have the legs for it.

Back in the 1980s, Austria dominated the British skiing market. But gradually the powerful allure of the high, snow-sure French mega-resorts began to exert itself. By 1995, France had taken the lead and has kept it ever since. But the pendulum is now swinging back, with the gap between the two countries gradually closing. Why? There are three key factors: lift systems – these days, the most efficient lift systems in Europe are not in France but in Austria; snowmaking, which in Austria is now top-notch, and means that skiers who want reliable snow can now get it even at low altitude; and on-the-spot prices. With exchange rates making any trip abroad a costly experience, differences between high and very high prices start to matter. And as our price survey shows, Austria is generally cheaper than France and sometimes much cheaper.

Being the land of cute valley villages and friendly wooded mountains does have a downside: resorts that conform to this pattern are at low altitude, and as a result don't offer reliably good natural snow. Of course, you may be lucky – and recent seasons have included some bumper natural snow years for much of Austria. But the snowmaking is key; most low resorts have radically increased their snowmaking capacity in the last decade, and in our Mayrhofen chapter you can see an extreme example of what it achieved during the famously tricky 2010/11 season. Of course, it does require low temperatures; but in midwinter, especially, lack of snow generally coincides with low night-time temperatures, even at low altitudes, and snowmaking comes into its own.

There are also some resorts that don't conform to the Austrian pattern, including some excellent high-altitude ski areas – notably Obergurgl, Ischgl and Obertauern – and some excellent glacier areas, including what we reckon are the world's best, at Hintertux and in the Stubai valley. Western Austria also has areas that get huge amounts of snow – Lech/ Zürs and especially Bregenzerwald, the snowiest corner of the Alps.

The improvement in Austrian lift systems over the last decade comes as a surprise to many people. When we invented our 'fast lifts' rating a few years back, we certainly got some surprises. The resorts with the highest proportions of fast lifts in their networks are Ischgl and Saalbach-Hinterglemm, both in Austria. Obergurgl also gets five stars, along with two French resorts and one Swiss.

The resorts of the SkiWelt are hugely popular with British skiers, and for good reason. For the Great British Intermediate, size matters, and the SkiWelt delivers size. With 279km of slopes, it is by a good margin the most extensive linked piste network in Austria, and we reckon the sixth largest in the Alps, which means the world. The map reproduced in the ad over the page shows what we're dealing with here.

We have chapters on two of the most popular resorts on the north side of the main mountain group (that is the left side as you look at the map) – Söll and Ellmau. Because Söll has traditionally been the British favourite, served by the largest number of tour operators, we deal with most of the less prominent resorts – Brixen, Hopfgarten, Itter and Westendorf – in the Söll chapter. In the Ellmau chapter we cover two small resorts nearby, Scheffau and Going.

Söll's popularity is understandable. It is a pleasant village with a good leisure centre, but for us the key to its attraction is Hohe Salve – the rounded but steep-sided peak reachable from Söll in only two gondola rides. Hohe Salve is the high-point of the whole area, and offers some genuinely testing slopes towards Söll and in the opposite direction.

But the great appeal of the SkiWelt lies in travel – skiing around a seemingly endless network of easy, pleasantly wooded slopes served by what is now an impressive lift system. In our 2011 edition we awarded the area four stars for fast lifts for the first time, reflecting the increased proportion of lifts that are gondolas or fast, detachable chairlifts.

Equally importantly, the area's snowmaking is now seriously impressive. Not only does the system cover three-quarters of the slopes, but they say they can cover half of those slopes from scratch in only three days. So even after a warm spell, the area can recover very quickly.

A key development in recent years was the construction of a proper link between Brixen, on the south side of the main SkiWelt area, and Westendorf. With a gondola to the top of Westendorf's main hill and an excellent red run back down, Brixen these days is arguably the best-positioned of all the SkiWelt resorts for full exploitation of the area.

This is partly because the SkiWelt is not isolated. Ski to the southern extremity of Westendorf's slopes, and you find buses to take you in only a few minutes to the lifts up to Pengelstein, one of the high-points of the Kitzbühel ski area, with another 170km of pistes. It can't be long before they build a lift link, and the combined area will then be able to claim 450km of linked pistes. A pass is available (the Kitzbüheler Alpen pass) that covers both areas, and some other areas as well.

Finally, there is the small matter of prices, and value for money. Like a number of other Austrian resorts, Söll and Ellmau fall into our 'green' category for resort prices, meaning that prices here for all aspects of a holiday are appreciably below the European average. Size + value – it's a compelling combination.

SNOWPIX.COM / CHRIS GILL

Friendly mountains wooded more or less to the top are typical of the SkiWelt; these are Westendorf's slopes, seen from Hohe Salve ↓

Introduction

103

Interactive resort shortlist builder at **www.wtss.co.uk**

REAL BIG
... AUSTRIA'S LARGEST INTERCONNECTED SKI AREA

2008/09, 2009/10 & 2010/11
SKIWELT VOTED
WORLD'S BEST SKI AREA

ADAC TOP SKIING AREA 2011
1. PLACE FOR THE BEST
VALUE FOR MONEY

SNOW GUARANTEED*

91 CABLE CARS AND LIFTS
279 KM OF SKI RUNS
70 REFRESHMENT STOPS

* OF THE 210 KILOMETRES OF SLOPES,
WHICH CAN BE ARTIFICIALLY SNOWED,
110 KM CAN BE WINTERISED IN JUST
3 DAYS.

SkiWelt
WILDER KAISER BRIXENTAL

www.skiwelt.at

SkiWelt Wilder Kaiser - Brixental
TEL +43 (0)5333 400
MAIL office@skiwelt.at

Brixen im Thale . Ellmau . Going
Hopfgarten . Itter . Kelchsau
Scheffau . Söll . Westendorf

In many resorts you have to deal with chaotic handling of the concept of 'ski routes'. If a resort's piste map explains what a ski route is (and some don't), it often says a ski route is a run that is marked and avalanche controlled but not groomed or patrolled. Officially, we are told, the rule throughout Austria is that a ski route is 'marked, protected against avalanche hazards and can be groomed and patrolled'. In practice, many routes are groomed; they may or may not be patrolled. This is madness. If such a run is groomed *and* patrolled, it is a piste, and should be identified as such so that people skiing solo can confidently go down it. If it is groomed *but not* patrolled, it opens up the insane possibility that people skiing solo might descend it by mistake.

These days, the thing that annoys us most about Austrian skiing is the strange business of opening hours, or strictly speaking closing hours. As spring approaches, lift closing times in the rest of the Alps drift towards 5pm or even later – we know of major high-altitude cable cars in Switzerland that in March run until 5.30pm, with the last piste patrol at 5.40. In Austria, basically things shut at around 4pm, even if there are three hours of daylight remaining. Nuts.

You're welcome to stay on the mountain drinking, and descend at leisure, and it has crossed our minds that the lift companies may be in the pay of the breweries. Instead of skiing on, people pack into mountain restaurants well before the end of the day and gyrate in their ski boots on the dance floor, on the tables, on the bar. There are open-air ice bars, umbrella bars and transparent 'igloo' bars in which to shelter from bad weather. Huge quantities of beer and schnapps are drunk, often to the accompaniment of German drinking songs or loud Europop music. In many resorts the bands don't stop playing until darkness falls, when the happy punters slide off in the general direction of the village to find another watering hole. After dinner the drinking and dancing starts again – for those who pause for dinner, that is.

Of course, not all resorts conform to this image. Lech and Zürs, for example, are full of rich, cool, 'beautiful' people enjoying the comfort of 4- or 5-star hotels. And villages such as Westendorf and Alpbach are pretty, quiet, family resorts. But lots of big-name places with the best and most extensive slopes are also big party towns – notably St Anton, Saalbach-Hinterglemm, Ischgl and Sölden.

Nightlife is not limited to drinking and dancing. There are lots of floodlit toboggan runs, and UK tour operator reps organise folklore, bowling, fondue, karaoke and other evenings.

One thing that all Austrian resorts have in common is reliably comfortable accommodation – whether it's in 4- or 5-star hotels with pools, saunas and spas or in great-value, family-run guest houses, of which Austria has thousands. Catered chalets and self-catering apartments are in general much less widely available.

The Germanic aversion to credit cards causes problems for many of our reporters. Many establishments do not accept cards – even quite upmarket hotels, as well as many ski lift companies. So check well in advance, or be prepared to pay in cash.

As other parts of Alpine Europe have cut out smoking in bars and restaurants, Austria has lagged behind, much to the displeasure of many British visitors. But there is progress. In 'multiple room establishments' the 'main room' now has to be non-smoking. In places with only one room, it's only in small places where you should now have to put up with smoke.

Salzburgerland's Ski Amadé lift pass is one of the world's biggest in terms of the amount of terrain and number of lifts covered. What's more, with a car you really could aim to get around most of the resorts it covers – they are clustered close together, no high passes are involved in getting from one resort to another, and many areas are geared to people arriving by car, with out-of-town lifts and car parks. (They are also conveniently close to Salzburg airport – we have taken early flights from the UK and been on the slopes here well before lunchtime; come departure day, we have skied until close of play, had a leisurely drive to the airport and still had time to kill before a flight home.)

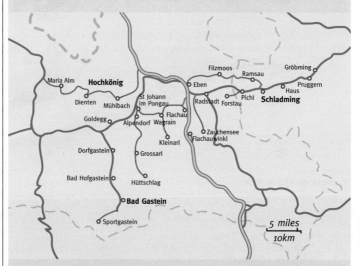

Some of the major resorts covered by the pass have their own chapters in the book. In the Schladming chapter we also cover the smaller linked resorts of Haus and Pichl, as well as Schladming's elevated satellite resort of Rohrmoos. Also close to Schladming is Ramsau in Dachstein, which has slopes at village level but also a lift up to the lip of the Dachstein glacier.

In the Bad Gastein chapter we cover not only the resorts in the Gastein valley but also the next-door valley of Grossarl, which shares a lift and piste network with Dorfgastein.

We also have a chapter on the major area of Hochkönig – an extensive network linking Mühlbach, Dienten, Hinterthal and Maria Alm.

Another big region is the Salzburger Sportwelt. The largest linked area here is the 200km three-valley system linking Wagrain to Flachau in one direction and to Alpendorf/St Johann im Pongau in the other. This area also embraces an extensive lift network linking Zauchensee, Flachauwinkl and Kleinarl, plus more modest lift systems at Filzmoos, Radstadt-Altenmarkt, Eben and Goldegg. Zauchensee often has the best snow in the region because of its height and north-facing slopes.

Considering the extent of the lift networks it covers (and the generally impressive efficiency of the lifts) the Ski Amadé pass is not expensive – 203 euros in high season last year. Prices on the spot are cheap as well. In our eating and drinking price survey, resorts in the Ski Amadé region came out among the cheapest in the Alps – with prices some 20% or even 30% cheaper than the average resort. This means big savings for families, in particular, in comparison with costs in more expensive resorts.

Introduction

Interactive resort shortlist builder at **www.wtss.co.uk**

85%
of the pistes are
serviced by
snow machines

GALSTERBERGALM 1986 m

HAUSER KAIBLING 2015 m

PLANAI 1894 m

HOCHWURZEN 1850 m

REITERALM 1860 m

FAGERALM 1885 m

ZAUCHENSEE 1350 m

GRAZ-KELN

ÖBLARN

PRUGGERN 680 m

GRÖBMING 776 m

AICH 750 m

ROHRMOOS

KEMAHHÖHE 1971 m

STODERZINKEN 2045 m

HAUS/ENNSTAL 752 m

SCHLADMING 745 m

FORSTAU 930 m

ALTENMARKT 856 m

PICHL 760 m   KLEMING 760 m   RADSTADT 862 m

MANDLING 820 m

RAMSAU AM DACHSTEIN 1108 - 1300 m

RITTISBERG 1582 m

ROSSBRAND 1600 m   TANNKOPPEN 1678 m

DACHSTEINGLETSCHER 2700 m

FILZMOOS 1057 m

NEUBERG

BISCHOFSMÜTZE

MAUTERNDORF

OBERTAUERN

GAMSKOGEL 2188 m

VILLACH-KL
ST. MICHAEL

GRAZ
TAMSWEG

SCHLADMING-DACHSTEIN
phone: +43 (0) 3687/23310
info@schladming-dachstein.com

FLACHAU, WAGRAIN, ST. JOHANN/ALPENDORF, ZAUCH
FLACHAUWINKL, KLEINARL, RADSTADT, ALTENMARKT, FIL
phone: +43 (0) 6457/2929, info@salzburgersportwelt.cc

Ski amadé

Austria's largest ski paradise -
much more than meets the eye!

Austria's largest ski paradise Ski amadé, **boasting 5 top ski resorts across 25 villages 270 modern lifts and 860 snow-sure pistes**, is waiting for you, all available on just one ski pass. Every element of your holiday blends perfectly together here: the fascinating mountain ranges, the natural charm of Austrian village life, unrivalled hospitality and delicious cuisine in the cosy mountain restaurants, all this within just one hour of Salzburg Airport! Simply put - much better value for money: special 4 for 3, Ladies' week and fantastic Easter packages are available!

Find out more and book online at **www.skiamade.com**

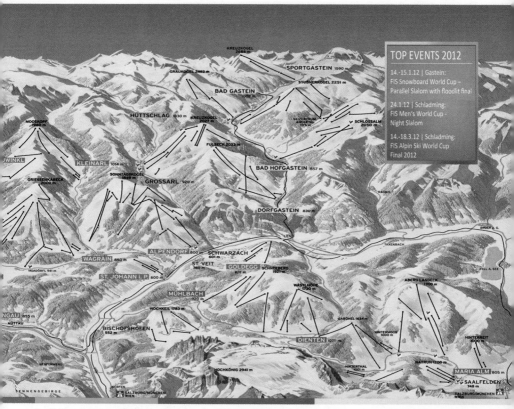

TOP EVENTS 2012

14.-15.1.12 | Gastein:
FIS Snowboard World Cup –
Parallel Slalom with floodlit final

24.1.12 | Schladming:
FIS Men's World Cup -
Night Slalom

14.-18.3.12 | Schladming:
FIS Alpin Ski World Cup
Final 2012

GROSSARLTAL	HOCHKÖNIG	GASTEIN
phone: +43 (0) 6414/281	phone: +43 (0) 6584/20388	phone: +43 (0) 6432/3393-0
info@sgrossarltal.com	info@hochkoenig.com	info@gastein.com

GETTING AROUND THE AUSTRIAN ALPS

Austria presents few problems for the car-borne visitor, because practically all the resorts are valley villages, which involve neither steep, winding approach roads nor high-altitude passes.

The dominant feature of the Tirol is the thoroughfare of the Inn valley, which runs from Landeck via Innsbruck to Kufstein. The motorway along it extends, with one or two breaks, westwards to the Arlberg pass and on to Switzerland. This artery is relatively reliable except in exceptionally bad weather – the altitude is low, and the road is a vital transport link that is kept open in virtually all conditions.

The Arlberg – which divides Tirol from Vorarlberg, but which is also the watershed between Austria and Switzerland – is one of the

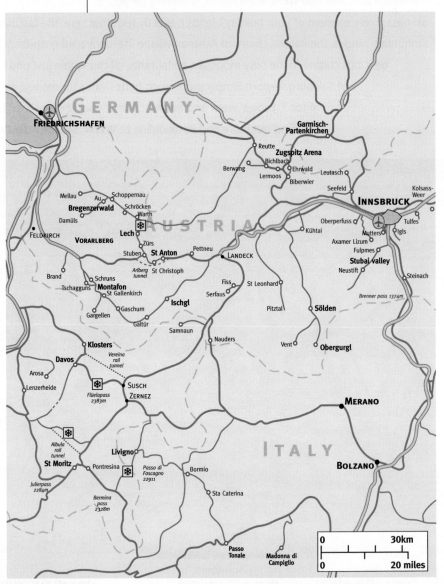

few areas where driving plans are likely to be seriously affected by snow. The east–west Arlberg pass itself has a long tunnel underneath it; this isn't cheap, and you may want to take the high road when it's clear, through Stuben, St Christoph and St Anton. The Flexen pass road to Zürs and Lech branches off northwards, just to the west of the Arlberg summit; this is often closed by avalanche risk even when the Arlberg pass is open.

All cars must display a motorway toll sticker, available at gas stations in and around Austria and at post offices and newsagents. There's a 10-day one for 4.50 euro and a two-month one for 11.50 euro. Throughout winter, whether in snowy conditions or not, cars must be equipped with winter tyres. Be aware that cars hired in Germany or Italy might not meet this requirement.

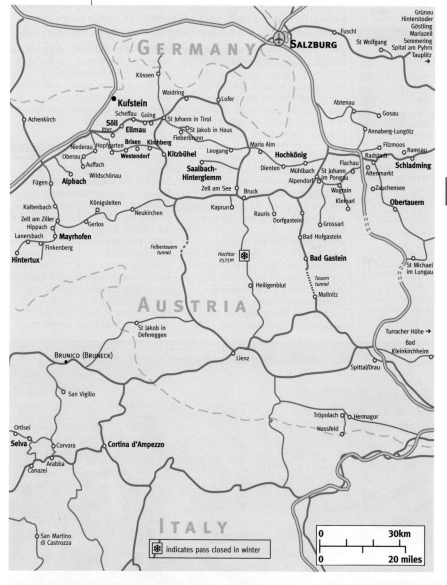

indicates pass closed in winter

0   30km

0   20 miles

Alpbach

*Small but perfectly formed: it's the pretty village rather than the
extent of the slopes that have attracted generations of Brits*

TOP 10 RATINGS

Extent	★
Fast lifts	★★★
Queues	★★★
Snow	★★
Expert	★
Intermediate	★★
Beginner	★★★★
Charm	★★★★★
Convenience	★★
Scenery	★★★

RPI   75

lift pass	£150
ski hire	£90
lessons	£80
food & drink	£115
total	**£435**

NEWS

2011/12: In low
season under 15s ski
for free if a parent
buys a weekly pass.
On two low-season
weeks, lodging, lift
pass and equipment
hire packages at 4
days for the cost of 3
are offered. There's
talk of a lift
connection with
Wildschönau but it
may not be finished
until 2012/13.

2010/11: A new
terrain park for all
levels was built.

➕ Charming, traditional, relaxed
village. Great for young children

➕ Handy, central nursery slopes

➕ Very low local prices – its RPI is
one of the lowest in the book

➕ Good, intermediate terrain, not
without challenges, but ...

➖ Slopes limited in extent and variety

➖ Main slopes are a shuttle-bus-ride
away (efficient service, though)

➖ Few long easy runs for beginners to
progress to

➖ Lower slopes can suffer from poor
snow, despite snowmaking help

This is an old British favourite – there is even a British ski club, the Alpbach
Visitors. The village is small, pretty and friendly, and inspires great loyalty in
regular visitors – one who has been going since 1983 claims only junior status.

THE RESORT

Alpbach is near the head of a valley,
looking south across it towards the
slopes of Wiedersbergerhorn. The Inn
valley is a few miles north, and trips
to Innsbruck and Salzburg are
possible. The Hintertux and Stubaier
glaciers are within reach. If you are
planning a tour, bear in mind that the
Kitzbüheler Alpen All Star pass covers
Alpbach and six other regions
including the Ski Welt (Söll, Ellmau
etc) and Kitzbühel. The local free guest
card is worth picking up from your
hotel too.

Village charm Alpbach is an
exceptionally pretty, captivating place;
traditional chalets crowd around the
pretty church, and the friendly nursery
slopes are only a few steps away.

Convenience The main village is the
place to stay for atmosphere and
après-ski but it involves using a free

shuttle-bus to and from the gondola at
Achenwirt, a mile away. The backwater
hamlet of Inneralpbach is more
convenient for the slopes, with its own
gondola up the mountain.

Scenery The pretty valley and low,
partly wooded ridges are picture-
postcard Tirol.

THE MOUNTAINS

Alpbach's main slopes are on two
flanks of the Wiedersbergerhorn.

Slopes The two gondolas from
Achenwirt and Inneralpbach take you
up to open, north-facing slopes above
the treeline, served by chairs and
drags. The runs are mostly of 200m to
400m vertical, but you can get more
by descending to the bottom of the
gondolas when snow is good down to
valley level. Behind Gmahkopf is a
short west-facing slope. A tiny
separate area at Reith is on the lift
pass and is 'well worth a morning's

WIEDERSBERGERHORN
2025m/6,640ft
Gmahkopf 1900m
Hornboden 1850m
Inneralpbach 1050m/3,440ft
1230m
Böglalm
1345m
REITH 1280m/4,200ft
Alpbach 1000m/3,280ft
Achenwirt 830m
Wölzenberg
Reith im Alpbachtal 670m/2,200ft

gondola
Slow chairs & drags
have no symbol

www.alpbachtal.com

alpbachtal
seenland

Alpbach Valley Austria

Your insider tip for skiing in one of the most authentic ski resorts of the Alps.
Alpbach is well known as Austria´s most beautiful village with its unique and
homogenous architectural style. Only 40 min. from Innsbruck airport.
Our tour operator partners: Inghams, Crystal, Thomson

Special Ski package 4:3

Only bookable via the tourist board Alpbachtal or any participating
accommodation. **Services**: 4 nights accommodation, 4-day skipass,
4-day ski equipment hire, Alpbachtal Seenland Card **for the price of 3!**
Validity: 8th – 15th January 2012 and 17th - 24th March 2012

Special skiing weeks for families

Free ski passes during low season for children up to the age of 15 (when
parents buy a 5- or 6-day ski pass, per parent one child gets a free pass)
Validity: 2nd December 2011 to 23rd December 2011 * 8th January 2012 to
27th January 2012 * 17th March 2012 to 15th April 2012

INFO & BOOKING

Alpbachtal Seenland Tourismus, Zentrum 1, A-6233 Kramsach/Tirol
Tel. +43 5336 600 600, Fax +43 5336 600 699, info@alpbachtal.at

KEY FACTS

Resort	1000m
	3,280ft
Slopes	670-2025m
	2,200-6,640ft
Lifts	21
Pistes	54km
	32 miles
Blue	28%
Red	63%
Black	9%
Snowmaking	80%

UK PACKAGES

Alpine Answers, Crystal, Inghams, Thomson

Phone numbers
From elsewhere in Austria add the prefix 05336; from abroad use the prefix +43 5336

TOURIST OFFICE

www.alpbachtal.at

DAVID MAXWELL LEES

Alpbach is a pretty village and great for beginners and families →

visit – well groomed and deserted', says a reporter. Access is by an eight-seat gondola. There's night skiing three times a week at Reith.

Fast lifts The only fast lifts are the two access gondolas – otherwise, it's all slow chairs and draglifts. A third gondola serves Reith.

Queues The gondolas make light work of any queues.

Terrain parks There's a new park for all abilities (see 'News') and a half-pipe on the Wiedersbergerhorn.

Snow reliability Alpbach cannot claim great snow reliability, but at least most of the Wiedersbergerhorn faces north, and 80% of the pistes are covered by snowmaking. The resort says this has helped to keep the runs to the valley open even in a poor snow year. Piste grooming is excellent.

Experts Alpbach isn't ideal, but the reds and the three blacks (often groomed) are not without challenge, and runs of 1000m vertical (when snow is good) are not to be sniffed at. There are a few off-piste routes and the schools take the top classes off-piste. One reporter 'skied with a guide for three hours in untracked powder'.

Intermediates There is fine intermediate terrain; the problem is that there's not much of it. This resort is for practising technique on familiar slopes, not high mileage.

Beginners Beginners love the sunny nursery slopes beside the village. But the main slopes are not ideal for confidence-building as most of them are red and there are only a few blues.

Snowboarding There's some good freeride terrain, plus a park and pipe.

Cross-country There are 20km of pretty cross-country trails that rise up beyond Inneralpbach.

Mountain restaurants There are several mountain restaurants – each worth a visit. Reporters recommend the Böglalm and 'great food and service' at the Dauerstoa Alm.

Schools and guides We've had good reports in the past on both main schools, Alpbach and Alpbach Aktiv; the Alpbach school boss is qualified to teach people with disabilities (and he himself has a disability).

Families Reporters find the compact, relaxed village and adjacent nursery slopes very child-friendly, with good ski kindergartens; babysitters can be arranged by the tourist office. And for some low-season dates children up to 15 get a free ski pass – see 'News'.

STAYING THERE

Hotels Of the smart 4-star places, the Alpbacherhof (5237) (spa, 'superb food and excellent service'), Alphof (5371) ('excellent, with friendly and welcoming staff') and ancient Böglerhof (5227) get most votes. The Berghof (5275) has been praised as 'an excellent 3-star; only 20 metres from the nursery slopes'. The 3-star Post (5203) is 'better than a lot of 4-stars'. The simpler Haus Thomas (5944), Haus Angelika (699 152 48202) and Haus Theresia (5386) have also been recommended. Pension Edelweiss (5268) is near the nursery slopes and offers B&B and 'clean, spacious, good value apartments'.

Apartments You can book some through the tourist office website.

Eating out Reader tips: the Post, Alphof, 'superb' Jakober in Alpbach, Wiedersbergerhorn in Inneralpbach, Rossmoos Inn (for its lively Tirolean evenings, 'superb' food) between the two. The toboggan run back to the resort has been recommended too.

Après-ski At peak times this is typically Tirolean, with lots of noisy teatime beer swilling in the bars of central hotels such as the Jakober and the Post. The latter has regular live music. Joe's Salett'l at Inneralpbach is popular. There are on-slope parties at the start and end of the season too.

Off the slopes There are pretty walks, tobogganing and trips to Innsbruck and Salzburg are possible. There is also an indoor ice rink (at Reith). The ski schools put on a weekly 'ski show'.

Bad Gastein

If you fancy 'taking the cure', there are few better resorts; even if you don't, you're likely to be impressed by the slopes

TOP 10 RATINGS

Extent	★★★
Fast lifts	★★★
Queues	★★★
Snow	★★★
Expert	★★★
Intermediate	★★★★
Beginner	★★
Charm	★★★
Convenience	★★
Scenery	★★★

RPI	90
lift pass	£180
ski hire	£95
lessons	£125
food & drink	£115
total	**£515**

NEWS

2010/11: In Dorfgastein a new blue slope opened in the mid-mountain area. A new snowshoe trail also opened. Elsewhere the ongoing improvements to snowmaking and piste widening continued.

+ Excellent, testing long runs for confident intermediates

+ Some relatively high slopes, snow-sure by Austrian standards

+ Lots of good, atmospheric, traditional mountain restaurants

+ Excellent thermal spas, but ...

− Main resorts are spa towns, lacking the usual Austrian resort ambience

− Bad Gastein itself has a steep, confined setting and narrow streets

− Valley slopes are split into five areas, and having a car helps

− Lacks genuinely easy runs

The Gastein valley is a bit different from Austrian ski resort norms. The slopes are quite testing – there are few blues, and some of those should be red. And the two main spa-town resorts are not from the usual mould, either; spacious Bad Hofgastein is preferable to steeply tiered, urban Bad Gastein. But little rustic Dorfgastein, down the valley, gets our vote. All three are covered here.

THE RESORT

Bad Gastein is an old spa town near the head of the Gastein valley. At its heart is the original spa area, laid out in a compact horseshoe on steep slopes. Above this, at the level of the railway and the gondola station, is a modern suburb with more lodgings.

The Stubnerkogel slopes above the town link with Bad Hofgastein, down the valley. Beyond that, a separate area of slopes above Dorfgastein links with Grossarl in the next valley. Up the valley is another separate area at Sportgastein. Various ski-bus routes

and trains connect the villages and lift stations, and 'run as per timetable' – though many bus services stop earlier than keen après-skiers would wish. Lots of resorts in this region are covered by the Ski Amadé lift pass (see p107), and easily reached.
Village charm The core is a curious mix of towny buildings – some grand, some modest. Away from here, the more modern hotels and guest houses have more of a normal ski resort feel.
Convenience The higher part of the resort is handy for the Stubnerkogel gondola, but the resort as a whole spreads widely, and the double chair

115

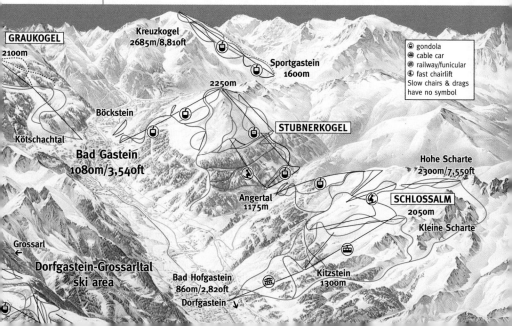

GRAUKOGEL
2100m

Kreuzkogel
2685m/8,810ft

Sportgastein
1600m

2250m

Böckstein

Kötschachtal

STUBNERKOGEL

Bad Gastein
1080m/3,540ft

Hohe Scharte
2300m/7,550ft

Angertal
1175m

SCHLOSSALM
2050m

Kleine Scharte

Grossarl
←

Dorfgastein-Grossarltal
ski area

Bad Hofgastein
860m/2,820ft

Kitzstein
1300m

Dorfgastein ↓

gondola
cable car
railway/funicular
fast chairlift
Slow chairs & drags
have no symbol

KEY FACTS

Resort	1080m
	3,540ft

The Gastein valley and Grossarl areas

Slopes	840-2685m
	2,760-8,810ft
Lifts	42
Pistes	201km
	125 miles
Blue	30%
Red	58%
Black	12%
Snowmaking	46%

Bad Gastein, Bad Hofgastein, Sportgastein only

Slopes	860-2685m
	2,820-8,810ft
Lifts	25
Pistes	112km
	70 miles

to the separate Graukogel area is on the opposite side of town.

Scenery The resort is set in virtually a gorge, steeply tiered and wooded. The slopes are higher than many Austrian resorts (particularly at Sportgastein), with wide views as a result.

THE MOUNTAINS

Most of the runs are on open slopes; this is a quite exposed region, and wind can affect both the snow and the lifts. Sportgastein is especially vulnerable. Graukogel is wooded. The piste map tries to cover all the areas and is difficult to follow and signposting 'is not a strong point', says a 2011 visitor.

Slopes From the Stubnerkogel gondola, a long blue run goes back to base, but most runs head for Angertal, which links with Bad Hofgastein.

Fast lifts There are quite a few gondolas, but also plenty of slow chairlifts and draglifts.

Queues There are few major problems.

Terrain parks There is a 'quiet and well-run' park on Stubnerkogel.

Snow reliability The slopes go a bit higher than many Austrian rivals – Sportgastein much higher – and there is snowmaking on crucial sections. 2011 reporters said the snow was better at Dorfgastein-Grossarl than at Stubnerkogel-Schlossalm.

Experts The few black runs are not severe, but many reds are long and satisfying. Graukogel has some of the most testing pistes. There is plenty of good off-piste – by the Jungeralm chair on the shady side of Stubnerkogel, for example. Sportgastein has an itinerary route from top to bottom.

Intermediates Confident intermediates, will find long, leg-sapping red runs in all sectors. The valley in general and Stubnerkogel in particular are not nearly so good for blue-run skiers. Sportgastein has a good range of runs, from gentle blues through easy reds to an easy black.

Beginners There are adequate nursery areas near the gondola station and at Angertal. But progression is awkward – the mountains are essentially steep. The few easy long runs are boring paths. There are no free lifts

Snowboarding The valley hosts snowboard events and there is good freeriding. Draglifts are dotted around.

Cross-country There are 90km of trails, but most are low down.

Mountain restaurants There are lots of pleasant huts doing decent food; but they can get crowded. Reader tips include Stubneralm, Jungerstube, Waldgasthof and Hirschenhütte.

Schools and guides Past reports on the school have been favourable.

Families Facilities are quite good. Angertal has a snow adventure park. Many of the huts have play areas too. There's also a 'Fun Center' for kids at Stubnerkogel, with playstations and other activities.

STAYING THERE

Most lodging is hotel-based.

Hotels There are lots of smart 4- and 3-star hotels with spa facilities. The Grüner Baum (25160) is a lovely retreat, but wildly inconvenient except for langlauf (though they do have a shuttle-bus). Reader tips include the quite grand Elizabeth Park (25510) and the 'quirky, friendly' Mozart (26860).

Eating out Choice is reasonable. The traditional Jägerhäusl offers 'lovely food, large portions, helpful staff'. The Amici serves 'great, good-value Italian'.

Après-ski The bars are lively at close of play; evenings are more subdued. The Silver Bullet and Haeggbloms are among the most popular. Bars for a quiet late drink include the Bellini bar and Ritz. There are a couple of discos and a casino.

Off the slopes The thermal spa/pool facilities are excellent and extensive; but expensive. There's ice climbing. Quite a few shops. Excursions to Salzburg are possible

Bad Hofgastein 860m

+ Sunny, spacious setting
+ Lovely long runs

− Lacks ski resort ambience
− Funicular from base can be crowded

Bad Hofgastein is a sizeable, spacious, quiet spa town set on flat ground in the widest part of the valley, with funicular access to the slopes.

Village charm The pedestrianised centre is compact and pleasant enough to stroll around, with lots of shops and restaurants. But it does feel like a town; there's little traditional Austrian rustic charm. There is a sizeable park next to the centre.

Convenience The resort spreads

UK PACKAGES
*Alpine Answers,
Crystal, Crystal Finest,
Ski Line, Ski Miquel,
STC, White Roc
Bad Hofgastein Crystal,
Crystal Finest,
Independent Ski Links,
Ski Club Freshtracks,
Ski Line, Skitracer, STC*

widely; much of the lodging is a long walk or ski-bus ride away from the funicular just outside the town. It's a longer ski-bus ride to Angertal.

Scenery Good valley views.

THE MOUNTAINS

Schlossalm is a broad, open bowl, with runs through patchy woods both to Bad Hofgastein and Angertal. As at Stubnerkogel, wind can be a problem.

Slopes The funicular to Kitzstein is followed by a cable car to the Schlossalm slopes. These link to Stubnerkogel via Angertal.

Fast lifts Getting up the mountain can be slow, and a few old chairs remain.

Queues The access lifts are queue-prone at peak times – and the cable car can be closed by wind.

Terrain parks There isn't one.

Snow reliability Snowmaking is fairly extensive, but snow-cover down to the bottom is unreliable, especially on the sunny Angertal slopes.

Experts There are no real challenges on the local pistes but there is ample opportunity to go off-piste.

Intermediates The Schlossalm slopes offer a good range of red runs, from easy to testing; the few blues are not all entirely easy. There are splendid long reds to the valley floor (we loved the away-from-the-lifts Hohe Scharte-Nord (10.4km long 1440m vertical).

Beginners There is a small nursery area at the funicular station. You have to catch a bus to the bigger nursery area at Angertal. And then you have few options for progression.

Snowboarding Good freeriding. Draglifts are dotted around though.

Cross-country Bad Hofgastein makes a fine base for cross-country when its lengthy valley-floor trails have snow.

Mountain restaurants Reader favourites are the self-service Aeroplanstadl and the table-service Pyrkerhof hotel. Other tips are Haitzingalm and Bärsteinalm.

Schools and guides 'Good teaching that pushed us,' says a recent report.

Families See Bad Gastein.

STAYING THERE

Hotels We enjoyed a stay two seasons ago at the 4-star Bismarck (66810) – excellent food, fairly central. Reader tips include the St Georg (61000; '200m to lift') and Palace (67150).

Apartments The Alpenparks resort is still 'excellent', says a repeat visitor.

Eating out There's plenty of choice.

Phone numbers
From elsewhere in Austria add the prefix 06434 (Bad Gastein), 06432 (Bad Hofgastein), 06433 (Dorfgastein); from abroad use the prefix +43 and omit the initial '0'

TOURIST OFFICE
For all resorts in the Gastein valley:
www.gastein.com

Piccola Italia does 'simple, tasty, good value' food. Other reader tips last year include the Salzburgerhof, the 'inexpensive' Chinese in the centre, and Dino's for pizza.

Après-ski Quiet by Austrian standards. The Aeroplanstadl on the hill and central Piccolo ice bar are popular at close of play. Head to Cafe Weitmoser, a historic little castle, for cakes. There are said to be a couple of disco bars.

Off the slopes The huge Alpen Therme Gastein spa has excellent pools etc. Other amenities include good shops, walking and a full-size ice rink.

Bad Gastein

117

DOWN-VALLEY VILLAGE – 830m

DORFGASTEIN

Dorfgastein is a quiet, rustic village. It has its own extensive slopes, shared with Grossarl in the next valley. A two-stage gondola and alternative chairlift start a little way outside the village. There is a nursery slope here, and another at the gondola mid-station. Like the other sectors, the mountain is essentially of red gradient, and best suits confident intermediates. On the front side there is one good long blue, but it doesn't go all the way to the valley. There is a terrain park. There are pleasant huts. We endorse readers' support for the excellent table-service Wengeralm – efficient, friendly service, jolly atmosphere and a slightly more wide-ranging menu than most. A 2011 visitor likes the Gipfstadl 'good food and excellent sun terrace'. The village ski schools get good reviews. Off-slope amenities are limited, but there's a pool with sauna and steam. Evenings are quiet. Reporters love the 4-star hotel Römerhof (7777) – 'superb food, great spa, extremely good value'.

Hot news in Austria's hottest resort, p177.

Interactive resort shortlist builder at **www.wtss.co.uk**

Ellmau

A good base on the extensive SkiWelt circuit, combining charm with reasonable convenience – good value too

TOP 10 RATINGS

Extent	★★★★
Fast lifts	★★★★
Queues	★★★★
Snow	★★
Expert	★
Intermediate	★★★★
Beginner	★★★★
Charm	★★★
Convenience	★★★
Scenery	★★★

RPI   85

lift pass	£190
ski hire	£70
lessons	£115
food & drink	£115
total	**£490**

NEWS

2011/12: Parents will be able to buy one pass between two, which either can use.

2010/11: An eight-pack, with child safety bar, replaced the Osthang quad from the bottom of the Eiberg quads up to Brandstadl.

+ Part of the SkiWelt, Austria's largest linked ski area

+ Excellent nursery slopes

+ Quiet, charming family resort – more appealing than Söll

+ Cheap, even by Austrian standards

+ Snowmaking is now more extensive and well used; even so ...

− Low altitude can mean poor snow

− Main lift a bus ride from village – though reachable via a draglift

− Runs on upper slopes mostly short

− Few challenges on-piste

− Limited range of nightlife

− The slopes can get crowded

− Appallingly inadequate piste map

If you like the sound of the large, undemanding SkiWelt circuit, Ellmau has a lot to recommend it as your base – quieter than Söll, but with more amenities than other neighbours such as Scheffau (covered at the end of the chapter). But consider Brixen, Hopfgarten and Westendorf too – covered in the Söll chapter.

THE RESORT

Ellmau sits at the north-eastern corner of the SkiWelt – an area of 279km of linked slopes that's an impressive 15km across. Other parts of it are covered in our chapter on Söll. You can also progress (via Brixen) to the slopes of Kitzbühel; these and various other ski areas within easy reach are covered by the Kitzbüheler Alpen AllStar ski pass.

Village charm Although sizeable, the village remains quiet, with traditional chalet-style buildings, welcoming bars and shops, and a pretty church.

Convenience Accommodation is scattered; there is some out by the funicular to the main slopes, but we prefer to stay in the compact centre of the village. There is a decent bus service but it doesn't cope well with high season demand.

Scenery The craggy Wilder Kaiser and the long SkiWelt ridge make a fine backdrop to the village.

THE MOUNTAINS

The piste map is hopelessly over-ambitious in trying to show the whole area in a single view. There's a mix of short runs at altitude and much longer ones to the villages.

Slopes The funicular railway on the

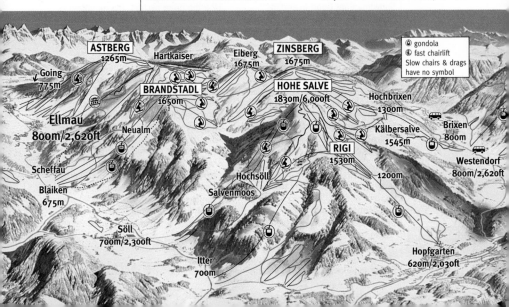

Good grooming and lots of snowmaking mean that the SkiWelt's largely intermediate pistes are normally kept in good condition →

SNOWPIX.COM / CHRIS GILL

KEY FACTS

Resort	800m
	2,620ft

Entire SkiWelt	
Slopes	620-1890m
	2,030-6,200ft
Lifts	91
Pistes	279km
	173 miles
Blue	44%
Red	46%
Black	10%
Snowmaking	75%

LIFT PASSES

SkiWelt Wilder Kaiser-Brixental

Prices in €

Age	1-day	6-day
under 16	20	98
16 to 17	32	156
over 18	40	195

Free under 7
Senior no deals
Beginner points cards
Notes
Covers Wilder Kaiser-Brixental area from Going to Westendorf, and the ski-bus; single ascent and part-day options; family discounts

edge of the village takes you up to Hartkaiser, from where a fine long red leads down to Blaiken (Scheffau's lift base station). Here, one of two gondolas takes you up to Brandstadl. Immediately beyond Brandstadl, the slopes become rather bitty; an array of short runs and lifts link Brandstadl to Zinsberg. From Zinsberg, long, south-facing pistes lead down to Brixen, where a gondola goes up to Choralpe in Westendorf's area and a lovely north-facing red piste comes back down. From Choralpe you can also head off towards the Kitzbühel slopes. Part-way down to Brixen you can head towards Söll, and if you go up Hohe Salve, you get access to a long, west-facing run to Hopfgarten.

Ellmau and Going share a pleasant little area of slopes on Astberg, slightly apart from the rest of the area, and well suited to the unadventurous and families. One piste leads to the funicular for access to the rest of the SkiWelt. The main Astberg chair is rather inconveniently positioned, midway between Ellmau and Going.
Fast lifts The main access lift is a fast funicular. Fast chairs are increasingly common on the upper slopes; last season's Osthang eight-pack moves the area to a ★★★★ rating.
Queues Lift upgrades have greatly improved this once queue-prone area and most reporters find few queues. But there are several bottlenecks at slow chairs around the mountain, and

when snow is poor the links between Zinsberg and Eiberg get crowded.
Terrain parks Ellmau has its own terrain park, the Kaiserpark, with beginner and expert boxes, rails and kickers, as well as a chill-out zone.
Snow reliability With a low average height, and important links that get a lot of sun, the snowmaking that the SkiWelt has installed is essential; the Ellmau-Going sector now claims 80% of slopes are covered. Snowmaking can, of course, only be used when temperatures are low enough. The north-facing Eiberg area above Scheffau holds its snow well. Grooming is 'excellent', and reports have praised 'ace' snowmaking.
Experts There are steep plunges off the Hohe Salve summit, a ski route from Brandstadl down to Scheffau and a little mogul field between Brandstadl and Neualm, but the area isn't really suitable unless you go off-piste.
Intermediates With good snow, the SkiWelt is a paradise for those who love easy cruising. There are lots of blue runs and many of the reds deserve a blue classification. It is a big area and you get a feeling of travelling around. In good snow the long red runs to the valley – down the Hartkaiser funicular, for example – are excellent. The main challenge arises

Don't miss the latest in Austria.
Check out p177.

Interactive resort shortlist builder at **www.wtss.co.uk**

when ice and slush can make even gentle lower slopes tricky. For timid intermediates the easy slopes of Astberg are handy.

Beginners Ellmau has an array of good nursery slopes covered by snow-guns. The main ones are at the Going end, but there are some by the road to the funicular. The Astberg chair opens up a more snow-sure plateau at altitude. The Brandstadl area has a section of short easy runs.

Snowboarding Ellmau is a good place to learn as its local slopes are easy.

Cross-country The SkiWelt area has a total of 170km of trails, including long and challenging ones, but trails at altitude are lacking.

Mountain restaurants There are many small places providing good-value food in pleasant surroundings. The Rübezahl Alm above Ellmau is one of our favourites – a lovely old hut with good food (the ribs have been recommended) and lots of different rooms and areas which make it very cosy; but it gets very busy. Other reporter tips include: the Jägerhütte (below Hartkaiser) for 'a lovely atmosphere and good food' before enjoying the 'quiet and pleasant' home run, and the 'jolly' Hartkaiser ('loos accessed by escalator!'). The Bergkaiser has 'efficient service, good value food' and the Blattlalm on Astberg 'super views'.

Schools and guides The four schools (counting one at Going) have good reputations – except that classes can be very large. We have no recent reports, but Top has been highly rated for children's lessons: 'All our children had a great time in different English-only speaking classes. It was a busy week, but most classes were small.'

Families Ellmau is an attractive resort for families, reporters agree: 'Loved by 14 families who ski with us each year.' Top ski school has been praised (see 'Schools'). Kindergartens seem to be satisfactory and include fun ideas such as a mini train to the lifts. Top's Kinderland has its own fun park and play areas. But we lack reports.

STAYING THERE

Ellmau is essentially a hotel and pension resort, though there are apartments that can be booked locally.

Hotels The Bär (2395) is an elegant, relaxed luxury place. Recommended by reporters for its friendly welcome and good spa. The Kaiserhof (2022) is another luxury option. The Sporthotel (3755) is 'incredible for the price', with 'huge five-course meals, gorgeous pool/spa facilities, huge lounge'. The Hochfilzer (2501) is central and well equipped (with outdoor hot tub, indoor pool, sauna, steam); the simpler Pension Claudia is under the same ownership and use of hotel facilities can be arranged. Kaiserblick (2230) has good spa facilities and is right by the piste.

Apartments There is a wide variety. The Landhof apartments have impressed a regular visitor – 'spacious, immaculate, well equipped' – with pool, sauna and steam room. The supermarket on the road to Going has been rated 'excellent'.

Eating out The jolly Gasthof Lobewein is a splendid, big, central chalet, with cheerful service in countless rooms and excellent food. The Ellmauer Alm has also been recommended (see below). A reporter's young kids loved the 'no nonsense food' in the Mexican.

Après-ski Bettina is good for coffee and cakes. Memory is the early-evening riotous party pub. Pub 66 and Ötzi have regular events such as karaoke and 'erotic dancers'. The Ellmauer Alm at the Going end of the

village has fun, live entertainment and is 'always good' with 'good service despite being very busy'. Tour operator reps organise events such as sleigh rides and tubing, and bowling and Tirolean folklore evenings in Söll. Ski Night and the Instructors' Ball Ellmau have 'a party atmosphere' each week. The toboggan run from the Astberg lift is also recommended.

Off the slopes A guest card entitles you to various discounts, including entry to the KaiserBad leisure centre. There are many excursions available, including to Innsbruck, Salzburg and Vitipeno. Valley walks are spoiled by the busy main road. Heading up to Hartkaiser by funicular railway to relax on the terrace 'was a highlight for our non-skiers', writes a reporter.

LINKED RESORT – 775m

GOING

Going is a tiny, attractively rustic village, ideal for families looking for a quiet time. It is well placed for the limited but quiet slopes of the Astberg and for the vast area of nursery slopes between here and Ellmau. Prices are low but, being at one extreme end of the Ski Welt, it's not an ideal base for covering the whole of the region on the cheap unless you have a car to speed up access to Scheffau and Söll. The Lanzenhof (2428) is a cosy central pension doing excellent traditional food in its woody dining rooms. Its wellness centre includes a sauna and a steam room.

Scheffau 745m

+ Plenty of cheap and cheerful pensions for those on a budget
+ Pretty village
+ Local slopes are some of the steepest in the area

– Little to amuse experts
– Not ideal for beginners either
– Not much to do off the slopes
– Quiet at night

Scheffau is one of the most attractive of the region's villages and centrally placed for quick access to most parts of the Ski Welt ski area.

Village charm It is a rustic little place with a pretty white church and spacious yet not sprawling. And it has a definite centre 1km off the busy main road (away from the slopes), which increases its charm at the cost of convenience.

Convenience The slopes and lifts at Blaiken (where there are several hotels) are a bus ride away.

Scenery Much like Ellmau and Söll.

THE MOUNTAIN

Scheffau is well placed for the most central section of pistes in the SkiWelt.

Slopes Two gondolas (one an eight-seater) give rapid access from Blaiken.

Fast lifts See Ellmau and Söll.

Queues The two gondolas shift weekend queues well at Blaiken.

Snow reliability Eiberg is the place to go when snow is poor.

Experts The local pistes are among the longest and steepest in the SkiWelt.

Intermediates The whole Ski Welt area is great for intermediates.

Beginners The nursery slope is in the village, nowhere near other slopes, making Scheffau a poor choice for mixed-ability parties; but a reporter rates the easy blues at Brandstadl as 'excellent' for beginner snowboarders.

Cross-country See Ellmau and Söll.

Mountain restaurants See Ellmau, Söll.

Schools and guides There are two. We lack recent reports though.

Families The non-ski nursery has a good reputation. There's a children's ski area and both schools have a 'Kinder-Kaiserland'.

STAYING THERE

Hotels Reporters recommend the 3-star Alpin (8556) – 'very helpful, friendly, good value restaurant'; pool, sauna and steam room. The central Gasthof Weberbauer (8115) is said to be 'friendly, quiet, with good food'. At the Blaiken gondolas, the Blaiken (8126) and Waldhof (8122) are good-value gasthofs (the latter 'worth a visit for the rustic loos alone').

Eating out There aren't many village restaurants. Donatello has been recommended for pizza and Gasthof Weberbauer for good varied food.

Après-ski 'Non-existent,' says one happy reporter, but there are a couple of bars. The Sternbar nearest to the gondolas is lively after the lifts close. There's bowling and tobogganing.

Off the slopes Walking apart, there is little to do. Tour operators organise trips to Innsbruck and Salzburg.

Phone numbers
From elsewhere in Austria add the prefix 05358; from abroad use the prefix +43 5358

TOURIST OFFICES

Wilder Kaiser
(Ellmau, Söll, Scheffau, Going)
www.wilderkaiser.info

SkiWelt
www.skiwelt.at

Ellmau

121

Interactive resort shortlist builder at www.wtss.co.uk

Hintertux / Tux valley

Small, unspoiled, traditional villages, high snow-sure glacier slopes and lots of other areas covered by the valley lift pass

TOP 10 RATINGS

Extent	★★★
Fast lifts	★★★
Queues	★★★
Snow	★★★★★
Expert	★★★
Intermediate	★★★
Beginner	★★
Charm	★★★
Convenience	★★
Scenery	★★★

RPI 85

lift pass	£190
ski hire	£80
lessons	£100
food & drink	£120
total	**£490**

NEWS

2011/12: A 10-person gondola is due to replace the double chair from Tuxer Fernerhaus on the glacier.

At Finkenberg, a six-pack is due to replace the Katzenmoos double chair, on the upper slopes of Penken.

2010/11: Work to improve snowmaking at Tuxer Fernerhaus (glacier area), and at Rastkogel above Lanersbach, was completed.

+ Hintertux has one of the best year-round glaciers in the world

+ Lanersbach's slopes form part of an extensive area, linked to Mayrhofen

+ Wide-ranging area lift pass

+ Some excellent off-piste

+ A choice of quiet, unspoiled, traditional villages to stay in

− Not the place for shops and throbbing nightlife

− Not ideal for beginners or timid intermediates

− Still some draglifts and slow chairs on the glacier slopes

− Glacier can be cold and bleak in midwinter

For guaranteed good snow, Hintertux is simply one of the best places to go. Its glacier is not only extensive; it arguably has the most challenging and interesting runs of any lift-served Alpine glacier area. But the quieter, friendlier, non-glacial slopes down the valley, linked to the slopes of Mayrhofen, are also well worth exploring (check out the Mayrhofen chapter).

The Tux valley, effectively the top end of Mayrhofen's Zillertal, offers a variety of small villages. At the end of the valley, directly below the glacier, is **Hintertux**; a few km down the valley, the major resorts are **Lanersbach** and next-door **Vorderlanersbach**. Lower down still – in the Zillertal, strictly speaking – is **Finkenberg**. There is also accommodation in Juns and Madseit, between Hintertux and Lanersbach.

The higher villages are linked by frequent free ski-buses. A cheap (one euro) night-bus also runs until 2am. Finkenberg is less well served.

There are some good rustic restaurants and bars and a few places along the valley with discos or live

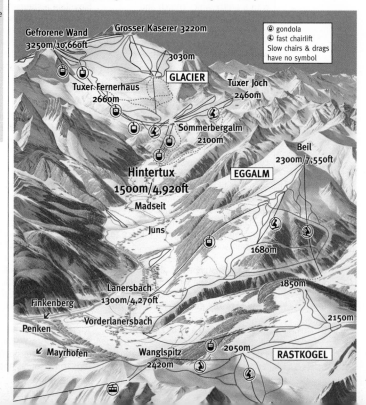

Gefrorene Wand 3250m/10,66oft

Grosser Kaserer 3220m

3030m

GLACIER

gondola
fast chairlift
Slow chairs & drags have no symbol

Tuxer Fernerhaus 2660m

Tuxer Joch 2460m

Sommerbergalm 2100m

Hintertux 1500m/4,920ft

Madseit

Beil 2300m/7,550ft

EGGALM

Juns

168om

1850m

Lanersbach 1300m/4,270ft

Finkenberg

Vorderlanersbach

2150m

Penken

↙ Mayrhofen

Wanglspitz 2420m

2050m

RASTKOGEL

KEY FACTS

Resort	1500m
	4,920ft

Ziller valley	
Slopes	630-3250m
	2,070-10,660ft
Lifts	171
Pistes	662km
	411 miles
Blue	26%
Red	63%
Black	11%
Snowmaking	75%

Ski and Glacier World Zillertal 3000	
Slopes	630-3250m
	2,070-10,660ft
Lifts	62
Pistes	225km
	140 miles
Blue	26%
Red	58%
Black	16%
Snowmaking	66%

Hintertux only	
Slopes	1500-3250m
	4,920-10,660ft
Lifts	22
Pistes	86km
	53 miles

TVB TUX-FINKENBERG

The major lift junction of Sommerbergalm is towards the bottom of this photo, with the glacier beyond and Tuxer Joch on the right ↓

music. But nightlife tends to be quieter than in many bigger Austrian resorts (Mayrhofen, for example).

All the major resort villages have gondola links into the local slopes: the Finkenberg gondola goes up to the Penken slopes shared with Mayrhofen; the Vorderlanersbach one goes to Rastkogel, which is linked with the Penken slopes; and the Lanersbach one goes to Eggalm, from which you can ski to Vorderlanersbach.

The Tux valley and Mayrhofen lifts now form what is called the Ski and Glacier World Zillertal 3000. The Superski lift pass also covers other Ziller valley resorts (look at the Mayrhofen chapter).

Hintertux 1500m

- ➕ Departure point for the excellent high glacier slopes
- ➕ Liveliest of the villages for après-ski
- ➖ Quiet later in the evening
- ➖ Remote setting
- ➖ Not much to do off the slopes

Life in Hintertux revolves around the glacier; staying at the base gets you up the mountain early, and means you don't have far to stagger after joining in the teatime revelry. But later on, it may feel too quiet for some.

Village charm The resort is little more than a small collection of hotels and guest houses, in traditional style. Well, two collections actually – see below.

Convenience The main village is a 15-minute walk away from the lifts, across a car park that fills with day-visitors' cars and coaches (especially when snow is poor in lower resorts); but there is a smaller group of hotels at the lift base – the obvious place to stay in our view.

Scenery There are fabulous views from the high-points of the glacier.

THE MOUNTAINS

Hintertux's slopes are fairly extensive and, for a glacier, surprisingly varied and occasionally challenging. Only the final ski route to the valley is in trees.

Slopes A series of three big twin-cable gondolas go from the base to the top of the glacier in around 30 minutes. The second and third stages are linked by a short slope at Tuxer Fernerhaus. A second smaller gondola also goes to Tuxer Fernerhaus, with a ten-seat gondola due to replace the Gefrorene Wand double chair above it for 2011/12. Above Tuxer Fernerhaus there are further chairs and draglifts with links across to another 1000m-vertical chain of lifts below Grosser Kaserer on the west. Behind Gefrorene Wand is the area's one sunny piste, served by a triple chair.

Descent to the valley involves a short six-pack ride to Sommerbergalm and then a ski route to the base.

At Sommerbergalm a fast quad chair serves short, easy slopes below Tuxer Joch and accesses a second ski route to the base, this one down a deserted valley.

Fast lifts There are high-capacity gondolas all the way to the top, but the shorter lifts serving most of the slopes are T-bars and slow chairs.

Queues The gondolas make light work of any queues when snow is poor elsewhere. But the main runs can get crowded, and then it is best to head

LIFT PASSES

Super-skipass Zillertal

Prices in €

Age	1-day	6-day
under 15	19	90
15 to 18	34	159
over 19	42	199

Free under 6
Senior no deals
Beginner no deals

Notes
1-day pass covers Hintertux glacier, Eggalm, Rastkogel and Penken areas; 4-day and over passes include all Ziller valley lifts; part-day and pedestrian passes available

over to the quieter Kaserer lifts, on skier's left.

Terrain parks Europe's highest World Cup half-pipe is on the glacier (a popular summer hang-out), and there is a terrain park for all levels with jumps, fun boxes and rails.

Snow reliability Snow does not come more reliable than this. Even off the glacier, the other slopes are high and face north, making for very reliable snow-cover. The runs from Tuxer Fernerhaus and Tuxer Joch down to Sommerbergalm have snowmaking, as does the longer ski route to the valley – bizarre, for a ski route.

Experts There is more to amuse experts here than on any other glacier, with a proper black run at glacier level and steep slopes beneath. A lot of the off-piste is little used.

Intermediates The area particularly suits good, confident intermediates. The long runs down from Gefrorene Wand and Kaserer are fun. And the ski routes to the valley are very satisfying. Moderate intermediates will love the slopes served by drags up on the glacier, and the Tuxer Joch area.

Beginners There is a short nursery slope at valley level, but then you're riding the gondola up to and back from Sommerbergalm, where there are blue runs served by drags. You'll need a full lift pass.

Snowboarding There are some great off-piste opportunities, but boarders complain about the number of T-bars.

Cross-country See Lanersbach.

Mountain restaurants There are two big, functional self-service places at the main lift junctions, but also more attractive options. The 100-year-old Spannagelhaus is a simple refuge with

self-service. Our favourite is the Gletscherhütte, at the top of the area – cosy inside, with good shielded terraces. Tuxer Joch Haus has great views of the glacier

Schools and guides The three schools serve all the resorts in Tux, but we lack reports. Tux 3000 has guiding, touring and freeriding programmes.

Families Most of the ski schools run classes for children from aged four, and lunch is provided. There's a children's fun area on the glacier.

STAYING THERE

Most hotels are large and comfortable and have spa facilities, but there are also more modest pensions.

Hotels If you are going to stay in a remote spot like this, you may as well go the whole hog and stay close to the lifts, rather than in the village proper. Our regular reporter uses the 4-star Neuhintertux (8580) ('unusually good half-board food, large spa and pool') or failing that the more intimate Vierjahreszeiten (8525) ('pleasant, good food, smaller spa').

Apartments There are plenty of self-catering apartments.

Eating out Restaurants are mainly hotel-based.

Après-ski There can be a lively après-ski scene both at mid-mountain (Sommerbergalm) and at the base; the Hohenhaus Tenne has several different bars and 'is great fun – the dance floor gets packed', the Rindererhof has a popular tea dance, and there are a couple of local bars.

Off the slopes The hotel spa facilities are excellent, including a thermal pool at the Kirchler, but there are many more options in Mayrhofen.

Lanersbach 1300m

+ Pleasant, compact village
+ Well placed for skiing the glacier or for the Mayrhofen slopes

- Village fairly quiet by Austrian standards
- Few easy local runs for novices

Lanersbach and neighbouring Vorderlanersbach are attractive bases for accessing both the glacier and the valley resorts.

Village charm Lanersbach is small, attractive, spacious and traditional. The quiet centre near the pretty church is delightfully unspoiled and is bypassed by the busy road up to Hintertux that passes the main lift. Vorderlanersbach is a mini version.

Convenience Lanersbach has everything you need in a resort. The centre is within walking distance of

the Eggalm gondola. Vorderlanersbach has its own gondola up to the Rastkogel area.

Scenery These are attractive villages in a long, pretty and varied valley.

THE MOUNTAINS

Slopes The slopes of Eggalm, accessed by the gondola from Lanersbach, offer a small network of pleasantly varied,

100%
SNOW GUARANTEE

www.tux.at

225 km of ski runs · 365 days of the year snowfun on the Hintertux Glacier

Rooms, Brochures, Information: Tourismusverband Tux-Finkenberg, A-6293 Tux, Lanersbach 472,
tel. +43/(0)5287/8506, e-mail: info@tux.at · info@finkenberg.at · **www.tux.at** · **www.finkenberg.at**

GETTING THERE

Air Salzburg 195km/120 miles (3hr); Munich 210km/130 miles (3hr30); Innsbruck 90km/55 miles (1hr45)

Rail Local line to Mayrhofen; regular buses from station

UK PACKAGES

Hintertux Snoworks
Finkenberg Crystal

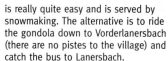

The peak of your emotions!

HOCHKÖNIG
The peak of emotions

150 km of connecting slopes + 33 modern ski lifts = One of the largest ski resorts in the Austrian alps and an exhilarating ski experience!

SNOWPIX.COM / CHRIS GILL

Fabulous blue runs (and a terrain park with a big pipe) on glacial slopes at the very top of the area ↓

intermediate pistes, usually delightfully quiet. You can descend on red or blue runs back to the village or to Vorderlanersbach, where a gondola goes up to the higher, open Rastkogel slopes; here, two fast chairlifts serve some very enjoyable long red and blue runs and link with Mayrhofen's slopes. The linking run is classified red but can get very mogulled, and many people opt to ride the jumbo cable car down; a short rope-tow cuts out the need to hike up to the top station. The lower half of the run back from Rastkogel to Eggalm is a ski route, but

is really quite easy and is served by snowmaking. The alternative is to ride the gondola down to Vorderlanersbach (there are no pistes to the village) and catch the bus to Lanersbach.

Fast lifts Gondolas are the access lifts and Eggalm has a newish six-pack.

Queues We have no reports of any problems. Indeed, Eggalm can be delightfully quiet.

Terrain parks The nearest parks are at Mayrhofen and Hintertux.

Snow reliability Snow conditions are usually good, at least in early season; by Austrian standards these are high slopes and snowmaking covers some runs on both Eggalm and Rastkogel. But Rastkogel is basically south-facing, so snow quality can suffer.

Experts There are no pistes to challenge experts, but there is a fine off-piste route starting a short hike from the top of the Eggalm slopes and finishing at the village.

Intermediates The local slopes suit intermediates best – and you have Mayrhofen's slopes to explore too.

Beginners Lanersbach has a nursery slope (as do Madseit and Juns) but there are few ideal progression slopes on Eggalm – most of the easy runs are on the higher lifts of the Rastkogel sector.

Snowboarding The area isn't great for novices – there are draglifts dotted around, some in key places.

Cross-country There are 28km of cross-country trails around Madseit and Vorderlanersbach.

Mountain restaurants There's no shortage but most, though fairly rustic, are self-service with simple food; the small Lattenalm on Eggalm is a table-service exception with splendid views of the Tux glacier.

Schools and guides There are three schools in the valley, but we lack recent reports on them.

Families The non-ski nursery takes children aged from one to three, and most of the schools take children from four upwards. There's a children's garden, including a carousel and a bob-run, on Eggalm.

STAYING THERE

Both villages are essentially hotel-based resorts.

Hotels The better places tend to be on the main road, but complaints of noise are few. The Lanersbacherof (87256) is a good 4-star with pool, sauna, steam and hot tub close to the lifts ('friendly, the food and wine are outstanding'). The 3-star Pinzger (87541) and Alpengruss (87293) are cheaper alternatives. In Vorderlanersbach the 3-star Kirchlerhof (8560) has been recommended; good spa.

Apartments Quite a lot are available.

Eating out Mainly hotel-based, busy, and geared to serving dinner early. The Forelle is noted for its trout dishes, not surprisingly.

Après-ski Nightlife is generally quiet by Austrian standards. Try the Kleine Tenne or Bergfriedalm – an old wooden building with traditional Austrian music. Gletscherspalte is a disco.

Off the slopes Facilities are fairly good for small resorts. Some hotels have pools, hot tubs and fitness rooms open to non-residents. Innsbruck and Salzburg are possible excursions

Finkenberg 840m

- ⊞ Fast lift access to the main slopes
- ⊞ Pleasant, uncrowded village that appeals to families but ...

- ⊟ Lodging sprawls along a steep and busy main road
- ⊟ No pisted runs to resort level

If you want to ski Mayrhofen's extensive area but avoid the après-ski crowds, Finkenberg makes a quieter alternative – and with direct access to the slopes.

Village charm The resort is no more than a collection of traditional-style hotels, bars, cafes and private homes. There is a pretty central area around the church.

Convenience Most of the buildings (and hotels) are spread along the busy, steep, winding main road up to Lanersbach. Beware slippery pavements. Some hotels are within walking distance of the gondola, and many of the more distant ones run their own minibuses; there is also an inefficient village minibus service.

Scenery Steep mountainsides rise up on both sides.

THE MOUNTAIN

Slopes A two-stage gondola gives direct access to the Penken slopes – and in good conditions you can ski back to the village on a ski route (though it is often closed).

Fast lifts See Mayrhofen.

Queues Few problems reported. The gondola to and from the Penken may have queues at peak times.

Terrain parks The Mayrhofen park is easily accessed.

Snow reliability The local slopes are not as well-endowed with snowmaking as those on Mayrhofen's side.

Experts Not much challenge, except off-piste and the Harakiri piste.

Intermediates The whole area opens up from the top of the gondola.

Beginners There are nursery areas at the top of the gondola, on Penken, but Mayrhofen is a more suitable base.

Snowboarding See Mayrhofen.

Cross-country Cross-country skiers have to get a bus up to Lanersbach.

Mountain restaurants See the Mayrhofen chapter.

Schools and guides The Finkenberg school has a good reputation.

Families The Finkenberg school takes children from age four.

STAYING THERE

Hotels The are several 4-stars. Sporthotel Stock (6775), owned by the family of former downhill champion Leonard Stock, is near the gondola station, and has great spa facilities. The Eberl (62667) has been recommended in the past, and the Kristall (62840) is 150m from the gondola with good wellness/spa facilities. The 3-star B&B hotel Harpfner (62094) is 'absolutely excellent and great value'.

Eating out Mainly in hotels, notably the Eberl. But Cafe Sennhütt'n is 'very good and reasonably priced'.

Après-ski The main après-ski spots are the lively Laterndl Pub at the foot of the gondola and Finkennest.

Off the slopes OK for the active: curling, ice skating, swimming and good local walks.

❋
Want to get other views?

Our website has an active forum, where readers swap experiences and views on resorts and other stuff. The WTSS editors join in, when they have time, so it's a good way to get their views.

Find out more at:

www.wtss.co.uk

Phone numbers
From elsewhere in Austria use the prefix 05287; from abroad use the prefix +43 5287

TOURIST OFFICE
www.tux.at

Hintertux

127

Interactive resort shortlist builder at www.wtss.co.uk

Hochkönig

A hidden gem: small unspoiled villages and a large uncrowded ski area, virtually unknown on the British market

TOP 10 RATINGS

Extent	★★★
Fast lifts	★★★
Queues	★★★★
Snow	★★★
Expert	★★
Intermediate	★★★★
Beginner	★★★
Charm	★★★
Convenience	★★
Scenery	★★★

RPI   90

lift pass	£190
ski hire	£110
lessons	£105
food & drink	£105
total	**£510**

NEWS

2011/12: In Dienten, a six-pack is due to replace a long T-bar from the valley towards Wastlhöhe, with a new ski route to connect the new lift to Hochkönigalm. Ski bridges over the village will mean that you no longer have to walk through it.

2010/11: A gondola opened from the bottom of the Aberg sector to the top of Gabühel, and a six-pack replaced the old chair and drag out of Hinterthal.

- Traditional resort villages
- Eating and drinking cheap by Alpine standards
- Plenty of uncrowded terrain

- Experts need off-piste guidance to get much out of the area
- Biggest resort, Maria Alm, not well connected to main lift system

This area links the cute, compact resort of Maria Alm to the sprawling village of Mühlbach via the small, rustic villages of Hinterthal and Dienten. The slopes in between are an undiscovered intermediate playground and in the last few years, the lift system has been vastly improved with the addition of fast new lifts in key places. Get there quickly before the crowds.

THE RESORT

There are several small, unspoiled villages dotted along a minor road. Maria Alm and Hinterthal are in the same valley. You go over one low pass to Dienten, and another to Mühlbach. **Village charm** Maria Alm and Hinterthal both benefit from being set off the valley road. Maria Alm is the most developed resort village. Hinterthal is smaller and more rustic. Dienten is smaller still; a road runs through it, but it's pretty quiet. Mühlbach, also spread along a through-road, is much bigger and less appealing. **Convenience** At Maria Alm you often have to take a bus to the main lift network in the morning, and always take one back at the end of the day. In Hinterthal the lift is at one end of the village. In tiny Dienten the lifts are central. The Mühlbach gondola is a bus ride from the village centre. **Scenery** The dramatic Hochkönig massif can be seen from many of the slopes (but you don't ski on it).

THE MOUNTAINS

There are 150km of pistes, on a par with well-known names such as Kitzbühel and Mayrhofen. **Slopes** The main slopes spread along a series of gentle peaks running east from Maria Alm to Mühlbach. Many of the runs are north-facing. Just to the west of Maria Alm is the tiny little area of Hinterreit, where international ski teams train. In good conditions, a red run leads from Maria Alm's local Natrun slopes (reached from the town centre by chondola) to the Aberg lift base and the main lift network, but it's sunny and not reliably open. Gondolas access Aberg and the link to Gabühel above Hinterthal and Dienten. Three further ascents and descents bring you to Mühlbach. A reporter says the piste map and signposting are 'not great'. **Fast lifts** Investment in the last few years means that, from the 2011/12 season, nearly all key links will be by modern gondolas or high-speed chairs. The main exception is the slow double

128

ⓖ	gondola
ⓖ⚫	chondola
④	fast chairlift
Slow chairs & drags have no symbol	

SCHNEEBERG 1820m/5,970ft

Sünnhütte 1750m/5,740ft

WASTLHÖHE 1730m/5,680ft

Bischofshofen

1560m

HOCHKEIL 1785m/5,86oft

Mühlbach 855m/2,810ft

Hochkönigalm

Dienten 1070m/3,510

KEY FACTS

Resorts	800-1070m
	2,620-3,510ft
Slopes	800-1900m
	2,620-6,230ft
Lifts	33
Pistes	150km
	93 miles
Blue	35%
Red	55%
Black	10%
Snowmaking	83%

UK PACKAGES

Maria Alm Neilson, Select Ski Chalets
Hinterthal, Hintermoos Elevation Holidays

Phone numbers
Elsewhere in Austria use the prefix 06584 (Maria Alm/Hinterthal), 06461 (Dienten), 06467 (Mühlbach); from abroad use +43 and omit the initial '0'

TOURIST OFFICE

www.hochkoenig.at

---

chair from Dienten to Gabühel.

Queues Not usually a problem.

Terrain parks There are three; the best are on Aberg and Sunnhütte but there is also one above Dienten.

Snow reliability The region claims to be in a 'snow pocket', with good conditions for its height. Snowmaking covers 83% of the pistes.

Experts There are several ungroomed ski routes, the best of which is in a huge bowl west of the Aberg area. 'There are lots of ways in, and I reckon the skiing's better than Vail's back bowls,' a local says. It's not well marked, and having a guide is useful. With a guide you can explore other excellent off-piste too – notably in the bowl above Hintermoos – including tree skiing. There are several genuine black pistes, though most have only occasional steep pitches.

Intermediates The area is great for adventurous intermediates, happy on red runs and easy blacks in varying conditions. Confirmed blue-run skiers, reluctant to take on challenges, are best off based in Mühlbach, with good runs at altitude and back to the valley.

Beginners All the villages have good nursery slopes, and there are fine progression runs in most sectors. Hinterthal lacks them, though.

Snowboarding Good for beginners and intermediates, but there are draglifts.

Cross-country Over 40km of tracks.

Mountain restaurants Lots of pleasant huts that are 'value for money'. Reporters praise Bergstadl, Thoraualm, Tischlerhutte (Aberg), Hochmaisalm (Hinterthal), Steinbockalm (Gabühel), Burgalm and Almhäusl (Dienten), Tiergartenalm (Sunnhütte).

Schools and guides All four main villages have schools, and many instructors speak good English. A past reporter judged Maria Alm's school 'great – catered well for all our levels'.

Families The kindergartens take children from age two, the schools from age four. Babysitting is available.

STAYING THERE

Hotels There are plenty of good hotels, many with spa facilities, especially in Maria Alm – there are half a dozen 4-star places here. In Hinterthal, Haus Salzburg (23497) is a chalet hotel run by an English couple (and has recently changed hands); and the 4-star Urslauerhof (8164) has a 'really impressive' spa. Between Maria Alm and Hinterthal, there are hotels on the slopes at Hintermoos. In Dienten the 4-star Vital Hotel Post (2030) gets another rave review this year: 'excellent, friendly staff, food is superb, excellent spa, good rooms'. Be aware that some 'Mühlbach' hotels are actually a few km out in the opposite direction to the main gondola.

Eating out In Maria Alm the 'friendly' Wirtshausl, the Almerwirt, Alpenland Sporthotel and the Dorfcafe have been recommended. In Hintermoos, the restaurant at the hotel Handlerhof has 'great food, good service'.

Après-ski Maria Alm is by far the most animated village. The Bachwirt and Dengl Alm are jolly, traditional bars. Almer Tenne has live music and a disco. Orgler Keller is good for a quieter time. The Almbar in Hinterthal can be lively and stays open late, as does the Haus Salzburg bar. Saustall is a decent 'pub' in Mühlbach.

Off the slopes Maria Alm has tobogganing, sleigh rides and nice walks. Several hotel pools are open to the public.

Ischgl

Ischgl is unique: high, snow-sure slopes, a superb lift system, and a traditional-style Tirolean village. Perfection? Well, not quite ...

RATINGS

The mountains

Extent	★★★★
Fast lifts	★★★★★
Queues	★★★★
Terrain p'ks	★★★★★
Snow	★★★★
Expert	★★★★
Intermediate	★★★★
Beginner	★★
Boarder	★★★★★
X-country	★★★
Restaurants	★★★★
Schools	★★★
Families	★★

The resort

Charm	★★★
Convenience	★★★
Scenery	★★★
Eating out	★★★★
Après-ski	★★★★★
Off-slope	★★★

RPI 105

lift pass	£190
ski hire	£145
lessons	£120
food & drink	£140
total	**£595**

NEWS

2011/12: A six-pack is due to replace the Sonnenlift T-bar, on the nursery slopes at Idalp. More snowmaking is planned.

Work will start in 2011 on a new Pardatschgrat gondola for 2012/13.

2010/11: A six-pack was installed from the Höllenkar valley (run 24) to the top of Greitspitz, serving the red and black pistes on its northern slopes.

On the Swiss side, a six-pack replaced the Mullerbahn quad from Alp Trida to Alp Bella.

- Compact, traditional-style village with a traffic-free core
- High slopes with reliable snow
- Broad area of slopes linked to Samnaun in Switzerland
- Superb modern lift system
- Après-ski like nowhere else, with an unmatched number of exceptionally lively places

- Village is densely developed, and has a rather urban, glitzy feel
- Not ideal for beginners or timid intermediates, for various reasons
- Few seriously steep runs
- Very little wooded terrain
- Treks to the gondolas for some
- Après-ski can be a bit tacky

Ischgl is at last becoming better known to Brits. It's about time – the mountain is one of Austria's best, and we love it (except in a snowstorm).

The village? We're less convinced. We visited last season as part of a Tirolean tour and, looking back, Ischgl came in seventh out of seven as a place to stay. Yes, it has clear merits. But it's all a bit high-pressure, with thousands of cars and scores of coaches piling in to its parking lots, and little room to breathe.

The alternative bases? Galtür (a bus ride away) is too quiet. Samnaun (linked, but in Switzerland) means appreciably higher prices. Ischgl it is, then.

THE RESORT

Ischgl is a compact village tucked away south of St Anton in the long, narrow Paznaun valley, on the Swiss border; the ski area is shared with Samnaun in Switzerland. The Silvretta ski pass also covers Galtür further up the valley (described at the end of this chapter) and Kappl and See down the valley (covered in the Resort Directory, at the back). All are worth a visit and would make cheaper, quieter bases. Frequent ski-buses link all of them. A car makes trips to St Anton viable.

VILLAGE CHARM ★★★
More town than village
The buildings are predominantly in traditional chalet style, with one or two modern exceptions, but this is no rustic backwater – the narrow streets

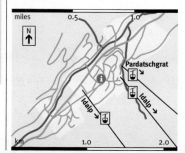

have a towny feel, and the style is swanky and brash rather than tasteful. There's a selection of lively bars and a better-than-usual selection of fashion shops – 'more luxury shops than Lech', an experienced observer of these matters points out. The narrow main street plus a couple of side streets are mostly traffic-free – the valley road up to Galtür bypasses the village.

CONVENIENCE ★★★
Beware of the bypass
As our village plan suggests, it is not a big place; but big enough for some of the lodgings to be a good walk from the nearest lift – beware lodgings the wrong side of the bypass road. You can leave your kit up at Idalp. Gondolas go up to mid-mountain from two points about 500m apart. The best location, overall, is on or near the main pedestrian street between the two. The eastern gondola station is separated from the main street by a low hill, but is reached by means of an underground moving walkway.

SCENERY ★★★
Good at the top
The wooded flanks of the valley rise steeply from the village, which gets almost no sun in January. But above the treeline, the Silvretta range is revealed in all its glory.

KEY FACTS

Resort	1400m
	4,590ft
Slopes	1400-2870m
	4,590-9,420ft
Lifts	41
Pistes	238km
	148 miles
Blue	20%
Red	64%
Black	16%
Snowmaking	
	800 guns

LIFT PASSES

VIP Skipass

Prices in €

Age	1-day	6-day
under 17	26	121
17 to 59	40	202
over 60	38	172

Free under 8

Beginner no deals

Notes

Covers all lifts in Ischgl and Samnaun and local buses; half-day pass and non-skier pass available; 2-day-plus pass available only to those staying in Ischgl or Mathon on presenting a guest card

Alternative passes

Regional pass covers Ischgl, Samnaun, Galtür, Kappl and See

THE MOUNTAINS

Ischgl is a fair-sized, relatively high, snow-sure area. Practically all the slopes are above the treeline, the main exception being the steep lower slopes above the village and a couple of short runs low in the Fimbatal.

The piste map is good. We have found signposting inadequate. What's more, the run numbering is lunatic: a run may have multiple tributaries, or may split part-way down, with the variants having the same number.

There are two varieties of ski route – plain and 'extreme' – clearly stated to be 'not monitored'.

EXTENT OF THE SLOPES ★★★★☆
Extensive cross-border cruising
The sunny **Idalp** plateau, reached by the 24-person Silvrettabahn from the western lift station and eight-seat Fimbabahn from the eastern one, is the hub of the slopes. It can be very crowded. Pardatschgrat, reached by the third gondola, is about 300m higher. From Idalp, lifts radiate to a wide variety of mainly north-west- and west-facing runs and the Swiss border.

The red runs back down to Ischgl provoke regular complaints. Neither is easy, conditions can be tricky, and countless imbeciles skiing too fast make these runs even more hazardous. Both have final stretches that probably should be black. The wide, quiet piste down the Velilltal looks better, but turns rather nasty lower down and joins the steep 'black' bottom part of run 1A. Quite a few people ride the gondolas down.

A short piste brings you from Idalp to the lifts serving the **Höllenkar** bowl, leading up to the area's south-western extremity and high point at Palinkopf. Runs of 900m vertical from here lead down to the **Fimbatal**. On the Swiss side, the hub of activity is **Alp Trida**, surrounded by south- and east-facing runs with great views. From here a scenic red goes down to Compatsch, for buses to Ravaisch (for the cable car back up) and Samnaun. From Palinkopf there is a long red run down a beautiful valley to Samnaun – not difficult, but very sunny in parts and prone to closure by avalanche risk. There is a long flat stretch at the end.

FAST LIFTS ★★★★★
One of the best
Ischgl is near the top of our fast league table. About 80% of its main lifts are fast – mainly fast chairs. Two more were installed this year; another six-pack is planned for 2011/12.

QUEUES ★★★★☆
OK up the mountain
Queues out of the valley are not the problem they once were, since two of the access lifts were upgraded. But peak-time queues still exist. A new jumbo gondola is under construction but not imminent. Crowds on the runs are an issue, especially at Idalp, and on the easier runs on the Swiss side.

TERRAIN PARKS ★★★★★
One of Europe's best
Ischgl is a top place for freestylers. The huge SnowArt park above Idalp, served by three chairlifts, is the big

In March, at least, there is some sun to be enjoyed in the village at close of play – outside the Kitzloch bar ➔

draw – 1600m long, and always well maintained. It has beginner, public and pro lines, revamped each year. Overall the park obstacles have an impressive creative flair. The big pro line consists of several 15m to 17m kickers, plus three corner jumps in a row. There is another park at Velillscharte and a small park on the Swiss side.

SNOW RELIABILITY ★★★★
Very good

All the slopes, except the runs back to the resort, are above 1800m, and many on the Ischgl side are north-west-facing. So snow conditions are generally reliable; many reporters comment on excellent early/late season conditions. Snowmaking now covers over half the slopes, including the descents to Ischgl and Samnaun. Grooming is good.

FOR EXPERTS ★★★★
Plenty to do

Ischgl can't compare with St Anton for exciting slopes. But by general Tirolean standards it serves experts well. All the blacks are genuine ones and in combination with testing reds offer excellent, challenging descents. Head first for Palinkopf, Greitspitz (with a new lift last season serving good

gondola
cable car
fast chairlift
Slow chairs & drags have no symbol

Lovely long run, with a jolly restaurant at the end, on the outskirts of Samnaun – so a great way to end the morning or the day

Greitspitz
2870m/9,420ft

Lange Wandba

Salaas

Greitspitz

Samnaun
1840m/6,040ft

Alp Trida
Sattel
2490m

Viderjoch II

Idjoch
2760m

Idjoc

Ravaisch

Pendelbahn

Luftseilbahn

Viderjoch I

Sattel

Flimjoch

Laret

Flimsattel

Velillscharte
2555m

Velill

Compatsch

Alp Trida
2265m

Marmotte

ALP TRIDA

Muller

Visnitz

Not a slow lift in sight in this sector – or in most other sectors, actually

Grivalea

Grivalea
2700m

2640m

blacks) and Pardatschgrat – piste 4 is a favourite. One of the branches of run 14a on Greitspitz (read our earlier remarks) includes a good steep pitch (70%, they claim). The wooded lower slopes of the Fimbatal are delightful in a storm. There is plenty of off-piste and powder doesn't get tracked out too quickly, particularly on the Swiss side. We had an excellent day last season, including exploration of the shady side of Velilltal. There are also ski routes. Ski route 39 from Palinkopf offers a testing 1000m descent.

FOR INTERMEDIATES ★★★★☆
Something for everyone
Most of the slopes are wide, forgiving and ideal for intermediates – and there are plenty of them.

At the tough end of the spectrum our favourite runs are those from Palinkopf down to Gampenalp at the edge of the ski area, with great views of virgin slopes. But there are lots of other options on Palinkopf, Greitspitz and Pardatschgrat. The reds down the beautiful Velilltal and the red from Greitspitz into Switzerland are great for quiet, high-speed cruising.

For easier motorway cruising, there is lots of choice, including the runs down around Alp Trida on the Swiss side – but these can get crowded.

FOR BEGINNERS ★★☆☆☆
Up the mountain
There are good, sunny, snow-sure nursery slopes served by drags and two fast chairs up the mountain at Idalp, but there are no special deals for beginners – you must buy a full lift pass to reach them. The blue runs on the east side of the bowl offer pleasant progression, and from there it's a small step to Switzerland.

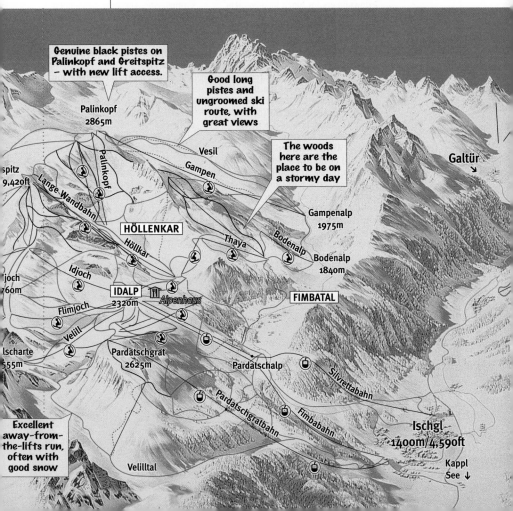

Genuine black pistes on Palinkopf and Greitspitz – with new lift access.

Good long pistes and ungroomed ski route, with great views

The woods here are the place to be on a stormy day

Palinkopf 2865m

Vesil

Gampen

Galtür

spitz 9,420ft

Lange Wandbahn

Palinkopf

HÖLLENKAR

Höllkar

Thaya

Bodenalp

Gampenalp 1975m

Bodenalp 1840m

joch 760m

Idjoch

IDALP 2320m

Alpenhaus

FIMBATAL

Flimjoch

Velill

Ischarte 555m

Pardatschgrat 2625m

Pardatschalp

Pardatschgratbahn

Silvrettabahn

Fimbabahn

Ischgl 1400m/4,590ft

Excellent away-from-the-lifts run, often with good snow

Velilltal

Kappl See ↓

SNOWPIX.COM / CHRIS GILL

If you were dreaming up the perfect mid-mountain lift base, it might look roughly like Idalp, at 2300m; you'd probably want to share it with fewer people, though ↓

FOR BOARDERS ★★★★★
Pretty much perfect
Ischgl has long been a popular spot for snowboarders, with its long, wide, well-groomed slopes served by snowboard-friendly gondolas and fast chairlifts. Although the off-piste terrain is less steep than in some other resorts, its above-the-treeline, easily accessible nature and good snow record makes for great riding for most ability levels. Ischgl is home to one of Austria's best terrain parks, and Silvretta Sports and Intersport Mathoy are recommended snowboard shops.

FOR CROSS-COUNTRY ★★★☆☆
Plenty in the valley
There are 24km of track in the valley between Ischgl, Galtür and Wirl. This tends to be shady, especially in early season, and is away from the main slopes, which makes meeting downhillers for lunch inconvenient.

MOUNTAIN RESTAURANTS ★★★★☆
Good modern choices
Mountain restaurants generally offer good quality and choice. But capacity can be stretched at peak times. They are clearly marked on the piste map.
Editors' choice On the Austrian side at Idalp, the Alpenhaus (6840) is very much a designer place, with both table-service (upstairs) and self-service areas. We're interested only in the former, obviously, although service is itself a bit slack. Food is good though, particularly the tarts, and the relaxed ambience is great. On the Swiss side at Alp Trida the Marmotte (+41 81 868 5221) wins no prizes for interior design but does good food in calm and comfortable surroundings.

Worth knowing about In the Fimbatal the 'lovely' Paznauner Thaya has self-service with famously good pizza, and table-service upstairs for 'fab chicken salad and spicy prawns'; often with live bands or throbbing disco music. Bodenalpe is a bit of a relic but has 'good, simple, cheap food'. From Gampenalp you can be towed 5km by snowmobile to the remote Heidelberger hütte – the way back is quite hard work, though. Above Idalp the glass-sided Pardorama complex is impressive, and less crowded than lower places. A 2011 visitor made it a regular haunt – 'very reasonable prices, excellent rösti'. Table-service (Mediterranean dishes) upstairs.

On the Swiss side the woody Alp Bella is good value and a consistent favourite with reporters for traditional food and 'old hut' atmosphere. This year's reports on the Alp Trida are enthusiastic. The new glass-sided Salaas is very stylish and spacious, but otherwise unremarkable.

SCHOOLS AND GUIDES ★★★☆☆
No worries
The school meets up at Idalp and starts at 10am. Recent reporters have been very happy, with instructors speaking 'sufficient English' and 'good advanced lessons'. One visitor's group was smaller than the 10-12 norm. The school also organises off-piste tours.

FOR FAMILIES ★★☆☆☆
High-altitude options
Idalp has a snow garden and childcare facilities; but small kids would be better off in Galtür or Kappl, where there are good play areas – see the end of this chapter.

SCHOOLS

Ischgl
t 5257/5404

Classes
5 days (3hr) €165
Private lessons
€110 for 90min; each
additional person €25

CHILDCARE

Kindergarten
t 5257/5404
Run by ski school at
Idalp: non-skiing
children 10am to
4pm, €40 per day
incl. lunch; ski-
kindergarten for ages
3 to 5 €55 per 4hr
day; lunch available

Ski school
Takes children from
the age of 5 (5 full
days €165)

GETTING THERE

Air Innsbruck 95km/
60 miles (1hr45);
Zürich 240km/150
miles (3hr30); Munich
300km/185 miles
(4hr)

Rail Landeck
(30km/19 miles);
frequent buses from
station

STAYING THERE

Chalets Ski Total broke into Ischgl last
season with the 58-bed chalet hotel
Abendrot, in a central position, and
has now added the 22-bed chalet Zita,
3 minutes from the Fimbabahn.
Hotels There is a good selection from
luxurious and pricey to simple B&Bs.
*****Trofana Royal (600) One of
Austria's most luxurious hotels, with
prices to match. A celebrity chef runs
the kitchen. Sumptuous spa facilities.
****Madlein (5226) Convenient, 'hip',
modern hotel. Pool, sauna, steam
room. Nightclub and disco.
****Elisabeth (5411) Right by the
Pardatschgrat gondola, with lively
après-ski. Pool, sauna and steam.
****Gramaser (5295) Formerly the
Grillalm and near the Trofana Royal.
We had a comfortable stay here in
2010; friendly staff and excellent food.
****Goldener Adler (5217) Central,
combining traditional ambience with
designer rooms; 'surprisingly good
food'. Sauna and spa.
****Jägerhof (5206) Friendly, good
food, large rooms. Sauna, steam, spa.
'Splendid food and wine.'
****Post (5232) 'Excellent central
position; very nice staff.' Spa centre.
****Christine (5346) The best B&B in
town? 'Huge rooms, central location,
helpful owners, splendid spa.'
****Lamtana (5609) Near the
Silvrettabahn. 'Spacious, modern
rooms.' Wellness area.
***Alpenglühn (5294) Convenient,
central and good value.
Apartments Some attractive
apartments are available. The Golfais
by the Pardatschgrat gondola and the
apartments in the hotel Solaria (with
use of its spa) have been suggested.

EATING OUT ★★★★☆
Plenty of choice
Most restaurants are hotel-based, but
not all. We enjoyed excellent, varied
meals at the popular Grillalm pizzeria
(hotel Gramaser). Reporters tip the
Salnerhof and Jagerhof ('splendid food
and wine') – offering five-course meals
and themed evenings. For lighter
meals try the Bära Falla ('great pizza
and Tirolean food') and Allegra
(burgers etc). The Trofana Alm, which
is as much a bar as a restaurant, and
the Kitzloch, with its galleries over the
dance floor, are best for grills and
fondue. For Italian, try the Toscana
('very good') and Salz & Pfeffer.

APRES-SKI ★★★★★
Very lively
Ischgl is the liveliest resort in the Alps,
we've concluded after a lot of in-depth
research. The fun starts in the early
afternoon – mountain restaurants such
as Paznauner Thaya slide into après
mode directly after lunch – and it
doesn't stop; lots of people are still in
ski boots late in the evening.
  The obvious ports of call in the
village are the Trofana Alm near the
Silvrettabahn and the Schatzi bar of
the hotel Elisabeth by the
Pardatschgratbahn – with scantily clad
dancing girls. Next door is Freeride,
new this year, with 'friendly staff, good
ski movies and no dancing girls'.
Across the river the Kitzloch offers not
only sunshine (check out our photo)
but also dancing on the tables in ski
boots. Niki's Stadl offers 'surreal
madness' thanks to its 'deranged DJs'.
Feuer & Eis and the basement
Kuhstahl are packed all evening – the
latter is one reporter's all-time
favourite après bar. The Golden Eagle
pub is popular with Brits looking for
somewhere to sit. We enjoyed a quiet
drink at the Kiwi and cocktails at
pricey Guxa.
  Later on, we had a splendid
evening dancing to a live band in the
huge Trofana Arena, which also has
pole dancing. The Coyote Ugly is
similarly popular. Other nightclubs
include: Pacha (as in Ibiza and
London), Living Room and Posthörndl,
with an ancient Rome theme.

OFF THE SLOPES ★★★☆☆
No sun but a nice pool
The village gets little sun in the
middle of winter, and the resort is best
suited to those keen to hit the slopes.

UK PACKAGES

Alpine Answers, Crystal, Crystal Finest, First Choice, Independent Ski Links, Inghams, Momentum, PowderBeds, Ski Expectations, Ski Independence, Ski Solutions, Ski Total, Skitracer, Snow Finders, STC
Galtür *Crystal, Inghams, Neilson, Ski Independence, STC*

ACTIVITIES

Indoor Silvretta Centre (bowling, billiards, swimming pool, tennis, sauna, solarium, massage), museums, concerts

Outdoor Ice rink, curling, sleigh rides, hiking tours, 7km floodlit toboggan run

Phone numbers
Calling long-distance
Add the prefix given below for each resort; when calling from abroad use the country code +43 and omit the initial '0'
Ischgl
05444
Galtür
05443

Samnaun (Switzerland)
From elsewhere in Switzerland add the prefix 081; from abroad use the prefix +41 81

TOURIST OFFICES

Ischgl
www.ischgl.com
Samnaun
(Switzerland)
www.samnaun.ch
Galtür
www.galtuer.com

But there's no shortage of off-slope activities. There are lots of maintained paths including many at altitude (the tourist office claims an astonishing 1140km in the valley), a 7km floodlit toboggan run and a splendid sports centre. And you can browse upmarket shops. It's easy to get around the valley by bus and the Smuggler's Pass for pedestrians enables them to use specially selected lifts.

LINKED RESORT – 1840m
SAMNAUN

Small, quiet duty-free Samnaun is in a corner of Switzerland more easily reached from Austria. We know of no UK tour operators going here, but a reporter this year reckons more Brits are finding their way here.

There are four small components, roughly 1km apart: Samnaun-Dorf, prettily set at the head of the valley is the main focus, with some swanky hotels and duty-free shops; Ravaisch, where the cable car goes up; tiny Plan; and the hamlets of Laret and Compatsch, at the end of the main piste to the valley. We've stayed happily on the edge of Dorf in the Waldpark B&B (8618310) and a 2011 visitor highly recommends the hotel Montana (8619000) for 'comfy rooms, fab pool, three great restaurants'. Other tips: 4-star Muttler (8618130) ('very good spa and complimentary ski bus'), and Des Alpes ('modern food'). There's a smart AlpenQuell spa-pool-fitness centre.

The Schmuggler Alm at the bottom of the long run from Palinkopf is a popular lunch and après-ski spot – a great place to end the day if you like 'cheesy euro-pop'. The Almraus (hotel Cresta) at Compatsch has been recommended for drinks. The school is 'first class', says a reporter.

UP-VALLEY VILLAGE – 1585m
GALTÜR

Galtür is a charming, peaceful, traditional village clustered around a pretty little church, amid impressive mountain scenery at the head of Ischgl's Paznaun valley. Many visitors find the resort very quiet – there are just a few shops, restaurants, and a 'fantastic bakery for coffee and cakes'.

Sunnier and cheaper than Ischgl, Galtür is a good base for families and mixed-ability groups. The free buses to Ischgl are regular and quick, but they get overcrowded at peak times even in January, and they stop at around 6pm. Taxis to Ischgl's nightlife are economic if shared.

Galtür's own slopes rise to 2295m above a lift base at Wirl, a short bus ride from the village. The Silvapark ski area has six 'sectors' to help guests make the most of the mountain; there are freestyle and family sectors, for example. The slopes can be bleak in poor weather, and are limited in extent. There are two fast chairs and a gondola, but still some long draglifts. Queues are rare. The slopes are fairly high, so pretty snow-sure; we had good snow on a warm March visit.

Most runs are classified red, though some would be blue elsewhere. Run 8 is a favourite of ours; a broad, long cruise with great views of the frozen dam below. The main blue piste can get crowded and has a steeper section at the top, but is a long, pretty cruise to the valley. There are some challenges – reds and a black served by the fast Ballunspitze chair are short and steep. And there are a couple of ski routes to try. The area on the far right of the piste map, served by a slow double chair and a T-bar, is quiet, shady and has some good off-piste in a bowl and among well-spaced trees. There's a terrain park, and a fine nursery area at the lift base.

The school is 'excellent and well organised' and offers small classes. Kinderland has its own tow, carousel, moving carpet and cartoon characters. Galtür has 74km of cross-country loops, some quite testing. The cosy, wooden Wieberhimml mountain hut is a lively, sunny spot for drinks. And we had good food at the table-service Panorama Tenne, beside the gondola. The Addis Abeba is a hip 'cube-style' bar near the Soppalift drag.

There are good hotels, including the 4-star Almhof (8253), Flüchthorn (8202), Ballunspitze (8214) and 3-star Alpenrose (8201).

Off-slope facilities are limited, apart from the impressive Alpinarium, an avalanche-protection structure and exhibition centre built after the avalanche that devastated the village in 1999. Much of the information is in German but it's worth a visit; they supply slippers if you turn up in ski boots. There's a sports centre with pool, tennis and squash – and night skiing and sledding on Wednesdays.

Kitzbühel

Despite the racy image, the slopes are mostly pretty tame; the town at the base, though, is something special – cute and lively

RATINGS

The mountains

Extent	★★★
Fast lifts	★★★★
Queues	★★★
Terrain p'ks	★★★
Snow	★★
Expert	★★★
Intermediate	★★★★
Beginner	★★
Boarder	★★
X-country	★★★
Restaurants	★★★★
Schools	★★★★
Families	★

The resort

Charm	★★★★
Convenience	★★
Scenery	★★★
Eating out	★★★★
Après-ski	★★★★
Off-slope	★★★★★

RPI   100

lift pass	£200
ski hire	£115
lessons	£120
food & drink	£125
total	**£560**

NEWS

2010/11: A 10-seat gondola and an eight-seat chair above it (both with heated seats) replaced the chain of slow Maierl chairs out of Kirchberg towards Ehrenbachhöhe.

➕ Extensive, attractive, varied slopes offering a sensation of travel – with trips to the SkiWelt also possible

➕ Beautiful medieval town centre

➕ Vibrant nightlife

➕ Lots to do off the slopes

➕ Plenty of cheap lodgings

➕ Excellent mountain restaurants

➖ Low altitude means snow is often poor low down (though snowmaking is fairly extensive)

➖ Surprisingly few challenges on-piste

➖ Disappointing nursery area

➖ Some crowded pistes

Kitzbühel is one of the big names of the ski world, largely thanks to its spectacular Hahnenkamm downhill race course – the most exciting on the World Cup circuit. Hahnenkamm race weekend is one of the key dates on the Alpine social calendar. But the place has powerful attractions for the rest of us, too.

We quite like the slopes, too – especially since the huge 3S cross-valley gondola made the link to Jochberg and Pass Thurn in 2004. The lift system as a whole is slowly being brought up to scratch – last season there was rejoicing in Kirchberg at the replacement, at last, of the infamous slow Maierl chairlifts.

It's just a pity the place isn't 300m higher. In countless visits over a 25-year period we've encountered good snow down to the village just once. Our advice is to book late, when you know the conditions are good.

THE RESORT

Kitzbühel is a large, animated valley town with its major ski area on one side and its minor one on the other. The major area, spreading south-west from the famous Hahnenkamm directly above the town, is shared with another substantial resort, Kirchberg, covered at the end of the chapter.

The 'excellent value' Kitzbüheler Alpen All Star lift pass covers seven separate ski areas in the region – see 'Lift passes'. One of those – the SkiWelt – is accessible by the Ki-West gondola, a short bus ride from Skirast.

VILLAGE CHARM ★★★★
A historic town

The largely car-free medieval centre is delightful. And many visitors love the sophisticated, towny ambience and swanky shops and cafes. But the resort spreads widely, and busy roads surround the old town. Visitors used to peaceful little Austrian villages are likely to be surprised by its urban feel.

CONVENIENCE ★★
Choose your spot carefully

A gondola from the edge of the town goes up to the Hahnenkamm, start of the main area of slopes. Across town,

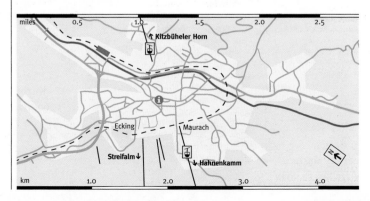

close to the railway station but some way from the centre, another gondola accesses the much smaller Kitzbüheler Horn sector.

The size of Kitz makes choice of location important. Many visitors prefer to be in the centre of town and close to the Hahnenkamm gondola. Beginners should bear in mind that the Hahnenkamm nursery slopes are often lacking in snow, and then novices are taken up the Horn. Some reporters say the free buses around

town get overcrowded. And the post bus service is said to be efficient yet often only goes as far as Jochberg and has limited service on Sundays.

SCENERY ★★★☆☆
Attractive valley views

Kitzbühel is set at a junction of broad, pretty valleys, among partly wooded mountains. There are good views from Pengelstein along both valleys and to the SkiWelt and beyond.

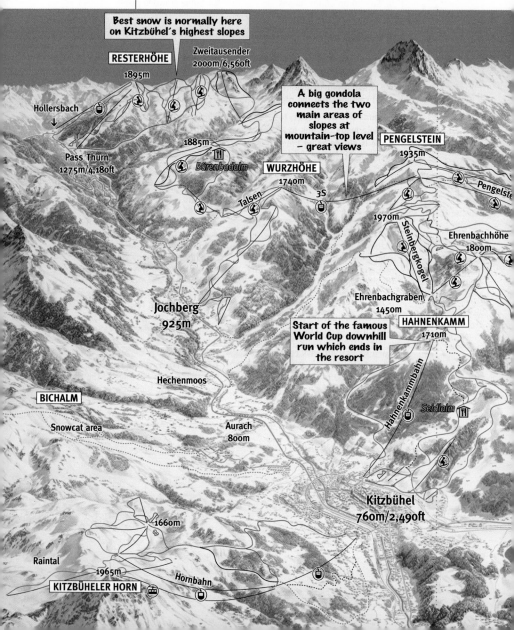

Best snow is normally here on Kitzbühel's highest slopes

RESTERHÖHE
1895m

Zweitausender
2000m/6,56oft

Hollersbach
↓

A big gondola connects the two main areas of slopes at mountain-top level – great views

PENGELSTEIN
1935m

Pass Thurn
1275m/4,18oft

1885m

Bärenbadalm

Talsen

WURZHÖHE
1740m

3S

Pengelste

1970m

Steinbergkogel

Ehrenbachhöhe
1800m

Jochberg
925m

Ehrenbachgraben
1450m

Start of the famous World Cup downhill run which ends in the resort

HAHNENKAMM
1710m

Hechenmoos

BICHALM

Snowcat area

Aurach
8oom

Hahnenkammbahn

Seidlalm

Kitzbühel
760m/2,490ft

1660m

Raintal

1965m

Hornbahn

KITZBÜHELER HORN

THE HAHNENKAMM DOWNHILL

Kitzbühel's Hahnenkamm Downhill race, held in mid-January each year (20 to 22 January in 2012), is the toughest as well as one of the most famous on the World Cup circuit. On the race weekend the town is packed and there is a real carnival atmosphere, with bands, people in traditional costumes and huge (and loud) cowbells everywhere. The race itself starts with a steep icy section before you hit the famous Mausfalle and Steilhang, where even Franz Klammer used to get worried. The course starts near the top of the Hahnenkamm gondola and drops 860m to finish amid the noise and celebrations right on the edge of town. The course is normally closed from the start of the season until after the race, but after the race weekend ordinary mortals can now try most of the course, if the snow is good enough – it's an unpisted ski route mostly. We found it steep and tricky in parts, even when going slowly – it must be terrifying at race speeds of 80mph or more.

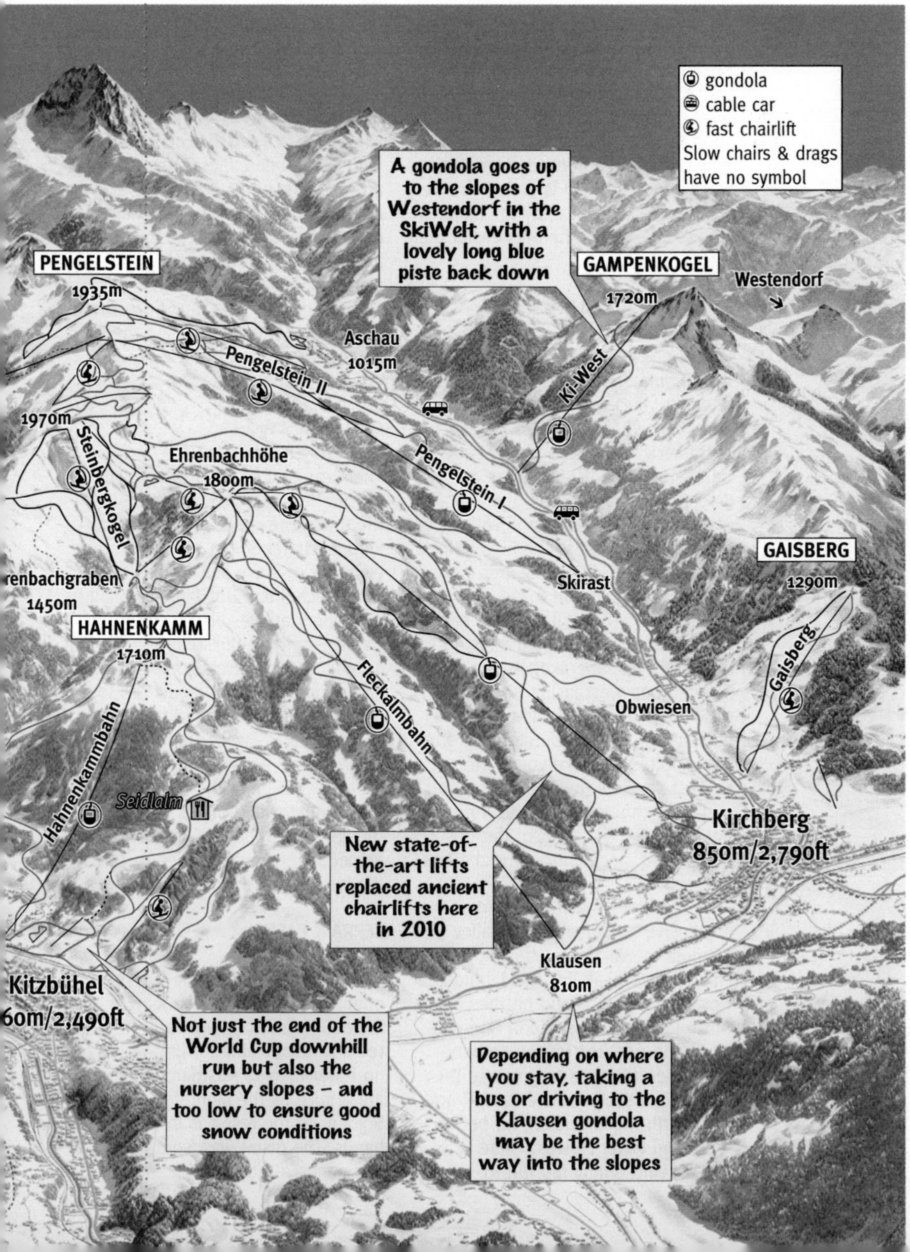

gondola
cable car
fast chairlift
Slow chairs & drags have no symbol

A gondola goes up to the slopes of Westendorf in the SkiWelt, with a lovely long blue piste back down

PENGELSTEIN
1935m

GAMPENKOGEL
1720m

Westendorf

Aschau
1015m

Ki-West

Pengelstein II

1970m

Pengelstein-I

Ehrenbachhöhe
1800m

Skirast

GAISBERG
1290m

renbachgraben
1450m

HAHNENKAMM
1710m

Obwiesen

Fleckalmbahn

Kirchberg
850m/2,790ft

Seidalm

New state-of-the-art lifts replaced ancient chairlifts here in 2010

Klausen
810m

Kitzbühel
6om/2,490ft

Not just the end of the World Cup downhill run but also the nursery slopes – and too low to ensure good snow conditions

Depending on where you stay, taking a bus or driving to the Klausen gondola may be the best way into the slopes

LIFT PASSES

Kitzbühel

Prices in €

Age	1-day	6-day
under 16	22	101
16 to 18	34	162
over 19	43	202

Free under 7
Senior 60+: day pass €32 on Tue & Thu; 80+: season pass €20
Beginner seven free lifts (three in Kitzbühel)
Notes
Covers all lifts in Kitzbühel, Kirchberg, Jochberg, Pass Thurn, Mittersill/Hollersbach; 50% reduction on pool entry with passes for 2 days or more; single ascent, hourly and pedestrian tickets; family reductions
Alternative passes
Kitzbüheler Alpen All Star Card covers seven ski areas – Kitzbühel, Schneewinkel (St Johann), Ski Welt, Alpbach, Wildschönau, Skicircus Saalbach, Zell-Kaprun; Salzburg Super Ski Card covers 22 ski areas in the Salzburg province

THE MOUNTAINS

Kitzbühel's extensive slopes – shared with Kirchberg and other villages – offer some open runs higher up but soon run into patchy forest lower down. Most face north-east or north-west. The piste map is praised as 'very clear and easy to use' by the majority. Many readers find the runs easier than their grades.

EXTENT OF THE SLOPES ★★★ ★ ★
Big but bitty
The slopes can be divided into several identifiable areas. The **Hahnenkamm** gondola takes you to the bowl of Ehrenbachgraben, a major lift bottleneck in the past but recently transformed by installation of not only a six-pack to Ehrenbachhöhe, the arrival point of lifts from Kirchberg, but also an eight-pack to the high-point of Steinbergkogel. Suddenly, this is a place you might want to do laps.

Beyond is the slightly lower peak of **Pengelstein**, with an eight-pack up to it from the Steinbergkogel area. Several long west-facing runs go down to Skirast, where there is a gondola back up, or to Aschau. Ski buses from these points will take you to the Ki-West gondola towards Westendorf and to Kirchberg. It takes up to an hour to reach the heart of the Westendorf slopes, including the bus connection.

Pengelstein is also the start of the impressive 30-person cross-valley 3S gondola to **Wurzhöhe** above Jochberg. This peak-to-peak link has fabulous views (especially if you hit the cabin with the partial glass floor) and is worth the ride just for the scenery.

Further lifts then take you to the **Resterhöhe** sector above Pass Thurn – well worth the excursion, for better snow and fewer crowds. There is a long, scenic, sunny red run to

Breitmoos, mid-station of the gondola up from Hollersbach, beyond Pass Thurn. Runs are otherwise short, but mostly served by fast chairs.

The **Kitzbüheler Horn** gondola second stage leads to the sunny Trattalm bowl, with an alternative cable car taking you up to the summit of the Horn, from where a fine, solitary piste leads down into the Raintal on the east side. There's a blue piste and two ski routes back towards town.

The separate **Bichlalm** area, which used to offer lift-served off-piste, has reopened for guided snowcat skiing. A new gondola is planned there, but a date is less definite.

FAST LIFTS ★★★★ ★
Much improved but...
There have been improvements in recent years, and last season's new lifts above Kirchberg put Kitzbühel into our ★★★★ category at last. But there are still lots of complaints from readers about slow old double chairs and too many T-bars in the Würzhöhe and Resterhöhe sectors. And the Horn has no fast lifts except the access gondola and a cable car.

QUEUES ★★★ ★ ★
Still some problems
There can still be peak time queues for the Hahnenkamm gondola out of the town. The chair upgrades at Ehrenbachgraben – a six-pack and an eight-pack – have solved the bottleneck there. But there can still be occasional queues elsewhere on the Hahnenkamm/Pengelstein sectors. And several 2011 reporters complained about 'dreadful' and 'regular 20 to 25 minute queues' for the old double chair G8 up to Zweitausender (unavoidable en-route to Resterhöhe). Both the Horn and the Hahnenkamm can have crowded pistes at times – though the gondola to Wurzhöhe has helped by encouraging people to use the Jochberg and Pass Thurn slopes.

TERRAIN PARKS ★★★ ★ ★
Double the fun
In order to attract a more freestyle-orientated clientele, Q parks was hired in 2008 to build a new park. The Q team is responsible for the design of no fewer than 10 Austrian parks in areas such as the Montafon and Sölden, so the resort is in good hands. The result was 'south' park, and aimed at advanced riders. But it is

↑ Pengelstein: the flash building on the left is the start of the 3S gondola to Wurzhöhe

KITZBÜHELER ALPEN MARKETING GMBH / SIMON OBERLEITNER

remote (on the Hanglalm run in the Resterhöhe sector). The park has several kicker lines, from big to huge, as well as advanced rails, a plethora of butter boxes and a visually pleasing wooden obstacle section. Pro riders love the park's centrepiece, a huge gap jump. The original park on the Kitzbüheler Horn has been renamed the Horn-Min-New-School-Park (snappy eh?) and is now specifically a beginner area and used by ski schools to introduce novices to freestyle. The park in nearby Westendorf is excellent – and is well worth the trip for freestyle aficionados.

SNOW RELIABILITY ★★☆☆☆
More snowmaking now
The problem is that Kitzbühel's slopes have one of the lowest average heights in the Alps and the Horn is also sunny. Even in an exceptionally good snow year some reporters complain of worn patches, ice and slush on the lower slopes. In a normal year, the lower slopes can be very tricky or bare at times (though the snow at the top is often OK). The expansion of snowmaking has improved matters when it's cold enough to make snow – runs down to Kitzbühel, Kirchberg, Klausen and Jochberg are covered. A 2011 visitor found conditions 'better than feared' because of this. But many slopes still remain unprotected. If snow is poor, head for Resterhöhe.

FOR EXPERTS ★★★☆☆
Plan to go off-piste
Steep slopes – pistes and off-piste terrain – are mostly concentrated in the Steinbergkogel-Ehrenbachgraben area, equipped with three fast chairs. Direttissima is seriously steep, but sometimes groomed – fabulous. The other blacks dotted around are easier. There are plenty of long, challenging reds. When conditions allow, there is plenty of gentler off-piste to be found – some of it safely close to pistes, some requiring a guide. And the long ski route from Pengelstein towards Jochberg is fabulous in good snow.

FOR INTERMEDIATES ★★★★☆
Lots of alternatives
The Hahnenkamm area is prime terrain but can get crowded. Good intermediates will want to do the World Cup downhill run, of course (see the feature panel earlier in the chapter). And the long blues of around 1000m vertical to Klausen, Kirchberg and Skirast are satisfying. The black to Aschau is not difficult, and a lovely way to end the day (check the bus times first).

The Wurzhöhe runs are good for mixed abilities, and the short, high runs at Resterhöhe are ideal if you are more timid. There are easy reds down

Interactive resort shortlist builder at www.wtss.co.uk

> **Not one but two glaciers on p177.**

SKI-DIRECT

Expert Advice

Lowest Prices

Group
Specialists

Open 7 Days

0844 553 3501
ABTA: D9779

SKI-DIRECT.CO.UK

UK PACKAGES

Alpine Answers, Alpine
Weekends, Carrier,
Crystal, Crystal Finest,
Elegant Resorts, First
Choice, Independent
Ski Links, Inghams,
Interactive Resorts,
Momentum, Neilson,
Ski Club Freshtracks,
Ski Line, Ski Solutions,
Skitracer, Snow
Finders, Snowscape,
STC, Thomson
Kirchberg Crystal, First
Choice, Neilson,
Snowscape

KITZBÜHELER ALPEN MARKETING
GMBH / STEFAN ASTNER
Few of the 56
mountain restaurants
have as spectacular
views as this one –
but they are one of
the reasons we
always enjoy visits to
Kitzbühel ↓

to Pass Thurn and Jochberg (but slow chairs back). The whole of this area tends to be much quieter than Hahnenkamm and Pengelstein. Much of the Horn is good cruising and the east-facing Raintal is excellent (though again, has a slow chair back).

FOR BEGINNERS ★★☆☆☆
Not ideal
The Hahnenkamm nursery slopes are no more than adequate, and prone to poor snow conditions – but at least they have some free lifts. There are nursery areas with free lifts at Jochberg, Pass Thurn and Aschau, too. The Horn has a high, sunny, nursery-like section, and quick learners will soon be cruising home from there on the long Hagstein piste. There are some easy runs to progress to if the snow is OK. Day and two-day lift passes just for the Horn slopes are now available. But there are better resorts to learn in.

FOR BOARDERS ★★☆☆☆
Gaining recognition
Kitzbühel was never known as a snowboarders' hub, but it is growing in popularity, year on year. The resort took a major step forward on the freestyle front in 2008 – see 'Terrain parks'; it now boasts two decent parks built for all levels of skill. (Be aware, though, that the advanced 'south' park is a long way from the resort, up at Pass Thurn/Resterhöhe.) There are some good off-piste runs and fun natural obstacles on the Hahnenkamm and around Pengelstein. All the major lifts are now gondolas or chairlifts – the area suits beginners and intermediates well.

FOR CROSS-COUNTRY ★★★☆☆
Plentiful but low
There are around 60km of trails scattered around, but most are at valley level and prone to lack of snow.

MOUNTAIN RESTAURANTS ★★★★☆
A highlight
There are many attractive restaurants – 'one of the reasons we keep going back', says one of our Kitz regulars. Pick up a copy of the local restaurant guide. Helpfully, they are named and marked on the piste map – 56 in total. **Editors' choice** On our most recent visit, we had a delicious lunch of oriental beef strip salad and crispy pork ribs at Bärenbadalm (0664 855 7994), halfway to Resterhöhe. This hut has a cool, modern bar area with flat screen TVs, a roaring log fire and comfy armchairs and sofas; you can eat there or in various dining areas with a more rustic feel. Endorsed by reporters. Seidlalm (63135), right by the lower part of the downhill course, is relatively quiet and delightfully rustic; praised by reporters, too. **Worth knowing about** In the Hahnenkamm sector we had a jolly meal at Berghaus Tyrol. Readers have also suggested Hahnenkammstüberl ('particularly good grostl') Melkalm, Hockeckhütte, Hochbrunn, Schutzhütte Steinbergkogel ('great freshly cooked food') and Ehrenbachgraben ('bright and modern'). On Pengelstein, the Usterweis is a nice woody place with a limited menu and Schroll has 'good food and service'. At Wurzhöhe/ Resterhöhe, try Hanglalm, Sonnalm, Bruggeralm or Panoramaalm. On the Horn, Hornköpfl-Hütte's good food and sunny terraces are praised. Gipfelhaus is quieter, with 'super views'.

SCHOOLS

Rote Teufel
t 62500
Alpin Experts
t 0664 125 5171
Element3
t 72302
Snowsports
t 0664 390 0090

Classes
(Rote Teufel prices)
6 days (2hr am and
pm) €180
Private lessons
€150 for 2hr

CHILDCARE

There is no non-ski
nursery, but
babysitters and
nannies can be hired

Ski school
From age 3 (6 days
€180 – Rote Teufel)

ACTIVITIES

Indoor Aquarena
Centre (pools, slides,
sauna, solarium, mud
baths, aerated baths,
underwater massage)
– discounted entry
with lift pass; tennis,
fitness centre, beauty
centre, climbing wall,
museums, casino,
cinema
Outdoor Ice rink
(curling and skating),
tobogganing,
ballooning, 65km of
cleared walking paths

GETTING THERE

Air Salzburg 75km/
45 miles (1hr30);
Munich 165km/
105 miles (2hr30);
Innsbruck 95km/
60 miles (1hr30)

Rail Mainline station
in resort. Post bus
every 15min from
station

SCHOOLS AND GUIDES ★★★★☆
Red Devils rule
The Kitzbühel Rote Teufel (Red Devils)
have absorbed several other local
schools (including the Total school).
The other schools emphasise their
small scale. Element3 is an adventure
company now offering ski/snowboard
classes. Reports please.

FOR FAMILIES ★☆☆☆☆
Not an ideal choice
It's a spread-out resort for a family.
Rote Teufel takes kids from age three.

STAYING THERE

Kitzbühel is essentially a hotel resort.
Chalets Crystal has a 35-bed chalet
close to the Hahnenkamm gondola.
Hotels There is an enormous choice.
★★★★★Tennerhof (63181) Luxurious
former farmhouse, with renowned
restaurant. Beautiful panelled rooms.
Relais et Châteaux.
★★★★★Schloss Lebenberg (6901)
Modernised 'castle' with smart
wellness centre; inconvenient location
but free shuttle-bus.
★★★★Golfhotel Rasmushof (652520)
Right on the slopes by the race finish
area, close to centre of town. 'Book a
room overlooking the slopes.'
★★★★Goldener Greif (64311) Elegant,
historic inn; vaulted lobby-sitting area,
panelled bar, sauna, steam.
★★★★Jägerwirt (6981) Modern chalet.
Not ideally placed, but has been
recommended.
★★★★Maria Theresia (64711) Central,
recently renovated. 'Food good, rooms
well-appointed and staff very helpful.'
★★★★Schwarzer Adler (6911) Traditional
hotel, near centre, highly praised by a
reporter. Pool.
★★★★Best Western Kaiserhof (75503)
By the Hahnenkamm gondola. 'Great
spa, pool – can't fault it.'
★★★★Schweizerhof (62735) Comfortable
chalet right by Hahnenkamm gondola.
★★★Edelweiss (75252) Close to centre.
'Most welcoming hotel we've ever
stayed at; supply bags for you to take
food from breakfast table for lunch.'
★★★Strasshofer (62285) Central.
'Friendly, good with children, quiet
rooms at back.' 'Excellent value.'
★★Mühlbergerhof (62835) Small,
friendly pension in good position.
Apartments Many of the best are
attached to hotels.

EATING OUT ★★★★☆
Something for everyone
There is a wide range of restaurants to
suit all pockets, including pizzerias
and fast-food outlets (even
McDonald's). The Neuwirt in the
Schwarzer Adler hotel is regarded as
the best in town and wins awards in
food guides. The Chizzo offers fine
dining in one of the oldest buildings
in Kitzbühel. Good, cheaper places
include the traditional Huberbräu-
Stüberl, Eggerwirt and, a little out of
town with great views, Hagstein
(traditional farm food). Goldene Gams
has both traditional and modern
dining rooms, plus a wide menu.
Barrique does 'great pizza'. On Fridays
you can dine at the top of the
Hahnenkamm gondola (Hochkitzbühel).
For something different take a taxi to
Rosi's Sonnbergstub'n. Choose the
speciality lamb or duck and expect to
be serenaded by Rosi herself.

APRES-SKI ★★★★☆
A main attraction
Nightlife is one of Kitz's great selling
points. There's something for all
tastes, from throbbing bars full of
teenagers to quiet places, nice cafes
and smart spots for fur-coat flaunting.
Immediately after the slopes close,
the town is jolly without being much
livelier than many other Tirolean
resorts. The Streifalm bar at the foot
of the slopes is popular, with 'white
pine and slate, open fire, widescreen
TV and Europop music'. 'The outside
bar at Chizzo was great fun,' says a
recent reporter whose favourite bar
was the Pavillion – 'great staff and a
great party atmosphere'. Praxmair,
Kortschak and Rupprechter ('great
place') are among the most
atmospheric cafes for tea-time cakes
and pastries. The lively Stamperl is
'classy and fun'. The Seidlalm has
Tirolean evenings (free) that reporters

have enjoyed. Lichtl's (with thousands of lights hanging from the ceiling) has karaoke. The Londoner Pub is a famous drinking place, well summarised by visitors as 'very crowded, very noisy and great fun', but the bar staff can be 'rude and sulky'. The Fonda has been recommended for the 'younger generation'. The Python, Highways and Take Five are the main discos.

The lift pass gives a reduction for the pools in the impressive Aquarena leisure centre. The Sports Park (with ice rink, ice hockey, bowling etc) is recommended. There's a museum (the one at the top of the Hahnenkamm is better says a reporter) and a casino. The railway makes excursions easy (eg Salzburg, Innsbruck).

Kirchberg 850m

- ➕ Easy access to SkiWelt as well as Kitzbühel's slopes
- ➕ Lively après-ski scene

- ➖ Sprawling village involving walks or bus rides to the lifts
- ➖ Not as cute as Kitzbühel

Kirchberg is handy for the SkiWelt slopes as well as those it shares with Kitzbühel. But it lacks Kitzbühel's car-free, medieval charm.

The local slopes (shared with Kitzbühel) are accessed via a choice of three gondolas (at the fringe of the village or a bus ride away at Klausen or Skirast). A bit further on from Skirast is a gondola into Westendorf's slopes and Brixen (a couple of miles away and with a gondola into the main SkiWelt slopes) can be easily reached by train or bus – see chapter on Söll for more on both of these.
Village charm The village is a large, busy, spread-out place; but has a pretty central square and church, as well as plentiful shops, bars and restaurants.
Convenience Many hotels and guest houses are close to the centre, which is a bus ride from the lifts.
Scenery Kirchberg sits at the junction of two pretty valleys – the one to Aschau is quiet and scenic.

THE MOUNTAIN
The local slopes are a mix of open runs higher up and pleasantly forested hillsides lower down.
Slopes A new gondola followed by an eight-seat chair provides fast access to Ehrenbachhöhe from the fringe of the village. Another gondola further out at Klausen goes to the same point. And yet another from Skirast goes towards Pengelstein – departure point of the cross-valley gondola towards the Resterhöhe slopes (at the far end of the Kitzbühel area). The separate small Gaisberg area on the other side of the valley has a couple of slopes and popular night skiing.
Fast lifts Most of the lifts on the Kirchberg side of the Kitzbühel area are now fast.

Queues We have no reports of recent problems locally.
Terrain parks See Kitzbühel.
Snow reliability Not a strong point.
Experts See Kitzbühel.
Intermediates Huge scope. The main slopes back to the resort are easy cruises when the snow is good.
Beginners There is a small nursery slope at the bottom of Gaisberg, with a free lift, but it's low so prone to poor snow. There are good progression runs down all the local gondolas.
Snowboarding The local blue runs make good novice terrain.
Cross-country There are lots of trails – but they can suffer from lack of snow.
Mountain restaurants There is a wide choice of huts throughout the region.
Schools and guides We lack recent reports on the local schools.
Families There are non-ski and ski kindergartens.

STAYING THERE
There's a wide choice.
Hotels There are plenty of central hotels and the 4-star Klausen (2128) is convenient for the gondola there.
Apartments There are some available.
Eating out Most restaurants are hotel-based, but there are a couple of pizzerias, a Chinese and a steakhouse.
Après-ski It's a pretty lively place, both at teatime and later on. The London Pub is the main après-ski venue. Boomerang has a sports bar and non-smoking lounge. Several places operate as discos later, and the VIP offers table-dancing.
Off the slopes There's floodlit tobogganing on Gaisberg, a leisure centre and some hotels have pools.

Weekly news updates and resort links at www.wtss.co.uk

Phone numbers
From elsewhere in Austria add the prefix 05356 for Kitzbühel and 05357 for Kirchberg; from abroad use the prefixes +43 5356 / +43 5357

TOURIST OFFICES
Kitzbühel
www.kitzbuehel.com
Kirchberg
www.kirchberg.at

Lech

If you can afford it, simply one of the best: a captivating village with exceptionally snowy slopes – plus St Anton just over the hill

RATINGS

The mountains

Extent	★★★★
Fast lifts	★★★★
Queues	★★★★
Terrain p'ks	★★★★
Snow	★★★★
Expert	★★★★
Intermediate	★★★★
Beginner	★★★★
Boarder	★★★★
X-country	★★★
Restaurants	★★★
Schools	★★★★
Families	★★★★★

The resort

Charm	★★★★
Convenience	★★★
Scenery	★★★
Eating out	★★★
Après-ski	★★★★
Off-slope	★★★

RPI 115

lift pass	£200
ski hire	£170
lessons	£125
food & drink	£155
total	**£650**

NEWS

2011/12: A chondola (fast hybrid lift of chairs and gondola cabins) will replace the Weibermahd quad above Oberlech.

The hotel Krone will undergo a major refurbishment.

+ Picturesque traditional village
+ Sunny but quite high slopes with excellent snow record
+ Sizeable area of intermediate pistes, plus extensive off-piste
+ Easy access by bus to the slopes of St Anton and other Arlberg resorts
+ Some very smart hotels
+ Lots of lovely heated chairlifts
+ Lively après-ski scene

– Pricey, by Austrian standards
– Surprisingly limited shopping
– Few non-hotel bars or restaurants
– Local traffic intrudes on main street
– Very few challenging pistes
– Nearly all slopes above treeline
– Blue runs back to Lech are rather steep for nervous novices
– Still a few slow, old lifts

Lech and its higher, linked neighbour Zürs are the most fashionable resorts in Austria, each able to point to a string of celebrity visitors, and to pull in Porsche-borne Germans by the thousand. Don't worry: we don't feel out of place here in our VWs, and neither would you.

The real point about Lech is that it offers excellent skiing on and off-piste (with one of the best snow records in the Alps) combined with a village that is a pleasure to inhabit – particularly if you can afford to stay in one of its lovely top hotels. And Zürs? In its bleak setting, it is never going to be a match for Lech; but the real problem is the through-traffic. The road to Lech needs to be buried in a tunnel. A whip-round among the owners of the four 5-star hotels should be enough to raise the necessary.

THE RESORT

Lech is an old farming village set in a high valley that spent long periods of winter cut off from the outside world until the Flexen Pass road through Zürs was constructed at the end of the 19th century. Even now, the road can be closed for days on end after an exceptional snowfall (a road tunnel is planned, but is not imminent).

Not far from the centre is the cable car up to Oberlech: a small, traffic-free collection of 4-star hotels set on the mountainside, with pistes running through it.

Zug is a hamlet 3km from Lech, with a lift into the Lech slopes. It's not ideal for sampling Lech's nightlife, but there is an evening bus service.

Lech is linked by lifts and runs to higher Zürs, described at the end of this chapter. There is a free, regular but often very crowded ski-bus service between the two resorts.

Buses (also crowded) run to St Anton, St Christoph and Stuben, too, all covered by the Arlberg pass. The post bus offers a less crowded option, but is not free. The Sonnenkopf area at Klösterle, reached by ski-bus from Stuben, is also covered – 'worth a trip' for its quiet, wide, woodland, intermediate runs, not least in bad weather.

VILLAGE CHARM ★★★★
Busy main street
The village is attractive, with upmarket hotels built in traditional chalet style, a gurgling river plus bridges, and a high incidence of snow on the streets. But don't expect a rustic idyll: away from the central area the place is fairly ordinary, and the appeal is somewhat dimmed by traffic on the main street, especially at weekends.

British visitors are not numerous, outnumbered 10:1 by Germans and 3:1 by Austrians.

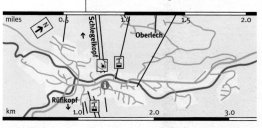

CONVENIENCE ★★★☆☆
It's a long village
The heart of the village is a short stretch of the main street beside the river, with most of the main hotels, the main shop (Strolz) and the Rüfikopf cable car, for access to the Zürs slopes. Just across the river are the chairlifts for Lech's main area of slopes. Chalets, apartments and pensions are dotted around the valley, and the village spreads for 2km. Some of the cheaper accommodation is quite a walk from the lifts.

Oberlech is a tiny place with pistes where you would expect streets, and an underground tunnel system linking the hotels and cable car station – used routinely to move baggage, and by guests in bad weather. The cable car works until 1am, allowing access to the mother resort's nightlife.

SCENERY ★★★☆☆
In a bright spot
Lech is in a fairly sunny position at the junction of two attractive valleys, with adequately impressive scenery, largely thanks to the Omeshorn looming to the south. It is high and open, with very few trees. From the top slopes, there are views to the Valluga above St Anton in one direction, and to Warth-Schröcken in the other.

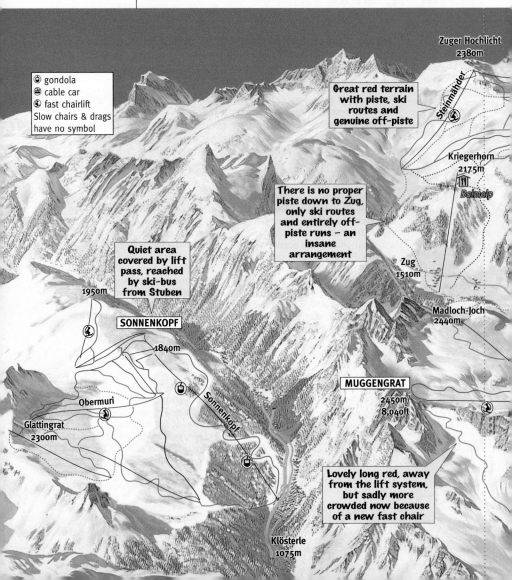

Zuger Hochlicht
2380m

⊕ gondola
⊜ cable car
④ fast chairlift
Slow chairs & drags
have no symbol

Great red terrain
with piste, ski
routes and
genuine off-piste

Steinmähder

Kriegerhorn
2175m

Balmalp

There is no proper
piste down to Zug,
only ski routes
and entirely off-
piste runs – an
insane
arrangement

Zug
1510m

Quiet area
covered by lift
pass, reached
by ski-bus
from Stuben

1950m

Madloch-Joch
2440m

SONNENKOPF

1840m

MUGGENGRAT

2450m/
8,040ft

Obermuri

Sonnenkopf

Glattingrat
2300m

Lovely long red, away
from the lift system,
but sadly more
crowded now because
of a new fast chair

Klösterle
1075m

THE MOUNTAINS

Practically all the slopes are treeless, the main exception being the lower runs just above Lech. Most are quite sunny – very few are north-facing.

The toughest runs are called 'ski routes' or 'high-alpine touring runs'.

The touring runs are simply off-piste runs that would not appear on the piste map at all in most resorts. No problem – if you fancy these runs, hire a guide.

The ski routes are marked, avalanche controlled but not groomed or patrolled. We applaud the clear explanation (lacking in many resorts), but we think many of these runs should be patrolled pistes. Ski routes form the only ways down to Zug, and thus are part of the Lech-Zürs-Lech circuit. And ski routes in several other areas are popular runs, treated like pistes. To add to the confusion, some of the routes are sometimes groomed (some were on our recent visits).

The piste map, which covers the whole of the Arlberg region in one view, is unclear and misleading in places – particularly around Oberlech.

Where is Austria's Golden Gate?
Answer on p177.

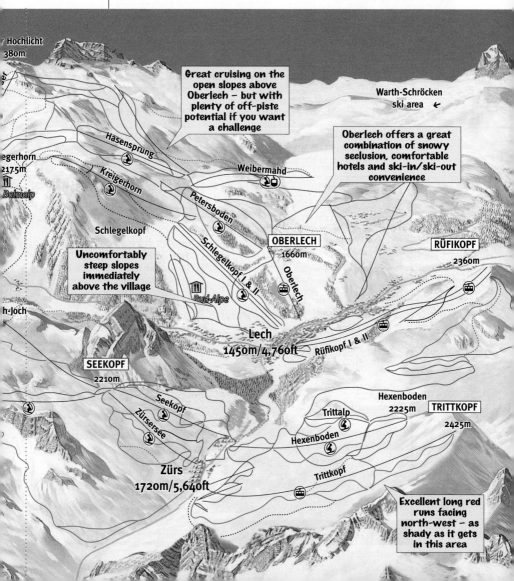

Great cruising on the open slopes above Oberlech – but with plenty of off-piste potential if you want a challenge

Warth-Schröcken ski area ←

Oberlech offers a great combination of snowy seclusion, comfortable hotels and ski-in/ski-out convenience

r Hochlicht
380m

Hasensprung

Weibermahd

egerhorn
2175m

Balmalp

Kreigerhorn

Petersboden

Schlegelkopf

OBERLECH
1660m

RÜFIKOPF
2360m

Oberlech

Uncomfortably steep slopes immediately above the village

Schlegelkopf I & II

Rud-Alpe

h-Joch

Lech
1450m/4,760ft

Rüfikopf I & II

SEEKOPF
2210m

Hexenboden
2225m

TRITTKOPF
2425m

Seekopf

Trittalp

Zürsersee

Hexenboden

Zürs
1720m/5,640ft

Trittkopf

Excellent long red runs facing north-west – as shady as it gets in this area

KEY FACTS

Resort	1450m
	4,760ft

Arlberg region

Slopes	1075-2650m
	3,530-8,690ft
Lifts	84
Pistes	280km
	174 miles
Blue	40%
Red	48%
Black	12%
Snowmaking	60%

For Lech-Zürs only

Slopes	1450-2450m
	4,760-8,040ft
Lifts	32
Pistes	117km
	73 miles
Blue	39%
Red	48%
Black	13%

They should really have one piste map for Lech-Zürs and separate ones for St Anton-St Christoph-Stuben and for Sonnenkopf. Piste marking is OK in general. But, confusingly, the same number is given to several pistes in places. Piste classification understates the difficulty of some pistes.

EXTENT OF THE SLOPES ★★★★
One-way traffic
The main slopes centre on **Oberlech**, 250m above Lech (just below the treeline), and can be reached by cable car or chairlifts. The wide, open pistes above here are perfect intermediate terrain and there is also lots of off-piste. Zuger Hochlicht, the high point in the sector, gives stunning views.

The **Rüfikopf** cable car takes Lech residents to the west-facing slopes of Zürs and the start of the Lech-Zürs-Lech circuit, which can only be done in a clockwise direction and is now called 'The White Ring'. This mountainside, with its high point at **Trittkopf**, is a mix of quite challenging intermediate slopes and flat/uphill bits. On the other side of Zürs the east-facing mountainside is of a more uniform gradient. Chairs go up to **Seekopf** with

intermediate runs back down.

A six-pack goes from Zürsersee up to **Muggengrat** (the highest point of the Zürs area). This has a good blue run back under it and the long, scenic, lift-free Muggengrat Täli red run back to Zürs – this used to be delightfully quiet but we've had reports of crowds since the six-pack arrived. It starts with a choice between a cat track and a mogul field, but develops into a fine, varied red with lots of nearby off-piste options on the way down; at the bottom you can take lifts up the other side or walk through the village to the Zürsersee chair back up to Seekopf.

From Seekopf you can ski down to the Madloch chair – slow and liable to closure by wind – which leads to the long, scenic ski route (often busy, with some tricky sections) back to the fringes of Lech, completing a clockwise circuit. You can peel off part-way down and head for Zug and the slow chairlift up to the Kriegerhorn above Oberlech.

FAST LIFTS ★★★★
Hotting up
A high proportion of lifts are now fast, including a new hybrid chondola for 2011/12, above Oberlech. Seven chairlifts have the luxury bonus of heated seats. But there are still a few slow, old lifts – Lech-Zürs is still some way behind Austrian pacesetters such as Ischgl and Saalbach in this respect.

QUEUES ★★★★
Still a few bottlenecks
There have been significant lift improvements and feedback is generally positive, but there are still one or two bottlenecks – the Schlegelkopf fast quad out of Lech and the crucial ('slow and cold') Madloch double chair at the top of the Zürs area generate peak-time queues on the Lech-Zürs-Lech circuit. Some readers mention the Rüfikopf cable cars to Zürs too. The resort proudly boasts that it limits numbers on the slopes to 14,000, to ensure a more enjoyable experience. Many reporters say that it works, and stress how much quieter Lech's slopes are than those over the hill in St Anton.

TERRAIN PARKS ★★★★
In Lech only
Snow Park is just above the Schlegelkopf and is one of the better terrain parks in Austria. There are over 20 features spread across easy,

LIFT PASSES

Arlberg

Prices in €

Age	1-day	6-day
under 16	27	127
16 to 19	41	184
20 to 64	45	212
over 65	41	184

Free no one, but day pass only €10 if under 8, €20 if over 75

Senior min. age for senior women is 60

Beginner points ticket

Notes Covers all St Anton, St Christoph, Lech, Zürs and Stuben lifts, and linking bus between Rauz and Zürs; also covers Sonnenkopf (10 lifts) at Klösterle, 7km west of Stuben (bus link from Stuben); single ascent, half-day and pedestrian options

SNOWPIX.COM / CHRIS GILL

Off-piste is plentiful, and excellent; taken from a ski route on Zuger Hochlicht, this shows ski routes and wider off-piste slopes on Kriegerhorn ↓

medium and pro lines, with kickers, two kinked boxes and a 9m-wide wall ride. The rails are also set in lines so you can hit several in a row. There's a fun box, 4m down rail and rainbow for beginners. There is also a designated Easy Park area made up of little banks and jumps, great for getting used to air time. See www.mellowparks.com.

SNOW RELIABILITY ★★★★
One of Austria's best
Lech and Zürs both get a lot of snow. Lech gets an average of almost 8m of snow between December and March, almost twice as much as St Anton, three times as much as Kitzbühel; but Zürs gets 50% more than Lech. The altitude is high by Austrian resort standards, and there is excellent snowmaking, helping to counter the sunny exposure. This combination, together with excellent grooming, means that the area normally has good coverage until late April.

FOR EXPERTS ★★★★
Off-piste is main attraction
There is only one (very short) black piste on the map, and there is no denying that for the competent skier who prefers to stick to patrolled runs the area is very limited. But the two types of off-piste route explained earlier offer lots to enjoy. There is plenty of excellent off-piste other than the marked ski routes, much of it accessed by long traverses – and the ski routes get heavily skied. By comparison with St Anton, fresh powder lasts well here.

Many of the best runs start from the top of the fast Steinmähder chair, which finishes just below Zuger

Hochlicht. Some routes involve a short climb to access bowls of untracked powder. From the Kriegerhorn there are shorter off-piste runs down towards Lech and a very scenic long ski route down to Zug (followed by a slow chair and a rope tow to pull you along a flat area). Most runs, however, are south- or west-facing and can suffer from sun. At the end of the season, when the snow is deep and settled, the off-piste off the shoulder of the Wöstertäli from the top of the Rüfikopf cable car down to Lech can be superb, as can Zuger Hochlicht. There are also good runs from the Trittkopf cable car in the Zürs sector, including a tricky one down to Stuben.

The steeper red runs (notably on Zuger Hochlicht and both sides of Zürs) are well worth a try, as is the lovely away-from-the-lifts Langerzug ski route back to Lech on the Rüfikopf side (steep start, then a gentle cruise, flattish run-out). And you'll want to visit St Anton during your stay, where there are more challenging pistes as well as more off-piste.

Heli-lifts are available to a couple of remote spots, at least on weekdays.

FOR INTERMEDIATES ★★★★
Flattering variety for all
The pistes in the Oberlech area are nearly all immaculately groomed blue runs, the upper ones above the trees, the lower ones in wide swathes cut through them. It is ideal territory for cruisers not wanting surprises.

Strong intermediates will want to do the circuit to Zürs and back. Whether it's wise for less confident intermediates to tackle the beautiful red ski route from Madloch depends,

MOMENTUM SKI

Weekend &
a la carte ski
holiday specialists

100% Tailor-Made

Premier hotels &
apartments

Flexible travel
arrangements

020 7371 9111
www.momentumski.com

SCHOOLS

Lech
t 2355

Oberlech
t 2007

Zürs
t 2611

**Omeshorn Alpincenter
Lech**
t 39880

Classes
(Lech prices)
6 days (2hr am and
2hr pm) €210
Private lessons
€245 for 4hr; each
additional person €20

UK PACKAGES

Alpine Answers, Alpine
Weekends, Crystal,
Crystal Finest, Elegant
Resorts, Erna Low,
Flexiski, Independent
Ski Links, Inghams,
Interactive Resorts,
Jeffersons, Kaluma,
Luxury Chalet
Collection, Momentum,
Oxford Ski Co, Powder
Byrne, Powder White,
PowderBeds, Scott
Dunn, Ski Club
Freshtracks, Ski
Expectations, Ski
Independence, Ski
Solutions, Ski Total,
Skitracer, Skiworld,
Snow Finders, STC,
Supertravel, White Roc
Oberlech Kaluma
Zürs Alpine Answers,
Alpine Weekends,
Carrier, Crystal, Crystal
Finest, Inghams,
Kaluma, Powder Byrne,
Scott Dunn, Ski
Solutions, STC

SKI amade
www.hochkoenig.at

*The peak of
your emotions!* HOCHKÖNIG
The peak of emotions

**150 km of connecting slopes
+ 33 modern ski lifts
= One of the largest ski resorts
in the Austrian alps and an
exhilarating ski experience!**

simply, on the conditions. It is not
steep, and part or all of it may be
groomed despite its non-piste status,
but parts can be heavily mogulled and
congested, and lots of people find the
run a struggle.

It's worth noting that the final blue-
run descents to Lech (as opposed to
Oberlech) are uncomfortably steep for
nervous novices.

More adventurous intermediates
will want to spend time on the fast
Steinmähder chair on Zuger Hochlicht
– a choice of satisfying pistes and ski
routes, and from there take the scenic
red run all the way to Zug (the latter
part on an easy ski route rather than a
piste). They may even want to give the
Langerzug ski route (see 'For experts')
a go. Lech is an excellent place to try
skiing deep snow for the first time.

Zürs has many more interesting red
runs, on both sides of the village. We
like the north-west-facing reds from
Trittkopf and the excellent Muggengrat
Täli (see 'Extent of the slopes').

FOR BEGINNERS ★★★★
Easy slopes in all areas
The main nursery slopes are at
Oberlech, but there is also a nice
dedicated area in Lech. There are
good, easy runs to progress to. You
can buy a points card rather than a
full lift pass.

FOR BOARDERS ★★★★
Easy riders, but mind the flats
Lech's upper-crust image has not stood
in the way of its snowboarding
development. It has some of the best
backcountry riding in Austria and is a
popular destination for freeriders. A
blend of impeccable piste grooming,
modern chairlifts and few draglifts
makes for nice learning conditions;
but beware of the west-facing slopes
at Zürs, which have many flat/uphill
sections.

FOR CROSS-COUNTRY ★★★
Picturesque valley trail
A 19km trail starts from the centre of
Lech and leads through the beautiful
but shady valley, along the Lech river
to Zug and back. Lunch at the Älpele
has been recommended. In Zürs there
is a 4km track to the Flexen Pass and
back.

MOUNTAIN RESTAURANTS ★★★
Still not a strong point
The restaurants of the hotels in Zürs
and Oberlech, in particular, have
traditionally dominated the lunch
scene here, but the options are
widening gradually. Restaurants are
clearly marked on the piste map
(except the ones in Oberlech, not
surprisingly).

Editors' choice Rud-Alpe (418250) is
not far above Lech, but far enough to
count as a mountain restaurant – it
would be an energetic non-skier who
walked up. It's a welcoming, rustic
place, lovingly built using timbers from
other old huts. We had excellent gröstl
and desserts there in 2011, efficiently
served in a cosy wood-built room. We
and reporters have also enjoyed the
modern, woody Balmalp, above Zug;
cool music (loud on the terrace,
quieter inside); simple food (pasta,
pizza, ribs, salad); 'stunning views',
'huge portions'.

Worth knowing about Kriegeralpe
above Oberlech is rustic and charming.
Above Zürs, Seekopf offers table
service and has been praised for
quality and price. At Oberlech there
are several big sunny terraces set
prettily around the piste. Quite often
you'll find a live band playing outside
one. Reader recommendations include
the Ilga Stüble, the lovely old Alter
Goldener Berg, the Mohnenfluh and
Burgwald.

SCHOOLS AND GUIDES ★★★★
Excellent in parts
The ski schools of Lech, Oberlech and
Zürs all have good reputations and the
instructors speak good English. Many
instructors are booked every year by
regular visitors. Group lessons are
divided into no fewer than nine ability
levels. We get good reports; one
regular visitor has been highly
satisfied over the past few years and
another reports 'excellent instruction
and attention'. The Omeshorn
Alpincenter school is an alternative
school, also with guiding.

CHILDCARE

Mini-clubs run 9am to 4pm, Sun to Fri
t 0664 123 9993
Miniclub Lech
From age 3
Little Zürs
From age 2
Kinderland Oberlech
From age 2
Babysitting list
Held by tourist office

Ski school
From 4½ to 14:
6 days €193

FOR FAMILIES ★★★★★
Oberlech's fine, but expensive

Oberlech makes an excellent choice for families who can afford it, particularly as its hotels are so convenient for the slopes. Reporters have praised the family-friendly approach and attention paid to children using the lifts: 'Mountain staff were really polite and helpful.' There's a kids' club in Oberlech and Goldener Berg has an in-house kindergarten. The Oberlech school is normally well-regarded (small groups, good English spoken), but has been criticised for poor organisation. Private lessons seem to have been more successful.

STAYING THERE

Chalets There are a few chalets run by UK tour ops, including two chalet hotels by Ski Total, one with pool, and two chalets in Zug by Skiworld, both with sauna.
Hotels There are four 5-stars, over 40 4-stars and countless other places.
LECH
★★★★★Arlberg (21340) Elegantly rustic central chalet, widely thought to be the best in Lech. Pool.

★★★★★Post (22060) Lovely old Relais & Châteaux place on the main street; pool, sauna. 'Remains fantastic. Very good bar and food, perfect service.'
★★★★Krone (2551) One of the originals, by the river. Repeatedly tipped over the years, and again in 2011. 'Marvellous location; rooms, food, staff excellent.' Small pool and spa. Due for major refurbishment for 2011/12.
★★★★Monzabon (2104) 'Excellent location, good food, helpful staff, attractive stube,' said a 2010 report. Pool, indoor ice rink.
★★★★Schwarzwand (2469) Perfectly positioned for beginners, by the separate nursery slope. Sauna, steam room, solarium. 'Food and service very high standard, and excellent value,' says our enthusiastic reporter.
★★★★Tannbergerhof (22020) Splendidly atmospheric inn on the main street, with outdoor bar and popular disco (tea time as well as later). Pool.
★★★Lärchenhof (2300) Neat B&B hotel with spa – 'excellent breakfast, nice modern rooms and friendly owners.'
OBERLECH
★★★★Bergkristall (2678) Smart, family-run, comfortable rooms, on slopes, hot tub, steam, sauna, solarium,

GETTING THERE

Air Zürich 200km/
125 miles (2hr30);
Innsbruck 120km/
75 miles (1hr30);
Friedrichshafen
130km/80 miles
(1hr45)

Rail Langen (17km/
10 miles); regular
buses from station;
buses connect with
international trains

ACTIVITIES

Indoor Sports park
(fitness studios,
tennis, bowling,
climbing wall, sauna),
hotel swimming
pools, museum,
galleries, library, ice
rink (in hotel
Monzabon)

Outdoor Cleared
walking paths, ice
rink, curling,
toboggan run (from
Oberlech),
snowshoeing, horse-
drawn sleigh rides

Phone numbers
From elsewhere in
Austria add the prefix
05583; from abroad
use the prefix +43
5583

TOURIST OFFICE

www.lech-zuers.at

massages. Own in-house nanny. Good reputation for food (including fresh fish daily); lovely lunch terrace.

****Burg** (22910) Smart, with pool, saunas, steam and famous outdoor umbrella bar.

****Montana** (2460) Welcoming chalet run by the family of Patrick Ortlieb, and reporters' favourite by a mile. 'Best hotel food ever, friendly and efficient service,' says a repeat visitor. Pool, smart wellness centre.

****Pension Sabine** (2718) Regular haunt of an American reporter – 'Excellent food, very friendly.'

Apartments There are lots available to independent bookers.

EATING OUT ★★★★★
Mainly hotel-based
There are over 50 restaurants in Lech, but nearly all of them are in hotels. Reporter recommendations include the Krone ('amazingly courteous service'), Post ('modern Austrian food'), Almhof Schneider ('traditional'), Don Enzo Due ('good pizzas') and Fux ('modern/Asian food; fine sushi, pork'). Hûs Nr 8 is one of the best non-hotel restaurants for traditional Austrian food. The Olympia has been suggested for cakes, coffee and 'excellent pork medallions', while the apple strudel at Backstüble is 'to die for'. Café Fritz is 'cosy and quite cheap for local standards'.

In Zug, the Rote Wand is excellent for traditional Austrian food, but is pricey. Reporters tip the 'cosy and pleasant' Alphorn and Klösterle ('tops all as far as food and charm is concerned; expensive').

APRES-SKI ★★★★★
Good but expensive
At Oberlech, the umbrella bar of the Burg hotel is popular at close of play, as is the champagne bar in hotel Montana. Readers also like the Ilga.

Down in Lech the outdoor bars of hotels Krone (in a lovely, sunny setting by the river) and Tannberghof (where there's an afternoon as well as a late-night disco) are popular. Later on, the Side Step disco (Krone hotel) and Archiv Bar liven up too. Readers also like the Fux Jazzbar (with live music and huge wine list).

Zug makes a good night out: you can take a sleigh ride for a meal at the Rote Wand, Klösterle or Auerhahn, and have drinks at the Vinothek wine bar at the s'Achtele restaurant.

After 7.30pm the free resort bus becomes a pay-for bus called James, which runs until 3am.

OFF THE SLOPES ★★★★★
At ease
Many visitors to Lech don't indulge in sports, and the main street often presents a parade of fur-clad strollers. The range of shopping is surprisingly limited – Strolz's plush emporium (including a champagne bar) right in the centre is the main attraction.

It's easy for pedestrians to get to Oberlech or Zug for lunch. The village outdoor bars are ideal for posing. There are 20km of walking paths – the one along the river to Zug is 'outstandingly' beautiful; the tourist office produces a good map. There's a sports centre (no pool).

The floodlit sledging run from Oberlech to town is popular with families and highly recommended.

LINKED RESORT – 1720m

ZÜRS

Some 10 minutes' drive towards St Anton from Lech is Zürs. Austria's first recognisable ski lift was built here in 1937. Zürs is a rare thing: a highly fashionable and expensive resort where the main occupation of visitors is skiing rather than parading. It has some excellent hotels (including four 5-stars); one inside them, all is well with the world. But the village as a whole doesn't have much appeal – it has nothing resembling a centre, few shops and a lot of intrusive traffic to/from Lech on the central through-road. We stayed at the 5-star Zürserhof (25130) and found it excellent – great service, food and spa facilities. There are nine 4-stars, and three humble 3-stars for the impoverished.

If you want to eat out in the evening, it will probably be in another hotel. Toni's Einkehr (a rustic hut at the foot of the Trittkopf slopes) is an exception and has been recommended. Nightlife is quiet. Vernissage is said to be the best nightspot. There's a disco in the Edelweiss hotel, a piano bar in the Alpenhof and the bar at the Hirlanda is 'pleasant'.

Many of the local Zürs instructors are booked up for private lessons for the entire season by regular clients; the last time we tried to get a private lesson here, the only available slots were over lunchtime.

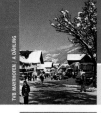

Mayrhofen

Large, lively resort with relatively reliable snow on local slopes and access to other good areas nearby, including a glacier

RATINGS

The mountains

Extent	★★★
Fast lifts	★★★★
Queues	★
Terrain p'ks	★★★★★
Snow	★★★
Expert	★★
Intermediate	★★★
Beginner	★★
Boarder	★★★★
X-country	★★
Restaurants	★★★
Schools	★★★★
Families	★★

The resort

Charm	★★★
Convenience	★
Scenery	★★★
Eating out	★★★
Après-ski	★★★★
Off-slope	★★★★

RPI 85

lift pass	£190
ski hire	£90
lessons	£80
food & drink	£120
total	**£480**

NEWS

2011/12: A six-pack is due to replace the Katzenmoos double chair on Penken, above Finkenberg.

2010/11: A hybrid gondola/chairlift replaced the triple chair just above the Penken gondola.

At Zell im Zillertal, a two-stage gondola replaced the Weisenalm lift from the valley and double chair above it. Snowmaking was improved too.

At Königsleiten a two-stage gondola opened from the village to a new restaurant at the top of the mountain. And another gondola replaced a quad on the Gerlos slopes.

➕	Good for confident intermediates
➕	High, snow-sure slopes by local standards – plus glacier nearby
➕	Several worthwhile nearby areas on the same lift pass
➕	Lively après-ski but it's easily avoided if you prefer peace
➕	Excellent children's amenities

➖	Long queues for the gondola to and from the main slopes
➖	Slopes can be crowded
➖	Many lodgings a bus ride from lifts
➖	Runs mostly short
➖	Few steep pistes, although they do include Austria's steepest
➖	No pistes to the valley from Penken

Like so many popular Tirolean resorts, Mayrhofen manages to meet the needs of young people bent on partying and families looking for a quieter time. What marks it out is its relatively high, relatively snow-sure slopes.

Bear in mind that you can access those slopes from quieter villages between Mayrhofen and Hintertux, covered in the Hintertux chapter. And don't forget that the valley lift pass covers lots of other places that are well worth exploring – it covers over 170 lifts and more than 640km of pistes.

Mayrhofen has long been a British favourite. We've had a few reports this year in response to our appeal last year, but would like more. If you go, do report.

THE RESORT

Mayrhofen is a fairly large resort sitting in the flat-bottomed, steep-sided Zillertal. Most shops, bars and restaurants are on one long street, with hotels and pensions spread over a wider area.

Free buses and trains linking the Zillertal resorts mean you can easily have an enjoyably varied week visiting different areas on the Ziller valley lift pass including the excellent glacier at Hintertux (which has its own chapter). At the end of this chapter we cover the Zillertal Arena area, which starts at Zell am Ziller. The other major Zillertal area is Hochzillertal/Hochfugen above Kaltenbach, dealt with in the Directory at the back of the book. There's a good train service to Salzburg, Innsbruck and Munich.

VILLAGE CHARM ★★★★★
Traditional and lively

As the village has grown, architecture has been kept traditional, and the place merges with the surrounding fields in a rather charming way. The resort has a well-deserved reputation for lively après-ski, but the central hotels are mainly slightly upmarket and overall the place feels pleasantly civilised. The valley road bypasses the village, but it is not traffic-free.

CONVENIENCE ★★★★★
Pick your spot

The original centre, around the church, tourist office and the road out to the bus/railway stations, is now on the edge of things. The main lift to the major Penken sector of slopes is set at the opposite end of the main street,

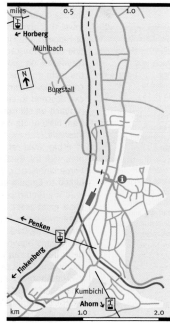

KEY FACTS

Resort	630m
	2,070ft

Ziller valley	
Slopes	630-3250m
	2,070-10,660ft
Lifts	171
Pistes	662km
	411 miles
Blue	26%
Red	63%
Black	11%
Snowmaking	75%

Mayrhofen-Lanersbach only (ie excluding Hintertux glacier)	
Slopes	630-2500m
	2,070-8,200ft
Lifts	53
Pistes	159km
	99 miles
Snowmaking	
	123 guns

LIFT PASSES

Superskipass Zillertal

Prices in €		
Age	1-day	6-day
under 15	19	90
15 to 18	33	159
over 19	42	199

Free under 6
Senior no deals
Beginner no deals
Notes
1-, 2- or 3-day passes cover Mayrhofen areas only; 4-day and over passes include all Ziller valley lifts; part-day and pedestrian passes available

1km away, and the Ahorn cable car is 200m further along, over the river. You can leave equipment at the lift station. The free bus service can be crowded, and it finishes early (5pm), so location is important. The most convenient area is on the main street, close to the Penken gondola station.

SCENERY ★★★
Views to the glacier
Mayrhofen is set between its two steep-sided mountains. From the top of each there are good views to the Hintertux glacier.

THE MOUNTAINS

Practically all Mayrhofen's slopes are above the treeline. Many are challenging reds, and some reporters note that the blues are not the easiest. Reporters praise signposting, but the piste map is poor, particularly around the complex Penken summit. We very nearly ended up in Finkenberg, with our car in Hippach.

As elsewhere in Austria, there are unexplained 'skiroutes', including all the runs to the valley. You may find some are groomed, but we presume all are unpatrolled. Take care.

EXTENT OF THE SLOPES ★★★
Fair-sized but inconvenient
The larger of Mayrhofen's two areas of slopes is **Penken-Horberg**, accessed by the main gondola from one end of town. It is also accessible via gondolas at Hippach and Finkenberg, both a bus ride away. You cannot get back to Mayrhofen on snow – you can catch the main gondola down or, if snow cover is good enough (it rarely is), you can descend to either Finkenberg or Hippach on ski routes. The buses back from Finkenberg run at only hourly intervals.

A big cable car links the Penken area with the **Rastkogel** slopes above Vorderlanersbach, which is in turn linked to **Egglam** above Lanersbach – read the Hintertux chapter. These links are a great asset, and the run to Egglam benefits from snowmaking now. Getting back from Rastkogel on skis means braving a busy red mogul field, but you can avoid it by taking the linking cable car down.

The **Ahorn** area is pleasant but very small, and tends to be neglected – except by the lift company, which a few years back equipped it with

Austria's largest cable car (carrying 160) for access and an eight-pack at altitude. Quite bizarre. There is a lovely, long red run to the valley.

FAST LIFTS ★★★★
Not enough to cope
Look at the map and a good proportion of the lifts are fast – gondolas and high-speed chairs. But given the queues (see below), more are needed to cope with the crowds.

Each of the main areas covered by the Ziller valley pass is large enough for an interesting day out.

QUEUES ★
Still a real problem
The Penken gondola cannot cope at peak times, morning and afternoon. Reports of queues of 45 or 60 minutes at the morning peak are still common. One way to deal with them is to stroll over to the queue-free Ahorn cable car and do a few warmup laps of 1300m vertical on that (maybe that's why they built it?). Alternatively, the gondolas out at Finkenberg and Hippach are less busy, and those at Lanersbach and Vorderlanersbach quieter still.

Up the mountain, the giant 150-er Tux cable car is not giant enough at times. Not surprisingly, with four gondolas moving people up from the valley, parts of Penken get crowded at times.

TERRAIN PARKS ★★★★★
Something for everyone
One of the finest parks in the Alps, the Vans Penken park (www.vans-penken-park.com) lies beneath the dedicated Sun-Jet chairlift on Penken. Naturally, it attracts business, and it can get crowded. There's a separate beginners' zone, kids' park, an intermediate line and a pro line of three tabletops ranging in length between 15m and 19m; plus a big hip jump at the end of the park. Every year there are more combinations of kinked, curved and flat boxes and rails in the jib line. A detailed plan of the park is distributed. The half-pipe is reasonably well maintained and not too big, making it perfect for learning the ropes. Experts should bear in mind the 360m-long super-pipe at Hintertux.

SNOW RELIABILITY ★★★
Good by Tirolean standards
The area is better than most Tirolean resorts for snow because the slopes

UK PACKAGES

Crystal, Crystal Finest, First Choice, Independent Ski Links, Inghams, Neilson, Ski Club Freshtracks, Ski Expectations, Ski Independence, Ski Line, Skitracer, Skiworld, STC, Thomson
Zell im Zillertal *Crystal*

GETTING THERE

Air Salzburg 175km/110 miles (2hr15); Munich 195km/120 miles (2hr45); Innsbruck 70km/45 miles (1hr15)

Rail Local line through to resort; regular buses from station

are relatively high – mostly above 1500m. Snowmaking covers the whole Ahorn area, all the main slopes on Penken-Horberg and some on Rastkogel and Eggalm. Hintertux is one of the best glaciers in the world.

FOR EXPERTS ★★★★★
Commit Harakiri
Austria's steepest piste, called Harakiri and under the Knorren chair, has a gradient of 78% (or 38°). It is certainly steep for a European piste; on both our recent visits, the run was mogul-free but rock hard; not surprisingly, it was delightfully deserted. It does offer a worthwhile challenge for the brave but is quite short. The black run under the Schneekar chair on Horberg is a good, fast cruise when groomed, but there are few other steepish pistes. The long unpisted trail to Hippach is quite challenging but rarely has good snow because of its low altitude. There is, however, quite a lot of decent off-piste to be found, such as from the Horbergjoch chair at the top of Rastkogel and under the cable car linking to Lanersbach.

FOR INTERMEDIATES ★★★★★
On the tough side
Most of Mayrhofen's slopes are on the steep side of the usual intermediate range – great for confident intermediates; many of the runs in the main Penken area are quite short, though, with verticals in the 300m/400m region. With access to the Lanersbach slopes, there is quite a bit of ground to cover, including delightfully quiet runs on Eggalm. Don't overlook Ahorn, mainly for its excellent run back to the valley. There are few really gentle blue runs, making the area less than ideal for nervous intermediates or near-beginners. The overcrowding on many runs can add to the intimidation factor. Ahorn offers a sanctuary, but is very limited.

FOR BEGINNERS ★★★★★
OK if it works for you
Despite its reputation for teaching, Mayrhofen is not ideal for beginners. You have to ride up the mountain to the nursery slopes, and there are no special lift passes so you'll need the full one. The Ahorn nursery slopes are excellent – high, extensive, sunny and crowd-free. But if you are with non-beginner mates they will want to be on Penken. There are very few easy blues to progress to.

Not one but two glaciers on p177.

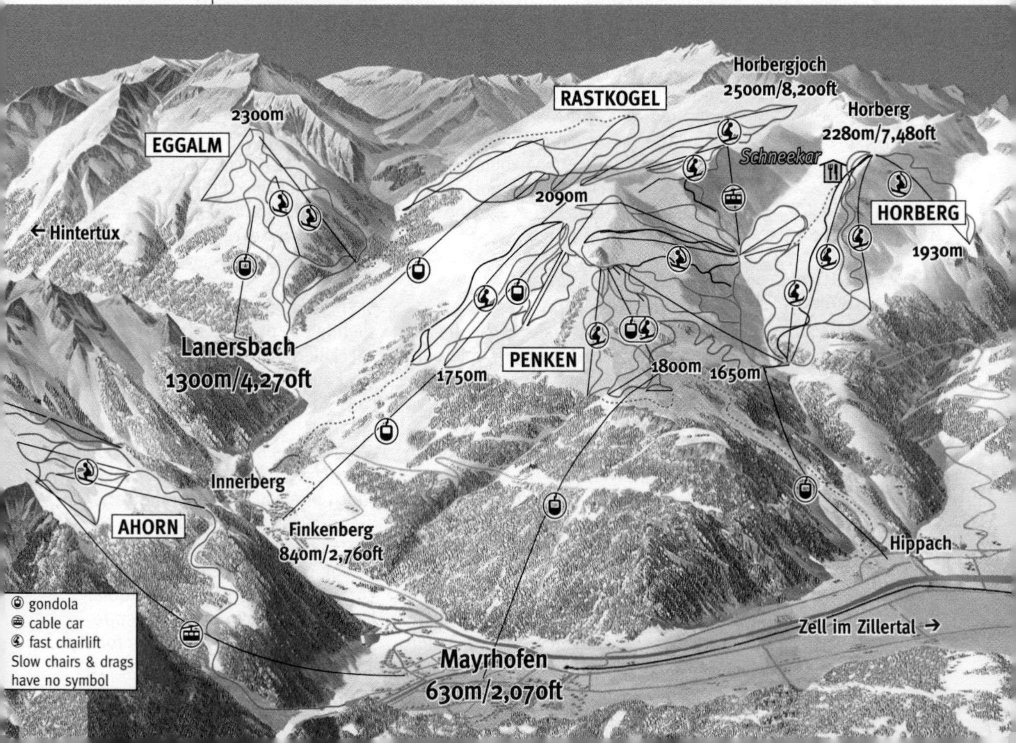

Weekly news updates and resort links at www.wtss.co.uk

↑ Snowmaking in Austria has really taken strides recently. This strip to the Ahorn cable car (in March 2011) was the best part of a metre deep.
SNOWPIX.COM / CHRIS GILL

SCHOOLS

Die Roten Profis (Manfred Gager)
t 63900

Total (Max Rahm)
t 63939

Mount Everest (Peter Habeler)
t 62829

Mayrhofen 3000 (Michael Thanner)
t 64015

Classes
(Roten Profis prices)
6 days (2½hr am or pm) €122

Private lessons
€119 for 2½hr for 1 person

FOR BOARDERS ★★★★☆
A popular hangout
Mayrhofen has long been popular with snowboarders. But beginners may have a hard time getting around, as the terrain tends to be relatively steep, the nursery slopes are inconvenient, and the area still has quite a few draglifts. Intermediates and upwards, however, will relish the abundance of good red runs and easily accessible off-piste. The terrain park is one of the best in Europe. The Snowbombing music festival is held here each year, as well as a 5-star TTR event, the Ästhetiker Wängl Tängl.

FOR CROSS-COUNTRY ★★☆☆
Head up the valley
There are 28km of trails in the area. Snow in the valley is not reliable but higher Vorderlanersbach has a much more snow-sure trail.

MOUNTAIN RESTAURANTS ★★★☆☆
Plenty of them
Most of Penken's many mountain restaurants are attractive but they can get crowded. They are clearly marked on the piste map.
Editors' choice The Schneekar (64940) at the top of the Horberg is our kind of place – beams and open fire inside, individual bookable tables on the terrace. Charming service, good view, excellent food. We had good hüttenflamkuchen (cheese, onion and bacon tart) here in 2011.
Worth knowing about The table-service Tappenalm below Horberg has 'great traditional food in bright surroundings'. Higher up, Grillhofalm is tipped as the 'cheapest we found and a great place to watch the park action'. The 'modern' Panorahma by the draglifts down from the Finkenberg gondola offers 'lovely pizzas' as well as wonderful views and 'world's best loos'. On Rastkogel, Berghaus Lämmerbichl is a 'good self-service'.

SCHOOLS AND GUIDES ★★★★☆
Excellent reputation
Mayrhofen's ski schools have good reputations, but we lack recent reports on most. However, an off-piste guide from the Mount Everest school provided 'good service and good value' for a 2011 visitor.

FOR FAMILIES ★★☆☆☆
Good but inconvenient
Mayrhofen majors on childcare and the facilities are excellent. But children have to be bussed around and ferried up and down the mountain.

STAYING THERE

Chalets There are several large places (ie, in or approaching the chalet hotel category). Skiworld has the Stoanerhof near the Ahorn cable car. Crystal has the Haus Tirol in the main street, close to the gondola. Inghams has the St Lukas, a short walk from the centre.
Hotels Note that the Penken gondola is 1km from the real centre, so 'central' does not mean 'close to lifts'. You can stay at the White Lounge ice-hotel on Ahorn, too.
★★★★★Elisabeth (6767) The only 5-star, slightly out of the centre.
★★★★Zillertalerhof (62265) 'Excellent food and service, great pool, sauna,' says a reader this year. Central.
★★★★Gutshof Zillertal (8124) A 2011 reporter was delighted to have found this place on the southern outskirts, which offers almost-free hire cars. 'Good meals, great deal.' Pool, spa.
★★★★Kramerwirt (6700) Lovely hotel, oozing character, central.
★★★★Strass (6705) By the gondola. Lively bars, disco, wellness centre, pool; but big, with low marks for style.
★★★★Neue Post (62131) An old

CHILDCARE

Wuppy's Kinderland
t 63612
Ages 3mnth to 7yr;
9am to 5pm, Mon-Fri
Crèche (Total school)
t 63939
From age 2; 9.30-3.30
Babysitting list
at tourist office

Ski school
All run classes for
children aged 4 or 5
to 14. Lunch can be
provided (6 days
including lunch €227)

ACTIVITIES

Indoor Adventure
pool, two hotel pools
open to the public,
massage, sauna,
squash, fitness centre,
climbing wall, tennis,
Outdoor Ice rink,
curling, 40km of
paths, snowshoeing,
paragliding,
tobogganing

Phone numbers
From elsewhere in
Austria add the prefix
05285 (Mayrhofen),
05282 (Zell), 05284
(Gerlos), 06564
(Königsleiten); from
abroad use the prefix
+43 and omit the
initial '0'

TOURIST OFFICES

Mayrhofen
www.mayrhofen.at

Zillertal Arena
Zell im Zillertal
www.zell.at
Gerlos
www.gerlos.at
Königsleiten
www.wald-
koenigsleiten.info

favourite, central. Pool, sauna, steam.
Apartments There are plenty available.

EATING OUT ★★★☆☆
Wide choice

There's a wide range of restaurants,
from local specialities to Chinese.
We've had good, satisfying meals at
the jolly, friendly Tiroler Stuben near
the station. Mo's is 'lively, with good
food', American-style. Wirtshaus zum
Griena is a lovely rustic old building
on the edge of town, with a traditional
menu – too much like a mountain
restaurant for our taste, but popular
with families. The Kramerwirt has
'excellent food with large portions'.

APRES-SKI ★★★★☆
Lively

Après-ski is a great selling point. At
close of play, the umbrella bar at the
top of the Penken gondola, the Ice Bar
at the hotel Strass and Brück'n Stadl
(Gasthof Brücke) get packed out.
Some of the other bars in the Strass
are rocking places later on, including
the Speak Easy Arena, with live music
and dancing until 4am. The Coup &
More has 'a lively atmosphere without
the rowdiness of some other places'.
Mo's American theme bar has live
music – 'lively but not too noisy'.
Scotland Yard is popular with Brits but
'expensive and tatty', reckons a 2011
visitor. For a quiet drink we head to
the bars of the big central hotels – the
Neuhaus or the Neue Post.

OFF THE SLOPES ★★★★☆
Good for all

Innsbruck and other resorts are easily
reached by train or bus. There are also
good walks and sports amenities,
including the swimming pool complex
– with saunas, solariums and lots of
other fun features. Pedestrians have
no trouble getting up the mountain to
meet friends for lunch. 'We had a non-
skier in our party and they found
plenty to do,' says a reporter.

DOWN-VALLEY AREA
ZILLERTAL ARENA

The Zillertal Arena was created in 2000
by linking the slopes of Zell im
Zillertal, a short drive down the valley
from Mayrhofen, to those above the
villages of Gerlos and Königsleiten.
They now share an area about as big
as the Mayrhofen-Lanersbach area. The
slopes are quite high, as in Mayrhofen,

but they also get a lot of sun, so the
snow message is a mixed one. The
slopes suit intermediates best. You
can really get a sense of travelling
around: the trip from one end to the
other is 17km and takes you over
several peaks and ridges. Our attempt
to explore it was spoilt by thick fog,
but a more fortunate reporter said:
'Starting from Zell, a return trip is a
full day's skiing. We did the tour over
two days to fit in all the other runs.'
Most runs are fairly short – the
longest, down to Gerlos, 4km.

Zell is the main town in the
Zillertal, and a real working town
rather than just a resort – it is a
sprawling place, and has the oldest
working brewery in the Tirol. There are
some good hotels, including the 4-star
Zapfenhof (2349) on the outskirts
(with pool) and the Brau (2313) in the
centre. The town is a bus ride from the
two gondolas into the ski area. You
have to ride these down as well as up
– there is no piste. Après-ski centres
around a few bars near the base of
the gondola.

Gerlos has the advantage of being
centrally situated in the ski area,
allowing you to explore in either
direction each day. It is a bustling
resort that straddles the road up to
the Gerlos pass and is a bus ride from
the gondola into the slopes. The home
slope benefits from top-to-bottom
snowmaking; there's a good local
terrain park, and a toboggan run.
Après-ski is lively and there are several
good local hotels, including the 4-star
Gaspingerhof (52160) with a very
smart spa.

Königsleiten is an unusual resort –
very spread-out, in a scenic wooded
setting above a dam; mostly small
chalets, but half a dozen hotels
including the 4-star Königsleiten
(82160). It has more extensive local
slopes than Gerlos, on either side of
the Gerlospass road, but less vertical.
On the north side, the runs are mostly
genuine reds, radiating from the peak
of Königsleitenspitze (2315m). The
lower southern sector has a row of
quad chairs serving easier slopes. A
new gondola from the village now
goes to the top of the mountain. The
Obermoser ski school has been
praised. But note that the draglift on
the village nursery slope is not
covered by the regional lift pass.

Both Gerlos and Königsleiten
attract a lot of Dutch visitors.

Obergurgl

A combination of high altitude and traditional Tirolean atmosphere keeps regulars going back, despite the drawbacks

RATINGS

The mountains

Extent	★★
Fast lifts	★★★★★
Queues	★★★★★
Terrain p'ks	
Snow	★★★★★
Expert	★★
Intermediate	★★★
Beginner	★★★★
Boarder	★★
X-country	★★
Restaurants	★★★
Schools	★★★★
Families	★★★★

The resort

Charm	★★★★
Convenience	★★★★
Scenery	★★★
Eating out	★★★
Après-ski	★★★★
Off-slope	★★

RPI   105

lift pass	£220
ski hire	£140
lessons	£110
food & drink	£120
total	**£590**

NEWS

2010/11: A new variant on the red from Hohe Mut opened.

There was also a new timed speed track by the Plattachbahn lift (Festkogl).

At Hochgurgl, snowmaking was extended and a new ice-bar opened beside the hotel Alpina.

KEY FACTS

Resort	1930m
	6,330ft
Slopes	1795-3080m
	5,890-10,100ft
Lifts	24
Pistes	110km
	68 miles
Blue	32%
Red	50%
Black	18%
Snowmaking	100%

➕ Glaciers apart, one of the most snow-sure resorts in the Alps; good for a late-season holiday

➕ Excellent area for beginners, timid intermediates and families

➕ Mainly queue- and crowd-free

➕ Traditional, quiet, chalet-style village with little traffic

➕ Jolly Tirolean teatime après-ski

➖ Limited area of slopes, with no tough pistes and no terrain park

➖ Exposed setting, with very few sheltered slopes for bad weather

➖ Little to do outside the hotels

➖ Village is fragmented, and lacking a real centre

➖ For a small Austrian resort, hotels are rather expensive

Obergurgl has never quite floated our boat. If we're going to a bleak, remote resort where there is little to do but ski, we'd rather go somewhere with rather more skiing to do.

But a loyal band of visitors go back time after time to Obergurgl or its higher satellite Hochgurgl, booking a year in advance to avoid disappointment, and it's not difficult to see why. If the list of plus-points above is what you're looking for, there really is nowhere else to beat it.

THE RESORT

Obergurgl is based on a traditional old village, set in a remote spot near the head of its valley – the highest parish in Austria and usually under a blanket of snow.

Although it's a small place, the village is split into three main parts. At the entrance to the resort is a cluster of hotels near the Festkogl gondola. The road then passes another group of hotels set on a little hill to the east, around the ice rink (beware steep, sometimes treacherous walks here). Finally you come to an attractive little square with the church, a fountain, and the focal hotel (Edelweiss und Gurgl). This is effectively the village centre, but it doesn't amount to much. There is an underground car park here. Even higher Hochgurgl, linked by a

mid-mountain gondola, is little more than a handful of hotels at the foot of its own area of slopes.

The lift pass is quite pricey, for a small resort. You can make it pricier still by paying 10 euro extra for a day in Sölden, a short bus ride down the valley (hourly buses).

VILLAGE CHARM ★★★★
On the quiet side
Obergurgl has no through traffic and few day visitors, so the place is calm and relaxed. The village 'centre' is mainly traffic-free, and entirely so at night. It's quite jolly immediately after the slopes close, but rather subdued later; most people stay in their hotels.

CONVENIENCE ★★★★
Lifts at both ends
Obergurgl is a small place, and there are lifts at both ends. The Hohe Mut gondola station is close to the 'centre', but nowhere is a long walk from a lift. Hochgurl looks like a convenient ski-in/ski-out resort, but nearly all the hotels are separated from the snow by roads and/or stairs.

SCENERY ★★★
High and bleak
Obergurgl's altitude and position mean the surrounding slopes are bleak. But it also means good panoramic views from the top of the lifts.

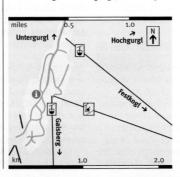

LIFT PASSES		
Obergurgl		
Prices in €		
Age	1-day	6-day
under 16	28	122
16 to 59	44	223
over 60	38	186
Free under 9		
Beginner no deals. (One free lift: Wiesenlift)		
Notes		
Covers lifts in Obergurgl and Hochgurgl, and local ski-bus; part-day passes and non-skier tickets available		

SNOWPIX.COM / CHRIS GILL

It's no exaggeration to say that, for many visitors, life revolves around the jolly Nederhütte. If you want a table for tea-time, it's best to get there by 11am and stay all day ↓

THE MOUNTAINS

Most of the slopes are very exposed – with few woodland runs to head to in poor conditions. Wind and white-outs can shut the lifts and, especially in early season, severe cold can limit enthusiasm. If the weather is bad but not that bad, another problem arises: in our view and that of many reporters, piste edge marking is dangerously slack. There are huge drop-offs that are not marked, and slopes seem to be marked either on one side only (often the uphill side) or in the middle only. Crazy. Reporters seem content with the piste map though. Classification of runs can overstate difficulty.

EXTENT OF THE SLOPES ★★★★★
Limited cruising
The total area of slopes is quite limited. A gondola links the Obergurgl and Hochgurgl ski areas at mid-mountain level. It closes absurdly early at 4pm. There are no piste links.

Obergurgl is the smaller of the two linked areas. It is in two sections, with a link at altitude in only one direction. The gondola from the village entrance and the Rosskar fast quad chair go to the higher **Festkogl** section. This is served by a short drag and a longer chair up to 3035m. From here you can head down to the gondola base or over to the **Hohe Mut** sector, also reached from the village via a gondola, which goes on to the sector high point at Hohe Mut. Lower down are slopes served by a slow quad and a six-pack.

There are two ski routes which were ungroomed on our recent visit but their status is not explained on the piste map. There's night skiing on 8km slopes, three times a week.

The slopes of **Hochgurgl** consist of high, gentle bowls, with fast lifts serving the main slopes above the village, but drags serving the more testing outlying slopes. From the top stations there are spectacular views to the Dolomites. A single run leads down through the woods to Untergurgl.

FAST LIFTS ★★★★★
Among the best
Most lifts are now high-capacity gondolas or fast chairs.

QUEUES ★★★★★
Few problems
Major lift queues are rare. 'Fantastic,' say reporters; 'surprisingly quiet and uncrowded, even in the Easter holidays'.

TERRAIN PARKS ★★★★★
There isn't one
There used to be a terrain park and pipe but these were scrapped.

SNOW RELIABILITY ★★★★★
Excellent
Obergurgl has high slopes and is arguably the most snow-sure of Europe's non-glacier resorts – even without its snowmaking, which the resort claims covers all the pistes. The resort has a long season by Austrian standards. Piste grooming is generally fine.

FOR EXPERTS ★★★★★
Not generally recommendable
There are few challenges on-piste – most of the blacks could easily be red, and where they deserve the classification it's only for short stretches (for example, at the very top of Wurmkogl). The ski routes are more challenging, particularly that from

Obergurgl

Interactive resort shortlist builder at **www.wtss.co.uk**

Hohe Mut when mogulled. There is a lot of easy off-piste to be found – the top school groups often go off-piste when conditions are right. Slopes around the Kirchenkar draglift are good for seeking out untracked powder. This is a well-known area for ski touring, and we have reports of very challenging expeditions on the glaciers at the head of the valley.

FOR INTERMEDIATES ★★★☆☆
Good but limited

There is some perfect intermediate terrain here, made even better by the normally flattering snow conditions. The problem is, there's not much of it. Keen piste-bashers will quickly tire of skiing the same runs and those who opted for the lift pass upgrade will be itching to catch the free bus to Sölden, down the valley.

Hochgurgl has the bigger area of easy runs, and these make good cruising. For more challenging intermediate runs, head to the Vorderer Wurmkogllift, on the right as you look at the mountain.

The Obergurgl area has more red than blue runs but most offer no great challenge to a confident intermediate. There is some easy cruising around mid-mountain on Festkogl. The blue run from the top of this sector to the village, via the Hohe Mut sector, is 1100m vertical. And there's another long enjoyable run down the length of the gondola, with a scenic black run and ski route variant (neither of them very steep) in the adjoining valley.

On Hohe Mut, there are very easy runs in front of the Nederhütte and back towards the village. The red run from Hohe Mut is narrow and in places winding – not recommended for timid intermediates.

FOR BEGINNERS ★★★★☆
Fine for first-timers

There is one free lift above the ski school; otherwise beginners need a full lift pass to get around. The inconveniently situated Mahdstuhl nursery slope above Obergurgl is adequate for complete beginners. And the gentle run under the gondola from the mid-station of the Hohe Mut gondola to the village is ideal to move on to as soon as a modicum of control has been achieved. The easy sheltered slopes that are served by the Bruggenboden chair are also suitable.

The Hochgurgl nursery slopes are an awkward walk from most of the hotels, but otherwise satisfactory. And there are good blue slopes to move on to.

The quality of the snow and piste preparation make learning here easier than in most lower Austrian resorts.

FOR BOARDERS ★★☆☆☆
Lacks challenge

Beginners can access most of the slopes without having to ride draglifts. There's some good off-piste potential for more advanced riders; a 2010 visitor singles out the area around the Steinmann chair low down in the Hohe Mut sector; but the lack of any terrain features or park is a major drawback for most.

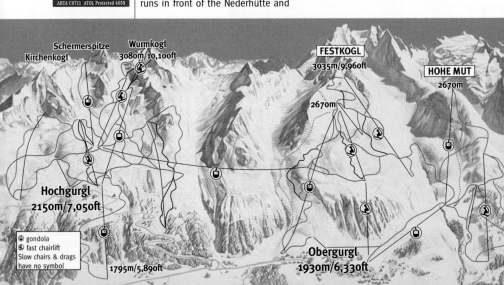

Schermerspitze
Kirchenkogl
Wurmkogl
3080m/10,100ft
FESTKOGL
3035m/9,960ft
HOHE MUT
2670m
2670m
2670m

Hochgurgl
2150m/7,050ft

Obergurgl
1930m/6,330ft

1795m/5,890ft

ⓖ gondola
ⓕ fast chairlift
Slow chairs & drags have no symbol

↑ You need to be sure-footed up here at Wurmkogl. In the distance are the slopes of Sölden

SNOWPIX.COM / CHRIS GILL

SCHOOLS

Obergurgl
t 6305

Hochgurgl
t 6265570

Classes
(Obergurgl prices)
6 days (2hr am and pm) €219

Private lessons
From €140 for 2hr;
€10 for additional person

CHILDCARE

Alpina and Hochfirst hotels
Kindergartens in these hotels

Kindergarten (ski school)
t 6305
From age 3; can include some skiing

Ski schools
From age 4 (6 days €219)

FOR CROSS-COUNTRY ★★☆☆☆
Limited but snow-sure
Three small loops, two at Obergurgl and one at Hochgurgl, amount to just 12km of trail. At Hochgurgl 1km is floodlit. All are relatively snow-sure and pleasantly situated but, like the slopes, very exposed in bad weather. Lessons are available.

MOUNTAIN RESTAURANTS ★★★☆☆
Fair choice
Hut choice is limited, but most reports are positive.
Editors' choice No contest, really. Hohe Mut Alm (639632) has table-service, fabulous glacier views from the big terrace, a woody interior, impressively efficient service, and good hearty food on our 2011 visit – endorsed by a reporter. But it gets packed early and doesn't take bookings. The jolly Nederhütte (6425), not far above village level, is hugely popular with readers: 'Great atmosphere, great traditional food'; 'excellent service, choice and reasonable prices'.
Worth knowing about The Top Mountain Star at Wurmkogl looks like an air traffic control tower, has great 360° views, a varied menu but a modern bar ambience. Kirchenkarhütte by contrast is a simple rustic hut – very small, and often crowded.

SCHOOLS AND GUIDES ★★★★☆
Positive reports
We continue to receive positive reports of the Obergurgl school and guides, with good English spoken, a maximum

of nine per group except at busy times and excellent lessons and organisation. Reporters find the instructors 'friendly, supportive and professional' and classes 'a very positive and pleasant experience'; 'superb' for children. Demand for private instruction appears to be increasing and it is advisable to book ahead during all peak periods.

FOR FAMILIES ★★★★☆
Check out your lodgings
Children's ski classes start at four years and children from age three can join Bobo's ski-kindergarten. There's lunchtime supervision for ski school and kindergarten children alike. Many hotels offer childcare of one sort or another (the Alpina has been particularly recommended) and Ski Esprit is a family-specialist UK chalet operator here.

STAYING THERE

Most tour operators feature hotels and pensions. Demand exceeds supply, and for once it is true that you should book early to avoid disappointment.
Chalets Ski Total has a big chalet here, and family-specialist sister company Esprit has two.
Hotels Accommodation is of high quality: most hotels are 4-stars, and none is less than a 3-star.

Psst! Wanna see Austria's best-kept secret? Check out p177.

Interactive resort shortlist builder at **www.wtss.co.uk**

Ski Expectations
01799 531888
skiexpectations.com

Europe's Top Resorts, the USA, & Canada

GETTING THERE

Air Innsbruck 95km/ 60 miles (2hr); Salzburg 285km/ 175 miles (4hr15); Munich 245km/ 150 miles (4hr30)

Rail Train to Ötz; regular buses from station

ACTIVITIES

Indoor Pools, saunas, whirlpools, steam baths and massage in hotels; bowling, indoor golf, indoor horseriding

Outdoor Natural ice rink, curling, snowshoeing, winter hiking paths, tobogganing

UK PACKAGES

Alpine Answers, Crystal, Crystal Finest, Esprit, First Choice, Independent Ski Links, Inghams, Interactive Resorts, Momentum, Neilson, PowderBeds, Ski Expectations, Ski Independence, Ski Solutions, Ski Total, Ski-Monterosa, Skitracer, Snow Finders, Thomson
Hochgurgl Crystal Finest, First Choice, Inghams, Neilson, Ski Expectations, Skitracer, Snow Finders, Thomson

Phone numbers
From elsewhere in Austria add the prefix 05256; from abroad use the prefix +43 5256

TOURIST OFFICE

www.obergurgl.com

OBERGURGL

****Alpina de Luxe (6000) Big, smart, excellent children's facilities. Pool and spa. 'Superb food, comfortable rooms, friendly staff.' 'Divine pool and spa, with Brit-friendly cozzie-on zone.'

****Bergwelt (6274) We stayed here in 2011. Very well run, with excellent food and charming service. Indoor, outdoor pools and spa facilities.

****Edelweiss und Gurgl (6223) The focal hotel; on the central square, near the main lifts. Pool and outdoor hot tub. 'Good marks for food, service, comfort and location.'

****Gotthard-Zeit (6292) Convenient for skiing, but uphill from the village. 'One of the best and friendliest hotels I have stayed in,' says a 2010 visitor. Spa and pool.

****Hochfirst (63250) 'Good location, very good food, great pool.' Five minutes from gondola. Ski-bus stop outside.

****Josl (6205) Uber-modern, convenient – close to the gondola. Big rooms, lots of storage, glass walls to bathrooms. Top floor has suite of saunas, steam rooms etc. We've stayed here and loved it.

***Pension Hohenfels (6281) Opposite the Festkogl gondola. Basic, but 'extremely friendly staff, very good breakfasts', says a 2010 visitor.

HOCHGURGL

*****Top Hotel Hochgurgl (6265) Relais & Chateaux – the only 5-star in the area. Good position.

****Riml (6261) Ski-in/ski-out location. 'Excellent pool, amazing wellness area, friendly staff, the most stunning hotel I've stayed in.'

****Sporthotel Olymp (6491) Near the Grosse Karbahn chair. 'Excellent food and service.'

Apartments The Lohmann (6201) is modern and well placed for the slopes. The 3-star Pirchhütt (6390) has apartments close to the Festkogl gondola.

EATING OUT ★★★☆☆
Wide choice, limited range
Hotel à la carte dining rooms dominate almost completely. The independent and rustic Krumpn's Stadl (where staff dress in traditional clothing) has a good choice, including rib specials. The Romantika at the hotel Madeleine and the Belmonte are popular pizzerias. For a varied menu, the two restaurants in the Edelweiss und Gurgl and the Josl (Austrian, vegetarian)

have been recommended. Other tips are the Hexenkuchl in the Jenewein (Austrian food) and the Angerer Alm at Hochgurgl for more of a gourmet offering. Some evenings you can eat on the hill, at Nederhütte (a fondue and live music evening, which 'rocks') or at David's Skihütte – both popular snowmobile destinations.

APRES-SKI ★★★★☆
Lively early, quiet later
Obergurgl is more animated than you might expect, at least in the early evening. Nederhütte at the Hohe Mut mid-station is the place to be when the lifts close, which in practice means getting there well before then ('get there at 2pm if you want a table inside'). It has live music and dancing (largely on the tables) several times a week, 'enjoyed by all age groups'. You ski home afterwards (or ride down on a snowmobile). All the bars at the base of the Rosskar and Hohe Mut lifts are also popular at close of play – try the Pic-Nic, or the Hexenkuchl at the Jenewein. The new ice dome bar outside the hotel Alpina was a popular attraction in 2011.

Later on, the crowded Krumpn's Stadl barn is the liveliest place in town with a DJ most nights. Josl's Keller is popular with all ages, with 'a western-style saloon downstairs and a posh wine bar upstairs'. You can usually find an atmospheric bar at one of the hotels. Reporters have enjoyed 'a great night out' at the Tuesday ski school display/mountain party/night ski on Festkogl.

Hochgurgl is very quiet at night except for live music in Toni's Almhütte bar (Sporthotel Olymp).

OFF THE SLOPES ★★★☆☆
Very limited
There isn't much to do during the day – hardly any shops, limited facilities of other kinds. There is an ice rink. Innsbruck is over two hours away by post bus. Sölden (20 minutes away) has a leisure centre and some shops. There are now buses every 15 minutes to Längenfeld (for the thermal spa). Pedestrians can ride gondolas to some of the restaurants for lunch, or walk part-way up the Hohe Mut area; there are 12km of 'pretty' hiking paths. The health suite at the hotel Hochfirst is said to be open to non-residents.

Obertauern

French-style convenience and snow-sure slopes meet Austrian après-ski – an unusual combination. Great for a short break

TOP 10 RATINGS

Extent	★★
Fast lifts	★★★★★
Queues	★★★★
Snow	★★★★
Expert	★★★
Intermediate	★★★★
Beginner	★★★★
Charm	★★
Convenience	★★★★
Scenery	★★★

RPI	95
lift pass	£180
ski hire	£105
lessons	£120
food & drink	£140
total	£545

NEWS

A 10-seat gondola is due to replace the Grünwaldkopfbahn quad from the valley to Treff 2000, but not until 2012/13.

+ Excellent snow record

+ Quite a lot of ski-in/ski-out lodging

+ Efficient modern lifts

+ Good mountain restaurants

+ Lively but not intrusive après-ski

− Village not notably charming, and spreads along the pass a long way

− Slopes limited in extent and, particularly, vertical

− Bleak, exposed setting

− Few off-slope diversions

Obertauern's combination of attractions is unique. If you're hooked on Austrian après-ski but looking for a change from slush and ice, moving up in the world by 1000m or so could be just the ticket. But note the minus points above.

THE RESORT

In the land of picture-postcard resorts grown out of rustic valley villages, Obertauern is different – a mainly modern development at the top of the Tauern pass. The slopes and lifts form a circuit around the village; lifts go up from the eastern fringes of the village itself, and from another major lift base about 1km west. There are big car parks at the lift bases for day visitors. **Village charm** Built in (high-rise) chalet style mixed with stylish modern architecture, the resort is not unattractive and has an up-market feel to it. Most accommodation is set either side of the through-road and sprawls some distance. Close to one end, another road leads off it at 90° and some of the best après-ski bars and smart ski shops are here – it is the nearest thing to a central focus. **Convenience** Check your location carefully – lifts go up either side of the access road at various points. **Scenery** The setting is satisfyingly rugged, with some long views from the high points of the area.

THE MOUNTAINS

Most of the slopes are above the tree-line, and bad weather can make skiing impossible (as we found in 2010). Reporters praise the signposting and map but give mixed views on piste classification. **Slopes** The circuit can be travelled either way in a couple of hours. The major share of the skiing is in the wide sunny basin to the north of the road and village. Visitors used to big areas will soon start to feel they have seen it all. Runs are short and vertical is limited – most major lifts are in the 200m to 400m range. There is floodlit skiing twice a week. **Fast lifts** There are fast chairs all over the place, and lifties reportedly manage to fill them. **Queues** Crowded pistes can be more of a problem than queues. The Sonnenlift chair can have problems at ski school time.

Wow! What's new in Austria?
See p177.

163

TVB OBERTAUERN

← The Zehnerkarspitze is a great hill, though not quite the precipice it seems in this shot

Terrain parks The small Longplay Park is above the Almrausche hut, on the far left on our piste map.

Snow reliability The resort has excellent snow reliability because of its altitude. Snowmaking covers 90% of the pistes. Grooming was criticised last year but a February 2011 visitor found it 'very good'.

Experts There are genuinely steep black pistes from the top Gamsleiten chair, but it is prone to closure. The icy race course under the Schaidberg-bahn is also a challenge. And try the black run from Seekarspitze and the ski route from Hundskogel (flat to start, steep moguls later). Some schools run off-piste guided groups.

Intermediates Most of the circuit is of intermediate difficulty. Stay low for easier pistes, or try the tougher runs higher up; you can't do the whole circuit without skiing reds.

Beginners There are good nursery slopes in several places, notably by the car parks at the western end of the resort. The Schaidberg chair leads to a high-altitude beginners' slope and there is an easy run down.

Snowboarding Draglifts are optional except for beginners. Blue Tomato is a specialist school.

Cross-country Obertauern has 26km of trails locally.

Mountain restaurants Mountain restaurants are numerous but often crowded. Reader favourites are the Hochalm for its lively party atmosphere, the Sonnhof ('good food brought very quickly'), the Kringsalm self-service and Treff 2000. Mankei Alm is cosy, with table service.

Schools and guides We have no recent reports of the six schools, but past reviews of both Krallinger and Koch have been positive.

Families The resort isn't particularly family-oriented and nursery slopes can be inconvenient, but most ski schools take children. The kindergarten takes children from 10 months to 4 years.

STAYING THERE

Hotels Practically all accommodation is in hotels (mostly 3-star and 4-star) and guest houses. Two places are regularly tipped by readers: the Latschenhof (7334) – 'best food in Austria', 'great spa, 50m from a run' – and the Marietta (7262) – 'friendly, well-run; lovely spa'.

Eating out The choices are mostly hotels (the Latschenhof is highly recommended). Some of the après-ski bars turn themselves into restaurants – the Almrausch does 'superb food'.

Après-ski There are several cute woody chalets at the base that throb at tea-time – Latsch'n Alm, Lürzer Alm, Gruber Stadl. WeltcupSchirm is a 'superb' lively umbrella bar. The Tauernkönig hotel has 'a cosy outdoor après area hidden away off the 8a home run'. Later on, Monkey's Heaven and the People bar have dancing. We had a quiet beer and used the free Wi-Fi in the modern, glass-fronted Mund Werk (part of a big ski shop).

Off the slopes There's an excellent, large sports centre (no pool). There are marked walks up to Kringsalm. Salzburg is an easy trip.

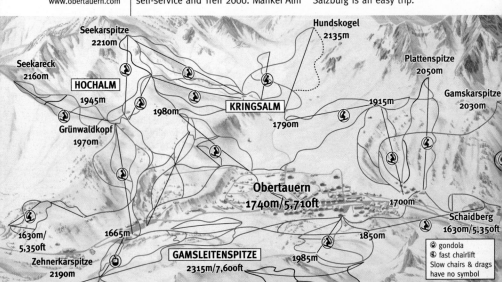

Obertauern.
Where snow is at home!

It's snowtime in Obertauern from late November to early May.

- Get the fantastic holiday feeling in one of the best skiing resorts of the Alps with a snow guarantee.
- Enjoy perfect winter sports conditions in a romantic atmosphere.
- Ski in – ski out: straight from your hotel onto the slope.

Obertauern at a glance:
100 km of slopes, 26 cable cars and lifts, night skiing, snowkiting school, 5 skiing and snowboarding schools, fun park for snowboarders.

Event dates:

▸ **24.11. – 11.12.2011: Int. Skicountdown**
Opening concert: Leningrad Cowboys LIVE on 26.11.2011

▸ **14.1. – 21.1.2012: Party Week for over 30s**
The ultimate Party-, Snow- & Chill-Out-Week in the Alps

▸ **19.4. – 22.4.2012: The Gamsleiten Criterion**
Austria's biggest treasure hunt with great prizes

Attractive package periods:

▸ **17.11. – 24.11.2011:** Opening Weeks

▸ **7.1. – 28.1.2012:** Powder Snow Weeks

▸ **24.3. – 31.3. / 14.4. – 1.5.2012:** Sun & Fun Weeks

Information and details: www.obertauern.com

Tourist Association Obertauern | Pionierstraße 1 | A-5562 Obertauern
Tel. +43(0)6456 / 7252 | Fax +43(0)6456 / 7252-9 | info@obertauern.com

www.obertauern.com

Saalbach-Hinterglemm

Lively, noisy, traditional-style villages and extensive, varied, prettily wooded slopes; pity they are mostly so sunny

RATINGS

The mountains

Extent	★★★
Fast lifts	★★★★★
Queues	★★★★
Terrain p'ks	★★★★
Snow	★★
Expert	★★
Intermediate	★★★★
Beginner	★★★
Boarder	★★★★★
X-country	★★
Restaurants	★★★★
Schools	★★★★
Families	★★★

The resort

Charm	★★★★
Convenience	★★★★
Scenery	★★★
Eating out	★★★
Après-ski	★★★★★
Off-slope	★★

RPI 90

lift pass	£200
ski hire	£110
lessons	£90
food & drink	£120
total	**£520**

166

➕ Large, well-linked, intermediate circuit, good for mixed groups

➕ Impressive lift system

➕ Saalbach is a pleasant, lively village, largely car-free in the centre

➕ Dozens of good mountain huts

➕ Extensive snowmaking but ...

➖ Most slopes are sunny as well as low, and the snow suffers

➖ Limited steep terrain

➖ Nursery slopes in Saalbach are sunny, and crowded in parts

➖ Both villages spread widely, with some lodgings far from central

➖ Both are noisy from 4pm and Saalbach can get rowdy at night

This year Saalbach-Hinterglemm virtually completes its mission to abolish slow lifts. At long last, the Bernkogel chairlift out of Saalbach is to be replaced. Our piste map has crammed into it an astonishing 33 fast lift symbols – marking detachable chairs, gondolas and cable cars. Leaving aside baby drags and the like, only three slow lifts remain. Amazing.

The valley has a lot going for it in other respects, too. Sadly, good snow isn't one of them. The altitudes are modest, but the bigger problem is that most of the slopes face south. The snowmaking is good enough to make a midwinter visit here a safe bet, but problems can arise as spring approaches.

THE RESORT

Saalbach and Hinterglemm are separate villages, their centres 4km apart, which have expanded along the floor of their dead-end east-west valley. They haven't quite merged, but some years back they adopted a single marketing identity. A 'ski-circus' links the two villages, with lifts and runs on both sides of the valley. At the eastern end is a link to Leogang in the next valley to the north.

Saalbach has a justified reputation as a party town – but those doing the partying seem to be a strangely mixed bunch. Big-spending BMW and Mercedes drivers staying in the smart, expensive hotels that line the main street share the bars with teenagers spending more on alcohol than on their cheap and cheerful pensions.

Hinterglemm is a more diffuse collection of hotels and holiday homes, where prices are lower and less cash is flashed.

Several resorts in Salzburgerland are reachable by road. The obvious nearby targets are Hochkönig to the north and Zell am See to the south. There are two regional passes to consider – read the 'Lift passes' panel in the margin.

VILLAGE CHARM ★★★★
Very appealing

Saalbach is an attractive, typically Tirolean village, with traditional-style (although mostly modern) buildings huddled together around a classic onion-domed church. Hinterglemm is less cute, with a more straightforward centre along a single main street. Both villages are free of through traffic.

Both villages are lively from mid-afternoon until the early hours. Saalbach in particular can get rowdy,

NEWS

2011/12: Access to the Hinterglemm slopes from Saalbach will be improved by an eight-seat gondola towards Bernkogel, replacing a famously slow and unreliable chairlift. The drags above are not being replaced until 2012, but there will be a new six-pack going on to Reiterkogel for the coming season.

There are plans to improve snowmaking.

2010/11: An eight-seat gondola with heated seats replaced the draglift serving the terrain park at Hinterglemm. The park was redesigned, and a short linking lift was installed from the village up to the new gondola base.

TVB SAALBACH-HINTERGLEMM

Mountain restaurants are impressive in quantity and quality; and you can stay in some, including the excellent Sonnhof, shown here ↓

with drunken revellers still in their ski boots late in the evening. If you are not among them, you might find this an undesirable feature.

CONVENIENCE ★★★★☆
Lifts near the centre

Saalbach is more convenient than most Austrian villages, with lifts into three sectors of the slopes starting close to the traffic-free village centre; the result, if staying centrally, is near to an ideal blend of Austrian charm with French convenience. Hinterglemm also has lifts and runs close to the centre, and offers quick access to some of the most interesting slopes – and, importantly, to most of the north-facing runs. In both villages, the amount of walking depends heavily on where you stay.

The valley bus service is fine, but not perfect: it finishes early, gets very busy at peak times and doesn't serve hotels in central Hinterglemm, or hotels set away from the main road. A Nightliner bus runs intermittently between the two resorts from 7.30pm to midnight (2am at weekends).

SCENERY ★★★☆☆
Pleasant rather than dramatic

The villages are flanked by modest, broad mountain ridges. The high points give more dramatic views of the mountains to the north.

THE MOUNTAINS

The runs form a 'circus' almost entirely composed of broad slopes between swathes of forest, so this is a good area in bad weather. Reporters comment on 'very good' signposting.

EXTENT OF THE SLOPES ★★★☆☆
User-friendly circuit

Travelling anticlockwise, you can make a complete circuit of the valley on skis, crossing from one side to the other at Vorderglemm and Lengau – if you wish you can stick to blues almost the whole way. Going clockwise, you have to do a shorter circuit – there is no lift at Vorderglemm – and there is more red-run skiing to do.

On the south-facing side, five sectors can be identified, each served by a lift from the valley – named on our map. The links across these slopes work well: when traversing the whole hillside you need to descend to the valley floor only once – at Saalbach, where the main street separates Bernkogel from Kohlmaiskopf. The Wildenkarkogel sector connects via Seidl-Alm to the slopes of **Leogang**; a small, high, open area served by fast lifts leads to a long, north-facing slope down to the base of an eight-seat gondola near Hütten, 3km from Leogang village.

Back in the main valley, the north-

KEY FACTS

Resort	1000m
	3,280ft
Slopes	930-2095m
	3,050-6,870ft
Lifts	55
Pistes	200km
	124 miles
Blue	45%
Red	48%
Black	7%
Snowmaking	90%

facing slopes are different in character: two widely separated and steeper mountains, one split into twin peaks. An eight-seat gondola rises from Saalbach to **Schattberg Ost**, where the high, open, sunny slopes behind the peak are served by a fast quad. The slightly higher peak of **Schattberg West** is reached by gondola from Hinterglemm. Another gondola makes the link from Schattberg Ost to Schattberg West. The second north-facing hill is **Zwölferkogel**, served by a two-stage eight-seat gondola from Hinterglemm. A six-pack and draglift serve open slopes on the sunny side of the peak, and a second gondola from the valley provides a link from the south-facing Hochalm slopes.

The Hinterglemm nursery slopes are well used, and floodlit every evening.

FAST LIFTS ★★★★★
The world's best

Saalbach-Hinterglemm has the highest proportion of fast lifts of any major resort in the world (over 90%). The already impressive lift system gained another gondola last season and two further upgrades are due for 2011/12 – both on Bernkogel (read 'News'). An efficient lift in that direction from Saalbach is way overdue, but we'll be interested to see how the drags above it (being replaced in 2012) cope with people flooding up the new gondola.

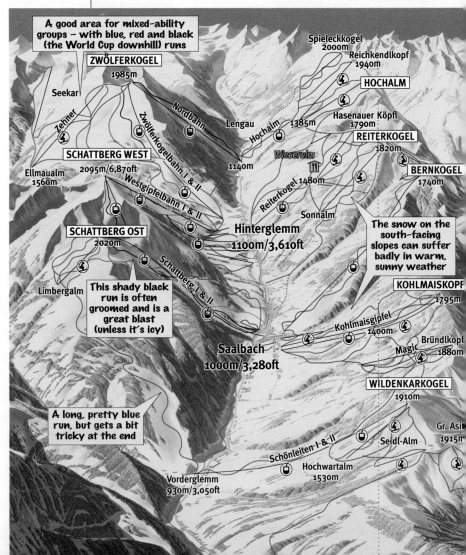

LIFT PASSES

Skicircus Saalbach Hinterglemm Leogang

Prices in €

Age	1-day	6-day
under 16	22	103
16 to 18	32	154
over 19	43	206

Free under 6
Senior no deals
Beginner points card
Notes
Covers Saalbach, Hinterglemm and Leogang, and the ski-bus; also Reiterkogel toboggan run at night; part-day and non-skier passes available

Alternative passes
Salzburg Super Ski Card covers 22 ski areas in the Salzburg province; Kitzbüheler Alpen All Star Card covers seven ski areas – Kitzbühel, Schneewinkel (St Johann), Ski Welt, Alpbach, Wildschönau, Skicircus Saalbach, Zell-Kaprun

QUEUES ★★★★
High season mostly
The lift system generally copes well, and we've had few complaints from reporters recently, even in high season. The new lift up Bernkogel from Saalbach should remove the main remaining bottleneck – although this season, it may just move it up the hill.

TERRAIN PARKS ★★★★
Now with its own gondola
The popular Nightpark just above Hinterglemm was completely redesigned for 2010/11, and is now served by a new heated gondola. The park is floodlit until 9.30pm and includes Big Air, kickers, wall-ride and rails, plus a beginner line. To improve access, a passenger lift up from Hinterglemm to the gondola was also installed. There's another park below Kl. Asitz towards Leogang.

SNOW RELIABILITY ★★
A tale of two sides
Most slopes are below 1900m and the south-facing slopes are in the majority; they can suffer when the sun comes out (we've encountered strips of machine-made snow amid green and brown fields). The north-facing slopes keep their snow better but can get icy. The long north-facing run down to Leogang often has the best snow in the area. Piste maintenance is good and snowmaking covers 90% of the area, including many top-to-bottom runs; but the fundamental problems won't go away.

FOR EXPERTS ★★
Little steep stuff
There are a few challenging slopes on the north-facing side. The long (4km) Nordabfahrt run beneath the Schattberg Ost gondola is a genuine black – a fine fast bash first thing in the morning if it has been groomed and is not icy. The Zwölferkogel Nordabfahrt at Hinterglemm is less consistent, but its classification is justified by a few short, steeper pitches. The World Cup downhill run from Zwölferkogel is interesting, as is the 5km Schattberg West–Hinterglemm red (and its scenic 'ski route' variant). Snow conditions and forest tend to limit the off-piste potential. Given decent snow, however, you can have a good time.

FOR INTERMEDIATES ★★★★
Paradise for most
The sunny side of the area is ideal for both the mileage-hungry piste-basher and the more leisurely cruiser, although many of the blues can be quite testing. For those looking for more of a challenge, the long red runs to the valley ranged along the north side are good fun. The otherwise delightful blue run from Bernkogel to Saalbach gets really crowded at busy times of day.

The north-facing area has some more challenging runs, with excellent relentless reds from both Schattberg West and Zwölferkogel, and a section of relatively high, open slopes around Zwölferkogel – good for mixed-ability

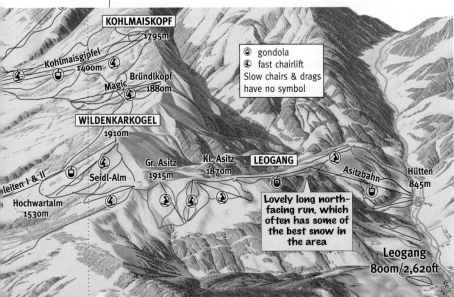

KOHLMAISKOPF
1795m

Kohlmaisgipfel
1400m

Bründlkopf
1880m

Magic

WILDENKARKOGEL
1910m

leiten I & II

Hochwartalm
1530m

Seidl-Alm

Gr. Asitz
1915m

Kl. Asitz
1870m

LEOGANG

Asitzbahn

Hütten
845m

gondola
fast chairlift
Slow chairs & drags have no symbol

Lovely long north-facing run, which often has some of the best snow in the area

Leogang
800m/2,620ft

↑ A valley of two halves – shady and fairly steep on the left, sunny and more gentle on the right; Saalbach is in the foreground, Hinterglemm further away, in the shade
TVB SAALBACH-HINTERGLEMM

GETTING THERE

Air Salzburg 90km/55 miles (2hr); Munich 225km/140 miles (3hr30)

Rail Zell am See 19km/12 miles; hourly buses

groups wishing to ski together. None of the black runs is beyond an adventurous intermediate, unless icy. The long, pretty blue to Vorderglemm gets you right away from lifts – but it gets a bit steep and tricky towards the end, and probably should be red.

Our favourite intermediate run is the long, off-the-main-circuit cruise to Leogang.

FOR BEGINNERS ★★★☆☆
Head for Hinterglemm
Saalbach's two sunny nursery slopes are right next to the village. The upper one is served by a short six-pack but gets a lot of through-traffic. There are short, easy runs to progress to at Bernkogel and Schattberg.

Hinterglemm's spacious nursery area is separate from the main slopes and preferred by reporters. It faces north, so lacks sun in midwinter but is more reliable for snow later on. There are lots of easy blue runs to move on to, especially on the south-facing side of the valley, but it pays to take advice on which are easiest.

FOR BOARDERS ★★★★★
Good all-rounder
Saalbach is great for boarding. Slopes are extensive, lifts are mainly chairs and gondolas, and there are pistes to appeal to beginners, intermediates and experts alike – with few flats to negotiate. For experienced boarders, there's off-piste terrain between the lifts if snow conditions permit.

FOR CROSS-COUNTRY ★★☆☆☆
Go to Zell am See
In mid-winter the 10km of valley trails get very little sun, and are not very exciting. There is a high trail on the Reiterkogel. But the area beyond nearby Zell am See is better.

Hot news in Austria's hottest resort, p177.

MOUNTAIN RESTAURANTS ★★★★☆
Excellent quality and quantity
The area is liberally scattered with huts – about 40 in total – most of them pleasant, lively, rustic places serving good food. All are marked and named on the piste map.
Editors' choice The Wieseralm (6939), at the heart of the Hinterglemm south-facing slopes, is a welcoming woody chalet doing table service of satisfying dishes; fine views from the terrace.
Worth knowing about Reporters regularly tip the Alte Schmiede above Leogang, a lovely wood hut with table service, a big fireplace, huge terrace and DJ; 'excellent' traditional and vegetarian meals, 'efficient staff'. A brewery museum/restaurant is due to open next door for 2011/12. Westernstadl on Bernkogel has a saloon theme, 'built around a stable with horses'; but also 'great food and friendly service'. Also tipped: Thurneralm on Bründlkopf.

SCHOOLS AND GUIDES ★★★★☆
More reports would be good ...
There's plenty of choice. We lack reports this year but past feedback on the Fürstauer school has been positive.

FOR FAMILIES ★★★☆☆
Hinterglemm tries harder
Saalbach doesn't go out of its way to sell itself to families, although it does have a ski kindergarten. Hinterglemm probably makes a better family base, with some good hotel-based nursery facilities – at the Theresia for example. And its nursery slope is better.

Saalbach-Hinterglemm

Interactive resort shortlist builder at **www.wtss.co.uk**

SCHOOLS

Saalbach

Fürstauer
t 8444

Snow Academy
t 668256

Hinterholzer
t 7607

Zink
t 0664 162 3655

Board.at
t 20047

easySki
t 0699 111 80010

Hinterglemm

Hinterglemmer
t 634640

Activ
t 0676 517 1325

Classes
(Fürstauer prices)
5 days (4.5hr) from
€158

Private lessons
From €139 for 3hr,
for 1 or 2 people;
extra person €15

CHILDCARE

Several hotels have
nurseries

Ski schools
Some take children in
mini-clubs from about
age 3 and can provide
lunchtime care; from
about age 4, children
can join ski school
(€218 for 6 days,
including lunch –
Fürstauer prices)

STAYING THERE

Chalets This isn't a major chalet resort,
but this year Inghams is introducing
an 80-bed chalet-hotel in a prime
position in Hinterglemm.

Hotels Both villages have lots of
hotels, mainly 3-star and above. Be
aware that some central hotels suffer
from disco noise, and front rooms
from street noise into the early hours.

SAALBACH

****Alpenhotel** (6666) Central place
with countless bars and restaurants,
open-fire lounge, nightclub; small
pool, hot tub.

****Kendler** (62250) Position second
to none, beside the Bernkogel lift.
Classy, expensive, good food.

****Kristiana** (6253) Near enough to
lifts but away from night-time noise.
Sauna, steam bath

****Saalbacher Hof** (71110) Major
central hotel, renovated in 2010, with
new restaurants and wellness centre.

***Haider** (6228) Best-positioned of
the 3-stars, right next to the main lifts.

***Peter** (6236) Main street location.
Recently renovated.

HINTERGLEMM

****Theresia** (74140) Hinterglemm's
top hotel, good for families. On road
to Saalbach, but at foot of a red run
and close to a draglift into the circus.
Superb food and friendly staff, say
past reports. Pool and spa.

***Sonnblick** (6408) Convenient 3-star
in a quiet location.

Apartments There's a big choice for
independent travellers.

At altitude Some mountain restaurants
have rooms. One reader greatly
enjoyed the 3-star Sonnhof (6295) at
the top of the Hochalmbahn, where
you get two six-packs all to yourself
for half an hour in the mornings (see
picture at start of this chapter).

EATING OUT ★★★★★
Wide choice of hotel restaurants

This is essentially a half-board resort,
with strikingly few restaurants other
than those in hotels. In Saalbach, the
Kohlmais Stub'n (Aparthotel Astrid) at
the foot of the slopes has friendly
service, a warm woody ambience and
creative, regional food. The hotel
Peter's restaurant, at the top of the
main street, is atmospheric and serves
excellent meat dishes cooked on hot
stones. Of the Alpenhotel's several
eateries, we've enjoyed pizza and
other stuff at La Trattoria, and like the
look of the Vitrine 'wok restaurant'.

APRES-SKI ★★★★★
It rocks from early on

'The best après-ski in the Alps,' claims
the resort website, and it is certainly
among the best. The site lists well
over 20 venues. Saalbach, in
particular, is very lively from mid-
afternoon until the early hours, and
can get positively wild.

On the hill above Saalbach, the
rustic Hinterhag Alm is an institution –
'Everybody meets here at 4pm' they
say, and that's how it seems; live
bands ensure a great atmosphere until
people start to slide down to the
already packed Bauer's Schi-Alm – an
old cow shed with attached umbrella
bars. Both are 'still over-the-top,
manic, noisy, drunken places, but
good fun'. There are alternatives:
Bäckstättstall and main bar of Berger's
Sporthotel have dancing when the lifts
close. Jack-in has Wi-Fi and big screen
TVs for the sports fans. Bobby's Pub
'resembles a drunken youth club –
with lots of falling over on karaoke
night', but is cheap, has bowling,
games machines, sport on TVs and
serves Guinness. A tireless reporter
tells us that 'you can just about hold a

ACTIVITIES

Indoor Swimming pools, sauna, massage, solarium, tennis, museum, gallery, bowling, casino

Outdoor Ice rink, curling, tobogganing, sleigh rides, snowshoeing, snowmobiling, quad bikes, ice karts, 40km of cleared paths, archery, paragliding

UK PACKAGES

Alpine Answers, BoardnLodge, Crystal, Crystal Finest, First Choice, Independent Ski Links, Inghams, Interactive Resorts, Neilson, PowderBeds, Rocketski, Select Ski Chalets, Ski Expectations, Ski Miquel, Skitracer, Snow Finders, Snowscape, STC, Thomson Leogang Zenith

Phone numbers
From elsewhere in Austria add the prefix 06541 (Saalbach), 06583 (Leogang); from abroad use the prefix +43 and omit the initial '0'

TOURIST OFFICES

Saalbach
www.saalbach.com

Leogang
www.leogang-saalfelden.at

conversation' in Zum Turm (a converted medieval jail) or Spitzbub (a converted garage), but recommends the Eva,Alm for a quiet drink. Later on, there are nightclubs under various central hotels, and several pole dancing dives.

We get fewer reports on the après-ski in Hinterglemm, which possibly attracts more families and fewer night-owls, but the Hinterhag role is clearly played by the lively and rustic goat-themed Goasstall. The hotel Dorfschmiede has a lively Harley-Davidson biker-themed bar. Later on, hit the Tanzhimmel and Hexenhäusl.

OFF THE SLOPES ★★☆☆☆
Surprisingly little to do
The resort is not very entertaining if you're not into winter sports. There are few shops other than supermarkets and ski shops. There are some walking paths, and a lift pass (67 euros) gives access to two lifts per day. Many good restaurants are reachable by lift, for lunchtime meetings. At Hinterglemm a new floodlit treetop walk has opened, and the Reiterkogel toboggan run is said to be great fun (and good value for multiple runs). There are excursions to Salzburg.

Leogang 800m

+ Unspoiled village, less expensive than Saalbach or Hinterglemm
+ Long, uncrowded, cruisey local slopes that keep their snow well

− Not an ideal base for most of the main piste circuit
− Village rather diffuse, lacking amenities, busy with through-traffic

Leogang may seem to offer a good budget base for skiing the slopes of Saalbach-Hinterglemm, but in practice it really suits best those who are content with the good local slopes, plus the runs to the east of Saalbach; getting to the best slopes beyond Hinterglemm takes quite a time.

Village charm The village is quietly attractive but is set on a busy through-road.
Convenience Lodging is widely scattered. For convenience it's best to stay in the hamlet of Hütten, near the gondola into the main ski area.
Scenery Leogang sits in a pretty valley beneath the impressive Birnhorn.

THE MOUNTAIN
The village is linked to the eastern end of the main ski circuit. The sunny slopes just over the ridge are fairly easily reached, but the more interesting slopes are a bit of a trek.
Slopes A gondola gets you into the ski area, followed by a series of chairlifts. The local slopes tend to be quiet.
Fast lifts Nursery slopes aside, all the lifts are fast.
Queues Few problems locally but a mid-February visitor found 20-minute queues at the Gr. Asitz chair to join the main circuit.
Snow reliability The local slopes have some of the best snow in the region, being north- and east-facing, with snowmaking on the run home.
Experts Not much challenge locally.
Intermediates Great long blue/red run cruise home from the top of the gondola. Plus the circuit to explore.
Beginners Good nursery slopes by the village, and short runs to progress to.

Snowboarding The whole area is great for boarding and there's a terrain park.
Cross-country There are 20km of trails, plus a panoramic high-altitude trail.
Mountain restaurants There are a couple of good local huts, including a real reader favourite (read the main text).
Schools and guides The Altenberger school has a good reputation.
Families There is a non-ski nursery, and children can start school at four years old.

STAYING THERE
Hotels The central 4-star Leonhard (8542) is recommended this year for 'great food, staff and spa'. The luxury Krallerhof (8246) has its own nursery lift that accesses the main lift station. The 4-star Salzburger Hof (7310) is a two-minute walk from the gondola; sauna and steam.
Apartments There are quiet apartments available.
Eating out Restaurants are hotel-based. The Kirchenwirt, upscale Krallerhof and much cheaper Hüttwirt have high reputations.
Après-ski The rustic old chalet Kraller Alm is very much the focal tea-time and evening rendezvous.
Off the slopes Very limited. There's night tobogganing. Excursions to Salzburg are possible.

Schladming

Pleasant old valley town in Styria, with a famous racing hill directly above, links to three other mountains and other areas nearby

RATINGS

The mountains

Extent	★★★
Fast lifts	★★★★
Queues	★★★★
Terrain p'ks	★★★
Snow	★★★★
Expert	★★
Intermediate	★★★★
Beginner	★★★
Boarder	★★★
X-country	★★★★
Restaurants	★★★★
Schools	★★★
Families	★★★★

The resort

Charm	★★★
Convenience	★★★
Scenery	★★★
Eating out	★★★
Après-ski	★★★
Off-slope	★★★

RPI 85

lift pass	£190
ski hire	£85
lessons	£105
food & drink	£100
total	**£480**

NEWS

2011/12: More car parking and a media building are planned beside Planet Planai.

More snowmaking is due on Hochwurzen.

2010/11: An eight-pack replaced the two top draglifts from Hauser Kaibling towards Planai. The Planet Planai skier services centre opened at the base.

The Reiteralm area was extended into the Preunegg valley by the addition of an eight-seat gondola and 2km-long red run with snowmaking. This tipped the resort into our ★★★ category for extent of slopes.

+ Ideal for intermediate cruising

+ Very sheltered slopes, among trees

+ Lots of good mountain restaurants

+ Appealing town with friendly people

+ Very cheap for meals and drinks

+ Extensive snowmaking and shady slopes mean generally good piste conditions, but ...

− The mainly north-facing runs can be cold in early season

− Slopes lack variety

− Very little to entertain experts

− Nursery slopes not central and may involve a bus ride

− Runs to valley level are not easy

− Après-ski not a highlight

One slope may be rather like another here, but with its four linked mountains Schladming offers the keen intermediate a real sense of travelling around on the snow. And its solid, valley-town ambience makes it a pleasant change from the Austrian rustic-village norm.

THE RESORT

The old town of Schladming sits at the foot of Planai, one of four linked ski mountains. It has a long skiing tradition: the town has hosted many World Cup races and is now gearing up to host the 2013 Alpine World Championships – starting with a new ultra-modern skier services building at the lift base, Planet Planai, not far from the focal square of the town.

From the western suburbs, slow chairlifts serve the next peak to the west, Hochwurzen, passing through Rohrmoos – a quiet, scattered village set on an elevated slope that forms a giant nursery area. From Hochwurzen you can progress to the most westerly of the four areas, Reiteralm. To the east of Schladming is the small, attractively rustic village of Haus, where a cable car and gondola go up to the highest of the four linked mountains, Hauser Kaibling.

Timetabled 'efficient' buses link the villages and lift bases. A night bus runs until 1am (3 euros).

There are several other separate mountains nearby covered by the local lift pass – including Fageralm (only slow chairlifts and T-bars, but lovely quiet, wide, easy cruising pistes and rustic huts – a very relaxing change of pace), Galsterbergalm, the Dachstein glacier and Stoderzinken. The Ski Alliance Amadé lift pass also covers many other resorts. A car is useful for getting the most out of this pass: trips are feasible to Bad Gastein, Wagrain/Flachau, Zauchensee and Hochkönig (and to Obertauern – not on the pass).

There are direct trains from Salzburg, so Schladming makes an excellent short break destination.

VILLAGE CHARM ★★★
Pleasant car-free centre
Most of Schladming's buildings are solid and traditional, and at its heart there's a pleasant, traffic-free main square, prettily lit at night, around which you'll find most of the shops, restaurants, bars and some appealing hotels. The busy main road bypasses the town.

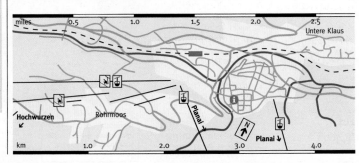

KEY FACTS

Resort	745m
	2,440ft

Schladming's four linked mountains

Slopes	745-2015m
	2,440-6,610ft
Lifts	45
Pistes	125km
	78 miles
Blue	34%
Red	62%
Black	4%
Snowmaking	99%

CONVENIENCE ★★★☆☆
Pleasantly compact
Much of the accommodation is close to the town centre; the sports centre and tennis halls are five minutes' walk away, as is the gondola to Planai. There is also accommodation out by the Planai-Hochwurzen lift link, and further down the valley (eg Pichl).

SCENERY ★★★☆☆
Four points of view
All four mountains are broadly similar, pleasantly wooded and share decent views along the Ennstal and to the more dramatic Dachsteingruppe, across the valley to the north.

THE MOUNTAINS

Most pistes are on the wooded north-facing slopes above the main valley, with some going into the side valleys higher up; there are a few short open slopes above the trees.

There's a confusing variety of piste maps. Even for the linked four-mountain area there are at least two, and when we visited there were maps for individual mountains too. All very confusing. As in many Austrian areas, you may also encounter multiple pistes identified by the same number. Add to this poor signposting, and finding your way around can be tricky.

EXTENT OF THE SLOPES ★★★☆☆
Four linked sectors
The pistes now total 125km in length – a modest figure, but enough to gain the resort our ★★★ rating. Each of the sectors has a variety of runs to

play on and you get a satisfying feeling of travelling around a lot. **Planai** is the main mountain, reached directly by gondola from the edge of the town centre. It is linked to **Hauser Kaibling** at altitude via the high, wooded bowl between them. But the links to **Hochwurzen** and **Reiteralm** are at valley level (and the first involves riding a gondola both ways). Our favourite area is Reiteralm – a hi-tech lift system and nicely varied terrain, extended down into Preuneggtal in 2011 by a new gondola and red runs.

Several lower runs go across poorly signposted roads – care is needed.

FAST LIFTS ★★★★☆
Some neglected links
Each linked sector has gondola access from the car parks at the bases, and there are now lots of fast chairs. But the slow chairlift from Schladming to Hochwurzen, and the one from Pichl to Reiteralm are obvious weaknesses.

QUEUES ★★★★☆
New lifts helping
Generally there are few problems. The main complaint is of big queues for the Planai gondola at peak times. New lifts between Hauser Kaibling and Planai should have helped there.

TERRAIN PARKS ★★★☆☆
Three to try
Planai has a park above Larchkogel, with medium and pro kicker lines, jumps, boxes and rails. Reiteralm's park is similarly well-equipped; there's also a half-pipe. Hochwurzen's Playground park is floodlit until 10pm.

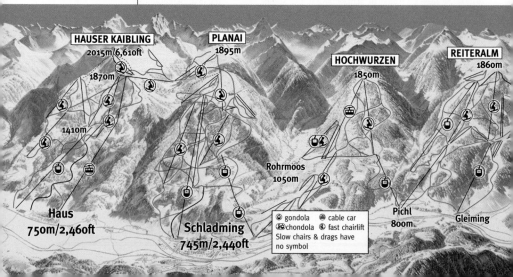

HAUSER KAIBLING
2015m/6,610ft
1870m
1410m
Haus
750m/2,460ft

PLANAI
1895m

HOCHWURZEN
1850m

REITERALM
1860m

Rohrmoos
1050m

Pichl
800m

Gleiming

Schladming
745m/2,440ft

gondola   cable car
chondola   fast chairlift
Slow chairs & drags have
no symbol

The scattered satellite village of Rohrmoos, reached by road or slow lift, is effectively a giant nursery slope at the foot of Hochwurzen →

SCHLADMING-ROHRMOOS
TOURISMUS / HERBERT RAFFALT

LIFT PASSES

Ski Alliance Amadé Ski Pass

Prices in €

Age	1-day	6-day
under 17	22	105
17 to 19	34	163
over 20	42	203
Free under 6		
Senior no deals		
Beginner no deals		

Notes
Day-pass price is for Planai-Hochwurzen, Reiteralm only; part-day tickets available; 2-day-plus passes cover the 860km of pistes and 270 lifts in five regions: Schladming-Dachstein; Gastein; Salzburger Sportwelt; Grossarl; Hochkönig

Alternative pass
Salzburg Super Ski Card: all lifts in Salzburgerland including Zell am See, Kaprun and Saalbach-Hinterglemm

SNOW RELIABILITY ★★★★
Excellent in cold weather
The northerly orientation of the slopes and good maintenance help keep the pistes in better shape than in some neighbouring resorts. The serious snowmaking operation makes it a particularly good choice for early holidays; coverage is comprehensive and the system is put to good use. But at this altitude poor conditions on the lower slopes are a natural hazard.

FOR EXPERTS ★★
Strictly intermediate stuff
Schladming's status as a racing venue doesn't make it macho. The steep black finish to the Men's Downhill course and the mogul runs at the top of Planai and Hauser Kaibling are the only really challenging slopes there. Reiteralm has two steep black runs (one very short) at the top and some good tree runs. Hauser Kaibling's off-piste is good, but limited.

FOR INTERMEDIATES ★★★★
Red runs rule
The area is ideal for intermediate cruising. The majority of runs are red but it's often difficult to distinguish them from some of the blues. One notable exception is the final very red section of the run below Rohrmoos; if in doubt, take the alternative blue.
New lifts have improved access to more challenging slopes at the top of Planai and Hauser Kaibling, as well as a short but pretty blue from the high point. The black racing pistes in these sectors, and the red that runs parallel to the Haus course, are ideal for fast cruising but can get very icy and tricky.

Hauser Kaibling has a lovely blue running from top to bottom, and Reiteralm has some gentle blues.

FOR BEGINNERS ★★★
Good slopes but poorly sited
The ski schools generally take beginners to the extensive but low-altitude Rohrmoos nursery area – fine if you are based there. For residents of central Schladming, it's a discouraging bus ride away.

FOR BOARDERS ★★★
Fine for all but experts
Schladming is popular with boarders. Most lifts on the spread-out mountains are gondolas or chairs, with some short drags around. The area is ideal for beginners and intermediates, except when the lower slopes are icy, though there are few exciting challenges for expert boarders bar the off-piste tree runs. The Blue Tomato snowboard shop runs the 'impressive' specialist snowboard school.

FOR CROSS-COUNTRY ★★★★
Huge network of trails
There are almost 500km of trails in the region, and the World Championships have been held at nearby Ramsau.

MOUNTAIN RESTAURANTS ★★★★
A real highlight
There are plenty of attractive rustic huts; most get enthusiastic reports. Some of the piste maps mark them.
On Hauser Kaibling, Kulmhoferhütte

Ski Austria's Big Three.
Where? See p177.

SCHOOLS
Tritscher
t 61142
Hopl (Hochwurzen-Planai)
t 23582
Blue Tomato (snowboard)
t 24223 16

Classes
(Tritscher prices)
5 days €164
Private lessons
€98 for 2hr; each
additional person €20

CHILDCARE
Mini club (Tritscher school)
t 22647
For ages 3 and 4
Nannies
Details at tourist
office

Ski school
From age 4 (€219 for
5 days including lunch
– Tritscher price)

ACTIVITIES
Indoor Swimming
pool, fitness club,
tennis, sauna
Outdoor Ice skating,
curling, tobogganing,
snowshoeing, sleigh
rides, 50km of cleared
paths, paragliding

GETTING THERE
Air Salzburg 95km/
60 miles (1hr15);
Munich 255km/160
miles (3hr30)
Rail Main line station
in resort

UK PACKAGES
Alpine Answers, Chalet
Group, Crystal, Crystal
Finest, Skitracer, Zenith

Phone numbers
From elsewhere in
Austria add the prefix
03687; from abroad
use the prefix +43
and omit the initial '0'

TOURIST OFFICE
www.schladming-
dachstein.at
www.skiamade.com

has a real mountain hut atmosphere, with fur-lined walls, as does Schoarlhütte ('good ribs'). For 'a very good gröstl' try Krummholzhütte. Harry's Lärchenpavillion is good for drinks and snacks.

On Planai, reporters love Onkel Willy's Hütte – 'lovely atmosphere, great staff', 'best food', 'great gulaschsuppe', 'top gröstl'. Schafalm has a wide menu and 'lovely pizza'. We've enjoyed good food at the pleasant Weitmoosalm.

On Hochwurzen, the large self-service Hochwurzenhütte and 'cosy' Hochwurzenalm just below it have been tipped. On Reiteralm the Schnepf'n Alm does 'outstanding food'. Gasselhöh Hütte is tipped for 'awesome' spare ribs.

On outlying Fageralm, we had delicious stew in the tiny Zeffererhütte, and a reporter had 'superb gröstl' at Unterbergalm.

SCHOOLS AND GUIDES ★★★★★
A choice – how was it for you?
There's a choice of school. We lack recent reports on adult lessons, but the Top school at Pichl has 'excellent' children's classes.

FOR FAMILIES ★★★★★
Rohrmoos is the place
The extensive gentle slopes of Rohrmoos are ideal for building up youngsters' confidence. There are snow gardens on Planai, Reiteralm and Hochwurzen.

STAYING THERE

Packaged accommodation is in hotels and pensions, but there are plenty of apartments for independent travellers.
Hotels Most lodging is mid-range but a few upmarket places exist.
★★★★Sporthotel Royer (200) Big and comfortable, a few minutes from the Planai gondola. Pool, sauna, steam.
★★★★Mitterhofer (22229) Out near the Planai-Hochwurzen lifts. Comfortable, good wellness area.
★★★★Almdorf-Reiteralm (72444) Ski-in/ski-out village at Hochalm, above Pichl. Individual chalets as well as hotel Edelweiss; restaurant, shop and spa facilities.
★★★★Raunerhof (7356) In Pichl. 'Superb position, friendly, good food.' No pool.
★★★Kirchenwirt (22435) Off the main square. 'A bit quaint, but great staff and excellent food,' says a 2011 visitor.

★★★Aqi (56600) Cool modern place, built in 2008 and supposedly the first of a chain. Opposite Planai gondola. 'Helpful staff, spacious quiet room, good food, breakfast plentiful.'
★★★Neue Post (22105) Large rooms, friendly, good food, central.
Apartments Schütter (23230) at Planai West are said to be spacious.

EATING OUT ★★★★★
Some good places
Most of the best places are in hotels. Tips include the Alte Post in the Posthotel for 'good food, first class service', and the Kirchenwirt and Neue Post hotels. Friesacher Lanstuberl is a good steakhouse near the church ('huge portions'). Maria's Mexican has 'fabulous food and service'. Biochi specialises in organic and vegan food. We liked the Lasser Cafe and the Stadttor for coffee and cakes, and the Schwalbenbräu brewery.

APRES-SKI ★★★★★
Hohenhaus gets lively
Some of the mountain huts have live or loud music in the afternoon. On Hochwurzen, Tauernalm at Rohrmoos 'has a good atmosphere'. In town, the focus is the huge Hohenhaus Tenne by the Planai gondola station, which has injected life into the Schladming après scene; fabulous main bar, dance floor and regular live music – 'lively and great fun'. Later on there's a disco and various other bars to entertain. Charly's Treff (with umbrella bar) opposite also gets busy. Many of the central bars stay open until the early hours; but this isn't Ischgl. Cult and Angels are nightclubs.

OFF THE SLOPES ★★★★★
A few things to do
The town has a few shops, museum, pool and an ice rink. Hochwurzen has a floodlit 7km toboggan run. Some mountain restaurants are accessible to pedestrians. Trips to Salzburg are easy.

LINKED RESORT – 750m

HAUS

Haus is a fairly self-contained village, with its own ski schools, kindergartens and railway station. Hotel prices are generally lower here. The user-friendly nursery slopes are between the centre and the gondola. Excursions are easy, but off-slope activities and nightlife are very limited.

Sölden

The resort could do with a bypass, but slopes reaching glacial heights and an ever-improving lift system more than compensate

RATINGS

The mountains

Extent	★★★
Fast lifts	★★★★
Queues	★★★
Terrain p'ks	★★★
Snow	★★★★★
Expert	★★★
Intermediate	★★★★
Beginner	★★★
Boarder	★★★★
X-country	★
Restaurants	★★★
Schools	★★★
Families	★★

The resort

Charm	★★
Convenience	★★
Scenery	★★★
Eating out	★★★
Après-ski	★★★★★
Off-slope	★★

RPI   100

lift pass	£220
ski hire	£140
lessons	£95
food & drink	£120
total	**£575**

NEWS

2010/11: Two new state-of-the-art gondolas, an eight-seater and a 24-person one above it, have replaced the bottom-to-top gondola on Gaislachkogl.

A new automated lift (Zentrum Shuttle) was built from the resort to the nursery slopes at Innerwald.

🞢 Excellent snow reliability, with access to two glaciers

🞢 Fairly extensive network of slopes suited to adventurous intermediates

🞢 Impressive lift system

🞢 Wide choice of huts for its size

🞢 Very lively après-ski/nightlife

🞢 Towny resort is spread along a road that is busy with through-traffic

🞢 Access lifts are a mile apart, and your hotel may be near neither

🞢 Main runs are all above the treeline – only a couple are sheltered

🞢 English not universally spoken

🞢 Town centre can get rowdy

'We were very surprised that we were the only people getting off the transfer coach in Sölden, while the other 50 went on to Obergurgl,' says a reporter this year. Yes: the resort's low profile in the UK is curious, given the powerful appeal of its snow-sure mountains and (if you like that kind of thing) its very lively après-ski scene. We always enjoy visits here, most recently in 2011, and so do the readers we hear from. And perhaps things are changing: two major chalet companies are offering big properties here for the coming season.

THE RESORT

Sölden is a long, towny place in the Ötz valley leading up to Obergurgl. Gondolas from opposite ends of town go up to the peak of Gaislachkogl and the lift junction of Giggijoch, with most of the shops, restaurants and hotels in between them. A road winds its way above the town through various rustic suburbs up to the satellite resort of Hochsölden – a group of 4-star hotels and little else.

When buying a six-day lift pass you can opt to pay 10 euro extra for a day in nearby Obergurgl (the hourly buses are included in the lift pass). You can also get buses up to the remote little village of Vent, and down the valley to Längenfeld where there is a big thermal spa. With a car you could make trips to St Anton or Ischgl.

VILLAGE CHARM ★★★★★
Not a strong point
Despite its traditional Tirolean buildings, a pretty church among them, Sölden is no charmer. There's a good selection of shops and bars, but the ambience is towny (prominent ads for strip clubs don't help), and it is strung along the valley road running through it, lacking a central focus. More seriously, the central strip is badly affected by traffic on the road. The place attracts a lively crowd, and the partying can spill into the street. Across the river there's a quieter area,

mainly of hotels and guest houses. Hochsölden offers splendid traffic-free isolation up the mountain.

CONVENIENCE ★★★★★
Lifts at either end
It's a long town, and the gondola stations are almost a mile apart. Not surprisingly, some of the lodgings are a good walk from the lifts. Don't dismiss places over the river from the main street – they aren't necessarily remote from the lifts. An efficient shuttle-bus serves the lifts. Hochsölden is basically ski-in/ski-out.

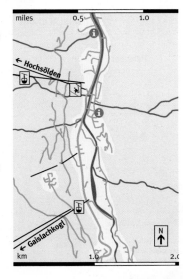

KEY FACTS

Resort	1380m
	4,530ft
Slopes	1350-3340m
	4,430-10,960ft
Lifts	34
Pistes	150km
	93 miles
Blue	46%
Red	34%
Black	20%
Snowmaking	67%

SCENERY ★★★☆☆
Get up on Gaislachkogl
Above Sölden's wooded valley setting is craggy and glacial terrain, and the top heights offer splendid wide views especially south to the Italian border.

THE MOUNTAINS

Practically all the slopes you spend your days on are above the treeline, though there are red and black runs through trees to the village.

We and reporters have found signposting slack in parts (notably on Gaislachkogl) and there have been several changes to the classification of runs recently. The standard issue piste map is absurd – multiple small maps squeezed on to a sheet cluttered with other information (read the next section). A smaller version is available too, although it's no clearer to read.

EXTENT OF THE SLOPES ★★★☆☆
Long run network
The ski area is not enormous, but it does go high. All sectors offer serious vertical and some long runs, which the piste map sets out in juicy and only occasionally misleading detail. It's 1880m vertical and a claimed 15km from the top of the glacier to the village; the runs from Gaislachkogl and Hainbachjoch are in the same league.

There are two similar-sized sectors above the town, linked by fast six-seater chairlifts out of the intervening Rettenbachtal. At the south end of town, a new gondola leads up to an impressive three-cable gondola above it to **Gaislachkogl**. The terrain above the mid-station is served by slow chairs. There are links south towards Gaislachalm and north towards the Rettenbachtal. Another gondola from the north end of the resort goes to **Giggijoch**. Fast lifts from here serve wide, open slopes below Rotkogljoch, from where a series of fast chairs and gondolas (one a cross-valley affair with no piste beneath it) leads to Sölden's glaciers – first the **Rettenbach**, and then the **Tiefenbach**. It may be a long journey (at least five lifts to reach the top) but with luck the reward will be quiet slopes with excellent powdery winter snow. Below Giggijoch, and reached by red and black runs, is Hochsölden – also reachable by a slow single-seat chair.

FAST LIFTS ★★★★☆
Well-linked system
There are still some slow lifts around – including (avoidable) T-bars on the glaciers, but most of the area is very well served by fast chairs and gondolas, and the resort hovers on the brink of a 5-star rating.

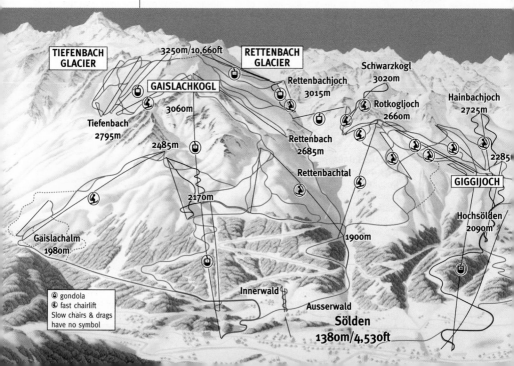

TIEFENBACH GLACIER

3250m/10,66oft

RETTENBACH GLACIER

GAISLACHKOGL

Schwarzkogl
3020m

Rettenbachjoch
3015m

Rotkogljoch
2660m

Hainbachjoch
2725m

3060m

Tiefenbach
2795m

2485m

Rettenbach
2685m

2285

2170m

Rettenbachtal

GIGGIJOCH

Gaislachalm
1980m

1900m

Hochsölden
2090m

Innerwald

Ausserwald

Sölden
1380m/4,53oft

ⓖ gondola
ⓕ fast chairlift
Slow chairs & drags have no symbol

the area, including all slopes on Giggijoch. Grooming is fine. Even in a generally poor season, such as 2011, you can generally count on coverage to resort level – we certainly found that on our March visit.

FOR EXPERTS ★★★☆☆
Off-piste challenges
None of the black pistes dotted around Sölden's map is serious, and some are silly; but there are quite a few non-trivial reds, notably on Gaislachkogl – with some steeper pitches above the mid-station – and the length and vertical of some of the runs present their own challenges. There are extensive off-piste possibilities.

FOR INTERMEDIATES ★★★★☆
Serious verticals
Most of Sölden's main slopes are genuine red runs ideal for adventurous intermediates; there are several easy blacks, too. Keen piste-bashers will love the serious verticals and long runs to be done.

There are two obvious targets for less confident intermediates. The long, quiet run above Gaislachalm, now reclassified blue, is great for cruising, and below it a gentle blue through the trees returns to the resort. And the blues above Giggijoch offer gentler gradients, but life can be complicated by crowds here. Less confident intermediates should beware the tricky red runs to town from Giggijoch and Rettenbachtal.

The glaciers are accessible to blue-run skiers, but it's best to return via the linking gondola to the Giggijoch slopes – the blue run down the Rettenbachtal is narrow (it's the summer glacier access road) and can get very busy, and it eventually turns into a red.

FOR BEGINNERS ★★★☆☆
Crowded nursery slopes
The beginners' slopes, served by a pair of parallel draglifts, are situated just above the village at Innerwald and reached by a new, free shuttle that replaces the old chairlift. Daily lift passes for the slope cost 10 euros. Progression to longer runs means using the gondola to go to and from the blues at Giggijoch; these are wide and gentle, although rather busy in places. Hochsölden is on a steep slope – avoid at all costs.

↑ The linking runs to and from the glaciers are blue, so even early intermediates can get up there
WENDY-JANE KING

LIFT PASSES

Sölden

Prices in €

Age	1-day	6-day
under 15	28	122
15 to 19	36	157
20 to 63	44	225
over 64	38	186

Free under 4; day pass 1 euro if under 8
Senior min. age for senior women is 59
Beginner no deals
Notes
Covers all Sölden lifts; part-day and pedestrian options

QUEUES ★★★☆☆
Giggijoch's not so great
The Giggijoch gondola out of town still generates big queues in the morning peak. If running, the nearby antique single chair to Hochsölden is worth seeking out to avoid them. By contrast, the new Gaislachkogl gondola was delightfully queue-free on our March 2011 visit. Key lifts to and from the glacier, such as the Einzeiger chair and Seiterkar chair (the only way back from the glacier), get busy. The chairs to Rotkogljoch are bottlenecks but shift crowds fast.

TERRAIN PARKS ★★★☆☆
Sufficiently equipped
The Swatch Snowpark above Giggijoch is well-established and regularly upgraded. As well as beginner, intermediate and pro kickers, there are waves, rails, various types of boxes and a wall ride. There's also a chill-out zone. The 'Swatch Shoot my ride' gives you the chance to watch and analyse your tricks on a big video wall at the bottom of the park. The Tiefenbach glacier has an early-season park.

SNOW RELIABILITY ★★★★★
Rarely a problem
The slopes are high and roughly east-facing; and there are two extensive glaciers. Snowmaking covers 67% of

SCHOOLS

Sölden-Hochsölden
t 2364

Yellow Power
t 2255

Freeride Center
t 0650 415 3505

Ski Aktiv
t 0664 441 5321

Vacancia Tirol
t 3100

Josef Fiegl
t 2118

Oetztal School
t 3281

Classes (Sölden prices) 5 days (4hr per day) €185

Private lessons €145 for 2hr for 1-2 persons; each additional person €30

UK PACKAGES

Crystal, Crystal Finest, Independent Ski Links, Neilson, PowderBeds, Ski Total, Skitracer, Skiworld, Snow Finders, STC

FOR BOARDERS ★★★★
Long, wide runs
Sölden is quite popular with boarders. The nursery slope involves drags, but after that draglifts can be avoided and you'll enjoy the wide, open blue runs above Giggijoch. Intermediates will relish the abundance of long runs and open terrain, and there's great freeriding for experienced boarders. There are some flat sections of piste in the Rettenbachtal and on the runs to resort. There's a decent terrain park.

FOR CROSS-COUNTRY ★
Little to entertain
There are a couple of loops by the river to Hof (back end of town) and another 5km trail to Rechenau.

MOUNTAIN RESTAURANTS ★★★
Few notable places
There are nearly 30 huts listed, all usefully marked on the piste map and summarised in a separate leaflet. Most offer traditional food. But those in the main area can get crowded. We like the rustic Gampe Thaya – simple food, table service, lovely terrace, cosy interior; a 2011 visitor warmly agrees. We've also enjoyed good käsespätzle at the peaceful Heidealm above Gaislachalm. Both places have fab views towards Obergurgl. Hühnersteign in the Rettenbachtal is 'cosy' and famous for its chicken (Hühne!), but was packed with Russian visitors on our visit – 'good food though', says a reporter. The self-service at Giggijoch is huge; the smaller Wirthaus table-service option looked nice. Below Hochsölden, a reader preferred the 'pleasant' Panorama Alm, which is bright with 'excellent food'.

SCHOOLS AND GUIDES ★★★
Wide choice, lacking feedback
Sölden has six schools; all restrict class sizes. We lack recent reports, though past reports have been positive. The new Ötztal school provides specialist race training.

FOR FAMILIES ★★
Few special facilities
Sölden does not go out of its way to cater to families. The intrusive main road traffic and possibly lengthy walks make it less attractive. But there are kindergartens at three schools and children can use the Innerwald slopes for a euro per day.

Half-way to the glaciers is this good little area beneath Schwarzkogl, with a wide blue on the left and an easy black on the right →
WENDY-JANE KING

CHILDCARE

Kindergartens (run by ski school)
t 2364
From age 6mnth to 3yr

Ski school
From 3 to 14, 10am to 3pm (6 days including lunch €256)

GETTING THERE

Air Innsbruck 85km/ 55 miles (1.15hr); Zürich 275km/170 miles (3.45hr); Munich 285km/175 miles (3hr)
Rail Train to Innsbruck or Öetz (30km); buses from station

ACTIVITIES

Indoor Freizeit Arena (swimming, sauna, fitness centre, bowling, ice rink, indoor tennis, volley ball)
Outdoor Sleigh rides, snowshoeing, tobogganing, paragliding, ice climbing, snow rafting, snow biking, snowmobiling, tubing, snow golf

Phone numbers
Except for the tourist office, from elsewhere in Austria add the prefix 05254; from abroad use the prefix +43 5254

TOURIST OFFICE

www.soelden.com

STAYING THERE

Most packaged accommodation is in hotels or pensions, but there are also apartments and now catered chalets run by UK operators.

Chalets Now Skiworld has a 30-bed chalet a short walk from the Giggijoch lift and the town centre, and Ski Total has its new chalet-hotel Hermann above the village, close to the piste from Giggijoch down to that lift (a free evening shuttle to the village will operate).

Hotels There is one 5-star hotel but most are good 3- or 4-stars. Take care if looking at very central places – there are noisy bars.

*****Central Spa (22600) Fairly central but also the biggest and best in town – the only 5-star; warmly welcoming; major spa, fitness room, pool.

****Bergland (22400) Hip, recently built place next to shuttle lift to Innerwald, with big 5th-floor spa, outdoor hot tub and decent pool.

****Erhart (2020) Across the river 500m from the Gaislachkogl gondola. 'Excellent location, superb food,' says a 2011 reporter. Spa/fitness facilities.

****Grauer Bär (2564) Near the Gaislachkogl lift. 'Large rooms, excellent food.' Spa area.

****Stefan (2237) Right next to the Giggijoch gondola. We have stayed happily here – good food. Fair-sized wellness area.

****Valentin (2267) Next to the Gaislachkogl lift. 'Reasonable prices; good food, small spa, no pool,' says a 2011 visitor.

Apartments The Gaislachkogl apartments (2246) are close to the gondola, with wellness facilities. Guests also get free entry to the Freizeitarena leisure centre.

EATING OUT ★★★★★
A reasonable choice
Many of the hotels have à la carte restaurants, serving traditional Austrian food. And there are various pizzerias and a steakhouse along the high street. We usually end up in the Tavola in the hotel Rosengarten, because it doesn't take reservations, and haven't been disappointed. s'Pfandl, above the town at Ausserwald, makes a jolly evening outing for traditional Tirolean food.

APRES-SKI ★★★★★
Throbbing until late
Sölden's après-ski is justly famous. It starts up the mountain, notably at Giggijoch, and progresses (possibly via Philipp's Eisbar at Innerwald) to packed bars in and around the main street. The hotel Liebe Sonne's Schirmbar is focal – lively and packed, usually overflowing into the road. Fire and Ice is a two-storey glass-fronted place that parties from 3pm to 3am. There are countless other places with live bands and throbbing discos, some with table dancing and/or striptease. Reader tips for quieter places include Grizzly's ('rustic interior, plenty of seats') and Die Alm ('sometimes with folk music').

OFF THE SLOPES ★★★★★
Disappointing for its size
There's a leisure centre, a swimming pool and an ice rink. Ice climbing and sleigh rides can be arranged. There's also a 5km floodlit toboggan run. A 2011 reporter enjoyed the Wednesday-night ski show on Gaislachkogl. Trips to Innsbruck are possible. Aqua Dome is a thermal spa centre at Längenfeld, now reached by regular buses (free with a lift pass).

Sölden

Interactive resort shortlist builder at www.wtss.co.uk

Söll

The ski area is big, but the attractive village is surprisingly small and intimate; shame it is not set right by the lifts

RATINGS

The mountains

Extent	★★★★
Fast lifts	★★★★
Queues	★★★
Terrain p'ks	★★★
Snow	★★
Expert	★
Intermediate	★★★★
Beginner	★★
Boarder	★★
X-country	★★★
Restaurants	★★★
Schools	★★★
Families	★★★

The resort

Charm	★★★
Convenience	★★
Scenery	★★★
Eating out	★★
Après-ski	★★★★
Off-slope	★★

RPI	85
lift pass	£190
ski hire	£85
lessons	£105
food & drink	£115
total	£495

NEWS

2011/12: The 3.5km toboggan run will be floodlit till 11pm every night. Parents will be able to buy one pass between two which either can use.

2010/11: An eight-pack, with child safety bar, replaced the Osthang quad from the bottom of the Eiberg quads up to Brandstadl.

182

➕ Part of the SkiWelt, Austria's largest linked ski and snowboard area

➕ Local slopes are north-facing, so they keep their snow relatively well

➕ Pretty village with lively après-ski

➕ Cheap, even by Austrian standards

➕ Snowmaking is now more extensive and well used; even so ...

➖ Low altitude can mean poor snow

➖ Long walk or inadequate bus service from the village to the lifts

➖ Runs on upper slopes mostly short

➖ Few challenges except Hohe Salve

➖ Not ideal for beginners

➖ The SkiWelt slopes can get crowded

➖ Appallingly inadequate piste map

Söll has long been popular with British beginners and intermediates, attracting both youths looking for fun and families looking for a quiet time. The resort is in fact far from ideal for beginners, but when the snow is good the SkiWelt can be a great area for intermediates who like easy cruising. Many visitors are surprised by the small size of the village (there aren't many shops) and the long trek out to the slopes. You may prefer to stay near the lifts and trek into the village in the evening. Or you may prefer, like us, to stay in one of the other SkiWelt resorts – Ellmau along the valley (which has its own chapter) or Westendorf over the hill (covered at the end of this chapter).

THE RESORT

Söll is a pleasant, friendly village, bypassed by the main valley road; although its chalets spread quite widely, the core is compact – you can explore it thoroughly in a few minutes.

It is part of the vast SkiWelt area with 279km of slopes. You can also progress (via Brixen) to the slopes of Kitzbühel; these and various other ski areas within easy reach such as Waidring, Fieberbrunn and St Johann are covered by the Kitzbüheler Alpen All Star ski pass.

VILLAGE CHARM ★★★
Follows tradition
Söll is quite attractive, with chalet-style buildings and a huge church near the centre (its graveyard prettily lit by candles at night).

CONVENIENCE ★★
Not for the slopes
The slopes are well outside the village, on the other side of a busy road crossed by a pedestrian tunnel. You can leave your equipment at the bottom of the gondola for a small charge. There is some accommodation out near the lifts, but most is in or around the village centre. From there, it's the ski-bus or a 15-minute walk to the lifts. A base on the far side of the village may mean that you can board the bus before it gets too crowded. But the bus does not serve every corner of the community.

SCENERY ★★★
Head for Hohe Salve
Söll sits in a woody valley, below the distinctive dome-shaped peak of Hohe Salve. From the top, there are good views to the whole SkiWelt and craggy Wilder Kaiser ridges.

THE MOUNTAINS

The SkiWelt is the largest piste network in Austria, linking eight resorts. It will easily keep an average intermediate amused for a week.

A recent visit confirmed our view that the piste map is hopelessly over-ambitious in trying to show the whole area in a single view; the result is a

K Hohe Salve

KEY FACTS

Resort	700m
	2,300ft

Entire SkiWelt	
Slopes	620-1890m
	2,030-6,200ft
Lifts	91
Pistes	279km
	173 miles
Blue	44%
Red	46%
Black	10%
Snowmaking	75%

LIFT PASSES

SkiWelt Wilder Kaiser-Brixental
Prices in €

Age	1-day	6-day
under 16	20	98
16 to 17	32	156
over 18	40	195

Free under 7
Senior no deals
Beginner points cards
Notes
Covers Wilder Kaiser-Brixental area from Going to Westendorf, and the ski-bus; single ascent and part-day options; family discounts
Alternative passes
Kitzbüheler Alpen All Star card covers seven ski areas: Schneewinkel (St Johann), Kitzbühel, SkiWelt, Wildschönau, Alpbachtal, Skicircus Saalbach-Hinterglemm and Zell am See-Kaprun

map that is appallingly inadequate, especially on the Zinsberg side of Hohe Salve and between Eiberg and Brandstadl. Not surprisingly, it generates a lot of complaints from reporters. A solution would be to have a series of smaller maps with a smaller overview map on each – or a big booklet-style publication with separate map for each sector.

Signposting is also criticised, but we found it OK once you realise that the signs point out the direction to the next lift you want and that the signs use the number of the lift to indicate the colour of the run.

EXTENT OF THE SLOPES ★★★★
Short run network
The SkiWelt is a big area but the peaks are not high – with the exception of Hohe Salve they are all under 1700m. In good snow there are long red runs to be done to the valley, but most of the skiing is on the upper slopes where most runs are very short (often less than 300m vertical).

A gondola takes all but complete beginners up to the mid-mountain shelf of Hochsöll, where there are a couple of short lifts and connections in several directions. These include an eight-seat gondola to the high point of Hohe Salve. From here there are runs down to Kälbersalve, Rigi and Hopfgarten. Rigi can also be reached by chairs and runs without going to Hohe Salve – to which it is itself linked by chairs. Rigi is also the start of runs down to Itter and to Hopfgarten. From Kälbersalve you can

head down south-facing runs to Brixen or up to Zinsberg and towards Ellmau. From Brixen, a gondola goes up to Choralpe in Westendorf's area and a lovely north-facing red piste comes back down. From Choralpe you can also head off towards the Kitzbühel slopes.

FAST LIFTS ★★★★
Gradual improvement
Lifts from the valley are mainly gondolas, with a growing number of fast chairs on the upper slopes; a new eight-pack that opened for 2010/11 (see 'News') shifted the resort to a ★★★★ rating, at last. But there are still plenty of slow lifts around.

QUEUES ★★★
Some high-season waits
Lift upgrades have greatly improved this once queue-prone area. Again, this year's reports (and most other recent ones) relate to January or March, and mention few problems except at weekends. But in peak season getting out of Söll at ski-school time in the mornings remains a problem, and there are still some bottlenecks around the mountain. When snow is poor, the links between Zinsberg and Eiberg get crowded.

TERRAIN PARKS ★★★
Local and floodlit
Söll has its own park below Hochsöll with beginner and expert lines; features include boxes, frames and rails. It's floodlit for night riding.

The SkiWelt has 279km of mainly gentle pistes and 70 mountain huts – perfect when there is this much fresh snow and blue sky →

SNOW RELIABILITY ★★☆☆☆
Erratic – but has artificial help
The SkiWelt has had some good seasons of late, with several reporters experiencing good fresh powder for much of their holidays. But it is not always like that, and with a low average height, and important links that get a lot of sun, the snow can suffer badly in warm weather. So the snowmaking that the SkiWelt has installed is essential. At 210km and covering about 75% of the area's pistes, it is Austria's biggest snowmaking installation. Reporters have been impressed by its use and by the grooming – endorsed by a 2011 reporter. We were there one January before any major snowfalls, and snowmaking was keeping the links open well. Warm weather is a more serious problem.

FOR EXPERTS ★☆☆☆☆
Not a lot
The two black runs from Hohe Salve towards Hochsöll and Kälbersalve and the black run alongside the Brixen gondola are the only challenging pistes. There are further blacks in Scheffau and Ellmau, but the main challenges are off-piste – from Brandstadl down to Söll, for example.

FOR INTERMEDIATES ★★★★☆
Mainly easy runs
When blessed with good snow the SkiWelt is a paradise for those who love easy cruising and don't mind short runs. It is a big area and you really get a feeling of travelling around. There are lots of blue runs and many of the reds could be blue. In general the most difficult slopes are those from the mid-stations to the valleys – to Blaiken, Brixen and Söll,

ASTBERG
1265m

Hartkaiser

Eiberg
1675m

ZINSB
1675

Astberg

BRANDSTADL
1650m

Tanzboden

Tanzbodenalm

HOHE SA
1830m/6,

Going
775m

Hartkaiser

Rübezahlalm

Ellmi's

Südhang

Aualm

Silleralm

Ellmau
800m/2,620ft

Neualm

Hohe Salve

Brandstadl I &II

Excellent long
runs when
snow is good
to valley level

Hochsöll

Hexen

Scheffau

Blaiken
675m

Hochsöll

Salvenmoos

Söll
700m/2,300ft

SalVista

gondola
fast chairlift
Slow chairs & drags
have no symbol

Itter
700m

for example. For more challenging reds head for Westendorf (and don't miss the excellent red back down from there to Brixen).

FOR BEGINNERS ★★★★★
Not ideal
The big area of nursery slopes between the main road and the gondola station is fine when snow is good – gentle, spacious, uncrowded and free from good skiers whizzing past. But it can get icy or slushy. In poor snow the Hochsöll area may be used. None of the lifts is free, but points cards are available. Progression to longer runs is likely to be awkward – there aren't many blue runs in this part of the SkiWelt. One is the narrow blue from Hochsöll, on which fast learners can get home when the run is not too icy.

FOR BOARDERS ★★★★★
Great cruising
Söll is a good place to try out boarding: slopes are gentle and there are plenty of gondolas and chairs. And it has its own terrain park. For competent boarders it's more limited – the slopes of the SkiWelt are tame.

FOR CROSS-COUNTRY ★★★★★
Neighbouring villages are better
Söll has 30km of local trails but they are less interesting than those between Hopfgarten and Kelchsau and around and beyond Ellmau. There is a total of 170km in the SkiWelt area. Lack of snow-cover can be a problem.

MOUNTAIN RESTAURANTS ★★★★★
Good, but crowded
There are quite a few jolly little chalets, but we've had complaints of insufficient seating and long queues.

ZINSBERG
1675m

Very sunny slopes, with the usual worries about the effect on snow conditions

Gondola and piste link mean access to Westendorf no longer relies on catching buses

HOHE SALVE
1830m/6,000ft

Zinsberg

Filzboden

Silleralm

ualm

Hochbrixen
1300m

Hochbrixen

Brixen
800m

Hohe Salve

Foisching

Kälbersalve
1545m

Westendorf
800m/2,620ft

RIGI
1530m

The highest and most testing slopes in the area, with some of the best snow

1200m

Hexen

ill

moos

Salvenbahn

Salvista

Hopfgarten
620m/2,030ft

↑ Brixen is long and strung out with a south-facing slope down from the main SkiWelt circuit

KITZBÜHELER ALPEN-BRIXENTAL / KURT TROPPER

CHILDCARE

Mini-club Hexenstube
t 0664 553 2937
9am–4.30; ages
6mnth to 4yr

Monti's Kinder-welt (bambinis)
t 5454
for ages 3 to 5

Ski school
Takes children from 5 to 14 for 4hr daily (5 days €145)

SCHOOLS

Söll-Hochsöll
t 5454

Knolln
t 0676 64 85060

Black Sheep Ski
t 066917 128571

Classes
5 4-hr days: €145
(Söll prices)

Private lessons
€55 for 1hr; each additional person €25

Editors' choice We've enjoyed lunch at Tanzbodenalm near Brandstadl (43150) – pleasantly woody, serving delicious deer stew; 'excellent service'. Another favourite is Rübezahlalm (see Ellmau).
Worth knowing about Just below Hochsöll the atmospheric converted cow shed Stöcklalm is recommended by reporters ('superb spit-roasted chicken'), as is the Hochsöll itself. The highly rated Hohe Salve (top of the gondola) offers a large revolving terrace and 'stunning views' (from the loos as well, say reporters). The Stoagrub'nhütte above Hopfgarten serves 'generous portions'. Other reporter recommendations include the Aualm below Zinsberg for cakes and glühwein, the 'pleasantly rustic' Neualm above Scheffau and, a bit lower down, Bavaria – which has a 'lovely comfy bar' and 'great value lunch specials'.

SCHOOLS AND GUIDES ★★★☆☆
A good reputation
The Söll-Hochsöll school has a fairly good reputation. A reporter and her family enjoyed 'very good' lessons; the children 'were confidently doing red runs by the end of the week', but groups were large ('up to 12'). Another visitor had a 'very good' carving clinic with Black Sheep Ski.

FOR FAMILIES ★★★☆☆
A range of options
Söll has fairly wide-ranging facilities – the focus is the Söll-Hochsöll school's Monti's Kinder-welt (and day care) at the gondola mid-station, which takes children from age three. It is well-

equipped with play areas and nursery slopes. There's a special kids-only drag and slope on the opposite side of the village to the main lifts.

STAYING THERE

Chalets Crystal has two big ones.
Hotels There is a wide choice of simple gasthofs, pensions and B&Bs, plus better-quality hotel accommodation – mainly 3-star.
★★★★Greil (5289) Attractive, but out of the centre and far from the lifts. A new indoor pool was built for 2010/11.
★★★★Postwirt (5081) Attractive, central, traditional, with stube; outdoor pool.
★★★★Alpenpanorama (5309) Far from lifts but with own bus stop; wonderful views; pleasant rooms.
★★★Bergland (5454) Well placed between the village and lifts. Has been refurbished.
★★★Tulpe (5223) Next to the lifts.
★★★Feldwebel (5224) Central.
★★★Hexenalm (5544) Next to the lifts.
★★★Eggerwirt (5236) 'Modern and comfortable.' Between centre and main road, bus stop outside.
Apartments The central Aparthotel Schindlhaus has nice accommodation. Some of the best apartments in town are attached to the Bergland hotel, and reporters have recommended the 'ideally located' Alpin apartments ('fabulous', 'outstanding in terms of cleanliness and space').

EATING OUT ★★☆☆☆
A fair choice
Some of the best restaurants are in hotels. The Greil and Postwirt

GETTING THERE

Air Salzburg 90km/
55 miles (1hr30);
Innsbruck 80km/
50 miles (1hr15);
Munich 260km/160
miles (3hr45)
Rail Wörgl (13km/
8 miles) or Kufstein
(15km/9 miles); bus
to resort

UK PACKAGES

*Crystal, First Choice,
Independent Ski Links,
Inghams, Interactive
Resorts, Neilson, Ski
Line, Skitracer, STC,
Thomson*
Hopfgarten *Contiki,
First Choice*
Westendorf *Crystal,
Inghams, Thomson*

ACTIVITIES

Indoor Swimming,
sauna, solarium,
massage, bowling,
squash
Outdoor Natural ice
rink (skating, curling),
sleigh rides, 3km of
floodlit toboggan
runs, walks,
snowshoeing, snow
tubing

('extensive and delicious New Year buffet') are good. The Schindlhaus is said to be the best, at least if you enjoy 'rich meat' dishes. Giovanni does excellent, large pizzas, while other places worth a visit include the Dorfstub'n (traditional and steaks) and the Venezia.

APRES-SKI ★★★★
Still some very loud bars
Söll is not as raucous as it used to be, but it's still very lively and a lot of places have live music.

The Salvenstadl (Cow Shed) bar is regularly recommended by reporters ('the best live music'). Moonlight at the gondola base is 'less Brit-dominated and has dancing on the tables even in low-season'. The Whisky-Mühle is a large disco that can get 'wild', especially after the bars close. Buffalo's is popular and the hotel Austria bar is 'boisterous' with pool tables and quiz evenings. Rossini is a 'lovely, modern bar', good for cocktails and live music.

Hot news in Austria's hottest resort, p177.

OFF THE SLOPES ★★
Not bad for a small village
You could spend a happy day in the splendid Panoramabad: taking a sauna, swimming, lounging about. There's 'great fun, good value' tobogganing from the top of the gondola. The large baroque church is worth a visit. Coach excursions include trips to Salzburg, Innsbruck and even Vipiteno, over the Brenner in Italy.

LINKED RESORT – 700m
ITTER

Itter is a tiny village half-way between Söll and Hopfgarten, with a gondola just outside the village that goes up to Hochsöll. There's a hotel and half a dozen gasthofs and B&Bs. The school has a rental shop, and there are nursery slopes close to hand but few easy longer runs to progress to in this part of the SkiWelt.

Hopfgarten 620m

⊞ Quick connection to highest slopes
⊞ Good base for cross-country

⊟ Home slope can suffer from sun
⊟ Not the best base for beginners

An unspoiled, friendly, traditional resort set off the main road with a two-stage gondola from town to the top of Hohe Salve.

Village charm The village is a good size: small enough to be intimate, large enough to have plenty of off-slope amenities.
Convenience Most hotels are within five minutes' walk of the gondola.
Scenery You get a different perspective of Hohe Salve from here.

THE MOUNTAIN
Hopfgarten is at the western extremity of the SkiWelt.
Slopes Two successive gondolas take you to Hohe Salve – the high point of the main SkiWelt circuit.
Fast lifts See Söll.
Queues We've had no reports of queues to leave the village since the eight-seat gondola was installed.
Terrain parks Söll has one.
Snow reliability The south-west-facing home slope is especially vulnerable in late season (but snowmaking is good).
Experts Experts should hire a guide and explore off-piste for excitement.
Intermediates When snow is good, the runs down to Hopfgarten and the

nearby villages of Brixen and Itter are some of the best in the SkiWelt.
Beginners There is a beginners' slope in the village, but it is sunny as well as low; lack of snow-cover means paying for a lift pass to higher slopes. There are few easy longer runs to progress to in this part of the SkiWelt.
Snowboarding See Söll.
Cross-country Hopfgarten is one of the best cross-country bases in the area. There are fine trails to Kelchsau (7km) and the Itter-Bocking loop (15km) starts nearby. Westendorf's trails are close. But all are at valley level.
Mountain restaurants See Söll.
Schools and guides Partly because Hopfgarten seems to attract large numbers of Australians, English is widely spoken in the two schools.
Families Hopfgarten is a family resort, with a nursery and ski kindergarten.

STAYING THERE
Cheap and cheerful gasthofs, pensions and little private B&Bs are the norm.
Hotels The comfortable Hopfgarten

(3920) and Sporthotel Fuchs (2420) are both well placed for the main lift.
Eating out Most of the restaurants are hotel-based, but there are exceptions, including a Chinese and a pizzeria.
Après-ski Après-ski is generally quiet, though a lively holiday can usually be

ensured if you go with Aussie-dominated tour operator Contiki.
Off the slopes Activities include swimming, riding, bowling, skating, tobogganing, paragliding and sleigh rides. You can go by train to Salzburg, Innsbruck and Kitzbühel.

Brixen im Thale 800m

- ☐ Ideal base for the whole of the Ski Welt and Kitzbühel slopes
- ☐ Main lifts go from one spot

- ☐ Home runs from main SkiWelt area suffer from too much sun
- ☐ Most lodgings involve bus rides

Great central location with gondolas into the main SkiWelt area on one side and into Westendorf's slopes and the link with Kitzbühel on the other.

Village charm The village is not particularly cute, but it is traditional in style and is pretty quiet now that it is bypassed by the main valley road.
Convenience The main hotels are near the railway station, a bus ride from the lift station, west of the centre.
Scenery Wide views from the slopes include the dramatic Wilder Kaiser.

THE MOUNTAIN
Slopes A gondola goes to Hochbrixen and the main SkiWelt slopes; lifts diverge for Hohe Salve and Söll, or Astberg and Ellmau. Another goes in the opposite direction up to Choralpe above Westendorf, which links to the slopes of Kitzbühel.
Fast lifts Much improved with several fast chairs having been installed up the mountain in recent years.
Queues Lift upgrades have improved the once queue-prone SkiWelt area.
Terrain parks There are good parks above both Westendorf and Söll.
Snow reliability Altitude is low, and the home runs from the main SkiWelt area are south-facing. But there is

snowmaking on these and many other slopes in the area.
Experts The black run alongside the Hochbrixen gondola is one of the few challenging pistes in the area.
Intermediates When snow is good, this is a great area. Brixen's local slopes suit confident intermediates best, on both sides of the valley. The north-facing red run back down from Choralpe in Westendorf's area is one of our favourites in the whole SkiWelt.
Beginners The nursery area is secluded, but a bus ride from the village. Progression runs are far from ideal, with no blues to the lift base.
Snowboarding See Söll and Westendorf.
Cross-country In addition to valley-floor trails, there's a 3km loop up the mountain at Hochbrixen.
Mountain restaurants The local slopes are well equipped.
Schools and guides The ski schools run the usual group classes, and mini-groups for up to six people.
Families There is a baby-sitting service and the ski school runs a kids' club.

STAYING THERE
Hotels There are plenty of hotels and pensions. The Alpenhof (88320) and Sporthotel (8191) are 4-stars with pool.
Eating out Most restaurants are hotel-based, but the Talhof is a highly recommended alternative.
Après-ski Not a highlight. There are two or three bars by the gondola station, of which the Brixner Stadl is a disco later on.
Off the slopes Activities include tennis, hotel-based spa facilities and days out to Salzburg and Innsbruck.

ALPEN MARKETING GMBH / HANNES DABERNIG

← Lots of villages in the SkiWelt are very pretty and based around beautiful onion-domed churches. This is Itter

Westendorf 800m

- ➕ Charming, traditional village
- ➕ Challenging local slopes
- ➕ Good local beginner slopes but ...
- ➖ Local slopes not ideal territory for progression from the nursery slopes
- ➖ Getting to main SkiWelt takes time

Quiet, attractive village with good local slopes for confident intermediates; easy access to Kitzbühel's slopes but slightly off the main SkiWelt circuit.

Village charm The village is small with traditional buildings, including an attractive onion-domed church. It has a relaxed, rustic atmosphere and was once declared 'Europe's most beautiful village' in a floral competition.

Convenience The centre is close to the nursery slopes, and a five-minute walk or free ski-bus ride from the main lifts.

Scenery The slopes here offer a bit more drama than some of the other hills nearby, and the views include the craggy Wilder Kaiser to the north.

THE MOUNTAIN

The local slopes are separated by one valley from the main SkiWelt circuit to the north and by another from the Kitzbühel slopes to the east. There's a pleasant mix of open and wooded slopes.

Slopes A two-stage gondola goes to Talkaser, one of the four minor peaks that make up the local area. From there, you can head for Choralpe and Brixen (via a splendid 5.5km-long red run of over 1000m vertical), or for Fleiding and Gampenkogel. All the local peaks have short east- or west-facing runs. A longer blue run of around 800m vertical goes from Gampenkogel to the Kitzbühel connection (which is a short shuttle-bus ride to the gondola at Skirast).

Fast lifts The two newish gondolas have vastly improved access but once up the mountain there are still a lot of slow lifts.

Queues We have no reports of any significant problems with queues.

Terrain parks There's an excellent park with something for all levels including jumps, boxes, kickers, rails and a half-pipe (www.boardplay.com).

Snow reliability Not a strong point of the region. But snowmaking is extensive and grooming excellent.

Experts The pistes are among the most testing in the SkiWelt area, and there is off-piste to be explored.

Intermediates Great for confident intermediates: nearly all Westendorf's terrain is genuinely red in gradient.

Beginners The village nursery slopes are extensive and excellent. There are a couple of genuine blues to progress to on the lower mountain, but further progression can be challenging.

Snowboarding Most lifts are chairs and gondolas and the park is great. But some runs have tedious flat sections.

Cross-country There are lots of trails, but snow-cover is unreliable.

Mountain restaurants There are good table- and self-service places. Ki-West, Schiwiege and Berggasthof Osl are the newest. Alpenrosenhütte, Brechhornhaus and the Gassnerwirt are popular.

Schools and guides A recent reporter's daughter made rapid progress with the Top School. Ski-Ideal and Westendorf are other options.

Families Westendorf sells itself as a family resort. The kindergarten takes children from the age of three.

STAYING THERE

There are plentiful hotels and guest houses, both near the centre and further afield.

Hotels: The Jakobwirt (6245) and Schermer (6268) are good 4-stars; the 3-star Post (6202) is 'basic and friendly' with 'good food'. No pool. Pension Cafe Elisabeth (8940) is central and recommended as 'very hospitable'. The small Glockenstuhl (6175) is a short walk away with a good spa. There are places out near the gondola.

Apartments The Schermerhof apartments (6979) are of good quality.

Eating out Most of the best restaurants are in hotels. Reporters also suggest the Wastlhof, Klinglers and Berggasthof Stimmlach (a taxi ride out).

Après-ski There are more lively spots than you might expect in a small, cute village. The Liftstüberl and Gerry's Inn are packed at close of play. Bruchtall 'caters for kids too'. The funky Moskito Cafe Bar and In's Moment have live music, and the Village Pub 'good Irish craic'. Karat is a smart lounge bar. There is at least one disco.

Off the slopes There are excursions to Innsbruck and Salzburg, plus pretty walks and sleigh rides.

Phone numbers
From elsewhere in Austria add the prefix 05358 (Wilder Kaiser), 05333 (Söll), 05332 (Hohe Salve), 05335 (Hopfgarten, Itter), 05334 (Brixen, Westendorf); from abroad use the prefix +43 and omit the initial '0'

TOURIST OFFICES

WILDER KAISER
(Söll, Scheffau, Going, Ellmau)
www.wilderkaiser.info

HOHE SALVE
(Hopfgarten, Itter)
www.hohe-salve.com

KITZBUHELER ALPEN
(Brixen, Westendorf)
www.kitzbuehel-alpen.com

SKIWELT
www.skiwelt.at

Interactive resort shortlist builder at **www.wtss.co.uk**

St Anton

If what you seek is dumps, bumps, boozing and bopping, there's nowhere quite like it – and with a neat Tirolean town as a bonus

RATINGS

The mountains

Extent	★★★★
Fast lifts	★★★
Queues	★★★
Terrain p'ks	★★★
Snow	★★★★
Expert	★★★★★
Intermediate	★★★
Beginner	★
Boarder	★★★★
X-country	★★
Restaurants	★★★
Schools	★★★
Families	★★★★

The resort

Charm	★★★★
Convenience	★★★
Scenery	★★★
Eating out	★★★★
Après-ski	★★★★★
Off-slope	★★

RPI 105

lift pass	£200
ski hire	£145
lessons	£125
food & drink	£135
total	**£605**

190

NEWS

2011/12: The Mooser hotel, adjoining the Mooserwirt bar, is due to open in December 2011, with luxury rooms and 10 suites, spa, pool and restaurant.

A smart new 4-star hotel (Anthony's) is to be built in the resort centre, on the site of several popular restaurants – we hear Funky Chicken has closed, Pomodoro pizza is to relocate.

➕ Varied terrain for experts and adventurous intermediates; lots of it, once you include Lech-Zürs, a bus ride away

➕ Heavy snowfalls, lots of snow-guns

➕ Car-free village centre retains solid traditional charm

➕ Very lively après-ski

➕ Improved lift system has cut queues from the base areas, but ...

➖ Some pistes are made dangerous by crowds and uncontrolled, inconsiderate skiers

➖ Slopes can be tough for near-beginners and timid intermediates

➖ Most tough runs are unpatrolled

➖ Snow quality can suffer from sun

➖ Resort sprawls, with long treks from some lodgings to key lifts and bars

➖ Centre can be noisy at night

St Anton is one of the world's best resorts for competent skiers and riders, particularly those with the energy to après-ski as hard as they ski. If you want to, you can party from 3pm to 3am. Good luck!

But the place doesn't suit everyone. If you are thinking of trying an Austrian change from a major French resort, or of going up a gear from Kitzbühel or Söll, be sure that you are not going to get thrown by blues that get heavily moggulled, and reds that might be black.

The resort now has impressive access gondolas to both sides of its ski area. As we have been saying for years, the urgent need is to deal with the dangerously busy run down from its main mountain by creating an alternative piste. There is a ski route already there; it just needs a bit of a makeover.

THE RESORT

St Anton is the western extremity of the Tirol, at the foot of the road up to the Arlberg pass. It is at one end of a lift network that spreads across to St Christoph and over the pass to Stuben. These two tiny villages are described at the end of the chapter.

The resort is a long, sprawling place, almost a town rather than a village, with mainly traditional-style buildings, squeezed into a narrow valley – there is only just room for the town, the bypass road, the river and the railway. St Anton spreads down the valley, thinning out before broadening again to form the suburb of Nasserein.

Development spreads up the hill to the west, towards the Arlberg pass – first to Oberdorf, then Gastig, 10 minutes' walk from the centre. Further up the hill are the suburbs of Stadle, Dengert and Moos – a long way out, but the latter two next to the slopes.

The ski pass covers Lech and Zürs, reached by regular free ski-buses from Alpe Rauz, where the slopes meet the Arlberg pass road, and the less well-known Sonnenkopf area above Klösterle. These buses can get crowded early and late in the day and often provoke complaints from reporters. The post bus offers a less crowded alternative, and means you can start or end your outing in St Anton; but it is not free. Taxis can be economic if shared. Serfaus, Ischgl and Sölden are feasible outings by car.

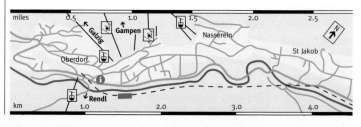

KEY FACTS

Resort	1305m
	4,280ft

Arlberg region	
Slopes	1075-2650m
	3,530-8,690ft
Lifts	84
Pistes	280km
	174 miles
Blue	40%
Red	48%
Black	12%
Snowmaking	60%

St Anton, St Christoph and Stuben	
Slopes	1305-2650m
	4,280-8,690ft
Lifts	42
Pistes	127km
	79 miles

VILLAGE CHARM ★★★★★
Traditional but lively

Although it is crowded and commercialised, St Anton is full of character, its traffic-free main street lined by traditional-style buildings. It is an attractively bustling place, day and night. Its shops offer little in the way of entertainment, but meet everyday needs well – a well-stocked Spar, for example, a watchmender who stocks batteries that fit our altimeters, and an excellent bookshop that sells good numbers of this book.

CONVENIENCE ★★★★★
Not bad for a large resort

The hub of the resort is at the western end of the main street, close to the base stations of the lifts to Gampen (a fast quad chair), to Galzig and to Rendl (modern gondolas). Staying on or close to this main street is ideal to keep treks to the lifts short.

Nasserein has an eight-seater gondola up to Gampen, and makes an appealing base for a quiet time. The nightlife action is a short bus ride or 15-minute walk away. Staying between the centre and Nasserein is fairly convenient too as the Fang chairlift gives access to the Nasserein gondola.

SCENERY ★★★★★
Head for the Valluga

St Anton squeezes into a narrow, partly wooded valley. The scenery becomes more impressive as you ride up the lifts, either towards the dramatic Valluga, or across the valley up to Rendl, which opens up a splendid panorama (shown partly over the page).

THE MOUNTAINS

The main slopes are essentially open: only the lower Gampen runs and the run from Rendl to the valley offer much shelter from bad weather.

St Anton vies with Val d'Isère for the title of 'resort with most underclassified slopes'. Many of the blue runs would be better classified as red; there are also plenty of reds that could be black; but paradoxically, none of the blacks is seriously steep, for reasons that we will explain.

The toughest runs are called 'ski routes' or 'high-alpine touring runs'.

The touring runs (at Rendl and Stuben) are simply off-piste runs that would not appear on the piste map at all in most resorts. No problem – if you fancy these runs, hire a guide.

The ski routes are marked, avalanche controlled but not groomed or patrolled. We applaud the clear explanation (lacking in many resorts), but we think many of these runs should be patrolled pistes. The ski routes in several areas (notably Schindler Spitze and Rendl) are popular runs, treated like pistes. To add to the confusion, some of the routes are sometimes groomed (some were on our recent visits).

The piste map is designed for marketing rather than navigation, covering the whole of the Arlberg region in one view; it is unclear and misleading in places. What's needed, really, is one piste map for St Anton-St Christoph-Stuben and separate ones for Lech-Zürs and for Sonnenkopf. The local cable TV shows the state of the pistes and queues – very useful.

SNOWPIX.COM / CHRIS GILL

On the left is the vast white bowl of Mattun, on the right Kapall with Gampen below, about on the treeline (seen from Rendl) →

EXTENT OF THE SLOPES ★★★★
Large linked area

St Anton's slopes fall into three main sectors, two of them linked. The major sector is that beneath the local high-spot, the **Valluga**, accessed by the jumbo gondola to Galzig, then a cable car. The tiny top stage of the cable car to the Valluga itself is mainly for sightseeing – you can take skis or a board up only if you have a guide to lead you down the tricky off-piste run to Zürs. The slightly lower station of Valluga Grat gives access to St Anton's famous high, sunny bowls, and to the long, beautiful red/blue run to Alpe Rauz. From here there's a six-pack, the Valfagehr, to return, or you can go on to explore the rather neglected slopes of **Stuben**, described at the end of the chapter. The run to Alpe Rauz and the high Valluga runs can also be accessed by riding the Schindlergrat triple chair, though some also involve a hike.

Other runs from Galzig go south-west to St Christoph and east into the Steissbachtal. Beyond this valley, with lift and piste links in both directions, is the **Kapall-Gampen** sector, reachable by chairlift from central St Anton or gondola from Nasserein. From Gampen at mid-mountain, pistes lead back to

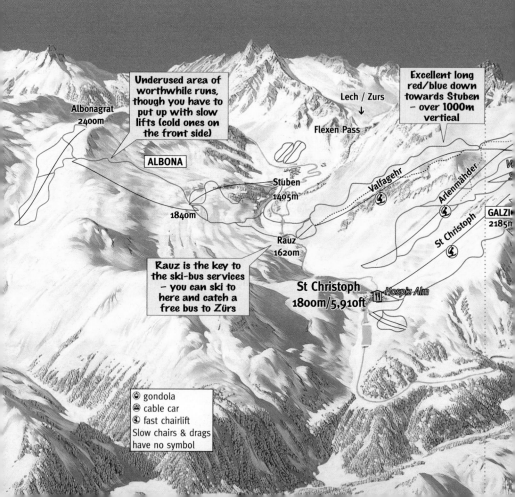

Albonagrat
2400m

Underused area of worthwhile runs, though you have to put up with slow lifts (cold ones on the front side)

ALBONA

1840m

Lech / Zurs ↓

Flexen Pass

Stuben
1405m

Rauz
1620m

Rauz is the key to the ski-bus services – you can ski to here and catch a free bus to Zürs

Excellent long red/blue down towards Stuben – over 1000m vertical

Valfagehr

Arlenmähder

St Christoph

GALZI
2185m

St Christoph
1800m/5,910ft

Hospiz Alm

🚡 gondola
🚠 cable car
🚡 fast chairlift
Slow chairs & drags have no symbol

St Anton and Nasserein. Or you can ride a six-pack on up to Kapall to ski the treeless upper mountain. The third main sector is **Rendl,** reached by a newish gondola which attracts more people to this once neglected sector. A handful of lifts serve the west-facing runs above the gondola, with a good north-facing piste to the valley.

FAST LIFTS ★★★
Fast access, patchy higher up
Access from the village is by smart gondolas or fast chairs. But while the Gampen and Galzig sector have a lot of fast chairs higher up, Rendl and Stuben still have a lot of slow ones.

QUEUES ★★★
Much improved, but ...
Queues are not the problem they once were. Our 2011 reporters had few problems and we didn't either on our

March visit. But there may be queues for key lifts at peak times, including the Valluga cable car from Galzig, the alternative Schindlergrat chair to Schindler Spitze and the Zammermoos chair out of the Steissbachtal (if you hit a serious queue it can be quicker to ski down to the Galzig gondola than to wait here).

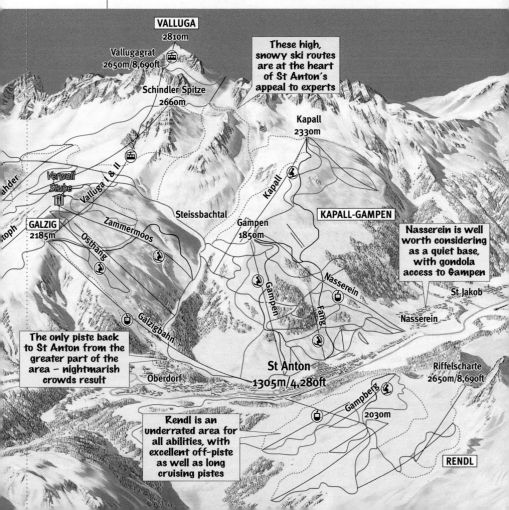

VALLUGA
2810m

Vallugagrat
2650m/8,690ft

Schindler Spitze
2660m

Kapall
2330m

These high, snowy ski routes are at the heart of St Anton's appeal to experts

Verwall Stube

Valluga I & II

Kapall

Steissbachtal

KAPALL-GAMPEN

GALZIG
2185m

Zammermoos

Gampen
1850m

Osthang

Nasserein

Nasserein is well worth considering as a quiet base, with gondola access to Gampen

St Jakob

Gampen

Fang

Nasserein

Galzigbahn

The only piste back to St Anton from the greater part of the area – nightmarish crowds result

Oberdorf

St Anton
1305m/4,280ft

Riffelscharte
2650m/8,690ft

Gampberg

2030m

RENDL

Rendl is an underrated area for all abilities, with excellent off-piste as well as long cruising pistes

↑ This is the bravo's way down from Schindler Spitze to join the long, long red/blue run to Alpe Rauz; Ulmer Hütte is beyond the chairlift

SNOWPIX.COM / CHRIS GILL

The lower runs are well equipped with snowmaking, which generally ensures the home runs remain open.

FOR EXPERTS ★★★★★
One of the world's great areas
St Anton vies with Chamonix, Val d'Isère and a handful of other resorts for the affections of experts. There are countless opportunities for going off-piste. The runs in the huge bowls below the Valluga are justifiably world-famous and immediately after a fresh snowfall, you can see tracks going all over the mountain; there are ski routes in the bowls too. Lower down, there are challenging runs in many directions from both Galzig and Kapall-Gampen. These lower runs can be doubly tricky if the snow has been hit by the sun.

Don't overlook the Rendl area, which has plenty of open space served by the top lifts, and several quite challenging runs. This is a great area for a mixed group and usually quieter than the main sector. The Sonnenkopf area, down-valley from Stuben, is even quieter and has several ski routes – and more serious off-piste, including an 'excellent' route to Langen. Read the Stuben section, too.

Perhaps more of a worry than the lift queues are the crowded pistes – see separate feature panel.

TERRAIN PARKS ★★★☆☆
Small, but perfectly formed
The 340m-long park on Rendl, just below the top of the gondola, has been vastly improved by Q-Parks (www.qparks.com). While it doesn't match Lech's park for quantity, it has lots of quality – including a jib line, and intermediate and pro tabletop jump lines, fun-cross for the kids, chill area and daily maintenance.

SNOW RELIABILITY ★★★★☆
Generally very good cover
If the weather is coming from the west or north-west (as it often is), the Arlberg region gets it first, and as a result St Anton gets heavy falls of snow – and neighbouring Lech and Zürs get even more. These resorts often have much better conditions than other resorts of a similar height, and we've had great fresh powder here as late as mid-April. But many slopes face south or south-east, causing icy or heavy conditions at times. As spring approaches, in particular, It's vital to time descents of the steeper runs off the Valluga to get decent conditions, or you can find yourself in trouble.

FOR INTERMEDIATES ★★★☆☆
Some real challenges
St Anton is well suited to good, adventurous intermediates. As well as lots of testing pistes, they will be able to try some of the ski routes in the Valluga bowls. The run from Schindler Spitze to Rauz is very long (over 1000m vertical), varied and ideal for good intermediates. Alternatively, turn off from this part-way down and take the Steissbachtal to the lifts back to Galzig or Gampen. The Kapall-Gampen section is also interesting, with sporty bumps among trees on the lower half. Good intermediates may enjoy the men's downhill run from the top of this sector to the town.

Timid intermediates will find St Anton less to their taste. There are few easy cruising pistes; most blue runs here would be red in most other resorts, and get bumpy, especially if there is fresh snow (the blue 1 home run often has testing moguls at the end of the day). The gentlest cruisers are the short blues on Galzig and the Steissbachtal but they get extremely crowded. The blue from Kapall to Gampen is wide and cruisey.

LIFT PASSES

Arlberg

Prices in €

Age	1-day	6-day
under 16	27	127
16 to 19	41	184
20 to 64	45	212
over 65	41	184

Free no one; day pass €10 if under 8, €20 if over 75

Senior min. age for senior women is 60

Beginner points ticket

Notes
Covers all St Anton, St Christoph, Lech, Zürs and Stuben lifts, and linking bus between Rauz and Zürs; also covers Sonnenkopf (10 lifts) at Klösterle, 7km west of Stuben (bus link from Stuben); single ascent, half-day and pedestrian options

The underrated Rendl area has a variety of trails suitable for good and moderate intermediates, including the long and genuinely blue Salzböden. The long treelined run to the valley (over 1000m vertical from the top) is the best run in the area when visibility is poor, but it has some awkward sections and can get very busy at the end of the day. You should take the bus to Lech-Zürs at least once during a week's stay.

FOR BEGINNERS ★☆☆☆☆
Far from ideal
The best bet for beginners is to start at Nasserein, where the nursery slope is less steep than the one close to the main lifts. There are further slopes up at Gampen and a short, gentle blue run at Rendl, served by an easy draglift. But there are no other easy, uncrowded runs for beginners to progress to. A mixed party including novices would be better off choosing a base in Lech or Zürs; those who want to explore St Anton can do so by getting on the bus.

FOR BOARDERS ★★★★☆
Freeriding heaven
For many, St Anton is the Mecca of Austrian freeriding. Excellent snowfall, countless steep gullies and backcountry powder fields with challenging terrain create a big draw for advanced riders. The Arlberg Snowboard Academy has a reputation for showing all levels where best to apply their skills – whether a beginner on the wide open pistes or a more advanced rider wanting guidance through trees or steeps.

FOR CROSS-COUNTRY ★★☆☆☆
A decent amount
Trails total around 40km and snow conditions are usually good.

MOUNTAIN RESTAURANTS ★★★☆☆
Lots of options
Editors' choice The Verwallstube at Galzig (2352501) is in a class of its own – an expensive table-service place with all the trimmings and splendid views. We've had seriously good lunches here a couple of times. We

OFF-PISTE RUNS IN ST ANTON

The Arlberg region is an off-piste skier's dream – renowned for its consistently high snowfall record and enormous diversity of terrain. We invited Piste to Powder Mountain Guides to give us an introduction to the possibilities. Remember you should never explore far off-piste without a guide.

Piste to Powder Mountain Guides

All day guiding 9am to 5pm. Choose from four skill levels. All safety equipment provided.

t 00 43 664 174 6282

info@pistetopowder.com

www.pistetopowder.com

Runs from Rendl
After initial practice close to the pistes, the natural progression is to go beyond the furthest lift to access the wide rolling bowls of powder of Rossfall.

More serious routes from Rendl take you well away from all lifts. The North Face, accessed from the Gampberg six-seat chair, offers challenging terrain to the intermediate/confident off-piste skier. The Riffel chairlifts access the imposing Hinter Rendl – a gigantic high-mountain bowl offering a huge descent down to St Anton, often in deep powder. A variant involves a climb to Rendl Scharte and a demanding descent with sections of 35° down the remote Malfontal to the village of Pettneu and a taxi back to St Anton.

Runs from Albona, above Stuben
Stuben's outstanding terrain, reached from the Albonagrat chair, is suited to the more experienced off-piste skier, as the descents are long. The open treelines of the Langen forest, where the powder is regularly knee to waist deep, form some of the world's finest tree skiing. A 30-minute climb from Albonagrat, with skis on your shoulder, opens up further outstanding terrain from Maroikopfe – either west, down undulating open slopes to Langen, or east, down steep 40° slopes to Verwalltal, where this glorious run ends with a glass of wine at an old hunting lodge.

Runs from the Valluga
The legendary runs from the summit cable car of the Valluga must be on the tick list of all keen and experienced off-piste skiers – the North Face, Bridge Couloir or East Couloir. Your pulse will race as you trace a steep ski line between cliff bands in the breathtaking scenery of the Pazieltal, leading down to Zürs. Here, at the top of the Madloch chairlift and after a short hidden climb, you can be roped down into the steep Valhalla Couloir, accessing 1200m vertical of open slopes ending in the hamlet of Zug, close to Lech.

Interactive resort shortlist builder at www.wtss.co.uk

BEWARE OF DANGEROUSLY OVERCROWDED PISTES

We have been saying for years that some of St Anton's pistes are often dangerously overcrowded – especially (but not only) the Steissbachtal (aka Happy Valley) and the home run below it. Bravos going recklessly fast add to the danger. So acute is this problem that several reporters have preferred to catch a bus home from Rauz or St Christoph. Other alternatives are to ride the gondola down from Galzig or to use the quite testing ski route beneath it. Our picture shows just one of several runs that feed into the home piste.

The run to Rauz can get very busy too; indeed editor Watts once abandoned skiing for the day because this piste was so crowded with reckless skiers that he felt he needed to look over his shoulder before making each turn – wing mirrors would have been handy.

We get a continual flow of similar complaints from visitors: 'people, people and, er, people everywhere; the pistes are simply dangerous'; 'the number of high-speed skiers can frighten you'; 'very crowded at end of day with reckless skiers and lots of moguls'. We could go on ...

If this was North America, the mountain would have been planned with enough pistes to cope with the people the lifts can carry and there would be high-profile staff on duty to give reckless skiers a dressing down (or worse). Why not here?

A KÄRKKÄINEN

SCHOOLS

Arlberg
t 3411
St Anton
t 3563
Alpine Faszination
t 0676 630 2136

Classes
(Arlberg prices)
6 days (2hr am and 2hr pm) €235
Private lessons
€162 for 2hr; each additional person €20

GUIDES

Piste to Powder
t 0664 174 6282

CHILDCARE

Kindergartens (run by ski schools)
t 2526 / 3563
From age 30mnth; must be toilet trained

Ski schools
Both Austrian schools take children aged from 5 (6 days including lunch €319)

often lunch on the fringe of St Christoph at the atmospheric, buzzing Hospiz Alm (3625), famed for its slide down to the toilets as well as its satisfying table service food and amazing wine cellar. Service gets stretched at times and it can be expensive. Recent visitors approve too: 'the ribs are great to share', 'delicious Tiroler gröstl'.
Worth knowing about The Rodelalm on Gampen is not marked on the piste map, but is beside black run 25 on the way to Nasserein. It's a pleasant, woody place; lovely beamed interior. We had good traditional food here and a reader enjoyed 'terrific roasted chicken'. On Galzig, the Ulmer Hütte, near the top of the Arlenmähder chair, has 'good service and food'. Just above the village, the après-ski bars (Mooserwirt, Griabli, Heustadl and Krazy Kanguruh) serve typical Austrian food and burgers. On Rendl, the self-service Rendl restaurant is revamped and spacious. We've had good food there in the past. Or head down the valley run to the small, rustic Bifang-Alm for regional specialities and excellent service.

SCHOOLS AND GUIDES ★★★☆☆
Mixed reports
The St Anton and the Arlberg schools are under the same ownership but operate separately. Reports on both schools complain of 'groups that were too large and the ability of pupils far too wide'. But past reporters have

Wow! What's new in Austria?
See p177.

been satisfied with beginner classes and off-piste guided groups with the Arlberg school.
Piste to Powder is a specialist off-piste outfit run by British guide Graham Austick. Past comments include: 'one of the best days ever on a mountain', 'a great operation', 'absolutely corking day with a great guide', 'exactly the right balance of instruction and guiding'. If you have particular ambitions, make sure your group is all of the required standard, though. We've had mixed reports of beginners to off-piste: some have been known to give up halfway through the day; others have had the 'best day ever'.

FOR FAMILIES ★★★★☆
Nasserein 'ideal'
The youth centre attached to the Arlberg school is excellent, and the special slopes both for toddlers (at the bottom) and bigger children (at Gampen) are well done. Children's instruction is reportedly very good ('Kids had a great week in the Arlberg school,' says a 2010 reporter). At Nasserein there is a moving carpet on the baby slope. There's also a good children's area by the Gampen fast quad. Nasserein makes a good base. Family chalet specialists Esprit Ski have their own facilities here.

STAYING THERE

There's a wide range of places to stay, from quality hotels to cheap and cheerful pensions and apartments, and a good choice of chalets.

Chalets This is by a wide margin Austria's catered chalet capital. Ski Total now leads the pack, with a dozen places ranging from six beds to the cool 32-bed Inge. Skiworld has 10 places, with 10 to 40 beds. Crystal has half a dozen properties. Inghams has several. Family specialist Esprit has two big chalets in Nasserein, one (new this year) right next to the gondola. Scott Dunn has some smooth places up on the western fringes. Flexiski has the absolutely central Amalien Haus.

Hotels There are dozens of 4- and 3-star places. For 2011/12, if all goes to plan, there will be two cool new places – the Mooser at the Mooserwirt and Anthony's in a prime spot in the centre.

*****Raffl's St Antoner Hof (2910) The one 5-star. Position less than ideal. Pool, sauna, steam.

****Bergschlössl (2220) Charming 10-room B&B right by lifts. 'Beautifully furnished, excellent value.'

****Best Western Alte Post (2553) Atmospheric central place with lively après-ski bar.

****Galzig (42770) Cool modern 'skihotel' by the lifts, tipped by a regular visitor.

****Montjola (2302) In Oberdorf. 'Good sized room, excellent food, shuttle bus,' says a 2011 reporter.

****Pepis Skihotel (283060) Stylish, modern B&B right by the Rendl lift; 'friendly and helpful staff, huge rooms with fab steam-shower rooms'.

****Post (2213) Century-old place bang in the centre, with 'beautiful spa and pool area'. 'Pick of the bunch,' says another reporter.

****Schwarzer Adler (22440) Centuries-old inn on main street. Varying bedrooms. 'Lovely' pool.

***Parseierblick (3374) In Nasserein. 'Loved it; next to lift; apartment fantastic for a family.'

***Nassereinerhof (3366) Close to the Nasserein gondola; sauna, steam room. 'Very pleasant, with good food.'

**Steffeler (2872) B&B in excellent central spot. Simple but welcoming; good breakfasts. Ideal.

Apartments There are plenty available, but few package deals. Past tips

GETTING THERE

Air Innsbruck 95km/ 60 miles (1hr15); Zürich 210km/ 130 miles (2hr45); Friedrichshafen 135km/85 miles (1hr45); Munich 210km/130 miles (3hr)

Rail Mainline station in resort

ACTIVITIES

Indoor Swimming pool (also hotel pools open to the public, with sauna and massage), fitness centre, tennis, squash, bowling, climbing wall, museum, library

Outdoor Cleared walking paths, natural ice rink (skating, curling), sleigh rides, snowshoeing, tobogganing, paragliding

include the Bachmann apartments in Nasserein and Haus Rali at the western end of St Anton.

EATING OUT ★★★★☆
Some excellent spots

There's a lot of half board lodging in St Anton, so the restaurant scene is not huge. Our standard port of call for a drink or two and a relaxed meal is the cool Hazienda – a basement place in the main street, with a wide-ranging menu (steaks, seafood, pasta); you can eat at the bar. For more of a blowout, it's up the hill to the village museum's restaurant – excellent, sophisticated food served in elegant panelled rooms. Ben.venuto out at the leisure centre is a cool place that gets rather overlooked. A 2011 reporter had 'excellent but expensive' traditional food and wine in the Train (hotel Manfred). Other favourites: Underground on the Piste ('great food, especially steaks'), Fuhrmannstube (traditional food) and Pomodoro for pizzas (due to reopen opposite its original site in 2011/12). In Nasserein, the Tenne was a hit with a 2010 visitor who went 'three out of six nights – good honest Austrian food, lovingly prepared'.

APRES-SKI ★★★★★
Throbbing till late

St Anton's bars rock from mid-afternoon until the early hours. A keen reporter notes that there is a lot of 'really fun live music' around.

Après-ski starts in a collection of bars on the slopes above the village. The Krazy Kanguruh is probably the most famous, but the Mooserwirt is the favourite with many reporters – 'brilliant atmosphere', 'pure fun'. It fills up as soon as the lunch trade finishes – reputedly dispensing more beer than any other bar in Austria. Griabli, opposite, is quieter, and the terrace

gives you a good view of the goings-on at the Mooserwirt; we enjoyed a live band there. The Heustadl has grown and is more cosmopolitan but still the place for 'great German cover bands'. The Sennhütte also has 'a fantastic atmosphere'. All this is followed by a slide down the piste in the dark.

The bars in town are in full swing by 4pm, too. Most are lively, with loud music; sophisticates looking for a quieter time are less well provided for. But Jacksy's, tucked away in a side street, is good for a quiet drink. And we like the Bodega tapas bar for pre-dinner drinks and, er, tapas; good atmosphere. Base Camp is a lot of fun, 'attracts a mixed crowd and ski instructors'. Underground on the Piste is 'the best party in St Anton'. Later on, the Piccadilly and Bar Cuba are popular clubs. Other tips: Scotty's (in Mark Warner's chalet hotel Rosanna), Kandahar ('sports TV and live bands') and, in Nasserein, the Fang House.

OFF THE SLOPES ★★☆☆☆
Some entertainment

We and reporters love the excellent Arlberg-well.com, a leisure centre with great indoor and outdoor pools – including one with jets that propel you around at lightning speed – plus three types of sauna and a huge steam room. A separate sports centre has indoor climbing and outdoor ice climbing walls. The village is lively during the day, but has few diverting shops. Getting to the other Arlberg resorts by bus is easy, as is visiting Innsbruck by train. Some of the better mountain huts are accessible by lift or bus. There are good walking trails to Pettneu and Verwall; it's worth considering Lech for 'more interesting walks'. The ski museum is open from 3pm to 10pm and is 'well worth the four euros entry'.

Phone numbers
From elsewhere in
Austria add the prefix
05446 (St Anton and
St Christoph), 05582
(Stuben); from abroad
use the prefix +43
and omit the initial '0'

TOURIST OFFICES

St Anton
www.
stantonamarlberg.com
St Christoph
www.tiscover.com/
st.christoph
Stuben
www.stuben.com

LINKED RESORT – 1800m
ST CHRISTOPH

St Christoph is a small collection of smart hotels, restaurants and bars just down from the summit of the Arlberg pass. There are decent beginner slopes served by draglifts and a fast quad chairlift to the heart of St Anton's slopes at Galzig, but the blue back down is not an easy run to progress to. St Christoph is quiet at night. You can't miss the huge 5-star Arlberg-Hospiz (2611). A more affordable but still excellent place is the 4-star Maiensee (21610), right on the slopes by the chair up to Galzig, with health and spa facilities and treatments. Inghams now has its flagship 135-bed chalet-hotel here – ski-in/ski-out, with good-sized pool.

LINKED RESORT – 1405m
STUBEN

Stuben is linked by lifts and pistes over the Arlberg pass to St Anton. It's a tiny, unspoiled village, with an old church, a few unobtrusive hotels, two or three bars and a few little shops. Heavy snowfalls add to the charm.

The Albona area makes a welcome change from the busy slopes of St Anton, with some lovely scenic runs. The shady slow chair from the village can be a cold ride, but blankets are available. The reward is north-facing slopes that hold powder well and some wonderful, deserted off-piste descents, including beautiful long runs down to Langen and to St Anton.

The Albonagratstube at the very top is a simple hut serving simple food. Lower down, the Albona self-service place gets packed, even on a quiet day. Reporters recommend heading back to the village for lunch at Willi's (pizza, ribs) or Berhaus Stuben ('excellent hearty Austrian food').

Stuben has sunny nursery slopes separate from the main slopes, but lack of easy runs to progress to makes it unsuitable for beginners. We've had good reports of the school: 'Hard to fault, really good teacher,' said one whose three children took classes.

Evenings are quiet, but several places have a pleasant atmosphere. The charming old Post (761) and Albona (712) are very comfortable. The Hubertushof (7710) is 'welcoming, efficient; excellent food and facilities'.

Interactive resort shortlist builder at **www.wtss.co.uk**

Stubai valley

Austria's biggest glacier area, they say, and certainly one of the best; down the valley, a string of appealing village bases

TOP 10 RATINGS

Extent	★★★
Fast lifts	★★★
Queues	★★★
Snow	★★★★★
Expert	★★★
Intermediate	★★★
Beginner	★★
Charm	★★★★
Convenience	★★
Scenery	★★★★

RPI	100
lift pass	£220
ski hire	£120
lessons	£100
food & drink	£120
total	**£560**

KEY FACTS

Resort	935-1000m
	3,070-3,280ft
Slopes	935-3210m
	3,070-10,530ft
Lifts	45
Pistes	147km
	91 miles
Blue	40%
Red	31%
Black	29%
Snowmaking	87%

200

+ High, snow-sure glacier slopes plus lower bad-weather options

+ Quiet, pretty Tirolean villages

− A lot of shuttling up and down the valley to and from the glacier

− Few challenging pistes

The Stubaier Gletscher ranks alongside Hintertux as one of the most extensive and rewarding glacier ski areas in the Alps. For the glacier, the obvious base is Neustift – the nearest major village, 20km away. But another 5km down-valley, Fulpmes is at the base of the Stubaital's best low-altitude area, Schlick 2000.

The 30km-long Stubai valley lies a short drive south of Innsbruck (there's also a tram as far as Fulpmes). The glacier is of course at the head of the valley. There are countless hamlets dotted along the valley; there is simple accommodation to be had in places like Falbeson (10km from the glacier) or Krössbach (15km). But three bigger villages – Neustift, Fulpmes and Mieders – have wooded ski areas, covered along with the glacier and linking buses by the Stubai lift pass. These resorts, described over the page, amount to a sizeable area of mostly intermediate terrain. All the villages have impressive toboggan runs – the valley has 11 in total.

The Stubaier Gletscher offers an extensive area of runs between 3200m and 2300m. Two gondolas go up from the huge car park at Mutterberg to a mid station at Fernau, and then to the two mid-mountain stations of Eisgrat and Gamsgarten. A third gondola from

Eisgrat goes to the top of the slopes, and there are three six-packs on other slopes supplemented by the numerous drags you expect on a glacier area.

The slopes are broken up by rocky peaks giving more sense of variety than is normal on a glacier. There are lots of fabulous long blue and red cruising runs. The two short black pistes are very much at the easy end of the spectrum. But for more challenges there are numerous ski routes (not explained, but presumably unpatrolled) in several areas. Much the toughest is the 4km Fernau-Mauer at the eastern extremity of the area – after the gentlest and widest of starts this drops steeply towards the Fernau mid station. There is also a lovely 10km ski route (Wilde Grub'n) from Gamsgarten to the valley – start with a cruise from the top of the glacier for a total of 1450m vertical. And there's proper off-piste to be explored. There are good beginner slopes at Eisgrat and Gamsgarten, where there is also a major children's learning area with associated childcare facilities.

The area is popular with snowboarders. There are lots of natural hits and kickers across the mountain, and the big terrain park has all the usual features.

Queues are not a serious problem. The gondola and Eisjoch six-pack can get busy at weekends.

Gamsgarten has a huge self-service restaurant, and excellent food in the table service part Zur Goldenen Gams. Eisgrat has a cool new building including a serious table-service section, Schaufelspitz. At Jochdohle, Austria's highest restaurant (3150m) gives stunning views. The Dresdner Hütte is a proper climbing refuge.

Après-ski starts up the mountain in the lively Gamsgarten bar and Ice Cube bar at Fernau.

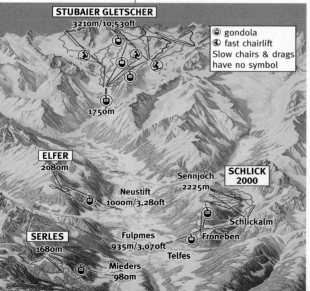

STUBAIER GLETSCHER
3210m/10,530ft

⚫ gondola
⚫ fast chairlift
Slow chairs & drags have no symbol

1750m

ELFER
2080m

Sennjoch
2225m

SCHLICK 2000

Neustift
1000m/3,280ft

Schlickalm

SERLES
1680m

Fulpmes
935m/3,070ft

Froneben

Telfes

Mieders
980m

stubai.at

moves YOU.

AUSTRIA'S LARGEST GLACIER SKI AREA
with guaranteed natural snow
THE MOST SNOW-SURE REGION
OF THE ALPS
from October - June
FAMILY AND CHILD FRIENDLY
Children under 10 travel free on all Stubai
mountain lifts (when accompanied by a
paying adult), excellent child care facilities
4 SKI AREAS
Stubai Glacier, Schlick 2000 Ski Centre,
Elfer and Serles runs
TYROL'S LARGEST TOBOGGANING ARENA
with 4 floodlit runs
SNOWPARKS
ONLY 20 MINUTES FROM INNSBRUCK

STUBAI PACKAGE
7 nights incl. breakfast
6 day Stubai Super Skipass
FROM EUR 439,00

Stubai valley

201

Interactive resort shortlist builder at **www.wtss.co.uk**

STUBAI TIROL TOURIST BOARD

Dorf 3 | 6167 Neustift im Stubaital | Austria
Tel. +43 (0)50 1881 0 | Fax +43 (0)50 1881 199
info@stubai.at | **www.stubai.at**

Tirol

↑ The restaurant at Gamsgarten is gigantic; the kids' area is pretty big, too; and yes, there is ice-climbing

NEWS

2010/11: At the glacier, the Eisgrat restaurant complex was rebuilt, including a smooth table-service section.

And there's a new family boardercross.

At Schlick 2000, the Panorama table-service restaurant opened downstairs at Kreuzjoch.

UK PACKAGES

Neustift Crystal, Crystal Finest, Interactive Resorts, Zenith
Fulpmes Crystal, Snowscape

Phone numbers
From elsewhere in Austria add the prefix 05226; from abroad use the prefix +43 5226

TOURIST OFFICE

www.stubai.at

NEUSTIFT
1000m

The major village closest to the glacier, 20km away. It's an attractive, traditional Tirolean village, with limited local slopes at Elfer.

The slopes at Elfer consist of a narrow chain of runs and lifts from Elferhütte at 2080m down to the village. The pistes are all red, and there's not much to entice experts, but it is a quiet place for intermediates to practise. This area is north-east-facing; there is a sunny nursery slope at village level, on the other side. There are some 27km of cross-country trails.

There is a big 5-star Relais & Chateaux hotel, and lots of 4-stars and 3-stars spread around the area. In the outlying hamlet of Neder, the glacier lift company runs the family-oriented 4-star Happy Stubai (2611).

Nightlife is focused on the Dorf and Bierfassl bars and the Nachtkastl and Rumpl discos. Most restaurants are hotel-based. Neustift has quite a lot to offer off the slopes: a leisure centre with two pools, saunas and bowling.

FULPMES
935m

Fulpmes (with its satellite village of Telfes) sits at the foot of Schlick 2000, the most extensive of the lower ski areas. It is an attractive, sizeable working village not dominated by skiing (there is a downside: the shops close early). The glacier is 25km away.
Uphill from the village a two-stage gondola takes you to Kreuzjoch

(2135m), opening up excellent views across the Stubaital and across the Schlick slopes to the dramatic Kalkkogel range. Most of the skiing is below the top gondola station – essentially a single open slope centred on a quad chair rising 580m, with draglifts serving the outermost runs. It is north-facing, so keeps snow well, and grooming is good. There are about five different pistes down, mostly of red difficulty with some easier blue options. There is also a ski-route – challenging at the best of times, very much so if snow is poor. And there is a fair amount of off-piste ('relatively safe', notes a regular).

Below the main slopes is a long easy run-out to the gondola mid-station at Froneben (1365m). This is the location of the nursery slopes, including Ronny's Kinderland, with moving carpets and fun features, and a couple of thumping après-ski bars. The blue run winding through woods to the village from here is good fun or tricky, depending on conditions and your competence. There is a terrain park. Queues are rare but the gondola gets busy at peak times.

There are some good huts, with table-service options at the top of the gondola and at Zirmachalm ('shared tables; great Gulaschsuppe'). You can be towed by snowcat to Galtalm, in woods below Kreuzjoch, for 'great food and views'.

There's a good choice of 3- and 4-star hotels, most with pools and spa facilities. The 4-star Stubaierhof (62266) is central. Café Dorfkrug has 'good quality food, friendly service and a great Austrian folk band'.

The nearest leisure centre is in Neustift, but Fulpmes has ice skating, snowshoeing and tobogganing.

MIEDERS
980m

Mieders is near the entrance to the Stubai valley, 15 minutes' drive from Innsbruck. It's an unspoiled village with its own tiny area of slopes.
The slopes of Serles are limited to four blues and two short reds. A gondola takes you to Kopponeck at 1680m, where a couple of T-bars serve the upper runs. There are a couple of mountain restaurants and 45km/ 28 miles of cross-country tracks above 1600m. The village has a small selection of hotels and guest houses.

Vorarlberg

Lech and Zürs are not the only resorts west of the Arlberg pass, above St Anton – the others include Europe's snowiest

Ski from St Anton to Stuben, and you cross over the Arlberg pass, moving from the Tirol to the province of Vorarlberg. Here, the melting snow drains into the Rhine, not the Inn and the Danube. It's a famously snowy area, catching the full force of storms sweeping in across the Bodensee. Fashionable and expensive Lech and Zürs are the resorts that are well known internationally, but there are small family resorts elsewhere that deserve attention.

Vorarlberg is small – the smallest 'land' in the Austrian federation (unless you count the city of Vienna). Its capital is Bregenz, down on the shores of the Bodensee.

Lech, Vorarlberg's best-known resort internationally, gets full coverage in its own chapter a few pages back, which also covers its linked close neighbour **Zürs**.

Those resorts aside, there are two main skiing regions, each of which is covered in its own chapter following this introductory one. Although very different in character, both areas have a handful of small resorts. Few UK tour operators go to these areas.

The **Montafon** valley, to the south-west of the Arlberg attracts a lot of visitors from Germany. They go particularly to the biggest ski area, shared by Gaschurn and St Gallenkirch, from where a new gondola will also access the Hochjoch area above Schruns for 2011/12. Golm above Vandans is less well known, and Gargellen is a bit of a backwater. At the top of the valley is famously good ski touring terrain.

Bregenzerwald, to the north-west of the Arlberg, is a delightfully unspoiled area, very proud of its cheeses – and it's here that two small resorts, Damüls and Warth, vie for the title of snowiest resort in the Alps. Warth is linked to Schröcken and, a couple of seasons ago, Damüls was linked to Mellau. The briefly named village of Au and next-door Schoppernau share the third-biggest ski area, Diedamskopf.

Then there are three other areas with some skiing to offer.

The **Alpenregion Bludenz**, west of the Arlberg, embraces Sonnenkopf above Klösterle – on the Arlberg lift pass, and therefore a popular outing from the Arlberg resorts – and the Brandnertal area shared between Brand (1035m) and Bürserberg (890m). This offers 55km of pistes with a top height of 2000m served by 14 lifts. Most of the skiing is easy, with open slopes above Brand and more woodland runs above Bürserberg. But all three runs to valley level are reds.

In the north-east corner of the province is a real curiosity. **Kleinwalsertal** is cut off from the rest of Austria, at the head of a German valley. It is close to one of the main German resorts, Oberstdorf, and is described briefly in the introduction to our section on Germany.

Finally, the **Bodensee-Vorarlberg** area in the north-west corner of Vorarlberg has some small areas. The largest, Laterns, has six lifts and 27km of runs, and a top height of 1780m.

GERMANY

FRIEDRICHSHAFEN

BREGENZ · Riefensberg
Alberschwende
Hittisau
Schwarzenberg · Egg · Oberstdorf
Andelsbuch
Bezau
Kleinwalsertal

Mellau · Au · Schoppernau
Laterns · Damüls · Bregenzerwald
Bodensee-Vorarlberg · Schröcken · Warth
FELDKIRCH · Lech
Bürserberg · BLUDENZ · Klösterle · Zürs · St Anton
Brand · Arlberg tunnel
Tschagguns · Schruns
Montafon
St Gallenkirch
Gaschurn
Gargellen · Galtür

AUSTRIA

SWITZERLAND

Klosters

5 miles
10km

Vorarlberg – Montafon

Extensive slopes in several areas covered by a single lift pass – and attractive places to stay, well off the beaten package path

RPI	90
lift pass	£180
ski hire	£85
lessons	£120
food & drink	£120
total	**£505**

NEWS

2011/12: A new gondola is planned from St Gallenkirch to the Hochjoch ski area, making it easy to get between the Hochjoch and Nova ski areas. At the top of this gondola, another new gondola is planned to take you to the high point of the ski area (replacing an old double chair). New slopes and hiking routes are due.

2010/11: At Gargellen, a six-pack with covers (Kristallbahn) was installed at the top of the gondola. A new beginner draglift also opened.

MONTAFON TOURISMUS

The Montafon valley has four ski areas covered by one lift pass ↓

The 40km-long Montafon valley contains no fewer than 11 resorts and four main lift systems. Packages from the UK are rare, but they exist – and for the independent traveller the valley is well worth a look, especially the biggest area (linking Gaschurn and St Gallenkirch) and high, tiny, isolated Gargellen.

The Montafon runs south-east from the medieval city of Bludenz – parallel with the nearby Swiss border. The shared valley lift pass covers the 'very reliable' post bus service and the Bludenz-Schruns trains, as well as all the lifts. So a car is not essential; but it helps. Parking is mostly free.

There are four separate ski areas in the valley. A fifth, the tiny Grabs area above Tschagguns, has closed.

Two areas – known jointly as Silvretta Montafon – are now under joint ownership and should be linked by the start of the 2011/12 season. The biggest of these (and the biggest area in the Montafon) is **Nova**, reached from either Gaschurn, towards the head of the valley, or St Gallenkirch. At St Gallenkirch, a new gondola to **Hochjoch** on the opposite side of the valley (and until now accessed only from Schruns, nearer the entrance to the valley) is planned for 2011/12.

Slightly nearer still to the valley entrance is Vandans, where a gondola goes up into the **Golm** area. Up a side valley near St Gallenkirch is tiny **Gargellen**, close to the Swiss border.

The valley road goes on from Gaschurn up to Partenen, where you can take a cable car up to Trominier, and then a minibus (covered by the

area pass) on up to Bielerhöhe and the Silvrettasee dam, at the foot of glaciers and Piz Buin (of sunscreen fame) – the highest peak in the Vorarlberg. Bielerhöhe is a great launch pad for ski tours, and there are high, snow-sure cross-country trails totalling 22km on and around the lake. And you can try the Silvetta Ski Safari to Galtür, near Ischgl, with the return to Bielerhöhe by snowcat – then a long descent back to Partenen; it cost 14.50 euros last season (more if you go with a ski school).

There are over 100km of cross-country trails along the main valley and in side valleys.

The top heights hereabouts are no match for the nearby Arlberg resorts; but there is plenty of skiing above the mid-mountain lift stations at around 1500m, and most of the slopes are not excessively sunny, so snow reliability (aided by snowmaking on quite a big scale) is reasonable. Grooming is 'excellent'. Practically all of the slopes are above the trees, so exposed in bad weather. Nearly all the pistes are accurately classified blue or red, but there is plentiful off-piste (and quite a few 'ski routes') to amuse experts. Reporters comment on crowd-free, varied slopes and generally efficient lift system.

There are separate piste maps for different areas (Golm and Gargellen each have their own, Nova and Hochjoch share one). And there are eight ski schools and seven ski kindergartens (which take kids from age two) in the valley.

Tobogganing is popular, with several runs – the 5.5km floodlit run on Nova being the most impressive.

For those with a car, there is accommodation in various smaller villages in addition to those dealt with below. Reporters suggest the Zum Guten Tropfen (8322) and Partenerhof (8319) in Partenen, and the Adler (67118) in St Anton im Montafon.

MONTAFON

Real mountains.
Real experiences.

Our visitors still care about perfect slopes. Not perfect hairstyles.

MOUNTAIN EXPERIENCES 2011/2012

Fancy a skiing holiday where sport and recreation are still paramount in a breathtaking natural setting? Discover a complete range of mountain experiences in the Montafon, one of the largest skiing areas in Vorarlberg.

Book a skiing holiday in the Montafon region. Now with attractive packages such as: **"Enjoy 7 days for the price of 5"** or **"The family-friendly Montafon"** (with free skiing and accommodation for children). For further details of our mountain experiences and packages please call +43 (0)5556 722530 or visit our site at www.montafon.at/en

The Montafon – a true region of sport in Vorarlberg:
www.vorarlberg.travel/en

HOCHJOCHTOTALE
The longest downhill run in Vorarlberg with an altitude difference of 1,700 m (5,800 feet!)

DIABOLO
The extremely steep slope with gradients of up to 70%

THE NIDLA OFF-PISTE SLOPE
The legendary deep-snow slope in Gargellen

KEY FACTS

Resorts	655-1425m
	2,150-4,680ft
Slopes	655-2395m
	2,150-7,860ft
Lifts	61
Pistes	219km
	136 miles
Blue	50%
Red	36%
Black	14%
Snowmaking	47%

UK PACKAGES

Crystal

VALLEY VILLAGE – 1000m

GASCHURN

A pleasant village, bypassed by the valley traffic, with a six-seat gondola to the Nova area of slopes – the valley's largest, with 114km of pistes. The lift network covers two parallel ridges running north-south, with most of the runs on their east- and west-facing flanks. The slopes are accessed from three points along the valley. A gondola from Gaschurn (prone to peak-season queues) takes you up to the east ridge. For some reason, the run back to Gaschurn is a ski route, not a piste. Another gondola from St Gallenkirch goes up to Valisera on the west ridge. Between the two villages, a double chairlift from a roadside station offers a third way up (and the floodlit toboggan run starts from the top of it). Snowmaking covers almost half the area, including runs down to two valley stations.

This is generally the most challenging area in the valley, with many red runs, and blues that are not entirely easy. Most of the slopes are above the treeline, typically offering a very modest 300m vertical. There is lots of off-piste potential, including steep (and quite dangerous) slopes down into the central valley. The map shows nine ski routes – completely unexplained, of course.

The NovaPark terrain park features a half-pipe and boardercross course.

We have a good report of the Gaschurn ski school: 'Excellent lessons, good English, small classes.'

There are lots of mountain restaurants, many impressive in different ways. At the top of the east ridge, the state-of-the-art Nova Stoba can seat over 1,500 people in various spaces, including splendid panelled rooms with table service. The big terrace bar gets seriously boisterous in the afternoons. At the top of the other ridge is the splendidly woody Valisera Hüsli ('great food'). The Brunellawirt does 'really good' chilli and goulash (and has live music at weekends). Zur Brez'n and Lammhütta on the ski route to Gaschurn are also worth trying.

The 4-star Posthotel Rössle (8333) is central, 190 years old and has a big pool and wellness centre. The Daneu (8338) has been recommended and is on the slopes 100m from the gondola. In the evenings, the Ausrutscher and Heuboda disco-bars are 'lively, with dancing and loud music'.

VALLEY VILLAGE– 900m

ST GALLENKIRCH

St Gallenkirch is strung along the main road and spoiled by traffic but will have the advantage of being at the centre of things when the new gondola to Hochjoch and its 44km of pistes open.
A gondola from St Gallenkirch goes up to Valisera on the west ridge of the

○ gondola
○ cable car
○ fast chairlift
Slow chairs & drags
have no symbol

Nova ski area (for a description of this, see Gaschurn opposite) and a blue run comes back down to the gondola base. It is planned that from the 2011/12 season a new gondola from the same area as the existing one will go up the opposite side of the valley to Grasjoch on the Hochjoch ski area (there will be no piste back). At Grasjoch another new gondola for 2011/12 is due to replace an old double chairlift and take you to the area's high point.

Hochjoch is a fair-sized area of easy blue runs, with occasional red alternatives. Apart from the new gondola and the fast Seebliga eight-pack, the rest of the lifts are slow chairs and drags. A reporter enjoyed 'excellent' guided off-piste here. The blue/red run from Kreuzjoch down to Schruns is a notable 12km long and 1700m vertical (and includes a section through the longest ski tunnel in the world – 473m). Snowmaking covers almost half the runs.

There are restaurants at strategic points. Wormser Hütte is a climbing refuge with 'stunning' views. Reporter tips are the 'cosy' Grasjoch Hütte, Schwartzkopfl for 'good goulash' and Kapell (self- and table-service). There is a children's play area called Hugo's Colourful Mountains at the top of the cable car from Schruns.

VALLEY VILLAGE – 700m
SCHRUNS

A working valley town, but quite a lively place, with access from points outside the town into both the Hochjoch and the Golm ski areas.
An old two-stage cable car and a gondola go up from separate bases outside town to the Hochjoch ski area (for a description of this see St Gallenkirch above).

Also accessible across the valley by a three-stage gondola from Vandans (or from a car park at the first mid-station) is the small Golm ski area (35km of pistes). This is 'good for morning sun' says a reporter and four chairs and a drag serve easy blue and red slopes above the trees. A six-pack goes to the top of the area, linked via a ski tunnel to slopes on the back of the hill, including the Diabolo black run (the steepest in the valley). Snowmaking covers many of the upper slopes and the run to the valley.

The town has a good range of

shops and restaurants, a car-free centre and a good bus service. As you are reminded frequently, Ernest Hemingway ensconced himself in Schruns in 1925/26, and his favourite drinking table in the hotel Taube (72384) can be admired. The Löwen (7141) and the Alpenhof Messmer (726640) are elegant, well-equipped 4-stars with big pools, the former a hub of the 'quite lively' après-ski scene. The 3-star Chesa Platina (72323) has been recommended ('old but spotless, welcoming, good value').

Après-ski is not the big deal it is in many Austrian resorts, but 'the bar terrace next to the gondola station gets quite lively, with loud music', and the Mo-Bar at the station and Einbahn Irish pub are popular, lively venues. Gasthaus zum Kreutz is 'by far the best for food', says a recent visitor. There's a big sports centre.

VALLEY VILLAGE – 1425m
GARGELLEN

A tiny, friendly village tucked up a side valley near the Swiss border, with a small (45km), varied and blissfully quiet piste network on Schafberg.
The modern eight-person gondola from the village seems rather out of place in this tiny collection of hotels and guest houses, huddled in a steep-sided, narrow valley. The runs it takes you to are gentle, with not much to choose between the blues and reds; but there is lots of off-piste terrain, plus ski routes. A special feature is the day tour around the Madrisa – a small-scale off-piste adventure taking you to Klosters in Switzerland. It involves a 300m climb, but is otherwise easy.

The high altitude of the village and north-east facing slopes make for reasonable snow reliability. And there is snowmaking on one of the several pistes to the valley, which include a couple of excellent, scenic away-from-the-lifts runs at the extremities of the area. With care you can ski to the door of some hotels, including the highly rated hotel Madrisa (6331) – 'superb staff, excellent facilities'. Behind the hotel is a rather steep nursery slope.

There are pleasant mountain huts: Schafberghüsli at the top of the gondola and two rustic huts at the treeline – the 'jolly' Obwaldhütte and the Kesslhütte. The Barga pizzeria at the foot of the Vergalden drag can also be reached by walkers.

Phone numbers
From elsewhere in Austria, add the prefix 05557 (Gargellen), 05556 (Schruns), 05558 (Gaschurn); from abroad, use the prefix +43 and omit the initial '0'

TOURIST OFFICES
Montafon
www.montafon.at
Gaschurn
www.gaschurn-partenen.com
St Gallenkirch
www.stgallenkirch.at
Schruns
www.schruns-tschagguns.at
Gargellen
www.gargellen.at

Interactive resort shortlist builder at **www.wtss.co.uk**

Vorarlberg – Bregenzerwald

An unspoiled region that is hardly heard of on the British market, with a lot of relatively small ski areas covered on one big pass

RPI	85
lift pass	£170
ski hire	£90
lessons	£110
food & drink	£115
total	**£485**

NEWS

2011/12: At Warth a new ski school building with play and climbing area for children (three to six years) is planned.

2010/11: At Damüls a new six-pack was installed, opening up another 4km or so of slopes. And snowmaking was increased around the link with Mellau. Tiny Bezau got a new cable car to replace its 50-year-old gondola, with a new 150-seat restaurant at the top station.

Bregenzerwald is tucked away between Germany and Switzerland at the western end of Austria, in Vorarlberg. Skirted by all the major road and rail links, it has remained remarkably unspoiled and is still primarily a farming community famous for its cheeses. But it is also the snowiest region in the Alps and has mountains rising up to over 2400m, with almost 260km of slopes served by almost 100 lifts above 22 villages. There is some seriously good skiing here, especially for intermediates, and the area is well worth considering for a quiet holiday exploring several different ski areas or for a family holiday. And prices are lower than in many better-known, more fashionable resorts.

Skiing began in Bregenzerwald in 1894 when the parish priest, Father Johann Müller, sent away to Norway for some newfangled 'Hickoryskis' and then careered down the slopes garbed in his flowing robes, amazing the local farmers. Until then, if you absolutely had to get around in winter, you wore a type of snowshoe. Father Johann established a trend that has transformed the region's economy.

This transformation has been greatly aided by abundant snowfall. One resort in the region (Warth) is supposed to have the best annual average snowfall in the Alps. Another (Damüls) is supposed to be the most snow-sure resort in the world. Eh? Let's just say the whole region gets huge amounts of snow. To put it in perspective: about four times as much

as Kitzbühel, three times as much as Chamonix and twice as much as St Anton and Val d'Isère.

There is a ski lift in almost every village. But few of the ski areas are large. They are all covered by the 3-Valley ski pass, which also covers two areas outside Bregenzerwald. The pass is valid in 31 ski areas and covers around 340km of slopes served by around 140 lifts. There are bus services between different resorts but having a car is useful (a 2011 reporter confirmed that getting around on buses is time consuming and some journeys involve changing buses). There are some excellent deals for families and nearly all the resorts offer activities other than skiing, with lots of cleared paths, tobogganing and cross-country skiing.

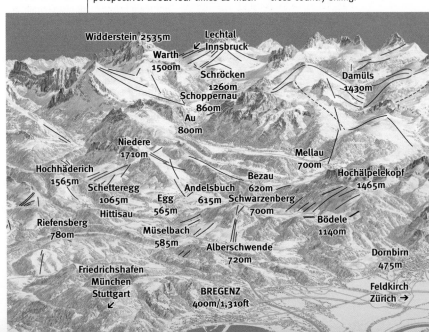

Widderstein 2535m
Lechtal
Innsbruck
Warth 1500m
Schröcken 1260m
Schoppernau 860m
Au 800m
Damüls 1430m
Niedere 1710m
Mellau 700m
Hochhäderich 1565m
Bezau 620m
Hochälpelekopf 1465m
Schetteregg 1065m
Andelsbuch 615m
Schwarzenberg 700m
Egg 565m
Hittisau
Bödele 1140m
Riefensberg 780m
Müselbach 585m
Alberschwende 720m
Dornbirn 475m
Friedrichshafen
München
Stuttgart
BREGENZ 400m/1,310ft
Feldkirch
Zürich →

↑ This is part of the Damüls ski area – now linked to Mellau to form the biggest ski area in the region with over 100km of pistes

SNOWPIX.COM / CHRIS GILL

THE BIGGEST SKI AREAS

Damüls and **Mellau** are now linked to form the biggest single ski area in Bregenzerwald, with 105km of runs between 700m and 2000m. Just under half of these are red runs, around a quarter are blue, and the rest are blacks and ski routes. And there's a good terrain park in Damüls. Altogether there are 31 lifts – these include two gondolas and 14 chairs (with six six-packs and a fast quad).

Damüls is quite high (the base area is at 1430m), and the sunny but snow-sure slopes go up to 2000m. Most runs are quite short, above the treeline and of genuine red steepness, and some of the blues are quite narrow; so it's best for adventurous rather than timid intermediates. On our 2009 visit, all of the ski routes we tried had been groomed and were of red run steepness – and some were busier than the pistes. Damüls also has 17km of sunny cross-country tracks and over 15km of winter walking trails.

Mellau's ski area is reached by an old gondola from the edge of the village and is on the more shady side of the mountain (most of the slopes are north-facing).

There's a steep black run that deserves its grading, as do the reds, and a ski route that is short but enjoyable (beware the drop on the right near the top, though). Most of the blues have fairly steep sections at the top – not good for timid intermediates. There's a long red through the trees right back to the village – enjoyable but narrow (it's a summer road for much of the way).

Damüls has no real village centre – it consists of a series of small collections of hotels (six 4-stars, nine 3-stars), inns and gasthofs, scattered along the edge of the slopes; most of the accommodation is ski-in/ski-out.

Mellau, on the other hand, is much lower but a proper little village, quiet and peaceful (it's bypassed by the valley road). There's little more to it than a few hotels – two 4-stars, three 3-stars – some gasthofs and a couple of bars. We enjoyed our 2009 stay at the 4-star Sonne Lifestyle (5518 2010) – modern, minimalist, wooden floors, spacious rooms, friendly staff, good food and spa facilities.

Warth and **Schröcken** are at opposite ends of their shared 66km of slopes, mainly between 1500m and 2000m and served by 15 lifts, including five fast chairs. Thanks to the exceptional snowfall record, the pistes are almost always in excellent condition (and the off-piste powder gets tracked out much less quickly than in the better-known resorts). The runs include several easy blacks and ski routes as well as reds and blues, and there's a terrain park. Most of the pistes are ideal for high-speed cruising and were very quiet on our January 2009 visit. Queues are rare.

Warth is only a few kilometres down the valley from the much better known Lech (see separate chapter). The road between the villages is closed in winter because of the danger of avalanches, but you can get good views of the Lech ski area from the top of the slopes, and you can ski there and back off-piste (the schools organise weekly excursions).

There are 21km of cross-country loops and 20km of walking trails.

The villages are small, pretty and unspoiled. There are six 4-star hotels, three 3-star hotels and one 2-star, plus inns and gasthofs. The 4-stars include the Walserberg (5583 3502) – with smart rooms and themed suites, saunas, steam room and fitness room – and the Sporthotel Steffisalp (5583 3699) with 'excellent' rooms in four

Phone numbers
From abroad use the
prefix +43 and omit
the initial '0'

different categories, a formal restaurant, après-ski hut and umbrella bar – and an 'impressive' spa area. Both of these are in Warth and right by the pistes and main lift (a fast quad, followed by a six-pack). Schröcken can be reached on skis only by a ski route, and there are no lifts there – you have to drive or catch a bus to the Hochtannberg pass, where a six-pack whisks you into the centre of the ski area.

Au and **Schoppernau** are neighbouring villages sharing the **Diedamskopf** ski area, which boasts Bregenzerwald's highest lift station at 2,060m and fabulous 360° views from the top. The sunny slopes (most are south or south-west facing) also have good views of the surrounding peaks and are popular with families. The eight lifts serve 44km of slopes, of which around 20% are red or black ski routes, 32% are blue pistes, 32% are red pistes and 16% are black pistes. The lifts include a two-stage gondola that takes you to the Panorama restaurant at the top.

The slopes suit good intermediates best; the blacks are quite serious, and some of the blues should be classified red, especially the blue from the top chair (which had moguls on it the afternoon we skied it). On the other hand, the reds in the Breitenalpe sector were easy and should really be classified blue. The runs are short, except for the 10km runs back to the valley station at 820m, which have a vertical of over 1200m. The lower section of this is served only by one red run and a ski route (the route was closed on our visit and the lowest section of the red run was stony; many people take the gondola down from mid-station). The rest of the pistes are above 1470m.

The resort claims that its Sajas terrain park – with varied features including rails, boxes and kickers – is the best in Bregenzerwald, and it attracts snowboarders and freestyle skiers from across Europe. There's night skiing twice a week.

At the top of the mountain, the Kids Adventure Land takes children aged three to eight years old.

Cross-country enthusiasts will find over 60km of trails. There are 40km of cleared walks and a natural ice rink.

The villages of Au and Schoppernau between them have 12 4-star and four 3-star hotels, plus gasthofs and plenty of dining options. Both are a ski-bus ride or drive from the ski area and are rather spread out. We preferred Schoppernau, which is off the main road, on the same side as the slopes, and has nice snowy lanes and snow-covered chalets.

SMALLER SKI AREAS

Andelsbuch and **Bezau** share the local **Niedere** ski area with eight lifts serving three short blue runs, a 7km-long red, a short black and several ski routes – 15km in total. It's a family ski area, and, given good snow, the ski routes offer more experienced skiers a challenge too. The top height is 1715m. The antiquated access gondola was pensioned off and replaced by a smart new cable car and top station restaurant for 2010/11. Andelsbuch has just one 3-star inn plus a few gasthofs, and Bezau has three 4-star hotels and one 3-star.

Alberschwende has 18km of runs, which are served by a chairlift and six T-bars, and it is popular with beginners. There are 16km of cross-country tracks and an ice rink. The village has a 4-star hotel and a 3-star, plus a few gasthofs.

Riefensberg has the tiny **Hochlitten** ski area, with just 5km of easy blue and red runs and four T-bars. It shares with neighbouring **Hittisau** the **Hochhäderich** ski area. This has 9km of runs (mainly blue and red but with a couple of blacks) served by four T-bars and a quad chair specially designed to be appropriate for children. It also has 16km of cross-country tracks at altitude and 12km of walking paths. Hittisau has two 4-star hotels and two 3-stars, while Riefensberg has two 2-star inns.

Egg is the biggest village in Bregenzerwald, with around 3,500 inhabitants and a small ski area at **Schetteregg**, which has six lifts serving 10km of easy blue and red runs between 1100m and 1400m. There are also 15km of cleared walks, one 3-star hotel, and six inns.

Schwarzenberg's local **Bödele** mountain has 24km of runs (mainly easy blues and reds) served by nine lifts (nearly all draglifts). There are also 16km of cross-country tracks and 30km of walking trails. Schwarzenberg has two 4-star and two 3-star hotels.

SKI Bregenzerwald

bregenzerwald

SKI Bregenzerwald Package:
4 nights' accommodation,
Sunday to Thursday or 3 nights'
accommodation, Thursday to
Sunday in the accommodation
category of your choice, plus
three-valley ski pass for three
days' varied skiing in all skiing
areas in the Bregenzerwald.

PRICE PER PERSON:
from € 284
in ****Hotels with half-board
from € 271
in ***Hotels with half-board

BOOKING:
8 January – 8 April 2012
(excl. 16 – 26 February)

INFORMATION AND BOOKING:
Bregenzerwald Tourismus
T +43(0)5512-2365
info@bregenzerwald.at
www.bregenzerwald.at/uk

Further info on Vorarlberg
www.vorarlberg.travel

VOR
ARL
BERG

Zugspitz Arena

Half a dozen family-friendly little resorts sharing a lift pass and (to a degree) proximity to the spectacular Zugspitze

RPI	85
lift pass	£190
ski hire	£105
lessons	£80
food & drink	£115
total	**£490**

KEY FACTS

Resorts	990-1340m
	3,250-4,400ft
Slopes	990-2960m
	3,250-9,710ft
Lifts	55
Pistes	148km
	92 miles
Blue	55%
Red	40%
Black	5%
Snowmaking	59%

UK PACKAGES

Berwang *First Choice*

SNOWPIX.COM / CHRIS GILL

Berwang is around 350m higher than other villages in the region – helping to give it a splendid winter-wonderland setting ↓

Zugspitz Arena is the name adopted by a group of small villages in the Tirol just to the west of Zugspitze, peak of the mighty Wetterstein massif which forms the border with Germany (Garmisch-Partenkirchen lies on the other side). They appeal particularly to families, who will be happy with limited and mainly gentle ski areas. There is the bonus of genuinely spectacular scenery.

Three of the Zugspitz Arena villages – Ehrwald, Lermoos and Biberwier – sit around the edge of a little plain, the Lermooser Moos, from which the Wetterstein massif rises dramatically 2000m to the peak of the Zugspitze. There is skiing on the Zugspitze itself (on glacier slopes on the German side of the border, but accessible via a spectacular cable car from the Austrian side), and each of the villages has its local slopes too. The other villages operating under the Zugspitz Arena banner – Berwang and Bichlbach – are a few miles to the west of the Moos.

The Top Snow Card covers all the 148km of slopes in the area plus Garmisch (on the German side of the Zugspitze). Garmisch has its own lifts up to the Zugspitze (including a cog railway), and challenging slopes lower down on the shady side of the Wetterstein massif. See our separate Garmisch chapter.

There are also over 110km of cross-country trails and 60km of cleared footpaths in the Zugspitz Arena area.

1000m

EHRWALD

Ehrwald is a pleasant village set right under the towering western wall of the Wetterstein massif, with easy access to three small ski areas.

There are two separate ski areas starting at valley level – Wetterstein and Ehrwalder Alm – and the Zugspitze glacier reached by cable car from a few km outside the village.

The mainly gentle **Wetterstein** slopes are accessed by a draglift from the village fringes, linking to the main Wetterstein triple chairlift, slightly further out. The runs total only 21km, with a top height of 1530m and longest run of under 500m vertical; and there's a half-pipe. Although it's a tiny area, there are two restaurants, with some après-ski animation.

The more rewarding **Ehrwalder Alm** slopes on the sunny side of the Wetterstein massif are accessed by an eight-seat gondola starting just outside the village. At the heart of the area is a broad, gentle nursery slope with several drags. From here a slow chair crosses a steep rocky mountainside to access good open red and blue slopes, one of which goes on into the woods to the Gaistal six-pack. The longer Ganghofer six-pack starts below the nursery slopes and serves two genuine red runs (one on the edge of the ski area beside scenic rocks) and a winding blue variant. There's a blue run back down the gondola. The lifts and runs are quite short – typically 300m to 400m vertical – but from the top there's a run of 7km (and over 800m vertical) to the base. The runs total 26km, mostly blue. The area has 80% snowmaking, including the valley run.

The terrain park in the centre of the slopes has easy, medium and pro lines of rails, boxes and kickers, and there's a half-pipe too.

A few km outside the village in the

opposite direction, a spectacular cable car climbs an impressive 1725m up to the peak of the **Zugspitze**, on the border with Germany. The Zugspitze is not remarkably high by Austrian standards, but it is the highest mountain in Germany and a major tourist attraction, with a museum at the peak as well as a restaurant. At the top, take an internal lift up, walk across into Germany, take another lift down and finally another cable car down to the glacial slopes of the Zugspitzplatt. This is a good area and covered in more detail in our Garmisch chapter.

There are two ski schools, Ehrwald Total and Intersport Tiroler.

The village spreads over a wide area but does have a pleasant central core around the church and a little open park nearby. Accommodation is dominated by 4-star hotels, but there are plenty of cheaper alternatives.

Twice a week the 3.6km home run from Ehrwalder Alm is floodlit for evening tobogganing, and the restaurants at the top and halfway down are kept open.

The Zugspitz Arena FamilienBad is a big, bright leisure centre with multiple pools, gym and massage. There's an ice rink and 15km of cross-country.

1005m

LERMOOS

Directly across the Moos from the Zugspitze, Lermoos and its slopes – arguably the best in the Zugspitz Arena area – offer great views of the dramatic Zugspitze.

Lermoos has lifts on the north-east-facing slopes of Grubigstein, a mainly wooded peak rising about 1000m above the village. The top height of 2060m, shady orientation and snowmaking on about two-thirds of the slopes means that (apart from the glacial Zugspitze) this is the most snow-sure of the local areas. The slopes total 33km.

A gondola from one end of the village and a six-pack from the other converge at mid-mountain. From here a fast quad leads to the main lift, a six-pack. This goes up over an extraordinary area of gigantic ready-made moguls – great fun for kids, given good snow – and serves a short but good red run and a winding blue as well as accessing further runs on a double chair and a long run back to the mid-station. This is an excellent descent, with the options of a decent black variant and a rather uninteresting ski route part-way down. The runs below mid-mountain are worthwhile, given good snow; you can descend the whole mountain, top to bottom, on red or blue runs. There are nursery slopes just above the village and at mid-mountain.

Lermoos is a slightly more compact, towny place than Ehrwald, more tightly focused on the main street running through it. This was an important thoroughfare until Fernpass traffic was banished to a tunnel in the 1980s, and is still far from traffic-free

There are several 3-star hotels, but notably three 'superior' 4-star hotels, which are quite different in style but equally impressive, and each a short walk from an access lift. The hotel Post (22810) is an ancient inn, greatly expanded over the years and entirely revamped in opulent fashion a few

years back. It offers 76 suites, and the facilities include a swanky 2,000m² spa, rated highly by our spa specialist. The terrace has the perfect view across the Moos to the Zugspitze. We found the food and service excellent. The Leading Family Hotel & Resort Alpenrose (2424) is an amazing place for families, but its facilities also include a cool, stylish wine bar, the Wine Lounge. The Mohre Life Resort (2362) is stylishly modern. Après-ski options include the Juxbar, Holzstadl and Lahme Ente.

A 3km toboggan run goes from Brettalm (1330m) to the valley. There's skating and curling on a natural open-air rink and 30km of hiking trails.

990m
BIBERWIER

The third of the villages around the Moos, Biberwier is set in the valley leading up to the Fernpass, with its own small area of slopes.
The mainly shady Marienberg slopes total 14km, more or less equally split into blue and red, with over a third covered by snowmaking. A six-pack serves a long blue slope at the bottom; a double chair up to 1675m serves a red run; above that two drags from the top height of 1790m serve blues, a red and two ski routes. Back at the base, the beginner lifts include an exceptionally long magic carpet. There's a boardercross course, half-pipe, snow tubing and snow biking. At altitude there are a couple of pleasant restaurants, and an umbrella bar next to the nursery slopes.

Like Lermoos, the village benefits from the tunnel keeping Fernpass traffic out of the centre. The best base is the solid old 3-star gasthof Goldenen-Löwen (2293).

Phone numbers
From elsewhere in Austria add the prefix 05673; from abroad use the prefix +43 5673

TOURIST OFFICES
Zugspitze
www.zugspitzarena.com
Ehrwald
www.ehrwald.com
Lermoos
www.lermoos.at
Biberwier
www.biberwier.at
Berwang
www.berwang.at
Bichlbach
www.bichlbach.at

1340m
BERWANG

Berwang is a quiet village tucked away in a slightly elevated valley, about 350m higher than the other villages in the region. The pistes total 36km, making it the most extensive network in the area, but most of the runs are short as well as easy.
The village enjoys a splendid winter-wonderland setting, with lifts rising on two sides, and slopes running down the very gentle valley. It looks an attractive place for a quiet family

holiday, although some of the accommodation is quite a walk from the lifts. On the sunny side, the Sonnalmbahn quad chair goes up to Hochalm where it meets the chondola up from Bichlbach; the shady runs to Bichlbach are about the best in the local area, giving over 500m vertical to the lift base station. All the runs from Hochalm have snowmaking. Across the village, drags go up the shady side. Runs down the valley dropping only about 50m in 1.5km bring you to further lifts, including the Rastkopf double chairlift to the area high-point at 1740m. From here there are blue and red runs. There are plenty of huts on the slopes.

The cross-country loops up here (totalling 25km) are separate from those down in the main valley, and look a bit more challenging.

There are three 4-star hotels, four 3-stars and lots of guest houses. The 4-star Kaiserhof (8285) is a giant family-oriented chalet-style place with pools and spa. There's a 1.5km toboggan run dropping 120m from Jägerhaus to Berwang, open most evenings; and skating and curling on a natural open-air rink. There are 25km of local footpaths.

1080m
BICHLBACH

Bichlbach is a quiet valley village with fast lift access to the slopes of higher Berwang (described above).
On the fringes of Bichlbach, the Tirol's first chondola lift goes up to Hochalm (1610m), for access to Berwang. You can ski to it from the top of the village nursery slope. There are three cross-country trails with one open for night skiing and a natural open-air ice rink.

995m
HEITERWANG

Another valley-level base for access to the Berwang slopes.
Heiterwang is a little way down the valley from Bichlbach, a short drive or bus ride from the chondola up to the Berwang slopes (it also has a short draglift and slope of its own). It's near a sizeable lake and is a major cross-country centre (it was the venue for the 2006 Austrian championships). There are about 40km of tracks between here and Bichlbach and night skiing is possible.

Zugspitz Arena
the perfect winter holiday destination.

Seven charming ski areas, car-free mobility, top-notch service and genuine Tyrolean hospitality.

Typical Zugspitz Arena: visitors to the area enjoy unique leisure opportunities with plenty of Tyrolean charm. **148 kilometres** of pistes and **55 mountain cableways** are spread over **seven diverse ski areas** - from glacier skiing on the Zugspitz plateau to the sun-kissed pistes of Biberwier, Berwang or Lermoos, there is something for absolutely everyone. From race carver to pleasure skier, from piste nipper to fledgling.

The ski area on the Zugspitze and 87 kilometres of covered pistes mean snow is guaranteed by the start of the winter season at the end of November.

Tirol
ZUGSPITZ ARENA

www.zugspitzarena.com

Interactive resort shortlist builder at **www.wtss.co.uk**

France

Last year around a third of British skiers and snowboarders chose France for their holidays – that's more than for any other country. It's not difficult to see what attracts us to France. The country has the biggest lift and piste networks in the world; for those who like to cover as many miles in a day as possible, these are unrivalled. Most of these big areas are also at high altitude, ensuring good snow for a long season. The best of them have state-of-the-art lift systems, too – but it's a myth that all French lift systems are wonderfully efficient. In quite a few big-name areas, draglifts and slow chairlifts still rule.

Another myth is that French resort villages are all soulless, purpose-built service stations, thrown up without concern for appearance during the boom of the 1960s and 1970s. We come back to this theme below. Many French resorts are now distinctly lively in the evening – a great change over the last 20 years. But there is little sign of French resorts developing the on-mountain afternoon party scene that is so common in Austria; Val d'Isère's Folie Douce has now been noisily replicated above Val Thorens and there's Rond Point at the top of Méribel, but no other examples spring to mind.

France may still lead the British market, but its share has dropped in the last couple of seasons. Although France is not expensive overall compared to its main Alpine rivals (as shown by our RPI figures), many French resorts are expensive for eating and drinking – especially major ones such as Val d'Isère, Courchevel and Méribel, where prices now far exceed their Austrian and Italian rivals. This leads to many complaints from reporters and is doubtless contributing to France's declining share of the British market. If it wasn't for the great job that UK tour operators do in keeping catered chalet holidays affordable, with lots of food and wine included in the price, the decline would be greater.

KEEPING COSTS DOWN

Chalet holidays are not the only way of economising, of course. Renting one of the new generation of genuinely comfortable and stylish apartments and catering for yourself is an attractive option – see our smart apartments chapter on page 40. Other ideas include staying in a relatively cheap valley town such as Bourg-St-Maurice or Brides-les-Bains and on-mountain picnic lunches, with which the Gill family experimented on their last stay in Courchevel.

ANY STYLE OF RESORT YOU LIKE

The main drawback to France, hinted at above, is the nature of some of the high-altitude purpose-built resorts. It's partly that the worst of them look hideous, but also that they were designed to cram in the maximum number of beds (and shops – we really hate the claustrophobic indoor malls) and that they are holiday camps rather than real communities. But even the worst places have learned from past mistakes, and newer developments are being built in a traditional chalet style. And the later generation of purpose-built resorts, such as La Rosière, La Tania and Arc 1950, are built in much more sympathetic style.

If you prefer, there are genuinely old mountain villages to stay in, linked directly to the big lift networks. These are not usually as

OT CHAMPAGNY-EN-VANOISE

← Extensive high-altitude, snow-sure slopes are what attract so many of us to French resorts – this is part of the La Plagne ski area

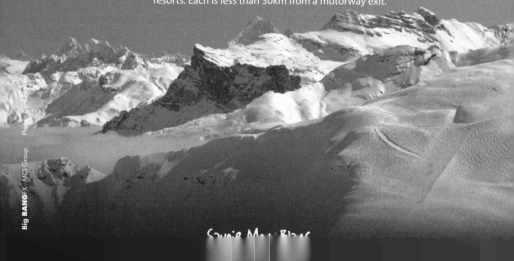

WITHOUT DOUBT, ONE OF THE WORLD'S BIGGEST SKI AREAS. BEYOND DOUBT, THE CLOSEST TO YOU.

EXCEPTIONAL SKIING

5 connected resorts, the Grand Massif, 4th biggest ski area in France, offers 265 km of pistes for all levels, from 720 to 2500 m in altitude, with panoramic views of the Mont Blanc range.

DIVERSE & COMPLEMENTARY

Its resorts are diverse and complementary! Morillon, Samoëns, Sixt and Les Carroz offer the authentically calm and convivial mood of traditional villages. Flaine, nestling at 1600m is a compact ski-in ski-out resort set in a rugged, snowy cirque. It shakes up this time-honoured image with its boldly modern architecture and works by leading contemporary artists.

RECORD SNOWFALLS... A WHITE PARADISE

The Grand Massif boasts one of the best snow records in the French Alps. The quality of snow is exceptional, thanks to the ideal orientation of the ski area. For those who love powder, Flaine is paradise on earth!

AN EASY-ACCESS SKI AREA

Fancy a week or just a weekend of winter sports? It couldn't be easier! The Grand Massif is just 55 minutes from Geneva airport and 2 hours from Lyon airport. Another key asset is its road network, which allows very easy access to all of the ski area's resorts. Each is less than 30km from a motorway exit.

Savoie Mont Blanc

Geneva

55 mn

FLAINE • MORILLON • SAMOËNS • SIXT • LES CARROZ

HAUTE-SAVOIE • **FRANCE**

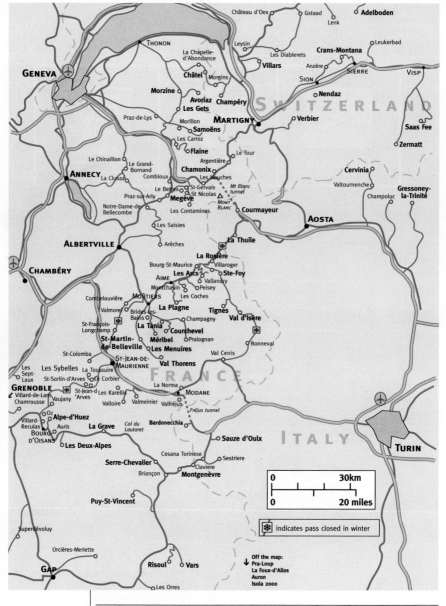

Getting around the French Alps

Pick the right gateway city as your initial Continental target – Geneva, Chambéry or Grenoble – and you can hardly go wrong. The only high pass you need worry about is on the approach to Serre-Chevalier and Montgenèvre – the 2060m Col du Lauteret; but even here the road is a major one, and kept clear of snow or reopened quickly after a fall (or you can fly to Turin and avoid that pass). Crossing the French-Swiss border between Chamonix and Verbier involves two closure-prone passes – the Montets and the Forclaz. When necessary, one-way traffic runs beside the tracks through the rail tunnel beneath the passes.

convenient for the slopes, but they give you a feel of being in France rather than in a winter-holiday factory. Examples include Montchavin or Champagny for La Plagne, Vaujany for Alpe-d'Huez, St-Martin-de-Belleville for the Trois Vallées, and Morillon or Samoëns for Flaine. There are also old villages with their own slopes that have developed as resorts while retaining at least some of their rustic ambience – such as Serre-Chevalier.

Two other resorts deserve a special mention. Megève is an exceptionally charming little town combining rustic style with sophistication. And then there is Chamonix, a big, bustling town sitting literally in the shadow of Mont Blanc, Europe's highest peak, and the centre of the most radical off-piste terrain in the Alps.

SKI SCHOOL COMPETITION
Gone are the days when the ESF was the only school in town. Most resorts now have lots of competing schools, which has lifted standards enormously. And many schools are now run and staffed by highly qualified British instructors – examples include New Generation and BASS, both of which have branches in several resorts and both of which reporters speak highly of.

PERFECT PISTES
France remains unusual among European countries in rating pistes on a four-point scale. The very easiest runs are classified green; except in Val d'Isère, they are reliably gentle. This is a genuinely helpful system, which ought to be used more widely. Some French resorts, sadly, make little use of it – notably Les Arcs and La Plagne.

PLAT DU JOUR
Despite the prices, France has advantages in the gastronomic stakes. Table service in mountain restaurants is common, and most places do food – often including a plat du jour – that is in a different league from what you'll find in Austria or North America. In the evening, most resorts have restaurants serving good traditional French food and regional specialities.

DRIVING AMBITION?
The French Alps are easy to get to by car. Starting on page 73 there is a chapter on driving to the French Alps. Driving is still popular, despite the growth of budget airlines; for self-caterers it has the advantage of being able to stock up in good-value valley supermarkets.

AVOID THE CROWDS
French school holidays mean crowded slopes, so they are worth avoiding. The country is divided into three zones, with fortnight holidays staggered between 11 February and 11 March 2012. Avoid 18 February to 4 March, in particular, when Paris is on holiday.

Introduction

Interactive resort shortlist builder at www.wtss.co.uk

Alpe-d'Huez

Impressive and sunny slopes above a hotchpotch of a purpose-built village, but with attractive alternative bases

RATINGS

The mountains

Extent	★★★★
Fast lifts	★★★
Queues	★★★★
Terrain p'ks	★★★
Snow	★★★★
Expert	★★★★
Intermediate	★★★★
Beginner	★★★★★
Boarder	★★★★
X-country	★★★
Restaurants	★★★★
Schools	★★★★
Families	★★★

The resort

Charm	★★
Convenience	★★★
Scenery	★★★★
Eating out	★★★★
Après-ski	★★★★
Off-slope	★★★★

RPI 100

lift pass	£200
ski hire	£130
lessons	£80
food & drink	£145
total	**£555**

KEY FACTS

Resort	1860m
	6,100ft
Slopes	1100-3330m
	3,610-10,920ft
Lifts	84
Pistes	250km
	155 miles
Green	31%
Blue	26%
Red	31%
Black	12%
Snowmaking	32%

222

- ➕ Extensive, high, sunny slopes, split interestingly into different sectors
- ➕ Vast, gentle, sunny nursery slopes
- ➕ Efficient access lifts from villages
- ➕ Some good mountain restaurants
- ➕ Livelier than many French resorts
- ➕ Pleasant alternative bases

- ➖ Some main intermediate runs get badly overcrowded in high season
- ➖ Many runs get too much sun
- ➖ Many of the tough runs are very high, and closed in bad weather
- ➖ Practically no woodland runs
- ➖ Sprawling, messy resort

There are few places to rival Alpe-d'Huez for extent and variety of terrain – in good wintery conditions it's one of our favourites. But as the season progresses the effects of the strong southern sun become more and more of a problem.

If you don't fancy staying in Alpe-d'Huez, think about the smaller bases described at the end of this chapter – especially Vaujany and Villard-Reculas.

THE RESORT

Alpe-d'Huez is a large, modern resort on a high, open, sunny plateau east of Grenoble. Although developed for skiing, it has grown in a seemingly unplanned, sprawling fashion.

The lift pass gives days in some other resorts. There are buses twice a week to Les Deux-Alpes, but the proper thing to do is go by helicopter – 'fantastic fun' (only 65 euros).

VILLAGE CHARM ★★
Bit of a hotchpotch

The nearest thing to a central focus is the main Avenue des Jeux in the middle, with an ice rink, indoor-outdoor swimming pool, shops, bars and restaurants. The buildings come in all shapes, sizes and designs but most new development is now in a pleasant chalet-style. Reporters have remarked on the warm welcome from the locals.

CONVENIENCE ★★★
Good in clusters

The resort spreads down a gentle slope in a triangular shape from the main lift station at the top corner. Very few lodgings are ski-in/ski-out. Access roads enter at the two lower corners.

Various 'quarters' have been identified – the main village is divided into three. Vieil Alpe includes the original chalet-style part, at the bottom of the slope; during the day there's a bucket-lift (with a piste beneath it) running through the resort from here to the main lifts. This seems handy, but it opens too late in the morning, builds queues at peak times and goes slowly; some people don't like jumping on and off, too. Then there are four satellite 'quarters'. These are a bit of a trek from the centre but have their own lifts, bars and restaurants. The one where you are most likely to be offered lodgings is Les Bergers, beyond the eastern entrance to the resort; a chalet suburb is expanding this quarter uphill – convenient for skiing but even more remote from the village centre. A reader points out that there are no proper footways from these quarters to the main resort centre.

The free ski-bus service around the resort is infrequent but reliable.

SCENERY ★★★★
Splendid panoramic views

The resort has a fabulous high setting on a sunny plateau. There are splendid views of the southern Alps.

miles	0.5	1.0	1.5	2.0

← Signal

Pic Blanc

Marmottes ↗

Les Bergers

L'Eclose

Signal de l'Homme ↗

km	1.0	2.0	3.0

NEWS

2011/12: A smart new hotel, the Alpenrose (yet to be given a star rating), is due to open in the quarter of Les Bergers, 250m from the lifts, and a CGH 4-star residence, Le Cristal de l'Alpe, is due to open in the centre of the village.

More free off-slope activities have been added to the Visalp lift pass, and the name has changed to Ski+. The Premium card is available as an extension, which includes equipment hire.

No wonder the day trip to Les Deux-Alpes by helicopter costs only 65 euro – look how close it is! ↓

THE MOUNTAINS

Practically all the slopes are above the treeline, and so there may be little to do when a storm socks in or the wind picks up. Piste classification is very unreliable and provokes regular complaints from readers. The main problem is that some of the blues are too tough, but in some areas it's the opposite – reds that might be blue.

EXTENT OF THE SLOPES ★★★★☆
Several well-linked areas
Alpe-d'Huez is a big-league resort, ranking alongside giants such as Val d'Isère or La Plagne for the extent and variety of its slopes. A notable feature is that it is possible to do many long runs with big verticals – the Sarenne run covered in our feature panel is an extreme example, but there are others.

The slopes divide into four sectors, with good connections between them. The biggest sector is directly above the village, on the slopes of **Pic Blanc**. The huge two-stage Grandes Rousses gondola, aka the DMC (a reference to its technology) and on the piste map marked as 'First Stage' and 'Second Stage', goes up from the top of the village. Above it, a cable car goes up to 3330m on Pic Blanc itself – the top of the small Sarenne glacier and start of the longest piste in the Alps (read our feature panel). The glacier is also reached via the Marmottes six-pack, then a two-stage gondola (the first stage of which also serves lower runs from Clocher de Macle).

The alternative from Pic Blanc is to take a 300m tunnel through the ridge to the front face, where a west-facing black mogul field awaits you.

Mega-resort skiing from a quiet base? Check out Vaujany p231.

The Sarenne gorge separates the main resort area from **Signal de l'Homme**. It is crossed by a down-and-up fast chairlift from the Bergers part of the village. From the top you can take excellent north-facing slopes towards the gorge, or head south to Auris or west to tiny Chatelard.

On the other side of town from Signal de l'Homme is the small **Signal** sector, reached by draglifts next to the main gondola or by a couple of chairs lower down. Runs go down the other side of the hill to the old village of Villard-Reculas. One blue run back to Alpe-d'Huez is floodlit twice a week.

The **Vaujany-Oz** sector consists largely of north-west-facing slopes, accessible from Alpe-d'Huez via red runs. At the heart of this sector is Alpette, the mid-station of the cable car from Vaujany. A disastrously sunny blue/red goes down from here to Oz, a much more reliable blue (which boarders will find a bit flat in places) goes north to the Vaujany home slopes around Montfrais, and a shady black plunges down to L'Enversin, just below Vaujany. Using different black, red and blue pistes and ending up at L'Enversin gives an on-piste descent of 2230m vertical from Pic Blanc – one of the biggest in the world. The links back to Alpe-d'Huez are by cable car from Alpette, or a gondola from Oz. You can also reach Oz from the top of the first stage of the DMC, followed by a long red run with a blue variant on the lower half. A gondola from Oz goes to Alpette.

FAST LIFTS ★★★☆☆
Efficient from the base
Gondolas and fast chairs are the main access lifts and serve most areas adequately, but there are lots of old chairs and draglifts scattered around.

QUEUES ★★★★☆
Generally few problems
Even in French holiday periods, there are few long hold-ups. Queues can build up for the lifts out of the village, but the DMC shifts its queue quickly and the bottom section can be avoided by taking alternative lifts. The Marmotte chairlift from the lower end of the village can cause bigger delays. The village bucket-lift is said to generate lengthy queues first thing.

Over much of the area a much greater problem than lift queues is that the main pistes can be unbearably crowded. We and many reporters rate the Chamois and Couloir runs from the top of the DMC among the most crowded we've seen, anywhere. Really, something needs to be done about these runs, which are just getting worse and worse. The reds to Vaujany and Oz can also be too busy for comfort – 'carnage all the way', said one reporter of the Oz run.

TERRAIN PARKS ★★★☆☆
A choice
There are two parks: one for novices near the bottom of the slopes, with various jumps and rollers ('excellent, the jumps were beautifully graded'); and a 1.5km advanced park near the Lac Blanc drag, with half-pipe, jumps, hips, rails, big air and a boardercross

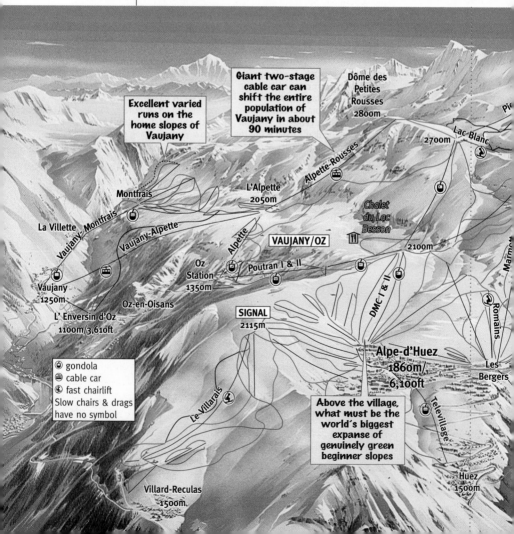

course ('good; fast and aggressive'). There's also a beginners' park above Vaujany. The ESF runs some freestyle courses for teenagers.

SNOW RELIABILITY ★★★★
Affected by the sun

Alpe-d'Huez is unique among major purpose-built resorts in the Alps in having mainly south- or south-west-facing slopes. The strong southern sun means that late-season conditions may alternate between slush and ice on most runs, with some lower runs closed altogether. There are shady slopes above Vaujany and at Signal de l'Homme. The glacier area is small.

In midwinter the runs are relatively snow-sure, thanks to extensive snowmaking on the main runs above Alpe-d'Huez, Vaujany and Oz. A reader

Mega-resort skiing from a quiet base? Check out Vaujany p231.

points out that the piste through the resort, down the bucket-lift, does not have snowmaking and often needs it.

Last season's difficult conditions resulted in an extreme range of conflicting views from readers on the resort's management of the pistes, particularly in January. We hesitate to draw conclusions, given the extraordinary circumstances, with rain falling in midwinter at one stage.

FOR EXPERTS ★★★★
Plenty of blacks and off-piste. There are long and challenging pistes as well as some serious off-piste routes (see feature box).

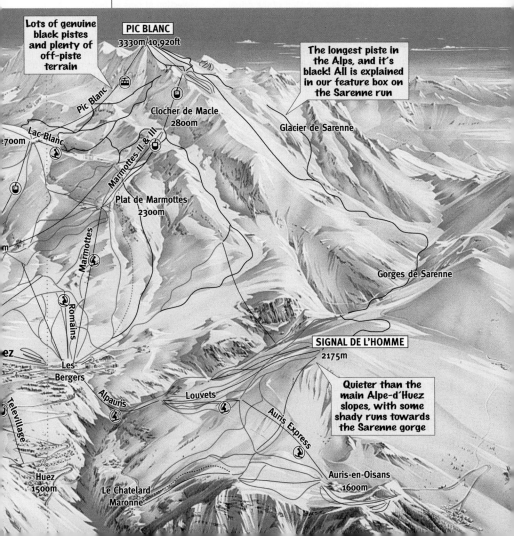

Lots of genuine black pistes and plenty of off-piste terrain

PIC BLANC
3330m/10,920ft

Pic Blanc

Clocher de Macle
2800m

The longest piste in the Alps, and it's black! All is explained in our feature box on the Sarenne run

Glacier de Sarenne

Lac-Blanc
700m

Marmottes II & III

Plat de Marmottes
2300m

Marmottes

Gorges de Sarenne

Romains

SIGNAL DE L'HOMME
2175m

Les Bergers

Alpauris   Louvets

Televillage

Auris Express

Quieter than the main Alpe-d'Huez slopes, with some shady runs towards the Sarenne gorge

Huez
1500m

Le Chatelard
Maronne

Auris-en-Oisans
1600m

It's no surprise that most ski runs that are seriously steep are also seriously short. The really long runs in the Alps tend to be classified blue, or red at the most. The Parsenn runs above Klosters, for example – typically 12km to 15km long – are manageable in your first week on skis.

So you could be forgiven for being sceptical about the 'black' Sarenne run from the Pic Blanc: even with an impressive vertical of 2000m, a run 16km in length means an average gradient of only 11% – typical of a blue run. But the Sarenne is a run of two halves. The bottom half is virtually flat (boarders beware), but the top half is a genuine black if you take the direct route – a demanding and highly satisfying run (with stunning views) that any keen, competent and fit skier will enjoy. The steep mogul field near the top can be avoided by taking an easier option (or by using the Marmottes III gondola); and the whole run can be tackled by an adventurous intermediate. It gets a lot of sun, so pick your time with care – there's nothing worse than a sunny run with no sun. Occasionally during the season you can ski the Sarenne by moonlight or wearing a head torch: take the last lift up, have a 'simple meal', then ski down with guides. The cost is 65 euros per person.

The black slope beneath the Pic Blanc cable car will be on your agenda. Despite improvements to the tunnel exit, the start of the actual slope is often awkward. The slope is of ordinary black steepness, but can be very hard in the mornings because it gets the afternoon sun. Get information on its condition. The long Sarenne run on the back of the Pic Blanc is described in the feature panel above.

Thanks to snowmaking, we've been able to ski the black Fare piste to L'Enversin on each of our last two visits – a highly enjoyable and varied long run, away from the lifts but not steep (really of red gradient with some blue sections, we thought). The Marmottes II gondola serves genuine black runs and a red from Clocher de Macle; Balcons is steep and quiet, often with good snow; Clocher de Macle is easier but busier; don't miss the beautiful, long, lonely Combe Charbonnière (but there's a fairly long traverse on moderately steep ground at the start). The Lièvre Blanc chairlift serves further testing slopes – Balme, looping away from the lifts, is a black, and one or two reds would be classified black in many resorts, especially when grooming is poor or non-existent. In good snow conditions, the steep La Fuma run down to Le Chatelard Maronne is worth trying. And the Col de Cluy from Signal de l'Homme is long and gets away from all the lifts.

The off-piste possibilities are immense, and some are described in the feature panel over the page. Some of these routes away from the lifts are shady, in contrast to the pistes of the main sector.

FOR INTERMEDIATES ★★★★☆
Fine selection of runs
Good intermediates have a fine selection of runs all over the area. In good snow conditions the variety of runs is difficult to beat.

Every section has some challenging red runs to test the adventurous intermediate. The Canyon run is one of the most challenging. There are lovely long runs down to Oz – the Champclotury blue from the mid-station of the gondola above Oz is a lovely, gentle run and usually quiet – and to Vaujany, with space for some serious carving. The Villard-Reculas and Signal de l'Homme sectors also have long challenging reds. Those at Signal de L'Homme are quieter, which keeps their snow better. The Chamois red from the top of the gondola down to the mid-station is quite narrow, and miserable when busy and icy and/or heavily mogulled. Fearless intermediates should enjoy the super-long Sarenne black run.

For less ambitious intermediates, there are usually blue alternatives, except on the upper part of the mountain. The main Couloir blue from the top of the big gondola is a lovely run, well served by snowmaking, but like the red Chamois it does get scarily crowded at times.

There are some great cruising runs above Vaujany; but the red runs between Vaujany and Alpe-d'Huez can be too much for early intermediates. You can travel via Oz on gondolas, if you are that keen to get around.

Early intermediates will also enjoy the gentle slopes leading back to Alpe-d'Huez from the main mountain, and the Signal sector. But the unreliable piste grading (see remarks

LIFT PASSES

Ski+

Prices in €

Age	1-day	6-day
under 13	33	161
13 to 64	42	215
over 65	33	161

Free under 5, over 72
Beginner four free lifts; Première Glisse pass covering 27 lifts; lesson and lift pass deals

Notes
Covers all lifts in Alpe-d'Huez, Auris, Oz, Vaujany and Villard-Reculas; half-day passes; discounts for families and regular visitors; 2-day-plus passes cover sports centre, ice rink, swimming pools, concerts, two museums; 6-day-plus passes allow one day's skiing at each of Serre-Chevalier, Puy-St-Vincent and the Milky Way in Italy, and two days in Les Deux-Alpes

Alternative passes
Alpe-d'Huez only, Auris only, Oz-Vaujany only, Villard-Reculas only

under 'The mountains') can make life scary for early intermediates, never knowing what to expect.

FOR BEGINNERS ★★★★★
Good facilities
The large network of green runs immediately above the village is as good a nursery area as you will find anywhere. The six-pack installed at Les Bergers several seasons ago has made that part much easier for novices too. Sadly, these slopes get very crowded and carry a lot of fast through-traffic. Both areas have been declared low-speed zones, but the restrictions are not policed and so achieve very little. Four beginner lifts are free and a special lift pass covers more lifts to progress to.

FOR BOARDERS ★★★★
Suits the adventurous
The resort suits experienced boarders well – the extent and variety of the mountains mean that there's a lot of good freeriding to be had; the off-piste is vast and varied and well worth checking out with a guide. There are quite a few flat areas to beware of though. The nursery slopes are excellent for learning but accessed mainly by draglifts (which can be avoided once a modicum of control has been achieved). Planète Surf is the main snowboard shop.

FOR CROSS-COUNTRY ★★★
High-level and convenient
There are 50km of trails, with three loops of varying degrees of difficulty, all at around 2000m and consequently relatively snow-sure.

MOUNTAIN RESTAURANTS ★★★★
Some excellent rustic huts
Mountain restaurants are generally good – even self-service places are pleasant, and there are more rustic

Mega-resort skiing from a quiet base? Check out Vaujany p231.

places with table service than is usual in high French resorts. But the restaurants in the more obvious positions get over-busy and some charge for the toilets. The piste map does not identify restaurants. Get hold of the resort's pocket restaurant guide, which covers 15 places, and marks them on a tiny piste map.
Editors' choice Compared with the main places, the cosy little Chalet du Lac Besson (0476 806537) is an oasis of calm – tucked away on the cross-country loops north of the DMC gondola mid-station (and reached by a special piste, the Boulevard des Lacs). Food and service are excellent. It's repeatedly endorsed by reporters.
Worth knowing about There are a couple of good spots low down – not mountain restaurants as such, but very popular targets nonetheless. The pretty little Forêt de Maronne hotel at Chatelard, below Signal de l'Homme, does good food and has 'very reasonable prices, charming staff'. The 'cosy' Bergerie at Villard-Reculas is an old farmhouse with 'outstanding' views, and 'inexpensive' food.

The Combe Haute, at the foot of the Chalvet chair in the gorge towards the end of the Sarenne run has reportedly been refurbished and now 'serves lovely food in charming, rustic surroundings', but gets busy. The Signal is quieter and has 'postcard views'. The Perce Neige, just below the Oz-Poutran gondola mid-station, has a 'great snug atmosphere' inside and a good terrace; the plats are 'excellent'.

The restaurants in the Oz and Vaujany sectors tend to be cheaper, but no less satisfactory. At Montfrais, the Airelles is a rustic hut, built into the rock, with a roaring log fire; we

Alpe-d'Huez

227

Interactive resort shortlist builder at **www.wtss.co.uk**

get repeated enthusiastic reports – 'lovely food, fast service, friendly staff'. Nearby, Au P'tit Truc is 'good value with well prepared food'. The Auberge de l'Alpette and the Grange at Alpette have also been tipped.

SCHOOLS AND GUIDES ★★★★
Plenty of choice
We get mixed reports on the ESF. This year, we hear of an excellent private lesson but a beginner class delivering 'minimal tuition'. Last year, a good off-piste group for a week, but intermediate classes spoilt by poor allocation of pupils to classes and an instructor with minimal English.

We lack recent reports on the competing smaller schools, but past reports have all been positive. Stance is run by two experienced instructors and specialises in teaching British clients. Masterclass is made up of British instructors and run by Stuart Adamson.

FOR FAMILIES ★★★★★
Positive reports
There's Les Intrépides day care centre for children aged six months to four years – 'first class'. The children's garden and nursery (for children aged six months to five years) at Vaujany have been recommended. Family specialist Esprit now operates here (read 'Chalets' in the next section).

STAYING THERE

There's quite a good range here. There is a Club Med in the Bergers quarter, which a 2010 reporter praised.
Chalets Quite a few options. Crystal leads the pack with half a dozen chalets plus a central 34-bed chalet-hotel. Skiworld has five chalets including one 30-bed property. Ski Total now has five chalets, two of them new this year. Inghams has taken on two chalets, one with outdoor hot tub. Family specialist Esprit now has a 60-bed chalet hotel in the old village.
Hotels There are more hotels than is usual in a high French resort – mainly 3-star – but we get few reports from readers. More reports welcome.
★★★★Au Chamois d'Or (0476 803132) The only 4-star. Good facilities, modern rooms, one of the best restaurants in town and well placed for the main gondola.
★★★Pic Blanc (0476 114242) Across the car park from Les Bergers lifts. Comfortable; on a recent visit we stayed in a big ('superior') room.

OFF-PISTE FOR ALL STANDARDS

There are vast amounts of off-piste terrain in Alpe-d'Huez, from fairly tame to seriously adventurous. Here we pick out just a few of the many runs to be explored – always with guidance, of course.

*There are lots of off-piste variants on both sides of the Sarenne run that are good for making your first turns off-piste. The **Combe du Loup,** a beautiful south-facing bowl with views over the Meije, has a black-run gradient at the top, and you end up on long, gentle slopes leading back to the Sarenne gorge. **La Chapelle Saint Giraud,** which starts at Signal de l'Homme, includes a series of small confidence-boosting bowls, interspersed with gentle rolling terrain.*

*For more experienced and adventurous off-piste skiers, the **Grand Sablat** is a classic that runs through a magnificently wild setting on the eastern face of the Massif des Grandes Rousses. This descent of 2000m vertical includes glacial terrain and some steep couloirs. You can either ski down to the village of Clavans, where you can take a pre-booked helicopter or taxi back, or traverse above Clavans back to the Sarenne gorge. In the **Signal** sector, there are various classic routes down towards the village of Huez or to Villard-Reculas.*

*The north-facing Vaujany sector is particularly interesting for experienced off-piste enthusiasts. Route finding can be very tricky, and huge cliffs and rock bands mean this is not a place to get lost. From the top of Pic Blanc, a 40-minute hike takes you to Col de la Pyramide at 3250m, the starting point for the classic route **La Pyramide** with a vertical of over 2000m. Once at the bottom of the long and wide Pyramide snowfield, you can link into the Vaujany pistes.*

The top of the resort from Signal, with the DMC leading off to the left, and the chalet-suburb above Les Bergers in the distance ➔

UK PACKAGES

Alpine Answers, Chalet Group, Club Med, Crystal, Erna Low, Esprit, First Choice, Independent Ski Links, Inghams, Interactive Resorts, La Source, Lagrange, Mountain Wave, Neilson, Powder White, Powder White Lite, PowderBeds, PV-Holidays.com, Richmond Holidays, Rocketski, Ski Collection, Ski Expectations, Ski France, Ski Independence, Ski Line, Ski Solutions, Ski Supreme, Ski Total, Skitracer, Skiweekends.com, Thomson, VIP, Zenith **Villard-Reculas** La Source
Oz-en-Oisans AmeriCan Ski, Erna Low, Independent Ski Links, Lagrange, Peak Retreats, Ski France **Vaujany** AmeriCan Ski, Erna Low, Peak Retreats, PowderBeds, PV-Holidays.com, Ski France, Ski Independence, Ski Peak

Phone numbers
From abroad use the prefix +33 and omit the initial '0' of the phone number

TOURIST OFFICE
www.alpedhuez.com

Apartments There are lots available, though few are notable. The big news is the opening for 2011/12 of the CGH residence Cristal de l'Alpe with pool, hot tubs, fitness stuff etc, and a prime central location. The P&V residence Ours Blanc and its Privilège variant are central and recently refurbished. Reporters have been happy with the Pierre & Vacances residence Les Bergers, with outdoor pool. Ski Collection and Erna Low offer these properties, and also have individual chalets to rent.

EATING OUT ★★★★
Good value
Alpe-d'Huez has dozens of restaurants, some of high quality; many offer good value by resort standards.
Widely thought to be about the best is Au P'tit Creux. We've had a fabulous meal here (foie gras, carré d'agneau, mango tatin) and over several years we've had rave reviews from reporters, too. This year's reporters tip more modest places – Smithy's Tavern ('great place for reasonably priced food – Tex-Mex'), Au Trappeur ('super and good value pizza'). A 2010 reporter who worked his way round the resort rated the set menu 'fantastic value' at the Grenier and also approved of the Genepi, the Pomme de Pin and the Taverne.

APRES-SKI ★★★★
Plenty going on
There's a wide range of bars, some of which get fairly lively later on. There are several British-run bars in chalet hotels. One is the Underground in Vieil Alpe – 'very pleasant, with live music every night', according to a reporter. Smithy's Tavern has 'plenty of atmosphere'. Other places tipped by reporters include Lounge21, O'Bar and the Pacific (sister bar to the one in Val d'Isère). There are reportedly three late-night places. The Sporting is 'a great bar with class bands' but has 'the highest prices'; the Igloo and the Caves des Alpes make up the trio.

OFF THE SLOPES ★★★★
Good by high-resort standards
There is a wide range of facilities, praised by recent non-skiers, including an indoor pool, a big and very popular indoor-outdoor pool ('warm, with friendly staff'), an Olympic-size ice rink and a splendid sports centre – all covered by the lift pass. There's also

Ski a high altitude resort with low prices – see p177

Ski a high altitude resort with low prices – see p177

an ice driving school and a toboggan run. You can try airboarding and snow biking on selected dates beside the Poutran lift. Visits to the Ice Cave are highly recommended by reporters. Shopping is not impressive.
The helicopter excursion to Les Deux-Alpes is exciting, though you may want to establish exactly where it drops you. There are well-marked walkers' trails (map available), the lifts 'cope well with pedestrians' and there's a special lift pass. The better mountain restaurants are widely spread though – and some are too remote for pedestrians. You can take a sleigh ride and weekly church organ concerts are free with your lift pass.

LINKED RESORT – 1500m

VILLARD-RECULAS

Villard-Reculas is a charming, secluded village just over the hill (Signal) from Alpe-d'Huez, complete with an old church and set on a small shelf wedged between an expanse of open snowfields above and tree-filled hillsides below. A fast quad up to Signal has increased the village's popularity as a base. Its visitor beds are mainly in self-catering apartments and chalets, booked either through the tourist office or La Source – an

229

Interactive resort shortlist builder at www.wtss.co.uk

ACTIVITIES

Indoor Sports centre (tennis, gym, squash, aerobics, swimming, shooting range, climbing wall, adventure trail), sauna, cinemas, concerts, theatre, library, museum

Outdoor Ice rink, curling, cleared walking paths, horse-drawn carriage rides, dog sledding, snowshoeing, snowmobiling, microlight flights, sightseeing flights, ice cave, skijoring, off-road vehicle tours, hang-gliding, paragliding, ice driving school, segway tours

GETTING THERE

Air Lyon 155km/ 95 miles (2hr30); Geneva 210km/ 130 miles (3hr30); Grenoble, 105km/ 65 miles (2hr15)

Rail Grenoble (63km/ 39 miles); daily buses from station

English-run agency that also runs a comfortable catered chalet in a carefully converted stone barn with outdoor hot tub (highly recommended by reporters – 'excellent food and hospitality, great ski guiding – personal service doesn't come any better'). There is a 2-star hotel (the Beaux Monts – 0476 804314), a 'nice' restaurant (Comptoir du Villard), pizza at L'étoile and a couple of bars. The village is very quiet in the evenings.

The local slopes have something for everyone, including a nursery slope at village level. But more than one reporter has warned that the blue runs above the village are not entirely easy, especially when snow is not good, making this an awkward place for beginners and near-beginners. A 2009 visitor found the ESF 'excellent'.

LINKED RESORT – 1350m
OZ-EN-OISANS STATION

The purpose-built ski station above the old village of the same name is a 'thriving small resort', says a reporter who has an apartment there. It has been built in an attractive style, with much use of wood and stone, and has nursery slopes, skating rink, bars, restaurants, supermarket and two mid-range hotels. The pool in the hotel Les Cristaux is open to all. But a reporter complains of a lack of nightlife.

Two gondolas whisk you out of the resort – one goes to Alpette, above Vaujany, the other goes in two stages to the mid-station of the DMC above Alpe-d'Huez. The main run home is

liberally endowed with snow-guns, but it needs to be. One clear advantage of staying here is that the slopes above Oz are about the best in the area when heavy snow is falling – and those based elsewhere may not be able to reach them.

The smart Chalet des Neiges apartments are in chalet-style buildings with pool, sauna, fitness area, bar and restaurant. Available through Peak Retreats and Lagrange.

LINKED RESORT – 1600m
AURIS-EN-OISANS 1600

Auris-en-Oisans 1600 is another tiny, purpose-built ski station – a series of wood-clad, chalet-style apartment blocks with a few shops, bars and restaurants set just above the treeline. It's a compact family resort, with a ski school, nursery and ski kindergarten. Beneath it is the original old village of Auris, with traditional buildings, a church and all but one of the resort's hotels. Staying here with a car you can drive up to the lift base or make excursions to other resorts.

Unsurprisingly, evenings are quiet. The Beau Site (0476 800639), which looks like an apartment block, is the only hotel in the upper village. A couple of miles down the hill, the traditional Auberge de la Forêt (0476 800601) feels like 'real' rural France.

Access to the slopes of Alpe-d'Huez is no problem (but returning to Auris may prove difficult for novices – the top of Signal de L'Homme is a bit steep). There are plenty of local slopes

---

Selected chalet in Villard-Reculas   ADVERTISEMENT

CHALET LA SOURCE *www.lasourcechalet.co.uk*   TEL & FAX 01707 655988

↑ VILLARD-RECULAS

Situated in the picturesque village of Villard-Reculas – an alpine secret in a spectacular setting with fast links to some of the best skiing in Europe.

La Source is a spacious, luxury-catered, owner-managed chalet offering accommodation for 2 to 16 people, and is perfect for those who appreciate imaginative cuisine and fine wine, with efficient and friendly service. La Source provides free airport transfers, local minibus and ski guiding.

email: Michael@lasourcechalet.co.uk

CHALET LA SOURCE ↑

Phone numbers
From abroad use the
prefix +33 and omit
the initial '0' of the
phone number

TOURIST OFFICES

Villard-Reculas
www.villard-reculas.
com

Oz-en-Oisans
www.oz-en-oisans.
com

Auris-en-Oisans
www.auris-en-oisans.
com

Vaujany
www.vaujany.com

---

to explore, for which there is a special lift pass. Most runs are intermediate, though Auris is also the best of the local hamlets for beginners.

LINKED RESORT – 1250m

VAUJANY

Vaujany is a quiet, rapidly growing village, perched on a sunny hillside opposite its own sector of the domain. Hydroelectricity riches continue to finance huge investment in lifts and other infrastructure.

A giant 160-person two-stage cable car whisks you up into the heart of the Alpe-d'Huez lift system. Alternatively, a two-stage gondola takes you less dramatically to the local slopes at Montfrais via a mid-station below the tiny hamlet of La Villette.

Accommodation is mainly in apartments, though there are hotels and catered chalets too.

As you enter the village, you come to a couple of small, simple hotels. The Rissiou is well run by British tour operator Ski Peak: delicious food and helpful staff. Ski Peak also has half a dozen comfortable catered chalets in Vaujany and La Villette; a minibus service for guests is available. Ski Peak also has several apartments. Pierre & Vacances has a modest residence here – available, along with several other options, through Peak Retreats (no relation).

You then come to a recently built complex around a small pedestrian square, Place Centre Village, with spacious, mid-range apartments built

in traditional style. There's a good ski shop, restaurants, food shops, a cafe/bar and a cavernous underground car park – and an escalator down to the nearby cable car and gondola stations. An elevator takes you further down the hill to the superb sports centre with 'fantastic pool and big slide'. We're told they are building an ice rink here, too.

An impressive enclosed escalator goes up the hillside past chalets and farm buildings to the top of the village, where sizeable apartment buildings are grouped around the Galerie Marchande – a small car-free zone with a small supermarket, a food shop, a couple of bars and a couple of restaurants. Since most of the visitor beds are up here, it is naturally the focus of evening activity.

There are no slopes leading directly to the village. But there is a 'pulse' gondola up from L'Enversin, below the village, where the Fare black run finishes (a great run and not steep – read 'For experts' earlier in this chapter), or you can take a blue to the mid-station of the Montfrais gondola and ride down the lower stage.

Beginner children are taken to a gentle roped-off area at the top of the gondola and adult beginners to the nursery slope at Alpette, the cable car mid-station. There's a good self-service restaurant with sunny terrace right by the children's learning area. The children's ski school was praised last year ('well organised by a local Brit') as is the nursery ('as good as it gets, good English spoken, not expensive').

Alpe-d'Huez

231

Interactive resort shortlist builder at **www.wtss.co.uk**

Selected chalets in Vaujany

Les Arcs

Three first-generation purpose-built villages plus a cute modern alternative – with an exceptional variety and extent of slopes

RATINGS

The mountains

Extent	★★★
Fast lifts	★★★
Queues	★★★★
Terrain p'ks	★★★★
Snow	★★★★
Expert	★★★★★
Intermediate	★★★★
Beginner	★★★
Boarder	★★★★
X-country	★★
Restaurants	★★
Schools	★★★★
Families	★★★★

The resort

Charm	★★
Convenience	★★★★
Scenery	★★★
Eating out	★★★
Après-ski	★★
Off-slope	★

RPI	100
lift pass	£210
ski hire	£125
lessons	£90
food & drink	£145
total	**£570**

NEWS

2011/12: The slow Mont Blanc chair from Arc 1600 and a drag lift above it are due to be replaced by a six-pack, going up to Les Deux Têtes. A new spa and swimming pool complex is planned for Arc 1950.

2010/11: A fixed-grip quad opened at the southern end of Plan-Peisey to improve access to the main lifts from there. And a new lift – a J-bar – replaced the chair serving the terrain park.

At Arc 2000, a rope tow was installed on the flat area below the Arcabulle chairlift and a covered moving carpet was added to the nursery slopes.

➕ Varied pistes, easy-to-reach off-piste

➕ Lots of genuinely challenging skiing

➕ Some excellent woodland runs

➕ Car-free, mainly convenient villages, including cute 1950

➕ Some quiet alternative bases

➕ Fast cable car link to La Plagne

➖ Original village centres lack charm, and aren't the most convenient

➖ Still lots of old chairlifts

➖ Fairly quiet nightlife

➖ Lots of flat linking runs

➖ Accommodation in high villages is nearly all in apartments

We've always liked Les Arcs' slopes: they offer long descents, plenty of steep stuff, and woods to head to in a storm. And for those who really like to travel on skis, the link to La Plagne takes you into the Three Valleys league.

We've never been keen on the functional main villages. We're aware that their various architectural styles are highly regarded by some; we're not among them, but our real objection is to their dreary, depressing mall-style shopping centres. Arcs 1600 and 1800 are not the most convenient of resorts, either. Newer Arc 1950 is something else: a resort that's not only more pleasant to inhabit than the others, but also very conveniently arranged.

THE RESORT

Les Arcs is made up of four modern resort units, all purpose-built, traffic-free and apartment-dominated.

Arc 1600 and 1800 stand a couple of km apart, roughly at the treeline on a broad, steepish mountainside overlooking the town of Bourg-St-Maurice (covered at the end of this chapter). Both consist mainly of large apartment blocks sitting below their slopes, with some development beside the slopes. 1600 was the first Arc, built at the top of a funicular railway up from Bourg. 1800 is much the largest of the villages.

Arc 2000 is quite separate – on the far side of the mountain ridge, at the bottom of a high, treeless bowl. It consists of half a dozen huge, linked apartment buildings, plus more recently built chalet-style apartment blocks. Just below Arc 2000 and linked to it by a short gondola, the newish mini-village of Arc 1950 is built in traditional style – more about this in the margin panel later in the chapter.

The numbers in the village names relate only loosely to their altitudes. 'Arc 2000' was meant to evoke the millennium – the future; its altitude is actually over 2100m.

At the southern end of the area is Peisey-Vallandry, from where a cable car links with La Plagne, covered by the Paradiski passes. Even from Arc 1950 you can be at the cable car in 20 minutes. At the northern end of the ski area, at much lower altitude, is the rustic hamlet of Villaroger. These outlying villages are described at the end of the chapter.

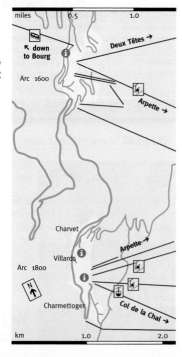

KEY FACTS

Resort	1600-2120m
	5,250-6,960ft
Slopes	1200-3225m
	3,940-10,580ft
Lifts	54
Pistes	200km
	124 miles
Green	1%
Blue	51%
Red	30%
Black	18%
Snowmaking	
	267 guns

Paradiski area	
Slopes	1200-3250m
	3,940-10,660ft
Lifts	135
Pistes	425km
	264 miles
Green	4%
Blue	52%
Red	28%
Black	16%
Snowmaking	
	626 guns

Day trips by car to Val d'Isère-Tignes are possible. La Rosière and Ste-Foy-Tarentaise are closer. Be warned: you have to pay for parking at Arcs 1950 and 2000 – the only free parking is throughout 1600 and before the entrance to 1800.

VILLAGE CHARM ★★☆☆☆
Head for 1950
Reporters repeatedly comment on the friendliness of the locals.

The apartment blocks of Arc 1600 and 1800 are low-rise, and not hugely intrusive seen from the slopes – they are much more conspicuous from below than from above. Arc 1600 is set in the trees and has a friendly, small-scale atmosphere; compact but limited. Bigger Arc 1800 has three main parts: Charvet and Villards are focused on small shopping centres, mostly open-air but still seeming claustrophobic. More easy on the eye is Charmettoger, with smaller, wood-clad buildings.

Arc 2000 consists of futuristic large blocks with swooping roof lines, plus some large chalet-style blocks.

Arc 1950 has been designed to be cute; its smaller apartment buildings have been finished in traditional style, and they are clustered around a pleasant, traffic-free square and street, which can both become quite lively at close of play.

CONVENIENCE ★★★★☆
Generally very good
Arcs 1600 and 1800 offer some very convenient lodgings, a few yards from the lifts, but also some that are less convenient than they look – you can walk miles within the apartment buildings to get to (and from) the snow. The central area in Arc 1600 is good for families: uncrowded, compact, and set on even ground. Arc 1800 is more spread out, and some lodging is further up the hill, well above the village itself. The main lifts depart from Villards.

Arc 2000 and Arc 1950 are compact, ski-in/ski-out places, with lifts starting below them as well as above. But getting around Arc 2000 on foot can be quite an effort, reporters tell us. All the bits of Arc 1950 we've looked at are genuinely ski-in/ski-out. You park directly under the apartment buildings, which is a rare bonus at the start and end of your stay.

SCENERY ★★★☆☆
Attractively varied
Arcs 1600 and 1800, and the slopes, enjoy views across the valley to Mont Blanc. The lower villages enjoy good views along the Nancroix valley and to La Plagne's splendid north face of Bellecôte. Higher up, Arc 2000 and Arc 1950 sit beneath the Aiguille Rouge, high-point of the slopes – great views from the top.

THE MOUNTAINS

Les Arcs' terrain is notably varied; it has a good mixture of high, snow-sure slopes and low-level woodland runs.

EXTENT OF THE SLOPES ★★★☆☆
Well planned and varied
Our rating relates to just the Les Arcs area; the whole Paradiski area easily scores five stars.

Arc 1600 and Arc 1800 share a west-facing mountainside laced with

OT LES ARCS / SEB LEON

Arc 1800 is the biggest of the resort 'villages', with the widest choice of bars and restaurants →

runs down to one or other village. At the southern end is an area of woodland runs above Peisey-Vallandry.

From various points on the ridge above 1600 and 1800 you can head down into the wide Arc 2000 bowl. From there, lifts take you to the high points of the area, the Aiguille Rouge and the Grand Col. As well as a variety of steep runs back to Arc 2000, the Aiguille Rouge is the start of an epic run (over 2000m vertical and 7km long) down to Villaroger.

The resort identifies nine black runs and one red as Natur' (never groomed) pistes – see 'For experts'.

On the lower half of the Aiguille Rouge is a speed-skiing run, which is sometimes open to the public.

FAST LIFTS ★★★☆☆
Still a way to go
Each of the four main villages has fast chair or gondola access to the slopes (and a new six-pack is planned from Arc 1600 for 2011/12). But there are still lots of old chairs – some of them very long and cold (one reader claims to have suffered frostbite in his glutei).

QUEUES ★★★★☆
Not without problems
Queues aren't generally an issue in low season, and peak-time queues are improving. But the lifts above Arc 2000 present problems, especially on sunny days. The Varet gondola to the shoulder of the Aiguille Rouge is always busy but shifts its queue quickly because it has lifties pulling people out of the queue to fill the cabins – excellent. Queues for the cable car to the top can be serious in clear weather; go at lunchtime, or late in the day, to avoid them. The Arcabulle has the potential for 'five-to-ten-minute waits'. At 1800 the Transarc gondola is queue prone, especially late in the day. At 1600 the Cachette chair has difficulty coping with morning crowds arriving on the funicular from the valley – but these

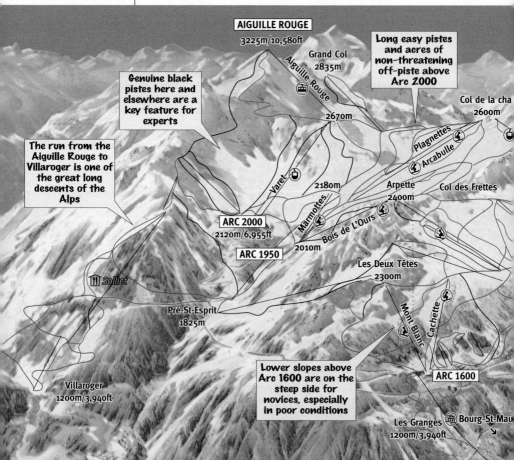

AIGUILLE ROUGE
3225m/10,58oft

Grand Col
2835m

Aiguille Rouge

2670m

Long easy pistes and acres of non-threatening off-piste above Arc 2000

Col de la cha
2600m

Genuine black pistes here and elsewhere are a key feature for experts

Plagnettes

Arcabulle

The run from the Aiguille Rouge to Villaroger is one of the great long descents of the Alps

Varet

2180m

Arpette
2400m

Col des Frettes

Marmottes

Bois de L'Ours

ARC 2000
2120m/6,955ft

ARC 1950

2010m

Les Deux Têtes
2300m

Solliet

Pré-St-Esprit
1825m

Mont Blanc

Cachette

Lower slopes above Arc 1600 are on the steep side for novices, especially in poor conditions

ARC 1600

Villaroger
1200m/3,94oft

Les Granges
1200m/3,94oft

Bourg-St-Mau

should be relieved by the new six-pack for 2011/12 (see 'News'). At Plan Peisey, morning queues for the chair (and for the Derby above it) are not unknown, partly because of arrivals on the cable car from La Plagne.

At peak periods the crowded pistes can be more of a problem than the queues are.

TERRAIN PARKS ★★★★
One excellent park
The Apocalypse Parc is between Arc 1600 and 1800, and served by a snowboarder-friendly J-bar lift. For years, this has been one of the most advanced parks in the Alps – on a par with the main park at Avoriaz. Three kicker lines are in place for all levels. There is a good rail and box line, a big wall ride, a spine jump and a large gap jump – variety and fun for all.

There is a boardercross below Col de la Chal and two smaller parks above Plan-Peisey.

SNOW RELIABILITY ★★★★
Good – plenty of high runs
A high percentage of the runs are above 2000m, and when necessary you can stay high by using lifts that start around that altitude. Most of the slopes face roughly west, which is not ideal. Those from the Col de la Chal and the long runs down to Villaroger are north-facing, and the blacks on the Aiguille Rouge are shady enough to keep their snow well. The limited

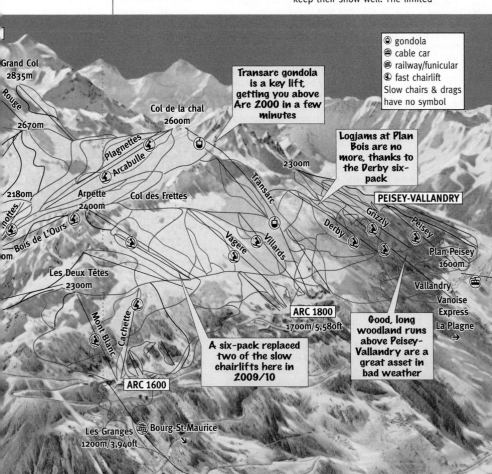

gondola
cable car
railway/funicular
fast chairlift
Slow chairs & drags have no symbol

Grand Col 2835m
Rouge 2670m
Col de la chal 2600m
2300m

Plagnettes
Arcabulle
Arpette 2400m
Col des Frettes
2180m
Bois de L'Ours
om
Les Deux Têtes 2300m
Transarc
Vagere
Villards
Derby
Grizzly
Peisey

Transarc gondola is a key lift, getting you above Arc 2000 in a few minutes

Logjams at Plan Bois are no more, thanks to the Derby six-pack

PEISEY-VALLANDRY

Plan-Peisey 1600m
Vallandry
Vanoise Express
La Plagne →

Good, long woodland runs above Peisey-Vallandry are a great asset in bad weather

ARC 1800
1700m/5,580ft

Mont Blanc
Cachette
ARC 1600

A six-pack replaced two of the slow chairlifts here in 2009/10

Les Granges
1200m/3,940ft
Bourg-St-Maurice

snowmaking is being gradually extended. Grooming is good: 'Despite hot sunny weather, the pisteurs worked miracles each night to make the lower slopes ready for action the next day,' says a 2011 reporter.

FOR EXPERTS ★★★★★
Challenges on- and off-piste
Les Arcs has a lot to offer experts – at least when the high lifts are open (the Aiguille Rouge cable car, in particular, is often shut in bad weather).

Most black runs are now Natur' runs and become huge mogul fields – while some reporters welcome this, the lack of many groomed blacks means that the steeper groomed reds can get very busy. One of the quieter reds (and one of our favourites) is the lower part of the epic Aiguille Rouge-Villaroger run which has remarkably varying terrain – the start is a narrow black shelf which can be awkward (but this can be avoided by taking the Lanchettes chair from Arc 2000). There is also a great deal of off-piste potential. There are steep pitches on the front face of the Aiguille Rouge and secluded runs on the back side, towards Villaroger. A short climb to the Grand Col accesses several routes, including a quite serious couloir and an easier option. From Col de la Chal there is an easy route down towards Nancroix. The wooded slopes above 1600 are another attractive possibility and there are open slopes beside the pistes all over the place.

FOR INTERMEDIATES ★★★★☆
Plenty for all abilities
One strength of the area is that most main routes have easy and more difficult alternatives, making it good for mixed-ability groups. An exception is the solitary Comborcière black from Les Deux Têtes down to Pré-St-Esprit, which has no nearby alternatives. This

long mogul-field justifies its classification and can be great fun for strong intermediates. Malgovert, from the same point towards Arc 1600, is a red Natur' piste and is tricky – it is narrow, as well as mogulled.

The woodland runs at either end of the domain, above Peisey-Vallandry and Villaroger, and the bumpy Cachette red down to 1600, also include some challenges. We especially like the Peisey-Vallandry area: its well groomed, treelined runs have a very friendly feel and are remarkably uncrowded much of the time, allowing great fast cruising. Good intermediates can enjoy the run to Villaroger.

The lower half of the mountainside above 1600/1800 is great for mixed-ability groups, with a choice of routes through the trees. The red runs from Arpette and Col des Frettes towards 1800 are quite steep but usually well groomed (except Clair Blanc).

Cautious intermediates have plenty of blue cruising terrain. Many of the runs around 2000 are rather bland and prone to overcrowding. Edelweiss is more interesting, with a short red alternative, and takes you to Arc 1950 from Col des Frettes. The blues above 1800 are attractive but also crowded. A blue favourite of ours is Renard, high above Vallandry – usually with excellent snow.

And, of course, you have the whole of La Plagne's slopes to explore.

FOR BEGINNERS ★★★☆☆
No long greens, but lots of blues
There are 'ski tranquille' nursery-slope zones above each of the three main Arcs, and at mid-mountain above Peisey-Vallandry; we and readers haven't found them always tranquil though we've had reports of some efforts to define and police them. Three of their serving lifts (one in each village) are free to use at weekends –

SCHOOLS

ESF Arc 1600
t 0479 074309

ESF Arc 1800
t 0479 074031

ESF Arc 2000
t 0479 074752

Arc Aventuras (ESI)
t 0479 076002

Darentasia
t 0479 041681

New Generation
t 0479 010318
0844 484 3663 (UK)
www.skinewgen.com

Initial-Snow
t 0673 514419

Privilege
t 0479 072338

Spirit 1950
t 0479 042572

Classes (ESF prices)
6 days (3hr am or
pm) €147

Private lessons
€150 for half-day
(4hr), for 1 or 2
people

'good for a warm-up on arrival day'. And two other lifts (at 1800 and Les Granges) are totally free. There are also a few enclosed learning areas with draglifts, used by the schools. Sadly, the resort does not use the valuable green-run classification common to most other French resorts. In all sectors there are long, wide blue runs to move on to, and some are gentle enough to be green. An example is Forêt down to Vallandry.

FOR BOARDERS ★★★★
A pioneering place
Ever since 1983 when Regis Rolland introduced the sport in the cult film Apocalypse Snow, Les Arcs has been a hot spot for snowboarders. It offers excellent freeriding, including steeps, gullies, trees, natural jibs and hits. And there are plenty of wide-open rolling slopes for intermediates and beginners too, especially at Vallandry and 1800. The terrain park is great and served by a snowboarder-friendly draglift. Most other lifts are chairs and gondolas. But beware of some long flat areas – especially at Arc 2000 and some linking blue runs (you may find it easier to take the wider reds).

FOR CROSS-COUNTRY ★★☆☆☆
Very boring locally
Short trails, mostly on roads, is all you can expect, but the pretty Nancroix valley's 40km of pleasant trails are easily accessible by free bus.

MOUNTAIN RESTAURANTS ★★☆☆☆
Not much choice high-up
They are mainly unremarkable.
Editors' choice Solliet (0668 960407) above Villaroger is a charming woody chalet with a warm ambience, table- or self-service and great views from the terrace. We had an excellent lunch here in 2010 after a change of owner.
Worth knowing about Chalets de l'Arc, just above Arc 2000, is a rustic place built in wood and stone. We were great fans in its early days, but on our last few visits (including 2011) we found the service rather slow, the welcome nominal and the food nothing special – we'd welcome your reports of 2012 meals.

The busy Cordée, just above Plan-Peisey, is consistently recommended for 'excellent food, first class service'. The restaurant at Col de la Chal was tipped last year for good service, food and views – even when busy. The little Blanche Murée is a pleasant, simple table-service place doing a good job in a chalet-style setting. The Arpette, above 1800, is a self-service that hits its target, as is the Poudreuse above Vallandry ('great burgers, friendly staff'). The tiny Bulle hut, near the Arcabulle chair, is fairly new – with 'excellent pizza at very reasonable prices', says a 2011 visitor.

The other good options are not very mountainous. At Pré-St-Esprit below Arc 2000, the 500-year-old Belliou la Fumée is set beside a car park; but it is charmingly rustic, and we've had good meals here. Reporters have enjoyed 'excellent' meals at the Ferme at Villaroger. If you want a top-notch meal and don't mind returning to resort level, go to Chalet d'Arcelle at 1600 (see 'Eating out').

SCHOOLS AND GUIDES ★★★★
Several, including a Brit school
British school New Generation are consistently recommended. A report this year is typical: 'Worth every cent – excellent instructor who suggested improvements that really made a difference.' 'Fourth year we have used them for private lessons, outstanding each time' was a response last year.

SNOWPIX.COM / CHRIS GILL

You get fine views
(including Mont Blanc)
from Arc 1950 ↓

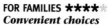
The ESF here is renowned for being
the first in Europe to teach ski
évolutif, where you start by learning
parallel turns on short skis, gradually
moving on to longer skis. Progress can
be spectacular, but classes can be
large. The Arc 2000 branch has had
glowing comments: 'our daughters had
an excellent instructor who really
moved them on', 'top guy; lots of fun'.
In Peisey, two young kids 'progressed
well and were in the park with
confidence'. Arc Aventures
(International school) was noted as
'good value' for an off-piste guide,
while Spirit in 1950 had 'friendly
teachers and not too big groups'.

FOR FAMILIES ★★★★
Convenient choices
Les Arcs is a good choice for families
wanting convenience. There is a
children's area at 1800, complete with
moving carpets, tobogganing and a
climbing wall. There are also a couple
of discovery pistes, at 1800 and 1600,
for children to find out about flora and
fauna of the Alps. The Pommes de Pin
facilities in Arc 1800 have received
favourable reports. Arc 1950 is
particularly family friendly – Spirit 1950
there reportedly provides good care
for smaller children, returning them
well fed and rested. Comments on
kids' ski classes have been positive.

STAYING THERE

Most resort beds are in apartments.
There is a long-established Club Med
presence in Arc 2000 and there's a
smarter one at Peisey-Vallandry.
Chalets There are lots of catered
chalets in the Peisey-Vallandry area –
see the end of this chapter. There are
also lots of chalet-apartments in smart
résidences with pools in Arc 2000 –
Skiworld, Ski Total ('very impressed
with attention to detail by staff,' says
a 2011 reporter), Inghams, Crystal and
family specialist Esprit feature these.
Skiworld also has three proper
individual chalets in 1800.
Hotels The choice of hotels in Les Arcs
is gradually widening.
★★★Golf (1800) (0479 414343) A pricey
3-star, with sauna, gym, covered
parking, kindergarten, spa, heated
pool. Accepts weekend bookings.
★★★Grand Paradiso (1800) (0479
076500) Locally judged to be worth
four stars rather than its actual three
('very comfortable, good food').
★★★Cachette (1600) (0479 077050)
Recommended, but expect lots of kids
– 1600's childcare facilities are here.
'Surprisingly good quality food.'
★★★Arcadien (1600) (0479 041600)
'Very reasonable, rooms relatively big.'
★★Aiguille Rouge (2000) (0479
075707) 'Stylish' bar. Free ski guiding.
★★Mélèzes (2000) (0479 075050)
'Fantastic value for a mixed family
group. Good food, great choices for
vegetarians.' Spa.
Apartments Beware – there are still
plenty of unbearably cramped
apartments in the older resort units.
But there are now lots of good,
modern developments available
through agencies such as Erna Low,

ARC 1950

Arc 1950, just below Arc 2000, is a self-contained mini-resort that was built in the last decade. It is high and relatively snow-sure, traffic-free (you park under your apartment building) and laid out very conveniently, with genuinely ski-in/ski-out lodgings. It is attractively built, with wood and stone chalet-style buildings grouped around a central square and street.

The accommodation is in apartments, spacious and well furnished by French standards – a reporter notes the Radisson is 'particularly spacious, with saunas and outdoor pools'.

There are just enough restaurants to get you through a week, plus a reasonable choice of après-ski bars, a tiny but well-stocked supermarket, a bakery, a gift shop, a crêperie, ski school and ski and board equipment shops.

Lagrange, Pierre & Vacances, Ski Collection, Ski Amis and Ski Independence. For Arc 1950, see the panel in the margin. In Arc 2000 the Chalet des Neiges, Chalet Altitude and Cimes des Arcs have well above average apartments. The Alpages de Chantel above Arc 1800 (now run by Pierre & Vacances) is attractive and comfortable, with pools, saunas and gyms. It is very convenient for skiing, but a bit isolated. The Roc Belle Face development opened a couple of seasons ago in central Arc 1600, built in tiers down the steep hillside. The Ruitor apartments, set among trees between Charmettoger and Villards (in 1800), are 'excellent in all respects'.

EATING OUT ★★★☆☆
Fair choice in Arc 1800

Arc 1800 has the best choice – about 15 restaurants; an ad-based (so not comprehensive) guide is given away locally. Reporters favour the Mountain Cafe, which has a varied menu ('good food, great buzz'), and San Diego ('consistently good, friendly service'). Tipped for tartiflette are the Laurus and Escale Gourmand.

Arc 1600's handful of restaurants include a couple of excellent ones. Chalet de L'Arcelle on the fringe of the village is a clear reporter favourite; it has a warm, quirky wood-and-stone interior and a mouth-watering carte – 'near Michelin one-star quality'. The Malouine has a 'largely Italian' menu and has improved under new management. The Cairn is 'simple, inexpensive' and reliable; the Arquebuse serves traditional food in 'a nice cosy setting'. For a quick snack, try the waffles at the Snack de l'Arbre.

In Arc 2000 Kilimandjaro has stood out in the past: 'Excellent food and wine; the tête de veau was a serious dish.' Chez Eux is 'a cheery place doing excellent pizzas'.

Arc 1950 has a reasonable choice for a small place. They get very busy, and we have some sympathy with the view of a reporter that the options are generally 'uninspiring'. But some receive positive reports. La Table des Lys ('very good food in a refined atmosphere') and Chalet de Luigi ('good selection of pastas') have been recommended.

APRES-SKI ★★☆☆☆
Arc 1800 is the place to be

Nightlife is not lively and mainly revolves around the bars. 1800 is the liveliest; some places have regular live music. The J.O. bar is open until the early hours and has a friendly atmosphere. Reporters like the friendly Red Hot Saloon for bar games, Chez Boubou at Charvet, the Jazz Bar in the hotel Golf ('great band, big sofas') and the cosy Etranger.

Although it's quieter, there are several options in 1600. The Abreuvoir, with live music and pool, is one reporter's 'favourite ski resort bar'. Stop by Chez Fernand for a friendly welcome, too. In Arc 2000 the Whistler's Dream, in the Chalet des Neiges, and the Bliss could be worth a try. At 1950, several places operate as bars; the Belles Pintes serves a 'great Guinness'. O'Chaud is 'the best' – open late, with live music or a DJ.

OFF THE SLOPES ★☆☆☆☆
Very limited

Les Arcs is not the place for an off-the-slopes holiday. There is very little to do, though several of the newer apartment blocks have pools; there are spa facilities at Arc 1950. There's bowling at 1800 and skating at 1800 and 2000. The cinemas have English films weekly. You can visit the Beaufort dairy and go shopping in Bourg-St-Maurice and there are a few walks – nice ones up the Nancroix valley.

Interactive resort shortlist builder at **www.wtss.co.uk**

ACTIVITIES

Indoor Squash (1800), saunas, solaria, multi-gym (1800), museums, cinemas, bowling (1800, 2000)

Outdoor Natural skating rinks (1800/2000), tobogganing, snowshoeing, dog sledding, cleared paths, paragliding, horse riding, skijoring, ice grotto

GETTING THERE

Air Geneva 160km/100 miles (3hr); Lyon 215km/135 miles (3hr); Chambéry 130km/80 miles (2hr)

Rail Bourg-St-Maurice; frequent buses and direct funicular to resort

LINKED RESORT – 1600m

PEISEY-VALLANDRY

Plan-Peisey and Vallandry are small, still-developing ski stations above the old village of Peisey, which has a bucket-lift up to Plan-Peisey. They sell themselves as Peisey-Vallandry, but the local cluster of villages, including one called Nancroix, is collectively known as Peisey-Nancroix. Got that?

The cable car to La Plagne starts from **Plan-Peisey** – one hotel, a few shops, bars and restaurants but no real focus other than the lift station. A six-pack takes you to the local slopes.

UK operator Ski Amis has a premium chalet here with a hot tub (it also has several self-catered chalets here). Ski Beat has 11 chalets (some with sauna) – 'I would recommend Chalet Marmotton and Ski Beat to anyone,' says a 2011 reporter. Family specialist operator Esprit has six neat chalets, each with hot tub. The hotel Vanoise (0479 079219) has a good

location, a pool and a fitness room: 'Staff were very friendly despite our appalling French, and the food was much better than expected,' says a 2011 visitor. The Arollaie is a smart, fairly new apartment development, with a small pool.

Of the restaurants, reporters like the rustic Solan ('rustic style but sophisticated inside with reasonable prices'), the Vache ('excellent food, relaxed friendly bar') and Chez Felix ('super food, popular with locals'). Après-ski is very quiet.

There is lodging down the hill in the characterful old village of Peisey, complete with fine baroque church. The other, mostly old, buildings include a few shops and a couple of bars and restaurants – a reader enjoyed the Ormelune. UK tour operator Mountain Heaven has a renovated old farm building run as a catered chalet with five en-suite rooms; there are three more in an annex, plus a sauna.

Phone numbers
From abroad use the prefix +33 and omit the initial '0' of the phone number

TOURIST OFFICES

Les Arcs/Bourg-St-Maurice
www.lesarcs.com

Peisey-Vallandry
www.peisey-vallandry.com

The Ancolie restaurant at Nancroix is worth the trip – a fabulous traditional auberge with welcoming hosts and excellent food. (Be aware that taxis will rip you off for the short journey if you're not careful.)

Vallandry is a few hundred metres away from Plan-Peisey and linked by shuttle-bus. A fast quad takes you into the slopes. There are lots of chalets and a small pedestrian-only square at the foot of the slopes with a small supermarket and a ski shop.

Ski Olympic's big piste-side chalet hotel La Forêt has 'outstanding food, good rooms, fabulous views, friendly and helpful staff'. The Orée des Cimes is a smart apartment development with a pool, sauna, steam and hot tub and great views; the Orée des Neiges is similar and new for 2011/12 with access to the Cimes leisure facilities.

There are several restaurants. The Caleche does 'large portions of Savoyard classics'. The Mont Blanc bar is cool – 'well worth the walk', and one of the cheaper options for lunch.

LINKED RESORT – 1200m
VILLAROGER

Villaroger is a charming, quiet, rustic little hamlet with three successive slow chairlifts going up to a point above Arc 2000; its slopes are not suitable for beginners. It has a couple of small bar-restaurants.

DOWN-VALLEY RESORT – 850m
BOURG-ST-MAURICE

With a funicular railway link to Arc 1600, Bourg-St-Maurice is marketed as part of Les Arcs, and does make a viable cheaper alternative to staying on the hill. But it is very different – not a ski resort, but a real valley town, with proper everyday shops and sizeable supermarkets. It is at the end of the TGV railway line, and therefore very appealing to rail travellers.

The funicular station is a walkable distance from the TGV platforms, but a drive or bus ride from most parts of Bourg. The advertised travel time is seven minutes, but that's for non-stop services, which in our experience are rare. In practice, staying in Bourg rather than Les Arcs costs you an hour a day in extra travelling time.

The plus side, of course, is that everything from accommodation to beer is cheaper. Depending on the time of the season and the exact comparison you make, you can rent an apartment for 30% to 60% less than the cost of a similar apartment on the hill. If you plan to ski Les Arcs (and La Plagne), you need to balance the cost savings against that lost hour a day.

But if you fancy a bit more variety, the appeal of Bourg-St-Maurice becomes clear. We spent a week here in 2010 and had a fab time skiing a different resort every day, from La Plagne to Val d'Isère. The more remote resorts are best accessed by car, though there are buses. But you can easily ski La Rosière (and linked La Thuile) by taking a bus to the chairlift above Séez which goes up into the slopes of La Rosière.

New two seasons ago, the Coeur d'Or apartments are comfortable without being indulgent. Close to the two major supermarkets, they are a walk from the town but a drive (or free shuttle bus ride) from the funicular.

A reporter reckons that the Angival (0479 072797), in a quiet back street, is 'the pick of the hotel crop'.

There are some good, unpretentious restaurants. Best in town (actually just outside the centre) is probably the Arssiban. In the main pedestrian street, the Tsablo and Montagnole do a good job, too.

Les Arcs

Interactive resort shortlist builder at www.wtss.co.uk

Avoriaz 1800

The 'ski to and from the door' purpose-built resort option on the French side of the big Portes du Soleil circuit

RATINGS

The mountains

Extent	★★★★★
Fast lifts	★★★★
Queues	★★★
Terrain p'ks	★★★★★
Snow	★★★
Expert	★★★
Intermediate	★★★★
Beginner	★★★★
Boarder	★★★★★
X-country	★★★
Restaurants	★★★★
Schools	★★★
Families	★★★★

The resort

Charm	★★
Convenience	★★★★★
Scenery	★★★
Eating out	★★★
Après-ski	★★★
Off-slope	★

RPI	95
lift pass	£200
ski hire	£125
lessons	£70
food & drink	£145
total	**£540**

NEWS

2011/12: New 5-star luxury Pierre & Vacances apartments (L'Amara – with spa, pool, saunas etc) are due to open in several linked buildings near the top of the resort. A new ice rink is planned for the centre. A five-hour pass, which lets you ski for any five consecutive hours in a day, is replacing the half-day pass.

2010/11: The Ardent gondola was revamped and now has a higher capacity. A boardercross course was built.

+ Good position on the main Portes du Soleil circuit, giving access to very extensive, quite varied runs

+ Very successful design – car-free, with ski-in/ski-out lodgings

+ Good children's facilities

+ Local slopes are among the best in the Portes du Soleil and generally have the best snow, but ...

– Linked resorts you visit present the risk of poor snow low down

– Architecture doesn't suit everyone

– Lacks a slick bag delivery system

– Can get very crowded at weekends

– Limited range of restaurants, very limited range of other amenities

– Most apartments are basic – but smart new ones for this season

Of the purpose-built resorts thrown up in the 1960s, Avoriaz is one of the better designed – genuinely convenient in most respects, completely car-free and visually striking rather than offensive. And it is set in the highest, most snow-sure part of the relatively low (but very extensive) Portes du Soleil ski area. At last, this season it is getting some 'luxury' apartments with a smart spa that might turn it into the sort of place we'd be happy to stay in for a week.

THE RESORT

Avoriaz 1800 is a purpose-built resort perched on a sloping shelf above a dramatic, sheer rock face.

It is entirely free of wheeled traffic; cars are left in paid-for parks at the edge of the village – book a space underground to avoid a chaotic departure if it snows. You drag your luggage to your apartment on a borrowed sled, or fork out for a ride on a snowcat or horse-drawn sleigh. (The problem of horse mess has been cut since horses wear 'nappies'.)

Avoriaz is on the main lift circuit of the Portes du Soleil – for an overview, look at our separate chapter. It has links to Châtel in one direction and to Champéry in Switzerland in the other – both covered in separate chapters.

It is above the valley resort of Morzine, to which it is linked by gondola (but not by piste). The slopes of Morzine and Les Gets, on the far side of Morzine, are not on the core circuit but are covered by the Portes du Soleil lift pass; both get their own chapters.

There are two hamlets on the fringes of the Avoriaz ski area with lifts into it – Ardent and Les Prodains. Both have some accommodation and are briefly described at the end of this chapter. Car trips to Flaine and Chamonix are possible.

VILLAGE CHARM ★★★★★
One of the best modern places

The village is all angular, dark, wood-clad, high-rise buildings – almost all apartments. It's not what you would call charming, but it is at least designed coherently. The snow-covered paths and pistes give the place quite a friendly Alpine feel, and both we and reporters have enjoyed the ambience, both day and night. Family-friendly events are laid on all season. A floodlit cliff behind the resort adds to its nocturnal charm. A recent reporter found the lifties 'friendly and helpful'.

CONVENIENCE ★★★★★
It doesn't get much better

As our scale plan suggests, it's a compact place, with everything close to hand (turn to the Chamonix chapter for a striking comparison). Wherever you stay, you should be able to ski from close to the door. The village is

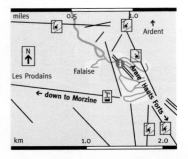

KEY FACTS

Resort	1800m
	5,910ft

Portes du Soleil

Slopes	950-2275m
	3,120-7,460ft
Lifts	196
Pistes	650km
	404 miles
Green	13%
Blue	40%
Red	37%
Black	10%
Snowmaking	
	800 guns

Avoriaz only

Slopes	1100-2275m
	3,610-7,460ft
Lifts	33
Pistes	70km
	45 miles
Snowmaking	
	126 guns

OT AVORIAZ 1800 / STÉPHANE LERENDU

Avoriaz is great for families – completely traffic-free and has an excellent Village des Enfants with its own chalet and slopes ↓

set on quite a slope; but elevators inside the buildings (and chairlifts outside, during the day) mean moving around is no problem except when paths are icy.

SCENERY ★★★☆☆
Cliff-top panorama
The village is high and its position on a sunny balcony gives good views. From the top of the lifts the mighty Dents Blanches range is clearly visible.

THE MOUNTAINS

The slopes closest to Avoriaz are bleak and treeless, but snow-sure. For notes on the main Portes du Soleil circuit see our special chapter on it.

Five runs – a blue, two reds and two blacks – are called 'snowcross' runs. We understand these are signed, ungroomed, patrolled and avalanche controlled. But a 2009 reporter found one was 'completely unmarked' (we've had no further reports of poor marking).

EXTENT OF THE SLOPES ★★★★★
360˚ choice
The village has lifts and pistes fanning out in all directions. Facing the village are the slopes of **Arare-Hauts Forts** and, when snow conditions allow, there are long, steep runs down to Les Prodains, way below the resort. The lifts off to the left go to the **Chavanette** sector on the Swiss border – a broad, undulating bowl. Beyond the border is the infamous Swiss Wall – a long, mogul slope with a tricky

start, but not the terror it is cracked up to be unless it's icy or you're on a snowboard. It's no disgrace to ride the chair down – lots of people do. At the bottom of the Wall is the open, gentle terrain of Planachaux, above Champéry, with links to the even bigger open area around Les Crosets and Champoussin.

Taking a lift up through the village of Avoriaz to the ridge behind it is the way to the prettily wooded **Lindarets-Brocheaux** valley, from where lifts go over to Châtel's Linga sector.

FAST LIFTS ★★★★☆
Good system here and at Linga
In the Avoriaz sector the lifts are impressively modern – hence our rating. On the Linga slopes, on the way to Châtel, you'll again be mainly riding fast lifts. But be warned: beyond Châtel, and in the opposite direction towards Champéry, it's like stepping back 20 years.

QUEUES ★★★☆☆
Main problems now gone
Most of the bad queues have been eliminated by newish fast lifts. The main long-standing problem is the queue for the cable car at Prodains, when snow attracts visitors from Morzine. Visitors report few other problems although one 2011 visitor found 'a 25-minute wait' at Les Lindarets to get back to Avoriaz and decided to ski to Ardent and get the bus. Peak-time crowds on the pistes (especially around the village) can be hazardous.

TERRAIN PARKS ★★★★★
Still leading the way
Avoriaz was one of the pioneers of
snowboarding in France, and the first
terrain park to be built in the country
was here in 1993. It is still leading the
way, and there are now five parks and
a super-pipe, all superbly maintained.
Check www.snowparkavoriaz.com for
details. Park lift passes are available.

The expert park is now at Arare and
the kicker and rail lines are superbly
shaped, designed and maintained. It
also has an airbag jump – 'the most
fun I had all trip', says a 2011 visitor.

Beginners and intermediates should
head to La Chapelle. This is a
500m-long park littered with jumps of
all sizes and fun little boxes, to suit all
levels of skiers and boarders. Parkway,
on the Trashers lift, is great for

beginners and kids. It has mini-jumps
and ride-on boxes, with green 'Go'
lights to press before you drop, a
smart safety-aware innovation.

The fourth park, The Stash in the
Lindarets valley, is a great innovation
imported from California – a wooded
mountainside, with three different
routes cut through the forest, and
wooden and natural elements bringing
all-mountain riding and freestyle
together – a recent visitor advises: 'Go
in the morning as there's more room
for manoeuvre and the snow is better.'
'First class; great fun; lived up to all
the hype,' says a 2011 reporter.

The fifth park is the Lil'Stash – a
mini version for younger kids. Just
above the village is a good super-pipe.
And there's a boardercross too.

SNOW RELIABILITY ★★★✩✩
High resort, low slopes
Although Avoriaz itself is high, its
slopes don't go much higher – and
some parts of the Portes du Soleil
circuit are much lower. Considering
their altitude, the north-facing slopes
below Hauts Forts hold snow well and
the snow in Avoriaz is usually much
better than over the border on the
south-facing Swiss slopes. But when
snow was sparse on one of our visits
we found the smooth, grassy, lower
slopes of Morzine-Les Gets better than
the rocky ones around Avoriaz, which
need more snow-cover. We've had
reports of poor piste maintenance.

FOR EXPERTS ★★★✩✩
Several challenging runs
Tough terrain is scattered about. The
challenging runs down from Hauts
Forts to Prodains (including a World
Cup downhill) are excellent. There is a
tough red and several long, truly black
runs including one of the 'snowcross'
runs we've talked about. Two chairlifts
serve the lower runs, which snow-guns
help to keep open. The Swiss Wall at
Chavanette will naturally be on your
agenda, and Châtel's Linga sector is
well worth a trip. The black runs off
the Swiss side of Mossettes and
Pointe de l'Au are worth trying, and
one reporter had a 'very good' day
here exploring off-piste with a guide.

FOR INTERMEDIATES ★★★★✩
Virtually the whole area
Although some sections lack variety,
the Portes du Soleil circuit through
Châtel, Morgins and Champéry is

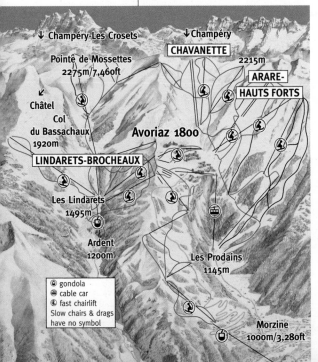

↓ Champéry-Les Crosets   ↓ Champéry

CHAVANETTE

Pointe de Mossettes
2275m/7,460ft

2215M

ARARE-
HAUTS FORTS

Châtel
Col
du Bassachaux
1920M

Avoriaz 1800

LINDARETS-BROCHEAUX

Les Lindarets
1495M

Ardent
1200M

Les Prodains
1145M

ⓖ gondola
ⓐ cable car
ⓕ fast chairlift
Slow chairs & drags
have no symbol

Morzine
1000m/3,280ft

Avoriaz 1800

Interactive resort shortlist builder at **www.wtss.co.uk**

LIFT PASSES

Portes du Soleil

Prices in €

Age	1-day	6-day
under 16	29	148
16 to 19	37	188
20 to 63	41	209
over 64	35	178

Free under 5
Beginner Special pass
€22 a day

Notes
Covers lifts in all
Portes du Soleil
resorts; 5-hour pass
available

Alternative passes
Avoriaz only

GETTING THERE

Air Geneva 90km/
55 miles (2hr); Lyon
215km/135 miles
(3hr30)

Rail Cluses (42km/
26 miles) or Thonon
(45km/28 miles); bus
and cable car to
resort

UK PACKAGES

Alpine Answers, Club
Med, Crystal, Erna Low,
First Choice,
Independent Ski Links,
Inghams, Interactive
Resorts, Lagrange,
Neilson, Powder White,
Powder White Lite,
PowderBeds,
PV-Holidays.com, Rude
Chalets, Ski Collection,
Ski France, Ski
Independence, Ski
Total, Skitracer,
Skiweekends.com,
Thomson, White Roc,
Zenith
Ardent Family Ski
Company

excellent for all grades of intermediates, provided snow is in good supply on the lower slopes. Timid types not worried about pretty surroundings need not leave the Avoriaz sector: there are quiet and scenic blues to Les Prodains and the Arare and Chavanette sectors are gentle, spacious, above-the-treeline bowls. The Lindarets area is also easy, with pretty runs through the trees, but several reporters complain about long flat sections. Further afield, Champoussin has a lot of easy runs, reached without too much difficulty via Les Crosets and Pointe de l'Au. Better intermediates have virtually the whole area at their disposal. The runs down to Pré-la-Joux and L'Essert on the way to Châtel, and those either side of Morgins, are particularly attractive – as are the long runs down to Grand-Paradis near Champéry when snow conditions allow. Brave intermediates may want to take on the Swiss Wall at Chavanette, but Pointe de Mossettes offers a less challenging route to Switzerland.

FOR BEGINNERS ★★★★☆
Convenient and good for snow
The nursery slopes seem small in relation to the size of the resort, but appear to cope. The slopes are sunny, yet good for snow, and link well to longer, easy runs. The main problem can be the crowded pistes.

FOR BOARDERS ★★★★★
Plenty to keep you busy all week
Avoriaz is great for expert riders. As well as state of the art 'conventional' parks, there's The Stash in the forest (see 'Terrain parks'). For safe freeriding after a dump, head for the ungroomed snowcross pistes. For something more extreme, the long cliff-band accessed from the Arare lift is perfect for cliff drops of all sizes. It is well worth

hiring a guide to exploit the off-piste riding. There are plenty of easy pistes (though some flat sections, especially in the Lindarets area), and very few draglifts, making this a good choice for beginners and intermediates too.

FOR CROSS-COUNTRY ★★★☆☆
Varied, with some blacks
There are 45km of trails, mainly between Avoriaz and Super-Morzine, with others around Lindarets and Montriond.

MOUNTAIN RESTAURANTS ★★★★☆
Good choice over the hill
Editors' choice The hamlet of Les Lindarets in the next valley consists of countless rustic restaurants – it is a popular tourist spot in summer. The jolly Crémaillière (0450 741168) has wonderful chanterelle mushrooms and great atmosphere. But on a good day it's difficult to beat the terrace of the, er, Terrasse (0450 741617) – a recent reporter agrees ('fine cooking, friendly efficient service').
Worth knowing about The rustic Grenouille du Marais has good food and views. The table-service Abricotine, Refuge des Brocheaux, Marmottes, Rhodos ('good menu, good service, pleasant atmosphere') and Pas de Chavanette (good views) have also been tipped.

SCHOOLS

ESF
t 0450 740565
Evolution 2 (L'Ecole de Glisse)
t 0450 740218
Alpine (AASS)
t 0450 383491

Classes
(ESF prices)
6 days (2½hr am and pm) €175
Private lessons
From €40 for 1hr, for 1 or 2 people

CHILDCARE

Les P'tits Loups
t 0450 740038
8.45 to 5.15; ages 3mnth to 5yr; 6 days €231 inc. lunch
Children's Village Annie Famose
t 0450 740446
From age 3; 9am to 5.30

Ski schools
Take children from 4 to 12 (6 days €160)

ACTIVITIES

Indoor Health centre 'Altiform' (sauna, gym, hot tub), cinema, bowling
Outdoor Dog sledding, tobogganing, mountain biking on snow, ice diving, walking, snowshoeing, paragliding, ski jöring, snowmobiling, sleigh rides, helicopter flights

Phone numbers
From abroad use the prefix +33 and omit the initial '0' of the phone number

TOURIST OFFICE

www.avoriaz.com

SCHOOLS AND GUIDES ★★★★★
Positive reports

We lack new reports on group lessons, but a 2011 visitor booked the ESF for three days' private off-piste lessons – 'he was a guide, spoke good English and found good off-piste'. One visitor had 'inspirational' snowboard lessons with former pro Angelique Corrèz-Hubert through the Ecole de Glisse. The Avoriaz Alpine Ski School has British instructors and has been highly recommended, especially for 'quite excellent children's lessons'.

FOR FAMILIES ★★★★★
'Annie Famose delivers'

With snow everywhere and not a wheeled vehicle to be seen, Avoriaz has obvious appeal. Then there's the Village des Enfants, which takes children from age three and is run by ex-downhill champ Annie Famose. Its facilities are excellent – a chalet full of activities and special slopes with fun things such as teepees.

STAYING THERE

Alternatives to apartments are few. **Chalets** Inghams has a chalet for 12. Ski Total has four neighbouring chalets including Marie in its Platinum range (lovely-looking with lots of wood and a sauna). All are ski-in/ski-out.
Hotels There is one good hotel. ***Dromonts** (0450 740811) Owned by a celebrity French chef and in the *Hip Hotels* guidebook. 'Bit expensive but very nice, with excellent food.'
Apartments Pierre & Vacances' new luxury Amara apartments (see 'News') should add a new dimension to Avoriaz – reports, please. Ski Collection is featuring these along with two other smart new developments – Crozats and Electra (both with sauna, steam, jacuzzi, fitness). Until now, recommendations have included Sepia, Falaise, Balcons du Soleil and Alpages, and standards have been fairly basic. P&V, PowderBeds, Erna Low and Crystal all offer a wide selection.

EATING OUT ★★★★★
Some interesting options

There are supposedly 20 restaurants in the resorts, but there isn't much variety and the number is barely adequate – they get very busy. The Table du Marché in hotel Dromonts (sister to similarly cool places in St Tropez and Marrakech) is the best in town, but of course pricey. We had an excellent meal in the cosy wood-panelled Salle à Manger at the Garde-Manger deli, serving three-course fixed-price menus changing daily. Chapka (see below) does appetising snacks. A recent reporter recommends Trappeurs ('perfect filet, huge portions and great choice'). Earlier reporter tips include: the Bistro, the Cabane, the Fontaines Blanches for Savoyard food, Douchka for its 'excellent' Moroccan lamb shank, Intrêts for pizza, pasta and Savoyard fare, Au Briska for a cosy night out and Falaise for pizza.

APRES-SKI ★★★★★
The bars are fun

A few bars have a good atmosphere, particularly in happy hour. Chapka is a hip bar with TV, live music and pool ('excellent service, great tapas, toilets immaculate'). Fantastique is a popular, simple bar. Yeti and Tavaillon are past reader tips. For late-night dancing, we're told the Place has bands.

OFF THE SLOPES ★★★★★
Not much at the resort

There's not a lot to keep non-skiers interested – few shops, and pedestrians are not allowed to ride the chairlifts. The Altiform Fitness Center has steam, saunas and hot tubs. A recent reporter enjoyed bowling. The smart new Aquariaz – a huge new swimming pool facility – should be opening in 2012.

LINKED RESORT – 1200m
ARDENT

Ardent is a very quiet little place at the foot of the gondola up to Les Lindarets. It has the basics of life, including a bar and a ski shop. The Family Ski Company has seven chalets here, the most remote 150m from the gondola, the nearest only 30m from it.

LINKED RESORT – 1145m
LES PRODAINS

Les Prodains, at the foot of the cliffs on which Avoriaz sits, has a cable car that is principally a quick way in and out of the resort, for Morzine-based people to get to the Portes du Soleil circuit, and for Avoriaz-based people to sample the bright lights of Morzine in the evening. But there are also some chalets and small hotels, and there are runs from Haut Forts.

Chamonix

HQ of French and arguably European mountaineering, with a magnetic attraction for tourists and off-piste thrill-seekers alike

RATINGS

The mountains

Extent	★★★
Fast lifts	★★★
Queues	★★
Terrain p'ks	★★★
Snow	★★★★
Expert	★★★★★
Intermediate	★★
Beginner	★★
Boarder	★★★
X-country	★★★
Restaurants	★★
Schools	★★★★★
Families	★★

The resort

Charm	★★★★
Convenience	★
Scenery	★★★★★
Eating out	★★★★★
Après-ski	★★★★
Off-slope	★★★★★

RPI	100
lift pass	£200
ski hire	£115
lessons	£110
food & drink	£155
total	**£580**

NEWS

2011/12: A new mountain restaurant is planned in the Balme area, above the Charamillon mid-station.

2010/11: At Flégère, 35 new snow-guns were installed along the Evettes green run link towards Brévent.

The Grands Montets terrain park was redesigned and now suits all levels. A new ARVA avalanche training park opened in the same sector.

➕ A lot of very tough terrain, especially off-piste

➕ Amazing cable car to the Aiguille du Midi, for the famous Vallée Blanche

➕ Stunning views wherever you are

➕ Other resorts covered on extended lift pass, notably sunny Courmayeur

➕ Town steeped in Alpine tradition

➕ Lots of affordable hotels; an excellent short break destination

➖ Several separate mountains, widely separated; mixed ability groups are likely to have to split up

➖ Bad weather can shut the best runs

➖ Still some old lifts, and queues in key spots

➖ It's a busy town, with lots of road traffic – not a relaxing place

➖ Shady and cold in midwinter

➖ Few good mountain restaurants

Chamonix could not be more different from the archetypal high-altitude, purpose-built French resort. It hasn't been designed to deliver the smoothest possible experience to the widest possible market. It hasn't been designed.

You don't have to be an expert to enjoy the place – editor Gill once got away with taking his blue-run-skiing wife and novice kids for a week here. But it is the expert and the adventurous would-be expert who really must give Chamonix a permanent place on their shortlist. Be warned, though: there are those who try it and never go home – including lots of Brits.

THE RESORT

Chamonix is a long-established, year-round tourist town that spreads for miles along the valley in the shadow of Mont Blanc.

On either side of the centre, just within walking distance, are base stations of the cable car to the Aiguille du Midi, for the famous Vallée Blanche glacier run, and a gondola to Le Brévent. A third high-altitude area, La Flégère, is reached by cable car from the nearby village of Les Praz. There are then three other major ski areas.

At the top of the valley are the villages of Le Tour, at the foot of the Balme slopes (with an alternative base at Vallorcine), and Argentière, beneath the Grands Montets – for many, the core of Chamonix's appeal. These villages are described at the end of

the chapter, but their slopes are taken in to the main part of the chapter.

Down the valley is Les Houches. This is entirely described at the end of the chapter; its lifts are not covered by the standard Chamonix pass.

Regular free ski-buses link all these points but can get very crowded and aren't always reliable. There are also hourly trains (free with a guest card, and recommended by reporters) to Argentière, Vallorcine and Les Houches (where the lifts are a long walk from the station).

The Unlimited lift pass covers not only Les Houches but also Verbier in Switzerland and Courmayeur in Italy. The first is a major expedition; the second is much more interesting, not least because the weather can be good in Italy when it is lousy in Chamonix. And there are free shuttle

KEY FACTS		
Resort	1035m	
	3,400ft	
Slopes	1035-3840m	
	3,400-12,600ft	
Lifts		44
Pistes		155km
		96 miles
Green		16%
Blue		36%
Red		32%
Black		16%
Snowmaking		
		125 guns

buses through the Mont-Blanc tunnel several times daily.

Having a car is useful in lots of ways, and makes that outing to Verbier a practical proposition.

VILLAGE CHARM ★★★★☆
Lots of atmosphere
It's a bustling place, with scores of hotels and restaurants and shops selling everything from tacky souvenirs to high-tech climbing gear. The car-free centre is full of atmosphere, with cobbled streets and squares, beautiful old buildings, a fast-running river and pavement cafes. Away from the centre, there are lots of apartment blocks. There are some disused buildings, and traffic clogs the streets at times.

CONVENIENCE ★☆☆☆☆
You don't come here for that
The obvious place to stay for the full experience is close to central Chamonix, where you can be a short walk from the gondola to Brévent. But most people just reconcile themselves to life on the buses or trains.

SCENERY ★★★★★
As dramatic as it gets
The mountains above Chamonix are not just high – the mighty Mont Blanc is the highest in Western Europe – they are also truly spectacular. The ride up to the Aiguille du Midi is breathtaking in every sense (we've known people need to lie down for a while at the top).

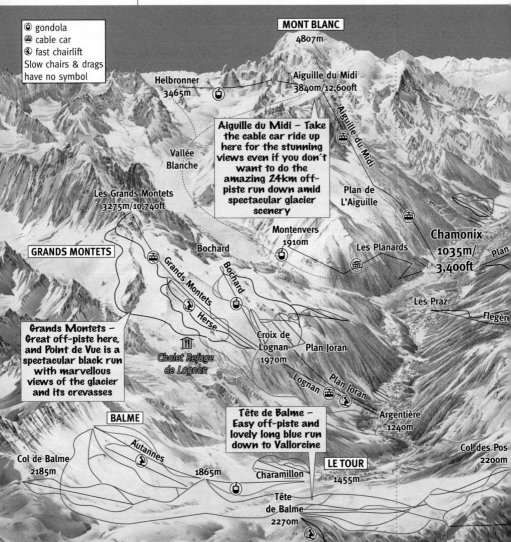

- gondola
- cable car
- fast chairlift
- Slow chairs & drags have no symbol

MONT BLANC
4807m

Helbronner
3465m

Aiguille du Midi
3840m/12,600ft

Aiguille du Midi

Aiguille du Midi – Take the cable car ride up here for the stunning views even if you don't want to do the amazing 24km off-piste run down amid spectacular glacier scenery

Vallée Blanche

Les Grands Montets
3275m/10,740ft

Plan de L'Aiguille

Chamonix
1035m/
3,400ft

Plan

Montenvers
1910m

Les Planards

GRANDS MONTETS

Bochard

Grands Montets

Bochard

Les Praz

Flégère

Herse

Grands Montets – Great off-piste here, and Point de Vue is a spectacular black run with marvellous views of the glacier and its crevasses

Chalet Refuge de Lognan

Croix de Lognan
1970m

Plan Joran

Plan Joran

Lognan

BALME

Autannes

Tête de Balme – Easy off-piste and lovely long blue run down to Vallorcine

Argentière
1240m

Col de Balme
2185m

1865m

Charamillon

LE TOUR
1455m

Col des Pos
2200m

Tête de Balme
2270m

THE MOUNTAINS

Practically all the slopes – with the notable exception of Les Houches – are above the treeline; there are some runs through woods to the valley, but the black ones from Brévent and Flégère, in particular, are often closed and unpleasantly tricky if open.

There is a valley piste map, also showing the individual areas. We've had mixed reports on signing, but complaints of poor marking ('virtually non-existent'; 'went off the edge of a cat-track in a near white-out'). In sectors other than Balme, classification of runs often understates difficulty – in particular, some of the blues would be classified red in other resorts.

EXTENT OF THE SLOPES ★★★
Very fragmented

There are several low beginner areas dotted along the Chamonix valley but there are five main areas.

The gondola for **Brévent** departs a short, steep walk or bus ride from the centre. There are runs on open slopes below the arrival point and a cable car goes on to the summit. There is a lift link to **Flégère**, also accessible via an inadequate old cable car from the village of Les Praz. These sunny areas give stunning views of Mont Blanc.

Up the valley at Argentière a cable car or chairlift take you up to **Les Grands Montets**. Chairs and a gondola serve open terrain above mid-mountain, but much of the best terrain

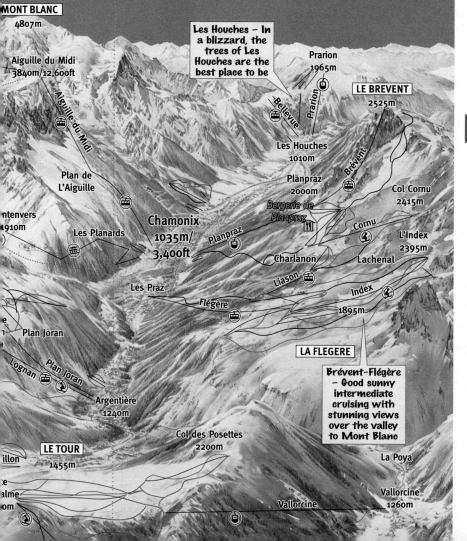

MONT BLANC
4807m

Aiguille du Midi
3840m/12,600ft

Aiguille du Midi

Les Houches – In a blizzard, the trees of Les Houches are the best place to be

Prarion
1965m

Bellevue

Prarion

LE BREVENT
2525m

Les Houches
1010m

Brévent

Plan de L'Aiguille

Planpraz
2000m

Col Cornu
2415m

ntenvers
1910m

Bergerie de Planpraz

Cornu

L'Index
2395m

Les Planards

Chamonix
1035m/
3,400ft

Planpraz

Charlanon

Lachenal

Les Praz

Liason

Index
1895m

Flégère

LA FLEGERE

Plan Joran

Lognan

Plan Joran

Brévent-Flégère – Good sunny intermediate cruising with stunning views over the valley to Mont Blanc

Argentière
1240m

Col des Posettes
2200m

La Poya

LE TOUR
1455m

illon

e
alme
om

Vallorcine

Vallorcine
1260m

↑ The peak on the left is the Grands Montets – adequately steep, as you can see; this is taken from the slopes of Balme

SNOWPIX.COM / CHRIS GILL

LIFT PASSES

Chamonix Le Pass

Prices in €

Age	1-day	6-day
under 16	35	175
16 to 64	41	205
over 65	35	175

Free under 4
Beginner no deals
Senior Over 75 50% of adult price

Notes
Covers Brévent, Flégère, Balme, Grands Montets except top cable car plus four small beginner areas; family reductions

Alternative passes
Mont-Blanc Unlimited (MBU) pass covers all the above plus Les Houches, Aiguille du Midi and Helbronner cable cars, Montenvers train, Lognan-Grands Montets cable car, and the Verbier (Switzerland) and Courmayeur (Italy) ski areas

is accessed by a further cable car of relatively low capacity, not covered by the standard lift pass (read 'Lift passes'). This shady area can be very cold in early season.

A little way further up the valley, the secluded village of Le Tour sits at the foot of the broad **Balme** area. A gondola goes up to mid-mountain, with a mix of drags and chairs above. There is also a lift up from Vallorcine.

FAST LIFTS ★★★☆☆
Not enough
Cable cars and gondolas serve each sector, but many need upgrading to be fully efficient. The handful of fast chairs are widely scattered.

QUEUES ★★☆☆☆
Ancient lifts, serious queues
Access to Brévent was transformed by the gondola upgrade in 2008. But this was only one of the valley's problem lifts. The ancient Flégère cable car can generate queues of an hour or more – to go down as well as up. The lifts out of Argentière build queues, and the chairlift appears to be on its last legs – it no longer operates from the main station, but starts a short way up the slope. At mid-mountain, the top cable car is a famous bottleneck. You can book slots in advance (on the spot or online), preferably the day before, or join the 'standby' queue, which we've found to be an effective alternative. There may be queues for the lift up to Balme at La Tour, too; it can be quicker to take the train to Vallorcine.

Crowded pistes can also be a problem in places – most notably at Lognan on the Grands Montets.

TERRAIN PARKS ★★★☆☆
In outlying areas
The Snow Bowl park on Grands Montets has been redesigned to incorporate features for all levels. The park is managed by the experienced HO5 crew, headed by ex-international pro Nico Watier. There are two main sections: the modules and a lower boardercross area, with courses for beginners and experts. Park features include kickers, seven rails and a step-up, step-down feature. The Fun Zone is designed for beginners wanting their first taste of air time. You can check the latest details at www.ho5park.com.

SNOW RELIABILITY ★★★★☆
Good high up; poor low down
The top runs on the north-facing Grands Montets slopes above Argentière generally have good snow, and the season normally lasts well into May. The risk of finding the top lift shut because of bad weather is more of a worry. There's snowmaking on the busy Bochard piste and the run to the valley. Balme has a snowy location, a good late-season record and snowmaking on the run down to the valley at Le Tour. The largely south-facing slopes of Brévent and Flégère suffer in warm weather, and the steep black runs to the resort are often closed. Don't be tempted to try these unless you know they are in good condition – they can be very tricky. Snowmaking was increased at Flégère this year to improve the link to Brévent. Some of the low beginners' areas have snowmaking. Piste grooming standards are generally respectable.

FOR EXPERTS ★★★★★
One of the great resorts

Chamonix is renowned for its extensive steep terrain and deep snow. To get the best out of the area you really need to have a local guide. There is also lots of excellent terrain for ski-touring on skins. Read the feature panel for more off-piste possibilities.

The Grands Montets cable car offers stunning views from the observation platform above the top station – if you've got the legs and lungs to climb the 121 steep metal steps. (But beware: it's 200 more slippery steel steps down from the cable car before you hit the snow.) The ungroomed black pistes from here – Point de Vue and Pylones – are long and exhilarating. The former sails right by some dramatic sections of glacier, with marvellous views of the crevasses.

The Bochard gondola serves a challenging red back to Lognan and a black to either Plan Roujon or the chairlift below. Shortly after you have made a start down the black, you can head off-piste down the Combe de la Pendant bowl.

At Brévent there's more to test experts than the piste map suggests – there are a number of variations on the runs down from the summit. Some are very steep and prone to ice. The runs in Combe de la Charlanon are quiet and include one red piste and excellent off-piste if the snow is good.

At Flégère there are further challenging slopes – in the Combe Lachenal, crossed by the linking cable car, say – and a tough run back to the village when the snow permits. The short draglift above L'Index opens up a couple of good steep runs (a red and a black) plus a good area of off-piste.

Balme boasts little tough terrain on-piste but there are off-piste routes from the high points to Le Tour, towards Vallorcine or into Switzerland.

FOR INTERMEDIATES ★★★★★
Plenty of better resorts

Chamonix is far from ideal for intermediates unless they relish challenging slopes and trying off-piste. If what you want is mile after mile of lift-linked cruisy pistes, go elsewhere.

For less confident intermediates, the Balme area above Le Tour is good for cruising and usually free from crowds. There are excellent shady, steeper runs, wooded lower down, on the north side of Tête de Balme, served by a fast quad. A lovely blue run goes on down to Vallorcine but it is prone to closure.

The other areas have some blue and red runs. Even the Grands Montets has an area of blues at mid-mountain. The step up to the red terrain higher

THE BEST OFF-PISTE SKIING IN THE WORLD?

Chamonix is renowned as an extreme sports Mecca, with arguably some of the best off-piste skiing in the world. And while thrill seekers and off-piste specialists are spoiled for choice, there is plenty for those looking for their first powder experience, too.

Les Houches and *Balme*, at opposite ends of the Chamonix Valley, are ideal for a first taste off the beaten track. The forested slopes of Les Houches are easy to navigate on bad-weather days, with gentle blue runs bringing you back to the valley. Balme's open slopes are perfect for a foray into deep snow in between the pistes, with firmer ground just a few reassuring metres away.

Snowboarders flock to *Flégère* after a snowfall, its array of boulders and drop-offs turning it into a massive terrain park. The open bowl of Combe Lachenal is easily accessed from the top of the Index lift, and the south-facing slopes of this ski area provide excellent spring skiing.

From the top of *Les Grands Montets* (3275m) skiing is mostly off-piste and on glacial terrain. The vast north-facing slope of the main face offers countless ways down, satisfyingly steep without being intimidating, with snow conditions that are often among the best in the valley. Off the back, there are several rewarding ways down to the Glacier d'Argentière. In the opposite direction you have access to the steep Pas de Chèvre run. Skiing under the colossal granite spire of Le Dru, with views of the Vallée Blanche, is an unforgettable experience. The Couloir du Dru and the Rectiligne are also on this face, reserved for the adventurous – with some slopes of 40/45˚.

These are just some of the off-piste options in the Chamonix valley, but the possibilities are endless. Together with heli-skiing on the Italian side of Mont Blanc and in neighbouring Switzerland, the wealth of off-piste on offer could keep you skiing for a lifetime. The Vallée Blanche is covered in a feature panel later in this chapter.

SCHOOLS

ESF
t 0450 532257

BASS
t 0845 468 1003 (UK)

Evolution 2
t 0450 555357

Gravity
t 0450 585092

Ski Sensations
t 0682 105922

Summits
t 0450 535014

Classes
6 half days: €190

Private lessons
€118 for 2hr, for 1 or 2 people

GUIDES

Compagnie des Guides
t 0450 530088

Chamonix Experience
t 0450 540936

up is quite pronounced, however.

If the snow and weather are good, confident intermediates can join a guided group and do the Vallée Blanche (read our feature panel).

FOR BEGINNERS ★★☆☆☆
Head for Le Tour
Chamonix is far from ideal for beginners too – there are countless better resorts in which to learn. There are limited but adequate nursery slopes either side of the town – Savoy, at the bottom of Brévent, and Les Planards on the opposite side (dark and cold in mid-winter). Moving on to longer runs means taking a lift up to Brévent or Flégère. La Vormaine, at Le Tour, is a much better bet: extensive, relatively high, sunny and connected to the slopes of the Balme area, where there are easy long runs to progress to. But it's 12km from Chamonix itself.

FOR BOARDERS ★★★☆☆
Leave it to the experts
The undisputed king of freeride resorts, Chamonix is a haven for advanced snowboarders who relish the steep and wild terrain. This means, however, that in peak season it's crowded and fresh snow gets tracked out very quickly. The rough and rugged nature of the slopes means it is not best suited for beginners, but for more experienced adventurous riders, willing to try true all-mountain riding. The easiest and arguably the most fun terrain is at the Balme area. If you do the Vallée Blanche, be warned: the usual route is flat in places. Check out former British champion Neil McNab's excellent extreme backcountry camps at: www.mcnabsnowboarding.com. Most lifts are cable cars, gondolas and chairs. However, there are quite a few difficult drags at Balme – though you can avoid these if you can hack the

cat tracks to take you to other lifts, says a reporter. There are terrain parks on Grands Montets and at Les Houches.

FOR CROSS-COUNTRY ★★★☆☆
A decent network of trails
Most of the 40km of prepared trails lie at valley level in and between Chamonix and Argentière. All the trails are shady and often icy in midwinter, and they fade fast in the spring sun. Catch the bus rather than ski between the Chamonix and Argentière areas, suggests a reporter, as the link is by 'steep and difficult trails'.

MOUNTAIN RESTAURANTS ★★☆☆☆
Mainly dull, lacking choice
Editors' choice On Brévent the Bergerie de Planpraz (0450 530542) is a wood and stone building with self- and table-service sections and good food; but it gets very busy. On the Grands Montets the tiny, rustic Chalet-Refuge de Lognan (06 8856 0354), off the Variante Hôtel run to the valley, has marvellous views and simple but satisfying food.
Worth knowing about On Brévent the little Panoramic at the top enjoys amazing views over to Mont Blanc, and the food is fine. There's a decent self-service place at Flégère. On the Grands Montets the Plan Joran has table- and self-service ('excellent pizzas'). There's also an indoor picnic area and good sunny terrace. Tucked away in the woods to skier's right of the home run, the Crémerie du Glacier is a cosy spot for a croûte. At Balme, at the top of the gondola from Le Tour, there's an adequate self-service and a picnic area. The charming Refuge du Col de Balme is a short hike beyond the lifts and offers a simple, rustic lunch spot.

SCHOOLS AND GUIDES ★★★★★
The place to try something new
The schools here are particularly strong in specialist fields – off-piste, glacier and couloir skiing, ski touring, snowboarding and cross-country. English-speaking instructors and mountain guides are plentiful.

At the Maison de la Montagne is the main ESF office and the HQ of the Compagnie des Guides, which has taken visitors to the mountains for 150 years. Both offer ready-made week-long 'tours' taking clients to a different mountain or resort each day.

CHILDCARE

Panda Club
t 0450 555357
From age 3

Piou Piou
0450 532257
Run by ESF; ages
from 3

Babysitter list
Available from the
tourist office

Ski schools
Take children aged 3
to 12 (6 half days
from €146 – ESF
price)

The slopes of Les
Houches give some
great views – this is
looking over the
village to the famous
aiguilles above
Chamonix ↓

For several years now there has been a branch of BASS here, with all British and Irish instructors, offering a range of options including a three-day off-piste package; reports welcome.

There are several other small, independent teaching and guiding operations.

FOR FAMILIES ★★✩✩✩
Very limited

Childcare is available from some of the ski schools. Evolution 2's Panda Club is used by quite a few British visitors; reports have been enthusiastic but the Argentière base can be inconvenient. Les Houches has better facilities, with a day care centre and children's club.

STAYING THERE

There is all sorts of accommodation, and lots of it.

Chalets Many chalets are run by small specialist operators. Quality tends to be high and value for money good. The big news this year is that Inghams are opening a 60-bed chalet-hotel overlooking the Savoy nursery slope at the bottom of Brévent, not far from the centre.

Hotels A wide choice, many modestly priced, the majority with no more than 30 rooms or so. Bookings for short stays are no problem – the peak season is summer. Momentum can fix whatever you want. Ski Weekends specialise in, er, weekends and offer Le Vert (see below) among others. Club Med has three linked buildings near the centre. Out at Le Lavancher is the 'hameau hôtelier' Les Chalets de Philippe (0607 231726) – a secluded cluster of lovingly furnished wooden chalets, most sleeping no more than three or four, with meals taken either in your own chalet on in a small central dining room.

*****Hameau Albert 1er (0450 530509) Smart, 100-year-old chalet-style Relais et Châteaux hotel with farmhouse annexe, now elevated to 5-star status. Restaurant with two Michelin stars. Pool.

****Mont-Blanc (0450 530564) Grand 19th-century place in a central location, currently closed for upgrading to 5-star status – re-opening 2012/13.

****Auberge du Bois Prin (0450 533351) A small modern chalet with a big reputation; great views; bit of a hike into town (closer to Brévent).

253

Chamonix

Interactive resort shortlist builder at **www.wtss.co.uk**

This is a trip you do for the stunning scenery. The views of the glacier and the spectacular rock spires beyond are simply mind-blowing. The standard run, although exceptionally long, is not steep – mostly gliding down gentle slopes (in places a bit too flat for snowboarders) with only the occasional steeper, choppy section to deal with. In the right conditions, it is well within the capability of a confident, fit intermediate. If snow is sparse, as it often is in early season, the run can be very tricky, with patches of sheet ice and exposed rocks, and narrow snow bridges over gaping crevasses. If fresh snow is abundant, different challenges may arise. Go in a guided group and check conditions before signing up at the Maison de la Montagne or other ski school offices. The trip is popular – on a busy day 2,500 people do it. To miss the crowds go very early on a weekday, or in the afternoon if you are a good skier and can get down quickly.

The cable car takes you to 3840m and the 3842 cafeteria (claimed to be Europe's highest restaurant) – check out the amazing view of Mont Blanc from here while you adjust to the dizzying altitude. Be prepared for extreme cold, too. A tunnel delivers you to the infamous ridge-walk down to the start of the run. Except at the start of the season, the walk is well prepared, with regular steps cut in the snow and fixed ropes to hang on to. If you have a backpack capable of carrying your skis, and crampons to give some grip, it's no problem; ask for them when you book your guide. Without those items, it can be tiring and worrying. Many parties rope up to their guides.

There are variants on the classic route, of varying difficulty and danger; on our last descent we did a mixture of the Petit Envers du Plan and the Vrai Vallée Blanche in 20cm of fresh snow under a blue sky with few other people around – it was absolutely magical, with hundreds of fresh-track turns among all that stunning scenery. Lack of snow often rules out the full 24km run down to Chamonix; a steep stairway (be warned: 311 steps) leading to a slow gondola links the glacier to the station at Montenvers, for the half-hour mountain railway ride down to the town.

GETTING THERE

Air Geneva 85km/ 55 miles (1hr15); Lyon 215km/ 135 miles (2hr45)

Rail Station in resort, on the St Gervais-Le Fayet/Vallorcine line. Direct TGV link from Paris on Friday evenings and at weekends

ACTIVITIES

Indoor Sports complex (swimming pool, sauna, steam room, tennis, squash, ice rink, fitness room, climbing wall), museums, library, cinemas

Outdoor Ice rink, snowshoeing, walking paths, tobogganing, dog sledding, paragliding

****Jeu de Paume** (Lavancher) (0450 540376) Alpine satellite of a chic Parisian hotel: a beautifully furnished modern chalet halfway to Argentière.
****Morgane** (0450 535715) Cool modern style; excellent restaurant, Michelin-starred; good location near Aiguille de Midi cable car; pool, sauna.
***Alpina** (0450 534777) Striking modern place just north of centre. Much the biggest in town – 138 rooms, most with balconies and mountain views. Sauna, hot tub.
***Croix-Blanche** (0450 530011) Small, simple hotel and brasserie in centre.
***Lanchers** (0450 534719) Near Flégère. Classic little 2-star hotel revitalised and upgraded to 3-star status by British owner – refurbished in 2009 and eight new rooms added in 2010. Tipped by readers for quality food and service.
***Mercure** (0450 530756) Next to the station. 'Comfortable rooms, friendly service, nothing too much trouble.' Has its own ski hire facilities.
***Prieuré** (0450 532072) Mega-chalet on northern ring-road – handy for drivers, quite close to centre. Sauna, hot tub.
***Vallée Blanche** (0450 530450) Smart, good-value B&B hotel, handy for centre and Aiguille du Midi.
Arve (0450 530231) Central, by the

river; small rooms. Smart restaurant.
Clubhouse (0450 984220) Boutique hotel in an art deco mansion, with a wide choice of ultra-modern rooms.
Le Vert (0450 531358) In Le Gailland, a mile from Chamonix, with en suite rooms for one to six people. 'Rocking bar, pool table, Sunday roast.'
Apartments Many properties in UK package brochures are in convenient but cramped blocks in Chamonix Sud. The Ginabelle is different – a Pierre & Vacances Premium residence near the station, with pool and fitness facilities, also available through Peak Retreats.

EATING OUT ★★★★★
Plenty of quality places
The top hotels all have excellent restaurants and there are many other good places. One or two advertising-based local guides give useful information.

It's some years since we ate at the hotel Morgane's Bistrot; it was excellent then, and now has a Michelin star. The Impossible is a favourite with us and with readers – a rustic chalet a short walk out of the centre with a varied menu; 'superb food, excellent value set menu, great wine list, friendly staff'. And we always enjoy the intimate Atmosphère, by the river, despite its two-sitting system. The 'cosy' Monchu does 'good Savoyard food and service at reasonable prices'. The Caleche gets booked up well ahead and is short on space but does 'excellent' traditional and more adventurous dishes.

Chamonix offers more variety than is normal in French resorts. Café de l'Arve is new at the hotel de l'Arve, offering a modern, creative menu. Alan Peru is a good Asian-fusion place that makes a refreshing change. Munchie is another ('small, good atmosphere').

Value-oriented reader tips include Pitz (pizza) and the Poele ('no frills, good basic food, good value').

APRES-SKI ★★★★✰
You have to know where to go
Chamonix attracts a lot of young Brits and Scans – blokes, mainly – wanting to après-ski hard after skiing hard. But it is not Austria, or even Méribel, where you can hear the top village bar as you ski home. It's a big town, and you have to know where to go. One exception is an obvious place at Flégère – the Rhododendrons, which has live music ('great atmosphere').

The tea-time après zone we hear most about is beside the train station. The Swedish-run Chambre Neuf gets 'packed, but not rowdy; live band from 5pm, dancing on the tables'. Elevation 1904, opposite, is a bit quieter.

Towards the river in Rue Whymper, the Lapin Agile is a relaxed wine bar doing Italian-style appetisers. Over the river to the left is Rue du Dr Paccard. The Pub gets packed with Brits ('on Burns night they piped in the haggis'). The Choucas opposite is equally popular for après and late night

action. Or turn right for the key Rue des Moulins. Bar'dUp is a small, relaxed place with live music and DJs. Mix is a 'wicked' cool DJ bar. Top tip for grown-ups is Privilege, a relaxed, woody, rustic-chic place with table service and live acoustic music. Soul Food is 'cool, French'.

Just outside the centre, MBC is a micro-brewery, now approaching its 10th anniversary; often has live bands. Real action enthusiasts may want to look at getting out of town to Le Vert.

There's a variety of nightclubs and discos. The Garage claims to be the biggest. The Cantina and the Choucas throb into the early hours, too.

OFF THE SLOPES ★★★★★
An excellent choice
There's more off-slope activity here than in many resorts. Everyone other than those with medical issues should ride the Aiguille du Midi cable car. Excursion possibilities are endless. The Alpine Museum is 'very interesting but all in French', the library has some English language books and there's a good sports centre with a pool, ice skating and ice hockey matches.

OUTLYING VILLAGE – 1240m

ARGENTIERE

This old village is in an impressive setting towards the head of the valley, 9km from Chamonix – the Glacier d'Argentière towers above it and the Aiguille du Midi and Mont Blanc still dominate the skyline.

There's a fair bit of modern development, and the road through to Le Tour, Vallorcine and Switzerland

UK PACKAGES

Argentière Action
Outdoors, Alpine
Answers, AmeriCan Ski,
BoardnLodge,
Collineige, Crystal,
Crystal Finest, Erna
Low, Independent Ski
Links, Interactive
Resorts, Lagrange,
Peak Retreats, Ski Club
Freshtracks, Ski France,
Ski Independence, Ski
Weekend,
TheWhiteChalet.com,
White Roc
Les Houches Alpine
Answers, Alpine Ski
and Golf Company,
AmeriCan Ski, Barrelli,
Bigfoot, Carrier, Erna
Low, Independent Ski
Links, Inghams,
Lagrange, Peak
Retreats, PowderBeds,
PV-Holidays.com, Ski
Collection, Ski
Expectations, Ski
France, Ski
Independence,
Skiweekends.com,
Zenith
Les Praz Bigfoot,
Chalet la Forêt
Vallorcine Erna Low,
Peak Retreats, Ski
Independence

Phone numbers
From abroad use the
prefix +33 and omit
the initial '0' of the
phone number

TOURIST OFFICES

Chamonix/Argentière
www.chamonix.com
Les Houches
www.leshouches.com

gets uncomfortably busy, but it still
has a rustic appeal.

The lifts to the Grands Montets are
about 600m from the slightly elevated
centre of the village. It's a fair hike,
but there are buses. Readers have
enjoyed the two central 2-star hotels –
the 'old fashioned, great value'
Couronne (0450 540002) and the
Dahu (0450 540155). But the two best
hotels, both 3-star, are out near the
lifts – the Grands-Montets (0450
540666), with pool, and the Montana
(0450 541499).

Le Cristal d'Argentière is a smart
Lagrange Prestige apartment
development, between the centre and
the lifts, with a decent pool (also
available through Peak Retreats).

There's a reasonable choice of
inexpensive, unpretentious restaurants
and bars in the central area. Best
known is the very popular Office,
offering a traditional Brit-pub
atmosphere and menu. Then there's
the Grenier ('amazing food'), Dahu,
Stone, Rusticana, Savoy, Rencard and
Slalom. More reports, please.

LE TOUR

Le Tour is a charming, unspoiled little
village 12km from Chamonix. The
valley's best nursery slopes are next to
the village, at La Vormaine. A gondola
from the edge of the village serves the
Balme slopes, an area of mainly easy
runs also reachable from Vallorcine.

VALLORCINE

Vallorcine is a small, but developing,
traditional mountain village over the
Col des Montets, near the Swiss
border and 16km from Chamonix. The
village shares with Le Tour the main
valley's Balme area.

A gondola and chairlift take you to
Tête de Balme. A gentle blue run leads
back to the village, but it is prone to
closure. There's a separate small area
of local slopes at La Poya.

Accommodation is mainly in
apartments. The newish 4-star L'Ours
Bleu, with pool and spa facilities, is
featured by Peak Retreats and Erna
Low. There's a limited choice of
restaurants and bars. The Buvette at
the station has been recommended for
drinks while waiting for the train back
to Chamonix (it takes 20 minutes).

LES HOUCHES

Les Houches is 6km down the valley
from Chamonix. The wooded slopes
are popular when bad weather closes
other areas, but are not covered by
the standard Chamonix pass. They
give great views of the looming Mont
Blanc massif.

It's a pleasant village, with an old
core around a pretty church, but
modern developments in chalet style
have spread along the road at the foot
of the slopes. Some of them are quite
a way from the widely separated lifts
going to opposite ends of the slopes –
a gondola and a queue-prone cable
car. On the mountain, all the lifts are
slow. There are some awkward links in
the network, and signing is poor.

There are nursery slopes and open,
gentle runs at the top of the main lifts
and long, worthwhile runs back
towards the village – blue, red and a
black that is Chamonix's World Cup
Downhill course: a fine intermediate
run, not deserving its black status.
There is a terrain park (Area 43) and a
chill-out zone. But there are lots of
draglifts and flat areas for boarders to
avoid. The ESF gets good reports for
children's classes – 'helpful, sensitive
to the child's need and flexible'.

Beyond the summit ridge is a very
gentle area with cross-country loops
and below that some pleasant, sunny
woodland runs with views across to
the slopes of Megève.

In good weather the slopes are
quiet, and the views superb from the
several attractive restaurants. The
Vieilles Luges is 'like a step back in
time; a great place'. Snow-cover on
the lower slopes is not reliable, but
there is a fair amount of snowmaking.

The village is quiet, but there are
some pleasant bars and restaurants.
Reporters have recommended the
3-star Hotel du Bois (0450 545035).
Granges d'En Haut (0450 546536) is
an exceptional development of luxury
chalets where you could self-cater but
there is also a smart restaurant; spa,
small pool. The hotel Bellevue, at the
top of the cable-car, which closed as a
hotel in the 1980s, has been rebuilt to
state-of-the-art eco-standards.

There are some good apartments
with pools, including CGH's Hameau
de Pierre Blanche (available through
Peak Retreats and Lagrange) and
Pierre et Vacances' Hauts de Chavants.

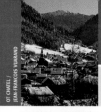

Châtel

A distinctively French base in an ideal position for exploring the huge Portes du Soleil circuit which spans the French-Swiss border

RATINGS

The mountains

Extent	★★★★★
Fast lifts	★★
Queues	★★★
Terrain p'ks	★★★
Snow	★★
Expert	★★★
Intermediate	★★★★
Beginner	★★★
Boarder	★★
X-country	★★★
Restaurants	★★★
Schools	★★★
Families	★★★

The resort

Charm	★★★
Convenience	★★
Scenery	★★★
Eating out	★★★
Après-ski	★★★
Off-slope	★★

RPI 95

lift pass	£200
ski hire	£115
lessons	£80
food & drink	£135
total	£530

NEWS

2011/12: The Rochassons double from Plaine Dranse to the link with Avoriaz is due to be replaced by a fast six-pack. Snowmaking is due to be increased in the terrain park and in the Plaine Dranse area. A five-hour pass, which lets you ski for any five consecutive hours in a day, is replacing the half-day pass.

➕ Very extensive, pretty, intermediate terrain on the Portes du Soleil

➕ Wide range of cheap and cheerful, good-value accommodation

➕ Pleasant, lively, French-dominated village, still quite rustic in parts

➕ Local slopes are among the best in the Portes du Soleil and relatively queue-free

➕ Easily reached. It's one of the shortest drives from the Channel, and close to Geneva

➖ Traffic congestion can be a problem at weekends and in peak season

➖ Both the resort and the slopes are low for a French resort, with the resulting risk of rain and poor snow, though snowmaking is now extensive

➖ Some main lifts are a bus ride from the village centre

➖ Best nursery slopes are reached by bus or gondola

Châtel offers an attractive blend of qualities much like that of Morzine – another established valley village in the Portes du Soleil. Morzine is a bit more polished, Châtel (with a claimed 30 working farms) more rustic. But its key advantage is that it is part of the main Portes du Soleil circuit. There is a gap in the circuit at Châtel, filled by buses; but this is more of an irritant to those passing through than for Châtel residents, for whom the excellent local bus services are part of the daily routine. On busy days it's worth trying the slopes of nearby La Chapelle-d'Abondance, which are pleasantly uncrowded.

THE RESORT

Châtel is a much expanded village near the head of the wooded Dranse valley, at the north-eastern limit of the huge French-Swiss Portes du Soleil ski circuit. It has two separate sectors of slopes, one linked to its French neighbour – high, purpose-built Avoriaz – and the other to two resorts in Switzerland: Morgins (on the Portes du Soleil circuit) and Torgon (not on the circuit).

A few kilometres down the valley is rustic La Chapelle-d'Abondance, with lifts into the Torgon slopes – covered at the end of this chapter.

VILLAGE CHARM ★★★
Rustic style, urban traffic
Châtel is still an attractive village, despite the inevitable expansion and reporters remark on the friendly locals. Modern, unpretentious chalet-style hotels and apartments rub shoulders with old farms where cattle still live in winter. But it is no rustic idyll: life revolves around two streets that are far from traffic-free: lots of visitors take cars, and the centre can get clogged with traffic – especially at weekends.

CONVENIENCE ★★
No perfect position
Although there is a definite centre, the village sprawls along the road in from lake Geneva and the diverging roads up the hillside towards Morgins and along the valley towards the Linga and Pré-la-Joux lifts. There is an excellent, frequent though sometimes crowded

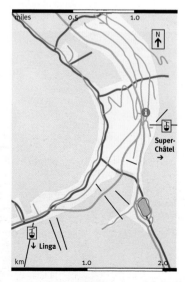

free bus service linking the sectors. Staying centrally helps with catching the ski-bus to the outlying lifts before it gets very crowded, and simplifies après-ski outings – the night bus finishes at 8pm most nights. But there is accommodation near the Linga lift, if first tracks are the priority.

SCENERY ★★★☆☆
Lots of variety
Châtel's broad valley setting is very scenic, with Linga providing a splendid backdrop and pleasantly woody slopes curving in both directions. The lifts above Torgon give great views over Lake Geneva. Around the Portes du Soleil circuit the dramatic Dents du Midi are constantly coming into view.

THE MOUNTAINS

Châtel sits between two sectors of the main Portes du Soleil circuit, each offering a mix of open and wooded slopes. For notes on the circuit see our special chapter on it.

EXTENT OF THE SLOPES ★★★★★
Two sectors to choose between
Directly above the village is **Super-Châtel** – an area of easy, open and lightly wooded slopes, accessed by a gondola or two-stage chair. From here you can embark on a clockwise Portes du Soleil circuit by heading to the Swiss resort of Morgins. Or you can head north for the slopes straddling a different bit of the Swiss border, above **Torgon** (great views of Lake Geneva).

An anticlockwise circuit starts outside the village with a lift into the

Linga sector – a gondola and newish six-pack from Villapeyron to Tête du Linga or a choice of fast chairs from Pré-la-Joux. The faster way to Avoriaz is via Pré-la-Joux, but the new chair means you can take the enjoyable Tête route without enduring a slow, cold chair ride. There is night skiing on the Linga run on Thursdays.

FAST LIFTS ★★☆☆☆
Luxurious Linga
Linga and the Plaine Dranse area are well served now that the Rochassons double is due to be replaced by a six-pack – but in the Super-Châtel sector the lifts beyond the access gondola are almost entirely slow chairs and drags, whether you head for Morgins or for Torgon. Hence our rating.

QUEUES ★★★☆☆
Bottlenecks have been eased
Queues have been eased throughout the Portes du Soleil in recent years by several fast new chairlifts. But queues form for the gondola to Super-Châtel when school parties gather and you can face queues to get down again if the sunny home slope is shut by poor snow. The slow Morclan chair at Super-Châtel has queues too, if the gondola is coming up full. Reporters have also found lengthy queues at the Tour de Don and Chermeu draglifts at certain times of day, causing difficulties for skiers rushing back to Super-Châtel to pick up children from ski school. A 2011 visitor has a gripe that the 'poor management of queues means that lifts go up at much less than full capacity at peak times'.

gondola
fast chairlift
Slow chairs & drags
have no symbol

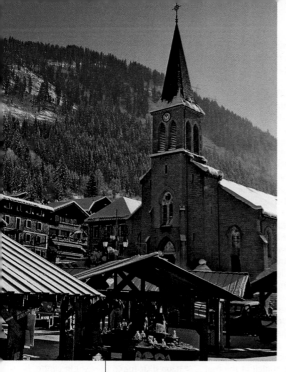

Interactive resort shortlist builder at www.wtss.co.uk

↑ Châtel is still an unpretentious mountain village at heart – this is the main square
OT CHATEL / JEAN-FRANÇOIS VUARAND

LIFT PASSES

Portes du Soleil

Prices in €

Age	1-day	6-day
under 16	29	148
16 to 19	37	188
20 to 63	41	209
over 64	35	178

Free under 5

Beginner points tickets for private village ski tows

Notes
Covers lifts in all Portes du Soleil resorts; 5-hour pass available

Alternative pass
Châtel only

TERRAIN PARKS ★★★
One size suits all
The Smooth Park at Super-Châtel has lines to suit both beginners and experienced freestylers, including rails, kickers, boxes, hips and boardercross.

SNOW RELIABILITY ★★
The main drawback
The main drawback of the Portes du Soleil as a whole is that it is low, so snow quality can suffer when it's warm. But a lot of snowmaking has been installed at Super-Châtel and on runs down to resort level. Linga and Pré-la-Joux are mainly north-facing and generally have the best local snow. The pistes to Morgins and towards Avoriaz get full sun.

FOR EXPERTS ★★★
Some challenges
The best steep runs – on- and off-piste – are in the Linga and Pré-la-Joux area. Beneath the Linga gondola and chair there's a pleasant mix of open and wooded ground, which follows the fall line fairly directly. And there's a serious mogul field between Cornebois and Plaine Dranse. Two pistes from the Rochassons ridge are steep and kept well groomed. On the way to Torgon from Super-Châtel, the Barbossine black run is long, steep and quite narrow and tricky at the top. There's

plenty of good lift-served off-piste to be explored with a guide: on a recent visit we did a great run from Tête du Linga over into the next (deserted) valley of La Leiche – see off-piste feature panel in Morzine chapter.

FOR INTERMEDIATES ★★★★
Some great local terrain
When conditions are right the Portes du Soleil is an intermediates' paradise. Good intermediates need not go far from Châtel to find amusement; Linga and Plaine Dranse have some of the best red runs on the circuit. The moderately skilled can do the Portes du Soleil circuit without problem, and will particularly enjoy runs around Les Lindarets and Morgins. Even timid types can do the circuit, provided they take one or two short cuts and ride chairs down trickier bits. But some blues are difficult when conditions are poor – in particular, one reporter witnessed skiers 'in tears' on the way down to Morgins from Châtel.

Visits to the Hauts Forts runs above Avoriaz are worthwhile. And note that the runs back to Plaine Dranse are real reds, and the Rochassons piste especially can get extremely busy at the end of the day.

Don't overlook the Torgon sector, which has some excellent slopes, including challenging ones.

FOR BEGINNERS ★★★
Three possible options
There are good beginners' areas at Pré-la-Joux (a bus ride away) and at Super-Châtel (a gondola ride above the village). And there are nursery slopes at village level if there is snow there. Reporters have praised the Super-Châtel slopes and lifts, which 'allow the beginner to progress' and 'safely practise' on gentle gradients away from the main runs. Getting up to them is a bit of an effort, though. The home run from Super-Châtel can be tricky – narrow, busy, steep at the end and often icy. The Pré-la-Joux slopes are less varied, with some steeper draglifts.

FOR BOARDERS ★★
Best for beginners – beware drags
Avoriaz is the hard-core destination in the Portes du Soleil. Châtel is not a bad place to learn or to go to as a budget option. But many lifts in the Super-Châtel sector are drags and reporters warn they can be a 'painful

SCHOOLS

ESF
t 0450 732264

Ecole de Ski Pro / skiing (ESI)
t 0450 733192

Henri Gonon
t 0450 732304

Ski Sensations
t 0450 813251

BASS
t 020 3286 3661 (UK)

Snow Ride (Ecole de Glisse)
t 0608 337651

Classes
(ESF prices)
6 half-days (2½hr am or pm) €123

Private lessons
€38 for 1hr, for 1 or 2 people

CHILDCARE

Mouflets Garderie
t 0450 813819
Ages 3mnth to 6yr;
8am to 7pm; full day with lunch €43

Club Piou Piou (Village des Marmottons)
t 0450 732264
Ages 3 to 6; 6 days €403 (with meals)

Le Jardin des Pitchounes
t 0450 813251
Ages 3 and 4

Ski schools
Generally take children from age 4 or 5 (ESF 6 half-days from €120)

GETTING THERE

Air Geneva 80km/ 50 miles (2hr)

Rail Thonon les Bains (40km/25 miles)

experience'. The Linga area has good, varied slopes and off-piste possibilities and more boarder-friendly chairlifts.

FOR CROSS-COUNTRY ★★★✩✩
Pretty, if low, trails
There are pretty trails (9km) along the river and through the woods on the lower slopes of Linga, but snow-cover can be a problem. When combined with La Chapelle-d'Abondance's trails, the total is 40km. The tourist office produces good maps with suggested routes and trail times.

MOUNTAIN RESTAURANTS ★★★✩✩
Some quite good local huts
A cluster of atmospheric huts can be found at Plaine Dranse – the Bois Prin, Tan ô Marmottes, Vieux Chalet ('low ceilinged, laden with teddies, run by a mad woman'), Chaux des Rosées, the 'excellent' Plaine Dranse self-service and Chez Denis have been recommended. In the Linga area the Ferme des Pistes is a cosy alpine barn, complete with stable-door. At Super-Châtel the Portes du Soleil at the foot of the Coqs drags is much better than the big place at the top of the gondola. The Escale Blanche is worth a visit. The chapter on Avoriaz has recommendations in the Lindarets valley, close by.

SCHOOLS AND GUIDES ★★★✩✩
Plenty of choice
There are six schools in Châtel, including a branch of BASS (British Alpine Ski & Snowboard School), which we have no reports of – please send one if you use them. The International school has been recommended by reporters, including visitors who had a private lesson that was 'one of our best ever' and a recent visitor's grandson who had 'so much more fun' than in previous lessons with the ESF. But the ESF has also been praised, with comments such as 'very helpful and customer-focused'.

FOR FAMILIES ★★★✩✩
Some good facilities
The Marmottons nursery has good facilities, including toboggans, painting, music and videos, and children (from three to six) are reportedly happy there. Ski Sensations has its own nursery area with a draglift and chalet at Linga.

STAYING THERE

This is emphatically a French resort. No big tour operators feature it.
Chalets A few catered chalets exist, including Chalet Le Dragon in La Chapelle-d'Abondance – see opposite.
Hotels Practically all the hotels are 2-stars, mostly friendly chalets, wooden or at least partly wood-clad. But there are some smarter places.
****Macchi (0450 732412) Smart, modern chalet, spacious comfortable rooms, 'excellent food'; small pool, spa; central.
***Fleur de Neige (0450 732010) Welcoming chalet on edge of centre; revamped for 2010/11; spa, sauna, steam, pool; Grive Gourmande restaurant is one of the best in town.
**Belalp (0450 732439) Simple chalet, small rooms, but 'very good food'.
**Choucas (0450 732257) Central location. 'Friendly owner.'
**Kandahar (0450 733060) One for peace lovers: a Logis by the river, a walkable distance from the centre.
**Lion d'Or (0450 813440) In centre, is fairly basic with a 'good atmosphere'.
**Rhododendrons (0450 732404) 'Great service, friendly, comfortable.'
**Tremplin (0450 732306) 'Excellent, good value. Owner cooks well but speaks no English.'
**Roitelet (0450 732479) 'Basic, good location, four-course dinner, made to feel part of the family.'
Apartments Many of the better places are available through agencies specialising in Châtel or in self-drive holidays. The Gelinotte (out of town but near the Linga lifts and children's village) and the Erines (five minutes from the centre; can also be provided catered) look good. The Avenières is right by the Linga gondola. Châtel's supermarkets are reported to be small and overcrowded, but there is a large supermarket out in the direction of Chapelle-d'Abondance.

EATING OUT ★★★✩✩
Fair selection
There is an adequate number and range of restaurants. The Macchi and Fleur de Neige hotels both have ambitious restaurants. We've also enjoyed the Table d'Antoine restaurant of the hotel Chalet d'Alizée, though it's a year or two since we were there. The rustic Vieux Four does ambitious dishes alongside Savoyard specialities and is approved by readers ('good

UK PACKAGES

Chalet Group, Connick, Interactive Resorts, Lagrange, Ski Addiction, Ski France, Ski Line, Ski Rosie, Skialot, Snow Finders, Snowfocus, Susie Ward **La Chapelle-d'Abondance** Chalet Le Dragon, Ski Addiction, Ski La Cote

ACTIVITIES

Indoor Spas in hotels, cinemas, library, bowling

Outdoor Ice rink, walks, cheese factory visits, ice diving, ice fishing, snowshoeing (special route map for Châtel and Morgins), paragliding

Phone numbers From abroad use the prefix +33 and omit the initial '0' of the phone number

TOURIST OFFICES

Châtel
www.chatel.com
La Chapelle-d'Abondance
www.lachapelle74.com

value and the best food we had all week'). The Poya is 'a blend of traditional and contemporary'. The Pierrier and the Fiacre ('pizzas good value') are more modest, everyday restaurants, good for families.

Out of town, the Ripaille, almost opposite the Linga gondola, is popular with locals and praised by reporters, especially for its fish. The hotel Cornettes in La Chapelle-d'Abondance is worth a trip (see right).

APRES-SKI ★★★★★
All down to bars
The Tunnel bar is very popular with the British and has a DJ or live music every night. The Avalanche is a very popular English-style pub with a 'good atmosphere and live music'. The Godille – close to the Super-Châtel gondola and crowded when everyone descends at close of play – has a more French feel. The 'small and cosy' Isba is the locals' choice, and shows extreme-sports videos. The bowling alley has a good bar.

OFF THE SLOPES ★★★★★
Less than ideal
Those with a car can easily visit places such as Geneva, Thonon and Evian. There are some pleasant walks, sleigh rides, you can visit the cheese factory or the two cinemas, or join in daily events organised by the tourist office.

The Portes du Soleil as a whole is less than ideal for non-skiers who like to meet their more active friends for lunch: they are likely to be at some distant resort at lunchtime and very few lifts are accessible to pedestrians.

DOWN-VALLEY VILLAGE – 1010m
LA CHAPELLE-D'ABONDANCE

This unspoiled, rustic farming community, complete with old church and friendly locals, is 5km down the valley from Châtel. It has its own quiet little north-facing area of easy wooded runs and a gondola on the outskirts links it to slopes between Torgon in Switzerland and Super-Châtel, and so the Portes du Soleil circuit. The Mousseron hut, near the Braitaz chairlift, is 'well worth a visit'.

Nightlife is virtually non-existent – just a few quiet bars, a cinema and torchlit descents. The Fer Rouge is a popular microbrewery, with live music.

The hotel Cornettes (0450 735024) is an amazing 2-star with 4-star facilities, including an indoor pool, a sauna, a steam room and hot tubs. It has been run by the Trincaz family since 1894 and has an atmospheric bar and an excellent restaurant with good-value menus. Look out for the showcases displaying puppets and dolls and for eccentric touches, such as ancient doors that unexpectedly open automatically.

Chalet Le Dragon is opposite the gondola into the main slopes and run as a catered chalet by its British owners. It has been fully renovated, with five bedrooms, new bathrooms and an outdoor hot tub. They run a minibus to and from other lifts too. A 2011 reporter was 'instantly wowed by the quality' and said it was 'the best chalet we have ever stayed in'.

Courchevel

Arguably the best of the half-dozen resorts that make up the famous Trois Vallées – with a choice of four different villages

262

RATINGS

The mountains

Extent	★★★★★
Fast lifts	★★★★
Queues	★★★★
Terrain p'ks	★★
Snow	★★★★
Expert	★★★★
Intermediate	★★★★★
Beginner	★★★★
Boarder	★★★★
X-country	★★★★
Restaurants	★★★
Schools	★★★★
Families	★★★★

The resort

Charm	★★
Convenience	★★★★
Scenery	★★★
Eating out	★★★★★
Après-ski	★★★★
Off-slope	★★★

RPI   120

lift pass	£220
ski hire	£150
lessons	£140
food & drink	£175
total	**£685**

NEWS

2011/12: A six-pack is due to replace the Plantrey fast quad at Courchevel 1850.

There are plans for new family fun zones above 1650 and 1550. Snowmaking is to be increased on the Murettes red run above Le Praz.

Among several hotel developments in 1850, a new complex (the K2), comprising seven luxury chalets, is due to open in December.

2010/11: Two 5-star hotels were elevated to the new 'Palace' category.

- ✚ Extensive, varied slopes
- ✚ Lots of slope-side accommodation
- ✚ Impressive snowmaking and piste grooming, and a decent lift system
- ✚ Partly wooded setting
- ✚ Choice of four very different villages
- ✚ Some great restaurants and top-notch hotels

- ▬ Unremarkable villages – downtown 1850, in particular, is disappointing
- ▬ Very high prices in 1850 and in mountain restaurants generally
- ▬ The French feel has been lost, with half the visitors now from abroad
- ▬ Not great for the indolent non-skier unless glitzy shops are your thing

Courchevel's ski area is the most compelling sector of the famous Trois Vallées, the biggest linked ski area in the world; if we're heading for the 3V, more often than not we'll head for Courchevel.

But it's not one destination, it's four. Swanky 1850 catches the headlines, with its airstrip, ritzy hotels and six Michelin-starred restaurants. The other villages – 1650, 1550 and 1300 – have none of 1850's pretensions and high prices.

There are plenty of afforable catered chalet holidays on sale here, even (thanks to the miracles worked by UK tour ops) in 1850. Sadly, there are no affordable lunches. So do lunch above La Tania, or above Les Menuires, or in St-Martin.

THE RESORT

Courchevel 1850 was one of the first French resorts to be purpose-built in the years immediately after World War Two. The other resort units were developed later, although they already existed as villages or hamlets.

A road winds up from 1300 (still more often referred to as Le Praz) past 1550 (the original Courchevel), through 1650 (formerly Moriond) to 1850. The numbers are not much of a guide to altitude; 1850 ought to be 1750, strictly speaking.

1850 is big enough to have several distinguishable quarters. The main lift base and the central area around it is La Croisette; the resort spreads widely across the hillside to the left through the chalet-filled suburbs of Cospillot and Nogentil to the Altiport, the resort's famously hazardous little airstrip. Above these suburbs is the Jardin Alpin, a forested area with some of the swankiest hotels (and more modest chalets and apartments), served by its own gondola. On the opposite, right-hand side of La Croisette is another little 'downtown' area, with the suburbs of Chenus above it and Plantret below.

The other resort villages are smaller and simpler. The main part of 1650 has grown up along the road up to

1850: on one side, at the foot of the slopes, is a series of apartment blocks, plus an area of more traditional development around the lift base area; and on the other side, individual chalets spreading down the hill. Then there is an area of more modern chalet development beside the

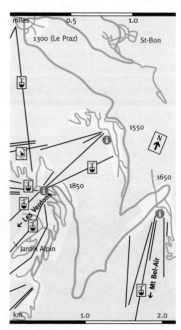

slopes, the upper part known as Belvedère. 1650 has its own distinct sector of slopes, connected to 1850. 1550 is a bit of a backwater, with a few blocks and many more individual properties, directly below 1850. Le Praz is an old village on a plateau at the bottom of wooded slopes.

La Tania, built for the 1992 Olympics and near Le Praz, gets its own chapter. With a car, Champagny is easily reached, linked to La Plagne.

VILLAGE CHARM ★★
Not a strong point

Courchevel 1850 has most of the smart hotels, nightlife and shops, and you would expect it to be a pretty smooth place in general. The reality is a let-down; when compared with other smart resorts, 1850 does not impress.

Although improvements are in train, the approach is dreary, and at La Croisette you are confronted by the backside of the main lift station building, complete with garage entrances. Past this point, things improve: the streets are lined by smart shops and jolly restaurants. But the nearest thing to a central focus is where a hairpin bend on the busy road through the resort to the affluent suburbs touches the slopes. The areas above the centre are more pleasant – in places, peacefully rustic.

Despite the through-road to 1850, central 1650 is more pleasant. Most visitors don't find traffic intrudes, and there is a quiet square off the main road with traditional-style buildings. There are plenty of quietly situated chalets. 1550 is a pleasantly quiet, spacious mini-resort, bypassed by the road to 1850. Le Praz suffers from through-traffic too, but away from the road is a low-key rustic place, with a friendly atmosphere, relatively unspoilt despite expansion for the Olympics – the ski jump is a prominent legacy.

CONVENIENCE ★★★★
Largely ski-in, partly ski-out

The villages all have lifts into the slopes, with much of the lodging close by, but in all cases you need to be careful about location if you want to avoid walks, sometimes with hills involved. 1850 has several pistes running through it, and a high proportion of ski-in/ski-out lodgings in all parts except the very centre, where you just plod to the lift base. 1550 and 1650 are essentially arranged

along the bottom of the slopes, with lifts immediately above most of the lodgings – so they may be ski-in, but are more likely to be plod-out. But both villages have some lodgings beside the home slope as well. 1650 has a lot of chalets well below the slopes, but has built impressive escalators up the steep hill to the lift base area. Le Praz is in general the least convenient place: the lifts start a short walk outside the village. Frequent free buses link the villages.

SCENERY ★★★
Go high for the best of it

Most of the villages enjoy a pretty woodland setting but the broad, open slopes above them have the best views to Mont Blanc and over the valley to Champagny and Bellecôte.

THE MOUNTAINS

Although there are plenty of trees around the villages, most of the slopes are essentially open, with the notable exception of the runs down to 1550 and to 1300, and the valley between 1850 and 1650.

Reporters have no complaints of the piste map or general signposting, but one 2011 visitor found information on piste closures at the top of lifts inadequate.

EXTENT OF THE SLOPES ★★★★★
Huge variety to suit everyone

A network of lifts and pistes spreads out from 1850. The main axis is the **Verdons** gondola, leading to a second gondola to La Vizelle and a nearly parallel cable car up to La Saulire. These high points of the **Saulire-Creux** sector give access to a wide range of terrain above Courchevel (including a number of couloirs), to Méribel and thus the whole of the Trois Vallées. Next to the Verdons gondola is the Jardin Alpin gondola, which serves the higher hotels until 8pm but also links to lifts and pistes beyond.

To the right looking up, the Chenus gondola goes towards the **Loze-Praz** sector, a second link with Méribel. Runs go back to 1850, and through the woods to La Tania and 1300.

There are various ways up from 1650 to the minor high-points of Bel Air and Signal, and on into the **Chanrossa** sector. This sector has links to Saulire-Creux at two points – Praméruel and Creux.

Le Ski
the chalet specialists

COURCHEVEL
VAL D'ISÈRE AND LA TANIA

❄ Five stunning new chalets
❄ Hot tub, pool, steam rooms, saunas
❄ Civilised Sunday flights to Chambéry
❄ Free ski guiding

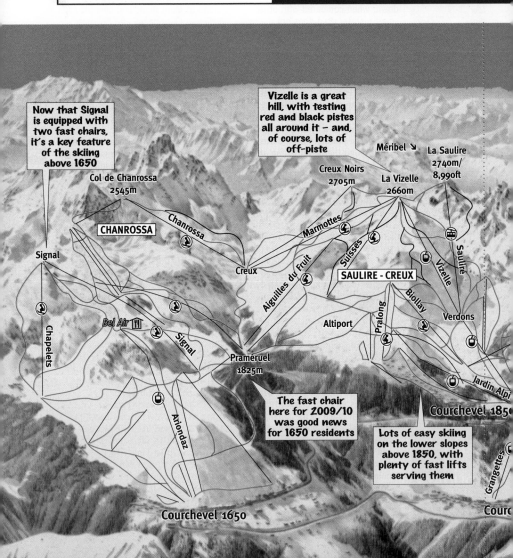

Now that Signal is equipped with two fast chairs, it's a key feature of the skiing above 1650

Vizelle is a great hill, with testing red and black pistes all around it – and, of course, lots of off-piste

Méribel ↘

La Saulire
2740m/
8,990ft

Creux Noirs
2705m

La Vizelle
2660m

Col de Chanrossa
2545m

Chanrossa

CHANROSSA

Creux

Marmottes

Suisses

Saulire

Vizelle

Signal

Aiguilles du Fruit

SAULIRE - CREUX

Chapelets

Bel Air

Signal

Prolong

Biollay

Verdons

Altiport

Praméruel
1825m

Jardin Alpi

Courchevel 185.

The fast chair here for 2009/10 was good news for 1650 residents

Lots of easy skiing on the lower slopes above 1850, with plenty of fast lifts serving them

Ariondaz

Grangettes

Courchevel 1650

Cour

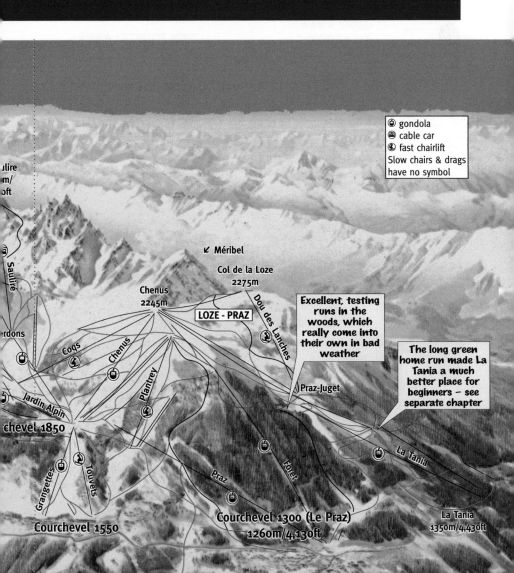

gondola
cable car
fast chairlift
Slow chairs & drags
have no symbol

↙ Méribel

Col de la Loze
2275m

Chenus
2245m

LOZE - PRAZ

Dou des Lanches

Saulire
m/
oft

rdons

Coqs

Chenus

Plantrey

Jardin Alpin

chevel 1850

Grangettes

Touvels

Praz

Excellent, testing
runs in the
woods, which
really come into
their own in bad
weather

The long green
home run made La
Tania a much
better place for
beginners – see
separate chapter

Praz-Juget

Forêt

La Tania

Courchevel 1550

Courchevel 1300 (Le Praz)
1260m/4,130ft

La Tania
1350m/4,430ft

GETTING THERE

Air Geneva 195km/ 120 miles (2hr45); Lyon 195km/ 120 miles (2hr30); Chambéry 110km/ 70 miles (1hr30)

Rail Moûtiers (24km/ 15 miles); transfer by bus or taxi

OT MERIBEL / JM GOUEDARD

Vizelle is a superb hill, with three fast lifts serving half a dozen testing pistes and acres of off-piste ↘

FAST LIFTS ★★★★☆
Plenty of them

You will occasionally find yourself on a slow chair, but there are only a couple of places where slow lifts are not avoidable. One is Col de la Loze; the other, more importantly, is the 1650 side of Chanrossa, where the best long, easy blues in the resort are served by drags. The piste map makes the distinction between slow and fast chairs, which helps. The Roc Mugnier six-pack has greatly improved access to 1650. A bit of history is being made this year, with a six-pack replacing the Plantrey chair, said to be the world's first detachable quad, installed 28 years ago.

QUEUES ★★★★☆
Not a problem

The list system is impressive, and even in peak season queues are minimal. But there can be a build-up at 1850 as the ski school gets going. The Biollay chair is very popular with the ski school (which gets priority) and is the main lift for the terrain park, so it can be well worth avoiding. At 1650, the gondola may have peak-time queues; an upgrade is in the pipeline.

TERRAIN PARKS ★★☆☆☆
Freestyle for all the family

Since slimming down the former Plantrey Snowpark beside 1850 and Loze Snowcross above the resort, the single Family Park below Verdons has been developed to offer something for everyone. Each year it gains more features. Reached by the Biollay chair or the Rocher de l'Ombre drag, it has lines to suit different levels, with a variety of jumps and obstacles including, at certain times, an airbag jump. Meanwhile, the Courchevel website still continues to describe the parks as they were in 2009, which gives a clue to the resort's attitude. Two smaller 'fun zones' are planned for 2011/12, above 1650 and 1550.

SNOW RELIABILITY ★★★★☆
Very good

The combination of Courchevel's northerly orientation, its height, an abundance of snowmaking and excellent grooming usually guarantees good snow down to at least 1850 and 1650. The snow is usually much better than in Méribel, where the slopes get more sun. The runs to 1300 are prone to closure in warm weather.

Courchevel's image is of upmarket luxury and pampered piste skiing. But it is a great resort for off-piste too. Manu Gaidet is a Courchevel mountain guide and a ski instructor with the Courchevel ESF. He is also one of the world's top freeriders, and won the Freeride World Championship three years running. We asked him to pick out a few of the best runs. Always go with a guide.

For a first experience off-piste, the Tour du Rocher de l'Ombre is great. Access is easy from the left of the Combe de la Saulire piste, and you are never far from the piste. It is very quiet, the slope is very broad and easy and you get a real sense of adventure as you plan your way between the rocks. And the view of the Croix des Verdons is impressive. Keep to the left for the best snow.

The Chanrossa chairlift opens up several routes. Les Avals is one of my favourites, involving a short climb to the ridge to the south. This run is not technically difficult and is particularly beautiful in spring conditions. Another possibility is to traverse towards the Aiguille du Fruit, and pick your spot to start skiing down to Creux. And there is Plan Mugnier, a shady run with normally very good snow, but more difficult – for experienced off-piste skiers only – and starting with a 20-minute hike.

Le Curé is in the Saulire area: this narrow gully starts under a towering rock and offers a steady 35° slope; it is only for expert skiers who don't mind climbing to the Doigt du Curé starting point.

ACTIVITIES

Indoor Ice rink, bowling, climbing wall, exhibitions, concerts, cinemas, language and computer courses; cookery courses, library; in hotels: health and fitness centres (swimming pools, saunas, steam room, hot tub, water therapy, weight training, massage)

Outdoor Hang-gliding, helicopter flights, paragliding, flying lessons, go-karts on ice, snowshoeing, snowmobile rides, ice karting, ballooning, walking on cleared paths, tobogganing

FOR EXPERTS ★★★★☆
Entertaining pistes, and ...

There is plenty to interest experts, even without considering the rest of the Three Valleys. The most obvious expert runs are the shady couloirs you can see on the right near the top of the Saulire cable car. All three main couloirs were once black pistes (some of the steepest in Europe), but only the Grand Couloir remains a piste – the widest and easiest of the three, but reached by a narrow, bumpy, precipitous access ridge.

The shady slopes of La Vizelle and Creux Noirs are not seriously steep, but all the runs – tough reds and not-tough blacks, offer a worthwhile challenge. If you like groomed blacks in the early morning, keep an eye on the grooming notices at lift bases to see when Suisses or M is groomed. Chanrossa often seems to have the most serious bumps. The blacks above Le Praz can be great fun, too – again, they are not seriously steep, but offer a vertical of almost 1000m.

There is a huge amount of off-piste terrain, including lots next to the pistes. The runs off Dou des Lanches through the trees down to La Tania and off the top of Creux Noir (via a little walk) down to join up with the Creux piste are recommended. The wooded areas in general are great for bad weather.

In good snow conditions you can ski all the way down (around 2000m vertical) from La Saulire to Bozelm.

There is plenty of other off-piste terrain in this valley to try with a guide – see the feature panel.

FOR INTERMEDIATES ★★★★★
Paradise for red-run skiers

For confident intermediates, Courchevel's local slopes are simply fabulous. Every sector has long, testing red runs and easy blacks, and there is abundant easy off-piste to experiment in. There are too many excellent runs to list; every high-point – Signal, Chanrossa, Vizelle, Creux Noirs, Saulire, Chenus, Loze – offers one, two, three, four notable descents.

For timid intermediates, we're not so enthusiastic. The red runs from Vizelle and Saulire can be quite testing, especially late in the day. But there are some excellent sectors to focus on. The long, narrow sector of blue slopes above 1650 is superb, and there is an array of excellent blue slopes above and below 1850 – the Biollay and Pralong fast chairs are the ones to head for here. On the ridge separating 1850 from La Tania, the Crêtes run and chair offer a great quiet area to build confidence on good snow. The runs on down to La Tania from here are long, rolling cruises, but how easy they are depends crucially on snow conditions.

FOR BEGINNERS ★★★★☆
Great graduation runs

There are excellent nursery slopes above both 1650 and 1850. At 1650, there are short drags right above the village. At 1850 there is a small but good beginner area in the Jardin Alpin, reachable by the gondola, and an excellent bigger one at Pralong, near the airstrip. Absolute beginners have to get to this by road. All together

Courchevel

267

Interactive resort shortlist builder at **www.wtss.co.uk**

Weekly news updates and resort links at www.wtss.co.uk

SCHOOLS

ESF in 1850
t 0479 080772

ESF in 1650
t 0479 082608

ESF in 1550
t 0479 082107

Supreme
t 0479 082787
(UK: 01479 810800)

New Generation
t 0479 010318
0844 484 3663 (UK)
www.skinewgen.com

Magic
t 0479 010181

Oxygène
t 0479 090399

BASS
t 0479 083387

RTM
t 0615 485904

Classes
(ESF 1850 prices)
6 days (2½hr am and
pm): €318

Private lessons
From €95 for 1½hr

GUIDES

Guides de Courchevel
t 0623 924612

there are seven free beginner lifts – an excellent arrangement. 1550 and 1300 have small nursery areas; but the former is quite steep. There are some excellent long runs to progress to.

FOR BOARDERS ★★★★
Upmarket all-rounder
Despite being an upmarket resort, Courchevel has always been popular with snowboarders. There are miles of well-groomed pistes, good freeride terrain and the lifts are in general very modern and quick, with few drags. The resort's freestyle facilities are not what you would call hard-core, though. The big snowboard hangout in 1850 is Prends ta Luge et Tire Toi.

FOR CROSS-COUNTRY ★★★★
Long wooded trails
Courchevel has a total of 60km of trails. 1300 is the most suitable village, with trails through the woods towards 1550, 1850 and Méribel. Given enough snow, there are also loops around the village.

MOUNTAIN RESTAURANTS ★★★
Fine if you can afford them
Mountain restaurants are plentiful and pleasant, but uncomfortably pricey. Fortunately, the local lift pass permits lunch above La Tania; of course the 3V pass gets you to Les Menuires. The piste map does not name restaurants.
Editors' choice The Bel Air (0479 080093), above 1650, has always stood out for its warm welcome, efficient service, good food, splendid tiered terrace and (by local standards) reasonable beer and cheap house wine. But even here the food is unpleasantly expensive; and while most reporters still approve, a repeat visitor in 2011 was disappointed and reckons the place is going downhill. Keep the reports coming. If we're feeding the family, we head for Bouc

Blanc, above La Tania.
Worth knowing about We had a good lunch at Pilatus, just below the Altiport; efficient table service and huge portions. The self-service Chenus is 'reasonably priced compared to other establishments'; 'good food and service'. The Soucoupe at Loze is a traditional place and 'a real treat'. There are some very good places on the pistes running down to Croisette. The traditional Bergerie is tipped. Chalet de Pierres is famously pricey, but we confess to calling in for an occasional treat, and a reporter confirms it is 'as good as ever'.

SCHOOLS AND GUIDES ★★★★
Plenty of choice
Courchevel's branches of the ESF add up to the largest ski school in Europe, with over 700 instructors. It is conscientiously managed, and works hard to ensure the language skills of its instructors. Complaints are rare. But we hear more about smaller schools.

Last season two of our editorial team were able to endorse the many positive reports we have received on New Generation (run by top British instructors): 'Brilliant. The instructor did just what we had hoped – building up our confidence so that we could then enjoy the ski area.' Reporters also praise another Brit-based outfit, RTM Snowboarding: 'Excellent. My private lesson was the best ever.' BASS is an established British school, operating in nine resorts including Courchevel and Méribel. Classes are small. Reports welcome.

Magic Snowsports Academy is run by an Anglo-French team and has native English-speaking instructors.

The Bureau des Guides runs all-day off-piste excursions. There's also an area at the foot of Les Suisses piste with transceiver practice and avalanche rescue sessions with dogs.

CHILDCARE

Village des Enfants (1850)
t 0479 080847
Ages from 18mnth

Les Ptits Pralins de Moriond (1650)
t 0479 063472
Ages from 18mnth

Maison des Enfants (1550)
t 0479 082107
Ages from 18mnth

Ski schools
Most offer lessons from age 3 or 4 (ESF 1850 prices €318 for 6 days)

OT COURCHEVEL / R&M GRAINGIER
The heart of 1850 – looking across the Croisette 'front de neige' from one downtown area to the other ↓

FOR FAMILIES ★★★★
Lots of suitable options

Courchevel is a good choice for families; there is lots of convenient lodging and gentle slopes. The 'Magnestick' system, to hold children securely on chairlifts, is being fitted to all fast lifts. The ESF Club des Piou-Piou at 1650 is reportedly 'very well run and a good introduction to skiing for children'. Several UK chalet operators run nurseries. Family specialist Esprit operates in 1850 – read 'Chalets', next.

STAYING THERE

Chalets There are lots available – specialist agents list dozens of them.

1650 is UK chalet central. Le Ski has operated here for almost 30 years and now has 11 chalets, from comfortable to classy. Among these are five small chalets in a single development added this year, with spacious lounges and a shared swanky spa area with hot tub and wave pool. Ski Olympic is also a 1650 specialist, with the central Avals chalet-hotel (complete with Rocky's bar) plus two large chalets. It's good to hear from a

reporter that the inimitable Dave and Megan, the longest-serving chalet hosts in the Alps, are still on top form in chalet Rikiki.

Skiworld has four chalets in 1650 too, including the traditional but smooth Estrella, with hot tub, and two in 1550. The biggest presence here is Ski Power with the 40-bed chalet-hotel Chanrossa as well as two chalets. It also has three properties down in 1300, where Crystal also has two.

Ski Total has a hotel-sized chalet bang in the centre of 1650, but most of its capacity is in 1850, where it has three chalets, one very central, and a fairly central 60-bed chalet-hotel.

Also in 1850, sister company Esprit, the family specialist, has a chalet-hotel with good pool right by the lifts at Pralong. Flexiski has the recently renovated chalet-hotel Saint Louis a short stride from the Bellecôte piste. We had an excellent short stay there last season. Inghams has three chalets, and a central 70-bed chalet-hotel; it has also added two chalets in 1650 this year.

There are some genuinely luxurious chalets in 1850 from operators like Consensio, Kaluma, and Supertravel.

Courchevel

Hotels There are more than 40 hotels in Courchevel, mostly at 1850 and many of them very swanky. Two were awarded the new 'Palace' rating this year – the Cheval Blanc and the Airelles – to distinguish them from the 5-star standard invented only a few years back; a dozen hotels now hold 5-star status. The prices of the top places give new meaning to the word 'exorbitant' – it is possible to pay £1,000 per person per night without too much difficulty, though you can of course pay a lot less. In our listings we concentrate on more affordable places – and are pleased to have a 2-star recommendation this year.

COURCHEVEL 1850
*****Sivolière (0479 080833) Chalet set among pines on the western edge of the village, with a reputation for friendly service despite the stars.
****Bellecôte (0479 081019) A bit of Alpine atmosphere as well as luxury. Close to the Bellecôte piste.
****Chabichou (0479 080055) Distinctive white building, right on the slopes; family-run, friendly and rustic, with very good food plus the option of a restaurant with two Michelin stars. New restaurant and spa due for 2012.
***Courcheneige (0479 080259) On the Bellecôte piste, with a rustic restaurant.
**Tovets (0479 080333) Good value hotel right at La Croisette. 'Spacious rooms, plentiful food, delightful staff, perfect location – why pay more?' says a 2011 visitor.
COURCHEVEL 1650
*****Manali (0479 080707) Smart and welcoming; slope-side, just above the gondola, with terrace; spa and pool (open to the public).
****Portetta (0479 080147) Neat place on the snow, with a good restaurant, pool – and the most civilised ski/boot room this side of the Atlantic.

Ski Collection
Major Resorts Great Prices

3 & 4 Star Self-Catering Ski Apartments

SkiCollection.co.uk
0844 576 0175
ABTA Bonded W5537

Phone numbers
From abroad use the prefix +33 and omit the initial '0' of the phone number

***Seizena** (0479 082636) Stylish and central (over road from the gondola).

COURCHEVEL 1550
***Flocons** (0479 080270) Handsome chalet near the Tovets six-pack and the piste from 1850.

COURCHEVEL 1300 (LE PRAZ)
***Peupliers** (0479 084147) Traditional, smart, good restaurant.

Apartments Courchevel may not be apartment-dominated, but there is plenty of choice. If you want to self-cater in real style, take a look at the chalets in the resort literature. Ski Amis has apartments in several parts of the resort. The best big residences are the Montagnettes Chalets de la Mouria above 1650 (apartments and semi-detached chalets), with sauna and hot tub, and the renovated Chalets du Forum in central 1850 – a Pierres & Vacances Premium residence. Erna Low has a good range of properties, including the very attractive Lofts above the Portetta hotel in 1650. Check out Ski Collection, too.

EATING OUT ★★★★★
Pick your price
You can eat very well here, but you have more choice if you have a fat wallet. A non-comprehensive pocket guide is distributed. In 1850 there are no fewer than three places with two Michelin stars – two of the swankiest hotels, and the more appealing Chabichou. Nearer to planet Earth are the one-stars – the Bateau Ivre, the Table du Kilimandjaro and the Strato.

In view of the prices it's perhaps not surprising that we are getting few reports these days. The Refuge is tipped this year – 'really good, with efficient service, generous portions, good Savoyard food'. Other recently tipped places include the Cloche ('traditional dishes at reasonable prices'); the 'refined' Cendree for excellent Italian food; the 'rustic' Anerie; the Chapelle for open fire grills; the self-explanatory Fromagerie; the 'delightful' Genepi; and the Saulire (aka Chez Jacques).

In 1650 the cosy Eterlou gets the readers' vote – 'warm, friendly, super food' – closely followed by the nearby Petit Savoyard (pizza as well as proper cooking).

In Le Praz, Michelin-starred Azimut is 'unpretentious, good value and always busy', says a seasoned observer. Bistrot du Praz is expensive but worth it, say reporters.

APRES-SKI ★★★★
Take your pick
At close of play there is no great on-mountain scene, unless you count a final glass or two of champagne or lovely cakes at Cap Horn or Chalet de Pierres. In 1850 there are bars around Croisette that may come to life. We hear that the Jump, once a pivotal place, is making a comeback. We get most reports these days on the 'relaxed, sometimes busy' Refuge. The new Kudeta (formerly Kalico) is Cuban-themed, often with live bands. We also had good food there.

But it's later on when things really get going. Kudeta's disco pumps until 4am, as does the Grange – a Moroccan-style place. There are some exclusive nightclubs, such as the Caves. The Mangeoire piano bar gets going late and is 'great fun' for live music. The Tremplin has karaoke. The Petit Drink specialises in wine and tapas. Oxygen is a cool lounge bar.

In 1650 there are several lively bars within a few yards of each other. The Bubble and Rocky's are Brit-run, and the Bubble and the Boulotte fill up with chalet staff letting down their hair and other things. A reporter tips instead the 'relaxing' Schuss and the 'cosy, refreshingly French' Cabane. The Funky Fox has pool, live music or DJs and the Club disco stays open late.

In 1550 there are a handful of bars that can develop a lively atmosphere – notably The Bar, and the bar of Ski Power's chalet-hotel Chanrossa.

OFF THE SLOPES ★★★
Not ideal
There is quite a bit to do, but the emphasis is very much on physical activities. A non-skiers' guide to paths and itineraries is distributed by the tourist office. A pedestrian lift pass for the gondolas and buses in Courchevel and Méribel makes it easy for non-skiers to get up the mountain to meet others for lunch. There is no public pool, and although some hotel pools are open to non-residents the prices are astronomical. Cinemas in 1850 and 1650 show English-speaking films. Snowshoeing among the trees and tobogganing from 1850 to 1550 are popular. And you can take joyrides from the altiport. There is a pocket shopping guide listing fashion and jewellery shops in 1850. The prices in these shops are stratospheric, and most of the customers are Russian.

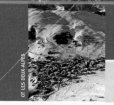

Les Deux-Alpes

*Sprawling resort with a high, narrow ski area that will disappoint
many intermediates; popular for summer skiing and boarding*

RATINGS

The mountains

Extent	★★★
Fast lifts	★★★★
Queues	★★
Terrain p'ks	★★★★★
Snow	★★★★
Expert	★★★★
Intermediate	★★
Beginner	★★★
Boarder	★★★★
X-country	★★
Restaurants	★★★
Schools	★★★
Families	★★★★

The resort

Charm	★★
Convenience	★★★
Scenery	★★★★
Eating out	★★★★
Après-ski	★★★★
Off-slope	★★

RPI 90

lift pass	£180
ski hire	£110
lessons	£80
food & drink	£135
total	£505

NEWS

2011/12: The Diable gondola is due to be replaced by a six-seat fast chairlift. At last! Snowmaking is to be introduced to the green run back to resort, Demoiselles. A new blue alternative is now planned, but it's not imminent.

2010/11: A new fast quad, Sautet, opened to link the area below Toura to the top of the Fée area. New signage was introduced for the whole ski area, with information boards at each major lift.

+ High, snow-sure, varied slopes, including an extensive glacier area

+ Lots of good off-piste terrain

+ Stunning views of the Ecrins peaks

+ Wide choice of affordable hotels

− Piste network modest by big resort standards, and congested in places

− Home runs are either steep and icy or dangerously overcrowded

− Virtually no woodland runs

− Spread-out, rather messy resort

We have a love-hate relationship with Les Deux-Alpes. We love the high-Alpine feel of its main slopes, and the good snow on the north-facing runs (as well as the glacier). But we're unimpressed by the limited extent of the pistes, and we hate the resulting congestion in peak season when the resort's 35,000 visitors are crammed on to them. And the village? Well, reports suggest it's no longer quite the lively place it was. Could it be that young Brits and Scans, more than most holidaymakers, are declining to pay French resort prices?

We've been complaining since 1994 about the dangerous home runs here. We hear, at last, that a blue alternative to the icy blacks and hideously crowded green is planned, possibly for 2012/13. Wonders will never cease.

THE RESORT

Les Deux-Alpes is a long, narrow village sitting on a high, remote col. It is modern, but seems to have grown haphazardly over the years without a coherent plan. Access is from the Grenoble-Briançon road to the north.

The six-day pass covers La Grave and gives two days in Alpe-d'Huez and days in Serre-Chevalier (an hour away over the Col du Lautaret) and other resorts. There are buses twice a week to Alpe-d'Huez, but a better plan is to splash 65 euro on doing it by helicopter. A car would be handy to make the most of these options, especially Serre-Che.

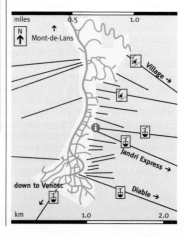

miles 0.5 1.0
N
Mont-de-Lans
Village →
i
Jandri Express →
down to Venosc
Diable →
km 1.0 2.0

VILLAGE CHARM ★★
Lively, but that's all

The village is a long, sprawling collection of apartments, hotels, bars and shops, most lining the two streets that form the one-way traffic system. There is a wide range of building styles, from old chalets through 1960s blocks to more sympathetic recent buildings. It looks better as you leave than as you arrive – all the balconies face south. The place has quite a buzz, in the early evening at least.

CONVENIENCE ★★★
Three main parts

Lifts are spread fairly evenly along the village. There is no clear centre, but three sectors can be identified. As you enter the village from the north, roads go off left up the hill to Les 2 Alpes 1800 – inconvenient for shopping and nightlife. Go straight on instead and you come to the effective centre, with the major gondola stations, outdoor ice rink and lots of shops and restaurants. At the far end of the resort is Alpe de Venosc, with many of the bars and hotels, the most character and the best shops. The free shuttle-bus saves some long walks.

SCENERY ★★★★
High southern peaks

The resort sits high among the southern Alps, with great views from the upper slopes of the Ecrins peaks.

272

↑ Car-free Les Deux-Alpes is not; but the place has quite a buzz in the early evening
OT LES DEUX ALPES

KEY FACTS

Resort	1650m
	5,410ft
Slopes	1300-3570m
	4,270-11,710ft
Lifts	51
Pistes	205km
	127 miles
Green	21%
Blue	47%
Red	21%
Black	11%
Snowmaking	
	211 guns

THE MOUNTAINS

There are trees immediately above the village, but the main slopes are virtually all above the treeline.

The piste map is inadequate, especially around mid-mountain. A few blue runs have short steep sections, and some runs are different colours on the map and on the mountain.

EXTENT OF THE SLOPES ★★★✫✫
Surprisingly small

For a big resort, Les Deux-Alpes has a disappointingly small area of pistes. The main area goes high and stretches a long way – the top is almost 8km from the village – but it is very narrow. We are unconvinced by the claimed extent of 205km. One reporter this year who took the splendid heli-trip to Alpe d'Huez (claimed extent 250km) was 'surprised and delighted' by how much bigger that ski area was.

The western side of Les Deux-Alpes, now branded **Vallée Blanche**, is served by lifts from various parts of town. It is relatively low (the top is 2100m) and has only short pistes back to town, which get the morning sun.

On the broad, gentle slope east of the resort are about ten beginner lifts, and above them a steep slope beneath the ridge of **Les Crêtes**. Lifts go up to the ridge from four points spread along the village. To get back to base you have a choice of one long, winding, narrow green run, often very crowded (and sometimes closed,

as it was during one reporter's 2011 visit), or four short black runs. These are usually mogulled (one is never groomed), and often icy at the end of the day (they get the afternoon sun). Many visitors ride down. It's this mess that the resort is at last planning to sort out with a new blue run.

The ridge has lifts and gentle runs along it, and behind it lies the deep, steep Combe de Thuit. Lifts span the combe to the mid-mountain station at **Toura**, at the heart of the slopes. We seem to spend a lot of time on three key fast chairlifts in this area, each serving decent runs – Bellecombes, at the top of the Combe de Thuit; Glaciers, carrying on towards the glacier; and Fée, on its own slightly separate hill (now reachable via the new Sautet chairlift). Other chairs go up towards the peak of La Toura serving short runs and terrain features.

The section of the mountain around Toura is very narrow – there is one main way down the mountain, and it gets crowded in the afternoon. You can avoid this by taking a long blue run around the La Fée sector, ending up in the Combe de Thuit, where chairs go up to Crêtes.

The top **Glacier du Mont de Lans** section has fine, easy runs with great views, served by an underground funicular and draglifts. There are steeper slopes off to the north, served by chairs. You can go from the top all the way down to Mont-de-Lans – a descent of 2270m vertical that we

FRANCE

274

believe is the world's biggest on-piste vertical. A walk (or snowcat tow) takes you to the slopes of La Grave.

FAST LIFTS ★★★★☆
Main lifts OK but ...
Les Deux-Alpes has some impressive lifts, with fast chair alternatives to the gondolas. But there are still a few draglifts and slow chairs around.

QUEUES ★★☆☆☆
Can be a problem
The village is large, and high-season queues for the gondolas in the morning can be serious. 2011 visitors reported waits of 45 minutes at the peak; one took to camping outside the lift station half an hour before it opened. The Diable gondola is due to

be upgraded to a six-pack for 2011/12, which will help but will not cure the problem. Up the mountain there are few problems, although the lifts in the Crêtes area get busy in peak season. The top lifts are prone to closure if it's windy, putting pressure on the lower lifts. We have repeated reports of queues for the gondolas back to the village when snow is poor low down.

TERRAIN PARKS ★★★★★
Europe's biggest summer park
The heavyweight terrain park is located above Toura in the winter, then shifts up to the glacier in the summer. The winter park is maintained to an excellent standard, and features a slopestyle line with three tables, rails, hips and boxes, a big air jump, half-pipe, kids-only mini park, beginner zone and rail zone, as well as a boardercross and a BBQ area. There's a 120m 4.5m-radius half-pipe.

The glacier park is probably the biggest and best park in Europe, with something for everyone (including beginners) – all serviced by the park's own draglift. This huge 800m-long playground has all manner of kickers, rails and obstacles. A second, smaller half-pipe is added for the summer. The boardercross course sits in its own area next to the park.

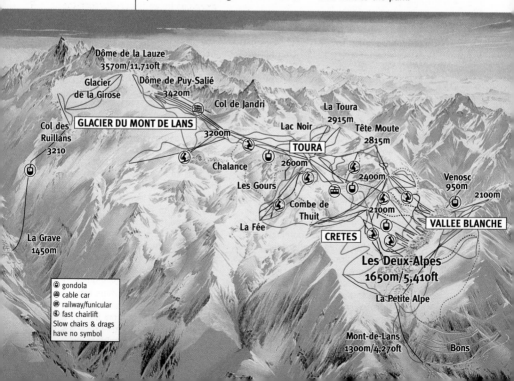

Dôme de la Lauze
3570m/11,710ft

Glacier de la Girose

Dôme de Puy-Salié
3420m

Col de Jandri

La Toura
2915m

Col des Ruillans
3210

GLACIER DU MONT DE LANS

3200m

Lac Noir

Tête Moute
2815m

Chalance

2600m

TOURA

Les Gours

2400m

Venosc
950m

2100m

Combe de Thuit

2100m

La Fée

VALLEE BLANCHE

CRETES

La Grave
1450m

2100m

Les Deux-Alpes
165om/5,41oft

La Petite Alpe

🚠 gondola
🚡 cable car
🚟 railway/funicular
🚠 fast chairlift
Slow chairs & drags have no symbol

Mont-de-Lans
1300m/4,270ft

Bons

The off-piste routes in Les Deux-Alpes are numerous and varied in difficulty. But never try them without the right equipment and a qualified guide.

*Both sides off the **Bellecombes** piste offer a wide range of varying terrain; it's important to take care here – there are several small cliff faces. For those keen to tackle couloirs this descent offers small ones that are ideal for your first attempts; they can be avoided, though.*

*Traversing across the top of the black Grand Couloir piste leads to the **North Rachas** area, with off-piste faces that normally offer good snow conditions all winter. The first large valley leads to three couloirs – one fairly broad and easy, the others much narrower and steeper. Traversing further leads to a much wider descent that avoids the three couloirs.*

*Strong skiers will enjoy the famous **Chalance** run (our favourite), which starts just below the glacier and descends 1000m vertical to the Gours run; there are several variations, mixing wide open slopes and rocky pitches. These faces are at times subject to quite a high avalanche risk.*

*Traversing above the north face of the Chalance leads to the couloir **Pylone Electrique** – a steep, narrow 200m-long couloir with the reward below it of an excellent wide powder field of moderate gradient. A rest on the Thuit chairlift is a must after this adrenalin-charged descent.*

*As well as these routes within the local lift network, there is a renowned descent to **St-Christophe** (you get a taxi back), and the famous **La Grave** terrain (see separate chapter) is easily accessed.*

LIFT PASSES

Super ski pass

Prices in €

Age	1-day	6-day
under 13	32	156
13 to 64	40	195
over 65	32	156

Free under 5, over 72

Beginner seven free lifts

Notes
Covers all lifts in Les Deux-Alpes; half-day and pedestrian passes; family rates; 6-day pass includes entry to swimming pool and ice rink and access to La Grave and two days in Alpe-d'Huez and one day in Serre-Chevalier, Montgenèvre and Sestriere

Alternative passes
Ski Sympa – covers 21 lifts

SNOW RELIABILITY ★★★★☆
Excellent on higher slopes
The snow on the higher slopes is normally very good, even in a poor winter. Above 2200m most of the runs are north-facing, and the top glacier section guarantees good snow. More of a concern is bad weather shutting the lifts, or very low temperatures at the top. But the runs just above the village from Les Crêtes face west, so they get a lot of afternoon sun and can be slushy or icy. Snowmaking covers some of the lower slopes – and is being extended to cover the home green run, at last. We have never found the snow on the Vallée Blanche sector good enough to ski.

FOR EXPERTS ★★★★☆
Off-piste is the main attraction
The area offers wonderful off-piste – see above. We especially like the long, deserted Chalance itinéraire, which is easier than it looks from the bottom.

A free weekly Freeride Attitude event promotes off-piste safety (see 'Schools and guides').

But there are few satisfying on-piste challenges. The black runs down to the resort are steep, but they often have poor snow conditions. Elsewhere, don't miss the black down the Bellecombe chair and its itinéraire variant (which often has better snow); the black and red runs down from the top of the Fée chair are enjoyable, and so is the red run served by the Super Diable chairlift.

FOR INTERMEDIATES ★★☆☆☆
Limited cruising
Les Deux-Alpes can disappoint keen intermediates because of the limited extent of the pistes. Avid piste-bashers will cover the pistes in a couple of days. A lot of the runs are either rather tough – some of the blues could be reds – or boringly bland. The runs higher up generally have good snow, and there is some great fast cruising, especially from the glacier to Toura and on the mainly north-facing pistes served by the chairlifts off to the sides. You can often pick gentle or steeper terrain in these bowls as you wish. The chairlifts at the glacier serve great carving pistes. If it's open, the Vallée Blanche area apparently has quite testing red runs.

Less confident intermediates will love the quality of the snow and the gentleness of most of the runs on the upper mountain. Their problem might lie in finding the pistes too crowded.

FOR BEGINNERS ★★★☆☆
Good slopes
The nursery slopes beside the village are spacious and gentle and seven lifts are free. The run along the ridge above them is excellent, too, except when it's crowded at the end of the day. The glacier also has a fine array of very easy slopes. A 2010 visitor notes that his eight-year-old could 'ski from the glacier to the village on greens and blues – a real sense of achievement for a child'.

Les Deux-Alpes

275

Interactive resort shortlist builder at **www.wtss.co.uk**

SCHOOLS

ESF
t 0476 792121

International
St-Christophe
t 0476 790421

European
t 0476 797455

Evolution2
t 0476 801798

Da Camp Freestyle
t 0476 792121

Classes
(ESF prices)
6 half days (2¼hr am
or pm) €150

Private lessons
€42 for 1hr for 1 or 2
persons

GUIDES

Bureau des guides
t 0476 113629

FOR BOARDERS ★★★★☆
Big appeal
Les Deux-Alpes has become a snowboard Mecca over the past few years in summer when the pros descend en masse. Its cheap and cheerful atmosphere counts for a lot – while the limited pisted slopes aren't as off-putting to boarders as to skiers. In town there are good trampoline facilities and a huge airbag to get a feeling of what air-time is all about. Although the focus is on the terrain park, the freeriding is not to be underestimated, with plenty of steep challenging terrain. Beginners will find the narrow, flat crowded areas mid-mountain and the routes down to the village intimidating. Most of the lifts on the higher slopes are chairs, and Primitive is a specialist snowboard school.

FOR CROSS-COUNTRY ★★☆☆☆
Needs very low-altitude snow
There are small, widely dispersed areas. Given good snow, Venosc, reached by a gondola down, has the only worthwhile picturesque ones. Total trail distance is 20km.

MOUNTAIN RESTAURANTS ★★★☆☆
A few good places
There are mountain restaurants at all the major lift junctions, but they are generally unremarkable.
Editors' choice Diable au Coeur (0476 799950) at the top of the Diable lift has excellent food (delicious confit de canard on our last visit) and service. Readers agree. The terrace gives good views, but sit as far as you can from the noisy adjacent chairlift machinery – instead be entertained by the 'enthusiastic people enjoying the hot tub'. The bigger but similarly excellent Chalet la Toura (0671 920768), in a fine position at Toura in the middle of the domain, is pleasantly woody, and serves good food.
Worth knowing about The Pano, at Toura, has 'a wide range of daily specials' and makes an attempt at Austrian-style on-mountain après, with a DJ and even a happy hour in the afternoon. There is a small table-service restaurant attached to the big self-service Les Glaciers at 3200m, though a 2011 visitor gave up waiting to be served – 'no staff in sight'. The Bergerie on the Pied Moutet slopes has been recommended for 'good local dishes and atmosphere'.

SCHOOLS AND GUIDES ★★★☆☆
Fair selection to choose fro n
There are plenty to choose between but we lack recent reports. There's a free Freeride Attitude off-piste safety course (held Mondays and Tuesdays between mid-January and mid-April) run by guides and patrollers who provide transceivers, shovels, probes etc and teach you how to use them.

FOR FAMILIES ★★★★☆
Fine facilities
The village nursery takes kids from six months to two years, the kindergarten from two to six years, and there are chalet-based alternatives run by UK tour operators. There are also seven free lifts at the village level and a kids' freestyle area. A 2009 reporter says 'There's a lot going on for kids at the foot of the slopes (kids' quad bikes, ice rink, pool) and good tobogganing terrain too.'

STAYING THERE

Les Deux-Alpes has plenty of that rarity in high-altitude French resorts, plenty of affordable hotels.
Chalets Several UK tour operators run catered chalets or chalet hotels. Skiworld has four varied chalets including one with outdoor hot tub. Crystal has half a dozen, again one or two with hot tubs. Mark Warner runs a chalet hotel with pool in a slope-side position on the road up to 1800.
Hotels There are about 30 hotels, of which the majority are 2-star or below.
★★★★Farandole (0476 805045) One of only two 4-stars. At the Venosc end.
★★★★Chalet Mounier (0476 805690) Smartly modernised and upgraded to a four-star. Good reputation for food. Pool, steam, sauna, hot tub. At the Venosc end of the resort.
★★★Mariande (0476 805060) Highly recommended by past reporters, especially for its excellent five-course dinners. At the Venosc end.
★★★Souleil'or (0476 792469) Looks like a lift station, but pleasant and comfortable. Rooms and food approved by past reporters. Central.
★★Lutins (0476 792152) Central, basic, convenient, clean and friendly.
★★Côte Brune (0476 805489) Slope-side, near Jandri Express. Large, basic, modern rooms.
Apartments There are plenty of them, but most are unremarkable, and some are about as simple as it gets these

Mid-mountain: the Toura lift station, with terrain parks beyond, Combe de Thuit down to the right, lifts going off to the glacier on the left →
OT LES DEUX-ALPES

CHILDCARE

Crèche Petit Bonhomme de Neige
t 0476 790262
Ages 6mnth to 2yr;
8.30-5.30
Garderie Bonhomme de Neige
t 0476 790677
Ages 2 to 6; 8.30-5.15
(also activity centre for ages 6 to 12)

Ski schools
Snow gardens for ages 3 to 6; classes for ages 6 to 12 (6 days €225 with ESF)

GETTING THERE

Air Lyon 160km/ 100 miles (2hr45); Grenoble 110km/ 70 miles (2hr15); Chambéry 135km/ 85 miles (2hr15); Geneva 220km/ 135 miles (3hr30)

Rail Grenoble (70km/43 miles); four daily buses from station

ACTIVITIES

Indoor Swimming pool, hot tub, sauna, sports centres (Club Forme, Acqua Center), squash, cinemas, games rooms, bowling, museums, library

Outdoor Ice rink, snowmobiling, paragliding, quad bikes, snowshoeing, ice climbing, sleigh rides, tobogganing

Phone numbers
From abroad use the prefix +33 and omit the initial '0' of the phone number

TOURIST OFFICE

www.les2alpes.com

days. MGM-style residences with pools are notably absent. One of the better residences is Goleon / Val Ecrin, at the entrance to the resort – two linked chalet-style buildings, with sauna and steam room. All the main French apartment agents have properties. Erna Low and Peak Retreats have a bigger range than most, including self-catered chalets.

Out of resort Close to the foot of the final ascent to Les Deux-Alpes are two small hotels, near-ideal for anyone thinking of visiting Alpe-d'Huez, La Grave and Serre-Chevalier – the cheerful Cassini (0476 800410) at Le Freney and the even more appealing Panoramique (0476 800625) at Mizoën – approved of by a past reporter for 'hearty food, informative Dutch hosts' and the 'wondrous' panorama.

An alternative is to stay in one of the hamlets close to the bottom of the gondola up from Venosc.

EATING OUT ★★★★
Plenty of choice
There are about 50 restaurants, including lots of simple places such as crêperies. Chalet Mounier's P'tit Polyte restaurant has a high reputation. La Grange, L'Alisier, The Patate, Cloche and Crêpes à Gogo ('great food, not just crêpes') and Etable ('best pizza ever') are reader recommendations. You can get a relatively cheap meal at Bleuets bar, the Vetrata or the Spaghetteria. One regular visitor says that Smokey Joe's Tex-Mex is the best value in the resort.

APRES-SKI ★★★★
Hit by exchange rate blues?
Les Deux-Alpes has long been one of the liveliest of French resorts, with plenty of jumping bars, several open

Ski a high altitude resort with low prices – see p177

until the early hours. But here, as in some other French resorts that have traditionally attracted a lot of young Brits and Scans on a budget, we detect a change, for the moment at least. Reporters tell us that in 2011 Smithy's Tavern wasn't the 'massive party venue' of earlier years, for example. All the same, there are still plenty of places to try – the resort website lists about 25. Among the bars favoured by this year's reporters are Pub le Windsor – a smaller, quieter place popular with locals; and the Polar Bear Pub – 'wood stove, serves Guinness'. Smokey Joe's is a popular central sports bar and the Secret has live music, big-screen TV and a wide choice of beers. The Red Frog shows sports. The main bar at 1800 is O'Brian's; the Tribeca pizzeria has 'a lovely ambience for grown-ups'.

The Avalanche is the main nightclub, at the Venosc end of town; up at 1800, Opéra is tipped by locals.

OFF THE SLOPES ★★★★★
Limited options
The pretty valley village of Venosc is worth a visit by gondola, and you can take a scenic helicopter flight to Alpe-d'Huez. There are lots of walks, a big outdoor pool and the Acqua Center has an indoor pool, sauna, steam and hot tub. Several mountain restaurants are accessible to pedestrians. The White Cruise in a snowcat takes you across the glacier and provides wonderful views. An exhibition on avalanches includes a simulator that lets you experience what it's like to be caught in one.

Interactive resort shortlist builder at www.wtss.co.uk

Flaine

Uncompromisingly modern, high-altitude resort sharing a big, broad area of varied slopes with more rustic alternatives

278

RATINGS

The mountains

Extent	****
Fast lifts	**
Queues	***
Terrain p'ks	***
Snow	****
Expert	****
Intermediate	*****
Beginner	*****
Boarder	***
X-country	**
Restaurants	**
Schools	***
Families	****

The resort

Charm	*
Convenience	*****
Scenery	****
Eating out	**
Après-ski	*
Off-slope	*

RPI	90
lift pass	£190
ski hire	£115
lessons	£70
food & drink	£150
total	**£525**

NEWS

2011/12: A new six-pack, the Désert Blanc, is due to replace the old Perdrix and Platé chairs. More snowmaking is to be added to the bottom of the Faust, Almandine and Serpentine runs.

2010/11: A new slope linked Forêt to Forum. The 3-star Terrasses de Veret apartments in Forêt and the 4-star Refuge du Golf above Hameau de Flaine opened.

- ✚ Big, varied area, with plenty of terrain to suit most levels of skill
- ✚ Reliable snow in the main bowl
- ✚ Compact, convenient, mainly car-free village, plus traditional villages on the lower fringes of the area
- ✚ Excellent facilities for children
- ✚ Very close to Geneva airport

- ▬ Some slow old chairlifts, though things are improving
- ▬ Austere 1960s buildings
- ▬ In bad weather, main Flaine bowl offers little to do, and links to outer sectors of the area may be closed
- ▬ Nightlife not a highlight
- ▬ Little to do off the slopes (in Flaine)

Flaine is best known as a convenient resort catering particularly well for families, but it has a much broader appeal than that. The Grand Massif is almost a match for Val d'Isère/Tignes in terms of extent, at least.

Flaine's family orientation is underlined by the domination of apartments. But you open up more lodging options by considering the outlying traditional villages – Samoëns (which has its own chapter) and Les Carroz and Morillon (covered here). They also have woodland slopes for bad-weather days.

THE RESORT

Flaine was built from scratch in the 1960s at the foot of a big snowy bowl. It's high, but not super-high (it is set among trees); the road in from Les Carroz actually involves a final descent from a col some 250m higher. The architecture of the main village is distinctive and uncompromising; it has its admirers, not including us.

The road in passes two satellite mini-resorts: Hameau de Flaine – lots of small chalets and the bigger new residence Refuge du Golf and Montsoleil, developed by Intrawest (of Arc 1950 fame) a few years back.

The Grand Massif ski area links Flaine with the lower, traditional villages mentioned above. A car gives you the option of visiting the Portes du Soleil, Megève, Chamonix or even Courmayeur in Italy.

VILLAGE CHARM *
Not to our taste
The concrete Bauhaus-style blocks that form the core of Flaine were supposed to exhibit 'the principle of shadow and light'. They look shocking from the approach road; from the slopes they are less obtrusive, blending into the rocky grey hillside. As a place to inhabit, Flaine has an austere feel, and some of the buildings are now looking tatty. For us, the outdoor sculptures by Picasso, Vasarely and Dubuffet do little

to improve things. In contrast, the Hameau de Flaine is built in a traditional chalet style, as is the Montsoleil development. The resort is supposed to be traffic-free, and for most purposes it is, although roads do penetrate the village.

CONVENIENCE *****
A fine example
The main resort is tiny. There are two parts: Forum is centred on a snow-covered square with buildings on three sides, the open fourth side blending with the slopes. Flaine Forêt is up the hillside, linked by lift, with its own bars and shops, and most of the apartments. There are children all over the place; they are catered for with play areas. Hameau de Flaine is about 1km from the slopes and main village, and has only one shop/bar/restaurant. Montsoleil is much nearer to the mother ship (a few hundred metres walk) and it has linking pistes. The bus service to/from these areas is good but stops early.

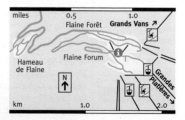

KEY FACTS

Resort	1600m
	5,250ft

Grand Massif (Flaine, Les Carroz, Morillon, Samoëns, Sixt)

Slopes	700-2480m
	2,300-8,140ft
Lifts	70
Pistes	265km
	165 miles
Green	12%
Blue	45%
Red	32%
Black	11%
Snowmaking	
	218 guns

For Flaine only

Slopes	1600-2480m
	5,250-8,140ft
Lifts	27
Pistes	140km
	87 miles
Green	13%
Blue	44%
Red	35%
Black	8%

LIFT PASSES

Grand Massif

Prices in €

Age	1-day	6-day
under 16	32	159
16 to 61	40	207
over 62	38	189

Free under 5, over 75
Beginner three free lifts

Notes
Covers all lifts in Flaine, Les Carroz, Morillon, Samoëns and Sixt; family discounts

Alternative passes
Flaine area only

SCENERY ★★★★
Good all around the Massif

The scenery is quite varied, with rocky ridges, partly wooded hillsides and splendid views from Les Grandes Platières and Tête des Lindars.

THE MOUNTAINS

The slopes in the Flaine bowl are mainly open, but the lowest slopes are wooded. Outside the bowl, above the other villages, it's the opposite – most of the runs are below the treeline.

The latest piste map is a vast improvement on the previous version, with a better attempt to define the individual bowls; but it is still difficult to read, and sometimes misleading.

EXTENT OF THE SLOPES ★★★★
A big white playground

Grand Massif is an impressive area; but the greater part of the domain lies outside the main Flaine bowl and the links can be closed by bad weather.

The **Grandes Platières** jumbo gondola speeds you in a single stage up the north-west-facing Flaine bowl to the high-point of the Grand Massif. A six-pack offers an alternative, going part-way up. There are essentially four or five main ways down the treeless, rolling terrain back to Flaine, or to chairs in the middle of the wilderness. On skier's right, the Cascades blue run leads away from the lift system behind the Tête Pelouse down to the outskirts of Sixt, dropping over 1700m in its exceptional 14km length. The gentle/flat top half is hard work, especially for boarders, and the run is scenic rather than exciting. At the end you can get a bus (often crowded) to the

lifts at Samoëns. Or spend some time exploring the slopes of Sixt – very quiet, with a non-trivial vertical.

On the near side of the Tête Pelouse, a broad catwalk leads to the experts-only **Gers** bowl. At the bottom, a flat trail links with the lower (more interesting) half of the Cascades run.

Back at Platières, an alternative is to head left down the lovely long red Méphisto to a quieter area of slopes beneath Tête des Lindars. This sector is also reachable by a second gondola from below the resort. The lower slopes are used as slalom courses.

The eight-seat Grand Vans chair, reached from Forum by means of a slow bucket-lift (or from Montsoleil via a short quad), gives access to the extensive slopes of **Les Carroz**, **Morillon** and **Samoëns** via the wide Vernant bowl, which is equipped with two fast chairlifts. An unusual feature of the area is that there are two points on the road between Les Carroz and Flaine where lifts go up into the slopes – Les Molliets and Vernant.

FAST LIFTS ★★
More being installed

Five fast lifts serve the main bowl and two there have been recent upgrades outside the bowl. But there are still a lot of slow old chairs and draglifts in the Grand Massif area, some of them in important spots. Most of the lifts up to Tête des Saix above Samoëns, for example, are slow

QUEUES ★★★
Still some problems

Many of the trouble spots are less acute than they once were, but the system can't cope with high-season

KERRY LEWIS

Flaine Forum in the foreground: the central square blends into the snow ➔

crowds. A February 2011 visitor had 'horrendous queues of between five and 30 minutes at every lift'. At other times, things are bearable. But towards the end of the day expect delays at the Vernant chair to get back to the Flaine bowl. Also expect crowds on the blue piste leading down to it and on the run back to Flaine under the Grand Vans chair. An alternative is to go down Les Molliets or Vernant, and catch a bus.

In the Flaine bowl, the Aup de Veran gondola still has queues, notably in the mornings. Queues elsewhere in the bowl can build up at weekends, when the lifts out are shut due to high winds or when it is warm and the lower resorts have poor snow.

TERRAIN PARKS ★★★☆☆
Cater for kids to experts
The main JamPark Pro (Jam = Jib and Air Maniacs) is in Flaine's Aujon area. It has a table, rails, kickers, a hip, a boardercross and a chill-out zone. Watch out for the draglifts round here, though. A 2010 reporter complains that the park is on the edge of the ski area and closes early. There is a kids' park in Morillon if snow permits.

SNOW RELIABILITY ★★★★☆
Usually keeps its whiteness
Most of the main bowl faces north or north-west, and keeps snow well. There is snowmaking on the greater part of the Tête des Lindars area and on the nursery slopes, and more is

The 14km-long, lift-free Cascades run to Sixt

Long, tricky draglift that serves a steep black run with great off-piste both sides

GERS

Grand Va
2205m

Vernants

1600m

Tête des Saix
2120m

A new six-pack two seasons ago above Samoëns 1600 – a huge improvement

Charlande Express

SAMOENS

Sixt
800m

Grand Massif 1600m

1500m

Saix

Sairon

Les Esserts

Good runs down the old gondola from Vercland, none down the newer one from close to Samoëns

Samoëns
720m/2,360ft

1100m

MORILLON

Morillon
700m/2,300ft

Morillon

Good cruising above Morillon – good on a bad weather day

due to be installed elsewhere for 2011/12 (see News). The runs towards Samoëns 1600 and Morillon 1100 are north-facing too, and some lower parts have snowmaking, but below these mid-stations the runs can be tricky or closed. The Les Carroz runs are west-facing and low, and can suffer from strong afternoon sun as a result, but a few runs have snowmaking. Grooming is excellent.

FOR EXPERTS ★★★★
Great fun with guidance
Flaine has some seriously challenging terrain. But much of it is off-piste and, although some looks like it can safely be explored without guidance, this impression is mistaken. The Flaine

bowl is riddled with rock crevasses and potholes, and should be treated with as much caution as you would use on a glacier.

All the black pistes on the map deserve their classification. The Diamant Noir, down the line of the main gondola, is tricky because of moguls, narrowness and other people, rather than great steepness; the first pitch is the steepest. To skier's left of Diamant Noir are several short, steep off-piste routes through the crags.

The Lindars Nord chair serves a shorter slope that often has the best snow in the area, and some seriously steep gradients but is 'poorly marked – mind the small cliffs'. Mind the chair doesn't whack you as you exit.

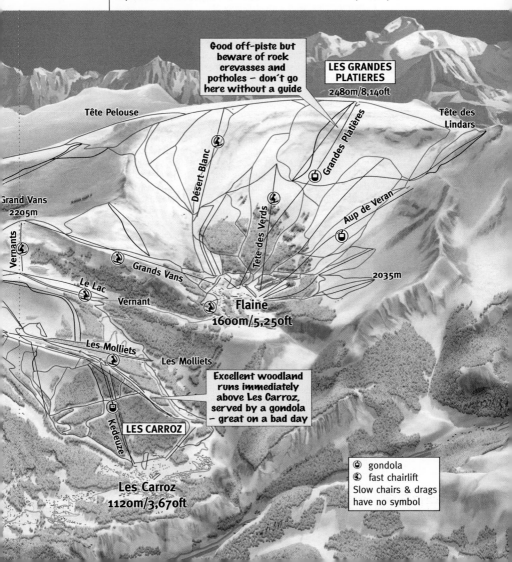

Good off-piste but beware of rock crevasses and potholes – don't go here without a guide

LES GRANDES PLATIÈRES
2480m/8,140ft

Tête Pelouse

Tête des Lindars

Désert-Blanc

Grandes Platières

Grand Vans
2205m

Aup de Veran

Tête des Verds

Vernants

Grands Vans

2035m

Le Lac

Vernant

Flaine
1600m/5,250ft

Les Molliets

Les Molliets

Excellent woodland runs immediately above Les Carroz, served by a gondola – great on a bad day

Kedeuze

LES CARROZ

Les Carroz
1120m/3,670ft

◉ gondola
④ fast chairlift
Slow chairs & drags have no symbol

GETTING THERE

Air Geneva 80km/
50 miles (1hr30)

Rail Cluses (30km/
19 miles); regular bus
service

UK PACKAGES

*Action Outdoors, Alpine
Answers, Classic Ski,
Crystal, Crystal Finest,
Erna Low, First Choice,
Independent Ski Links,
Inghams, Lagrange,
Neilson, Powder White,
PowderBeds,
PV-Holidays.com, Ski
Club Freshtracks, Ski
Collection, Ski France,
Ski Independence,
Skitracer, Ski Weekend,
Skiweekends.com,
Thomson, Zenith*

ACTIVITIES

Indoor Sauna,
solarium, gymnasium,
massage, cinema,
climbing wall,
bowling, cultural
centre with art gallery
and library

Outdoor Ice rink,
snowshoeing, dog
sledding, walking,
snowmobiling,
paragliding, helicopter
rides, quad bikes, ice
driving, snow kiting

TOURIST OFFICE

Flaine
www.flaine.com

The Gers draglift, outside the main bowl, serves great on- and off-piste expert terrain in a north-facing bowl (of about 550m vertical) that normally has good snow top to bottom. The Onyx piste is a proper black and nearby off-piste slopes reach 45°. There are more adventurous ways in from the Grand Vans and Véret lifts. Further serious black pistes go down from Tête des Saix towards Samoëns.

There are some scenic off-piste routes from which you can be retrieved by helicopter – such as the Combe des Foges, next to Gers.

FOR INTERMEDIATES ★★★★★
Something for everyone
Flaine is ideal for confident intermediates, with a great variety of pistes (and usually the bonus of good snow, at least above Flaine itself). The diabolically named reds that dominate the Flaine bowl tend to gain their status from short steep sections rather than overall difficulty. The relatively direct Faust is great carving territory and Méphisto is popular with lots of reporters. There are gentler cruises from the top – Cristal, taking you to the new Désert Blanc chair and Serpentine all the way home. The blues beneath Tête des Lindars are excellent for confidence building, but the drag serving them is not.

The connection with the slopes outside the main bowl is a blue run that can be tricky because of crowds, narrowness or poor snow. Once the connection has been made, however, all intermediates will enjoy the long tree-lined runs down to Les Carroz, as long as the snow is good. The Morillon slopes are also excellent intermediate terrain – the long green Marvel run to Morillon 1100 is an easy cruise with signs along it explaining the local wildlife (in English as well as French).

FOR BEGINNERS ★★★★★
Fairly good
There are excellent nursery slopes right by the village, served by free lifts which make a pass unnecessary until you are ready to go higher up the mountain. The area is roped off, but it is still used as a short cut back to the village by other skiers (a new piste for 2010/11 should have reduced this problem – reports please). There are some gentle blues to progress to on skier's right, beneath Tête Pelouse. Progress to the gentle blues in the

Tête des Lindars area is not easy due to several steep draglifts. An alternative is to get the bus to a gentle, quiet green at Vernant.

FOR BOARDERS ★★★
Beware the draglifts
Flaine suits boarders quite well – there's lots of varied terrain and plenty of off-piste with interesting nooks and crannies, including woods outside the main bowl. The key lifts are now chairs or gondolas (but beware the draglifts marked as difficult on the piste map plus the Aujon draglift, which serves the terrain park but strangely isn't marked as difficult). Black Side is the local specialist shop, with a cafe and bar in the central Forum.

FOR CROSS-COUNTRY ★★
Very fragmented
The Grand Massif claims 64km of tracks but only about 13km of that is around Flaine itself. The majority is on the valley floor and dependent on low snow. Extensive tracks between Morillon and Les Carroz include some tough uphill sections.

MOUNTAIN RESTAURANTS ★★
Back to base, or quit the bowl
The piste map marks restaurants but does not name them. In the Flaine bowl, there are only two options above the resort's upper outskirts – Grands Platières, which gets mixed reviews, and the rustic Blanchot, just

← There is some excellent and relatively safe off-piste terrain within the lift system

SCHOOLS

ESF
t 0450 908100

International
t 0450 908441

Moniteurs indépendants
t 0450 937978

Flaine Super Ski
t 0681 061906

Flaine Ski Clinic
t 0666 139281

Freecimes
t 0664 118329

François Simond
t 0450 908097

Bruno Uyttenhove
t 0610 183082

Hameau Master Class
t 0450 908716

Mountain Experience
t 0603 294486

ZigZag (Morillon)
t 0686 660721

Classes (ESF prices)
6 (3hr) half days
€145

Private lessons
From €41 for 1hr

GUIDES

Mountain guide
t 0450 900655

CHILDCARE

Les Petits Loups
t 0450 908782
Ages 6mnth to 3yr

Rabbit Club
t 0450 908100
From 3yr; 9am-5pm

La Souris Verte
t 0450 908441
Ages from 3

Hotel MMM Le Flaine
t 0492 126262
Ages 18mnth to 14yr

Ski school
For ages 3 to 11:
€123 for 6 (3hr) half days (ESF prices);
English-speaking tuition: Catherine Pouppeville (0609 266008)

---

above the treeline on skier's right. This has a restaurant and a snack bar – both generally approved by reporters. At Forum level, across the piste from the gondola, are two attractive, simple chalets – the Michet and the Eloge. Up the slope a bit, the Cascade is self-service but with a good terrace.

Outside the Flaine bowl, we're regular visitors to the remote Gîte du Lac de Gers (0450 895514 – book in advance and ring for a snowcat to tow you up from the Cascades run) – simple, hearty food but splendid isolation. A 2011 visitor confirms the 'food is still good', but found the service extremely slow. The friendly and rustic Igloo above Morillon has 'great food'; we've had an excellent plat du jour there. The Combe has been recommended in the past. The woody Chalet les Molliets is generally well liked – 'atmospheric, cosy', 'copes with groups well', 'excellent plats'.

SCHOOLS AND GUIDES ★★★☆☆
Mixed reports
A 2010 reporter who used the ESF got 'the best instructor we've ever had'. However, in the past one reader found that classes were 'far too big – 20 in a couple of cases'. A beginner boarder enjoyed an 'excellent' week with the International school. The competition-oriented Super Ski has 'small classes, good instruction'.

FOR FAMILIES ★★★★☆
Parents' paradise?
Flaine prides itself on being a family resort, and the number of English-speaking children around is a bonus. There are some free children's lift passes available in low season weeks. The International school offers classes for three- to five-year-olds. Crystal's 'well-organised and popular' hotel Le Totem has good childcare facilities.

STAYING THERE

Accommodation is overwhelmingly in self-catering apartments.
Hotels The hotels now seem to be called 'club' hotels and (except for Crystal's Totem – see 'For families') are marketed by big French agencies – but also bookable through UK operators such as Erna Low. B&B is available at the Cascade restaurant, up the hill.
Apartments Top option, underlined now by the award of the new 5-star status, is the ski-in/ski-out Montsoleil/

Terrasses d'Eos residence – a Pierre & Vacances Premium property, outside the village: comfortable, good outdoor pool, sauna, steam, hot tub – but no restaurant or bar. In Flaine Forêt, P&V also has the Forêt. Lagrange has several properties, including attractive chalets out at Hameau – also the location of the recently built Refuge du Golf, with pool. All these options are available through Ski Collection.

EATING OUT ★★☆☆☆
Limited choice
The choice is adequate, no more. Reporters are most enthusiastic about the Ancolie in Hameau – 'first class food', 'brilliant open fire chalet atmosphere' and 'friendly staff and very comfortable bar'. They will ferry you to and from your residence. The 'lively' Brasserie les Cîmes has 'very good food, prices' and 'quick service'. The Grange has been tipped, too.

A couple of places on the slopes just outside the village are open in the evening (including the Michet – see 'Mountain restaurants').

APRES-SKI ★☆☆☆☆
Signs of life
You can eat and drink into the early hours here if you move around a bit – but you don't have much choice of venue. The White pub has a big screen TV, rock music and punters trying to get pints in before the end of happy hour. The Flying Dutchman is lively early on, with karaoke and themed evenings, but 'tends to wind down around 11pm'. The Perdrix Noire has an English pub atmosphere. The bar at the bowling alley is popular with families, and stays open late – 'the only place still serving food until 3am'. There's one nightclub, but drinks are reportedly 'very expensive' and the music 'not up to much'.

OFF THE SLOPES ★☆☆☆☆
Curse of the purpose-built
Flaine is not recommended for people who don't want to hit the slopes. But there is a great ice driving circuit where you can take a spin (literally) in your car or theirs. Snowmobiling and dog sledding are popular, and there's a cinema and a gym. Shopping is limited.

> **Ski a high altitude resort with low prices – see p177**

Ski a high altitude resort with low prices – see p177

Flaine

Interactive resort shortlist builder at www.wtss.co.uk

UK PACKAGES

Les Carroz 360 Sun and Ski, AmeriCan Ski, Crystal Finest, Erna Low, Peak Retreats, Powder White, PowderBeds, PV-Holidays.com, Ski France, Ski Independence, Skiology.co.uk
Morillon Alps Accommodation, AmeriCan Ski, Chalet Group, Erna Low, Lagrange, Peak Retreats
Sixt AmeriCan Ski, Peak Retreats

Phone numbers
From abroad use the prefix +33 and omit the initial '0' of the phone number

TOURIST OFFICES

Les Carroz
www.lescarroz.com
Morillon
www.ot-morillon.fr

LINKED RESORT – 1120m

LES CARROZ

This is a sizeable, sprawling place (bigger than Flaine) – a sunny, traditional family resort with the lived-in feel of a real village where life revolves around the central square, with its cafes and restaurants. Traffic can be busy at peak times though.

The gondola starts a steep 300m walk up from the centre – the nursery drag is a help or you can catch the free ski-bus (though we're told it finishes too early). This lift serves some excellent slopes in the woods above the village, so this is a great place in bad weather. It's a good place for novices, with a beginner area at the top of the gondola, a wide green to progress to and a very gentle blue run back from Les Molliets. There is regular praise for the ESF: one recent reporter had 'the best advanced class ever' while his young daughter 'wants to go back to her caring instructor'. The ski school's torchlit descent is 'not to be missed' – ending with vin chaud and live jazz in the square.

There are half a dozen hotels, of which the pick are beside the Timalets red home run. The Servages d'Armelle (0450 900162) is a beautifully furnished little 4-star with seven rooms and three suites, housed in two old chalets, with a 'superb' restaurant. Milkhotel (0450 900618) is the new name for the renovated Bois de la Char, highly recommended this year – 'well managed, perfectly situated, excellent value; good set menu'. Les Fermes du Soleil is a chalet-style Pierre & Vacances Premium residence with pool, hot tubs etc, close to the centre. Les Chalets de Jouvence is a similar CGH complex. Both available through Peak Retreats.

A visitor this year who tried several restaurants tips La Spatule – 'massive salads, good crêpes and steaks'.

There is more après-ski animation than in Flaine but things are much quieter later on. The Marlow pub is popular at close of play; Pointe Noire, next door, is cheaper and more animated; Carpe Diem gets busy when the other places close and 'has more character than the others'.

LINKED RESORT – 700m

MORILLON

Morillon is a small, quiet, traditional old village, with a few cafes, restaurants, bars, supermarket and shops spread out along the road through. Newer buildings are in chalet style and quite attractive. There's a 3-star hotel, the Morillon (0450 901032). A gondola goes up to the mid-mountain mini-resort of Morillon 1100 (aka Les Esserts), with slope-side apartments at the foot of wide, gentle and tree-lined slopes – popular with families and novices. A choice of red and blue runs go to the valley. These runs are low and good snow is not reliable, although the area as a whole is north-facing and keeps snow well.

Morillon 1100 has the essentials of life – two ski schools, three ski shops, a bakery, supermarket, a couple of restaurants and the Madison pub with 'live music and quizzes'. Recent reporters have been impressed by the ZigZag school.

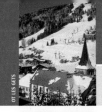

Les Gets

Traditional-style village with a very French feel, providing serious competition for its more established linked neighbour, Morzine

TOP 10 RATINGS

Extent	★★★★★
Fast lifts	★★
Queues	★★★
Snow	★★
Expert	★★★
Intermediate	★★★★
Beginner	★★★★
Charm	★★★★
Convenience	★★★
Scenery	★★★

RPI	90
lift pass	£200
ski hire	£115
lessons	£70
food & drink	£135
total	**£520**

NEWS

2010/11: The Chavannes gondola was refurbished with new six-seat cabins and the base station improved for ground-level entry. A new boardercross course opened on the Chavannes sector and the Jib park was improved. More snowmaking was installed in the Chavannes and Ranfoilly areas. A new lift pass for five consecutive hours starting any time has replaced the half-day pass.

Extent rating
This relates to the whole Portes du Soleil area.

Piste map
The whole local area is covered by the map in the Morzine chapter.

OT LES GETS / N JOLY

The local slopes offer great groomed cruising ➔

➕ Good-sized, varied and treelined slopes shared with Morzine

➕ Attractive chalet-style village

➕ Relatively short drive from the UK

➕ Few queues or crowds locally

➕ Part of the vast Portes du Soleil ski pass region, but ...

➖ It's quite a long way to the main Portes du Soleil circuit at Avoriaz

➖ Modest altitude means there is always a risk of poor snow

➖ Few challenging pistes

➖ Slow, old chairs in some sectors

➖ Weekend crowds

Les Gets is an attractive, small, family-friendly resort with a very French feel to it, partly because of appetising food and wine shops lining the main street. The area of slopes that it shares with Morzine offers the most extensive local network in the Portes du Soleil, and in some respects Les Gets is the better base for that area. But if you intend to visit the main Portes du Soleil circuit repeatedly, it makes sense to stay closer to it in Morzine.

THE RESORT

Les Gets is an attractive, sunny village of traditional chalet-style buildings, on the low pass leading to Morzine. The main road bypasses the village centre.

The local pass saves a fair bit on a Portes du Soleil pass, and makes a lot of sense for many visitors.

Village charm The village has a quiet ambiance that appeals to families, though it does liven-up at weekends. The main street is lined with attractive food and other shops and restaurants. The centre is gradually becoming more pedestrian-friendly too, and a popular outdoor ice rink adds to the charm.

Convenience Although the village has a scattered appearance, most facilities are close to the main lift station – and the free 'petit train' road-train shuttle is a cute way of travelling around. There are also free conventional buses around the village and buses to Morzine at one euro per journey. You can store skis and boots at the Perrières ski shop.

Scenery Good views from the high points – from Mont Chéry you get a great panorama of the village and slopes, with Mont Blanc beyond.

THE MOUNTAINS

Les Gets is not an ideal base for the Portes du Soleil, but its local slopes are extensive.

Slopes The main local slopes – accessed by a refurbished gondola and fast chair-lift from the nursery slopes beside the village – are shared with Morzine, and are mainly described in that chapter. On the opposite side of Les Gets is Mont Chéry, accessed by a gondola followed by a chair or drag. The slopes include some of the most challenging in the area, and are usually very quiet. Both sectors offer wooded and open slopes. Signage is considered 'very good'.

Fast lifts The village lifts are gondolas, but there are a lot of slow, old chairs both on Mont Chéry and in some sectors of the Morzine slopes.

Queues See the Morzine chapter. Mont Chéry is crowd-free.

Snow reliability The nursery slopes benefit from a slightly higher elevation than Morzine, but otherwise our

KEY FACTS

Resort	1170m
	3,840ft

Portes du Soleil	
Slopes	950-2275m
	3,120-7,460ft
Lifts	196
Pistes	650km
	404 miles
Green	13%
Blue	40%
Red	37%
Black	10%
Snowmaking	
	800 guns

Morzine-Les Gets only	
Slopes	1000-2010m
	3,280-6,590ft
Lifts	52
Pistes	110km
	68 miles
Snowmaking	
	387 guns

UK PACKAGES

Alpine Answers, Alpine Elements, AmeriCan Ski, Chalet Group, ChaletBook, Crystal, Esprit, Ferme de Montagne, First Choice, Independent Ski Links, Interactive Resorts, Lagrange, Luxury Chalet Collection, Mountain Wave, Oxford Ski Co, Peak Retreats, Reach4theAlps, Ski Expectations, Ski Famille, Ski France, Ski Independence, Ski Total, Skitracer, Ski Weekend, Snow Finders, VIP

Phone numbers
From abroad use the prefix +33 and omit the initial '0' of the phone number

TOURIST OFFICE

www.lesgets.com

general reservations about the lack of altitude apply. You may get rain. The runs to the resort have snowmaking. The front slopes of Mont Chéry face south-east – bad news at this altitude (and it meant they were closed for much of last season, says a reporter); but the other two flanks are shadier. Grooming is good ('Pisteurs worked wonders; could ski back to resort in March in a poor snow year and warm temperatures,' says a 2011 visitor). The grassy slopes don't need much snow-cover and in a sparse snow year you may do better here than in higher, rockier resorts such as Avoriaz.

Terrain parks There's a new boardercross on Chavannes plus a jib park with boxes and rails and the small Cross District park for beginners.

Experts Black runs on the flank and back of Mont Chéry are quite steep and often bumped. In good snow there's plenty to do off-piste, including some excellent wooded areas.

Intermediates High-mileage piste-bashers might prefer direct access to the main Portes du Soleil circuit, but the local slopes have a lot to offer, with excellent reds on Mont Chéry.

Beginners The village nursery slopes are convenient. A bigger and more snow-sure area has been created at Chavannes, with four free lifts. There are lots of easy runs to progress to – including the Bleuets on Chavannes.

Snowboarding The local slopes are good for beginners and intermediates.

Cross-country There are 12km of good, varied loops locally.

Mountain restaurants See Morzine for places on the shared slopes. On Mont Chéry, reporters enthuse about the Grande Ourse, run by an English family and offering snacks and 'very special' table-service lunches – 'excellent steaks'. A 2011 visitor raves about Lhottys at the top of the Nauchets chairlift for its 'peasant-style mountain soup – to die for'.

Schools and guides You're spoilt for choice. BASS (the British Alpine Ski & Snowboard School) operates here. Les Gets Snowsports is also British-run and 'excellent'. And a reporter says the instructors at Ecole de Ski 360 spoke 'very good' English and her six-year-old daughter was 'cruising down the main slopes on day two'.

Families This is a good resort for families. There are comprehensive facilities, including an American Indian-themed trail area on Chavannes with

teepees, activities and a warpaint workshop – called the Grand Cry Territory – and family-specialist tour operators Esprit Ski and Ski Famille offer holidays here.

STAYING THERE

There is a good selection of chalets and mid-range hotels.

Chalets A 2011 reporter has stayed four years in a row at Ski Famille's 'jolly nice' Le Marjorie chalet; Ski Famille has seven other chalets here too. Esprit Ski has four in one building (along with its own crèche). Ski Total also has four (three with outdoor hot tub, one with a sauna). Private catered Chalet le Frene has been praised.

Hotels We loved the Ferme de Montagne (0450 753679) and so have reporters. It's a kind of cross between a small hotel and a chalet – a beautifully renovated farmhouse with eight luxury bedrooms, gourmet food, ski guiding, sauna, steam, outdoor hot tub, massage therapist; right on the edge of town at La Turche. Of the 3-stars, the Crychar (0450 758050), 100m from central Les Gets at the foot of the slopes, is one of the best. Other reader tips are the 3-star Nagano (0450 797146), the 4-star Marmotte with spa (0450 758033) and the 3-star Alpages (0450 758088).

Apartments Lagrange has the central Sabaudia apartments and the brand new Les Fermes Emiguy in its Prestige range (both with pool, hot tub, sauna etc). Peak Retreats also offers Les Fermes Emiguy as well as other apartments and several self-catered chalets (some luxurious).

Eating out The Ferme de Montagne (see 'Hotels') serves excellent cuisine in lovely surroundings. The Tourbillon and Choucas ('fabulous house red') have been recommended. Try the Tyrol for pizza, the rustic Vieux Chêne for Savoyard specialities.

Après-ski Après-ski is quiet, especially on weekdays. But there are half a dozen bars; the obvious first target is the Irish Pub and the Black Bear above it. The Igloo disco is popular.

Off the slopes There's an outdoor ice rink and bowling. There are good shops, a cinema and an intriguing Mechanical Music Museum. Husky sleigh rides, snowshoeing and parapenting are possible. It's feasible to visit Geneva, Lausanne and Montreux from here, too.

Le Grand Massif

Big area of varied slopes shared by hugely contrasting resorts from the rustic to the uncompromisingly concrete

The Grand Massif is a big area of varied, mainly snow-sure slopes best known in the UK for its modern resort of Flaine. For any keen skier, it deserves serious consideration as an alternative to more popular giant ski areas such as the Trois Vallées, Espace Killy, Paradiski and Portes du Soleil. It has slopes to suit every ability level from beginner to expert, and some compelling rustic bases that Francophiles may find more attractive than Flaine.

The Grand Massif is one of the nearest major ski areas to Geneva airport and ideal for short breaks as well as week-long stays. The best-known resort on the UK market is family-friendly **Flaine**. This uncompromisingly concrete resort was conceived in the 1960s, and its core is made up of Bauhaus-style blocks around a traffic-free square. It is not to everyone's taste (including ours) but has more appealing chalet-style developments built more recently away from the centre. It is covered in its own chapter.

That chapter also covers two more sympathetic and French-feeling alternative bases. **Les Carroz** is a sizeable, sprawling, sunny, traditional family resort (bigger than Flaine) where life revolves around the village square with its pavement cafes and restaurants. A gondola 300m from the centre goes up to the slopes. **Morillon** is a small, quiet, traditional old village, with a few cafes, restaurants,

bars, a supermarket and shops spread out along the road. A gondola goes up to the mid-mountain mini-resort of Morillon 1100, with slope-side apartments at the foot of wide, gentle and tree-lined slopes.

Samoëns is an attractive ancient village complete with traffic-free centre, stone fountain, ancient linden tree, a fine church and other medieval buildings. Two gondolas a bus ride from town take you into the slopes. It is covered in its own chapter. **Sixt** is a small, rustic village 6km away from Samoëns at the end of a 14km run from Flaine and with its own small ski area. Buses run to Samoëns.

All the villages have good beginner slopes; the area as a whole is ideal for intermediates, but it also has a lot that will keep experts happy. The slopes reach almost 2500m, and many are north-facing so keep their snow well. But the runs down to the old villages can be patchy.

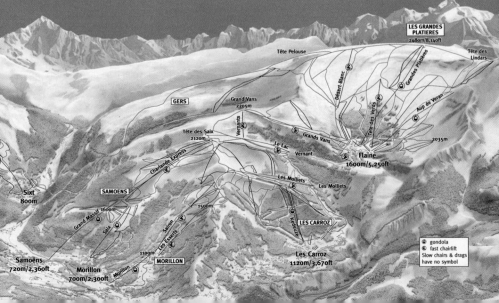

LES GRANDES PLATIERES 2480m/8,140ft · Tête Pelouse · Tête des Lindars · GERS · Grand Vans 2205m · Grandes Platières · Aup de Veran · Tête des Saix 2120m · Vernants · Grands Vans · Tête des Verds · Désert Blanc · 2035m · Le Lac · Vernant · Flaine 1600m/5,250ft · Charlande Express · Les Molliets · Les Molliets · Sixt 800m · SAMOENS · Grand Massif 1600m · Saix · 1500m · LES CARROZ · Les Esserts · Seiron · Kedeuze · 1100m · Samoëns 720m/2,36oft · MORILLON · Morillon 700m/2,300ft · Les Carroz 1120m/3,670ft · Morillon · gondola · fast chairlift · Slow chairs & drags have no symbol

La Grave

A world apart: an unspoiled mountain village beneath high, untamed off-piste slopes, some of them extreme and hazardous

TOP 10 RATINGS

Extent	★
Fast lifts	
Queues	★★★★
Snow	★★★
Expert	★★★★★
Intermediate	★
Beginner	★
Charm	★★★
Convenience	★★★
Scenery	★★★★

RPI	95
lift pass	£200
ski hire	£100
lessons	£95
food & drink	£135
total	**£530**

NEWS

La Grave does not change much, and that is half the charm of the place.

- ➕ Legendary off-piste mountain
- ➕ Usually crowd-free
- ➕ Usually good snow conditions
- ➕ Link to Les Deux-Alpes
- ➕ Easy access by car to other resorts

- ➖ Poor weather means lift closures – on average, two days per week
- ➖ Suitable for experts only
- ➖ Through-traffic detracts from Alpine village atmosphere
- ➖ Nothing to do off the slopes

La Grave enjoys cult status among experts. It has around 500 visitor beds and just one serious lift serving a high, wild and almost entirely off-piste mountainside. The result: an exciting, usually crowd-free area. Strictly, you ought to have a guide, but in good weather many people go it alone.

THE RESORT

La Grave is a small, unspoiled village built along the road up to the Col du Lautaret. A car is useful for access to Les Deux Alpes down the valley, Serre-Chevalier over the pass.

Village charm The centre has a rustic feel, some welcoming hotels and friendly inhabitants. But it is a bit plain, and traffic on the through-road can be intrusive.

Convenience The single serious lift starts a short walk below the centre.

Scenery La Grave is set on a steep hillside facing the impressive glaciers of majestic La Meije. Great views.

THE MOUNTAIN

A slow two-stage 'pulse' gondola (with an extra station at a pylon halfway up the lower stage) ascends into the slopes and finishes at 3200m. Above that, a short walk and a draglift give access to a second drag serving twin blue runs on a glacier slope of about 350m vertical – from here (after another walk) you can ski to Les Deux-Alpes. But the reason that people come here is to explore the legendary slopes back towards La Grave. These slopes offer no defined, patrolled, avalanche-protected pistes – but there are two marked itinéraires (with several variations usefully marked on the 'piste' map) of 1400m vertical down to the pylon lift station, or 1750m all the way down to the valley.

Slopes The Chancel route is mostly of red-run gradient; the Vallons de la Meije is more challenging but not too steep. People do take these routes without a guide or avalanche protection equipment, but we couldn't possibly recommend it.

There are many more demanding runs away from the itinéraires, including couloirs that range from the straightforward to the seriously hazardous, and long descents from the glacier to the valley road below the village, with return by taxi, bus, or strategically parked car. The dangers are considerable (people die here every year), and good guidance is essential. You can also descend a 'spectacular' valley southwards to St-Christophe, returning by bus and the lifts of Les Deux-Alpes.

Fast lifts There aren't any, and there's no need for any.

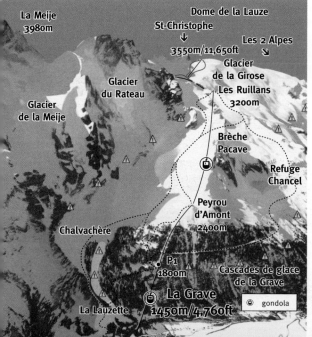

La Meije 3980m · Dome de la Lauze · St-Christophe ↓ 3550m/11,650ft · Les 2 Alpes ↘ · Glacier de la Girose · Glacier du Rateau · Les Ruillans 3200m · Glacier de la Meije · Brèche Pacave · Refuge Chancel · Peyrou d'Amont 2400m · Chalvachère · P1 1800m · Cascades de glace de la Grave · La Grave 1450m/4,760ft · La Lauzette · ⊙ gondola

↑ You get a fair idea of the village and the setting from this shot, but not of the skiing, behind the first ridge or out of the frame to the right

OT LA GRAVE / ETIENNE GIROUD

KEY FACTS

Resort	1450m
	4,760ft
Slopes	1450-3550m
	4,760-11,650ft
Lifts	4
Pistes	5km
	3 miles
Green/Blue	100%

The figures relate only to pistes; practically all the skiing – at least 90% – is off-piste

Snowmaking	none

UK PACKAGES

Alpine Answers, Independent Ski Links, Lagrange, Mountain Tracks, Peak Retreats, Pure Powder, Ski Club Freshtracks, Ski Weekend

Phone numbers
From abroad use the prefix +33 and omit the initial '0' of the phone number

TOURIST OFFICE

www.lagrave-lameije.com

Queues Normally, there are queues only at weekends. March is reportedly the busiest month, when queues can be serious. If snow conditions are poor, queues can build up for the gondola down from the lower stations.
Terrain parks There aren't any.
Snow reliability The chances of powder snow on the high, north-facing slopes are good, but if conditions are tricky, there are no pistes to fall back on apart from the three short blue runs at the top of the gondola.
Experts La Grave's uncrowded off-piste slopes have earned it cult status among hard-core skiers. Only experts should contemplate a stay here – and then only if prepared to deal with bad weather by sitting tight or struggling over the Col du Lautaret to the woods of Serre-Chevalier.
Intermediates The itinéraires get tracked into a piste-like state, and adventurous intermediates could tackle the Chancel. Most folk will soon tire of the three blue runs at the top of the gondola. The valley stations of Villar d'Arène and Lautaret, around 3km and 8km to the east respectively, and Le Chazelet, 3km to the north-west, offer very limited slopes with a handful of runs.
Beginners Novices tricked into coming here can go up the valley to the beginner slopes at Villar d'Arène, or to Le Chazelet, which has a newish fast quad and two snow-guns.
Snowboarding There are no special facilities for boarders, but advanced freeriders will be in their element on the open off-piste powder.

Cross-country There is a total of 20km of loops in the area.
Mountain restaurants Surprisingly, there are three. The excellent, tiny Refuge Chancel, where supplies and waste are backpacked in and out, is the pucka La Grave experience; call in during the morning to see what's cooking, and book.
Schools and guides There are claimed to be 30 or so guides, offering a wide range of services through their bureau. 'Excellent' is the usual verdict. See also 'Hotels' below.
Families Not really a family resort, but the tourist office knows of babysitters.

STAYING THERE

There are very few choices.
Hotels There are several simple options. The Brit-run 2-star Edelweiss (0476 799093) has 'quite basic' rooms but does 'excellent' food and has a 'legendary' wine list. The Skiers Lodge/ Hotel des Alpes (0476 110318) offers all-inclusive week-long packages including guiding. A past reporter had an 'excellent' week.
Apartments Bookable through the tourist office.
Eating out Most people eat in their hotels, though there are alternatives.
Après-ski The central Cafe des Glaciers, and the Castillan are the standard teatime venues. The bars of the Edelweiss and Skiers Lodge have live music. The Vieux Guide gets crowded later.
Off the slopes Anyone not using the slopes will find La Grave much too small and quiet.

Megève

One of the traditional old winter holiday towns; best for those who enjoy relaxed cruising and spectacular views

RATINGS

The mountains

Extent	★★★★★
Fast lifts	★
Queues	★★★★
Terrain p'ks	★★★
Snow	★★
Expert	★★
Intermediate	★★★★
Beginner	★★★
Boarder	★★
X-country	★★★★
Restaurants	★★★★
Schools	★★★
Families	★★★

The resort

Charm	★★★★
Convenience	★★
Scenery	★★★★★
Eating out	★★★★
Après-ski	★★
Off-slope	★★★★

RPI	95
lift pass	£170
ski hire	£125
lessons	£80
food & drink	£165
total	**£540**

NEWS

2010/11: There is a new moving carpet at the Caboche nursery slopes/toboggan area on Rochebrune. It is free to use (although the access lifts are not).

Two chairs on Rochebrune (Petit Rochebrune and Grands Champs) were fitted with the child safety feature, Magnestick.

➕ Extensive easy slopes

➕ Scenic setting, with splendid views

➕ Charming old town centre

➕ Some very smart hotels and shops

➕ Great mountain restaurants

➕ Good for weekends

➕ Great when it snows – woodland runs with no one on them

➕ Plenty to do off the slopes

➖ Low altitude of slopes means a risk of poor snow, though the grassy terrain does not need much cover.

➖ Lots of slow, old lifts remain

➖ Three separate mountains, only two linked (and by lift but not by piste)

➖ Few challenging pistes, though good off-piste available

➖ Very muted après-ski scene

➖ Meals and drinks pricey

Megève has a medieval heart but it was, in a way, the original purpose-built French ski resort – developed in the 1920s as an answer to Switzerland's irritatingly fashionable St Moritz. Although Courchevel long ago took over as France's swankiest resort, Megève's smart hotels still attract fur coats and fat wallets. Happily, you don't need either to enjoy the place. And make no mistake – it is highly enjoyable; just look at that list of plus points above.

This is one of our favourite places to be in falling snow, when Megève regulars take one look and retreat to their duvets. But when the sun's out and we want to zip around the 325km of pistes, we get very frustrated by the preponderance of slow lifts. The area still ranks close to the bottom of our fast lifts league table. The resort's managers still have a lot to learn from St Moritz.

THE RESORT

Megève is in a lovely sunny setting and has a beautifully preserved, partly medieval centre. Visitors are mainly well-heeled French couples and families, who come here for an all-round holiday.

The skiing divides into three sectors. One is directly accessible by lifts from close to the centre and from the southern edge of town, another from an elevated suburb or from an out-of-town lift base. The third involves buses, for most people.

There are several alternative bases (which offer some good-value lodging) on the fringes of the area. St-Gervais and Le Bettex above it have gondola access (St-Gervais is described at the end of this chapter). But beware slow access lifts from otherwise attractive spots. The slopes also link with La Giettaz; this has interesting local terrain, but is out on a limb and not a sensible base.

The Evasion Mont Blanc lift pass also covers Les Contamines. A car is handy for outings here, and perhaps for using the Princesse gondola.

VILLAGE CHARM ★★★★
Old France at its best
Megève's charming old centre is pedestrianised and comes complete with open-air ice rink, horse-drawn sleighs, cobbled streets and a fine church. Lots of smart clothing, jewellery, antique, gift and food shops add to the chic atmosphere. The main Albertville road bypasses the centre, and there are expensive underground car parks. But the resort's clientele

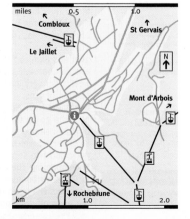

KEY FACTS

Megève

Resort	1100m
	3,610ft
Slopes	850-2355m
	2,790-7,730ft
Lifts	84
Pistes	325km
	202 miles
Green	17%
Blue	30%
Red	40%
Black	13%
Snowmaking	
	485 guns

LIFT PASSES

Evasion Mont Blanc

Prices in €

Age	1-day	6-day
under 15	30	144
15 to 59	38	180
over 60	34	162

Free under 5, over 80
Beginner three free lifts; Rochebrune pass covers 6 lifts; three other limited passes, each covering one or two lifts

Notes
Covers lifts at Les Contamines as well as those of the Megève pass (see list below)

Alternative passes
Megève pass (covers Megève, La Giettaz, Combloux, St-Gervais and St-Nicolas); Jaillet-Combloux-Giettaz only pass; pedestrian pass

---

arrives mainly by car, and the resulting traffic jams and fumes can be a problem in high season and on some weekends.

CONVENIENCE ★★★★★
Stay close to a lift

Unless you have a car, staying close to one of the main lifts makes a lot of sense. Some of the best hotels are above the centre, close to the Mont d'Arbois gondola. Some lodgings are a long walk from the lifts, but the ski-buses are free.

SCENERY ★★★★★
Beautiful town, beautiful views

The resort enjoys a splendid position between its three attractive mountains, with wonderful views of Mont Blanc from much of the ski area.

THE MOUNTAINS

The slopes are largely below the treeline – this is a great resort in poor weather – though there are extensive open areas, particularly higher up in the Mont d'Arbois sector.

Pistes tend to be overclassified – many of the reds would be blue elsewhere. The piste map is badly designed and difficult to follow in many areas, notably around the summit of Mont d'Arbois.

EXTENT OF THE SLOPES ★★★★★
More than enough for a week

Each of the three mountains has a worthwhile amount of terrain, and they add up to a great deal of skiing.

The town is most directly linked with the **Rochebrune** sector – a

gondola goes up from the centre of town, and a cable car from the southern edge. A network of gentle, wooded, north-east-facing slopes, served by drags and mainly slow chairlifts, leads to the high point of Côte 2000, which often has the best snow in Megève. The minor peak of Alpette was the starting point for Megève's historic downhill course, now abandoned.

At just above resort level the Rocharbois cable car goes across the valley to link Rochebrune to the gondola for the bigger **Mont d'Arbois** sector, starting from an elevated suburb of the resort. The Princesse gondola starting a couple of miles north of the town (with extensive free car parking) offers another way up. The slopes above the resort are sunny, but there are north-east-facing slopes to Le Bettex and on down to St-Gervais. A two-stage gondola returns you to the top. You can work your way over to Mont Joux and up to the small Mont Joly area – Megève's highest slopes. And from there you can go to the backwater village of St-Nicolas-de-Véroce (there's a splendid red run along the ridge with wonderful views of Mont Blanc).

The third area is **Le Jaillet**, accessed by gondola from just outside the north-west edge of town, or much more slowly from the separate village of Combloux. In the other direction is the high point of Le Christomet, which is linked to the slopes of Le Torraz, above tiny **La Giettaz**. The slopes of Le Torraz are worth visiting, not least for the spectacular views from the summit.

SNOWPIX.COM / CHRIS GILL

Mountain restaurants are a highlight, and this is one of our favourites – Auberge du Christomet in the sector of Le Jaillet →

FAST LIFTS ★☆☆☆☆
Still too many slow ones
Megève continues to lag behind its
rivals in the uplift business. Gondolas
and cable cars provide the main
access, and fast chairs are dotted
around – but overall three out of four
lifts are slow. Slow lifts provoke more
complaints from readers than queues
or crowds.

QUEUES ★★★★☆
Few weekday problems
Megève is relatively queue-free during
the week, except at peak holiday time.
But school holidays and sunny Sunday
crowds can mean some delays. The
long, steep Lanchettes and Roche Fort
drags between Côte 2000 and the rest
of the Rochebrune slopes can have
'ridiculously long waits' – as does the

cable car linking the two mountains.
Crowded pistes at Mont Joux and Mont
d'Arbois can also be a problem. And
on a snowy day the slopes can be
delightfully quiet as the pampered
clientele stay in bed, leaving the fresh
snow to you and us.

TERRAIN PARKS ★★★☆☆
Four, surprisingly
You wouldn't have thought there was
much call for terrain parks from
Megève's clientele – but the place has
four. The Waidzai park is located by
the Grands Champs chairlift in the
Rochebrune area. However, it is small
with a few medium jumps and rails for
beginners and teenagers. There is a
500m-long boardercross course and a
freestyle airbag nearby. Six snow-guns
ensure good snow cover throughout

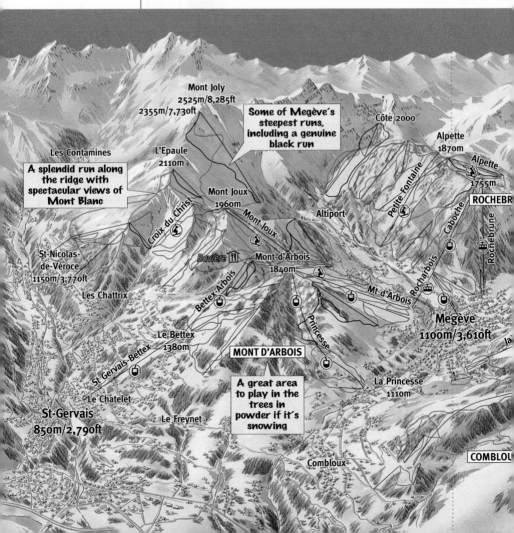

the season. There is also a park on Mont d'Arbois by the Mont Joux chair, with a good line of jumps for all ability levels. These are flanked by a host of rails and boxes and a boardercross. Combloux also has a park and La Giettaz a smaller park, albeit with a real multitude of jump sizes and a few rails. Both have boardercross.

SNOW RELIABILITY ★★☆☆☆
The area's main weakness
The problem is that the slopes are low, with very few runs above 2000m, and partly sunny – the Megève side of Mont d'Arbois gets the afternoon sun. So in a poor snow year, or in a warm spell, snow on the lower slopes can suffer badly. Fortunately, the grassy slopes don't need much depth of

snow. We and reporters found excellent conditions during the February 2011 drought, with piste preparation of a high standard. The resort has an extensive snowmaking network, but that can't work in warm weather.

FOR EXPERTS ★★☆☆☆
Off-piste is the main attraction
One of Megève's great advantages for expert skiers is that there is not much competition for the powder – many days after a fresh dump you can often make first tracks on challenging slopes.

The Mont Joly and Mont Joux sections offer the steepest slopes. The top chair here serves a genuinely black run, with some serious off-piste off the back of the hill, and the

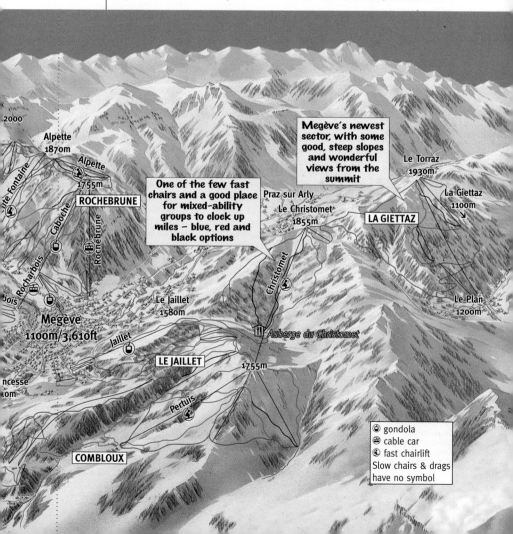

Megève's newest sector, with some good, steep slopes and wonderful views from the summit

One of the few fast chairs and a good place for mixed-ability groups to clock up miles – blue, red and black options

Alpette 1870m
Alpette 1755m
ROCHEBRUNE
Rochebrune
Caboche
Rocharbois
ute fontaine
bois
Megève 1100m/3,610ft
Jaillet
Le Jaillet 1580m
LE JAILLET
1755m
Pertuis
ncesse
om
COMBLOUX

Praz sur Arly
Le Christomet 1855m
Christomet
Auberge du Christomet

Le Torraz 1930m
La Giettaz 1100m
LA GIETTAZ
Le Plan 1200m

2000

🚠 gondola
🚡 cable car
🚟 fast chairlift
Slow chairs & drags have no symbol

ACTIVITIES

Indoor Sports centre (tennis, ice rink, climbing wall, swimming pool, sauna, solarium, gym), beauty treatments, health and fitness centres, bowling, museum, library, cinemas, casino, language courses, concerts and exhibitions, bridge, painting courses

Outdoor Cleared paths, snowshoeing, ice rink, curling, dog sledding, paintballing, horse-drawn carriage rides, adventure park, sightseeing flights, paragliding

UK PACKAGES

Alpine Answers, AmeriCan Ski, Carrier, Erna Low, Flexiski, Lagrange, Luxury Chalet Collection, Momentum, Oxford Ski Co, Peak Retreats, PowderBeds, PV-Holidays.com, Simon Butler Skiing, Ski Collection, Ski Expectations, Ski France, Ski Independence, Ski Solutions, Ski Weekend, Snow Finders, Stanford Skiing, White Roc **St Gervais** AmeriCan Ski, Chalet Group, Erna Low, Holiday in Alps, Lagrange, Mountain Tracks, Peak Retreats, PowderBeds, Ski Club Freshtracks, Ski France, Ski Weekend, Snowcoach, Zenith **Combloux** Erna Low, Peak Retreats

slightly lower Epaule chair has some steep runs back down and also accesses some good off-piste, as well as pistes, down to St-Nicolas. The steep area beneath the second stage of the Princesse gondola can be a play area of powder runs among the trees. Cote 2000 has a small section of steep runs, including good off-piste.

The terrain under the Christomet chair can be a good spot to practise off-piste technique, given decent snow.

FOR INTERMEDIATES ★★★★
Superb if the snow is good
Good intermediates will enjoy the whole area – there is so much choice it's difficult to single out any particular sectors. Keen skiers are likely to want to focus on the fast lifts, and happily several of these serve excellent terrain – the Princesse and Bettex gondolas on Mont d'Arbois, the Fontaine and Alpette chairs on Rochebrune and the Christomet chair in the Le Jaillet sector. But don't confine yourself to those – there are lots of other interesting areas, including the shady north-east-facing slopes on the back of Mont d'Arbois and Mont Joux and the front of Rochebrune, and the genuinely red/black slopes of La Giettaz. The slopes above Combloux are well worth exploring, particularly the quiet reds and black served by the Jouty chairlift.

Megève is also a great area for the less confident. There are long, easy blue runs in all sectors. A number of gentle runs lead down to Le Bettex and La Princesse from Mont d'Arbois, while nearby Mont Joux accesses long, problem-free runs to St-Nicolas. Alpette and Cote 2000 are also suitable. As is most of Le Jaillet, especially the long easy runs down to Combloux.

FOR BEGINNERS ★★★
Good choice of nursery areas
There are beginner slopes at valley level, and more snow-sure ones at altitude on each of the main mountains. There are also plenty of very easy green runs to progress to.

FOR BOARDERS ★★
Beginner friendly
Boarding doesn't really fit with Megève's traditional, rather staid, upmarket image. But freeriders will find lots of untracked off-piste powder for days after new snowfalls. It's a good place to try snowboarding for

the first time, with plenty of fairly wide, quiet, gentle runs and a lot of chairlifts and gondolas. The draglifts around are generally avoidable. There are no specialist schools, but all the ski schools offer boarding lessons. There are four terrain parks.

FOR CROSS-COUNTRY ★★★★
An excellent area
There are 43km of varied trails spread throughout the area. Some are at altitude, making meeting with Alpine skiers for lunch simple.

MOUNTAIN RESTAURANTS ★★★★
Something for all budgets
Megève has some chic, expensive, gourmet mountain huts but plenty of cheaper options too. The Stanford Skiing website has a really useful guide to the restaurants. The piste map is of no help whatever.
Editors' choice On Mont d'Arbois, the Ravière (0450 931571), tucked away in the woods near the Croix chair, is a tiny rustic hut that does a set meal; booking essential. One 2011 reporter was unimpressed, though. The same reporter endorses the Auberge du Christomet (0450 211134), at the foot of the Christomet chair on Le Jaillet ('it's perfect'). It has a lovely setting with fabulous views and a cosy rustic interior; it is accessible by car, and gets booked out well in advance.
Worth knowing about The possibilities seem to be almost endless.

Mont d'Arbois is well endowed. The Igloo at the top has become Vertigo, and we hear it now has a comfortable bar as well as the attractive restaurant. The famously expensive Idéal is said to be excellent. Coming down to earth, there are several modest, small places worth seeking out. We liked Sous les Freddy's, near the Arbois chair; very good meat platter and home-made desserts. Reports on the Gouet, on the Gouet piste, are good – 'friendly family service with great mountain fare'. The Refuge de Porcherey above St-Nicolas offers 'lovely food and ambiance'. The Espace at Mont Joux is 'friendly, reasonably priced'. At the bottom of the Communailles lift, O'Communailles is very welcoming – varied menu and efficient service. Alpage is also tipped.

On Rochebrune/Cote 2000 the Alpette is the prestige place – 'good for a blowout'. Radaz has 'a sunny location, outstanding lasagne and good value plats du jour'. Super

SCHOOLS

ESF
t 0450 210097
International
t 0450 587888
Freeride
t 0680 306898
Summits
t 0450 933521
Agence de Ski
t 0450 891273
BASS
t 0845 468 1003 (UK)
Revolution Glisse
t 0667 608964
Ski Pros
t 0681 610615
Ski Technique
t 0616 766 948

Classes (ESF prices)
5 mornings (2.5hr)
€149
Private lessons
€42 for 1hr

GUIDES

Compagnie des Guides
t 0450 215511

CHILDCARE

Meg'Accueil
t 0450 587784
From age 1
P'tites Frimrousses du Mont d'Arbois
t 0450 211869
Ages 12mnth to 3yr
Club des Piou-Piou
t 0450 589765
Ages 3 and 4

Ski schools
From age 5 (ESF prices): 5 mornings (2hr) €122

GETTING THERE

Air Geneva 90km/ 55 miles (1hr15); Lyon 180km/ 110 miles (2hr30)

Rail Sallanches (12km/7 miles); regular buses from station

Megève at the top of the cable car is 'pricey but good', with 'great ambiance'. On the back of the hill, Chalet Forestier is an atmospheric hut with 'reliable plat du jour'.

On Le Jaillet, Face au Mont Blanc at the top of the gondola does a great fixed-price buffet. Auberge Bonjournal towards La Giettaz has a cosy, rustic interior, 'good food and friendly staff'.

SCHOOLS AND GUIDES ★★★★★
Good private lessons
The ESF has lots of competition here, not only from the International school but also from smaller French schools and some British-run outfits. These tend to be more expensive. We've had good reports on Ski Technique. BASS has a branch here, and offers a range of clinics, typically with a maximum group size of 6 or 8. Reports welcome.

Expeditions to the Vallée Blanche (in Chamonix) and to heli-skiing (in Italy) can be arranged, and mountain guides are available (we've had a great morning powder skiing in the trees with Alex Périnet: 0685 428339).

FOR FAMILIES ★★★★★
Language problems
The kindergartens offer a wide range of activities. But lack of English-speaking staff could be a drawback. The slopes are family-friendly and the schools rated by reporters. There are snow gardens in the main sectors.

STAYING THERE

There is an impressive range of accommodation in the area.
Chalets Stanford is the Megève specialist; for a cheap and very cheerful base, you won't do better than its Sylvana – a creaky, unpretentious old hotel, run along chalet lines, close to the Rochebrune cable car and to the centre of town.
Hotels Megève offers a range of exceptionally stylish and welcoming hotels, mainly quite small and built in chalet style. We don't list the three lovely 5-star places – they are of course expensive, and we never get reports on them.

★★★★Flocons de Sel (0450 214999)
Food-oriented eight-room place in a cluster of chalets secluded a few km out. 'Pampering as good as it gets, amazing staff, best food ever,' says a reporter. Two Michelin stars. Spa.
★★★★Chalet St Georges (0450 930715)
Central, close to the gondola. Warmly welcoming, with 24 rooms and suites.
★★★★Fer à Cheval (0450 213039)
Rustic-chic at its best, with a lovely wood interior. 300m from the church square. Spa and pool.
★★★Coin du Feu (0450 210494)
23-room chalet midway between Rochebrune and Chamois lifts.
★★★Coeur de Megève (0450 212530)
Central, very close to the gondola.
Apartments Loges Blanches is central and smart, with pool and restaurant; bookable via Ski Collection. Pierre et Vacances has two properties. Stanford also has an apartment and an eight-bed self-catering chalet.

EATING OUT ★★★★★
Very French
There are lots of upmarket restaurants, many of them in the better hotels. The gastro guide favourites – the Michelin-starred Roches Fleuries and the Flocons de Sel (read 'Hotels') – are a drive out of town. The Flocons has a more modest branch – Flocons Villages, near the Jazz Club – that is highly recommended by locals.

The 'very French and friendly' Chamois is the place for a fondue and other regional specialities. Other recommended places include Cintra, for seafood, and Bistrot for good value local specialities.

APRES-SKI ★★★★★
Strolling and jazz
Megève is a pleasant place to stroll around after the lifts close, but exciting it isn't. If there are lively bars for a post-piste beer, they have eluded us. And those looking for loud disco-bars later may be disappointed. Club de Jazz (aka the 5 Rues) is our choice – a very popular, if rather expensive, jazz club-cum-cocktail bar, that gets some big-name musicians and opens from tea-time to late. The Kitschen bar

Megève

Interactive resort shortlist builder at **www.wtss.co.uk**

ST-GERVAIS

St-Gervais is a handsome 19th-century spa town set in a narrow river gorge, on the far side of Mont d'Arbois from Megève, with access to the shared slopes via a gondola from just outside the town.

Although definitely a town, it's a pleasant place, with interesting food shops, cosy and sophisticated bars (we liked the trendy Pur bar for cocktails and upmarket nibbles), newly renovated thermal baths and an Olympic ice rink. Prices are noticeably lower than in Megève. The resort has a train station and there are regular and convenient bus services. There is also a mountain railway up to the ridge to the east of the town.

The lodgings are mostly modest – there are half a dozen 2-star hotels, and only two 3-stars. Two hotels convenient for the gondola are the Liberty Mont Blanc (0450 934521), a pleasantly traditional 2-star with pool, and the 3-star Carlina (0450 934110), with a small pool and sauna. The unclassified Féline Blanche (0450 965870) is a hip boutique place with just ten rooms done out in black and white. The basic 2-star Val d'Este (0450 936591) has one of the best restaurants in town (Le Serac).

Holiday in Alps has a large selection of apartments and self-catered chalets to rent. Fermes de St Gervais is a smart Lagrange Prestige residence with a pool, a mile out of town. These and other apartments are also available through Peak Retreats.

The gondola from town goes to Le Bettex, a small mid-mountain development of hotels, restaurants, excellent nursery area and well-organised ski school – recommended by a reporter. It's a good base for families wanting quiet, slope-side convenience. We enjoyed staying recently at the 3-star Arbois-Bettex (0450 931222), with pool, spa and good restaurant, popular with families; and dining at the lovely rustic Chalet Rémy – traditional food, friendly.

On the opposite side of St-Gervais is a rack-and-pinion railway, which in 1904 was intended to go to the top of Mont Blanc but terminates at the ridge that forms part of the ski area of Les Houches (described in the Chamonix chapter); but sadly there are no lift pass sharing arrangements.

---

is lively, Brit-run, 'serves tapas with a French twist'. The Cocoon is another Brit favourite, with live music and sports TV. The casino is more slot machines than blackjack tables. Palo Alto has two discos.

OFF THE SLOPES ★★★★
Lots to do
There is a 'fantastic' sports centre with a fitness room and pool (being renovated), an outdoor ice rink, cinemas and a market on Fridays. Trips to Annecy and Chamonix are possible. Walks are excellent, with 50km of marked classified paths. Meeting friends on the slopes for lunch is easy.

Phone numbers
From abroad use the prefix +33 and omit the initial '0' of the phone number

TOURIST OFFICES
Megève
www.megeve.com
St-Gervais
www.st-gervais.net

Weekly news updates and resort links at **www.wtss.co.uk**

Les Menuires

The bargain base for the Trois Vallées – with increasing amounts of stylish accommodation as well as the original dreary blocks

TOP 10 RATINGS

Extent	★★★★★
Fast lifts	★★★★
Queues	★★★★
Snow	★★★★
Expert	★★★★
Intermediate	★★★★★
Beginner	★★★
Charm	★
Convenience	★★★★★
Scenery	★★★

RPI | 100

lift pass	£220
ski hire	£120
lessons	£80
food & drink	£135
total	**£555**

NEWS

2011/12: Two new apartment complexes will open in Reberty/ Les Bruyères.

2010/11: A moving carpet was installed at Reberty 1850.

A short blue run was created by the Sunny Express, avoiding the steeper Boyes slope.

The Becca fun zone was revamped and gained snowmaking.

WENDY-JANE KING

La Croisette, the heart of Les Menuires. Convenient and safe for kids, but not really our cup of tea ↓

➕ Speedy, mostly queue-free access to the huge Trois Vallées area

➕ Lots of slope-side accommodation, with traffic well separated

➕ Low prices by local standards

➕ French atmosphere

➖ Big, dreary blocks and gloomy indoor shopping malls in centre

➖ Main intermediate and beginner slopes get a lot of sun

➖ Some slopes can get very crowded

Les Menuires arguably has the best position in the Three Valleys, and we've warmed to it as better (and better-looking) lodgings have continued to be built. With our RPI confirming it as the most affordable major resort in the area, we now view Les Menuires as a very attractive proposition – especially the traditional-style bits we've christened collectively 'Belles-Menuires'.

THE RESORT

Les Menuires is a purpose-built resort, dominated by large apartment blocks, with about 60% of the visitors French. It has excellent links to Val Thorens in the same valley, and to the Méribel valley. The core of the resort is La Croisette, a horseshoe of blocks plus a low-rise shopping mall below the main lifts. Recent development has added various suburbs to the original core, and a second lift base across the mountainside at Les Bruyères.

Village charm The original buildings that surround the main lift base are among the most brutal examples of the monolithic architecture of the 1960s/70s. They still dominate, which is why we retain the 1-star rating. But the resort is trying hard to smarten up. A couple of the original buildings have been demolished (as we advised over a decade ago) and replaced by chalet-style blocks. Recent developments are all in stone-and-wood traditional style.

Read our Belles-Menuires feature at the end of the chapter.

Convenience For most visitors, the resort is very conveniently arranged – a great deal of the accommodation is ski-in, and much of it ski-out. Stay in the central area, and nothing is more than a stroll away. Stay in some of the outposts, and it may be different. They have their own shops and bars, but if you want more choice, you are reliant on buses that are 'infrequent and slow, especially in the evenings'. In the mornings, too, you may have some hiking to do if you want to start from a lift other than the nearest one.

Scenery The scenery can be rather bleak, but there are grand views from the peaks of the ski area.

THE MOUNTAINS

Les Menuires is set at about the treeline, with almost all open slopes.

The latest piste map meets with reader approval. Signing is good, with clear directions at key points.

Slopes The major part of the network spreads across the broad, west-facing mountainside between Les Menuires and St-Martin, with links to the

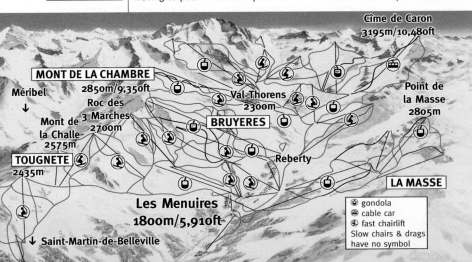
Méribel valley at four points and to Val Thorens at the southern end. A gondola and a fast chair go up from La Croisette, and the same from Les Bruyères. A chair and gondola to the separate sector of La Masse, across the valley, start below the village.

Fast lifts Les Menuires now has a good supply of fast chairs or gondolas.

Queues Not usually a problem; most of our 2011 reporters comment on few queues. But the Bruyères gondola (for access to Val Thorens) and Mont de la Chambre chair may get busy at peak times. Crowded slopes are more of a problem in general, particularly those leading down to the resort centre.

Terrain parks The newly revamped Becca park and ski-cross area above Reberty has rails, slides and big air; there's a learner area.

Snow reliability La Masse's height and orientation ensure good snow for a long season. The west-facing slopes have lots of snowmaking but the snow lower down is often icy or slushy.

Experts The upper slopes of La Masse are virtually all of stiff red/soft black steepness – great fast cruises when groomed. There is also a huge amount of off-piste, including the Vallon du Lou south of La Masse.

Intermediates With good snow, the slopes above the village, virtually all blue and red, have a lot to offer. Don't miss La Masse – the blacks are not super-steep – but beware the steep Masse draglift. One lift – the Bruyères gondola – is all it takes to get to Val Thorens or the Méribel valley.

Beginners The resort has improved its nursery areas, now with six free moving carpets. There is a special lift

pass for beginners. Snow quality on the nursery slopes is a concern. There is a green run to the village from the Roc des 3 Marches chair, and lots of easy blues to progress to, but they are prone to crowds.

Snowboarding There are few drags but some flattish sections of piste.

Cross-country The 28km of prepared trails are along the valley between St-Martin and Les Menuires.

Mountain restaurants There are some excellent spots – good news for people based in Courchevel and Méribel in search of an affordable lunch. The consistent favourite is the Grand Lac, a big chalet in a fine spot at the bottom of the Granges chair – 'great choice, healthy portions, friendly service, reasonably-priced'. Way across the hill, the Alpage is similarly praised. The Sonnailles, off the valley bottom Cumin run, is another favourite. In the almost-a-mountain-restaurant category, the Ferme, piste-side at Reberty 2000, is excellent. Consider the slope-side hotel terraces up here, too, particularly the Ours Blanc.

Schools and guides ESF gets mixed reviews. SnowBow, a branch of the Internationale school has been recommended. A group of instructors operating here and in St-Martin under the startling name of Ski School offer private lessons only in English and are reported to be 'really good'.

Families Good facilities. There are kids' 'villages' with indoor and outdoor facilities at both La Croisette and Les Bruyères. The chalet operators in Reberty operate their own nurseries. There are fun parks, tubing, and kids' snow scooters and quad bikes.

Cîme de Caron
3195m/10,480ft

MONT DE LA CHAMBRE
2850m/9,350ft

Méribel

Roc des
3 Marches
Mont de 2700m
la Challe
2575m

TOUGNETE
2435m

Val-Thorens
2300m

BRUYERES

Reberty

Point de
la Masse
2805m

LA MASSE

Les Menuires
1800m/5,910ft

Saint-Martin-de-Belleville

gondola
cable car
fast chairlift
Slow chairs & drags
have no symbol

↑ The fisheye lens distorts things, but you can see there's quite a bit of skiing

KEY FACTS

Resort	1800m
	5,910ft

Three Valleys

Slopes	1260-3230m
	4,130-10,600ft
Lifts	173
Pistes	600km
	373 miles
Green	16%
Blue	40%
Red	34%
Black	10%
Snowmaking	
	2091 guns

Les Menuires / St-Martin only

Slopes	1400-2850m
	4,590-9,350ft
Lifts	33
Pistes	160km
	99 miles
Green	16%
Blue	45%
Red	31%
Black	8%
Snowmaking	50%

Phone numbers
From abroad use the prefix +33 and omit the initial '0' of the phone number

TOURIST OFFICE

www.lesmenuires.com

STAYING THERE

Les Menuires itself consists mainly of large apartment blocks. Reberty has hotels and chalets, as well as apartment residences.

Chalets Quite a few operators have chalets in the resort's more appealing slope-side suburbs – read our Belles-Menuires feature, over the page.

Hotels There are good places on the slopes at Reberty/Les Bruyères. The Kaya (0479 414200) is the resort's only 4-star – attractively smart and modern. The Isatis (0479 004545) is a chalet-style 3-star right at the Bruyères gondola – 17 suites, all with hot tubs. We stayed here happily in 2011. The bigger 3-star Ours Blanc (0479 006166) is up the slope in Reberty.

Apartments There are lots of new developments in chalet style, most of them covered by our Belles-Menuires feature. In the suburb of Preyerand, just below the main resort centre, is the chalet-style CGH residence Les Clarines, with spa and pool. Ski Amis has units in all parts of the resort.

Eating out We had very good traditional and gourmet meals at the Cocon des Neiges (hotel Isatis). Up the slope in Reberty, the piste-side Ferme is very popular for its food (steaks etc), atmosphere and good-value menus. The K (hotel Kaya) is a good gourmet option. Other recent tips include the 'efficient, jolly' Chouette ('great crêpes'), the Marmite de Géant ('excellent Savoyard and more adventurous dishes') and the Vieux Grenier ('lots of choice', 'great atmosphere' but 'slow service').

Après-ski It's pretty quiet in the evening. A reporter favourite for close-of-play beers, sometimes with live music, is the Chouette at Les Bruyères. There is no shortage of bars in La Croisette, but many are in the dreadfully claustrophobic mall, which for some of us rules them out. The Grotte de Yeti in Preyerand does a 'spectacular flaming pyramid of vodka shots', and the cabaret at Medz'é-ry is 'unusually' entertaining, we're told. There are discos in both La Croisette and Les Bruyères.

Off the slopes The resort does make an effort on this front. There is a big and seriously impressive sports/spa/fitness centre. The various outdoor activities include a 4km-long toboggan run down the Roc des 3 Marches gondola. Engine-driven options include microlight flights. But this is basically a destination for skiers and boarders, and not very appealing for others.

Les Belles-Menuires

La Plagne has its Belle-Plagne – why shouldn't Les Menuires have its Belles-Menuires? Or should it be Beaux-Menuires? Whatever ... We've made up this name to represent the attractive, chalet-style suburbs of Les Menuires – places where Méribel habitués might be happy.

These suburbs aren't simply built in chalet style – they also contain actual chalets, most of them operated by British firms who advertise on this spread and are marked, approximately, on our map. They are concentrated up the slope in Reberty 2000, or down in Les Bruyères, a micro-resort complete with ice rink and swimming pool – and a major lift, the Bruyères gondola. The area shown also has the resort's best hotels, some smart apartment residences (read the margin panel), and an excellent slope-side restaurant, the Ferme.

Down the valley, on the opposite side of the resort centre are further traditional-style, small-scale, relatively upmarket developments (read the left margin panel).

↑ Reberty 2000 has an excellent piste-side restaurant, the Ferme, and an adequate small supermarket; and lots of chalets

OT LES MENUIRES / P ROYER

DOWN THE HILL

Below the main resort centre in Le Bettex, Ski Amis has a cluster of smart, independent chalets with outdoor hot tubs and saunas, 150m from the piste and the Bettex chairlift. A blue piste from the top of that takes you to the Tortollet chair to get up to Les Menuires and the Rocher Noir chair for La Masse.

Weekly news updates and resort links at www.wtss.co.uk

Reberty, Les Bruyères, Le Bettex

APARTMENTS

In Reberty 2000, the Chalets du Soleil is an offshoot of the next-door 4-star hotel Kaya. Newly built up here for 2011/12 and in the same ownership is Chalet Julietta, with wellness facilities.

Slightly lower down, Alpages de Reberty is a Pierres & Vacances Premium residence with pool, sauna etc.

La Sapinière includes the Montagnettes residence Hameau de la Sapinière, with sauna and hot tub, and the residence Montalys, with spacious apartments and restaurant.

Down in Les Bruyères, a new development for 2011/12 is Les Chalets du Mont Vallon, with pool, gym, sauna and a serious restaurant.

All the specialists in French apartments offer these and other residences – Ski Collection, Lagrange, Erna Low.

Catered chalets run by British operators

Ski Amis ▲
Ski Famille ▲
Family Ski Co ▲
Ski Olympic ▲
Powder N Shine ▲

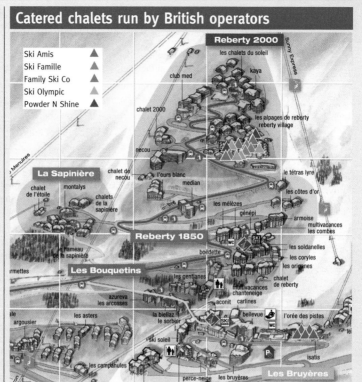

Designed with the family in mind
www.familyski.co.uk
family ski company

Les Menuires

301

Interactive resort shortlist builder at www.wtss.co.uk

Selected chalets in Les Menuires

ADVERTISEMENT

SKI AMIS *www.skiamis.com*

T **0203 411 5439**

- Chalets de Bruyeres – 5 chalets for 12-16 people – ski-in/ski-out
- Chalets de Bettaix – 4 chalets for 8-10 people
- Hot-tubs, free WIFI, satellite TV
- Excellent catering with full English breakfast every day, afternoon tea and three course evening meal
- Unlimited good quality wine

sales@skiamis.com

↑ CHALETS DE BETTAIX

SKI AMIS

CHALETS DE BRUYERES ↑

Méribel

The enduring British favourite: a comfortable, upmarket chalet-style resort in the centre of the incomparable Trois Vallées

302

- ➕ Central to the Trois Vallées, the biggest lift network in the world
- ➕ Pleasant chalet-style architecture
- ➕ Impressive lift system
- ➕ Very lively après-ski scene
- ➕ Excellent piste maintenance and snowmaking; nevertheless …

- ➖ Snow on the west-facing side suffers from afternoon sun
- ➖ Sprawling main village
- ➖ Expensive, particularly for food and drink
- ➖ Full of Brits
- ➖ Some pistes can get crowded

A loyal band of regular visitors just love Méribel, and it's not difficult to see why. For keen piste-bashers who like to rack up the miles but dislike tacky post-war resorts, it's difficult to beat: unlike other modern purpose-built resorts, Méribel has always insisted on chalet-style architecture.

Other 3V resorts have the edge in some respects. For better snow opt for Courchevel or Val Thorens. For lower prices, Les Menuires. For a more compact village and a lower concentration of Brits, go virtually anywhere.

THE RESORT

Méribel was founded in 1938 by a Brit, Peter Lindsay, and has retained a strong British presence and influence ever since. It occupies the central valley of the Trois Vallées network. It consists of two main resort villages.

The original resort is built on a steepish west-facing hillside with the home piste running down beside it to the main lift stations in the valley bottom, slightly below the village centre. The resort now spreads widely away from the centre and the piste; various quarters can be identified – among them Mussillon, beside the road in to the resort, where many individual chalets are located. A road winds up from the centre to the top of the main village. From there, one road goes on through woods to the outpost of the Altiport (a snow-covered airstrip) while another goes under the home piste to a more recently developed area, Belvedere.

The satellite resort of Méribel-Mottaret, a mile or two up the valley, is centrally placed in the Trois Vallées ski area, offering quicker access to Val Thorens in particular. The hamlet of Méribel-Village, on the road from Méribel to Courchevel, has developed into a pleasant, quiet micro-resort. It is at the bottom of a blue run from Altiport, with a fast quad giving access to the other slopes.

You can stay in the valley below

Méribel, in the spa town of Brides-les-Bains – see the end of this chapter – or in the village of Les Allues at a mid-station of the gondola from Brides.

A car is useful for outings to other resorts in the Tarentaise; you can access La Plagne via Champagny. But it can be useful around the village too.

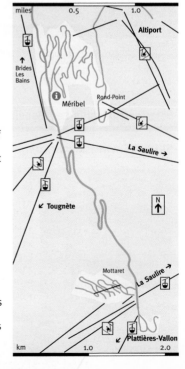

KEY FACTS

Resort	1400-1700m
	4,590-5,580ft

Three Valleys	
Slopes	1260-3230m
	4,130-10,600ft
Lifts	173
Pistes	600km
	373 miles
Green	16%
Blue	40%
Red	34%
Black	10%
Snowmaking	
	2091 guns

Méribel only	
Slopes	1400-2950m
	4,590-9,680ft
Lifts	50
Pistes	150km
	93 miles
Green	12%
Blue	47%
Red	31%
Black	10%
Snowmaking	
	728 guns

LIFT PASSES

Three Valleys

Prices in €

Age	1-day	6-day
under 13	36	177
13 to 64	47	235
over 65	40	200

Free under 5, over 75
Beginner mini-pass
for two beginner
areas
Notes
Covers Courchevel, La
Tania, Méribel, Val
Thorens, Les Menuires
and St-Martin; family
reductions; pedestrian
and half-day passes
Alternative passes
Méribel and Méribel-
Mottaret only with
one-day Three Valleys
extension available

Chalets, chalets,
chalets; we're
guessing this must be
Méribel-Village or
some even more
remote backwater →

VILLAGE CHARM ★★★☆☆
Built with style
Méribel is one of the most tastefully
designed of French purpose-built
resorts. The buildings are wood-clad,
chalet-style and mainly low-rise, and
they include a lot of individual chalets
as well as big chalet-shaped blocks of
apartments. Mottaret lacks these
smaller chalets, and looks more block-
like as a result, despite wood cladding
on its apartment buildings. Even so,
it's more attractive than many other
resorts built for slope-side
convenience. It has far fewer shops
and bars and much less après-ski than
Méribel itself, and nothing like the feel
of a village – it has no real centre.

CONVENIENCE ★★★☆☆
Shuttle to the slopes, usually
Although some lodgings are right on
the piste beside the village, many
depend on using free (and now
'excellent') public buses or private
minibuses to and from the slopes.
There are collections of shops and
restaurants at a couple of points on
the road through the resort – Altitude
1600 and Plateau de Morel – so you
are not obliged to descend to the
centre every evening.
    Méribel-Village is a small place; it
has some luxury chalets and
apartments, but has very limited
amenities – a bread shop, a small
supermarket, fitness centre, bar,
pizzeria and a couple of restaurants.
    Mottaret has spread up both steep
sides of the valley, though most of the
blocks are on the east-facing side.

Many lodgings are ski-in/ski-out, but
not all. Both sides are served by lifts
for pedestrians – but the gondola up
the east-facing slope stops at 7.30pm
and it's a long, tiring walk up.

SCENERY ★★★☆☆
Head for Vallon
The village is attractively set in
woodland, below long craggy ridges –
a satisfying although unspectacular
scene. But there are wonderful glacial
views from Mont du Vallon at the head
of the valley.

THE MOUNTAINS
Most of the slopes are above the
treeline, but there are some sheltered
runs for bad-weather days. Piste
classification is not always reliable – a
problem compounded by exposure of
many slopes to the sun. Signposting is
now excellent. The piste map is
adequate; but it could be so much
better if it covered the two sides of
the valley separately.

EXTENT OF THE SLOPES ★★★★★
Centre of a huge area
Leaving aside the rest of the Trois
Vallées, this is a big area. Lifts go up
to nine high-points on the ridges
above the resort – two entry points to
the Courchevel valley, no less than six
entry points to the Belleville valley
shared by St-Martin, Les Menuires and
Val Thorens, and Mont du Vallon, a
very worthwhile cul de sac.
    On the morning-sun side, chairs go
up to the first two links with St-Martin,

and some relatively quiet slopes back towards Méribel. To the left, a gondola and then a six-pack go from Méribel to **Tougnète**, for both Les Menuires or St-Martin. You can also head down to **Mottaret** from here. From there, a fast chair then a drag take you to Belleville entry point number four.

South of Mottaret are some of the best slopes in the valley, in the **Plattières-Vallon** sector at the head of the valley. The Plattières gondola ends at the fifth entry point to the Belleville valley. To the east of this is the big stand-up gondola to the top of Mont du Vallon. The Côte Brune fast quad from near this area goes up to Mont de la Chambre, the sixth link with the next valley, and the only one giving direct access to Val Thorens.

On the afternoon-sun side, gondolas leave both Méribel and Mottaret for **Saulire,** the main link to Courchevel 1850. The other link is from Altiport, via a slow chairlift to Col de la Loze.

FAST LIFTS ★★★★★
Highly efficient system
Modern chairs and gondolas serve either side of the valley, with good links into the rest of the Three Valleys.

QUEUES ★★★★☆
3V traffic a persistent problem
The area is generally queue-free most of the time, but as more and more visitor beds are added to the Trois Vallées resorts, new bottlenecks emerge. The lift company could

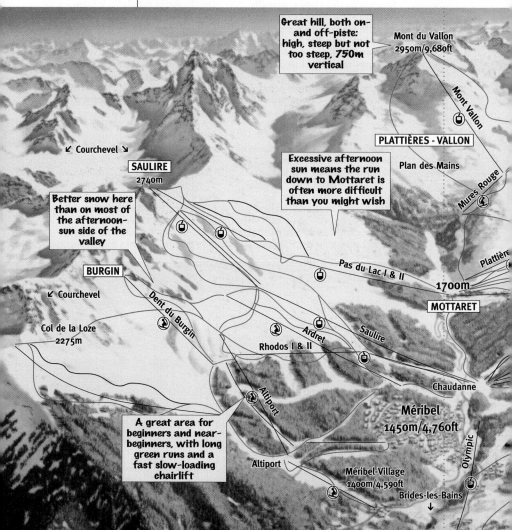

Great hill, both on- and off-piste: high, steep but not too steep, 750m vertical

Mont du Vallon
2950m/9,68oft

PLATTIÈRES - VALLON

Mures Rouge

Plan des Mains

Excessive afternoon sun means the run down to Mottaret is often more difficult than you might wish

Courchevel

SAULIRE
2740m

Better snow here than on most of the afternoon-sun side of the valley

Plattières

Pas du Lac I & II

1700m

BURGIN

Courchevel

Dent du Burgin

MOTTARET

Col de la Loze
2275m

Ardret

Saulire

Rhodos I & II

Chaudanne

Altiport

Méribel
1450m/4,76oft

A great area for beginners and near-beginners, with long green runs and a fast slow-loading chairlift

Altiport

Olympic

Méribel-Village
1400m/4,59oft

Brides-les-Bains

achieve a lot by employing lifties to usher people into half-empty cabins. If Les Arcs can do it ....

We and reporters alike have found that the six-pack above the Tougnète gondola is a serious bottleneck – it comes nowhere near coping with the combination of people coming up the gondola and people descending the four good pistes above.

The Plattières gondola and the Côte Brune chair, serving great terrain and accessing Val Thorens, both attract crowds – though the fast Combes and Chatelet chairs are a viable alternative to the former. Both of the main gondolas for Courchevel from Méribel and Mottaret can build queues.

In this central valley the most serious problems result from the tidal flows of people passing through in the morning (when the tide coincides with the start of ski school) and in the late afternoon, when crowds on the runs to Mottaret can also be a problem.

Most people returning from Val Thorens form a queue for the Plan des Mains chair so as to avoid the flat start of the 'blue' Ours valley run. Confident skiers should use our trick instead: by-pass Plan des Mains by traversing above it, off-piste.

TERRAIN PARKS ★★★★☆
Two comprehensive areas
Méribel has two decent parks. The main Moonpark is accessed by the Arpasson draglift and covers over 10 hectares, spilling over onto the Grive slope. In charge are the respected Ho5

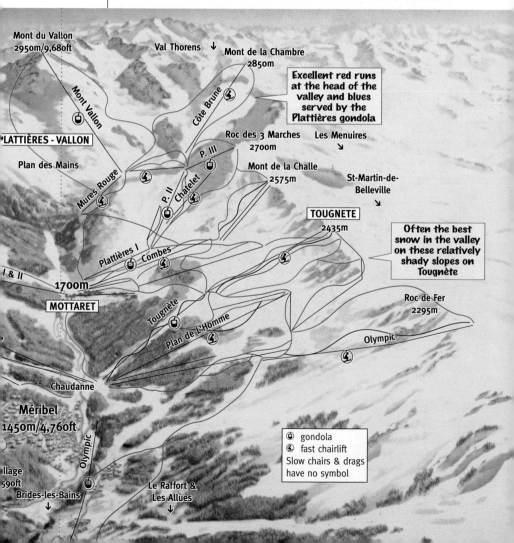

SNOWPIX.COM / CHRIS GILL

Not trivial for a blue run, eh? This is Lièvre, approaching the base of the Tougnète gondola ↓

crew. There's a triple kicker line for all levels with smooth take-offs, quite advanced rails and big spine jump. There is a step-up to step-down obstacle, S-box, wooden goal post feature, 'chill and grill' BBQ zone and a boardercross. The Magic ski school gives free freestyle lessons in the park on Wednesdays. Kids get their own area, P'tit Moon, with mini jumps, boxes and even a small boardercross. The other full park is at Plattières, newly redesigned and including two half-pipes and boardercross.

SNOW RELIABILITY ★★★
Not the best in the Three Valleys
Méribel's slopes aren't the highest in the Three Valleys, and they mainly face roughly east or west; the latter (the

runs down from Courchevel) get the full force of the afternoon sun. In late season you soon get into the habit of avoiding this side in the morning, when it is still rock-hard having frozen overnight. Skiers coming over from Courchevel can get a real shock. The run down from Saulire to Mottaret is a particular problem – often like concrete for its whole 1000m vertical; in our countless visits over many years, we've never found this run enjoyable. The slopes above Altiport get less direct sun and generally have decent snow, and the morning-sun side can be excellent. At the southern end of the valley, a lot of runs are north-facing and keep their snow well, as do the runs on Mont du Vallon.

Snowmaking has been increased to the point where the lower runs have substantial cover. Lack of snow is rarely a problem. Grooming was reportedly 'good' this year. A daily map is available at the tourist office showing which runs were groomed overnight.

FOR EXPERTS ★★★★
Exciting choices
The size of the Trois Vallées means experts are well catered for. In the Méribel valley, Mont du Vallon has lots to offer. The long, steep Combe Vallon run here is classified red; it's a wonderful, long, fast cruise when groomed (which it normally is), but presents plenty of challenge when mogulled. And there's a beautiful off-piste run in the next valley to the main pistes, leading back to the bottom of the gondola.

A good mogul run is down the side of the double Roc de Tougne draglift which leads up to Mont de la Challe. And there are steep, unrelenting runs from Tougnète back to Méribel – the upper Ecureuil piste is now a black while the adjacent Combe Tougnète is

Méribel has a lot of very good off-piste to discover. Here, we pick out some of the best runs for skiers with at least some off-piste experience. Don't tackle them without guidance.

The run from near Roc de Fer to Le Raffort, a mid-station on the gondola from Brides-les-Bains, is an adventure with exceptional views. You ride the Olympic chairlift, go along the ridge, then ski a gentle bowl to finish among the trees.

The wide, west-facing slope above Altiport is enjoyable when the snow is fresh – varied terrain, from average to steep, some open some wooded, reached from the Tétras black run.

There are lots of runs suitable for more accomplished off-piste skiers. One is the Cairn, from the Mouflon piste at the top of the Plattières gondola; it starts in a fairly steep couloir and becomes wider, with a consistent pitch, until you reach the Sittelle piste.

The Roc de Tougne draglift accesses some challenging runs. To the right of the Lagopéde red piste is an area guides call the Spot – a rather technical and steep descent to the Sittelle piste. Alternatively, a 15-minute hike brings you to the Couloir du Serail, leading to the Mouflon red piste – a favourite because of the vertical, the constant pitch and the quality of snow.

Some of the best routes in the Méribel valley are accessed from the other valleys. The Col du Fruit is a classic, far away from the lifts and resorts. You ride the Creux Noirs chairlift in Courchevel, then walk along the ridge for 15 minutes before descending through the national park to Lac de Tueda and the cross-country tracks ... 800m of flat ground from the Mottaret lifts. Some of the best snow is accessed from the 3 Vallées 2 chairlift at Val Thorens. Ducking the rope at the top takes you into varied terrain mixing couloirs and gentle slopes, with exposures from north-east to north-west. Eventually you join the red Lac de la Chambre piste.

now a red. At the north end of the valley the Face run was created for the women's downhill race in the 1992 Olympics. Served by a fast quad, it's a splendid cruise when freshly groomed (with good views over the village).

Nothing on the Saulire side is as steep as on the other side of the valley. The Mauduit red run is quite challenging, though – it used to be classified black.

Throughout the area there are good off-piste opportunities – read our feature panel, and the other Trois Vallées resort chapters.

FOR INTERMEDIATES ★★★★★
Paradise found
Méribel and the rest of the Trois Vallées form something close to paradise for intermediate skiers and riders; there are few other resorts where a keen piste-basher can cover so many miles so easily and with such satisfaction. Virtually every slope in the region has a good intermediate run down it, and to describe them all would take a book in itself.

For less adventurous intermediates, the run from the second station of the Plattières gondola above Mottaret back to the first station is ideal, and used a lot by the ski school. It is a gentle, north-facing, cruising run and is generally in good condition. But

below that the run can get tricky, bumpy and very crowded later in the day. The red run into Mottaret on the other side of the valley also gets dangerously icy and crowded. Something should be done to tackle these two problems, which spoil an otherwise ideal intermediate area.

Even early intermediates should find the runs over into the other valleys well within their capabilities, opening up further vast amounts of intermediate runs. In Courchevel or Val Thorens you also get the bonus of better snow.

Virtually all the pistes on both sides of the Méribel valley will suit more advanced intermediates. Few of the reds are easy.

FOR BEGINNERS ★★★★
Strengths and weaknesses
Méribel continues to improve its appeal to beginners. At the core of this appeal is an excellent long green slope – gentle, wide, tree-lined – at Altiport (where one of the editors of this book learned to ski, [cough] years ago). This is a lift or bus-ride above the resort, which is not ideal, but there are green runs from the top and bottom of the slope back to the village. And now a green-run link is being created from the mid-station of the Saulire gondola, so that novices

Interactive resort shortlist builder at **www.wtss.co.uk**

will be able to ski all the way down
from that point. The main slope is
served by a drag which is one of six
free lifts in the resort, and by a fast
chair going a bit higher which is not
free. But there is a special beginner's
lift pass.

There is a small nursery slope at
Rond-Point, at the top of the village,
which is mainly used by the children's
ski school.

At Mottaret, facilities are less
impressive, but adequate. There are
three enclosed beginner areas ('zen
zones') – one beside the village has a
new covered magic carpet at the
bottom, with the upper part served by
the free village gondola, and there are
two higher zones reached via the
Plattières gondola; there is no green
piste back to the village, and novices
should not even think about
attempting the busy, tricky blue.

FOR BOARDERS ★★★★
Loved by Brits
Méribel is a favourite for British
snowboarders. The terrain is good and
varied, with a worthwhile number of
tree runs. Mont du Vallon has some
very good steep freeriding that stays
relatively untracked. There are lots of
red runs here for intermediates and
gentle blues and greens for beginners.
Most lifts are chairs or gondolas but
beware of flat sections on the main
routes to and from Val Thorens – avoid
the Ours blue run down to Mottaret
from Mont du Vallon, which is very
hard work. Specialist shops include
Avalon Rider (in central Méribel).

FOR CROSS-COUNTRY ★★★
Scenic routes
There are about 33km in the Méribel
valley. The main area is in the forest
near Altiport and great for trying cross-
country for the first time. There's also
a loop around Lake Tueda, in the

nature reserve at Mottaret, and for the
more experienced an itinéraire from
Altiport to Courchevel.

MOUNTAIN RESTAURANTS ★★★
A disappointing choice
There are few places worth singling
out here, and there aren't enough
restaurants to meet the demand, so
many places get crowded. Restaurants
are not named on the piste map.

We've had a good lunch in the
table-service part of Plan des Mains,
and we're told the self-service has
improved but would welcome more
reports. The Chardonnet, mid-station
of the Pas du Lac gondola, is 'a real
find' and popular for its steak tartare
prepared at the table, says a 2011
visitor. The Coeur de Cristal, low down
beside the Adret chair, does 'very nice,
well presented food'. The
Rhododendrons, at the top of the
Altiport drag, is a popular spot for its
large terrace but gets mixed reviews.

This is one of the few resorts where
we can be persuaded to descend to
resort level for lunch on one of three
slope-side hotel terraces – the Adray
Telebar, the Allodis or the Altiport. All
thoroughly excellent. Above Mottaret,
the Grain de Sel gets a reader vote –
twice for the 'best burgers'.

SCHOOLS AND GUIDES ★★★★
Some excellent options
The ESF is by far the biggest school,
with over 450 instructors. It has an
international section with instructors
speaking good English. It offers useful
options, such as off-piste groups, heli-
skiing on the Italian border and Three
Valleys tours. Magic Snowsports
Academy, the second largest school, is
run by an Anglo-French team and has
a number of native English-speaking
instructors.

New Generation, a British school
that operates in Courchevel, La Tania

and Méribel, gets excellent reports –
for example, 'patient and clear', 'all
excellent instructors', 'the perfect
amount of jokes, drills, talks and
brilliant skiing'.

BASS is an established British
school, operating in nine resorts
including Courchevel and Méribel.
Classes are small. Reports welcome.

Snow Systems, with about 15
instructors, is clearly very efficient at
prompting clients to report to us. We
don't mind that – the many reports we
receive are clearly genuine. An
example from the 2011 crop: 'The
patience and quality of tuition was
superb, ensuring my first ski trip was
a success.' Snow D'Light is similarly
energetic, or was – we have no reports
this year.

FOR FAMILIES ★★★☆☆
A popular chalet choice
Méribel is a sensible choice for
families wanting a chalet holiday. What
it lacks in convenience it gains in an
impressive area, with gentle beginner
slopes. 'Magnestick' child safety
systems will now be fitted to all fast
chairlifts in the area. Some of the
children's classes have received good

reports (see 'Schools'). But we rarely
get reports on childcare facilities – no
doubt many readers use the facilities
of chalet operators.

STAYING THERE

Chalets Méribel has more chalets on
the British market than any other
resort. The specialist agents list scores
of options. What really distinguishes
Méribel is the range of recently built
luxury chalets. Many have saunas, hot
tubs or both. Some are well located,
but many rely on minibus services.

The widest choice is from Ski Total,
with 13 properties in the mid-to-large
size range. Two are new this year, and
deservedly get Total's top Platinum
rating. Hot tubs, of course, and cinema
and billiard room in the case of chalet
Isba. Skiworld has 11 chalets of
various sizes, including two swanky
places with sauna and hot tub.

Purple Ski has five top-notch and
highly individual chalets – in good
positions, with lovely interiors, and
outdoor hot tubs. Alpine Action has
seven smart-looking chalets (one new
for 2011/12) in various parts of the
resort (including Méribel Village and a

Méribel

309

Interactive resort shortlist builder at **www.wtss.co.uk**

CHILDCARE

Les Saturnins
t 0479 086031
Ages 18mnth to 3yr

Kids Etc
t 0622 626903
07763 945192 (UK)
From 18mnth to 10yr

Les Piou Piou
t 0479 086031 (Mér)
t 0479 004949 (Mot)
Ages 3 to 5; 9am-5pm

Childminder list
Available from the
tourist office

Ski school
The ESF runs classes
for ages 5 to 13: 6
half-days (2½hr) from
€120

couple close to the resort centre), most with saunas, some with hot tubs.

Inghams has added four chalets this year to give a total of five, plus a 60-bed chalet-hotel in a prime spot near the lifts at Chaudanne. Ski Beat has five chalets, one with sauna and one close to the centre.

Ski Olympic has two properties including the smooth Parc Alpin at 1600 with 12 luxurious rooms (all with plasma screen TVs), dinky swimming pool and sauna. Crystal has three chalets. Meriski is a Méribel specialist.

Family specialist Esprit has a 60-bed chalet-hotel in a good slope-side position, up at Rond Point – 'excellent; childcare beyond exemplary', says a 2011 guest.

Hotels Méribel doesn't compete with Courchevel in the fancy hotel stakes, but has some excellent places. Of course, they're not cheap.

****Grand Coeur (0479 086003) Our favourite almost-affordable hotel in Méribel. Just above the village centre. Welcoming, mature building with plush lounge. Huge hot tub, sauna etc.

****Mont-Vallon (0479 004400) The best hotel at Mottaret; good food, and excellently situated for the Three Valleys' pistes. Pool, sauna, squash, fitness room etc.

***Altiport (0479 005232) Smart and luxurious hotel, isolated at the foot of the Altiport lifts. Convenient for Courchevel, not for Val Thorens. Extensively refurbished for 2010/11.

***Allodis (0479 005600) Out of town at Belvedere, but ski-in/ski-out and excellent in every other way. Seriously good restaurant, superb service, nice terrace and valley views.

***Arolles (0479 004040) On the piste at the top of Mottaret, with the 'best ever staff, food from good to superb, lovely lounge'. Pool and sauna.

**Adray Télébar (0479 086026) Welcoming piste-side chalet with pretty, rustic rooms, good food and popular lunch terrace. New spa, restaurant and lodges for 2010/11.

Apartments The two most impressive larger residences are Pierre & Vacances Premium properties – Les Fermes de Méribel is a classic tasteful MGM

Selected chalets in Méribel

ACTIVITIES

Indoor Parc Olympique (ice rink, swimming pool, climbing wall), fitness centres in hotels, bowling, library, cinemas, casino, museum, heritage tours

Outdoor Flying lessons and excursions, snowmobiles, snowshoeing, sleigh rides, cleared paths, paragliding, segway riding

GETTING THERE

Air Geneva 190km/ 120 miles (2hr45); Lyon 190km/120 miles (2hr30); Chambéry 100km/ 60 miles (1hr30)

Rail Moûtiers (18km/11 miles); regular buses

Phone numbers
From abroad use the prefix +33 and omit the initial '0' of the phone number

TOURIST OFFICE

www.meribel.net

development of six large chalets with the usual good pool, gym etc in Méribel-Village. Les Crêts is a big residence up at Mottaret. These properties are available through various agents including Ski Collection. Ski Amis has a good range of apartments in various areas. Erna Low has some appealing chalets.

EATING OUT ★★★★☆
New places to try
There is a reasonable selection of restaurants, from ambitious French cuisine to pizza and pasta. For the best food, in plush surroundings, you won't beat the top hotels – we've had top-notch meals at the Grand Coeur and Allodis. The Zinc brasserie and Escale gourmet restaurant are new at the highly regarded Altiport hotel. We've also enjoyed the Kouisena, with its very rustic, intimate interior and open-fire cooking of good meat. For the 'all French' experience and fine food, the Orée du Bois is suggested this year. In Mottaret, tucked away near the Plattières lift, Zig Zag is a good cheaper option (bar/traditional).

Just outside Méribel-Village, the Plantin is a lovely chalet doing a wide range of dishes. In the village, the unpretentious Brit-run Lodge du Village (pasta, Tuscany specials) serves 'some of the tastiest food in the Three Valleys', and at prices that are modest by local standards.

APRES-SKI ★★★★★
Méribel rocks – loudly
Méribel's après-ski revolves around British-run places, and is far more animated than is usual in most French resorts. (Not that our readers have much time for this sort of thing, to judge by reports.) We're told the Arpasson hut (Tougnète) now has 'blaring music' in an attempt to create some on-mountain action. At the top of the village, the 'legendary' Rond Point is as lively as they come, packed from happy hour 4pm-5pm – live music, toffee vodka and crowd-surfing are the norm. Or you could try Jack's, not far from the main lift stations. Aviatic is a new bar/club at the Altiport hotel. The ring of bars around the main square do good business at teatime. The Doron attracts a younger crowd for videos, pool and 'good live bands' all evening. The Poste injects a bit of French cool into the scene ('good drinks, nice young crowd').

Later on, Dick's Tea Bar is the focus – now revamped and with a new gastro-pub (The Den) next door. But they are away from the centre and slopes.

In Mottaret the bars at the foot of the pistes get packed at tea time.

In Méribel-Village, the bar at Lodge du Village has live music at teatime a couple of nights a week.

OFF THE SLOPES ★★★☆☆
Quite a bit to do
The Olympic Centre has the ice rink where the Olympic events were held in 1992 and where you can watch regular hockey matches. It also has bowling, a climbing wall, a gym, a good public pool and a spa – these last two irritatingly separate, a reporter points out. You can take joyrides in the little planes that operate from the altiport. There are pleasant marked walks in several areas – eg between Méribel and the altiport area; down through hamlets to Les Allues (return by bus or gondola); and at Plan de Tueda, beyond Mottaret – 'gorgeous'. There is a pedestrian's lift pass, and accessible restaurants to meet friends for lunch. Both villages have a cinema. There are very few shops other than ski shops, even in Méribel itself.

Down-valley town – 600m
BRIDES-LES-BAINS

Brides-les-Bains is an old spa town way down in the valley. For the Méribel events in the 1992 Olympics the competitors were accommodated here and ferried up on a newly built gondola. It offers a quieter, cheaper alternative base, with some simple hotels, good-value apartments, adequate shops and restaurants. Skiweekends.com runs a chalet hotel here. The 3-star hotel Amelie (0479 553015) is near the spa and gondola ('delicious food, great atmosphere'). There is a casino, but evenings are distinctly quiet. We have reports of one lively bar. The gondola ride to and from Méribel is supposed to take 25 minutes, but may take 40. It arrives at a point irritatingly short of the main lifts up the mountain. It also closes rather early, at 5pm. But in good conditions you can ski off-piste to one or other of the mid-stations at the end of the day (or in exceptional conditions down to Brides itself). Given a car, Brides makes a viable base for visiting other resorts.

Interactive resort shortlist builder at **www.wtss.co.uk**

Montgenèvre

The snowiest part of the Milky Way circuit reaching across to Sauze d'Oulx in Italy – now with through-traffic buried in a tunnel

RATINGS

The mountains

Extent	★★
Fast lifts	★★
Queues	★★★
Terrain p'ks	★★★
Snow	★★★★
Expert	★★
Intermediate	★★★★
Beginner	★★★★★
Boarder	★★★
X-country	★★★
Restaurants	★★
Schools	★★★
Families	★★★★

The resort

Charm	★★★
Convenience	★★★
Scenery	★★★
Eating out	★★
Après-ski	★★★
Off-slope	★

RPI   85

lift pass	£170
ski hire	£95
lessons	£80
food & drink	£130
total	**£475**

NEWS

2011/12: The Montquitaine double chair from Claviere towards Montgenèvre is due to become a fast quad. A new luxury hotel, the Anova, with a pool, spa, bar and restaurant is due to open.

2010/11: A roller coaster run – the Monty Express – was created from the top of the Chalvet gondola, and, at 1400m, is claimed to be the longest in France.

New 4-star apartments Le Chalet des Dolines opened, including a pool, sauna and spa.

+ Good snow record means local snow is often the best in the Milky Way area

+ Plenty of intermediate cruising and good, convenient nursery slopes

+ A lot of accommodation close to the slopes, and some right on them

+ Great potential for car drivers to explore other nearby resorts, but …

– Italian Milky Way resorts such as Sauze d'Oulx are not easy to explore without road transport

– Lots of slow lifts and mainly short runs in local area

– Local mountain restaurants poor

– Little to challenge experts on-piste

– Limited, mostly unsophisticated restaurants and après-ski places

Montgenèvre is set on a minor pass between France and Italy (hence the good snow record) at one end of the big cross-border Milky Way network. On snow, it's a time-consuming trek from here to and from Sestriere and Sauze d'Oulx at the far end. So unless you have transport it's best to focus on the local slopes shared with Claviere (in Italy).

The village is pleasant – and now largely traffic-free thanks to a bypass. It is edging out of the cheap-and-cheerful category with the development of the Hameau de l'Obélisque quarter, containing two very smart hotels and some smart apartments. A new leisure centre is planned for two years' time.

THE RESORT

Montgenèvre is a small roadside village set on a high pass only 2km from the Italian border.

On the village side of the col are the south-facing slopes of Le Chalvet (there are plans to link it to the adjacent 3000m peak of Mt Chaberton in a couple of years' time). The more extensive north-facing slopes of Les Gondrans are across the main road, with nursery slopes at the bottom. Both sectors have piste links with Claviere, gateway to the other Italian resorts of the Milky Way – Sansicario, Sestriere and Sauze d'Oulx. But it takes ages to get to those resorts on skis; best to drive or join a group going by private bus.

Serre-Chevalier and Puy-St-Vincent, with lift pass sharing arrangements, are easily reached by car. Different lift pass options cater for most needs.

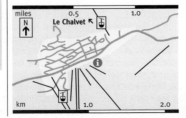

VILLAGE CHARM ★★★
Rustic with no through traffic

Cheap and cheerful cafes, bars and restaurants line the road running along the bottom of the nursery slopes, now happily free of through traffic. And a couple of narrow parallel roads with a few bars and restaurants and a church lie behind it. The old buildings give it a rustic and lived-in feel. The friendly natives and generally good snow add to the charm factor. The smart new Hameau de l'Obélisque development of wood-clad chalet-style apartments and hotels at the eastern end of the village is a complete contrast.

CONVENIENCE ★★★
Never far from a lift

Most of the accommodation is less than five minutes from a lift. But the main gondolas are at opposite ends of the village. Some of the newer accommodation in Hameau de l'Obélisque is right on the slopes and convenient for both sectors. The free bus service is 'really unreliable', says a 2011 reporter.

SCENERY ★★★
Look north or south

The area is broken up by rocky outcrops and woods, with good views from both sides of the valley.

Montgenèvre

KEY FACTS

Resort	1850m
	6,070ft

Montgenèvre-Monts de la Lune (Claviere)

Slopes	1760-2630m
	5,770-8,630ft
Lifts	32
Pistes	110km
	68 miles
Green	13%
Blue	34%
Red	36%
Black	17%
Snowmaking	55%

For the whole Milky Way area

Slopes	1390-2825m
	4,560-9,270ft
Lifts	72
Pistes	400km
	249 miles
Blue	25%
Red	55%
Black	20%
Snowmaking	60%

GETTING THERE

Air Turin 100km/ 60 miles (1hr30); Grenoble 170km/ 105 miles (3hr); Lyon 235km/145 miles (3hr)

Rail Briançon (12km/ 7 miles) or Oulx (15km/9 miles); buses available from both five times a day

THE MOUNTAINS

The slopes of Montgenèvre and Claviere offer lots of variety – some high and open, some wooded lower down. Run classification on the local map, the Milky Way map and on the mountain have differed in the past, which can be confusing. And many of the runs are overgraded, with 'blacks that are tough reds and reds that are tough blues', says a 2011 reporter. Signposting is 'mainly adequate except on the homeward trek from Monti della Luna', says a 2011 visitor.

EXTENT OF THE SLOPES ★★★★★
Nicely varied

Our stars are based on the local slopes; the Milky Way as a whole easily gets a ★★★★★ rating.

The north-facing slopes above Montgenèvre divide into two sectors. The high, open slopes of **Les Gondrans** are reached by the Chalmettes chondola from the west end of the village; a green run brings you back. The lower, steeper wooded slopes of **Le Prarial** are reached by chairlifts – the Prarial from the slopes directly in front of the village, or the Tremplin from a point well to the east.

From both of these sectors you can descend into a valley separating them from the peak of l'Aigle. This has no skiing, but there are links below it and behind it into Italy and the **Monti della Luna** slopes of Claviere.

The sunny sector behind the village of Montgenèvre – **Le Chalvet** – has long been accessed by a gondola from the east end of the village. A more recently added alternative access is the Serre Thibaud chondola, starting next to the aforementioned Tremplin chair. This chondola has opened up new blue and black runs into the main Chalvet bowl and into the valley beyond the Col de l'Alpet. The Chalvet runs are mainly on open slopes above the gondola; there are blue and green runs back to Montgenèvre, and a blue run to Claviere (it's a long slog across the village to get up the other side).

FAST LIFTS ★★★★★
Still a way to go

The main lifts out of the village are a chondola and a gondola. But slow chairs and drags predominate on the upper slopes.

QUEUES ★★★★★
Few problems

Recent reporters have found the resort queue-free, even at New Year and Easter. But a 2011 visitor found home runs 'busy – we saw several injuries'.

TERRAIN PARKS ★★★★★
Various facilities

There's a half-pipe and a jump with an airbag to cushion landings on the lower slopes of the Gondrans sector and boardercross runs in both sectors.

SNOW RELIABILITY ★★★★★
Excellent locally

Montgenèvre has a generally excellent snow record, receiving dumps from westerly storms funnelling up the valley to the col. The high north-facing

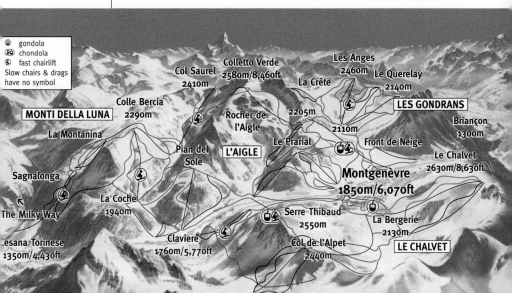

gondola
chondola
fast chairlift
Slow chairs & drags have no symbol

Col Saurel 2410m
Colletto Verde 2580m/8,460ft
Les Anges 2460m
Le Querelay 2140m
La Crête
MONTI DELLA LUNA
Colle Bercia 2290m
Rocher de l'Aigle
2205m
2110m
LES GONDRANS
Briançon 1300m
La Montanina
Pian del Sole
L'AIGLE
Le Prarial
Front de Neige
Le Chalvet 2630m/8,630ft
Sagnalonga
La Coche 1940m
Montgenèvre 1850m/6,070ft
The Milky Way
Serre Thibaud 2550m
La Bergerie 2130m
Cesana Torinese 1350m/4,430ft
Claviere 1760m/5,770ft
Col de l'Alpet 2440m
LE CHALVET

slopes naturally keep their snow better than the south-facing area. Snow-guns now cover 55% of the area, including most lower slopes; its use is 'intensive and very effective', says a reporter.

FOR EXPERTS ★★☆☆☆
Limited, except for off-piste
There are very few challenging pistes locally. Many of the runs are overclassified. There is, however, ample off-piste terrain. On the Gondrans side, there's a 'freeride zone' of ungroomed slopes that are avalanche controlled. Also on this side, the Rocher de l'Aigle area and the open sections around Col Saurel and between La Montanina and Sagnalonga in Italy are good powder areas. One reporter was taken on long off-piste runs off the back of Les Gondrans by ESF instructors. On the Chalvet side, the remote north-east-facing bowl beyond the Col de l'Alpet is superb in good snow and has black pistes, too. Heli-skiing can be arranged in Italy.

FOR INTERMEDIATES ★★★★☆
Plenty of cruising terrain
The overclassified blacks are just right for adventurous intermediates, though none holds the interest for very long. The pleasantly narrow treelined runs to Claviere from Pian del Sole, the steepest of the routes down in the Chalvet sector and the runs off the back of Col de l'Alpet are all fine in small doses. Average intermediates will enjoy the red runs, though most are short. On the major sector, both the runs from Colletto Verde can be great fun. Getting to Cesana via the lovely sweeping run starting at Colle Bercia, and heading home from Pian del Sole, are both easier than the classifications suggest, and can be tackled by less adventurous intermediates, who also have a wealth

of cruising terrain high up at the top of Les Gondrans. The runs down to the village are easy cruises.

FOR BEGINNERS ★★★★★
One of the best places to learn
There is an excellent, large, gentle nursery slope area at the foot of the Gondrans sector, with a moving carpet and draglift; and it is fenced off so that you don't get speeding skiers going through it. The moving carpet and a draglift outside the nursery area are free to use, so a full pass is not needed for complete beginners. Progression to longer runs could not be easier, with long, very easy green runs in both sectors. Les Gondrans is particularly good.

FOR BOARDERS ★★★☆☆
Something for everyone
There's plenty to attract boarders to Montgenèvre. There are good local beginner slopes and long runs on varied terrain for intermediates. The only real drawback is that a fair number of the lifts are drags and there are some flat sections (especially getting to and from Sestriere). There are some excellent off-piste areas with a few natural hits for more advanced boarders and a dedicated freeride area in the Gondrans sector. Snow Box is a specialist shop.

FOR CROSS-COUNTRY ★★★☆☆
Travel to the best of it
The 17km of local trails offer ample variety. But the best area is the 60km of trails in the unspoiled Clarée valley, starting an 8km drive away in Les Alberts at the bottom of the pass road's winding ascent from Briançon.

MOUNTAIN RESTAURANTS ★★☆☆☆
Head for Italy
The options on Montgenèvre's local slopes are few, and unremarkable; but reporters have enjoyed the table-service Bergerie (Chalvet sector) for 'good food, no crowds, marvellous views'. In the Claviere sector there is a slightly wider choice of atmospheric little huts; Baita La Coche is 'very friendly' with 'great food'.

SCHOOLS AND GUIDES ★★★☆☆
Encouraging reports
Reports are few. Those on the ESF are usually positive: 'friendly, helpful, with good English'. 'We had a four and six year old with us – both loved their

UK PACKAGES

AmeriCan Ski, Carrier, Crystal, Crystal Finest, Erna Low, Go Montgenevre, Independent Ski Links, Lagrange, Neilson, Peak Retreats, PowderBeds, Rocketski, Ski Etoile, Ski France, Ski Independence, Skitopia, Skitracer, Thomson, Zenith **Claviere** Crystal, First Choice, Independent Ski Links, Rocketski, Skitracer

ACTIVITIES

Indoor Cinema, exhibition hall

Outdoor Natural ice rink, snowshoeing, snowmobiling, walking, tobogganing

Phone numbers
From abroad use the prefix +33 and omit the initial '0' of the phone number

TOURIST OFFICE

Montgenèvre
www.montgenevre.com

Claviere
www.claviere.it

OT MONTGENEVRE / ANNIE BENE

The north-facing Les Gondrans sector has excellent beginner slopes; and the village feels more rustic than it looks in this photo ↓

classes,' says a 2011 visitor. A beginner reporter joined the A-Peak school and thought they were 'very good'.

FOR FAMILIES ★★★★
Hugely improved
With the intrusive main road traffic removed, Montgenèvre is now a fine family resort. The beginner area has the Mini-Club Les Marmottes and a snow garden for young children. There is also a childcare centre. Le Chalvet has a play area at the gondola top.

STAYING THERE

Development of Hameau de l'Obélisque, at the east end of the resort, has introduced a bit of class.
Chalets A few operators have catered chalets here, including Crystal and Zenith. And Pot de Miel is a B&B run on chalet lines (with optional evening meals) by an Australian woman and her French ski instructor husband.
Hotels Two smart places.
★★★★Chalet Blanc (0492 442702) Very comfortable, lovely soft duvets and pillows, smart bathrooms – we enjoyed our 2011 stay here. Spa.
★★★★ Anova (0680 438930) New for 2011. 40 rooms and suites. Pool, spa.
Apartments There are some smart 4-star developments with pool and spa at Hameau de l'Obélisque – the Hameau des Airelles ('spacious apartments') and Chalet des Dolines are available through Peak Retreats.
At altitude The Sporthotel Sagnalonga is halfway down the piste to Cesana, reached by chairlift or snowmobile. Even in peak weeks you get the surrounding slopes to yourself until skiers based elsewhere arrive mid-morning. We lack recent reports.

EATING OUT ★★☆☆☆
Mainly no-frills
With about ten no-frills places in the village, the choice is no more than adequate. For gourmets there is La Cloche – reports please. Reader tips: Graal ('out-of-this-world burgers'), Capitaine ('magnificent calzone pizza'), Caesar ('lively vibe, food was well cooked and reasonably priced') and Estable ('a great find, full of locals').

APRES-SKI ★★★☆☆
Mainly bars
The range is limited – 2011 visitors found it quiet ('not the place for lively nightlife'). The Refuge and the Jamy are the focal cafe-bars at tea time. The Graal is a friendly, unsophisticated place with big TVs; the Ca del Sol bar is a cosy place with an open fire.

OFF THE SLOPES ★☆☆☆☆
Limited
The Monty Express 1400m-long two-seater roller coaster ride starts at the top of the gondola up Chalvet. For 2011/12 we're told the ski school will organise torchlit walks with a snack in a teepee. A bus trip down to the beautiful old town of Briançon is possible.

LINKED RESORT – 1760m
CLAVIERE

Claviere is over the border in Italy – a small, traditional village, barely a mile from Montgenèvre – but an 'expensive' taxi ride or 15-minute walk away for evenings out. It's no great beauty but visitors seem to like its quiet, relaxed ambience, especially now the main road by-passes it. Montgenèvre's slopes are as easily reached as those on the Italian side of the border, thanks to recent lift additions. The nursery slope is small and steep but usually uncrowded and snow-reliable. A 2011 reporter praises the ski school: 'very good instructors and all the kids progressed well'. Readers tip several restaurants: the Kilt ('excellent pizzas, sensible prices, very friendly'), Da Sandro ('best meal of the week') and Gran Bouc ('good food and service, but a bit pricey'). Après-ski is quiet; Baita La Coche mountain hut 'can do hot chocolates and crêpes in the evening and lay on snowcat transport'. The bar at the Roma hotel 'has good prices and Sky Sports'. Pub Gallo can be lively later on.

Morzine

A large, lively, year-round resort with its own attractive slopes and linked by lift to the main Portes du Soleil circuit

RATINGS

The mountains

Extent	★★★★★
Fast lifts	★★
Queues	★★★
Terrain p'ks	★★
Snow	★★
Expert	★★★
Intermediate	★★★★
Beginner	★★★
Boarder	★★★★
X-country	★★★★
Restaurants	★★★
Schools	★★★
Families	★★★★

The resort

Charm	★★★
Convenience	★★
Scenery	★★★
Eating out	★★★
Après-ski	★★★★
Off-slope	★★★

RPI 95

lift pass	£200
ski hire	£100
lessons	£100
food & drink	£135
total	**£535**

NEWS

2011/12: A new indoor swimming pool should be open by December 2011. Nine more snow-guns are planned for the Pléney and Nyon sectors.

2010/11: A new six-pack to the top of Chamossière replaced the triple chair and Blanchots draglift. Eleven new snow-guns were installed on the Pléney and Nyon sectors. A new lift pass for five consecutive hours starting any time has replaced the half-day pass.

Extent rating
This relates to the whole Portes du Soleil area.

➕ Larger local piste area (shared with Les Gets) than other resorts in the vast Portes du Soleil area

➕ Good nightlife by French standards

➕ Quite attractive summer-resort town

➕ Few queues locally, in general

➕ Lots of treelined runs

➖ Just off the Portes du Soleil circuit

➖ Bus ride or long walk to lifts from much of the accommodation

➖ Low altitude means an enduring risk of rain and poor snow

➖ Few tough pistes for experts

➖ Weekend crowds

Morzine is a long-established year-round resort, popular for its easy road access, traditional atmosphere and gentle wooded slopes; bad weather rarely causes problems (except that it rains here not infrequently). For keen piste-bashers wanting to ski the Portes du Soleil circuit regularly, the main drawback is that you're slightly off the main circuit.

This problem can be solved by taking a car or using a tour operator who will drive you around. The little-used Ardent gondola, a short drive from Morzine, is a particularly neat option, giving the alternative of a shorter circuit that misses out Avoriaz, where the worst crowds tend to be found.

THE RESORT

Morzine is a well established mountain resort, as popular in summer as in winter, sprawling along both sides of a river gorge – though with the centre emphatically on the west side, at the foot of the local slopes. These are shared with slightly higher Les Gets (covered in a separate chapter). Across town is a gondola forming the link with a chain of lifts leading to Avoriaz on the Portes du Soleil circuit.

Our view that the resort suits car

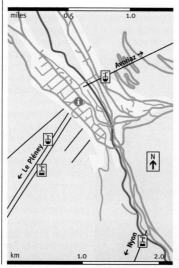

drivers is widely shared. But the roads are busy and the one-way system takes some getting used to. Car trips to Flaine and Chamonix are feasible.

VILLAGE CHARM ★★★
Quietly attractive
The resort consists of chalet-style buildings large and small; they look cute under snow, and as that snow disappears towards spring the village quickly takes on a spruce appearance. Morzine is a family resort, and village ambience tends to be fairly subdued; but there is plenty of après-ski action – and a 2011 reporter enjoyed the daily events – 'well run and free'. A 2010 visitor commented on how friendly everyone was.

CONVENIENCE ★★
It's a big resort ...
Morzine is a town where getting from A to B can be tricky. The best plan is to stay in or near the centre of town, a short walk from one or both of the gondolas. Restaurants and bars line the streets up to the lifts to Le Pléney, where a busy one-way street runs along the foot of the slopes. Accommodation is widely scattered, but a very good multi-route bus service (including two electric buses) links all parts of the town to the lifts, including those for Avoriaz. There's a bus to Les Gets too.

SCENERY ★★★☆☆
Quite good from the tops
Despite their modest top heights, the local peaks of Pointe de Nyon and Chamossière are not without drama (or impressive views, including Mont Blanc), and the slopes below them are attractively wooded.

THE MOUNTAINS

The local slopes are mainly wooded, with some open areas higher up. The piste map is fine, but several reporters have criticised signposting and links between pistes. And in a bad snow year, several 2011 visitors complained about a lack of info on which runs were open or closed.

EXTENT OF THE SLOPES ★★★★★
Good local area, plus the PdS
Our rating is for the whole Portes du Soleil linked area, the bulk of which is reached via Avoriaz. Morzine is not an ideal base for the main circuit, but its local area of slopes – which it shares with Les Gets – is very satisfactory.

A gondola rises from the edge of central Morzine to **Le Pléney**. (The parallel cable car is for the hotel up there and ski school kids only, unless the gondola breaks down.) Numerous routes return to the valley, including a run down to Les Fys – a quiet lift junction at the foot of the **Nyon-Chamossière** sector where the area's most challenging slopes are; Chamossière is served by a six-pack but Nyon still has a slow chair. This sector can also be accessed by a cable car starting a bus ride from Morzine. A

slow chair from Les Fys along with a fast one from Le Grand Pré, further up the valley, connect with the sector of **Les Chavannes**, above Les Gets. At the far end of this sector, the bowl beneath Le Ranfoilly forms a sub-sector, where no fewer than five chairlifts have their base stations clustered together.

Beyond Les Gets, **Mont Chéry** is notably quiet, and well worth a visit.

Across town from the Le Pléney sector – a handy 'petit train' shuttle service runs between the two – is a gondola leading (via another couple of lifts and runs) to Avoriaz and the main Portes du Soleil circuit. You take the gondola down at the end of the day to get back to Morzine (there's no piste back). Alternatives are a bus ride or short drive to either Les Prodains, from where you can get a (queue-prone) cable car to Avoriaz or a chair into the **Hauts Forts** slopes above it, or to Ardent, where a gondola accesses Les Lindarets for lifts towards Châtel, Avoriaz or Champéry. There's floodlit skiing every Thursday and a torchlit descent every Tuesday.

FAST LIFTS ★★☆☆☆
More fast chairs needed
The main access lifts are gondolas, cable cars or fast chairs, but higher up things are not so good: only Chamossière, Le Ranfoilly and La Rosta have a decent supply of fast chairs. Elsewhere, slow chairs and drags dominate.

OT MORZINE / V PORET

Most of Morzine's slopes are wooded but some of the steeper, higher slopes are more open ↓

GETTING THERE

Air Geneva 95km/
60 miles (1hr30);
Lyon 215km/
135 miles (3hr)

Rail Cluses or Thonon
(30km/19 miles);
regular bus
connections to resort

QUEUES ★★★☆☆
Only peak season problems

Queues aren't normally a problem
except during peak holiday seasons
and at weekends. Then queues can
form for both the gondolas out of the
resort (and for the gondola back down
from Avoriaz at the end of the day) –
and for the cable car from Les

Prodains to Avoriaz. Bottlenecks may
also form when everyone returns from
Les Gets – notably at Le Grand Pré.
Once you are up the mountain, queues
are not usually a problem.

TERRAIN PARKS ★★☆☆☆
Lots to choose from

There is a park below Pointe de Nyon
and parks and a boardercross in Les
Gets (see Les Gets chapter). Or you
can try one of the five excellent terrain
parks in Avoriaz.

SNOW RELIABILITY ★★☆☆☆
A weakness at resort level

Morzine has a very low average height,
and it can rain here when it is snowing
higher up (almost every year some
reporters mention days of rain). But
because you ski on grassy pastures
you need relatively little depth of
snow to be able to ski. Snowmaking

Good, challenging runs
both on- and off-piste

Chamossière
2000m

Le Ranfoilly
1825m

Pointe de Nyon
2010m/6,590ft

La R
166

NYON-CHAMOSSIERE

Ranfoilly

Chez
Nannon

Des Têtes

Charniaz

Nauchets

Grains-d'Or

LES CHAVANNES

Pointe
de Nyon

Nyon
1420m

Le Grand Pré

Nyon

Belvédère

Tu

Les Fys

1510m

LE PLENEY

Les Ge
1170m/3,8

The gondola is a
link to Avoriaz
from the centre of
town. But you have
to catch it down
too – there's no
piste back

← Avoriaz

Pléney

Super-Morzine

Morzine
1000m/3,280ft

Lovely easy blue
run away from
all the lifts

has been increased, most noticeably on runs at Nyon, Le Pléney and the home runs. Grooming is good.

FOR EXPERTS ★★★☆☆
A few possibilities
The runs from Pointe de Nyon and Chamossière are quite challenging, as are the black runs down the back of Mont Chéry and the Hauts Forts blacks at Avoriaz. There is plenty of off-piste scope – see feature panel overleaf.

FOR INTERMEDIATES ★★★★☆
Something for everyone
Good intermediates will enjoy the challenging red and black down from Chamossière. Mont Chéry, on the other side of Les Gets, has some fine steepish runs which are usually very quiet. Those looking for something less steep have a great choice. Le Pléney has a compact network of pistes that are ideal for groups with mixed abilities: there are blue and red options from every lift. One of the easiest cruises on Le Pléney is a great away-from-it-all, snow-gun-covered blue (Piste B) from the top to the valley lift station. Heading from Le Ranfoilly to Le Grand Pré on the blue is also a nice cruise. And the slopes down to Les Gets from Le Pléney are easy when conditions are right (the slopes face south). The Ranfoilly and Rosta sectors have easy blacks and cruisey reds served by fast chairs. And, of course, there is the whole of the extensive Portes du Soleil circuit to explore by going up the opposite side of the valley.

FOR BEGINNERS ★★★☆☆
Good for novices and improvers
The wide village nursery slopes are convenient, and benefit from snow-

La Rosta
1665m

Pointe de la Turche

Grains-d'Or

ES CHAVANNES

Perrières

Les Perrières

La Turche

Les Gets
1170m/3,840ft

Mont Chéry

If you're driving, park here and take the fast chair into the slopes

Underused, quiet sector with some of the steepest runs in the area and great red run cruising

MONT CHERY
1825m

Col de l'Encrenaz
1435m

gondola
cable car
fast chairlift
Slow chairs & drags
have no symbol

guns, though crowds are reported to be a problem ('insanely busy in French holiday weeks – 10-minute queues for the magic carpet'). There are excellent progression runs on Le Pléney, at Nyon, and at Super-Morzine.

FOR BOARDERS ★★★★
Great for park and ride
Morzine is very popular with boarding seasonaires because of the extensive slopes, proximity to the excellent terrain parks in Avoriaz and the lower prices here. Former British champ Becci Malthouse is one of the people running the British Alpine Ski & Snowboard School. The slopes in Morzine are great for all abilities and have very few draglifts. But a reporter complained of irritating flat areas. Plenty of tree-lined runs make for scenic and interesting snowboarding and the more adventurous should hire a guide to explore off-piste.

FOR CROSS-COUNTRY ★★★★
Good variety
There are around 70km of varied cross-country trails, not all at valley level. The best section is in the pretty Vallée de la Manche beside the Nyon mountain up to the Lac de Mines d'Or, where there is a good restaurant. The Pléney-Chavannes loop is pleasant and relatively snow-sure.

MOUNTAIN RESTAURANTS ★★★
Some excellent huts
Editors' choice We have had several very enjoyable Savoyard lunches at the rustic Chez Nannon (0450 792115), near the top of the Troncs chair between Nyon and Chamossière – cosy inside and a nice terrace. A 2011 reporter agrees: 'One of the finest places to eat in the Alps.' We are still looking forward to trying the Pointe de Nyon (0450 044564), which was built a few years ago and has impressed several reporters ('sublime beef bourgignon').
Worth knowing about The nice little Atray des Neiges at the foot of the d'Atray chair does 'delicious crêpes'. The 'good value' Raverettes crêperie at Nyon has a 'warm, friendly atmosphere'. The Wetzet at Ranfoilly does 'great mid-morning chocolate'. The Vaffieu above the Folliets chair has been praised for its 'excellent Savoy specialities'. And the Mouflon at the top of Rosta has 'great pizzas' and 'fab views'.

OFF-PISTE RUNS IN THE PORTES DU SOLEIL AREA

The Portes du Soleil offers a lot of great lift-served off-piste. Here is a small selection. Like all serious off-piste runs, these should only be done with a guide.

Morzine – Nyon/Chamossière area
From the Chamossière chairlift, heading north brings you to two runs – one on the same north-west slope as the pistes, the other via a col down the north-east slope to the Nyon cable car in the Vallée de La Manche – a wild area, with a great view of Mont Blanc at first.

Avoriaz area – two suggestions
From the Fornet chairlift on the Swiss border, you head west to descend a beautiful, unspoiled bowl leading down to the village of L'Erigné. In powder snow you descend the west-facing slopes of the bowl; when there is spring snow, you traverse right to descend the south-facing slopes. Medium-pitch slopes, for skiers and snowboarders.

From the top of the Machon chairlift you traverse west, beneath the peaks of Les Hauts Forts, across Les Crozats de la Chaux – a steep, north-facing slope. You then turn north to descend through the forest to the cable car station at Les Prodains. Testing terrain, for very good skiers. And beware that the traverse can be dangerous following a snowfall.

Châtel area
From the top of the Linga chair, head north-west to cross the ridge on your right at a col and then head down the La Leiche slope to the draglift of the same name. It's a north-facing slope, starting in a white wilderness, taking you through trees back to civilisation. Steep slopes – for good skiers only.

SCHOOLS

ESF
t 0450 791313

Easy 2 Ride (E2SA) – International
t 0450 790516

Snow School
t 0486 688840

BASS
t 0871 780 1500 (UK)

Mint Snowboard
t 0450 841388

Classes
(ESF prices)
6 half days (2½hr am or pm) €125

Private lessons
From €37 for 1hr for 1 to 3 people

GUIDES

Mountain Office
t 0450 747223

CHILDCARE

L'Outa nursery
t 0450 792600
Ages 3mnth to 6yr

Club des Piou-Piou
t 0450 791313
From age 3; with ESF instruction and lunch

Cheeky Monkeys
t 0450 750548
Ages from 3mnth

Jack Frost's
t 07817 138678 (UK)
Ages from 3mnth

Ski school
ESF takes children from age 4: 6 half days €116

ACTIVITIES

Indoor Ice rink, fitness centre, sauna, hot tub, yoga, library, cinemas

Outdoor Snowshoeing, helicopter flights, snowmobiles, ice diving, ballooning, tobogganing, paintballing, paragliding

TOURIST OFFICE

www.morzine-avoriaz.com

SCHOOLS AND GUIDES ★★★★★
Good reports of most
Reporters praise the British Alpine Ski & Snowboard School (BASS) ('instructors very nice and helpful'), the Snow School ('taught my parents, who are in their mid-60s, and they're loving it') and the ESF (one group was 'full of praise for their instructor and doing well by the end of the week'). And there's E2SA (International) to try.

FOR FAMILIES ★★★★★
A fine family choice
Morzine caters well for families. On the mountain there are gentle, sheltered slopes and play areas. And there are plenty of other activities. Club des Piou-Piou is run by the ESF school and takes children from three to 14 years old. 'Excellent – my children, six and three, were happy,' says a 2010 visitor. Above Les Gets, at Chavannes, there is a big children's area. Day care is provided by several organisations.

STAYING THERE

The tour operator market concentrates on hotels and chalets.
Chalets There's a wide choice, but position varies enormously; check this carefully before booking. Mountain Heaven has a six-bedroom, all-en-suite place with an outdoor hot tub close to the Nyon cable car.
Hotels The handful of 3-star hotels includes some quite smart ones; and there are dozens of 2-stars and 1-stars.
***Airelles** (0450 747121) Central 3-star close to Pléney lifts. Good pool.
***Champs Fleuris** (0450 791444) Comfy 3-star next to Pléney lifts. Pool.
***Dahu** (0450 759292) 3-star linked to centre by footbridge over river; good restaurant; pool, sauna, steam, hot tub. Shuttle to lifts.
***Tremplin** (0450 791231) Next to the lifts. Small but 'comfortable' rooms.
***Bergerie** (0450 791369) Rustic B&B chalet, in centre. Friendly staff. Outdoor pool, sauna, massage.
***Chalet Philibert** (0450 792518) Traditional, small chalet-style hotel, with 18 rooms. Fairly central.
***Côtes** (0450 790996) On the edge of town. Pool, sauna, gym, bowling.
Equipe (0450 791143) One of the best 2-stars; next to the Pléney lift. 'Nice food, tiny pool.'
Soly (0450 790945) 'Great value, loads of car parking, fabulous and generous portions of food.'

Apartments. Aiglon de Morzine has 12 luxury units and is central – bookable through Erna Low.

EATING OUT ★★★★★
A reasonable choice
There is a fair choice, including some fine hotel restaurants but also traditional and Italian fare. The best place in town is probably the Atelier in the hotel Samoyède, which offers traditional and modern cuisine. The hotel Rhodos has a 'child-friendly restaurant, with a good choice of meals' and the Airelles and Dahu are other hotel-based options. The Flamme is highly rated ('amazing duck and salads; one of our group was made speechless by his dish'). The unpretentious Etale is popular and does 'very good pizzas'. The Tyrolien has been praised for steaks and grilled meats and the 'traditional' Kinkerne is 'friendly and does excellent salads'. Several 2011 visitors like the Chamade – 'gourmet food at moderate prices'; 'food and service excellent'.

APRES-SKI ★★★★★
One of the livelier French resorts
Nightlife is good by French resort standards, and several places around the base area get busy as the slopes empty. The Crépu is pleasantly quiet early on but livens up late and has a 'very good atmosphere' and several screens to show sport. Other options include Bar Robinson and the Dixie, with sport on TV, MTV, a cellar bar and some live music. Between the slopes and the centre, and all in the same building are: the Cavern, which is popular with seasonaires; the Coyote for arcade games and DJ; and the Boudha, with Asian decor and recommended by a reporter. The Opéra and Laury's are late-night haunts.

OFF THE SLOPES ★★★★★
Quite good; excursions possible
There are two cinemas, an excellent ice rink, a new indoor pool and lots of pretty walks ('booklet available from tourist office, but some walks are difficult to find and some cross pistes, which can be dangerous'). Visitors have enjoyed visits to the cheese factory and watching ice hockey. Morzine has a good range of shops. Buses run to Thonon for more shopping, and car owners can drive to Geneva, Annecy or Montreux.

Paradiski

Les Arcs and La Plagne are pretty impressive resorts in their own right; the ability to explore both is just the icing on the cake

KEY FACTS

Paradiski area

Slopes	1200-3250m	
	3,940-10,660ft	
Lifts		135
Pistes		425km
		264 miles
Green		4%
Blue		52%
Red		28%
Black		16%

December 2003 saw the opening of the world's largest cable car – a double-decker called the Vanoise Express holding 200 people – crossing a wooded valley to link Les Arcs and La Plagne, and thus to form Paradiski, one of the biggest joint ski areas in the Alps. When it opened, we were a bit sceptical about its value, particularly in view of the sheer width of the La Plagne area. But we're now quite used to staying in Arc 1950 and having lunch above Champagny, or staying in Belle-Plagne and having lunch above Arc 2000.

The Vanoise Express cable car spans the 2km-wide valley between Plan-Peisey (on the edge of the Les Arcs area) and a point 300m above Montchavin (on the edge of the La Plagne area).

The linking of these two major resorts is good news for the great British piste-basher who likes to cover as much ground as possible. For those who like a bit of a challenge, getting from your home base to both far-flung outposts of the area – Villaroger in Les Arcs and Champagny in La Plagne – would make quite a full day.

The link is also good for experts. Those based in either resort can more easily tackle the north face of La Plagne's Bellecôte, finishing the run in Nancroix. Those based in La Plagne who are finding the piste skiing a bit tame can easily get across to Les Arcs' excellent Aiguille Rouge.

If you want to make the most of the link it's sensible to stay near one of the cable car stations. But it's easily accessible from many other bases too.

On the Les Arcs side, **Plan-Peisey** and nearby **Vallandry** are in pole position. They are basically small, low-rise, modern developments, but built in a much more sympathetic style than the original Les Arcs resorts. They are quiet places to stay, but are expanding rapidly and a few UK operators have chalets there. You can also stay in the unspoiled old village of **Peisey**, 300m below and linked by bucket-lift to Plan-Peisey. These places are covered at the end of the Les Arcs chapter.

It's easy to get to the cable car station at Plan-Peisey from the main resort parts of Les Arcs. One lift and one run is all it takes to get there from **Arc 1800**, which is the biggest of the main resort units. From quieter **Arc 1600**, along the mountainside from 1800, it takes two lifts. **Arc 2000** and the stylish **Arc 1950** development seem further away, over the ridge that separates them from 1600 and 1800; but all it takes is one fast chair to the ridge and one long run down the other side. In the valley bottom beyond Arc

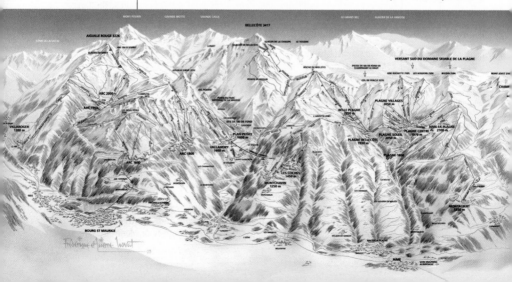

LIFT PASSES

Paradiski
Covers lifts in whole Paradiski area.
6-day pass €249 (over 65 and under 14 €187).

Paradiski Découverte
Covers lifts in Les Arcs area or La Plagne area plus one day Paradiski extension.
6-day pass €229 (over 65 and under 14 €172)

2000, the hamlet of Villaroger is not an ideal starting point.

On the La Plagne side, the obvious place to stay is **Montchavin**, which is below the Vanoise Express station. Montchavin is a carefully developed old village with modern additions built in traditional style. **Les Coches**, across the mountain from the station, is most easily reached with the help of a lift. It is entirely modern, but built in a traditional style. From either village, one lift brings you to the Vanoise Express cable car.

The other parts of La Plagne are some way from the cable car. But one long lift is all it takes to get from monolithic **Plagne-Bellecôte** up to L'Arpette, from which point it's a single long descent. The most attractive of the resort villages, **Belle-Plagne**, is

only a short run above Plagne-Bellecôte. From the villages further across the bowl – **Plagne-Villages**, **Plagne-Soleil**, dreary **Plagne-Centre**, futuristic **Aime-la-Plagne** – you have to ride a lift to get to Plagne-Bellecôte. From **Plagne 1800**, below the bowl, add another lift. From the villages beyond the bowl – rustic, sunny **Champagny-en-Vanoise** and expanding **Montalbert** – it's going to be pretty hard work, but it's certainly possible.

RIDING THE VANOISE EXPRESS

The cable car ride from one resort to the other takes less than four minutes. The system is designed to be able to operate in high winds, so the risk of getting stranded miles from home is low. It can shift 2,000 people an hour, and although end-of-the-day crowds could be a snag in theory, they don't seem to be a problem in practice.

The lift company offers a six-day pass covering the whole Paradiski region, perhaps most likely to appeal to people based in the villages close to the lift. It's not cheap. But there is also a pass (Paradiski Découverte) that includes just one day in the other resort during the validity of the pass. Alternatively, you can buy a one-day extension to a Les Arcs or La Plagne six-day lift pass, as and when you fancy the outing.

Paradiski

323

SNOWPIX.COM / CHRIS GILL

This is the Les Arcs end of the Vanoise Express at Plan-Peisey. The ride to La Plagne takes less than four minutes ➜

La Plagne

Villages from the rustic to the futuristic, spread over a vast area of intermediate terrain – mainly high and snow-sure

RATINGS

The mountains

Extent	★★★★
Fast lifts	★★
Queues	★★
Terrain p'ks	★★★★
Snow	★★★★
Expert	★★★★
Intermediate	★★★★★
Beginner	★★★★
Boarder	★★★
X-country	★★★★
Restaurants	★★★★
Schools	★★★
Families	★★★★

The resort

Charm	★★
Convenience	★★★★★
Scenery	★★★
Eating out	★★★
Après-ski	★★★
Off-slope	★

RPI 105

lift pass	£210
ski hire	£120
lessons	£105
food & drink	£150
total	**£585**

NEWS

2011/12: A new six-pack is due to replace the slow Verdons Sud chair from the Champagny sector to Les Verdons above Plagne-Centre.

A three-year renovation plan is kicking off in the shopping malls in Plagne-Centre. A new swimming pool and spa complex is due to be completed in Montchavin, by the main chair.

2010/11: A new black piste linked Col de la Chiaupe, at the bottom of the glacier area, to Les Bauches.

The Les Coches-Montchavin blue run was made easier.

- ➕ Extensive and varied intermediate pistes, plus excellent off-piste
- ➕ Good nursery slopes
- ➕ High and fairly snow-sure
- ➕ Wide choice of resort villages – high or low, convenient or cute
- ➕ Wooded runs of lower satellite resorts are great in poor weather
- ➕ Cable car link to Les Arcs from one of those satellite villages

- ➖ Few steep pistes
- ➖ Still lots of slow old chairlifts
- ➖ Serious high season queues
- ➖ Pistes get very crowded in places
- ➖ Lower villages can have poor snow – sunny Champagny especially
- ➖ Brutal architecture in some villages
- ➖ No long green runs
- ➖ Upscale accommodation still rare

With 225km of its own slopes, of which almost 80% are blue or red, La Plagne is an intermediate's paradise, even if you don't use the link to Les Arcs. For experts, it has the attraction that the huge area of off-piste doesn't get skied out too quickly. But the shortage of challenging pistes is a definite drawback, and it's sad to note that two of the most rewarding black pistes (dropping 800m vertical from the glacier) were wiped from the map two seasons ago.

Plagne-Bellecôte, effectively the hub of the lift and piste network, has had lift queues as long as we can remember; so, when snow is poor lower down, has the Bellecôte gondola to (and from) the glacier. You would hope that as the resort celebrates its 50th birthday this season, it would sort these problems out – but no. At least it is starting to sort the dire shopping malls of Plagne-Centre.

THE RESORT

La Plagne consists of no fewer than eleven separate 'villages'. Each is a self-sufficient mini-resort, though they vary widely in character. They divide basically into two groups: seven units purpose-built at altitude in a broad bowl, on or above the treeline; and four real villages, adapted and expanded for skiing, at lower altitude on the fringes of the area.

At the heart of the high-altitude area, Plagne-Centre is aptly named: it is the focal point for shops and après-ski. Directly below Centre is the chalet-filled suburb of Plagne 1800, spread across a steep hillside. A short lift ride away from Centre are the slightly higher units of Aime-la-Plagne, Plagne-Soleil and Plagne-Villages. Over a low ridge, beyond the last two, are Plagne-Bellecôte and Belle-Plagne above it.

Outside the main bowl, at the northern edge of the area, are Les Coches and Montchavin. At the southern edge is rustic Champagny. Beyond Aime-la-Plagne, at the western edge, is growing Montalbert. These are described later in the chapter.

A free bus system between the core villages within the bowl runs until after midnight. Lifts between some resort units run until 1am.

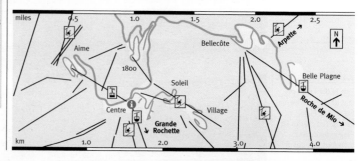

↑ Some of the blue runs can get pretty tricky – and very crowded
SNOWPIX.COM / CHRIS GILL

KEY FACTS

Resort	1800-2100m
	5,900-6,890ft

La Plagne only	
Slopes	1250-3250m
	4,100-10,660ft
Lifts	81
Pistes	225km
	140 miles
Green	8%
Blue	53%
Red	25%
Black	14%
Snowmaking	
	359 guns

Paradiski area	
Slopes	1200-3250m
	3,940-10,660ft
Lifts	135
Pistes	425km
	264 miles
Green	4%
Blue	52%
Red	28%
Black	16%
Snowmaking	
	626 guns

A cable car from Montchavin links to Les Arcs via Peisey-Vallandry. Day trips by car to Val d'Isère-Tignes or the Three Valleys resorts are possible. Staying in Champagny means quick access by car or taxi to Courchevel.

VILLAGE CHARM ★★☆☆☆
Take your pick
The high-altitude villages vary quite a lot in character; our rating relates to Belle-Plagne and Plagne 1800, where most Brits go. The first unit to be built, in the 1960s, was Plagne-Centre. Typical of its time, it has ugly square blocks and dreary indoor 'malls' that house shops, bars and restaurants. At last, as the resort celebrates its 50th birthday, a three-year renovation project is being started to improve the malls, with better access, lighting and leisure areas. More recent developments are more stylish, but they can't compete with Centre in terms of facilities. Plagne 1800 is all in chalet style, so is visually inoffensive. Aime-la-Plagne, in stark contrast, is a group of monolithic blocks given a nominal chalet-roof shape. Plagne-Soleil and Plagne-Villages mainly consist of small-scale apartment buildings finished in chalet style. The apartment buildings of Plagne-Bellecôte form a gigantic wall at the foot of the slopes leading down to it. By contrast, Belle-Plagne just above is built in a pleasant chalet style, and has a mini-resort centre, though few shops.

CONVENIENCE ★★★★★
No worries at altitude
The high-altitude villages are mostly ski-in/ski-out – but much of Plagne 1800 presents challenges because of its steep setting, which has to be negotiated on foot. At Plagne Bellecôte you'll walk further inside your apartment building than outside. Belle-Plagne is now quite large, and spread over a steepish hillside that provokes complaints from readers who find its multiple levels exhausting. Readers find Plagne-Soleil works well.

SCENERY ★★★☆☆
Look to the horizon
The scenery makes an attractive and varied backdrop to the less attractive core villages. And Mont Blanc looms big on the horizon, especially from Montchavin and Les Coches.

THE MOUNTAINS

The majority of the slopes in the main bowl are above the treeline, though there are trees scattered around most of the resort centres. The slopes outside the bowl are open at the top but descend into woodland – and are the best place to be in bad weather.

Some runs are more difficult than their classification suggests, while others are easier – note our warning in 'For intermediates'. Piste names and classification seem to alter regularly. Signposting is fine though piste marking can be a bit vague in places.

LIFT PASSES

La Plagne

Prices in €

Age	1-day	6-day
under 14	33	157
14 to 64	43	209
over 65	33	157

Free under 6
Beginner 17 free lifts
Senior pass for 1-15
days for €6 if over 72
Notes
Covers all lifts in La
Plagne areas;
individual village-area
and half-day passes;
Paradiski extension

Paradiski Découverte

Prices in €

Age	6-day
under 14	172
14 to 64	229
over 65	172

Free under 6
Beginner no deals
Notes
Covers all lifts in La
Plagne areas with one
day in Paradiski

Paradiski

Prices in €

Age	1-day	6-day
under 14	37	187
14 to 64	49	249
over 65	37	187

Free under 6
Beginner no deals
Senior pass for 1-15
days for €9 if over 72
Notes
Covers all lifts in Les
Arcs area and La
Plagne area; family
reductions

EXTENT OF THE SLOPES ★★★★
Multi-centred; can be confusing

Our rating relates to just the La Plagne area; the whole Paradiski area easily scores five stars.

La Plagne's pistes spread over a wide area that can be broken down into seven sectors. From Plagne-Centre you can take a lift up to **Le Biolley**, from where you can head back to Centre, to Aime-la-Plagne or progress to **Montalbert**. But the main lift out of Plagne-Centre leads up to **La Grande Rochette**. From here there are good sweeping runs back down and an easier one over to Plagne-Bellecôte, or you can drop over into the sunny **Champagny** sector, for excellent long runs and great views of Courchevel.

From Plagne-Bellecôte and Belle-Plagne, you can head up to **Roche de Mio**, and have the choice of a gondola or two successive fast chairs (the first of which also accesses Champagny). From Roche de Mio, runs spread out in all directions – towards La Plagne, Champagny or **Montchavin/Les Coches**. This sector can also be reached by taking an eight-seat chair from Plagne-Bellecôte to L'Arpette.

From Roche de Mio you can also take a gondola down then up to the **Bellecôte glacier**. It is prone to closure by high winds or poor weather. The top chair is often shut in winter – but if open, it offers excellent snow and stunning views. The black piste below Col de la Chiaupe (new for last season) means that you can descend from the glacier on-piste to Les Bauches without riding the gondola back up to Roche de Mio; if you go all the way to Montchavin, it's 2000m vertical.

The piste map marks three draglifts (in the Biolley/Montalbert sectors) as 'difficult', and they are. Plagne-Centre has a night skiing slope.

FAST LIFTS ★★
Slipping behind again?

Years ago La Plagne fell behind its French mega-resort rivals in lift investment; there have been spurts of improvements, but now the area is again slipping behind. Happily, many key lifts are fast, and the Montchavin/Les Coches sector is pretty much sorted, but once you start to really explore other sectors of the slopes you find lots of old chairs and draglifts – above Les Bauches, around Centre and above Montalbert, for example.

QUEUES ★★
Obvious bottlenecks remain

La Plagne's lift and piste network has some fundamental flaws – in particular, moving across the area often involves passing through Plagne-Bellecôte – where long queues ('horrendous', 'worst in years') build in high season. The Roche de Mio gondola is especially bad ('20 to 40 minutes' in 2011), but the chairs towards Centre and Montchavin are not queue-free. What's needed is some lifts from Belle-Plagne, higher up.

Plagne-Centre also has problems; even the Bergerie six-pack builds queues (but they move quickly). The gondola to the glacier is queue-prone when snow is poor lower down – to get back up to Roche de Mio as well as to the glacier (we saw horrendous queues to get back at the end of the day on our March 2011 visit).

In the Champagny sector, the Verdons Sud chair up to Les Verdons has been another serious bottleneck, but is due to be replaced by a six-pack for 2011/12. One Easter skier had days out in Courchevel: 'The contrast was startling,' he says.

Crowds on the pistes are now as much of a problem as lift queues. The worst-affected area is from Roche de Mio down to Belle-Plagne and Plagne-Bellecôte (we went off-piste to avoid dangerously crowded pistes here on our 2011 visit). The slopes outside the main bowl are quieter, except runs to Montchavin late in the day.

TERRAIN PARKS ★★★★
Lots of choices

With no fewer than five terrain zones, freestylers are well catered for. There is a 90m long, 3.5m high half-pipe at Plagne Bellecôte (plus an FIS-approved super-pipe, which hosts the World Cup but isn't open to the public). Belle-Plagne is home to the big park, split into beginner and more advanced zones, with a mix of jumps, boxes, rails, tables and other obstacles, plus an airbag. Then there are three boardercross courses dotted around.

SNOW RELIABILITY ★★★★
Generally good except low down

Most of La Plagne's runs are snow-sure, being at altitudes between 2000m and 2700m on the largely north-facing open slopes above the purpose-built centres. The two sunny runs to Champagny are something else

– one is often closed, the other (Les Bois) is kept open as much as possible with lots of artificial snow. Snowmaking on runs to all the villages is being improved. On our March 2011 visit we found most of the pistes in great condition, despite the lack of natural snowfall.

FOR EXPERTS ★★★★☆
Few steep pistes; good off-piste
The two long, steep and bumpy black runs from Bellecôte to a lift below Col de la Chiaupe were returned to off-piste status in 2009/10 – not surprising given that they were rarely open, but a shame all the same. The new piste linking this area to Les Bauches and Montchavin doesn't really deserve its black status.

Up on the glacier Chiaupe merits its black status for a short stretch, but really the tough piste skiing is now confined to the Biolley sector. On the back of the hill, the Coqs and Morbleu blacks are seriously steep, Palsembleu less so. From the very top of this sector, Etroits owes its black status to a quite short pitch that is both steep and narrow, but is otherwise harmless. The long Emile Allais red down to the La Roche chair is north-facing, often quiet and great fun in good snow.

But experts will get the best out of La Plagne if they hire a guide and explore the vast off-piste potential – which takes longer to get tracked out than in more 'macho' resorts. The glacier and Biolley sectors have some excellent off-piste terrain. More serious undertakings include numerous runs from the glacier to Les Bauches (a drop of over 1400m). For the more experienced, the north face of Bellecôte presents a splendid challenge with usually excellent snow at the top. You can descend to Peisey-Nancroix (a drop of 2000m), enjoy a splendid lunch at the charming, rustic Ancolie (a real favourite of ours) and

La Plagne

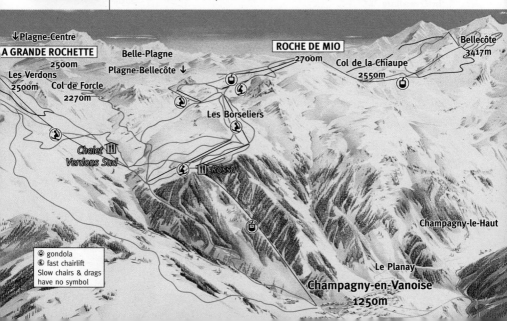

↓Plagne-Centre
A GRANDE ROCHETTE
2500m
Les Verdons
2500m   Col de Forcle
2270m

Belle-Plagne
Plagne-Bellecôte ↓

ROCHE DE MIO
2700m   Col de la Chiaupe
2550m

Bellecôte
3417m

Les Borseliers

Chalet
Verdons Sud

Rossa

Champagny-le-Haut

Le Planay
Champagny-en-Vanoise
1250m

then catch a taxi or free bus to the Vanoise Express cable car. Another beautiful and out-of-the-way run starts with a climb and goes over the Cul du Nant glacier to Champagny-le-Haut.

FOR INTERMEDIATES ★★★★★
Great variety

Virtually the whole of La Plagne's area is a paradise for intermediates, with blue and red runs wherever you look. The main drawback is that many of them get overcrowded at times.

For early intermediates there are plenty of gentle blue motorway pistes in the main La Plagne bowl, and a long, interesting (but often very crowded) run from Roche de Mio to Belle Plagne, the Tunnel (going through, er, a tunnel). The blue runs either side of Arpette, on the Montchavin side of the main bowl, are glorious cruises – but beware, the blues further down towards Montchavin are quite challenging. The easiest way to and from Champagny is

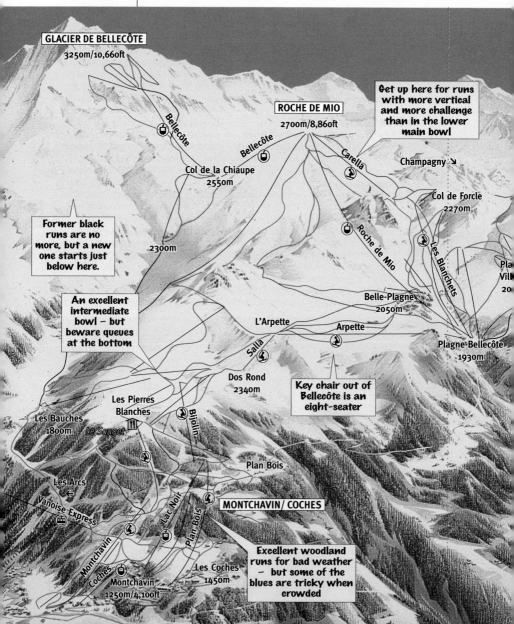

GLACIER DE BELLECÔTE
3250m/10,66oft

ROCHE DE MIO
2700m/8,86oft

Get up here for runs with more vertical and more challenge than in the lower main bowl

Bellecôte

Bellecôte

Carella

Champagny ↘

Col de la Chiaupe
2550m

Col de Forcle
2270m

Roche de Mio

Les Blanchets

Pla
Vil
20

Former black runs are no more, but a new one starts just below here.

2300m

Belle-Plagne
2050m

An excellent intermediate bowl – but beware queues at the bottom

L'Arpette

Arpette

Plagne-Bellecôte
1930m

Salla

Dos Rond
2340m

Key chair out of Bellecôte is an eight-seater

Les Pierres Blanches

Bijolin

Les Bauches
1800m

Le Sauget

Plan Bois

Les Arcs

Vanoise Express

Lac Noir

Plan Bois

MONTCHAVIN/ COCHES

Montchavin

Coches

Les Coches
1450m

Montchavin
125om/4,10oft

Excellent woodland runs for bad weather – but some of the blues are tricky when crowded

If the thrills of a day on the slopes aren't enough, you can round it off by having a go on the bobsleigh run built for the 1992 Winter Olympics. The floodlit 1.5km run has 19 bends, generating forces as high as 3g.

You can go in a driverless bob-raft (38 euros) reaching 50mph, which most people find quite exciting enough. Then there's the faster solo mono-bob (103 euros); we found this a great thrill – we had to close our eyes on the sharper bends. Fastest of all is the 'taxi-bob' (108 euros), where three of you are wedged in a real four-man bob behind the driver – advertised speed 68mph. Be sure your physical state is up to the ride; there are minimum age limits. The run is open on certain days only – book ahead. Additional insurance is available. One visitor loved the ride, but found the staff rude and impatient: 'They rushed us through, despite the fact that we were early.'

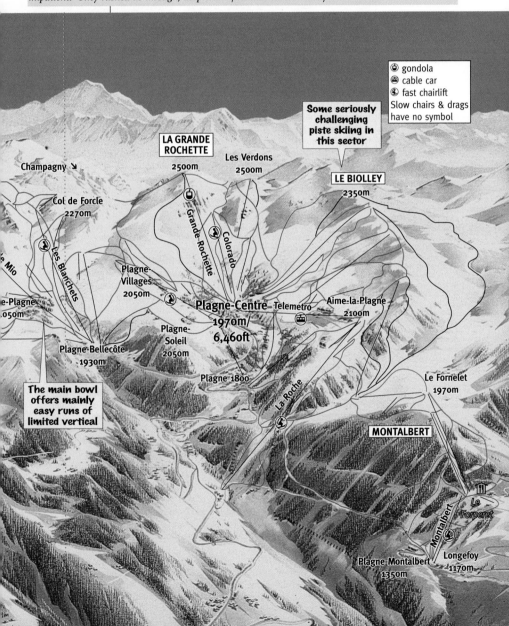

UK PACKAGES

*Action Outdoors, Alpine
Answers, Alpine
Elements, Chalet
Group, Club Med,
Crystal, Crystal Finest,
Erna Low, Esprit, First
Choice, Independent
Ski Links, Inghams,
Interactive Resorts,
Lagrange, Mark
Warner, Mountain
Heaven, Mountain
Wave, Neilson, Oxford
Ski Co, Powder White,
Powder White Lite,
PowderBeds,
PV-Holidays.com, Silver
Ski, Ski Amis, Ski Beat,
Skibug, Ski Club
Freshtracks, Ski
Collection, Ski
Expectations, Ski
France, Ski Hiver, Ski
Independence, Ski Line,
Ski Olympic, Ski Soleil,
Ski Solutions, Ski
Supreme, Skitracer, Ski
Weekend,
Skiweekends.com,
Skiworld, Snow
Finders, Snowchateaux,
SnowCrazy, Solo's,
Thomson, VIP*
Montchavin *Chill
Chalet, Lagrange, Peak
Retreats, Ski Hiver, Ski
Soleil, Snowchateaux*
Les Coches *Erna Low,
Family Ski Company,
Ice and Fire,
Independent Ski Links,
Interactive Resorts,
Lagrange,
Mountainsun, Peak
Retreats, PowderBeds,
PV-Holidays.com, Ski
France, Ski
Independence, Ski Line,
Snowchateaux*
Montalbert *Lagrange,
Mountain Heaven, Ski
Amis*
Champagny *Barrelli,
Erna Low, Independent
Ski Links, Lagrange,
Peak Retreats, Ski
France, Ski
Independence*

from the Roche de Mio-Col de Forcle
area. Warning: the Mira piste from
Grande Rochette back towards Plagne-
Centre is the steepest blue run we
have ever encountered – it should
without question be red; lower down
it turns into an excellent cruise. (The
resort tells us the Mira piste is being
improved for 2011/12 – reports please).
Verdons, nearby, is a great cruise too.

Better intermediates have lots of
delightful long red runs to try. There
are challenging red mogul pitches
down from Roche de Mio to Les
Bauches (a drop of 900m) – the first
half is a fabulous varied run with lots
of off-piste diversions possible; the
second half, Les Crozats, is classified
black, and can be tricky if snow is less
than ideal. The Sources red to Belle
Plagne is a good run, too.

The Champagny sector has a couple
of tough reds – Kamikaze and Hara-
Kiri – leading from Grande Rochette.
And the long blue cruise Bozelet has
one surprisingly steep section. The
long Mont de la Guerre red, with
1250m vertical from Les Verdons to
Champagny, is a fine away-from-all-lifts
run with a decent red-gradient stretch
half-way down, but long flattish tracks
at the start and finish. There are
further excellent red slopes in the
other outlying areas – including the
winding, treelined Les Coches.

FOR BEGINNERS ★★★★
Comprehensive facilities
La Plagne is a good place to learn,
with 17 free lifts in the whole area;
each village has at least one. There
are good facilities for beginners,
provided you go to the right bits, and
generally good snow. There are
beginner areas in Centre, 1800, Aime
and Bellecôte; and in Montchavin, Les
Coches and Montalbert. But there are
no long green runs to progress to from
the nursery slopes. Although a lot of
the blue slopes are easy, you can't
count on that; some, as we note
above, are quite testing.

FOR BOARDERS ★★★
Something for everyone
With such a huge amount of terrain,
there is something for everyone.
Expert freeriders should hire a guide
to explore the off-piste. Although this
is a great place for beginners and
intermediates, with huge wide-open
rolling pistes, there are a lot of flattish
areas, especially above Belle-Plagne,
in the middle of the Tunnel run and
the blue run linking from Les Bauches
to Montchavin – make sure to get
enough speed there. Most draglifts
have been replaced, and others can be
avoided; the more difficult ones are
marked on the piste map. The park
caters for all levels and there are three
boardercross runs – see 'Terrain parks'.

FOR CROSS-COUNTRY ★★★★
Open and wooded trails
There are 80km of prepared cross-
country trails scattered around. The
most beautiful of these are the 22km
of winding track set out in the sunny
valley around Champagny-le-Haut. The
north-facing areas have more wooded
trails that link the various centres.

OT LA PLAGNE / ELINA SIRPARANTA

SCHOOLS

ESF (Belle Plagne)
t 0479 090668
Schools in all centres
Oxygène (Plagne-Centre)
t 0479 090399
El Pro (Belle-Plagne)
t 0479 091162
Reflex (Plagne 1800)
t 0613 808056
Evolution 2 (Montchavin-Les Coches)
t 0479 078185

Classes (ESF prices)
6 days from €217
Private lessons
From €180 for 2.5hr for up to 5 people

CHILDCARE

Les P'tits Bonnets (Plagne-Centre)
t 0479 090083
Marie Christine (Plagne-Centre)
t 0479 091181
Ages 2 to 6
ESF nurseries (ages from 18 mnth or 2yr):
Aime 0479 090475
Belle 0479 090668
Bellecôte 0479 090133
Snow gardens run by ESF: ages from 3 to 5

Ski schools
Children's classes are available up to 13 or 16yr depending on the village: 6 days €259 (ESF prices)

MOUNTAIN RESTAURANTS ★★★★
An enormous choice
Mountain restaurants are an attraction of the area: numerous and varied – and crowded only in peak periods. But all our favourites are outside the main bowl, above the satellite villages.
Editors' choice We've had excellent meals at Chalet des Verdons Sud (0621 543924) above Champagny; reporters agree – appetising food and good service, on a big terrace with a fine view or in the warmly woody interior. Above Montalbert, the Forperet (0479 555127) is an old farm, doing super home-made dishes. We had an excellent tartiflette there (as did a reporter). The rustic Sauget (0479 078351), above Montchavin, is a great place to hole up in poor weather for some highly traditional dishes.
Worth knowing about Readers' tips include Plein Soleil at Plan Bois ('a bit cramped but excellent food'), Roc des Blanchets above Champagny ('stunning location, great food'), Borseliers above Champagny ('excellent variety of local dishes, reasonably priced plat du jour and big sun terrace'), Bergerie above Plagne Village ('for the occasional free post lunch genepi'), Chalet des Glaciers on the, er, glacier ('tiny hut with hearty soup in a bread bowl; outside seating only'). In Bellecôte, the takeaway kiosk McCotes does 10 euro meal deals for burger, frites and a drink – 'once we found this place we didn't eat anywhere else'. Above Montchavin, the Cristal des Neiges serves 'filling and tasty' food.

SCHOOLS AND GUIDES ★★★
Better alternatives to ESF
Each centre has its own ESF school and we had positive reports in 2011. Champagny: 'For the near beginner in our group, the lessons were fun, and the instructor built up a real sense of camaraderie among the diverse group.'

Belle Plagne (arranged by Ski Esprit): 'My four-year-old had positive and encouraging instructors, and progressed well.' There are some very worthwhile alternatives too. The Oxygène school in Plagne-Centre was said to be 'superb', 'brought us on by stretching us over more and more difficult terrain'. Reflex based in 1800 and Evolution 2 based in Montchavin have had good past reviews. Antenne Handicap offers private lessons for skiers with any kind of disability.

FOR FAMILIES ★★★★
Good facilities
Children are well catered for with facilities in each of the villages. The nursery at Belle-Plagne is 'excellent, with good English spoken'. The one in Les Coches is not apparently (see 'Les Coches'). Several UK chalet operators run childcare services – Esprit was particularly highly recommended by a 2011 reporter ('excellent from start to finish'). One or two reporters were concerned by the crowded pistes.

STAYING THERE

Chalets There are lots of catered chalets. Many are in apartments, but there are lots of proper little chalets in 1800 which is where most large UK tour operators have places, including Inghams and Crystal. Mountain Heaven has a mid-sized, all en suite place in a good location at 1800. Ski Beat has 13 chalets, mainly in 1800 and nine with saunas. Skiworld has ten chalets dotted around several parts of the resort. Family specialist Esprit has the exceptionally cool chalet hotel Deux Domaines, in a great position at Belle-Plagne, with good pool and spa and 'excellent' childcare facilities that got a rave review from a 2011 reporter. In Centre, there is a ski-in chalet hotel run by Ski Olympic ('great team,

↑ Lots of high, snow-sure intermediate slopes are one of the resort's main attractions

SNOWPIX.COM / CHRIS GILL

service and food'). See also our descriptions of lower villages.

Hotels There are very few, and most are of 2-star or 3-star grading.

****Carlina (0479 097846) Beside the piste below Belle-Plagne and recently upgraded from 3- to 4-star. Pleasant rooms, good restaurant, pool and spa centre. Family-friendly. We've enjoyed our stays here. Endorsed by a satisfied reader last year.

***Araucaria (0479 092020) Very modern 3-star at Plagne-Centre.

***Balcons (0479 557655) 3-star at Belle-Plagne. Pool.

Apartments There is a wide choice, including lots of smart new developments, most with pools, available through operators such as Ski Collection, Peak Retreats, Ski Amis, Pierre & Vacances, Ski Independence, Lagrange and Erna Low. Chalets les Montagnettes in Belle-Plagne are spacious with good views. The Nereides residence up here was fully refurbished a few years ago. In Plagne-Soleil the Granges du Soleil is very comfortable and has excellent views. Up at Aime is the Pierre & Vacances Premium residence Hauts Bois – 'excellent, with a decent pool'. Lagrange has two Prestige residences here: Aspen in Plagne-Villages and Chalets Edelweiss (seven chalet-style buildings sharing a pool) – right by the lift out of 1800.

EATING OUT ★★★☆☆
A reasonable choice
There is a decent range of casual restaurants including pizzerias and traditional Savoyard places. In Belle-Plagne, the Face Nord is recommended for 'excellent local cuisine and service'. The Matafan served up a hearty meal of grilled meats and good desserts on our recent visit and we enjoyed a very tasty three course meal at the hotel Carlina's restaurant 'C', which is also recommended for lunch. Down in Bellecôte, the Ferme does 'superb Savoyard food'.

Reader recommendations in Plagne-Centre include the Maison (steaks) and Scotty's for 'friendly service and good food'. The Refuge is charmingly rustic.

In Plagne-Villages, the Casa de l'Ours does pizzas and steaks. In Plagne-Soleil, Monica's is 'excellent, and good value'.

In Plagne 1800, we had a good evening at Petit Chaperon Rouge – friendly, cosy atmosphere in a wooden chalet that serves local specialities at reasonable prices; the Loup Blanc is popular for 'fine steaks and pizza'.

At Aime-la-Plagne, the rustic old chalet Au Bon Vieux Temps on the slopes is open in the evening, and there's the Arlequin – a 'proper' restaurant, but family-friendly.

APRES-SKI ★★★☆☆
Bars, bars, bars
Though fairly quiet during low season, La Plagne has plenty of bars, catering particularly for the younger crowd.

In Belle-Plagne, the Tête Inn, the Cheyenne and Maître Kanter are the main bars. In Plagne-Centre, the Igloo Igloo has an 'icy decor'. The PlanJA is popular and has English cider, apparently. Scotty's is 'lively'. The Mine is the focal point in Plagne 1800 – complete with old train and mining artefacts: 'good beer and live music'.

Interactive resort shortlist builder at **www.wtss.co.uk**

ACTIVITIES

Indoor Sauna and solarium in most centres, squash (1800), fitness centres (Belle-Plagne, 1800, Centre, Bellecôte), library (Centre), climbing wall, bowling

Outdoor Heated swimming pool, bobsleigh, marked walks, tobogganing, paragliding, helicopter rides, snowmobiles, ice climbing, ice rink, ice karting, snow quad bikes, snowshoeing, dog sledding, air boarding, zip slide

Phone numbers
From abroad use the prefix +33 and omit the initial '0' of the phone number

TOURIST OFFICES

La Plagne
www.la-plagne.com

Montchavin-Les Coches
www.montchavin-lescoches.com

Champagny
www.champagny.com

Mama Mia's is a fun spot. Plagne Soleil has Monica's pub ('superb value food and drink'). Aime-la-Plagne is quiet. There are discos at Plagne-Centre and at Belle-Plagne.

OFF THE SLOPES ★★★★★
OK for the active
As well as the sports and fitness facilities, there are plenty of winter walks along marked trails. It's also easy to get up the mountain on the gondolas, which both have restaurants at the top. There's an ice grotto on the glacier. Plagne 1800 has bowling and tubing. The Olympic bobsleigh run is a popular evening activity (see feature box). There are cinemas at Aime, Bellecôte and Plagne-Centre. Excursions are limited.

LINKED RESORT – 1250m
MONTCHAVIN
Montchavin is based on an old farming hamlet and has an attractive traffic-free centre. There are adequate shops, a kindergarten and a ski school. The local slopes have quite a bit to offer – pretty, sheltered runs, well endowed with snowmaking, with nursery slopes at village level. The blue home runs can be quite tricky. Après-ski is quiet, but the village doesn't lack atmosphere and has a couple of nice bars, a nightclub, cinema and night skiing (and a new swimming pool and spa complex for 2011/12). Hotel Bellecôte (0479 078330) is convenient for the slopes.

LINKED RESORT – 1450m
LES COCHES
Les Coches is a little way above Montchavin, across the hillside, and shares the same slopes. It is a sympathetically designed, quiet, modern mini-resort with a traffic-free centre. The hillside setting makes for some steep walks. There are nursery slopes across the mountainside, linked by bucket lift. It has a kindergarten. But we have a scathing report from one visitor. Family Ski Company may be a better bet; it has two piste-side chalets close to the village centre. Ice and Fire has a smart-looking 24-bed chalet on the piste with a sauna and offers bathrobes as standard. The Chalets de Wengen is a trio of comfortable chalet-style apartment buildings sharing a pool.

Dining out options approved by readers include the Poze (pizza), the Savoy'art ('stunning interior'), and Taverne du Monchu.

LINKED RESORT – 1350m
MONTALBERT
Montalbert is a traditional but much expanded village with a nice little front de neige area, with a choice of restaurant terraces. The lift out of the village is a fast one, but your progress to the main bowl depends on two further slow ones. The local slopes are easy and wooded. Restaurant choice is adequate, Abreuvoir has 'reasonable prices in happy hour and friendly staff', Tourmente is a popular pub with a pool table and the Code is a 'racy but rocking' nightclub. The Aigle Rouge (0479 547843) is a simple hotel. Ski Amis has a central, all en suite, seven-room chalet with all the trimmings here, and various self-catering options. Mountain Heaven has a duplex apartment run as a catered chalet (strongly recommended by a 2011 reporter); and self-catering apartments in several modern developments; the best of the apartments are notably spacious by French standards, and well furnished.

LINKED RESORT – 1250m
CHAMPAGNY
Champagny is a small, charming village in a pretty, wooded, sunny setting, with its modern expansion done sensitively. It is remote from the link to Les Arcs and the red run to the village that is most reliably open is rather steep and narrow for nervous intermediates (but you can ride the gondola down). It is well placed for an outing by taxi or car to Courchevel.

The Glières (0479 550552) is a rustic old hotel with varied rooms, a friendly welcome and good food. The Ancolie (0479 550500) is smarter, with modern facilities. The Alpages de Champagny has 'generous-sized apartments', a pool and sauna. The Club Alpina apartments next to the gondola have been recommended.

The village is quiet in the evenings, but readers tip a few restaurants: Poya ('superb atmosphere, friendliness and food'), Bouquetin ('uncomplicated ingredients expertly cooked') and Rochers, near the church ('lovely food, good value').

Portes du Soleil

Low altitude, largely intermediate circuit of slopes straddling the French-Swiss border, with a variety of contrasting resorts

KEY FACTS

Slopes	950-2275m
	3,120-7,460ft
Lifts	196
Pistes	650km
	404 miles
Green	13%
Blue	40%
Red	37%
Black	10%
Snowmaking	
	800 guns

The Portes du Soleil vies with the Trois Vallées for the title 'World's Largest Ski Area', but its slopes are very different from those of Méribel, Courchevel, Val Thorens and neighbours. The central attraction is an extensive circular tour, straddling the French-Swiss border, taking you through two French resorts and several small Swiss ones – great for keen intermediates who like a sensation of travel while skiing. You can travel the circuit in either direction and longer or shorter variations are possible – including or excluding the Champéry slopes.

We have separate chapters on all the major Portes du Soleil resorts. On the French side, purpose-built **Avoriaz** usually has the best snow on the circuit. The circuit breaks down at the traditional village of **Châtel** – you take a bus between the resort's two sectors of slopes. **Morzine** and **Les Gets** are also traditional villages; they are off the main circuit but share the biggest area of local slopes in the region.

On the Swiss side, **Champéry** is a classic, charming mountain village with slopes that you can choose to include or exclude from the circuit. Nearby are the tiny, purpose-built satellite stations of **Champoussin** and **Les Crosets**. Then there is the larger, traditional village of **Morgins**. There's a short walk across the village here – less of an effort if you are travelling the circuit clockwise.

The lifts you ride doing the circuit vary widely. In the Avoriaz sector and in the Linga sector of Châtel the lifts are mainly modern and fast. On the far side of Châtel and on the Swiss side of the network, drags and old chairlifts dominate, and progress is slow.

The slopes are low by French standards, with top heights in the range 2000m to 2275m, and low points where snow may be particularly poor in Morgins and Châtel (1200m). In general, you can expect better snow on the north-facing French side of the link with Avoriaz than on the Swiss side, where the slopes basically face east and south.

Until 2007 there was a booklet-style map covering the whole of the Portes du Soleil. But now each resort has its own map showing local lifts and pistes – you have to pick these up along the way. But at least last season they all had the same map of the whole circuit on the back.

335

SNOWPIX.COM / CHRIS GILL

Puy-St-Vincent

Underrated small modern resort with limited but varied slopes –
good for young families who haven't been spoilt by mega-resorts

TOP 10 RATINGS

Extent	★★
Fast lifts	★★
Queues	★★★
Snow	★★★
Expert	★★★
Intermediate	★★★
Beginner	★★★
Charm	★★
Convenience	★★★★★
Scenery	★★★★

RPI   75

lift pass	£130
ski hire	£95
lessons	£75
food & drink	£120
total	**£420**

NEWS

2010/11: Two fixed-grip (ie slow) quads were installed on the upper slopes: one replaced the Rocher Noir draglift, the other replaced the Pendine double chair.

336

+ Mostly convenient resort with friendly locals and great for families

+ Some great cross-country routes

+ Low prices overall

− Slopes limited in extent

− Few alternatives to apartments

− Queues and crowds in peak season

− Limited facilities and diversions

Puy-St-Vincent's ski area may be limited, but it offers a decent vertical and a lot of variety, including a bit of steep stuff. Provided you pick your spot with care, it makes an attractive choice for a family not hungry for piste miles.

THE RESORT

Puy-St-Vincent proper is an old mountain village, but most people stay in one of the purpose-built ski-stations. Station 1400 is a small development by the chairlift just along the mountainside from Puy-St-Vincent proper; the major part, Station 1600, with long, low, white 1970s-style apartment blocks arranged across the hill, is a few hairpins further up. Spreading up the hillside from 1600 are newer chalet-style developments – sometimes referred to as Station 1800. The three developments are linked by free buses till 8pm.

The six-day pass allows a day in Pelvoux, a short bus ride away (and in several more distant major resorts); this small area has quiet, very rewarding blue, red and black runs, and a vertical of over 1000m.

Village charm The main resort of 1600 is functional rather than charming. We and our reporters have found PSV a very friendly, welcoming resort.

Convenience 1600 is compact, with its few shops, bars and restaurants lining the foot of the slopes – ideal for families. Much of the lodging is ski-in/ski-out; one main lift starts just below the village, which helps. 1800 is fine for the slopes but has no supermarket or bars, one restaurant and the bus stops at 8pm, so a night out in 1600 means an uphill slog home.

Scenery The resort has a lovely woody position above the valley; great views from the top to the Ecrins mountains.

THE MOUNTAINS

Within its small area, PSV packs in a lot of variety. A few reporters have judged some blue runs a bit tough.

Slopes There are gentle slopes between 1600 and 1400, but most of the runs are above 1600. A fast quad goes up to the treeline at around 2000m. The top lift is a (slow) quad to La Pendine at 2700m, serving open slopes. More lifts serve further open

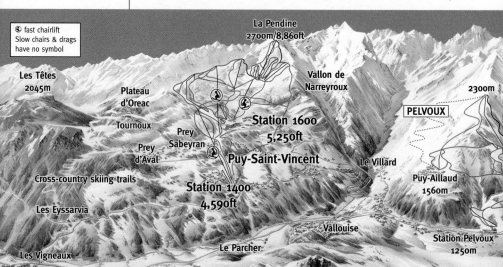

⚙ fast chairlift
Slow chairs & drags have no symbol

La Pendine
2700m/8,860ft

Les Têtes
2045m

Plateau
d'Oreac

Vallon de
Narreyroux

2300m

Tournoux

PELVOUX

Prey
Sabeyran

Station 1600
5,250ft

Prey
d'Aval

Puy-Saint-Vincent

Le Villard

Cross-country skiing trails

Station 1400
4,590ft

Puy-Aillaud
1560m

Les Eyssarvia

Les Vigneaux

Vallouise

Le Parcher

Station Pelvoux
1250m

KEY FACTS

Resort	1400-1600m
	4,590-5,250ft
Slopes	1250-2700m
	4,100-8,860ft
Lifts	12
Pistes	75km
	47 miles
Green	18%
Blue	41%
Red	35%
Black	6%
Snowmaking	13%

UK PACKAGES

Erna Low, Lagrange, Ski Collection, Ski France, Snowbizz, Zenith

Phone numbers
From abroad use the prefix +33 and omit the initial '0' of the phone number

TOURIST OFFICE

www.paysdesecrins.com

---

runs here, and access splendid cruising runs that curl around the edges of the area into the woods.
Fast lifts The key lifts out of the resorts are fast chairs.
Queues Reporters complain of crowds during French school holiday periods, but few problems at other times.
Terrain parks There is a park and boardercross on Pendine.
Snow reliability The slopes face north-east and are reasonably reliable for snow. Snowmaking covers much of the slopes at 1600 and runs to 1400.
Experts The two black runs are short but genuinely black, often with moguls. There are good off-piste opportunities in the high bowl and lower down in the trees, and longer routes to be tackled with guidance.
Intermediates Size apart, it's a good area for those who like a challenge – but there aren't many very easy runs.
Beginners A day pass is available for the drag on the small nursery area at 1400. Progression is not ideal: there is a long green from 2000m but it crosses several other pistes and is very busy as it approaches the resort.
Snowboarding There are slopes to suit all levels, but still some draglifts.
Cross-country The 30km of cross-country trails include some varied routes between 1400m and 1700m.
Mountain restaurants The woody, self-service Etoile des Neiges on the lower slopes has an open fire and is tipped for 'fantastic food and friendly staff'. The modern Bartavelles at the top of the chair from 1600 has great views and self- and table-service sections.
Schools and guides As well as the ESF there is a large International school run in partnership with tour operator Snowbizz. We have very positive reports: 'fun, friendly, knowledgeable'; 'excellent off-piste guiding'.

Families From all points of view the resort suits families well. Snowbizz runs its own crèche: 'Large, light and airy, caring staff, lots of toys. Our boys did not want to come home at night.'

STAYING THERE

Most accommodation is in self-catering apartments at the foot of the slopes.
Hotels There are three hotels in 1400. We'd stay at the 3-star St-Roch: right by the lift, great views over the valley, good food, very friendly. The Pendine is just over the road, the Aigliere a bus ride away – both 2-stars.
Apartments Peak Retreats features three smart residences with pools and saunas at 1800. Snowbizz has very family-friendly places right by shops and slopes at 1600.
Eating out There's a fair choice in 1600. Petit Chamois serves 'generous portions' and caters well for kids. The three hotel restaurants in 1400 have all been recommended.
Après-ski Après-ski is confined to a few bar-restaurants in 1600 and the hotel bars in 1400.
Off the slopes Village diversions are very limited, but there are 20km of walks, snowshoeing, parapenting, tobogganing and skating. The cinema doesn't show English-speaking films.

Puy-St-Vincent

337

OT DU PAYS DES ECRINS / M DURAND

The foot of the slopes at 1600. The chalet-style buildings higher up are 1800 →

OT ST-LARY-SOULAN

The Pyrenees

An underrated region with decent skiing and boarding at lower prices than the Alps and villages that remain distinctly French

RPI	85
lift pass	£170
ski hire	£120
lessons	£90
food & drink	£115
total	£495

It is certainly true that ski areas in the French Pyrenees can't compete in terms of extent with the mega resorts of the Alps. But don't dismiss them: they have considerable attractions, including price – hotels and apartments can cost half as much as in the French Alps, and meals and drinks are cheaper. Provided the snow is good and you're not in search of steep mogul fields and wild après-ski, there is a surprising amount of variety packed into some of these smaller areas.

UK PACKAGES

Les Angles *Lagrange, Ski Collection, Ski France*
Barèges *Borderline*
Cauterets *AmeriCan Ski, Lagrange, Ski Collection*
Font-Romeu *Lagrange, PV-Holidays.com, Ski Collection, Ski France, Zenith*
La Mongie *Lagrange, PV-Holidays.com, Ski Collection*
St-Lary-Soulan *AmeriCan Ski, Lagrange, PV-Holidays.com, Ski Collection, Ski France, Zenith*

338

The Pyrenees are serious mountains, with dramatic, picturesque scenery, and are worth considering for beginners, intermediates and quiet family holidays at a lower cost. The resorts are attractively French, and many have a rustic, rural Gallic charm. You'll find a mix of traditional villages and charmless purpose-built satellites.

Access has improved, with low-cost airlines using Toulouse and handy little Lourdes – just 30 minutes' easy drive to Cauterets. Note that some high col roads in the Pyrenees are closed all winter; others can be for days on end. So touring resorts from one base is less easy than in the Alps, especially getting to Spanish resorts.

Snowmaking has been improved, and there's plenty of skiing above

2000m. Late season is more of a problem, when the strong southern sun gets to work; conditions can deteriorate quickly, but we have enjoyed splendid April snow-cover.

The locals like to visit at weekends, so the slopes can get busy. Queues are rare outside peak holidays though, and a lot of locals do cross-country rather than downhill. British visitors are still relatively few, so English is less widely spoken in the ski schools.

Resorts are grouped in three main regions: the eastern Pyrenees, the central Haute Pyrenees and the western Pyrenees. La Mongie and St-Lary-Soulan are in the central area. Cauterets is further west. And Font-Romeu and Les Angles are further east (and east of Andorra).

KEY FACTS

Resort	935m
	3,070ft
Slopes	1730-2415m
	5,680-7,920ft
Lifts	11
Pistes	36km
Snow-guns	Some

TOURIST OFFICE

www.cauterets.com

Cauterets

- ☒ Charming, old spa town
- ☒ Serious cross-country trails
- ☒ Plentiful off-slope diversions

- ☐ Downhill slopes very limited
- ☐ Long gondola ride to/from slopes
- ☐ Quiet at night

Cauterets is good for a short break; it's a relaxing old town, easy to reach, and its small downhill ski area suits a couple of days – try the cross-country too.

Many of Cauterets' buildings are well-preserved examples of the 19th century, and very French. The spas are a popular attraction for visitors; the new Bains du Rocher opened for 2011. British-run Mulcares in the Pyrenees

offers central apartments and there is a wide choice of hotels. The town's position at the head of a wide, sunny valley means traffic is rarely a problem, despite its appeal as a large year-round tourist destination.

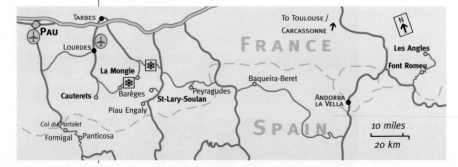

The skiing takes place in a high, open and treeless bowl, the Cirque du Lys, reached by a long gondola from town; you have to ride it down as well as up. There is parking up at Le Courbet (1360m), from where a short gondola departs for the slopes – though this was closed on our 2010 visit. The 36km of varied slopes radiate around the bowl, between 1730m and 2415m. The area just above the gondola top station is ideal for children and beginners, and newly revamped for 2011. There are some gentle blue runs for progression. But it does get busy at weekends, as does the main restaurant – a self-service. Cauteret's jewel, though, is its cross-country, a long drive or bus ride from town at Pont d'Espagne. It's one of the best we've seen, and amid beautiful scenery and impressive waterfalls – plenty of people agree, judging by the popular large car park at the base.

St-Lary-Soulan

➕ One of biggest Pyrenean ski areas
➕ Attractive, traditional village

➖ Few challenges on-piste
➖ No runs back to the resort

St-Lary combines an attractive, traditional village with one of the largest ski areas in the French Pyrenees – fine for intermediates wanting a sense of travel.

If you stay in the village, you ride a cable car or gondola both ways. Or you can stay up at purpose-built St-Lary 1700 (Pla-d'Adet) or 1900 (Espiaube), both served by buses.
Village charm St-Lary is pleasant enough, with an attractive church, wood and stone buildings, and charming terraced restaurants.
Convenience Accommodation spreads widely from the centre along a river towards the hamlet of Soulan. Staying close to one the two lifts is best.
Scenery The rocky ridges and open slopes give fine views.

THE MOUNTAIN
The slopes cover three main sectors and most runs are above the treeline.
Slopes A cable car and gondola go up to an area of short slopes at St-Lary 1700. From there you can head for 1900 and a gondola towards a more varied area of intermediate slopes.
Fast lifts Apart from the three above, most lifts are slow chairs and drags.
Queues We have no recent reports, but the newish gondola should have eased queues out of the village.
Terrain parks There are a couple of parks, boardercross and a pipe.
Snow reliability Reasonable; many slopes are north-east facing, almost half with snowmaking.
Experts The few black runs are not very challenging but there's off-piste at Courne Blanque and Soum de Matte.
Intermediates The area best suits intermediates, with a good mix of red and blue runs.
Beginners The nursery slopes and longer easy runs are at St-Lary 1700, but there is no special lift pass.
Snowboarding There are good cruising runs, though still some old draglifts.
Cross-country Not the best choice.
Mountain restaurants Choice is limited and 'disappointing'.
Schools and guides The four schools offer the usual options, though good spoken English cannot be guaranteed.
Families St-Lary is a good family resort, with kids' snow gardens, mini-terrain park and family fun area. The

The Pyrenees

Interactive resort shortlist builder at **www.wtss.co.uk**

day care centre at 1700 takes children from 18 months to six years old.

STAYING THERE
Hotels There are good value 2- and 3-star hotels. The 3-star Pergola is 'charming with a good restaurant'. **Apartments** 4-stars with pool, sauna, steam, hot tub include l'Ardoisière (800m from the gondola), Cami Real (central) and Chalets de l'Adet (on the slopes). Pierre & Vacances has the 3-star Rives de l'Aure (near cable car).

Ski Collection, Lagrange and Zenith have a good selection of places.
Eating out There's a fair choice, from pizzerias to grills. Our favourite is the Grange (local gourmet dishes). Other tips: the Gros Minet, Maison du Cassoulet and Pergola.
Après-ski Nightlife is quiet, but there are a few bars. Try the Fitzroy or Top Ski at 1700 (music and tapas).
Off the slopes There's a spa centre, skating, dog sledding, snowmobiling, snowshoeing, a cinema, a museum.

KEY FACTS

Barèges-La Mongie	
Resort	1800m
	5,910ft
Slopes	1400-2500m
	4,590-8,200ft
Lifts	39
Pistes	100km
Snow-guns	172 guns

TOURIST OFFICE
Domaine Tourmalet
uk.n-py.com
La Mongie
www.bagneresde
bigorre-lamongie.com

La Mongie

➕ One of biggest Pyrenean ski areas
➕ Convenient, slope-side village

➖ Purpose-built resort lacking charm
➖ Open, treeless slopes; lots of drags

La Mongie offers extensive and fairly snow-sure slopes, as well as some of the steepest slopes in the Pyrenees. Shame about the village.

La Mongie is a purpose-built, modern resort on one side of the high Col du Tourmalet pass (closed in winter). On the other side is Barèges, with which it shares the slopes. The centre has little charm but is convenient, with lifts and pistes radiating around it and good restaurant terraces from which to gaze at the scenery. Look up and you'll see the Observatory on Pic de Midi. The slopes span four valleys, but with the most variety above La Mongie. The

black runs are considered some of the toughest in the French Pyrenees. The open bowls give good scope for intermediates, but it's a long way to the gentle treelined runs above Barèges. And there are few huts. You can stay in Barèges, a spa town and one of the oldest ski areas in France; but the village has little to commend it. The shady main street has drab, rather neglected buildings. And the lift base is a drive away at Tournaboup.

KEY FACTS

Resort	1775m
	5,820ft
Slopes	1775-2215m
	5,820-7,270ft
Lifts	23
Pistes	58km
Snow-guns	80%

TOURIST OFFICE
www.font-romeu.fr

Font-Romeu

➕ High, fairly snow-sure slopes
➕ Popular family resort

➖ Limited in extent, with shortish runs
➖ Weekend crowds

With Font-Romeu you can choose from a delightful old village or a purpose-built station at the foot of the woody, cruisey slopes. Beginners are well catered for.

The old village, complete with 12th century church and contrasting modern National Scientific Centre, is linked to the slopes by a gondola that you ride down as well as up. Alternatively, you can stay at Pyrenees 2000 – a purpose-built development at the foot of the lifts, and a short bus ride away.

The slopes span three partly wooded hills, with a good mix of runs. There are a couple of free beginner lifts and good progression to gentle greens. There is a local lift pass, but the Neiges Catalan pass also covers Les Angles (see below) and seven other resorts in the eastern Pyrenees.

KEY FACTS

Resort	1650m
	5,410ft
Slopes	1650-2375m
	5,410-7,790ft
Lifts	19
Pistes	50km
Snow-guns	363 guns

TOURIST OFFICE
www.lesangles.com

Les Angles

➕ Sheltered, treelined slopes
➕ Good, gentle beginner terrain but ...

➖ English less widely spoken here
➖ Shortish runs that lack challenge

Les Angles is a small but charming stone village, complete with old church. The slopes are limited but relatively snow-sure and family-friendly.

Les Angles offers high but mainly wooded slopes that cover a broad hillside. Most runs are short and intermediate; over half are classified red, but there is a good proportion of gentler terrain. There are nursery

slopes at village level and at 1800m – reached by car or free ski-bus. There is a decent terrain park and 36km of cross-country trails. Font-Romeu is 16km away. Off-slope diversions are few, but dog sledding is possible.

La Rosière

A friendly, family-oriented little resort in a panoramic setting; the link to La Thuile in Italy adds much-needed interest to the skiing

TOP 10 RATINGS

Extent	★★★
Fast lifts	★
Queues	★★★★
Snow	★★★
Expert	★★
Intermediate	★★★
Beginner	★★★★★
Charm	★★★
Convenience	★★★
Scenery	★★★★

RPI · 80

lift pass	£160
ski hire	£100
lessons	£75
food & drink	£130
total	**£465**

NEWS

2010/11: Another 10 snow-guns were installed. The free bus service was improved.

KEY FACTS

Resort	1850m
	6,070ft

Espace San Bernardo (La Rosière and La Thuile)

Slopes	1175-2610m
	3,850-8,560ft
Lifts	38
Pistes	160km
	99 miles
Green	10%
Blue	31%
Red	40%
Black	19%
Snowmaking	24%

- ➕ Pleasant, compact, friendly resort in a sunny setting – good for families
- ➕ Good beginner slopes
- ➕ Fair-sized area of slopes if you include linked La Thuile in Italy
- ➕ Heli-skiing in Italy from the border
- ➕ Fine panoramic views
- ➕ Big dumps of snow when storms sock in from the west, but ...

- ➖ When storms do sock in, both local slopes and the link can be bleak – or closed
- ➖ Sunny slopes are affected by sun as the season progresses
- ➖ Mainly slow old lifts
- ➖ Local pistes rather limited and lacking variety
- ➖ Limited village diversions

La Rosière is very different from its famous neighbours such as Val d'Isère-Tignes and Les Arcs – much smaller, quieter, sunnier; more friendly, too, say reporters. Many reporters are also more impressed than we are by the skiing, which mainly consists of several short runs down a single open slope, served by slow lifts. Happily, you can quite easily reach some of the slopes of La Thuile – more interesting, and served by better lifts.

THE RESORT

La Rosière has been developed in traditional chalet style high up on the road that climbs from Bourg-St-Maurice towards the Petit-St-Bernard pass to Italy. In winter the road ends at a car park below the main lifts in La Rosière. The resort has several identifiable parts, but the key distinction is between the main village and the developing satellite of Les Eucherts, a short bus ride – or a 'pleasant' floodlit forest walk – to the east. This is more or less self-sufficient, but offers less choice of everything than the main village.

Village charm The resort is attractively built in traditional styles; it is quiet, with a few shops and friendly locals; don't expect much lively nightlife. It is centred on the road through to the lift station car park; so although there is no real through-traffic, the centre is far from traffic-free.

Convenience It's a small place, where you may have only a short stroll to a lift, but big enough for many locations to require use of a free shuttle bus. The satellite of Les Eucherts has its own fast chair into the slopes.

Scenery La Rosière's home slopes are south-facing, with great views over the Isère valley to Les Arcs and La Plagne.

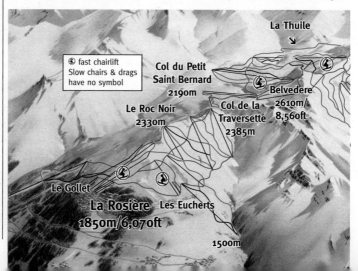

④ fast chairlift
Slow chairs & drags have no symbol

La Thuile ↘

Col du Petit Saint Bernard
2190m

Le Roc Noir
2330m

Col de la Traversette
2385m

Belvedere
2610m/
8,56oft

Le Gollet

La Rosière
1850m/6,07oft

Les Eucherts

1500m

OT LA ROSIERE / ANNE ROYER-
BADERSPACH
The main village is on
the left, partly in the
trees, and Les
Eucherts is beyond
them on the right ↓

THE MOUNTAINS

La Rosière and La Thuile in Italy share
a big area of slopes called Espace San
Bernardo. The link with Italy's slopes is
prone to closure because of high
winds or heavy snow. There are few
treelined runs.

Slopes Two fast chairs, one at the
main village and one at Les Eucherts,
take you into the slopes; then a
parallel series of lifts serve the main
mountainside, at the far end of which
is the Col de la Traversette, departure
point for Italy. West of the village is a
separate sector with red and black
runs descending through woods to the
Ecudets chair – and a blue on down to
the village of Seez (at about 900m)
when snow is good.

Fast lifts Only the two main village
chairs, serving blue runs, are fast; all
the red runs are served by slow lifts.
One or two reporters have noted that
these lift rides can be cold affairs if a
wind is whistling over the pass.

Queues Reporters stress the lack of
queues, even at peak times. If better
weather on the Italian side sends
crowds flocking over the border,
expect some queues on the way back.

Terrain parks There are three
'snowzones' – a terrain park just above
the village centre, a boardercross at
the far end of the slopes, and a
freeride area on skier's right below Roc
Noir. One reader was disappointed to
find the parks closed throughout his
March 2011 visit.

Snow reliability The slopes get a lot of
snow from storms pushing up the
valley, but conditions can be badly
affected by sun or wind.

Experts There are a couple of short,
easy but worthwhile black runs – we
particularly like Ecudets, down the
eponymous chairlift – and lots of safe
off-piste between the pistes and in the
designated freeride area around the
top of the Ecudets chair. There is more
serious, easily accessed off-piste
terrain just outside the lift network.
And there's heli-skiing from just over
the Italian border.

Intermediates The main area is a
broad open mountainside offering
straightforward red pistes, mostly at
the easy end of the spectrum and

UK PACKAGES

A Mountain Chalet, Alpine Answers, BoardnLodge, Chalet Group, Crystal, Erna Low, Esprit, Independent Ski Links, Interactive Resorts, Lagrange, Mountain Heaven, Peak Retreats, PowderBeds, PV-Holidays.com, Ski Amis, Ski Beat, Ski Collection, Ski Expectations, Ski France, Ski Independence, Ski Olympic, Ski Solutions, Skibug, Skitracer, Skiworld, Snow Finders, SnowCrazy

mostly short, with verticals in the range 300m to 450m. The exception is the Marmotte red, dropping over 800m to the chairlift below Les Eucherts. More interesting than anything on the main slope is the lovely wooded Fontaine Froide red, dropping 750m vertical to the Ecudets chair. Keen intermediates will want to make multiple trips to the fast lifts and more varied terrain above the pass, on the Italian side of the border.

Blue-run skiers are effectively confined to the pistes near the village, served by the two fast lifts. Not surprisingly, they get quite busy. The longer blues running across the main slope are just tracks from A to B, so not of much interest. The outing to Italy involves a red run at the start; it is not especially tricky; but be aware that the two draglifts that follow total almost 3km in length.

Beginners There are good nursery slopes and short lifts near the main village (three are free to use) and near Les Eucherts. The blue runs above the village are excellent for progression.

Snowboarding Most of the lifts are chairs, making the place good for novices. And the sunny slopes are

good for gentle freeriding when the snow is soft.

Cross-country There are 7km of trails.

Mountain restaurants There are only two, both self-service. Plan du Repos, in the heart of the slopes, is pleasant enough, with 'pretty good grub'.

Schools and guides We have had consistently good reports of the ESF – 'very good teachers', 'cater very well for English-speaking skiers', say 2011 visitors. Evolution 2 has had mixed reviews in the past; but a 2011 reporter praises her instructor for being 'knowledgeable and patient'. The Elite school offers clinics and private lessons.

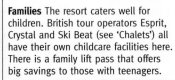

Weekly news updates and resort links at www.wtss.co.uk

Phone numbers
From abroad use the prefix +33 and omit the initial '0' of the phone number

TOURIST OFFICE
www.larosiere.net

Families The resort caters well for children. British tour operators Esprit, Crystal and Ski Beat (see 'Chalets') all have their own childcare facilities here. There is a family lift pass that offers big savings to those with teenagers.

STAYING THERE

Chalets This is now a major chalet resort, with a surprising number of properties. Many are located in Les Eucherts. The biggest operator is family specialist Esprit, with 13 units of all shapes and sizes, plus its usual comprehensive childcare ('staff were brilliant'). Ski Beat has nine purpose-built places, with two shared saunas. Mountain Heaven has a splendid-looking penthouse, with six en-suite rooms and an outdoor hot tub, as well as four other chalets. Ski Olympic has a chalet hotel and four chalets (including two with access to a pool, sauna, steam and hot tub). Skiworld has five smart mid-sized properties. Crystal has a cluster of four chalets in Les Eucherts.

Hotels There are a couple of 2-star hotels in the village, and more lower down the hill. Chalet Matsuzaka (0479 075313) is a Japanese-influenced 10-room 4-star at Les Eucherts.
Apartments Many of the best places are in Les Eucherts. Ski Amis has a wide range of properties with up to four bedrooms. Mountain Heaven has a smart-looking penthouse apartment. The major French self-catering operators have properties here. The CGH residence Cîmes Blanches – smart, with a 'lovely' pool, hot tub, sauna and steam room – is available through Peak Retreats and Lagrange. Pierre & Vacances has the simpler Vanoise. For those who don't take self-catering too literally Montagne Saveurs is an outfit delivering 'fantastic food'.
Eating out Out of the dozen or so restaurants, readers' current favourites are the 'excellent, very welcoming' Genepi, the 'cosy' Ancolie in Les Eucherts and the 'atmospheric' Grange.
Après-ski Confined to a few bars in the village. The Petit Danois is 'lively' and 'always full'. Bar Fusion is popular too, but quieter, say reporters. The Moobar at Les Eucherts is also tipped.
Off the slopes It's improving, but there's not a huge amount to amuse the non-skier – cleared walks, snowshoeing and paragliding, with ten-pin bowling and ice skating at Les Eucherts. There is a 'tiny' cinema. Lunch with skiing friends will have to be in the village; but keen skiers may want to visit La Thuile more than once – and when they do, they won't be tempted to come back for lunch.

Selected chalet in La Rosière

MOUNTAIN HEAVEN *www.mountainheaven.co.uk*　　T **0151 625 1921**

The Penthouse, possibly the best chalet in La Rosiere!
* Sleeps 12 – 14 people in 6 large en-suite bedrooms
* Superb position close to the slopes, bowling alley and ice skating rink
* Outdoor hot tub
* Fantastic food and wine
* Large lounge/dining area with open fireplace
* WIFI and wall mounted LCD TV
* Stunning uninterrupted views
* Personalised service with everything pre-booked for you

↑ THE LOUNGE/DINING AREA

THE PENTHOUSE OFFERS STUNNING VIEWS ↑

Samoëns

Characterful but inconvenient base for the extensive and varied Grand Massif, shared with Flaine, Morillon and Les Carroz

TOP 10 RATINGS

Extent	****
Fast lifts	**
Queues	****
Snow	***
Expert	****
Intermediate	*****
Beginner	**
Charm	****
Convenience	*
Scenery	****

RPI   90

lift pass	£190
ski hire	£105
lessons	£70
food & drink	£150
total	**£515**

PISTE MAP

Samoëns is covered on the Flaine map

OT SAMOËNS

When we've visited, the market has been out on the fringe of the village. The church is shown in the right spot, though ↓

➕ Lovely historic village, with traffic-free centre and weekly market

➕ Lifts into big, varied area shared with Flaine and Les Carroz

➕ Glorious views from top heights

➕ Very close to Geneva airport

➖ Main access lift is way outside the village, and has no return piste

➖ Not the best base for beginners

➖ Limited choice of central bars and restaurants

The impressive Grand Massif area is chiefly associated in Britain with high, purpose-built, apartment-dominated Flaine; but the network (described mainly in the Flaine chapter) can also be accessed from lower, traditional villages. And the cutest of these, if not the most convenient for skiing, is Samoëns.

THE RESORT

Samoëns is an attractive 'Monument Historique' – once a thriving centre for stonemasons, with their work much in evidence.

Village charm The resort has a small traffic-free centre of narrow streets lined by appealing food shops, and a pretty square (sadly not traffic-free) with a stone fountain, an ancient linden tree, a fine church and other medieval buildings. Also nearby is a nominally car-free area of modern development. The place as a whole retains the feel of 'real' rural France and makes a compelling base for families. There is a weekly market for your cheese supplies.

Convenience Slope access is by one of two gondolas, both a drive or 'reliable and frequent' bus ride from the village: an old one across the valley and a newer one nearer to the village. Back to the old gondola, there are only red and black runs that can be tricky or closed – and there are no

runs to the new one. So it's a gondola then a bus at the end of the day. Not a problem, but not convenient.

Scenery The village has a pretty valley setting, with attractively woody ridges and glorious views from the tops.

THE MOUNTAINS

Most of the skiing directly above Samoëns is on open slopes beneath the peak of Tête des Saix.

Slopes The two gondolas from the valley arrive at separate points on the 'hilly plateau' of Samoëns 1600. This mini-resort is also reachable by road. A six-pack installed two seasons ago now whisks you up to Tête des Saix, from which point you can proceed towards Flaine via a narrow, crowded piste followed by a fast chair in the Vernant bowl. Or you can turn right to descend to Morillon or Les Carroz.

Fast lifts Mountain access is now respectably quick, but the area as a whole has many slow lifts still.

Queues We have had reports of annoying waits for the main gondola

KEY FACTS

| Resort | 720-1600m |
| | 2,360-5,250ft |

Grand Massif ski area
(Samoëns and all
linked resorts)

Slopes	700-2480m
	2,300-8,140ft
Lifts	70
Pistes	265km
	165 miles
Green	12%
Blue	45%
Red	32%
Black	11%
Snowmaking	
	218 guns

Massif ski area
(excluding Flaine)

Slopes	700-2120m
	2,300-6,700ft
Lifts	43
Pistes	125km
	78 miles

UK PACKAGES

Alps Accommodation,
AmeriCan Ski,
BoardnLodge, Chalet
Bezière, Chalet Group,
Chez Michelle, Erna
Low, Independent Ski
Links, Lagrange, Peak
Retreats, Powder
White, PowderBeds, Ski
Expectations, Ski
France, Ski
Independence, Zenith

Phone numbers
From abroad use the
prefix +33 and omit
the initial '0' of the
phone number

TOURIST OFFICE

www.samoens.com

at peak periods, but not recently.
Queues at 1600 for access to Tête des
Saix are 'transformed' by the new six-
pack; but the narrow piste towards
Vernant is more crowded than ever.
Terrain parks The main park is in
Flaine.
Snow reliability The slopes above
Samoëns face due north, so above
1600 snow is fairly reliable. There is
snowmaking around 1600, but one
January visitor this year was appalled
by the state of the blue run from Tête
des Saix, which lacked snowmaking
and as a result was 'icy, with lots of
stones'.
Experts The upper pistes on Tête des
Saix are among the most testing in the
Grand Massif, and there is lots of good
off-piste in the region.
Intermediates Samoëns normally
makes a satisfactory base for all but
the most timid intermediates, who
might be better off in Morillon. But
note the comments above on snow
conditions on Tête des Saix. From
there you have a choice of good long
runs in various directions. In good
snow the valley runs to Vercland are
highly enjoyable – the black is little
steeper than the red, and used less.
Beginners Beginners buy a special
pass and go up to 1600, where they
will find gentle, snow-sure slopes –
excellent when not crowded – but no
long green runs to progress to.
Morillon is a better bet. And the
nursery slopes at Sixt are quiet.
Snowboarding Beware draglifts on the
nursery slopes.
Cross-country There are trails on the
flat valley floor around Samoëns, and
more challenging ones up the valley
beyond Sixt and up at Col de Joux
Plane (1700m).
Mountain restaurants Several options
at Samoëns 1600. We enjoyed
excellent service and pork provençal
at the newish Lou Caboëns, a small,

woody table-service place. Mimy's is
tipped for its 'massive burger in a
lovely crusty roll'. The Pré d'Oscar is a
handy spot for a drink at the end of
the day.
Schools and guides We've had good
reports of the ZigZag school ('great
attitude, patience, encouragement').
Families The Loupiots nursery takes
kids from three months to six years
old, and ski lessons are available. The
ZigZag school offers multi-activity
courses.

STAYING THERE

Alps Accommodation is a British-run
Samoëns specialist with over 35
chalets and apartments available.
Chalets Samoëns doesn't seem to
figure in the programmes of major
chalet operators, but we continue to
get glowing reports of owner-run
chalet Bezière ('outstanding',
'enormous bedrooms, food absolutely
excellent').
Hotels There are five 2-star and 3-star
places. We and readers have enjoyed
the 3-star Neige et Roc (0450 344072),
a walk from the centre – 'friendly staff,
big spa area' and 'haute cuisine'. Avoid
the annexe, though.
Apartments Self-catering is mostly in
small-scale developments, and quite a
lot of it in individual chalets. The
Fermes de Samoëns is a smart
Lagrange Prestige residence (with
pool). Similarly attractive options
available through Peak Retreats are
the CGH residence Reine des Près and
the Ferme de Fontany.
Eating out The Table de Fifine is a
short drive from the centre, but a fine
spot for a proper dinner – beautiful
wooden interior and 'good quality,
imaginative menu'. The formerly
'excellent' Muscade et Basilic has
changed hands and is now La
Mezzanine. A 2011 reporter rates the
Bois de Lune 'excellent'. The Louisiane
has 'great' pizza.
Après-ski Nightlife is quiet and
reporters complain there is little choice
of bars; Irish pub Covey's ('doubled in
size and still the liveliest') and Savoie
are the reader favourites.
Off the slopes Samoëns offers quite a
range of activities. Snowmobiling up at
Samoëns 1600 is wilder than is usual
in the Alps. There's dog sledding and a
reader recommends the snowshoeing.
There is an outdoor, covered ice rink,
hosting regular hockey matches, and a
sports and cultural centre.

SNOWPIX.COM / CHRIS GILL

Serre-Chevalier

Odd mixture of ancient and modern villages sit beneath an extensive and varied mountain with lots of woodland runs

RATINGS

The mountains

Extent	★★★★
Fast lifts	★★
Queues	★★★
Terrain p'ks	★★★
Snow	★★★
Expert	★★★
Intermediate	★★★★
Beginner	★★★★
Boarder	★★★★
X-country	★★★
Restaurants	★★★★
Schools	★★★★
Families	★★★

The resort

Charm	★★★
Convenience	★★★
Scenery	★★★
Eating out	★★★★
Après-ski	★★
Off-slope	★★★

RPI	90
lift pass	£190
ski hire	£105
lessons	£80
food & drink	£135
total	**£510**

NEWS

2011/12: At Le Monêtier base area, the old restaurant has been demolished and a new one is being built. And there are plans for more smartening up of the base area in the next two years. There are also plans for a new table-service restaurant beside the Chapka hut above Le Monêtier.

2010/11: A new six-pack, Vallons, has improved access from Villeneuve to Le Monêtier. More snowmaking was installed.

In Briançon, the Aigle-Bleu apartments opened near the gondola.

+ Big, varied mountain

+ Lots of good woodland runs

+ One of the few big French areas based on old villages with character

+ Good-value and atmospheric old hotels, restaurants and chalets

+ Very friendly and welcoming locals

– Busy road runs along the valley and right through Le Monêtier

– A lot of indiscriminate new building took place in the 1960s and 70s

– Still too many drags and slow chairlifts

– Limited nightlife

This is one of our favourite places. It is one of the few French resorts offering the ambience you might look for in a summer holiday – a sort of Provence in the snow, with lots of small family-run hotels and restaurants in old stone buildings. And the slopes are set apart from the French norm by the quantity of woodland runs – though there are high, open bowls, as well. You really get a sense of travelling around too, because the slopes are split into distinctly different segments. And there are some good (and affordable) mountain restaurants. What's more the snow is reliably good too. And, unlike in many French resorts, the locals are noticeably friendly and welcoming. But the list of minus points above is not inconsiderable. And if you are looking for luxury and sophistication, there are many resorts that will suit you better.

THE RESORT

Serre-Chevalier is made up of a string of 13 villages set on a valley floor with a busy main road.

The valley runs roughly north-west to south-east, below the north-east-facing slopes of the mountain range that gives the resort its name. From the north-west – coming over the Col du Lautaret from Grenoble – the three main villages are spread over a distance of 8km – Le Monêtier (or Serre-Che 1500), Villeneuve (1400) and Chantemerle (1350). Finally, at the extreme south-eastern end of the valley, is Briançon (1200) – not a village but a town (the highest in France). As well as the main villages there are nine smaller villages, some of which give their names to the communes: Villeneuve is in the commune of La Salle les Alpes, for example. Confusing.

The resort is not at all fashionable and there are no 4- or 5-star hotels. But there are more hotels here in the modestly priced Logis de France 'club' than in any other ski resort. This is a family resort, and it gets especially busy in the February/March French school holidays.

Ski-buses are covered on all lift passes. These circulate around and between the villages, taking in the lift bases along the valley. The local navettes stop soon after the lifts close, but the valley buses now run free night services till 11.30pm.

A six-day area pass (or rather your receipt for that pass) covers a day in each of Les Deux-Alpes, Alpe-d'Huez, Puy-St-Vincent, Montgenèvre/the Milky Way. All of these outings are possible by bus, but are easier by car. The road from Grenoble and Lyon passes over the Col du Lautaret, which may require chains and is very occasionally closed.

347

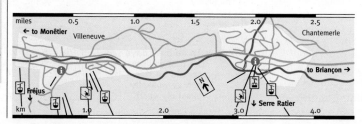

VILLAGE CHARM ★★★☆☆
Some quaint old parts

Each of the parts of Serre-Chevalier is based on a simple old village, with narrow cobbled streets lined by small shops, cosy bars, hotels and traditional restaurants that give each village a very French feel. Around these older parts there is a lot more modern development ranging in style from brash to brutal. And it is not a smart resort in any sense; even the older parts are roughly rustic rather than chocolate-box pretty. (A ban on corrugated iron roofs would help.) But when blanketed by snow the older villages and hamlets do have an unpretentious charm, and we find the place as a whole easy to like.

Le Monêtier is the smallest, quietest and most unspoiled of the main villages, with new building which is mostly in sympathetic style. But it is the most seriously affected by traffic – it is bisected by the road to Grenoble, which skirts the other villages; pedestrians stroll about, hoping the cars will avoid them.

Because the resort is so spread out, the impact of cars and buses is difficult to escape, even if you're able to manage without them yourself. But reporters seem happy to put up with the road and its traffic.

Briançon's 17th-century fortified upper quarter is a delight, with its traditional shops, auberges, pâtisseries and restaurants; it is now a UNESCO World Heritage Site. By contrast, the wide selection of modern facilities around the town's lift station, including good-value lodging and a casino, has little character.

Every year reporters stress how

- ⓖ gondola
- 🚠 cable car
- ④ fast chairlift
- Slow chairs & drags have no symbol

L'Eychauda
2660m/8,730ft

Serre-Chevalier
2490m/8,170ft

Prorel
2565m/8,410ft

Grand Serre

Prorel

Grand Alpe

Foret

Combes

BRIANCON

CHANTEMERLE

Bivouac de la Casse

L'Aravet
2000m

Casse de Boeuf

Pra Long
1625m

Great views over Briançon on the lovely long red down the gondola

Chalet Hotel

Serre Ratier
1905m

Grand Alpe I & II

Tronçon

Aravet

Prorel

Briançon
1200m/3,940ft

Even on busy days the fast cruises served by this chair are usually blissfully quiet

Chantemerle
1350m/4,430ft

KEY FACTS		
Resort	1200-1500m	
	3,940-4,920ft	
Slopes	1200-2735m	
	3,940-8,970ft	
Lifts		63
Pistes		250km
		155 miles
Green		22%
Blue		28%
Red		37%
Black		13%
Snowmaking		
		75%

friendly and welcoming the locals are – hardly the norm in France. We were struck by this on our recent visit too.

CONVENIENCE ★★★☆☆
Good access but expect a walk

All of the main villages have lift access, either by gondola, cable car or fast chairs, to different parts of the ski area. Briançon has a gondola from the bottom of town; your hotel could be next to it, or miles from it. Villeneuve, too, has lodgings close to its multiple access lifts, but the old village is across the valley from the lifts. The nearby hamlet of Le Bez makes a peaceful and more convenient alternative – with its own gondola. In Chantemerle the old sector is not far distant from the lifts. But a lot of accommodation is further away across the main road and can be quite a long walk from the lifts. Le Monêtier has one main access lift, reached from the village by bus or a 10-minute walk (downhill in the morning, uphill at the end of the day and tricky when ice is around, though you can leave your skis and boots at the lift base).

SCENERY ★★★☆☆
Six good viewpoints

The Serre-Chevalier range is not notably dramatic seen from the valley, though there are great views from Briançon's old town. And from each of the area's six main summits there are fine views of the rugged 4000m-high Ecrins massif.

THE MOUNTAINS

Trees cover almost two-thirds of the mountain, providing some of France's best bad-weather terrain (we once had a great day here when all the upper lifts were closed by high winds).

Reporters speak favourably of the improved piste signposting, but several 2011 visitors still find the Villeneuve area confusing. Piste classification is not reliable, and tends to exaggerate difficulty. Our 2011 reporters are almost unanimous in viewing most blacks as over-rated, and the same can be said of many reds.

The piste map shows several 'brut de neige' areas – basically, runs that are left ungroomed.

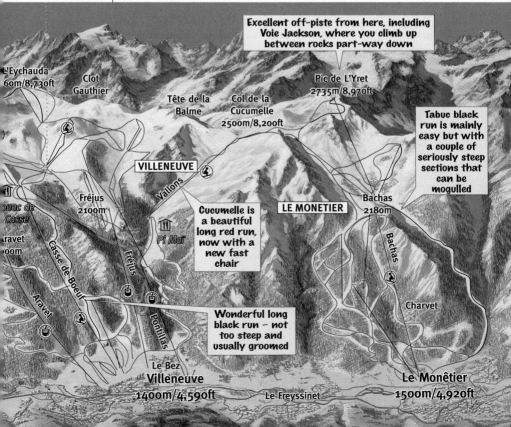

LIFT PASSES

Grand Serre-Che

Prices in €

Age	1-day	6-day
under 12	34	160
12 to 64	42	200
over 65	33	180

Free under 6, over 75
Beginner limited pass in each area: eg Villeneuve €16

Notes
Covers all lifts in Briançon, Chantemerle, Villeneuve and Le Monêtier; 6 days or more passes give one day in each of Les Deux-Alpes, Alpe-d'Huez, Puy-St-Vincent and Voie Lactée (Milky Way); reductions for families

Alternative passes
Individual areas of Serre-Chevalier

SNOWPIX.COM / CHRIS GILL

Although the lifts out of the valley are powerful, there are still quite a lot of slow old lifts higher up the slopes ↓

EXTENT OF THE SLOPES ★★★★
Interestingly varied and pretty
Serre-Chevalier's 250km of pistes are spread across four main sectors above the four main villages and you get a real feeling of travel as you move from one to another. The sector above **Villeneuve** is the most extensive, reaching back a good way into the mountains and spreading over four or five identifiable bowls. The main mid-station is Fréjus. This sector is linked at altitude and mid-mountain to the slightly smaller **Chantemerle** sector. The onward link from Chantemerle to **Briançon** is over a high, exposed col via a six-pack. In the opposite direction, the link between Villeneuve and **Le Monêtier** has been greatly improved by the new Vallons six-pack built up the Cucumelle valley for 2010/11. Skiing from Le Monêtier to Villeneuve involves a red run, so timid intermediates may prefer to use the bus service.

FAST LIFTS ★★
Improvements, but slowly
A range of big lifts gets you out of the valley and progress has been made in upgrading some of the higher lifts. But there are still many old, slow lifts at altitude that hinder progress.

QUEUES ★★★
Still some bottlenecks
There are few problems getting out of the villages now, but there can be queues further up. Queues on the way to Le Monêtier have been relieved by the new Vallons six-pack for 2010/11 (see 'News'). In the opposite direction, the slow Yret chair from Bachas above Le Monêtier provokes complaints, as does the Cibouit chair from Bachas. Other bottlenecks include the Fréjus chair above the Pontillas gondola from Villeneuve, the Crêtes draglift it links with and the Côte Chevalier chair which links the area above Villeneuve to Chantemerle.

When the resort gets busy in the French school holidays, head for (slow) Aiguillette chair at Chantemerle (see 'For intermediates'). And consider riding the gondolas down to avoid busy home runs.

TERRAIN PARKS ★★★
Fully featured
The main parks are strategically positioned to be easily reached from both Chantemerle and Villeneuve. Legendary French ripper Guillaume Chastagnol and the Serre Che Brigade have been building and improving the freestyle infrastructure here for several years. The Altitude snowpark is situated under the Forêt chair (and has a dedicated draglift). It incorporates about 30 different features and the obligatory chill-out and BBQ area. The park is clearly marked out in three zones for all levels, including 13 tables, wall ride, rails, kickers and log-jibs. A major focus has been placed on the beginner area, which makes it a great learning park. A boardercross accessible by the Grande Serre or Combes lifts is 'good, fast and flowing' says a reporter. An innovative feature is Mélèzone, beside the Champcella drag lift. Featuring various fun jibs built from larch wood in a natural, wooded setting, it also has a picnic area and educational exhibit on the local conifer varieties. There's also a small, fun boardercross near the top of the Combes and Grand Serre chairs.

SNOW RELIABILITY ★★★
Good – especially upper slopes
Most slopes face north or north-east and so hold the snow well, especially high up (there are lots of lifts starting at altitudes above 2000m). The weather pattern is different from that

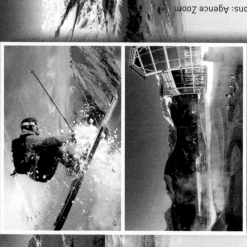

of the northern Alps and even that of Les Deux-Alpes or Alpe-d'Huez, only a few miles to the west. Serre-Che can get good snow when there is a shortage elsewhere, and vice versa as was proved in 2011 when Serre-Che had good snow while other resorts were struggling. Some upper lifts may be prone to closure by high winds.

Snowmaking was increased last year and now covers 75% of the pistes, including long runs down to each village. Piste grooming is generally excellent.

FOR EXPERTS ★★★★★
Deep, not notably steep

There is plenty to amuse experts – except those wanting extreme steeps.

The broad black runs down to Villeneuve (Casse du Boeuf – our favourite) and Chantemerle (Luc Alphand) are only just black in steepness. They are regularly groomed, and great fun for a fast blast, with their gradient sustained over an impressive vertical of around 800m. But one or the other may be closed for days on end for racing or training. The rather neglected Tabuc run, sweeping around the mountain away from the lifts to Le Monêtier, has a couple of genuinely steep pitches (which may be heavily mogulled) but is mainly a cruise. For other steepish runs, look higher up the mountain to slopes served by the two top lifts above Le Monêtier and the three above Villeneuve. The runs beside these lifts – on- and off-piste – form a great playground in good snow.

There are huge amounts of off-piste terrain throughout the area – both high-up and in the trees above Villeneuve and Chantemerle. We've enjoyed the La Voie Jackson run accessed from the Yret chair above Le Monêtier, which includes a short climb between rocks to a deserted open bowl. The Cucumelle valley at the western side of the Villeneuve sector offers plenty of gentle off-piste which is now much easier to exploit with the new chairlift in place.

There are plenty of more serious off-piste expeditions, including: Tête de Grand Pré to Villeneuve or Le Monêtier and Couloir de Roche Corneille to Le Monêtier (both a climb

from Cucumelle); off the back of L'Eychauda to Puy-St-André (isolated, beautiful, taxi ride home); l'Yret to Le Monêtier via Vallons de la Montagnolle; Tabuc also to Le Monêtier (steep at the start in a big bowl, very beautiful). The experts' Mecca of La Grave is nearby.

FOR INTERMEDIATES ★★★★★
Ski wherever you like

Serre-Chevalier's slopes ideally suit intermediates, who can buzz around without worrying about nasty surprises on the way. On the trail map red runs far outnumber blues – but most reds are at the easy end of the scale and the grooming is usually good, so even nervous intermediates shouldn't have problems with them. The broad, open bowls above Grande Alpe and Fréjus offer lots of options. And the runs on skier's right on the lower slopes above Le Monêtier are gentle, quiet and wind prettily through the woods.

There's plenty for more adventurous intermediates, though. Cucumelle on the edge of the Villeneuve sector is a beautiful long red that is now served by a new chairlift. The red runs off the little-used slow Aiguillette chair in the Chantemerle sector are worth seeking out – quiet, enjoyable fast cruises. Other favourites include Aya and Clos Galliard at Le Monêtier, and the wonderful long run from the top to the bottom of the gondola at Briançon (with great views of the town).

If the reds are starting to seem a bit tame, there is plenty more to progress to. Unless ice towards the bottom is a problem, the usually well-groomed blacks on the lower mountain should be on the agenda; try them early in the day when they are uncrowded and freshly groomed.

FOR BEGINNERS ★★★★★
All four areas OK

All four sectors have nursery areas and lift passes covering a handful of lifts in each. Chantemerle's area is small, so you generally go up to Serre Ratier or Grand Alpe – both rated as good by a beginner reporter. There are some easy high runs to progress to; Villeneuve has excellent green runs above Fréjus. But below here, the green paths to Chantemerle and Villeneuve down from mid-mountain are narrow, and not enjoyable when the runs become hard and others are speeding past.

Le Monêtier has nursery slopes at

resort level, which beginners have recommended for 'better snow and fewer people' than in the other villages. There are no long green runs here, but genuine blue runs on both lower and upper mountain.

FOR BOARDERS ★★★★
Plenty of scope for experts
The term 'natural playground' could have quite easily been coined in Serre-Chevalier. The slopes are littered with natural obstacles that seem made for confident snowboarders. Try the Cucumelle slope and the areas around the Rocher Blanc lift at Prorel for such terrain. For less expert boarders, the many draglifts can be a problem, as can the flat areas. There's a good terrain park for all abilities and Generation Snow in Chantemerle is a school that offers everything from beginners' lessons to freestyle courses.

FOR CROSS-COUNTRY ★★★
Excellent if the snow is good
There are 35km of tracks along the valley floor, mainly following the gurgling river between Le Monêtier and Villeneuve and going on up towards the Col du Lautaret.

MOUNTAIN RESTAURANTS ★★★★
Some good places
Mountain restaurants are quite well distributed (and, usefully, marked clearly on the piste map).
Editors' choice At the top of the cable car and chair from Chantemerle, Chalet Hotel Serre Ratier (0492 205288) has a delightful large terrace and pretty indoor dining room, good service and delicious food. Just above the Casse du Boeuf quad from Villeneuve, the Bivouac de la Casse (0492 248772) is an attractive chalet with both self- and table-service (inside and out). We were mightily impressed by both the food and service, and recent reporters endorse our view ('great plat du jour'). Shame about the plastic chairs on the terrace though. Pi Maï (0492 248363) in the hamlet of Fréjus is cosy on a bad day and charming on a sunny day, and it offers excellent food such as steaks and tartiflette. But both Bivouac de la Casse and Pi Maï are relatively expensive.
Worth knowing about The 'charming' Echaillon, just below the Bivouac, is a lofty chalet with open fire and a table-service section doing 'excellent confit de canard'. The Bercail, near the top

SCHOOLS

ESF In all centres
t 0492 241741

Génération Snow
(Chantemerle)
t 0492 242151

Evasion (Chantemerle)
t 0492 240241

Buissonnière
(Villeneuve)
t 0492 247866

New Generation
t 0479 010318
0844 484 3663 (UK)
www.newgen.com

Insight
t 0679 068683

Experience
(Chantemerle)
t 0492 435871

Ski Connections
(Villeneuve)
t 0492 462832

Internationale
(Le Monêtier)
t 0683 670642

Classes (ESF prices)
6 half days from €144

Private lessons
From €46 for 1hr

of the Aravet lift, is an unusual mixture – table-service except that you go and order your food and pay self-service style, then it's cooked fresh and delivered to your table. The Aravet in the same area does 'deliciously thin and crispy pizzas – very, very good'. Above Chantemerle, we loved the small table-service Troll – great good-value food and very jolly service. The Grand Alpe self-service is spacious, and a bit cheaper than most places.

In the Briançon sector, the 'attractive' Pra Long chalet at the gondola mid-station has good views and food in both table- and self-service sections. The little Chalet de Serre Blanc, just down from the top of Prorel, has superb views but gets mixed reports.

Above Le Monêtier the tiny Peyra Juana on a blue run near the bottom does 'superb food' and now has an enlarged terrace; a reporter insists that you should visit 'if only to hear a marmot wolf-whistle as you enter the toilet'. The self-service Chapka (formerly Bachas) at mid-mountain does 'simple, tasty food' and has a 'welcoming central fire'. Both get packed on bad-weather days.

SCHOOLS AND GUIDES ★★★★
Nearly all good

For years we have been recommending British instructor Gavin Crosby, operating as EurekaSki. He now runs a branch of another British outfit that is an established reader favourite in other resorts, New Generation. Gavin gets good reports time after time: 'fantastic', 'consistently good', 'quickly identified what I needed to work on'. Classes with a maximum size of six (for adults and children) range from beginner to off-piste adventure. We've skied with Gavin a couple of times, and have been greatly impressed. Book well in advance to avoid disappointment. Meanwhile, Gavin's wife Mel offers a kind of concierge service for visitors under the EurekaSki name – see 'Staying there'.

Another British-run school, Ski Connections, also receives positive reports: 'Had the perfect combination of fun, challenge and learning, a great leap forward.' A 2011 reporter enthuses: 'Their all-inclusive bundle of ski hire, lift pass and lessons was very good value for beginners.'

We have received a number of reports on the Ecole de Ski

↑ As well as easy blue runs (don't worry: they are not all this narrow), there's good off-piste to be explored with a guide
SNOWPIX.COM / CHRIS GILL

GUIDES

Montagne Aventure (Chantemerle)
t 0492 247440
Bureau des Guides
t 0492 247590
Montagne à la carte (Villeneuve)
t 0492 247320
Montagne et Ski (Le Monêtier)
t 0492 244681

CHILDCARE

Les Schtroumpfs
t 0492 247095
Ages 6mnth upwards;
9am-5pm
Micro-crèche
t 0492 490086
From 3mnth
Les Poussins
t 0492 240343
Ages 8mnth upwards;
9am-5pm
Les Eterlous
t 0492 244266
Ages 9mnth to 6yr;
9am-5pm

Ski school
Snow gardens for ages 3 to 5; from age 5 children can join ski school classes (ESF 6 half-days €144)

Buissonnière over the years – most of them full of praise ('I learnt 10 times more because of the personal service,' says a reporter). Two absolute beginners in one visitor's group were 'satisfied' with their snowboard lessons with Generation Snow.

A 2011 reporter enjoyed a private lesson with Brit Darren Turner of Insight: 'He was able to cope with a range of abilities and help us all.'

The ESF is improving. A 2011 visitor says, 'unrecognisable from the ESF of yore, English speaking instructors always available', while another found they'd take groups out with 'as few as two students'. And a 2010 reporter says three groups of kids 'had a great time' in their classes. Local chalet-operator Hannibals has reported happy clients with the Chantemerle school. We have positive feedback on the Internationale school: 'My six- and 14-year-old nephews made a huge amount of progress, and my parents (both beginners, aged 68 and 70) were reasonably confident by the end of the week.'

FOR FAMILIES ★★★☆☆
Facilities at each village

Serre Chevalier is popular with French families and there are good family-friendly events and activities. For childcare, Les Schtroumpfs in Villeneuve was 'brilliant, and the baby loved it'. There is a micro-crèche (Les P'tits Loup) in Villeneuve too, taking children from three months to six years. EurekaSki can arrange private nannies and babysitting.

STAYING THERE

There is a wide choice of lodging but, as we have noted elsewhere, very little of it has any claim to luxury. Resort-based EurekaSki (www.eurekaski.com) can simplify life by arranging accommodation, passes, equipment rental, childcare, transfers etc.
Chalets Several operators offer catered chalets or chalet-hotels. Hannibals has two chalets including Marmottes, a well-renovated old farmhouse in old Chantemerle, five minutes from the lifts, with rooms all en suite. In Villeneuve, Zenith has two chalets, including the ski-in/ski-out Ridon and Crystal has three. In Le Monêtier, Ski Miquel has a chalet and a chalet-hotel.
Hotels One of the features of this string of little villages is the range of attractive family-run hotels – many of them members of the generally reliable Logis de France consortium.
LE MONÊTIER
★★★Auberge de Choucas (0492 244273) Smart but small wood-clad rooms; serious restaurant. We have enjoyed a stay there.
★★Europe (0492 244003) Simple well-run Logis in heart of old village, with pleasant bar and good food.
★★Alliey (0492 244002) 'Excellent rooms with an indoor/outdoor pool and spa.' Good restaurant.
VILLENEUVE
★★★Christiania (0492 247633) Civilised, family-run hotel on main road, crammed with ornaments.
★★Vieille Ferme (0492 247644) Stylish conversion on the edge of the village.

GETTING THERE

Air Turin 120km/ 75 miles (1hr45); Grenoble 150km/ 95 miles (2hr45); Lyon 200km/125 miles (3hr15)

Rail Briançon (6km/ 4 miles); regular buses from station

UK PACKAGES

Action Outdoors, Alpine Answers, Alpsholiday, AmeriCan Ski, Chalet Group, Club Med, Crystal, Erna Low, First Choice, Hannibals, Independent Ski Links, Interactive Resorts, Lagrange, Neilson, Peak Retreats, PowderBeds, PV-Holidays.com, Rocketski, Ski Expectations, Ski France, Ski-in.co.uk, Ski Independence, Ski Miquel, Ski Solutions, Skitopia, Skitracer, Snow Finders, Thomson, Zenith **Briançon** BoardnLodge

ACTIVITIES

Indoor Swimming pools, sauna, fitness centres, thermal baths, museums, cinemas, libraries

Outdoor Ice rinks, paragliding, cleared paths, snowshoeing, skijoring, ice driving, ice climbing, snowkites, horse-drawn carriage rides

Phone numbers From abroad use the prefix +33 and omit the initial '0' of the phone number

TOURIST OFFICE

www.serre-chevalier. com

*Chatelas (0492 247474) Prettily decorated simple chalet by river in old part of town.

CHANTEMERLE

**Boule de Neige (0492 240016) In the old centre. Good past reports.

*Ricelle (0492 240019) Charming, but across the valley from the slopes in Villard-Laté. Good food.

Maison du Bez (0492 248696) Ski-in/ ski-out, traditional, 'quirky, with cosy lounge'. Sauna.

Apartments There is an increasing supply of high-quality residences. In the Lagrange Prestige range is Le Hameau du Rocher Blanc, by the slopes in Chantemerle (pool, gym, sauna, steam). This and L'Adret in Chantemerle (formerly a Best Western Premier hotel, 300m from the lifts, with spacious apartments and a small indoor-outdoor pool) is also bookable through Peak Retreats and Erna Low. Pierre & Vacances has two properties, both approved by recent reporters. In Le Monêtier the Arts et Vie is modern, right on the slopes and good value. The hotel Alliey has apartments too.

At altitude Pi Maï (0492 248363) above Villeneuve and the Chalet Hotel Serre Ratier (0688 017704) above Chantemerle have rooms (see also 'Mountain restaurants').

EATING OUT ★★★★☆
Unpretentious and traditional

In Le Monêtier, there are several good hotel-based options. At the upper end, the Maison Alliey (hotel Alliey) has a good reputation, and we've had an excellent dinner at the Auberge du Choucas. The Europe has reliable cooking at more modest prices. Reporter tips include the Brasera for a 'good' pizzeria; the Kawa and the Belotte – 'good staff, good value'.

In Villeneuve, two 2011 reporters recommend the 'atmospheric' Refuge where the Alps Bell ('cooking meat on a hot cast-iron bell') is popular. A 2010 visitor's favourite was the Petit Pont, with 'steaks to die for'. The Frog is Scottish-run, and 'better than its name suggests'. Other reader tips include the 'good-value' Marotte, a tiny stone building with classic French cuisine, the 'excellent' Manouille doing mountain dishes and more ambitious stuff and the Bidule (seafood/fish) over in Le Bez.

In Chantemerle, we've had delicious dinners at the unpretentious Loup Blanc. Reporters approve, and also

like the 'charming' Petit Chalet, 34 (fondue), Cabassa (pizza), Batchi, and the 'cool' Triptyque (traditional French dishes and 'fabulous buffalo burgers').

In Briançon, the Péché Gourmand takes top slot; the location in the new part of town is ordinary, but the menu prices are accordingly modest. In the historic old town, tips are Lou Grand Caire (mountain specialities) and Pied de la Gargouille (open-fire grills).

APRES-SKI ★★☆☆☆
Quiet streets and few bars

Nightlife seems to revolve around bars, scattered through the various villages, and some reporters complain that the resort is too quiet.

In Le Monêtier the British-run Bar de l'Alpen has live music, sports TV, free nibbles and welcoming staff. In Villeneuve, head for the Grotte at the foot of the slopes (live music, happy hour and 'good bar food' – later on it 'doubles up as a nightclub'). Loco Loco in the old village is 'a funky little bar' that gets lively too. The Frog is popular with Brits, while the Cocoon has 'a good local atmosphere'. In Chantemerle the newish Station at the foot of the pistes is popular with Brits – Sky Sports and 'entertainment every evening; pub food is good'; the 'smart' Piano Bar on the main road gets a mention. In Briançon, there's a lively tea-time scene (assisted by a happy hour) at the bar next to the gondola; the Eden has been mentioned, and Spirit and Due are in the old town.

OFF THE SLOPES ★★★☆☆
Try the hot baths

The old town of Briançon is well worth a visit. There is a leisure complex with pools, sauna, hot tub and steam room. Briançon also has an ice hockey team – their games make 'a good night out'. In Le Monêtier there's a large, thermal spa complex, Les Grands Bains ('superb tonic for tired limbs'), with indoor and outdoor pools, saunas, steam rooms, a 'chill-out' music grotto and a waterfall (some areas only for the over-18s). The hotel Alliey has a pool and spa. There is a public swimming pool and health spa near the hotel Sporting in Villeneuve. Each of the villages has a cinema and an ice rink, and there is good walking on 'well-prepared trails'. You can also learn to drive a piste grooming machine, hot air ballooning is available.

OT STE-FOY / MARK JUNAK

Ste-Foy-Tarentaise

Tasteful, modern mini-resort appealing to families and experts – and to motorists as a base for expeditions to nearby mega-resorts

TOP 10 RATINGS

Extent	★
Fast lifts	★★
Queues	★★★★★
Snow	★★★
Expert	★★★★
Intermediate	★★★
Beginner	★★
Charm	★★★
Convenience	★★★
Scenery	★★★

RPI	75
lift pass	£100
ski hire	£105
lessons	£90
food & drink	£135
total	£430

NEWS

2011/12: The smart new Etoile des Cîmes apartments will open.

2010/11: There were 10 new snow-guns.

KEY FACTS

Resort	1550m
	5,090ft
Slopes	1550-2620m
	5,090-8,600ft
Lifts	7
Pistes	32km
	20 miles
Green	6%
Blue	24%
Red	47%
Black	23%
Snowmaking	10 guns

+ Safe untracked powder within the lift system, and epic runs outside it
+ Good base for visits to Val d'Isère/ Tignes and Les Arcs
+ Quiet, even in peak periods, but ...

– Too quiet for some visitors: very little après-ski and few restaurants
– Very limited piste network
– Mainly slow chairlifts with no covers; only one fast quad

Ste-Foy is a small, attractive, unpretentious resort built in the last few years, at the foot of what started life as a cult off-piste mountain. It remains excellent for experts but now attracts many others, including families. Keen piste-bashers will want to travel to big resorts nearby – easily done by car.

THE RESORT

Ste-Foy itself is a village straddling the busy road up from Bourg-St-Maurice to Val d'Isère. Its slopes start at Ste-Foy-Station (aka Bonconseil), set 4km off the main road. With a car you can visit some excellent restaurants close by and explore nearby resorts – Val d'Isère, Tignes, Les Arcs, La Plagne and La Rosière. With a Ste-Foy pass you can buy day passes for these resorts at about half price.

Village charm Ste-Foy-Station is a complete resort in miniature, with a limited choice of bars and restaurants, a small supermarket and a newsagent; and these are surrounded by a cluster of chalets and chalet-style apartment blocks, all in the traditional Savoyard style of wood and stone but without a real central focus. Lots of properties have been bought by the Brits and the Dutch: 'the atmosphere is very British', says a 2011 reporter.

Convenience No accommodation is far from the lifts or nursery slope.

Scenery The Tarentaise mountains give a dramatic backdrop to Ste-Foy's pleasant setting among the trees.

THE MOUNTAIN

There is an attractive mix of wooded slopes above the village and open slopes higher up.

Slopes The slow quad from the village takes you up to a tiny mid-mountain station with two tiny restaurants at Plan Bois. A second goes on to the treeline, and a third to Col de l'Aiguille accesses slopes of almost 600m vertical above the treeline. The two black runs from this chair form the basis of two unexplained special off-piste zones; we're told they are avalanche controlled and that the Crystal Dark/Off Tracks one is only open when the snow conditions and weather are right. Slightly further

OT STE-FOY / A ROYER

There's a great fenced-off beginner area with moving carpets that are free to use right at the base ↓

357

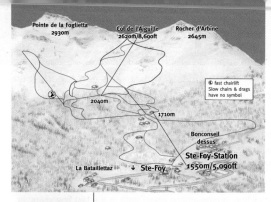

Pointe de la Foglietta 2930m
Col de l'Aiguille 2620m/8,600ft
Rocher d'Arbine 2645m

fast chairlift
Slow chairs & drags have no symbol

2040m

1710m

Bonconseil dessus

2040m

Ste-Foy-Station 1550m/5,090ft

La Bataillettaz ↓ Ste-Foy

peak retreats
the french alps specialist

Quality
self-catering
chalets &
apartments and
hand picked
hotels

0844 576 0173

peakretreats.co.uk
ABTA W5537

UK PACKAGES

Alpine Answers, Alpine
Elements, Alpine
Weekends, AmeriCan
Ski, Chalet Group,
Chalet One, Erna Low,
Independent Ski Links,
Inspired to Ski,
Lagrange, Mountain
Tracks, Oxford Ski Co,
Peak Retreats,
PowderBeds, Première
Neige, Richmond
Holidays, Ski
Collection, Ski France,
Ski Independence, Ski
Weekend, SnowCrazy

Phone numbers
From abroad use the
prefix +33 and omit
the initial '0' of the
phone number

TOURIST OFFICE

www.saintefoy.net

down the hill is a less steep zone,
Shaper's Paradise. The two lower
chairs serve a few pleasant runs
through trees and back to the base
station. A six-pack serves a blue run to
the east of the main area.
Fast lifts Just one fast chair.
Queues Despite all the new building
and slow lifts, reporters hardly ever
find queues at Ste-Foy ('not even New
Year week', says a 2011 reporter).
Terrain parks In Shaper's Paradise you
are encouraged to build features.
Snow reliability The slopes face
roughly north-west. Snow reliability
can suffer on the sunnier bits,
especially as there is snowmaking only
on the run down to the resort.
Experts Experts can have great fun on
and between Ste-Foy's black and red
runs, exploring lots of easily accessible
'tremendous' off-piste and trees,
including the special zones mentioned
above. The lack of crowds means you
can still make fresh tracks days after a
storm. There's more serious off-piste
on offer too, for which you need a
guide. There are wonderful runs from
the top of the lifts down through
deserted old villages, either to the
road up to Val d'Isère or back to the
base, and a splendid route down to
the tiny village of Le Crot. The ESF
runs group off-piste trips, with
transport back to base from the village
of Le Miroir, where the route ends.
There's also a Bureau des Guides,
which can arrange heli-skiing in Italy,
including a route which also brings
you back to Le Miroir.
Intermediates The piste skiing is
limited in extent, but you can enjoy
900m vertical of uncrowded reds and
blues on the upper slopes. The red
from the Col de l'Aiguille is a superb
test for confident intermediates, who
would also be up to the off-piste
routes, especially the Monal route
back to base.

Beginners There are nursery slopes
with free moving carpets in the village.
You can progress to a long green run
off the first chair, then blues higher up
– but they are not the easiest.
Snowboarding Great freeriding terrain,
with lots of trees and powder between
the pistes to play in, plus a dedicated
freestyle area for building kickers.
Cross-country No prepared trails.
Mountain restaurants There are two
rustic restaurants at Plan Bois. Tiny
Les Brevettes is cosy but cramped –
'great if you can get in' – while Chez
Léon is much more spacious. But
many people head back to the base,
where the Maison à Colonnes gets
good reports.
Schools and guides We lack recent
reports. K Spirit is an alternative to
the ESF. Off-piste guides are plentiful.
Families Les P'tits Trappeurs take
children from age three to 11. UK tour
operator Première Neige also runs a
nursery, the Cub Club ('nannies were
lovely; our kids didn't want to leave').

STAYING THERE

Hotels Recommended places: Auberge
sur la Montagne (0479 069583), near
the bottom of the access road to Ste-
Foy station; tiny, rustic Ferme du
Baptieu (0479 069752) just above Ste-
Foy village; the smartly refurbished
Monal (0479 069007) in the village.
Chalets and apartments Première
Neige has a handful of catered chalets
and lots of apartments. Peak Retreats
has apartments in the smart new
Etoile des Cîmes and the Fermes de
Ste-Foy (both with pool, hot tub,
sauna, steam, fitness).
Eating out In Ste-Foy-Station the
Bergerie does excellent food and
Maison à Colonnes is 'simple and
good'; 'one of the best pierrades I can
remember', says a 2011 visitor. In the
village of Le Miroir, Chez Merie is
excellent (for lunch as well as dinner).
In Ste-Foy village, La Grange is 'the
best restaurant this Francophile has
ever eaten in', says a regular reporter.
Après-ski Pretty quiet. Reporters
enjoyed the Iceberg piano bar. The
Pitchouli is the place to go for a drink
later on. The bar of the hotel Monal
can get busy, too; tastings are held in
the cellar wine bar there.
Off the slopes There's little to do off
the slopes, but snowshoeing and dog
sledding are available. The pool/spa at
the Balcons de Ste-Foy apartments are
open to non-residents for a fee.

St-Martin-de-Belleville

Explore the Three Valleys from a traditional old village – and so avoid the Méribel crowds who descend on it for lunch

➕ Attractively developed traditional village with pretty church

➕ Access to the whole Trois Vallées

➕ Long, easy intermediate runs on rolling local slopes

➕ Extensive snowmaking keeps runs open in poor conditions, but ...

➖ Snow on runs to the resort suffers from afternoon sun, and altitude

➖ No green runs for novices

➖ Taxing climb up from the lower part of the village to the one access lift

➖ Limited village facilities and diversions

St-Martin is a lived-in, unspoiled village with an old church (prettily lit at night), small square and buildings of wood and stone, a few miles down the valley from Les Menuires. As a quiet, relatively inexpensive, attractive base for exploration of the Three Valleys, it's unbeatable. But it is quiet.

THE RESORT

St-Martin was a backwater farming village until the 1980s, when chairlifts linked it to the slopes of Méribel and Les Menuires.

Village charm St-Martin is a pleasant old village, set on a steep slope, with its extensive modern developments all in traditional style. The main feature remains the lovely 16th-century church – prettily floodlit at night.

Convenience The village is small – you can walk around it in 20 minutes – but the main lift is above the centre and we get complaints about the hike up from those based lower down. There are some good local shops and a few 'touristy' ones.

Scenery St-Martin has one of the more attractive locations in the valley, set among quiet, lightly wooded slopes.

THE MOUNTAINS

The whole of the Three Valleys can easily be explored from here. The piste map for Les Menuires covers this area.

Slopes A gondola followed by a fast quad (a cold ride in the mornings) take you to a ridge from which you can access Méribel on one side and Les Menuires on the other.

Fast lifts Fast lifts get you into the slopes of Les Menuires or Méribel.

Queues Queues at the village gondola are not unknown.

Terrain parks None locally, but you can get to those above Les Menuires and Méribel relatively easily.

Snow reliability The local slopes get the full force of the afternoon sun, and the village is quite low. The home run is kept open by snowmaking to the bottom, but conditions are often poor.

you are based near the gondola. Piou Piou club at the ESF takes children from three months to five years old. There are babysitters.

STAYING THERE

For a small village there's a good variety of accommodation.

Chalets The Brit-run Alpine Club (not really a club) has two chalets in carefully renovated old farmhouses: Ferme de Belleville (central location) and Abode – in the quiet hamlet of Villarabout, combining original features with a modern interior. We've had good reports on food and service in the past. The company runs a minibus to and from the gondola.

Hotels There are several 3-stars, on which we lack recent reports. The Alp Hôtel (0479 089282) in pole position by the gondola is being refurbished by new owners for 2011/12.

Apartments The stylish CGH residence Chalets du Gypse is well placed beside the piste above the village, with a smart pool, hot tubs etc; available through Peak Retreats. Ski Amis has an appetising range of properties, mostly very central.

Eating out There is a good choice for a small village, no doubt due in part to the healthy lunchtime trade. The Montagnard, on the snow, is an atmospheric converted barn doing a good range of dishes. One regular visitor now prefers the Lachenal, a simple hotel in the village ('excellent lamb'). The Voûte is still recommended for pizza and more serious dishes. The Eterlou does 'great grills'. The Ferme de la Choumette, slightly out of the village, is a working farm and cheesery – 'delicious food'. The Ferme Auberge Chantacoucou in Le Chatelard is similar, but we're told is 'even better'. The Bouitte, up the road in St-Marcel, has two Michelin stars; we and a reporter had splendid meals there in 2011; yes, it is very expensive.

Après-ski Choice is limited. The Dahlia, at the bottom of the gondola, is popular for après-ski drinks. As we go to press the future of Pourquoi Pas? is uncertain; but for quiet evening drinks try Bar Joker or the Billig.

Off the slopes Options are limited. The village has a sports hall, an 'excellent' museum and musical events in the church. And there's dog sledding, snowshoe trips, and pleasant walks. Pedestrians can ride lifts to and from Méribel.

KEY FACTS

Resort	1400m
	4,590ft

Three Valleys	
Slopes	1260-3230m
	4,130-10,600ft
Lifts	173
Pistes	600km
	373 miles
Green	16%
Blue	40%
Red	34%
Black	10%
Snowmaking	
	2091 guns

Les Menuires / St-Martin only	
Slopes	1400-2850m
	4,590-9,350ft
Lifts	33
Pistes	160km
	99 miles
Green	16%
Blue	45%
Red	31%
Black	8%
Snowmaking	50%

UK PACKAGES

Alpine Club, Chalet Group, Crystal, Erna Low, First Choice, Independent Ski Links, Kaluma, Oxford Ski Co, Peak Pursuits, Peak Retreats, PowderBeds, Ski Amis, Ski France, Ski Independence, Ski l'Alpage, Skitracer, Snow Finders

Phone numbers
From abroad use the prefix +33 and omit the initial '0' of the phone number

TOURIST OFFICE

www.st-martin-belleville.com

Experts Locally there are large areas of gentle and often deserted off-piste. The descent from Roc de Fer to the village of Béranger is recommended. Head to La Masse for steep slopes.

Intermediates The local slopes are pleasant blues and reds, mainly of interest to intermediates. It's a pity that the main blue home run includes an awkward section above the mid-station – steep, narrow, often icy and congested. The alternative is to use the Méribel lifts to access the Verdet blue – an easy cruise, usually very quiet. One of our favourite runs is the rolling, wide Jerusalem red.

Beginners Not ideal – there's a small nursery slope but no long green runs to progress to. The blue run down the gondola is fairly gentle, though.

Snowboarding There is some great local off-piste freeriding available.

Cross-country There are 28km of trails in the Belleville valley.

Mountain restaurants Reporters love the Grand Lac (read the Les Menuires chapter). There are three atmospheric old places to try lower on the home run: the reliable Loy ('friendly staff, good meals') currently has the edge over the Chardon Bleu and the small, woody Corbeleys. Just above the village is the Ferme de la Choumette (read 'Eating out').

Schools and guides Reports on ESF lessons are generally positive. A potential problem is that when demand is low you may have to go to Les Menuires to find a class of the right level. A group of instructors operating here and in Les Menuires under the startling name of Ski School offer private lessons only in English, and are reported to be 'really good'.

Families One of our growing band of regular reporters on St-Martin has five children and seems to find it near-ideal, not least because it is so small and safe. There are steep walks unless

La Tania

A well-placed budget base for the slopes of Courchevel and Méribel – and a pleasant place, for a modern apartment-based resort

TOP 10 RATINGS

Extent	★★★★★
Fast lifts	★★★★
Queues	★★★★
Snow	★★★
Expert	★★★★
Intermediate	★★★★★
Beginner	★★★
Charm	★★★
Convenience	★★★★
Scenery	★★★

RPI 105

lift pass	£220
ski hire	£130
lessons	£100
food & drink	£135
total	**£585**

NEWS

2011/12: The new crèche/medical centre planned for last season should be open.

2010/11: There is a new beginner area at the top of the gondola, served by a moving carpet.

Snowmaking was increased on the Plan Fontaine green run.

➕ Part of the Trois Vallées – with good access to Courchevel and Méribel

➕ Long runs through woods to the village – a great place in a storm

➕ Attractive, small, traffic-free village

➕ Much improved snowmaking but ...

➖ At this altitude, snowmaking is vital

➖ Limited village diversions

➖ Village nursery slope gets through-traffic (but higher one does not)

➖ Remote from the highest and most snowsure slopes of the Trois Vallées

La Tania is a good-value, family-friendly base from which to explore the slopes of its swanky neighbours, Courchevel and Méribel. Trips to the far end of the huge Trois Vallées are possible, but it is hardly the ideal starting point.

It is a purpose-built resort, and at 1350m about the lowest you'll find; its wood-clad buildings sit comfortably in a pretty woodland setting – quite a contrast to the bleakness of classic French ski stations.

THE RESORT

La Tania is set just off the minor road linking Le Praz (aka Courchevel 1300) to Méribel. Free buses go to Courchevel. For evenings on the town, Méribel is slightly nearer than Courchevel 1850.

Village charm The village has grown into a quiet, attractive, car-free collection of mainly ski-in/ski-out chalets and apartments. There are a few lively bars and restaurants, but nightlife is still relatively low-key.

Convenience It's a small place – you can walk around the village in a couple of minutes – but big enough to have all the basic amenities (except a pharmacy). A gondola from one end of the village leads up into the slopes, and you should be able to ski back to

a point close to your doorstep. And the lower nursery slope is central.

Scenery The resort is prettily set among the trees. But Col de la Loze makes a better viewpoint, overlooking Courchevel's slopes.

THE MOUNTAINS

The slopes immediately above La Tania and nearby Le Praz are wooded, and about the best place in the whole Three Valleys to spend your time in bad weather. Above mid-mountain, the slopes are open.

Slopes The gondola out of the village goes to Praz-Juget. From here draglifts go on up to Chenus or to Loze and the slopes above Courchevel 1850, and a fast quad goes to the link with Méribel via Col de la Loze. From all these points, varied, interesting

361

FRANCE

362

KEY FACTS

Resort	1350m	
	4,430ft	
The Three Valleys		
Slopes	1260-3230m	
	4,130-10,600ft	
Lifts		173
Pistes		600km
		373 miles
Green		16%
Blue		40%
Red		34%
Black		10%
Snowmaking		
		2091 guns
Courchevel/		
La Tania only		
Slopes	1260-2740m	
	4,130-8,990ft	
Lifts		59
Pistes		150km
		93 miles
Green		16%
Blue		38%
Red		37%
Black		9%
Snowmaking		44%

intermediate runs take you back into the La Tania sector.

Fast lifts Our rating is for the whole Courchevel area lift system. The lifts above La Tania are not great – the gondola is not super-quick, and the alternative is long draglifts that are labelled 'difficile'.

Queues The slopes above La Tania are relatively crowd-free, but there may be morning queues for the village gondola in peak season. The problem seems to be that it opens just in time for the ski school to pour on to it through their priority couloir, leaving everyone else waiting ('up to 30 minutes', says a February 2011 visitor).

Terrain parks There is no local terrain park or half-pipe, but you can get to Courchevel's 'central park' easily.

Snow reliability Good snow-cover down to Praz-Juget is usual all season. Snowmaking covers the green run and the whole of the blue run back to the village; if, despite this, the runs are icy in the afternoon, you have the option of riding the gondola down.

Experts The mountainside above La Tania is steep enough to be interesting without being scary. The Dou des Lanches chairlift serves a lot of good off-piste terrain as well as the eponymous easy black piste. The Jean Blanc and Jockeys blacks from Loze to Le Praz are challenging more because of length than gradient.

Intermediates There are two lovely, long, undulating intermediate runs back through the trees to La Tania – though there's little difference in gradient between the blue and the red, and timid intermediates may want to use the Plan Fontaine green. On the higher slopes you have a choice of three or four pistes. Both the red Lanches and the black Dou des Lanches are excellent and challenging (the latter is often groomed). The Crêtes blue run and associated slow chair form an excellent, under-used area for building confidence – high, sunny, with good snow.

Beginners There is a good beginner area and lift right in the village, and

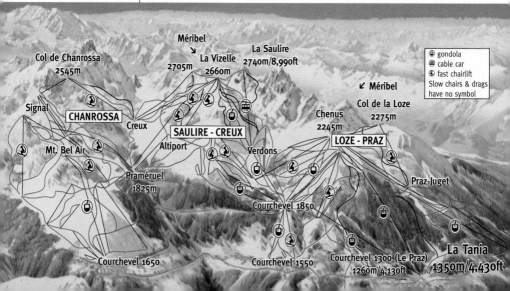

children are well catered for. But there's a lot of through traffic on the main slope. A new and more snow-sure area opened at the top of the gondola (Praz-Juget) for 2010/11, with access to the Plan Fontaine green run to the village – a long easy slope to progress to. This is an excellent arrangement; but the step up to the blue home run is quite a big one.

Snowboarding It's easy to get around on gondolas/chairs, avoiding drags.

Cross-country There are 66km of trails in the Courchevel/La Tania area, many of them through the woods.

Mountain restaurants Bouc Blanc (0479 088026), near the top of the gondola out of La Tania, is a favourite – if we're feeding the family, we'll bring them here rather than pay Courchevel prices. It has friendly table service in a wood-clad dining room, good food (reliable plat du jour) and a big terrace. Reporters regularly endorse our view, but occasionally find service stretched. The tiny Roc Tania, up at Col de la Loze, is very pretty inside.

Schools and guides Reports of the ESF vary. Magic Snowsports Academy delivered the goods for a family last year: 'Kids loved the lessons and they changed the groups over the first two days to make sure groups were of a similar standard.' Highly regarded British school New Generation gets excellent first reports from its new La Tania branch: 'A highly motivated and very friendly team, excellent coaching; the sense of enjoyment is evident in the instructors,' says a 2011 customer.

Families La Tania is popular with

families looking for a quiet and convenient base, and a child-friendly atmosphere – 'excellent for our three-family group of 14, including all ability levels'. Chez Nounours kindergarten takes both skiing and non-skiing children from three years old. The Jardin des Neiges takes skiing children from the age of four. UK tour operators Le Ski and Ski Beat both operate nurseries. A list of babysitters (for children over six months old) is available from the tourist office.

STAYING THERE

Chalets There are lots of catered chalets here, mostly dotted around in the woods above the resort centre. Ski Amis has seven chalets – including four mid-sized ones added last year that look very impressive (all with hot tub and Wi-Fi). One has the company's premium level of service. Their chalet Balkiss is 'very comfortable, with excellent food and brilliant service', enthuses a 2011 reporter. Major Courchevel operator Le Ski has three

La Tania

363

OT LA TANIA / PIERRE SEJALON

See how they made the roof lines kind of echo the slope of the hills, and the shape of the trees? An age-old trick rediscovered in the late 1980s →

Phone numbers
From abroad use the
prefix +33 and omit
the initial '0' of the
phone number.

chalets here; a small one in a great piste-side location, and two largish ones that are particularly child-friendly, with family rooms – and they run a large crèche. Alpine Action has three smart chalets near the centre, two with outdoor hot tubs. Ski Beat has six chalets, most with balconies or terraces, one with sauna. Ski Power has five mid-sized chalets, including one wood-built property with outdoor hot tub. Crystal has a 16-bed chalet.

Hotels The Montana (0479 088008) is a 'good value, comfortable and friendly' slope-side 3-star next to the gondola, with sauna and fitness club.

Apartments There are plenty of options from the major French specialist agencies – Peak Retreats, Lagrange, Erna Low. Ski Amis has a broad range of properties. Pierre & Vacances has several residences including the recently refurbished Christiania. There is a deli, a bakery, and small supermarket.

Eating out There's no doubt about the favourite among our reporters: the Taïga, over the road from the main village, is 'friendly' and 'reasonably priced', with 'a serious chef'. The Ski Lodge does good-value fast food. The Marmottons is popular and 'reasonably priced'. We've had an excellent meal at the Michelin-starred Farçon, but the bill was a bit shocking. It feels a bit out of place here, frankly.

Après-ski It's quite lively at close of play, but again the choice is limited. The Ski Lodge has long been the focal après-ski place and has live bands – 'lively, friendly and cheapest for a beer'. The Chrome bar has regular live music. For a quieter time, the hotel Montana bar is worth trying.

Off the slopes The place is very small and limited. However, snowmobile trips, tobogganing, snowshoeing and paragliding are possibilities. The hotel Montana has a fitness club with a swimming pool. There are some cleared paths and snowshoe routes. Non-skiers can go up the gondola or take the bus to Courchevel to meet skiing friends for lunch.

Selected chalets in La Tania

SNOWPIX.COM / CHRIS GILL

Tignes

Stark apartment blocks and a bleak, treeless setting are the prices you pay for the high, snow-sure slopes and varied terrain

NEWS

Building work is under way in the transformation of the old village of Les Boisses into the new ski station of Tignes 1800, with the first phase due to open at the end of 2012.

2011/12: Le Jhana, a new CGH residence, is due to open in Val Claret.

2010/11: A new 18-person gondola, Boisses, replaced the old double chairlift from Tignes-les-Boisses (now Tignes 1800).

➕ Good snow guaranteed for a long season – about the best Alpine bet

➕ One of the best areas in the world for lift-served off-piste runs

➕ Huge amount of varied terrain, with swift access to Val d'Isère

➕ Lots of accommodation close to the slopes

➕ Efforts to make the resort villages more welcoming are paying off

➖ Resort architecture not to everyone's taste (including ours)

➖ Bleak, treeless setting – many lifts prone to closure by storms

➖ Still a few long, slow chairlifts

➖ Beginners need an area pass to get to long green runs

➖ Limited, but improving, après-ski

The appeal of Tignes is simple: good snow, spread over a wide area of varied terrain, shared with Val d'Isère. The altitude of Tignes is crucial: a forecast of 'rain up to 2000m' means 'fresh snow down to village level in Tignes'.

We prefer to stay in Val, which is a more human place. But in many ways Tignes makes the better base: appreciably higher, more convenient, surrounded by intermediate terrain, with quick access to the Grande Motte glacier. And the case gets stronger as results flow from Tignes' campaign to reinvent itself in a more cuddly form. The place is a lot less hostile to the visitor than it once was.

And the lift system has improved too with a burst of fast new chairs on the western side of the Tignes bowl a few years ago. But investment has stalled since then and there are still a few key links that need upgrading.

THE RESORT

Tignes was created before the French discovered the benefits of making purpose-built resorts look acceptable. But things are improving, and the villages are gradually acquiring a more traditional look and feel.

Tignes-le-Lac is the hub of the resort, split into two sub resorts: Le Rosset and Le Bec-Rouge. It's at the point where these two meet – a snowy pedestrian area, with valley traffic now passing through a tunnel beneath – that the lifts are concentrated: a powerful gondola towards Tovière and Val d'Isère and a fast six-pack up the western slopes. There is also a suburb built on the lower slopes known as Les Almes. A nursery slope separates Le Rosset from the fourth component part, the group of apartment blocks called Le Lavachet, below which there are good fast lifts up both sides.

Val Claret is 2km up the valley, beyond the lake. From there, fast chairs head up to the western slopes, towards Val d'Isère and to the Grande Motte. An underground funicular also accesses Grande Motte.

Beside the road along the valley to the lifts is a ribbon of development in traditional style, named Grande Motte (after the peak). Val Claret is built on two levels, which are linked by a couple of (unreliable) indoor elevators, stairs and by hazardous paths.

Down the valley from the main villages are two smaller places. Tignes-les-Boisses, quietly set in the trees

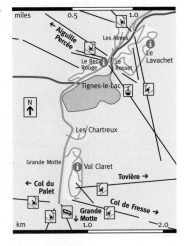

beside the road up, is in the process of a 150-million euro redevelopment, with a new MGM eco-resort opening at the end of 2012. It is being re-branded Tignes 1800 and is due to be complete by the end of 2014. Tignes-les-Brévières is a renovated old village at the lowest point of the slopes – a favourite lunch spot, and a friendly place to stay (but there's no bus service with other Tignes 'villages').

VILLAGE CHARM ★☆☆☆☆
Functional, not fancy
Some of Tignes-le-Lac's smaller buildings in the central part have been

successfully revamped in chalet style. But the place as a whole is dreary, and the blocks overlooking the lake from Le Bec-Rouge will remain monstrous until the day they are demolished. A recent reporter described it as 'absolutely hideous – in a way, it is so hideous that it is quite wonderful'. But some attractive new buildings are being added both in the centre and on the fringes. The main part of Val Claret, Centre, is an uncompromisingly 1960s-style development on a shelf above the valley floor.

So, if it's more charm you seek, stay in Les Brévières.

KEY FACTS

Resort	2100m
	6,890ft

Espace Killy	
Slopes	1550-3455m
	5,090-11,340ft
Lifts	88
Pistes	300km
	186 miles
Green	15%
Blue	42%
Red	26%
Black	17%
Snowmaking	
	821 guns

Tignes only	
Slopes	1550-3455m
	5,090-11,340ft
Lifts	47
Pistes	150km
	93 miles

> At the top, the best snow in Espace Killy. Lower down, the lovely red back to Val Claret can be very crowded – try the scenic Génépy blue instead

LA GRANDE MOTTE
3455m/11,340ft

GLACIER

Col de la Leisse

Panoramic
3015m

COL DE FRESSE

Grande Motte

Vanoise

Borsat

Val d'Isère

TOVIERE
2705m

Fresse

les Lanches

Grande Motte

Tichot

Bollin

Tommeuses

Tufs

Aeroski

Val Claret

Lavachet

Tignes-le-Lac

Daille

> The only run from Tovière to Tignes-le-Lac is a black, and the blue run to Val Claret gets very busy. Accessing Tignes from Col de Fresse is more relaxing

Le Lavachet

Tignes
2100m/6,890ft

ⓖ	gondola
ⓒ	cable car
ⓡ	railway/funicular
ⓕ	fast chairlift
	Slow chairs & drags have no symbol

FRANCE

Weekly news updates and resort links at www.wtss.co.uk

CONVENIENCE ★★★★☆
Good all rounder

Location isn't crucial, as a regular free bus service connects all the villages (except Les Brévières) – though in the day the route runs along the bottom of Val Claret, leaving Val Claret Centre residents with a climb.

SCENERY ★★★☆☆
Great from the glacier

Tignes is in a high, bleak, treeless bowl; when the sun shines the rugged mountain terrain is splendid, especially from the glacial heights of the Grande Motte.

THE MOUNTAINS

The area's great weakness is that it can become unusable in bad weather. There are no woodland runs except immediately above Tignes 1800 and Tignes-les-Brévières. Heavy snow produces widespread avalanche risk and wind closes the higher chairs.

Piste classification here isn't perfect but it is more reliable than in Val d'Isère, and signposting is clear. But we've had complaints that lift and piste closing time information is unreliable (and sometimes different on the piste map and at the lift) and, in

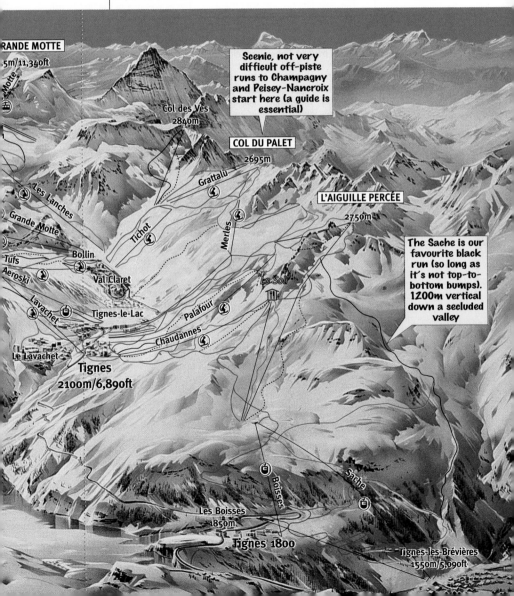

GRANDE MOTTE
5m/11,340ft

Scenic, not very difficult off-piste runs to Champagny and Peisey-Nancroix start here (a guide is essential)

Col des Vés
2840m

COL DU PALET
2695m

Grattalu

Les Lanches

Grande Motte

Tichot

Merles

L'AIGUILLE PERCÉE
2750m

Tufs

Bollin

Aeroski

Val Claret

La Sol

The Sache is our favourite black run (so long as it's not top-to-bottom bumps). 1200m vertical down a secluded valley

Lavachet

Tignes-le-Lac

Palafour

Le Lavachet

Chaudannes

Tignes
2100m/6,890ft

Boisses

Sache

Les Boisses
1850m

Tignes 1800

Tignes-les-Brévières
1550m/5,090ft

last season's poor snow conditions, that information on which runs were closed was inadequate.

EXTENT OF THE SLOPES ★★★★★
High, snow-sure and varied
Tignes and Val d'Isère share a huge area of slopes known as L'Espace Killy. Locally, Tignes' biggest asset is the **Grande Motte** – and the runs from, as well as on, the glacier. An underground funicular from Val Claret whizzes you up to over 3000m in seven minutes. There are blue, red and black runs to play on up here, as well as beautiful long runs back to the resort.

The main lifts towards Val d'Isère are efficient: a high-capacity gondola from Le Lac to **Tovière,** and a fast chair from Val Claret to **Col de Fresse.** You can head back to Tignes from either: the return from Tovière to Tignes-le-Lac is via a steep black run but there are easier blue runs to Val Claret.

Going up the opposite side of the valley takes you to a quieter area of predominantly east-facing slopes split into two main sectors, linked in both directions – **Col du Palet** and **l'Aiguille Percée.** A few years ago, this whole mountainside was at last given some of the fast lifts it had needed for years – but investment has stalled and some chairs still need modernising. These include the Col des Ves chair, at the south end of the Col du Palet sector, which serves one of the six 'naturides' (see 'For experts'). You can descend from l'Aiguille Percée to Tignes-les-Brévières or Tignes 1800 on blue, red or black runs. There are efficient gondolas back (including a new one last season from Tignes 1800), but the chairs above them are old and slow and need upgrading.

FAST LIFTS ★★★★★
Improved but not good enough
Fast chairs and gondolas get you up the mountain from most parts of the resort. And there are some fast chairs higher up too. But a few key slow ones remain that could do with being upgraded (including the chairs mentioned above and the one to l'Aiguille Percée above Tignes-le-Lac).

QUEUES ★★★★★
Very few
If snow low down is poor, the Grande Motte funicular generates queues; the fast chairs in parallel with it are often quicker, despite the longer ride time.

These lifts jointly shift a lot of people, with the result that the red run down to Val Claret can be unpleasantly crowded (the roundabout Génépy blue is a much quieter option). The worst queues now are for the cable car on the glacier – half-hour waits are common. Of course, if higher lifts are closed by heavy snow or high winds, the lifts on the lower slopes have big queues. Otherwise there are usually very few problems; crowded pistes are more of an issue.

TERRAIN PARKS ★★★★★
X Games standard but...
Tignes was one of the first French resorts to build a terrain park and will be hosting its third successive European Winter X Games from 14 to 16 March 2012. The Swatch Snowpark is beneath the Grattalu chair on Col du Palet and has rails and kickers split into green, blue and red levels, plus a boardercross course and a free airbag jump. In the summer the park doubles in size and moves up to the Grande Motte for freestyle camps. The 120m long winter half-pipe is right at the bottom of the mountain in Val Claret, which means if it's open and you have the energy to hike, you can ride it for free. There is also a mini park at town level in Le Lac, so a day's freestyle for free is definitely an option.

Despite (or maybe because of) hosting the X Games (or possibly due to the poor snow conditions), this year we've had further reader criticism of facilities ('there weren't many rails open and it's not very big – the better park is in Val d'Isère').

SNOW RELIABILITY ★★★★★
Difficult to beat
Tignes has all-year-round runs (barring brief closures in spring or autumn) on its Grande Motte glacier. And the resort height of 2100m generally means good snow-cover right back to base for most of the long winter season – November to May. The west-facing runs down from Col de Fresse and Tovière to Val Claret suffer from the afternoon sun, although they now have serious snowmaking. Some of the lower east-facing and south-east-facing slopes on the other side of the valley can suffer late in the season, too. Grooming is 'excellent' – in last season's challenging conditions, 'a lot of wonderful work was done to keep pistes open and in good condition'.

FOR EXPERTS ★★★★★
An excellent choice

Tignes has converted many of its black runs into 'naturides', which means they are never groomed (a neat way of saving money!) but they are marked, patrolled and avalanche protected. Many of them are not especially steep (eg the Ves run – promoted from red status and renamed after the local freeride hero Guerlain Chicherit). Perhaps the most serious challenge is the long black run from Tovière to Tignes-le-Lac, with steep, usually heavily mogulled sections (the top part, Pâquerettes, is now a naturide, but the bottom part, Trolles, is a normal black). Parts of this run get a lot of afternoon sun. Our favourite black run (still a 'normal' black) is the Sache, from l'Aiguille Percée down a secluded valley to Tignes-les-Brévières. It can become very heavily mogulled, especially at the bottom – you can avoid this section by taking the red Arcosses piste option part-way down.

But it is the off-piste possibilities that make Tignes such a draw for experts and the schools organise off-piste groups. See the feature box overleaf for a few of the off-piste runs.

The bizarre French form of heli-skiing is available here: mountaintop drops are forbidden, but from Tovière you can ski down towards the Lac du Chevril to be retrieved by chopper.

FOR INTERMEDIATES ★★★★★
One of the best

For keen intermediate piste-bashers who like varied terrain, the Espace Killy is one of the world's best areas.

Tignes' local slopes are ideal intermediate terrain. The runs on the Grande Motte glacier nearly always have superb snow. The runs from the top of the cable car are bizarrely classified red and black, but they are wide and mostly easy on usually fabulous snow and could easily be blues. The Leisse run down to the chairlift of the same name is classified black and can get very mogulled but usually has good snow. The red run all the way back to town is a delightful long cruise – though often crowded. The roundabout blue (Génépy) is much gentler and quieter.

From Tovière, the blue 'H' run to Val Claret is an enjoyable cruise and generally well groomed. But again, it can get very crowded.

Tignes has fabulous lift-served off-piste – some, like this, on public view, some much more remote; the schools run guided groups ↓

There is lots to do on the other side of the valley and the runs down from l'Aiguille Percée to Tignes 1800 and Tignes-les-Brévières are scenic and fun. There are red and blue options as well as the beautiful Sache black run – adventurous intermediates shouldn't miss it. The runs from l'Aiguille Percée to Le Lac are gentle, wide blues.

FOR BEGINNERS ★★✩✩✩
Good nursery slopes, but...
The nursery slopes of Tignes-le-Lac and Le Lavachet (which meet at the top) are excellent – convenient, snow-sure, gentle, free of through-traffic and served by a slow chair and a drag. The ones at Val Claret are less appealing: an unpleasantly steep slope within the village served by a drag, and a less convenient slope served by the fast Bollin chair. All of these lifts are free.

Although there are some fairly easy blues on the west side of Tignes, for long green runs you have to go over to the Val d'Isère sector. You need an Espace Killy pass to use them, and to get back to Tignes you have a choice between the blue run from Col de Fresse (which has a tricky start) or riding the gondola down from Tovière. And in poor weather, the high Tignes valley is an intimidatingly bleak place – enough to make any wavering beginner retreat to a bar with a book.

FOR BOARDERS ★★★★★
One of the best
Tignes has always been a popular destination for snowboarders. Lots of easily accessible off-piste and lower prices than Val d'Isère are the main attractions, and quite a few top UK snowboarders make this their winter home. There are a few flat areas (avoid Génépy and Myrtilles), but lift system relies more on chairs and gondolas than drags. There are long, wide pistes to blast down, such as

Grattalu, Carline and Piste H, with acres of powder between them to play in. And the backside of Col de Fresse in Val d'Isère is a natural playground. There are three specialist snowboard schools (Snocool, Surf Feeling and Alliance) and a Welsh-run snowboarder chalet (www.dragonlodge.com). Go to the Snowpark shop in Tignes-le-Lac for all your equipment needs.

FOR CROSS-COUNTRY ★★★✩✩
Interesting variety
The Espace Killy has 44km of cross-country trails, including 20km of tracks on the frozen Lac de Tignes, along the valley between Val Claret and Tignes-le-Lac, at Tignes 1800 and Les Brévières and up on the Grande Motte.

MOUNTAIN RESTAURANTS ★★★✩✩
A couple of good places
The mountain restaurants are not a highlight – a regular hazard of high, purpose-built resorts, where it's easy to go back to the village for lunch. **Editors' choice** Lo Soli (0479 069863) at the top of the Chaudannes chair is a clear favourite. The terrace shares with the adjacent self-service Alpage a superb view of the Grande Motte; reporters endorse our opinion: 'excellent food, ambience and service'; 'did us proud, with epic hot chocolates and enjoyable tartiflette'. The table-service bit of the Panoramic (0479 066011) at the top of the funicular competes: 'wonderful views, very good spaghetti bolognese (enough to share), excellent puddings'. **Worth knowing about** At the top of the Tichot chair from Val Claret, the Palet has a 'decent choice, big portions'. On the nursery slope above Val Claret, the 'expensive' Chalet du Bollin has been recommended for its casserole served from the pot: 'The portion was huge! Excellent.' The big Panoramic self-service at the top of the funicular gets

Tignes is renowned for offering some of the best lift-served off-piste skiing in the world. There is a tremendous choice, with runs to suit all levels, from intermediate skiers to fearless freeriders and off-piste experts. Here's just a small selection. Don't go without a guide.

*For a first experience of off-piste, **Lognan** is ideal. These slopes – down the mountainside between the pistes to Le Lac and the pistes to Val Claret – are broad and not very difficult.*

*One of our favourite routes is the **Tour de Pramecou**. After a few minutes' walking at the bottom of the Grande Motte glacier, you pass around a big rock called Pramecou. There is then a multitude of possibilities, varying in difficulty – so routes can be found for skiers of different abilities.*

***Petite Balme** is a run for good skiers only – access is easy but leads to quite challenging north-facing slopes in real high-mountain terrain, far from the pistes.*

*To ski **Oreilles de Mickey** (Mickey's Ears) you start from Tovière and walk north along the ridge to the peak of Lavachet, where you get a great view of Tignes. The descent involves three long couloirs, narrow and pretty steep, which bring you back to Le Lavachet.*

*The best place to find good snow is the **Chardonnet** couloirs – they never get the sun. The route involves a 20-minute walk from the top of the Merles chairlift.*

*The **Vallons de la Sache** is one of the most famous routes – a descent of 1200m vertical down a breathtaking valley in the heart of the National Park, overlooked by the magnificent Sache glacier. Starting from l'Aiguille Percée you enter a different world, high up in the mountains, far away from the ski lifts. You arrive down in Les Brévières, below the Tignes dam.*

*One of the big adventures is to go away from the Tignes ski area and all signs of civilisation, starting from the Col du Palet. From there you can head for **Champagny** (linked to La Plagne's area) or **Peisey-Nancroix** (linked to Les Arcs' area) – both very beautiful runs, and not too difficult.*

Tignes

Interactive resort shortlist builder at www.wtss.co.uk

SCHOOLS

ESF
t 0479 063028

Evolution 2
t 0479 083529

Snocool
t 0479 243094

333
t 0479 062088

Alliance
t 0645 120824
0844 484 9390 (UK)

New Generation
t 0479 010318
0844 484 3663 (UK)
www.skinewgen.com

BASS
t 0679 512405

Ali Ross Skiing Clinics
t 01997 421909 (UK)

Classes (ESF prices)
6 half days: from
€140

Private lessons
From €46 for 1hr

GUIDES

Bureau des Guides
t 0479 064276

Tetra
t 0631 499275

crowded, but has great views from its huge terrace and 'good portions'.

There are lots of easily accessible places for lunch in the resorts. One ski-to-the-door favourite of ours in Le Lac is the hotel Montana, on the left as you descend from l'Aiguille Percée ('more competitively priced than others'). Others are the Ferme des 3 Capucines a short walk down from the bottom of the Chaudannes and Paquis chairs and the Arbina (see 'Eating out' for more on these two). The Chalet du Pain is recommended for a 'quick cheap lunch', while the Jam Bar is a 'tiny cafe with brilliant freshly made pasta sauces, great bruschetta and the best coffee'. In Val Claret the Taverne des Neiges is 'lively' with 'good food and service'; Pignatta serves 'quality and value succulent pizzas'; the Aspen Cafe does 'big American-diner style portions for reasonable prices' and Carline is 'nothing fancy but convenient and quick'.

At the extremity of the lift system, Les Brévières makes an obvious lunch stop. A short walk round the corner into the village brings you to places much cheaper than the two by the piste. Sachette, for example, is crammed with artefacts from mountain life and offers 'lots of good cheese

dishes'. The Armailly is 'heartily' recommended for its 'fabulous Beaufort tart'. The Etoile des Neiges serves 'great, typical Savoyard food' but service can be 'poor'.

SCHOOLS AND GUIDES ★★★★
Plenty of choice
There are over half-a-dozen schools, including three specialist snowboard schools, plus various independent instructors. A reporter recommends Ali Ross Skiing Clinics (pre-booking required) – 'a great character who achieved results'. Reporters advise that at busy times pre-booking is 'essential' for normal schools as well. ESF gets mixed reviews: one 2010 reporter's group abandoned their group lessons mid-way through the week because they were so bad; but a 2011 visitor had a 'fantastic' day's guiding with 'some good snow in challenging spring conditions'.

New Generation, a British-run school with branches in several other resorts, opened in Tignes three seasons ago. A recent reporter had 'an excellent one-on-one private lesson, and came away very happy'. BASS (British Alpine Ski & Snowboard School) has a branch here and a reporter enjoyed 'excellent, small

CHILDCARE

Les Marmottons
t 0479 065167
Ages 30mnth to 10yr

Ski schools
Evolution 2 takes children from age 5 and ESF takes children from age 4 (6 days €249)

GETTING THERE

Air Geneva 225km/140 miles (3hr30); Lyon 230km/145 miles (3hr15); Chambéry 145km/90 miles (2hr15)

Rail Bourg-St-Maurice (30km/19 miles); regular buses or taxi from station

group clinics'. We regularly have glowing reports of a British-run snowboarding outfit, Alliance: 'tuition was appropriate to our requirements, and very passionate and sincere – we improved our confidence and skills greatly'; 'excellent instruction'.

The highlight of a 2011 visitor's holiday was a two-hour private lesson he and his daughter had with 333's principal Fred – 'even held our hands through the turns'. Another reporter's teenage sons had 'outstanding tuition and lots of varied skiing' on an Ultimate Snowsports course.

Reports on Evolution 2 have been positive: 'private lessons were excellent value for money; the instructor was very friendly, spoke excellent English and really took us to task on technique – our skiing improved as a result'; 'very happy with the children's lessons booked through Ski Esprit'. The off-piste 'Tarentaise Tour' has also been praised ('a superb long day, with an enthusiastic guide').

FOR FAMILIES ★★★✩✩
Good reports
We have had good reports on the Marmottons kindergartens – 'brilliant', said a father of a four year old – and the Spritelets ski classes arranged by Esprit Ski and Evolution 2: 'She loved her class and could snowplough by the end of the week.' British-run t4Nanny (www.tnanny.com) was recommended – 'flexible and terrific'. Family specialist tour operator Esprit Ski runs chalets and comprehensive childcare here.

All three main styles of lodgings are available through tour operators. More luxury options are appearing.
Chalets The choice of catered chalets is increasing, though they are mainly in Le Lac. Ski Olympic's chalet hotel Rosset has been recommended by reporters; their other chalets look good too. Skiworld has 11 chalets from luxury (some with sauna and hot tub) to budget and a swanky chalet hotel with pool and sauna – Chalet Annapurna was 'highly recommended'. Ski Total has 14 chalets including some very smart places with pool, hot tub and sauna – Chalet Anne-marie is 'strongly recommended'. Family specialist Esprit has seven chalets here, including the smart, modern 24-person Corniche with sauna, steam and hot tub. Crystal has eight places from smart to budget, plus a Riders' Lodge for boarders and freestyle skiers that sleeps around 30. A regular reporter this year recommends Chalet Chardon run by small tour operator Snowstar: 'used to be Robert Maxwell's private apartment; lovely large lounge with floor-to-ceiling windows and a great view of the lake'.
Hotels The few hotels are small and concentrated in Le Lac.
***Campanules (0479 063436) Smartly rustic chalet in upper Le Lac, with good restaurant. One reporter was impressed enough to suggest that it deserved a 4-star rating.
***Village Montana (0479 400144) Stylishly woody, on the east-facing slopes above Le Lac, with a 4-star suites section. Outdoor pool, sauna, steam, hot tub. 'Not cheap but first class hotel with accommodating staff.'
***Lévanna (0479 063294) Central in Le Lac – comfortable, with a 'generous hot tub'; a reporter found 'friendly staff but a woeful lack of them'.
***Diva (0479 067000) Biggest in town (121 rooms). On lower level of Val Claret, a short walk from lifts. 'Very comfy rooms, excellent meals.' Sauna.
***Marais (0479 064006) Prettily furnished, simple hotel in Tignes 1800.
***Refuge (0479 063664) Oldest hotel in Tignes (Le Lac). 'Well-run.'
**Arbina (0479 063478) Well-run place close to the lifts in Le Lac, with lunchtime terrace, crowded après-ski bar and one of the best restaurants.
Génépy (0479 065711) Simple Dutch-run chalet in Les Brévières.

UK PACKAGES

Action Outdoors, Alpine Answers, Alpine Elements, Carrier, Chalet Group, Club Med, Crystal, Crystal Finest, Erna Low, Esprit, First Choice, Friendship Travel, Hundred Hills, Independent Ski Links, Inghams, Inspired to Ski, Interactive Resorts, Lagrange, Mark Warner, Mountainsun, Neilson, Oxford Ski Co, Peak Retreats, Powder White, Powder White Lite, PowderBeds, PV-Holidays.com, Ski Amis, Ski Club Freshtracks, Ski Collection, Ski Expectations, Ski France, Ski Independence, Ski Line, Ski Olympic, Ski Solutions, Ski Supreme, Ski Total, Skitracer, Ski Weekend, Skiworld, Snow Finders, Snoworks, Snowpod, Snowstar, Thomson

ACTIVITIES

Indoor Wellness and fitness centres (pools, saunas, Turkish baths, hot tub, spa and beauty treatments, weight training), multi-sports hall, yoga, squash, climbing wall, cinema, library, bowling, heritage centre
Outdoor Dog sledding, mountaineering, ice climbing, ice driving, ice diving, ice rink, paragliding, snowmobiling, snowshoeing, ice karting, biking on snow, helicopter flights

Phone numbers
From abroad use the prefix +33 and omit the initial '0' of the phone number

TOURIST OFFICE

www.tignes.net

Apartments There are lots of apartments in all price ranges. Ski Collection has some good-looking options and Ski Amis does self-catered places here too. The growing number of smart places include Ferme du Val Claret, Nevada and Pierre et Vacances' Ecrin des Neiges in Val Claret, and Télèmark and Residence Village Montana in Le Lac. In Les Brévières, the Belvédère has very smart large apartments and chalets with three to six bedrooms. All the above have access to pool, sauna etc, but at extra cost in some cases. The Chalet Club in Val Claret is a collection of simple studios, but it has a free indoor pool, sauna and a restaurant and bar.

The supermarket at Le Lac is reported to be 'comprehensive but very expensive' – 'stock up in Bourg'.

EATING OUT ★★★★
Good places scattered about

The options in Le Lavachet are rather limited, though a recent reporter enjoyed the Grenier with its 'excellent cold meats and tartiflette' and another the 'novel experience' of eating with over-wintering farm animals on display through a viewing window at the 'atmospheric' and 'very reasonably priced' Ferme des 3 Capucines (we had a good lunch here on our last visit too). And we have very positive reports of the good-value, British-run Brasero: 'This restaurant is establishing a good reputation in Tignes; the food was quite simply excellent. We were made to feel very welcome.' Finding anywhere with some atmosphere is difficult in Le Lac, though the food in some of the better hotels is good, and the Chaumière in the Village Montana had 'good food and terrific service'. The upstairs restaurant at the Arbina is endorsed again by 2011 reporters: 'very good service and excellent food; the 30 euro three-course fixed menu is good value'. The 'atmospheric' Escale Blanche is popular with 'great food', but reporters disagree over its value. Repeated visitors have enjoyed 'traditional' food at the Eterlou, but the service 'went downhill after we complained about the house wine'.

In Val Claret the Caveau is recommended for a special treat – 'superbly presented food and good service in an intimate cellar setting'. Pepe 2000 has 'reasonable prices and helpful staff' and 'very decent for

standard fondues, raclettes etc'. A 2010 reporter had 'the best meal of week: huge caesar salad with lots of chicken and croutons' at the Pignatta.

APRES-SKI ★★★
Hidden away

Reporters agree that there is plenty going on if you know where to find it. Val Claret has some early-evening atmosphere, and happy hours are popular. Reporters differ on the merits of the Crowded House (popular with Brits). The Drop Zone has live music, 'a good atmosphere and a dance floor that fills up pretty quickly'. Grizzly's is 'cosy and atmospheric, but you pay for the ambience'; 'very cool'. The 'whisky lounge' in the Couloir is a 'great place to relax'. A 2011 reporter 'always ended the night in the Melting Pot' and avoided the 'seedier' Blue Girl.

Le Lac is a natural focus for immediate après-ski drinks. The 'lively' Loop, with pool table, has a 'two for one' happy hour from 4pm to 6pm ('I was delighted with the size of the reasonably priced gin and tonic'), while the Embuscade is 'very friendly'. The bar of the hotel Arbina is our kind of spot – cosy with friendly service. It's a great place to sit outside and people-watch. The Alpaka Lodge bar is popular with Brits and 'a pleasant spot, especially if you manage to grab one of the sofas by the fire'. TC's bar is 'very friendly, with good music'. Bagus Bar is 'rocking'. Jack's and the Dock are popular late haunts.

Vincents in Les Brévières is 'lively', with lots of drinking, singing and sometimes live music'.

OFF THE SLOPES ★★
Good leisure centre

Despite the range of alternative activities, Tignes is a resort for those who want to use the slopes, where anyone who doesn't is liable to feel like a fish out of water. Some activities do get booked up quickly as well – a reporter said it was impossible to find a free dog sledding slot in April. The ice skating on the lake includes a 500m circuit as well as a conventional rink. This and the pools of the Lagon leisure centre (various pools, slides, wellness and fitness facilities) which is praised by reporters are free to use with a lift pass for two days or more. The museum in the Maison de Tignes is 'good'. A reporter's kids 'really enjoyed' the bowling at Tignes-le-Lac.

COURCHEVEL / J. KELAGOPIAN

Les Trois Vallées

With the swankiest resort in the Alps at one end, and the highest at the other: the biggest lift-linked ski area in the world

Despite competing claims, notably from the Portes du Soleil, in practical terms the Trois Vallées cannot be beaten for sheer quantity of lift-served terrain. There is nowhere like it for a keen skier or boarder who wants to cover as much mileage as possible while rarely taking the same run repeatedly. It has a lot to offer everyone, from beginner to expert. And its resorts offer a wide range of alternatives – not only the widely known attractions of the big-name mega-resorts but also the low-key appeal of the smaller villages.

What's more, the area undersells itself. It should actually be known as the Quatre Vallées, since its expansion south into the Maurienne.

The runs of the Trois Vallées and their resorts are dealt with in six chapters. The four major resorts are Courchevel, Méribel, Les Menuires and Val Thorens, but we also give chapters to St-Martin-de-Belleville, a village down the valley from Les Menuires, and La Tania, a modern development between Courchevel and Méribel.

None of the resorts is cheap, but of the major resorts **Les Menuires** is clearly the cheapest. The centre of the resort is an eyesore, but new developments have been built in a much more acceptable style, and two

of the original buildings have been demolished to make way for new ones in a much more sympathetic style – something we suggested over a decade ago. Les Menuires has an excellent position for exploration of the Trois Vallées as a whole.

Down the valley from Les Menuires is **St-Martin-de-Belleville**, a charming traditional village that has been expanded sympathetically. It has good-value accommodation and lift links towards Les Menuires and Méribel.

Up rather than down the Belleville valley from Les Menuires, at 2300m,

Val Thorens is the highest resort in the Alps, and at 3230m the top of its slopes is the high-point of the Trois Vallées. The snow in this area is almost always good, and it includes two glaciers where good snow is guaranteed. But the setting is bleak and the lifts are vulnerable to closure in bad weather. The purpose-built resort is very convenient. Visually it is not comparable to Les Menuires, thanks to the smaller-scale buildings and more traditional styles.

Méribel is a multi-part resort. The highest component, **Méribel-Mottaret**, is about the best placed of all the resorts for getting to any part of the Trois Vallées system. **Méribel** itself, 200m lower, is a British favourite. It is the most attractive of the main Trois Vallées resorts, built in chalet style on a steep hillside. Parts of the resort are very convenient for the slopes and the village centre; parts are not. The growing hamlet of **Méribel-Village** has its own chairlift into the system. You can also stay down in the valley town of **Brides-les-Bains**.

Courchevel has four parts. 1850 is the most fashionable resort in France, and among the most expensive resorts in the Alps (though it doesn't have to cost a fortune to stay there). The other parts – 1300 (Le Praz), 1550 and 1650 – are much less expensive. Many people rate the slopes around Courchevel the best in the Three Valleys, with runs to suit all standards.

La Tania was built for the 1992 Olympics, just off the minor road linking Courchevel to Méribel. It has now grown into an attractive, car-free collection of chalets and apartment blocks set among the trees, and is popular with families. It has a good nursery slope and good intermediate runs in the woods above.

Val d'Isère

One of the great high mega-resorts, particularly (though not only) for experts – with a very attractive town at the base

RATINGS

The mountains

Extent	★★★★★
Fast lifts	★★★★
Queues	★★★★
Terrain p'ks	★★★
Snow	★★★★★
Expert	★★★★★
Intermediate	★★★★★
Beginner	★★★
Boarder	★★★★
X-country	★
Restaurants	★★★
Schools	★★★★★
Families	★★★★

The resort

Charm	★★★
Convenience	★★★
Scenery	★★★
Eating out	★★★★★
Après-ski	★★★★
Off-slope	★★

RPI   100

lift pass	£210
ski hire	£125
lessons	£80
food & drink	£165
total	**£580**

NEWS

The resort seems to be concentrating more on swish hotels than new lifts – how times have changed. No new lifts since 2008/09, but four hotels have been promoted to 5-star status in the last couple of years (including the Blizzard and the Christiania most recently). And the Becca restaurant in Le Laisinant has become the second restaurant in the resort to be awarded a Michelin star.

+ Huge area shared with Tignes, with lots of runs for all abilities

+ One of the great resorts for lift-served off-piste runs

+ Once the snow has fallen, high altitude of slopes keeps it good

+ Wide choice of schools, especially for off-piste lessons and guiding

+ For a high Alpine resort, the town is attractive, very lively at night, and offers a good range of restaurants

+ Wide range of package holidays – including some comfortable chalets

– Some green and blue runs are too challenging, and all runs back to the village are tricky

– You're quite likely to need buses at the start and end of the day (but they are very frequent and efficient)

– Most lifts and slopes are liable to close when the weather is bad

– At times seems more British than French – especially in low season

– Eating and drinking expensive – among the four priciest resorts in France for this

Val d'Isère is one of the world's best resorts for experts – attracted by the extent of lift-served off-piste – and for confident, mileage-hungry intermediates. You don't have to be particularly adventurous to enjoy the resort; but it would be much better for novices if the piste classifications were more reliable.

The drawbacks listed above are mainly not serious complaints, whereas most of the plus-points weigh heavily in the balance. For a combination of seriously impressive skiing and captivating village ambience, there aren't many places we'd rather go.

THE RESORT

Val d'Isère spreads along a remote valley, which is a dead end in winter. The road in from Bourg-St-Maurice brings you dramatically through a rocky defile to La Daille – a convenient but hideous slope-side apartment complex and the base of lifts into the major Bellevarde sector of the slopes.

Turn right at the centre and you drive under the nursery slopes and lifts to a lot of new development. Continue up the main valley instead, and you come to Le Laisinant, a peaceful little outpost with a fast lift out of the valley, and then to Le Fornet, the fourth major lift station.

The developments up the side valley beyond the main lift station – in Le Châtelard and La Legettaz – are mainly attractive, and some offer ski-in/ski-out convenience. La Daille and Le Fornet have their (quite different) attractions for those less concerned about nightlife. A car is of no great value around the resort. The supermarkets have been praised for 'enticing pre-cooked food'.

VILLAGE CHARM ★★★

Developing nicely

The outskirts of Val proper are dreary, but as you approach the centre the improvements put in place over the last 20 or so years become evident: wood- and stone-cladding, culminating in the tasteful pedestrian-only Val Village complex. Many first-time visitors find the resort much more pleasant than they expected.

KEY FACTS

Resort	1850m
	6,070ft

Entire Espace Killy area	
Slopes	1550-3455m
	5,090-11,340ft
Lifts	88
Pistes	300km
	186 miles
Green	15%
Blue	42%
Red	26%
Black	17%
Snowmaking	
	821 guns

Val d'Isère only	
Slopes	1785-3300m
	5,860-10,830ft
Lifts	46
Pistes	150km
	93 miles

OT VAL D'ISERE / JP NOISILLIER / NUTS.FR

The village spreads a long way down the valley; you can see why they need their good bus service from this picture ↓

CONVENIENCE ★★★★★
Mostly fine
There is a lot of traffic around, but the resort has worked hard to get cars under control and has made the centre more pedestrian-friendly. The location of your accommodation isn't crucial, unless you want to ski from the door or be close to a nursery slope. The main lift stations are served by very efficient free shuttle-buses; but in peak periods you may have to let a few full ones pass before there's space to board. But in the evening frequency plummets and dedicated après-skiers will want to be near the centre.

SCENERY ★★★★★
Valley deep, mountain high
The resort sprawls along a steep-sided river valley, beneath a series of high and partly-wooded mountain ridges. There are splendid views from the Pissaillas glacier.

THE MOUNTAIN

Although there are wooded slopes above the village on all sectors, in practice most of the runs here are on open slopes above the treeline, and a lot of lifts can close in bad weather. Several visitors confirm that piste grooming is good but reporters still complain about poor signing. And Val d'Isère vies with St Anton for the title of 'resort with most under-classified slopes'. Many blue and some green runs (including runs to the valley) are simply too steep, narrow and even bumpy; in other resorts they would be reds, or even blacks; we have a hefty file of complaints from readers who agree with our judgement. The piste map has 'quiet skiing' zones marked on it. The local radio (96.1 FM) carries weather reports in English as well as in French.

EXTENT OF THE SLOPES ★★★★★
Vast and varied
Val d'Isère's slopes divide into three main sectors, two reachable from the village. **Bellevarde** is the mountain that is home to Val d'Isère's two famous downhill courses: the OK piste that is used for the World Cup every December and the Face piste that was used for the 1992 Winter Olympics and the 2009 World Championships. You can reach Bellevarde quickly by underground funicular from La Daille or the powerful Olympique gondola from near the centre of town. From the top you can descend to the valley, play on a variety of drags and chairs at altitude or take a choice of lifts to Tignes' slopes (see separate chapter).

Solaise is the other mountain accessible directly from the village. The Solaise fast quad takes you a few metres higher than the parallel cable car. Once up, a short drag or rope tow takes you over a plateau and down to a variety of chairs that serve this very sunny area of predominantly gentle pistes. From near the top of this area you can catch the fast Leissières chair

Col Pers – one of our favourite off-piste runs, from the glacier down to Le Fornet

Worth getting up here for the snow and the views

3300m/10,830ft

GLACIER DE PISSAILLAS

Cascade

2950m

COL DE L'ISERAN
2765m

2900m

Leissières

Cugnaï

Man

Pyramides

Vallon de L'Iseran

Glacier

Madeleine

2325m

Laisinant

Fornet

Edelweiss

SOLAISE
2560m

Le Fornet
1930m

Good shady red run served by the Laisinant fast chair

Le Châte

No easy way back to the village from Solaise

Solaise

Le Laisinant

Val d'Isère
1850m/6,070ft

gondola
fast chairlift
Slow chairs & drags
have no symbol

ISSAILLAS

Good area of varied intermediate runs at altitude, with a couple of fast chairs

The blue from here is the easiest and least crowded intermediate route to Tignes

Glacier de la Grande Motte

DE RAN

55m

2900m

Cugnai

Excellent runs down to the Manchet chair – though affected by sun later in the season

Lots of long, high easy runs – but also lots of slow old lifts

COL DE FRESSE
2770m

Glacier

Madeleine

Manchet

Le Manchet
1940m

Grand Pré

Borsat

Tignes

Fresse

TOVIERE
2705m

BELLEVARDE
2705m

Marmottes

Tommeuses

SE

Loyes

Le Châtelard

L'Olympique

Solaise

The world's trickiest green run – narrow in parts and crowded and mogulled at the end of the day

Bellevarde

Funival

Daille

al d'Isère
om/6,07oft

The 1992 Winter Olympic men's downhill course is now a genuine black run and often mogulled from top to bottom

La Daille
1785m/5,86oft

(which climbs over a ridge and down the other side) to the third main area, in the valley running up to the **Col de l'Iseran**. This area can also be reached by the fast chair from Le Laisinant or by cable car from Le Fornet. At the top here is the **Glacier de Pissaillas**.

FAST LIFTS ★★★★
Access all areas
High capacity lifts provide good access from the valley and there are lots of fast chairs higher up. But there are still a few slow chairs and draglifts around.

QUEUES ★★★★
Few problems
Queues to get out of the resort have been kept in check by lift upgrades and additions. At Solaise the slow Lac chair back up to the Tête Solaise can

generate queues, but a recent reporter praises 'the good queueing systems, with each chair filled to capacity'. Crowded pistes in high season is a more common complaint than queues.

TERRAIN PARKS ★★★
Beginners and experts welcome
Above the La Daille gondola and served by the Mont Blanc chairlift lies the DC Valpark (www.valdiserevalpark. com). Maintenance can be a bit hit or miss – but an April 2011 reporter said: 'My son really enjoyed messing about in the park which, all credit to those responsible, was kept open and maintained as well as possible in warm conditions.' There are 18 table jumps and 25 boxes and rails of all shapes and sizes. Plus a large hip, 3m wall ride and four kicker lines, with up to five jumps in a row ranging from 3m in the blue line to 20m in the pro line. Head to Tignes for a half-pipe.

SNOW RELIABILITY ★★★★★
One of the best
In years when lower resorts have suffered, Val d'Isère has rarely been short of snow. Even in a poor snow year like last season, decent skiing was still available in April. Once a big dump of snow has fallen, the resort's height means you can almost always get back to the village. But even more

---

THE BEST LIFT-SERVED OFF-PISTE IN THE WORLD?

Few resorts can rival the extent of lift-served off-piste skiing in Val d'Isère. Here is a selection of what's on offer. But don't try any of it without a guide and essential safety equipment.

*Some runs are ideal for adventurous intermediates looking to try off-piste for the first time. The **Tour du Charvet** goes through glorious scenery from the top of the Grand Pré chairlift on the back of Bellevarde. For most of the way it is very gentle, with only a few steeper pitches. It ends up at the bottom of the Manchet chair up to the Solaise area. The **Pays Désert** is an easy run with superb views on the Pissaillas glacier, high above Le Fornet and reached by traversing away from the pistes above cliffs from the top of the lift system. You end up at the Pays Désert T-bar.*

*For more experienced off-piste skiers, **Col Pers** is one of our favourite runs. Again, it starts a traverse from the Pissaillas glacier. You go over a pass into a big, fairly gentle bowl with glorious views and endless ways down. If there is enough snow, you drop down into the Gorges de Malpasset and ski over the frozen Isère river back to the Fornet cable car. If not, you can take a higher route.*

Cugnai is a wide, secluded bowl reached from the chair of the same name at the top of the Solaise sector. A steep (37 degree) slope at the far end descends beneath a sheer black rock wall and then narrows into a gully to the valley floor, leading to the Manchet chair.

*Banane is reached via the Face de Bellevarde piste and is a long and impressive run (37 to 40 degrees) with spectacular views over the Manchet valley. For a real challenge intrepid experts should try the **Couloir des Pisteurs**, which requires a 20-minute climb from the Tour de Charvet. The view from the top is simply stunning. A very narrow steep couloir (44 degrees) bounded by rock faces brings you out on to a wide open slope above Le Grand Pré, right opposite Bellevarde.*

Then there's the whole of Tignes' extensive off-piste to explore of course.

LIFT PASSES

Espace Killy

Prices in €

Age	1-day	6-day
under 14	36	178
14 to 64	45	223
over 65	36	178

Free under 5, over 75
Beginner five free lifts on nursery slopes

Notes
Covers Tignes and Val d'Isère; half-day and pedestrian passes; family discounts; 5-day-plus passes valid for one day in the Three Valleys, one day in Paradiski (La Plagne-Les Arcs)

Alternative pass
Val d'Isère only

important is that in each sector there are lots of lifts and runs above mid-mountain, between about 2300m and 2900m. Many of the slopes face roughly north. And there is access to glaciers at Pissaillas or over in Tignes, although both take a while to get to.

FOR EXPERTS ★★★★★
One of the world's best
Val d'Isère is one of the top resorts in the world for experts. The main attraction is the huge range of beautiful off-piste possibilities – see the feature panel on the left.

There may be better resorts for really steep pistes – there are certainly lots in North America – but there is plenty of on-piste action to amuse most experts, despite the small number of blacks on the piste map. And some of these have been converted to 'naturides', which means they are never groomed (a neat way of saving money!) but they are marked, patrolled and avalanche protected. Many reds and blues are also steep enough to get mogulled.

On Bellevarde the famous Face run is the main attraction – often mogulled from top to bottom, but not worryingly steep. Epaule is the sector's other black run – where the moguls are hit by long exposure to sun and can be slushy or rock hard (it is prone to closure for these reasons too). Most of the blacks on Solaise and above Le Fornet are now 'naturides'.

Wayne Watson of off-piste school Alpine Expérience puts a daily diary of off-piste snow conditions and runs on the web at www.alpineexperience.com.

FOR INTERMEDIATES ★★★★★
Quantity and quality
Val d'Isère has just as much to offer intermediates as experts. There's enough here to keep you interested for several visits – though pistes can

be crowded in high-season, and the less experienced should be aware that many runs are under-classified.

In the Solaise sector is a network of gentle blue runs, ideal for building confidence. And there are a couple of beautiful runs from here through the woods to Le Laisinant – ideal in bad weather, though prone to closure in times of avalanche danger.

Most of the runs in the Col de l'Iseran sector are even easier – ideal for early and hesitant intermediates. Those marked blue at the top of the glacier could really be classified green.

Bellevarde has a huge variety of runs ideally suited to intermediates of all levels. From Bellevarde itself there is a choice of green, blue and red runs of varying pitch. The World Cup downhill OK piste is a wonderful rolling cruise when groomed. The wide runs from Tovière normally offer the choice of groomed piste or moguls.

A snag for early intermediates is that runs back to the valley can be challenging. The easiest way is down to La Daille on a green run which would be classified blue or red in most resorts. It gets very crowded and mogulled by the end of the day. None of the runs from Bellevarde and Solaise back to Val itself is easy. Many early intermediates ride the lifts down.

FOR BEGINNERS ★★★☆☆
OK if you know where to go
The nursery slope right by the centre of town is 95% perfect; it's just a pity that the very top is unpleasantly steep. The lifts serving it are free.

Once off the nursery slopes, you have to know where to find easy runs; many of the greens should be blue, or even red. One local instructor admits: 'We have to have green runs on the map, even if we don't have so many green slopes – otherwise beginners wouldn't come to Val d'Isère.'

Val d'Isère

Interactive resort shortlist builder at **www.wtss.co.uk**

SCHOOLS

Alpine Expérience
t 0479 062881

BASS
t 0679 512405

Development Centre (TDC)
t 0615 553156

ESF
t 0479 060234

Evolution 2
t 0479 007729

Misty Fly Snocool
t 0479 419577

Mountain Masters
t 0479 060514

New Generation
t 0479 010318
0844 484 3663 (UK)
www.skinewgen.com

Oxygène
t 0479 419958

Progression
t 0621 939380

Ski Concept
t 0479 401919

Ski-lesson.com
t 0615 207108

Snow Fun
t 0479 061979

Top Ski
t 0479 061480

Val Gliss
t 0479 060072

Martin Mckay
t +44 (0)7710 237094

Classes (ESF prices)
6 days (3hr am, 2½hr pm) €391

Private lessons
From €43 for 1hr

GUIDES

Mountain guides
t 0687 528503

Tetra
t 0631 499275

A good place for your first real runs off the nursery slopes is the Madeleine green run on Solaise – served by a six-pack. The Col de l'Iseran runs are also gentle and wide, and not overcrowded. There is good progression terrain on Bellevarde, too – though getting to it can be tricky. From all sectors, it's best to take a lift back down to the valley.

FOR BOARDERS ★★★★
Watch out for flats
Val d'Isère's more upmarket profile attracts a different kind of holiday boarder from Tignes; the resort is, perhaps, seen as Tignes' less hard-core cousin. But the terrain here is great for freeriders. The easier slopes are suitable for beginners, and there are now very few draglifts. But there are quite a few flat areas where you'll end up scooting or walking. Specialist snowboard shops are Misty Fly and Quiksilver Boardriders.

FOR CROSS-COUNTRY ★★★★★
Limited
There are a couple of loops in each of three areas – towards La Daille, on Solaise and out past Le Laisinant. More picturesque is the one going from Le Châtelard (on the road past the main cable car station) to the Manchet chair. But keen cross-country enthusiasts should go elsewhere.

MOUNTAIN RESTAURANTS ★★★★★
Acceptable – but expensive
For such an upmarket resort, there are surprisingly few enjoyable places to eat on the mountain. The major places are self-service and at the top of lifts. But everywhere gets busy and high-season service can be poor. And most places are 'hideously expensive', says a 2011 reporter. Apart from prices, reporters' main gripe is having to pay to use the loos in many mountain restaurants, even if you eat there.

Editors' choice The wood-and-stone Edelweiss (0610 287064), above Le Fornet, is our favourite for the best food and ambience. We've eaten there several times and had delicious lamb, duck and fish; reporters regularly send us rave reviews too ('Echo all you say; duck burger with foie gras is to die for,' says a 2011 visitor). It's a bit cramped inside and if it's a nice day, we much prefer the sunny terrace.

Worth knowing about On Bellevarde, the Fruitière at the top of the La Daille gondola is kitted out with stuff from a dairy. Reporters used to rate it highly but it crams in too many people, and a 2011 reporter thought it 'overrated and not pleasant'. More reports please. The busy table-service Trifollet halfway down the OK run 'always has a good plat du jour'. The Marmottes, near the base of the chair of the same name, is consistently recommended by readers and one of the cheapest places to eat – an efficient self-service with a big sunny terrace, helpful staff and good food ('decent goulash and spag bol without requiring a second mortgage'). And the Tanière (popular with locals) set between the two chairs going up Face de Bellevarde has been recommended.

On Solaise, reader tips include Tête de Solaise self-service at the top of the Solaise chair ('good choice and big portions'). The Datcha at the bottom of the Glacier Express has a small table-service section ('all the dishes were tasty and reasonably priced by Val d'Isère standards'). Bar de L'Ouillette, at the base of the Madeleine chairlift is 'small and friendly' and 'advertises its free loos!'.

Above Le Fornet, the Signal at the top of the cable car has self- and table-service sections and a take-away snack bar – 2011 reporters recommend all three. You'll find us upstairs in the table-service section ('nice atmosphere, sensational food'; 'pricey but not bad value'). The snack bar served 'huge baguettes big enough to share, making a very cheap lunch'.

Of course there are lots of places in the resort villages. Arolay at Le Fornet is 'excellent for both lunch and dinner, with a lovely terrace', and Atelier d'Edmond (decorated like a carpenter's workshop and opposite the Fornet cable car) is 'serious (expensive) dining with impeccable service, good for a treat'. The terrace of hotel Brussel's in Val d'Isère, right by the nursery slopes, has 'good food and excellent service'. The Sun Bar at the base of the Olympique cable car is 'surprisingly good value', as is the Tartine, used by many ski instructors. The Barillon, at the foot of La Daille, is a 'good value' snack bar. In town, 'the Perdrix Blanche set menu is excellent'.

SCHOOLS AND GUIDES ★★★★★
A very wide choice
There is a huge choice of schools, guides and private instructors – just look at the list in the margin on the left. But as they all get busy, at peak periods it's best to book in advance. Practically all the schools run off-piste

groups at various levels of competence, as well as on-piste lessons. A recent visitor had 'a great time' with her off-piste ESF group: 'spoke good English, was safety conscious, found lots of interesting and challenging skiing'.

New Generation, a British-run school, has a branch here. Reports are very positive: 'the morning we had was one of the highlights of our holiday – lots of fun and we learned a lot too'; 'worth every euro; they managed to find fresh powder wherever we went'. Private lessons with BASS (British Alpine Ski & Snowboard School) were 'the best any of us have ever had' and 'gave a real confidence boost to our most nervous skier'. The Development Centre is a group of British instructors who offer intensive clinics for all levels of skier, and have been highly praised.

Mountain Masters is a group of British and French instructors and guides, and a reporter said: 'They knew exactly how to take me over that seventh-week plateau.' Progression is a British-run school with a maximum group size of six or eight: 'great progress in the space of one lesson'.

Val d'Isère

383

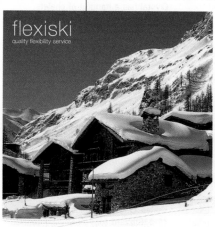

Interactive resort shortlist builder at www.wtss.co.uk

CHILDCARE

Le Village des Enfants
t 0479 400981
Ages 18mnth to 13yr

Le Petit Poucet
t 0479 061397
Ages from 3; 9am-5.30

Babysitter list
Contact tourist office

Ski schools
Most offer classes for ages 5 up (ESF prices €391 for 6 days)

GETTING THERE

Air Geneva 230km/145 miles (3hr30); Lyon 240km/150 miles (3hr15); Chambéry 145km/90 miles (2hr15)

Rail Bourg-St-Maurice (30km/19 miles); regular buses from station

We've heard from satisfied pupils of Snow Fun and Evolution 2. Reporters consistently praise Bernard Chesneau of Ski Mastery. Misty Fly is a specialist snowboard school.

Alpine Expérience and Top Ski specialise in guided off-piste groups – an excellent way to get off-piste safely without the cost of hiring a guide as an individual. We have had great mornings out with both; reporters recommend both too. Heli-skiing trips can be arranged from over the border in Italy – heli-drops are banned in France. Henry's Avalanche Talk at Dick's Tea Bar (every Tuesday last season – see www.henrysavalanchetalk.com for 2011/12) was 'very engaging and interesting', says a reporter.

FOR FAMILIES ★★★★
Good tour op possibilities
Many people prefer to use the facilities of UK tour operators such as family specialist Esprit Ski. But there's a 'children's village' for children from 18 months to 13 years, with supervised indoor and outdoor activities on the village nursery slopes. And Petit Poucet takes children from age three and will pick them up and take them home at any time during the day.

STAYING THERE

More British tour operators go to Val (and Méribel) than anywhere else. Val d'Isère à la Carte specialises in arranging tailor-made holidays there.
Chalets This is Planet Chalet, with properties at every level of the market. Many of the most impressive are in the side valley running south from the village – some in the elevated enclave of Les Carats. YSE is a Val d'Isère specialist, with 21 varied chalets – from swanky apartments for four or six to proper big chalets. Le Ski has nine chalets, including six splendid all-en-

suite places grouped together just up from the main street (with a big outdoor hot tub) and two luxurious chalets for eight nearby (which have huge living room windows and share another outdoor hot tub); all eight have a free pick-up and drop-off service and free WiFi. Skiworld has 10 varied chalets from smart to budget plus a smart chalet hotel with sauna, steam, hot tub. Ski Total has 18 smart places, including three very swanky ones in their Platinum range – one with outdoor hot tub, two with saunas – and a chalet hotel at La Daille. Ski Beat has five units in a grand chalet overlooking the piste at La Daille. Crystal has a handful of chalets, including two smart central ones with saunas in their Finest range. Ski Power has an atmospheric chalet hotel and some smaller chalets. Esprit, the family specialist, has a central chalet hotel. Flexiski has a central six-bedroom chalet, available for three and four nights as well as week-long bookings.
Hotels There are over 30, with increasing numbers at the luxury end: four 5-stars and five 4-stars.
*****Barmes de L'Ours (0479 413700) The best in town. Close to slopes and centre. Rooms are in a different style on each floor. Excellent pool.
*****Christiania (0479 060825) Big chalet. Chic but friendly. Pool, sauna.
*****Blizzard (0479 060207) Central. Comfortable. Indoor-outdoor pool and sauna. Good food and lively bar.
****Aigle des Neiges (0479 061888) Highly rated refurbished version of former Latitudes. Central. Sauna.
****Auberge St Hubert (0479 060645) On main street. Two 2011 reporters praise it – 'very friendly family hotel'.
****Avenue Lodge (0479 065530) Central and new. 'Very modern decor, comfortable rooms,' says a reporter.
****Tsanteleina (0479 061213) On the main road. 'Courteous staff, welcoming

ACTIVITIES

Indoor Sports centre (with pools, climbing wall, fitness, gym, sauna, steam, squash), fitness and health clubs, yoga, cinema, bridge, chess

Outdoor Ice rink, walking, snowshoeing, snowmobiles, ice climbing, dog sledding, ice driving, paragliding, microlight flights, helicopter flights, igloo evenings

UK PACKAGES

Action Outdoors, Alpine Answers, Alpine Elements, Alpine Weekends, Carrier, Chardon Mountain Lodges, Club Med, Crystal, Crystal Finest, Elegant Resorts, Erna Low, Esprit, First Choice, Flexiski, Friendship Travel, Hundred Hills, Independent Ski Links, Inghams, Interactive Resorts, Jeffersons, Lagrange, Le Ski, Luxury Chalet Collection, Mark Warner, Momentum, Mountain Wave, Neilson, Oxford Ski Co, Powder White, Powder White Lite, PowderBeds, PV-Holidays.com, Scott Dunn, Ski Amis, Ski Beat, Ski Club Freshtracks, Ski Collection, Ski Expectations, Ski France, Ski Independence, Ski Line, Ski Power, Ski Solutions, Ski Supreme, Ski Total, Skitracer, Ski-Val, Ski Weekend, Skiweekends.com, Skiworld, Snow Finders, Snoworks, Supertravel, Thomson, Val d'Isère A La Carte, VIP, White Roc, YSE

Phone numbers
From abroad use the prefix +33 and omit the initial '0' of the phone number

TOURIST OFFICE

www.valdisere.com

bar area, but not outstanding food.'
***Kandahar** (0479 060239) Smart, newish building above Taverne d'Alsace on main street.
***Sorbiers** (0479 062377) Modern but cosy chalet, not far out. 'Clean, comfortable, good-sized rooms.'
***Samovar** (0479 061351) In La Daille. Traditional, with good food. 'Very friendly and helpful staff.'
Danival (0479 060065) B&B, piste-side location. 'Very reasonable.'
Galise (0479 060504) Central, family-run B&B. 'Comfortable, quiet.'
Apartments There are thousands of apartments available. Among the best are Chalets du Jardin Alpin at the foot of Solaise and Chalets du Laisinant (at Le Laisinant), and Pierre & Vacances' Balcons de Bellevarde at La Daille and Chalets de Solaise (with outdoor pool) close to the centre. Ski Collection, Ski Amis, Ski Independence, Erna Low and local agency Val d'Isère Agence (0479 067350) have good selections.

EATING OUT ★★★★★
Plenty of good places
The 70-odd restaurants offer a wide variety of cuisines; there's a free Guide des Tables booklet covering some, but many worthwhile places are missing.

At the top end, La Becca at Le Laisinant has a 30-year-old chef from a local family and was awarded a Michelin star in 2011 – we can't wait to try it. The Table de l'Ours, in the Barmes de l'Ours hotel, also has a Michelin star. The Grande Ourse, by the nursery slope, is another place to head for a top-of-the-range meal ('very good food, service, and ambience'). The hotel Aigle des Neiges restaurants are rated highly by locals. Arolay and L'Atelier d'Edmond at Le Fornet are worth making the journey to (see 'Mountain restaurants').

There are plenty of pleasant mid-priced places. We always enjoy the unchanging Taverne d'Alsace. The Barillon de la Rosée Blanche is 'a little gem, astonishing value, great steaks, fab frog's legs'. Bar Jacques is 'small, very welcoming with excellent food and set menu', recommended again in 2011. Casserole and Pré d'Aval have both been recommended for their 'good-value set menus'. Corniche has a 'lovely traditional ambience' and 'good service and range of well-cooked food'. Chez Paolo has 'excellent' pizza and pasta; Casa Scara 'good food'; Canyon 'caters to all

pockets'; but service at these last two has been criticised. The Grand Cocor has 'nice pizza'; 1789 has 'great service, excellent meals and is value for money'.

APRES-SKI ★★★★
Very lively
Nightlife is surprisingly energetic, given that most people have spent a hard day on the slopes. There are lots of bars, many with happy hours and then music and dancing later on.

The Folie Douce, at the top of the La Daille gondola, has become an Austrian-style tea-time rave, with music and dancing on tables; you can ride the gondola down. The Tipi bar on the Glacier run on Solaise is a 'nice place to stop for an afternoon drink – open air with rug-covered loungers'. At La Daille the bar at the Samovar hotel is 'a good spot for a beer after skiing'. In downtown Val, Blue Note (opposite the ESF) 'offers free après-ski nibbles and a warm welcome'. Bananas is a cosy wooden chalet with a nice terrace (but on our last visit was needing a refurb and had filthy toilets). At Café Face the 'early beer prices start at 2 euros and increase hourly'. The Moris pub (live music at tea time and later) and Saloon (under hotel Brussel's) fill up as the slopes close; the 'friendly' Boubou and Bar Jacques are popular with locals. The Pacific Bar has sport on big-screen TVs. The basement Taverne d'Alsace is quiet and relaxing, as are Bar XV, the first-floor bar of the hotel Blizzard and Wine Not (with a 'great choice' of wines by the glass).

Later on, Dick's Tea Bar is the main disco. Doudoune is 'more expensive but nicer'. Graal is 'usually good'.

OFF THE SLOPES ★★
A reasonable amount to do
A new sports centre opened two seasons ago with two pools, sauna, steam, gym, climbing wall and is 'fantastic'; a lift pass for two days or more gets you one free swim. There's an outdoor ice rink and ice driving, and the range of shops is better than in most high French resorts. There are few mountain restaurants easy for pedestrians to get to. A reporter says the nature walk from Le Fornet to Pont St Charles in late season is fascinating.

Ski a high altitude resort with low prices – see p177

Val Thorens

Europe's highest resort, with guaranteed good snow – and other attractions: stylish lodgings and good restaurants among them

RATINGS

The mountains

Extent	★★★★★
Fast lifts	★★★★★
Queues	★★★
Terrain p'ks	★★★★
Snow	★★★★★
Expert	★★★★
Intermediate	★★★★★
Beginner	★★★★
Boarder	★★★★
X-country	★
Restaurants	★★★★
Schools	★★★
Families	★★★

The resort

Charm	★★
Convenience	★★★★★
Scenery	★★★
Eating out	★★★★
Après-ski	★★★★
Off-slope	★★

RPI   100

lift pass	£220
ski hire	£125
lessons	£80
food & drink	£155
total	**£580**

NEWS

2011/12: A new jumbo gondola is planned above the Portette chair, opening up new runs on the front of the mountain and off-piste on the back.

The 4-star hotel Altapura is due to open in December 2011. The resort's first 5-star apartment residence, Montana Plein Sud, is also due to open.

2010/11: Two new green runs were created in the free nursery area, and a red run was added above Plein Sud.

A three-in-one pass was introduced for non-skiers, combining lift pass, six-day use of the leisure centre and a toboggan ride.

+ Extensive slopes for all abilities, locally and in the vast Trois Vallées
+ The highest resort in the Alps, and one of the most snow-sure
+ Compact, with ski-in/out lodgings
+ Convenient, gentle nursery slopes
+ Decent range of hotels for a high, purpose-built resort

– Not a tree in sight
– Away from the 'front de neige', not an attractive place to walk around
– Not ideal for non-skiers
– Some very crowded pistes and dangerous intersections
– Queues for the justifiably popular Cîme de Caron cable car

For the enthusiast looking for the best snow available, it's difficult to beat Val Thorens. For a late trip, in particular, it's the best base in the wonderful Trois Vallées. But we normally prefer a cosier base lower down. That way, if a storm socks in, we can play in the woods; if the sun is scorching, we have the option of setting off for Val Thorens.

There's good news this year: a big new gondola opening up an entirely new bit of the mountain – not something that happens every year.

THE RESORT

Val Thorens is a classic purpose-built resort, high above the treeline at the head of the valley it shares with Les Menuires and St-Martin. Buses to/from Les Menuires are not free for skiers and boarders (some are for walkers).

VILLAGE CHARM ★★
Functional but pleasantly so
Seen from the slopes, the resort is not as ugly as many of its rivals, and it has more of a lively ski-resort buzz than most people expect. The buildings are mainly medium-rise and wood-clad; some are distinctly stylish. But many are designed with their smart 'fronts' facing the slopes, and look very dreary from the streets. And the place lacks a focus. The streets are supposedly traffic-free; most visitors' cars are banished, except on Saturday. Workers' cars still generate a fair amount of traffic, though, and Saturdays can be mayhem. You're advised to book parking in advance.

CONVENIENCE ★★★★★
Ski through the centre
It's a compact village with lots of ski-in/ski-out lodging. At its heart is the snowy Place de Caron, on the slope side rather than the street side of the central buildings, where pedestrians mix with skiers and boarders. Many of the shops and restaurants are clustered here, along with the best hotels; the sports and leisure centres are nearby. The resort is basically divided in two by a little slope (with a moving carpet lift) that leads down from here to the broad main nursery slope running the length of the village. The upper half of the village is centred on the Place de Péclet, where there is one of two shopping malls. A road runs across the hillside from here to the chalet-style Plein Sud area, where many of the most recent apartments have been built. You can ski to and from some of these places, but it's often very tricky and two reporters this year complain of icy, uncleared paths. There is a free but infrequent ski-bus. The main feature of the lower half of the village is the Rue du Soleil winding down from the bus station.

SCENERY ★★★
Panoramas on high
The resort sits on a sunny, west-facing slope. The views are good from the village, fabulous from the high point at Cîme de Caron.

KEY FACTS

Resort	2300m
	7,550ft

Three Valleys

Slopes	1260-3230m
	4,130-10,600ft
Lifts	173
Pistes	600km
	373 miles
Green	16%
Blue	40%
Red	34%
Black	10%
Snowmaking	
	2091 guns

Val Thorens-Orelle only

Slopes	1800-3230m
	5,900-10,600ft
Lifts	31
Pistes	140km
	87 miles
Green	12%
Blue	38%
Red	39%
Black	11%

THE MOUNTAINS

The main disadvantage of Val Thorens is the lack of trees. Heavy snowfalls or high wind can shut practically all the lifts and slopes, and even if they don't close, poor visibility can be a problem. Some blue runs are pretty tough.

EXTENT OF THE SLOPES ★★★★★
High and snow-sure
The resort has a wide piste going right down the front of it, leading down to a number of different lifts. The big **Péclet** gondola heads more or less east from the resort and rises 700m to the Péclet glacier, with a choice of red runs down. One links across to a wide area of runs beneath the ridge directly south of the resort, the high point of which is the **Pointe de Thorens**. Lifts go up to two points on the ridge, to be joined by a third – the resort's fourth jumbo gondola – for 2011/12. You can take red or blue runs into the 'fourth valley', the Maurienne, from

one of the points on the ridge – the Col de Rosaël, served by the Grand Fond jumbo gondola.

Above **Orelle** in the Maurienne valley two successive slow chairs go up to 3230m on the flanks of Pointe du Bouchet – the highest lift-served point in the Three Valleys, with stunning views. The former black run off the back of here is now off-piste due to crevasse and avalanche danger. The way back to Val Thorens via Col de Rosaël has been greatly improved – the fourth valley is now open to blue-run skiers, although a 2011 visitor found it narrow and poorly marked.

The 150-person cable car to **Cîme de Caron** is one of the great lifts of the Alps, rising 900m in no time at all. It can be reached by skiing across from mid-mountain, or via the Caron gondola that starts below the village. From the top there is a choice of red and black pistes down the front, or a black into the Maurienne. Nearby, the relatively low **Boismint** sector is underused, but is actually a very respectable hill with a total vertical of 860m.

Chairlifts heading north from the resort serve sunny slopes above the village and also lead to the link to the Méribel valley. Les Menuires can be reached via these lifts; the alternative Boulevard Cumin along the valley is nearly flat, and can be hard work.

FAST LIFTS ★★★★★
Very few slow ones
Recent investment means the lift system is impressive, with jumbo gondolas and fast chairs in most of the key places. It's quite surprising that none of the chairs has bubbles. Moving carpets have replaced old draglifts on the nursery slopes.

QUEUES ★★★★★
Persistent at the Cîme de Caron
Serious peak-time queues for the Cîme de Caron cable car are just a fact of life. You can plug in your iPod and accept the wait, or get there early to avoid it. We think it's time a ticket system was operated here, so that you could ski while you wait. The chairlifts below the village are prone to queues – the Plein Sud chair (especially in the afternoon) and the Deux Lacs chair further down the slope. A reporter this year also fingers the Moutière chair,

OT VAL THORENS / M BERENGUER

← Val Thorens has successfully avoided the monolithic style used in some rival resorts

Val Thorens

further down still. The Rosaël chair back from the fourth valley is now a six-pack, which seems to have eased the bottleneck there. So the place is not without its problems. And when snow is in short supply elsewhere, the pressure on the Val Thorens lifts can increase markedly.

Crowded pistes, especially around the village, are a bigger problem than queues – compounded by people going too quickly. We have noticed this on recent visits and lots of reporters have commented on it too. We agree with a reporter this year who suggests that it is time the resort imposed slow skiing zones around the village – and policed them. Gendarmes on the slopes may not sound appealing, but the problem is serious.

TERRAIN PARKS ★★★★
Well-designed
The terrain park on the 'Plateau' has been improving year-on-year. It is accessible via various chairlifts, and has a nice open layout. There are four different areas that range from beginner to pro, with all sorts of kickers, rails and box combinations. The hip/corner jump is excellent. The boardercross has some great banked turns, and lots for beginners. A dedicated draglift ensures quick rotations of the park. The whole park is well maintained, and new obstacles are often built for local competitions. The park also has a giant airbag jump, to test your aerials before you put them to proper use on the snow. There is a second boardercross in the 'fourth'

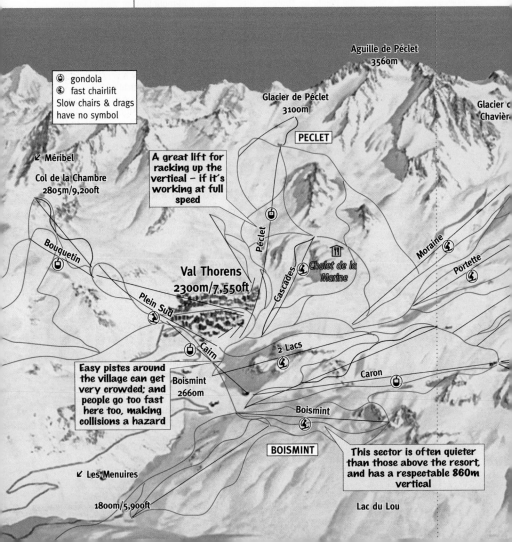

gondola
fast chairlift
Slow chairs & drags
have no symbol

Aguille de Péclet
3560m

Glacier de Péclet
3100m

Glacier de Chavière

PECLET

Méribel
Col de la Chambre
2805m/9,200ft

A great lift for racking up the vertical – if it's working at full speed

Péclet

Bouquetin

Moraine

Portette

Val Thorens
2300m/7,550ft

Cascades

Chalet de la Marine

Plein Sud

Cairn

2 Lacs

Caron

Easy pistes around the village can get very crowded; and people go too fast here too, making collisions a hazard

Boismint
2660m

Boismint

BOISMINT

This sector is often quieter than those above the resort, and has a respectable 860m vertical

Les Menuires

1800m/5,900ft

Lac du Lou

valley. Neighbouring Les Menuires has a good park, at Reberty.

SNOW RELIABILITY ★★★★★
One of the best
Few resorts can rival Val Thorens for reliably good snow-cover, thanks to its altitude and generally north-facing slopes. Snowmaking covers a lot of the key pistes, including the crowded south- and west-facing runs on the way back from the Méribel valley and in the Orelle sector. But the terrain is rocky and needs a lot of snow for good coverage – we have found the higher runs patchy in some early season visits when snow throughout the Alps has been slow to arrive, and at times like that the off-piste terrain is obviously hazardous. The resort

offers a 'snow guarantee' that at least 70% of the area's lifts will be open, with free skiing days on a future visit if this guarantee is not met.

FOR EXPERTS ★★★★
Lots to do off-piste
Val Thorens' local pistes are primarily intermediate terrain; many of the blacks could easily be classified red instead. The fast Cascades chair serves a short but steep black run that quickly gets mogulled. The pistes down from the Cîme de Caron cable car are challenging, but not seriously steep, and there's a good, sunny black run off the back into the fourth valley.

The Falaise and Variante runs from Col de Rosaël can get heavily mogulled and challenging; Chamois

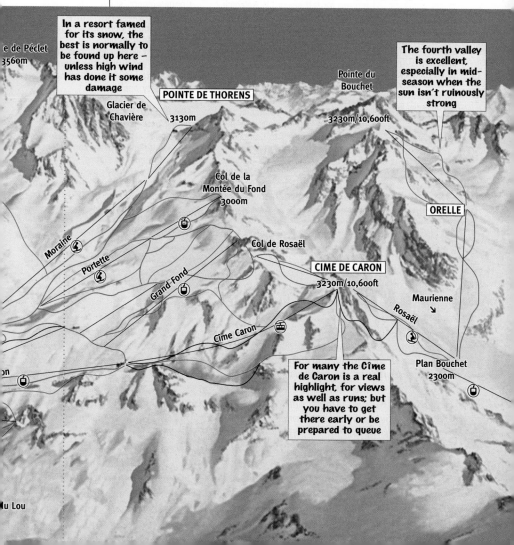

In a resort famed for its snow, the best is normally to be found up here – unless high wind has done it some damage

e de Péclet
3560m

Glacier de Chavière

POINTE DE THORENS
3130m

Col de la Montée du Fond
3000m

Moraine

Portette

Grand Fond

Col de Rosaël

Cîme Caron

Pointe du Bouchet

3230m/10,600ft

ORELLE

CIME DE CARON
3230m/10,600ft

Maurienne

Rosaël

Plan Bouchet
2300m

The fourth valley is excellent, especially in mid-season when the sun isn't ruinously strong

For many the Cîme de Caron is a real highlight, for views as well as runs; but you have to get there early or be prepared to queue

u Lou

LIFT PASSES

Three Valleys

Prices in €

Age	1-day	6-day
under 13	36	177
13 to 64	47	235
over 65	40	200
Free under 5, over 75		
Beginner Nine lifts for 50% of Val Thorens day rate		

Notes Covers Courchevel, La Tania, Méribel, Val Thorens, Les Menuires and St-Martin; family reductions; pedestrian and half-day passes

Alternative pass Val Thorens-Orelle only; Vallée de Belleville only

has been reclassified blue though. The sunny Goitshel run, one of the routes from the Méribel valley, is one of the easiest blacks we've come across, but it can get crowded and be icy in the morning, so the creation of a parallel red run for last season is welcome.

There is a huge amount of very good off-piste terrain to explore with a guide – read our feature panel. But it does require good snowfall – note our remarks on snow, above.

FOR INTERMEDIATES ★★★★★
Great in good weather
The scope for intermediates in the Trois Vallées is enormous. A keen intermediate can get to Courchevel 1650 at the far end in only 90 minutes or so, if not distracted on the way.

The local slopes in Val Thorens are some of the best intermediate terrain in the region. Most of the pistes are

easy reds and blues (the runs on the top half of the mountain are steeper than those back into the resort) and made even more enjoyable by the excellent snow.

The snow on the red Col run is normally some of the best around. The blue Moraine below it is gentle and popular with the schools. The Grand Fond gondola serves a good variety of red runs. The red and blue runs from the Péclet gondola are excellent. The Pluviomètre from the Trois Vallées chair is a glorious varied run, away from the lifts. Adventurous intermediates shouldn't miss the Cîme de Caron runs. The black run is not intimidating – it's very wide, usually has good snow, and is a wonderful fast cruise when freshly groomed (though reports suggest this is less likely than it was). Don't neglect the excellent, quiet Boismint area next door to Caron, either.

Blue-run skiers can now venture to the fourth valley, with the return run improved to become a blue (though not an easy one).

FOR BEGINNERS ★★★★
Good late-season choice
The slopes at the foot of the resort are very gentle and provide convenient, snow-sure nursery slopes, with moving carpet lifts and new green runs. These are free, and there is a cheap pass for three serious lifts on the lower slopes

FABULOUS OFF-PISTE IN VAL THORENS

Val Thorens offers a huge choice of off-piste. And because of the high altitude, the snow stays powdery longer here than in lower parts of the Trois Vallées.

For those with little off-piste experience, the Pierre Lory Pass run is ideal. It is a very large and gentle slope, and you access the pass by doing an easy traverse on the Chavière glacier from the top of the Col chairlift. When you arrive at Pierre Lory Pass there are breathtaking views of the Aiguilles d'Arves in the Maurienne valley, and you will be just above the glacier du Bouchet, which you then ski down, rejoining the lift system at Plan Bouchet.

For those with more off-piste under their belt already, the Lac du Lou is a famous off-piste run of 1400m vertical. It is easily accessible from the Cîme de Caron. The many ways into this long, wide valley allow plenty of variety and opportunities for making first tracks; because many of the slopes face north or north-west it is not unusual to find good powder most of the ski season, even in late April. The views are stunning and you'll notice the quietness and vastness of the whole valley.

La Combe sans Nom in the fourth valley, also accessible from the Cîme de Caron cable car, usually offers superb skiing and snowboard conditions. There's a choice of south-, west- and, on the far side, some east-facing slopes, which makes for excellent spring skiing conditions.

For the more adventurous there are many options, including hiking up from the Col chairlift to a long run over the Gébroulaz glacier down to Méribel-Mottaret.

But don't even think about doing any off-piste runs without a fully qualified guide or instructor. Route finding can be difficult, there can be avalanche danger, and hidden hazards such as cliffs and crevasses lurk.

– an excellent package. There are no
long green runs to progress to, but the
blues immediately above the village
are easy. The resort's height and
bleakness make it cold in midwinter,
and intimidating in bad weather.

FOR BOARDERS ★★★★
Reliable all season
Val Thorens has always been popular
with snowboarders; it is the highest
and most snow-sure of the Three
Valleys resorts, and has a younger feel
in comparison with Courchevel and
Méribel – though it's almost as pricey.
Being far above the treeline, the
slopes are rather bleak; however, there
are great steep runs, gullies and
groomed pistes for all levels. The
terrain park is worth a visit. The lifts
are mainly chairs and gondolas.

FOR CROSS-COUNTRY ★☆☆☆☆
Go to Les Menuires
There are no cross-country trails in Val
Thorens. Your best bet is the 28km
link between Les Menuires and
St-Martin-de-Belleville.

MOUNTAIN RESTAURANTS ★★★★☆
Lots of choice
For a high modern resort, the choice
of restaurants is good, and improving.
The piste map names the restaurants,
unlike those of the other valleys. It's
such a simple thing ...
Editors' choice We've had several good
lunches in the rustic table-service
section of the Chalet de la Marine
(0479 000186), repeatedly endorsed
by readers. It has a big terrace with
'funky' music. The self-service section
below has a wide choice. The Plein
Sud has become an imitation of Val
d'Isère's famous Fruitière/Folie Douce;
interesting menu, well executed when
we had lunch in 2010; much less
atmospheric than the original, but also
much less frenetic. Reports, please.
Worth knowing about The Marine has
a clear challenger among reader
reports. The Chalet des 2 Ours is
repeatedly recommended for food
('great homemade pasta'), service and
views. The rustic Chalet des 2 Lacs is
also a reader favourite, but a regular
visitor found service slack this year.

SCHOOLS AND GUIDES ★★★☆☆
Good reports
Prosneige is a small school that limits
class sizes to 10, and gets good
reports. A 2010 reporter's son made

'great progress; friendly, patient
instructors with a good understanding
of individual needs'. The ESF offers a
wide choice of private and group
classes, including freestyle and
freeride courses. Recent reports are
positive; 'highly recommended', says a
reporter of her off-piste group. Ski
Cool class sizes are also guaranteed
not to exceed 10. There are several
guiding outfits.

FOR FAMILIES ★★★☆☆
Coolly efficient
There is a children's area, Espace
Junior, beside the 2 Lacs chairlift and a
good family toboggan run. The tourist
office produces a handy family guide
to weekly activities. The Prosneige
school takes children from age five,
and recent reporters have been 'very
happy' with the standard of instruction
and care provided. We lack reports on
the ESF nursery.

STAYING THERE

Accommodation is of a higher
standard than in many purpose-built
resorts – more comfortable as well as
more stylish.
Chalets Most of the properties
operated as catered chalets are
apartments in quite big developments,
mainly the relatively new ones above
the resort centre. This has the
advantage that you often have the use
of a pool in the residence. There are
no notably swanky places.
  Skiworld has 15 units, quite a few
new for this season. The best have
quite grand, high-ceilinged living
rooms. Crystal has seven units and
Inghams five.
  Ski Total has five newish units that
are more like actual chalets – two
units in one chalet, three units in the
other; both have shared saunas. And it
has added a standalone chalet to the
programme this year with use of the
pool at the nearby Chalet des Neiges
residence.
Hotels Unusually for a high, purpose-
built resort, there are plenty of hotels,
and there's a Club Med, too. A new
4-star, the Altapura, is due to open in
December 2011, with indoor/outdoor
pool etc.
★★★★Fitz Roy (0479 000478) The sole
4-star is smart, with good service and
lovely rooms. Good restaurant with
flexible half-board menu. Pool. Well
placed at the heart of things.

UK PACKAGES

Action Outdoors, Alpine Answers, Alpine Elements, Club Med, Crystal, Crystal Finest, Erna Low, First Choice, Flexiski, Independent Ski Links, Inghams, Interactive Resorts, Lagrange, Neilson, Powder White, Powder White Lite, PowderBeds, PV-Holidays.com, Ski Amis, Ski Club Freshtracks, Ski Collection, Ski Expectations, Ski France, Ski Independence, Ski Line, Ski Solutions, Ski Supreme, Ski Total, Ski Weekend, Skitracer, Skiworld, Thomson **Orelle** Peak Retreats, Zenith

ACTIVITIES

Indoor Sports centre (spa, sauna, fitness room, hot tub, tennis, squash, swimming pool, volleyball, table tennis, badminton, football), cinema, bowling, concerts

Outdoor Paragliding, sightseeing microlight flights, snowmobiles, snowshoeing, walks, tobogganing, ice driving, paintball

Phone numbers
From abroad use the prefix +33 and omit the initial '0' of the phone number

TOURIST OFFICE
www.valthorens.com

***Val Thorens** (0479 000433) Next door to Fitz Roy.
***Sherpa** (0479 000070) Highly recommended by past reporters. Ski-in/ski-out, but a hike from the centre.
***Val Chavière** (0479 000033) 'Friendly, fab position, good set menu,' says a 2011 reporter.
Apartments Val Thorens now has lots of smart chalet-style developments. These and many other residences are offered by UK operators and agents including Ski Amis, Erna Low, Pierre & Vacances, Lagrange and Ski Collection.

In the Plein Sud area, above the main village, are several chalet-style residences; some have a pool. Among the best are Chalet Altitude and Chalet Val 2400, sharing a pool. The Balcons de Val Thorens gained a new spa with pool last season. Many properties up here claim to be ski-in and possibly ski-out, but a couple of reporters have confirmed our own suspicion that access can be tricky in practice.

There are three Montagnettes residences, of which the clear leader is the hotel-style Oxalys, with pool, hot tubs, separate spa for those in the best apartments and a superb restaurant (read 'Eating out'); some of the units here are very impressive.

Opening for 2011/12 is the Montana Plein Sud residence, claiming the newly invented 5-star status.

EATING OUT ★★★★☆
Star quality
Val Thorens has something for most tastes and pockets. The resort's excellent 'Practical Booklet' includes a very helpful guide, with photos and some idea of the cuisine.

Top of the range is the restaurant in the residence Oxalys, with two Michelin stars. We had a delicious and very inventive meal here; expensive, but worth it. The Fitz Roy and Val Thorens hotels also have serious restaurants. The Epicurien has gastro ambitions, too.

There are plenty of more modest places. The Galoubet was one reader's 'restaurant of the year' for choice, quality and service. For Savoyard stuff there's the Fondue ('friendly, intimate'), Auberge des Balcons ('nice food, attentive staff'), Chaumière ('good value, rustic') and the 'friendly' Cabane. The Vieux Chalet has a varied menu, including seafood and duck. The Blanchot is a stylish wine bar with a simple but varied carte.

APRES-SKI ★★★★☆
Livelier than you might expect
Val Thorens is more lively than most high-altitude ski-stations. The action now starts up the hill at the Folie Douce or on the terrace of Club Med in the village. The Red Fox up at Balcons is crowded at close of play, with karaoke. The Frog and Roastbeef at the top of the village claims to be the highest pub in Europe and is a cheerful British ghetto – 'great burgers too'. The Saloon is lively and the Downunder bar is new (formerly the Viking). Quieter bars include the cosy Rhum Box Cafe (aka Mitch's). Later on, the Malaysia cellar bar rocks from 11pm until the early hours with 'top quality' live bands and dancing.

OFF THE SLOPES ★★☆☆☆
Could be worse
Val Thorens is not ideal for non-skiers. But there's a sports centre with small pool, saunas, hot tubs, gym etc and a leisure centre with bowling lanes (pricey) and pool tables. Free weekly concerts are held in the church (highly recommended by a reporter), there's a small cinema, twice-weekly street markets, and an ice-driving course. The toboggan run (longest in France) is 'great fun' for all ages. You can get to some mountain restaurants, and the panorama from the Cîme de Caron is not to be missed. Buses to Les Menuires / St-Martin are free on Wednesdays, for access to the market. The Monday night welcome festivities are well done.

OUTLYING RESORT – 900m
ORELLE

Ski off-piste beyond the runs of the fourth valley, and you end up at Orelle, at the bottom of the gondola. Orelle isn't a recognisable resort, but offers good accommodation at a bargain price. A couple of hairpins up the hill from the lift base (there's a frequent ski-bus) is Hameau des Eaux, a smart complex of 200 apartments in eight chalet-style buildings, sharing a spa with decent pool – available through Peak Retreats and Zenith. It includes a small convenience store and a restaurant. The small town of St-Michel is 6km away.

Ski a high altitude resort with low prices – see p177

Vars / Risoul

Two high, purpose-built resorts in an attractive setting, with a traditional French atmosphere and a big linked area of slopes

TOP 10 RATINGS

Extent	★★★
Fast lifts	★
Queues	★★★★
Snow	★★★
Expert	★★
Intermediate	★★★★
Beginner	★★★★
Charm	★★
Convenience	★★★★
Scenery	★★★

RPI   80

lift pass	£160
ski hire	£95
lessons	£85
food & drink	£120
total	**£460**

NEWS

2011/12: In Risoul, the slow Razis chair (which accesses the Vars sector) is due to become a fast quad.

2010/11: In Risoul, a new two-person roller-coaster track opened.

➕ Attractive, family-friendly resorts

➕ Fair-sized, uncrowded area of slopes

➕ High resorts, reasonably snow-sure, but with lots of treelined runs

➕ Among the cheapest resorts in the French Alps

➖ Still mainly draglifts and slow old chairs, though a few fast ones

➖ Few on-piste challenges for expert skiers and boarders

➖ Little to do off the slopes

➖ Fairly remote location

Were they nearer Geneva, Vars and its linked neighbour Risoul might be as well known as Les Arcs and Flaine. The slopes of their shared Forêt Blanche area are equally extensive, and the villages are more attractive than either. We visited last season and loved it, despite the seriously flawed lift system, which is probably the most antiquated in these pages. All a question of priorities ...

THE RESORT

Vars and its linked neighbour Risoul are the most southerly French resorts to get a chapter in this book. Airport transfers can take some time.

Vars includes several small, old villages on or near the approach road, chief among them Vars-Ste-Marie. There are lifts on the fringe of this village, but the focus for most visitors is higher, purpose-built Vars-les-Claux. **Village charm** Vars-les-Claux has a lot of flat-roofed apartment blocks, which look worse from up the mountain than in the village, when it feels much nicer and you can see the smaller chalet-style buildings as well. Reporters like its pleasant, relaxed atmosphere. **Convenience** It's a small place, but spread along a winding, quite steep road, with two main clusters of shops, bars, restaurants and lodgings – the

original focus is at the base of the main gondola; Point Show is 10 minutes' walk up the hill. Each has nursery slopes and fast lifts into the slopes. Buildings spread beyond these points, varying in convenience. **Scenery** Pretty wooded slopes surround the village, and Pic de Chabrières has fine views.

THE MOUNTAINS

There are slopes on both sides of the village, linked by pistes and by chair at the lower end of Vars-les-Claux.

Some reporters have found piste classification variable, and the map unclear on the links between resorts. **Slopes** The wooded, west-facing Peynier area is the smaller sector, and reaches only 2275m. The main slopes are in an east-facing bowl with links to the Risoul slopes at three points. There's also a speed-skiing course.

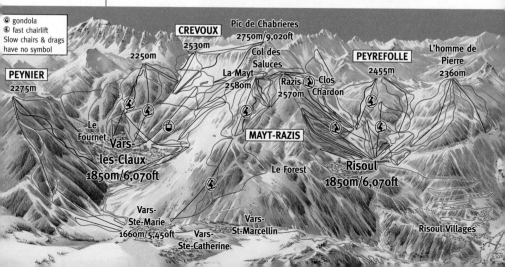

Key:
- ⊙ gondola
- ❹ fast chairlift
- Slow chairs & drags have no symbol

PEYNIER
2275m

CREVOUX
2530m

Pic de Chabrieres
2750m/9,020ft

Col des Saluces

La Mayt
2580m

Razis
2570m

Clos Chardon

PEYREFOLLE
2455m

L'homme de Pierre
2360m

Le Fournet

Vars-les-Claux
1850m/6,070ft

MAYT-RAZIS

Le Forest

Risoul
1850m/6,070ft

Vars-Ste-Marie
1660m/5,450ft

Vars-Ste-Catherine

Vars-St-Marcellin

Risoul-Villages

KEY FACTS

| Resort | 1850m |
| | 6,070ft |

The entire Forêt Blanche ski area

Slopes	1660-2750m	
	5,450-9,020ft	
Lifts	51	
Pistes	185km	
	115 miles	
Green	17%	
Blue	42%	
Red	32%	
Black	9%	
Snowmaking		
	116 guns	

OT RISOUL

Risoul's buildings are very attractively wood-clad ↓

Beneath it are easy runs, open at the top but dropping into trees.

Fast lifts After the three fast lifts out of the village it's draglifts and slow chairs unless you head down to Vars-Ste-Marie or over to Risoul.

Queues Queues are rare outside the French holidays, and even then Vars is not as busy as most family resorts.

Terrain parks Last season, there were five freestyle areas.

Snow reliability Not bad: the altitudes are quite high, the orientation mostly easterly; and snowmaking is plentiful.

Experts There is little to challenge experts, on-piste, but there is plenty of off-piste terrain (and great off-piste tree skiing in Risoul too).

Intermediates Fine intermediate slopes, with a good mix of decent reds

and easy blues. Jas du Boeuf from La Mayt is a gentle cruise. The Olympique red run from the top of La Mayt to Ste-Marie delights most reporters and is a very respectable 920m vertical. If you can face the slow chairlifts and tricky drags, there are good treelined runs in the separate Peynier sector.

Beginners There are three free lifts on good slopes in central Vars, with lots of progression runs throughout the area. Quick learners will be able to get over to Risoul by the end of the week.

Snowboarding There is good freeriding but beginners might find the number of draglifts a problem.

Cross-country There are 35km of cross-country trails in the whole domain.

Mountain restaurants We lack reports but most places are self-service.

Schools and guides A 2010 reporter had 'great' private lessons with ESF.

Families The ski school runs a nursery for children from two years old and there is a ski kindergarten.

STAYING THERE

Hotels The Ecureuil (0492 465072) is an attractive, modern B&B chalet. Ste-Marie has a Logis de France – the Vallon (0492 465472).

Apartments Ski Collection features four apartment complexes, including the 4-star Hameau des Rennes. P&V has a couple of places – the Albane was liked by a reporter and has a pool.

Eating out There is a choice of simple, good-value places. The Après Ski at Point Show is worth a look, as is the Chaudron in Ste-Marie.

Après-ski Après-ski is animated at tea time. Later on, nightlife revolves around one or two bars.

Off the slopes There's tobogganing, ice skating, 35km of walking paths, a cinema, leisure centre, snowmobiling, snowshoeing and dog sledding.

Risoul 1850m

+ Uncrowded slopes
+ Some good off-piste terrain

- Still lots of difficult draglifts
- Limited mountain restaurants

Risoul 1850 is a modern ski station, purpose-built from the late 1970s onwards at the top of a winding road up from the original village of Risoul.

It is a quiet, apartment-based resort, popular with families – but not exclusively so.

Village charm Many of the original resort buildings are bulky eight- or nine-storey buildings, but wood-clad with some traditional style. Newer developments are attractive and chalet-style, made of wood and stone. The busy little main street, with a small range of shops, bars and restaurants, is far from traffic-free. But the locals offer a friendly and welcoming atmosphere.

Convenience The village meets the mountain in classic French purpose-built style, with sunny restaurant terraces facing the slopes and a compact centre. But some lodgings are a short but 'knackering' uphill walk away, if you miss the last lift.

Scenery Risoul has a pleasantly woody setting beneath its slopes; reporters often comment on great views.

THE MOUNTAINS

The upper slopes are open, but those back to Risoul are prettily wooded, and good for bad-weather days.

Slopes The slopes, mainly north-facing, spread over several minor peaks and bowls, and connect with neighbouring Vars at two points.

Fast lifts There are four fast chairs accessing a good number of runs, but still lots of tricky 'difficile' draglifts.

Queues Queues are rare and the slopes generally uncrowded. In January you get pistes to yourself at times.

Terrain parks There's a decent park with jumps and rail lines, air bag, big air and boardercross ('good fun'). There are also two half-pipes.

Snow reliability Snow reliability is reasonably good; the slopes are all above 1850m and mostly north-facing. Snowmaking is fairly extensive.

Experts Risoul's main top stations access a couple of steepish descents. And there's some good off-piste terrain – including excellent widely spaced tree skiing on not very steep slopes and areas accessed through gates that are closed when there's an avalanche risk (though these are not marked or explained on the piste map).

Intermediates There are decent reds and blues in all sectors. Almost all Risoul's runs return to the village, making it difficult to get lost.

Beginners Three free lifts serve good, convenient, nursery slopes. There are lots of easy pistes to move on to.

Snowboarding There is a lot of good freeriding to be done throughout the area, although beginners might not like the large proportion of draglifts.

Cross-country There are 35km of cross-country trails in the whole domain. A trail through the Peyrol forest links the two resorts together.

Mountain restaurants Choice is limited. But the self-service Tetras is a small, attractive hut, with 'good food, friendly staff', says a visitor who went there every day of his trip.

Schools and guides Reports on the ESF have been positive and we had an excellent ESF guide on our visit.

Families Risoul is very much a family resort. Both ski schools operate ski kindergartens, slightly above the village, reached by a child-friendly lift.

STAYING THERE

Most visitors stay in apartments.

Hotels The Chardon Bleu (0492 460727) is right on the slopes. You can also stay overnight up at the Tetras mountain refuge (0492 460983).

Apartments We enjoyed the 4* Balcons de Sirius units with a good pool and sauna; Antarés is similar. Ski Collection has these and another property.

Eating out There's a decent choice offering fairly good value. Readers tips: Chérine (pizza, pasta), Marmite ('superb steaks and friendly staff') and Entre Pot ('very friendly, fantastic food'). We tried L'Extrad, which served huge portions (enough for two) of hearty mountain food.

Après-ski Nightlife is livelier than most people expect. There are several bars and two clubs. Try the Caribbean-themed Babao and the Chalet or Eterlou for a quieter drink.

Off the slopes Limited. We enjoyed the guided night-time snowmobiling on adventurous and varied terrain. There's also tobogganing and skating. Excursions to Briançon are possible.

Phone numbers
From abroad use the prefix +33 and omit the initial '0' of the phone number

TOURIST OFFICES

Vars
www.vars-ski.com

Risoul
www.risoul.com

Germany

Germany isn't a big destination for UK-based skiers. Over the page is a chapter on Garmisch-Partenkirchen, by far the most important downhill resort in Germany – famously the venue for the 1936 Olympics (when downhill racing was introduced, and Adolf Hitler got the facilities built on time). 75 years later it hosted the 2011 World Championships. On this page, a non-comprehensive tour of the country's main skiing regions.

THE ALPS

Allgäu This region claims 300km of downhill runs and an amazing 800km of cross-country trails. The main lift systems operate under the regional name Das Hoechste. Highest of all is Nebelhorn (2225m) reached from the nice little town of **Oberstdorf** by a two-stage cable car to the main slopes (served by two chairs), with a third stage to the top for Germany's longest piste (7.5km). Oberstdorf is probably best known as the resort which racks off the annual Four Hills ski jumping tournament held over each New Year period. The Post hotel has been praised for 'good, substantial, reasonably-priced' meals. South of Oberstdorf you enter **Kleinwalsertal**, which belongs to Austria, strangely. The Kanzelwand slopes link with Fellhorn to form Germany's 'biggest and most modern' area, with three six-packs, two gondolas and nine other lifts. Walmendingerhorn, a little further up the valley, and Ifen are smaller areas and the Allgäu has lots of other resorts such as Oberjoch and Pfronten.
Bavarian Alps Garmisch-Partenkirchen is covered over the page. **Mittenwald** (915m) is a cute town in a spectacular setting. The cable car to Karwendel accesses an epic ski route dropping 1300m in 6km. Across the valley seven lifts serve modest slopes up to 1350m.

The other resorts are on the fringes of the Alps, with less dramatic scenery. **Oberammergau** (835m and famous for its once-a-decade Passion Play) is another cute town, with a gondola to Laber (1685m) that accesses a long ski route and a direct black piste; across town a chairlift serves Kolbensattel (1270m). There are more extensive slopes on Brauneck above **Lenggries** (680m) – 34km of pistes with a top height of 1710m, and 18 lifts including a gondola.

There are other small resorts, some near the infamous Berchtesgaden.

THE REST

Black Forest In the south-west corner: a lot of cross-country, but downhill too. Feldberg reaches 1500m with 31 lifts and 55km of pistes.
Harz A low mountain range, south of Hanover. A handful of small resorts, the biggest being Braunlage.
Sauerland Low mountains east of Düsseldorf. Some 300km of cross-country. Winterberg has 21 lifts, Willingen a gondola and 11 drags.
Saxony On the border with the Czech Republic: a handful of low, small resorts, the most compelling at Fichtelberg above Oberwiesenthal.
Thüringer Wald North-east of Frankfurt: extensive cross-country, and a bit of easy downhill. The best-known resort is Oberhof.

GARMISCH-PARTENKIRCHEN

← It can't be often there's this much snow in downtown Garmisch; but good snow is pretty much guaranteed on the Zugspitze in the distance

WEBSITES

Allgäu
www.english.allgaeu.info
www.das-hoechste.de
Bavarian Alps
www.karwendelbahn.de
www.laber-bergbahn.de
www.brauneck-bergbahn.de
Black Forest
www.blackforest-tourism.com
Harz
www.harzinfo.de
Sauerland
www.wintersport-arena.de
Saxony
www.oberwiesenthal.com
www.fichtelberg-ski.de
Thüringer Wald
www.oberhof.de

397

Garmisch-Partenkirchen

Twin resort towns sprawling at the foot of Germany's highest mountain, reaching glacial heights on the Austrian border

TOP 10 RATINGS

Extent	★
Fast lifts	★★
Queues	★★★
Snow	★★★
Expert	★★★★
Intermediate	★★★
Beginner	★
Charm	★★★
Convenience	★★
Scenery	★★★★

RPI   80

lift pass	£180
ski hire	£100
lessons	£75
food & drink	£105
total	£460

KEY FACTS

Resort	710m
	2,330ft
Slopes	720-2720m
	2,360-8,920ft
Lifts	30
Pistes	48km
	30 miles
Blue	16%
Red	71%
Black	13%
Snowmaking	47%

- **+** Weather-proof combo of fair-sized glacier and woods lower down
- **+** Some spectacular views
- **+** Some excellent, challenging runs
- **+** Good-value hotels, cheap for eating and drinking, good for short breaks

- **–** Except on glacier, very few long easy runs – beginners and timid intermediates beware
- **–** Many of the best runs descend to low altitude, where conditions are rarely good
- **–** Glacier access takes time

Garmisch is Germany's leading ski resort. It has two separate ski areas: one at low altitude with mainly tough runs, the other on a glacier with gentler terrain. It has plenty to amuse confident skiers for a couple of days, and with short transfers from Munich it makes a good short-break destination.

THE RESORT

Garmisch and Partenkirchen are separate towns that have merged as they have spread to fill the broad, flat valley bottom beneath the Zugspitze, while keeping their centres distinct.

There are smaller resorts on the Austrian side of the Zugspitze (see our chapter on Zugspitz Arena in the Austria section). These and the Garmisch ski areas are covered by the Top Snow Card.

Village charm Each half of the resort is a sizeable town – spacious and pleasant but not notably captivating.

Convenience You'll need to use trains, buses or cars at both ends of the day. The Zugspitze railway starts next to the main station, more or less between the two town centres; it goes to the glacier via the other lift bases.

Scenery The Wetterstein massif, of which the Zugspitze is the peak, is impressive, and there are great panoramic views from the top – plus some dramatic scenery lower down.

THE MOUNTAINS

The glacier is quite separate from the lower slopes, which the resort calls the 'Classic' area. In fact, that area also divides into two parts, awkwardly linked – a higher, almost treeless part (Alpspitz) and a lower, heavily wooded part (Hausberg-Kreuzeck). Piste marking is slack.

Slopes The **Hausberg-Kreuzeck** sector directly above the resort is accessed by two gondolas; these start a few km out of town and are served by the railway. These lower lifts have decent verticals and serve long runs; the lifts higher up are all much shorter. An inconspicuous narrow path and a rope tow form the link between this sector and the base of the higher **Alpspitz** sector, more directly reached via the Alpspitz cable car. Although the altitude is modest, this sector feels like high-mountain terrain, with dramatic scenery – Dolomite-like on the isolated Osterfelder and Bernadein runs, on skier's right.

There are two routes to the glacier: the railway from town that serves the 'Classic' area lift bases continues and tunnels slowly through the mountain, emerging in the middle of the glacier; or the cable car from Eibsee that climbs 1950m to the Zugspitze – from there you have to ride another cable car down to the slopes. Although the Zugspitze is not notably high (2960m), its isolated position gives great views.

Above the main lift junction are typical blue glacier slopes served by multiple drags. Below it and spreading across the bowl is a range of good red runs and some good off-piste terrain served by three drags and one six-seater chairlift. None of these lifts rises more than 350m vertical, but in other respects it's a good area.

Fast lifts Access lifts are fast, but after that it's mainly drags and slow chairs. On the glacier drags also dominate.

Queues Fine weekends attract crowds from Munich; but at other times we don't expect problems.

Terrain parks On the glacier there is a 700m-long park with expert and novice lines, with kickers, boxes and rails in each.

Snow reliability The glacier area is small and remote, so conditions lower

Zugspitze 2960m/9,710ft

ZUGSPITZPLATT 2720m/8,920ft

ALPSPITZ

Osterfelderkopf 2050m

Ehrwald ↓

Eibsee

1720m

HAUSBERG-KREUZECK

Kandahar

Kreuzeck 1650m

Alpspitzbahn

Hausberg 1310m

Kreuzeckbahn

Grainau 750m

Hausbergbahn

gondola
cable car
railway/funicular
fast chairlift
Slow chairs & drags
have no symbol

Garmisch-Partenkirchen
710m/2,330ft

Wank 1780m

down are important. The lower main area is shady, but some of the best runs descend to valley level – ie to 720m. Despite comprehensive snowmaking, conditions at these altitudes can be poor even when there's great snow higher up, as we confirmed one January visit.

Experts The long runs to the valley are challenging enough to amuse most experts, particularly the excellent Kandahar downhill race course. The final pitch of this takes real bottle when icy at the end of the day. Higher up, there are off-piste opportunities in the Alpspitz sector and on the glacier.

Intermediates For confident skiers it's fine, but this is not a hill where timid intermediates can build confidence.

Beginners Learn elsewhere. The nursery slopes are fine but up the mountain and there is no beginner pass. And the only easy runs to move on to are busy links between Kreuzeck and Hausberg (or on the glacier).

Snowboarding There are drags in all sectors, though many can be avoided. Getting up to the park on the glacier involves a drag.

Cross-country There are several trails along the valleys, of varying difficulty.

Mountain restaurants The glass-sided Gletschergarten (glacier), has a roof that opens on sunny days and offers 'consistently excellent' Punjabi-Arabic-Mediterranean fusion dishes. The Hochalm below Alpspitz does good value chilli and pasta. The Bayernhaus is worth a stop on the gentle blue run 6 from Hausberg ('good cakes').

Schools and guides We lack reports.

Families The Kinderland centre at Hausberg looks good, with magic carpet and snow sculptures.

STAYING THERE

Hotels There is one 5-star – Reindl's Partenkirchner Hof (943870), well placed for the rail stations – and lots of 4-stars and 3-stars. Tips are the 3-star Garmischer Hof (9110) and Atlas Post (7090), and the 4-star Zugspitze (9010). Rates are low in Alpine terms.

Apartments Can be booked via the tourist office.

Eating out Plenty of choice. Gasthof Fraundorfer ('awesome') and the upscale Alpenhof do hearty Bavarian food. Spago's Italian is 'superb'.

Après-ski There are bars at the lift bases where you can enjoy waiting for the next train home, and in town there are lots of cosy bars such as Zirbel Stube. Peaches is a lively bar.

Off the slopes There's lots to do, both outdoors and indoors. Walks include one through the Partnachklamm gorge – 'very easy and spectacular' – and paths on the lift-served hill across town from the slopes, called Wank.

Interactive resort shortlist builder at www.wtss.co.uk

Italy

Italy has a lot going for it as a destination: it offers great value for money (over half the Italian resorts fall into our green category – the cheapest – for their RPI); the atmosphere is jolly; it has good (and affordable) food and wine; the scenery, especially in the Dolomites and Courmayeur, is simply stunning; the lift systems include some of the most modern in Europe; the snowmaking is state-of-the-art (and they use it well); the grooming is top-notch; and most of the slopes are ideal for intermediates.

Italian resorts vary as widely in their characteristics as they do in location – and they are spread along the full length of the Italian border, from Sauze d'Oulx to the Dolomites.

A lot of Italian runs seem flatteringly easy. This is partly because grooming is immaculate and partly because piste classification seems to overstate difficulty. Nowhere is this clearer than in the linked slopes of La Thuile (in Italy) and La Rosière (in France), where you move from Italian motorways to French moguls.

Many Italians based in the cities ski at weekends, and it's very noticeable that many resorts are busy only then, and become peaceful once the weekend invaders retreat. It's a great advantage for those of us who are there for the whole week. This pattern is especially noticeable at the chic resorts, such as Cortina, Courmayeur and Madonna, and resorts that have not yet found international fame such as those in the Monterosa region. On the other hand, it doesn't really happen in parts of the Dolomites favoured by German visitors – like Brits, they tend to go for a week.

In general, Italians don't take their skiing or boarding too seriously. A late start, long lunch and early finish are the norm – leaving the slopes delightfully quiet for the rest of us. Mountain restaurants are reasonably priced, and there are welcoming places almost everywhere, encouraging leisurely lunching. Our reporters' standard complaint about the primitive hole-in-the-ground loos in mountain restaurants (and sometimes in resorts, too) is becoming less common. A persistent drag, though, is the ludicrous system in many self-service places where you have to queue to pay and then queue again to acquire your food or drink.

One thing that Italian resorts do have to contend with is erratic snowfall. While the snow in the northern Alps tends to come from the west, Italy's snow tends to come from storms arriving from the south. So it can have great conditions when other countries are suffering; or vice versa. Italian resorts have extensive snowmaking, and our observation is that they tend to use it more effectively than other Alpine countries. We have skied in Courmayeur and in the Dolomites when little natural snow has fallen, and in each case there has been excellent cruising on man-made snow.

Italy seems to have been in the grip of 'legislation fever' for the last few years, with mixed results. Italian bars and restaurants are now smoke-free, a huge improvement. And it is now compulsory for children (under 14, we understand) to wear helmets on the slopes. But many areas have also made it illegal to go off-piste near their pistes, or to go off-piste at all, or to go off-piste outside defined

VAL GARDENA MARKETING

← The scenery surrounding many Italian resorts is stunning; this is the attractive little town of Ortisei near Selva in the Dolomites

routes or without a guide or without transceiver, shovel and probe. We've tried to get to the bottom of these developments; but a prompt, clear, accurate response to a slightly technical question such as this is not a speciality of Italian tourist bodies. Some resorts tell us there are national laws; others, that it's a regional matter; others, that it's a local matter. Of course, there is then the matter of whether the law is applied and how it is policed. Where we have a clear view of the situation in a given resort, we've included that in the relevant chapter. We'll continue to investigate, and post the results on our website. Thankfully, we have no evidence of any interference in off-piste skiing in the Aosta valley, which is Italy's off-piste/heli-skiing HQ.

DRIVING IN THE ITALIAN ALPS

There are four main geographical groupings of Italian resorts, widely separated. Getting to some of these resorts is a very long haul, and moving from one area to another can involve very long drives (though the extensive motorway network is a great help).

The handful of resorts to the west of Turin – Bardonecchia, Sauze d'Oulx, Sestriere and neighbours in the Milky Way region – are easily reached from France via the Fréjus tunnel, or via the good road over the pass that the resort of Montgenèvre sits on.

Further north, and somewhat nearer to Turin than Milan, are the resorts of the Aosta valley – Courmayeur, Cervinia, La Thuile and the Monterosa area are the best known. These (especially Courmayeur) are the easiest of all Italian resorts to reach from

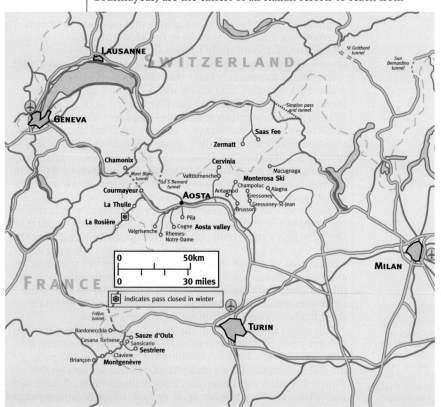

Britain or from Geneva airport (via the Mont Blanc tunnel from Chamonix in France). The Aosta valley can also be reached from Switzerland via the Grand St Bernard tunnel. The approach is high and may require chains. The road down the Aosta valley is a major thoroughfare, but the roads up to some of the other resorts are quite long, winding and (in the case of Cervinia) high.

To the east is a string of scattered resorts, most close to the Swiss border, many in isolated and remote valleys involving long drives up from the nearest Italian cities, or high-altitude drives from Switzerland. The links between Switzerland and Italy are more clearly shown on our larger-scale Switzerland map at the beginning of that section of the book than on the map of the Italian Alps included below. The major routes are the St Gotthard tunnel between Göschenen (near Andermatt) and Airolo – the main route between Basel and Milan – and the San Bernardino tunnel reached via Chur.

Finally, further east still are the resorts of the Dolomites. Getting there from Austria is easy, over the Brenner motorway pass from Innsbruck. But getting there from Britain is a very long drive indeed – allow at least a day and a half. We wouldn't lightly choose to drive there and back for a week's skiing, except as part of a longer tour including some Austrian resorts. It's also worth bearing in mind that once you arrive in the Dolomites, getting around the intricate network of valleys linked by narrow, winding roads can be a slow business – it's often quicker to get from village to village on skis. Impatient Italian driving can make it a bit stressful, too.

Interactive resort shortlist builder at www.wtss.co.uk

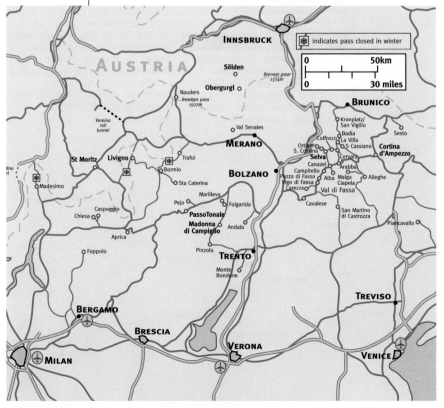

Aosta valley

The Aosta valley can reasonably claim to contain the best skiing that Italy has to offer – it certainly includes the highest

Aosta is a mid-sized city that is the capital of an autonomous (ie largely independent) region north of Turin called Valle d'Aosta. The valley has high mountains on both sides, and comes to an abrupt stop at Monte Bianco. Courmayeur – the resort at the foot of Europe's highest mountain – is well known in the UK, as is Cervinia, up a long side valley on the Swiss border (and linked to Zermatt). These two get their own chapters, as do less well known La Thuile, linked across the French border to La Rosière, and Monterosa Ski. But the valley has many more resorts worth knowing about.

It's perhaps not surprising that the valley has managed to retain a degree of independence. It shares a long border with France, and French was the dominant language for centuries until Italian was imposed in the Fascist period in the early 20th century. The region was even French territory for a time. Almost all place names and local surnames are French in origin. These days, street signs are bilingual.

A Valle d'Aosta lift pass is available covering all the resorts in the region; a useful starting point is the related website www.skivallee.it.

MAJOR RESORTS

We devote separate chapters in the book to three individual resorts.

Courmayeur is one of the Italian resorts best known in Britain – a charming, lively old village with a big cable car into a small but quite interesting ski area with some great off-piste runs outside it – and access to the famous Vallée Blanche glacier.

Not far down the valley, a road branches off south-west for the Petit St Bernard pass leading to Bourg St Maurice, in France. In winter the road is closed – and in fact becomes a piste leading down to the small resort of **La Thuile**. Its lifts and pistes link with those of La Rosière, in France.

Much further down the valley, beyond Aosta, a long side valley leads northwards towards the Swiss border, and climbs through Valtournenche to the valley's other well-known resort, **Cervinia**. This exceptionally high resort was developed in the Fascist era around the small old climbing village of Breuil, at the foot of Monte Cervino – better known to us as the Matterhorn. Its high, treeless ski area is linked to that of Zermatt in Switzerland.

aosta-valley.co.uk

↑ The treeline at Pila
is exceptionally high,
so most of the slopes
are wooded
BRIAN WALKER

UK PACKAGES

Gressoney St Jean
Alpine Answers
Pila *Crystal, First
Choice, Independent
Ski Links, Interski,
Pilaski, Ski Supreme,
Ski Yogi, Thomson*

For contact details of
relevant tourist offices
and lift companies go
to www.wtss.co.uk

MONTEROSA SKI

We have a fourth full chapter devoted
to Aosta valley skiing: it covers not a
single resort but the ski area called
Monterosa Ski. This is a three-valley
system to the east of the Cervinia
valley, linking the village of Champoluc
in the western Val d'Ayas to Gressoney
la Trinité in the central valley and so
to Alagna in the eastern valley, which
is outside the Aosta region and
reached by a quite different route from
the east. The main Monterosa Ski area
combines a network of pistes covering
a huge area of mountain with an
exceptional range of off-piste and heli-
skiing terrain.

A short way down the Val d'Ayas
from Champoluc is **Antagnod** (1710m).
It's a family-oriented resort with a
great view of Monte Rosa itself. As
well as good nursery slopes with
moving carpets it has two chairlifts,
the major one rising 575m to a top
height of 2305m and serving blue and
red runs to the village; total 14km of
pistes. Further down the valley is
Brusson (1330m). This is a major
venue for international cross-country
races along the valley, back towards
Antagnod. There is sunny downhill
skiing up a side valley at **Estoul**
(1800m) – easy red slopes (total 9km)
served by two chairlifts, the major one
rising 500m vertical to a top height of
2235m.

Gressoney Saint Jean (1390m) is an
old village with a rich heritage in the
central valley of the Monterosa Ski
area. It's equally good for cross-
country and downhill skiing. Outside
the village at Bieltshocke is a well-
equipped nursery slope and a chairlift
rising 675m to a top height of 2025m
serving not only blue and red slopes
but also a short black run (total 7km
of pistes).

All of these resorts offer 100%
snowmaking on their pistes.

GRAN PARADISO/RUITOR AREA

Gran Paradiso, less often called by its
French name Grand Paradis, is a
glacier-draped 4000m peak south of
Aosta – the only such peak entirely in
Italy. Surrounding it is a national park
of the same name, and on the fringes
of the park are two small resorts. Ice
climbing and ski touring are popular
activities in and around the park.

Cogne (1535m) is the main resort
for exploration of the park in summer,
and has a privileged position only a
few km from the peak of Gran
Paradiso itself, with the slightly lower
peak of La Grivola even closer. It is a
major centre for cross-country skiing,
with 70km of trails along the valley;
international races include the Marcia
Gran Paradiso. The downhill slopes
above the village offer 9km of runs; a
pulse gondola takes you up to 2060m,
and a chairlift then to 2250m. At the
base is another chairlift and a moving

405

Interactive resort shortlist builder at www.wtss.co.uk

The Aosta Valley Italy

Ski in renowned Italian resorts across four famous peaks.
Discover amazing off-piste, big powder and epic heliskiing.
Enjoy the finest Italian food, culture and accommodation.

All at permanently off-peak prices, less than 2 hours from Geneva, Turin and Milan. To discover Italy's best kept secret, visit the brand new website.

carpet. There are three 4-star hotels, and over 20 3-star and 2-star ones.

Rhêmes Notre Dame (1725m) is a small village with a handful of 2-star and 3-star hotels in a quiet valley with a fine view up to the peaks on the French border. It has a tiny amount of lift-served downhill skiing. Skin up to the head of the valley and descend into France, and with luck you'll end up near Val d'Isère.

The next valley to the west of Val di Rhêmes is **Valgrisenche**, also the name of a small village (1665m) immediately below the glacial slopes of Tête du Ruitor. There are cross-country loops around the village and short, mainly red downhill runs (totalling 12km) served by two draglifts – plus a nursery slope.

But the area is justifiably best known for heli-skiing from a base at Bonne, just above the village of Valgrisenche. The head of the valley is reputed to have a particularly snowy micro-climate, and there are about 20 established heli-drop points on the surrounding peaks, with runs into France as well as Italy. They claim their runs typically offer verticals of 1300m to 1800m. You can do it by the day if there is availability, as well as in multi-day packages. And you can be ferried by chopper from/to Cervinia or Courmayeur.

AOSTA/PILA

Aosta – a substantial city rich in Roman and medieval remains – is very unusual in also being a ski resort, of a kind. No, there are no pistes to the city, but it does have a gondola going up to ski slopes from quite close to the centre; this takes you in 20 minutes to the very worthwhile slopes of the small resort of Pila. It's 30 minutes by road.

It's perfectly viable to base yourself in Aosta and ski Pila, either every day or mixing it up with visits to other Aosta Valley resorts. If you take a car, you can have a great time like this, getting to all the places covered in this chapter while still having the convenience of the home slopes of Pila not far away.

Aosta seems a dreary place as you approach, but it has a pleasant traffic-free old centre, with cobbled streets and impressive squares lined by smart shops and cafes. There are 3-star and 4-star hotels within walking distance

of the gondola base station, but the chain hotels tend to be further away. There is a good choice of restaurants which cater mainly for locals rather than holidaymakers. As well as the aforementioned remains, there are churches to visit, and a large museum. Prices of everything are low by ski resort standards. The main drawback of staying down here, apart from the hour a day you'll spend travelling up and down, is that you can expect queues for the gondola to descend at the end of the day.

Pila (1800m) is a modern ski station, looking much like a French purpose-built resort, with 2,000 beds in hotels and apartments. The central areas are car-free, and much of the accommodation is ski-in/ski-out. There is not much more to the place except a couple of small convenience stores, a few bars and ski shops.

Chairlifts (some fast, most slow) and a cable car fan out from the resort serving an interesting mix of slopes totalling 70km. The treeline is notably high, at about 2300m, and most runs are below it, making this an excellent bad-weather resort. From the top heights there are grand views to Mont Blanc in the west and the Matterhorn in the east.

There are runs for all standards, but mostly they are reds, ranging from easy to stiff. The few blacks, above the treeline at the top of the area, don't amount to much, but there is quite a bit of off-piste. There are two short beginner lifts, but progression to longer runs means using a central run, which when the resort is busy is unpleasant. Most of the slopes face north or east of north, and the altitude is respectable (top height 2740m), so with extensive snowmaking and good grooming conditions are reliably good.

Like so many other Aosta Valley resorts, Pila is pretty quiet during the week but can be hectic at weekends – and it does attract lots of British school groups who may clog up some of the beginner runs at times.

SMALLER RESORTS

There are lots of other, smaller resorts in the Aosta valley region that are worth considering for a quiet skiing holiday: Chamois, Champorcher, Col de Joux, Crevacol, La Magdeleine, Ollomont, Torgnon and Valsavarenche. Go to: aosta-valley.co.uk.

SNOWPIX.COM / CHRIS GILL

Cervinia

One of a kind, this: for extensive, snow-sure, sunny, easy skiing, there is nowhere to match Cervinia. Good for late season holidays

RATINGS

The mountains

Extent	★★★
Fast lifts	★★★★
Queues	★★★★
Terrain p'ks	★★★★
Snow	★★★★★
Expert	★
Intermediate	★★★★
Beginner	★★★★★
Boarder	★★★★
X-country	★
Restaurants	★★★
Schools	★★★★
Families	★★

The resort

Charm	★★
Convenience	★★★
Scenery	★★★★
Eating out	★★★★
Après-ski	★★
Off-slope	★

RPI   90

lift pass	£180
ski hire	£110
lessons	£90
food & drink	£120
total	**£500**

aosta-valley.co.uk

NEWS

2011/12: Work to renovate the Plateau Rosa cable car is due for completion. More snowmaking is also due to be installed.

2010/11: A short new black run (59) was created from the Pancheron chair above Plan Torrette. Below it, red run 9 has become a designated 'slow ski' zone. And red run 24 from the same lift was remodelled, with a short new black variant. At Plan Maison a boarder-cross course and a new children's area with moving carpet lift opened.

➕ Miles of long, consistently gentle runs – ideal for intermediates wary of steep slopes or bumps

➕ Slopes are sunny, but high and pretty snow-sure

➕ Impressive scenery

➕ Excellent village nursery slope

➕ The link with Zermatt in Switzerland provides more great runs, views and lunches but ...

➖ Bad weather can close not only the Zermatt link but most of the higher lifts, severely limiting your options

➖ Very little to interest those looking for challenges

➖ Not a notably attractive village

➖ Few off-slope amenities

➖ Steep climb to the main gondola – though there is a chairlift alternative

If there is a better resort than Cervinia for those who like cruising on motorways in spring sunshine, we have yet to find it. And then there's the easiest of Zermatt's slopes just over the Swiss border.

And for the rest of us? Well, to be frank, the rest of us are better off elsewhere. In particular, those with an eye on bumps or powder over in Zermatt should probably think about residing there, not here. Despite major lift improvements in Zermatt, access to its best slopes is still a time-consuming business. And that's assuming the exposed, 3300m-high link is open.

The village was branded Cervinia when it was developed for skiing, but these days harks back to its mountaineering roots by prefixing that with its original name, Breuil. Ever heard of that? No, quite. So we'll stick with Cervinia.

THE RESORT

Cervinia is on the Italian side of the Matterhorn (or Monte Cervino in Italian), at the head of a long valley off the Aosta Valley. At weekends, the resort can fill up with visitors from Turin. At other times (January especially), it can be full of Russians.

The slopes link to Valtournenche further down the valley (covered by the lift pass) and at high altitude to Zermatt in Switzerland (covered by a daily supplement, or a more expensive weekly pass – take your passport).

Day trips by car are possible to Courmayeur, La Thuile and the

Monterosa Ski resorts of Champoluc and Gressoney. A six-day Cervinia Valtournenche pass covers two days in these other resorts. Or you can buy an Aosta Valley pass for the week and optionally add two days in Zermatt.

VILLAGE CHARM ★★
Somewhat lacking
The old climbing village grew into a ski resort (in the years before and after WW2) in a haphazard way, and the result is a bit of a mess – neither pleasing to the eye nor as offensive as the worst of the French purpose-built resorts. The centre is compact and traffic-free, and a pleasant enough place to walk around. But ugly apartment blocks and hotels spoil the views from the slopes.

CONVENIENCE ★★★
Up or down
As our plan makes clear, this is not a big place but location is still worth considering carefully. The main lift, a gondola to Plan Maison, starts a hike up from the south end of the village – irritating for some, 'truly awful' for others. But there is an alternative six-

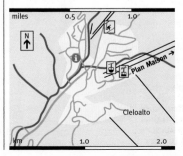

pack from the nursery slopes, next to the village centre, making this the obvious place to stay – especially now that it leads to another six-pack. Footpaths can be 'lethally slippery'.

There are also developments above the main village, closer to the gondola. Some hotels run their own shuttle-bus and there's an efficient public bus from the Cieloalto complex, well to the south of the main village.

SCENERY ★★★★☆
Monte Cervino rules

The Matterhorn is less special from the Italian than from the Swiss side, but Cervinia's setting is impressive by normal standards, with the peak towering above the village, and fine views from the slopes.

THE MOUNTAINS

Cervinia's main slopes are high, open, sunny and mostly west-facing. It's an unpleasant place when the weather is bad, and the top lifts forming the link with Zermatt are often closed because of high winds (sometimes for days).

Piste marking is praised by readers. The piste map covers both Cervinia and Zermatt fairly clearly. The two resorts' maps are very similar, but not quite identical. Both currently show planned cable cars from Furggsattel to Plateau Rosa and from there to the Klein Matterhorn, but we're told these are not imminent.

The high number of red runs on the piste map is misleading: most of them could be classified blue.

M. Cervino
Matterhorn
4478m

Schwarzsee
2585m

Zermatt
←

Trockener Steg
2940m

Theodulpass
3300m

Rifugio Teodulo

Crowds permitting, this is a great lift for racking up some vertical

Plateau Rosa
3480m/11,420ft

Plateau Rosa

Colle Sup.
Cime Bianche
2980m

Bontadini

Forner

Plan Maison

PLAN MAISON

Very easy cruising from top to bottom of the mountain (1240m vertical) in this sector

LAGHI CIME BIANCHE
2810m

Laghi Cime Bianche

Chalet Etoile

Fast new six-pack for last season makes this good little sector a more attractive place to play

Plan Torrette
2470m

Plan Maison
2555m

Plan Maison

E Cretaz

Cretaz

CIELOALTO

gondola
cable car
fast chairlift
Slow chairs & drags have no symbol

Fast chair here – plus the new one above it – makes this a good alternative route up the mountain and makes the area close to the nursery slopes a good place to stay

Cervinia
2050m/6,730ft

EXTENT OF THE SLOPES ★★★★★
High, wide and easy

Cervinia has the biggest, highest, most snow-sure area of easy, well-groomed pistes we've come across. The area has Italy's highest pistes and some of its longest. At the top you are 6km as well as 1400m vertical from the village.

A deep gorge splits the slopes into two main sectors. Looking up the hill, the lifts from the village take you into the left-hand sector at first.

A gondola takes you to the mid-mountain base of **Plan Maison**. We've rarely seen the parallel cable car working, but a regular visitor assures us it does move occasionally. A more convenient alternative for many is the six-pack from the village nursery slopes to Plan Torrette, where a six-

pack now serves the good slopes under the Matterhorn – and gives pretty quick access to Plan Maison.

Above Plan Maison, a chain of three fast quads goes on up to Theodulpass, slightly the lower of two links with the slopes of Zermatt. From Plan Maison you can instead take a gondola across to **Laghi Cime Bianche**, and the right-hand sector. From there a jumbo cable car goes up to Plateau Rosa, the other link with Zermatt. This is the start of the splendid, wide Ventina run back to the cable car station (or on down to the village).

Part-way down you can branch off left for **Valtournenche**. The slopes here are served by three fast chairlifts, above a modern gondola from the village – but the final lift back to

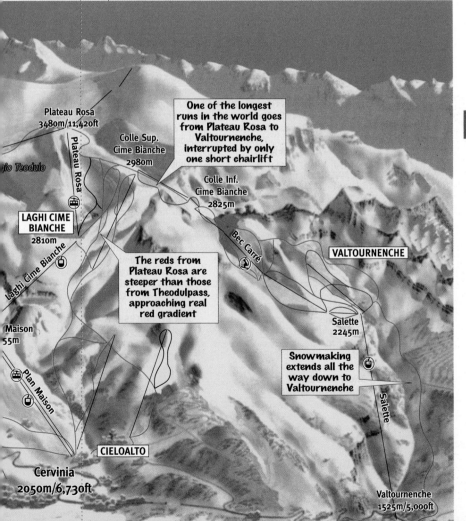

Plateau Rosa
3480m/11,420ft

Plateau Rosa

Rio Teodulo

Colle Sup.
Cime Bianche
2980m

Colle Inf.
Cime Bianche
2825m

> One of the longest runs in the world goes from Plateau Rosa to Valtournenche, interrupted by only one short chairlift

LAGHI CIME BIANCHE
2810m

Laghi Cime Bianche

Bec Carré

VALTOURNENCHE

> The reds from Plateau Rosa are steeper than those from Theodulpass, approaching real red gradient

Maison
55m

Plan Maison

Salette
2245m

> Snowmaking extends all the way down to Valtournenche

Salette

CIELOALTO

Cervinia
2050m/6,730ft

Valtournenche
1525m/5,000ft

Resort	2050m
	6,730ft

Cervinia/ Valt'nenche	
Slopes	1525-3480m
	5,000-11,420ft
Lifts	23
Pistes	150km
	93 miles
Blue	30%
Red	59%
Black	11%
Snowmaking	50%

Cervinia/ Valt'nenche/ Zermatt combined	
Slopes	1525-3820m
	5,000-12,530ft
Lifts	58
Pistes	350km
	217 miles
Blue	23%
Red	57%
Black	20%
Snowmaking	59%

THE ZERMATT CONNECTION

Getting to Zermatt's classic terrain on the Rothorn/Stockhorn sectors is much quicker than it once was, thanks to the Furi to Riffelberg gondola, built in 2006. Getting there and back by mid-afternoon is now no problem. But don't expect to spend very long on those Triftji moguls. On the way back there may be long queues for the Klein Matterhorn cable car and for the alternative long, slow T-bars. Allow plenty of time – and beware closure of the top lifts by high winds.

Cervinia is still a long draglift. From top to bottom the run down is not far short of 2000m vertical and a claimed 13km in length, interrupted only by a quad chairlift part-way.

There is also the very small, little-used **Cieloalto** area at the bottom of the Ventina run, served by a slow old chair to the south of the village. This has some of Cervinia's steeper pistes, and the only trees in the area.

FAST LIFTS ★★★★☆
Farewell to slow chairs
Cervinia's long lift modernisation process was completed for the 2010/11 season with the replacement at long last of the two old chairs above Plan Torrette by a six-pack.

QUEUES ★★★★☆
Very few problems
In general, neither we nor readers have complaints about queues in the main area of slopes. The gondola and six-pack out of the resort cope even at peak times, but the chair above Plan Maison does still get busy. Lifts at Valtournenche can be a 'problem' on peak weekends, says a 2010 visitor. Of course, the lower lifts may be busy when upper lifts are shut by wind.

TERRAIN PARKS ★★★★☆
One of Italy's best
The 'Indian' terrain park by the fast Fornet chair is one of the best parks in Italy. Run by *Snowboard Italy*'s former editor, new creative obstacles are introduced every year. The park has been shaped so that riders can hit an easy line or an intermediate line. There is also an expert tabletop line, culminating in a 20m monster. The Italian flag down-rail is a good feature for intermediate and advanced riders, while the variety of bonk posts encourages you to try all the latest tricks. Helmets are compulsory. There is no half-pipe, but Zermatt's pipe is only just over the border.

SNOW RELIABILITY ★★★★★
A question of altitude
This is not a notably snowy corner of the Alps, and the slopes get the afternoon sun. But snow is usually good from early to late season thanks to altitude (these slopes are among the highest in the Alps), good grooming and snowmaking on most key runs from top to bottom – down to Valtournenche as well as Cervinia.

FOR EXPERTS ★☆☆☆☆
Forget it
This is not a resort for experts. There are a few black runs scattered here and there, but they are not reliably open and most of them would be classified red elsewhere; we have only one sighting of moguls, on the new black above Plan Torrette. Accessible off-piste terrain is limited, and high winds can play havoc with fresh snow. But of course there is some off-piste potential – above Plan Torrette for example – and of course conditions are sometimes brilliant, and you then have the advantage that the snow can remain untracked for ages. Heli-skiing with guides can be arranged.

Many reporters head over to Zermatt for more challenging slopes – look at the 'Zermatt connection' box in the margin.

FOR INTERMEDIATES ★★★★☆
Miles of long, flattering runs
Virtually the whole area can be covered comfortably by average intermediates. From top to bottom there are wide, gentle, smooth runs. But strong intermediates will get bored quickly, and be itching to be off to Zermatt. The area on the right as you look at the mountain is best for more adventurous intermediates. The Ventina red is a particularly good fast cruise. You can use the cable car to do the top part repeatedly. The reds served by the new Pancheron chair at Plan Torrette are also a bit more interesting than the norm, and tend to be attractively quiet.

The runs towards Valtournenche are great cruises and very popular with reporters. The 13km run all the way down is very satisfying, through splendid rocky scenery.

FOR BEGINNERS ★★★★★
Gentle progress
A limited day pass covers the good village nursery slope, with its long moving carpet, and the adjacent chairlift. Complete beginners start there and graduate to the fine flat area around Plan Maison and the gentle blue runs above. Fast learners will be going all the way from top to bottom of the mountain in a few days.

FOR BOARDERS ★★★★☆
Easy cruising
The wide, gentle and well-groomed slopes, generally good snow and lack

Cervinia

There are lodgings right by the nursery slope and the six-pack to Plan Torrette; the Plan Maison gondola is not nearly so convenient →

of many draglifts make Cervinia pretty much ideal for beginner and early intermediate boarders. But there are some long, flat parts to beware of (notably around Plan Maison). Serious boarders will enjoy the terrain park, and there's an exclusive park pass that cost 26 euros a day last season; they could also try heli-boarding.

FOR CROSS-COUNTRY ★☆☆☆☆
Hardly any
There are only two short trails (both 3km or so); this is not a good cross-country resort.

MOUNTAIN RESTAURANTS ★★★☆☆
OK if you know where to go
There are some good places if you know where to go. Toilet facilities are a traditional cause of complaints from reporters, but several have now been improved. You can, of course, head over to Zermatt for lunch.
Editors' choice Chalet Etoile (0166 940220), on a blue run above Plan Maison is an old favourite, happily supported by a continuing flow of reader reports – 'great food, lovely setting'. There's an improved self-service section too. The much simpler Rifugio Teodulo (0166 949400) at Theodulpass is another good option – excellent pasta.
Worth knowing about Recent reporters tip Plan Torrette ('amazing food',

'welcoming staff'), which has both table and self-service parts. Readers regularly recommend the Bontadini ('good food and superb view'). Other reporter tips include the 'bright and cheerful' Ventina self-service, 'cosy' Rifugio Guide de Cervino. The British-run Igloo, above Valtournenche, has its supporters ('great desserts').

The restaurants are cheaper and less crowded in the Valtournenche sector. Tips above Salette include Lo Baracon dou Tene – 'excellent location, service and food' – and the Motta – 'basic but good value'.

SCHOOLS AND GUIDES ★★★★☆
Generally positive reports
Cervinia has three main schools, Cervino, Breuil and Matterhorn-Cervinia. A 2010 snowboarder made 'good progress' in a private lesson with the Breuil school, and the Cervino school has received favourable reports recently: 'excellent off-piste week', said one reporter who was staying with Club Med (they use Cervino instructors); 'well organised, learnt a lot', said another.

FOR FAMILIES ★★☆☆☆
No recent reports
The Cervino ski school runs a ski kindergarten that looks very appealing. And there's a babysitting and kindergarten area at Plan Maison.

GETTING THERE

Air Turin 120km/ 75 miles (2hr); Geneva 185km/ 115 miles (2hr45)

Rail Châtillon (27km/17 miles); regular buses from station

ACTIVITIES

Indoor Swimming pools and saunas in hotels, fitness centre, squash

Outdoor Natural ice rink, hiking, snowmobiling, snow-biking, mountaineering, snowshoeing, ice karting, ice climbing, airboarding, snow dinghies, kite skiing

Phone numbers
From abroad use the prefix +39 (and do **not** omit the initial '0' of the phone number)

TOURIST OFFICE

www.montecervino.it
www.cervinia.it

STAYING THERE

Chalets Inghams is opening the 25-bed chalet-hotel Dragon for 2011/12, in a great position close to the nursery slope.

Hotels There are almost 50 hotels, mostly 2- or 3-stars. Choose your location with care, or look for a place with its own shuttle bus.

****Hermitage** (0166 948998) Small, luxurious Relais et Châteaux just out of the village on the road to Cieloalto. Pool. Minibus to the lifts. Great views.

****Excelsior Planet** (0166 949426) Near the nursery slopes. Pool, spa and minibus to the lifts.

****Sertorelli Sport Hotel** (0166 949797) At south end of village. Completely renovated in 2009. Small pool, saunas, steam and hot tub.

****Europa** (0166 948660) Well placed near nursery slope. Pool. Repeated recommendations, particularly for 'exceptionally helpful staff'.

***Edelweiss** (0166 949078) At south end of village. Quirky place, but 'couldn't have better hosts'.

***Mignon** (0166 949344) Central – 50 yards from the lifts. Good past reports.

***Miravidi** (0166 948097) Central and recently updated hotel. 'Looked after us superbly,' says a 2010 visitor.

***Serenella** (0166 949041) 'Very Italian feel (and food), brilliant location, friendly, excellent value.'

Apartments There are many apartments, but few are available via UK tour ops. The Escargot ones in Cieloalto are 'very spacious'.

At altitude Up at Plan Maison, Lo Stambecco (214 4115) is a 50-room 3-star hotel ideal for early starts.

EATING OUT ★★★★☆
Plenty to choose from
Cervinia's 50 or so restaurants allow plenty of choice, but one reader notes that prices climb steeply once you leave pizza territory. Reader favourites include: the Matterhorn, with a varied menu, including vegetarian dishes – 'friendly, good value', 'lively; children welcome'; the Grotta – 'very friendly, extensive menu, delicious food'; Jour et Nuit for its steaks – 'amazing', 'best of the week'; and the Copa Pan bar's basement restaurant – 'good food, lively'. Recommended pasta/pizza-oriented spots include Vieux Grenier, Lino's and Falcone. Dinner at Baita Cretaz, just above the village, makes a change.

APRES-SKI ★★☆☆☆
Disappoints many Brits
Plenty of Brits come here looking for action but find there isn't much to do except tour the bars. 'Take a good book,' said one reporter. At tea time you can do worse than to hit the 'great cakes' at the Samovar. The hotel Grivola's bar, next to the Vieux Grenier restaurant, is attractively woody, friendly and lively. The Copa Pan is lively (starting with a happy hour), with great music ('really liked it, difficult to leave'). The Dragon Bar is popular with Brits and Scandinavians and has satellite TV and videos; the Yeti is popular too (another happy hour ensures that) and serves 'great free nibbles with drinks'. Other recommendations include Hostellerie des Guides (with mementos of the owner's Himalayan trips). Discos liven up at weekends when the Italians arrive – Bianconiglio can be 'a bit cheesy, but it's great on Friday night', said one reporter.

OFF THE SLOPES ★☆☆☆☆
Little attraction
There is little to do for those who don't plan to hit the slopes. Amenities include hotel pools, a fitness centre and a natural ice rink. There are few diverting shops. The walks are disappointing. Few mountain restaurants are reachable by gondola or cable car, and most of those are not special.

LINKED RESORT – 1525m

VALTOURNENCHE

Some 500m lower than Cervinia and 9km down the access road, Valtournenche offers lower prices and a rather more traditional style, and is well worth considering as a base unless Zermatt is high on your agenda (getting to the border takes longer from here than from Cervinia). The village spreads along the busy, steep road up to Cervinia; it is reported to be 'not so much quiet as dead' in the evening.

A gondola leaves from the edge of the village, and fast lifts predominate above that. The epic run back from Plateau Rosa on the Swiss border is a great way to end the day.

There's a fair selection of simple hotels; some have shuttles to the lift. The 3-star Bijou (0166 92109) is 'very friendly but not cheap'.

Cortina d'Ampezzo

The scenery will take your breath away even if the slopes don't; take your posh frocks to feel part of the high-season scene

RATINGS

The mountains

Extent	★★★
Fast lifts	★★★
Queues	★★★★
Terrain p'ks	★★
Snow	★★★
Expert	★★
Intermediate	★★★
Beginner	★★★★★
Boarder	★★★
X-country	★★★★★
Restaurants	★★★★
Schools	★★★
Families	★★

The resort

Charm	★★★★
Convenience	★
Scenery	★★★★★
Eating out	★★★★★
Après-ski	★★★
Off-slope	★★★★★

RPI	105
lift pass	£220
ski hire	£125
lessons	£120
food & drink	£125
total	**£590**

NEWS

2011/12: In the Cinque Torri sector, a new double chairlift is planned from mid-mountain to the top to replace the ancient single-person chair and subsequent rope tow.

2010/11: A new 500m-long terrain park aimed at beginners and intermediates opened at Socrepes. Part of the Vitelli piste at Faloria became a designated 'slow ski' zone with benches and chill-out areas. Rifugio Averau at the top of Cinque Torri re-opened after renovation.

➕ Magnificent Dolomite scenery and a quite exceptional setting

➕ Marvellous nursery slopes and good long cruising runs

➕ Access to the vast area covered by the Dolomiti Superski pass

➕ Attractive although rather towny resort, with lots of upmarket shops

➕ Good off-slope facilities

➕ No crowds or queues

➖ Several separate areas of slopes – though well linked by buses

➖ Erratic snow record

➖ Expensive by Italian standards

➖ Still quite a few slow lifts

➖ Gets very crowded in town and in restaurants during Italian holidays

➖ Few tough runs

If you like lazy days centred around indulgent lunches on sunny terraces, gazing at scenery that is just jaw-droppingly wonderful, this is the place. The town is ringed by dramatic, pink-tinged cliffs and peaks soaring above the slopes, giving picture-postcard views wherever you look. Every time we go back, the memory has faded and our jaws drop again.

Cortina is Italy's most fashionable resort, with all that entails – in high season, when the money is in town, a lot of strolling, people-watching, serious shopping and lengthy lunching goes on. The majority of Italian visitors don't go near the slopes except to drive up to a 'mountain restaurant' for lunch. Which is good for the rest of us because it means the slopes stay uncrowded.

Like most such swanky resorts, Cortina attracts more skiers driving Fords than driving Ferraris, even if few of the Fords are Cortinas. So it is not literally exclusive – and ordinary mortals will feel at home here. As an occasional change from serious ski resorts, we love it.

THE RESORT

Cortina is a sizeable town spread across a wide, impossibly scenic bowl. Although it runs World Cup races, and leapt to international prominence as host of the 1956 Winter Olympics, it relies for its appeal on other things – 70% of all Italian visitors don't step on to the slopes. People leave the slopes early, and by 5pm hardly anyone is still in ski gear. In the high season the streets are packed with people parading up and down in their furs and baubles, shouting into their mobile phones and walking their tiny dogs.

Unlike most of the Dolomites, Cortina is pure Italy. The Veneto region has none of the Germanic traditions of the Südtirol, only a few miles away. And reporters have found the place friendly and welcoming.

San Cassiano is a short drive to the west, with links from there to Corvara and the other Sella Ronda resorts.

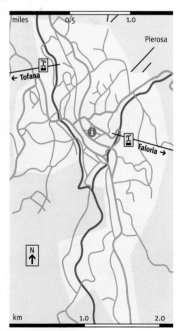

KEY FACTS

Resort	1225m
	4,020ft
Slopes	1225-2930m
	4,020-9,610ft
Lifts	37
Pistes	115km
	71 miles
Blue	50%
Red	35%
Black	15%
Snowmaking	95%

UK PACKAGES

Alpine Answers,
Crystal, Momentum,
Mountain Tracks, Ski
Club Freshtracks, Ski
Solutions, Ski
Weekend, Ski Yogi,
Snow Finders,
Thomson, White Roc,
Zenith

VILLAGE CHARM ★★★★☆
Bella Italia

The centre is the traffic-free Corso Italia, which is full of chic designer clothes shops, jewellery and antique shops, art galleries and furriers – finding a ski shop can be tricky. The picturesque church tower adds to the atmosphere.

Surrounding the centre is a busy one-way system, which struggles to cope with the traffic at weekends.

CONVENIENCE ★☆☆☆☆
Widely scattered

Staying centrally is best: the lifts to the two main areas of slopes are at opposite sides of town (and a fair way from the centre, though the distances are walkable). Other lifts are bus, car or taxi rides away. There are plenty of hotels in the centre but some are scattered around the outskirts. The top ones have their own shuttles, of course. The town bus service is efficient and 'very punctual' too; it is free to ski pass holders.

A car can be useful, especially for getting to the outlying ski areas and to make the most of other areas on the Dolomiti Superski pass.

SCENERY ★★★★★
Stand and admire

Cortina is surrounded by some of the most stunning mountain scenery in the skiing world – the Dolomite mountains are magnificent, with their pink-tinged cliffs and peaks rising up from pretty wooded valleys. They look particularly spectacular at sunset.

THE MOUNTAINS

There is a good mixture of slopes above and below the treeline. Reporters consistently praise quiet slopes, at least in the areas close to the town, but complain about signs, piste classification and marking, and the piste map.

EXTENT OF THE SLOPES ★★★☆☆
They add up ...

All Cortina's smallish, fragmented areas are a fair trek from the town centre. The highest is **Tofana**, accessed by successive cable cars starting from near the ice rink. The largest is **Pomedes**, accessed by the first cable car mentioned above followed by a blue piste, or by a tricky black piste from Tofana, or by chair and draglifts a bus ride away from the centre.

On the opposite side of the valley is the tiny **Mietres** area. A two-stage cable car from the east side of town leads to the **Faloria** area, from where you can head down to chairs that lead up into the limited but dramatic runs beneath **Cristallo**.

Other areas are reachable by road – in particular the road west over Passo Falzarego. First, there's the small but scenic **Cinque Torri** area. Excellent north-facing cruising runs are accessed by a fast quad, followed by a new double chair (see 'News'). From the top, you can go over the ridge to a sunny, panoramic red run on the back of the hill or to a chair which accesses another red run to the tiny – north-facing – **Col Gallina** area. From here you can take a blue back to Cinque Torri or a cable car from Passo

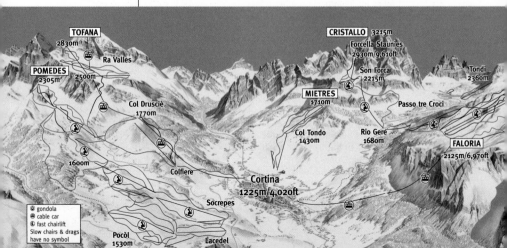

LIFT PASSES

Dolomiti Superski

Prices in €

Age	1-day	6-day
under 16	32	163
16 to 59	46	233
over 65	41	210

Free under 8

Senior must be over 65 before the beginning of the season

Beginner no deals

Notes
Covers 450 lifts and 1220km of piste in the Dolomites, including all Cortina areas

Alternative passes
Cortina d'Ampezzo (Cortina, San Vito di Cadore, Auronzo and Misurina)

Falzarego up to Lagazuoi that serves an excellent red/blue run back to the base station and accesses the famous 'hidden valley' run to the fringe of the Alta Badia area. (More on this in the Sella Ronda chapter.)

One way to tour the area is to use special ski itineraries (maps are available). 'Skitour Olympia' takes you on the 1956 Olympic courses.

FAST LIFTS ★★★★★
Some in each sector
The main access lifts are cable cars and there are fast chairs scattered throughout each sector, but a lot of slow old lifts remain too.

QUEUES ★★★★★
No problem
Most Italian visitors rise late, lunch at length and leave the slopes early. That means few lift queues and generally uncrowded pistes. One visitor, however, reported crowded runs at Cinque Torri, even in low season. He speculates that the crowds came from the Sella Ronda resorts, taking in Cinque Torri before riding the cable car to Lagazuoi for the famous 'hidden valley' run. Queues can form for this cable car, not surprisingly.

TERRAIN PARKS ★★★★★
New challenges for all
A new 500m-long park opened in Socrepes in 2010 for both beginners and intermediates. It has kickers,

boxes, rails, and a wall ride. Helmets are compulsory. The original park at Faloria may not be built for 2011/12.

SNOW RELIABILITY ★★★★★
Lots of artificial help
The snowfall record is erratic – it can be good here when it's poor on the north side of the Alps, and vice versa. But 95% of the pistes are covered by snowmaking, so cover is good if it is cold enough to make snow. As so often, it's the black runs that are most vulnerable when natural snow is short – several are south-facing, and liable to closure. Grooming is excellent.

FOR EXPERTS ★★★★★
Normally rather limited
Decent amounts of natural snow are the key factor – not only to provide plentiful off-piste (which will offer fresh tracks for days on end) but to ensure adequate snow cover on the few black runs that there are (some of which get a lot of sun). They include the excellent Forcella from Tofana to Pomedes: deservedly classified black, it goes through a gap in the rocks, and gives wonderful views of Cortina way down in the valley below. Cortina's most serious challenge is the Staunies run at the top of the Cristallo area – a south-facing couloir that we have never found open (tougher than it looks from below, warns a reporter). There are short but genuinely black runs below Pomedes and Duc d'Aosta.

Interactive resort shortlist builder at www.wtss.co.uk

GETTING THERE

Air Venice 160km/
100 miles (2hr15).
Treviso 130km/
80 miles (2hr). Sat
and Sun transfers for
hotel guests (advance
booking required);
35-minute heli-
transfers from Venice

Rail Calalzo (35km/
22 miles) or Dobbiaco
(32km/20 miles);
frequent buses from
station

DEE CHILTON

Looking down from
Lagazuoi to Passo
Falzarego; you catch
this cable car up to
reach the start of the
'hidden valley' run ↓

There are some excellent red runs
too, notably at Pomedes and Faloria.
Heli-skiing is available.

FOR INTERMEDIATES ★★★☆☆
Fragmented and not extensive
To enjoy Cortina you must like cruising
in beautiful scenery, and not mind
doing runs repeatedly.

The runs at the top of Tofana are
short but normally have the best
snow. The highest are at over 2800m
and mainly face north. But be warned:
the only way back down is by the
tricky black run described above or by
cable car. The reds in the linked
Pomedes area offer good cruising and
some challenges.

Faloria has a string of fairly short
north-facing runs – we loved the Vitelli
red run, round the back away from the
lifts. And the Cristallo area has a long,
easy red run served by a fast quad.

It is well worth making the trip to
Cinque Torri for fast cruising on usually
excellent north-facing snow. And do
not miss the wonderful 'hidden valley'
red run from the Passo Falzarego cable
car (see the Sella Ronda chapter).

FOR BEGINNERS ★★★★★
Wonderful nursery slopes
While there are no special deals for
beginners, the Socrepes area has
some of the biggest nursery slopes
and best progression runs we have
seen. Points cards are issued by the
day too. You'll find ideal gentle terrain
on the main pistes but some of the
blue forest paths can be icy and
intimidating.

FOR BOARDERS ★★★☆☆
Wide slopes and plenty of chairs
Despite its upmarket chic, Cortina is a
good resort for learning to board. The
Socrepes nursery slopes are wide,
gentle and served by a fast chairlift.
And progress on to other easy slopes
is simple because you can get around
in all areas using just chairs and cable
cars – although there are drags, they
can be avoided. Boarderline is a
specialist snowboard shop that
organises instruction as well as
equipment hire. In a normal snow year
there is little off-piste, but there are
some nice trees and hits under the top
chair at Cinque Torri.

FOR CROSS-COUNTRY ★★★★★
One of the best
Cortina has around 70km of trails
suitable for all standards, mainly in
the Fiames area, where there's a cross-
country centre and a school. Trails
include a 30km itinerary following an
old railway from Fiames to Cortina,
and there is a beginner area equipped
with snowmaking. Passo Tre Croci
offers more challenging trails, covering
10km. A Nordic area pass is available.

MOUNTAIN RESTAURANTS ★★★★☆
Good, but get in early
Many restaurants can be reached by
road or lift, and fur coats arrive as
early as 10am to sunbathe, admire the
views and idle the time away on their
mobile phones. In some places, skiers
are decidedly in the minority. Although
prices are high in the swishest
establishments, we've found plenty of
reasonably priced places, serving
generally excellent food. Reporters
stress the consistently high standard.

In the Socrepes area, the Rifugio
Col Taron and the Rifugio Pomedes
have received good reports. The Piè
de Tofana and El Faral are also good.
And Baita Son dei Prade above Pocol
is 'never too crowded, wonderful
lasagne', says a recent reporter.

There are good restaurants at Cinque Torri – the Scoiattoli, Rifugio Averau and Rifugio Fedare are all recommended. Rifugio Lagazuoi, a short hike up from the top of the Passo Falzarego cable car, also has great views.

SCHOOLS AND GUIDES ★★★☆☆
Mixed reports
Of the several ski schools, we've had mixed reports of the Cortina school over the years – though we lack recent reports. The Guide Alpine offers off-piste and touring.

FOR FAMILIES ★★☆☆☆
Some good lift pass deals
Families will find a wide choice of lift pass deals and discounts for children and there are a couple of snow gardens. But don't count on good spoken English. And the fragmented slopes can make for stressful days with children.

STAYING THERE

Hotels dominate the market but there is some accommodation to rent.
Hotels There's a big choice, from 5-star luxury to 1-star and 2-star pensions.
★★★★★Cristallo (0436 881111) Top of the market. A hike from the town centre and Faloria lift, but there is a shuttle, of course. Pool, sauna, steam.
★★★★★Miramonti Majestic (0436 4201) Spectacularly grand hotel, 2km south of town. Pool, sauna, steam, hot tub.
★★★★Poste (0436 4271) At the heart of the town, on the car-free Corso Italia. Large rooms, some with spa baths. An established reader favourite, though we lack recent reports.
★★★★Ancora (0436 3261) Elegant public rooms. On the traffic-free Corso Italia.
★★★★Parc Victoria (0436 3246) Rustic and family-run with small rooms but good food, at the Faloria end of town.
★★★★Park Faloria (0436 2959) Near ski jump, splendid pool, good food.
★★★Columbia (0436 3607) B&B hotel a walk from Tofana lift but a bit of a hike from town. Recommended recently – 'very helpful staff'.
★★★Menardi (0436 2400) Welcoming roadside inn, a long walk from the town centre.
★★★Olimpia (0436 3256) Comfortable B&B hotel in centre, near Faloria lift.
★★★Des Alpes (0436 862021) On the edge of town. Hot tub. Has been praised for service and friendly staff.

★★Montana (0436 862126) Good value, central B&B.
Apartments There are some chalets and apartments – usually well outside the town centre – available for independent travellers.

EATING OUT ★★★★★
Huge choice
There's an enormous selection of restaurants, both in town and a little way out, doing mainly Italian food. The very smart and expensive El Toulà is in a beautiful old barn, just on the edge of town. A recent reporter enjoyed two good visits to the Pontejel (hotel Astoria) – 'excellent lamb'. Many of the best restaurants are further out: the Michelin-starred Tivoli, the Meloncino al Cameneto, the Leone e Anna, the Rio Gere (game dishes) and the Baita Fraina (pasta and meats).

APRES-SKI ★★★☆☆
Lively in high season
Cortina is a lively social whirl in high season, with lots of well-heeled Italians staying up very late.
The Lovat is one of several high-calorie teatime spots. There are many good wine bars: Enoteca has 700 wines and good cheese and meats; Osteria has good wines and local ham; and Villa Sandi and LP26 have been recommended. Past reporters have enjoyed the hospitality of the hotel Poste. The liveliest bar is the Clipper, with a bobsleigh by the door. Discos liven up after 11pm.

OFF THE SLOPES ★★★★★
A classic resort
Cortina attracts lots of people who don't use the slopes, unless you count strolling across them – despite a lack of published information there are good and popular walks to be done in several sectors, particularly Pocol and Socrepes. The shopping is 'fabulous'; as well as high fashion 'you can get anything and everything at the Co-operativa di Cortina'. Mountain restaurants are accessible by road. And there's plenty more to do, such as swimming and skating. There is a Planetarium near the ice rink and an observatory at Col Druscié. There's polo on the snow occasionally. Excursions to Venice are easy. You can visit the First World War tunnels at Lagazuoi.

Courmayeur

A seductive old village on the sunny side of spectacular Mont Blanc, best combined with visits to neighbouring resorts

RATINGS

The mountains

Extent	★★
Fast lifts	★★★
Queues	★★★★
Terrain p'ks	★★
Snow	★★★★
Expert	★★★
Intermediate	★★★★
Beginner	★
Boarder	★★★
X-country	★★★
Restaurants	★★★★
Schools	★★★★
Families	★★

The resort

Charm	★★★★
Convenience	★
Scenery	★★★★
Eating out	★★★★
Après-ski	★★★★
Off-slope	★★★

RPI 90

lift pass	£190
ski hire	£105
lessons	£90
food & drink	£120
total	**£505**

aosta-valley.co.uk

NEWS

2011/12: A couple of new pistes are planned, vaguely. And a slick new nightclub.

2010/11: Two new mountain restaurants opened at Plan Checrouit.

MOMENTUM SKI

Weekend & a la carte ski holiday specialists

100% Tailor-Made

Premier hotels & apartments

No. 1 specialists in Courmayeur

020 7371 9111
www.momentumski.com

+ Charming old village – car-free centre with stylish shops and bars

+ Stunning views of Mont Blanc

+ Some good off-piste and heli-skiing – and access to the famous Vallée Blanche run to Chamonix

+ Comprehensive snowmaking

+ Some great mountain restaurants

– Small area of slopes (we're sceptical about the claimed 100km of piste)

– Lots of drawbacks for beginners

– No really tough pistes

– No pistes back to the village, only to Dolonne (where you catch a bus)

– Often crowded at weekends

Courmayeur is a great place for a short midweek break (or a day trip to escape bad weather in Chamonix), and we always look forward to a quick visit here. Excellent restaurants both on and off the mountain plus village bars among the most civilised in the skiing world are factors, we admit. The skiing is tricky to recommend, though. Its pistes are best suited to competent intermediates, who are likely to have an appetite for mileage that Courmayeur will arouse but not satisfy. Happily, the lift pass covers two days elsewhere in the Aosta Valley – check out our chapter; La Thuile is the obvious target, but there are other possibilities, at least if you have a car.

THE RESORT

Courmayeur is a traditional old mountaineering village that has retained much of its character.

La Thuile is an easy drive or bus ride away; Aosta/Pila and Chamonix are not far, and Cervinia is reachable.

VILLAGE CHARM ★★★★
Attractive and sophisticated
The village has a charming traffic-free core of cobbled streets and well-preserved old buildings. As the lifts close, the central Via Roma comes alive: people pile into the many bars, or browse the smart clothes shops and tempting delis (there's also a good bookshop). At weekends the fur coats of Milan and Turin lend a sophisticated air. An Alpine museum and a statue of a long-dead mountain rescue hero add to the historical feel.

Away from the centre it's a resort of parts. There are pleasant woody suburbs, but also a lot of conspicuous modern apartment blocks.

CONVENIENCE ★
Buses to the lifts
A huge cable car on the southern edge of the village will take you to and from Plan Checrouit, at the heart of the slopes. You cannot ski back to the village, but you can ski to the base of

the alternative gondola from Dolonne (across the valley); parking is much easier there, too. Buses serve both lift stations but readers have found services poor. Many hotels run shuttles, and most will take you to Dolonne. Drivers can also go to Entrèves, up the valley, where there is a large car park at the cable car. Most people leave their gear in lockers up

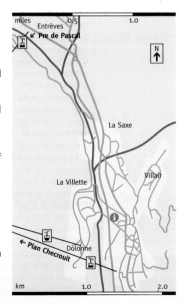

↑ Courba Dzeleuna is a key link between the two sectors – and has a great view of the head of Val Veny and the Ghiacciaio del Miage

WENDY-JANE KING

KEY FACTS

Resort	1225m
	4,020ft
Slopes	1210-2755m
	3,970-9,040ft
Lifts	18
Pistes	100km
	62 miles
Blue	27%
Red	59%
Black	14%
Snowmaking	70%

the mountain or at a lift base.

Buses, infrequent but timetabled, go to La Palud, just beyond Entrèves, for the Monte Bianco cable car to Punta Helbronner and the Vallée Blanche run to Chamonix.

Taxis are easily arranged for evening outings to valley restaurants.

SCENERY ★★★★☆
Mont Blanc rules
The high glacial slopes of the Mont Blanc massif overlook Courmayeur's slopes. The views from the high points at Cresta d'Arp and Cresta Youla, especially, are stunning.

THE MOUNTAINS

The slopes above the focal point of Plan Chécrouit are mainly wide open, but there are also wooded areas, particularly on the back side of the hill. Signposting of pistes is adequate and the piste map has been revised to show lift names and direction.

EXTENT OF THE SLOPES ★★☆☆☆
Small but interestingly varied
There are two distinct sectors, separated by a rocky ridge. The routes between the two can be a bit confusing at first.

We have asked the tourist office to show us the basis of Courmayeur's claimed 100km of piste, without result.

Above Plan Chécrouit, the east-facing **Chécrouit** area, accessed mainly by the Chécrouit gondola, catches morning sun and has open, above-the-treeline slopes. The 25-person Youla

cable car goes (infrequently) to the top of Courmayeur's pistes. A further tiny cable car to Cresta d'Arp serves only long off-piste runs (a guide is no longer compulsory to ride this lift).

Most people follow the sun over to the north-west-facing slopes of **Val Veny** in the afternoon. These are interesting, varied and treelined, with great views of Mont Blanc and its glaciers. The Val Veny slopes are also accessible by cable car from Entrèves, a few miles outside Courmayeur.

A little way beyond Entrèves is La Palud, where a cable car goes up in three stages to Punta Helbronner, at the shoulder of **Mont Blanc** for the famous Vallée Blanche run to Chamonix. You avoid the scary ridge walk that forms the start on the Chamonix side (but also miss out on some of the more interesting and steeper variants of the run). On the Italian side of Mont Blanc there are tougher off-piste runs – notably the Toula glacier route beside the cable car. Obviously, these glacier runs require guidance. There are buses back from Chamonix.

FAST LIFTS ★★★☆☆
A mixed bag
The main access lifts are cable cars or a gondola. On the hill, there are fast lifts in most key spots, but the ancient Bertolini chair on the Val Veny side cries out for an upgrade.

QUEUES ★★★★☆
Much improved
These days, queues are generally not a problem unless conditions trigger a weekend influx. There may still be queues to descend at the end of the day if the run to Dolonne lacks snow. On the back of the hill, Zerotta is a bottleneck – we waited 15 minutes in March 2011. The infrequent Youla cable car may require patience – it's worth it only for those heading off-piste.

TERRAIN PARKS ★★☆☆☆
Small one at Dolonne
There is a small park for beginners and intermediates at Dolonne, with jumps, two rails, boardercross and a new big airbag for 2011.

SNOW RELIABILITY ★★★★☆
Good for most of the season
Courmayeur's slopes are not high – mostly between 1700m and 2250m. Those above Val Veny face north or

LIFT PASSES

Courmayeur

Prices in €

Age	1-day	6-day
under 14	30	124
14 to 64	42	206
over 65	30	124

Free under 8

Beginner three free nursery lifts (but you have to pay for the gondola to reach them)

Notes
Covers Courmayeur and the Mont Blanc cable cars; 3- or 4-hour passes; some single ascent passes; weekly passes allow two days in another Aosta valley resort

Alternative passes
Non-skier; Mont Blanc Unlimited (includes Chamonix valley and Verbier); Valle d'Aosta (covers Valle d'Aosta ski areas + La Rosière + Alagna + Valesia)

ACTIVITIES

Indoor Hotel swimming pools, Alpine museum, library, sports centre with climbing wall, ice rink, curling, fitness centre, indoor golf, squash, tennis

Outdoor Walking, snowshoeing, golf on snow, dog sledding, ice climbing

north-west, so they keep their snow well, but the Plan Checrouit side is too sunny for comfort in late season. There is snowmaking on most main runs, including the red run to the valley. So good coverage in early and mid-season is virtually assured – we've been there in a snow drought and enjoyed decent skiing entirely on man-made snow. Grooming is good.

FOR EXPERTS ★★★☆☆
Off-piste is the only challenge

Courmayeur has few challenging pistes. The black runs on the Val Veny side are not severe, but moguls are allowed to develop. If you're lucky enough to find fresh powder, you can have fantastic fun among the trees.

Classic off-piste runs go from Cresta d'Arp, at the top of the lift network, in three directions: a clockwise loop via Arp Vieille to Val Veny, with close-up views of the Miage glacier; east down a deserted valley to Dolonne or Pré-St-Didier; or south through the Youla gorge to La Balme, near La Thuile.

The possibilities on Mont Blanc are considerable, some described above. A day trip to Chamonix is appealing.

There are also heli-drops, including

a wonderful 20km run from the Ruitor glacier into France – you ride the lifts back up from La Rosière and descend to La Thuile (then take a taxi back).

FOR INTERMEDIATES ★★★★☆
Good reds, but limited extent

It's an intermediate's mountain, for sure, laced with interestingly varied, genuine red runs. But it is small; the avid piste-basher will ski it in a day. There are some good long runs – it's 700m vertical from Col Checrouit to Zerotta, and 1400m vertical from Cresta Youla to Dolonne – but they are few. On the steeper Val Veny side of the ridge there are challenges to be found – while the reds and blues cut across the mountain, a row of easy blacks go down more directly.

For the timid intermediate, on the other hand, the area is short of confidence-building blue runs. There is basically one long blue on each side of the ridge, reached from Plan Checrouit via the six-seater Pra Neyron chair; that on the Val Veny side is better for the challenge-averse. Many of the reds, particularly up around Col Checrouit, and down to Plan Checrouit, do have the merit that they are

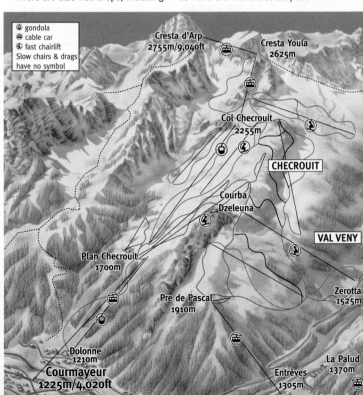

gondola
cable car
fast chairlift
Slow chairs & drags have no symbol

Cresta d'Arp
2755m/9,040ft

Cresta Youla
2625m

Col Checrouit
2255m

CHECROUIT

Courba
Dzeleuna

VAL VENY

Plan Checrouit
1700m

Pre de Pascal
1910m

Zerotta
1525m

Dolonne
1210m

Courmayeur
1225m/4,020ft

Entrèves
1305m

La Palud
1370m

No fur coats in the Via Roma? Obviously a weekday, then →

WENDY-JANE KING

SCHOOLS

Monte Bianco
t 0165 842477

Courmayeur
t 0165 848254

Classes
(Monte Bianco prices)
5 days (2hr per day)
€187
Private lessons
From €40 for 1hr;
additional person €12

GUIDES

Guides Courmayeur
t 0165 842064

GETTING THERE

Air Geneva 100km/
60 miles (1hr30);
Turin 150km/95 miles
(2hr)

Rail Pré-St-Didier
(5km/3 miles); regular
buses from station

generally wide, which helps a lot.

Adventurous, fit intermediates can try the off-piste Vallée Blanche run to Chamonix, and the local heli-skiing.

FOR BEGINNERS ★☆☆☆☆
Lots of drawbacks
Of course, you can learn to ski here, but you have obstacles in your path. There is a free lift on the beginner slope at Plan Checrouit, but you pay to get up to it, and it gets crowded. There is another up on the ridge, which again means paying for access. The best starting point for beginners is at the top of the Entrèves cable car, where there is a beginner slope with magic carpet, and easy longer runs on the Peindeint chair. As we explain under 'Intermediates', there are few other genuinely easy longer runs to progress to once off the nursery slope.

FOR BOARDERS ★★★☆☆
Mainly intermediate fun
Courmayeur's pistes suit intermediates well, and most areas are easily accessible by cable cars, chairs and gondolas (though the beginner slopes employ drags). A past reporter enthused about 'an above-average number of lumps and bumps to the side of the piste for playful frolics'. For the more adventurous, there are good off-piste routes. There's a small park and boardercross for novices at Dolonne.

FOR CROSS-COUNTRY ★★★☆☆
Beautiful trails
There are 30km of trails. The best are the five covering 20km at Val Ferret, served by bus. Dolonne has a couple of short trails.

MOUNTAIN RESTAURANTS ★★★★☆
A very good choice
The area is lavishly endowed with establishments ranging from rustic little huts to a large self-service place. Most huts do table service of delicious pizza, pasta and other dishes. But there are also plenty of snack bars.
Editors' choice On our March 2011 visit we had splendid meals at Chiecco (0338 7003035) at Plan Checrouit, a small hut with a welcoming host and a very varied menu – including fantastic chicken curry and a wild boar stew. Fine choice of local wines too. An old favourite of ours is Maison Vieille (0337 230979), a cosy, rustic place with jolly service and excellent pasta.

Worth knowing about Another favourite at Plan Checrouit is the Christiania (book a table downstairs to escape the crowds). Nearby, the Chaumière pizzeria has replaced Etoile Ski; family-run, serving 'good pizza and roast chicken' on 'one of the best terraces in Courmayeur'. Alpetta was also new for 2010/11, serving homemade pastas and burgers – 'great for families'. Reporters also like the Baita self-service for low prices and Bar du Soleil for more of those good views. At Col Checrouit, Chez Croux serves 'the best cakes and hot drinks on the mountain'. There is another clutch of worthwhile places in Val Veny: we enjoyed the smartly rustic Grolla for steaks and salads. The Petit Mont Blanc is also popular ('fabulous roast suckling pig').

SCHOOLS AND GUIDES ★★★★☆
Good private lessons
A 2011 report on private lessons with the Monte Bianco school is fairly enthusiastic. The Courmayeur school has 'a more snowboardy and young funky image'. There is a thriving guides' association ready to help you explore the area's off-piste; it has produced a helpful booklet showing the main possibilities. We had a super day in 2011 with solo guide Gianni Carbone (www.giannicarbone.com), who was patient and reassuring.

423

Interactive resort shortlist builder at **www.wtss.co.uk**

CHILDCARE
Fun park Dolonne
9am-4.30

Mini club Biancaneve (Monte Bianco school)
Ages 0 to 10

Ski-tots (Mammolo) (Monte Bianco school)
Lessons (2hr per day) for 3 and 4 year olds

Ski schools
Take children from age 5

UK PACKAGES
Alpine Answers, Alpine Weekends, Crystal, Crystal Finest, First Choice, Flexiski, Friendship Travel, Independent Ski Links, Inghams, Inspired to Ski, Interactive Resorts, Interski, Just Skiing, Mark Warner, Momentum, Ski Club Freshtracks, Ski Expectations, Ski Line, Ski Solutions, Skitracer, Ski Weekend, Skiweekends.com, Ski Yogi, STC, Thomson, Tracks European Adventures, White Roc

Phone numbers
From abroad use the prefix +39 (and do **not** omit the initial '0' of the phone number)

TOURIST OFFICE
www.courmayeur.it
www.lovevda.it

FOR FAMILIES ★★★★★
Some facilities
There is a children's playground at Dolonne and a nursery at Plan Checrouit for children up to 10 years.

STAYING THERE
Courmayeur's long-standing popularity ensures that there's a wide range of packages on offer (including some excellent weekend deals), mainly in hotels. Momentum Ski is an agent specialising in Courmayeur and can fix pretty much whatever you want here.
Chalets Some UK operators have catered chalets.
Hotels There are over 50 hotels, spanning the star ratings.
★★★★★Royal e Golf (0165 831611) Large, grand place in centre just off Via Roma. Outdoor pool, sauna, piano bar.
★★★★Gran Baita (0165 844040) Luxury place with antiques. Panoramic views. Pool and sauna.
★★★★Auberge de la Maison (0165 869811) Small, atmospheric hotel in Entrèves; owned by the same family as Maison de Filippo (see 'Eating out').
★★★★Cresta e Duc (0165 842585) Recently renovated. In centre. 'Great management and service.'
★★★★Villa Novocento (0165 843000) A short walk from the centre. Elegant lobby, good food and breakfasts.
★★★Pilier d'Angle (0165 869770) Friendly, cosy hotel in Entrèves; rooms and self-contained chalets. Good restaurant and wellness centre.
★★★Bouton d'Or (0165 846729) Small, friendly B&B hotel near main square. Heartily endorsed in 2011 for 'great breakfasts, amazing service'; '3-star hotel with friendly 5-star service'.
★★★Courmayeur (0165 846732) Near cable car. 'Very friendly, small rooms.'
★★★Maison Saint Jean (0165 842880) Central, family-run, pool and sauna.
★★Scoiattolo (0165 846721) Spacious rooms; near main square.
Apartments The 3-star Grand Chalet (0165 841448) is central with spacious apartments. Hot tub, steam and sauna are also available for non-residents.
At altitude Visiting Courmayeur and not staying in the charming village seems a bit perverse – if you're that keen to get going in the morning, this is probably not your ideal resort. But up the cable car at Plan Checrouit, the 1-star Christiania (0165 843572) has simple rooms; the 3-star Baita (0165 846542) is smarter.

EATING OUT ★★★★★
Jolly Italian evenings
There is a great choice of places. A handy promotional booklet describes many of them (in English). In downtown Courmayeur, we've been impressed by the traditional Italian cuisine of both Pierre Alexis and Cadran Solaire. Reporters regularly recommend the Piazzetta for pizza and seafood pastas. The long-established Tunnel pizzeria is 'still good'. Al Camin is a 'meat lover's paradise'. Mont-Fréty is now a smart, modern place and 'a favourite of the Milan set'; but it failed to impress a 2011 visitor. In Entrèves, the touristy but very jolly Maison de Filippo is rightly famous for its fixed-price, 36-dish feast. For a gourmet treat take a taxi to the Clotze in Val Ferret (same management as Chiecco – see 'Mountain restaurants'), for good homemade pastas and desserts; meat and seafood specials.

APRES-SKI ★★★★★
Stylish bar-hopping
Courmayeur has a lively evening scene – at weekends, at least – centred on stylish bars with comfy armchairs or sofas, often serving free canapés in the early evening. We like the Privé (great cocktails) and the back room of the Caffè della Posta. Bar Roma seems increasingly reliant on its impressive free buffet to pull in the crowds these days. A reader preferred the 'friendly' Petit Bistro bar. The Cadran Solaire is where the big money from Milan and Turin hangs out. The American Bar has good live music. Later on, try Covo nightclub in Entrèves (free shuttle bus service). A smart new club is due to open for 2011/12, below Dolonne.

OFF THE SLOPES ★★★★★
Lots on for non-slope users
The resort attracts many non-skiing Italians, who focus on showing off their togs and buying more of them in the abundant boutiques. You can go by cable car up to Punta Helbronner, by bus to Aosta, or up the main cable car to Plan Checrouit where there are countless spots to meet friends for lunch. The huge sports centre is good (but has no pool). Don't miss a visit to the thermal baths at Pré-St-Didier – with over 40 spa 'experiences' including saunas, waterfall and outdoor thermal pools. The Parco Avventura (10km from town) has a 'great' ropes course.

Livigno

Lowish prices and highish altitude – a tempting combination, especially when you add in a quite pleasant Alpine ambience

RATINGS

The mountains

Extent	★★
Fast lifts	★★★★
Queues	★★★★
Terrain p'ks	★★★★
Snow	★★★★
Expert	★
Intermediate	★★★
Beginner	★★★★
Boarder	★★★★
X-country	★★★★
Restaurants	★★★
Schools	★★★
Families	★★

The resort

Charm	★★★
Convenience	★★
Scenery	★★★
Eating out	★★★
Après-ski	★★★
Off-slope	★★

RPI   80

lift pass	£190
ski hire	£85
lessons	£90
food & drink	£100
total	**£465**

NEWS

2010/11: The Livigno Express transfer service now serves Innsbruck airport every Saturday. And opening times for the Munt la Schera tunnel from Switzerland were extended to 24 hours at weekends.

KEY FACTS

Resort	1815m
	5,950ft
Slopes	1815-2795m
	5,950-9,170ft
Lifts	30
Pistes	115km
	71 miles
Blue	26%
Red	57%
Black	17%
Snowmaking	70%

➕ High altitude plus snowmaking means reliable snow

➕ Large choice of beginners' slopes

➕ Impressive modern lift system

➕ Cheap by the standards of high, snow-sure resorts

➕ Lively, friendly, quite smart village with some Alpine atmosphere

➕ Long, snow-sure cross-country trails

➖ No challenging pistes, and off-piste without a guide officially banned

➖ Bleak setting, susceptible to white-outs and lift closures

➖ Very long transfers – over five hours for some reporters

➖ Village is very long and straggling – with no buses later in the evening

➖ Nightlife can disappoint

Livigno's recipe of a fair-sized mountain, high altitude and fairly low prices is uncommon, and obviously attractive. As a relatively snow-sure alternative to the Pyrenees or to the smallest, cheapest resorts in Austria, Livigno may make your shortlist. But don't expect rock-bottom prices, and do make sure the rest of the Livigno formula suits you – some of the drawbacks we list are enough to spoil a holiday. Experts, for a start, should go elsewhere.

THE RESORT

Livigno is set in a wide, remote valley near the Swiss border; the airport transfers are long and winding. The Alta Valtellina lift pass covers Bormio (about an hour's bus ride – free with the lift pass) and Santa Caterina (another 20 minutes). The Livigno pass gets you half-price on one day in St Moritz – an excursion not easily done from any other major resort.

VILLAGE CHARM ★★★★★
Pleasant enough
Hotels, bars, specialist shops and supermarkets line a single long, pedestrian-friendly street. The buildings are small in scale and mainly traditional in style, giving the village a pleasant atmosphere.

CONVENIENCE ★★★★★
Stay near the centre
It's a long, spread-out place. The original hamlet of San Antonio is the nearest thing Livigno has to a centre, and the best all-round location. Here, the main street and those at right angles, linking it to the busy bypass road, are nominally traffic-free, but actually are just through-traffic-free. The busy road that skirts the centre becomes intrusive in the hamlets of Santa Maria, 1km to the north, and San Rocco, a bit further away to the south (and a bit uphill).

Lifts along the length of the village access the western slopes of the valley (Costaccia and Carosello). The main lift to the eastern (Mottolino) slopes is across the flat valley floor from the centre – an inconvenient walk away.

You may make heavy use of the free bus services. They run every 15 minutes, but get overcrowded at peak times and stop at 8pm. While finding the services 'regular' and 'efficient', a 2011 visitor also found the routes difficult to understand. Taxis (including minibuses for groups) are an affordable alternative.

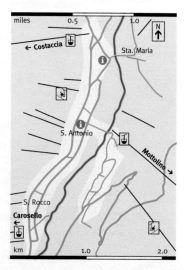

LIFT PASSES

Livigno

Prices in €		
Age	1-day	6-day
under 15	32	131
15 to 64	39	190
over 65	32	131
Free under 8		
Beginner points card		

Notes
Covers Livigno only;
half-day passes and
reduced Saturday
passes; family
reductions; 50%
discount on day pass
at St Moritz with
3-day-plus passes

Alternative passes
Alta Valtellina pass
covers Livigno,
Bormio and Santa
Caterina

SCENERY ★★★☆☆
Bleakness a feature
Livigno's high position and long ridges
provide attractive views from both
sides of the valley – but it can feel
bleak and isolated.

THE MOUNTAINS

The slopes are on either side of the
valley and are mainly above the
treeline. It's not a good place in bad
weather. Signposting is very good, but
the piste map does not identify runs.
Night skiing is available on Thursdays.

EXTENT OF THE SLOPES ★★☆☆☆
Widely spread
The slopes are more extensive than in
many other budget destinations, but
it's not a huge area and lots of the
runs are very similar to each other.

A two-stage gondola at the north
end of the village takes you up to
Costaccia, where a long fast quad
chairlift goes along the ridge towards
the **Carosello** sector. The blue linking
run back from Carosello to the top of
Costaccia is flat in places and may
involve energetic poling if snow
conditions and the wind are against
you. Carosello is more usually
accessed by the optimistically named
Carosello 3000 gondola at San Rocco,
which goes up, in two stages, to
2750m. Most runs return towards the
village, but there are a couple on the
back of the mountain, on west-facing
slopes, served by a six-pack.

The ridge of **Mottolino** is reached
by an efficient gondola from Teola, a
tiresome walk or a bus ride across the

valley from San Antonio. From the top,
you can descend to fast quads on
either side of the ridge, or take a very
slow antique chair along the ridge.

We don't show on our map a low-
level link from the nursery drags at the
bottom of Carosello to those below
Costaccia; it's more of a walk than a
run – not recommended for boarders.

FAST LIFTS ★★★★☆
A positive attraction
The lift system is impressively modern,
with fast chairs and gondolas covering
both sectors – though draglifts still
serve the valley nursery slopes.

QUEUES ★★★★☆
Few problems these days
Queues are generally not a problem.
Delays can occur at the main gondolas
at peak times, such as the Carosello
3000. A bigger problem is that winds
can close the upper lifts, causing
crowds lower down.

TERRAIN PARKS ★★★★☆
Serious facilities
The main park behind Mottolino is an
impressive freestyle zone for all levels.
It also plays host to the World Rookie
fest and River Jump contest – both on
the Ticket to Ride calendar. It has
kicker lines for all levels and a hip.
This is bordered by a big super-pipe,
often used as a training ground by
pros, and there are advanced rails in
and around the jumps as well. In 2010
a huge airbag jump was added –
perfect for trying out backflips and
other advanced tricks.

Livigno's second park is at

Weekly news updates and resort links at www.wtss.co.uk

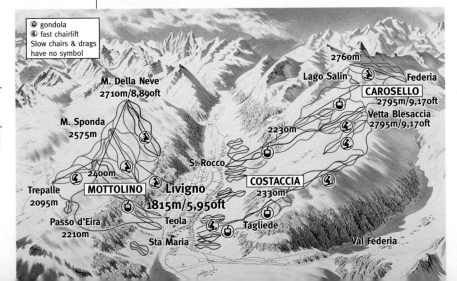

- ⓖ gondola
- ⓕ fast chairlift
- Slow chairs & drags
  have no symbol

M. Della Neve
2710m/8,890ft

M. Sponda
2575m

2400m

Trepalle
2095m

MOTTOLINO

Passo d'Eira
2210m

Livigno
1815m/5,950ft

Teola

Sta Maria

S. Rocco

2230m

2760m

Lago Salin

Federia

CAROSELLO
2795m/9,170ft

Vetta Blesaccia
2795m/9,170ft

COSTACCIA
2330m

Tagliede

Val Federia

↑ It's a broad valley, and a long, long village; we're looking here at the Carosello/Costaccia slopes

APT LIVIGNO / MARCO PAGANI

GETTING THERE

Air Bergamo 190km/120 miles (3hr45); Brescia 225km/140 miles (4hr45); Innsbruck 180km/110 miles (3hr15); Zürich 190km/120 miles (3hr30)

Rail Tirano (48km/ 30 miles); Zernez (Switzerland, 28km/ 17 miles); regular buses from station, weekends only

Carosello 3000. It also caters for all standards and includes another huge airbag jump. The two other parks – Amerikan, beside the Amerikan lift in San Rocco, and the Del Sole area near the centre of town – are aimed at novices and juniors.

SNOW RELIABILITY ★★★★☆
Very good, despite no glacier
Livigno's slopes are high (you can spend most of your time around 2500m) and, with snow-guns on the lower slopes of Mottolino and Costaccia, the season is long.

FOR EXPERTS ★☆☆☆☆
Not recommended
There are several black runs on Mottolino, but they are really no more than stiff reds, and regularly groomed. And going off-piste without a guide is now officially banned, though you see a lot of tracks between the pistes.

FOR INTERMEDIATES ★★★☆☆
Flattering slopes
Good intermediates will be able to have serious fun on the groomed blacks on Mottolino, as well as the wide choice of reds. The woodland black run from Carosello past Tea da Borch is narrow in places and can get mogulled and icy in the afternoon. Moderate intermediates have virtually the whole area at their disposal. The long run beneath the Mottolino gondola is one of the best, and there is also a long, varied, under-used blue

going less directly to the valley. Leisurely types have several long cruises available; the blue beneath the fast chair at the top of Costaccia is a splendid slope.

FOR BEGINNERS ★★★★☆
Excellent but scattered slopes
A vast array of nursery slopes including those along the sunny lower flanks of Costaccia, are excellent for novices – although some of the slopes at the northern end are steep enough to cause difficulties. There are lots of longer runs to progress to.

FOR BOARDERS ★★★★☆
Spacious but on-piste
It is a shame that off-piste without a guide is now officially banned. So you are technically confined to the pistes, which are in general big, wide, open and rolling motorways. But you do see a lot of people riding between the pistes, despite the prominent signs telling you not to. Beginners be warned: practically all the smaller lower slopes are serviced by drags. But the resort still attracts good numbers of beginners, and Madness is a specialist snowboard school.

FOR CROSS-COUNTRY ★★★★☆
Good snow, bleak setting
Long snow-sure trails (40km in total) follow the valley floor, making Livigno a good choice, provided you don't mind the bleak scenery. There is a specialist school, Livigno 2000.

Livigno

Interactive resort shortlist builder at **www.wtss.co.uk**

SCHOOLS

Centrale
t 0342 996276

Azzurra
t 0342 997683

Livigno Italy
t 0342 996767

Livigno Galli Fedele
t 0342 970300

Madness Snowboard
t 0342 997792

New
t 0342 997801

Classes
(Centrale prices)
6 days (2hr per day)
€108
Private lessons
€36 for 1hr; each
additional person €8

CHILDCARE

Lupogno Kinder Club
t 0342 996276
Ages 3 and over; Sun
to Fri; 8.30 to 3.30
M'eating Point
t 0342 997408
**Spazio gioco Per i
bimbi**
t 0342 970711

Ski school
Takes children from
age 4 (6 2hr days
€108)

ACTIVITIES

Indoor Aquagranda
wellness park
(swimming pool,
sauna, fitness rooms),
badminton, billiards,
bowling, basketball
Outdoor Cleared
paths, ice rink,
snowshoeing, horse
riding, tobogganing,
dog sledding, go-karts
on ice snowmobiling,
ice driving

UK PACKAGES

*Independent Ski Links,
Inghams, Neilson,
Skitracer*

Phone numbers
From abroad use the
prefix +39 (and do **not**
omit the initial '0' of
the phone number)

TOURIST OFFICE

www.livigno.eu

MOUNTAIN RESTAURANTS ★★★★★
No more than adequate

On Mottolino, the large M'eating Point refuge at the top of the gondola has a 'lively, overcrowded' self-service section that can be 'slow, resulting in cold food'. We've mixed reports of the small – and peaceful – table-service section: 'very average', says one; 'well-flavoured spaghetti', says another. Lower down are the rustic restaurants at Passo d'Eira and at Trepalle, where the Trela pizzeria and restaurant has been recommended (best to book). Carosello has a popular but 'acceptable' self-service place and a table-service wine bar and restaurant below. Tea da Borch, in the trees lower down, has a Tirolean-style atmosphere. In the Costaccia sector a reporter reckons the food at the Costaccia restaurant to be only average, while another remarks on the new and 'very clean' toilets. The Berghütte just above the nursery slopes in the Tagliede area is small and rustic, with 'good' food but a 'limited' menu.

SCHOOLS AND GUIDES ★★★★★
Short but sweet classes

Reports on the schools have generally been good, praising instruction and English. Classes are rated great value for money, but are mornings only (as is usual in Italy).

FOR FAMILIES ★★★★★
Not bad for Italy

The schools run classes for children from the age of four, and the Centrale school offers all-day non-skiing care for children from the age of three; the staff speak English. Beware the long, winding airport transfers.

STAYING THERE

Livigno has an enormous range of hotels and a number of apartments. There are some attractively priced catered chalets from UK operators.
Hotels There is a wide choice.
★★★★Intermonti (0342 972100) Modern with pool and other mod cons; on the Mottolino side of the valley.
★★★★Camana Veglia (0342 996310) Charming old wooden chalet. Popular restaurant, well placed in Santa Maria.
★★★Steinbock (0342 970520) Nice little place, far from major lifts.
★★★Loredana (0342 996330) Modern chalet on the Mottolino side.
★★★Montanina (0342 996060) Very

central, family run, 'friendly staff'.
★★★Larice (0342 996184) Stylish little B&B well placed for Costaccia lifts.
★★★Champagne (0342 996437) Pleasant B&B close to centre.
★★Silvestri (0342 996255) Comfortable place in the San Rocco area.
Apartments Available locally and from tour operators; a 2010 reporter was impressed with his 'massive' apartment from Neilson.

EATING OUT ★★★★★
Value for money

Livigno's restaurants are mainly traditional, unpretentious places, many hotel-based. Over the years we've had countless recommendations for where to eat. The latest recommendations include: Paprika ('good flavour, good value'), Scala ('fish a speciality; flavour, service and ambiance excellent'), the Garden Hotel ('tasty lunch, professional service, best meal in Livigno') and the Pastorella Hotel ('food very tasty, quiet attentive service'). The Rusticana is a good-value pizzeria and Pesce d'Oro specialises in seafood.

APRES-SKI ★★★★★
Lively, but disappoints some

The scene is quieter than some people expect – and the best places are scattered about, so the village lacks evening buzz. At tea time Tea del Vidal, at the bottom of Mottolino, is the place to be – 'après-ski is tame everywhere else', says one visitor – and it gets lively at the Stalet bar at the base of the Carosello gondola ('very friendly and warm') and at the central umbrella bar. Nightlife gets going after 10pm. The Kuhstall under the Bivio hotel is an excellent cellar bar with live music, as is the Helvetia, over the road. The San Rocco end is quietest, but Daphne's is 'one of the few lively bars in Livigno', Miky's is 'vibrant and very busy', and Marco's is popular. Kokodi is the main disco.

OFF THE SLOPES ★★★★★
New spa fails to impress

A 2011 visitor to the new thermal spa/wellness centre rated it 'not a patch on Bad Gastein and twice the price'. Other visitors have enjoyed the dog sledding, and tobogganing is also popular. And you can go bowling and ice-driving. Walks are uninspiring. There's duty-free shopping, of course – and trips to Bormio and St Moritz.

Madonna di Campiglio

MADONNA TOURIST OFFICE

A fashionable resort amid stunning scenery – a bit like Cortina, in other words, but with a more compelling ski area

TOP 10 RATINGS

Extent	★★★
Fast lifts	★★★
Queues	★★★
Snow	★★★
Expert	★★
Intermediate	★★★★
Beginner	★★★★
Charm	★★★
Convenience	★★★
Scenery	★★★★

RPI   95

lift pass	£210
ski hire	£110
lessons	£100
food & drink	£125
total	£545

NEWS

2011/12: The long-awaited gondola link between the Cinque Laghi sector of slopes and Pinzolo, due last season, is expected to open. On Grostè the Boch chair is to be replaced by a fast quad, with an additional blue run.

2010/11: Above Madonna, several new pistes were created. A new terrain park was built at Pradalago.

A new fixed-grip quad chairlift opened above Marilleva, between Val Panciana and Doss della Pesa.

At Pinzolo, an eight-person gondola opened, starting from Tulot (just outside the town) and serving new, good-looking black and red runs.

+ Pleasant, stylish town in a splendid setting in the Brenta Dolomites

+ Extensive, mainly intermediate slopes, including those of Folgarida, Marilleva and now Pinzolo

− Resort spreads miles along valley, away from the compact centre

− Tough pistes are few, and widely separated around a big area

− Quiet in the evenings

Campiglio may come second to Cortina for glitz and scenery, but the slopes around it are more extensive, and better linked. The outlying sectors, including Pinzolo, offer some of the best skiing, and it all adds up to a good-sized area.

THE RESORT

Campiglio is a towny, fashionable resort, set in a broad valley that includes a pretty frozen lake. It seems now to be attracting lots of Russian visitors at certain times of year.

Village charm Campiglio has a traditional style with a pleasant core (bypassed by through-traffic) where there are lots of smart shops. The place is busy all day, and promenading is an early evening ritual.

Convenience The centre is fairly compact: the lifts to the Cinque Laghi and Pradalago sectors bracket most of the main hotels, and are about a five-minute walk apart. Five minutes outside the centre is a gondola to the Grostè sector. But the resort then spreads about 3km down the valley, while up the valley is the outlying suburb of Campo Carlo Magno, where there are further major lifts up to Grostè and Pradalago. The free ski-bus is said to have improved of late; some hotels run their own shuttles.

Scenery The resort has a splendid setting, with the dramatic cliffs of the Brenta group to the south-west.

[Resort map showing Madonna di Campiglio ski area]

Legend:
- ◉ gondola
- ◉ fast chairlift
- Slow chairs & drags have no symbol

Passo Grostè 2505m/8,220ft

GROSTÈ

Monte Spinale 2100m

Doss del Sabion 2100m

Val d'Agola

Pinzolo 770m

1540m

Malga Grual

800m

Madonna di Campiglio 1520m/4,990ft

CINQUE LAGHI 2150m

PRADALAGO 2145m

Doss della Pesa 2155m

MONTE VIGO 2180m

Campo Carlo Magno 1680m

Monte Spolverino 2090m

Orti

1860m

1888m

Folgarida 1400m

Marilleva 1400m

1300m

↑ The close-up views of the Brenta group from the Cinque Laghi sector are superb

TRENTINO SPA / ALESSANDRO TROVATI

Weekly news updates and resort links at **www.wtss.co.uk**

THE MOUNTAINS

The upper slopes are open, the lower slopes attractively wooded. Many runs classified red could be blue.

Slopes The Pradalago sector is linked via Monte Vigo to the slopes of Folgarida and Marilleva, and the new gondola from Cinque Laghi will access the slopes of Pinzolo. Reporters have been very impressed by immaculate grooming.

Fast lifts Most of the key lifts are fast chairs and gondolas.

Queues Rarely a problem except at ski school time.

Terrain parks The Ursus park, at Grostè, includes boardercross, half- and quarter-pipes, rails, a fun box and a kicker. There's a special boarders' pass for the area. There is also a beginner park in the Pradalago sector.

Snow reliability Although many of the runs are sunny, they are at a fair altitude, and there has been hefty investment in snowmaking. As a result, snow reliability is reasonable.

Experts As elsewhere in Italy, off-piste is formally banned, but the ban is often ignored. The trees under the Genziana chair are a good spot for untracked snow. There are genuine black pistes dotted around – basically, one per sector, including the outlying resorts. Few of the local reds present much challenge – the 3 Tre race course is one.

Intermediates Grostè and Pradalago have long, easy runs, and timid intermediates will love them. Cinque Laghi, Campiglio's racing mountain, is a bit tougher, as are the runs at Folgarida, Marilleva and Pinzolo, which keen intermediates should explore.

Beginners The nursery slopes at Campo Carlo Magno are excellent, but do involve a bus ride. The draglift here is not covered by the main lift pass – you have to buy a separate day ticket when you get there. Progression to longer runs is easy.

Snowboarding The resort is popular with boarders and some major events have been held here.

Cross-country There are 22km of pretty trails through the woods.

Mountain restaurants Reports are all positive, but some reporters wish there were more little rustic places. Some of the best are mountaineering/walking refuges. Recommendations on Grostè: Boch, Stoppani ('elegant dining, fabulous views'), Chalet Fiat Albergo Dosson ('modern, stylish, excellent food'), Graffer ('lovely position, very reasonable prices, efficient service') and Malga Montagnoli; on Pradalago: Viviani Pradalago ('best pasta') and Cascina Zeledria ('cook your own on a hot rock before being towed back to the piste').

Schools and guides There are seven schools – Nazionale is the main one. Language has been a problem in the past, but we are assured that Nazionale and Rainalter in particular have English-speaking instructors.

Families Very limited. The ski schools take children from about three. The Rainalter Ski School offers a baby club arranging non-ski activities for children between three and eight years.

KEY FACTS	
Resort	1520m
	4,990ft
Madonna, Folgarida, Marilleva, Pinzolo combined area	
Slopes	800-2505m
	2,620-8,220ft
Lifts	62
Pistes	150km
	93 miles
Blue	40%
Red	45%
Black	15%
Snowmaking	95%

Phone numbers
From abroad use the prefix +39 (and do **not** omit the initial '0' of the phone number)

TOURIST OFFICE

www.campiglio.to

STAYING THERE

There is a wide choice of hotels and some self-catering.

Hotels Of the 4-stars, we enjoyed the Carlo Magno (0465 441010) on our last visit, and a 2011 reporter recommends the Lorenzetti (0465 441404) for 'the excellent food and glorious views'. Of the 3-stars, the central St Hubertus (0465 441144) has been praised. A visitor praises the Arnica B&B (0465 442227) chiefly for its helpful English-speaking owner.

Eating out There are around 20 restaurants. Reader recommendations include Antico Focolare ('spectacular ravioli in creamy nut sauce'), Le Roi ('crowded with happy people – great pizza and pasta') and, for a gourmet treat, the 'amazing' Da Alfiero.

Après-ski Cafe Campiglio, Bar Suisse and Cafe Nardis are busy as the slopes close. Bar One at the bottom of Spinale is more 'conveniently placed but not so popular'. Later in the evening Des Alpes Mood Club, Cliffhanger and also Zangola (out of town) are possibilities. Cantina del Suisse has live music some evenings.

Off the slopes There's not a huge amount to do. Skating on the lake and snowshoeing are popular, and the local Alpine guides offer ice climbing.

LINKED RESORT – 1400m
MARILLEVA

Marilleva is a modern resort consisting of several 1960s-style, ugly but functional, low-rise concrete buildings (most of them well screened by trees, thankfully) built on a mid-mountain shelf at 1400m and reached by road or gondola from the lower part of the resort at 900m, on the valley floor.

The shady slopes above Marilleva include excellent long, testing reds from Monte Vigo, served by a gondola and a six-pack and various shorter blues. There's also a serious black run served by a two-stage chair to Doss della Pesa. The Orso Bruno mountain restaurant offers 'fantastic views, good food and reasonable prices'.

LINKED RESORT – 1400m
FOLGARIDA

Folgarida is also purpose built and set above the floor of the Val di Sole, but it is beside the road over to Campiglio, and is much more traditional in style

than Marilleva. The main part of the resort is clustered below the gondola base station at 1400m. It feels a bit upmarket, with smart hotels and a few shops, but there are few other amenities. A 2011 reporter rates it excellent for families, with 'friendly, helpful locals'. You may encounter some fur-clad patrons, or in January families from Eastern Europe. A 2009 reporter judged the 4-star hotel Caminetto 'almost perfect'. There's a smaller area of development at 1300m, by another gondola station.

The slopes down to Folgarida are gentler than those above Marilleva, though they include an easy black, and one reader found some of the blues rather tricky.

Midway between Marilleva and Folgarida, an eight-person gondola runs from the valley village of Daolasa up to Val Mastellina, the top section serving a long, sweeping red with lovely views of the Val di Sole below.

LINKED RESORT – 770m
PINZOLO

Pinzolo is the main town of the Val Rendena, south-west of Madonna di Campiglio, and a 20-minute drive away. A long (and long-planned) gondola link with the Cinque Laghi slopes of Campiglio is due for 2011/12.

From Pinzolo, a gondola followed by a fast chair take you to the area's high point of Doss del Sabion (2100m), where there are great views of the Brenta massif. It's a challenging area, mainly consisting of genuine blacks (groomed when we visited), genuine reds, and reds that are occasionally of black steepness. The Tulot gondola opened in 2010 serves a new black/red run of almost 900m vertical to the base station, just outside the town. Many of the slopes are shady, so keep their snow well.

Madonna di Campiglio

431

Interactive resort shortlist builder at **www.wtss.co.uk**

SNOWPIX.COM / CHRIS GILL

Monterosa Ski

One of Europe's best-kept secrets: three unspoiled villages, long easy pistes and excellent, uncrowded off-piste terrain

aosta-valley.co.uk

NEWS

2011/12: At Gressoney, a new gondola is to replace the existing one from Stafal to Gabiet.

2010/11: Developments focused on remodelling some slopes and improving snowmaking efficiency.

- ✚ Fabulous off-piste and heli-skiing, for both intermediates and experts
- ✚ Slopes usually very quiet weekdays
- ✚ Panoramic views
- ✚ Good snow reliability and grooming
- ✚ Quiet, unspoiled villages
- ✚ Lovely long runs and a sensation of travel from place to place, but ...

- ▬ Virtually no choice of route when touring the three valleys on-piste
- ▬ Few challenges (or moguls) on-piste
- ▬ High winds can close links
- ▬ Few off-slope diversions
- ▬ Can be surprisingly busy at weekends
- ▬ Limited après-ski

Monterosa Ski's three resorts – Champoluc, Gressoney la Trinité and Alagna – are popular with weekenders from Milan and Turin. But they are little-known internationally, and retain a friendly, small-scale, unspoiled Italian ambience that we (and a growing band of readers) like a lot. And like La Thuile, another Aosta Valley resort, they are crowd-free at half-term.

The three-valley network of slopes is anything but small-scale: Alagna and Champoluc are an impressive 17km apart – slightly further apart than Courchevel and Val Thorens. But a glance at the piste map reveals that the Italian network is skeletal compared with the full-bodied Trois Vallées. More about this later. Outside the piste network is a lot of great off-piste terrain that has long attracted experts. Most of it is again lift-served thanks to the cable car that opened in 2009 following closure of the ancient Punta Indren lift.

THE RESORT

There is one main village in each of the area's three valleys. Champoluc in the western Val d'Ayas and Gressoney in the central valley are both about an hour's drive up from the Aosta valley, to the south. Alagna is even more remote, and approached by a quite different route from the east. Like most Italian resorts, the villages really come to life only at weekends.

Down-valley from Gressoney la Trinité is Gressoney St Jean. Down-valley from Champoluc are Antagnod and Brusson. All have small slope areas covered by the Monterosa Ski lift pass. Antagnod is used by local instructors on bad-weather days and has some good off-piste.

Trips to Cervinia, La Thuile, Courmayeur and Pila are possible by car. An Aosta Valley pass covering all of them is available.

Village charm All three villages are small-scale and pleasantly rustic, without being picture-postcard pretty.

Champoluc is strung out along the road running up the valley from the centre, which is more or less devoid of bars and inviting shops.

Gressoney la Trinité is a quiet, neat little village, with cobbled streets, wooden buildings and an old church – but also many disused buildings.

Alagna is a secluded village with a solid church and some lovely old wooden farmhouses built in the distinctive Walser style.

Convenience In Champoluc you can get up the hill via the village gondola, starting from a kind of micro-resort several minutes' walk up the road (you can store kit there overnight), or a newish funicular starting further up the valley at Frachey.

Gressoney la Trinité is about 800m from the base station of a slow chairlift into the local slopes, where there are a few convenient hotels. The lifts for the other valleys go from the mini-resort of Stafal at the head of the valley. But its lodgings are quite widely spread away from the lifts.

Alagna is streets ahead of its neighbours in this respect: the gondola starts from the village square.

Scenery Some of the highest peaks in the Alps surround Monterosa Ski – a string of peaks over 4000m, and some over 4500m; the panoramic views from restaurant terraces are fabulous.

KEY FACTS

Slopes	1200-3275m
	3,940-10,740ft
Lifts	23
Pistes	135km
	84 miles
Blue	17%
Red	71%
Black	12%
Snowmaking	97%

THE MOUNTAINS

The slopes offer an attractive mix of woodland runs low-down, particularly at Gressoney, and open slopes higher up; but the latter dominate, and the top lifts can be closed by wind. Run classification generally exaggerates difficulty. Signposting is excellent ('impossible to get lost' says one reporter).

Slopes The slopes span vast distances, but don't add up to a huge amount of piste skiing. The claimed total of 135km for the linked area (excluding the separate smaller ski areas down-valley from Champoluc and Gressoney) doesn't convince many readers, or us. It is based on figures that look dodgy – the red Pistone Betta down to Stafal, for example, is a lovely long cruise; but is it 10.5km long for a drop of 550m? More like half that, we reckon.

The main three-valley network is very simple. Starting from Frachey, up the valley from Champoluc, or from Alagna at the opposite end, you ride two or three lifts up to the first ridge, ski down to Stafal, ride two or three lifts up to the second ridge, ski down. All the descents are gloriously long; the run from Passo Salati to Alagna is a claimed 13.5km, 1760m vertical and a lovely easy black for the first half and a tough red for the lower half. But there is little choice of route along the way. Added to this core are the local slopes of Champoluc and Gressoney. (Alagna has no such additional area of slopes, which is a real drawback.)

The gondola from Champoluc goes up to Crest, a mid-mountain nursery area with a further gondola and chairlift above it climbing a further 700m to Colle Sarezza. This area is linked to the runs above Frachey (and the link to Stafal) via a steep, narrow, bumpy red run – very difficult for timid intermediates, who are better off starting at Frachey.

At Gressoney, a pair of chairlifts go up from two points serving wooded runs of 400m/500m vertical, with piste links across the mountainside to Gabiet where you can join the three-valley link towards Alagna, or descend to Stafal to go towards Champoluc.

Fast lifts The lifts are virtually all chairs and gondolas; most of the important chairs are fast, the one out of Gressoney being an exception.

Queues Problems generally occur only at weekends and peak periods, when pistes can get crowded and the gondola and cable car from Alagna can build queues. The gondola out of Stafal was queue-prone too, but is being upgraded. The double chair on the way from Frachey to Champoluc can have long afternoon queues.

Terrain parks Gressoney has a boardercross but there's no park. Big air jumps are sometimes built near the top of the gondola from Champoluc.

Snow reliability Generally good, thanks to altitude and extensive snowmaking, which impresses reporters. Grooming is very thorough – one or two reporters have complained that 'to find bumps you have to go off-piste'.

gondola
cable car
fast chairlift
Slow chairs & drags have no symbol

Colle della Bettaforca 2725m

Indren 3275m/10,740ft

Passo Salati

ALAGNA

Bocchetta delle Pisse 2400m

GRESSONEY

CHAMPOLUC

Stafal
S. Anna

Gabiet 2320m

Pianalunga 2045m

Frachey 1620m

Colle Sarezza 2700m

Orsia

Punta Jolanda 2280m

an Pera 2310m

Champoluc 1580m/5,180ft

Crest 1980m

Ostafa 2420m

Gressoney La Trinité 1640m/5,380ft

Alagna 1200m/ 3,940ft

Antagnod 1720m

2235m

Gressoney St Jean

Estoul 1735m

Weissmatten

Experts The attraction is the off-piste, with great runs from the high points of the lift system and some excellent heli-drops. Among the adventures we've enjoyed here was a heli-drop on Monte Rosa, skiing down to Zermatt and returning off-piste from Cervinia. The opening of the new lift to Punta Indren in 2009 has restored some sorely missed off-piste opportunities. But guides can take you to plenty of places lower down too, including the excellent Mandria forest area above Frachey. There is good, shady, easily accessible off-piste beside the long run from Passo Salati towards Alagna.
Intermediates There are excellent, long cruising runs from the ridges down into the valleys. Down towards Alagna, the black Olen piste (which is more like a tough red and was classified red originally) is a great blast, as is the tough red Alagna piste below it. There isn't much other sustained on-piste challenge for more demanding intermediates – take a guide and explore the gentler off-piste. But timid intermediates should beware of the run from Colle Sarezza mentioned under 'Slopes' above.
Beginners The high nursery slopes at

Crest above Champoluc, served by two moving carpets, are better than the lower ones at Gressoney. But neither has ideal gentle runs to progress to.
Snowboarding There's a boardercross at Gressoney and great freeriding.
Cross-country There are long trails: 25km around Gressoney St Jean, 17km in Champoluc; Brusson, in the Champoluc valley, has the best trails in the area (38km).
Mountain restaurants The mountain restaurants are generally simple but good value. There are plenty of them and readers enthuse about most (but not about the squat toilets).

In the Val d'Ayas, there are two notably charming places serving excellent food in beautifully renovated old wooden buildings – Rascard Frantze above Champoluc and Stadel Soussun above Frachey. Other recent reader tips include: the Belvedere, the Ostafa ('great pasta'), the modern Campo Base ('good curry, the best hot chocolate'), and Lo Retsignon ('good views'; 'good value food and sandwiches'). In the Gressoney valley tips include the Sitten ('great views, excellent pasta') and Gabiet ('good pasta and cakes, fab bombardinos'),

Champoluc *Alpine Answers, Crystal, Inghams, Interactive Resorts, Momentum, Mountain Wave, Ski 2, Ski Club Freshtracks, Ski Expectations, Ski Solutions, Ski Yogi, Snow Finders, White Roc*
Gressoney la Trinité *Alpine Answers, Crystal, Crystal Finest, Inghams, Momentum, Mountain Tracks, Ski Club Freshtracks, Skitracer, Ski Yogi, Snoworks*
Alagna *Alpine Answers, Mountain Tracks, Ski Club Freshtracks, Ski-Monterosa, Ski Weekend*

Phone numbers
From abroad use the prefix +39 (and do **not** omit the initial '0' of the phone number)

www.monterosa-ski.com/en

both above Stafal, also the Bedemie ('excellent value pasta and tarts, service a little slow') and Morgenrot above Orsia ('smart with good service and food'), the Alpen Lys above the Passo Salati gondola at Punta Indren ('good-value, simple food') and the Punta Jolanda – formerly the Chamois ('great venison stew and polenta, wonderful views'). In the Alagna valley top slot goes to the splendid Rifugio Guglielmina just below the ridge ('excellent food', 'outstanding views'). Lower down, Alpen Stop at Pianalunga, the Baita just below and Shoppf Vittine are recommended.
Schools and guides We have had mixed reports on the Italian ski schools – we've a report of a beginner with the Stafal school having a 'disastrous' lesson with one instructor but three 'excellent' lessons with another. We have had good reports of the ski school run by tour op Ski 2 ('good, friendly instructors'), and of the Monterosa mountain guides.
Families Facilities are limited. Talk to your tour operator.

STAYING THERE

A growing list of tour operators feature the area. We've had good reports of Monterosa specialists Ski 2 ('great from pick-up to drop-off').
Hotels For a small place, Champoluc has a striking range of attractive hotels. We have lots of favourable reports on the 3-star Champoluc (0125 308088) – 'very friendly, excellent position' – despite complaints that the spa facilities cost extra, and on the central, 3-star, creaky old Castor (0125 307117) – 'great atmosphere, good food, helpful, friendly staff'. The central Relais des Glaciers (0125 308182) is a 'comfortable and well appointed' 4-star with 'excellent if limited' menus each night. One luxury option is the 4-star Breithorn (0125 308734), just up the road, but a recent reporter found the rooms very small and the service lacking. In 2010 we enjoyed the friendly 4-star La Rouja (0125 308767) with 13 rooms clad in local wood. Two mountain restaurants have charming rooms – Stadel Soussun (0348 6527222) and Rascard Frantze (0125 941065).
At Gressoney la Trinité, right by the Punta Jolanda lift are the 3-star Dufour (0125 366139), the 'welcoming and friendly' Residence (0125 366217) with steam and sauna and the modern Val

Verde (0125 366148) with hot tub and sauna. In the village, Lo Scoiattolo (0125 366313) is run by 'lovely cheerful people' who will ferry you to the lift. In a peaceful setting between Stafal and Gressoney is the Anderbätt (0125 366600) – a 'really lovely, friendly' restaurant with six rooms. At Stafal are the Rédél Näscht (0347 797360), a 'fabulous' little B&B run by a 'super-friendly family', and the 'small and charming' Chalet du Lys (0125 366086), with 'excellent' food.
In Alagna, try the 4-star Cristallo (0163 922822), the 3-star Monterosa (0163 923209) – 'did the perfect job for the price but the evening meal was very basic' – or the Residence Mirella (0163 91286) – 50m from the lifts and above the village bakery ('superb' breakfasts, not surprisingly). The Rifugio Guglielmina (0163 91444) up at 2880m has cosy rooms.
Eating out Most restaurants are in hotels, but there are a few stand-alone places. Reader recommendations include: in Champoluc, the Osteria Il Balivo ('terrific food and atmosphere') and Atelier Gourmand ('fantastic wines') – both on Route Ramey – and the Grange up at Frachey; in Stafal, the Capanna Carla; in Alagna, the Unione ('excellent pasta and steaks') and Dir und Don pizzeria/grill ('good value/service').
Après-ski The evenings are generally quiet, at least during the week. In Champoluc, the bar of the hotel Castor is cosy and popular with resort workers; the Golosone is a small, atmospheric, distinctly Italian wine bar; the Galion opposite the gondola is busy as the lifts close; the West Road pub in the hotel California has karaoke some nights. At weekends, the Gram Parsons disco beneath the California gets going. Gressoney is even quieter; in Stafal the Giovanni is a 'great place for a decent beer as you finish for the day'. In Alagna, the Mirella (see 'Hotels'), the Caffè della Guide and the Luisa ('cheapest drinks') have been recommended. The An Bacher Wi wine bar gets good reports.
Off the slopes There is an outdoor ice rink at Champoluc, but little else.

Passo Tonale

An excellent place to learn or to build confidence at moderate cost, with its appeal broadened by the link with Ponte di Legno

TOP 10 RATINGS

Extent	★★
Fast lifts	★★★★
Queues	★★★★
Snow	★★★★
Expert	★
Intermediate	★★★
Beginner	★★★★★
Charm	★★
Convenience	★★★
Scenery	★★★

RPI   70

lift pass	£170
ski hire	£75
lessons	£50
food & drink	£100
total	**£395**

NEWS

There are plans for new lifts on the Presena Glacier for 2012/13.

2010/11: A new mountain hut, Rifugio Passo Paradiso, opened beside the Paradiso gondola top station.

The Skiline system, to track progress around the slopes, was introduced.

KEY FACTS

Resort	1885m	
	6,180ft	

Passo Tonale and Ponte di Legno combined area

Slopes	1120-3015m	
	3,670-9,890ft	
Lifts		30
Pistes		100km
		62 miles
Blue		17%
Red		66%
Black		17%
Snowmaking		100%

- ➕ Good-value, mid-market lodgings
- ➕ Sunny but snow-sure slopes
- ➕ Plenty of uncrowded, easy runs, immediately above the village
- ➕ Link to Ponte di Legno adds attractive, steeper, treelined runs

- ➖ Not much locally for experts or keen intermediates
- ➖ Local slopes are above the treeline and unpleasant in bad weather
- ➖ Linear village strung along the pass road is no beauty

Passo Tonale's blend of attractions makes it a great place for beginners and timid intermediates. It's a more interesting destination for the more adventurous now that it is linked to the slopes above Ponte di Legno.

THE RESORT

Village charm The resort was developed mainly for skiing, along a road over a pass; many of the buildings are in chalet style, but it lacks a focus, and traffic intrudes.

Convenience Tonale is fairly compact, with its hotels, shops, bars and restaurants spread along the bottom of the main slope area – so the nearest lift is generally not far away.

Scenery The setting can feel rather bleak, but Ponte di Legno's woods offer an attractive contrast – and there are some wide views.

THE MOUNTAINS

The home slopes are entirely above the treeline, and bad weather can mean white-outs and closures. The Tonale slopes are linked to the lower ones of Ponte di Legno, which are generally steeper and quieter than Passo Tonale's main area. The regional pass covers Marilleva, 30 minutes east

(free daily bus), and linked Madonna di Campiglio. Another pass gives a day or two in Aprica, 45 minutes west.

Slopes Tonale's slopes are spread over two main sectors on opposite sides of the pass. The broad, south-facing area is much the larger, starts right at the village and is served by a well-laid-out mix of chairs and drags. Most runs are short, with limited vertical. The north-facing Presena area is steeper, narrower and taller. First, there is an eight-seat gondola; then a double chairlift; and at the top, on the Presena glacier, two draglifts.

Ponte di Legno is reached by a blue/red run through the trees (mostly wide and easy but including a short much steeper section) followed by an (easy) black run that you can't avoid on the Ponte di Legno side. Or you can ride the gondola there.

Fast lifts The lift system is impressive, with seven fast chairs in the main local areas of slopes.

Queues High-season visitors in 2011

- 🚠 gondola
- 🚞 railway/funicular
- 🚡 fast chairlift
- Slow chairs & drags have no symbol

Cima Presena 3015m/9,890ft
Corno Lacoscuro 3160m/10,360ft
PRESENA
2120m
1905m/6,250ft
Passo Paradiso 2585m
Corno d'Aola 1920m/6,300ft
Valbione 1500m
Vermiglio 1260m/4,140ft
Passo Tonale 1885m/6,180ft
Ponte di Legno 1255m/4,120ft
Passo Contrabbandieri 2575m
2180m
2210m
Maga Valbiolo 2245m
2500m
2525m

↑ The runs on the glacier are short but sweet, with no great difference between black and red variants
ED FERRARI

UK PACKAGES

Crystal, First Choice, Independent Ski Links, Inghams, Neilson, Skitracer, STC, Thomson

Phone numbers
From abroad use the prefix +39 (and do **not** omit the initial '0' of the phone number)

TOURIST OFFICE

www.passotonale.it
www.adamelloski.com
www.valdisole.net

found no queues, and even at the busiest time they are not a problem.
Terrain parks There's a park with kickers and boxes (no half-pipe was built in 2011) and a beginners' park. Both are served by the fast Valena chair at Passo Tonale.
Snow reliability The Presena slopes are high and shady, so they are fairly snow-sure. But the sunny main slopes can suffer in late season. The comprehensive snowmaking has impressed reporters.
Experts This isn't a resort for experts (see 'Intermediates'). But in good conditions there are epic off-piste runs from the glacier, including the impressive 16km Pisgana run towards Ponte di Legno (a vertical of 1650m).
Intermediates The south-facing slopes offer gentle terrain ideal for cruising; many of these runs are graded red but are really no more than gentle blue gradient. We particularly enjoyed the 4.5km Alpino piste down a deserted valley to the village. Adventurous intermediates will find the Presena area worth a visit. The glacier runs are short, but offer good snow; the black is scarcely distinguishable from the reds. Below that the run beneath the chair is no more than a cat-track, but the black beneath the gondola is a rewarding run, at the easy end of the black spectrum. The red runs at Ponte di Legno are excellent, deserving their classification.
Beginners It's an excellent resort for novices. The sunny lifts on gentle

slopes right by the village are ideal, and there are plenty of easy, wide blue runs to move on to (usually with good snow) in order to gain confidence.
Snowboarding The gentle slopes and ability to get around mainly on chairlifts mean the area is good for beginner and intermediate boarders.
Cross-country There are 44km of trails at Passo Tonale, in the valley and at altitude at Ponte di Legno.
Mountain restaurants Readers have generally been unimpressed with the mountain restaurants but pleased with the 'very reasonable' prices. La Baracca (with table- and self-service sections) at the foot of the slopes is 'the best – the ski-in terrace a bonus'. Past recommendations include Scorpion Bay and the Nigritella in the main area of slopes and the 'rustic' Capanna Valbione at Ponte di Legno. We've no reports of the new Rifugio Passo Paradiso (see 'News').
Schools and guides A 2010 visitor judged his private lesson to be 'of a much higher standard than elsewhere'; some past reporters have criticised standards of spoken English.
Families There's a kindergarten at hotel Miramonti for ages four to 12; the ski school takes kids from four.

STAYING THERE

Passo Tonale has long been popular with tour operators.
Hotels There are around 30, most of them 3-stars, including the slope-side Sporting (0364 903781) with 'excellent food'. We've also had a glowing report on the location, rooms, owners and 'amazing' food of the Edelweiss (0364 903789). The 4-star Miramonti (0364 900501) has a pool, spa and good location.
Apartments There are 1,400 beds in apartments, a few on the UK market.
Eating out Mainly hotel restaurants, including the 'good value' Torretta ('best in town with a genuine pizza oven'). But reporters have generally found the standard of food disappointing.
Après-ski There are quite a few spots to try. Reader recommendations include the Magic Pub, El Bait ('great', 'free après snacks'), Nico's Bar, Heaven (in Sport Hotel Vittoria) and the Miramonti and Paradiso discos.
Off the slopes If you don't intend to hit the slopes, we wouldn't recommend Tonale – though there's snowmobiling, snowshoeing, skating.

SAUZE D'OULX TOURIST OFFICE

Sauze d'Oulx

A lively village beneath an attractive area of slopes forming part of the extensive Milky Way; but non-trivial drawbacks persist

438

NEWS

2011/12: There are plans to move two high-speed quads (Triplex and Pian della Rocca) on the upper part of Sauze's ski area to make moving around the mountain easier and to replace two existing slow chairs.

2010/11: Three blue slopes (Cresta, Boursailles, Boulevard) on Monte Fraiteve were improved or built to create better links in this area. Bar Marmotta near the Triplex chair reopened. And Cafe della Seggiovia replaced the Lounge Bar in the village.

➕ Extensive and uncrowded slopes – great intermediate cruising

➕ Mix of open and treelined runs is good for all weather conditions

➕ Entertaining nightlife

➕ Part of the Milky Way network, spreading across the border into France, but ...

➖ Full exploration of the Milky Way area really requires a car or taxis

➖ Erratic snow record and far from comprehensive snowmaking

➖ Still some ancient slow lifts

➖ Several drawbacks for beginners

➖ Steep walks around the village, and an inadequate shuttle-bus service

➖ Crowds at weekends in season

➖ Few challenging pistes

➖ Still very British-dominated

Skiers with long memories are inclined to dismiss Sauze as lager-lout territory. In the 1980s and maybe 1990s the tabloids mined a rich vein here of young Brits behaving badly. That view is out of date; there are still lots of lively bars and shops festooned in English signs, and lots of young Brits working in them, but it is a much more civilised place. The resort's Italian clientele is more in evidence, especially at weekends (Sauze is the closest decent-sized ski area to Turin), and when we visit we find ourselves liking Sauze more than we expect to – as do many reporters.

But Sauze still has a problem: investment, lack of. With its acutely unreliable natural snow, it needs the kind of comprehensive snowmaking that many other major Italian resorts now enjoy. And the rate of progress in upgrading lifts needs a serious boost, as well.

THE RESORT

Sauze d'Oulx sits on a sloping mountain shelf facing north-west to the mountains bordering France.

It is a mid-sized resort – a big village rather than a town – but it spreads quite widely. Out of the bustle of the centre, there are secluded apartment blocks in quiet, wooded areas and a number of good restaurants also tucked away.

The Via Lattea (Milky Way) lift pass covers not only next-door Sestriere and Sansicario, easily reached by lift and piste, but also the more remote area of slopes around the French border, above Claviere and Montgenèvre. These resorts are much more easily reached by car, or by taxi.

VILLAGE CHARM ★★☆☆☆
Falling behind?
The village has an attractive old core, with narrow, twisting streets and houses roofed with huge stone slabs. But most of the resort is modern and undistinguished, made up of block-like hotels relieved by the occasional chalet, spreading down the steep hillside from the slopes. It rather gives the impression of falling behind the times, with little sign of investment in smart, woody hotels and apartments.

There is a central car-free zone, but at both ends of the day the rest of the village can be congested. The roads have few pavements and can be icy.

Despite the decline in lager sales, the centre is still lively at night; the late bars are usually quite full, and, in a good season, the handful of discos do brisk business – at the weekend, at least. Noise can be a problem in the early hours.

VIA LATTEA

Sportinia: a sunny mid-mountain clearing with a nursery slope area, hotels and restaurants ↓

CONVENIENCE ★★☆☆☆
Uphill struggles

The Clotes chair, for the left-hand side of the network, is at the top of the village, up a short but steep hill. Some hotels are above this lift, and in good snow offer ski-in/ski-out convenience – but most are not. There is a moving carpet that cuts out part of the climb. The Sportinia chair, for the heart of the slopes, is a strenuous and hazardous walk (often on slippery roads) further out. But you can ride the Clotes chair and ski across to the Sportinia one. There is a free ski-bus service.

The smaller, lower village of Jouvenceaux is worth considering as a base, with a fast lift into the slopes and good red run back down.

SCENERY ★★★☆☆
Plenty of trees

The scenery is attractively woody, especially low down and along the Val di Susa. The sunny, open slopes higher up give wide panoramic views of the mountains bordering France.

THE MOUNTAINS

Sauze's mountains provide excellent intermediate terrain. The higher slopes are open, the lower ones pleasantly wooded. The piste classification changes from year to year, so not surprisingly the signs on the ground don't always match the piste map. As in many Italian resorts, pistes tend to be overclassified, with reds that should be blues and blacks that should be reds. Piste marking may be absent. And signposting isn't great; reporters remark on the lack of large-scale maps at the top of lifts. Despite improvements, the piste map is still very difficult to follow.

EXTENT OF THE SLOPES ★★★★☆
Big and varied enough for most

Sauze's local slopes are spread across a broad wooded bowl above the resort, ranging from west- to north-facing. The main lifts are chairs, slow from the top of the village up to **Clotes** and fast from the western fringes to **Sportinia** – a sunny mid-mountain clearing in the woods, with a ring of restaurants and hotels and a small nursery area. You can get from Clotes to Sportinia using the high Triplex chairlift; this was prone to closure by high winds, though this may be sorted with its planned new position (see News). There is also an easy blue piste link from Clotes to the bottom of the Sportinia chair.

The high point of the system is **Monte Fraiteve**. From here you can travel west on splendid broad, long runs to **Sansicario** – and on to a two-stage gondola near **Cesana Torinese** that links with **Claviere** and then **Montgenèvre**, in France, at the far end of the Milky Way (both are reached more quickly by car).

M Fraiteve is the main way to

LIFT PASSES

Via Lattea

Prices in €

Age	1-day	6-day
over 8	34	180

Free under 8; over 75

Beginner Restricted day pass (€24)

Notes
Covers lifts in Sauze d'Oulx, Sestriere, Sansicario, Cesana and Claviere; half-day passes

Alternative passes
International (covers all the above plus Montgenèvre)

ITALY

440

Sestriere. There is a red piste all the way down, but the slope faces south; the bottom section is rarely open – expect to ride the gondola down.

FAST LIFTS ★★★☆☆
Few and far between
Fast lifts are in a minority. There are still a lot of drags and old, slow chairlifts. Things are improving slowly but serious investment is needed to update the lift system.

QUEUES ★★★☆☆
Weekend problems
There can be queues on Saturdays when the hordes from Turin flock in. And crowds on the piste can be a problem then too ('dangerously overcrowded' and 'I was relieved to ski home in one piece' said a 2011 reporter). But during the week the slopes are usually quiet – though recent changes around M Fraiteve may have increased congestion there at peak times. Regulars will be glad to hear of the planned removal of the two ancient Rocce Nere chairs to Col Basset, which were painfully slow and prone to breakdown. Elsewhere, there can be irritating waits at Sportinia, especially when school classes set off, or just after lunch. The quad out of the village to Clotes can still generate queues.

TERRAIN PARKS ★☆☆☆☆
Maybe
The location and size of the park has changed from year to year – but for the last two years has been at Sportinia. Don't count on it opening though: in the past we've had reports of it being closed with little explanation. There is a park at Sansicario too.

SNOW RELIABILITY ★★☆☆☆
Can be poor, affecting the links
The area is notorious for erratic snowfalls, suffering droughts with worrying frequency – though recent seasons have been pretty good. Snowmaking has been increased throughout the area (including the Sportinia nursery slopes) but coverage is still far from complete. In thin years, reporters have been impressed by the efforts to keep runs open in poor conditions ('they worked miracles'). Grooming is in general 'immaculate' .

FOR EXPERTS ★★☆☆☆
Head off-piste
There are black runs but most of them do not deserve their classification. One of the steeper slopes is shown on the piste map as a mogul field – a sunny slope down the Moncrons draglift. We're told the black Malafosse run is not fiercely steep, but is narrow and very isolated. There are plenty of

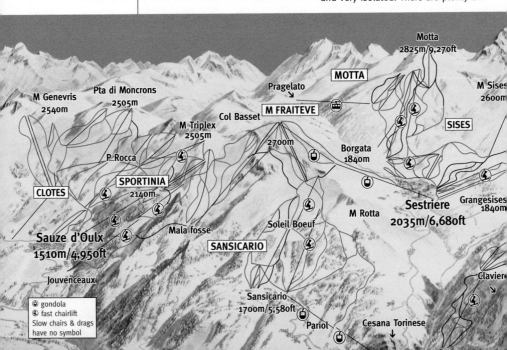

SCHOOLS

Sauze Sportinia
t 0122 850218

Sauze d'Oulx
t 0122 858084

Sauze Project
t 0122 850654

Classes
(Sauze Sportinia
prices)
6 3hr days: €180

Private lessons
€35 for 1hr

GUIDES

Marco Degani
t 0335 398984

CHILDCARE

Ski school
6 half days €180
(Sportinia prices)

off-piste opportunities within the lift network – between the pistes and down lift lines.

FOR INTERMEDIATES ★★★★☆
Splendid cruising terrain

The whole area is ideal for confident intermediates who want to clock up the kilometres. For the less confident, the piste map doesn't help because it picks out only the very easiest runs in blue – when actually there are many others that are manageable.

The Moncrons sector at the east of the area is served only by drags but offers some wonderful, uncrowded cruising, some of it above the treeline. In the central part of the slopes there are some good long descents – red 11 is about 1000m vertical.

At the higher levels, where the slopes are above the treeline, the terrain often allows a choice of route. Lower down are pretty runs through the woods, where the main complication can be route-finding. The mountainside is broken up by gullies, limiting the links between pistes that appear to be quite close together.

The long runs down to Jouvenceaux are splendid, flattering intermediate terrain, as are those below Sportinia.

The slopes above Sansicario are also excellent, including the amiable Olympic Women's Downhill and the particularly fine red run, away from the lifts, down to Pariol, the mid-station on the Cesana-Sansicario gondola. These runs are affected by the afternoon sun, though. You can now get to and from the Sansicario sector more easily, thanks to recent lift re-arrangements on M Fraiteve.

FOR BEGINNERS ★☆☆☆☆
Not a good choice

You might think a resort like this, with cheap accommodation and gentle terrain, would cater well for beginners, but you would be wrong. The main nursery area up at Sportinia has only a short moving carpet lift, and is reached by a chairlift. There is a day pass covering these plus two other lifts, but there is no suitable longer lift-served slope to progress to. You can leave your skis and boots at Sportinia and take the chairlift back down. There is a slope at village level with a free moving carpet, but the slope is too steep for complete beginners. Equally importantly, the mornings-only classes don't suit

everyone. Once off the nursery slopes, the main problem is that virtually all of the runs are classified red, whether they deserve it or not.

FOR BOARDERS ★★
Too many drags

A recent reporter found little to interest adventurous boarders and 'far too many drags' – which is a serious drawback for novice riders too. But competent intermediates will enjoy cruising on the well-groomed pistes. Don't count on finding a terrain park.

FOR CROSS-COUNTRY ★☆☆☆☆
You're on your own

There are no prepared loops in Sauze.

MOUNTAIN RESTAURANTS ★★★☆☆
Some pleasant possibilities

There are about 15 restaurants locally. They are generally pleasant, but can get very busy; few are particularly special. Stupidly, only some are marked on the piste map. There are several places at Sportinia; the Rocce Nere is repeatedly praised ('excellent food and service' confirms a 2011 reporter); the Capanna Kind is a bit pricier, and views differ on whether it delivers. The 'cosy' Ciao Pais above Clotes does a 'tasty porcini mushroom pasta'. And the hotel Capricorno below it is the place for a serious table-service lunch. It is not cheap, and midweek in low season it can be deserted. Clot Bourget is recommended for 'fast service, best pizzas on the slopes and good value'. The rustic Bar Clotes is 'a great end-of-day-bar'. The Fontaine at Jouvenceaux is good for 'a quiet drink and snack'.

SCHOOLS AND GUIDES ★★☆☆☆
More reports, please

A 2011 visitor 'highly recommends' a private lesson with Roger Goodfellow of the Sauze d'Oulx school and who has been in Sauze for 30 years – 'we were of slightly different abilities but the lesson improved us all markedly'.

FOR FAMILIES ★★☆☆☆
Tour operator alternatives

You might want to look at the nursery facilities offered by major UK tour operators in the chalets and chalet-hotels that they run here. All the schools take children from four years, and spoken English should be OK. The moving carpet on the village nursery slope is a great aid to sledging.

GETTING THERE

Air Turin 90km/ 55 miles (1hr30)

Rail Oulx (5km/ 3 miles); frequent buses

UK PACKAGES

Crystal, First Choice, Independent Ski Links, Inghams, Mountain Wave, Neilson, Ski Line, Skitracer, Solo's, Thomson
Sansicario Crystal, Thomson

ACTIVITIES

Indoor Sauna, solarium, massage

Outdoor Ice rink, snowmobiling, snowshoeing, walking

Phone numbers
From abroad use the prefix +39 (and do **not** omit the initial '0' of the phone number)

TOURIST OFFICE

Sauze d'Oulx, Cesana Torinese (Sansicario)
www.turismotorino. org
www.vialattea.it
www.comune. sauzedoulx.to.it

STAYING THERE

All the major mainstream operators offer hotel packages here.
Hotels Simple 2-star and 3-star hotels form the core, with a couple of 4-stars and some more basic places.
****Torre (0122 859812) Cylindrical landmark 200m below the centre. Excellent rooms, mini-buses to lifts. Pool, spa, hot tub, sauna, steam.
****Relais des Alpes (0122 859747) 'Large rooms, food excellent with friendly restaurant staff.'
***Gran Baita (0122 850183) Comfortable place in quiet, central backstreet, with excellent food and good rooms, some with sunset views.
***Stella Alpina (0122 858731) Between main lifts. Well run by Anglo-Italian family; 'cannot fault food, service and location – highly recommended', 'very good value'.
***Terrazza (0122 850173) In a quiet part of town, near the Clotes chair.
**Biancaneve (0122 850160) Pleasant, with smallish rooms. Near the centre.
**Hermitage (0122 850385) Neat chalet-style hotel beside the piste.
**Villa Cary (0122 850191) Comfortable 2-star, repeatedly recommended by an annual visitor for 'excellent food and service'.
**Albergo Martin (0122 858246) Basic, comfortable 2-star in Jouvenceaux. Shuttle to resort. 'Excellent value, helpful staff, good breakfast.'
Chalets Perhaps surprisingly, of the big tour operators only Neilson has a catered chalet here.
Apartments Plenty are available, some through UK operators.
At altitude The 4-star Capricorno (0122 850273), up at Clotes, is the most attractive and expensive hotel in Sauze – a charming little chalet beside the piste, with only nine bedrooms. Not quite in the same league are the places up at Sportinia – though reporters have enjoyed them.

EATING OUT ★★★☆☆
Caters for all tastes and pockets
Sauze has over 30 restaurants. Typical Italian banquets of five or six courses can be had in places such as the Cantun – on the menu are unusual dishes such as venison with onion jam. Del Falco (fine meats and pasta dishes) has been praised as 'the best in town – terrific'. In the old town there are several cutely rustic places. Paddy McGinty's does Mexican and steaks. Sugo's Spaghetti House has 'a good atmosphere' and the Pizza House 'serves excellent pizza, good value'.

APRES-SKI ★★★★☆
Suzy does it with more dignity
If you're used to Austrian resorts you may be disappointed by the lack of open-air bars at the foot of the slopes, but in other respects Sauze's bars now impress most reporters, young and old. Choice is wide, with multiple happy hours, free antipasti in some places. The popular Assietta has lots of entertainments later on.

The Scotch bar in the hotel Stella Alpina is popular for English beer with a 'friendly welcome'. The Village Cafè, in a basement at the foot of the slopes, is 'big, friendly, fun'. And Miravallino is a smart, lively bar where every night there is a different entertainment (karaoke, bar games etc) – 'happy hour is fantastic' says a 2011 reporter. Max's ('happy hour lasts for four hours!') and Scatto Matto are both popular for 'excellent food, service and ski videos'. Try the Derby (below the hotel) for a quiet, civilised drink – log fire, sofas, but also video screens. Il Lampione in the old town has a 'chilled out atmosphere and excellent beer'. Osteria dei Vagabondi is the only live music venue (it starts late and prices are a bit higher here).

Other reader recommendations: the intimate, atmospheric bar Moncrons, which holds regular quiz nights, and the Cotton Club, 'an attractively woody late-night bar' which sounds like it is spoilt by video screens.

OFF THE SLOPES ★☆☆☆☆
Go elsewhere
Shopping is limited, there are no gondolas or cable cars for pedestrians and there are few off-slope activities. Turin and Briançon are worth visiting.

LINKED RESORT – 1700m
SANSICARIO

Sansicario is ideally placed for exploration of the whole Milky Way. It is a modern, purpose-built, self-contained but rather soulless little resort, mainly consisting of apartments grouped around the small shopping precinct. The 45-room Rio Envers (0122 8113337) is a comfortable, expensive 4-star hotel. There are taxi-bob rides on the Olympic bobsleigh run, between Sansicario and Cesana.

Sella Ronda

Endless intermediate slopes amid spectacular scenery, and a choice of attractive valley villages with a distinctive local culture

NEWS

2011/12: The Bamby quad between San Cassiano and La Villa is to be upgraded to a six-pack. A new quad is to replace one of the double chairs from Passo Campolongo to Monte Cherz. A new terrain park is planned at Corvara, with a line for kids plus a couple of easy to medium lines.

2010/11: The Prè Ciablun quad chair opened in the Corvara/San Cassiano area. In La Villa, the Rua triple chair was upgraded to a quad. In Canazei the Hexen Club opened – including a nightclub.

TOURIST OFFICE

www.dolomitisuperski.com
www.sella-ronda.info

Strategically placed benches are not uncommon in these parts, for obvious reasons. This is the Gruppo del Sella from above Colfosco →

+ Vast network of connected slopes – suits intermediates particularly well

+ Stunning, unique Dolomite scenery

+ Lots of mountain huts with good food as well as fab views

+ Relatively low prices

+ Extensive snowmaking – one of Europe's best systems – but ...

− They need it: natural snowfall is erratic in this southerly region

− Few tough pistes, and off-piste is not only very limited but banned, strictly speaking

− Mostly short runs with limited vertical (with notable exceptions)

− Crowds on the Sella Ronda circuit

− Still some old draglifts

The Sella Ronda is an amazing circular network of lifts and pistes taking you around the Gruppo del Sella – a mighty limestone massif with villages scattered around it. The spectacular Dolomite scenery is like something Disney might have conjured up for a movie or a theme park. But the geology that provides the visual drama also dictates the nature of the slopes. Sheer limestone cliffs rise out of gentle pasture land, which is where you spend your time. The skiing is relaxing, not exciting.

The scale of it is some compensation; the distances you can cover on skis are huge – in overall dimensions, the network exceeds even the famed Three Valleys in France. In addition to the main Sella Ronda circuit, major lift systems lead off it at three main points along the way: Selva (covered in the chapter after this), Corvara and Arabba (both covered in this chapter).

This is one of the few destinations where we pray for sun; snow would interfere with our scenery-gazing without bringing any real benefit – off-piste is off the agenda, and the snowmaking delivers reliably good piste conditions.

KEY FACTS

Sella Ronda
The linked lift
network of Val
Gardena, Alta Badia,
Arabba, and the
Canazei and
Campitello slopes of
Val di Fassa

Slopes	1005-3250m
	3,300-10,660ft
Lifts	179
Pistes	433km
	269 miles
Blue	38%
Red	53%
Black	9%
Snowmaking	90%

KEY FACTS

Resort	1600m
	5,250ft
Slopes	1600-2380m
	5,250-7,810ft
Lifts	26
Pistes	62km

Phone numbers
From abroad use the
prefix +39 (and do **not**
omit the initial '0' of
the phone number)

TOURIST OFFICE
www.arabba.it

CHOOSING A BASE

For good skiers, one of the best bases is Selva – covered in the next chapter along with Santa Cristina and Ortisei further down the Val Gardena. Another option for good skiers is Arabba.

Corvara is perhaps the best all-round bet – well placed for access to Selva, Arabba, the Sella Ronda circuit, the Alta Badia area and excursions to Cortina (and the famous 'hidden valley' run – see feature panel). Colfosco is just next door. San Cassiano and La Villa are slightly off the Sella Ronda circuit.

Canazei and Campitello have their own modest ski areas, and reasonable access to Selva and Arabba.

Your choice might be influenced by travel plans. There are countless possible arrival airports, and various transfer routes; some can take four or five hours, including interminable winding mountain roads.

The Dolomiti Superski pass covers not only the Sella Ronda resorts but dozens of others. The lift system logs your lift rides – so you can go online to check your distance and vertical.

The vast network of slopes requires a vast selection of piste maps – 12 Superski ones in all, plus locally produced ones for some resorts. Pick up local maps as you progress.

Arabba

➕ Some of the best steep pistes in the area – shady too
➕ Quick access to Marmolada glacier

➖ Not a good base for novices, with more blacks than blues locally
➖ Off-slope activities are limited

Arabba is a small, quiet but fast-growing village appealing particularly to people looking for more challenging terrain than this region normally offers.

Village charm The village is small and traditional in style. There are some shops, bars and restaurants, but this is not a place for lively nightlife.
Convenience It's a small place, but staying in the older part involves an uphill walk to reach the ski area, which provokes a few complaints from reporters. A newer area of hotels and chalets has developed higher up, better placed for the lifts and slopes.
Scenery Arabba is beautifully positioned between the stunning Gruppo del Sella and the Marmolada glacier, with great views at altitude.

THE MOUNTAIN

Arabba's local slopes are some of the highest in the region, and mainly above the trees.
Slopes The two-stage double-cable gondola and the cable car beside it rise almost 900m vertical to the high point at Porta Vescovo (2475m). From here a choice of runs return to the village or you can head off around the Sella Ronda circuit. From the mid-station of the gondola, chairs take you to Passo Padon and onwards to the Marmolada glacier. This is an excellent outing, despite the queues described later. The views from the top at 3270m are spectacular, and the 1500m vertical red run to Capanna Bill is splendid, with great snow on the top sections.

From the other side of the village, a fast quad gets you on the way to Burz,

Passo di Campolongo and Corvara.
Fast lifts Access to and from the village is by fairly new fast lifts.
Queues The outing to Marmolada can be troublesome on a busy day, involving the bottleneck of the Sass de la Vegla double chair. Despite upgrades, there may be long waits for the Marmolada cable cars.
Terrain park Head for San Cassiano.
Snow reliability Arabba offers some of the most snow-sure slopes in the Sella Ronda region. Good snow is far from assured, but snowmaking is extensive and the main runs are north-facing.
Experts Arabba has steep slopes to match those of Val Gardena. The north-facing blacks and reds from Porta Vescovo offer genuine challenges and there is some tempting off-piste terrain too – but look at the off-piste feature panel.
Intermediates The local slopes suit adventurous intermediates best. Most are quite challenging and those on the main circuit suffer from crowds.
Beginners It is not a good choice for beginners. There is a small nursery slope near the Burz chair, but access to longer easy runs is tricky.
Snowboarding Porta Vescovo offers some decent challenges. Most of the lifts are fast chairs or gondolas.
Cross-country There is one loop at village level.
Mountain restaurants There's lots of choice, from rustic huts to larger

places. Most are lively and many have great views – in this respect, Luigi Gorza at the top of the Porta Vescovo lifts takes some beating, but the food 'isn't great'. The smart new self-service Cesa da Fuoch at the mid-station has 'excellent and reasonable fresh cooked pasta'; the Rifugio Plan Boé, between Arabba and Campolongo, has 'good food and service'. Below Marmolada, a 2011 visitor had a 'good value' meal at Passo Fedaia, and Capanna Bill lower down is a cosy spot. Rifugio Fodom just below Passo Pordoi is 'really busy but great fun'.

Schools The local Arabba school offers group and private classes. We have no recent reports.

Families The kindergarten at the ski school takes children from two years.

STAYING THERE

New accommodation has been built at the top end of town, closer to the lifts.

Chalets Ski Total has the dinky six-bed chalet Heidi and three slightly larger places. This season Inghams is introducing three chalets sleeping 10 to 18 people.

Hotels There are about a dozen hotels. The favourite of one regular visitor is the 4-star Grifone (0436 780034) out at Passo Campolongo – 'remote, but food and service superb; excellent bar and health club/pool'. In the village, we've had good reports in the past on the 3-star Portavescovo (0436 79139) and the 4-star Sporthotel (0436 79321).

Apartments Self-catering accommodation is available.

Eating out Restaurant choice is limited. The central hotels all have busy restaurants (see above). Reporters consistently praise Miky's Grill in the

THE SELLA RONDA CIRCUIT

You can ski around the huge Sella massif in either direction by following very clear coloured signs; it's easily managed in a day by even an early intermediate. The clockwise route is slightly quicker and offers more interesting slopes, but is much busier – so many reporters prefer the anticlockwise route, despite a tedious series of five lifts from Corvara. Some resort piste maps include a Sella Ronda map; most take something close to a bird's eye topographical view. (Bizarrely, at least one puts south at the top.) A very detailed topo map is available from the tourist offices (and some lift stations).

The runs total around 23km and the lifts around 14km. There is one bit where no skiing is possible: you ride the Borest chair at Corvara in both directions. The lifts take a total of about two hours (plus any queuing). We've done the circuit in just three and a half hours excluding diversions and hut stops; five or six hours is a realistic time when things are crowded.

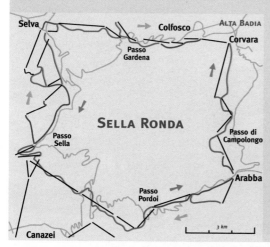

If you set out early and make good time, you can divert from the circuit, notably at Selva and Arabba. Less confident intermediates could explore the Alta Badia area, east of Corvara.

Not everyone likes it. You may find that 'it's a bit of a slog', 'too busy and crowded', 'over-hyped', and over-regimented' and 'not a relaxing business when it's busy'. And boarders should be aware that there are quite a few flat bits.

If you pick your time – low season or a Saturday, in good weather – and start early, we reckon it's worth doing.

hotel Mesdì ('good value'; 'very good quality steaks and meat; mixed grill a speciality'). And reporters rate again Al Table as 'friendly and good value', serving everything from 'simple pasta and great pizzas to well-cooked steak'. The Alpenrose hotel will send its horse-drawn sleigh to pick you up if you book a table in its Stube Ladina ('good food and surroundings'). You can go up to Rifugio Plan Boé by snowmobile for dinner and dancing.

Après-ski The après-ski is limited. There are three bars and, according to recent reports, the central Bar Peter seems to be the focus – 'a little too bright, noisy and euro-poppy', says a 2011 visitor. Reporters also mention the Stube ('the closest in Arabba to a village bar, but clears out at 8pm') and the Treina. Cosy hotel bars are other options in the village. The atmospheric Rifugio Plan Boé up the mountain is good for a last drink on the piste – assuming you like 'loud 70s, 80s and Europop music'.

Off the slopes Off-slope diversions are few. There are some shops and cafes, and there's an ice rink. Snowmobiling and snowshoeing are available.

Corvara

➕ One of the best locations, where Alta Badia meets the Sella Ronda
➕ Pleasant, lively village
➕ Local slopes suit novices, but ...

➖ Few challenges locally
➖ Alta Badia still has plenty of drags and slow chairlifts

Corvara rivals Selva from most points of view, that of experts being a notable exception; for families and novices it takes some beating – though nearby Colfosco merits consideration too.

Village charm The place is lively and family-friendly, with a pleasant centre that is bypassed by through traffic.
Convenience The main shops and some hotels cluster around a small piazza, but the rest of Corvara sprawls along the valley floor, so you may have some walking to do.
Scenery There are impressive rock faces and spires all around the village, notably the distinctive Sassongher.

THE MOUNTAIN
Corvara is well positioned, with village lifts heading off to reasonably equidistant Selva, Arabba and San Cassiano. The local slopes are gentle and confidence-boosting.
Slopes Lifts go off in three directions. A long gondola heads south towards Boé and the clockwise Sella Ronda circuit. Two successive fast quads head west towards Colfosco and the

The Alta Badia – the area around La Villa, including Badia, San Cassiano, Corvara and Colfosco – has gradually built up a culture of top-flight cooking, and is now starting to capitalise on its success in doing so. For many years, its top hotels have run excellent gourmet restaurants, but now the tourist office has developed an excellent scheme to encourage serious cooking in mountain restaurants, too. This involves pairing up mountain restaurant chefs with 'starred' chefs from resort restaurants in the area, plus their chums from around Europe.

There are three local 'starred' restaurants. The chef from the Rosa Alpina hotel in San Cassiano is teamed up with Ütia Bioch up at 2080m. The chef from the Ciasa Salares hotel partners Ütia Col Alt. The guy from the restaurant at La Perla in Corvara works with Ütia I Tabla. Then chefs from Milan, Slovenia, Lugano, St Moritz, Munich etc are paired with seven other mountain restaurants.

The deal is that each restaurant offers a single dish created by its partner chef, costing little or nothing more than other dishes on the menu but offering something special – certainly something you wouldn't expect to find in a rustic mountain restaurant. When we visited in 2011, we ate at I

Tabla, where we had superb knuckle of pork in honey with thyme-scented polenta and chanterelles.

A wine from Südtirol is suggested for each dish. The tourist office produces a handsome pocket-sized brochure listing the restaurants and the special dishes. It sponsors other foodie schemes too – for example, a series of mountain restaurants between La Villa and Santa Croce, above Badia, form a 'gourmet skitour', detailed in another little brochure.

These schemes encourage variety and quality in mountain nosh; we approve.

TOURIST BOARD ALTA BADIA

Sella Ronda

447

Interactive resort shortlist builder at **www.wtss.co.uk**

anticlockwise route. The area around both lifts can get congested at peak times. A slow chair or a gondola take you into the slopes shared with San Cassiano and La Villa.
Fast lifts New fast lifts are gradually improving the area.
Queues We regularly have reports about long waits for the Borest chair between Corvara and Colfosco (which forms part of both Sella Ronda circuits), but otherwise there are few problems.
Terrain park There is a terrain park on the Ciampai run above San Cassiano.
Snow reliability As in the rest of the Sella Ronda area, natural snowfall is erratic, but snowmaking and grooming are excellent.
Experts Very few of Corvara's slopes offer any real challenges. The short black above Boé is really no more than a red. The wooded runs down to La Villa include a just-about-genuine

SNOWPIX.COM / CHRIS GILL

← Arguably the best base in the area – Corvara, with the distinctive peak of Sassongher in the background

black. Otherwise, you're off to Selva or Arabba. Look at the feature panel for off-piste runs.
Intermediates There's a vast network of slopes ideal for cruising and confidence-boosting. On one side is

the network of rolling hills shared with San Cassiano; on the other, above Colfosco, the more dramatically set Val Stella Alpina, off the Sella Ronda circuit, plus the long, gentle runs from Passo Gardena – essentially one long nursery slope. The red underneath the Boé cable car that goes off towards Arabba is usually uncrowded and retains good snow. The adventurous can head for the steeper, wooded pistes going down to La Villa.
Beginners There's a decent nursery area and lots of easy runs to progress to on both sides of the village
Snowboarding Novices can make rapid progress on gentle slopes. A few awkward draglifts remain, but most can be avoided.
Cross-country The Alta Badia area offers 38km of trails, including a 16km valley loop on the way to Colfosco.
Mountain restaurants Look at our gourmet feature panel, and at the San Cassiano section, where we cover places between the two resorts.
Schools There's a local branch of the Alta Badia school – reports welcome.
Families Kinderland takes children from the age of three.

STAYING THERE

Stay near the main square at the top end of the village to be near the lifts.
Hotels There are some deeply comfortable 4-stars. La Perla (0471 831000) is one of our all-time favourites, offering superb food and service in a relaxed atmosphere and perfect position. The Col Alto (0471 831100) is a regular haunt of a trusted reporter, endorsed by a 2011 visitor – 'huge bedrooms, outstanding food and the best wellness centre I've seen'. The Posta Zirm (0471 836175) also has a large spa; but we lack recent reports.

Eating out A reasonable choice. Most of the hotels have restaurants – the Stüa de Michil in La Perla hotel has a Michelin star, and greatly impressed us – superb food and a warm atmosphere. See also San Cassiano.
Après-ski The fashionable place to go at close of play these days seems to be L'Murin, a rustic outbuilding of La Perla. We've no recent reports on the famous tea-dance scene in the basement of the Posta Zirm.
Off the slopes There's a covered ice rink, indoor tennis courts, an outdoor climbing wall and snowshoeing.

San Cassiano

KEY FACTS

Resort	1540m
	5,050ft
Slopes	1330-2530m
	4,360-8,300ft
Lifts	52
Pistes	130km
Snow-guns	392 guns

Phone numbers
From abroad use the prefix +39 (and do **not** omit the initial '0' of the phone number)

TOURIST OFFICE
www.altabadia.org

➕ Local Alta Badia slopes are friendly, extensive and scenic
➕ Small, quiet village with some notably good hotels

➖ Lifts and pistes are outside village
➖ Slightly off the Sella Ronda circuit
➖ Alta Badia still has plenty of drags and slow chairlifts

If you prefer San Cassiano to Corvara it's likely to be because you particularly like one of its excellent hotels – or because you want a quiet time.

San Cassiano is a pleasant little village with some good hotels, sharing slopes with Corvara and La Villa.
Village charm It's a quiet, civilised resort, without much animation. It is bypassed by the road to Cortina.
Convenience Most hotels are close to the village centre – around a 5-minute walk from the gondola and slopes (but most of the better hotels have their own shuttle-buses).
Scenery The village is set in an attractive, tree-filled valley. The views from the slopes are superb.

THE MOUNTAIN
The local slopes adjoin the main Sella Ronda circuit.
Slopes A gondola starting just outside the village rises to Piz Sorega. From the top, fast chairs form the links with Corvara and La Villa, or you can head for Pralongia and the long runs home. Most of the area has very gentle slopes, ideal for easy cruising.
Fast lifts Essentially well-connected, but some old chairs and drags remain.
Queues Few problems, thanks to continual lift upgrades.

THE 'HIDDEN VALLEY'

If you like runs in spectacular scenery well away from all signs of civilisation, don't miss the easy red run from Lagazuoi, reached by cable car from Passo Falzarego. The pass is easily accessible from Armentarola, close to San Cassiano – shared taxis run a shuttle service (5 euros each) to the pass from here. There's also a bus from San Cassiano (but it is reported to be 'very crowded and slow').

The run is one of the most beautiful we've come across, and delights most reporters. Views from the top of the cable car are splendid, and the run passes beneath sheer, pink-tinged Dolomite peaks and frozen waterfalls. Because the cable car has low capacity, the run is never crowded. Make time to stop at the atmospheric Rifugio Scotoni near the end ('thoroughly enjoyable').

At the bottom, it's a long skate to a horse-drawn sled with ropes attached, which tows you back to Armentarola (for a couple of euros). This is more of a challenge than the run, and the risk of a pile-up if someone falls has concerned some reporters. We're told there is a bus alternative. At Armentarola there is a draglift up to a run back to San Cassiano.

ALAN LIPTROT

OFF-PISTE

Off-piste skiing is generally prohibited in the Sella Ronda area – as in many Italian areas. This doesn't stop people doing it where the temptation arises. And it doesn't rule out some spectacular routes, away from the pistes, where it's accepted you can safely go with guidance.

There are some well known routes on the Sella massif, reached via the cable car from Passo Pordoi. There are fairly direct descents back to the pass (the very sunny Forcella) or down the Val Lasties towards Canazei. But the classic run is the Val Mesdì, a long, shady couloir down to Colfosco, reached by hiking across the massif. Marmolada, the highest peak of the Dolomites, is the other obvious launching point. It offers a range of big descents on and off the glacier.

There is a mountain guides office in the centre of Corvara (www.altabadiaguides.com).

Terrain park You'll find boardercross, jumps, rails and humps.

Snow reliability The Dolomites have an erratic snowfall record, but snowmaking and grooming are excellent.

Experts Experts would be wise to stay elsewhere. There are steeper runs at La Villa, but it's a bit of a trek to Selva or Arabba.

Intermediates Pretty much ideal if you love easy cruising on flattering, well-groomed runs. The red option back to the valley is a serious red though. There's relatively quick access to the famous 'hidden valley' run (described in our feature panel).

Beginners There are nursery slopes a short bus ride away at Armentarola, and at the top of the gondola – not ideal. But there are plenty of long, easy slopes to progress to.

Snowboarding Endless carving on quiet pistes and there's a terrain park.

Cross-country There are 27km of trails.

Mountain restaurants Look at our gourmet feature panel. There are countless options on the slopes between San Cassiano and Corvara. Most are woody and cosy in traditional style, but Las Vegas is a wild exception – cool, minimalist, with huge windows to make the most of the views. We haven't had lunch here, but we have enjoyed a superb dinner. I Tablà is quite a plain little place but does excellent food – and a reader notes that it offers 'outstanding value'. Punta Trieste is recommended again this year – 'excellent pasta but so, so busy'. Other reader tips include Club Moritzino above La Villa ('fine wines,

delicious cheeses, charming host'), Marmotta ('lovely – old skis and photos'), Col Alt ('excellent venison') and Bioch ('outstandingly tasty pasta'). Pralongià is 'a great place for a last drink'.

Schools Last season a snowboarder in a reporter's party 'had private lessons and the instructor was excellent' and a beginner 'progressed very quickly' – more reports welcome.

Families The school offers the usual arrangements for children and there are several kids' parks.

STAYING THERE

Hotels The Rosa Alpina (0471 849500) is a splendid place – genuine comfort, great food, good spa. Its three restaurants include the St Hubertus, which has two Michelin stars. The Fanes (0471 849470) is a smart chalet-style place with indoor-outdoor pool and a spa. You can stay up the mountain at the modern, trendy Las Vegas restaurant (0471 840138).

Eating out As well as the Rosa Alpina's St Hubertus, two restaurants in the area have one Michelin star; one, the Siriola in the hotel Ciasa Salares, is in Armentarola, just up the road; for the other see Corvara. Las Vegas will take you up the mountain in a snowcat for dinner (you can ride back down or ski in front of the cat's headlights).

Après-ski It starts up the mountain with loud music at Las Vegas. A reporter recommends the Ütia Bioch on the home run and skiing down after dark. Nightlife is very limited.

Off the slopes There are some lovely walks amid the stunning scenery.

Other resorts

LINKED RESORT – 1645m

COLFOSCO

Colfosco is a smaller, quieter satellite of Corvara, 2km away. It has a fairly compact centre with a group of large hotels spread along the road from Corvara towards Passo Gardena and Selva, enjoying splendid views of the Gruppa del Sella. On the snow it's connected to Corvara by the two-way Borest chairlift. In the opposite direction, a gondola goes towards Passo Gardena. There are excellent nursery slopes and the runs back from Passo Gardena are easy, long cruises, making this a great base for novices. Check out our Corvara entry too.

LINKED RESORT – 1435m

LA VILLA

Like San Cassiano, La Villa is a bit detached from the Sella Ronda circuit. But it's a much busier place, with the road from Brunico and Bolzano running through it. It's more conveniently arranged, with lifts and pistes on both sides of the village, and nursery slopes dotted around. A recent visitor complains of inadequate rental shops, and poor spoken English both there and in the ski school. We've had repeated glowing reports on the hotel Antines (0471 844234) – 'one of the best, with an outstanding restaurant'; 'very friendly staff'.

SNOWPIX.COM / CHRIS GILL

The red run from the top of Marmolada is a glorious broad affair; it gets steeper lower down, with a black variant in theory ↓

LINKED RESORT – 1325m
BADIA

This small roadside village (formerly known as Pedraces) is out on a limb beyond La Villa, so is difficult to recommend as a base for the region as a whole. But some will find it more interesting now that there is a free bus link with Piccolino (20 minutes), where a gondola goes into the Plan de Corones/Kronplatz ski area. The village has its own one-run ski area with a fast quad and a slow double chair to Santa Croce (2045m) where there is a famous old rifugio with 'fabulous views' (and a tiny church).

LINKED RESORT – 1465m
CANAZEI

Canazei is a sizeable, bustling roadside village of narrow streets, rustic buildings, traditional-style hotels and little shops, set beneath a heavily wooded mountainside.

The village itself is slightly off the main Sella Ronda circuit, but its main slopes form part of it. A 12-person gondola (powerful, but queue-prone) rises 470m to Pecol, at the foot of the slopes of Belvedere. These are linked in one direction to the slopes of Passo Pordoi and Arabba, and in the other to

Passo Sella and Col Rodella (above Campitello), and then on to Selva. A red run returns to Canazei, but it gets the afternoon sun and is often closed.

The Belvedere slopes are open and sunny, with modest verticals of about 450m. Almost all are graded red; this exaggerates the difficulty of some, but rules the resort out for timid intermediates and beginners – the nursery slope, across the valley from the village, is inconvenient, too.

The grand 4-star Schloss Hotel Dolomiti (0462 601033) in the centre is one of the oldest hotels. The 4-star La Perla (0462 602453), also central, is praised by a 2011 visitor for 'great food and value, and amazing spa'.

There are numerous restaurants, and the après-ski is surprisingly animated. The Rose Garden and Osteria, at the bottom of the home run, and the Paradis (a converted barn – 'great fun') are popular at close of play. The 'friendly' International bar and ice cream parlour is quieter. La Stua di Ladins serves local wines and the Husky sometimes has live music.

Off-slope entertainment consists of beautiful walks and shopping. There's also a pool, sauna and Turkish baths.

LINKED RESORT – 1445m
CAMPITELLO

Campitello is a pleasant, unremarkable village a short way down the valley from Canazei – smaller, quieter and cheaper, and still unspoiled. There are no pistes to the valley but a cable car rises 1000m up to Col Rodella and the slopes above Passo Sella. At the start of the day this lift can build queues even in January, and in high season they can be 'massive' – it's quicker to get the bus up to Canazei's gondola. There is no nursery slope. Après-ski is quite lively – the Da Giulio bar gets packed.

VAL GARDENA TOURIST OFFICE

Selva / Val Gardena

Pleasant village amid spectacular Dolomite scenery, well placed for skiing on and off the vast Sella Ronda lift network

The mountains

Extent	★★★★★
Fast lifts	★★★★
Queues	★★★
Terrain p'ks	★★★
Snow	★★★★
Expert	★★★
Intermediate	★★★★★
Beginner	★★★
Boarder	★★★
X-country	★★★★★
Restaurants	★★★★★
Schools	★★★
Families	★★

The resort

Charm	★★★
Convenience	★★★
Scenery	★★★★★
Eating out	★★★
Après-ski	★★★
Off-slope	★★★

RPI 90

lift pass	£220
ski hire	£100
lessons	£95
food & drink	£105
total	**£520**

NEWS

2011/12: The Sasso Levante triple chair at Passo Sella is due to be replaced with a fast quad.

2010/11: The old Rasciesa single-seat chairlift was replaced by a new funicular from the base at Ortisei to Rasciesa. It serves a 6km toboggan run and a red piste that links to a cable car up to Seceda.

+ A key resort of the Sella Ronda region, with all the usual plus points: extent, snowmaking, scenery, mountain huts

+ Excellent local slopes, with big verticals by Sella Ronda standards

+ Mix of open and wooded slopes

+ Excellent nursery slopes

+ Attractive but strung-out village in a lovely wooded setting

– Some of the minus points of the Sella Ronda region too, notably: erratic natural snowfall, crowds on the main Sella Ronda circuit

– No easy long runs immediately above Selva – buses or taxis are needed for access to them up at Plan de Gralba

– Busy road through the village

Selva is one of three sizeable resorts near the head of Val Gardena (a name well known to 'Ski Sunday' viewers) and one of the main bases to consider for a visit to the unique Sella Ronda region described in the chapter before this one. Selva remains one of our favourite bases in the area, essentially because of the local slopes, including two race courses through woods to the valley that are among the most satisfying runs in the area – not least because they offer decent verticals. Beginners and timid intermediates, though, are probably better off staying in Corvara or Colfosco, described in the Sella Ronda chapter.

THE RESORT

Selva is a long roadside village at the head of the Val Gardena, almost merging with the next village down-valley, Santa Cristina. Appreciably further down-valley is Ortisei.

For many years this area was part of Austria, and it retains a Tirolean charm. German is more widely spoken than Italian, and many visitors are German, too. Most places have two names: Selva is also known as Wolkenstein and the Gardena valley as Gröden. We do our bit for Italian unity by using the Italian place names. The local language, Ladin, also survives – giving a third name to some places. Not surprisingly, visitors find all this confusing. The valley is famed for wood carvings, which are on display (and sale) wherever you look.

VILLAGE CHARM ★★★★★
Pity about the traffic
The village has traditional Tirolean-style architecture and an attractive church, but is a sprawling place and suffers from through-traffic (and a lack of parking facilities).

Despite the World Cup fame of Val Gardena, Selva is neither upmarket nor brash. It's a good-value, civilised, low-key resort – relaxed and family-friendly in many respects, once you get away from the intrusive through-road.

CONVENIENCE ★★★★★
Choose your spot with care
From the village, gondolas rise in two directions. The Ciampinoi gondola goes south from near the centre of the village to start the anticlockwise Sella Ronda route. The Dantercëpies gondola, for the clockwise Sella Ronda

451

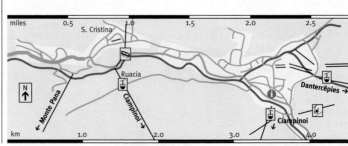

route, starts above the village at the top of the nursery slopes (but accessible via a central chairlift and a short run down). The most convenient position to stay is near this chair or one of the gondolas.

There are local buses until early evening – seven euros for a weekly card. In the past they have generated all sorts of complaints from reporters but the flow seems to have dried up. There's a night bus between Selva and Ortisei. All the 4-star hotels run their own free shuttle-buses.

Ortisei, the main town of Val Gardena, and S Cristina, are described at the end of the chapter. Another possible (cheaper) base is the village of Siusi, down at around 1000m.

SCENERY ★★★★★
Pretty in pink
The village enjoys a lovely setting under the impressive pink-tinged walls of Sassolungo and the Gruppo del Sella – a fortress-like massif 6km across that lies at the hub of the Sella Ronda circuit (see separate chapter).

THE MOUNTAINS

Selva's own slopes cover both sides of the valley. The lower slopes are wooded, with open slopes higher up.

The local piste map exists in several variations, which reporters find confusing. The maps show neither names nor numbers for the runs. Piste signing provokes some criticism.

Good, long blue runs for beginners to progress to – but you have to catch a bus from Selva to avoid a tricky red from Ciampinoi

Lovely long reds; the one on skier's right of the gondola used to be the Women's Downhill run

Efficient underground train links the gondolas for the Ciampinoi and Seceda sectors

ⓖ gondola
ⓒ cable car
ⓡ railway/funicular
ⓕ fast chairlift
Slow chairs & drags have no symbol

Marmolada 3340m
Sassolungo/Langkofel 3180m
Gruppo del Sella / Sella Gruppe 3150m
Canazei 1465m
PASSO SELLA 2245m
Sella Ronda
Sella Ronda
Sole
Piz Seteur
Sotsaslong
Comici I
Piz Sella
Piz Sella
2255m
PLAN DE GRALBA
Plan de Gralba 1800m
CIAMPINOI
Ciampinoi
DANTERCĒPIES
2300m
Dantercēpies
Sochers
Saslong
Selva/Wolkenstein 1565m/5,130ft
Vallunga
Col Raiser
Col Raiser
SECE

The Dolomiti Superski pass covers not only Selva and the Sella Ronda resorts but dozens of others. It's an easy road trip to Cortina. You can check your lift rides, skiing distance and vertical descended online.

EXTENT OF THE SLOPES ★★★★★
High-mileage excursions
The **Ciampinoi** gondola accesses several shady pistes, including the famous World Cup Downhill run, leading back down to Selva and Santa Cristina. In the opposite direction, runs go on to **Plan de Gralba** – and to the anticlockwise Sella Ronda circuit.

On the other side of the valley, the **Dantercëpies** gondola serves lovely red runs back to Selva and accesses the clockwise Sella Ronda circuit.

The sunny **Seceda** area is accessed by a gondola on the outskirts of Santa Cristina. This is also accessible by descending from Ciampinoi to ride a slick underground train across the valley. Runs descend to Santa Cristina or to Ortisei – a red run of about 7km. And from Ortisei a gondola on the other side of the valley takes you to and from **Alpe di Siusi** – a gentle elevated area of quiet, easy runs, cross-country tracks and walks. This area can also be accessed by road or gondola from the village of Siusi, way off to the west. You can move between Alpe di Siusi and Monte Pana (which is connected to Ciampinoi) by bus, but it's a slow affair.

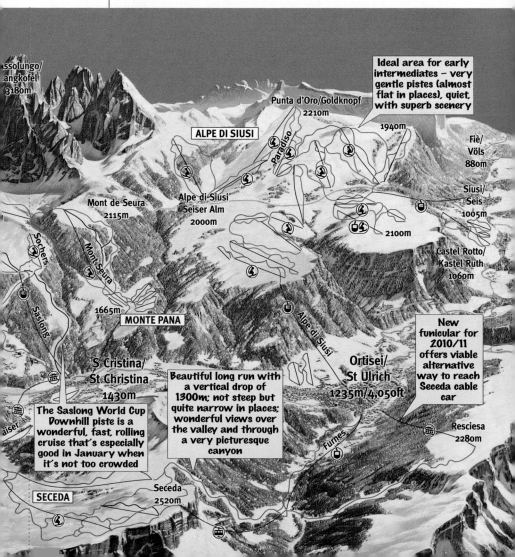

ssolungo/
angkofel
318om

Punta d'Oro/Goldknopf
2210m

Ideal area for early intermediates – very gentle pistes (almost flat in places), quiet, with superb scenery

ALPE DI SIUSI

Paradiso

1940m

Fiè/
Völs
88om

Mont de Seura
2115m

Alpe di Siusi
Seiser Alm
2000m

Siusi/
Seis
1005m

2100m

Castel Rotto/
Kastel Ruth
1060m

Sochers

Mont Seura

1665m

MONTE PANA

Alpe di Siusi

New funicular for 2010/11 offers viable alternative way to reach Seceda cable car

Saslong

S Cristina/
St Christina
1430m

Beautiful long run with a vertical drop of 1300m: not steep but quite narrow in places; wonderful views over the valley and through a very picturesque canyon

Ortisei/
St Ulrich
1235m/4,05oft

Resciesa
2280m

aiser

The Saslong World Cup Downhill piste is a wonderful, fast, rolling cruise that's especially good in January when it's not too crowded

Furnes

Seceda
2520m

SECEDA

FAST LIFTS ★★★★☆
Getting better
The main access lifts are gondolas, and there are lots of fast chairs above them. But there are still a few slow chairs and drags – the area only just scrapes into our 4-star category.

QUEUES ★★★☆☆
Still some problems
New lifts are vastly improving the area as a whole, but for most of the season the gondolas out of the village build 'morale-sapping morning queues'; the drags up to the Dantercëpies gondola may hold you up, too. There are bottlenecks on the main Sella Ronda circuit. The gondola out of Ortisei for Seceda ensures that the cable car above it is over-busy in the mornings. And there are double chairs on Alpe di Siusi that need upgrading.

TERRAIN PARKS ★★★☆☆
Facilities spread around
There are parks at Passo Sella by the Cavazes Grohmann chair, Piz Sella by the Comici chair ('excellent', says a 2010 reporter) and at Alpe di Siusi by the Laurin chair.

SNOW RELIABILITY ★★★★☆
Excellent when it's cold
The slopes are not high – there are few above 2200m and most are between 1500m and 2000m. Natural snowfalls are erratic, but Selva's slopes are well covered by snowmaking. During severe droughts we have enjoyed excellent pistes here, and our reporters are regularly impressed – 'a revelation', 'wonderful', 'stunning', 'unbelievable coverage and quality'. Problems arise only if it is too warm to make snow.

FOR EXPERTS ★★★☆☆
A few good runs
There are few challenges, essentially no moguls (the blacks all get groomed) and a low likelihood of powder. There are few major off-piste routes because of the nature of the terrain and off-piste is prohibited in places; see the off-piste panel in the Sella Ronda chapter.

The Val Gardena World Cup piste, the Saslong, is one of several steepish runs between Ciampinoi and both Selva and Santa Cristina. It is kept in racing condition, but it is open to the

LIFT PASSES

Dolomiti Superski

Prices in €

Age	1-day	6-day
under 16	32	163
16 to 59	46	233
over 65	41	210

Free under 8

Beginner no deals

Senior over 65 before the beginning of the season

Notes

Covers 1220km of piste and 450 lifts in the Dolomites, including all Sella Ronda resorts

Alternative pass

Val Gardena-Alpe di Siusi only

ALAN LIPTROT

← Sassolungo and Sassopiatto form an extraordinary backdrop to the Alpe di Siusi area; we skied it in 2011 and they were lost in cloud (sob ...)

---

public much of the time and makes a wonderful fast cruise – it's one of our favourite runs. The long red runs from Dantercëpies are entertaining, too.

FOR INTERMEDIATES ★★★★★
Fast cruising on easy slopes

There is a huge amount of skiing to do, in several areas.

Competent intermediates will love the red and black descents from Dantercëpies and Ciampinoi to Selva (but more timid intermediates may find them too steep and/or crowded).

The blue runs in the Plan de Gralba area are gentle; the red run to get there from Ciampinoi is a real obstacle – it's steep and crowded and can be icy – but reporters find it worth the struggle. The quiet runs at Mont de Seura, above Monte Pana, are worth exploring.

The broad Alpe di Siusi above Ortisei is ideal for confidence-building. The red runs that dominate the map are rarely red in practice, and they are crowd-free (and impossibly scenic). Runs are mostly of limited vertical, the main exception being the red from Punta d'Oro – 500m vertical.

The Seceda sector has good red and blue runs at altitude, and splendid runs to the valley – an easy blue/red to Santa Cristina and the beautiful red Cucasattel, passing through a natural gorge to Ortisei.

FOR BEGINNERS ★★★☆☆
Great slopes, but ...

The village nursery slopes below the Dantercëpies gondola are excellent – spacious, convenient, and kept in good condition. There are lots of gentle, long runs to progress to, but they are at Plan de Gralba and Alpe di Siusi and reached by bus or taxi.

FOR BOARDERS ★★★☆☆
Limited options

Selva attracts few boarders. There's little to challenge experts, and off-piste opportunities are limited, but the nursery slopes are good and there are lots of gentle runs to progress to. The main valley lifts are all gondolas or chairs. There are three terrain parks and a couple of half-pipes.

FOR CROSS-COUNTRY ★★★★★
Beautiful trails

There are 115km of trails, all enjoying wonderful scenery. The 12km trail up the Vallunga-Langental valley is

particularly attractive, with neck-craning views all around. Almost half the trails have the advantage of being at altitude (so better snow as well as better views), running between Monte Pana and across Alpe di Siusi.

MOUNTAIN RESTAURANTS ★★★★★
A real highlight

There are lots of huts all over the area, and virtually all of them are lively, with helpful staff, good food, lots of character and modest prices. 'Not a bad one all week' is a typical reporter's comment, leading us to bestow a rare 5-star rating.

In the Dantercëpies sector, the Panorama is a small, cosy, rustic suntrap at the foot of the drag near the top, tipped for its coffee, chocolate and cakes as well as views. Not far away at the bottom of the Val double chair, the Ciampac is 'brilliant for coffee or lunch in the sun'. While at the top of the Costabella chair, Rif Pastura is a great place for lunch or 'chocolate to die for' later.

In the Plan de Gralba area the Rif Emilio Comici is atmospheric, with a big terrace. Valongia does 'the best kaiserschmarren'. Piz Seteur has 'superb lasagne' (and check out 'Après-ski'). At Passo Sella, Rif Friedrich August has Highland cattle strolling around outside, and closely related steaks on sale inside.

In the Seceda sector there are countless options. Baita Gamsblut is a 'super rustic hut with a good menu and a warm, friendly atmosphere'. Daniel's Hütte is 'very cosy in a storm, with excellent food and good service'. The small Curona is a favourite of one repeat visitor ('friendly; best strudel'). The Mastle hut is recommended again for 'the best pizza of our stay'. On the long Cucasattel run, Val d'Anna is another reader favourite ('the very best cakes and pastries').

From the countless options, our Alpe di Siusi specialist picks out Laurinhütte ('welcoming, excellent food, great views'), Zallinger Hütte ('charming – a great find') and Mont Seuc, at the top of the Ortisei gondola – 'perfect for watching the cliffs slowly turn red while sipping a drink'.

SCHOOLS AND GUIDES ★★★☆☆
No worries

Racing star from the 1990s Peter Runggaldier seems to have merged his Ski Academy with the resort's main

Selva / Val Gardena

Interactive resort shortlist builder at **www.wtss.co.uk**

The lower half of the Seceda area above Ortisei is prettily wooded, with distant views of Gruppo del Sella →

SCHOOLS

Selva Gardena – Ski Academy Peter Runggaldier (Ski Factory)
t 0471 795156
2000
t 0471 773125
Top School Val Gardena
t 0471 794099

Classes (Selva prices)
6 half days (full day on final session)
€183

Private lessons
€40 for 1hr

GUIDES

Val Gardena Mountain Guide Association
t 0471 794133

CHILDCARE

Selvi mini club
0471 795156
Ages 0 to 4yr; 9am to 4pm, Sun to Fri
Casa Bimbo (at S Cristina)
0471 793013
From 0 to 3yr

Ski school
For age 4 to 12:
6 days (10am to 4pm) from €317, lunch included (Selva school price)

Selva Gardena school, which has been recommended by several readers – most recently for children's classes. Reports on the 2000 school are mixed.

FOR FAMILIES ★★★★★
It's all down to the detail
At first sight, in general, the village does not seem ideal for families. It's a sprawling place requiring use of not entirely efficient buses, with a busy through-road. But make the right arrangements and pick your location with care, and you can have very successful family holidays here. An obvious first step is to look at UK tour operators with their own nursery facilities, of which Esprit is the clear leader (see below).

STAYING THERE

Chalets There is a fair choice of catered chalets, including some good ones with en suite bathrooms, and some with childcare – specialist Esprit has two large properties and three smaller ones.
Hotels There are about 20 4-star hotels in Selva, about 40 3-stars and numerous lesser hotels. It is not a small place. Few of the best are well positioned – though they generally operate shuttle-buses.
★★★★Aaritz (0471 795011) Best-placed 4-star, opposite the gondola.
★★★★Gran Baita (0471 795210) Large, luxurious sporthotel, with lots of mod cons including pool. A few minutes' walk from centre and lifts.
★★★★Granvara (0471 795250) Just out of town but free shuttle, great views, pool and a spa.
★★★★Mignon (0471 795092) Good value, close to lifts – 'comfortable, with fantastic dinners, friendly staff'.
★★★★Oswald (0471 795151) One Californian reader's top choice in Europe. 'Good rooms, fantastic food, very helpful staff.' Near a ski-bus stop and with its own shuttle.
★★★★Savoy (0471 795343) Next to the 'slow but quiet' Ciampinoi chairlift. One reader's regular favourite – 'amazing food, comfortable rooms plus great indoor/outdoor swimming pool'.
★★★Des Alpes (0471 772700) Good location at a bus stop, 'warm, friendly staff and ample four-course meals'.
★★★Linder (0471 795242) An established reader favourite in a central location. 'Cosy, comfortable, very welcoming family, fantastic food

and great free guiding.' Pool and spa.
★★★Miara (0471 794627) Next to the Ciampinoi gondola. 'Modern, quiet, with friendly helpful owners.'
★★★Pralong (0471 795370) Uphill walk from the centre, but 'one of the best we've visited', said a reporter.
★★★Solaia (0471 795104) Superbly positioned for lifts and slopes.
★★★Stella (0471 795162) Tipped in 2009 for great location right at the Sella Ronda lifts and 'very good food'.
★★★Gardena (0471 793313) in Santa Cristina was recommended last year. 'Excellent food, newly refurbished, very well appointed rooms.'
Villa Seceda (0471 795297) A 'friendly' B&B near the nursery slopes,
Apartments We have had excellent reports of the Villa Gardena and Isabell apartments.

EATING OUT ★★★★★
Adequate choice
The better restaurants are mainly based in hotels or, ironically, B&B guest houses. Reader tips include: Armin's Grillstube ('inexpensive and cosy cellar restaurant'), the Sal Fëur in the Garni Broi ('best meal we had all week'), the Bula ('fabulous pasta and pizza, very welcoming'), the Rino and the Bellavista for pizza, and the Costabella for Tirolean specialities. The hotel Des Alpes gets mixed reviews – maybe avoid the budget menu.

Air Verona 215km/
135 miles (2hr45);
Bolzano 55km/
35 miles (1hr);
Treviso 200km/
125 miles (3hr30);
Brescia 240km/150
miles (3hr30); Milan
340km/210 miles
(4hr30); Innsbruck
120km/75 miles
(1hr45)

Rail Chiusa (27km/
17 miles); Bressanone
(35km/22 miles);
Bolzano (40km/
25 miles); frequent
buses from station

Alpine Answers,
Crystal, Crystal Finest,
Esprit, First Choice,
Independent Ski Links,
Interactive Resorts,
Momentum, Mountain
Wave, Ski Solutions,
Ski Total, Skitracer, Ski
Yogi, Snow Finders,
STC, Thomson
Ortisei Crystal,
Inghams, Ski
Expectations, Thomson
S Cristina Ski Club
Freshtracks

In Val Gardena:

Indoor Swimming
pool, sauna, bowling,
ice rink, climbing wall,
fitness centre, tennis,
museum, library,
chess

Outdoor Sleigh rides,
snowshoeing,
tobogganing, ice
climbing, ice rink,
paragliding, extensive
cleared paths

Phone numbers
From abroad use the
prefix +39 (and do **not**
omit the initial '0' of
the phone number)

www.valgardena.it

APRES-SKI ★★★☆☆
Not without action

At close of play some of the mountain
restaurants offer distractions. Piz
Seteur is one place where you can
expect a bit of a buzz. At the base, the
Stua is a popular last stop (and if you
settle in for the evening, live music
may arrive mid-evening; 'fairly-priced
drinks') and Kronestube has been
recommended previously ('good
atmosphere'). Café Mozart on the main
street 'serves the best hot chocolate in
the world and cakes to match'. The
hotel Sochers is said to be good for a
quiet drink. Later on the village streets
are fairly quiet, but there are places to
go. Goalie's Irish bar, with its hockey
memorabilia, was recommended last
year for 'a quieter drink in a relaxed
atmosphere'. 'Keep an eye out for the
dancing girls at Salto's,' says a 2010
reporter. There are several places with
DJs open until about 1am – notably
the Laurinkeller and the 'very German'
Luislkeller – 'bonkers', says a recent
reporter, with 'a DJ so bad he's good'.
The serious nightclub is the Dali, with
dance music for 'a younger clientele'.

OFF THE SLOPES ★★★☆☆
Good variety

There are many spectacular walks to
be done on Alpe di Siusi and Rasciesa,
in particular. There's a sports centre,
snowshoeing, tobogganing and sleigh
rides. One reporter enjoyed an
organised bowling night, another a
'fun night' with the locals watching ice
hockey – quite a big deal in these
parts. There are buses to nearby
Ortisei and more distant Bolzano, with
a museum featuring 5,000-year-old
Oetzi the Ice Man, among many
attractions. And coach excursions to
Cortina and Verona. A group of hotels
has formed Val Gardena Active,
offering free excursions run by
'impressive' guides. Pedestrians can
reach numerous good restaurants by
gondola or cable car.

S CRISTINA

A few km downvalley from Selva, at
the bottom of the race course from
Ciampinoi, S Cristina is a pleasant
village well worth considering as an
alternative base. It has gondolas
towards Ciampinoi and Seceda (their
base stations linked by an
underground funicular), and a slow

chairlift up to a ring of nursery slopes
at Monte Pana (but no piste back).
There is accommodation up here, too.
There's a good range of hotels in the
village from 5-star down, and
countless B&Bs.

ORTISEI

Ortisei is an attractive, prosperous
market town with a life of its own
apart from tourism. It's full of lovely
buildings, pretty churches, smart
shops and tempting cafes, and has an
interesting museum, a large hot-spring
swimming pool and an ice rink. The
valley road follows the river, bypassing
the centre. The local slopes offer an
astonishing six toboggan runs, one
from Rasciesa 6km long and accessed
by funicular – as well as vast amounts
of easy skiing. They aren't on the main
Sella Ronda circuit. If you plan to do
much skiing at or beyond Selva, plan
on using the ski-buses to S Cristina or
Selva.

The gondola to the Seceda slopes
is easily reached from the centre by a
300m-long series of moving walkways
and escalators. Alternatively, you can
reach the top of that gondola, and the
start of the Seceda cable car, by riding
the Rasciesa funicular and descending
a red piste.

The gondola for Alpe di Siusi is a
similar distance out, across the river –
a footbridge from the centre is the
best approach, going over the valley
road too. Note that if you are moving
from one area to another it is quite a
walk between the two.

The nursery area, school and
kindergarten are also over the river,
along with a fair range of
accommodation. The fine public indoor
pool and ice rink are also here.

There are hotels and self-catering
accommodation to suit all tastes and
pockets and many good restaurants,
mainly specialising in local dishes. The
3-star hotel Dolomiti Madonna (0471
796207) is recommended this year
despite its location at the very end of
the town – 'delightful evening meals'.
A regular rates the 5-star Gardena
Grödnerhof (0471 796315) above the
'well-situated' 5-star Adler (0471
775000) due to its 'outstanding food,
nicer guest rooms, unbeatable ski
guide and fewer people'. Après-ski is
quite jolly, and many bars keep going
till late.

SESTRIERE: TOURIST OFFICE

Sestriere

Altitude is the main attraction of this, Europe's first purpose-built resort; some would say it's the only attraction

458

TOP 10 RATINGS

Extent	★★★★
Fast lifts	★★★
Queues	★★★
Snow	★★★★
Expert	★★★
Intermediate	★★★★
Beginner	★★★
Charm	★
Convenience	★★★
Scenery	★★★

RPI   85

lift pass	£170
ski hire	£105
lessons	£95
food & drink	£105
total	**£475**

NEWS

2010/11: The blue Boursaille run on the Sauze side of Monte Fraiteve was improved to provide a better link with Sauze d'Oulx.

KEY FACTS

Resort	2035m
	6,680ft
Milky Way	
Slopes	1390-2825m
	4,560-9,270ft
Lifts	72
Pistes	400km
	249 miles
Blue	25%
Red	55%
Black	20%
Snowmaking	60%

Sestriere-Sauze	
d'Oulx-Sansicario	
Slopes	1390-2825m
	4,560-9,270ft
Lifts	41
Pistes	300km
	186 miles
Snowmaking	38%

PISTE MAP

Sestriere is covered on the Sauze d'Oulx map

+ Local slopes suitable for most levels, with some tougher runs than in most neighbouring resorts

+ Part of the extensive Milky Way area, with Sauze d'Oulx and Sansicario only one lift away

+ Snowmaking covers all but one or two marginal slopes, but ...

– It needs to, given the very erratic local snowfall record

– The village is a bit of an eyesore

– For a purpose-built resort, not conveniently arranged

– Weekend and peak-period queues

– Little après-ski during the week

Sestriere was built for snow – high, with north-west-facing slopes – and it has very extensive snowmaking, too. So even if you are let down by the notoriously erratic snowfalls in this corner of Italy, you should be fairly safe here – certainly safer than in Sauze d'Oulx, over the hill. All of which makes Sestriere a great weekend away for the residents of Turin. As a holiday destination for residents of Tunbridge Wells, it doesn't have such a strong case.

THE RESORT

Sestriere was the first purpose-built resort in the Alps, developed by Fiat's Giovanni Agnelli in the 1930s.
Village charm The resort sits on a broad, sunny and windy col, and neither the site nor the village, with its rows of apartment blocks and two round towers, looks very hospitable – though improvements were made for the 2006 Winter Olympics.
Convenience The village is not huge, and some accommodation is close to the snow – it depends where you stay; but basically the buildings are on one side of the col and the skiing is on the other, and some of the walks between the two are non-trivial. The slightly lower satellite of Borgata is less convenient for nightlife and shops. The valley town of Pragelato is a viable base, with its cable car link up to the Motta slopes.
Scenery The Motta slopes are high and rolling, with extensive views across the Milky Way and its part-wooded slopes to the mountains on the French border.

THE MOUNTAINS

The local skiing is on shady slopes, mainly open with some woodland, facing the village. Sestriere is at one extreme of the big Franco-Italian Milky Way area – though the slopes around the border are best reached by road.
Slopes The local slopes, served by drags and chairs, are in two main sectors: Sises, directly in front of the

village, and Motta, above Borgata; Motta is more varied and bigger, with more vertical. Across the valley, a gondola goes up from a car park west of the village to M Fraiteve, for access to Sauze d'Oulx, Sansicario and the rest of the Milky Way. For the return to Sestriere there are blue and red runs from M Fraiteve – but both are sunny, and you usually have to ride the gondola down. Signposting and piste marking are poor and the piste map difficult to follow – reporters complain about all three.
Fast lifts The lifts are mainly modern, though there are still some inadequate, 'painfully slow', old ones, both here and over in Sauze.
Queues The main lifts can have queues on sunny weekends when people flock up from Turin. Now that all the lifts out of Sestriere, Sauze and Sansicario meet at M Fraiteve the summit area is 'very congested' at peak times, says a repeat visitor, and there may be serious queues for the gondola down.
Terrain parks There wasn't one in Sestriere last season – but there were in Sauze d'Oulx and Sansicario.
Snow reliability The Italian part of the Milky Way gets notoriously unreliable snowfalls, but Sestriere has comprehensive snowmaking. When combined with its altitude and orientation, this means you can count on good cover on the pistes. Don't expect powder, though.
Experts There is a fair amount to amuse – steep pistes served by the

↑ Sestriere is no beauty and is dominated by apartment blocks and these two round towers

VIA LATTEA

Schools and guides A 2011 reporter says the adults in his group 'thought there was a lot of standing around' but the children 'seemed to progress well'.

Families There are no special facilities for children.

STAYING THERE

Most accommodation is in apartments.

Hotels There are a dozen hotels, mostly 3-star or 4-star; a repeated criticism from reporters is that some of those with 4 stars deserve only 3. The central hotel du Col (0122 76990) offers an 'ideal location', 'good food, very clean and excellent staff'. The Biancaneve (0122 755176) has 'great food, good service'. The Cristallo (0122 750190) has also been recommended for its position and food. The Pragelato Village Resort Spa (0122 740001) is 'outstanding' says a 2011 reporter – 'spacious chalets, high spec, comfy' – with cable car access to slopes but beginners and timid intermediates 'need to take a 20-minute bus ride to town'. The Shackleton Mountain Resort (0122 750773) is a smart, modern complex with pool and wellness centre. Just out of the village is the luxurious Principi di Piemonte (0122 750740).

Apartments The Villagio Olimpico apartments built for the 2006 Olympics is reasonably central and 'good value, spacious rooms, with good facilities'.

Eating out There are plenty of options. The rustic Antica Spelonca in Borgata has been recommended for 'great local dishes'. Other reader tips include Pinky ('renowned for pizza and pasta but steak to die for'), Last Tango and Ritrovo.

Après-ski The quietness of the place during the week, when the Italians are absent, disappoints some visitors. Pinky is a popular bar and restaurant, with low sofas in the classic Italian casual-chic style. Other reader tips for a good atmosphere include Brahms, Pub Black Pepper and the Tabata disco.

Off the slopes There's more to do than most visitors realise. There are some smart shops, a fitness centre, an ice rink, a sports centre and pool, and other diversions such as dog sledding. Outings are possible to nearby Pragelato and to Turin – only 100km away by road.

drags at the top of both sectors, three now designated as mogul fields. Given good snow, there is some decent off-piste. Don't count on it, though.

Intermediates Both sectors also offer plenty for confident intermediates, who can also explore practically all of the Milky Way areas, conditions permitting. The runs in the Motta sector offer more of a challenge than elsewhere.

Beginners The terrain is good for beginners, with several nursery areas and the gentlest of easy blue runs down to Borgata. A special day pass covers use of five lifts. But there is a lack of easy runs to progress to.

Snowboarding Competent intermediates will enjoy cruising the pistes and the draglifts are largely avoidable. But there was no terrain park last season.

Cross-country There are three loops covering about 12km.

Mountain restaurants The woody Raggio di Sole at Anfiteatro offers 'good local food, and good music'. Despite its valley-bottom location, Il Capret at Borgata is popular with readers – 'very friendly staff, reasonable prices, clean toilets'.

La Thuile

A revitalised mining town and a modern lift-base complex, with extensive, easy slopes linked with La Rosière in France

TOP 10 RATINGS

Extent	★★★
Fast lifts	★★★
Queues	★★★★
Snow	★★★★
Expert	★★
Intermediate	★★★★
Beginner	★★★★
Charm	★★★
Convenience	★★★
Scenery	★★★

RPI	85
lift pass	£160
ski hire	£100
lessons	£95
food & drink	£120
total	£475

aosta-valley.co.uk

NEWS

2010/11: Snowmaking was increased and a new kindergarten (Il Bosco Incantato) opened. Children's lift passes were improved: free if under eight and discounts for under-14s.

- ➕ Fair-sized area linked to La Rosière in France
- ➕ Strikingly crowd-free slopes
- ➕ Excellent beginner and easy intermediate slopes

- ➖ The tough runs are low down, and most low, woodland runs are tough
- ➖ The French link is exposed to bad weather, and the return is slow
- ➖ Not the place for lively après-ski

La Thuile has a lot going for it. If you are limited to school holidays and have had enough of the peak-season crowds over the hill in France, it could be just the job – provided a quiet village appeals to you as much as quiet slopes.

THE RESORT

La Thuile is a bit like a French purpose-built resort, with the modern Planibel complex at the base, but with a distinctly Italian old quarter nearby. The pass includes two days in other Val d'Aosta resorts, and free buses run twice daily to nearby Courmayeur.

Village charm Many people find the Planibel complex rather soulless, and prefer to stay in the old village. Much of it has been restored and new buildings tastefully added.

Convenience The Planibel complex is right by the main lift, with lodgings, a leisure centre, bars, restaurants and shops – including an excellent bomb shop and good supermarket. There are also a few other hotels around the base area. The main old village spreads over a wide area across the river (served by a regular free bus).

Scenery The scenery is varied, with open bowls and lower wooded slopes overlooked by the nearby Mont Blanc massif. Good views into France.

THE MOUNTAINS

La Thuile has quite extensive slopes linked to those of La Rosière via slopes above the Petit San Bernard pass (which are poorly covered on the over-compressed piste map). Many runs marked red deserve no more than a blue rating. Strong winds can close high lifts, including the link.

Slopes The lifts out of the village (a gondola and a fast chair) take you to Les Suches, with shady black runs going back down directly to the village through the trees, and reds taking a more roundabout route. From here chairs take you to Chaz Dura for access to a variety of gentle bowls facing east and slightly more testing slopes on the back of the ridge, above the Petit St Bernard pass. From there two chairs go up to the shoulder of Belvedere, launch pad for La Rosière. Immediately above the lift base is the small, sheltered Maison Blanche area.

Fast lifts The key lifts are fast chairs and a gondola.

Queues Short queues may form at the gondola first thing, but not at the chair. There are no problems once you are up the hill. A 2011 reporter confirms our earlier findings: 'Even at half-term it is like low season.'

Terrain parks A new park opened in the Maison Blanche area last season.

Snow reliability Most of La Thuile's slopes are north- or east-facing and above 2000m, so the snow keeps well. There's also a decent amount of snowmaking; grooming is fine too.

Experts The black pistes down through the trees from Les Suches – the Diretta, Berthod, Muret – are serious stuff, as well as two steepish blacks at Maison Blanche. The black slopes down to the pass are easier – only

Chaz Dura 2580m

Col de Fourclaz
2610m/
8,560ft

Arnouvaz
Cerellaz

Les Suches
2200m

La Rosière

La Thuile
1440m/4,720ft

- ⓖ gondola
- Ⓔ fast chairlift
- Slow chairs & drags have no symbol

La Thuile

↑ The return from La Rosière involves this long, long exposed drag; just hope there isn't an east wind blowing …
BRIAN WALKER

KEY FACTS

Resort	1440m
	4,720ft

Espace San Bernardo (La Rosière and La Thuile)	
Slopes	1175-2610m
	3,850-8,560ft
Lifts	38
Pistes	160km
	99 miles
Green	10%
Blue	31%
Red	40%
Black	19%
Snowmaking	24%

UK PACKAGES

Alpine Answers, Crystal, First Choice, Independent Ski Links, Inghams, Interski, Just Skiing, Neilson, Ski Club Freshtracks, Ski Solutions, Skitracer, Thomson, Tracks European Adventures

Phone numbers
From abroad use the prefix +39 (and do **not** omit the initial '0' of the phone number)

TOURIST OFFICE

www.lathuile.it

just genuine, but there is also plenty of off-piste here; fast quads mean you can do quick circuits in this area. Don't hope for moguls on-piste.

Heli-lifts are available. The Ruitor glacier offers a 20km run to Ste-Foy in France, a short taxi ride from La Rosière for the lifts for La Thuile.
Intermediates The slopes above Les Suches consist almost entirely of gentle blue and red runs, ideal for cruising and carving but free of challenges. There are also long reds through the trees back to the resort – easy but pleasant. The red runs on the back side of the top ridge, down towards the Petit St Bernard pass, are less gentle. The pass road forms the roundabout San Bernardo red to the village, taking 11km to drop only 600m; avoid in fresh snow.

The skiing in La Rosière is more testing – mostly genuine red runs, sometimes with moguls, and with snow more affected by sun. The route back starts with a genuine red, and involves long, exposed draglifts.
Beginners There are no free lifts, but a day pass (5 euros) allows use of the moving carpet on the village nursery slope. There is also a nursery area up at Les Suches and long easy blues above there, ideal for progression. You ride the gondola down.
Snowboarding These are great slopes for learning. You need ride only chairlifts and the gondola, and most of the slopes are easy. For the more experienced there are great tree runs, good freeriding and some good carving runs. But there are some frustratingly flat sections too.
Cross-country La Thuile has four loops of varying difficulty on the valley floor, adding up to 16km of track.
Mountain restaurants There is a reasonable choice of places. Our favourite is Maison Carrel off run 30 – an excellent table-service place with

floor to ceiling windows doing a good range of dishes at reasonable prices ('fantastic pizza and gnocchi'); it gets busy, and service can be stretched. But we have still to try Chalet de Cantamont on run 16, said to be a 'super, friendly' hut, with 'excellent' food. The self-service Mélèze, at the top of the gondola, is 'very welcoming' with 'reasonably priced' food. And the San Bernardo serves 'excellent sausage and polenta'. The Off Shore, above Arnouvaz, is a small, 'cosy' place selling drinks and snacks The Roxi bar at the foot of the Fourclaz chair does 'lovely' hot pork rolls.
Schools and guides A repeat visitor in 2011 confirms that the instructors are enthusiastic and friendly and generally speak good English, though he found his private lesson this year 'a bit' pricey.
Families There is a nursery area, with mini-club and snow garden. The village kindergarten – Il Bosco Incantato – takes children from three to 11, and the Planibel hotel runs an all-day club for children aged four to 12. Children over five can join adult ski classes.

STAYING THERE

Hotels The 4-star Planibel (0165 884541) is large and characterless, but readers like its ideal location, pools and gym, and a 2011 reporter speaks of 'excellent rooms and beautifully presented buffet meals'. The B&B hotel du Glacier (0165 884137), a short walk above the lifts, gets repeated rave reviews, mainly thanks to its energetic owner Susanna. The Miramonti (0165 883084), in the old village (shuttle on demand), recently refurbished in traditional style, offers 'excellent food and service'.
Apartments Reporters say that the furniture and fittings in the Planibel apartments are in need of upgrading, but that they are spacious and good value – 'perfectly adequate'.
Eating out Reader tips include the Grotta ('very friendly, good pizza, pasta, fondue'), Pizzeria Dahü ('good value') and the Coq Maf ('best steak in 37 years of skiing').
Après-ski Nightlife is quiet. The Konver music cafè is open until late, with a regular DJ.
Off the slopes There are few shops; the Planibel complex has a pool and there are marked walks. Pedestrians can ride up the gondola for lunch, but can't reach the best spots.

Switzerland

Switzerland is home to some of our favourite resorts. Only three resorts in this book are awarded ✹✹✹✹✹ for both resort charm and spectacular scenery – the essentially traffic-free Swiss villages of Zermatt, Mürren and Wengen, pictured on the left. Many other Swiss resorts are not far behind in the charm and scenery stakes. Many resorts have impressive slopes, too – including some of the biggest, highest and toughest runs in the Alps – as well as a lot of good intermediate terrain. For fast, queue-free lift networks, Swiss resorts are not known as pacesetters – too many historic cable cars and mountain railways for that. But the real bottlenecks are steadily disappearing. And there are compensations – the world's best mountain restaurants, for one, and pretty reliable accommodation too.

Until recently, one of the drawbacks of Switzerland was that smoking was allowed in public areas. But now nearly every canton that matters has banned smoking except in dedicated smoking rooms, and all hotels, restaurants and bars will have smoke-free areas.

People always seem to think Switzerland is expensive. It's never going to be cheap, but whether it is actually expensive depends hugely on exchange rate fluctuations. For many years, we tried to get across the fact that it was no more expensive than France. But not any longer; things have changed.

As most people know only too well, in the last four years the pound has fallen against the euro by about 40%. But in the same period it has fallen against the Swiss franc by a massive 85%. If you skied in Switzerland last season, you know the result: prices are not just high, they are ridiculously high. Our price survey shows that food and drink now costs Brits as much in the cheapest Swiss resort, Meiringen, as in the most expensive French resort, Courchevel. Overall holiday costs are less unreasonable: when you add in the cost of lifts, ski hire and lessons, a few Swiss resorts work out close to the European average. But most are way, way above it, and Swiss resorts dominate the above-average category in our price index results. Until the exchange rate improves, most people will simply go elsewhere.

Many Swiss resorts have a special relationship with the British, who invented downhill skiing in its modern form in Wengen and Mürren by persuading the locals to run their mountain railways in winter, to act as ski lifts, and by organising the first downhill races. An indication of the continuing strength of the British presence in these resorts is that Wengen has an English church.

While France is the home of the purpose-built resort, Switzerland is the home of the mountain village that has transformed itself from traditional farming community (or health retreat) into year-round holiday resort. Many of Switzerland's most famous mountain resorts are as popular in the summer as in the winter, or more so. This creates places with a more lived-in feel to them and a much more stable local community.

Many villages are still dominated by a handful of families lucky or shrewd enough to get involved in the early development of the area. This has its downside as well as advantages. The ruling families have been able to stifle competition and bar newcomers

JUNGFRAU REGION MARKETING AG

← No one does chocolate-box car-free mountain villages like the Swiss; this is downtown Wengen

from taking a slice of their action. Alternative ski schools – to compete with the traditional, nationally organised school, resulting in continuing pressure to raise standards – are still less common than in other Alpine countries, for example. But this grip has at last started to weaken.

The quality of service throughout Switzerland is generally high. The food is almost universally of good quality and much less stodgy than in neighbouring Austria. Even the standard rustic dish of rösti is haute cuisine compared to Austrian sausages. And in Switzerland you get what you pay for: the cheapest wine, for example, is not cheap, but it is reliable.

Perhaps surprisingly for such a traditional, rather staid skiing nation, Switzerland has gone out of its way to attract snowboarders. Davos may hit the headlines mainly when it hosts huge economic conferences, but yards from the conference hall there are dudes getting big air on the Bolgen slope's training kickers. Little-known Laax claims one of Europe's best terrain parks.

Switzerland, like Italy, doesn't have much time for tree-huggers who object to the impact of helicopters on wildlife. Heli-skiing is not unrestricted, but it is available, whereas in Austria it is confined to Lech-Zürs and in France it is confined to retrieval of clients from valley bottoms – you can't be deposited on a peak.

GETTING AROUND BY TRAIN

The Swiss railway network is famously extensive and reliable. The trains run like clockwork to the advertised timetable – if you think a Swiss train is late, make sure your watch is right before you complain. (There is, however, some truth in the cynical view that the trains are able to run on time because the timetables incorporate long stops at stations.)

The rail network is a perfectly viable means of reaching many

SWISS RAIL PASSES

These are the main options – there are others. On any of the passes listed, children under 16 accompanied by at least one parent travel free.

Swiss Pass *Covers unrestricted travel on most of the Swiss railway network, buses and postal buses during the period of validity – 4, 8, 15 or 22 days; or one month. Prices: 4 days from £167; 8 days from £240*

* *Includes panoramic rail routes as well as using trams and buses in 38 towns*

* *50% discount for using most of the mountain railways*

* *Free entrance to about 400 museums*

* *15% discount for two and more adults travelling together*

Swiss Transfer Ticket *Permits travel from the Swiss border or airport and your destination, out and back, by the most direct route. Valid for one month. You can use two different airports. Prices: from £80*

Swiss Flexi Card *Permits unrestricted travel across Switzerland, like the Swiss Pass, on 3, 4, 5 or 6 days of your choice during a one-month period of validity – on days when you choose to use the card, you just write the date on the card. On days when you choose not to use up one of the 3, 4, 5 or 6 days, the card gets you a discount of 50%. There's 15% discount for two and more adults travelling together. Prices: 3 days from £160; 6 days from £253*

Swiss Card *An extension of the Transfer Ticket. As well as travel to and from your destination, you get a 50% discount on all rail, bus and boat fares during the one-month period of validity – and on some cable car fares. Prices: from £115*

What mountains. What space. What light!

resorts. There are often linking services that run to the top of the mountain, doubling as ski lifts, too. We did a week-long tour of Valais resorts last season to see how it worked in practice. Our feature panel explains the main rail passes you might use.

Our tour took us first from Geneva to Crans-Montana, then on to the Aletsch Arena area at the far eastern end of the Valais – look for the resorts of Riederalp and Bettmeralp on our map. Next, we backtracked to Zermatt, and before returning to Geneva we left the rail network to try the postbus services to and from Saas-Fee – a resort inexplicably not served by a railway.

Things went pretty smoothly, but not perfectly. At Sierre, where we were to change to the funicular for Crans, we failed to detect the shuttle-bus and had quite a walk from one station to the other. We were surprised to find that our tickets were not valid for the cable-car up to Riederalp. And we were repeatedly disappointed by the inadequate luggage space, even in first-class carriages. We would use the railways again if visiting resorts like Riederalp and Zermatt where you can't take cars. And our postbus adventure went to plan, too, with the most satisfactory luggage space of the trip.

GETTING AROUND BY CAR

Access to practically all Swiss resorts is fairly straightforward when approaching from the north – just pick your motorway. But many of the high passes that are perfectly sensible ways to get around the country in summer are closed in winter, which can be inconvenient if you are moving around from one area to another.

There are very useful car-carrying trains in various places; they can cut out huge amounts of driving. One key link is between the Valais (Crans-Montana, Zermatt etc) and Andermatt via the Furka tunnel, and another is from Andermatt to the Grisons (Laax, Davos etc) via the Oberalp pass – closed to road traffic in winter but open to trains except after very heavy snowfalls. Another rail tunnel that's very handy is the Lötschberg, linking Kandersteg in the Bernese Oberland with Brig in the Valais. The recently opened Lötschberg Base Tunnel is lower, longer and faster, but it takes only passenger and freight trains.

St Moritz is more awkward to get to than other major resorts. The main road route is over the Julier pass. This is normally kept open, but at 2285m it is naturally prone to heavy snowfalls that can shut it for a time. Fallbacks are car-carrying rail tunnels under the Albula pass and the Vereina tunnel from near Klosters.

These car-carrying rail services are generally painless. Often you can just turn up and drive on. But carrying capacities are obviously limited. Some services (eg Oberalp) carry only a handful of cars, and booking is vital. Others (eg Furka, Lötschberg, Vereina) are

SWISS TOBOGGAN RUNS

The Austrians might dispute it, but Switzerland seems to do tobogganing on an unmatched scale. It isn't just the famous Cresta run at St Moritz (check out that chapter for more information), it's that so many resorts have epic runs. The longest in the world, they say, is at Grindelwald – 15km from the Faulhorn via Bussalp to the resort; it's fantastically scenic, being surrounded by famous peaks, but it does involve a 2hr30 hike from the top of the First gondola.

There are plenty of other extraordinary runs, without the hiking penalty. Fiesch in the little-known Aletsch Arena area has a 13km run, Saas Grund below Saas Fee has one of 11km. Even macho Verbier has a 10km run from Savoleyres, dropping 850m.

ALP VILLAGE
SA

BUY DIRECT FROM THE DEVELOPER

LUXURY SWISS SKI CHALETS IN THE VERBIER SKI REGION

Alp Village SA is a Swiss developer specialising in building high quality chalets and apartments in the resorts of Veysonnaz, Nendaz and Les Collons which all connect to 410km of pistes in Verbier:

"Chalets du Rhone" - At 1650m on the old ski piste below Les Collons, traditional style 4, 5 and 6 bedroom chalets priced from 920,000 Sfrs.

"Pieds des Pistes Chalets" - Just 200m from the chairlift at 1550m three bedroom chalets from 675,000 Sfrs.

"Ski-in, Ski-out Chalets" - Directly on the ski slopes in Les Collons. These luxury five bedroom chalets priced from 2.2m Sfrs.

"Matterhorn Village" - Six modern style chalets in Les Collons designed by local architect, Eric Papon using traditional materials but with a stunning modern twist. Prices from 2.2m Sfrs.

"Ski Heaven" - Stunning apartment building with spa in Veysonnaz. Two, three and four bedroom apartments from 600,000 Sfrs.

Please contact us, or visit our web site to view the latest developments.

ALP VILLAGE SA
1987 HEREMENCE, VALAIS, SWITZERLAND
TEL +44 208 458 5889 INFO@ALP-VILLAGE.COM
WWW.ALP-VILLAGE.COM

much bigger operations with much greater capacity – but that's a reflection of demand, and at peak times there may be long queues – particularly for the Furka tunnel from Andermatt, which Zürich residents use to get to the big Valais resorts. There is a car-carrying rail tunnel linking Switzerland with Italy – the Simplon. But most routes to Italy are kept open by means of road tunnels. Read the Italy introduction for more information.

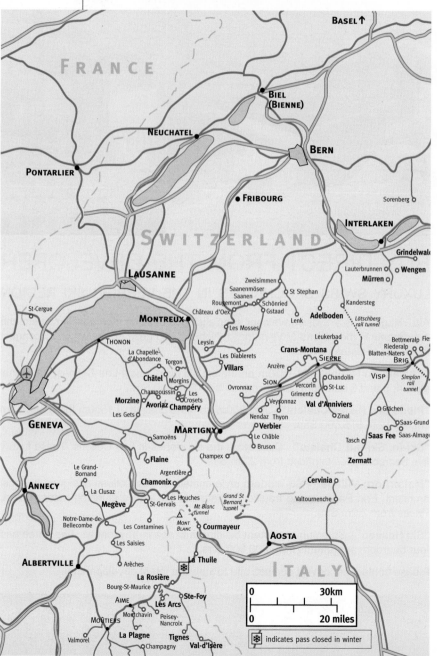

BASEL ↑

FRANCE

BIEL (BIENNE)

NEUCHATEL

BERN

PONTARLIER

FRIBOURG

Sorenberg

INTERLAKEN

SWITZERLAND

Grindelwald

Lauterbrunnen   Wengen

LAUSANNE

Zweisimmen

Mürren

Saanenmöser
Saanen
Rougemont   Schönried   St Stephan

St-Cergue

Kandersteg

Château d'Oex   Gstaad

MONTREUX

Les Mosses   Lenk   Adelboden   Lötschberg rail tunnel

Leysin

Leukerbad   Bettmeralp   Fies
Riederalp

THONON

Crans-Montana   Blatten-Naters

La Chapelle-d'Abondance   Les Diablerets

SIERRE   BRIG

Torgon

Villars   Anzère   Chandolin   VISP   Simplon rail tunnel

Châtel   Morgins

SION   Vercorin   St-Luc

Champoussin   Les Crosets

Ovronnaz   Grimentz   Veysonnaz

Morzine   Avoriaz   Champéry

Val d'Anniviers   Glächen

Les Gets   Nendaz   Thyon   Zinal

Saas-Grund

GENEVA   MARTIGNY   Verbier

Samoëns   Le Châble   Tasch   Saas Fee   Saas-Almage

Bruson

Flaine   Champex   Zermatt

Le Grand-Bornand   Argentière

ANNECY   Chamonix   Cervinia

La Clusaz   Les Houches   Grand St Bernard tunnel

Megève   St-Gervais   Mt Blanc tunnel   Valtournenche

Notre-Dame-de-Bellecombe   Les Contamines   MONT BLANC   Courmayeur

Les Saisies   AOSTA

ALBERTVILLE   Arêches

La Thuile

La Rosière   ITALY

Bourg-St-Maurice   Ste-Foy

AIME   Les Arcs

Montchavin   Peisey-Nancroix

MOÛTIERS

Valmorel   La Plagne   Tignes

Champagny   Val-d'Isère

0		30km

0		20 miles

❄ indicates pass closed in winter

To use Swiss motorways you have to buy an annual permit to stick on your windscreen. Permits cost SF40 and are valid for 14 months – from December to the end of January. They are sold at the border and are, for all practical purposes, an inescapable purchase. This isn't unreasonable – it's difficult to avoid using motorways if you're driving serious distances within the country. But you could always try ....

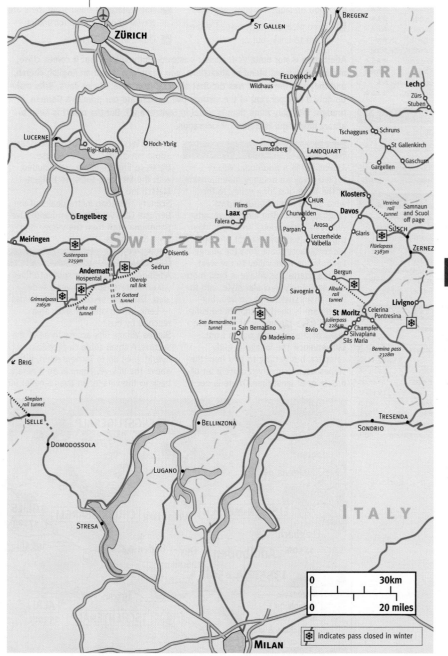

Interactive resort shortlist builder at **www.wtss.co.uk**

Adelboden

Traditional village with plenty to do off the snow – but also with extensive, varied and scenic slopes, some also accessible from Lenk

TOP 10 RATINGS

Extent	★★★
Fast lifts	★★★
Queues	★★★
Snow	★★★
Expert	★★
Intermediate	★★★
Beginner	★★★★
Charm	★★★★
Convenience	★★
Scenery	★★★★

RPI 120

lift pass	£210
ski hire	£145
lessons	£110
food & drink	£210
total	**£675**

NEWS

2010/11: An avalanche safety centre opened on Tschentenalp. The proposed large spa and wellness complex is on hold, awaiting further funding.

KEY FACTS

Resort	1355m
	4,450ft
Slopes	1070-2360m
	3,510-7,740ft
Lifts	56
Pistes	185km
	115 miles
Blue	41%
Red	52%
Black	7%
Snowmaking	60%

470

+ Chalet-style mountain village in a splendid setting

+ Good off-slope facilities

+ Some pleasantly uncrowded slopes linked to Lenk, but ...

− The slopes are fragmented and widely spread; access can be slow

− Not a place for bumps but there are plenty of off-piste opportunities

− Quiet, limited nightlife

Adelboden is not quite your classic postcard-pretty village, but it comes close, and offers a good blend of attractions. 100 years ago it had an English church, and they say the priest was the first ski instructor here. These days, Brits make up only a few per cent of the visitors (we have found our primitive German brought into play more than is usual in Switzerland). But the resort is keen to attract more, and it merits consideration.

THE RESORT

Adelboden is a traditional village tucked away on a sunny mountainside at the head of a long valley to the west of the much better known Jungfrau region. The Jungfrau resorts (Wengen, Mürren etc) are within day-trip range. Its major sector of slopes is indirectly accessible from the village of Lenk, in the next valley to the west.

Village charm The village is built more or less entirely in chalet style, and the long, main street (not car-free, but nearly so) is lined by chalets housing shops. It's a pity many of them have racks of cheap goods out in front.

Convenience The village is fairly compact, but getting to and from the slopes usually involves quite a bit of hassle or at least time. There is no

perfect location, unless you are clear about which lift you plan to use. Buses to Engstligenalp are included with the lift pass, those to Elsigen-Metsch are not.

Scenery The 3000-metre peaks of the Bernese Oberland make an impressive panorama both from the village and from the slopes.

THE MOUNTAINS

Adelboden's slopes are split into five varied sectors, spread over a wide area. The main sector stretches across to Lenk, which offers a sixth area reached by bus.

Slopes Village lifts access three of the sectors. A small cable car/gondola hybrid goes up to Tschentenalp, just above the village. There is an itinerary back to the village. An even smaller lift

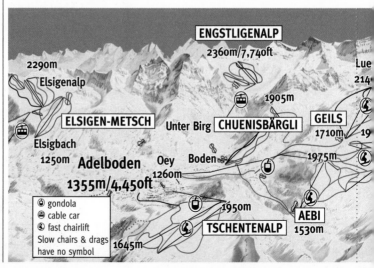

ENGSTLIGENALP
2360m/7,740ft

2290m
Elsigenalp

1905m

Lue
214

ELSIGEN-METSCH   Unter Birg CHUENISBÄRGLI   GEILS
1710m   19

Elsigbach
1250m   Adelboden   Oey   Boden
1260m
1355m/4,450ft

1975m

⚡ gondola
🚡 cable car
⚡ fast chairlift
Slow chairs & drags have no symbol

1645m

1950m

TSCHENTENALP   1530m

AEBI

↑ Fine views of Chuenisbärgli (and distant views of Engstligenalp) from the restaurant at the top of Tschentenalp
SNOWPIX.COM / CHRIS GILL

goes down to Oey, where a proper gondola goes up to the Chuenisbärgli sector and then on to the major sector (in two further stages, taking 15min in total). This major sector has no single name; on our map we show the three main subsectors – Geils, Aebi and Metsch (on the Lenk side of the ridge). There is a pretty run home to Oey.

Engstligenalp, a flat-bottomed high-altitude bowl, is reached by a cable car 4km south of the resort; Elsigen-Metsch (with another cable car) is 5km away to the north-east.

Fast lifts The main lifts are gondolas and fast chairs, but there are still a fair few slow lifts.

Queues The main access gondolas get busy at peak times, but the minibus service to Geils is an alternative. The two main lifts out of Geils to the ridge above Lenk can develop queues. A January 2011 visitor found queues at the Bühlberg chair due to all the school groups using it, and crowded slopes. The little lift linking Oey to the main street is a real bottleneck; public and hotel buses offer a way round it.

Terrain parks The Gran Masta Park at Hahnenmoos has jumps, big air, rails, snack bar and chill-out zone. There's a boardercross run at Silleren, and skiercross at Elsigen.

Snow reliability Despite unremarkable top heights, most slopes are above 1500m, so snow reliability is reasonable. North-facing Tschentenalp and Luegli usually have the best snow. Snowmaking covers over half the main pistes. Grooming is good.

Experts The black pistes generally merit the rating, at least in parts, and are great fun unless you crave bumps – they are groomed regularly. Off-piste possibilities are good and don't get tracked out quickly; the Lavey and Luegli chairs in the Geils bowl access routes to Adelboden and Lenk. Engstligenalp has off-piste potential – and is a launching point for tours.

Intermediates All five areas deserve exploration by intermediates. There is a lot of ground to be covered in the main sector; at Geils and Aebi the runs are mainly excellent wide reds, but on the sunny Metsch side there is great blue cruising. Tschentenalp is quieter, and worth a visit.

Beginners There are good nursery slopes in the village and at the foot of nearby sectors. At Geils and Metsch there are glorious long, easy runs to progress to. Engstligenalp is 'superb'.

Snowboarding There are still lots of draglifts. Two specialist schools offer lessons and there's a freeride zone at Engstligenalp.

Cross-country There are extensive trails along the valley towards Engstligenalp where there is a high altitude, snow-sure circuit.

Mountain restaurants There are plenty of pleasant spots. Newly renovated TschentenAlp has superb views, a traditional menu and Argentinian BBQ.

Schools and guides The Adelboden school is the main one, but we have no new reports.

Families The resort sets out to cater for families, and seems to succeed,

with lots of facilities including several toboggan runs. Several hotels offer childcare.

STAYING THERE

There is locally bookable self-catering, and some 30 pensions and hotels (mainly 3- and 4-star).

Hotels The central 4-star Cambrian (673 8383) is 'brilliant: excellent quality and value for money, with friendly staff'. Pool and smart spa. The little Bären (673 2151) is a simple but captivating wooden chalet. The Beau-Site (673 2222) has a good, central location ('excellent breakfast, worth paying for a better room upstairs'); so does the Viktoria-Eden (673 8888).

Eating out The choice is not enormous. The Bären has 'good prices, excellent food'; Kreux does 'delicious pizza and meringue'. Guests on half board can 'dine around' at affiliated hotels twice a week – an excellent arrangement.

Après-ski There are several tea rooms and bars to head for at close of play, including some in central hotels. Most recently favoured by reporters is the Time Out bar ('good atmosphere'). The village seems pretty quiet later on.

Off the slopes The leisure arena offers curling and skating, ten-pin bowling and climbing walls. Some hotel pools are open to the public. There are several toboggan runs of up to 5km. Some mountain huts are reachable on foot and there are 'good, well-marked' hiking paths. Special lift passes are available for walkers, but a reader found individual rides expensive.

SNOWPIX.COM / CHRIS GILL

In the main sector practically all the slopes are above the trees; on the treeline here is Geils, with the village way off in the distance beyond it →

Andermatt

A slow-paced, old-fashioned resort with some great steep, high terrain on- and off-piste (and the snowfall to go with it)

Extent	★★
Fast lifts	★
Queues	★★
Snow	★★★★
Expert	★★★★
Intermediate	★★
Beginner	★
Charm	★★★★
Convenience	★★★
Scenery	★★★

RPI	115
lift pass	£200
ski hire	£100
lessons	£135
food & drink	£210
total	£645

NEWS

Work has started on a huge luxury development on the outskirts of the village, with the flagship hotel Chedi and many designer apartments expected to open in 2013.

KEY FACTS

Resort	1445m
	4,740ft
Slopes	1445-2965m
	4,740-9,730ft
Lifts	20
Pistes	125km
	78 miles
Blue	22%
Red	46%
Black	32%
Snowmaking	36%

+ Attractive, traditional village

+ Excellent snow record

+ Some good steep pistes, off-piste terrain and ski-touring opportunities

+ Good access from Zürich

− Not a resort for beginners, or mileage-hungry intermediates

− Limited off-slope diversions

− English not universally spoken

− Busy at weekends

Little old Andermatt seems about to be overwhelmed by construction of what amounts to a whole new village on the outskirts of the original, with countless luxury hotels and apartments. For the moment, at least, the appeal of the tall, steep, snowy, largely off-piste Gemsstock is undiminished, and unthreatened. How quickly the quiet, traditional village will alter remains to be seen.

THE RESORT

Andermatt gets a lot of weekend business, but at other times can seem deserted. East-west links with the Grisons and the Valais rely on car-carrying trains. The lift pass also covers the slopes of Sedrun – 20 minutes away and a popular excursion (see the Directory) – and linking trains. The small Winterhorn area has closed.

Village charm The town is quietly attractive. Charming wooden houses and handsome churches line the main street that runs from the central river bridge to the cable car.

Convenience The centre is compact, but the lifts are widely separated, on opposite sides of the town; take your choice. Buses run in the main season, but a car can be handy at other times.

Scenery The local Gemsstock peak is well defined and higher than its neighbours, with rugged steep terrain.

THE MOUNTAINS

Andermatt's local skiing is split over two unlinked mountains, both limited in extent. Most slopes are above the trees and piste marking is slack – bad news in a resort prone to white-outs.

Slopes A two-stage cable car from the edge of the village serves the open, steep, north-facing and usually empty slopes of Gemsstock. Across town is the gentler, sunny Nätschen area.

Fast lifts Apart from the Gemsstock cable car, there are no fast lifts.

Queues The Gemsstock cable car can generate queues on fine weekends.

Terrain parks Gemsstock has one.

Snow reliability The area has a justified reputation for reliable snow. Nätschen gets a lot of sun. Piste grooming is generally good.

Experts It is most definitely a resort for experts. The north-facing bowl beneath the top Gemsstock cable car

473

WENDY-JANE KING

The gentle slopes of Nätschen get the sun, while the steeper slopes of Gemsstock basically don't →

UK PACKAGES

Alpine Answers, Mountain Tracks, Ski Club Freshtracks, Ski Solutions, Ski Weekend

Phone numbers From elsewhere in Switzerland add the prefix 041; from abroad use the prefix +41 41

TOURIST OFFICE

www.andermatt.ch

is a glorious, long, steep slope (about 900m vertical), usually with excellent snow, down which there are countless off-piste routes, an itinerary and a piste. Outside the bowl, the Sonnenpiste is a fine open red run curling away from the lifts to the mid-station, with more off-piste opportunities. From Gurschen to the village there is a black run, not steep but often tricky. Routes outside the bowl go down the Felsental or Guspis valleys towards Hospental, or steeply into the deserted Untertal, to the east (ending in a bit of a walk). Nätschen has black pistes, and off-piste terrain, including worthwhile itinerary routes.

Intermediates Intermediates needn't be put off Gemsstock: the Sonnenpiste can be tackled, and at mid-mountain there are some short blues and an easy but longer black run (the latter served by a tricky draglift). Nätschen's sunny mountain is well worth a visit, as are the red runs of Sedrun.

Beginners Not ideal; but the lower half of Nätschen has a long, easy blue run.

Snowboarding The cable car accesses some great freeride terrain.

Cross-country There are 28km of loops along the valley.

Mountain restaurants Choice is limited. On Gemsstock, Gadäbar by the Lutersee T-bar is a quieter, simple alternative to the busy Gurschen hut.

Schools and guides Bergschule Uri/ Mountain Reality, a guiding outfit run by local big wheel Alex Clapasson, is very pricey. The Swiss ski school has

cheaper options. Andermatt Xperience is an alternative and Snowlimit is a specialist snowboard school.

Families There are friendly slopes at Nätschen; the Swiss school does classes. Family passes are available.

STAYING THERE

Andermatt's accommodation is mostly in cosy 2- and 3-star hotels.

Hotels River House (887 0025) is a stylish, upmarket B&B in a 250-year-old building, with eight individually designed rooms. And see 'Eating out'. Gasthaus Sternen (887 1130) is an attractive central chalet with a cosy restaurant and bar. The 3-star Sonne (887 1226), towards the Gemsstock lift, is a lovely old place.

Apartments The hotel Monopol (887 1575) has apartments.

Eating out Alte Apotheke at the River House has been well supported (meat and fish dishes with a 'modern twist'). Café Toutoune (cafe, restaurant and lounge bar) is a smart recent addition, with a Mediterranean/veggie bias. Gasthaus Tell and the Sonne are more traditional alternatives.

Après-ski We like the cosy bar at River House for tea and cake (live music later on). Reader tips include the Curva at the hotel Monopol and the Spycher. The Picadilly/Gotthard bars liven up at weekends.

Off the slopes There's a toboggan run at Nätschen. The fitness centre at the hotel Drei König is open to the public. There are maintained footpaths.

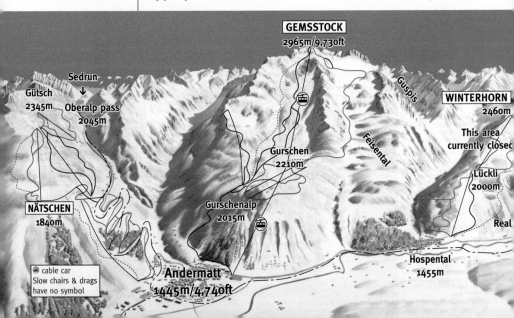

Champéry

Picture-postcard village that few UK tour operators feature these days, with access to the Portes du Soleil circuit

TOP 10 RATINGS

Extent	★★★★★
Fast lifts	★
Queues	★★★★
Snow	★★
Expert	★★★
Intermediate	★★★★
Beginner	★★
Charm	★★★★
Convenience	★
Scenery	★★★★

RPI	120
lift pass	£210
ski hire	£145
lessons	£110
food & drink	£210
total	£675

NEWS

2011/12: In Les Crosets, the slow Grand Conche chair which links to the Avoriaz slopes is due to be replaced by a fast six-pack. This will make a welcome speedy route to Avoriaz as an alternative to the nearby Mossettes fast chair.

2010/11: A new avalanche awareness and safety information park opened. It's free to enter but you need your own transceiver etc. A new indoor climbing wall opened at the Palladium. And a backpacker hotel, Le Petit Baroudeur, opened.

- ➕ Charmingly rustic mountain village
- ➕ Quick access to the Franco-Swiss Portes du Soleil piste circuit
- ➕ Quiet, relaxed – yet plenty to do off the slopes

- ➖ Local slopes suffer from the sun
- ➖ No runs back to the village
- ➖ Lift system is antiquated
- ➖ Not good for beginners

Champéry is great for intermediate skiers looking for a quiet time in a lovely place. Access to the Portes du Soleil circuit is not bad: Avoriaz is fairly easy to get to – and there may be good snow there when Champéry is suffering.

THE RESORT

Champéry is on the Swiss side of the Portes du Soleil region, with fairly quick links to Avoriaz in France, and to the Lindarets valley separating Avoriaz from Châtel.

Village charm The village is friendly and relaxed, with classic old wooden chalets and a charming atmosphere.

Convenience Champéry's slopes are mainly high above the village, reached by a cable car which starts at the railway station, down a steepish hill, away from the main street. The village spreads over quite an area, but there is a free shuttle-bus.

Scenery The resort sits beneath the dramatic Dents du Midi – impressive both from the village and the slopes.

THE MOUNTAINS

Once you get up to them, the local slopes are open, friendly and relaxing.

Slopes Champéry's sunny slopes are part of the big Portes du Soleil circuit, which links resorts in Switzerland and France. See our special chapter on the Portes du Soleil in the France section. The village cable car or a fast six-seat chairlift from Grand Paradis, a short free bus ride from Champéry, go up to the edge of the bowl of Planachaux. If snow is good, there are a couple of

The resort sent us this photo to show off its Superpark. Can you spot it? Ah well, at least it shows some nice scenery →

pistes back to Grand Paradis – one curling well away from the lift system – with an efficient bus service back to the village, but no pistes back to Champéry. With a couple of lift rides you can end up at the French border.

Fast lifts A real drawback for the Swiss side of the Portes du Soleil is that there are very few fast lifts, especially above Champoussin and Morgins – where ancient draglifts and slow chairs prevail. There are plans to modernise the system, but hold-ups getting the necessary permission.

Queues If snow is poor, expect end-of-day queues for the cable car down to the village. Few other problems.

Terrain parks The Superpark is a good terrain park at Les Crosets. Its features include kickers, rails, jibs, spines, boxes and a chill-out area. There are other (excellent) parks in Avoriaz.

Snow reliability The snow on the north-facing French side of the link with Avoriaz is usually better than on the Swiss side, which basically faces east but includes some south-facing slopes. The Champéry area would benefit from more snowmaking.

Experts Few local challenges and badly placed for most of the tough Portes du Soleil runs. The Swiss Wall, on the Champéry side of Pas de Chavanette, is long and bumpy, and provides great amusement when riding the chairlift that rises above it; but is not terrifyingly steep. There's scope for off-piste on the broad slopes of Les

Crosets and Champoussin, and good terrain across the border at Pas de Chavanette where the slopes are less sunny and snow is often better.

Intermediates Confident intermediates have the whole Portes du Soleil at their disposal. Locally, the runs home to Grand Paradis are good when the snow conditions allow. Les Crosets is a junction of several fine runs. There are slightly tougher pistes from Mossettes and Pointe de l'Au, leisurely cruising above Champoussin, and delightful treelined meanders from La Foilleuse to Morgins. From Col des Portes du Soleil a long blue run goes down a quiet, wooded valley to Morgins; but after a good descent to the rustic Tovassière restaurant the run is a path dropping only 200m in 4km.

Beginners Far from ideal. The Planachaux runs, where lessons are held, are steepish and small (as well as remote from the village) and some of the local blue runs are verging on red steepness.

Snowboarding Not ideal for beginners (see above) and there are several draglifts (some quite steep). Good terrain parks in Les Crosets and Avoriaz for intermediates and experts though, and some good powder areas between pistes.

Cross-country It's advertised as 10km – not a lot – with 4km floodlit every night, but the snow is unreliable.

Mountain restaurants There are about 15 in this sector of the Portes du

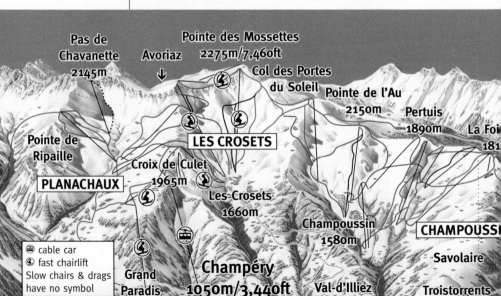

UK PACKAGES

Alpine Answers, Chalet Group, Erna Low, Independent Ski Links, PowderBeds, Scott Dunn, Ski Freedom, Ski Independence, Ski Weekend, White Roc
Les Crosets *Mountain Lodge*
Morgins *Chalet Group, Ski Morgins, Ski Rosie*

Phone numbers
From elsewhere in Switzerland add the prefix 024; from abroad use the prefix +41 24

TOURIST OFFICES

Champéry
www.champery.ch
Les Crosets / Champoussin / Val-d'Illiez
www.valdilliez.ch
Morgins
www.morgins.ch

Soleil, between Champéry and Morgins, marked but not named on the piste map. Chez Coquoz near the Planachaux chair offers a warm welcome, excellent food (try the lamb shank) and a knockout Valais wine list (we loved the Cornalin). The tiny Lapisa on the way to Grand Paradis is delightfully rustic – they make cheese and smoke meat on the spot.

Schools and guides We get few reports. At least the Swiss school faces healthy competition from the Freeride Co and Redcarpet Snowsport School.

Families Champéry wouldn't be high on our shortlist for a family trip, given the lack of slopes at village level.

STAYING THERE

A few UK tour operators offer packages here.

Hotels There's a handful of 3-star and 2-star hotels, and more than the usual number outside the star system. The 3-star Beau Séjour (479 5858) has been revamped into a 'boutique hotel'; the 3-star National (479 1130) has 'excellent food, very friendly and helpful staff'; and the Auberge Le Paradis (479 1167) is 'charmingly rustic but noisy'.

Apartments The Lodge (494 4424) has very smart, spacious apartments with good views and contemporary decor.

Eating out Mitchell's is stylish and modern, and we had a good meal there on our last visit a few years back. Local culinary star Denis Martin

has a Michelin star for his pricey c21 restaurant; you can also eat tapas-sized dishes in the Centre wine bar. Other reader tips are the bistro in the hotel National, the Farinet and Le Pub.

Après-ski Mitchell's, with big sofas and a fireplace, is popular at tea time. There are a few bars, and the Crevasse and Farinet are nightclubs.

Off the slopes Walks are pleasant and the railway allows lots of excursions. There's ice climbing and snowshoeing. The Palladium at the bottom of the village incorporates the Swiss national ice sports centre with various other facilities including pool and tennis.

LINKED RESORT – 1660m
LES CROSETS

A good base for a quiet time and slopes on the doorstep. The 3-star Télécabine hotel (479 0300) has 'basic rooms but extremely helpful staff, and the five-course dinner is delicious'.

LINKED RESORT – 1580m
CHAMPOUSSIN

A good family choice – no through traffic, on the slopes – is the 3-star Alpadze Lou Kra, which used to be the Royal Alpage Club hotel (pool, gym, two restaurants – 476 8300).

LINKED RESORT – 1350m
MORGINS

Over the hill from the other resorts covered here and close to Châtel in France, Morgins is a fairly scattered, but attractive, quiet resort with a gentle nursery slope right in the village. The hotel Reine des Alpes (477 1143) is well thought of.

DOWN-VALLEY VILLAGE – 950m
VAL-D'ILLIEZ

About 4km down the valley from Champéry, and in a similar position facing the Dents du Midi, Val-d'Illiez has no lifts or slopes, but makes a viable base – there are buses and trains up to Champéry. The road up to Les Crosets and Champoussin branches off here. Down in the valley bottom is the Thermes Parc thermal spa. The hotel du Repos (477 1414) is comfortable, woody and British-run; in the centre, opposite the station, with a piano bar, a bar/bistro and a trattoria as well as a dining room.

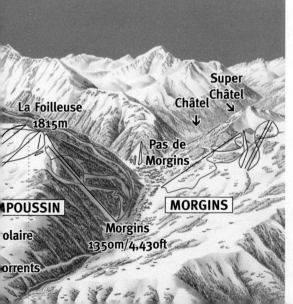

La Foilleuse 1815m

Super Châtel
Châtel

Pas de Morgins

POUSSIN

olaire

orrents

MORGINS

Morgins
1350m/4,430ft

SNOWPIX.COM / CHRIS GILL

Crans-Montana

An increasingly stylish big-town base with a fabulous panoramic view and sun-soaked slopes

TOP 10 RATINGS

Extent	★★★
Fast lifts	★★★★
Queues	★★★
Snow	★★
Expert	★★
Intermediate	★★★★
Beginner	★★★
Charm	★★
Convenience	★★
Scenery	★★★★

RPI 135

lift pass	£250
ski hire	£160
lessons	£120
food & drink	£240
total	**£770**

NEWS

2011/12: The Chetzeron mountain restaurant plans to open smart lodging above the restaurant for December 2011.

The City Ski Champs, in association with Momentum Ski, will be held here in March 2012.

2010/11: A fast quad replaced the Cry d'Er/ Bella-Lui cable car and T3 draglift. The terrain park moved from Aminona to Cry d'Er.

KEY FACTS

Resort	1500m	
	4,920ft	
Slopes	1500-3000m	
	4,920-9,840ft	
Lifts	28	
Pistes	140km	
	87 miles	
Blue	39%	
Red	50%	
Black	11%	
Snowmaking	35%	

➕ Large, varied piste area

➕ Splendid setting and views

➕ Excellent, gentle nursery slopes

➕ Decent cross-country trails

➕ Very sunny slopes, but ...

➖ Snow is badly affected by the sun

➖ Large, busy, urban resort

➖ For many people, life revolves around driving or buses

➖ Few challenges except off-piste

Crans-Montana isn't really our kind of place. We're too fussy about snow, for a start. (Maybe you are too: we don't get many reports.) But we have to admit we loved some of the very smart new lodgings we sampled last winter. And some of the mountain restaurants. Perhaps we're softening ...

THE RESORT

Set on a broad shelf facing south across the Rhône valley, Crans-Montana is really two towns, their centres a mile apart and their fringes merging. The resort is reached by road or by a funicular railway from Sierre. There are also places to stay at the other base stations, a mile east at Les Barzettes (aka Les Violettes, strictly the name of the hill above) and further out at Aminona. Outings to Zermatt, Saas-Fee and Verbier are possible.
Village charm Both Crans and Montana are emphatically towns rather than villages, with little traditional Alpine character and a lot of traffic. But the wooded setting softens the urban feel of the main centres. Crans is the more upmarket part, with fancy shops, an

increasing number of 5-star hotels and improved pedestrian-friendly centre.
Convenience The towns spread widely away from their respective gondola stations and many visitors need to use their cars or the free half-hourly shuttle-bus; it can get crowded.
Scenery The panoramic views over the Rhône valley to the peaks bordering Italy are breathtaking.

THE MOUNTAINS

There's a pleasant mix of open and wooded runs offering few challenges. Pistes are not named or numbered on the piste map and only occasionally on the ground. Weird. Virtually all the runs are red, but many are gentle and wide enough to be blue.
Slopes The slopes are spread over a broad mountainside, with lifts from

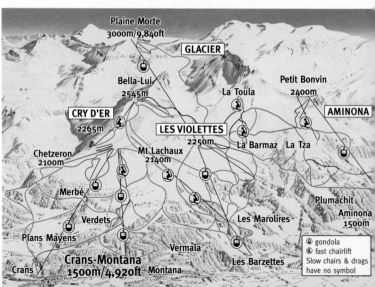

Plaine Morte 3000m/9,840ft
GLACIER
Bella-Lui 2545m
La Toula
Petit Bonvin 2400m
CRY D'ER 2265m
LES VIOLETTES 2250m
La Barmaz La Tza
AMINONA
Chetzeron 2100m
Mt Lachaux 2140m
Merbé
Plumachit
Aminona 1500m
Verdets
Les Marolires
Plans Mayens
Vermala
Les Barzettes
Crans-Montana 1500m/4,920ft
Crans Montana

🚠 gondola
🚡 fast chairlift
Slow chairs & drags have no symbol

Cabane CAS at Les Violettes is perched above the Valais trench, looking across to the peaks on the border with Italy →

SNOWPIX.COM / CHRIS GILL

four valley bases. Gondolas from Crans and Montana meet at Cry d'Er – an open bowl descending into patchy forest. A third gondola accesses the next sector, Les Violettes. A six-pack from the mid-station here links with Cry d'Er. Above Les Violettes, a jumbo gondola goes up to the Plaine Morte glacier. The fourth sector is served by a gondola from Aminona. Some of the runs down to the valley are narrow woodland paths.

Fast lifts A few slow lifts remain; the slow chair up from La Barmaz to Les Violettes is a particularly weak point.

Queues Our recent visits have been queue-free.

Terrain parks The Aminona park and boardercross have relocated to Cry d'Er, still with features for all levels.

Snow reliability The runs on the Plaine Morte glacier are very limited, and nearly all the other slopes get a lot of direct sun. There is snowmaking on the main runs but the condition of the runs (as opposed to the depth of snow) depends heavily on the weather.

Experts There are few steep pistes and the only decent moguls are on the short slopes at La Toula. There's plenty of off-piste, particularly beneath La Toula, La Tza and Chetzeron – the best place to go in a storm. There are more adventurous routes outside the lift network – Les Faverges is a beautiful, easy valley bringing you to Aminona.

Intermediates There's a lot to do, including some notably long runs. The 12km run from Plaine Morte to Les Barzettes starts with top-of-the-world views and powder, and finishes among pretty woods. The Piste Nationale downhill course is a good fast cruise.

Beginners There are excellent nursery areas at resort level (on the golf course) and at mid-mountain (near the mid-station of the Montana gondola, though there is nothing on the piste map to suggest it). No special passes.

Snowboarding Despite the resort's mature image, boarding is popular. The Avalanche Pro is a specialist shop and school. There are few draglifts.

Cross-country There are 19km of trails, plus a glacier trail (limited opening).

Mountain restaurants The piste map marks 25 huts (although some are just bars). The best are above swanky Crans, of course. Our traditional favourite is Merbé, but we have lately fallen for the smart, cool Chetzeron – all steel, glass, wood and stone, and good food at prices no higher than

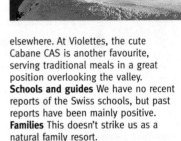

elsewhere. At Violettes, the cute Cabane CAS is another favourite, serving traditional meals in a great position overlooking the valley.

Schools and guides We have no recent reports of the Swiss schools, but past reports have been mainly positive.

Families This doesn't strike us as a natural family resort.

STAYING THERE

Hotels and apartments are plentiful. Crans Luxury Lodges (480 3508) are five new slope-side chalets above Les Barzettes, combining chalet-style privacy with deep comfort and hotel service. We loved them.

Hotels There are some very swanky lodgings. We are now torn between two dinky little places – 5-star LeCrans (486 6060), way above the town, with chalet-style suites, and off-the-star-scale Pas de l'Ours (485 9333) – chic but welcoming, on the edge of town.

Eating out There is a good variety of places, from French to Lebanese. Among the best is the Bistrot in the Pas de l'Ours hotel.

Après-ski At close of play, Dutch-run bar/restaurant Zerodix at the Crans lift base is the happening place. After that, you're on your own. We'll be in the bar of LeCrans, with luck.

Off the slopes There are swimming pools (in hotels), two ice rinks, dog sledding, tubing, tobogganing, 65km of walks, a cinema and a casino. Sierre and Sion are close.

479

Interactive resort shortlist builder at **www.wtss.co.uk**

Davos

A grey urban sprawl at the centre of a glorious Alpine playground
(for skaters and langlaufers as well as downhillers)

RATINGS

The mountains

Extent	★★★★
Fast lifts	★★★★
Queues	★★★
Terrain p'ks	★★★★
Snow	★★★★
Expert	★★★★
Intermediate	★★★★★
Beginner	★★
Boarder	★★★★★
X-country	★★★★★
Restaurants	★★★
Schools	★★★
Families	★★

The resort

Charm	★★
Convenience	★★
Scenery	★★★★
Eating out	★★★
Après-ski	★★★
Off-slope	★★★★★

RPI	130
lift pass	£240
ski hire	£130
lessons	£135
food & drink	£230
total	**£735**

➕ Very extensive slopes

➕ Some superb, long, and mostly easy pistes away from the lifts, with trains to bring you back to base

➕ Lots of accessible off-piste terrain, with several marked itineraries

➕ Good cross-country trails

➕ Plenty to do off the slopes

➖ Davos is a huge, busy place with dreary block-style buildings, lacking ski-resort atmosphere

➖ Five separate areas of slopes

➖ Lots of T-bars on outlying mountains

➖ The only piste back to town from the main Parsenn area is a black

One of your editors learned to ski in Davos, so it has a special place in our affections. Many return visits have confirmed the appeal of its slopes, which are both distinctive and extensive and have revealed its considerable off-piste potential. But the town/city (it could never be called a village) does not get any easier to like. Davos may be the more convenient base for access to most of the mountains it shares with Klosters, but Klosters has the welcoming, intimate feel of a ski resort, and Davos does not.

THE RESORT

Davos is set in a high, broad, flat-bottomed valley, with its lifts and slopes either side. Arguably it was the very first place in the Alps to develop its slopes. The railway up the Parsenn was one of the first built for skiers (in 1931), and the first draglift was built on the Bolgen nursery slopes in 1934. You can reach the resort by train, but the trip from Zürich airport involves two changes. The Davos Express coach transfer service is a recommended alternative. There is also a transfer service from Friedrichshafen airport.

Trips are possible by car or rail to St Moritz (via the Vereina rail tunnel) and Arosa, and by road to Laax-Flims and Lenzerheide – but none of them is quick enough to have wide appeal.

VILLAGE CHARM ★★
City in the mountains
The resort is more like a city than a village, and plagued by traffic. It started life as a health resort and many of its massive luxury hotels were built as sanatoriums. Sadly, that's just what they look like and ski resort ambience is notably lacking. It is now well known for its conference and sporting facilities too.

CONVENIENCE ★★
Take the train
The resort has two main centres, Dorf and Platz, about 2km apart. Transport is good, with buses around the town as well as the railway linking Dorf and Platz to Klosters and other villages. Readers suggest arming yourself with train and bus timetables. Easiest access to the main Parsenn area is from Dorf, via the funicular railway; Platz is better placed for Jakobshorn, the sports facilities, smarter shopping and the evening action.

SCENERY ★★★★
Pick your viewpoint
It's an area of grand, wide views across the broad, deep, wooded valleys from one sector of the slopes to another, and to high peaks beyond.

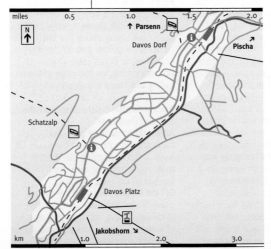

2011/12: On Jakobshorn, the Brämabüel draglift up from Jschalp is to be replaced by a high-speed quad – the small mountain's fifth fast chair.

2010/11: The second stage of the Parsenn funicular from mid-mountain to Weissfluhjoch was upgraded and now goes much more quickly.

KEY FACTS

Resort	1550m
	5,090ft
Slopes	810-2845m
	2,660-9,330ft
Lifts	55
Pistes	307km
	191 miles
Blue	20%
Red	44%
Black	36%
Snowmaking	16%

IAN ASHMORE

Davos has a lot of slopes above the treeline. But not all its cable cars are as small as this one ↓

THE MOUNTAINS

Davos shares its slopes with the famously royal resort of Klosters, which gets its own chapter. They have something for everyone, though experts and nervous intermediates need to choose their territory with care. Piste classification is questionable; many blue and red runs are of similar pitch. The piste map generally looks clear, but tries to cover too much ground in a small space – at some points, it is simply misleading and distances are unclear. Signposting is generally fine, but reporters have complained that the lower parts of the long runs to Küblis and Serneus are poorly marked.

EXTENT OF THE SLOPES ★★★★
Vast and varied
You could hit a different mountain around Davos nearly every day for a week. The out-of-town areas tend to be much quieter than the ones directly accessible from the resort.

The Parsennbahn funicular from Davos Dorf takes you to mid-mountain, where a choice of a six-pack or a further, newly renovated funicular take you on up to the major lift junction of Weissfluhjoch, at one end of the **Parsenn**. The only run back to town is a sunny black that can have poor snow (a reporter recommends catching the funicular down or skiing to Klosters and catching the train at the end of the day if conditions are poor). At the other end of the wide, open Parsenn bowl is Gotschnagrat,

reached by cable car from the centre of Klosters. There are exceptionally long intermediate runs down to Klosters and other villages (see feature panel later in chapter).

Across the valley, **Jakobshorn** is reached by cable car or chairlift from Davos Platz; this is popular with snowboarders but good for skiers too. **Rinerhorn** and **Pischa** are reached by bus or (in the case of Rinerhorn) train.

Pischa is now a designated freeride area, with half the runs left ungroomed and just three main lifts. Several of the runs here are now marked as unpatrolled as well as ungroomed – a very unusual arrangement for runs going down beside a lift, and one we don't like. But reporters tell us that these runs are sometimes groomed, and then have blue markers, not yellow.

Last season the little **Schatzalp** area above Platz, closed for several years, partly reopened – but is not covered by the main lift pass.

Beyond the main part of Klosters, a gondola goes up from Klosters Dorf to the sunny, scenic **Madrisa** area.

FAST LIFTS ★★★★
Key ones are fine but ...
The main lifts from the valley are mostly gondolas or cable cars. Higher up, Jakobshorn is very well served for fast chairs and Parsenn reasonably so (hence the 4-star rating). But the upper lifts on Madrisa, Rinerhorn and Pischa are entirely T-bars except for one slow double chair on Madrisa.

QUEUES ★★★
Few problems
Davos has improved its key lifts and generates relatively few complaints. This year's reporters had very few problems, even at half term. But there can still be lengthy queues at the cable car out of Klosters and the Totalp chair on the mountain at Parsenn at peak times and weekends. Crowded pistes have raised concern – in the Parsenn sector around Weissfluhjoch especially. In contrast, the Jakobshorn is said to be quiet.

TERRAIN PARKS ★★★★
Entry level to Olympic standard
Three of the local mountains have terrain parks but Jakobshorn is the focus of the action with the big Jatz Park. At 2300m, with snowmaking to be sure, it's open from mid-November

Interactive resort shortlist builder at www.wtss.co.uk

to the very end of the season (May in 2011) and looked after by a small team that takes pride in what it does. Four lines (including kickers from 2m to 18m, rainbow rail, down rails and a spine feature with wall ride and tyre bonk) provide something for everyone, although it's clear the better features are geared towards higher end riders. Jakobshorn is also home to a super-pipe – Europe's largest and used for several events including the O'Neill Evolution 6* TTR. There's floodlit riding twice a week. For smaller crowds, though a less well-maintained park, head to Pischa – next to the Mitteltäli lift you'll find an array of rails and kickers – or Madrisa, where there's a beginner park by the Glatteggen lift. There are three boardercross courses,

one on Parsenn, one on Pischa, one on Madrisa. There is also a mini-park for children next to the Trainer lift on Rinerhorn.

SNOW RELIABILITY ★★★★
Good, but not the best

Davos is high by Swiss standards. Its mountains go respectably high, too – though not to glacial heights. Not many of the slopes face directly south, but Pischa does suffer from excessive sun. Snow reliability is generally good higher up. It can be poor lower down. Snow-guns cover a few of the upper runs on the Parsenn, several on the Jakobshorn, and the home runs from the Parsenn to Davos Dorf and Klosters. Piste grooming is generally good; but some runs on Parsenn are

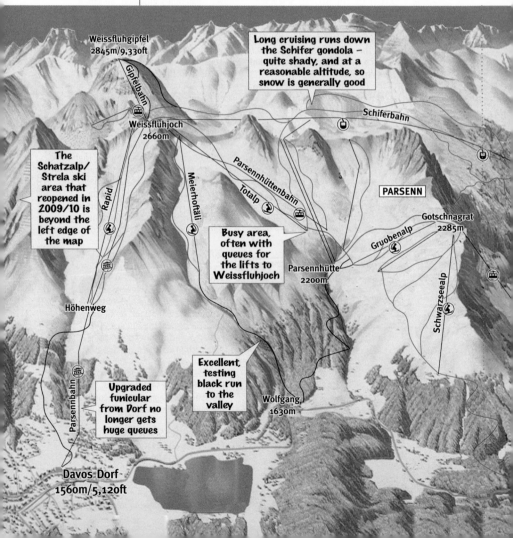

Weissfluhgipfel
2845m/9,33oft

Long cruising runs down
the Schifer gondola –
quite shady, and at a
reasonable altitude, so
snow is generally good

Gipfelbahn

Schiferbahn

Weissfluhjoch
2660m

The
Schatzalp/
Strela ski
area that
reopened in
2009/10 is
beyond the
left edge of
the map

Rapid

Meierhoftäli

Parsennhüttenbahn

Totalp

PARSENN

Busy area,
often with
queues for
the lifts to
Weissfluhjoch

Gruobenalp

Gotschnagrat
2285m

Parsennhütte
2200m

Schwarzseealp

Höhenweg

Parsennbahn

Upgraded
funicular
from Dorf no
longer gets
huge queues

Excellent,
testing
black run
to the
valley

Wolfgang,
1630m

Davos Dorf
1560m/5,12oft

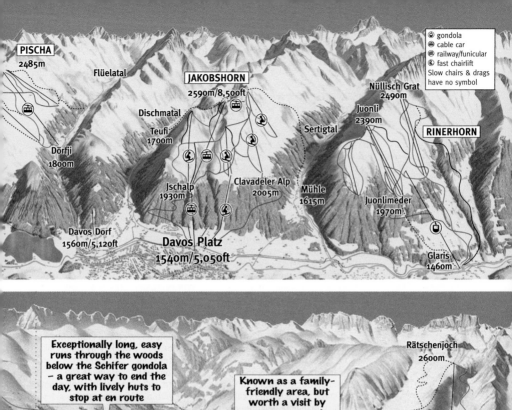

PISCHA
2485m

Flüelatal

JAKOBSHORN
2590m/8,500ft

Dischmatal

Teufi
1700m

Dörfji
1800m

Jschalp
1930m

Clavadeler Alp
2005m

Davos Dorf
156om/5,120ft

Davos Platz
1540m/5,050ft

Sertigtal

Nüllisch Grat
2490m

Juonli
2390m

RINERHORN

Mühle
1615m

Juonlimeder
1970m

Glaris
1460m

gondola
cable car
railway/funicular
fast chairlift
Slow chairs & drags
have no symbol

Exceptionally long, easy runs through the woods below the Schifer gondola – a great way to end the day, with lively huts to stop at en route

Known as a family-friendly area, but worth a visit by anyone – experts included

Rätschenjoch
2600m

Schaffürggli
2395m

Küblis
810m

Saas

Schifer
156om

...nagrat
...5m

MADRISA
189om

Serneus
990m

Klosters cable car is queue-prone in the mornings – more of a problem for those based here than those based in Davos

Madrisabahn

Beautiful long run away from lifts; the lower black section isn't difficult in good snow conditions (it used to be red)

Gotschnabahn

Klosters Dorf
1125m

Schlappin

Klosters
1190m/3,900ft

gondola
cable car
railway/funicular
fast chairlift
Slow chairs & drags
have no symbol

JAN ASHMORE

It's a big town with block-style buildings. This photo is taken from Jakobshorn; the funicular on the far side goes to Schatzalp ↓

said to be 'poorly maintained' – in particular, the super-long runs to the valley.

FOR EXPERTS ★★★★
Plenty to do, given snow

The appeal of this area for experts depends to a considerable degree on the snow conditions. Although there are challenges to be found at altitude, most of the rewarding runs descend through the woods to valley level, and are not reliable for snow. The black pistes include some distinctive, satisfying descents. The Meierhoftälli run to Wolfgang is a favourite – quite steep, narrow and 'exciting'. The run from Parsennhütte to Wolfgang is less challenging; it probably owes its black status due to one short 'tricky' section.

There are also some off-piste itineraries – runs that are supposedly marked but not patrolled. At one time, these runs were a key attraction for adventurous skiers not wanting to pay for guidance, but over the decade to 2005 no fewer than 10 of them disappeared from the map, including the infamous Gotschnawang run down the top stage of the Klosters cable car and its less fearsome neighbours, Drostobel and Chalbersäss. Many of these abandoned runs have had piste status at some time in the past, and are not difficult to follow if you know what you are doing. Two of the most satisfying itineraries that remain are long ones from the top of Jakobshorn, both with decent restaurants at the end. The start of the run to Mühle is not obvious, which has led more than one reporter into difficulty; once found, the run is 'nowhere steeper

than a tough red'. The run to Teufi is more often closed: it goes first down a steep 200m gully, but thereafter is 'not difficult'.

There is also excellent 'proper' off-piste terrain, for which guidance is more clearly needed. Reporters have enjoyed heading away from the pistes above Serneus and Küblis. The long descent from Madrisa to St Antönien, north of Küblis, is popular, not least for the 'spectacular' views along the way. And there are some short tours to be done. Arosa can be reached with a bit of help from a train or taxi, and from there you can go on to Lenzerheide, but you'll need a train back. From Madrisa you can make circular tours to Gargellen in Austria.

FOR INTERMEDIATES ★★★★★
A splendid variety of runs

For intermediates this is a great area. There are good cruising runs on all five mountains, so you would never get bored in a week. This variety of different slopes, taken together with the wonderful long runs to the Klosters valley, makes it a compelling area with a unique character.

As well as the epic runs described in the feature panel there is a beautiful away-from-the-lifts run to the valley from the top of Madrisa back to Klosters Dorf via the Schlappin valley (it's an easy black – classified red until the mid-1990s).

The Jakobshorn has some genuine challenges, notably by the Brämabüel drag. Rinerhorn is more of a cruise. Pischa is the gentlest of the Davos mountains but now branded as freeride territory; in good snow it should be a decent spot for first attempts at skiing ungroomed stuff.

FOR BEGINNERS ★★★★★
Platz is the more convenient

There are no free lifts but each sector offers day or half-day passes. The Bolgen nursery slope beneath the Jakobshorn is adequately spacious and gentle, and a bearable walk from the centre of Platz. Dorf-based beginners face more of a trek out to Bünda though – unless staying at the hotel of the same name. There are easy runs to progress to, spread around all the sectors. The Parsenn sector probably has the edge, with long, easy intermediate runs in the main Parsenn bowl, as well as in the valleys down from Weissfluhjoch. And there is a

THE PARSENN'S SUPER-RUNS

The runs from Weissfluhjoch that head north, on the back of the mountain, make this area special for many visitors. The pistes that go down to Schifer and then on to Küblis and Serneus, and the one that curls around to Klosters, are a fabulous way to end the day, given good conditions. The run to Saas used to be a red piste but is now marked as an ungroomed and unpatrolled route.

The runs are classified red. They are not steep, but the latter parts can be challenging because of the snow conditions – they get heavily skied, they are not reliably groomed, and by the end you are at low altitudes. Signposting is not always good, either. What marks these runs out is their sheer length (10-12km) and the resulting sensation of travel they offer – plus a choice of huts in the woods at Schifer and lower down on the way to Klosters. You can descend the 1100m vertical to Schifer and take the gondola back up. Once past there, you're committed to finishing the descent.

If you are based in Davos, the return journey is by train (included in the lift pass).

ACTIVITIES
Indoor Fitness centres, tennis, squash, swimming pools, climbing wall, sauna, solarium, massage, wellness centres, ice rink, cinema, casino, galleries, museums, libraries, horse-riding school, golf driving range
Outdoor Over 110km of cleared paths, ice climbing, snowshoeing, tobogganing, ice rink, curling, sleigh rides, hang-gliding, paragliding

UK PACKAGES
Alpine Answers, Alpine Weekends, Crystal, Crystal Finest, Flexiski, Headwater, Inghams, Luxury Chalet Collection, Momentum, Neilson, Oxford Ski Co, Ski Club Freshtracks, Ski Safari, Ski Solutions, Skitracer, Ski Weekend, Swiss Travel Service, Switzerland Travel Centre, White Roc

GETTING THERE
Air Zürich 165km/ 105 miles (2hr30); Friedrichshafen 150km/95 miles (2hr30)
Rail Stations in Davos Dorf and Platz

dedicated slow (or 'chill-out') skiing piste alongside the Parsennbahn too – though a 2011 reporter says that people still speed through it.

FOR BOARDERS ★★★★★
Epic
Davos is a Mecca for keen snowboarders. And Jakobshorn is the favoured mountain for many of them, with its top-notch park and super-pipe. It's also a great area to learn on. Rinerhorn has trees galore and pistes like rollercoaster rides. Pischa is the freeride hill with huge marked off-piste areas – one reporter says, 'There are no problems with crowds. The powder is amazing, and there are endless kicker-building spots with loads of windlips and cliff drops.' And Parsenn has a boardercross, night riding and is host to international freeride competitions on the face beneath the Weissfluhgipfel, but watch out for the flats on the runs down to the Schifer gondola. And if you have a family in tow, the kids can stay out of trouble in the beginners' parks at Madrisa or Rinerhorn. Synergy Snowsports is a specialist school and Top Secret Davos is a specialist shop and school. There are several cheap hotels geared to boarders, notably the Bolgenhof near the Jakobshorn, the Snowboardhotel Bolgenschanze and the Snowboarders Palace.

FOR CROSS-COUNTRY ★★★★★
Long, scenic valley trails
Davos is a popular spot for langlauf. It has a total of 123km classic and skating trails running along the main valley and reaching well up into the side valleys of Sertigtal, Dischmatal and Flüelatal. There is a cross-country ski centre and special ski school on the outskirts. Trails are free.

MOUNTAIN RESTAURANTS ★★★★★
Stay high or go low
Most high-altitude restaurants are dreary self-service affairs – but there are good table-service exceptions. Overall, reports are mixed – 'lacking inspiration', 'expensive', and 'decent food' were all comments this year. Our favourite has been Bruhin's at Weissfluhgipfel; this has now changed hands and is called Weissfluhgipfel (417 6644) – a 2011 reporter says the cooking is still 'at the same excellent level though its prices are high'. The Gruobenalp at Gotschnagrat is 'welcoming, with perfect sausage dishes and strudel', says a repeat visitor. Above it, the Gotschnagrat is 'friendly, with decent mountain fare'. There are other compelling places lower down in the Parsenn sector. Readers enjoy the Höhenweg at the Parsennbahn mid-station for 'excellent pizzas' and 'quick service, even when busy'. There are several rustic 'schwendis' in the woods on the way down to the Klosters valley: the cosy Chesetta and its terrace get good reviews. Blockhütte Erezsäss has a 'wide choice and great views' too. These are fun places to end up as darkness falls – some sell wax torches for your final descent.

On Jakobshorn the Jatzhütte is unusual, with changing decor such as mock palm trees, parrots and pirates – and serves 'delicious soups'. Chalet Güggel is recommended by two reporters this season: 'excellent'; 'rustic charm and efficient service'.

On Pischa, the Mäderbeiz at Flüelamäder is an 'extremely pleasant' and spacious woody hut. And on Rinerhorn, try the Hubelhütte.

There are several handy valley restaurants; the Kulm at Wolfgang is rated 'one of the best'.

SCHOOLS

Swiss Davos
t 416 2454
Top Secret
t 413 4043
Planetskier
t 079 776 4655
Pat. Skilehrer Rageth
t 416 3901
Snow & You
t 079 636 7030
Synergy Snowsports
t UK 0141 416 3525

Classes
(Swiss prices)
6 4hr days SF375
Private lessons
Half day SF220 for
1-2 persons

CHILDCARE

Kinderland Pischa
t 416 1313
Ages from 3; 10.30 to
4pm
Bobo Club
t 416 2454
Ages 4 to 10;
10am-noon, 2pm-4pm
Babysitter list
At tourist office

Ski school
Takes ages 5 to 14 (6
days SF375)

Phone numbers
From elsewhere in
Switzerland add the
prefix 081; from
abroad use the prefix
+41 81

TOURIST OFFICE

www.davos.ch

SCHOOLS AND GUIDES ★★★★★
Decent choice
There are several options but we lack recent reports – more welcome. The main Swiss school has received favourable past reports, notably for kids' classes. Top Secret offers small groups (maximum of six). Swissfreeride is a guiding company offering all-inclusive off-piste weeks. Synergy Snowsports provides enthusiastic guiding and instruction by Brits.

FOR FAMILIES ★★★★★
Not ideal
Davos is a rather spread-out place in which to handle a family. The kids' ski school operates a Disney-themed slope at Bolgen. We're told the nursery is 'well organised, but even the best instructors may slip into German'. Kinderland Pischa offers childcare, and there is a snow garden on Rinerhorn. But Madrisa-Land at Klosters is a more comprehensive facility.

STAYING THERE

Although most beds are in apartments, hotels dominate the UK market.
Hotels A dozen 4-stars and about 30 3-stars form the core. The tourist office runs a central booking service.
*****Flüela (410 1717) The more atmospheric of the 5-star hotels, in central Dorf. Pool.
**** Sheraton Waldhuus (417 9333) Convenient for langlaufers. Quiet, modern, tasteful. Pool and spa facility. 'Bucolic setting, ideal for families.'
****Sunstar Park (413 1414) At far end of Davos Platz. Pool, sauna, spa. Recommended by reporters.
****National (415 1010) Five minutes from centre of Davos Platz. 'Good service and five-course dinners.'
***Davoserhof (417 6777) Our favourite. Small, old, beautifully furnished, excellent food; in Platz.
***Panorama (413 2373) In central Platz. Piano bar.
***Ochsen (417 6777) Good-value; with triple- and four-bedded rooms as well as doubles and singles.
**Alte Post (417 6777) In central Platz. Traditional; popular with boarders.

EATING OUT ★★★★★
Wide choice, mostly in hotels
In a town this size, you need to know where to go. For a start, get the tourist office's pocket guidebook. The more ambitious restaurants are mostly in

hotels. There are two good Chinese places – the lavish Zauberberg in the Europe and the Goldener Drachen in the Grischa. The Carretta is good for home-made pasta and the small and cosy Gentiana for fondues and gamey dishes (with an upstairs stübli). One of the cheaper options is Cioccolino – good for 'quick and tasty pizza'. Excursions out of town are popular. The Höhenweg (at the mid-station of the funicular) is open some evenings, but you have to pay to ride the funicular. Schatzalp (also reached by a funicular) and the Schneider have been recommended.

APRES-SKI ★★★★★
Generally quiet
At tea time, mega-calories are consumed at the Weber and at Schneider's. The Scala (hotel Europe) has a popular outside terrace. Nightlife is generally quiet. The rustic little Chämi bar is lively and popular with locals. The smart Ex-Bar attracts a mixed age group. Nightclubs tend to be sophisticated, expensive and lacking atmosphere during the week. The pick are the Cabanna (in the hotel Europe), Cava Davos (next to the Europe) and Rotliechtli. Bolgenschanze and Bolgen-Plaza attract lots of boarders. There's a casino.

OFF THE SLOPES ★★★★★
Great, apart from the buildings
Looks aside, Davos has lots to offer the non-skier/rider. The towny resort has shops and other diversions, and transport along the valley and up on to the slopes is good – though the best of the mountain restaurants are well out of range. The sports facilities are excellent. Europe's biggest natural ice rink is supplemented by artificial rinks, indoor and outdoor. Spectator events include speed skating as well as ice hockey. The Eau-là-là leisure centre incorporates pools and wellness facilities. There are lots of walks on the slopes, around the lake and along the valleys (special map available). There's tobogganing on Rinerhorn and Schatzalp (both floodlit), but the best in the area is the longer run on Madrisa. A 2011 reporter recommends the 'extraordinarily scenic, cheap and easy' day trips by train to St Moritz, Scuol (for the spa) and Preda-Bergün for the 6km toboggan run. Another reader recommends the local museums and galleries.

ENGELBERG TOURIST OFFICE

Engelberg

A high, distinctive mountain with some classic off-piste runs, above a solid valley town dominated by an ancient monastery

TOP 10 RATINGS

Extent	★★
Fast lifts	★★★
Queues	★★
Snow	★★★
Expert	★★★★
Intermediate	★★★
Beginner	★★
Charm	★★
Convenience	★
Scenery	★★★★

RPI 110

lift pass	£210
ski hire	£100
lessons	£130
food & drink	£190
total	**£630**

NEWS

2010/11: A new snowcross bike park was built at Trübsee.

KEY FACTS

Resort	1050m
	3,440ft
Slopes	1050-3030m
	3,440-9,940ft
Lifts	24
Pistes	82km
	51 miles
Blue	33%
Red	57%
Black	10%
Snowmaking	40%

➕ Easily reached from Zürich airport

➕ Reliable snow on the high, shady slopes of Titlis

➕ Some classic off-piste runs

➖ Fragmented slopes, some poor links

➖ Ski-bus needed from most lodgings

➖ Limited piste area, mostly above the trees

Quick access and abundant lodgings make Engelberg great for short breaks. And Titlis is a compelling mountain, particularly for experts. When you're after a quick weekend fix of powder, the towny nature of the resort is not a problem.

THE RESORT

The resort was named after the 12th-century Benedictine monastery (Engelberg means the mountain of the angel) that dominates the town as you look down from the lifts. It was very popular with Brits in the early 1900s.
Village charm The place is more of a town than a village. Its grand Victorian hotels, some recently renovated, have been joined by chalet-style buildings and concrete blocks. There is one traffic-free cobbled street.
Convenience It's a free shuttle-bus, (which one reporter found busy and we found not working on an early December visit), or longish walks to the lifts from most hotels.
Scenery There's lots of visual drama from the high, glacial slopes.

THE MOUNTAINS

The mainly treeless, shady slopes of Titlis rise almost 2000m above the town. The separate slopes of Brunni are sunnier and gently wooded.
Slopes The pistes in the main area are

limited and fragmented by the glaciers and rugged terrain.

There are two main sectors, both above the treeline: Titlis-Stand and Jochpass. A gondola goes up via Gerschnialp to Trübsee, whence two successive cable cars go up to Stand (with chairlifts going up in parallel) and then Klein Titlis – the second one rising above glacial crevasses and rotating 360° on the way. From Trübsee, you can also head for Jochpass via a two-way chairlift to Alpstübli. At Jochpass the top is served by a fast six-pack, with another couple of chairs lower down. The much smaller Brunni area is reached by a cable car from the other side of town. There's also a kids'/nursery area behind the monastery.
Fast lifts High-capacity cable cars and gondolas provide the main access.
Queues Big queues form for the gondola out of town at weekends and in peak season (half-hour waits are reported). The old lifts in parallel may operate but 'do little to help'. Pistes can get uncomfortably busy too.

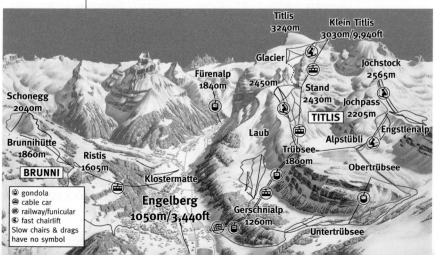

Titlis 3240m · Klein Titlis 3030m/9,940ft · Glacier 2450m · Fürenalp 1840m · Jochstock 2565m · Schonegg 2040m · Stand 2430m · Jochpass 2205m · TITLIS · Laub · Alpstübli · Engstlenalp · Brunnihütte 1860m · Ristis 1605m · Trübsee 1800m · Obertrübsee · BRUNNI · Klostermatte · Engelberg 1050m/3,440ft · Gerschnialp 1260m · Untertrübsee

- ◎ gondola
- ⊜ cable car
- ⊛ railway/funicular
- ⚡ fast chairlift
- Slow chairs & drags have no symbol

UK PACKAGES

Alpine Answers, Chalet
Espen, Crystal,
Inntravel, Momentum,
Mountain Tracks,
Neilson, PowderBeds,
Ski Club Freshtracks,
Ski Independence, Ski
Safari, Ski Solutions,
Ski Weekend, Ski-
Monterosa, Skitracer,
STC, White Roc

Phone numbers
From elsewhere in
Switzerland add the
prefix 041; from
abroad use the prefix
+41 41

TOURIST OFFICE
www.engelberg.ch

Terrain parks The park is at Jochpass, with jumps, kickers and rails.

Snow reliability The high, north-facing slopes of Titlis and Jochpass keep their snow well and have a long season. The resort says 50% of the resort is snow-sure, including glacial runs and those with snowmaking.

Experts There is lots of superb off-piste for experts who hire a guide. The classic Laub run is 1000m vertical down an immensely wide face with a consistent pitch and magnificent views of town. We enjoyed even more the less popular 2000m vertical Galtiberg run, which starts over glaciers and ends among streams and trees, with a bus back to town. The easily accessed off-piste at the top of Titlis looks great but takes you close to crevasses; don't go without a guide. There are few black pistes; the itinerary from Titlis to Stand is steep and often mogulled.

Intermediates Most runs are steep reds and there are few easy cruises. The good snow on the reds at the top of the rotating cable car, along with the views, make it worth the trip to the top (catch the cable car down to avoid the itinerary mentioned above). The Jochpass area is often quieter than Titlis, with enjoyable blue and red runs, including lovely long ones down to the valley gondola station.

Beginners There's a good isolated beginner area at Gerschnialp, served by draglifts, and smaller areas at Trübsee and Untertrübsee. You have to use lifts to and from these slopes (limited passes are available for the beginner lifts plus access lifts); and there are few longer easy runs to progress to – all far from ideal.

Snowboarding The beginner area is served by draglifts, so it's not ideal. But there is excellent freeriding if you hire a guide. Beware of the flat start to the runs down from Jochpass.

Cross-country There are 40km in total with valley trails and loops at altitude. A 1.5km World Cup route is floodlit two nights a week.

Mountain restaurants An impressive choice. Our favourite, and that of last year's reporters, is Skihütte Stand, a woody table-service place beside the cable car to Titlis: 'good main courses, friendly service'. Jochpass has less atmosphere, but 'prompt service'. Try Untertrübsee for meringues. The Trübsee hotel has table-service ('food and service excellent, quiet even on a busy day') and self-service sections.

Schools and guides There are four schools: Swiss ski and snowboard, Prime, Boardlocal and Active Snow Team. The local guiding outfit is Outventure.

Families Gobi's Winterland at Brunni is best for families, with play areas and lifts. Special passes are available. The ski school takes children from age three, and the kindergarten from two. Some hotels offer childcare, and the tourist office has details of babysitters.

STAYING THERE

There are lots of hotels, B&Bs and apartments.

Hotels The 3-star Edelweiss (639 7878) is 'excellent for families with young children'. The Schweizerhof (637 1105) is centrally located with 'good food and service, spacious rooms'. The Ski Lodge (637 3500) is popular with 'friendly staff' (avoid rooms above the bar, say reporters), as is The Alpenclub (637 1243) – a central guest house with a good restaurant.

Eating out There is a huge variety of restaurants – more than 50 – from traditional Swiss to Tex-Mex (at the Yucatan), Chinese (Moonrise), and Indian (Chandra at the Terrace hotel). We had splendid chicken/veal dishes at the hotel Central; large portions, very well presented. The Ski Lodge is 'one of the best' (gourmet duck, salmon).

Après-ski The liveliest venues are the Yucatan (main square) and the Chalet (bottom of the gondola); both have popular happy hours. But a recent visitor found the Yucatan 'quiet mid-week, with slow service'. The Ski Lodge bar is 'pleasant'. For dancing, try Eden or the Spindle nightclub. A trip up to the elevated Terrace hotel for a 'preprandial G&T' has been recommended.

Off the slopes The 12th-century monastery and its cheese-making factory and shop are worth a visit. And there's a fair collection of shops. It's worth taking a trip up the rotating cable car for the views and a tour of the ice grotto. There are many walking and snowshoeing trails, an igloo bar at Trübsee (you can stay the night there), tubing, sledging and a good sports centre. Up the valley, a gondola goes up to Fürenalp, where there is walking, tobogganing and snowshoeing. Lucerne is reachable by train for day trips.

Grindelwald

Traditional mountain town set beneath the towering Eiger and with an old cog railway still the main way up to the slopes

RATINGS

The mountains

Extent	★★★
Fast lifts	★★★
Queues	★★
Terrain p'ks	★★★
Snow	★★
Expert	★★
Intermediate	★★★★
Beginner	★★★
Boarder	★★★
X-country	★★
Restaurants	★★★
Schools	★★★
Families	★★

The resort

Charm	★★★★
Convenience	★★
Scenery	★★★★★
Eating out	★★★
Après-ski	★★★
Off-slope	★★★★

RPI · 120

lift pass	£240
ski hire	£120
lessons	£115
food & drink	£220
total	**£695**

NEWS

2011/12: More snowmaking is planned in the Eigergletscher and Männlichen areas. The First Flyer zip wire is now included in the lift pass.

2010/11: Capacity on the upper section of the First gondola was raised by 50%.

➕ Dramatically set, beneath the north face of the Eiger

➕ Lots of long intermediate runs

➕ Pleasant old village with long mountaineering history

➕ Fair amount to do off the slopes, including splendid walks

➖ Slow, queue-prone trains and gondolas to access the main slopes

➖ Few challenging pistes for experts

➖ A fair trek to visit Mürren

➖ Natural snow-cover unreliable (but substantial snowmaking now)

➖ Village gets little midwinter sun

For stunning views from the town and the slopes, there are few places to rival Grindelwald. The village is nowhere near as special as Mürren or Wengen, just over the hill, but it does provide direct access to Grindelwald's own First slopes. The main access lifts are appalling, taking half an hour to ride even if you don't have to queue (for the gondola) or wait (for the train). Grindelwald regulars accept all this as part of the scene. We're not Grindelwald regulars.

THE RESORT

Grindelwald is a long village set along a road that runs across a hillside facing the towering north wall of the Eiger, which means that the resort gets very little sun in January. Its main slopes are shared with Wengen; and there is a separate area of sunny slopes on First. Getting to the tougher, higher slopes of Mürren on snow and lifts is a lengthy business (around three hours to the top). Trips to other resorts are not very easy.

VILLAGE CHARM ★★★★
Not quite in the Wengen league
The central buildings are mainly in traditional chalet style, in keeping with its long mountaineering history. And the station and cog railway add to the olde-worlde charm. The village can feel very jolly at times (eg during the snow carving festival in January, when huge sculptures are created). Sadly, traffic intrudes on the main road.

CONVENIENCE ★★
Not a strong point
The most convenient places to stay are in the centre near the main station or at Grund, departure point of the main access lifts and arrival point of the main home piste, about 80m vertical lower. If you stay in the centre, you can also take the train up, but you need to catch it back up from Grund on the way home too. Staying near the centre means the gondola up the First area is a walkable distance. At the foot of First are nursery slopes, ski school and kindergarten. Buses link the lift stations – at times these get congested, but the service has 'greatly improved' says a 2011 visitor.

SCENERY ★★★★★
Unrivalled
The mountains in these parts are legendary among climbers – from all over the slopes there are superb views, not only of the Eiger but also of the Wetterhorn and other peaks.

THE MOUNTAINS

The major area of slopes is shared with Wengen and offers a mix of a few wooded runs and much more extensive open slopes higher up. The smaller First area is mainly open; at the top on skier's left is a protected area for chamois and you can spot lots of them there.

Piste marking and piste map are poor; reporters find the Männlichen slopes, in particular, confusing.

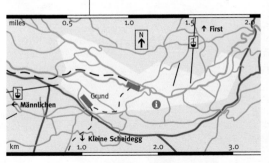

KEY FACTS

Resort	1035m
	3,400ft

Jungfrau region	
Slopes	945-2970m
	3,100-9,740ft
Lifts	44
Pistes	213km
	132 miles
Blue	33%
Red	49%
Black	18%
Snowmaking	40%

First-Männlichen-Kleine-Scheidegg	
Slopes	945-2485m
	3,100-8,150ft
Lifts	32
Pistes	161km
	100 miles
Snowmaking	65%

EXTENT OF THE SLOPES ★★★★★
Broad and mainly gentle

From Grund, near the western end of town, you can get to **Männlichen** by an appallingly slow two-stage gondola or to **Kleine Scheidegg** by an equally slow cog railway (with some trains starting in the centre of town). The slopes of the separate south-facing **First** area are reached by a long, slow gondola starting a walk or short bus ride east of the centre.

FAST LIFTS ★★★★★
Better high up

Getting up from the village is slow but new fast chairlifts continue to improve the area higher up – most recently the Eigernordwand six-pack from below Kleine Scheidegg to Eigergletscher.

QUEUES ★★★★★
Can be dreadful at the bottom

These days visitors generally find few problems once they are on the mountain, but the train and the Männlichen gondola at Grund can be crowded at peak periods. Waiting times for the gondola can be very bad in high season, especially on Saturdays, when children up to 15 ski for free if an accompanying adult buys a day pass. And the gondola goes very slowly, too. One reporter also found 'big queues to download at the end of the day' when the lower runs were closed. The increased capacity on the First gondola should have eased congestion there, though.

TERRAIN PARKS ★★★★★
First things first

There is a terrain park on First with rails, boxes, kickers and jumps for different abilities; plus a separate 100m super-pipe.

SNOW RELIABILITY ★★★★★
Improved snowmaking helps

Grindelwald's low altitude means that natural snow is often in short supply or in poor condition. First is a bit higher than the Männlichen area, and may have better snow in midwinter; but it is sunny, and less snow-sure as spring approaches. A lot of snowmaking has been added recently too, and the resort claims that more than 65% of its slopes are now covered. When we were there in 2009, it had not snowed for a few weeks and a warm Föhn wind had melted a lot of snow, but most slopes were in good condition. Piste maintenance gets mixed reviews.

FOR EXPERTS ★★★★★
Few on-piste challenges

The area is quite limited for experts, but there is some fine off-piste if the snow is good. Heli-trips are organised. We and readers have enjoyed the splendid Bort Direct black run on First. This turns into a downhill route between Bort and town and is quite tough, especially when the snow has suffered from the sun.

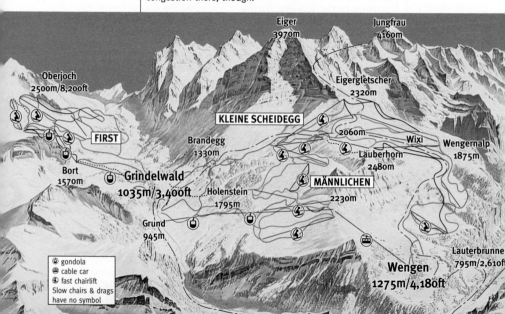

gondola
cable car
fast chairlift
Slow chairs & drags have no symbol

Non-skiers can enjoy lots of cleared paths with magnificent views. This photo is of a path on the First area →

JUNGFRAU REGION MARKETING AG

LIFT PASSES

Jungfrau

Prices in SF

Age	1-day	6-day
under 16	31	157
16 to 19	50	251
20 to 61	62	314
over 62	56	283

Free under 6 (if with parent)

Beginner points card

Notes
Covers Wengen, Mürren and Grindelwald, trains between them and Grindelwald ski-bus; day pass price is for First-Kleine Scheidegg-Männlichen area only

Alternative passes
Grindelwald and Wengen only; Mürren only; non-skier pass

SCHOOLS

Swiss
t 854 1290

Buri Sport
t 853 3353

Swiss Kleine Scheidegg
t 855 1545

Felix Ski Paradies
t 853 1288

Privat
t 853 0473

Altitude
t 853 0040

Classes (Swiss prices)
5 (4hr) days SF415

Private lessons
From SF85 for 1hr for 1 or 2 persons

FOR INTERMEDIATES ★★★★☆
Ideal intermediate terrain
In good snow, First makes a splendid intermediate playground, though the general lack of trees makes the area less friendly than the larger Kleine Scheidegg-Männlichen area. Nearly all the runs from Kleine Scheidegg are long blues or gentle reds. On the Männlichen there's a choice of gentle runs down to the mid-station of the gondola – and in good snow, down to the bottom. For tougher pistes, head for the top of the Lauberhorn lift and the runs to Kleine Scheidegg, or to Wixi (following the World Cup downhill course). The north-facing run from Eigergletscher served by the Eigernordwand six-pack often has the best snow late in the season.

FOR BEGINNERS ★★★☆☆
Depends where you go
The Bodmi nursery slope at the bottom of First is scenic but not particularly convenient. ('The chore of getting to and from it with small children was too much,' said one reporter.) Snow quality can also suffer from the sun and the low altitude, and fast skiers and tobogganers racing through are off-putting. Kleine Scheidegg has a better, higher beginner area and splendid, long runs to progress to, served by the railway. To save a full lift pass cost there is a points card available, but no free lifts.

FOR BOARDERS ★★★☆☆
Best for intermediates
Intermediates will enjoy the area most, while experts will hanker for Mürren's steep, off-piste slopes. First is the main boarders' mountain, not only because of the terrain park and big pipe but also because of the open freeride terrain near the top. There are still a few drags dotted around.

FOR CROSS-COUNTRY ★★☆☆☆
Okay but shady
There are 15km of prepared tracks. Almost all of this is on the valley floor, so it's shady in midwinter and may have poor snow later on.

MOUNTAIN RESTAURANTS ★★★☆☆
Wide choice
See the Wengen chapter for additional options. Brandegg, on the railway, is regularly recommended ('excellent, friendly welcome' and 'wonderful' apple fritters and doughnuts). Other reader tips include: Jägerstubli, off the Rennstrecke piste ('excellent value', 'amazing veal stew'); Café Génépi on First for Flammenkuchen (thin pizza); and Berghaus Aspen just above Grund ('best-ever rösti'). On First we enjoyed Bort, where the old building houses a restaurant built in contemporary style. One reader loved the tiny Alpweg, not for the food but for a welcoming, local atmosphere – 'where the locals break out into song and yodelling'.

SCHOOLS AND GUIDES ★★★☆☆
Reports please
We lack recent reports on the ski schools – more welcome. The Privat school offers off-piste guiding.

FOR FAMILIES ★★☆☆☆
Lacks convenience but ...
It's not a convenient place for families (see 'For beginners'). Snowli Children's Club based at Bodmi (First) takes kids from three years old and operates a bus from the village. Kinderclub Sunshine is a nursery and play area at the top of Männlichen.

Grindelwald

Interactive resort shortlist builder at www.wtss.co.uk

CHILDCARE

Kinderclub Sunshine
t (0)79 632 8178
Ages from 6mnth;
9am-4pm

Snowli Kinderclub
t 854 1290
From age 3 (from
6mnth on Fri by
arrangement); 9.30-
4pm

Felix Ski Paradies
t 853 1288
From age 3
10am-3pm

Ski schools
Take children from
age 3 or 4 (5 half
days SF190)

UK PACKAGES

Alpine Answers,
Crystal, Elegant
Resorts, Inghams,
Momentum, Neilson,
Powder Byrne,
PowderBeds, Ski Club
Freshtracks, Skitracer,
Swiss Travel Service,
Switzerland Travel
Centre, Thomson,
White Roc

GETTING THERE

Air Zürich 160km/
100 miles (2hr45);
Bern 70km/45 miles
(1hr30); Basel
165km/105 miles
(2hr30)

Rail Station in resort

ACTIVITIES

Indoor Sports centre
(pool, sauna, steam,
fitness), ice rink,
curling, museum,
cinema

Outdoor 80km of
cleared paths, ice
rink, tobogganing,
snowshoeing, ice
climbing

Phone numbers
From elsewhere in
Switzerland add 033.
From abroad use the
prefix +41 33.

TOURIST OFFICE

www.grindelwald.com

STAYING THERE

The hotels UK tour operators offer are mainly at the upper end of the market. **Hotels** There's a 5-star, seven 4-stars and plenty of more modest places.
*****Grand Regina (854 8600) Big and imposing; right next to the station. Nightly music in the piano bar. Recommended for excellent service, good pool and spa facilities.
****Belvedere (888 9999) Over 100 years old, comfortable, family-run, friendly, close to the station. Pool, steam, sauna, hot tub. Great views of the Eiger from south-facing rooms.
****Schweizerhof (854 5858) Close to the station. Pool.
****Spinne (854 8888) Central. A reporter highly recommended this as 'friendly, with good rooms'.
***Gletschergarten (853 1721) Out past First gondola. 'Friendly, good English spoken, four-course meals.'
***Hirschen (854 8484) Family-run; by nursery slopes. Good food.
***Derby (854 5461) Popular, modern, next to station, with 'first-class' service, good food and great views.
***Eigerblick (854 1020) A bit away from the station but praised for its service. Huge bedrooms.
*Wetterhorn (853 1218) Cosy, simple chalet way beyond the village, with great views of the glacier. Rooms were refurbished for 2010/11.
Apartments Readers recommend those in the Hirschen and Eiger hotels.
At altitude The Berghaus Bort (853 1762), at the gondola station in the middle of the First area, has everything from single rooms to dormitories.

EATING OUT ★★★☆☆
Hotel based

There's a wide choice of good hotel restaurants such as the Hirschen; Challistübli in the Kreuz; Schmitte in the Schweizerhof; and the Alte Post. The Kirchbühl is good for vegetarians. Hotel Spinne has an Italian option and the candlelit Rôtisserie. Onkle Tom's Hütte has been recommended for

pizza. The rustic Rancher bar is worth a visit for an evening meal of 'meats, cheese and potatoes served in drawstring sacks'. A 2011 reporter recommends the Steinbock ('good food, reasonable prices, pizza cooked in wood oven, busiest place in town').

APRES-SKI ★★★☆☆
Getting livelier

Tipirama (a wigwam at Kleine Scheidegg) is a fun place immediately after skiing (but 'becoming a bit tatty'), sometimes with DJs and live bands. There are various (mainly open air) bars to stop in on the way down to Grund. The liveliest are the Rancher (on run 22), attracting a young crowd; Holzerbar (on run 21); the tiny Holdrio (relatively cheap beer) and the Aspen hotel (just below). In town, the terrace of the C&M Café und Mehr is good for coffee and cake. Later on, there's live music in several bars and hotels, such as the Challibar (hotel Kreuz); but it isn't a place for bopping until dawn. The Espresso bar in the Spinne hotel seems to be the liveliest and the Hotel Eiger has the 'good fun' Gepsi-Bar. Later on, people head for the Mescalero (in the Spinne) and Plaza (in the Sunstar) clubs.

OFF THE SLOPES ★★★★☆
Plenty to do, easy to get around

There are many cleared paths with magnificent views and a special (but pricey) pedestrian lift pass. Many of the mountain huts are accessible to pedestrians. A trip to Jungfraujoch is spectacular (see below), and train trips are easy to Interlaken and Bern. Tobogganing is big here; there are over 50km of runs, including Europe's longest (12.5km); but it starts a 2hr30 walk from the top of the First gondola. First also has the First Flyer – a zip-wire affair – free if you have a ski pass. There's a cinema, ice hockey and curling to watch, an indoor rope park and an excellent sports centre with pool. Scenic flights from Männlichen are popular – see Wengen chapter.

THE JOURNEY TO THE TOP OF EUROPE

From Kleine Scheidegg you can take a train through the Eiger to the highest railway station in Europe – Jungfraujoch at 3450m. The journey is a bit tedious – you're in a tunnel except when you stop to look out at magnificent views from two galleries carved into the sheer north face of the Eiger. At the top is a big restaurant complex, an 'ice palace' carved out of the glacier and fabulous views of the Aletsch glacier (a UNESCO World Heritage Site). The cost in 2010/11 was SF55.50 with a Jungfrau lift pass for three days or more.

Klosters

*Ski the extensive slopes of Davos from a traditional village base –
with Davos traffic at last banished to a bypass*

TOP 10 RATINGS

Extent	★★★★
Fast lifts	★★★★
Queues	★★
Snow	★★★★
Expert	★★★★
Intermediate	★★★★★
Beginner	★★★
Charm	★★★★
Convenience	★★
Scenery	★★★★

RPI   125

lift pass	£240
ski hire	£110
lessons	£130
food & drink	£230
total	**£710**

NEWS

2011/12: On Jakobshorn, the Brämabüel draglift up from Jschalp is to be replaced by a high-speed quad – the small mountain's fifth fast chair.

2010/11: The second stage of the Parsenn funicular from mid-mountain to Weissfluhjoch was upgraded and now goes much more quickly.

➕ Extensive slopes shared with Davos

➕ Some lovely long intermediate runs

➕ Lots of accessible off-piste terrain

➕ Some cute mountain restaurants

➕ Pleasant traditional village, these days bypassed by the valley traffic

➖ The slopes are spread over six widely separated areas

➖ Preponderance of T-bars is a problem for some visitors

➖ Queue-prone cable car

➖ Maybe too quiet for some visitors

In a word association game, 'Klosters' might trigger 'Prince of Wales'. The resort has even named its queue-prone cable car after him. Don't be put off: Klosters is not particularly exclusive, and makes an attractive alternative to towny Davos, with which it shares its slopes – more so since 2005, when a bypass road removed the intrusive Davos and Vereina tunnel traffic from the village.

THE RESORT

Klosters is a sizeable village with a relaxed Alpine atmosphere.
Village charm Klosters Platz is the main focus – a comfortable, quiet collection of upmarket, traditional-style hotels around the railway station. Traffic bound for Davos and the Vereina rail tunnel takes a bypass.
Convenience The cable car up the wooded slopes of Gotschna starts in the heart of the Platz. The village spreads along the valley road, fading into the countryside; then you come to the even quieter village of Klosters Dorf, and the gondola to Madrisa. Local train and bus services are good.
Scenery The contrast between steeply wooded valleys and high, craggy peaks is impressive.

THE MOUNTAINS

Most of the runs are on open slopes above steeper woodland.
Slopes A cable car from the railway station in Platz takes you to the Gotschnagrat end of the Parsenn area shared with Davos. These slopes are dealt with in the Davos chapter. A gondola from Dorf takes you up to the scenic Madrisa area, which we deal with here. There's also a little slope at Selfranga (floodlit some evenings), a suburb of Platz.
Fast lifts Apart from the gondola, Madrisa is poorly served.
Queues Queues for the Gotschna cable car can be a problem at weekends and peak times. One reporter noted the area busier in January than in previous years too.

493

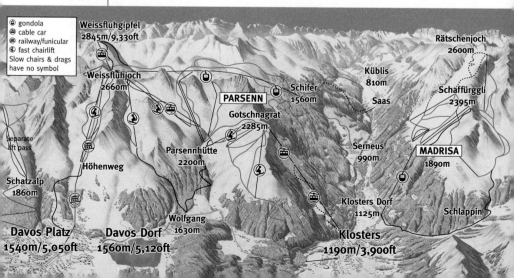

gondola
cable car
railway/funicular
fast chairlift
Slow chairs & drags
have no symbol

Weissfluhgipfel
2845m/9,330ft

Rätschenjoch
2600m

Weissfluhjoch
2660m

PARSENN

Schifer
1560m

Küblis
810m

Saas

Schaffürggli
2395m

Gotschnagrat
2285m

Parsennhütte
2200m

Serneus
990m

MADRISA
1890m

Separate
lift pass

Höhenweg

Schatzalp
186om

Klosters Dorf
1125m

Schlappin

Wolfgang
1630m

Davos Platz
1540m/5,050ft

Davos Dorf
1560m/5,120ft

Klosters
1190m/3,900ft

KEY FACTS

Resort	1190m
	3,900ft
Slopes	810-2845m
	2,660-9,330ft
Lifts	55
Pistes	307km
	191 miles
Blue	20%
Red	44%
Black	36%
Snowmaking	16%

UK PACKAGES

Alpine Answers, Carrier, Crystal Finest, Flexiski, Independent Ski Links, Inghams, Luxury Chalet Collection, Momentum, Neilson, Oxford Ski Co, Powder Byrne, Pure Powder, Ski Club Freshtracks, Ski Expectations, Ski Independence, Ski Safari, Ski Solutions, Skitracer, Ski Weekend, Snow Finders, STC, Swiss Travel Service, Switzerland Travel Centre, White Roc

Phone numbers
From elsewhere in Switzerland add 081; from abroad use the prefix +41 81

TOURIST OFFICE

www.klosters.ch

Terrain parks Madrisa has a beginners' park and a boardercross course.

Snow reliability It's usually good higher up. The home runs are quite low, but now have snowmaking, and piste grooming is 'good'.

Experts The lift-served off-piste possibilities are the main appeal, on Madrisa as elsewhere in the region – and on 'family-friendly' Madrisa it doesn't get skied out so quickly.

Intermediates Madrisa is not huge, but it is all excellent intermediate terrain. The black run to the valley is not difficult unless conditions make it so.

Beginners There is a slope between Dorf and Platz, plus Selfranga; but Madrisa's higher slopes are more appealing. No special lift-pass deals.

Snowboarding Local slopes are good, but more boarders stay in Davos.

Cross-country There are 35km of free trails and lots more up at Davos; a Nordic ski school offers lessons.

Mountain restaurants There are some atmospheric huts on the home run from the Parsenn – see Davos chapter. On Madrisa the best option is the woody Erika at Schlappin, halfway down the black run to the valley – 'excellent atmosphere and food'.

Schools and guides There is a choice. Saas is well regarded for good, English-speaking instructors and 'fun' private lessons, though one group got two instructors during their week. Adventure-Skiing has historically been praised for private guiding.

Families Madrisa-Land adventure park has lots to offer children, including disabled visitors. New features were added last year. Access is free to kids under six years old. The ski schools offer 'excellent' children's classes too.

STAYING THERE

Hotels For most people, central Platz is the best location. Here, the smart Chesa Grischuna (422 2222) is 'small and personal'. In 2009 we stayed at the comfortable and welcoming 3-star Rustico (410 2288) – see 'Eating out'. The readers' favourite is the 4-star Alpina (410 2424) – 'good food and location'. The panelled old Wynegg (422 1340) is a perennial British favourite, with excellent food. The 4-star Silvretta Park Hotel (423 3435) is 'very kid friendly'. In Dorf the Sunstar Albeina (423 2100) has a 'lovely location, is very comfortable'.

Apartments Apartments are available through local agencies.

Eating out Good restaurants abound, but there are few cheap and cheerful places. Top of the range is the Walserhof, with a Michelin star ('one of the best meals we've had'). We enjoyed Asian fusion at the Rustico hotel (the owner's wife is Asian). Al Berto serves 'wonderful' pizza. Other tips: Casanna at Platz for steaks, Chesa Grischuna for 'fabulous venison' and good wines, and Fellini pizzeria.

Après-ski Gaudy's umbrella bar at the foot of the slopes is popular. In the village, the Chesa Grischuna has live music. The bar at the Alpina and the Wynegg are popular too. The Casa Antica is a small disco.

Off the slopes Klosters is an attractive base for walking (there's a special map available) and cross-country skiing. Tobogganing is popular – there is an exceptional 8.5km run from Madrisa to Saas. There is an ice rink, and some hotel pools are open. See Davos chapter for ideas for train outings.

Laax

Contrasting villages beneath high, wide, sunny slopes – well known to Swiss weekenders, and becoming known more widely

495

TOP 10 RATINGS

Extent	★★★★
Fast lifts	★★★★
Queues	★★★★
Snow	★★★
Expert	★★★
Intermediate	★★★★★
Beginner	★★★★
Charm	★★★
Convenience	★★★
Scenery	★★★

RPI | **120**
lift pass | £250
ski hire | £105
lessons | £140
food & drink | £200
total | **£695**

NEWS

2011/12: A six-pack is due to replace two draglifts above Laax, from Alp Dado to the ridge above Crap Sogn Gion. New blue runs are planned for this area too.

2010/11: Capacity was increased on the gondola out of Flims and on the Laax cable car. And a 2.5km long freestyle slope was built from Crap Sogn Gion to Curnius.

Europe's first indoor Freestyle Academy opened at the Laax base station.

Rocksresort at Laax opened its last (eighth) lodgings unit.

KEY FACTS

Resort	1100m
	3,610ft
Altitude	1100-3020m
	3,610-9,910ft
Lifts	27
Pistes	220km
	137 miles
Blue	29%
Red	32%
Black	39%
Snowmaking	11%

➕ Extensive, varied slopes ideal for intermediates, shared with Flims

➕ Generally efficient lift system, but with some long ride times

➕ One of Europe's best terrain parks

➖ Sunny orientation can spoil snow

➖ Bus rides or long walks from some lodgings to the lifts

➖ Nightlife subdued in parts, intrusively noisy in others

Laax, marketed in the past (and still in the summer) as Flims, is in terms of area and piste km one of Switzerland's biggest resorts. It is now managed in a very dynamic, focused way, and is finding an international market as a result – we now get a substantial flow of reports from readers, mostly enthusiastic.

THE RESORT

Laax is a resort of parts. Laax Dorf is a rustic village; just outside it is a big, busy lift base/hotel/parking complex, called Laax, of which the newly completed Rocksresort development is a part. The slopes spread across to lift bases at Flims Dorf and Falera.
Village charm Laax Dorf is pleasantly traditional, with quiet suburbs set around a lake. Laax is modern and more youth-oriented. Flims Dorf is traditional but unremarkable, spread along the road through (though a bypass takes the through-traffic). Flims Waldhaus is a more appealing leafy suburb with upscale secluded hotels. Falera, once a quiet hamlet, has been much expanded in traditional style.
Convenience It depends where you stay. The smart hotels in Waldhaus run courtesy buses and there are 'quick and efficient' free ski-buses.
Scenery There are grand panoramic views to the peaks on the Italian border from the upper slopes.

THE MOUNTAINS

The slopes are mostly open; there are not many woodland runs, but some are quite long. The resort piste map also shows unexplained 'freeride runs' (dotted on our map); we hear they are avalanche-protected, but not all are patrolled. Readers complain of poor lift/run status info at the base. Many of the black runs could be red.
Slopes There are long gondolas into the slopes from both Flims Dorf and Laax (beside a cable car of exceptional length). Above mid-mountain, there is a complex web of lifts and runs. The glacier is limited; but it accesses superb long runs to Alp Ruschein.

Fast lifts Some slow lifts remain.
Queues There may be queues for the village lifts at peak times, for the isolated chair at Alp Ruschein, and for the glacier drags. High winds can close the upper lifts.
Terrain parks The park at Crap Sogn Gion is one of Europe's best, and certainly impresses readers. There are four areas, two big pipes, plus a new 'excellent' freestyle slope to Curnius. Regular high-profile competitions are held here. The glacier has an early season park, too. A new indoor Freestyle Academy offers tuition.
Snow reliability Upper runs are fairly snow-sure. The lower ones can suffer from sun, even early in the season; key ones have snowmaking. The runs from Cassons and the glacier are prone to closure.
Experts The black pistes present few challenges, but the freeride runs add a lot of excellent terrain – timing your descents can be crucial, though, to avoid rock-hard moguls. There are huge amounts of off-piste terrain, notably from La Siala and Cassons.
Intermediates A superb area. Reporters are often surprised by the extent, length and variety of the slopes. The bowl below La Siala is huge and gentle. For the more confident, there are plenty of reds and some easy blacks. The sheltered Grauberg valley is a favourite – long and fast. The long black run from the glacier is steep only at the top. The Downhill piste from Crap Sogn Gion is excellent. Some of the freeride runs are great for trying off-piste, but some are steep.
Beginners OK in midwinter; later on the village slopes suffer from the sun. There is a pass covering access to and use of the Spaligna drag just above

UK PACKAGES

*Alpine Answers,
Crystal, Crystal Finest,
Erna Low, PowderBeds,
Powder Byrne, Ski Club
Freshtracks, Ski
Expectations, Skitracer,
Ski Weekend, Snow
Finders, Swiss Travel
Service, Switzerland
Travel Centre*
Flims *Alpine Answers,
Crystal, Crystal Finest,
Independent Ski Links,
Momentum, Ski Safari,
Ski Solutions, Skitracer,
Ski Weekend,
Switzerland Travel
Centre, White Roc*

Phone numbers
From elsewhere in
Switzerland add the
prefix 081; from
abroad use the prefix
+41 81

TOURIST OFFICE

Flims, Laax and Falera
www.laax.com

Flims and the Falera chairlift, but no special pass for the excellent beginner slopes up at Crap Sogn Gion, high above Laax. The Foppa and Curnius areas have good, easy progress runs.

Snowboarding Hugely popular. Apart from the top terrain park, there's good freeriding. Many linking pistes have flat/uphill stretches – plan carefully.

Cross-country There are 60km of trails.

Mountain restaurants The piste map describes the main ones – helpfully identifying the more ambitious places. In this category are the two we hear most about – Startgels (aka Alpenrose) for its views, fine grills and Italian specials, and Tegia Larnags, a 'charming' farmhouse with typically Swiss dishes. Tegia Curnius is a popular self-service. Also tipped: Tegia Miaz ('excellent meats') and Foppa ('excellent schnitzel and ravioli').

Schools and guides The school is run by the lift company, USA-style. Recent reports speak of 'flexible, considerate' instructors speaking excellent English.

Families There are 'Wonderlands' at all three bases. We have had rave reviews of both the childcare and ski classes.

STAYING THERE

Hotels At Laax the 'design hotel' Signina (927 9004) at Rocksresort has 'truly exceptional service', 'good breakfasts, wonderful pool'. The Laaxerhof (920 8200) is 'almost ski-out/in', has 'good rooms' and 'great food and staff' in its stubli. Laax Dorf offers the charming little Posta Veglia (921 4466). In Flims Dorf the cheap and cheerful Arena (920 9393), with 'great location, terrace and bar' suits boys' trips (see 'Après-ski'). In Waldhaus the Cresta (911 3535) has 'excellent food, service and top spa facilities'. The Adula (928 2828) is similarly praised by a regular visitor.

Apartments The tourist office has a long list of available apartments.

Eating out In Laax, Rocksresort places include Nooba ('excellent Asian food, friendly staff'), and the smart Grandis (fine wines and BBQ specialities). In Laax Dorf the Posta Veglia has a lovely old stube, with a plainer room behind. In Flims, a regular tips the two à la carte restaurants of the hotel Adula.

Après-ski There are busy bars at the lift bases at close of play. Later on, clubs at the hotel Arena and the Riders Palace at Laax throb until late.

Off the slopes There's a big sports centre on the edge of Flims, with ice rink, and 60km of 'really excellent' marked walks. Shopping is limited. Outings to historic Chur are easy.

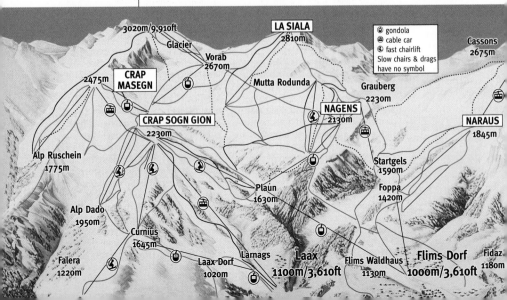

Meiringen

Modest area of varied, scenic slopes above a traditional valley town, ideal for those with a sweet tooth

TOP 10 RATINGS

Extent	★
Fast lifts	★★★★
Queues	★★★★
Snow	★★
Expert	★★
Intermediate	★★★
Beginner	★★★
Charm	★★★
Convenience	★★★
Scenery	★★★★

RPI   95

lift pass	£180
ski hire	£80
lessons	£100
food & drink	£180
total	**£540**

NEWS

Snowmaking improvements planned for last season are now expected for 2011/12.

KEY FACTS

Resort	600m
	1,970ft
Slopes	1060m-2435m
	3,480-7,990ft
Lifts	18
Pistes	60km
	37 miles
Blue	36%
Red	59%
Black	5%
Snowmaking	16%

+ Unspoiled valley town with access to quiet, crowd-free slopes

+ Great views towards the Jungfrau area and the nearby lakes

+ Cheap by Swiss resort standards

+ Plenty to do off the slopes

+ Very sunny slopes, but ...

− Snow is badly affected by the sun

− It's very much a red-run mountain, with few pistes that are genuinely easy or particularly challenging

− Slopes are reached by bus or cable car from Meiringen, with no runs back to the valley (though there are hotels on the mountain, too)

Even if you haven't heard of Meiringen, you've certainly heard of its most famous product, the meringue; the sugary dessert is said to have been created here and named after the town. Its ski area is unlikely to achieve the same fame, but it's a scenic and interesting mountain – aka Hasliberg – that will appeal to confident intermediates looking for an escape from crowds. At these altitudes the sunny orientation is a real worry as spring approaches, though.

THE RESORT

Meiringen is an old town in the broad Haslital – the valley name is used in promoting tourism in the area – at the eastern end of the Bernese Oberland (which has Interlaken and the better-known Jungfrau area at its heart). It is about 90 minutes' drive from Zürich or Bern, and is also on the railway line from Interlaken.

The almost eponymous sweet treat is of course widely available in the town's restaurants and cafes. And it is not Meiringen's only claim to international fame: Sherlock Holmes and his arch enemy Moriarty died in the final Holmes novel at the Reichenbach Falls across the valley.

The ski area is at Hasliberg, the collective name for a few small villages on the sunny mountain balcony above the town. You can park up here (better for day trips), or take a bus or cable car up from Meiringen.

Outings to the Jungfrau resorts of Wengen, Mürren and Grindelwald are possible, via Interlaken.

Village charm The resort lacks the charm of a classic chocolate-box Swiss village; many of the buildings are block-like. But there is a cute little church with a 14th-century tower and wooden spire, shops and restaurants along the main street. Much of the area is pleasantly woody.

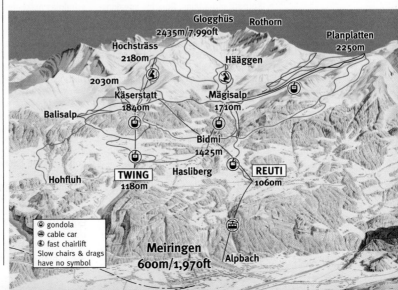

Glogghüs 2435m/7,990ft Rothorn
Planplatten 2250m
Hochsträss 2180m
Hääggen
2030m
Käserstatt 1840m Mägisalp 1710m
Balisalp
Bidmi 1425m
Hohfluh
TWING 1180m Hasliberg REUTI 1060m
Meiringen 600m/1,970ft Alpbach

◉ gondola
▣ cable car
④ fast chairlift
Slow chairs & drags have no symbol

↑ When the cloud clears, the views from Mägisalp across the Haslital to the Jungfrau peaks are splendid
SNOWPIX.COM / CHRIS GILL

Convenience Although the town is spacious, most of the hotels and guest houses are near the railway station and around the main street. There are free ski-buses to the cable car station at Alpbach and up to the slopes at Hasliberg, where you can also stay.

Scenery The slopes themselves are quite scenic, but it is the fabulous views that mark the place out – of the Brienzersee to the west, the famous peaks of the Bernese Oberland to the south-west and (from Planplatten) Engelberg's Titlis to the east.

THE MOUNTAINS

The slopes are on a broad, sunny mountainside (facing generally south-west) beneath the Glogghüs and Rothorn mountains. Roughly speaking the upper half of the slopes are open, the lower half wooded. There are no runs down to Meiringen itself. Piste marking is poor – route finding can be tricky, especially in poor visibility.

Slopes The slopes are spread across two main sectors; each has a lift base area at around 1100m (about 500m above the town), with a mid-mountain lift junction higher up, just above the treeline at 1700m/1800m.

The cable car up from Meiringen arrives at **Reuti**, from where two successive eight-seat gondolas take you up to Bidmi and then Mägisalp, above the treeline. From Mägisalp, another gondola goes to panoramic Planplatten, or two successive quads (the lower one is fast) take you to the highest point in the ski area at the shoulder of Glogghüs.

The other lift base at **Twing** (aka Wasserwendi) is reached by road. From here, a six-seat gondola goes up to Käserstatt. Gentle, rolling terrain extends from here to Balisalp, with a long drag for the return. A six-pack goes on up to Hochsträss. Up here, there are red-run links in both directions between the two sectors; at lower altitude there are blue-run links via Bidmi to Twing (one using a slow double chair up to Käserstatt) but there is no blue run link from the Twing sector to Reuti. There is night skiing at Käserstatt.

Fast lifts For a small area there is a good proportion of fast lifts – mainly well-linked gondolas.

Queues Queues are rare and the gondolas make light work of shifting peak-time crowds. The weak point is the slow double chair connecting Bidmi and Käserstatt.

Terrain parks Mägisalp had a good terrain park, pipe and boardercross, but they were not built last season.

Snow reliability The slopes are quite high and enjoy a good snow record, but they mostly face south-west, which means the effect of the sun is about as severe as it gets. The slopes from Planplatten are an exception, facing north of west. Snowmaking covers the main slope from Hääggen to Bidmi and the nursery slopes there. The run from Käserstatt to Bidmi is also covered. More is planned for 2011/12.

Experts Experts will find little to challenge them on-piste; the former World Cup downhill black run from Planplatten is a bit more challenging than the reds, but not much more. But there is plenty of off-piste terrain to explore within the lift system, and opportunities to go outside it – major routes into the long Gental to the east of the piste network, for example. There's an avalanche transceiver test centre offering advice too.

Intermediates Most of the pistes are justifiably classified red, with some decent vertical from the high points. There are lovely descents through the woods to Bidmi from both sides of the area. In good conditions, a run leading away from the lifts goes down to Hasliberg Hohfluh, from where buses take you back to the gondolas. It's a less satisfactory area for blue-run skiers. The blues in the Reuti sector probably should be red, which means you are more or less confined to the runs from Käserstatt to Balisalp (a lovely gentle area, but not huge) or on down to Twing – a great way to end the day, with grand views of the lake.

Beginners The nursery slopes at Bidmi are ideal; broad and gentle. And the long blue runs down to Balisalp are ideal for progression. Where you go next is the problem (as explained above). The nursery lifts are free to use, but you still need to pay to reach them.

Snowboarding The area is popular with snowboarders. World Cup freestyle and ski cross events are held here. There are lots of natural gullies and bowls to be explored with a guide and Bidmi has good novice terrain. But there are flat, scoot sections too.

Cross-country There are 35km of trails in the Haslital. The Gadmen circuit is 15km, along a pretty river valley. Part of the loop is floodlit some nights.

Mountain restaurants There is a good choice of huts, plus several snack bars. The Alpen tower at Planplatten has spectacular panoramic views and opens early for a breakfast buffet. There's a splendid terrace and table- or self-service indoors, with a wide choice on the menu. Both Käserstatt and Mägisalp have a Berghaus with table- and self-service areas; we had good meals at the latter. Bidmi has a large family-friendly place, but also the rustic Bärgbeizli hut. The cosy Hääggenstubeli has traditional home-made dishes and cakes.

Schools and guides The Swiss school is the main one, also offering heli-skiing. Castor mountain guides operate off-piste tours.

Families Meiringen is great for families, provided you don't mind schlepping the kids up and down the mountain repeatedly. There are comprehensive facilities. Ski häsliland at Bidmi is a large area with kids' snow gardens, carousel, special family restaurants and fun areas. There is a children's terrain park at Käserstatt, with lots of fun features. The Swiss school takes children from five years old.

STAYING THERE

At present no UK operators feature Meiringen. There is a choice of hotels, including one 4-star; most are central.

Hotels The 3-star Park Hotel du Sauvage (972 1880) is one of the oldest and most elegant in the resort, with pool and sauna. By contrast the 3-star Victoria (972 1040) is a designer hotel in an art deco style, with a wellness centre. Of the other 3-stars, the Sherlock Holmes (972 9889) has a quiet location near the cable car, with a pool, sauna and restaurant; and the chalet-style Alpbach (971 1831) is similarly well-placed with stylish suites and a gourmet restaurant.

Apartments There are plenty of apartments available in Meiringen.

At altitude There are several hotels up the mountain at Twing and Reuti. The Reuti (917 1832) has simple lodging, with family rooms. Nearby is the larger 3-star Viktoria (972 3072).

Eating out Most of the restaurants are hotel-based, but offer a wide range of cuisine. Among the best in town is the restaurant at the hotel Victoria, specialising in French and Asian dishes and with a Michelin entry. There are a couple of pizzerias.

Après-ski Après-ski is quite lively up the mountain. There are a couple of umbrella bars and Berghaus Käserstatt has a big terrace and regular live music. The Kuhstall at Mägisalp is popular. In town, nightlife is quiet and relaxed, mostly confined to hotel bars. The Lyon's pub is a sports bar.

Off the slopes Meiringen has plenty of attractions. Pedestrians can get around the ski area easily by gondola (go to the Alpen tower for great views), and there are more than 40km of walking tracks on the Hasliberg plateau. The snowshoeing is good, as are the two 3km toboggan runs. There's a cinema, fitness centre, ice rink and indoor pool – and, of course, the Sherlock Holmes museum. Excursions to Interlaken or Lucerne are possible by train.

Phone numbers
From elsewhere in Switzerland add the prefix 033; from abroad use the prefix +41 33

TOURIST OFFICE
www.haslital.ch

Meiringen

499

Interactive resort shortlist builder at www.wtss.co.uk

Mürren

The dinky, car-free mountain village where the British invented downhill ski racing; stupendous views from one epic run

RATINGS

The mountains

Extent	★
Fast lifts	★★★★
Queues	★★★
Terrain p'ks	★★
Snow	★★★
Expert	★★★
Intermediate	★★★
Beginner	★★
Boarder	★★
X-country	★
Restaurants	★★
Schools	★★★
Families	★★★

The resort

Charm	★★★★★
Convenience	★★★
Scenery	★★★★★
Eating out	★★
Après-ski	★★
Off-slope	★★★

RPI 125

lift pass	£240
ski hire	£135
lessons	£110
food & drink	£220
total	**£705**

NEWS

2011/12: The mountain restaurant at Birg is due to reopen in December 2011 after refurbishment and will be a table-service restaurant with a sun terrace.

- ✚ Tiny, charming, traditional village, with 'traffic-free' snowy paths
- ✚ Stupendous scenery, best enjoyed descending from the Schilthorn
- ✚ Good sports centre
- ✚ Good snow high up, even when the rest of the region is suffering

- ▬ Extent of local pistes very limited, no matter what your level of expertise
- ▬ Lower slopes can be in poor condition
- ▬ Quiet, limited nightlife

Mürren is one of our favourite resorts. There may be other mountain villages that are equally pretty, but none of them enjoys views like those from Mürren across the deep valley to the rock faces and glaciers of the Eiger, Mönch and Jungfrau: simply breathtaking. Then there's the Schilthorn run – 1300m vertical with an unrivalled combination of varied terrain and glorious views.

But our visits are normally one-day affairs; week-long guests are likely to want to explore the extensive intermediate slopes of Wengen and Grindelwald, across the valley. And that takes time.

It was in Mürren that the British more or less invented modern skiing. Sir Arnold Lunn organised the first ever slalom race here in 1922. Some 12 years earlier his father, Sir Henry, had persuaded the locals to open the railway in winter so that he could bring the first winter package tour here. Sir Arnold's son Peter has been a regular visitor since he first skied here in November 1916.

THE RESORT

Mürren is one of a trio of resorts set amid the fabulous scenery of the Jungfrau group. It has an amazing position, set on a shelf high above the valley floor, across from Wengen, and can be reached only by cable car from Stechelberg or from Lauterbrunnen (via Grütschalp, where you change to a train). To get to Wengen, you go down to Lauterbrunnen and catch the cog railway up. You can then ski to Grindelwald, but getting to the First area is a long trek.

VILLAGE CHARM ★★★★★
Picturesque and peaceful
You can't fail to be struck by Mürren's beauty and tranquillity. Paths and narrow lanes weave between little wooden chalets and a handful of bigger hotel buildings – all normally blanketed by snow.

Mürren's traffic-free status is being somewhat eroded; there are now a few delivery vehicles. But it still isn't plagued by electric carts and taxis in the way that many other traditional 'traffic-free' resorts are. Even Wengen seems busy by comparison.

CONVENIENCE ★★★
Small enough not to matter
The village is so small that location is not a concern. Nothing is more than a few minutes' walk.

SCENERY ★★★★★
Glorious panorama
The views from the village and from the Schilthorn are magnificent. The grandeur of the Eiger, Mönch and Jungfrau across the valley as you descend the slopes is outstanding.

THE MOUNTAINS

Despite its small size, Mürren's ski area is interestingly varied. The lower slopes are below the treeline, but in practice it is an inhospitable area when the weather is bad.

EXTENT OF THE SLOPES ★
Small but interesting
Mürren's slopes aren't extensive. But there is something for everyone, including a vertical of some 1300m to the village. There are three connected areas around the village. The biggest is **Schiltgrat**, served by a fast quad chair at the south end of the village. A short funicular goes from the middle

KEY FACTS

Resort	1650m
	5,410ft

Jungfrau region

Altitude	945-2970m
	3,100-9,740ft
Lifts	44
Pistes	213km
	132 miles
Blue	33%
Red	49%
Black	18%
Snowmaking	40%

Mürren-Schilthorn only

Slopes	1650-2970m
	5,410-9,740ft
Lifts	12
Pistes	53km
	33 miles

ACTIVITIES

Indoor Alpine Sports Centre: swimming pool, sauna, solarium, steam bath, massage, fitness room; tennis, gymnasium, squash

Outdoor Ice rink, curling, tobogganing, cleared paths, snowshoeing

of the village to the nursery slope at **Allmendhubel** – from where you can link to the slightly higher **Maulerhubel**. Runs go down from here to Winteregg and a newish fast quad.

Much more interesting are the higher slopes reached by cable car to **Birg**. Below Birg, the Engetal area has several snow-sure slopes served by chairs. A further cable car goes up to the Schilthorn and its revolving restaurant, Piz Gloria, which featured in the James Bond film *On Her Majesty's Secret Service*. In good snow you can ski (via a short chairlift) right down to Lauterbrunnen – almost 16km and 2175m vertical (below Winteregg, it's mostly narrow paths); an annual race for amateurs called the Inferno is run in January over this route (but competitors can't use the chairlift).

FAST LIFTS ★★★★
New chairs in place
Cable cars are the main access to Mürren's highest slopes, and chairlifts are gradually being updated.

QUEUES ★★★
Generally not a problem
Mürren doesn't get as crowded as Wengen and Grindelwald, except on sunny Sundays. But there can be queues for the cable cars to Birg and Schilthorn; the top stage has only one cabin, so capacity is limited.

TERRAIN PARKS ★★
Affirmative
There is a terrain park on the lower slopes of Schiltgrat, with jumps, a couple of pipes and chill-out bar area.

SNOW RELIABILITY ★★★
Good on the upper slopes
The Jungfrau region does not have a good snow record – but we've always found Mürren has the best snow in the area. When Wengen-Grindelwald (and Mürren's lower slopes) have problems, the Schilthorn and Engetal slopes often have packed powder snow because of their height and orientation – facing roughly north-east to east. The runs from below Engetal to Allmendhubel and parts of the lower slopes have snowmaking.

FOR EXPERTS ★★★
One wonderful piste
The run from the top of the Schilthorn starts with a steep but not terrifying slope, in the past generally mogulled but now more often groomed. It flattens into a schuss to Engetal, below Birg. Then there's a wonderful,

You almost feel you can reach out and touch the Eiger, Mönch and Jungfrau across the valley →
ALAN LIPTROT

GETTING THERE

Air Zürich 155km/ 95 miles (3hr); Bern 65km/40 miles (2hr); Basel 160km/100 miles (2hr45)

Rail Lauterbrunnen; transfer by mountain railway and cable car

LIFT PASSES

Jungfrau

Prices in SF

Age	1-day	6-day
under 16	31	157
16 to 19	50	251
20 to 61	62	314
over 62	56	283

Free under 6 (if with parent)
Beginner points card
Notes Covers Wengen, Mürren and Grindelwald, trains between them and Grindelwald ski-bus; day pass price is for Mürren-Schilthorn area only
Alternative passes Grindelwald and Wengen only; Mürren only; non-skier pass

SCHOOLS

Swiss
t 855 1247

Classes
5 half-days SF170
Private lessons
SF140 for 2hr for 1-2 persons

UK PACKAGES

Inghams, Ski Line, Ski Solutions, Swiss Travel Service
Lauterbrunnen Ski Miquel

wide run with stunning views over the valley. Chairlifts allow you to play on these upper runs before resuming your descent to the village. Below the Engetal lifts you hit the Kanonenrohr (gun barrel). This is a narrow shelf with solid rock on one side and a steep drop on the other – protected by nets. After an open slope and scrappy zigzag path, you arrive at the 'hog's back' below Allmendhubel and can descend towards the village on either side of the low peak.

From Schiltgrat a short, serious mogul run – the Kandahar – descends towards the village, but experts are more likely to be interested in the off-piste runs into the Blumental – from here (the north-facing Blumenlucke) and from Birg (the sunnier Tschingelchrachen) – or the more adventurous runs from the Schilthorn top station.

FOR INTERMEDIATES ★★★☆☆
Limited, but Wengen nearby
Keen piste-bashers will want to make a few trips to the long cruising runs of Wengen-Grindelwald. The best easy cruising run in Mürren is the north-facing blue down to Winteregg. The reds on the other low slopes can get mogulled, and snow conditions can be poor. The runs up at Engetal, below Birg, normally have good snow, and you can choose your gradient.

Competent, confident intermediates can consider tackling the Schilthorn.

FOR BEGINNERS ★★☆☆☆
Not ideal, but adequate
The nursery slopes at Allmendhubel, at the top of the funicular, are on the steep side. And there are only two or three easy runs to graduate to, for which you'll need to buy full or daily passes or use a points card.

FOR BOARDERS ★★☆☆☆
Tough going for intermediates
The major lifts are snowboard-friendly cable cars and chairlifts. The terrain above Mürren is suitable mainly for good freeriders – it's steep, with a lot of off-piste. Intermediates will find the area tough and limited; nearby Wengen is gentler and larger.

FOR CROSS-COUNTRY ★☆☆☆☆
Forget it
There's a 12km loop along the Lauterbrunnen valley. But snow is unreliable at valley height.

MOUNTAIN RESTAURANTS ★★☆☆☆
Nothing outstanding
Piz Gloria revolves once an hour, displaying a fabulous 360° panorama of peaks and lakes. We don't like the ambience here, but reporters have enjoyed the 'amazingly tasty' and 'surprisingly good value' meals. Other reader tips include the small, rustic Schilthornhütte, by the Engetal chairs, and the rustic, secluded Suppenalp lower down in the Blumental – but it gets no sun in January. Gimmeln is self-service with a large terrace,

CHILDCARE

Kinder Paradis
t 856 8686
Ages 3 to 8yr; 9.30-
12noon; 1.30-4.30;
SF78 for one day inc.
lunch

Babysitter list
Available from tourist
office

Ski school
Takes age 5 and over
(5 2hr days SF170)

Phone numbers
From elsewhere in
Switzerland add the
prefix 033; from
abroad use the prefix
+41 33

TOURIST OFFICE
www.mymuerren.ch
www.muerren.ch

famous for its apple cake. The restaurant at Birg is being revamped – see 'News'.

SCHOOLS AND GUIDES ★★★★★
No recent reports
We lack recent reports. But the school has a long tradition of teaching Brits.

FOR FAMILIES ★★★★★
Adequate
Mürren is attractive for a quiet family holiday, but facilities are limited. There is a nursery slope with a rope tow. The Kinder Paradis nursery takes children from three years old, the ski school from the age of five and there is all-day childcare in the sports centre.

STAYING THERE

Hotels There are fewer than a dozen. ****Eiger** (856 5454) Chalet style; next to station. Widely recommended for good blend of efficiency and charm. Good food; pool.
***Alpenruh** (856 8800) Attractively renovated chalet next to the cable car. Food and service praised. Sauna.
***Edelweiss** (856 5600) 'Great, friendly service, very good rooms,

excellent views, good wholesome food, highly recommended.'
***Jungfrau** (856 6464) Perfectly placed for families, in front of the baby slope and close to the funicular.
Alpenblick (855 1327) Simple, small, modern chalet near the station.
Apartments There are plenty of chalets and apartments in the village for independent travellers to rent.

EATING OUT ★★★★★
Mainly in hotels
The main alternative to hotels is the rustic Stägerstübli – a bar as well as a restaurant, and popular with locals, serving regional dishes. There is a children's menu too. The Eigerstübli (hotel Eiger) is good for fish and meat options; the Edelweiss, Bellevue and Alpenruh have received good reports from readers, too.

APRES-SKI ★★★★★
Not entirely devoid of life
The tiny Stägerstübli is cosy, and the place to meet locals. The Bliemlichäller disco in the Blumental hotel caters for kids, the Tächi bar in the Eiger for a more mixed crowd.

OFF THE SLOPES ★★★★★
Tranquillity but not much else
There isn't a lot to amuse people who don't hit the slopes apart from the scenery and a very good sports centre with an outdoor ice rink. There are lots of prepared winter walking trails, which a reporter thoroughly enjoyed. Excursions to Bern and Interlaken are easy, and skiers can easily return to the village to meet non-skiers for lunch. The only problem for non-skiers with meeting for lunch at the top of the cable car is the expense of it.

DOWN-VALLEY VILLAGE – 795m

LAUTERBRUNNEN

This is a good budget base, with a bit of resort atmosphere and access to both Wengen (until late) and Mürren. We've happily stayed at two hotels – the 3-star Schützen (855 3026) and 2-star Oberland (855 1241), also recommended for its food; the 3-star Silberhorn (856 2210) has been highly recommended by a past reporter for its five-course dinners. The Horner hotel bar has 'only a telly and plastic dartboard', but is fine for a pub atmosphere. Ski Miquel's chalet hotel is said to be of an 'excellent standard'.

SNOWPIX.COM / CHRIS GILL

Saas-Fee

For practical purposes, the highest skiing in the Alps, plus a cute old village at the base; great for an early/late break

NEWS

2011/12: No big changes. The lift company must be saving up to build its planned gondola from the car parks to Längfluh and on to Feechopf at 3888m.

2010/11: Saas-Almagell gained a new panoramic mountain restaurant (Heidbodme), along with a new kids' club at the ski school.

KEY FACTS

Resort	1800m	
	5,910ft	
Slopes	1800-3500m	
	5,910-11,480ft	
Lifts	22	
Pistes	100km	
	62 miles	
Blue	25%	
Red	50%	
Black	25%	
Snowmaking	18%	

➕ Most runs are at exceptionally high altitude, and snow-sure; great for early or late-season trips

➕ Traditional, car-free village, with clear attractions for families

➕ Dramatic setting amid high peaks and glaciers

➕ Good off-slope facilities

➖ Small area of slopes

➖ Mainly easy runs, with little to amuse experts (glacier limits off-piste exploration)

➖ Many visitors face some long walks around the village

➖ Shady and cold for much of winter

➖ Bad weather can shut the slopes

Saas-Fee is one of our favourite places – a sort of miniature Zermatt without the conspicuous consumption. As well as the charm factor there's the super-reliable snow: you spend most of your days here at an altitude – between 2500m and 3500m – that is unrivalled in the Alps. It's a compelling combination.

We tend to drop in here for a day or two at a time, so the limited extent and challenge of the slopes is not a worry; if we were here for a week, we'd soon be taking trips to Saas-Grund and even Zermatt. But if you don't mind skiing the same flattering slopes every day, Saas-Fee takes some beating.

THE RESORT

Saas-Fee is a high-altitude mountain village of narrow streets, lined by attractive old chalets and free of cars (parked at the resort entrance). It's not free of traffic, though: electric taxis and trucks are not the nuisance that they are in Zermatt, but they do provoke complaints from readers.

The worthwhile slopes of Saas-Almagell and Saas-Grund are not far away, and you can buy a lift pass that covers all three resorts and linking buses. Trips to Zermatt are time-consuming but possible, and with a six-day lift pass the day pass for Zermatt costs just SF30. Tour ops sometime arrange excursions.

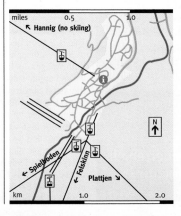

miles   0.5   1.0
↖ Hannig (no skiing)

N ↑

↖ Spielboden
↙ Felskinn
↓ Plattjen

km   1.0   2.0

VILLAGE CHARM ★★★★★
Unpretentious rural idyll

Despite expansion, Saas-Fee still feels like a village, with cow sheds still in evidence. It doesn't have much of a central focus, but we'll forgive that; it's a charming place just to stroll around and relax in – at least when the spring sun is beating down (it's a chilly place in midwinter). There are some smart hotels (plus many more modest ones) and good bars and restaurants.

CONVENIENCE ★★
A hike maybe

Although it's a small village, it's about 2km long, and the slopes and most of the lifts are at one end. There are free but limited public mini-buses and a road-train, and the bigger hotels run their own taxis. But most people, most of the time, just walk everywhere. The biggest lift – the Alpin Express gondola – starts from a more central location. And you can store your gear near the lifts, which helps.

SCENERY ★★★★
The Pearl of the Alps

Saas-Fee has stunning views up to a ring of 4000-metre peaks – on a sunny day the restaurant terraces by the nursery slopes at the south end of the village are a magnet. Higher up, the views are even better.

LIFT PASSES

Saas-Fee

Prices in SF

Age	1-day	6-day
under 16	38	194
17 to 18	57	290
19 to 64	67	341
over 65	61	307

Free under 10

Beginner pass for village lifts only

Notes
Covers lifts in Saas-Fee only; single and return tickets available on most main lifts; also afternoon passes

Alternative passes
Whole valley pass; separate passes for each of the other Saastal ski areas (Saas-Grund, Saas-Almagell, Saas-Balen); non-skier single fares

THE MOUNTAINS

The upper slopes are largely gentle, while the lower mountain, below the glacier, is steeper and rockier, needing good snow-cover. There is very little shelter in bad weather: during and after heavy snowfalls you may find yourself limited to the nursery area.

Take it easy when climbing out of the top lift station at 3500m: some people can't handle the thin air.

Some of the red runs on the glacier would be better classified as blue.

Saas-Fee is one of the leading resorts for ski touring; the extended Haute Route from Chamonix via Zermatt ends here.

More than one reporter has thought the lift pass expensive for a relatively small area. Quite a few big Swiss areas charge less.

EXTENT OF THE SLOPES ★★☆☆☆
A glacier runs through it
There are two routes up to the main **Felskinn** area. The 30-person Alpin Express gondola, starting across the river from the centre of the village, takes you there via a mid-station at Morenia. The alternative is a short drag across the nursery slope at the south end of the village, and then the Felskinn cable car.

From Felskinn, the Metro Alpin underground funicular hurtles up to **Allalin**. From below here, two draglifts access the high point of the area.

Also from the south end of the village, a gondola leaves for Spielboden. This is met by a cable car that takes you up to **Längfluh**.

Between Felskinn and Längfluh is an off-limits glacier area. A very long draglift from Längfluh takes you to a point where you can get down to the Felskinn area. These two sectors are served mainly by draglifts, and you can get down to the village from both.

Another gondola from the south end of the village goes up to the separate, small area of **Plattjen**.

FAST LIFTS ★★★★☆
Too many T-bars
The area is a strange mixture of powerful fast lifts and a lot of 'ghastly long and cold T-bars', as a 2010 reporter put it; there are only two chairlifts. Blame the glaciers, on which it's tricky to build chairlifts. Our rating may look mysterious, but over half the lifts are fast, which puts Saas-Fee comfortably into the 4-star range.

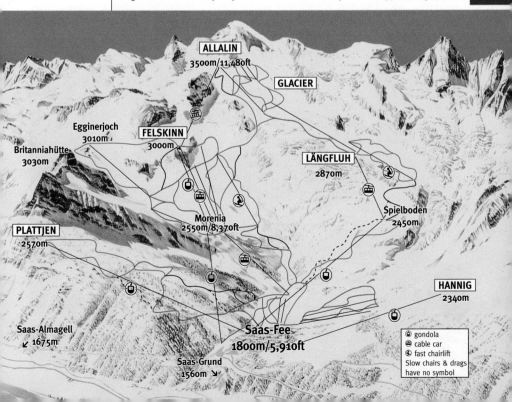

ALLALIN 3500m/11,480ft
GLACIER
Egginerjoch 3010m
FELSKINN 3000m
Britanniahütte 3030m
LÄNGFLUH 2870m
PLATTJEN 2570m
Morenia 2550m/8,370ft
Spielboden 2450m
HANNIG 2340m
Saas-Almagell 1675m
Saas-Fee 1800m/5,910ft
Saas-Grund 1560m

gondola
cable car
fast chairlift
Slow chairs & drags have no symbol

Air Sion 75km/
45 miles (1hr45);
Geneva 225km/
140 miles (3hr30);
Zürich 250km/
155 miles (4hr);
Milan 200km/
125 miles (3hr30)

Rail Brig (38km/
24 miles) or Visp;
regular buses from
station

SNOWPIX.COM / CHRIS GILL

Some bits of glacier
are skiable, other bits
are emphatically not.
Beyond the crevasses,
Morenia and the main
area of slopes, seen
from Längfluh ↓

QUEUES ★★★☆☆
Still peak season problems
We had no problems with queues in
February and March 2011, and no
reports from readers of particular
problems. But at peak holiday periods,
you may meet long queues for the
Felskinn cable car ('an hour to reach
Felskinn'). There may also be queues
up at Längfluh and for the highest
draglifts. Crowds on the home run
from Morenia can be a problem at the
end of the day, and when bad weather
closes higher lifts.

TERRAIN PARKS ★★★★★
Well developed
The 42 Crew (www.42crew.ch) who run
the show here are renowned for
building great parks. The big Morenia
park has a plethora of kickers, rails
and boxes, and a truly world-class
half-pipe. Shapers are constantly
changing the rail and box lines to
keep the park creative as well as
adding interesting obstacles like a
gondola roof jib. There is also a
dedicated female kicker line. Beginners
may be best off starting out in the
snow-skate park in Stafelwald, near
the nursery slopes. You'll find plenty
of entry-level jumps and rails here. In
summer, you will often see pro riders
honing their skills.

SNOW RELIABILITY ★★★★★
A question of altitudes
Most of Saas-Fee's slopes face north
and many are above 2500m, making
this one of the most reliable resorts
for snow in the Alps. The glacier is
open most of the year. Lower down,
on the runs back to the resort, snow
quality and cover can be more patchy,
but snowmaking now seems adequate.
Grooming is also adequate.

FOR EXPERTS ★★☆☆☆
Not a lot to keep your interest
There is not much steep stuff – the
handful of short, sharp pitches dotted
around the area just merit their black
classification. The slopes around the
top of Längfluh can provide good
powder, and there are usually moguls
above Spielboden. There is excellent
tree skiing on Plattjen but it requires
serious depths of snow to cover the
very rocky terrain. On the main sector,
the glacier puts limits on the off-piste
even with a guide – crevasse danger is
extreme. But there are extensive
touring possibilities.

FOR INTERMEDIATES ★★★★☆
Great for gentle cruising
For early intermediates and those not
looking for much of a challenge, Saas-
Fee is ideal. For long cruises, head for

SCHOOLS

Swiss
t 957 2348

Eskimos
t 957 4904

Optimum Snowsports
t 957 2039

Classes
5 3hr days SF193

Private lessons
SF80 for 1hr

CHILDCARE

Kindergarten Ferien-Kinderparadies
t 957 4057
Ages 18mnth to 6yr;
9am to 5pm

Swiss
t 957 2348
From age 3; 9.45 to
3.30 (half skiing, half
activities)

Ski school
From age 5 (5 3hr
days SF193)

UK PACKAGES

Alpine Answers, Alpine
Life, Crystal, Crystal
Finest, Erna Low,
Esprit, Family Ski
Company, Independent
Ski Links, Inghams,
Interactive Resorts,
Momentum, Neilson,
Oxford Ski Co,
PowderBeds, Ski
Expectations, Ski
Independence, Ski Line,
Ski Safari, Ski
Solutions, Ski Total,
Skitracer, Skiweekends.
com, Snow Finders,
Swiss Travel Service,
Switzerland Travel
Centre, Thomson

Allalin. The top of the mountain, down as far as Längfluh in one direction and Morenia in the other, is ideal, with gentle reds leading to even gentler blues, and usually excellent snow.

The reds around mid-mountain are a bit more challenging, notably at Längfluh. The descents from Allalin to the village offer a leg-testing 1700m vertical. The lower runs have steepish, tricky sections and can have poor snow, and the blues here are mainly narrow paths – timid intermediates might prefer to take a lift down from mid-mountain. Don't ignore the rather neglected Plattjen, which is basically of red-run gradient.

FOR BEGINNERS ★★★★★
A great place to start
There's a superb, large, out-of-the-way nursery area at the edge of the village, as snow-sure as any you will find. Those ready to progress can head for the gentle blues between Felskinn and Morenia. A useful beginners' pass covers all the short village lifts.

FOR BOARDERS ★★★★☆
Backed from the beginning
Saas-Fee has backed snowboarding from its inception and provides year-round riding. The terrain suits intermediates and beginners best; there's little to satisfy experts and the glacier limits freeriding, but carvers will find wide, well-groomed pistes to shred down. The main access lifts are gondolas, cable cars and a funicular, but nearly all the rest are T-bars. The high altitude and the glacier mean the resort is a favourite for early-season and summer riding. The Popcorn bar and shop is the favourite spot for après-snowboard beers.

FOR CROSS-COUNTRY ★★★☆☆
Good local trail and lots nearby
There is a nice short (6km) trail at the edge of the village and 26km down in the Saas valley.

MOUNTAIN RESTAURANTS ★★☆☆☆
Head to Plattjen
The restaurants at the main lift stations are functional; at least the food at the self-service Morenia is 'cooked fresh while you wait'. **Editors' choice** The Vernissage Berghaus Plattjen (just down from the top of Plattjen), in the Ferienart hotel stable, is in a league of its own – great Alpine atmosphere, delicious hearty food and excellent service; great glacier views from a tiny terrace. **Worth knowing about** The best bet within the main piste network is the cosy Gletschergrotte, slightly off the run from Spielboden (watch for signs on the left) – but 'be prepared for a wait'. Higher up, the Gletscherwelt at Längfluh has a great view of the glacier and its crevasses from its large terrace. A 15-minute trek from the pistes at Felskinn brings you to Britanniahütte, a real climbing refuge with great views; understandably, food is simple.

SCHOOLS AND GUIDES ★★★★☆
Good reports
Optimum Snowsports, Saas Fee's first British-run school, opened in 2009 and this year we have a glowing report on both kids' classes and adult private lessons: 'a truly inspiring and talented instructor'. Recent visitors said of the Swiss school: 'efficient and fun for kids', 'a great success for our seven year old'.

FOR FAMILIES ★★★★☆
Safely suitable
The village and its gentle nursery slopes form a great environment for families. The kids' fun park proved a 'great introduction' for one toddler. Several hotels have an in-house kindergarten. There's a day care centre for children from six months to six years and there's also a babysitting service. Child-friendly operators Esprit and Family Ski both have chalets here.

WORLD'S HIGHEST REVOLVING LUNCH?

If you fancy 360° views during lunch, head up to the world's highest revolving restaurant at Allalin, where you can get a different vista with starters, mains and pud. Only the bit of floor with the tables on it revolves; the stairs stay put (along with the windows – watch your gloves). The other two revolving cafes in the Alps are also in Switzerland – at Mürren and Leysin – and we rate the views there better. But it's an amusing novelty that most visitors enjoy; lunch is OK too, but a recent reporter said that service was 'slow' by 'staff who didn't seem to care'. To reserve a table next to the windows phone 957 1771.

↑ The village does get some sun, as the season progresses; this is early February, mid-afternoon, taken from the lower slopes of Plattjen
SNOWPIX.COM / CHRIS GILL

ACTIVITIES

Indoor Bielen leisure centre (swimming, hot tub, steam bath, whirlpool, solarium, sauna, aerobics, massage, tennis, badminton, gym, aqua fitness), museums

Outdoor 30km of cleared paths, ice rink (skating, curling, snow bowling), tubing, tobogganing, snow-shoeing

Phone numbers
From elsewhere in Switzerland add the prefix 027; from abroad use the prefix +41 27

TOURIST OFFICE

www.saas-fee.ch

STAYING THERE

Chalets Although quite a few UK tour operators sell holidays to Saas-Fee, there are surprisingly few chalet holidays. Ski Total has a 50-bed chalet hotel in a prime spot, over the street from the nursery slopes. Look also at 'For families', above.
Hotels There are over 50.
*****Ferienart (958 1900) Central top hotel. Superb blend of comfort, service and relaxed style. Half-board food about the best we've had.
***Allalin (958 1000) 'Large rooms, outstanding food, fantastic staff,' says a 2010 reporter.
****Golfhotel Saaserhof (958 9898) Good location near lifts. 'Outstanding – excellent service and food.'
***Bristol (958 1212) 'A quiet, quality hotel; beside the nursery slopes,' says a recent visitor. Highly recommended.
***Waldesruh (958 6464) Close to the Alpin Express. 'Family run and family friendly.'
***Europa (958 9600) Near the Hannig gondola. 'Clean, comfortable'; 'good food'; 'gorgeous wellness facilities'.
**Belmont (958 1640) The most appealing of the hotels looking directly on to the nursery slopes.
Fletschhorn (957 2131) Upmarket, elegant chalet in the woods. Original art and individual rooms. A trek from

the village and lifts, but great food.
Hohnegg (958 1070) Small, more rustic alternative to the Fletschhorn, in a similarly remote spot.
Apartments A reporter recommends the 'great and convenient' Perla apartments, near the main gondola.

EATING OUT ★★★★
Good variety
Gastronomes will want to head for the Michelin-starred and expensive Fletschhorn – 'the best meal I've ever had', says a reporter. We like the woody Bodmen, which has great food and a varied menu. The hotel Ferienart operates several good restaurants including the serious Vernissage, the Mandarin (Thai) and Del Ponte (pizza). Don Ciccio's is 'child-friendly' and does 'great pizzas and veal'. The Vieux Chalet is tipped this year for fondue. Zur Mühle and the hotel Tenne have been recommended.

APRES-SKI ★★★★
Excellent and varied
If you want an end of day beer in the sun, grab it up at Plattjen; for much of the season the village is back in the shade again by close of play. Despite this, the terraces of Zur Mühle and the Black Bull in the main street are always buzzing; NoOne's has 'lively music and is good for the first après beer'. Later on, Nesti's and the Alpen-Pub keep going till 1am. Popcorn is a long-time favourite for many visitors. The Metro-Bar is said to feel like a 19th-century mine shaft. Why-Not is the place for a Guinness and the Happy bar's happy hours are popular. The 'relaxing' Living Room in the hotel Dom has 'modern' sofas and a giant fountain. Poison is the place to drink shots and party the night away, while Night-Life disco 'livens up late'.

OFF THE SLOPES ★★★★
A mountain for pedestrians
The whole of the Hannig mountain is dedicated to walking, snowshoeing, paragliding and tobogganing. The splendid Bielen leisure centre boasts a 25m pool, indoor tennis courts and a sunbed area. The Feeblitz 'roller-coaster-style' bob ride, right beside the Alpin Express, is very popular and good fun. The museums are interesting – kids can make bread at the bakery one. If you like ice caves, don't miss the world's largest. The tourist office organises daily walks.

St Moritz

One of a kind: a panoramic high-altitude playground that has as much going on off the slopes as on

NEWS

2011/12: New panoramic cabins with windows to floor level are planned for the Diavolezza cable car, and it will be closed for fitting them from 26 November 2011 until 11 February 2012.

2010/11: The hotel on Muottas Muragl (non-skiing mountain) reopened following renovation, with new restaurants, lounge and terrace.

+ Wonderful panoramic scenery

+ Extensive intermediate slopes

+ High, and fairly snow-sure

+ Off-slope activities second to none (and a whole mountain dedicated to non-skiing activities)

+ Some good mountain restaurants, some with magnificent views

− A sizeable town, with little traditional Alpine character and some big block buildings

− Several unlinked mountains

− Runs on home mountain all fairly easy and most lacking variety

− Can be pricey, as you'd expect from such a fashionable resort

St Moritz is Switzerland's definitive 'exclusive' winter resort: glitzy, fashionable and, above all, the place to be seen – a place for an all-round winter holiday, with an unrivalled array of wacky diversions such as polo, golf and cricket on snow, and countless festivals. It has long been popular with upper-crust Brits, who stay in the top hotels in order to go sledging. Well, OK: in order to descend the world-famous Cresta Run. But, like all such self-consciously smart resorts, it makes a perfectly good destination for anyone. And it offers some bargain holidays – see the advert near the start of the Switzerland section of this book. It also has some seriously good slopes to enjoy.

The town of St Moritz is far from chocolate-box pretty. But if, like us, you can look beyond the urban environment and big buildings, you will appreciate the beauty of St Moritz's spectacular setting. Our progress on the mountains here is regularly interrupted by the need to stand and gaze. We've had no reader reports this year; please do report if you visit in 2011/12.

509

THE RESORT

St Moritz is at the heart of the upper Engadin – the remote, high valley of the En, which flows on into the Austrian Tirol as the Inn (as in Innsbruck). The valley bottom is filled by a chain of lakes, one of which separates the two parts of St Moritz. On a steep hillside above the lake, St Moritz Dorf is the fashionable main town. Beside the lake is the more ordinary spa resort, St Moritz Bad. The skiing is in several separate sectors; only one, Corviglia, is reachable directly from the resort; the higher, wider Corvatsch is a bus ride away.

In winter the lake is used for eccentric activities including horse and greyhound racing, show jumping, polo, 'ice golf' and even cricket. And there's a whole mountain (Muottas Muragl) set aside for not skiing – see 'Off the slopes'. The upper Engadin makes a superb setting for walking and cross-country skiing, which is very big here; the Engadin Ski Marathon is held every March – over 12,000 take part.

The home slopes are shared with Celerina, down the valley (see end of chapter). And there are other possible bases – Sils Maria, for example, has

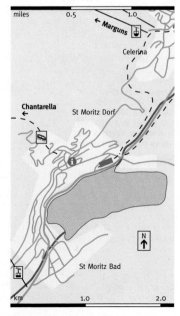

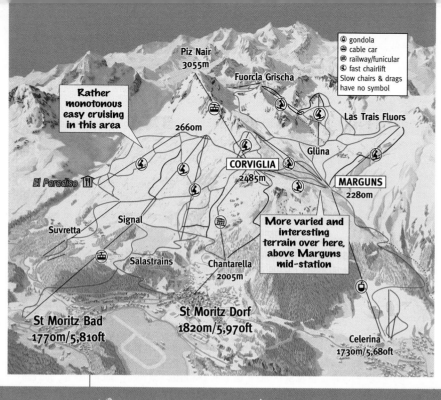

Rather monotonous easy cruising in this area

Piz Nair
3055m

Fuorcla Grischa

gondola
cable car
railway/funicular
fast chairlift
Slow chairs & drags have no symbol

Las Trais Fluors

2660m

Glüna

CORVIGLIA
2485m

MARGUNS
2280m

El Paradiso

Signal

Suvretta

Salastrains

Chantarella
2005m

More varied and interesting terrain over here, above Marguns mid-station

St Moritz Bad
1770m/5,810ft

St Moritz Dorf
1820m/5,970ft

Celerina
1730m/5,680ft

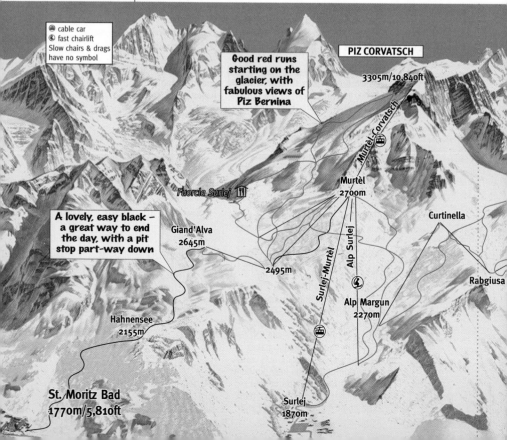

cable car
fast chairlift
Slow chairs & drags have no symbol

PIZ CORVATSCH

Good red runs starting on the glacier, with fabulous views of Piz Bernina

3305m/10,840ft

Murtèl-Corvatsch

Fuorcla Surlej

Murtèl
2700m

Curtinella

A lovely, easy black – a great way to end the day, with a pit stop part-way down

Giand'Alva
2645m

2495m

Surlej-Murtèl

Alp Surlej

Rabgiusa

Hahnensee
2155m

Alp Margun
2270m

St. Moritz Bad
1770m/5,810ft

Surlej
1870m

KEY FACTS

Resort	1770m
	5,810ft
Slopes	1730-3305m
	5,680-10,840ft
Lifts	56
Pistes	350km
	217 miles
Blue	20%
Red	70%
Black	10%
Snowmaking	30%

For Corviglia only

Slopes	1730-3055m
	5,680-10,020ft
Lifts	22
Pistes	100km
	62 miles

good access to the big Corvatsch sector of the slopes via Furtschellas.

There are good rail links from Zürich, but it's quicker to drive. A car is handy, too: the valley bus service is free with a lift pass; but it gets crowded at peak times. And a car greatly speeds up visits to the more distant mountains. Trips are possible to Davos and other resorts, including Austrian and Italian ones; St Moritz lift passes get you a half-price one in Livigno, for example. The proximity of Italy means lots of Italian visitors and workers, food and wine.

VILLAGE CHARM ★★★★★
Urban glitz instead
In the main resort towns there is little traditional Alpine character; St Moritz is very much a glitzy town rather than a cute village. St Moritz Dorf has two main streets – lined with boutiques selling Rolex, Cartier, Hermes – a few side lanes and a small main square. St Moritz Bad is less urban, and less prestigious. Many of the buildings in both parts of the resort are block-like.

Interesting, varied intermediate terrain on this side of the sector

Furtschellas 2800m

Rabgiusa

hella

Val Fex

FURTSCHELLAS 2310m

Excellent winding run to the valley – best done early in the day on good snow with no crowds

Sils-Furtschellas

Sils Maria 1795m ↘

CONVENIENCE ★★★★★
Bad is good – or better, at least
It's a perfectly convenient resort if you are content to ski Corviglia, stay in central Dorf and ride the funicular, or stay on the edge of Bad and use the Signal cable car. But both parts of the resort spread widely away from these lifts, and you will probably want to ski other mountains, for which transport is needed. For keen skiers, Bad is the better base – you can ski back to it from the big Corvatsch sector. If this is all too much for you, the local heli-skiing outfits will drop you at the top of the lifts. It's that kind of place.

SCENERY ★★★★★
Fabulous panoramas
The lake-filled valley, with 4000m peaks forming the Italian border to the south, provides mesmerising views from Corviglia, and the close-up views of Piz Bernina from Corvatsch are stunning. Should we award 5 stars?

THE MOUNTAINS

There are lots of long, wide, well-groomed runs with varied terrain – practically all on open slopes above the trees. The 350km of pistes are in three separate areas, covered on three very clear piste maps; our maps show only the two main areas (Corviglia and Corvatsch) close to St Moritz. Every Friday, from 7pm to 2am, the 4.2km piste down from the middle station on Corvatsch is floodlit.

EXTENT OF THE SLOPES ★★★★★
Big but broken up
From St Moritz Dorf a two-stage railway goes up to **Corviglia**, a lift junction at the eastern end of a sunny and rather monotonous area of slopes facing east and south over the main valley. The peak of Piz Nair, reached from here by cable car, separates these slopes from the less sunny and more varied ones in the wide bowl above **Marguns** – and gives fabulous views across the valley to Piz Bernina. From Corviglia you can (snow permitting) head down easy paths to Dorf and Bad; you'll probably pass through Salastrains – just above Dorf, with nursery slopes, restaurants and two hotels. There is a red run from Marguns to Celerina.

From Surlej, a few miles from St Moritz, a two-stage cable car takes you to the north-facing slopes of

↑ There's plenty to do here other than ski – all amid stunning views of mountains and frozen lakes

Weekly news updates and resort links at www.wtss.co.uk

LIFT PASSES

Upper Engadin

Prices in SF

Age	1-day	6-day
under 13	24	122
13 to 17	48	240
Over 18	72	358

Free under 6
Senior no deals
Beginner no deals

Notes
Covers all lifts in Corviglia, Corvatsch, Diavolezza-Lagalb and Zuoz, and includes the Engadin bus services and certain stretches of the Rhätische Bahn railway; 1-day price is for Corviglia only

Alternative passes
Half-day and day passes for individual areas within Upper Engadin

Corvatsch, which reach glacial heights. From the mid-station at Murtèl you have a choice of reds to Stüvetta Giand'Alva and Alp Margun. From the latter you can work your way to **Furtschellas**, also reached by cable car from Sils Maria. If you're lucky with the snow, you can end the day with the splendid Hahnensee run, from the northern limit of the Corvatsch lift system at Giand'Alva down to St Moritz Bad – a black-classified run that is of red difficulty for 95% of its 6km length. It often opens around noon, when the snow softens. It's a five-minute walk from the end of the run to the cable car to Corviglia.

The third area consists of two peaks on opposite sides of the road to the Bernina pass and Italy, about 20km away (a 50-minute bus ride). **Diavolezza** (2980m) has excellent north-facing pistes of 900m vertical, down its cable car (which will be closed from late November 2011 till 11 February 2012 –see 'News'). **Lagalb** (2960m) is a smaller area with quite challenging slopes – west-facing, 850m vertical – served by a smaller cable car. From late February these cable cars run until 5pm.

FAST LIFTS ★★★★☆
Plenty of options
St Moritz has invested heavily in upgrading lifts, especially on Corviglia and Marguns, where there are fast chairs all over the place. Corvatsch still has some T-bars, though. The area as a whole has a lot of modest-sized

cable cars – both for getting out of the resort and for access to peaks.

QUEUES ★★★☆☆
Not much of a problem
Queues for the cable cars are not unknown, and we had a high-season report of a one-hour queue to get out of Bad in 2009/10. But reporters have generally had good experiences lately and say that the slopes tend to be quiet early and late in the day.

TERRAIN PARKS ★★★★☆
World class facilities
The Crowland Park on Corviglia is easily reached from Celerina as well as St Moritz. The park was designed with female pro skiers and snowboarders and advanced riders in mind, and is home to some of the biggest contests for women. There are three lines, the hardest including a big 12m tabletop jump, plus a brilliant 400m easy line. There are many rails and boxes of all sizes, and a boardercross course. New for last season was the Engadinsnow Park at Corvatsch. There are two kicker lines, two jib lines, beginner boxes, a 25m table plus a quarter-pipe.

SNOW RELIABILITY ★★★★☆
Improved by good snowmaking
This corner of the Alps has a rather dry climate, but the altitude means that any precipitation is likely to be snowy. The top runs at Corvatsch are glacial and require good snow depths to be safe. There is snowmaking in each sector, and grooming is excellent.

GETTING THERE

Air Zürich 220km/
135 miles (3hr15);
Friedrichshafen
210km/130 miles
(2hr45); Upper
Engadine airport
5km/3 miles

Rail Mainline station
in resort

UK PACKAGES

Alpine Answers, Alpine
Weekends, Carrier, Club
Med, Crystal, Crystal
Finest, Elegant Resorts,
Flexiski, Inghams,
Jeffersons, Luxury Chalet
Collection, Momentum,
Oxford Ski Co,
PowderBeds, Scott
Dunn, Ski Independence,
Ski Line, Ski Safari, Ski
Solutions, Skitracer,
Swiss Travel Service,
Switzerland Travel
Centre
Celerina Switzerland
Travel Centre

FOR EXPERTS ★★★★
Dispersed challenges
Few of the black runs are genuinely steep; those at Lagalb and Diavolezza are the most challenging. But there is good off-piste terrain, and it doesn't get tracked out. There is an excellent north-facing slope immediately above Marguns, for example. There are tough routes from Piz Nair and the Corvatsch summit. More serious expeditions can be undertaken – eg the Roseg valley from Corvatsch.

Out at Diavolezza, a very popular and spectacular off-piste glacier route goes off the back beneath Piz Bernina to Morteratsch. There's a 30-minute plod at first, then it's downhill, with splendid views. It is not difficult, but may take you close to crevasses; we wouldn't do it without a guide – and we are told you can join guided groups on the spot at 1pm. On the front of the mountain, the Gletscher chair accesses an excellent shady run down Val d'Arlas. And across at Lagalb, a route goes steeply off the back down towards La Rosa.

There are a couple of firms offering heli-drops on Fuorcla Chamuotsch, for runs back to the Engadin valley down Val Suvretta or Valletta dal Guglia.

FOR INTERMEDIATES ★★★★
Good but flattering
St Moritz is great for intermediates. Most pistes on Corviglia are very well groomed, easyish reds that could well have been classified blue – ideal cruising terrain, or monotonous, depending on your view. The Marguns bowl is more interesting, including some easy blacks and the pleasant Val Schattain run away from the lifts.

The Corvatsch-Furtschellas area is altogether more varied, interesting and challenging, as well as higher and wider. There are excellent red runs in both parts of the area, including descents to the two valley stations – particularly the Furtschellas one; do these in the morning, and return to St Moritz Bad via the lovely Hahnensee run – an easy black. The runs from the Corvatsch top station are genuinely red in parts, with fabulous views of Piz Bernina.

Diavolezza is mostly intermediate stuff, too. There is an easy open slope at the top, served by a fast quad, and a splendid long intermediate run back down under the lift. The link to Lagalb requires use of parts of a black run,

but it is of red gradient. (Plans to improve this link seem to have stalled.) Lagalb has more challenging pistes – two reds and a genuine black.

FOR BEGINNERS ★★
Not ideal
Beginners start up at Salastrains or Corviglia, or slightly out of town at Suvretta. Celerina has good, broad nursery slopes at village level and a child-friendly lift. But progression from the nursery slopes to longer runs is rather awkward – there are few blue runs without a difficult section. Nor are there any free lifts; but there are various 'selected' day, or part-day, lift passes available.

FOR BOARDERS ★★★★
Very welcoming
The terrain in St Moritz is boarder-friendly and there's a special boarder's booklet. Freeride tours are available through the ski schools and the best freeride terrain is on Diavolezza and Corvatsch, but there are several draglifts on Corvatsch. Apart from those, most of St Moritz's lifts are chairs, gondolas, cable cars and trains; beginners will enjoy the rolling blue runs, and intermediates will relish the red runs. The great thing for freeriders is that most people tend to stay on-piste in this resort, leaving terrain untracked for days after a snowfall. There's a very good and varied park on Corviglia. The World Snowboard Tour stops off at the new park on Corvatsch. Playground in Paradise is a specialist board shop.

FOR CROSS-COUNTRY ★★★★★
Excellent
This is one of the premier regions in the Alps, with 180km of trails, some floodlit, amid splendid scenery and with fairly reliable snow. A reporter recommends lessons at the Langlauf Centre near the hotel Kempinski. But the best bases are outside St Moritz.

MOUNTAIN RESTAURANTS ★★★
Some special places
Mountain restaurants are plentiful, and include some of the most glamorous in Europe. Not surprisingly, prices can be high. The piste maps have pictures and phone numbers of the restaurants. **Editors' choice** El Paradiso (833 4002), secluded at the extreme southern end of Corviglia, has it all: breathtaking views, a tastefully renovated, slightly

SCHOOLS

Swiss
t 830 0101

Suvretta
t 836 6161

Private
t 852 1885

Classes
(Swiss prices)
5 days SF330

Private lessons
From SF100 for 1hr

CHILDCARE

Salastrains
t 830 0101
Run by Swiss school

Schweizerhof hotel
t 837 0707
From age 3; 9.30-
6pm; Mon-Sat

**Palazzino – in
Badrutt's Palace Hotel**
t 837 1000
Ages 3 to 12; 9.30 to
7pm; SF50 per day for
non-residents

**Kempi Kids Club – in
Kempinski Hotel**
t 838 3838

Ski school
Ages from 5; 5 days
SF330

---

trendy interior, great service and top-notch food. Fuorcla Surlej (842 6303, though we doubt they'll take a reservation), on the Fuorcla run from the Corvatsch glacier, could not be more different: a remote refuge serving basic food very slowly. But the view from the ramshackle 'terrace' is among our top three in the world.

Worth knowing about On Corviglia, the top lift station houses several restaurants run under the umbrella title of Mathis Food Affairs, including the famously swanky Marmite. The Chasellas is also recommended, particularly for strudel. Lej de la Pêsch, behind Piz Nair, is a cosy spot, better for a snowy day than a sunny one. On the Corvatsch side, the rustic Alpetta has been recommended. Hahnensee, on the run of that name to Bad, is a splendid place to pause in the sun.

SCHOOLS AND GUIDES ★★★★★
Internal competition
There are two main schools, the 'very good' Swiss school (St Moritz) and the 'excellent' Suvretta attached to the eponymous hotel. Some other hotels have private instructors, too. The St Moritz Experience runs heli-trips.

FOR FAMILIES ★★★★★
Choose a hotel with a nursery
There's a kindergarten and children's restaurant at Salastrains, and we'd be inclined to stay up there if you can afford it. Some hotel nurseries are open to non-residents.

STAYING THERE

There is a Club Med, which is 'good value' and has its own restaurants on the main slope sectors. The tourist office can provide a list of apartments.
Hotels Over half the hotels are 4-stars and 5-stars – Switzerland's highest concentration. We were persuaded by a reader to list one of the 5-stars; the others – the all-suite Carlton, the Kulm with its Cresta Run connections, the

Gothic Badrutt's Palace, the Kempinski are the others but we don't like the compulsory jacket and tie rules.
★★★★★Suvretta House (818 363636) The 5-star for skiers, in a secluded location with its own branch of the lift system. 'Splendid views, magnificent fitness centre and pool – difficult to fault, except that jackets and ties are required after 6pm.'
★★★★Bären (830 8400) Heartily recommended in the past. 'More welcoming than the glitzier places, top-notch staff and very good food.'
★★★★Schweizerhof (837 0707) 'Relaxed' hotel in central Dorf, five minutes from the Corviglia lift. Après-ski hub.
★★★★Monopol (837 0404) Good value (for St Moritz); in centre of Dorf. Repeatedly approved by readers. Good spa facilities.
★★★Sonne (838 5959) 'Very comfortable and generous rooms' in Bad, not far from the lake.
★★★Laudinella (836 0000) In Bad. Austere decor; six different restaurants. 'Comfortable rooms, helpful staff.' Fitness facilities limited and not free.
★★★Nolda (833 0575) One of the few chalet-style buildings, close to the cable car in Bad.
At altitude The 3-star chalet-style Salastrains (830 0707) is on the lower slopes of Corviglia and has great views. Muottas Muragl (842 8232), at over 2500m on the non-skiing mountain, was fully renovated for last season and has even better views.

EATING OUT ★★★★★
Mostly chic and expensive
A lot of restaurants here are very pricey. Of course you can eat more cheaply, and that often means eating basic Italian. The hotels Laudinella and Sonne, in Bad, both have wood-fired pizza ovens, approved of by a reader (with pizzas and pasta dishes for around SF15 to 20). The Laudinella has five other restaurants too. The Cascade in Dorf seems to have moved upmarket since we were last there but

THE CRESTA RUN

No trip to St Moritz is really complete without a visit to the Cresta Run. It's the last bastion of Britishness (until recently, payment had to be made in sterling) and male chauvinism (women need an invitation from a club member). Any adult male can pay around £350 for five rides (helmet and lunch at the Kulm hotel included). You lie on a toboggan (called a 'skeleton') and hurtle head-first down a sheet ice gully from St Moritz to Celerina. Watch out for Shuttlecock corner – that's where most of the accidents happen.

↑ The Corviglia ski area, with the edge of the frozen lake in the foreground
ENGADIN ST MORITZ / SWISS-IMAGE.CH / MAX WEISS

ACTIVITIES

Indoor Swimming pool, sauna, solarium, golf range, tennis, squash, fitness centre, health spa, casino, cinema, museums

Outdoor Ice rink, curling, snowshoeing, sleigh rides, tobogganing, hang-gliding, bobsleigh rides, Cresta Run, 150km cleared paths

Phone numbers
From elsewhere in Switzerland add the prefix 081; from abroad use the prefix +41 81

TOURIST OFFICES

St Moritz
www.stmoritz.ch
Celerina
www.engadin.
stmoritz.ch/celerina/

they still do some pasta dishes for under SF30. We liked the three smooth, expensive restaurants in the Chesa Veglia (an ancient 'rustic' outpost of Badrutt's hotel) – 'excellent food, service and ambience', confirms a reporter. A top, world-class restaurant is Bumanns Chesa Pirani, a fine old house out of town in La Punt. We also liked the rustic Landhotel Meierei, by the lake.

An evening up at Muottas Muragl, between Celerina and Pontresina, offers spectacular views, a splendid sunset and dinner.

APRES-SKI ★★★☆☆
Caters for all ages
There's a big variety of après-skiing age groups here. The fur coat count is high – people come to St Moritz to be seen. For tea and good cakes head for Hanselmann's. The Roo bar outside the hotel Hauser hotel is 'a comfortable après-ski spot' with a terrace.

Bobby's Pub attracts a young crowd, as does the loud music of the Stübli, one of three bars in the hotel Schweizerhof: the others are the Mulibar, with a trendy chill-out setting and dancing, and the chic Piano Bar. The Cresta, at the Steffani, is popular with the British, while the Cava below it is louder, livelier and younger. We don't get many reports on the late-night scene, but the Diamond Club has been mentioned. The two most popular discos are Vivai (expensive), and King's at Badrutt's Palace (even

more expensive; jackets and ties required). If you need to liberate even more cash, try the casino.

OFF THE SLOPES ★★★★★
Excellent variety of pastimes
Even if you lack the bravado for the Cresta Run, there is lots to do. In midwinter the snow-covered lake provides a playground for events such as polo, horse racing and cricket, but then activities are limited as the lake starts to thaw. There's an annual 'gourmet festival', with chefs from all over the world. The Engadin museum is said to be 'very interesting'. And the shopping is simply 'incredible' if your plastic remains flexible.

There are extensive well-marked walking trails, which a reporter loved (a map is available). Muottas Muragl is a mountain set aside for not skiing – with funicular access to snowshoeing, tobogganing, an igloo village and restaurants – all with stunning panoramic views.

Some hotels run special activities, such as a curling week. Other options are hang-gliding and indoor tennis. Several reporters rave about the views from the Bernina Express train to Italy, with 'amazing bends and scenery'. Another visitor highly recommends a trip by train to Scuol for the 'fabulous spa with lots of great facilities; buy the combi pass covering the train, bus and spa entrance'. There's an 'excellent' public pool in Pontresina.

LINKED RESORT – 1730m
CELERINA

At the bottom end of the famous Cresta Run, Celerina is an appealing base if you want a quiet time – it is unpretentious and villagey, but lacks a central focus (and has very few shops). It has good access to the Corviglia/Marguns sector – a gondola to Marguns. It spreads quite widely, with a lot of second homes, many owned by Italians (the upper part is known as Piccolo Milano). There are some appealing small hotels – reporters like Chesa Rosatsch (837 0101) – and a couple of bigger 4-stars. The modern Inn Lodge (834 4795) has rooms and dormitories for the budget-conscious. The food at the Chesa Rosatsch attracts non-resident diners and has been recommended. The Freestyle School (opened in 2010) focuses on park practice.

COEUR DU VALAIS

Val d'Anniviers

Exceptionally cute, unspoiled villages beneath high, snow-sure slopes. Sounds perfect? Well, there are some drawbacks ...

TOP 10 RATINGS	
Extent	★★
Fast lifts	★
Queues	★★★★
Snow	★★★★
Expert	★★★★
Intermediate	★★★
Beginner	★★★
Charm	★★★★★
Convenience	★★
Scenery	★★★★

RPI	100
lift pass	£190
ski hire	£105
lessons	£75
food & drink	£210
total	£580

NEWS

2010/11: At Zinal, the Sorebois hut was revamped downstairs to offer a buffet-style dining area and kids' play zone.

516

- ➕ Charming unspoiled villages
- ➕ Excellent, extensive off-piste
- ➕ Reliable snow-cover
- ➕ No crowds, few queues
- ➕ Four varied ski areas offering good intermediate cruising, but ...

- ➖ Each area has very limited pistes
- ➖ Lots of slow chairs and draglifts
- ➖ Very quiet villages; dead, even
- ➖ Almost entirely open slopes
- ➖ Timetabled buses or ideally a car needed to get between the areas; and the roads are not the best.

In some ways, Val d'Anniviers is in a bit of a time warp. There is plenty of modern accommodation, and some modern lifts in key spots, but most of the villages have unspoilt rustic cores, and you spend a lot of time riding draglifts. Approach the area with the right attitude and you'll probably find it all quite a refreshing change from high-pressure resorts with high-speed everything.

The Val d'Anniviers runs almost due south from the huge trench of the Valais at Sierre. The resort villages are all at least 1000m above Sierre, and the road up has in places been carved out of sheer rock faces. This may help to explain why the valley has been rather neglected by the international travel trade.

The main villages present plenty of chocolate-box photo opportunities, with lots of old wooden houses and barns, narrow paths and lanes, and few shops. Most of the lodging is in more modern, less photogenic areas spreading around these old village cores, but the development is generally tasteful and low-rise, and the atmosphere relaxed.

There are five resort villages. On the morning-sun side of the valley, the slopes of Zinal are linked to those of Grimentz by a long, isolated black run. Vercorin is a smaller separate area, with a lift direct from the Valais bottom. On the afternoon-sun side, the slopes of Chandolin and St-Luc are properly linked at high and low altitude, and are marketed as one.

Except at Vercorin, nearly all the slopes are above the treeline and there's a lot of skiing above 2400m, which usually means good snow. All of the individual areas are small, but they add up to a decent amount.

Buses (free with a lift pass) link the villages and lift bases – the little town of Vissoie is the hub, where you change services. You need to plan times carefully, but a 2011 reporter happily used them to get around.

1650m / 2000m

ST-LUC / CHANDOLIN

These are the sunniest of the main ski resort villages and their slopes are well linked to form the biggest ski area. St-Luc also has the attraction of a fabulous, characterful old hotel.
A funicular goes up from the edge of St-Luc and a high-speed chair from the edge of Chandolin. Both are served by the free ski-buses. The 65km of slopes face west to south-west, so the snow suffers from the sun. Apart from Chandolin's fast quad, there is only one other chair – the other 11 lifts are all drags.

The pistes suit beginners and intermediates best; there are no black runs, though there are three short itinerary routes – among them is one that we reckon is the steepest marked run in the Alps – and a gnarly freeride area where competitions are held. There are some testing reds, but in general the slopes are gentle, easy cruising territory. A highlight is the long, easy red run from Bella Tola at 3000m away from all the lifts down to the Tipi bar and ski-bus stop – a great way to end the day. There's a good beginner area and a terrain park near the top of the St-Luc funicular.

There are some good mountain restaurants with fine views. Above Chandolin the tiny Illhorn has a limited menu but a cosy panelled room (and fab pear tart); the Tsapé is a smart, stark place, high-up, with 'good local cuisine'; above St-Luc, the Bella Tola is a traditional, table-service hut.

alpine answers co.uk

GREAT SKI HOLIDAYS SINCE 1992

020 7801 1080

ABTA & ATOL PROTECTED

Both Chandolin and St-Luc are fairly spread out. But St-Luc has a cute, compact old centre with a small outdoor après-ski bar. The 4-star hotel Bella Tola (475 1444) is just a few strides from here. Built in 1859, it has been beautifully renovated by its current owners, with a fine spa, great sunny terrace, and good restaurant serving notably 'excellent fish dishes'.

1670m
ZINAL

This small village near the head of the valley doesn't have the charm of the other villages. It has a small area of slopes with stunning views of high peaks including the Matterhorn.
A modern cable car goes to Sorebois at 2440m, the hub of the ski area. Most of the slopes face roughly east and keep their snow well.

The runs are mainly short (some only 200m or 300m vertical) but include some good reds – our favourites are those from Combe Durand at the edge of the ski area, served by a steepish draglift that also accesses a freeride area. The one fast chairlift serves wide and gentle blue runs, ideal for novices. The two short black runs are really of red steepness. There is a longer red run (with a black variant on the lower part) back to the village. And there's great off-piste in bowls between the pistes. From the top of the area, Piste du Chamois is a real highlight – a long, easy black run down a shady deserted bowl with lots of accessible off-piste, ending with a woodland path to Grimentz.

Zinal is popular with families and there's a good beginner area and children's snow garden.

There are only two huts. On weekends and holidays the Sorebois self-service now offers an 'all you can eat' buffet in a newly revamped area downstairs; 'good quality, with hot/ cold food and desserts'.

Zinal has a handful of hotels. The central 2-star Pointe de Zinal (475 1164) does excellent food.

1570m
GRIMENTZ

Grimentz has a richly deserved reputation for its extensive off-piste. And it has a small area of varied pistes above its very cute old village.
The village is spread out on quite a steep slope and a lot of new building is going on, and here (more than in the other villages) there is a separation between the cute old centre – lots of tiny old barns and narrow paths – and the skiers' accommodation. Much of this is conveniently close to the gondola up to Bendolla at 2130m – but some is less conveniently placed on the opposite side of the old village.

Bendolla has a good, roped-off beginner area, and above it are two main sectors. On the right as you look up are easy blue and red runs. On the left are steeper and quieter runs, including two blacks, one of which goes from the top to almost the bottom of the mountain (1300m vertical) and is interestingly varied. The main run to the village is quite

Val d'Anniviers

517

Interactive resort shortlist builder at **www.wtss.co.uk**

Combe Durand

Corne de Sorebois
2895m

2440m

ZINAL

2880m

Zinal
1670m/5,48oft

Piste du Chamois

Bella Tola
3000m/
9,840ft

Mottec

GRIMENTZ

2770m

Grimentz
1570m/5,15oft

2130m

Roc d'Orziva
2855m

247om

St-Jean

Mt Major
2375m

Tignousa
2180m

St-Luc
1650m/5,410ft

ST LUC-CHANDOLIN

Vissoie

Illhorn
2600m

VERCORIN

Chandolin
2000m/6,560ft

Vercorin
1340m/4,400ft

Chalais

To
Geneva
→

🚠 gondola
🚡 cable car
🚞 railway/funicular
🚦 fast chairlift
Slow chairs & drags
have no symbol

Sierre
560m/1,84oft

Phone numbers
From elsewhere in Switzerland add the prefix 0848 (for Coeur du Valais) and 027 (for everywhere else); from abroad use the prefix +41 and omit the initial '0'

TOURIST OFFICES

Val d'Anniviers
www.sierre-anniviers.ch
Grimentz
www.grimentz.ch
St-Luc
www.saint-luc.ch
Vercorin
www.vercorin.ch
Zinal
www.zinal.ch
Chandolin
www.chandolin.ch
Coeur du Valais
www.coeurduvalais.ch

WENDY-JANE KING

Bendolla, at the top of the Grimentz gondola, has good beginner and kids' facilities ↓

steep, but you can ride the gondola.

The real attraction for experts is the extensive off-piste. We did a great run with a guide off the back of Roc d'Orzival: a huge, ski-anywhere bowl that goes on for hundreds of turns before dropping into an area of widely spaced trees and a long run-out.

The International ski school has received very positive past reports.

The functional main restaurant is mainly self-service, with a small table-service section that serves good food. Readers favour the more traditional Etable du Marais below Grands Plans ('fantastic, huge rösti'). We've had good pasta at the Orzival.

As the lifts close, Chez Florioz on the piste just above the village is the place for a drink – very welcoming host. The best restaurants are probably those in the main hotels. But we have also enjoyed an excellent meal at Arlequin (a pizzeria). Bar le Country is a lively sports bar.

We have had comfortable stays and good food at the two 3-star hotels – the Alpina (476 1616) almost opposite the gondola and the less convenient Cristal (475 3291).

UK tour operator Mountain Heaven's Cole Ridge catered chalet is on the slopes, with outdoor hot tub, sauna and stunning views. They also have some smart, central self-catered chalet-apartments. Grimentz Location has apartments and chalets to rent.

1340m
VERCORIN
The smallest area of slopes, and not so easily reached from other resorts.
The pretty village of Vercorin, perched on a shelf overlooking the Rhône valley, is reached by a winding road or by a cable car from just outside Sierre. The slopes suit intermediates best.

Interactive resort shortlist builder at **www.wtss.co.uk**

Verbier

Big, chalet-style resort that attracts powder hounds from all over the world – and big-spending night owls from Geneva

RATINGS

The mountains

Extent	★★★★★
Fast lifts	★★★★
Queues	★★★
Terrain p'ks	★★★
Snow	★★★
Expert	★★★★★
Intermediate	★★★
Beginner	★★
Boarder	★★★
X-country	★
Restaurants	★★★
Schools	★★★★★
Families	★★★

The resort

Charm	★★★
Convenience	★★
Scenery	★★★★
Eating out	★★★★
Après-ski	★★★★★
Off-slope	★★★

RPI	135
lift pass	£270
ski hire	£145
lessons	£125
food & drink	£240
total	**£780**

NEWS

2011/12: There are plans for a new fast six-seat chair (Mayentzet) to replace two successive slow chairs from just above the top of the nursery slopes to Les Ruinettes. More snowmaking is planned, and a new restaurant is due to be built at La Chaux. A planned new lift from Les Esserts to Savoleyres has been postponed to 2012/13.

2010/11: The Mont-Fort cable car was upgraded with new panoramic cabins, but the lift capacity remains the same. The Médran lift station was renovated and new facilities added.

+ Extensive, challenging slopes with a lot of off-piste and long bump runs

+ Upper slopes offer a real high-mountain feel, plus great views

+ Sizeable, animated village in a sunny, panoramic setting

+ Lively, varied nightlife

+ Much improved lift system, piste grooming and signposting, but...

– Piste map and piste naming still have a long way to go

– Some overcrowded pistes and areas

– The 4 Valleys network is much less wonderful than it looks on paper

– Sunny lower slopes will always be a problem, even with snowmaking

– Some long walks/rides to lifts

– Expensive bars and restaurants

For serious off-piste routes and for mogul fields, Verbier is one of the world's cult resorts. For vibrant nightlife, too, it is difficult to beat. At first, with its claimed 410km of pistes, Verbier also seems to rank alongside the French mega-networks as a dream resort for keen piste skiers who like to ski for a week without doing the same run twice. But if the French 3 Vallées floats your boat, you may be sorely disappointed by the Swiss 4 Vallées. The network is an inconveniently sprawling affair, with lots of tedious links.

Verbier's local pistes leave a lot to be desired, too: in comparison with the slopes of somewhere like Courchevel, they are distinctly limited. A good intermediate skier could cover them in a day. This is partly because many of the runs that could and should be black pistes are classified as unpatrolled itinéraires – something that we have been moaning about for years.

THE RESORT

Verbier enjoys an impressive setting on a wide, sunny balcony facing spectacular peaks. It's a fashionable, informal, very lively place that teems with cosmopolitan visitors. Most are younger than visitors to other big Swiss resorts.

The resort is at one end of a long, strung-out series of interconnected slopes, optimistically branded the 4 Valleys and linking Verbier to Nendaz, Veysonnaz, Thyon and other resorts. These other resorts have their own pros and cons. All are much less lively in the evening than Verbier, appreciably cheaper places to stay, and some are more sensible bases for those who plan to stick to pistes rather than venture off-piste – the Veysonnaz-Thyon sector, in particular, is much more intermediate-friendly than Verbier. As bases for exploration of the whole 4 Valleys, only tiny Siviez is much of an advance on Verbier. You can also stay down in the valley village of Le Châble, which has a gondola up to Verbier and on into the slopes. Across the valley, Bruson is

more attractive as a place to visit for a day than to stay in. For more on these alternatives, see end of the chapter.

Chamonix and Champéry are within reach by car. But a car can be a bit of a nuisance in Verbier itself. Parking is tightly controlled; your chalet or hotel may not have enough space for all guests' cars, which means a hike from the free parking at the sports centre or paying for garage space.

Danni Sports was praised by a 2011 reporter: 'Extremely helpful and friendly, good choice of equipment for hire, and they do a half-price ski-service happy hour mid-week.'

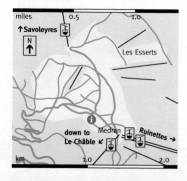

KEY FACTS

Resort	1500m
	4,920ft

4 Valleys area	
Slopes	1500-3330m
	4,920-10,930ft
Lifts	89
Pistes	410km
	255 miles
Blue	39%
Red	44%
Black	17%
Snowmaking	11%

Verbier, Bruson and Tzoumaz/Savoleyres sectors only (covered by Verbier pass)	
Slopes	1500-3025m
	4,920-9,920ft
Lifts	39
Pistes	203km
	126 miles
Blue	49%
Red	27%
Black	24%
Snowmaking	13%

VERBIER ST-BERNARD / FRANÇOIS PERRAUDIN

Challenging and extensive off-piste – that's Verbier's raison d'être ↓

VILLAGE CHARM ★★★★★
Busy upmarket chalet town
The resort is an amorphous sprawl of chalet-style buildings. Most of the shops and hotels (but not chalets) are set around the Place Centrale and along the sloping streets stretching both down the hill and up it to the main lift station at Médran, 500m away. At close of play this street, in particular, is buzzing with après-ski activity. These central areas get unpleasantly packed with cars at busy times, especially weekends, which rather detracts from the ambience.

CONVENIENCE ★★★★★
Pick your spot
It's a sprawling resort where most people suffer some inconvenience. But most people just get used to using the 'OK' free buses, which run efficiently on several routes until 8pm. Some areas have quite an infrequent service.

The Médran lift station is a walkable distance from the Place Centrale, so staying between the two has attractions. If nightlife is not a priority, staying somewhere near the upper (north-east) fringes of the village may mean that you can almost ski to your door – plus there is a piste linking the upper nursery slopes to the one in the middle of the village. Skiing from the door is less likely. More chalets are built each year, with many newer properties inconveniently situated along the road to the lift base for the secondary Savoleyres area, about 1.5km from Médran.

SCENERY ★★★★★
A circle of Alpine peaks
Verbier is surrounded by stunning Alpine scenery; from the top of Mont-Fort there are impressive views in all directions, including Mont Blanc to the west and the Matterhorn to the east.

THE MOUNTAINS

Essentially this is high-mountain terrain. There are wooded slopes directly above the village, but the runs here are basically just a way home at the end of the day. There is more sheltered skiing in other sectors – particularly above Veysonnaz.

The piste signposting has been improved and the piste map now has some (but not all) runs named – but in type too small to read. What's more, the piste names are still not posted on the mountain. So it's less of a shambles than it was, but still a shambles. And readers still complain: 'poorly signed', 'spent ages looking at the map with print too small to read', 'need more big maps at top of runs' and 'map fails to adequately show up and down' are recent reports.

EXTENT OF THE SLOPES ★★★★★
Very spread out
Savoleyres is a small area effectively isolated from the major network, reached by a gondola from the north-west end of the village. This area is underrated and generally underused. A new access gondola from the central nursery slopes is planned, but not

until 2012/13. It has open, sunny slopes on the front side, and long, pleasantly wooded, shadier runs on the back. You can take a catwalk across from Savoleyres to the foot of Verbier's main slopes.

These are served by lifts from Médran, at the opposite end of the village. Two gondolas rise to Les Ruinettes and then a gondola and chairlift continue on to **Les Attelas**. From Les Attelas a small cable car goes up to Mont-Gelé, for steep off-

piste runs only. Heading down instead, you can go back westwards to Les Ruinettes, south to La Chaux or north to Lac des Vaux. From Lac des Vaux chairs go to Les Attelas and to Chassoure, the top of a wide, steep and shady off-piste mogul field going down to **Tortin**, with a gondola back.

You can also ride a chondola from Les Ruinettes to the sunny, easy slopes of La Chaux. At the bottom of these slopes a jumbo cable car goes up to **Col des Gentianes** and the

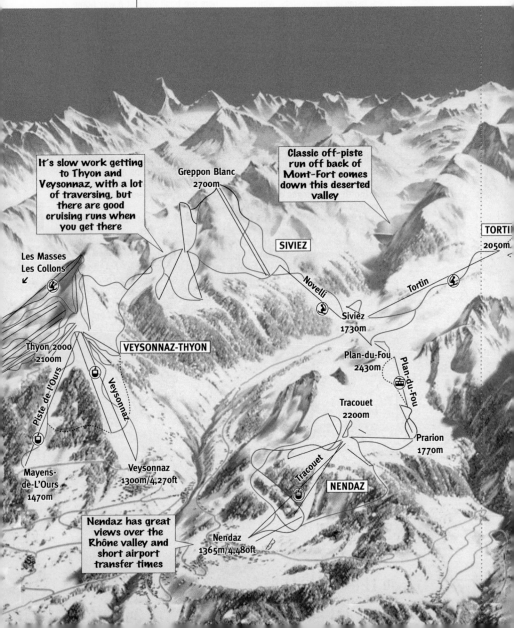

It's slow work getting to Thyon and Veysonnaz, with a lot of traversing, but there are good cruising runs when you get there

Classic off-piste run off back of Mont-Fort comes down this deserted valley

Greppon Blanc
2700m

SIVIEZ

TORTI
2050m

Les Masses
Les Collons

Novelli

Tortin

Siviez
1730m

Thyon 2000
2100m

VEYSONNAZ-THYON

Plan-du-Fou
2430m

Plan-du-Fou

Piste de l'Ours

Veysonnaz

Tracouet
2200m

Prarion
1770m

Mayens-de-L'Ours
147om

Veysonnaz
1300m/4,27oft

Tracouet

NENDAZ

Nendaz has great views over the Rhône valley and short airport transfer times

Nendaz
1365m/4,48oft

glacier area. The lovely, often quiet, red run back down to La Chaux is one of our favourites. A second, much smaller cable car (now with new panoramic cabins) goes up from Gentianes to the **Mont-Fort** glacier. From the top, there's only a long, steep black run back down. From Gentianes you can head down on another off-piste route to Tortin; the whole north-facing run from the top to Tortin is almost 1300m vertical. A cable car returns to Col des Gentianes.

Below Tortin is the gateway to the rest of the 4 Valleys, **Siviez**. From here, a ridiculously outdated chair goes off into the long, thin **Nendaz** sector. A fast quad heads the other way towards **Veysonnaz-Thyon**, via a couple of drags and a lot of catwalks.

Allow plenty of time to get to and from these remote corners – the taxi-rides home are expensive.

The slopes of **Bruson**, across the valley from Verbier, are described briefly at the end of this chapter.

MONT-FORT
3330m/10,930ft

Mont-Fort

The dotted lines going down the Gentianes and Chassoure lifts are itinéraires, officially unpatrolled. But most good skiers treat them as pistes, which is what they should be

Col des Gentianes
2950m

Lovely red run that is often quiet

Col des Gentianes

Mont-Gelé
3025m

3 Jumbo

Mont-Gelé

La Chaux
2260m

Chassoure
2740m

LES ATTELAS

TORTIN
2050m

Chassoure

L. des Vaux I   2730m

Attelas

Chaux Express

Lac des Vaux
2545m

Funispace

Bruson

Col des Mines
2320m

LES RUINETTES   2200m

Our favourite run in Verbier: the Vallon d'Arby itinéraire

Chez Dany

Mayentzet

Le Châble

Vallon d'Arby

Médran I & II

Excellent and rather neglected intermediate runs, especially on the back

SAVOLEYRES

Verbier
1500m/4,920ft

Taillay

Savoleyres

Savoleyres
2355m

○ gondola
● cable car
⊗ chondola
Ⓢ fast chairlift
Slow chairs & drags have no symbol

La Tzoumaz

Savoleyres

La Tzoumaz
1500m/4,920ft

OFF-PISTE FOR ALL

Verbier has some of the best, most extensive and most varied off-piste in the world, and major freeride competitions are held there every year. Here, we pick out just a few of the off-piste runs on offer. See 'For experts' for the status of itinéraires; for the other runs here you should hire a guide.

The Col des Mines and Vallon d'Arby itinéraires, accessible from Lac des Vaux, are relatively easy, though there may be some unnerving moments on the traverse to the point where they split. The first is a long, open slope back to Verbier and the latter a very beautiful run in a steep-sided valley down to La Tzoumaz and the Savoleyres lifts. Further afield, the long Eteygeon itinéraire from Greppon Blanc above Siviez is 'wonderfully varied and should not be missed', says a reporter; it ends up on the road and you catch a bus back to Les Masses (see end of chapter).

Stairway to Heaven is usually quiet (we were the only people on it on a March visit) and its snow is kept in good condition by the lack of crowds and its shady orientation. It starts a short ski, pole and steep climb from Col des Gentianes. Then you drop over the ridge into a deserted valley, and it's a long, relatively easy ski down to Tortin, pretty much parallel to the Gentianes itinéraire.

The Mont-Gelé cable car offers some of the most amazing terrain accessible anywhere by lift, with long runs down to Siviez on steep but open slopes, before a scenic traverse and schuss along the valley. Or go down the opposite side of the mountain through the steep rock face towards Lac des Vaux (not a route for the faint hearted). The many couloirs accessible from Attelas can also be fantastic. There are serious adventures to be had off the back of Mont-Fort – we loved it (except for the long walk out past Lac de Cleuson); it's a vast bowl and we found fresh powder, even though it hadn't snowed for days; you end up at Siviez.

FAST LIFTS ★★★★
Locally fine

The main access lifts are gondolas and chairs. Further afield, more upgrades are needed to improve links throughout the 4 Valleys (especially between Siviez and Veysonnaz-Thyon, where a 2011 reporter found a key draglift out of action necessitating 'a steep 50m walk up to the piste').

QUEUES ★★★
Not the problem they were

Queues have been greatly eased by investment in powerful new lifts and have barely been a problem for reporters over the past couple of years. There may be queues at Médran if Sunday visitors fill the gondola from Le Châble, but they shift quickly.

Queues still occur for outdated lifts in the outlying 4 Valleys resorts, and the quad at Siviez gets busy at peak times and if the weather is poor. Savoleyres is generally queue-free.

TERRAIN PARKS ★★★
Expert and beginner options

The Swatch Snowpark, Verbier's main freestyle area, is at La Chaux. It has four separate lines: soft, medium, hard and rail. Features are varied with boxes and rails of all types and a skate-style pyramid. To try out new moves, hit the giant airbag jump, complete with a video screen for watching your performance. There is

also a boardercross and a chill-out zone with deckchairs, DJs and BBQ. Freestyle coaching (check www. snowschool.ch) is available. Helmets are mandatory.

SNOW RELIABILITY ★★★
Improved snowmaking

The slopes of the Mont-Fort glacier always have good snow. The runs to Tortin are normally snow-sure, too. But nearly all of this is steep and mogulled, and much of it is formally off-piste. Most of Verbier's main local slopes face south or west and are below 2500m – so they can be in poor condition at times. Snowmaking covers the whole main run down from Les Attelas to Médran. La Chaux, the nursery slopes and some of the Savoleyres sector are also well-served. At Veysonnaz-Thyon snowmaking now covers 80% of the area. We have been very impressed with its use on the runs down to Mayens-de-L'Ours and to Veysonnaz. Piste grooming is good throughout the 4 Valleys.

FOR EXPERTS ★★★★★
The main attraction

Verbier has some superb tough slopes, many of them off-piste and needing a guide – see feature panel above. There are few conventional black pistes; most of the runs that might have this designation are now defined as itinéraires – which means they are

LIFT PASSES

4 Valleys/Mont-Fort

Prices in SF

Age	1-day	6-day
under 14	34	174
14 to 19	54	278
20 to 64	67	348
over 65	54	278

Free under 6; over 77
Beginner limited pass

Notes
Covers all lifts and ski-buses in Verbier, Mont-Fort, Bruson, La Tzoumaz, Nendaz, Veysonnaz and Thyon; part-day passes; family reductions

Alternative passes
Verbier only; La Tzoumaz/Savoleyres only; Bruson only

GETTING THERE

Air Geneva
160km/100 miles
(2hr15)

Rail Le Châble (7km/
4 miles); regular
buses to resort or
gondola

'marked, not maintained, not controlled'. But they are closed if unsafe or if snow-cover is insufficient. We'd like to see them given official black piste status, so you know clearly where you stand. The blacks that do exist are mostly indistinguishable from nearby reds. The front face of Mont-Fort is an exception: a long mogul field, with a choice of gradient from steep to intimidatingly steep. The World Cup run (Piste de l'Ours) at Veysonnaz is a steepish, often icy red, ideal for really speeding down when in good nick. The two most popular itinéraires to Tortin are both excellent in their different ways. The one from Chassoure starts with a rocky traverse at the top and is then normally one huge, steep, wide mogul field. The north-facing one from Gentianes is longer, less steep, but feels much more of an adventure (keep left for shallower slopes and better snow).

FOR INTERMEDIATES ★★★★★
Hit Savoleyres – or Veysonnaz

Many mileage-hungry intermediates find Verbier disappointing. The intermediate slopes in the main area are concentrated between Les Attelas and the village, above and below Les Ruinettes, plus the little bowl at Lac des Vaux and the sunny slopes at La Chaux. This is all excellent and varied intermediate territory, but there isn't much of it; to put it in perspective, this whole area is no bigger than the tiny slopes of Alpbach, and it is used by the bulk of the visitors staying in one of Switzerland's largest resorts. So it is often crowded, especially the otherwise wonderful sweeping red

from Les Attelas to Les Ruinettes. There is excellent easy blue run skiing at La Chaux, including a 'slow skiing' piste. Getting back from La Chaux to Les Ruinettes is easy: as well as the chondola, there is a short piste from the top of the lift avoiding the steepest section down.

The under-used Savoleyres area has good intermediate pistes, usually better snow and fewer people. It is also a good hill for mixed abilities, with variations of many runs. There is a blue run linking this sector to the Médran lift base, but the way down to that link from the top is not easy.

The Veysonnaz-Thyon and Nendaz sectors are worth exploring (those not willing to take on the itinéraires can ride the lifts down).

FOR BEGINNERS ★★★★★
OK but not ideal

There are sunny nursery slopes close to the middle of the village and at Les Esserts, at the top of it. These are fine provided they have snow, and they are well-equipped with snowmaking. Day passes covering these two areas cost SF29 in 2010/11 (free for children). For progression, a local Verbier pass is available. There are easy blues at La Chaux and on the back of Savoleyres.

FOR BOARDERS ★★★★★
Extreme freeride heaven

Verbier has become synonymous with extreme snowboarding and is generally seen as a freeriders' resort, with powder, cliffs, natural hits and trees all easily accessible. Not surprisingly, it is on the Freeride world tour (see www. freerideworldtour.com). For years the

SCHOOLS

Swiss
t 775 3363

Fantastique
t 771 4141

Adrenaline
t 771 7459

Altitude
t 771 6006

New Generation
t 771 1181 /
+33 479 010318

European Snowsport
t 771 6222

Powder Extreme
t 479 8771
020 8123 9483 (UK)

Warren Smith Ski Academy
t 01525 374757 (UK)

Classes
(Swiss prices)
6 half days SF280

Private lessons
From SF170 for 2hr
for 1 or 2 people

GUIDES

Bureau des guides
t 775 3370

Olivier Roduit
t 771 5317

Bec des Rosses has been home to Verbier Extreme – the most high-profile event of its kind. There is a lot of steep and challenging terrain to be explored with a guide, but the pistes and itinéraires will provide most riders with plenty to think about. Chairlifts and gondolas serve the main area, with no drags. The area is far from ideal for beginners and timid intermediates, who should stick to the lower blue runs and the Savoleyres area, but there are several draglifts there. There is a good terrain park.

FOR CROSS-COUNTRY ★☆☆☆☆
Little on offer
There's a 4km loop in Verbier, 10km at Les Ruinettes-La Chaux and 8km down the valley in Champsec and Lourtier.

MOUNTAIN RESTAURANTS ★★★☆☆
Surprisingly uninspiring
There are too few huts so they get too crowded. The standard of food and service gets mixed reviews.
Editors' choice In the main area, the rustic Chez Dany (771 2524) – aka Restaurant de Clambin – is a classic old chalet on the itinéraire on the southern fringe of the area.
Worth knowing about Some reader favourites are far-flung. One of the most frequently recommended is the Chottes between Siviez and Veysonnaz-Thyon ('continues to please, both inside and out, good pasta'). At Les Collons the Cambuse has 'excellent food and is not too expensive'. At Siviez, Chez Odette has been recommended.

Closer to home, past reporters have favoured the rustic Marmotte and the Namasté on Savoleyres and the Sonalon, on the fringe of the village (good views and French cuisine), but we lack recent reports.

The huge self-service at the top of Savoleyres has 'good value' Italian and

traditional dishes. The Croix de Coeur is an attractive 15-sided building with great views from the terrace, but a limited menu. The Poste hotel by the Tzoumaz chair takes some beating for value and lack of crowds.

Back in the main sector, the restaurants at Les Ruinettes were smartened up three years ago with new terraces and menus – the Cristal offers fine dining under the former chef of Chalet d'Adrien but the self-service section was 'poor'. The Olympique at Les Attelas includes a good table-service restaurant. The Cabane Mont-Fort is a proper mountain refuge off the run to La Chaux from Col des Gentianes – and gets packed. Chalet Carlsberg has a good position at La Combe and impressed us with fast and efficient service. Carrefour, near the top of the nursery slopes, does 'great food, worth a visit'. Mayens, accessible from both the main Verbier slopes and the Col des Mines has 'great views and reasonable prices'. The baguette kiosk at the bottom of Médran 'holds its own against Pret a Manger'.

SCHOOLS AND GUIDES ★★★★★
Good reports
There's no shortage of schools to choose between. New Generation, well established and a reader favourite in several top French resorts, has its first Swiss branch in Verbier. We were very impressed with our mountain guide from Adrenaline and it has had good reviews for its private lessons. We have had good reports of Altitude: 'excellent for children'; 'booked five 3hr off-piste lessons and were the only two in the group'. The Swiss School has been recommended – 'good fun, valuable tuition'. British instructor Warren Smith runs his Ski Academy here and Powder Extreme specialises in off-piste. We have skied with both

Verbier

Interactive resort shortlist builder at www.wtss.co.uk

CHILDCARE

Schtroumpfs
t 771 6585
Ages 3mnth to 3yr;
8.30 to 5.30

Kids Club
t 775 3363
From age 3; 9am-4.30

Ski school
Takes children aged 4
to 13 (6 half days
SF280)

outfits and thought them good. A 2010/11 customer on Warren Smith's course felt misled by the pre-course marketing but found her skiing 'more relaxed and fluent' after the course.

FOR FAMILIES ★★★
Good for childcare

The nursery slopes are central, and the Swiss school's facilities are good. There are considerable reductions on the lift pass price for families too. The possibility of leaving very young babies at the Schtroumpfs nursery is valuable. In the past, a visitor has recommended the nanny services provided by Chalet Services Verbier.

STAYING THERE

There are surprisingly few apartments and B&Bs, though there are inexpensive B&Bs in Le Châble. Hotels are pricey for their gradings.

Chalets Verbier is the chalet-party capital of Switzerland, with some very luxurious places. Ski Verbier has an impressive portfolio at the top of the market. Ski Total has two chalet hotels and three chalets – all very smart and with facilities such as pool, sauna, steam. Skiworld has a large central chalet with jacuzzi and sauna. Inghams has five chalets (two close to the Médran lift station) and a chalet-hotel in the main square. Crystal Finest has two smart chalet-apartments in a new building near Médran.

Hotels There is a 5-star, five 4-stars, nine 3-stars and a few simpler places.

*****Chalet d'Adrien (771 6200) Relais & Chateaux. A beautifully furnished low-rise 29-room chalet, with top-notch cooking. In a peaceful setting next to the Savoleyres lift, with great views. Neat spa/gym/pool.

****Nevaï (775 4000) Modern, minimalist, trendy, next to Farm Club (same ownership). Après-ski bar.

****Montpelier (771 6131) Very comfortable, but out of town (free courtesy bus). Pool.

****Vanessa (775 2800) Central, with spacious apartments as well as rooms; all were refurbished for 2009/10.

***Rotonde (771 6525) Much cheaper; well positioned between centre and Médran; some budget rooms.

***Poste (771 6681) Midway between centre and Médran; pool. Some rooms small. Recommended by a reporter for its 'pleasant atmosphere'.

***Farinet (771 6626) Central, British-owned, with a focal après-ski bar.

***Au Vieux Valais (775 3520) Charming old chalet with friendly service at entrance to resort. We have stayed there recently and enjoyed it.

Apartments There are surprisingly few on the UK market. Ski Expectations has a conveniently-located, Swiss-owned 4-bedroom chalet and studio apartment. Ski Verbier has some nice-looking places.

EATING OUT ★★★★
Plenty of choice

There is a wide range of restaurants; many are listed in a free pocket guide, which would be much more useful if it gave some clues about price.

The 5-star Chalet d'Adrien is one of the best gourmet places in town (one Michelin star). We had an excellent meal in the Nevaï hotel. King's (under the same ownership) is another of our favourites – innovative food in a stylish, club-like setting. We've also had good meals in the stylish, 'quiet and sophisticated'

Ski a high altitude resort with low prices – see p177

Millénium. The traditional, small Ecurie does 'excellent steaks'. The Rouge Restaurant and Club specialises in fish and local dishes.

For Swiss specialities, try the Relais des Neiges ('quieter than many; excellent food'), the Caveau, Vieux Verbier by the Médran lifts or Esserts by the nursery slopes. The ever-popular Fer à Cheval does reasonably priced pizza and other simple dishes. Downstairs in the Pub Mont-Fort you can get good value gastropub food. The 'hanging meat' has to be tried at Al Capone's, out near the Savoleyres gondola – also known for its pizzas; we had excellent pizzas at Borsalino, near the centre of town.

You can be ferried by snowmobile up to Clambin or the Marmotte for a meal, followed by a torchlit descent.

APRES-SKI ★★★★★
Throbbing but expensive
On the slopes, popular stops include the Rocks bar at Ruinettes, either of the tents of 1936 or the Chalet Carlsberg (with a pay-as-you-soak hot tub). In town, the Offshore Cafe at Médran is ever-popular for people-watching, milk shakes and cakes. The Big Ben pub is lively. The Nevaï hotel has live music on its terraces and the Rouge at the bottom of the golf course has a popular sun deck.

Then if you're young, loud and British, it's on to the Pub Mont-Fort – there's a widescreen TV for live sport. The Nelson and Fer à Cheval are popular with locals. The Farinet has won awards for its après-ski and rocks to live bands regularly ('beer, band and bop were great'). Or you can sip cocktails in its lounge bar next door.

After dinner the Pub Mont-Fort is again popular (the shots bar in the cellar is worth a visit). Crock No Name is a cool 'sophisticated' cocktail bar with a blues band or a DJ. T-Bar shows

live rugby and football. King's is a quiet candlelit cellar bar with 60s decor – 'hip crowd, good music'. New Club is a sophisticated piano bar, with comfortable seating and a more discerning clientele. The Farm Club is seriously expensive – on Friday and Saturday packed with rich Swiss paying SF220 for bottles of spirits.

The Coco Club, Casbah and Coup d'Etat are nightclubs.

OFF THE SLOPES ★★★☆☆
A few things to do
Verbier has an excellent sports centre (with pool, saunas, hot tubs), dog sledding between Les Ruinettes and La Chaux and some nice walks. Montreux is an enjoyable train excursion from Le Châble, and Martigny is worth a visit for the Roman remains and art gallery. Reporters have recommended the spa complex at Lavey-les-Bains. Various mountain restaurants are accessible to pedestrians – a walker's pass covers most of the local lifts. There are toboggan runs on Savoleyres.

LINKED RESORT – 1365m
NENDAZ

Nendaz is little known in Britain but is a major resort, with over 17,000 beds (practically all in apartments). Most of the resort is modern, built in traditional chalet style and has great views across the Rhône valley.

It's a sizeable and sprawling place and the centre is busy with traffic. The local bus services are reliable, but get oversubscribed at peak times. There are 100km of walks, an ice rink, fitness centre, climbing wall, squash courts.

A 12-person gondola takes you to the top of the local slopes at Tracouet. This is a splendid, sunny little shelf with gentle slopes and long, shady red and blue runs back down to Nendaz. But getting to and from the rest of the 4 Valleys can be a slow business and key links on the way have no snow-making and can be closed. Getting back involves taking an itinéraire (or riding a cable car down) followed by a black run – tricky for intermediates. Many people prefer to drive/bus to Siviez, and start/finish skiing there.

UK chalet company Ted Bentley has four chalets, all with outdoor hot tubs. There are a couple of small 3-star hotels – the 'basic but pleasant' Mont-Fort (288 2616) is 150m from the lifts

ACTIVITIES

Indoor Sports centre (swimming pools, ice rink, curling, squash, sauna, solarium, steam bath, hot tub), cinema, museums, galleries

Outdoor 25km of cleared walking paths, paragliding, snowshoeing, ice climbing, dog sledding, tobogganing

Verbier is the chalet capital of Switzerland, with lots of very smart places to stay ➜

Interactive resort shortlist builder at **www.wtss.co.uk**

Alpine Answers, Alpine Weekends, Belvedere Travel, Bramble Ski, Carrier, Chalet Group, Chalets Unlimited, Crystal, Crystal Finest, Elegant Resorts, Erna Low, First Choice, Flexiski, Independent Ski Links, Inghams, Inspired to Ski, Interactive Resorts, Jeffersons, Kaluma, Luxury Chalet Collection, Momentum, Mountain Beds, Mountain Tracks, Oxford Ski Co, Powder White, PowderBeds, Ski Expectations, Ski Freedom, Ski Independence, Ski Line, Ski Safari, Ski Solutions, Ski Total, Skitracer, Ski Verbier, Ski Weekend, Skiweekends.com, Skiworld, Snow Finders, Snoworks, STC, Supertravel, V-Ski, VIP, White Roc
Nendaz *Alpine Answers, Crystal, Erna Low, First Choice, Lagrange, Ski Independence, Skiworld, Ted Bentley*
Veysonnaz *Crystal, Erna Low, Luxury Chalet Collection, Oxford Ski Co*

– and a plentiful supply of apartments (Skiworld has a new 3-bed one right opposite the gondola).

There's quite a wide choice of restaurants including Tex-Mex, pizzas, Thai and sushi, as well as steaks and local mountain food. Chez Edith, out of town on the way to Siviez was recommended by a local.

LINKED RESORT – 1730m
SIVIEZ

Siviez, a small huddle of buildings in an isolated spot, is effectively a junction of the slopes of Verbier, Nendaz and Veysonnaz-Thyon. It is the best base from which to explore the whole 4 Valleys lift network, though lodging is limited to apartments and the 3-star hotel Siviez (which takes large group bookings only). There are daytime buses to/from Nendaz. The long and gentle blue run through the sheltered valley from Tortin is super beginner progression territory. Being set a little way down the valley from Tortin, at the foot of the steep itinéraires from Chassoure and Mont-Fort, means it is also an excellent base for doing the tough skiing of Verbier – you can end the day with a descent of 1600m vertical from Mont-Fort; no noise in the evenings; perfect.

LINKED RESORT – 1300m
VEYSONNAZ

Veysonnaz is a small, family resort, sunny in the afternoon, at the foot of an excellent, long red slope from the ridge above Thyon. A second excellent

(though often icy) red, regularly used for major races, descends to the isolated lift base of Mayens-de-l'Ours.

The resort is spread widely across and down the hillside, with extensive views across the Rhône valley. The original attractive old village, complete with church, is two hairpin bends below Veysonnaz Station, the lift base and the main focus of the place for the visitor. The link up to Thyon is an eight-seat gondola, but progress from there towards Verbier is a slow business. Taking a car means you can drive to Siviez for much quicker access to the Verbier slopes. Shuttle-buses serve the lifts, but they are not super-frequent and do not run on Saturdays.

Veysonnaz Station has the essential facilities – half a dozen bars and cafes, four restaurants, a disco or two and a 'good' wellness centre with swimming pool and spa facilities (closed Saturdays). There are adequate shops, including a butcher and baker.

Accommodation is mainly in apartments – substantial chalet-style buildings dotted along the road the lift base is on. There are plenty of smaller chalets, too. There are two 3-star hotels next to the gondola station: the Chalet Royal (208 5644) has 'stunning views', though not from all rooms, and 'generally good' food. The Magrappé (208 5700) is more the focus of lively après-ski. There are some B&Bs.

There are two schools: Swiss and Neige Adventure. And there is a children's day care centre on the mountain. There is a 5km cross-country trail along the mountainside, with grand views.

Phone numbers
From elsewhere in
Switzerland add the
prefix 027; from
abroad use the prefix
+41 27

TOURIST OFFICES

**Verbier / Le Châble
(Bruson) / La Tzoumaz**
www.verbier-st-
bernard.ch

Nendaz / Siviez
www.nendaz.ch

Veysonnaz
www.veysonnaz.ch

**Thyon 2000 /
Les Collons**
www.thyon-region.ch

LINKED RESORT – 2100m

THYON 2000

Thyon 2000 is a functional, purpose-built collection of plain, medium-rise apartment blocks just above the treeline at the hub of the Veysonnaz-Thyon sector of the 4 Valleys. It has the basics of resort life – supermarket, newsagent, a couple of restaurants, an indoor pool, a disco. A free shuttle-bus runs to Les Collons. There's a fair-sized terrain park and boardercross, 'good' children's snow-garden and a kindergarten, as well as a ski school. The slopes are ideal for families and beginners, with two nursery lifts close to the accommodation. The lift network shared with Les Collons and Les Masses is elderly and slow (though gradually being improved). Snowmaking is extensive.

LINKED RESORT – 1800m

LES COLLONS

Some 300m below Thyon, at the foot of a broad, east-facing slope, Les Collons is a couple of strings of chalet-style buildings spread along two roads following the hillside, 50m vertical apart; a lot of building has been going on here recently.

Three draglifts go up towards Thyon from the upper level of the resort, and a chairlift from the lower level takes you above Thyon. There's 6km of cross-country. A free shuttle-bus runs to Thyon.

Most accommodation is in apartments, but there are also a couple of modest hotels – including the 3-star Cambuse (281 1883) just below one of the lift bases.

There's a wider range of bars, restaurants and other diversions than in Thyon, plus a 1km toboggan run through the woods above the village. Prepared walking trails add up to a modest 7km.

LINKED RESORT – 1515m

LES MASSES

Half-a-dozen hairpins down the mountainside from Les Collons, Les Masses is no more than a hamlet at the base of the double chairlifts that form the southern limit of the Thyon-Veysonnaz slopes. The home run is a red. Accommodation is in apartments. There is a grocery and a restaurant.

LINKED RESORT – 1500m

LA TZOUMAZ

This tiny hamlet sits in a quiet valley on the shady, wooded side of Verbier's Savoleyres slope sector. There are a handful of small hotels, shops and restaurants, forming a very quiet place to stay and ski this underrated sector. An 'efficient' free bus serves the lifts. A newish gondola and a couple of fast chairs serve most of the slopes here. The 10km toboggan run back to the base area is one of the longest in the region; we're told by the tourist office that it is 'a professional run, not suitable for children under seven and helmets are recommended'.

LINKED RESORT – 820m

LE CHÂBLE

Le Châble is a busy roadside village in the valley, at the bottom of the hairpin road up to Verbier. It is linked to Verbier by a queue-free gondola that goes on (without changing cabins) to Les Ruinettes, which means access to the slopes can be just as quick as from Verbier. Buses run late too. Le Châble is on the rail network, and is also convenient for drivers who want to visit other resorts. And it is handy for Bruson. There are several modest hotels, of which the 2-star Giétroz (776 1184) is the pick. The Tsâna restaurant is 'well presented; good meat, very good wines'.

OUTLYING RESORT – 1000m

BRUSON

Bruson is a small village on a shelf just above Le Châble, across the valley from Verbier, and reached by a short free bus ride. Its lifts are covered by the Verbier pass. From the village a slow chair goes up over gentle east-facing slopes to Bruson les Forêts (1600m). The open slopes above here are served by a quad chair up to a ridge, on the far side of which is a short draglift serving a tight little bowl. In addition to the intermediate pistes served by these lifts there are large areas of underused off-piste terrain, notably through woods on the front side accessed by the drag on the back. The off-piste down the back towards Orsières is good; you return by train. It is a great place to escape the crowds for a day – and maybe find powder when Verbier is skied out.

Villars

Traditional year-round resort with local low-altitude slopes, a cog railway and a much needed but far-flung glacier

TOP 10 RATINGS

Extent	★★★
Fast lifts	★★
Queues	★★★
Snow	★★
Expert	★★
Intermediate	★★★
Beginner	★★★★
Charm	★★★
Convenience	★★
Scenery	★★★

RPI	115
lift pass	£230
ski hire	£110
lessons	£115
food & drink	£210
total	**£665**

+ Pleasant, year-round resort
+ Fairly extensive intermediate slopes
+ Close to Geneva airport

− Unreliable snow-cover, although snowmaking is getting better
− Short runs on the upper slopes
− Little to amuse experts on piste

Villars is popular with second-home owners because of its closeness to Geneva airport. For many keen skiers, its low altitude and far from snow-sure slopes will rule it out. But for a varied family holiday it has its attractions.

THE RESORT

Villars sits on a sunny shelf, looking across the Rhône valley to the Portes du Soleil. Its home slopes link to those of Les Chaux, above the delightfully rustic village of Gryon. You can get a whole area pass covering Les Diablerets (linked by lifts and pistes) and also Leysin and Les Mosses, both of which are easy outings by rail or road. It also covers Glacier 3000, the small glacier area beyond Les Diablerets, halfway to Gstaad. Getting to and from the glacier is a long, slow business though – buses between it and Les Diablerets are infrequent, and it's a 10-minute walk to the Isenau area to ski down to the glacier lift. Outings to Verbier are easily possible.

Village charm Villars is more like a town than a village, with sprawling suburbs of smart chalets and several international schools. The focus is a longish, traffic-filled but pleasant high street lined with a variety of shops.

Convenience A slow cog railway goes from the main street up to the slopes around Bretaye. A gondola at the other end of town is quicker. It's best to stay near to one of these or at a hotel with its own shuttle-bus, since ski-buses can be infrequent and crowded.

Scenery The scenery is more dramatic than you might expect.

Floriettez 2120m/6,960ft
Cabane 2525m
Sex Rouge 2970m/9,740ft
Gstaad Reusch ↓
Isenau 1760m
GLACIER 3000
Vers L'Eglise
MEILLERET 1950m
Col du Pillon 1545m
Croix des Chaux 2020m/6,630ft
Petit Chamossaire 2035m/6,680ft
Laouissalet
Les Diablerets 1200m/3,940ft
LES CHAUX 1750m
Chaux de Conches
Grand Chamossaire 2120m
Chaux Ronde 1985m
Alpe des Chaux 1515m
Roc d'Orsay 2000m
BRETAYE 1810m
Sodoleuvre
Col de Soud 1525m
La Rasse 1350m
Villars 1300m/4,270ft
Barboleuse 1200m/3,940ft
Gryon 1115m/3,660ft

⊚ gondola
⊜ cable car
⊛ fast chairlift
Slow chairs & drags have no symbol

Bretaye can be reached by cog train; the slopes above are prettily dotted with trees →

WENDY-JANE KING

NEWS

2011/12: A six-pack is planned to replace the two-seat chair to Petit Chamossaire.

2010/11: Snow-guns now cover the lower slopes from Col de Soud to the resort, and the link with Gryon via La Rasse.

A new mountain hut (The Etable) opened on the Sodoleuvre slope above Gryon.

KEY FACTS

Resort	1300m
	4,270ft

Villars, Gryon and Les Diablerets, but excluding Glacier 3000

Slopes	1115-2120m
	3,660-6,960ft
Lifts	34
Pistes	100km
	62 miles
Blue	37%
Red	53%
Black	10%
Snowmaking	12%

Phone numbers
From elsewhere in Switzerland add the prefix 024; from abroad use the prefix +41 24

TOURIST OFFICE

www.villars.ch

THE MOUNTAINS

There's a good mix of wooded and open slopes throughout the area, but the piste map and signing are poor.

Slopes The cog train goes up to the col of Bretaye, which has intermediate slopes on either side. To the east, open slopes go to La Rasse and the link to Les Chaux. There used to be a piste down from Chaux Ronde, but this is now an itinerary; it has a tricky section at the top that is often closed. There's an alternative blue run from Bretaye. From Les Chaux there are runs to Barboleuse above Gryon, with a gondola back up. The gondola from Villars takes you to Roc d'Orsay, from where you can head for Bretaye or back to Villars. A long, slow, two-way chairlift links to Les Diablerets. The glacier has very gentle slopes at the top, but there is a splendid run down the Combe d'Audon (red whenever we've skied it, but apparently now black) with a dramatic cliff face rising up on the right. You can descend to the valley or part way down catch a fast chair back up (that serves another splendid red run).

Fast lifts Fast lifts exist, but so do old chairs and drags.

Queues The lifts at Bretaye get busy mainly at peak times, but the new six-pack to Petit Chamossaire should cut queues there. The buses and train can get overcrowded.

Terrain parks Chaux Ronde has a park, Diablerets a half-pipe and small park.

Snow reliability Low altitude and sunny slopes mean snow reliability isn't good – though on such gentle, grassy terrain, deep snow-cover isn't needed. New snowmaking on the runs back to town and at La Rasse is a welcome improvement.

Experts Little on-piste challenge but some good off-piste with a guide.

Intermediates The local slopes offer a good variety. Les Chaux has some steeper slopes and a lovely long cruisy blue to Barboleuse. The run from Meilleret to Les Diablerets is a delightful long cruise that can be deserted first thing in the morning.

Beginners The nursery slope behind the station is free to use. There is another at Gryon. There are gentle but often crowded runs at Bretaye.

Snowboarding There are a few tricky draglifts but good intermediate slopes.

Cross-country There are 50km of trails; those up the valley past La Rasse are long and pretty. There are more in the depression beyond Bretaye.

Mountain restaurants They are often oversubscribed. We hear most about Lac des Chavonnes (a short walk below Petit Chamossaire) and the Col de Soud for 'very good food, great service'. The Golf Club does 'delicious tartiflette'. At Gryon, we like the relatively quiet Des Chaux at Les Chaux and Refuge Frience (it's a walk back to the T-bar though). The Etable is a newly converted farmhouse at Sodoleuvre above La Rasse.

Schools and guides Past reports of both the Swiss and Villars schools have been positive.

Families La Trottinette non-ski nursery takes children up to six.

STAYING THERE

Hotels We enjoyed staying at the 4-star central Golf (496 3838) – big rooms, spa facilities. Nearby is the 3-star Alpe Fleurie (496 3070). The 4-star Eurotel Victoria (495 3131) is near the gondola.

Eating out Cookie out past Barboleuse does traditional and Asian-fusion food (with Indian food in a tent in the garden). Francis does 'good pizza' and the Sporting traditional dishes/grills.

Après-ski The rustic Buvette d'Arrivée on the home run above the top of town is popular at close of play, as is the Sporting. The Moon Boot Lounge is a newish cocktail bar.

Off the slopes Activities include paragliding, snowshoeing, skating and swimming. There are 'excellent' walks and rail trips.

Wengen

A charming old village, stunning scenery, an old cog railway and gentle intermediate slopes make for a relaxing and leisurely holiday

RATINGS

The mountains

Extent	★★★
Fast lifts	★★★
Queues	★★★
Terrain p'ks	★
Snow	★★
Expert	★★
Intermediate	★★★★
Beginner	★★★
Boarder	★★
X-country	★
Restaurants	★★★★
Schools	★★★
Families	★★★★

The resort

Charm	★★★★★
Convenience	★★★
Scenery	★★★★★
Eating out	★★
Après-ski	★★
Off-slope	★★★★

RPI   125

lift pass	£240
ski hire	£120
lessons	£120
food & drink	£220
total	**£700**

NEWS

2011/12: More snowmaking is planned in the Eigergletscher and Männlichen areas. There are plans to upgrade the Wixi chair to near the top of the Lauberhorn from a double to a six-pack, but not until 2012/13 at the earliest.

- ➕ Some of the most spectacular scenery in the Alps
- ➕ Small, traditional, nearly traffic-free Alpine village
- ➕ Lots of long, gentle runs, ideal for intermediates
- ➕ Nursery slopes in heart of village
- ➕ Calm, unhurried atmosphere
- ➕ Good resort for families and groups that include non-skiers. It's easy to get around on mountain railways

- ➖ Limited terrain for experts and adventurous intermediates
- ➖ Natural snow unreliable (but substantial snowmaking now)
- ➖ Trains to slopes are slow and there are still a few old lifts
- ➖ Getting to Grindelwald's First area can take hours
- ➖ Subdued in the evening, with little variety of nightlife

Given the charm of the village, the friendliness of the locals and the drama of the scenery, it's easy to see why many people love Wengen – including large numbers of Brits who have been going for decades. It's great for a relaxing time, for those who don't take their skiing too seriously, for families and for mixed groups of intermediates and non-skiers.

Keen piste-bashers should not underestimate the drawbacks. If you're used to modern mega-resorts, you'll find Wengen a huge contrast, and may have difficulty adjusting. But the spectacularly scenic Jungfrau region is one that every keen skier should experience; and to experience all of it Wengen, centrally placed between Mürren and Grindelwald, is the best base.

THE RESORT

Wengen is one of three resorts close together in the Jungfrau region. It is set on a sloping shelf above the Lauterbrunnen valley, opposite Mürren, and reached only by a cog railway, which carries on up to Kleine Scheidegg and the slopes shared with Grindelwald. Access to Mürren involves a train down to Lauterbrunnen, a cable car up and then another train (or a bus from Lauterbrunnen to a different two-stage cable car to Mürren). Access to the First area of Grindelwald is an even longer process, including skiing down to Grindelwald and crossing town. The Jungfrau lift pass covers all of this. Outings further afield aren't really worth the effort.

VILLAGE CHARM ★★★★★
Almost traffic-free
The village was a farming community long before skiing arrived; it is still tiny, but dominated by sizeable hotels, mostly of Victorian origin. So it is not exactly chocolate-box pretty, but it is charming and relaxed, and almost traffic-free. There are electric hotel

taxi-trucks and a few ordinary, engine-driven taxis. (Why, we wonder?)
The short main street is the hub. Lined with chalet-style shops and hotels, it also has the ice rink and village nursery slopes right next to it.

CONVENIENCE ★★★
Compact, but hilly in parts
Wengen is small, so location isn't as crucial as in many resorts. But those who don't fancy a steepish morning climb should avoid places down the hill, below the station. The ridge where the slopes of Wengen meet those of Grindelwald is reached either by train or by cable car – much quicker. Both stations are central. There are hotels on the home piste, convenient for the slopes.

SCENERY ★★★★★
Three of the best are here
The views across the valley are stunning. They get even better higher up, when the famous trio of peaks comes fully into view – the Mönch (Monk) in the centre protecting the Jungfrau (Maiden) on the right from the Eiger (Ogre) on the left.

miles   0.5

Männlichen

N ↑

Lauterbrunnen

down to

Kleine Scheidegg

km   0.5

KEY FACTS

Resort	1275m
	4,180ft

Jungfrau region

Slopes	945-2970m
	3,100-9,740ft
Lifts	44
Pistes	213km
	132 miles
Blue	33%
Red	49%
Black	18%
Snowmaking	40%

First-Männlichen-
Kleine Scheidegg
only

Slopes	945-2485m
	3,100-8,150ft
Lifts	32
Pistes	161km
	100 miles
Snowmaking	65%

LIFT PASSES

Jungfrau

Prices in SF

Age	1-day	6-day
under 16	31	157
16 to 19	50	251
20 to 61	62	314
over 62	56	283

Free under 6 (if with parent)

Beginner points ticket

Notes
Covers Wengen, Mürren and Grindelwald, trains between them and Grindelwald ski-bus; day pass price is for First-Kleine Scheidegg-Männlichen area only

Alternative passes
Grindelwald and Wengen only; Mürren only; non-skier pass

THE MOUNTAINS

Although Wengen is famous for the fearsome Lauberhorn Downhill course – the longest and one of the toughest on the World Cup circuit – its slopes are best suited to early intermediates. Most of the Downhill course is now open to the public and the steepest section (the Hundschopf jump) can be avoided by an alternative red route. Most of Wengen's runs are gentle blues and reds, ideal for cruising.

Piste marking and piste map are poor; reporters find the Männlichen slopes, in particular, confusing. And following heavy snowfalls in 2009, one visitor found piste markers had disappeared under the deep snow – 'a potentially dangerous, not to mention avoidable, problem'.

EXTENT OF THE SLOPES ★★★★★
Picturesque playground
Most of the slopes are on the Grindelwald side of the mountain. From the railway station at Kleine Scheidegg you can head straight down to Grindelwald or work your way across to the top of the Männlichen. This area is served by a drag and several chairlifts, and can be reached directly from Wengen by the cable car. There are a few runs back down towards Wengen from the top of the Lauberhorn, but there's really only one below Wengernalp.

FAST LIFTS ★★★★★
OK except for the train
The fast cable car and slow train are the main access lifts; new fast chairs replacing old lifts have improved things higher up; the latest is the Eigernordwand six-pack from below Kleine Scheidegg (on the Grindelwald side) to Eigergletscher.

QUEUES ★★★★★
Village crowds, better higher up
Both the train and the cable car can be crowded at peak periods. It is best to avoid travelling up at the same time as the ski school. Queues up the mountain have been alleviated a lot in the last few years by the installation of fast chairs, and recent reporters have experienced few problems in midweek. But weekends can be busy, especially on the Grindelwald side of the hill – and on Saturdays children up to 15 can ski free if an accompanying adult buys a day pass.

TERRAIN PARKS ★★★★★
No longer nearby
There has been a small park at Wengernalp in the past, but it wasn't built last year and there are no plans for it this year. The nearest parks are at First and Mürren – each a fair trek.

SNOW RELIABILITY ★★★★★
Improved snowmaking helps
Most slopes are below 2000m, and the few runs on the Wengen side of the ridge are sunny; the long blue run back to the village is particularly vulnerable. But a lot of snowmaking has been added recently, with more due for 2012. Some 60% of the slopes in the Kleine Scheidegg-Männlichen area are now covered. When we were there in 2009, it had not snowed for a few weeks and a warm Föhn wind had melted a lot of snow, but most slopes were in good condition. Piste maintenance gets mixed reviews.

FOR EXPERTS ★★★★★
Few challenges
Wengen is quite limited for experts. The only genuine black runs in the area are parts of the Lauberhorn World Cup Downhill and a couple of pistes from Eigergletscher towards Wixi including Oh God (which used to be off-piste). There are some decent off-piste runs such as White Hare from under the north face of the Eiger and more adventurous runs from the Jungfraujoch late in the season (see the Grindelwald chapter for more about going to the Jungfraujoch). The new Eigernordwand six-pack 'makes good off-piste more accessible', says a 2011 visitor.

For more serious challenges it's well worth going to nearby Mürren, around an hour away. Heli-trips are organised if there are enough takers.

FOR INTERMEDIATES ★★★★★
Wonderful if the snow is good
Wengen and Grindelwald share superb intermediate slopes. Nearly all are long blue or gentle red runs (though there are genuine reds too); see the Grindelwald chapter. The run back to Wengen is a relaxing end to the day, as long as it's not too crowded and the snow is OK (it can be patchy).

For tougher pistes, head for the top of the Lauberhorn chair and then the runs to Kleine Scheidegg, or to Wixi (following the start of the Downhill course). You could also try the north-facing run from Eigergletscher, which often has the best snow late in the season, and now has better access with its new six-pack.

FOR BEGINNERS ★★★☆☆
Not ideal
There's a nursery slope in the centre of the village – convenient and gentle, but it gets afternoon sun and at this modest altitude the snow can suffer. There's a beginners' area at Wengernalp and another on the Grindelwald side of Kleine Scheidegg, but to get back to Wengen you either have to take the train or tackle the run down, which can be tricky, with some flat sections. None of these areas offers free lifts, but there are alternatives to buying a full week's pass (such as a points card). There are plenty of good, long, gentle runs to progress to on the slopes above Grindelwald.

FOR BOARDERS ★★☆☆☆
Best for beginners
Wengen is not a bad place for gentle boarding – the nursery area is not ideal, but beginners have plenty of slopes to progress to, with lots of long blue and red runs served by the train and chairlifts. Getting from Kleine Scheidegg to Männlichen means an unavoidable draglift, though. And the slope back to Wengen is narrow and almost flat in places, so you may have to scoot. For the steepest slopes and best freeriding, experts will want to head for Mürren.

FOR CROSS-COUNTRY ★☆☆☆☆
There is none
There's no cross-country in Wengen itself, which seems a shame given the nature of the resort. There are 12km of tracks down in the Lauterbrunnen valley, where the snow is unreliable.

MOUNTAIN RESTAURANTS ★★★★☆
Plenty of variety
Editors' choice The Jungfrau hotel at Wengernalp (855 1622) is an old favourite of ours, with superb views from the sunny terrace; the menu is limited, but the rösti is excellent. You also get magnificent views from the narrow balcony of Wengen's highest restaurant, Eigergletscher.
Worth knowing about The station buffet at Kleine Scheidegg receives repeated rave reviews ('good food and friendly service') but gets packed. The Grindelwaldblick is a worthwhile trudge uphill from Kleine Scheidegg, for 'a tasty and good value lunch with generous portions and attentive service'. The Allmend, near the top of the Innerwengen chair and the train stop, has wonderful views of the valley from the terrace and been noted for friendly service, but has 'no buzz', said a visitor last year. For restaurants above Grindelwald, see that chapter.

Wengen

535

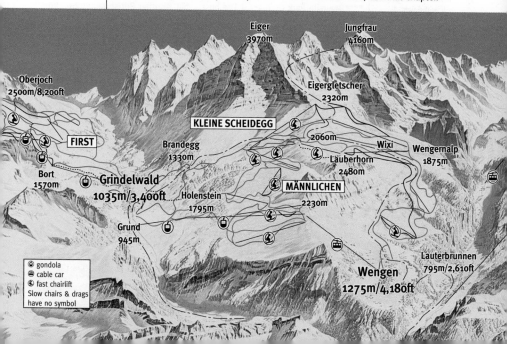

SCHOOLS

Swiss
t 855 2022

Privat
t 855 5005

Altitude
t 853 0040

Classes
(Swiss prices)
6 3hr days SF270

Private lessons
From SF149 for 2hr

CHILDCARE

Playhouse
t 856 8585
Age 2-7; 8.30-5pm;
Sun-Fri

Kinderhort Sunshine
t 854 1290
Ages from 6mnth to
8yr; 8.45-5pm

Babysitters
List available from
tourist office

Ski school
The Swiss school
takes ages 3 up
(6 3hr days SF270)

SNOWPIX.COM / CHRIS GILL

The Männlichen cable
car to goes to the top
of the ridge in this
photo and the train to
Kleine Scheidegg goes
off to the right ↓

SCHOOLS AND GUIDES ★★★★★
Healthy competition
We have no reports this year, but
views on the Swiss school are
generally positive – for 'excellent'
organisation and a friendly approach
to classes. Private lessons with the
Privat school have also been
recommended. Guides are available for
heli-trips and off-piste.

FOR FAMILIES ★★★★★
Conveniently placed
It is an attractive and reassuring
village for families. The nursery slope
is in the centre and there are two
kindergartens. There is a list of
babysitters available at the tourist
office. A reporter praised the children's
ski school classes: 'The best so far by
a mile. My four year old really enjoyed
all the activities.' The train gives easy
access to higher slopes.

STAYING THERE

Most accommodation is in hotels.
There is only a handful of catered
chalets (none especially luxurious).
Self-catering apartments are few, too.
   Staying down in Lauterbrunnen will
halve your accommodation costs and
give faster access to Mürren (see
Mürren chapter).
Hotels There are about two dozen
hotels, mostly 4-star and 3-star, with a
handful of simpler places.
★★★★Beausite Park (856 5161) The best

in town reputedly. Good pool, steam,
sauna, massage. But poorly situated at
top of nursery slopes – a schlep up
from main street.
★★★★Wengener Hof (856 6969) No
prizes for style or convenience, but
recommended for peace, helpful staff,
spacious rooms with good views. 'A
truly warm welcome, excellent food.'
★★★★Sunstar (856 5200) Family-
friendly, modern, on main street right
opposite the cable car. Comfortable
rooms. Pool with views.
★★★★Silberhorn (856 5131)
Comfortable, modern and central.
'Great views, quality five-course meals,
and attractive spa,' says a 2010 visitor.
★★★★Caprice (856 0606) Small, smartly
furnished, chalet-style, just above the
railway. Sauna and massage.
'Comfortable and friendly'; 'fabulous
views, excellent food'. Kindergarten.
★★★★Regina (856 5858) Grand Victorian
hotel with piano bar, sun terrace, spa
and fitness room – 'tremendous food
and service though drinks are
expensive', says a 2011 visitor.
★★★Belvédère (856 6868) Some way
out, buffet-style meals, family-friendly,
spacious rooms and grand art nouveau
public rooms. 'Highly recommended.'
★★★Alpenrose (855 3216) Long-
standing British favourite; eight
minutes' climb to the station. Small,
simple rooms, but good views and
food; friendly staff.
★★★Falken (856 5121) Further up the
hill. Another British favourite – 'the

There's a very strong British presence in Wengen. Many Brits have been returning for years to the same rooms in the same hotels in the same week, and treat the resort as a sort of second home. There is an English church with weekly services, and a British-run ski club, the DHO (Downhill Only) – so named when the Brits who colonised the resort persuaded the locals to keep the summer railway running up the mountain in winter, so that they would no longer have to climb up in order to ski down again. That greatly amused the locals, who until then had regarded skiing in winter as a way to get around on snow rather than a pastime to be done for fun. The DHO is still going strong.

GETTING THERE

Air Zürich 155km/ 95 miles (3hr); Bern 65km/40 miles (2hr); Basel 160km/100 miles (2hr45)

Rail Station in resort

UK PACKAGES

Alpine Answers, Club Med, Crystal, First Choice, Inghams, Neilson, PowderBeds, Ski Club Freshtracks, Ski Line, Ski Solutions, Skitracer, STC, Swiss Travel Service, Switzerland Travel Centre, Thomson

ACTIVITIES

Indoor Swimming pools (in hotels), sauna, solarium, whirlpool, massage (in hotels)

Outdoor Ice rink, curling, 50km of cleared paths, tobogganing, ice climbing, snowshoeing, paragliding

Phone numbers
From elsewhere in Switzerland add the prefix 033; from abroad use the prefix +41 33

TOURIST OFFICE

www.wengen.ch

service was first class and the live jazz pianist had the place rocking'.

Apartments The hotel Bernerhof's decent Résidence apartments are well positioned just off the main street, and the hotel facilities are available for guests to use.

At altitude You can stay at two points up the mountain reached by the railway: the expensive Jungfrau hotel (855 1622) at Wengernalp – with fabulous views – and at Kleine Scheidegg, where there are rooms in the big Bellevue des Alpes (855 1212) and dormitory space above the Grindelwaldblick restaurant (855 1374) and the station buffet.

EATING OUT ★★☆☆☆
Mainly hotel-based

Most restaurants are in hotels. They offer good food and service but a 2011 reader laments lack of other places to eat. The Silberhorn offers varied and 'excellent' five-course meals. The Bernerhof has good-value traditional dishes. The little hotel Hirschen has good steaks. The Residence Brunner servers 'sumptuous four-course meals and delicious home-made soups'. The hotel Regina's 'food is excellent but they won't serve tap water'. There's no shortage of fondues in the village, and several bars do casual food. Da Sina does steaks and Italian food and has been recommended. Cafe Gruebi is not to be missed for 'the most wonderful cakes'. The Jungfrau at Wengernalp has an excellent restaurant – but you have to get back on skis or on a toboggan.

APRES-SKI ★★☆☆☆
It depends on what you want

People's reactions to the après-ski scene vary widely, according to their expectations and their appetites.

If you're used to raving in Kitzbühel or Les Deux-Alpes, you'll rate Wengen dead, especially for young people. If you've heard it's dead, you may be pleasantly surprised to find that there is a handful of small bars that do

good business both early and late in the evening. On the mountain, Tipirama (a wigwam at Kleine Scheidegg) is a fun place immediately after skiing ('vibrant and welcoming' but 'becoming a bit tatty'), sometimes with DJs and live bands. We've had mixed reviews of the Start Bar on the Lauberhorn ('fun', 'fantastic views and live music at weekends' but 'very unfriendly service and expensive'). The bar at the Bumps section of the home run is a popular final-run stop-off. Further down, the snow bar at the Residence Brunner was 'enjoyable', and in the village the tiny, 'always welcoming' Pickel Bar (formerly Eiger) is popular at the end of the day. The small, traditional Tanne is 'relaxed, friendly, and cocktails and champagne are popular' – but it can get crowded. The 'animated' Sina's, a little way out by Club Med, has 'realistic pricing', big-screen TV, a live DJ and special evenings such as karaoke and quiz nights. Rock's with its plasma screens showing Sky Sports has been recommended. There are discos and live music in some hotels.

OFF THE SLOPES ★★★★☆
Good for a relaxing time

With its unbeatable scenery and pedestrian-friendly trains and cable car (there's a special – but pricey – pass for pedestrians), Wengen is a superb resort for those who want a relaxing holiday. It's easy for mixed parties of skiers and non-skiers to meet up for lunch on the mountain. There are some lovely walks, and ice skating, tobogganing and curling are popular. Several hotels have health spas. The cinema often shows English-language films. Excursions to Interlaken and Bern are possible by train, as is the trip up to the Jungfraujoch (see the Grindelwald chapter). From Männlichen there are scenic flights giving splendid close-up views of the mountains and glaciers, either by helicopter or much cheaper small plane.

Wengen

537

Interactive resort shortlist builder at **www.wtss.co.uk**

Zermatt

A magical combination of nearly everything you could want from a ski resort, both on and off the slopes

RATINGS

The mountains

Extent	★★★★
Fast lifts	★★★★★
Queues	★★★
Terrain p'ks	★★★
Snow	★★★★
Expert	★★★★
Intermediate	★★★★
Beginner	★★
Boarder	★★★
X-country	★
Restaurants	★★★★★
Schools	★★★
Families	★★

The resort

Charm	★★★★
Convenience	★★
Scenery	★★★★★
Eating out	★★★★★
Après-ski	★★★★★
Off-slope	★★★★

RPI   135

lift pass	£280
ski hire	£145
lessons	£125
food & drink	£230
total	**£780**

NEWS

2011/12: There are several lift/piste developments in the pipeline, but nothing confirmed.

2010/11: The Blauherd restaurant was renovated as a new smart bar-lounge area (Blue Lounge), with a larger terrace. The Sunnegga hut became a self-service to offer more capacity.

538

- ➕ Wonderful, high and extensive slopes in four varied areas
- ➕ Spectacular high mountain scenery
- ➕ Charming, if rather sprawling, old mountain village, largely traffic-free
- ➕ Reliable snow at altitude
- ➕ World's best mountain restaurants
- ➕ Nightlife to suit most tastes
- ➕ Smart shops
- ➕ Linked to sunny Cervinia in Italy
- ➕ Extensive helicopter operation

- ➖ Main lifts may be a long walk, or a crowded bus or taxi ride from home
- ➖ Far from ideal for novices, despite recent efforts to improve matters
- ➖ High prices for everything, including lift pass (one of Europe's priciest)
- ➖ Slow train up to Gornergrat
- ➖ Some lift queues at peak periods
- ➖ Annoying electric taxis in 'car-free' streets detract from ambience
- ➖ Few options to ski in bad weather; can be really windy or cold too

Our verdict is short and simple: you must try Zermatt before you die. There is nowhere else to match it. Its drawbacks are non-trivial but, for us and for virtually all our reporters, these pale into insignificance compared with its attractions. Editor Watts regularly takes his holiday here. Enough said.

THE RESORT

Zermatt started life as a simple farming village, developed as a mountaineering centre in the 19th century, then became a winter resort. Summer is still as big as winter here.

The village is car-free, but not traffic-free – electric buggies operating either as hotel shuttles or as public taxis zip around the streets. Residents can drive up to Zermatt, but the rest of us must park at Täsch (or more distant Visp) and arrive by train. At Täsch there's a big car park (SF14.50 a day) and you can wheel luggage trolleys on and off the trains.

Zermatt mainly attracts a well heeled international clientele; the clientele is also relatively, er, mature for what is quite a sporty resort.

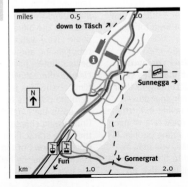

VILLAGE CHARM ★★★★☆
Old and new in harmony

The resort is a mixture of ancient chalets and barns, grand 19th-century hotels and modern buildings, most in traditional style but some decidedly funky. The oldest, most charming part of the village has narrow lanes and old wooden barns with slate roofs, many of them supported on stone 'legs'. But modern-day Zermatt sprawls along both sides of the river with a lot of new building at both ends and up the sides of the mountains that rise steeply on each side.

Arriving at the station, it all seems very towny, especially if there is no snow on the ground. The centre doesn't have the relaxed, rustic feel of other car-free resorts, such as Wengen and Saas-Fee. The main street running away from the station is lined with luxury hotels, restaurants, banks and glitzy shops. The electric taxis are intrusive, especially at busy times.

CONVENIENCE ★★☆☆☆
Lifts at opposite ends

The village is small enough to get around on foot in the evenings, but not in ski boots and carrying skis. There is a free ski-bus service; it is inadequate at peak times, though one 2011 visitor reckoned it had improved.

You arrive at a fair-sized square at the north end of the resort, where you

KEY FACTS

Resort	1620m
	5,310ft

Zermatt only	
Slopes	1620-3820m
	5,310-12,530ft
Lifts	35
Pistes	200km
	124 miles
Blue	16%
Red	60%
Black	24%
Snowmaking	65%

Zermatt-Cervinia-Valtournenche combined	
Slopes	1525-3820m
	5,000-12,530ft
Lifts	58
Pistes	350km
	217 miles
Blue	22%
Red	60%
Black	18%
Snowmaking	59%

find ranks of electric taxis and hotel shuttles and horse-drawn sleighs.

The cog railway to the Gornergrat sector starts from near the main station. The Sunnegga underground funicular for the Rothorn sector is a few minutes' walk away, but the lifts to Furi and the other sectors (and the link to Cervinia) are over 1km away.

Staying near the lifts to Furi gives swift access to three of the four sectors. But a more central location can combine proximity to the Gornergrat and Sunnegga railways, and to most of the resort's shops, bars and restaurants.

Some accommodation is up the steep hill across the river in Winkelmatten – you can ski back to it (or close to it) from all areas, and it has its own reliable bus service.

SCENERY ★★★★★
On a grand scale

Zermatt's emblematic, unmistakable Matterhorn is not visible from central parts of the village – if you want the famous view from your balcony, stay on the east side of the village, or at the south end – but once you are on the slopes its unreal profile dominates the views. The cable car trip up to the Klein Matterhorn opens up vast panoramas, as well as close-up glacier views.

THE MOUNTAINS

539

Practically all of the slopes are above the treeline – the runs served by the Sunnegga funicular are the main exception, and these and in a path to the village.

A single piste map covers both Cervinia and Zermatt fairly clearly, and lists recommended 'ski safari' routes of either 10,500m or 12,500m vertical; but if you want lift names you'll have to get hold of the Cervinia version. Both resorts' maps currently show planned cable cars from Furggsattel to Plateau Rosa and from there to the Klein Matterhorn, but we're told these are not imminent.

In each sector there are runs marked in yellow on the resort map and dotted on ours, called 'itinéraires' on the piste map or 'freeride' runs on the Cervinia one. We'll call them itineraries. The terms are not explained on the maps – a ridiculous and dangerous state of affairs. They are probably not patrolled – if skiing alone, take care.

On Thursdays, you can get first tracks from Trockener Steg. For 30SF, you can take the lift at 7.40am, about an hour ahead of the herd, and have a buffet breakfast at Ice Pizzeria. We prefer our normal routine of the 8am train to Gornergrat.

Once a month there are moonlight descents from the Klein Matterhorn with the ski patrol, including an Asian meal at the smart self-service restaurant at the top, for SF87.50.

We have been impressed by service improvements over the years: polite and helpful lift staff; big boards at the bottom of each sector indicating which lifts and pistes are open in all sectors; useful announcements in English on the train and some cable cars; and free tissues at most lift stations.

EXTENT OF THE SLOPES ★★★★☆
Beautiful and varied

Zermatt's slopes divide naturally into four main sectors. The resort likes to identify more sectors on its maps. But at least it gave up, last season, branding most of them as various forms of 'paradise' (although it didn't communicate this to the publishers of the Cervinia piste map).

The **Rothorn** sector is reached by an underground funicular to Sunnegga starting by the river, not far from the

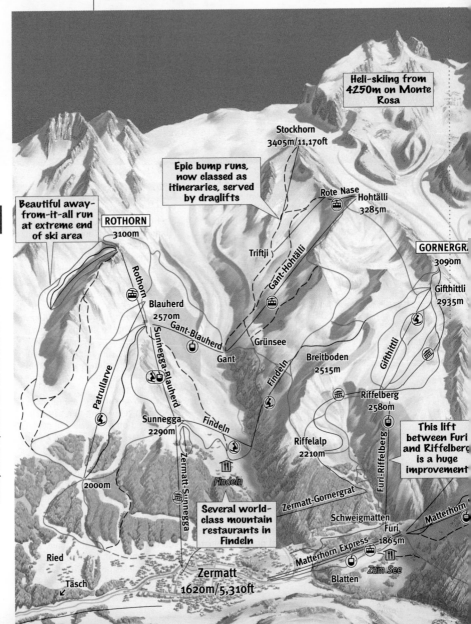

centre of the village. The main nursery area is just below Sunnegga, reached by a miniature funicular. A hybrid chondola goes from here to Blauherd, where a cable car goes up to Rothorn.

The second main area, **Gornergrat**, is reached from Zermatt by cog railway trains that take 30 or 40 minutes to the top – arrive early to get a seat (best on the right-hand side to enjoy the fabulous views). We love getting the 8am train with the lifties and restaurant staff. It arrives at the top just as they drop the rope to open the pistes, and you have the slopes to yourself for an hour or two.

The Rothorn and Gornergrat sectors, separated by the Findel valley, are linked by pistes and itineraries descending to two lift stations.

The Matterhorn Express gondola from the south end of the village goes first to Furi (where you can change to another gondola to go to Riffelberg, for Gornergrat) and on to the small but worthwhile **Schwarzsee** area.

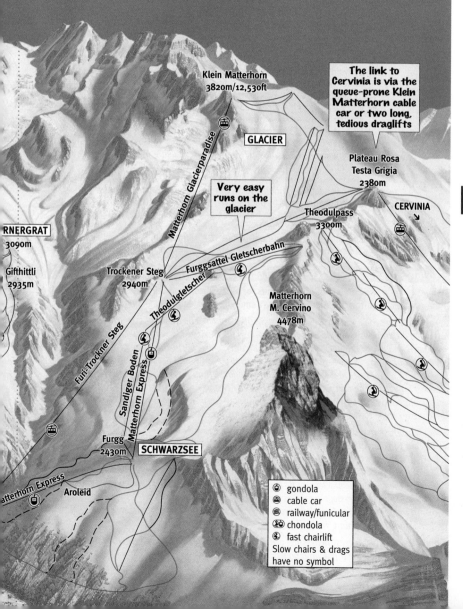

Klein Matterhorn
3820m/12,530ft

The link to Cervinia is via the queue-prone Klein Matterhorn cable car or two long, tedious draglifts

GLACIER

Plateau Rosa
Testa Grigia
2380m

CERVINIA

Very easy runs on the glacier

Theodulpass
3300m

RNERGRAT
3090m

Gifthittli
2935m

Matterhorn Glacierparadise

Furggsattel Gletscherbahn

Trockener Steg
2940m

Theodulgletscher

Matterhorn
M. Cervino
4478m

Furi-Trockner Steg

Sandiger Boden

Matterhorn Express

Furgg
2430m   **SCHWARZSEE**

atterhorn Express

Aroleid

⊙ gondola
⊜ cable car
⊛ railway/funicular
⊛⊙ chondola
⊛ fast chairlift
Slow chairs & drags
have no symbol

The same gondola goes on up to Trockener Steg, focal point of the third major sector, the super-high **Glacier**. This can also be reached by a jumbo cable car from Furi – quicker if you time it right, and less liable to closure by wind. Above Trockener Steg another cable car makes a spectacular ascent to Klein Matterhorn. When you arrive, you walk through a long tunnel, to emerge on top of the world for the highest piste in Europe; you can dine and stay up here too. This area links to Cervinia – you peal off left from the glacier at one of two points.

There are pistes back to the village from all sectors – though some can be closed or tricky due to poor snow conditions. They can be hazardous at the end of the day, due to crowds and speeding skiers – note our remarks under 'For intermediates'.

FAST LIFTS ★★★★★
Huge improvements
All Zermatt's four sectors are well-connected by fast chairs, gondolas, big cable cars or mountain railways. There are of course slow lifts in places, but most can be avoided.

QUEUES ★★★☆☆
Main problems being solved
Zermatt has improved its lift system hugely in recent years, eliminating major bottlenecks. Again, all this year's reporters are generally positive, but a couple of problems remain.

The Klein Matterhorn cable car has queues much of the time (up to an hour mid-morning; quieter in the afternoon) – one regular reporter recommends jumping this queue occasionally by splashing out 200 francs a head for a 20-minute heli-lift to Plateau Rosa incorporating a close-up tour of the Matterhorn – 'fantastic; one of the highlights of my life'.

The gondola to Trockener Steg is prone to closure in high winds, putting pressure on the alternative cable-car in these conditions.

A real bottleneck is Gant in the Findel valley – notably the old, slow gondola to Blauherd. Half-hour waits are common here in high season. There are plans to construct a piste from Gant down the valley to the lower chairlift base so that the

OFF-PISTE RUNS FROM THE ACCESSIBLE TO THE EPIC

Zermatt offers a wide variety of off-piste runs for all abilities, from off-piste beginner to expert. And if the runs reached from the lift system aren't enough, heli-skiing is available (and popular).

Zermatt's 'itineraries' (explained, as far as possible, under 'The mountains') open up a lot of ungroomed terrain. If you love long mogul pitches, those in the Gornergrat sector served by the Stockhorn and Triftji draglifts are the stuff of dreams. Being north-facing and high, this area keeps good snow long after a new snowfall (but it needs deep snow, and does not normally open until February, or even March). The itineraries carry on down from the Triftji T-bar to Gant, but snow quality can deteriorate on this lower part. There are two wonderful itineraries from Rothorn, with spectacular views (though again they need good snow-cover to be really enjoyable). At Schwarzsee there are a couple of steep north-facing gullies through the woods.

Away from the marked runs, there are marvellous off-piste possibilities from the top lifts in each sector, but they are dangerous, because of rocky and glacial terrain; guidance is essential. Stockhorn is a great starting point; descending towards Gant, one special run goes down 'the lost valley'; going in the other direction, there is an excellent descent to the Gornergletscher, ending at Furi. Be warned: getting off the end of the glacier can be tricky – it may involve walking along narrow rocky paths above long drops or side-stepping down steep slopes, depending on snow levels (we've encountered both). In the Schwarzsee sector there are many good slopes, including 'innru waldieni', right underneath the Matterhorn, reached from the Hörnli T-bar.

Zermatt is the Alps' biggest heli-skiing centre; at times the helipad has choppers taking off every few minutes. There are only a few drop points. The classic run is from over 4250m on Monte Rosa and descends over 2300m vertical through wonderful glacier scenery to Furi; note our warning above.

and quite a lot of snowmaking. Three of the four sectors go up to over 3000m, and the Glacier area has summer skiing. There are loads of runs above 2500m, many of which are north-facing, guaranteeing decent snow except in freak years.

There is snowmaking, in all four sectors, on at least some pistes from above 3000m right down to resort level. Coverage is gradually being increased. On repeated March visits we have been impressed with the use of snowmaking on the runs to resort level. Piste grooming is generally excellent.

FOR EXPERTS ★★★★☆
Head off-piste
There is some great off-piste when conditions are right – see our feature panel – but Zermatt doesn't get huge snowfall, so you can't always count on it, particularly early in the season. There are few challenging pistes. That's one of the consequences of designating their toughest regularly skied runs as itineraries (see under 'The mountains'). The handful of black runs marked on the piste map are not worthy of their classification; the one with the steepest pitches (Blauherd-Patrullarve) is also very wide.

FOR INTERMEDIATES ★★★★☆
Mile after mile of beautiful runs
Zermatt is ideal for adventurous intermediates. Many of the blue runs tend to be at the difficult end of their classification. Reds vary unhelpfully: some are quite tough; some ought to be blue. Few are really what you might call 'cruising' runs.

Among our favourites in the Gornergrat sector are the very beautiful reds down lift-free valleys from both Gornergrat (Kelle) and Hohtälli (White Hare) to Breitboden – we love these first thing in the morning, before anyone else is on them. The steepest part of Kelle has been reclassified black, but an easier red variant bypasses it. From Breitboden you can go on down to Gant, or to Riffelalp on a run that includes a narrow wooded path with a sheer cliff and magnificent views to the right.

On the Rothorn sector, the 5km

Zermatt

543

Interactive resort shortlist builder at www.wtss.co.uk

LIFT PASSES

gondola can be retired, but the timing is uncertain.

The top section of piste from Hohtälli can get dangerously busy ('awful crowds on a narrow red that was bumped by mid-morning').

TERRAIN PARKS ★★★☆☆
Better in summer than winter
There's a detectable lack of enthusiasm in the resort's attitude to an amenity which obviously is of no interest to 99% of visitors. Gravity Park, next to the Furggsattel six-seat chair, is still 'pants' according to reporters this year ('no real signposting to indicate difficulty, no music, no atmosphere, no one in it'). Things improve in the summer, when the park moves up to Plateau Rosa and a six-man crew shape the 600m park daily. A nicely integrated 120m-long super-pipe sits next to an array of kickers, rails, a quarter-pipe, wall ride, mail box and tree jib.

SNOW RELIABILITY ★★★★☆
Generally good
Zermatt has rocky terrain and a relatively dry climate. But it also has some of the highest slopes in Europe,

SCHOOLS

Swiss
t 966 2466

Stoked
t 967 7020

Summit
t 967 0001

European Snowsport
t 967 6787

Adventure
t 967 5020

Almrausch
t 967 0808

AER
t 967 7067

Prato Borni
t 967 5115

Classes (Swiss prices)
5 days (10am to 3.30
with lunch break)
SF345

Private lessons
SF170 for 2hr for 1 or
2 people

GUIDES

Alpin Center
t 966 2460

Kumme/Tufternkumme run – from Rothorn itself to the bottom of the Patrullarve chair – also gets away from the lift system and has an interesting mix of straight-running and mogul pitches (but it gets a lot of sun and lacks snowmaking).

In the Glacier sector the reds served by the fast quad chair from Furgg are gloriously set at the foot of the Matterhorn. The Furggsattel chair from Trockener Steg serves more pistes with stunning views, notably the 1100m-vertical Matterhorn piste – blue in gradient for most of its great length, but classified red because of a short, steep pitch near the end which causes problems for many skiers.

For timid intermediates, the best runs are the blues from Blauherd on Rothorn, and above Riffelberg on Gornergrat, and in good weather the super-high runs between Klein Matterhorn and Trockener Steg. Of these, the Riffelberg area often has the best combination of good snow and easy cruising, and is understandably popular with the ski schools.

In the Glacier sector most of the runs, though marked red on the piste map, are very flat and represent the easiest slopes Zermatt has to offer, as well as the best snow. Even an early intermediate can make the trip to Cervinia, crossing at Theodulpass rather than taking the more challenging run from Plateau Rosa.

Beware the black run from Furgg to Furi at the end of the day. It is not steep, but gets chopped up, mogulled in places and very crowded. A much more relaxed alternative is the scenic Weisse Perle run from Schwarzsee (the Stafelalp variant is even more scenic but has a short uphill and steep downhill sections).

FOR BEGINNERS ★★★★★
Still far from ideal
These days the resort makes an effort to cater for beginners – there are beginner areas dotted around on all four sectors, and a main one has been developed (with three moving carpets and two rope tows) at Leisee and reached by a short funicular from Sunnegga. There is now a half-price pass to get you to and from that area, which is a step forward. But this year, as last, we have reports from readers

THE WORLD'S BEST MOUNTAIN RESTAURANTS ★★★★★

The choice of restaurants is enormous, the standard high. We list here only a selection. It is best to book. The tourist office restaurant directory has photos but does not indicate prices. Beware: some places don't take cards.

Below Sunnegga, down at Findeln, are several attractive, expensive, rustic restaurants sharing a great Matterhorn view. Chez Vrony (967 2552) has long been one of our (and readers') favourites; service can be stretched but is reliably friendly, and the food excellent. We hope Vrony's flirtation with a two sitting system is over. We regularly get enthusiastic reports on the Adler (967 1058), with its outdoor BBQ – 'delicious food', 'impeccable service' – and Findlerhof (967 2588) – 'wonderful pasta with mussels'. The Paradies (967 3451) is also recommended. Further up the Findel valley, in a beautiful, isolated situation off the run from Rothorn, Fluhalp (967 2597) is another favourite – excellent food and service, often with live music on the huge terrace. Up at Blauherd, the old self-service place has become Blue Lounge – a cool modern bar serving tapas to jazz and other music. Lower down, Tuftern famously does 'slabs of bread and cheese on a terrace with a great view'. On Gornergrat, the Alphitta (967 2114) below Riffelalp is 'a lovely spot'.

In sharp contrast to all the rustic huts, at Trockener Steg we recommend highly the relatively new Ice Pizzeria (967 1812) – a smart, modern table-service place with great views. Higher up, the secluded Gandegghütte (079 607 8868) has stunning views and good, simple food; no milk, so no hot choc though. Over at Schwarzsee, the Stafelalp (967 3062) is a reader favourite – glorious position, 'excellent food; friendly, prompt service'.

At Furi, restaurant Furri (966 2777) does a 'great apple strudel', and Simi (967 2695), tucked away, does 'great grills on its open fire'. Just above Furi, Aroleid (967 2658) is a reader favourite – 'tops for rösti'. Below Furi, there are countless places to pause on the way home, though they are not ideally placed for lunch (unless you are calling it a day). Zum See (967 2045) is a charming old hut, reputedly the best restaurant on the mountain – we've certainly eaten well there. Below it, Blatten (967 2096) serves 'one of the best strudels'. And Marmottes (967 8282) is a newish little hut with a serious menu; the food pleased our first reporter on the place.

↑ The terraces at Findeln give the classic lunchtime view – this is Chez Vrony

SNOWPIX.COM / CHRIS GILL

CHILDCARE

Kinderparadies
t 967 7252
Ages from 3mnth;
9am-5pm
**Kinderclub Pumuckel
(Hotel Ginabelle)**
t 966 5000
Ages from 30mnth
Schwarzsee (Stoked)
t 967 7020
Ages from 3yr
**Nico Kids Club
(Schweizerhof hotel)**
t 966 0000
Ages from 2 to 8;
8.30-6pm; Sun-Fri
Snowli Village (Swiss)
t 966 2466
Ages 4 to 5: SF435
for 5 days
Private babysitters
List at tourist office

Ski school
From age 6; 5 full
days incl. lunch SF388
(Swiss prices)

who judge this small area inadequate, and press for a return to a 1-star rating for Zermatt in this respect. Apart from the merits of this area, it's a real drag for beginners to have to get themselves up the mountain. And progression to longer runs is awkward – the Zermatt slopes as a whole are very challenging for near-beginners, which includes fast learners who are ready to quit the nursery slopes after a couple of days. Of course you can learn to ski here, but given a choice we would go elsewhere.

FOR BOARDERS ★★★☆☆
Some good angles
The slopes are best for experienced freeriders and there's a terrain park above Trockener Steg. There are adequate beginner areas, complete with moving carpet lifts, which we've seen many beginner snowboarders having lessons on. The main lifts are boarder-friendly: train, funicular, gondolas, cable cars and fast chairs, and there aren't too many flat bits. Stoked is a specialist school.

FOR CROSS-COUNTRY ★☆☆☆☆
Fairly limited
There are 12km trails from Täsch to Randa (don't count on good snow). There are also 'ski walking trails', which we believe combine the two activities – best tackled as part of an organised group.

SCHOOLS AND GUIDES ★★★☆☆
Competition paying off
The main Swiss school seems to have improved since competing schools were permitted, and our most recent report was positive. We get more reports on other schools, though. Summit and European Snowsport are staffed mainly by Brits. We've had mixed reports on Summit recently – some criticisms of beginner lessons, but enthusiasm for an intermediate class. Stoked snowboard school is made up of talented young instructors, some of whom are British and all of whom speak good English. Group sizes are said to be small. Again, we have had mixed reports. Our most recent reporter on Prato Borni this year was very happy.

FOR FAMILIES ★★☆☆☆
Good hotel nurseries
The prices, the general inconvenience of the place and the challenges facing beginners and near-beginners work against families. But, as our margin panel shows, there are plenty of facilities for children and we don't doubt that they are thoroughly well run. The tourist office has a list of babysitters. And families do have successful holidays here, some repeatedly. Choose your location with care, says one reader. Another notes that the number of hotels offering family suites is a plus-point.

Interactive resort shortlist builder at **www.wtss.co.uk**

UK PACKAGES

Alpine Answers, Alpine Weekends, Carrier, Crystal, Crystal Finest, Elegant Resorts, Elysian Collection, Flexiski, Independent Ski Links, Inghams, Interactive Resorts, Lagrange, Luxury Chalet Collection, Momentum, Mountain Tracks, Neilson, Oxford Ski Co, Powder Byrne, PowderBeds, Pure Powder, Scott Dunn, Ski Club Freshtracks, Ski Expectations, Ski Independence, Ski Line, Ski-Monterosa, Ski Safari, Ski Solutions, Ski Total, Skitracer, Skiweekends.com, Snow Finders, Supertravel, Swiss Travel Service, Switzerland Travel Centre, Thomson, VIP, White Roc, Zenith

STAYING THERE

Chalets Several operators have places here; many of the most comfortable are in apartment blocks. Ski Total has a remarkable 19 properties – mostly with 6 or 8 beds, a couple with more.
Hotels There are over 100 hotels, mostly comfortable and traditional-style 3-stars and 4-stars, but taking in the whole range. What distinguishes Zermatt is the number of 'hip' places, many of which are listed below.
*****Mont Cervin** (966 8888) Biggest in town. Elegantly traditional.
*****Zermatterhof** (966 6600) Traditional 'grand hotel' style, with piano bar.
*****Omnia** (966 7171) Designer hotel, minimalist, central, reached by a lift in a rock, smart fitness centre.
****Coeur des Alpes** (966 4080) Smart, modern B&B place at south end of town; relaxed, friendly feel.
****Alex** (966 7070) Close to train stations. An old favourite, though few recent reports. Large pool, etc.
****Beau Site** (966 6868) Grand place over the river with Matterhorn views. 'Simply the best we've stayed at.'
****Cervo** (968 1212) Hip place opened in 2009 with rooms, suites, chalets for up to 10. Ski to the door – at the end of the piste from Rothorn.
****Europe** (966 2700) Superb place over the river from the church, with fab modern rooms in new extension. We stayed here in 2011. Great food, relaxed atmosphere, charming people.
****Julen** (966 7600) Charming, modern-rustic chalet over the river.
****Matterhorn Focus** (966 2424) Super-stylish B&B place designed by Heinz Julen, right by the Matterhorn lifts. 'Exceptionally good.'
****Mirabeau** (966 2660) Heartily tipped by two reporters in 2011 – 'outstanding food, friendly staff, excellent spa – made our holiday'.

****Monte Rosa** (966 0333) Well-modernised original Zermatt hotel in centre; full of climbing mementos. 'Wonderful,' says a 2011 report.
****Sonne** (966 2066) In quiet setting; 'superb' wellness centre. 'They couldn't be more friendly, very good food,' says a repeat guest.
***Alpenroyal** (966 6066) We have repeated praise this year for 'comfort, service, food and location'.
***Butterfly** (966 4166) Near the train stations. 'Very comfortable, friendly, and good five-course meals.'
Atlanta (966 3535) No frills, but 'clean, warm, friendly and serves wholesome food'; close to centre, with Matterhorn views from some rooms.
Apartments There are lots. We have repeatedly enjoyed staying in the amazingly cheap apartments of the hotel Ambassador (966 2611), with free use of all its facilities such as a pool and sauna, but they are overdue for a refurb. The Alex Lodge apartments in Winkelmatten (owned by Alex of hotel Alex) look very luxurious. Ski Solutions has a decent selection.
At altitude There are several hotels on the hill, of which the pick is the 5-star Riffelalp Resort (966 0555), at the first stop on the Gornergrat railway, with pool, spa and its own evening trains. Highly recommended – luxurious, but 'not at all stuffy'.

EATING OUT ★★★★★
Huge choice
There are over 100 restaurants to choose from: top-quality haute cuisine, through traditional Swiss food, Chinese, Japanese and Thai to egg and chips. There is even a McDonald's. The tourist office produces a directory, with photos. One reader reckons that you pay a lot less in restaurants at the south end of the village, well away from the centre.
   One of our favourites is the Pipe – a tiny place with interesting Asian/African/Caribbean fusion dishes, 'still superb' according to a reader in 2010. We've also enjoyed the Schwyzer Stübli (local specialities and live Swiss music and dancing); good value Mexican and Swiss dishes at the Weisshorn, endorsed by a reader ('very good food, friendly service, shame about the decor'); and decent Thai food at Rua Thai. Sparky's pub/restaurant is praised for its 'basic but nourishing food', which includes vegetarian options, stews and curries.

GETTING THERE

Air Geneva
240km/150 miles
(4hr); Zürich
265km/165 miles
(4hr30); Sion 80km/
50 miles (2hr)

Rail Station in resort

ACTIVITIES

Indoor Sauna, tennis,
squash, hotel
swimming pools
(some open to
public), fitness centre,
climbing wall,
museums, cinema

Outdoor Ice rinks,
curling, 45km cleared
paths, snowshoeing,
tobogganing,
helicopter flights, ice
climbing

Phone numbers
From elsewhere in
Switzerland add the
prefix 027; from
abroad use the prefix
+41 27

TOURIST OFFICE

www.zermatt.ch

And the restaurant at the cool hotel Cervo sounds appetising, with tapas, game and fish dishes – 'a welcome addition serving a modern take on mountain food'. 'Absolutely rammed' Grampi's is tipped again this year, for 'good pizza'.

Other reader tips include: Casa Rustica ('good Swiss food'); Klein Matterhorn for fish/pasta ('superb food'); Schäferstube ('some of the best lamb dishes in the village'); Stockhorn ('simple food done well'); and the dear old Whymper-Stube ('great food, very friendly service, reasonable prices').

APRES-SKI ★★★★★
Something for everybody

There's a good mix of sophisticated and informal fun, though it helps if you have deep pockets. Promenading the main street checking out expensive clothes and watches is a popular early-evening activity.

There are lively places to pause on your final descent. On the way back from Rothorn, Othmar's Skihütte and Olympia Stübli have great views, and the funky new Cervo where the piste ends has a 'great bar with live music'. Caffè Snowboat (near the Sunnegga funicular) is a small, modern place, with a terrace and lounge bar. On the way back from Furi there are lots of options, some described under 'Mountain restaurants'. Very near the end of the run, Hennu Stall blasts out loud music and attracts huge crowds – live bands play most days. 'Possibly my favourite mountain bar of all,' says one fan; 'awful service from surly Brits' is an opposing view.

For a lively bar through the evening you won't beat the Papperla Pub – 'rocks from 4.30pm', 'great atmosphere'. The long-established North Wall doesn't get many mentions in reports but still seems to be the season-worker favourite. Potters Bar (geddit?) is a relaxed British pub.

There are plenty of quieter places. The Vernissage is our favourite – unusual, stylish and modern, with the projection room for the cinema built into the upstairs bar and displays of art elsewhere; 'great ambience and decor'. Elsie's famous bar is wood-panelled and atmospheric; it attracts an older crowd, but gets seriously busy early and late. Reader tips include Brit-run Sparky's ('best priced beer in town'), the Little Bar (crowded if there are ten people in) and the

cosy/cramped Hexen. Of the hotel bars, the Alex has 'comfy sofas, good service and a pool table' and the Pollux is 'reliably good'.

Later on, the hotel Post complex has something for everyone, from a quiet, comfortable bar (Papa Caesar's) to a lively disco (Broken), live music (Pink) and various restaurants. The T-Bar draws a young crowd for dancing and live bands. At Grampi's ('very lively later in the evening'), the 'very entertaining' Elton John act seems to be still pulling in the crowds; there is a disco below. The Schneewittchen nightclub (Papperla) is 'still heaving at 3.30am', say reporters.

OFF THE SLOPES ★★★★☆
Considerable attractions

Zermatt is an attractive place to spend time. As well as expensive jewellery and clothes shops, there are interesting places selling food, wine, books and art. It is easy (but costly) for pedestrians to get around on the lifts and meet others for lunch, and there are some nice walks – a special map is available. If the weather is good, the Klein Matterhorn cable car is an experience not to be missed: there is a small self-service restaurant at the top as well as a viewing platform and an ice cave, with 'incredible carvings'. Be aware that the air is thin up there, though. The Matterhorn Museum in the village is worth seeing. You can take a helicopter trip around the Matterhorn (see 'Queues'). There is a cinema, and free village guided tours. For an icy experience, visit (or stay at) the Igloo above Riffelberg.

DOWN-VALLEY VILLAGE – 1450m
TÄSCH

Täsch, where visitors must leave their cars, is just a 12-minute train ride from Zermatt, so makes a viable base. There are several 3-star hotels charging half the Zermatt price. The Täscherhof (966 6262) – 'fine, comfortable and with a reasonably priced restaurant' – and the Walliserhof (966 3966) – 'a very good option' – have been recommended by past reporters. Täsch is very quiet in the evening, but it's no problem to spend evenings in Zermatt – trains run until 12.30am Monday to Wednesday, and hourly all night from Thursday to Sunday. And taxis can operate up to the edge of Zermatt.

USA

Most people who give it a try find America is pretty seductive, despite the relatively small sizes of its ski areas. What got the US started in the UK market was its (generally) reliable snow, and that remains a key factor. Other factors are the relatively deserted pistes, the quality of accommodation, the excellent, varied resort restaurants, the high standards of service and courtesy, and the immaculate piste grooming. Depending on the resort, you may also be struck by the cute Wild West ambience and the superb quality of the snow. Of course, US skiing does have some distinct disadvantages, too. Read on.

We have organised our American chapters in regional sections – California, Colorado, Utah, Rest of the West and New England.

Most American resorts receive serious amounts of snow – typically in the region of 6m to 12m (or 250 to 500 inches, as they measure it there) in a season; that's around double the 3m to 6m that resorts like Chamonix, St Anton and Val d'Isère in Europe average. It tends to arrive in more frequent falls than in Europe too, so your chances of hitting fresh snow are appreciably higher. And most resorts have serious snowmaking facilities that are used well – laying down a base of snow early in the season, rather than patching up shortages later. There are wide differences in quantity and quality of snowfall, both between individual resorts and between regions.

The classification of pistes (or trails, to use the local term) is different from that in Europe. Red runs don't exist. The colours used are combined with shapes. Green circles correspond fairly closely to greens in France and easy blues in the rest of Europe. American blue squares correspond to blues and easy reds in Europe; the tougher ones are sometimes labelled as double squares, or as blue-black squares. Then there are black diamond runs, which is where things get interesting. Single diamonds correspond fairly closely to European blacks and really tough reds. But then there are multiple diamonds. Double-diamond runs are seriously steep – usually steeper than the steepest pistes in the Alps. A few resorts have wildly steep 'extreme' double diamonds, or triple diamonds.

549

PATROLLED AND AVALANCHE-CONTROLLED OFF-PISTE

One of the great attractions of North American resorts to us is that they have patrolled and avalanche-controlled ungroomed terrain that would be classified as off-piste in Europe. Each resort has a 'ski area boundary'; this may be marked by signs on the trees bordering the trails or there may be a rope running right round the ski area boundary. The 'boundary' may be moved depending on snow conditions, and anywhere within the boundary is known as 'in-bounds' and is patrolled and avalanche controlled. In-bounds terrain includes areas between marked and groomed trails and often big areas of ski-anywhere bowls or steep couloirs (or chutes, to use the local term). In Europe such terrain is normally off-piste, and we recommend you ski it only with a qualified local guide; in North America it is safe to ski it without that expense. North America also has what it calls backcountry, which is the area outside the ski area boundary (and which you are often forbidden to access except through gates placed at various points on the boundary). This is not controlled or patrolled and should be treated like European off-piste and skied only with a guide.

← Quiet slopes, few lift queues, frequent dumps of snow – these are just three of the reasons we love skiing in the USA

The most obvious drawback to the US is that many resorts have slopes that are very modest in extent compared with major Alpine areas. But usually there are other resorts nearby – so if you are prepared to travel a bit, you won't get bored. Roads are good and car hire is cheap (watch out for extra insurance charges, though). But if snow is expected, you will need a 4WD or snow chains (you'll have to buy them – we've yet to find a US rental company that will provide them). It's also true that in many resorts the mountains are slightly monotonous, with countless similar trails cut through the forest. You don't usually get the spectacular mountain scenery and the distinctive high-mountain runs of the Alps. But the forest runs do offer good visibility in bad weather, and unlike in Europe, it's normal to be able to ski in among the trees themselves (or glades as they call them) – great fun in fresh snow.

GREAT GROOMING AND DESERTED SLOPES

Piste grooming is taken very seriously – most US resorts set standards that only the best Alpine resorts seem to be able to match. Every morning you can expect to step out on to perfect 'corduroy' pistes. But this doesn't mean that there aren't moguls – far from it. It's just that you get moguls where the resort says you can expect moguls, not everywhere.

The slopes of most US resorts are blissfully free of crowds – a key advantage that becomes more important as the pistes of Europe become ever more congested. If you want to ski quickly and safely with less fear of collisions, head for the States.

Ski schools offer consistently high standards, but work in a way that seems strange to Europeans – and disappointing to many. Your group will often have different instructors from day to day. Your classmates will vary too – people don't sign up for a week, but only for one or two lessons as they feel the need. But at least you don't have to join ski school to get to know the mountain: most resorts offer free guided tours of the area once or twice a day (usually carried out by volunteers who get a free lift pass in return); and many have 'mountain hosts' on hand to help you find your way. Piste maps are freely available at lift stations, and signposting is generally exemplary.

Lifts are generally efficient, and queues are orderly and short, partly because spare seats are religiously filled with the aid of cheerful, conscientious attendants who ask 'How are you today?' or urge you to 'Have a nice day' every time you get on a lift. You'll also find that Americans on chairlifts with you will be keen to talk to you on the way – weird to European eyes, but we like it. First-time visitors are surprised that some chairlifts in the States do not have safety bars; even on a chair that has a bar, you will find Americans curiously reluctant to use it, and eager to raise it as soon as the top station is in view. They worry about being trapped, not falling off. The lifts close irritatingly early – as early as 3pm in some cases (and some upper lifts might start closing as early as 1.30pm). That may explain another drawback of America – the dearth of decent mountain restaurants. The norm is a monster self-service refuelling station – designed to minimise time off the slopes. Small restaurants with table service and decent food are rare.

US resort towns vary widely in style and convenience, from cute restored mining towns to purpose-built monstrosities. Two important things the resorts have in common are high quality,

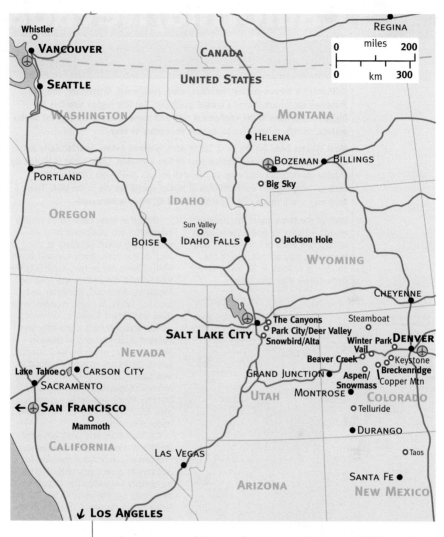

spacious accommodation and restaurants that are reliably good and varied in cuisine. Young people should be aware that the rigorously enforced legal age for drinking alcohol is 21; even if you are older, carry evidence of age, especially if you look younger than you are.

Crossing the pond is no longer cheap and neither are extras such as lift passes, ski hire and ski school – all these are generally much more expensive than in Europe. But eating and drinking is relatively cheap. Take a look at our price panels for each resort for an idea of what to budget for. With lift passes, in many resorts you can save huge amounts by buying in advance through tour operators or websites. Strangely, you can often also save money by buying discounted lift passes from local stores rather than at the official ticket office.

In the end, your reaction to skiing and snowboarding in America may depend on your reaction to America. If repeated exhortations to have a nice day wind you up – or if you like to ride chairlifts in silence – you'd better stick to the Alps. We love skiing there.

California/Nevada

California? It means surfing, beaches, wine, Hollywood, Disneyland and San Francisco cable cars. Nevada means gambling. But this region also has the highest mountains in the continental USA and some of America's biggest winter resorts, usually reliable for snow from November to May.

Most visitors head for the Lake Tahoe area, mapped below. Spectacularly set high in the Sierra Nevada 320km east of San Francisco, Lake Tahoe is ringed by skiable mountains containing 14 downhill resorts and seven cross-country centres – the highest concentration of winter sports resorts in the USA. Then, a long way south (more often reached from LA), there is Mammoth.

Each of the three major 'destination' resorts – Heavenly and Squaw Valley, at opposite ends of Lake Tahoe, and Mammoth, way off our map to the south – is covered in its own chapter immediately after this page.

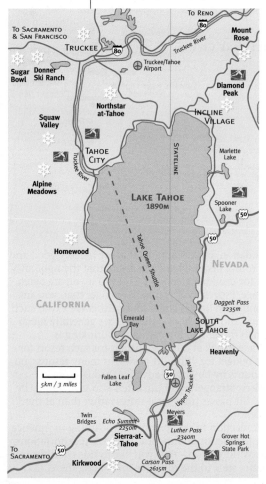

The other main Lake Tahoe resorts (shown on our map) each have an entry in the resort directory at the back of the book. Many are well worth visiting for a day or two, especially the four second-division resorts – Alpine Meadows, Kirkwood, Northstar and Sierra-at-Tahoe. We also enjoyed Sugar Bowl and Mount Rose.

Californian resorts often have the deepest accumulations of snow in North America, which Rockies powder connoisseurs are inclined to brand as wet 'Sierra Cement'. The snow can be heavy. But mostly the snow is fine, at least by Alpine standards – we've had truly fabulous powder days in all the major resorts here.

Californian resorts don't have the traditional mountain-town ambience that can add an extra dimension to holidays in other parts of the States, particularly Colorado. The recently developed car-free plaza in South Lake Tahoe called Heavenly Village and the pedestrian Village at Mammoth – both linked to the slopes by gondola – haven't achieved a great deal in this respect. But Squaw Valley and Northstar have both developed attractive base villages.

You could visit all these resorts by car (best to have a 4WD) from a single base at Heavenly or somewhere thereabouts; but a two-centre holiday also including some time at the north end of the lake would be better – Squaw would be our choice. A lift pass covering seven resorts around the lake and another valid at seven northern resorts are both available through tour operators (also see www.skilaketahoe. co.uk and www.gotahoenorth.com), though there is some sense in buying by the day according to the weather.

552

HEAVENLY SKI RESORT / SCOTT MARKEWITZ

Heavenly

Heavenly is unique: one of America's biggest mountains, with fabulous lake and 'desert' views, above a tacky casino town

RATINGS

The mountains	
Extent	***
Fast lifts	****
Queues	****
Terrain p'ks	*****
Snow	****
Expert	***
Intermediate	****
Beginner	****
Boarder	****
X-country	**
Restaurants	*
Schools	****
Families	**
The resort	
Charm	*
Convenience	*
Scenery	****
Eating out	****
Après-ski	***
Off-slope	***

RPI	135
lift pass	£340
ski hire	£115
lessons	£180
food & drink	£125
total	**£760**

NEWS

2011/12: Many of the upper runs on the California side are being substantially widened. A new ski school building for children and a new kids' adventure zone are to open at Adventure Peak.

2010/11: The Tamarack Lodge mountain restaurant opened at Adventure Peak, with terrace, food court and bar.

- + Spectacular views of Lake Tahoe and Nevada from slopes
- + Fair-sized mountain that offers a sensation of travelling around
- + Large areas of widely spaced trees – fabulous in fresh powder
- + Some serious challenges for experts
- + Numerous other worthwhile resorts within an hour's drive
- + Good snow record plus impressive snowmaking facilities
- + Unique nightlife in town at base

- − Town at base, South Lake Tahoe, is a messy, traffic-ridden place
- − No trail back to Heavenly Village at the base of the gondola
- − Lifts vulnerable to wind closure
- − Pronounced step from easy groomed blues to mogulled blacks
- − If natural snow is poor, most of the challenging terrain may be closed
- − Mountain restaurants dire (though new one in 2011 an improvement)
- − Very little traditional après-ski

With a top height of 3060m and vertical of 1060m, Heavenly is the highest and biggest of the resorts around famously deep, pure and beautiful Lake Tahoe. It has the best lake views, too. But anyone drawn by the scenic setting is likely to be dismayed by the barren base town of South Lake Tahoe, straddling busy US Highway 50. You could stay out of town, close to one of the other lift bases.

And the skiing? If your taste is for easy Alpine blacks or tough reds, just be sure you are ready to step up to ungroomed stuff – you'll find the blues tame.

THE RESORT

South Lake Tahoe, on the shore of the lake, is primarily a summer resort. It straddles the California-Nevada border, and its economy is based on gambling, which Nevada permits. The central Stateline area is dominated by a handful of high-rise hotel-casinos built on the Nevada side of the line.

These brash but comfortable hotels offer good-value rooms (subsidised by the gambling), swanky restaurants and various entertainments. Picking your way between the slot machines in ski gear, carrying skis or board, is weird.

Near the casino area is the small Heavenly Village, purpose-built around the main lift base. There are other lift base areas (with lodgings) on both California and Nevada sides of the hill.

Other resorts around the lake are easily visited from a base here, and lift passes that cover several areas are

VAIL RESORTS INC / COREY RICH

The Heavenly Flyer is the latest way to take in those amazing lake views →

KEY FACTS

Resort	1900m
	6,230ft
Slopes	2000-3060m
	6,570-10,040ft
Lifts	30
Pistes	4,800 acres
Green	20%
Blue	45%
Black	35%
Snowmaking	73%

available. A car is handy to explore them (although buses, some free, are available) and to get to many of the best restaurants, but parking can be expensive. Boat services to or from Squaw seem to have expired.

The obvious gateway airport is San Francisco, but Reno is much closer, and the road up less likely to be affected by snow.

VILLAGE CHARM ★✩✩✩✩
The highway rules

From a distance the casinos look like a classic American downtown area, which you'd expect to be full of shops and bars. But there's hardly any of that – just the seriously busy and pedestrian-hostile Highway 50. The rest of the town spreads for miles along the road – dozens of low-rise hotels and motels (some quite shabby), stores, wedding chapels and so on. The general effect is less dire than it might be, thanks to the camouflage of tall trees. Heavenly Village provides a downtown après-ski focus (basically just one bar), but is otherwise not a great success.

CONVENIENCE ★✩✩✩✩
Gamble on the gondola?

The central area close to Heavenly Village and the gondola looks the obvious place to stay, despite the lack of trails down to it. Some of the casino-hotels are within five minutes' walk of the gondola, but others are a hike away. There are lodgings close to the other lift bases – California Lodge, up a heavily wooded slope 2km out of South Lake Tahoe, and the more remote Nevada bases, Boulder Lodge and Stagecoach Lodge. And there are cheaper places literally miles from a lift, and used largely by people with cars. There are free shuttle-buses. You can ski down at the end of the day to all these other bases.

SCENERY ★★★★✩
Splendid panoramas

The views over Lake Tahoe, ringed by snow-capped mountains, are spectacular. The casinos are a conspicuous part of those views from the lower slopes, though not from above mid-mountain; the long Ridge Run, across the top, is good for lake views. In the other direction the slopes overlook wild and arid Nevada – sufficiently arid to be classified as desert, though the Sahara it ain't.

THE MOUNTAIN

Practically all of Heavenly's slopes are cut through forest, but in many areas the forest is not dense and there is excellent tree skiing. The trail map gives a good indication of the density of trees. As elsewhere in the US, this 'off-piste' terrain is 'patrolled' but only by hollering – ineffective if you are unconscious; don't ski the trees alone.

Two days a week, am and pm, there are free and 'excellent' mountain tours led by forest rangers.

EXTENT OF THE SLOPES ★★★✩✩
Interestingly complex

The mountain is complicated, and getting from A to B requires more careful navigation than is usual on American mountains. Quite a few of the links between different sectors involve long, flat tracks.

There is a clear division between the California side of the mountain (above South Lake Tahoe) and the Nevada side. If lift closures leave you on the wrong side, it's not a big deal – the bus rides don't take long.

The gondola from South Lake Tahoe goes to one end of the California side. There is no skiing back to the town. At the other end of this side, the steep lower slopes are served by the Aerial Tramway (cable car) and Gunbarrel fast chair from California Lodge. The much more extensive upper slopes are served by four fast chairs, one going up to the Skyline trail to the Nevada side.

The Nevada side is more fragmented, but the central focus is East Peak Lodge. Above it is an excellent intermediate area, served by two fast quad chairs, with a downhill extension served by the Galaxy chair. From the fast Dipper chair back up, you can access the open terrain of Milky Way Bowl, leading to the seriously steep chutes of Mott and Killebrew Canyons, served by the Mott Canyon chair. Below East Peak Lodge are runs down to Nevada's two bases, Stagecoach and Boulder – the latter often quiet because its chairs are slow.

FAST LIFTS ★★★★✩
California does it better

Most people can spend practically all their time on fast chairs. The Mott Canyon chair is slow, but that's a niche market. The main weaknesses are the slow chairs up from Boulder Lodge.

QUEUES ★★★★
Gondola up and down

Most reporters have had few other problems, often commenting on uncrowded slopes. The gondola can have queues to go up and particularly to go down – and because of this you'll see signs advising you to get back to the gondola ridiculously early. Pay no attention – have a beer or two at the top while waiting for the queue to dissipate. Or forget the gondola and head for one of the other bases, and jump on a shuttle. Other lifts that people use to get back to the top of the gondola can also be busy at peak times – Groove and Sky Express among them. One 2010 visitor reports crowds around the lifts from East Peak Lodge on the Nevada side too. Some lifts, including the gondola, also seem prone to closure because of wind.

TERRAIN PARKS ★★★★★
Splendid for all abilities

Heavenly has something for everyone – all sensibly located on the California slopes. The Groove Park, at the top of the lifts up from California Lodge, has beginner features such as small jumps and boxes for novice park riders. Intermediates should head to Player's Park off the Canyon chair; this is a great progression area, with three lines, a collection of intermediate rails, boxes, wall rides, recycled features, jibs and bonks. High Roller Park, near the top of the Canyon chair, serves expert riders; there is a large double-jump line – with jumps exceeding 20m in length – as well as large boxes, rails, wall rides and recycled features that often elevate 1m–3m off the snow. Ante Up Park under the Tamarack chair is intended for advanced and intermediates; all its features use recycled materials.

SNOW RELIABILITY ★★★★
No worries for intermediates

Heavenly averages an impressive 360 inches per year, but depth isn't everything. The weather here is much less consistent than further inland, so you can't count on ideal conditions even with abundant snow and with the benefit of impressive snowmaking. One January 2011 visitor got warm days and cold nights, spelling ice. Generally, the grooming is excellent, and overcomes these problems. A useful TV programme, *Another Heavenly Morning*, covers snow conditions.

↑ Just look at those perfectly spaced trees – on the Nevada side of the hill (the clouds are over the desert)
TANYA BOOTH

SCHOOLS

Heavenly
t 775 586 7000

Classes
3-day learn-to-ski package (includes equipment and pass) $430
Private lessons
From $425 for 3hr

CHILDCARE

Day Care Center
t 775 586 7000
Ages 6wk to 6yr; 8.30-4pm; from $125 including lunch; discount if booked ahead

Ski school
For ages 4 to 13 (snowboarding 5 to 13); full day (including 5hr of teaching, equipment, pass and lunch) from $180

FOR EXPERTS ★★★★★
Some specific challenges

The black runs under the California base lifts – including the Face and Gunbarrel (often used for mogul competitions) – are seriously steep. We've seen lots of people struggling on the top-to-bottom icy bumps. Many of the single diamonds higher up are at the easy end of the range. Ellie's, at the top of the mountain, may offer continuous moguls too, but was groomed and a great fast cruise when we last skied it. Skiways Glades, to skier's right of that, offers friendly, widely spaced trees; further right still are two newish trails, the Pinnacles. Lower down, a trusted reader raves about Maggie's Canyon.

On the Nevada side there are some excellent single-diamond glade areas too – notably to skier's left of the slow North Bowl chair. And there is some really steep stuff. Milky Way Bowl provides a gentle single-diamond introduction to the double-diamond terrain beyond it: the chutes in the otherwise densely wooded Mott and Killebrew Canyons are seriously steep and narrow. They are accessed through roped gateways, and are not to be underestimated. The Mott Canyon chair is slow, but you may not mind. Good natural snow is needed for the Canyons to be enjoyable (or open).

FOR INTERMEDIATES ★★★★★
Lots to do

The California side offers a progression from the relaxed cruising of the long Ridge Run, starting right at the top of the mountain, to more challenging blues dropping off the ridge towards

Sky Deck. More confident intermediates will want to spend time on the Nevada side, where there is more variety of terrain, more carving space and some great longer cruises down to the lift bases. But really strong intermediates looking for challenges need to be prepared to step up to the tree runs – maybe starting with Powderbowl Woods or The Pines – or to the blacks, which are often mogulled.

FOR BEGINNERS ★★★★★
An excellent place to learn

There are excellent beginner areas at the top of the gondola, at California Lodge and at Boulder Lodge (in Nevada). On the California side there are gentle green runs to progress to at the top of the cable car. Package deals of tuition and lift ticket are worth looking into.

FOR BOARDERS ★★★★★
Perfect playground – nearly

Heavenly has several terrain parks, and the resort's naturally varied terrain makes a perfect playground for advanced freeriders. Intermediates will have fun too, especially if there's powder in the trees. And there are good areas for beginners. But beware of the many flat spots where you'll have to scoot. Boardinghouse at Heavenly Village is the local snowboard-only shop.

FOR CROSS-COUNTRY ★★★★★
A separate world

The serious stuff is around the lake – notably at the Spooner Lake: over 80km of prepared trails.

GETTING THERE

Air San Francisco 320km/200 miles (3hr45); Reno 90km/55 miles (1hr30); South Lake Tahoe, 15min

UK PACKAGES

Alpine Answers, AmeriCan Ski, American Ski Classics, Crystal, Crystal Finest, Erna Low, Funway Holidays, Independent Ski Links, PowderBeds, Ski Independence, Ski Line, Ski Safari, Ski Solutions, Skitracer, Skiworld, Supertravel, Virgin Snow

ACTIVITIES

Indoor Casinos, spas, swimming pool, full hockey-size ice rink, galleries, cinema, museums

Outdoor Lake cruises, snowmobiling, gondola rides, helicopter tours, sleigh rides, dog sledding, hot springs, small ice rink, ballooning, snowshoeing, zip-line, factory outlet shops

Phone numbers
Different area codes are used on the two sides of the stateline; for this chapter, therefore, the area code is included with each number

From distant parts of the US, add the prefix 1. From abroad, add the prefix +1

TOURIST OFFICE

www.skiheavenly.com

MOUNTAIN RESTAURANTS ★☆☆☆☆
Dire – but new one helps
The on-mountain catering is grossly inadequate, especially in bad weather. However, a new restaurant, Tamarack Lodge, opened at the top of the gondola last season and reporters are united in welcoming it: 'a great improvement', 'fairly standard food but quality fine, and the place is large and comfortable'. Gunbarrel Grill in Lakeview Lodge at the top of the tram gets a mention for its 'excellent' buffet. The other options are outdoor decks serving BBQs and pizzas (hugely unenjoyable in a blizzard, as we can testify) and grossly overcrowded cafeterias. East Peak Lodge offered a reporter 'as bad an example of piste food as I ever hope to encounter'.

SCHOOLS AND GUIDES ★★★★☆
Small groups if you're lucky
A 2010 reporter sums up recent views well: 'Excellent tuition for all levels, with everyone progressing well; the beginners were skiing black-diamond tree runs by the end of the week.' Groups are generally small.

FOR FAMILIES ★★☆☆☆
Hardly heavenly
Heavenly offers various children's programmes and facilities. A new kids' ski school building and adventure zone are due to open at Adventure Peak for 2011/12, and Adventure Peak is home to family activities such as tubing as well.

STAYING THERE
Accommodation in the South Lake Tahoe area is abundant and ranges from the huge casinos to quite small motels.
Hotels Of the main casino hotels, Harrah's (775 588 6611) and Harveys (775 588 2411) are the closest to the gondola. Rooms booked on the spot are expensive; packages are cheaper.
Embassy Suites (530 544 5400) Luxury suites close to the gondola. Breakfast and après cocktails included.
Inn by the Lake (530 542 0330) 'Posh motel', less convenient but 'big rooms, nice view'. Hot tub, pool.
Station House Inn (530 542 1101) A Best Western; 'comfortable and well maintained'; 'excellent choice of full cooked breakfasts'.
3 Peaks Resort (530 544 4131) Convenient, with large rooms. Pool.

Timber Cove Lodge (530 541 6722) Bland but well run, with lake views from some rooms.
Lakeland Village (530 544 1685) Wide range of 'very comfortable' lodgings. A 2011 reporter rated his townhouse there 'very large and comfortable'.
MontBleu Resort (775 588 3515) 'Cheap rooms; can be noisy at night.'
Apartments Plenty of choice.

EATING OUT ★★★★☆
Good value and choice
There's a huge variety, at least if you are prepared to drive (and not drink). The casino hotels' all-you-can-eat buffets offer fantastic value and variety, and there are 'gourmet' choices too – try 19 Kitchen and Bar on the 19th at Harveys – 'great steaks'. LewMarNel's at the Station House Inn serves good fish, pasta, steak and veal ('delicious filet mignon'). Evan's American Gourmet Cafe does 'wonderful fresh food' and has an extensive wine list. The Stateline Brewery does 'excellent pub fare'.The Brit-style Tudor pub near the Inn by the Lake serves 'great burgers and steaks'. Other reporter tips include Hunan Garden for Chinese, Fresh Ketch at Tahoe Keys Marina ('good fish; went twice and loved it') and Zephyr Cove Resort. Heidi's serves a 'vast' breakfast, or try Nikki's Chaat (Indian), the Blue Angel or the Driftwood Cafe.

APRES-SKI ★★★☆☆
Some improvement
The close-of-play scene has looked up in recent years: there is an Austrian-style umbrella bar near the top of the gondola and Fire+Ice at the foot of it (with an outdoor seating area with open fires and heaters). Both get busy. Whiskey Dick's, on the main highway, has regular live music. Later on, the casinos have shows, occasionally with top-name entertainers.

OFF THE SLOPES ★★★☆☆
Luck be a lady
If you want to get away from the bright lights, try a boat trip or a hot-air balloon ride. Pedestrians can use the cable car or the gondola to share the lake views. Adventure Peak, at the top of the gondola, has tubing, snow biking and tobogganing, and the Heavenly Flyer zip-line. There are lots of snowshoe trails. The leisure centre has a proper swimming pool, and a hockey-size ice rink.

Mammoth Mountain

A big, sprawling mountain above a car-oriented, sprawling but pleasantly woody resort, a six-hour drive from Los Angeles

RATINGS

The mountains

Extent	★★★
Fast lifts	★★★★
Queues	★★★★
Terrain p'ks	★★★★★
Snow	★★★★
Expert	★★★★
Intermediate	★★★★
Beginner	★★★★
Boarder	★★★★★
X-country	★★★★
Restaurants	★★
Schools	★★★★
Families	★★★★

The resort

Charm	★★
Convenience	★★
Scenery	★★★
Eating out	★★★★★
Après-ski	★★★
Off-slope	★

RPI 125

lift pass	£280
ski hire	£120
lessons	£205
food & drink	£110
total	**£715**

NEWS

2011/12: The three-person slow Chair 5 will be replaced by a fast quad – good news for bad weather days.

2010/11: A new pedestrian bridge connecting the Village Ski Back Trail to The Village at Mammoth opened. And the Ski Back Trail that it serves was improved again.

➕ One of North America's bigger ski hills, with something for everyone

➕ Mix of open Alpine-style bowls and classic American wooded slopes

➕ Impressive snowfall record

➕ Uncrowded slopes most of the time

➕ Mightily impressive terrain parks

➕ Good views by US standards

➖ Mammoth Lakes is a rather straggling place with no focus, where life revolves around cars

➖ Most, though not all, lodgings are miles from the slopes

➖ Weekend crowds in high season

➖ Trail map and signing inadequate

➖ Wind can be a problem

Mammoth may not be mammoth in Alpine terms – from end to end, it's less than one-third of the size of Val d'Isère/Tignes, in area more like one-sixth – but it is big enough to amuse many people for a week.

These days there is something resembling a village to stay in – The Village, a typically careful Intrawest confection of lodgings, restaurants and shops. But most people stay elsewhere – in hotels, condos and houses spread around the vast wooded area of Mammoth Lakes – and never go near it. Pick your location carefully, and you can walk to a lift; get a car, and you open up lots of options.

THE RESORT

The mountain is set above Mammoth Lakes, a small year-round resort that spreads over a wide area of woodland. The drive up from Los Angeles takes around six hours (more in poor conditions). You pass through the Santa Monica mountains close to Beverly Hills, then the San Gabriel mountains and Mojave Desert (with the world's biggest jet-plane parking lot) before reaching the Sierra Nevada.

The Mammoth lift pass also covers June, a small mountain half an hour's drive north, with deserted slopes. See feature box, later in this chapter.

VILLAGE CHARM ★★
Good first impressions

The place is entirely geared to driving, with no discernible centre – hotels, restaurants and little shopping centres are scattered along the four-lane highway called Main Street and Old Mammoth Road, which crosses it. The resort buildings are generally timber-clad in traditional style – even McDonald's has been tastefully designed – and are set among trees, so although it may be short on village ambience, the place has a pleasant enough appearance – particularly when under snow. The Village is car-free, and neatly designed, but we hear the shops are struggling.

CONVENIENCE ★★
Canyon Lodge is closest

The town meets the mountain at two lift bases, both a mile or two from most of the hotels and condos.

The major base is Canyon Lodge, with a big day lodge; there are hotels, condos and individual homes in the area below the lodge. The Village is linked to Canyon Lodge by a gondola, so is a fairly convenient base. You can now ski back on a green run too – though it is very flat in parts. The minor base is Eagle Lodge (also known as Juniper Springs, strictly is the name of the adjacent condos).

A road skirts the mountain to two other major base areas: Mill Cafe, and Main Lodge, a mini-resort with a big day lodge. You can stay here, in the Mammoth Mountain Inn; but you are then four miles from the 50+ restaurants in Mammoth Lakes.

Shuttle-buses run on several colour-coded routes serving the lift bases; easy to use as 'stops are all perfectly placed and numbered'. Night buses run until midnight. But a car is useful.

SCENERY ★★★
Hint of the Alpine

The resort has a sheltered, wooded setting below contrasting Alpine style ridges. From the top there are great views north-east into Nevada, and of the jagged Minarets to the west.

Steep open slopes at the top, wooded at the bottom, and lightly wooded in between →

MAMMOTH MOUNTAIN / PEATROSS

KEY FACTS

Resort	2425m
	7,950ft

Mammoth only	
Slopes	2425-3370m
	7,950-11,050ft
Lifts	28
Pistes	3,500 acres
Green	25%
Blue	40%
Black	35%
Snowmaking	
	33%

June Mountain only	
Slopes	2290-3075m
	7,510-10,090ft
Lifts	7
Pistes	500 acres
Green	35%
Blue	45%
Black	20%
Snowmaking	none

THE MOUNTAIN

The 28 lifts access an impressive area, suitable for all abilities. The highest runs are open, the lower ones sheltered by trees, with lightly wooded slopes at mid-mountain that are great on a stormy day.

Finding your way around is not easy at first. The chairlifts are either named or numbered (the traditional practice was to give them numbers), but the trails are still ill defined: the map shows trails by means of isolated symbols, not continuous lines, and signposting of runs on the mountain is sporadic. On the lower part of the mountain this is mainly an inconvenience. But higher up there are real dangers in poor visibility. The map uses six classifications, including green/black and blue/black – a good idea, but somewhat pointless when you often end up on the wrong trail.

A reporter this year rates the free tours by mountain hosts excellent.

EXTENT OF THE SLOPES ★★★★★
Interesting variety
From **Main Lodge** the two-stage Panorama gondola goes via McCoy Station right to the top. There are countless ways down the front of the mountain, which range from steep to very steep – or vertical if the wind has created a cornice, as it often does. Or you can go off the back of the hill, down to **Outpost 14**, whence Chair 14 or Chair 13 brings you back to lower points on the ridge. The third option is to follow the ridge, which curls around

and eventually brings you down to the Main Lodge area – though you wouldn't know it from studying the trail map. This route brings you past an easy area served by a double chair, and a very easy area served by the Discovery fast quad.

McCoy Station can also be reached using the Stump Alley fast chair from **Mill Cafe**, on the road up from town. The fast Gold Rush quad, also from Mill Cafe, takes you into the more heavily wooded eastern half of the area. This has long, gentle runs served by lifts up from **Canyon Lodge** and

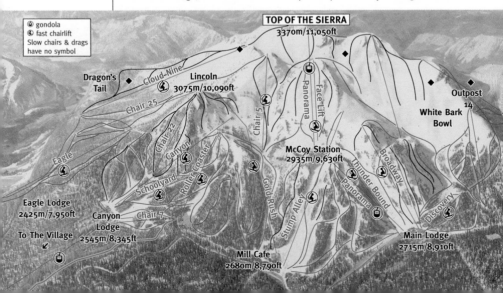

MAMMOTH MOUNTAIN

The lightly wooded slopes around mid-mountain are excellent when the weather is less benign than this ↓

Eagle Lodge and seriously steep stuff as well as some intermediate terrain on the subsidiary peak known as Lincoln, served by lifts 25 and 22.

FAST LIFTS ★★★★
Where it counts
There is plenty of choice from every base: all the main access lifts are fast chairs or gondolas. The Outpost area is the least well served.

QUEUES ★★★★
Normally quiet slopes
Mammoth's lifts and slopes are usually very quiet, with few queues. The lift system is fairly impressive, but even that can struggle when there's an invasion from Los Angeles on fine peak-season weekends. To avoid them, try the blissfully uncrowded June Mountain, half an hour away.

TERRAIN PARKS ★★★★★
Difficult to beat
Mammoth's world-class Unbound Terrain Parks areas are made up of no fewer than seven parks. There are over 50 jumps, 65 jibs and three half-pipes in 90 acres of freestyle territory. Easiest is the Disco park at Main Lodge, with small low-to-the-snow rails and boxes. Next is the beginner-friendly Wonderland park, located by Chair 7. It has a fun mini-pipe, various micro-scale rails, boxes and mini-jumps, and a great atmosphere. For intermediate to advanced riders South Park, Jibs Galore (Chair 4) and Forest Trail (Chair 6) Park are playgrounds offering a bewildering choice of rails

and kickers. Alternatively, take on the X-Course boardercross (Chair 4). Finally Main Park, situated off Chair 6 above Main Lodge, is huge; everything here is up to pro standard. Kickers range from 18m to 24m long and border the famous super-duper pipe (183m long, with 7m walls) that looms over the car park and dwarfs the super-pipe beside it; it is cut daily. Main Park is serviced by a fast chairlift, allowing for a full lap time of only eight minutes. The Art Park features paintings and photographs as tributes to local legend the late Jeff Anderson and is located on the Round Robin run near Canyon Lodge and Chair 16. The parks can get very crowded at weekends – try neighbouring June Mountain for a quiet and highly regarded alternative.

SNOW RELIABILITY ★★★★
A long season
Mammoth has an impressive snow record – an annual average of 385 inches, which puts it ahead of major Colorado resorts and about on a par with Jackson Hole. Its slopes are appreciably higher than those of the Tahoe resorts, and it has an ever-expanding array of snow-guns, so it enjoys a long season. The mountain faces roughly north-east; the relatively low and slightly sunny slopes down to Eagle Lodge are affected by warm weather before others. Strong winds are not uncommon on the upper mountain and the snow quality can be affected. But you may find powder is just shifted down the hill. Grooming is generally good.

June Mountain, a scenic half-hour drive from Mammoth, is in the same ownership and covered by the lift pass. It makes a pleasant haven if Mammoth is busy. When Mammoth isn't busy, June is quite simply deserted; we've skied run after run without seeing anyone other than lifties. Quite, quite weird.

A double chair goes up from the car park at 2290m over black slopes (often short of snow) to a lodge, June Meadows Chalet. A quad chair serves a gentle blue-run hill, and a double chair goes over very gentle green runs to a quad serving short but genuinely black slopes on June Mountain itself (3100m). There are three freestyle areas, a super-pipe and a jib park.

FOR EXPERTS ★★★★
Some very challenging terrain

The steep double-diamond chutes strung across the width of the mountain top provide wonderful opportunities for experts. Fortunately for the rest of us there are three or four broad single-diamond slopes, requiring rather less bottle.

There is lots of challenging terrain lower down, too, much of it lightly wooded and therefore good to ski in bad conditions; Chair 5, Chair 22 (the top of which is higher than the very top of Heavenly) and Broadway are often open in bad weather when the top is firmly shut, and their more sheltered slopes may in any case have the best snow. There are plenty of good slopes over the back towards Outpost 14, too.

Many of the steeper trails are short by Alpine standards (typically under 400m vertical), but despite this we've had some great powder days here.

FOR INTERMEDIATES ★★★★
Lots of great cruising

Although there are exceptions, most of the lower mountain, below the treeline, is intermediate cruising territory and generally flattering.

As you might hope, the six-point trail difficulty scale – which we haven't tried to replicate – is a good guide to what you'll find on the mountain.

Some of the mountain's longest runs, blue-blacks served by the Cloud Nine Express and Chair 25, are ideal for good intermediates. There are also some excellent, fairly steep woodland trails down to Mill Cafe. Most of the long runs above Eagle Lodge, and some of the shorter ones above Canyon Lodge, are easy cruises. There is a variety of terrain, including lots of gentle stuff, at the western extremity of the slopes (the right hand side of the trail map), both on the front side and on the back side.

FOR BEGINNERS ★★★★
Good, gentle slopes

Chair 7 and the Schoolyard Express chair at the Canyon Lodge base and Discovery Chair at Main Lodge serve quiet, gentle green runs – perfect terrain for novices, and the American skiing product at its best. These lifts, plus two others, are included in a beginner lift pass. Excellent instruction and top-notch piste maintenance usually make progress speedy, delighting reporters.

FOR BOARDERS ★★★★★
Great parks and terrain

Regularly voted one of the best snowboard resorts in the USA by *Transworld Snowboarding* magazine readers, Mammoth has encouraged snowboarding since its early days. A huge amount has been spent on the terrain parks, and this tends to overshadow just how good the mountain's natural terrain really is. Almost entirely serviced by hassle-free fast chairs and gondolas, this is a snowboarder's heaven. There are bowls, chutes, tree runs and cliffs dotted around the mountain, something for everybody. There are heaps of not-so-steep and wide runs for beginners on the lower parts of the resort. The terrain parks are about the best you will find. Wave Rave snowboard shop has a big selection of gear.

FOR CROSS-COUNTRY ★★★★
Very popular

Two specialist centres, Tamarack (31km) and Sierra Meadows (ungroomed), provide lessons and tours. A recent reporter enjoyed an 'excellent outing' there: 'gorgeous vistas gliding through the forest around mountain lakes'. And there are lots of ungroomed tracks, including some through the pretty Lakes Basin area.

Mammoth Mountain

561

Interactive resort shortlist builder at www.wtss.co.uk

SCHOOLS

Mammoth Mountain
934 2571

Classes
Half-day (9.30-12pm)
$135
Private lessons
$160 for 1hr for up to
five people

CHILDCARE

Small World
t 934 0646
Ages newborn to 8yr;
8.30-4.30 $119

Ski school
Takes ages 5 to 12.
Full day $179 inc
lunch, lift, rental
(9am-3pm)

GETTING THERE

Air Los Angeles
494km/307 miles
(5hr); Reno
275km/175 miles
(4hr15)

ACTIVITIES

Indoor Fitness
centres, spas,
museum, art galleries,
cinema, theatre

Outdoor Tubing, ice
skating, gondola
rides, snowmobiling,
snowshoeing

UK PACKAGES

*AmeriCan Ski, American
Ski Classics,
Independent Ski Links,
Ski Independence, Ski
Line, Ski Safari, Ski
Solutions, Skitracer,
Skiworld, Snow
Finders, Virgin Snow*

Phone numbers
From distant parts of
the US, add the prefix
1 760; from abroad,
add the prefix +1 760

TOURIST OFFICE

www.mammoth
mountain.com

MOUNTAIN RESTAURANTS ★★★★★
Back to base ...
There are really only two or three lunch options on the hill. Top of the Sierra Cafe and Market is small and 'very functional' but has 'views to die for'. McCoy Station at mid-mountain offers a wide choice – Waffle'wich was added in 2011 – and the table-service Parallax next door is pleasant, with a splendid view from its picture windows. A fair-weather option is the primitive outdoor BBQ at Outpost 14, on the back of the hill, and 2011 saw the introduction of the Roving Mammoth, a snowcat that drives around the mountain selling burritos and stuff – cool, eh?

SCHOOLS AND GUIDES ★★★★★
Come on, people?
We have no recent reports. But there is a choice of performance classes, such as 'camps' for experts or women.

FOR FAMILIES ★★★★★
Family favourite
Mammoth is keen to attract families. The focal point is the Small World childcare centre, with comprehensive facilities for children up to eight years old. Working closely with them is the Woollywood school, based in the Panorama gondola station and offering various tuition packages. There are other kids' schools at the Canyon and Eagle Lodges.

STAYING THERE

A good choice of hotels (none very luxurious or expensive) and condos. The condos tend to be out of town, near the lifts or on the road to them.
★★★Mammoth Mountain Inn (934 2581) Good value, but way out of town at Main Lodge.
★★★Alpenhof Lodge (934 6330) Comfortable and centrally located. Shuttle-bus stop and plenty of restaurants nearby.
Westin Monache Resort (934 0400) Condo hotel near The Village gondola, with restaurant, hot tubs and pool.
Quality Inn (934 5114) Good main street hotel with a big hot tub.
Sierra Nevada Lodge (934 2515) Central; recently renovated. Spa.
Apartments The Village Lodge is close to many restaurants and shops; Juniper Springs Resort is near the Eagle base; both are high quality. Other comfortable options are the

Seasons 4 Resort (close to the Village), the 1849 Condos (Canyon Lodge area) and the nearby Mammoth Ski and Racquet Club.

EATING OUT ★★★★★
Outstanding choice
Mammoth has 50+ restaurants offering a wide choice from typical American to Japanese. There's a local menu guide covering many but not all.

The chalet-style Lakefront in the Tamarack Lodge is one of the best, with great views and 'a real French feel and fabulous food', enthuses a recent reporter. Readers also like Giovanni's Italian for 'excellent' pizza and pasta. Slocums Grill is a popular steakhouse ('excellent meals'). Angels has 'good value ribs and steaks'. Chart House serves 'excellent' seafood dishes. For 'good home cooking' the meat loaf or prime rib at the Stove is reportedly worth a try. And we've had excellent dinners at Skadi and Whiskey Creek.

Other possibilities include Shogun for Japanese or Gomez's for Tex-Mex. For a hearty breakfast, try the, er, Breakfast Club. The Side Door cafe is an appealing eatery in The Village. The Parallax at McCoy Station opens for snowcat dinners up the mountain.

APRES-SKI ★★★★★
Lively at weekends
At the close of play, the Yodler at Main Lodge is still the liveliest spot – a renovated chalet (originally brought from Switzerland, so they say). Tusks at Main Lodge and the Dry Creek bar in the Mammoth Mountain Inn across the road are the other choices.

Nightlife revolves around a handful of bars, livening up at weekends. Reporters favour the Clocktower Cellar, Whiskey Creek (stays open late), Grumpy's sports bar and quieter Slocums. In The Village, Hawaiian-style Lakanuki's and the Auld Dubliner Irish bar are worth a look. An après-ski bus runs from Main Lodge to The Village, connecting with the town buses.

OFF THE SLOPES ★★★★★
Mainly sightseeing
There are various outdoor activities, including skating. There are pleasant drives; Mono Lake is worth a visit, and the town of Bishop is a 40-minute drive south. There is factory shopping nearby too, and the World War II centre at Manzanar on the road to Los Angeles has been recommended.

Squaw Valley

The site of the 1960 Olympics has become the most compelling resort in the Tahoe area, for novices and experts at least

- ➕ Lots of challenging terrain
- ➕ Impressive snow record
- ➕ Superb beginner slopes
- ➕ Convenient, pleasant, purpose-built village at the base

- ➖ Not for mile-hungry intermediates
- ➖ Lifts prone to closure by wind
- ➖ Adventurous skiers need guidance to really exploit the area
- ➖ Limited range of village amenities

When Intrawest built a neat little base village a few years back, Squaw became our favourite place to stay at Tahoe. It won't suit everyone, of course. And we would always combine it with a stay at the other end of the lake, to ski Heavenly and the resorts south of the lake. Oh, and pray for good weather.

NEWS

2011/12: All trails have been given names and classified for difficulty, and signposting is now being installed. Amazing.

2010/11: Grooming was improved, and the Olympic House, Olympic Village and Gold Coast Lodges were given facelifts. The Belmont terrain park became a kids' adventure area.

THE RESORT

Squaw is the major resort at the north end of Lake Tahoe. Since construction of the car-free Village here has become more attractive (particularly if you have a car), but it is still also popular as a day trip from South Lake Tahoe and Heavenly. There are shuttle-buses. There are other lodgings around the valley, and at Tahoe City.

Village charm The Village is very small and limited in what it offers, but works well. And the older base developments next to it are not unpleasant. One recent reporter notes empty retail units, which is bad news.

Convenience The Village and adjacent lodgings are at the base of the main lifts. The self-contained, luxurious, conference-oriented Resort at Squaw Creek hotel has its own chairlift into one end of the network.

Scenery There are fabulous views of Lake Tahoe from Squaw Peak.

THE MOUNTAINS

One of the attractions of the area is that the slopes are lightly wooded. The resort has until now been stupidly unhelpful about navigation. Only now are conventional named, classified trails being shown on the mountain map. And proper matching signs on the ground are now being installed.

Slopes There are several distinct sectors. A gondola and a big cable car rise 600m to the twin stations of Gold Coast and High Camp (linked by the Pulse gondola). Above them is a wide area of beginner slopes, and beyond that the three highest peaks of the area, with lifts of modest vertical – much the biggest is on Squaw Peak's Headwall six-pack: 535m.

From High Camp you can descend into a steep-sided valley from which the Silverado chair is the return.

Two other peaks are accessed directly from the village. A fast quad

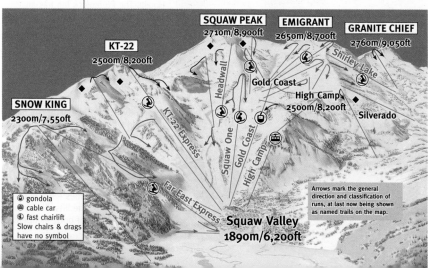

SQUAW PEAK 2710m/8,900ft
EMIGRANT 2650m/8,700ft
GRANITE CHIEF 2760m/9,050ft
KT-22 2500m/8,200ft
Shirley Lake
Headwall
Gold Coast
High Camp 2500m/8,200ft
SNOW KING 2300m/7,550ft
KT-22 Express
Squaw One
Gold Coast
Silverado
High Camp
Far East Express
Squaw Valley 1890m/6,200ft

Arrows mark the general direction and classification of runs, at last now being shown as named trails on the map.

ⓖ gondola
ⓒ cable car
ⓕ fast chairlift
Slow chairs & drags have no symbol

UK PACKAGES

AmeriCan Ski, American Ski Classics, Crystal, Funway Holidays, Independent Ski Links, PowderBeds, Ski Independence, Ski Safari, Skitracer, Skiworld, Supertravel, Virgin Snow

Phone numbers
From distant parts of the US, add the prefix 1 530; from abroad, add the prefix +1 530

TOURIST OFFICE

www.squaw.com

TANYA BOOTH

The slopes are lightly wooded more or less to the top, which is a great help in heavy snowfall ↓

serves steep KT-22; a slow triple goes to rather neglected Snow King.

Squaw's cable car runs in the evenings to serve the floodlit slopes (including a 5km run to the base area), and terrain parks and the dining facilities at High Camp.

Fast lifts There are fast lifts in each sector, but also slow old chairs.

Queues Few problems usually, but the weather and weekend invasions are key factors.

Terrain parks Riviera Park offers intermediate and expert jump lines, a night-accessible pipe with 5.5m walls, and big jib features. The Rail Yard is constantly updated with innovative features. There are other peak season parks, when conditions permit, and parks designed for kids and novices.

Snow reliability An impressive 450 inches on average, plus snowmaking.

Experts The possibilities for experts on KT-22, Squaw Peak and Granite Chief – plus the Silverado valley – are huge, with lots of steep chutes and big mogul fields; many extreme skiing and boarding movies are made here. But at first it is very difficult to identify routes that are safe, and easy to get yourself into tricky spots – to get the most out of the area, get a guide.

Intermediates Blue-run skiers have a choice of some lovely cruises in the Emigrant and Snow King sectors and a three-mile top-to-bottom run. But there is not much more groomed cruising, so keen piste-bashers will find the area limited. There is, however, lots of steep blue and easy black terrain in which to develop

deep-snow or mogul skills – particularly around the Siberia, Solitude and Granite Chief lifts.

Beginners The Papoose nursery area has a gentle slope served by a double chairlift – a special beginner package, with lift pass, is available. There's a superb choice of easy runs to progress to at altitude, notably at High Camp.

Snowboarding This is one of the most snowboarder friendly resorts around. The higher areas are full of steep and deep gullies, cliff drops, kicker building spots and tree runs, and the parks are kept in excellent shape.

Cross-country There are 18km of groomed trails at Squaw Creek.

Mountain restaurants The mid-mountain facilities are uninspiring, except in terms of views.

Schools and guides The school runs 'Go with a Pro' adult group lessons morning and afternoon. There are specialist workshops and free orientation tours – but they are only an hour long.

Families Squaw offers slope-side convenience and a children's on-slope play area at the Papoose base. Squaw Kids takes children from three years.

STAYING THERE

Hotels The PlumpJack Inn (583 1576) is our favourite – comfortable, stylish, central. The Resort at Squaw Creek (583 6300) offers luxury rooms, an outdoor pool and hot tubs, and 'fantastic buffet breakfasts'.

Apartments The Village has well-appointed ski-in/ski-out condos.

Eating out For a tiny place, choice is adequate in the Village and the nearby older buildings – notably Olympic House. The PlumpJack Inn has an excellent restaurant. More routine places include the Auld Dubliner pub ('good Guinness stew'), Fireside (pizza/pasta) and Mamasake (sushi). You can eat up at High Camp.

Après-ski The Olympic House (revamped for 2010/11, we are told) has several venues. In the Village, the places above mostly function as bars, too: Auld Dubliner has live music on a Friday, but is 'dead during the week'. Uncorked at Squaw Valley is a wine bar with live music and weekly wine tastings.

Off the slopes High Camp has an ice rink and other activities – not much use if wind closes the lifts. The Trilogy Spa offers a range of body-pampering treatments.

Colorado

Colorado is the most popular American destination for UK visitors. And justifiably so: it has the most alluring combination of attractive resorts, slopes to suit all abilities and excellent, reliable snow – dry enough to justify its 'champagne powder' label. It also has direct scheduled BA flights to Denver (though no longer charter flights).

Colorado has amazingly dry snow. Even when the snow melts and refreezes, the moisture seems to be magically whisked away, leaving it soft and powdery. Even the artificial snow is of a quality you'll rarely find in Europe. And like most North American rivals, Colorado resorts generally have excellent, steep, ungroomed areas that you can ski safely without a guide.

The resorts vary enormously. If you want cute restored buildings from the mining boom days of the late 1800s, try the dinky old towns of Telluride or Crested Butte or the much bigger Aspen. Other resorts, such as Aspen's modern satellite Snowmass, major on convenience. Some – such as Vail and Beaver Creek – deliberately pitch themselves upmarket, with lots of glitzy, expensive hotels, while others –

such as Breckenridge and Winter Park – are much more down to earth.

You could consider renting a car and touring several resorts – maybe cutting costs by staying in the valley.

Six of the major resorts get write-ups in this section. The others with blue circles in the map below have entries in the resort directory at the back of the book – of these Steamboat, Copper Mountain, Keystone, Crested Butte and Telluride have proper resort villages while the others cater mainly for day skiers.

Many Colorado resorts are extremely high. As a result, lowlanders going there are at risk of altitude sickness, which can put you out of action for days. On our tours, we start in one of the lower resorts – or spend a night in Denver to acclimatise.

One of the great things about skiing in North America is that wild, ungroomed terrain such as the Hanging Valley area of Snowmass is avalanche controlled and patrolled – and so you don't need to hire a guide to explore it ↓

565

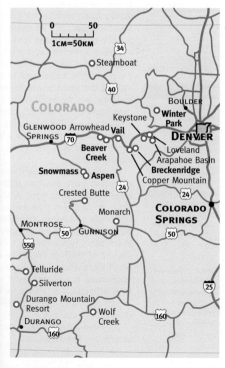

Aspen

Don't be put off by the ritzy image – with a fun, historic town and quiet, extensive slopes, this is America's best resort

RATINGS

The mountains

Extent	★★★★
Fast lifts	★★★★
Queues	★★★★
Terrain p'ks	★★★★★
Snow	★★★★★
Expert	★★★★★
Intermediate	★★★★★
Beginner	★★★★★
Boarder	★★★★
X-country	★★★★
Restaurants	★★★
Schools	★★★★★
Families	★★

The resort

Charm	★★★★
Convenience	★★
Scenery	★★★
Eating out	★★★★★
Après-ski	★★★★
Off-slope	★★★★

Our extent rating relates to the whole Aspen-Snowmass area. Aspen alone would rate ★★

566

RPI	150
lift pass	£340
ski hire	£185
lessons	£215
food & drink	£125
total	**£865**

NEWS

2011/12: At Tiehack on Buttermilk, a new high-speed quad is due to replace the existing slow lifts, cutting ride time by 60%. The gladed terrain it serves will be improved. And the Merry-Go-Round restaurant at mid-mountain on Aspen Highlands is due to reopen after a $6m makeover.

2010/11: There are now free tours of Highland Bowl on Wednesdays at 11am for skiers and riders confident on double black diamond terrain.

- ➕ Notably uncrowded slopes
- ➕ Attractive, characterful old mining town, with lots of smart shops
- ➕ Great range of restaurants
- ➕ Excellent Aspen Highlands and Snowmass just up the road
- ➕ Extensive slopes to suit every standard, but...
- ➖ Slopes split over four separate mountains (including Snowmass), served by efficient, free buses
- ➖ Expensive, and tending to become more so as cheap places disappear
- ➖ A bit isolated from the rest of Colorado, if you're set on a two-centre trip

A 2011 editorial visit confirmed that Aspen is still our favourite American resort. It has everything we look for – except, obviously, convenience. Our affection depends heavily on the presence of Aspen Highlands, a little way down the valley, and on Snowmass, considerably further down the valley (covered in a separate chapter). So most days you have to ride a bus; that doesn't worry us, and doesn't seem to worry readers who report on the place – one besotted reporter went for the fifth time a few seasons ago. (We don't get many reports, and would welcome more – whether you are besotted or not.)

Many rich and some famous guests jet in here, and for connoisseurs of cosmetic surgery the bars of the top hotels can be fascinating places. And the place does seem to be drifting even further upmarket. But, like all other 'glamorous' ski resorts, Aspen is actually filled by ordinary holidaymakers. Don't be put off.

THE RESORT

In 1892 Aspen was a booming silver-mining town, with 12,000 inhabitants, six newspapers and an opera house. But the town's fortunes took a nosedive when the silver price plummeted in 1893, and by the 1930s the population had shrunk to 700 or so, and the handsome Victorian buildings had fallen into disrepair. Development of the skiing started on a small scale in the late 1930s. The first lift was opened shortly after the Second World War, and Aspen hasn't looked back.

Aspen Mountain is right above the town. And there are three other ski areas nearby (all covered by the ski pass). Around 3km from Aspen are Buttermilk and Aspen Highlands. Buttermilk has the Inn at Aspen hotel at the base. Highlands has a limited amount of lodgings (including the very smart Ritz Carlton Club). Snowmass, 14km away, is a proper resort with great attractions as a base for families, in particular, and it gets its own chapter.

All three outlying areas are served by efficient free buses.

VILLAGE CHARM ★★★★
Smart old town

Aspen's historic centre – with a typical American grid of streets – has been preserved to form the core of the most fashionable ski town in the Rockies. There's a huge variety of restaurants, bars, shops and art galleries – some very upmarket.

A mixture of developments spreads out from the centre, ranging from the homes of the super-rich through surprisingly modest hotels and motels to mobile homes for the workers. Though the town is busy with traffic, it moves slowly, and pedestrians effectively have priority in much of the central area.

↓ Aspen Mountain

LIFT PASSES

Four Mountain Pass

Prices in US$

Age	1-day	6-day
under 13	66	336
13 to 17	91	486
18 to 64	100	540
over 65	91	486

Free under 7
Senior over 70: $379 for unlimited period
Beginner included in price of lessons

Notes
Covers Aspen Mountain, Aspen Highlands, Buttermilk and Snowmass, and shuttle-bus between the areas. Large savings if you purchase in advance online or through certain tour operators

ASPEN / DANIEL BAYER

Aspen Highlands runs are often deserted; and the views of the Maroon Bells are the stuff of postcards ↓

CONVENIENCE ★★★★★
Better by bus

Aspen is very unusual in being a cute old town with a major lift close to the centre: the Silver Queen gondola straight to the top of Aspen Mountain is only yards from some of the top hotels, restaurants and shops that make Aspen what it is. Downtown Aspen is quite compact by American resort standards, but it spreads far enough to make the free ski-bus a necessity for many visitors staying less centrally. You also need buses to get to the other mountains, of course. Generally, they work well. But they can get crowded, and you may need to keep an eye on the timetables.

SCENERY ★★★★★
Beautiful Bells

The views from the upper part of Highlands are the best that Aspen has to offer – the famous and distinctive Maroon Bells that appear on countless postcards. Buttermilk enjoys great views of Pyramid Peak (Colorado's most difficult 14,000ft mountain to climb) and the Maroon Creek valley.

THE MOUNTAINS

Most of the slopes are in the trees. All the mountains have free guided tours at 10.30, given by excellent volunteer ambassadors. The ratio of acres to visitor beds is high, and the slopes are usually blissfully uncrowded. Signposting could be better where runs merge. A reporter found piste classification 'inconsistent' between mountains. Plum TV channel offers up-to-date slope information.

EXTENT OF THE SLOPES ★★★★★
Widely dispersed

Each of the four mountains is worth a visit – though novices should note that Aspen Mountain has no green runs. Much the most extensive mountain in the area is at Snowmass – see separate chapter. Note that our extent rating is based on the total skiable area including Snowmass.

Once you are up the gondola, a series of chairs serves the ridges of **Aspen Mountain**. In general, there are long cruising blue runs along the valley floors and short, steep blacks down from the ridges.

Buttermilk is the smallest, lowest and least challenging mountain, accessed by a fast quad from the fairly primitive main base lodge. The runs fan out from the top in three directions – back to the base, down to Tiehack and down to West Buttermilk (with fast quads back from all three).

Aspen Highlands consists essentially of a single ridge served by three fast quad chairs, with easy and intermediate slopes along the ridge itself and steep black runs on the flanks – very steep ones at the top. And beyond the lift network, a free snowcat ride leads to Highland Bowl, where gates access a splendid open bowl of entirely double-black gradient.

FAST LIFTS ★★★★★
Serving bottom to top

Each mountain has a few key fast chairs or a gondola up to the top stations; the other lifts are slow chairs.

QUEUES ★★★★★
Few problems

Major queues are rare on any of the mountains. At Aspen Mountain, the gondola can still have delays at peak times. The alternative is the slow Shadow Mountain chair, with a short uphill walk to reach it. Aspen

Aspen

Interactive resort shortlist builder at www.wtss.co.uk

GET THE BEST OF THE SNOW, ON- AND OFF-PISTE

Aspen offers special experiences for small numbers of skiers or riders.

Fresh Tracks *The first skiers to sign up each day get to ride the gondola up Aspen Mountain at 8am the next morning and get first tracks on perfect corduroy or fresh powder. Free but numbers are limited! Take your time over the descent, though: if you get back to the base before the normal lift opening time, you'll have to wait, like everyone else.*

Powder Tours *Spend the day finding untracked snow in 1,500 acres of backcountry beyond Aspen Mountain, with a 12-passenger heated snowcat as your personal lift. You're likely to squeeze in about 10 runs in all. You break for lunch at an old mountain cabin. Costs $390 per person.*

Sundeck
3415m/11,200ft

The fast Ajax chair serves a good high area of blues and easy blacks

Good cruising served by this unusual chair – a fast double

Copper Bowl

Gentleman's Ridge

3080m/10,110ft
Face of Bell

Bell is an excellent hill for those not up to the double-diamond runs that dominate other black areas

Nose of Bell

Silver Queen

Ruthie's

ASPEN MOUNTAIN

Long top-to-bottom cruises down Spar Gulch and Copper Bowl

Aspen
2425m/7,950ft

gondola
fast chairlift
Slow chairs & drags
have no symbol

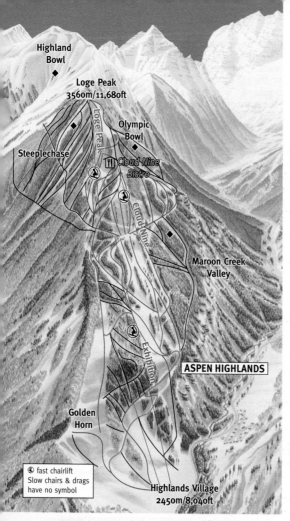

Highland Bowl

Loge Peak
3560m/11,68oft

Olympic Bowl

Steeplechase

Cloud Nine Bistro

Maroon Creek Valley

ASPEN HIGHLANDS

Golden Horn

Exhibition

Cloud Nine

Loge Peak

④ fast chairlift
Slow chairs & drags have no symbol

Highlands Village
2450m/8,04oft

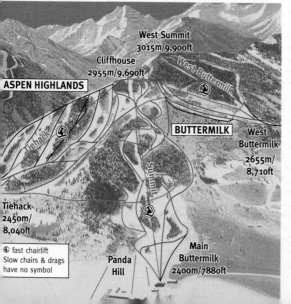

West Summit
3015m/9,900ft

Cliffhouse
2955m/9,69oft

West Buttermilk

ASPEN HIGHLANDS

Tiehack

BUTTERMILK

West Buttermilk
2655m/8,71oft

Summit

Tiehack
2450m/8,04oft

④ fast chairlift
Slow chairs & drags have no symbol

Panda Hill

Main Buttermilk
2400m/788oft

Highlands is almost always queue-free, even at peak times (and was deserted when we were there in mid-February last season). The lift out of Main Buttermilk sometimes gets congested.

TERRAIN PARKS ★★★★★
X Games standard
Aspen has two pipe and park mountains – Snowmass (see separate chapter) and Buttermilk. Buttermilk Park is famous as the home of the Winter X Games, and stretches over 3km from the top to the bottom of the mountain – it is said to be the longest in the world. It has over 100 features, the X Games slope-style course and a world-class super-pipe that's over 150m long with 6.7m walls. The Ski & Snowboard Schools Park and Panda Pipe are for beginner freestylers.

SNOW RELIABILITY ★★★★★
Rarely a problem
Aspen's mountains get an annual average of 300 inches of snow – not in the front rank, but not far behind. In addition, all areas have substantial snowmaking. Immaculate grooming adds to the quality of the pistes, and the light traffic can only help.

FOR EXPERTS ★★★★★
Buttermilk is the only soft stuff
There's plenty to choose from – all the mountains except Buttermilk offer lots of challenges.

Aspen Mountain has a formidable array of double black diamond runs. From the top of the gondola, Walsh's, Hyrup's and Kristi are on a lightly wooded slope and link up with Gentleman's Ridge and Jackpot to form the longest black run on the mountain. A series of steep glades drops down from Gentleman's Ridge. The central Bell ridge has less extreme single diamonds on both its flanks, including some delightful lightly wooded areas. On the opposite side of Spar Gulch is another row of double blacks, collectively called the Dumps, because mining waste was dumped here.

At Highlands there are challenging runs from top to bottom of the mountain. Consider joining a guided group as an introduction to the best of them. Highland Bowl, beyond the top lift, is superb in the right conditions: a big open bowl with pitches from a serious 38° to a terrifying 48°. The trail map very usefully lists all the runs and gives the

Interactive resort shortlist builder at **www.wtss.co.uk**

KEY FACTS

Resort	2425m
	7,950ft

Aspen Mountain

Slopes	2425-3415m
	7,950-11,210ft
Lifts	8
Pistes	675 acres
Green	0%
Blue	48%
Black	52%
Snowmaking	31%

Aspen Highlands

Slopes	2450-3560m
	8,040-11,680ft
Lifts	5
Pistes	1,028 acres
Green	18%
Blue	30%
Black	52%
Snowmaking	11%

Buttermilk

Slopes	2400-3015m
	7,880-9,900ft
Lifts	9
Pistes	470 acres
Green	35%
Blue	39%
Black	26%
Snowmaking	23%

Total with Snowmass

Slopes	2400-3815m
	7,880-12,510ft
Lifts	43
Pistes	5,305 acres
Green	10%
Blue	45%
Black	45%
Snowmaking	12%

UK PACKAGES

Alpine Answers, AmeriCan Ski, American Ski Classics, Carrier, Crystal, Crystal Finest, Elegant Resorts, Erna Low, Frontier, Funway Holidays, Independent Ski Links, Momentum, Oxford Ski Co, PowderBeds, Scott Dunn, Ski Expectations, Ski Independence, Ski Line, Ski Safari, Ski Solutions, Skitracer, Skiworld, Snow Finders, Supertravel

average and steepest pitch angles and orientation of each – the north-facing runs are the longest hikes. There are free snowcat rides from the top of the lifts to the first access gate of Highland Bowl, but if these are not operating, it's a 20-minute hike. All the further gates require more hiking.

Left of the bowl, the Steeplechase area consists of a number of parallel natural avalanche chutes, and their elevation means the snow stays light and dry. The Deep Temerity lift (vertical 520m) adds a useful amount of skiable vertical to these runs and to Highland Bowl. The Olympic Bowl area on the opposite flank of the mountain has great views of the Maroon Bells and some serious moguls. The Thunderbowl chair from the base serves a nice varied area that's often underused.

FOR INTERMEDIATES ★★★★★
Grooming to die for
Most intermediate runs on Highlands are concentrated above the mid-mountain Merry-Go-Round restaurant, many served by the Cloud Nine fast quad chair. But there are good slopes higher up and lower down – don't miss the vast, neglected expanses of Golden Horn, on the eastern limit of the area.

Aspen Mountain has its fair share of intermediate slopes, but they tend to be tougher than on the other mountains. Copper Bowl and Spar Gulch, running between the ridges, are great cruises early in the morning but can get crowded later. Upper Aspen Mountain, at the top of the gondola, has a dense network of well-groomed blues served by the Ajax fast chair. The unusual Ruthie's chair – a fast double, apparently installed to rekindle the romance that quads have destroyed – serves more cruising runs.

Buttermilk offer good, easy slopes to practise on, and can be extraordinarily quiet. And good intermediates should be able to handle the relatively easy black runs – when groomed, these are a real blast. Buttermilk is also a great place for early experiments off-piste.

See the Snowmass chapter too.

FOR BEGINNERS ★★★★★
Can be a great place to learn
Buttermilk is a superb mountain for beginners. West Buttermilk has beautifully groomed, gentle, often

deserted runs, served by a quad. The easiest slopes of all, though, are at the base of the Main Buttermilk sector – on Panda Hill. Despite its macho image and serious double diamond terrain, Highlands boasts the highest concentration of green runs in Aspen, served by the fast Exhibition chair.

FOR BOARDERS ★★★★
Loads of scope
There is a huge amount of terrain to explore, which will satisfy all levels of boarder – especially when you include Snowmass (see our separate chapter). The hills are free of draglifts and have few flat sections. Buttermilk is the least testing of the mountains, with gentle carving runs and freeriding – but it's also home to the most serious terrain park.

FOR CROSS-COUNTRY ★★★★
Backcountry bonanza
There are 90km of groomed trails between Aspen and Snowmass in the Roaring Fork valley – the most extensive maintained cross-country system in the US. And the Ashcroft Ski Touring Center maintains around 35km of trails around Ashcroft, a mining ghost town. The Pine Creek Cookhouse (925 1044) does excellent food and is accessible only by ski, snowshoe or horse-drawn sleigh. Aspen is at one end of the famous Tenth Mountain Division Trail, heading 370km northeast almost to Vail, with 12 huts for overnight stops.

MOUNTAIN RESTAURANTS ★★★
Good by American standards
Surprisingly, Highlands and Snowmass (see separate chapter) have good table-service places and Aspen Mountain doesn't.

Editors' choice At Highlands, Cloud Nine bistro (544 3063) is the nearest thing in the States to a cosy Alpine hut, with excellent food – thanks to an Austrian chef. Not wildly expensive, either – $31 for two courses (daily changing set menu). We had a great late lunch there in 2011 (delicious elk stew) and the place had turned into an Austrian-style après-ski venue by the time we left – dancing on the tables in ski boots and lots of alcohol being consumed (very un-American).

Worth knowing about On Aspen Mountain there's the Sundeck self-service – about as good as an American self-service restaurant gets –

The Sundeck at the top of Aspen Mountain is about as good as a self-service US resort restaurant gets; great views of Aspen Highlands too →

ASPEN / DANIEL BAYER

SCHOOLS

Aspen
t 923 1227

Classes
Full day (5hr) $129
Private lessons
$459 for 3hr for up to 5 people

CHILDCARE

Snow Cubs
t 923 1227
Ages 8wk to 4yr
Grizzlies
t 923 1227
Ages 5 and 6
All-day babysitting services
Several

Ski school
Ages 7 to 12, $104 per day (9.30 to 3.15, lunch included)

GETTING THERE

Air Aspen 6km/
4 miles (15mins);
Eagle 110km/
70 miles (1hr45);
Denver 360km/
225 miles (4hr45)

Rail Glenwood Springs
(63km/39 miles)

light and airy with great views across to Highland Bowl. Bonnie's self-service is another option, but 'disorganised' says a 2011 reporter – we much preferred the terrace to the inside on our 2011 visit. On Aspen Highlands, the mid-mountain Merry-Go-Round self-service restaurant will have been completely refurbished for 2011/12 – reports please. On Buttermilk the mountaintop Cliffhouse specialises in a Mongolian barbecue stir-fry.

SCHOOLS AND GUIDES ★★★★★
One of the best?
Aspen's school is highly regarded, and group classes are usually small and of a high standard. A 2011 reporter said: 'My wife had three days of lessons and although not cheap, there were three in her group one day, two the next and she was the only pupil the third. So almost private instruction and with the same instructor for the three days.' The school also runs various specialist programmes – for women and seniors, for example.

FOR FAMILIES ★★★★★
Choice of nurseries
Aspen caters well for families, with Buttermilk the focus for lessons. Children are bussed to and from the mountain's impressive Fort Frog. And the kids' trail map is a great idea. We get few reports, but the childcare arrangements usually receive excellent reviews. But Snowmass has clear advantages for young families.

STAYING THERE

Hotels There are places for all budgets. Most smaller hotels provide a good free après-ski cheese and wine buffet. Skiworld and Ski Independence feature a range of good hotels.
*****St Regis Aspen (920 3300) Opulent city-type hotel, near gondola. With a fancy spa facility.
*****Hyatt Grand Aspen (429 9100) A grand place, near the gondola.
*****The Little Nell (920 4600) Stylish, modern hotel right by the gondola, with popular bar. Fireplaces in every room, outdoor pool, hot tub, sauna. Smart condos too.
*****Jerome (920 1000) Step back a century: Victorian authenticity combined with modern-day luxury. Several blocks from the gondola.
****Lenado (925 6246) Smart modern B&B place with open-fire lounge, individually designed rooms.
***Aspen (925 3441) Spacious, basic rooms; pool; hot tub; 10 minutes' walk to gondola. Near bus stop.
***Molly Gibson Lodge (925 3434) Various room styles, all 'great value'. Pool, hot tub, bar. Opposite hotel Aspen.
***Aspen Mountain Lodge (925 7650) Small, friendly, in a quiet location.
***Limelight Lodge (925 3025) Recently rebuilt in modern style, moderately priced, central. Pool, tubs.
***The Sky (925 6760) Hip, swanky New York-style hotel in great location by gondola.

Indoor Club & Spa (sauna, swimming, weights, aerobics, steam, hot tubs); Recreation Center (pool, ice rink), galleries, cinemas, theatre, museum

Outdoor Snowshoeing, ice skating, snowmobiling

Phone numbers
From distant parts of the US, add the prefix 1 970; from abroad, add the prefix +1 970

www.aspensnowmass.com

ASPEN / DANIEL BAYER

We're not sure what this chap is on. But he's about to arrive at the Ajax Tavern in downtown Aspen at the foot of Aspen Mountain ↓

**St Moritz Lodge (925 3220) Rooms and suites at the west end of town. Pool. 'Great staff, lovely hot tub.'
**Mountain Chalet (925 7797) Cosy lodge five minutes from gondola. Pool, sauna, steam and games room.
Apartments The standards here are high, even in US terms. Many of the smarter developments have their own free shuttle-buses. The Gant, Aspen Square and 'lovely' Aspen Meadows Resort have been recommended.

EATING OUT ★★★★★
Dining dilemma
Aspen has an excellent blend of upmarket places and cheaper options. Some giveaway magazines include menu guides and there are basic listings at www.eataspen.com. Every year brings a raft of closures and new ventures and we welcome your reports.

Top of the range places include: Il Mulino (an outpost of a classy Italian restaurant in New York) in the Little Nell residences; Syzygy, Piñons and, in the Little Nell hotel, Montagna (all with innovative American cooking); Matsuhisa (Asian and seafood); and the Rustique Bistro, Brexi Brasserie and Cache Cache (all French).

You can eat more cheaply at a lot of the more up- and mid-market places by eating at the bar rather than in the restaurant – basically, you get smaller portions of the food that is served in the restaurant, but the downside is that you can't book a table. We did this very satisfactorily on our 2011 visit at Jimmy's (American, seafood), Cache Cache (French), L'Hosteria and Campo de Fiori (both Italian).

Mid-market and cheaper choices receiving favourable past reports include Little Annie's, Asie, Elevation, Mezzaluna, Hickory House and New York Pizza; there's a McDonald's.

APRES-SKI ★★★★
Lots of options
As the lifts shut, a few bars at the bases get busy – notably Out of Bounds at Highlands and Ajax Tavern ('very lively upmarket crowd') in Aspen. The Terrace Bar at the Little Nell is a great place for gazing at facelifts; 39 Degrees at the Sky hotel has a chic atmosphere and outdoor heaters by the pool.

Later on, wine connoisseurs could try Victoria's Espresso & Wine Bar. Many of the restaurants are also bars – Jimmy's (spectacular stock of tequila) and Mezzaluna, for example. The J-bar of the Jerome hotel dates back to 1889 and has a traditional feel. Aspen Billiards adjoining the fashionable Cigar Bar is an upscale venue for playing pool. The Aspen Brewing Company is the local micro-brewery and has a Tasting Room.

For music and dancing, head for Belly Up or the Regal Watering Hole. Or you can get a week's membership of the famous members-only Caribou club.

OFF THE SLOPES ★★★★
Silver service
Aspen has lots to offer, especially if your credit card is in good shape. There are literally dozens of art galleries, as well as the predictable clothes and jewellery shops. There are plenty of shops selling affordable stuff. Glenwood Springs is worth a visit for its hot-spring outdoor pool. The Aspen Recreation Center at Highlands has a huge swimming complex and an indoor ice rink. Hot-air ballooning is possible too. The best mountain restaurant is awkward for pedestrians to get to.

Beaver Creek

Exclusive and very pricey modern resort with quiet, varied slopes. Good for a pampered stay or a day trip from Vail

TOP 10 RATINGS

Extent	★★
Fast lifts	★★★★★
Queues	★★★★★
Snow	★★★★★
Expert	★★★★
Intermediate	★★★★
Beginner	★★★★★
Charm	★★
Convenience	★★★★
Scenery	★★★

RPI 140

lift pass	£290
ski hire	£160
lessons	£215
food & drink	£125
total	**£790**

NEWS

2011/12: The Rose Bowl triple chairlift is to be replaced by a fast quad.

They take pampering seriously here: immaculate grooming, mountain-top boards listing groomed runs, speed control by aircraft and radar. But there's nowhere decent for lunch – weird ↓

➕ The slopes can be very quiet, on weekdays at least

➕ Mountain has it all, from superb novice runs to daunting moguls

➕ Fast chairlifts all over the place

➕ Compact, traffic-free village centre

➖ Lacks any Wild West or genuine US town atmosphere

➖ Very expensive

➖ Disappointing mountain restaurants

➖ Not much going on at night

'Not exactly roughing it' is the strangely coy slogan of Vail's kid sister resort, discreetly underlining its status as about the smoothest resort in the US. We don't find the exclusive resort village particularly appealing, but the mountain certainly is. We wouldn't dream of visiting Vail without spending a day or two here. A pity that it's impossible to get a decent lunch on the hill.

THE RESORT

Beaver Creek, 16km to the west of Vail, was developed in the 1980s and is unashamedly exclusive. The lift system spreads across the mountains to Bachelor Gulch, a small collection of relatively new condos and houses and a Ritz-Carlton hotel, and to Arrowhead, a slope-side hamlet that is less pricey than Beaver Creek. Below here is the valley town of Avon, where there are free car parks for day visitors (parking in the resort itself is expensive and limited); you can take a free shuttle to the village or a fast chair up to Bachelor Gulch. A gondola links the Riverfront area of Avon to this chair.

Day trips to Vail, Breckenridge and Keystone (all covered by the lift pass) and Copper Mountain are possible.

Village charm The village centres on a small, smart, modern pedestrian area with upmarket shops, open-air ice rink and heated pavements.

Convenience There are top-quality hotels and condos right by the slopes and escalators up from the centre.

Scenery The scenery is pleasantly woody, rather than dramatic.

THE MOUNTAINS

All the slopes are below the treeline, though there are some more open areas. Free two-hour mountain tours are held every day at 10am. At the top of most main lifts is a big piste map board (and lights showing which runs have been groomed – a great idea that we haven't seen before). They take their 'slow skiing zones' seriously here too – with big banners across the piste warning that skier speed is monitored by aircraft and by radar! **Slopes** The slopes immediately above Beaver Creek divide into two sectors, each accessed by a fast quad chair – one centred on Spruce Saddle, the other Bachelor Gulch (which links to Arrowhead). Between these are Grouse Mountain and Larkspur Bowl, again with fast quads. Off to the left is another varied sector which will be served by a new fast quad for 2011/12. **Fast lifts** Nearly all key lifts are now fast chairs and beginners get their own gondola.

Queues Queues aren't normally a problem, but improved lift access from the valley may be attracting more visitors. One recent reporter had 'a 10-minute wait' at the main Centennial chair and another found it 'busier than Vail at Spring Break'. But on all our visits (including February 2011) the slopes have been blissfully deserted.

Terrain parks Park 101 is a small beginners' park, Zoom Room has

KEY FACTS

Resort	2470m
	8,100ft
Slopes	2255-3485m
	7,400-11,440ft
Lifts	17
Pistes	1815 acres
Green	19%
Blue	43%
Black	38%
Snowmaking	33%

UK PACKAGES

Alpine Answers,
AmeriCan Ski, American
Ski Classics, Carrier,
Crystal, Crystal Finest,
Elegant Resorts,
Frontier, Funway
Holidays, Independent
Ski Links, Oxford Ski
Co, PowderBeds, Ski
Independence, Ski Line,
Ski Safari, Skitracer,
Skiworld, STC,
Supertravel

Central reservations
phone number
496 4500

Phone numbers
From distant parts of
the US, add the prefix
1 970; from abroad,
add the prefix +1 970

TOURIST OFFICE

beavercreek.snow.com

intermediate-level features and Rodeo has big hits for advanced riders. There's a 110m-long half-pipe, off Barrel Stave. Parkology is a park and pipe programme for kids.

Snow reliability An impressive snow record (average 310 inches) and snowmaking means you can relax. But Grouse Mountain can have thin cover (some call it Gravel Mountain).

Experts There is plenty of satisfying steep terrain. In the Birds of Prey and Grouse Mountain areas most runs are long, steep and mogulled (but watch the grooming map and boards – when one of these is groomed it makes a great fast cruise; the Birds of Prey race course is groomed every Saturday night we're told). Grouse and Stone Creek Chutes have great steep glades.

Intermediates There are marvellous long, quiet, cruising blues everywhere you look, including top-to-bottom runs with a vertical of 1000m.

Beginners There are excellent nursery slopes at resort level – served by a short gondola – and more at altitude. And there are plenty of easy longer runs to progress to.

Snowboarding Good riders will love the excellent gladed runs and perfect carving slopes. The resort is great for beginners, too, with special teaching methods and equipment that they claim will help you learn quicker.

Cross-country There's a splendid, mountain-top network of tracks at McCoy Park (over 32km), reached via the Strawberry Park lift.

Mountain restaurants Spruce Saddle at mid-mountain is the main place – a food court in an airy log building, but it can get very busy. Red Tail Camp is basic; decent BBQs. Spago at Bachelor Gulch is the best bet for table service.

Schools and guides We've had very good reports over the years.

Families Small World Play School looks after non-skiing kids from two months to six years from 8.30 to 4pm. At the top of the Buckaroo gondola are adventure trails and a tubing park.

STAYING THERE

Hotels Lots of upmarket places, such as the Ritz-Carlton and Park Hyatt. The Osprey, Charter and Pines Lodge combine hotel facilities with luxury condo convenience.

Apartments Elkhorn Lodge, Oxford Court, St James Place and SaddleRidge are slope-side condos. For cheaper luxury, consider staying in Arrowhead.

Eating out SaddleRidge is plush and packed with photos and Wild West artefacts. Toscanini, the Golden Eagle Inn, Dusty Boot, and Beaver Creek Chophouse have been recommended. Spago offers fine dining at Bachelor Gulch. You can take a sleigh ride to dine at a swanky log cabin on the slopes. Or try the valley towns; a reader recommends Outback in Avon for 'excellent steaks'. The resort runs shuttle buses between Beaver Creek and Avon daily from 8am-10pm.

Après-ski Try the Coyote Cafe and McCoy's (live bands) and the 8100 Mountainside Bar.

Off the slopes Smart shops and galleries, an ice rink, ballooning, dog sledding, snowshoeing and concerts.

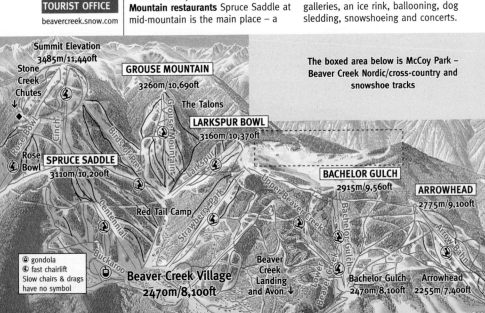

Summit Elevation
3485m/11,440ft
Stone Creek Chutes

Rose Bowl

GROUSE MOUNTAIN
3260m/10,690ft

The Talons

LARKSPUR BOWL
3160m/10,370ft

SPRUCE SADDLE
3110m/10,200ft

Red Tail Camp

The boxed area below is McCoy Park –
Beaver Creek Nordic/cross-country and
snowshoe tracks

BACHELOR GULCH
2915m/9,560ft

ARROWHEAD
2775m/9,100ft

gondola
fast chairlift
Slow chairs & drags
have no symbol

Beaver Creek Village
2470m/8,100ft

Beaver Creek Landing
and Avon ↓

Bachelor Gulch
2470m/8,100ft

Arrowhead
2255m/7,400ft

VAIL RESORTS INC / BOB WINSETT

Breckenridge

A sprawling resort with a cute 'Wild West' core, beneath a wide, varied mountain; increasing amounts of slope-side accommodation

NEWS

2011/12: This season Breckenridge will be celebrating its 50th anniversary, with lots of promotions and events running throughout the winter.

2010/11: More luxury condos, One Ski Hill Place, opened at the Peak 8 base, along with a bar and restaurant. Gold Runner Alpine Coaster – a bit like a toboggan run on tracks – also opened at Peak 8.

The Freeway terrain park gained a new super-pipe. And the Village at Breck reopened following a facelift.

- ➕ Slopes have something for all abilities – good for mixed groups
- ➕ Cute Victorian Main Street, with mainly sympathetic new buildings
- ➕ Plenty of lively bars and restaurants
- ➕ Shared lift pass with four other worthwhile resorts nearby
- ➕ Efficient lifts mean few queues
- ➕ Some slope-side accommodation
- ➕ One of the nearest major resorts to Denver; so a short transfer, but ...

- ➖ At 2925m the village is one of the highest you will encounter, with a risk of altitude sickness if you go there directly from the UK
- ➖ Very prone to high winds, affecting particularly the high, exposed advanced slopes
- ➖ On-piste terrain not very extensive by Alpine standards; few long runs
- ➖ Lack of good, central hotels
- ➖ Main Street is a thoroughfare – always busy with traffic

A repeat visit last season confirmed that we like Breckenridge a lot. The town is attractive and lively, with Wild West roots and lots of places to eat and drink. And the slopes are fabulous for beginners. And for experts too, provided the ungroomed top slopes are open – as they were on our 2011 visit, when we whooped it up in fresh powder in the bowls above Peak 7. Sadly, they are too often closed by high winds – as we've found on previous visits. Intermediates more interested in mileage than challenges should plan to explore other resorts (covered by the lift pass) by car or bus too; they'll find Breck too limited for a week. And heed our warning about altitude sickness: at almost 3000m this is the highest resort to get a full chapter in this book – and the skiing goes up to almost 4000m. Like many readers, editor Gill has been affected by altitude sickness here, and now always spends time in a lower resort before hitting Breckenridge; a night or two in Denver is an alternative way to cut the risk.

THE RESORT

Breckenridge was founded in 1859 and became a booming gold-mining town. Old clapboard buildings line much of Main Street and the streets nearby have been well renovated. Small shopping malls and other buildings have been added in similar style. But there are some (rather out-of-place) modern buildings too.

The resort is in the same ownership as Vail, Beaver Creek and Keystone. A multi-day lift ticket covers all these plus Arapahoe Basin. All of them plus Copper Mountain can be reached by bus (free except for the trips to Vail or Beaver Creek).

VILLAGE CHARM ★★★☆☆
A festive treat

The town centre is lively in the evening – particularly at weekends – with lots of people strolling around the shops on their way to or from 100-plus restaurants and bars. Christmas lights and decorations remain throughout the season, giving the town a festive air. This is enhanced by a number of festivals such as Ullr Fest – honouring the Norse God of Winter – and snow sculpture championships.

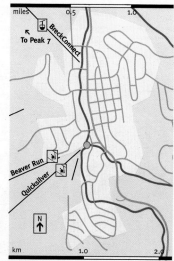

KEY FACTS

Resort		2925m
		9,600ft
Slopes	2925-3915m	
	9,600-12,840ft	
Lifts		30
Pistes	2,358 acres	
Green		14%
Blue		31%
Black		55%
Snowmaking		24%

CONVENIENCE ★★★☆☆
Slope life or nightlife

There is a lot of slope-side lodgings, including smart recent developments at the bases of Peaks 7 and 8. But there is also some inconveniently distant from both Main Street and the lift base-stations. Hotels and condos are spread over a wide area and linked by regular, free shuttle-buses (less frequent in the evening – worth staying centrally if you plan to spend much time in Main Street). There are a couple of supermarkets – one just behind Main Street, the other on the outskirts and a long walk if you don't have a car.

SCENERY ★★★☆☆
Peak after peak

This is high country; on a clear day above the treeline there are extensive views of Colorado's highest summits – many of which reach over 4000m.

THE MOUNTAINS

The slopes are mainly cut through the forest but there is quite a lot of steeper skiing above the treeline (and prone to closure by high winds).

The resort used to have some runs classified as blue-black. They have now scrapped these and made them single black diamond – a real backward step because the old blue-blacks (mainly on Peak 10) are still great intermediate cruises and the new black classification may put people off from trying them.

EXTENT OF THE SLOPES ★★☆☆☆
Small but fragmented

There are four sectors, linked by lift and piste. Two fast chairlifts go from one end of the town up to **Peak 9**, one accessing mainly green runs on the lower half of the hill, the other mainly blue runs higher up. From there you can get to **Peak 10**, with black runs (including former blue-blacks) served by one fast quad.

The **Peak 8** area – tough stuff at the top, easier lower down – can be reached by a fast quad from Peak 9. The base lifts of Peak 8 at the Bergenhof can also be reached by the slow Snowflake lift from the suburbs, or by gondola from the fringes of town – where there's ample parking. The six-pack serving the lower slopes of **Peak 7** can be accessed from Peak 8 and from the gondola's mid-station.

The higher open slopes on Peaks 7 and 8 are accessed by a T-bar – a rarity in these parts – reachable from either base, and by the Imperial fast quad at the top of the Peak 8 lift network. The resort claims a top height of 3960m, but that involves a hike of 45m vertical at the very top.

FAST LIFTS ★★★★☆
Good coverage

Breckenridge's gondola and nine fast chairlifts cover all four sectors and provide good access from either end of town – the slow Snowflake chair in between is an obvious exception.

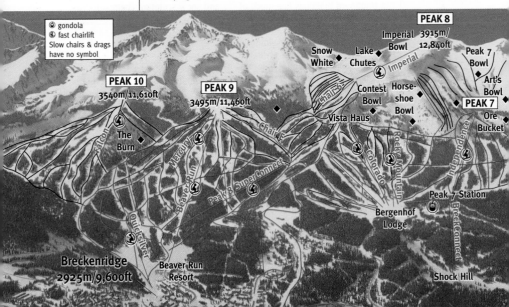

gondola
fast chairlift
Slow chairs & drags have no symbol

PEAK 8

Imperial 3915m/
Bowl 12,840ft

Snow   Lake   Peak 7
White   Chutes Bowl

Imperial

Art's
Bowl

PEAK 10   Contest Horse-
3540m/11,610ft   Bowl   shoe   PEAK 7
        Bowl
PEAK 9   Vista Haus   Ore
3495m/11,460ft   Bucket

The
Burn

Peak 7 Station

Bergenhof
Lodge

Breckenridge
2925m/9,600ft   Beaver Run
Resort   Shock Hill

LIFT PASSES

Breckenridge

Prices in US$

Age	1-day	6-day
under 13	49	294
13 to 64	92	552
over 65	82	492

Free under 5
Beginner included in price of lessons

Notes
Covers Breckenridge, Keystone and Arapahoe Basin, plus 3 days (on a 6-day pass) at Vail and Beaver Creek; prices are high-season rates paid in the resort; the best prices for international visitors can be obtained if they pre-book through a UK tour operator (it is not necessary to buy a complete holiday package to obtain these prices)

QUEUES ★★★★
Peak times possibly

You do get queues at peak times but the fast chairs and the lifties making sure they are filled make light work of peak-time crowds. The old Chair 6 on a powder day and the Snowflake chair that gives access to Peak 8 for thousands of condo-dwellers can generate queues. But recent reporters have had no complaints.

TERRAIN PARKS ★★★★★
Something for everyone

The main focus is Peak 8, with three parks for different ability levels. Freeway is one of the best parks in North America, featuring a series of big jumps, obstacles and a super-pipe – 'massive, steep, well kept, awesome'. Next to it, Park Lane is a big intermediate-level park. And Trygves has gentle jumps and rollers for beginner freestylers. On Peak 9 are two more parks and a pipe: Eldorado is for beginners; Bonanza is for intermediates; Gold King Pipe is a stepping stone to the super-pipe. See www.breck1080.com.

SNOW RELIABILITY ★★★★★
Ample quantities

With its high altitude, Breckenridge boasts a great natural snow record – annual average 300 inches. That is supplemented by substantial snowmaking (used mainly early in the season to form a good base). There are a lot of east- and north-east-facing slopes, which hold snow well. But high winds can remove or spoil the snow, notably on exposed upper runs.

FOR EXPERTS ★★★★
Lots of short but tough runs

A remarkable 55% of the runs are classified black – that's a higher proportion than famous 'macho' resorts such as Jackson Hole, Taos and Snowbird. And a good proportion are classified as 'expert' (double-diamond) or 'extreme' terrain. But most runs are short – most of the key lifts offer verticals of around 300m.

Peak 8 is at the core of the tough skiing. The lightly wooded slopes served by Chair 6 are a good place to start – picturesque and not too steep. Below, steeper runs lead further down to the junction with Peak 9. Above, the Imperial quad accesses huge amounts of above-the-treeline terrain and longer runs. You can hike up to the double-diamond Imperial Bowl, and the 'extreme' Lake Chutes and Snow White areas to the left of the photo on this page. Or you can traverse round the back towards Peak 7 and double-diamond runs in the bowl on the right of the photo (we had a great time in fresh snow there on our 2011 visit); the T-bar on Peak 8 accesses the lower parts of these runs (single-diamonds) and the double-diamond Horseshoe and Contest bowls. On the lower, wooded part of Peak 8 is a worthwhile area of single diamonds.

Peak 9's wooded North Slope under Chair E is excellent – shady, sheltered and steep – we've had great runs down Devil's Crotch, Hades and Inferno. Peak 10 has easy black runs (former blue-blacks) down the central ridge, but more challenging stuff on both flanks. To skier's left is a lovely, lightly wooded area called The Burn.

FOR INTERMEDIATES ★★★★
Nice cruising, limited extent

Breckenridge has some good blue cruising runs for all intermediates. But dedicated piste-bashers are likely to find the runs short and limited in variety. Peak 9 has the easiest slopes. It is nearly all gentle, wide, blue runs at the top and almost flat, wide, green runs at the bottom. And the ski patrol is supposed to enforce slow-speed skiing in certain areas.

Peak 10 has a number of easy, normally groomed, black runs that used to be classified blue-black, such as Crystal and Centennial, which make for good fast cruising. Peaks 7 and 8 both have a choice of blues on trails cut close together in the trees.

SCHOOLS

Breckenridge
t 496 4700

Classes
Half day $85

Private lessons
$460 for 3hr for up to
3 people

VAIL RESORTS INC

Part of the charm of
Breckenridge is its
beautifully restored
old houses and new
additions built in
sympathetic style ↓

Adventurous intermediates can also try some of the high bowl runs and more gentle gladed runs such as Ore Bucket glades on the fringe of Peak 7 and the runs beneath Chair 6 on Peak 8.

FOR BEGINNERS ★★★★★
Excellent
The bottom of Peak 9 has a big, virtually flat area and some good, gentle nursery slopes. There's then a good choice of green runs to move on to. Beginners can try Peak 8 too, with another selection of green runs and a choice of trails back to town. There is a special beginner package available (see 'Schools and guides').

FOR BOARDERS ★★★★★
One of the best
Breckenridge is pretty much ideal for all standards of boarder and hosts several major US snowboarding events. Beginners have ideal nursery slopes and greens to progress to. Intermediates have great cruising runs, all served by chairs. The powder bowls at the top of Peaks 7 and 8 make great riding and can be accessed via the Imperial quad, so avoiding the awkward T-bar. Boarders of all levels will enjoy the choice of excellent terrain parks. Nearby Arapahoe Basin is another area for hard-core boarding in steep bowls and chutes.

FOR CROSS-COUNTRY ★★★★
Specialist centre in woods
Breckenridge's Nordic Center is prettily set in the woods between the town

and Peak 8 (served by the shuttle-bus). It has 32km of trails and 16km of snowshoeing trails. A further 22km of cross-country is on the golf course.

MOUNTAIN RESTAURANTS ★★
Improved by more base options
Of the self-service places above base level, Peak 9 restaurant is the 'best of a mediocre bunch'. Both Ten Mile Station, where Peak 9 meets 10, and the dreary Vista Haus on Peak 8 are food-court operations. But they get nightmarishly busy at weekends. Sevens is a smart table-service restaurant at the Peak 7 base; the food is OK but nothing special. The new Ski Hill Grill at the base of Peak 8 has a smart decor with lots of stone and a 'good variety' of self-service food (including Asian fusion). Several places offer 'Lunch for Less': $9.95 (plus tax) buys you something like soup, a sandwich and a soft drink.

SCHOOLS AND GUIDES ★★★★★
Excellent reports
Reporters have praised small classes doing what the class, not the instructor, wants ('you can buy three days of lessons and take them whenever you want', 'friendly, first-class instruction'). The good-value beginner package which includes lessons, equipment rental and lift pass is also highly recommended. Special clinics include women's and telemark. The school's full day Adventure Sessions offer guided instruction for intermediates and experts.

CHILDCARE

Children's Centers
t +1 888 576 2754
All-day care from 8am to 4pm for children from age 8wk to 3yr – reservation recommended

Resort sitters
t 513 4445

Summit sitters
t 453 7097

Ski school
For ages 3 to 13, 9am to 3.30 daily ($150 for full day)

GETTING THERE

Air Denver 165km/ 105 miles (2hr15)

UK PACKAGES

Alpine Answers, AmeriCan Ski, American Ski Classics, Crystal, Crystal Finest, Erna Low, Frontier, Funway Holidays, Independent Ski Links, Inghams, Interactive Resorts, Oxford Ski Co, PowderBeds, Ski Expectations, Ski Independence, Ski Line, Ski Safari, Ski Solutions, Skitracer, Skiworld, Snow Finders, STC, Supertravel, Thomson, Virgin Snow
Frisco AmeriCan Ski

ACTIVITIES

Indoor Spas, theatre, cinema, museum, galleries, ice rink, recreation centre (pool, gym, tennis, climbing wall) on the outskirts of town – accessible by bus

Outdoor Horse-drawn sleigh rides, dog sledding, ice rink, snowshoeing, tobogganing

Phone numbers
From distant parts of the US, add the prefix 1 970; from abroad, add the prefix +1 970

TOURIST OFFICE

www.breckenridge. snow.com

FOR FAMILIES ★★★★
Excellent facilities

Past reports on the children's school and nursery have been full of praise. The Mountains of Discovery programme aims to combine teaching and fun on the slopes (for kids aged three to 13 years).

STAYING THERE

Chalets Several tour operators have very comfortable chalets. Skiworld has three smart places, all with outdoor hot tubs, and Crystal Finest features a swanky privately-run place with hot tub near Peak 8.

Hotels There's a noticeable lack of good places close to Main Street.
★★★★Great Divide Lodge (547 5725) A short walk to the slopes and a bearable walk to Main Street, but dreary. Pool, tub, sauna. 'Good value.'
★★★★Lodge & Spa at Breckenridge (453 9300) Stylish luxury spa resort set out of town among 32 acres, with great views. Private shuttle-bus. Pool, tub, steam, sauna and massage.
★★★★Beaver Run (453 6000) Huge, slope-side resort complex with 520 spacious rooms. Pools, hot tubs.
★★★★Barn on the River (453 2975) B&B on Main St. Hot tub.
★★★Little Mountain Lodge (393 2271) Luxury B&B near ice rink.
★★★Village (453 5192) Central. 'Good value with spacious rooms.' Had a facelift over summer 2010.

Apartments There is a huge choice. Mountain Thunder Lodge (near the gondola and the supermarket), Main Street Station (near the Quicksilver lift) and One Ski Hill Place at Peak 8 are recommended at the luxury end. A regular visitor also recommends for location, quality and value the recently refurbished Village at Breckenridge, Trails End, Corral, One Breckenridge Place and Saddlewood. A cheaper option is Der Steiermark (Peak 9 base). River Mountain Lodge is praised for 'quality, cost and location'.

EATING OUT ★★★★★
Over 100 restaurants

There's a wide range, from typical US food to fine dining. At peak times they get busy and many don't take bookings. The Breckenridge Dining Guide lists the full menu of most.

Recent visitors confirmed the attractions of the Hearthstone (modern American cuisine in a beautiful 100-year-old house): 'excellent; beautifully cooked steak'. For no-nonsense grills-and-fries in a pub ambience, we've enjoyed both the Brewery (famous for mega 'appetisers', such as buffalo wings, and splendid beers) and the Kenosha steakhouse. Reader tips: Whale's Tail ('great seafood and fish'), Mi Casa ('lively Mexican'), South Ridge (predominantly fish – 'good atmosphere'), Downstairs at Eric's (classic American), Michael's (extensive Italian menu), Steak & Rib ('bit of an institution; stacks of photos and memorabilia') and Spencer's (out at Beaver Run resort – 'excellent quality and value'). The Blue Moose does the usual killer breakfasts; Cool River cafe has some healthier options.

APRES-SKI ★★★
The best in the area

There's not much tea-time animation at the lift bases. Maggie's at the base of Peak 9 'has music on the terrace but doesn't stay open much beyond 5pm' says a 2011 reporter. Park Avenue Pub, just off Main Street, and the Brewery were lively on our recent visits. Later on we've enjoyed the Gold Pan saloon (reputedly the oldest bar west of the Mississippi); reader tips include the Liquid Lounge and Fatty's sports bar. Cecilia's serves good cocktails, Burke and Riley's is an Irish bar, Downstairs at Eric's a disco sports bar, Three20South has live bands.

OFF THE SLOPES ★★★
Pleasant enough

Breckenridge is a pleasant place to wander around, with plenty of souvenir and gift shops plus a free 'excellent' museum. Silverthorne (about 30 minutes away by free bus) has bargain factory outlet stores.

NEARBY TOWN – 2765m

FRISCO

Staying in Frisco makes sense for those touring or on a tight budget. It's a pleasant small town with bars, restaurants and good value lodgings. Hotel Frisco (668 5009) is 'comfortable and convenient'. The Lake Dillon Lodge (668 5094) is handy for the bus. Restaurants include Backcountry Brewery, Tuscato (Italian), Blue Spruce Inn ('best food in town, in an old low-ceilinged cabin'), the Boatyard (pizzas) and Food Heads World Cafe ('good duck and steak').

Breckenridge

Interactive resort shortlist builder at www.wtss.co.uk

Snowmass

Aspen's modern satellite – with impressively varied and extensive slopes, and a smart new fledgling Base Village

TOP 10 RATINGS

Extent	★★★★
Fast lifts	★★★★★
Queues	★★★★
Snow	★★★★★
Expert	★★★★★
Intermediate	★★★★★
Beginner	★★★★★
Charm	★★
Convenience	★★★★
Scenery	★★★★

RPI   150

lift pass	£340
ski hire	£185
lessons	£215
food & drink	£120
total	**£860**

NEWS

2011/12: Work has begun to replace Café Suzanne at the top of the Elk Camp gondola with a new much bigger restaurant due to open for 2012/13.

2010/11: There was a new super-pipe and a new beginner pipe.

+ Varied mountain, with the biggest vertical in the US at 1340m

+ Aspen's three mountains are also accessible by free bus

+ Uncrowded slopes

+ Lots of slope-side lodgings

– Limited dining, shopping and nightlife

– Diversions of Aspen town are a bus ride away

The slopes of Snowmass suit all standards and are a key part of the attraction of nearby Aspen as a destination. As a base, Snowmass has obvious appeal for families wanting easy cruising on their doorstep; its appeal is starting to broaden as more shops and restaurants open at the new Base Village – but the recession has slowed the planned development.

THE RESORT

Snowmass is a modern, purpose-built resort, with low-rise buildings set alongside the gentle home slope. Within these buildings is Snowmass Village Mall. Further down the hill is a new Base Village.

Village charm The new Base Village is adding a bit of style to what is a rather plain modern resort.

Convenience Much of the lodging is ski-in/ski-out and Snowmass Village Mall has a small cluster of shops and restaurants. Efficient free bus services (crowded at times) link Snowmass with Aspen's mountains and town – the one to Aspen runs to 2am.

Scenery The views from the high-points are long but not dramatic.

THE MOUNTAIN

Snowmass is big by US standards – almost 8km across, with the biggest vertical in the US. Most of the slopes are in the forest; higher ones are open or only lightly wooded.

Slopes Chairlifts and a gondola diverge from the base to go up to two high-points at either end of the ski area – Elk Camp and Sam's Knob. Links higher up go to the two sectors in the middle, High Alpine and Big Burn, where a draglift goes to the high-point of the whole lift system on The Cirque. Signage is 'very good at all intersections and top of lifts', says a 2011 visitor.

Fast lifts Most of the key lifts are fast, including the chairlift from Two Creeks

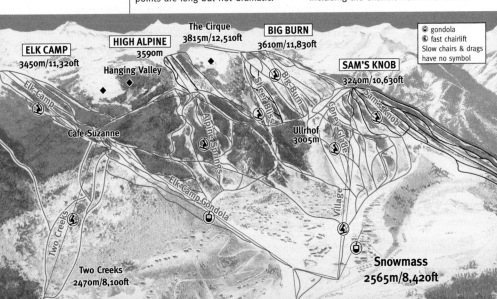

KEY FACTS

Resort	2565m
	8,420ft

Snowmass only	
Slopes	2470-3815m
	8,100-12,510ft
Lifts	21
Pistes	3,132 acres
Green	6%
Blue	50%
Black	44%
Snowmaking	7%

See Aspen chapter for statistics on other mountains – star rating for extent includes them all

UK PACKAGES

Alpine Answers, AmeriCan Ski, American Ski Classics, Carrier, Crystal, Ski Independence, Ski Safari, Supertravel

Phone numbers
From distant parts of the US, add the prefix 1 970; from abroad, add the prefix +1 970

TOURIST OFFICE

www.aspen snowmass.com

(nearer Aspen and with free slope-side parking). But there are still a couple of long, slow chairs that can be cold in midwinter.

Queues Any problems can usually be avoided. A recent reporter noted short queues for the Cirque draglift. The home slope gets very crowded.

Terrain parks Snowmass has a 6.7m super-pipe, a 3.6m beginner pipe and three parks: Lowdown (beginner), Makaha (intermediate) and Snowmass (expert), with about 90 features in total including jibs, rails and jumps.

Snow reliability With 300 inches a year plus snowmaking, it's good.

Experts There's great terrain, although the steep runs tend to be short. Consider joining a guided group as an introduction. Our favourite area is around the Hanging Valley Wall and Glades – beautiful scenery and steep wooded slopes. The other seriously steep area is The Cirque, reached by draglift from Big Burn to the area's highest point. From here, the Headwall is not terrifyingly steep, but there are also narrow, often rocky, chutes – Gowdy's is one of the steepest. The runs funnel into a pretty, lightly wooded valley.

Intermediates Excellent – the best mountain in the Aspen area for intermediates (and by far the biggest). All four sectors have lots to offer. Highlights include: the top slopes on Big Burn – a huge, varied, lightly wooded area, including the Powerline Glades for the adventurous; long, top-to-bottom cruises from Elk Camp and High Alpine; regularly groomed single-black runs from Sam's Knob. Long Shot is a glorious, normally ungroomed, 5km run, lost in the forest

---

and ending at Two Creeks, and well worth the short hike up from the top of Elk Camp.

Beginners In the heart of the resort is a broad, gentle beginners' run. An even easier slope (and less busy) is the wide Assay Hill, at the bottom of Elk Camp. There's also a beginner area served by three lifts at Elk Camp Meadows, at the top of the Elk Camp gondola. From Sam's Knob there are long, gentle cruises back to the resort.

Snowboarding A great mountain, whatever your boarding style.

Cross-country Excellent trails between here and Aspen – see Aspen chapter.

Mountain restaurants There are three table-service places (very unusual for America): Gwyn's High Alpine (established over 30 years), Lynn Britt Cabin (old log cabin, elegant table settings) and Sam's Smokehouse (newish, big windows, great views) – all do good food. And Up4Pizza is a 'little gem', says a recent visitor.

Schools and guides We've had mixed reports. A 2011 visitor had 'two different teachers' with 'no real enthusiasm or feedback' but his son had the 'same teacher, very enthusiastic, good feedback – my son enjoyed it and his skiing improved'.

Families Snowmass is a family-friendly resort. The Treehouse adventure centre at Base Village is a very impressive facility and there are special trails and trail maps for children.

STAYING THERE

Most accommodation is self-catering.

Hotels The focal hotel is the huge Silvertree (923 3520). A 2011 visitor raves about the Stonebridge Inn (923 2420) 'excellent bar and restaurant; awesome outdoor pool and hot tubs'. The luxury Viceroy (923 8000) is at Base Village.

Apartments Capitol Peak and Hayden Lodge are luxury condos at Base Village. Tamarack Townhouses and Crestwood Condos are popular.

Eating out The Brothers' Grille in the Silvertree hotel has mixed reviews, but the Eight K restaurant in the Viceroy has 'innovative fine dining'. Past reader tips include Il Poggio (Italian) and Artisan. Base Camp has reasonable prices and Buchi is a Japanese restaurant.

Après-ski Try Base Camp (live music) or, at Base Village, Sneaky's Tavern.

Off the slopes There's snowshoe trails, snowcat rides and dog sledding.

Vail

A vast, swanky resort with some very swanky hotels at the foot of one of the biggest (but also busiest) ski areas in the States

RATINGS

The mountains

Extent	★★★★
Fast lifts	★★★★★
Queues	★★
Terrain p'ks	★★★★★
Snow	★★★★★
Expert	★★★★
Intermediate	★★★★★
Beginner	★★★
Boarder	★★★
X-country	★★★
Restaurants	★★
Schools	★★★★★
Families	★★★★

The resort

Charm	★★★
Convenience	★★★
Scenery	★★★
Eating out	★★★★★
Après-ski	★★★
Off-slope	★★★

RPI 135

lift pass	£290
ski hire	£160
lessons	£215
food & drink	£115
total	**£780**

NEWS

2011/12: The 10th, a much-needed new table-service restaurant, is due to open at Mid-Vail.

2010/11: The High Noon Express fast quad replaced the existing slow chair on the Sun Up and Sun Down back bowls. More luxury accommodation opened.

+ One of the biggest areas in the US – great for confident intermediates, especially

+ The Back Bowls are big areas of treeless terrain – unusual in the US

+ Fabulous area of ungroomed, wooded slopes at Blue Sky Basin

+ Largely traffic-free resort centres, very pleasant in parts – but ...

– Resort is a vast sprawl

– Slopes can be crowded by American standards, with serious lift queues

– Inadequate mountain restaurants

– Blue Sky Basin and the Back Bowls may not be open in early season; warm weather can close the Bowls

– Expensive with lots of luxury lodgings but few budget options

We always enjoy skiing Vail; it's a big mountain with a decent vertical, and Blue Sky Basin adds hugely to its attractions. But it is far from being our favourite American mountain. In an American resort you expect the runs to be pretty much crowd-free – and in any resort, these days, you expect 20-minute lift queues to be a thing of the past. In these respects, Vail disappoints.

A repeat visit in 2011 confirms that when the budget runs to a swanky billet in Vail Village or the new Lionshead area, we're happy enough with the resort, too; it is a pleasant place to wander around. But we're not enthusiastic about Vail Village's pseudo-Tirolean style, and the rest of the huge resort has stylish architecture but lacks character. In the end, we reckon Vail can't compete with more distinctively American resorts based on old mining or cowboy towns.

THE RESORT

Vail is an enormous resort, stretching almost four miles along the I-70 freeway running west from Denver. Beaver Creek, 16km away, is covered by the lift pass and is easily reached by bus. Breckenridge and Keystone – both owned by Vail Resorts and covered by the lift pass – and Copper Mountain are possible excursions.

VILLAGE CHARM ★★★
No real identity
Standing in the centre of Vail Village, surrounded by chalets and bierkellers, you could be forgiven for thinking you were in the Tirol – which is what Vail's founder, Pete Seibert, intended back in the 1950s. But this is now just one part of a huge resort, built mostly in anonymous (but smart) modern style.

CONVENIENCE ★★★
There's always the bus
The vast village has a free and efficient bus service which makes choice of location less than crucial. But the most convenient – and expensive – places to stay are in the mock-Tirolean Vail Village, near the Vista Bahn fast chair, or at Lionshead, near the gondola – a recently redeveloped area that now has smart lodgings such as the Ritz-Carlton and Arrabelle at Vail Square. There is a lot of accommodation further out – some on the far side of the I-70.

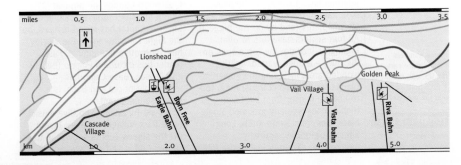

↑ Lionshead, near the base of the gondola, has been redeveloped with smart new buildings and luxury lodgings

KEY FACTS

Resort	2500m
	8,200ft
Slopes	2475-3525m
	8,120-11,570ft
Lifts	31
Pistes	5,289 acres
Green	18%
Blue	29%
Black	53%
Snowmaking	9%

SCENERY ★★★★★
Unusual for America
Vail's main mountain is densely wooded on the front side. But go over the ridge and the bowls at the back are splendidly wide and mainly open – unusual for America.

THE MOUNTAINS

You get a real sense of travelling around Vail's mountains – something missing in many smaller American resorts. Some of the runs (especially blacks) are overclassified and we've had mixed reports on trail signposting. There are free mountain tours at 10.30 and separate tours of Blue Sky Basin at 11am every day. The slopes have yellow-jacketed patrollers who stop people speeding recklessly.

EXTENT OF THE SLOPES ★★★★★
Something for everyone
Vail has the second biggest area of slopes in the US (Big Sky/Moonlight Basin has 223 acres more). They can be accessed via three main lifts. From Vail Village, the Vista Bahn fast chair goes up to the major mid-mountain focal point, Mid-Vail; from Lionshead, the Eagle Bahn gondola goes up to the Eagle's Nest complex; and from the Golden Peak base area just to the east of Vail Village, the Riva Bahn fast chair goes up towards the Two Elk area.

The front face of the mountain is largely north-facing, with well-groomed trails cut through the trees. At altitude the mountainside divides into three bowls – Mid-Vail in the centre, with Game Creek to the south-west and Northeast Bowl to the, er, north-east. Lifts reach the ridge at three points, all giving access to the **Back Bowls** (mostly ungroomed and treeless) and through them to **Blue Sky Basin** (mostly ungroomed and wooded, with a 'backcountry' feel).

FAST LIFTS ★★★★★
Plenty of them
There are lots of fast lifts on both sides of the mountain. All three of Blue Sky Basin's lifts are fast chairs.

QUEUES ★★★★★
Can be bad
The front side of Vail has some of the longest lift lines we've hit in the US, especially at weekends because of the influx from nearby Denver. Even on a mid-December visit we hit big queues. Mid-Vail is a bottleneck that is difficult to avoid; 20-minute waits are common (and 45 minutes is not unheard of). The Northwoods chair is another hot-spot and the Eagle Bahn gondola can have 'queues of up to 20 minutes virtually all day'. But other reporters have been luckier ('occasional' queues and 'max 10 minutes at the bottom').

TERRAIN PARKS ★★★★★
Three to choose between
There are three parks. Beginner and intermediate freestylers will want to explore the Bwana and Pride parks,

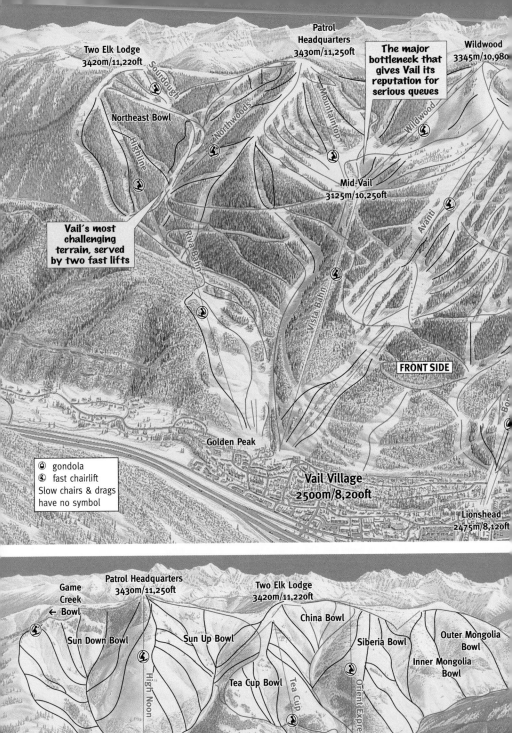

Two Elk Lodge
3420m/11,220ft

Patrol Headquarters
3430m/11,250ft

The major bottleneck that gives Vail its reputation for serious queues

Wildwood
3345m/10,980

Northeast Bowl

Sourdough

Northwoods

Mountaintop

Wildwood

Mid-Vail
3125m/10,250ft

Avanti

Highline

Vail's most challenging terrain, served by two fast lifts

Riva Ridge

Vista Bahn

FRONT SIDE

Golden Peak

Vail Village 2500m/8,200ft

ⓖ gondola
ⓕ fast chairlift
Slow chairs & drags
have no symbol

Lionshead
2475m/8,120ft

Game Creek
← Bowl

Patrol Headquarters
3430m/11,250ft

Two Elk Lodge
3420m/11,220ft

China Bowl

Sun Down Bowl

Sun Up Bowl

Siberia Bowl

Outer Mongolia Bowl

Inner Mongolia Bowl

Tea Cup Bowl

Tea Cup

High Noon

Orient Express

BACK BOWLS

2865m/9,400ft

3000m/9,840ft

Pete's

2915m/9,560ft

Skyline

Blue Sky Basin

ⓕ fast chairlift
Slow chairs & drags
have no symbol

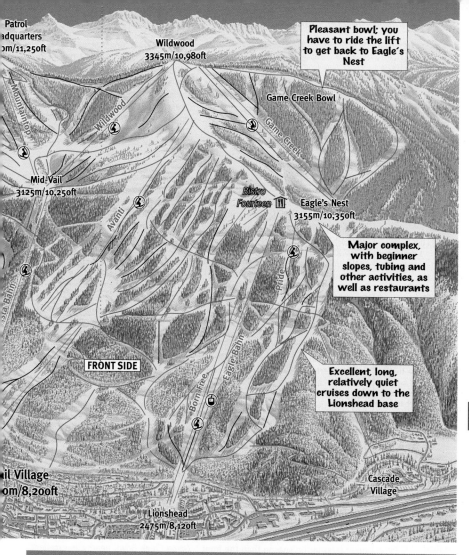

Patrol
adquarters
om/11,250ft

Wildwood
3345m/10,980ft

Pleasant bowl: you have to ride the lift to get back to Eagle's Nest

Game Creek Bowl

Mountaintop

Wildwood

Game Creek

Mid-Vail
3125m/10,250ft

Avanti

Bistro
Fourteen

Eagle's Nest
3155m/10,350ft

Major complex, with beginner slopes, tubing and other activities, as well as restaurants

La Bahn

Pride

Born Free

Eagle-Bahn

FRONT SIDE

Excellent, long, relatively quiet cruises down to the Lionshead base

il Village
om/8,200ft

Cascade
Village

Lionshead
2475m/8,120ft

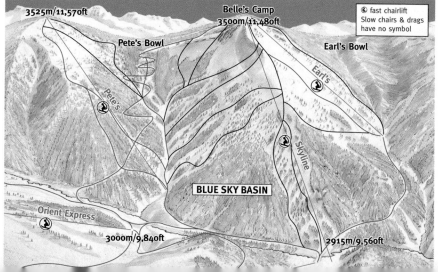

3525m/11,570ft

Belle's Camp
3500m/11,480ft

Pete's Bowl

Earl's Bowl

④ fast chairlift
Slow chairs & drags
have no symbol

Pete's

Earl's

Skyline

BLUE SKY BASIN

Orient Express

3000m/9,840ft

2915m/9,560ft

LIFT PASSES

Colorado

Prices in US$

Age	1-day	6-day
under 13	61	366
13 to 64	97	582
over 65	87	522

Free under 5
Beginner included in price of lessons

Notes
Covers all Vail, Beaver Creek, Breckenridge and Keystone resorts, plus Arapahoe Basin; prices quoted are ticket window prices; the best prices for international visitors can be obtained if they pre-book through a UK tour operator (it is not necessary to buy a complete holiday package to obtain these prices)

UK PACKAGES

Alpine Answers, AmeriCan Ski, American Ski Classics, Carrier, Crystal, Crystal Finest, Elegant Resorts, Erna Low, Frontier, Funway Holidays, Independent Ski Links, Interactive Resorts, Momentum, Oxford Ski Co, PowderBeds, Ski Expectations, Ski Independence, Ski Line, Ski Safari, Ski Solutions, Skitracer, Skiworld, Snow Finders, STC, Supertravel, Thomson

located under the Eagle Bahn gondola on Bwana run. Here, a selection of small to medium sized jumps and boxes gradually become more challenging as you progress through each park. More advanced riders will be best served at the Golden Peak Terrain Park. Located halfway down the Riva Bahn chairlift, the park is home to various high-profile events and is often in the top ten in terrain park lists and polls. There are over 40 features, including a huge triple-jump line, a quarter-pipe, mini pipe and log rail park – all built in nice fluid lines. A water tank feature, superdome and big wall ride are all signature features, as is the Landing Pad airbag jump. The super-pipe boasts 5.5m walls, and is 137m long.

SNOW RELIABILITY ★★★★★
Excellent, except in the Bowls
As well as an exceptional natural snow record (average 348 inches), Vail has extensive snowmaking, normally needed only in early season. Both the Back Bowls and Blue Sky Basin usually open later in the season than the front mountain. Blue Sky is largely north-facing (and wooded) and keeps its snow well. But the Bowls are sunny, and in warm weather snow can deteriorate to the point where they are closed or a traverse is kept open to allow access to Blue Sky Basin; for the best snow, head skier's right from the top of the Game Creek chair, where the sun has least effect because the runs are east-facing. Grooming is excellent.

FOR EXPERTS ★★★★⚡
Lots of variety
Vail's Back Bowls are vast areas, served by four chairlifts and a short draglift. You can go virtually anywhere you like in the half-dozen identifiable bowls, trying the gradient and terrain of your choice. There are interesting,

lightly wooded areas, as well as the open slopes that dominate the area. Some 87% of the runs in the Back Bowls are classified black but are not particularly steep, and they have disappointed some of our expert reporters. The snow can deteriorate rapidly in warm, sunny weather.

Blue Sky Basin has much better snow than the Back Bowls and some great adventure runs in the trees – some widely spaced, some very tight, some on relatively gentle terrain, some quite steep. All the runs funnel into the same run-out so you can't get lost.

On the front face there are some genuinely steep double black diamond runs, which usually have great snow; they are often mogulled, but they are sometimes groomed to make wonderful fast cruising. The fast Highline lift – on the extreme east of the area – serves three black runs. Prima Cornice, served by the Northwoods Express, is one of the steepest runs on the front of the hill.

If the snow is good, try the back-country Minturn Mile – you leave the ski area through a gate in the Game Creek area to descend a powder bowl and finish on a path by a river – ending up at the atmospheric Saloon. Go with a local guide.

FOR INTERMEDIATES ★★★★★
Ideal territory
The majority of Vail's front face is great intermediate terrain, with easy cruising runs. Above Lionshead, especially, there are excellent long, relatively quiet blues – Bwana, Born Free and Simba all go from top to bottom. Game Creek Bowl, nearby, is excellent, too. Avanti, underneath the chair of the same name, is a nice cruise.

As well as tackling some of the easier front-face blacks, intermediates will find plenty of interest in the Back Bowls. Some of the runs are groomed and several are blue, including Silk Road, which loops around the eastern edge, with wonderful views. Some of the unpisted slopes are ideal for learning to ski powder. Confident intermediates will also enjoy Blue Sky Basin's clearly marked blue runs and the easier ungroomed runs there (Cloud 9 is a lovely gentle area of groomed glades; In the Wuides is a bit steeper but still lovely).

↑ The front side of Vail mountain has lots of runs cut through the trees – from great groomed cruisers to steep bump runs

TANYA BOOTH

Interactive resort shortlist builder at www.wtss.co.uk

SCHOOLS
Vail
t 496 4800

Classes
Full day (9.45-3.30)
$135
Private lessons
$710 for 1 day

CHILDCARE
Small World
t 754 3285
Ages 2mnth to 6yr;
8am to 4pm;
reservation
recommended

Ski school
Ages 3 to 12; full day
including lift pass and
lunch from US$169
per day

FOR BEGINNERS ★★★☆☆
Good but can be crowded
There are fine nursery slopes at resort level and at altitude, and easy longer runs to progress to. But they can be rather crowded.

FOR BOARDERS ★★★☆☆
Big isn't always best
The terrain is about as big as it comes in America. Beginners will enjoy the front side's gentle groomed pistes (but not the crowds), good for honing skills and serviced by fast chairlifts. But beware of flat areas, especially at the top of the Wildwood and Northwoods lifts, and cat tracks. The back bowls will keep most expert and intermediate riders busy for days. Blue Sky Basin is definitely worth checking out, with its acres of natural trails, gladed trees and cornices. There are three terrain parks too.

FOR CROSS-COUNTRY ★★★☆☆
Go for Golden
Vail's cross-country areas (17km) are at the foot of Golden Peak and at the Nordic Center on the golf course. There are 10km of snowshoe trails too.

MOUNTAIN RESTAURANTS ★★☆☆☆
Surprisingly poor
Vail's mountain restaurants are disappointing for such a big, upscale resort. The major self-service restaurants can be unpleasantly crowded from 11am to 2pm.
Editors' choice The table-service Bistro Fourteen (754 4530) at Eagle's Nest – an airy room doing good food at not

exorbitant prices. We look forward to trying the new Mid-Vail table-service.
Worth knowing about There are self-service places at several major lift junctions. Two Elk is a huge, airy place that many visitors find satisfactory; but it can get very crowded. Try Wildwood Smokehouse for BBQs, Buffalo's for 'sandwich-soup combos'. Several places offer 'Lunch for Less': $9.95 (plus tax) buys you something like soup, a sandwich and a soft drink. You can take your own food and cook it on free BBQs at Belle's Camp at the top of Blue Sky Basin (take your own booze too).

SCHOOLS AND GUIDES ★★★★★
Among the best in the world
The school has an excellent reputation and we've had glowing reports in the past: 'excellent'; 'the best ski lesson I've ever had'. But we lack recent reports. You can sign up for lessons on the mountain. The school's full day Adventure Sessions offer guided instruction for intermediates and experts.

FOR FAMILIES ★★★★☆
Good all round
The main children's centre is at Golden Peak and takes kids aged 3-15; the nursery takes kids from two months to six years. There are splendid areas with adventure trails and themed play zones, such as the Magic Forest and Chaos Canyon. There's even a special kids' cafe area at Mid Vail. There are kids' snowmobiling and trampolines at Adventure Ridge.

↑ Blue Sky Basin is our favourite area, with lots of powdery, ungroomed, wooded terrain
TANYA BOOTH

GETTING THERE

Air Eagle 55km/
35 miles (45mins);
Denver 195km/
120 miles (2hr15)

ACTIVITIES

Indoor Athletic clubs and spas, massage

Outdoor Tubing, ski biking, snowmobiling, snowshoe excursions, bungee trampolining, dog sledding

Central reservations phone number
t 496 4500

Phone numbers
From distant parts of the US, add the prefix 1 970; from abroad, add the prefix +1 970

TOURIST OFFICE

vail.snow.com

STAYING THERE

There's a big choice of packages to Vail and it's easy to organise your own visit too, with regular airport shuttles.

Chalets Ski Independence has a smart one with some big bedrooms (and a couple of smaller ones) and an outdoor hot tub across I-70. Skiworld has a couple of smart ones with outdoor tubs in East Vail.

Hotels Vail's hotels are nearly all upmarket and expensive (becoming even more so with the opening of the luxurious Ritz-Carlton, Four Seasons and Solaris hotels last season). Other 5-star places include the Vail Cascade (with its own lift into the slopes), the plushly Bavarian Sonnenalp and the brilliantly convenient Lodge at Vail (right by the Vista Bahn). Other slightly more affordable places include:
****Marriot Mountain Resort At Golden Peak. Impressive spa.
****Manor Vail Resort At Golden Peak. Suites with sitting area, fireplace, kitchen, terrace. Hot tub and pools.
***Evergreen Lodge Between village and Lionshead. More affordable than others. Outdoor pool, sauna and hot tub. Sports bar. 'Excellent value for money and spacious rooms.'
Apartments There's a wide range from standard to luxury. The Racquet Club at East Vail has lots of amenities. At Vail Village, Mountain Haus is central and high quality. Vail Cascade Resort and Spa is good value, including breakfast and use of the hotel's leisure facilities. And Manor Vail might be a preferred family choice – it's beside the children's ski school. Good value

places at Lionshead include: Village Plaza Inn, Vantage Point, the Antlers, Enzian, Westwind and Vail 21.

EATING OUT ★★★★★
Endless choice
Whatever kind of food you want, Vail has it – but most of it is expensive.

Fine-dining options include the Wildflower (in the Lodge), Centre V (French-inspired; in the Arrabelle), the Tour (modern French) and Ludwig's (in the Sonnenalp). For Alpine ambience try the Alpenrose II and Pepi's in the hotel Gramshammer. You can take the gondola up to Eagle's Nest and be driven by snowcat to the Game Creek Club for dinner (it's a private members' club at lunch times); three-course set menu $82 (plus tax) last season.

For more moderate prices, we've found Blu's 'contemporary American' food satisfactory; Billy's Island Grill does steaks; and Campo de Fiori is an excellent Italian. Bart & Yeti's is good for local ales and no-frills, hearty American food. The Chophouse at Lionshead serves seafood and steaks. Reader recommendations include Sweet Basil ('delicious food; good atmosphere') and Lancelot ('for steaks and seafood') both at Vail Village, May Palace (Chinese) and Nozawa (Asian) in West Vail, Sapphire (seafood), Montauk (seafood), Los Amigos (Mexican), Russell's, Vendetta's and Pazzo's ('great pizzas, good value').

APRES-SKI ★★★☆☆
Fairly lively
Lionshead is quiet in the evenings; but Garfinkel's has a DJ, sun deck and happy hour. The Red Lion in Vail Village is 'cheap and good fun' with live music, big-screen TVs and huge portions of food. The George models itself on an English-style pub. Pepi's is popular and Los Amigos is lively at four o'clock. The Tap Room in the Vista Bahn building is a relaxed woody bar. We enjoyed comedy and music at the Club.

You can have a good night out at Adventure Ridge at the top of the gondola. As well as restaurants and bars, there's lots to do on the snow.

OFF THE SLOPES ★★★☆☆
A lot to do
Getting around on the free bus is easy, and there are lots of activities. The factory outlets at Silverthorne are a must if you can't resist a bargain.

Winter Park

A radical alternative to the run of Colorado resorts, for those more interested in snow and space than in après-ski amusements

RATINGS

The mountains

Extent	★★★
Fast lifts	★★★★
Queues	★★★★
Terrain p'ks	★★★★★
Snow	★★★★★
Expert	★★★★
Intermediate	★★★★
Beginner	★★★★★
Boarder	★★★
X-country	★★★★
Restaurants	★★★
Schools	★★★★★
Families	★★★★

The resort

Charm	★★
Convenience	★★★
Scenery	★★★
Eating out	★★
Après-ski	★
Off-slope	★

RPI 130

lift pass	£310
ski hire	£150
lessons	£165
food & drink	£100
total	£725

NEWS

2010/11: All six terrain parks were improved with new features. A new fun tree run for kids, Dilly Dally Alley, was developed. The Lodge at Sunspot at the top of Winter Park Mountain was given a facelift inside and out. And the Private Lesson Center opened – combining private lessons with lift queue priority, ski lockers, boot driers and an upmarket lounge.

The small village at the base doesn't amount to much and most accommodation is a shuttle-bus ride away →

➕ The best snowfall record of all Colorado's major resorts

➕ Good terrain for all abilities

➕ Quiet on weekdays

➕ Leading resort for teaching people with disabilities to ski and ride

➕ Largely free of inflated prices and ski-resort glitz

➖ 'Village' at the lift base is still very limited and dead in the evening

➖ Town is a bus ride away and lacks the usual shops and restaurants

➖ Trails tend to be either easy cruises or stiff mogul fields

➖ Some tough terrain liable to closure by bad weather

Winter Park's ski area – developed for the recreation of the citizens of nearby Denver, and still owned by the city – is world class. When Intrawest (developers of resorts such as Whistler) got involved a few years ago, there was the prospect of a world-class resort being developed at the base, too. But things have stalled and further expansion plans now seem to have been put on hold.

For the present, there's only a small, very quiet 'village' at the base and most lodging, shops and restaurants are a bus ride away. If that doesn't matter to you, Winter Park is well worth considering.

THE RESORT

Winter Park started life in the 19th century: when the Rio Grande railway was built, workers climbed the slopes to ski down. One of its mountains, Mary Jane, is named after a legendary 'lady of pleasure', who is said to have received the land as payment for her favours. The resort (at 2745m) is one of the highest to get a chapter in this book (only Breckenridge is higher) so there is a risk of altitude sickness if you go straight there from the UK. And the approach road from Denver is even higher – crossing the Continental Divide at Berthoud Pass (3450m) – and Alpine in character. Don't plan on driving over in the dark. Having a car makes day trips to Denver and to resorts such as Copper Mountain, Breckenridge (see separate chapter) and Keystone possible.

You can stay at the small 'village' at the base of the slopes or in the town of Winter Park, linked by shuttle-bus.

VILLAGE CHARM ★★
Old or new?
Most accommodation is in spacious condos scattered around either side of US highway 40, the road through the

KEY FACTS

Resort	2745m
	9,000ft
Slopes	2745-3675m
	9,000-12,060ft
Lifts	25
Pistes	3,060 acres
Green	8%
Blue	36%
Black	56%
Snowmaking	10%

town of Winter Park. Drive into the town at night, and the neon lights make it seem like a real ski resort town – but in the cold light of day it's clear that the place doesn't amount to much, though the locals are 'friendly'. It even lacks a proper supermarket – the nearest is a drive or free bus ride away at Fraser.

Stylish lodgings have been developed at or near the foot of the slopes, to form a very small car-free mini-resort known as The Village at Winter Park. Confusingly, an area between the mountain and the town is known as Old Town.

CONVENIENCE ★★★★★
Walk or ride
If you stay in the 'village' you are right by the slopes. Shuttle-buses run between town and the lift base, and hotels and condos also have shuttles.

SCENERY ★★★★★
See the Continental Divide
You are almost on the Continental Divide here, with views of the rolling hills in the other direction from the top of Parsenn Bowl.

THE MOUNTAINS

There's a good mix of terrain that suits all abilities – when it's all open. There are guided tours at 10am and 1pm ('guide was knowledgeable and friendly', says a 2011 reporter). Route finding can be tricky in places.

EXTENT OF THE SLOPES ★★★★★
Interestingly divided
Winter Park's ski area is big by US standards. There are five distinct, but well-linked, sectors. From the main base, a fast quad takes you to the peak of the original **Winter Park** mountain. From there, you can descend in all directions. Runs lead back towards the main base and over to the **Vasquez Ridge** area on the far right, served by the Pioneer fast quad.

You can also descend to the base of **Mary Jane** mountain, where four chairs up the front face serve tough runs; other chairs serve easier terrain on the flanks. From here you can head for the **Parsenn Bowl** on the Panoramic Express chair for intermediate terrain above and in the trees. From Parsenn, conditions permitting, you can hike for

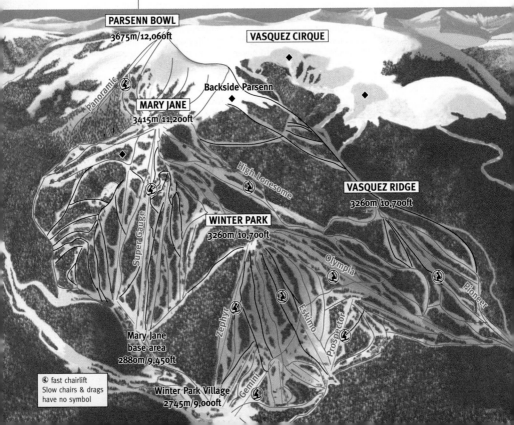

SKIING AND BOARDING FOR THE DISABLED

Winter Park is home to the US National Sports Center for the Disabled (NSCD) – the world's leading centre for teaching skiing and snowboarding to people with disabilities. If you are disabled and want to learn to ski or snowboard, there's no better place to go. It's important to book ahead so that a suitably trained instructor is available. The NSCD can help with travel and accommodation arrangements. See www.nscd.org.

UK PACKAGES

Alpine Answers, AmeriCan Ski, American Ski Classics, Crystal, Erna Low, Funway Holidays, Independent Ski Links, Interactive Resorts, PowderBeds, Ski Independence, Ski Safari, Ski Solutions, Skitracer, Skiworld, Snow Finders, Supertravel, Thomson, Virgin Snow

up to half an hour to access advanced and extreme terrain at **Vasquez Cirque**. You can return to Parsenn Bowl using the Eagle Wind chair, saving a long run-out to the Pioneer lift.

FAST LIFTS ★★★★
Adequately covered
Fast chairs have gradually replaced old lifts, though a few slow ones remain.

QUEUES ★★★★
Quiet during the week
During the week the mountain is generally quiet. However, the Zephyr Express can get busy at peak times: 'Get up the mountain before 9am to avoid queues,' says one reporter; 'Wait an hour after lift starting times,' says another. But there can be weekend crowds and queues (including at Discovery Park, says a 2011 visitor).

TERRAIN PARKS ★★★★★
Parks for all standards
All six parks were upgraded last season and new rails were installed. The flagship Rail Yard park, with 30 features including big jumps, jibs, boxes, a host of variously shaped rails and quarter-, half- and super-pipes, is enough to challenge most experts. It runs down much of the front of Winter Park mountain for 1.3km. Halfway down it crosses a bridge so that those on the Village Way green run can cross the park safely. At the bottom are the huge features of Dark Territory, open to special pass holders only (you need to pay $20, sign a waiver and watch a safety video to get the pass). For those who prefer smaller hits, there are the Re-Railer and Gangway parks for intermediates nearby. There's also the beginner-intermediate Ash Cat on the Jack Kendrick green run plus the Starter park under Prospector Express and the Bouncer park in the 'village' – both for beginners. Check them out at www.rlyrd.com.

SNOW RELIABILITY ★★★★★
Among Colorado's best
Winter Park's position close to the Continental Divide, gives it an average yearly snowfall of 30 inches – higher than most major Colorado resorts. Snowmaking covers a lot of Winter Park mountain's runs.

FOR EXPERTS ★★★★
Some hair-raising challenges
Mary Jane has some of the steepest

mogul fields, chutes and hair-raising challenges in the US. On the front side is a row of long black mogul fields that are quite steep enough for most of us. There are some good genuine blacks on Winter Park mountain, too.
Some of the best terrain is open only when there is good snow and/or weather – so it's especially unreliable early in the season. The fearsome chutes of Mary Jane's back side – all steep, narrow and bordered by rocks – need a lot of snow and are accessed by a control gate. Parsenn Bowl has superb blue/black gladed runs and black diamond gladed runs on the back side down to the Eagle Wind chair. Vasquez Cirque, the least reliably open area, has excellent ungroomed expert terrain but not much vertical before you hit the forest.

FOR INTERMEDIATES ★★★★
Choose your challenge
From pretty much wherever you are on Winter Park mountain and Vasquez Ridge you can choose a run to suit your ability. Most blue runs are well groomed every night, giving you perfect early morning cruising on the famous Colorado 'corduroy' pistes. Black runs, however, tend not to be groomed, and huge moguls form. If bumps are for you, try Mary Jane's front side. If you're learning to love them, the blue/black Sleeper enables you to dip in and out.
Parsenn Bowl has grand views and several gentle cruising pistes as well as more challenging ungroomed terrain. There are blue and blue-black runs and glades here, offering a nice range of gradients. It's also an ideal place to try powder for the first time. But when it's actually snowing you are better off riding lower lifts, sticking to the powdery edges of treelined runs for better visibility. The blue-black Hughes is a great thrash home at close of play.

FOR BEGINNERS ★★★★★
About the best we've seen
Discovery Park is a 25-acre dedicated area for beginners, reached by a high-speed quad and served by two more chairs. As well as a nursery area and longer green runs, it has an adventure trail through trees. And the Sorensen Park learning zone at the base area is good too. There are lots of long green runs, but some are perilously close to being flat.

Winter Park

Interactive resort shortlist builder at **www.wtss.co.uk**

SCHOOLS

Winter Park
t 1 800 729 7907
National Sports Center for the Disabled
t 726 1540
Special programme for disabled skiers and snowboarders

Classes (Winter Park prices)
Half day (2½hr) $75
Private lessons
$385 for 3hr for 1 to 3 people

CHILDCARE

Wee Willie's
t 1 800 420 8093
Ages 2mnth to 6yr; $100 per day; 8am to 4pm

Ski school
Takes ages 3 to 14 ($135 per day including lift ticket, helmet and GPS tracking)

GETTING THERE

Air Denver 165km/ 105 miles (2hr15)
Rail Denver, Sat and Sun only

ACTIVITIES

Indoor Fitness clubs, hot tubs, museum
Outdoor Ice rink, snowshoeing, ski bikes, snowcat tours

Central reservations
toll-free number (from within the US)
1 800 979 0332

Phone numbers
From distant parts of the US, add the prefix 1 970; from abroad, add the prefix +1 970

TOURIST OFFICE

www.skiwinterpark.com

FOR BOARDERS ★★★★★
Beware the moguls and flats
There is some great advanced and extreme boarding terrain and a high probability of fresh powder to ride. And the terrain parks are great. The resort is also good for beginners and intermediates, with excellent terrain for learning. A good school provides classes for all levels, including learning to jump and ride rails. But there are quite a few flat spots to beware of, and a lot of the steep runs have huge moguls, which many boarders find tricky.

FOR CROSS-COUNTRY ★★★★★
Lots of it nearby
There are several areas nearby (none actually in the resort) with over 200km of groomed trails plus backcountry tours and generally excellent snow.

MOUNTAIN RESTAURANTS ★★★★★
Some good facilities
The highlight is the Lodge at Sunspot, at the top of Winter Park mountain. This wood and glass building has a welcoming bar with a roaring log fire and table- and self-service sections – but it gets very busy. Lunch Rock Cafe at the top of Mary Jane has 'excellent views', does quick snacks and has a deli counter. And there is a self-service (with 'reasonable prices' but 'limited choice' say recent reporters) at Snoasis, by the beginner area. Otherwise, it's down to the bases. The Club Car at the base of Mary Jane offers table service and a varied menu.

SCHOOLS AND GUIDES ★★★★★
Very good reports
A recent reporter with a school party said, 'I would like to stress how good, helpful and flexible the ski school is.' 'Three people in our group had lessons, and the improvement in all was quite startling to see,' said another visitor. As well as standard classes there are themed lessons such as bumps, women-only, telemark clinics and three-day steep and deep camps.

FOR FAMILIES ★★★★★
Some of the best
Wee Willie's Child Care at the base area houses day-care facilities, taking kids from two months to six years, and is the meeting point for children's classes, which have their own areas.

STAYING THERE

Chalets Skiworld has a lovely log-cabin with outdoor hot tub ('the best we've ever stayed in – very spacious, wi-fi, bus stop outside', says a 2011 visitor).
Hotels There are a couple of hotel/ condo complexes with restaurants and pools near, but not in, the new Village.
★★★Iron Horse Resort 'Wonderful; ski-in/ski-out; great restaurant.' Outdoor pool and hot tubs, steam room.
Vintage Hotel Linked by the car park bucket lift to the 'village'. 'Nice hotel, amazing value,' says a reporter. But a 2011 visitor found the 'bar closed at 9pm'. Outdoor pool and tub, sauna.
Apartments The Zephyr Mountain Lodge, Fraser Crossing and Founders Pointe are swish places in the 'village'. There are a lot of comfortable condos in or on the way to town. Reader tips: Beaver Village, Sawmill Station, Red Quill, Meadowridge, Crestview Place.

EATING OUT ★★★★★
A real weakness
There isn't the range of places you get in most 'destination' resorts. For 'fine dining' you have to drive 13km to Devil's Thumb Ranch. Get hold of the giveaway Grand County menu guide. In town, reporters are keen on Deno's (seafood, steaks etc), New Hong Kong ('excellent' Chinese), Gasthaus Eichler (German-influenced food), Shipwreck Landing North ('food is the best in Winter Park'), Carlos and Maria's (Tex-Mex), Fontenot's (Cajun), Hernando's (pizza/pasta). Crooked Creek Saloon, a drive away at Fraser, has a good local atmosphere and typical American food.

APRES-SKI ★★★★★
If you know where to go ...
At close of play, there's action in the 'village' at the Derailer Bar ('the best and cheapest') and Doc's Roadhouse, and at the Club Car at the base of Mary Jane – but reporters say they close too early. The Cheeky Monk serves 'good Belgian beer'. Later on, Deno's and the Winter Park Pub in town are the main hot spots. Moffat Station micro brewery has good beer.

OFF THE SLOPES ★★★★★
Mainly the great outdoors
Reporters enjoy the floodlit tubing at Fraser, skating at the base area rink and snowmobiling to the Continental Divide. The Silverthorne factory outlet stores are 90 minutes away.

Utah

'The Greatest Snow on Earth' is Utah's marketing slogan. And it's not far from the truth: some Utah resorts do get huge amounts of snow – usually light, dry powder. If you like the steep and deep, you should at some point make the pilgrimage here. And if you like a beer or two après-ski, don't be put off by the image of a 'dry' Mormon state – getting alcohol has never been a problem (and the laws were greatly relaxed in July 2009, anyway). But boarders beware: two of its top resorts don't allow snowboarding.

The biggest dumps fall at Alta (which bans boarding) and Snowbird. Their average of 500 inches of snow a year (twice as much as some Colorado resorts) has made them the powder capitals of the world. Park City, 45 minutes' drive away, is the main 'destination' resort of the area, and a sensible holiday base; upmarket Deer Valley (which also bans boarding) is next door; and The Canyons is only a short drive away. Although only a few miles from Snowbird/Alta as the crow flies, these resorts get 'only' 300 to 350 inches of snow. We have separate chapters on these five resorts.

Of course, you're not guaranteed fresh powder. We've occasionally been disappointed. But we've had some memorably snowy visits, too. We spent a week in Park City in 2008, and it

virtually never stopped snowing. Every day we had fresh, knee-high powder. We never made it to Alta or Snowbird: the access road to them was often closed by avalanche danger – but in any case the snow on the three local mountains was awesome.

Other resorts worth visiting (covered in the resort directory at the end of the book) include **Brighton** and **Solitude**, in the valley next to Alta/Snowbird and blessed with similar amounts of snow. The snow gets tracked out less quickly because the resorts attract far fewer experts. The main claim to fame of **Sundance** is that it's owned by Robert Redford; it averages 320 inches of snow. It was unknown **Snowbasin** (400 inches), well to the north, that hosted the Olympic downhill events in 2002. **Powder Mountain** (500 inches), a bit further north, is aptly named. A few seasons ago the resort started all-day guided snowcat tours, which were so popular that the available terrain has been increased to 3,000 acres.

Until July 2009 the sale and consumption of alcohol was tightly controlled in Utah, the Mormon state. Until then, to get a drink in bars and clubs dedicated to drinking (as opposed to restaurants) you had to pay a fee to become a member or be the guest of a member. At some places you had to order food in order to get an alcoholic drink. These rules have now been scrapped. There are still differences between bars and restaurants, but effectively you don't need to worry about them, and as long as you are over 21 (and can prove it – eg by showing your passport) you should have no problem getting alcoholic drinks between 10am and midnight or 1am. The amount of spirits allowed in a drink has been increased too.

593

TOURIST OFFICE

Ski Utah
www.skiutah.com

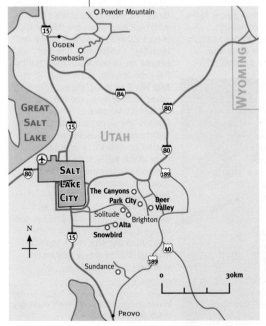

Alta

Cult powder resort linked to Snowbird but with less brutal architecture and a friendlier, old-fashioned feel

594

TOP 10 RATINGS

Extent	★★★
Fast lifts	★★★★
Queues	★★★
Snow	★★★★★
Expert	★★★★★
Intermediate	★★★
Beginner	★★★
Charm	★★
Convenience	★★★★
Scenery	★★★

RPI	125
lift pass	£280
ski hire	£180
lessons	£150
food & drink	£110
total	**£720**

NEWS

2011/12: There are plans to widen a blue run back to the bottom of the Collins lift.

2010/11: Work continued on improvements to the Albion Base, including better access from the Transfer tow to the Sunnyside lift.

➕ Phenomenal snow and steep terrain mean cult status among experts (there's great beginner terrain, too)

➕ Linked to Snowbird, making it one of the largest ski areas in the US

➕ Ski-almost-to-the-door convenience

➖ 'Resort' is no more than a scattering of lodges, so not much après-ski atmosphere, and few off-slope diversions

➖ Limited groomed runs for intermediates

Alta and Snowbird are the powder capitals of the world (the snow here is as plentiful, frequent and light as it comes), and add up to a great area for adventurous skiers (much less so for boarders, who are banned from Alta). Of the two, Alta is our preferred base – it has a friendlier, small-scale feel.

THE RESORT

Alta sits at the craggy head of Little Cottonwood Canyon, 2km beyond Snowbird and less than an hour's drive from downtown Salt Lake City. Both the resort and the approach road are prone to avalanches and closure: visitors can be confined indoors for safety.

Village charm Where once there was a bustling and bawdy mining town, there is now just a strung-out handful of lodges and parking areas.

Convenience Life revolves around the two separate lift base areas – Albion and Wildcat – linked by a bi-directional rope tow along the flat valley floor. There are about a dozen places to stay, all convenient for the lifts.

Scenery Alta is recognised for its impressively rugged scenery and challenging, sparsely wooded ridges.

THE MOUNTAINS

Alta's slopes are lightly wooded, with some treeless slopes. Check out the separate chapter for the linked Snowbird slopes. Unlike most US resorts, Alta does not differentiate between single and double black diamond trails – regrettable, we think.

Slopes The dominant feature of Alta's terrain is the steep end of a ridge that separates the area's two basins. To the left, above Albion Base, the slopes stretch away over easy green terrain towards the blue and black runs from Point Supreme and from the top of the Sugarloaf quad (also the access lift for Snowbird). To the right, above Wildcat Base, is a more concentrated bowl with blue runs down the middle and blacks either side, served by the fast two-stage Collins chair. The two sectors are linked at altitude, and by a flat rope tow along the valley floor.

Fast lifts Fast chairs depart from each base; another forms the link with Snowbird's ski area.

Queues The slopes are normally uncrowded and queues rare. But it is said to be difficult to board the Collins chair at the mid-station at times because of everyone skiing to the base and boarding there.

Terrain parks There isn't one.

Snow reliability The quantity and quality of the snow – an average 500 inches a year – and the northerly orientation put Alta in the top rank. And last season was a near-record, with over 700 inches.

ALTA SKI AREA

← Vast amounts of ungroomed terrain covered in vast amounts of powder – that's what you go to Alta and Snowbird for

KEY FACTS

Resort	2600m
	8,530ft
Alta and Snowbird combined area see Snowbird	

Alta only	
Slopes	2600-3215m
	8,530-10,550ft
Lifts	11
Pistes	2,200 acres
Green	25%
Blue	40%
Black	35%
Snowmaking	Some

UK PACKAGES

Skitracer

Phone numbers
From distant parts of
the US, add the prefix
1 801; from abroad,
add the prefix +1 801

TOURIST OFFICE

www.alta.com

Experts Even before the Snowbird link Alta had cult status among local experts, who flocked to the high ridges after a fresh snowfall. There are dozens of steep slopes and chutes.
Intermediates Adventurous intermediates happy to try ungroomed slopes and learn to love powder will love Alta too. There is also suitable terrain in Snowbird. But if it is miles of perfectly groomed piste you are after, there are plenty of better resorts.
Beginners Albion has a nursery area and gentle lower slopes, with a beginner lift pass covering three lifts. The Sunnyside lift is free to use after 3pm. But it's hard to recommend such a narrowly focused resort to beginners.
Snowboarding Boarding is banned (but allowed in Snowbird and guided snowcat boarding is available nearby).
Cross-country 5km of groomed track.
Mountain restaurants There's one in each sector, offering mainly fast food. Alf's on the Albion side has 'fast service' and a wide choice. The 'nice, light and airy' Watson Shelter on the Wildcat side has self- and table-service sections. Or head back to the base.
Schools and guides The ski school specialises in powder lessons – though there are regular classes, too.
Families Day care for children from six weeks to nine years is available at the Children's Center at Albion Base.

STAYING THERE

None of the hotels is luxurious in US terms but most get booked up by repeat visitors; unusually for the US, most operate half-board deals, with dinner included.
Hotels The venerable Alta Lodge (742 3500) has comfortable rooms and an atmospheric bar, and has developed a cult following among American visitors by operating a bit like a catered chalet, serving a four-course dinner menu at shared or private tables. Rustler Lodge (742 2200) is more luxurious, with a big outdoor pool, but impersonal. The comfortable, modern and conveniently located Goldminer's Daughter (742 2300) and the basic Peruvian Lodge (742 3000) are cheaper. The Snowpine Lodge (742 2000) is convenient, has a sauna and has been recommended.
Eating out It is possible, but eating in is the normal routine.
Après-ski This rarely goes beyond a few drinks in one of the hotel bars. The Goldminer's Daughter Saloon is the main après-ski bar for the amusement of day visitors, with a pool table etc.
Off the slopes There are few options other than snowshoeing, a sightseeing trip to Salt Lake City, or the Cliff Lodge spa down the road at Snowbird.

POINT SUPREME
3200m/10,500ft
Catherine's Area
East Castle
Devil's Castle 3185m/10,450ft
Mineral Basin/ Snowbird
MOUNT BALDY
3375m/11,070ft
Snowbird
Baldy Shoulder
Ballroom
Peruvian Ridge
Sugarloaf
East Greeley
Collins
Sunnyside
Collins
Wildcat Area
⑭ fast chairlift
Slow chairs & drags have no symbol
Albion Base
Wildcat Base
2600m/8,530ft

Canyons

One of the five biggest ski areas in the US, with a small purpose-built resort at the base of the slopes on the edge of Park City

TOP 10 RATINGS

Extent	★★★
Fast lifts	★★★
Queues	★★★★
Snow	★★★★
Expert	★★★★
Intermediate	★★★★
Beginner	★★
Charm	★★
Convenience	★★★★
Scenery	★★★

RPI	130
lift pass	£290
ski hire	£180
lessons	£165
food & drink	£110
total	**£745**

NEWS

2010/11: A new fast quad opened up the resort's ninth peak, Iron Mountain, with 300 acres of varied terrain. Another quad opened from the resort to a point near the top of the Sun Peak lift; it increases capacity from the base by almost 50%. The terrain park was relocated and is now a mile long. A new mountain hut, Cloud Dine, opened on Dream Peak.

+ Relatively extensive area of slopes

+ Modern lift system with few queues

+ Very easy access to Park City and Deer Valley ski areas

+ Convenient purpose-built resort developing at the base, but ...

− Village is limited

− Snow on the many south-facing slopes is affected by sun

− Many runs are short

− Few green runs suitable for those progressing from nursery slopes

Canyons has the potential to become the most extensive ski area in the US (and already claims it is among the five biggest), with nine linked mountains. Anyone having a holiday in adjacent Park City should plan to visit. Staying in the village at the base is not something we'd be keen on, though.

THE RESORT

Canyons has been transformed over the past decade or so. The area of the slopes has more than doubled, and a car-free village built at the base.
Village charm The village has a few shops, restaurants and bars as well as accommodation. And the new Ski Beach is an outdoor bar/café area at the foot of the slopes. But it doesn't add up to a very appealing place to spend time, and we would much rather stay in central Park City.
Convenience Staying at the base is convenient for Canyons but not especially for the other local Park City and Deer Valley slopes. If you stay in Park City, regular shuttle-buses run to the car park below Canyons village, from which you get a cabriolet lift up.
Scenery A series of broad, long ridges are separated by valleys and most of the area is fairly densely wooded.

THE MOUNTAINS

Canyons gets its name from the valleys between the nine mountains that make up the ski area.
Free daily mountain tours start at 10.30, and a First Tracks programme runs three times a week where former Olympic medallists guide you around the slopes before they officially open.
Slopes Red Pine Lodge, at the heart of the slopes, is reached by an eight-seat gondola from the village. A new fast quad reaches a higher point. From the top of both lifts you can move in either direction across a series of ridges and valleys. Runs come off both sides of each ridge and generally face north or south. Most runs are quite short (less than 500m vertical), with some long, quite flat run-outs. If you return to the resort from the Sun Lodge area, you need to take a rope tow, which some people find awkward.

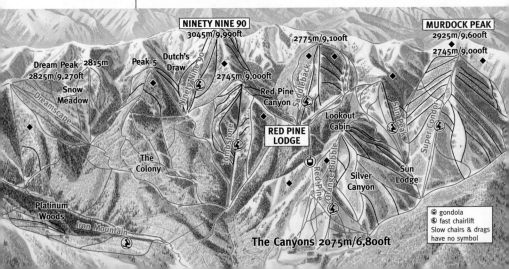

NINETY NINE 90
3045m/9,990ft

2775m/9,100ft

MURDOCK PEAK
2925m/9,600ft

2745m/9,000ft

Dream Peak 2815m
2825m/9,270ft

Peak 5

Dutch's Draw

2745m/9,000ft

Snow Meadow

Ninety Nine 90

Red Pine Canyon

Saddleback

Dreamscape

Lookout Cabin

Super Condor

Tombstone

Sun Peak

RED PINE LODGE

The Colony

Red Pine

Dragon Bubble

Silver Canyon

Sun Lodge

Platinum Woods

Iron Mountain

The Canyons 2075m/6,800ft

Ⓖ gondola
Ⓕ fast chairlift
Slow chairs & drags
have no symbol

interest. From the Super Condor and Tombstone fast chairs there are excellent double blue square runs. The Dreamscape area can be quiet, and is great for early experiments in off-piste powder. Getting back from here you ski through The Colony – an area of huge homes for the super-rich.

Beginners There are good areas with moving carpets up at Red Pine Lodge. But the run you progress to is rather short and gets very busy.

Snowboarding Except for the flat run-outs from many runs, it's a great area, with lots of natural hits. Canis Lupus is a mile-long, natural half-pipe with numerous obstacles ('fantastic fun').

Cross-country None in resort. The Park City golf course has 20km and the Homestead Resort course 12km.

Mountain restaurants Red Pine Lodge is a large, attractive building with a busy cafeteria, table-service restaurant and big deck. Reporters have found the Sun Lodge quieter. The table-service Lookout Cabin has wonderful views. Cloud Dine is another option that opened last season. The Dreamscape and Tombstone Grill snack huts offer simple food outdoors.

Schools and guides No recent reports; but as well as the usual classes, there are special clinics. Children's classes are for ages four to 14.

Families There's day care in the Grand Summit Hotel for children from six weeks to six years, and at the school for ages two and three years.

STAYING THERE

Hotels The luxurious Grand Summit, Waldorf Astoria and Silverado Lodge have pools and hot tubs.

Apartments The Escala (with pool and hot tubs) and Westgate Resort and Spa are pricey and luxurious. Of the cheaper places Timberwolf condos have been recommended; other options include Bear Hollow, Hidden Creek, Red Pine and Sundial.

Eating out The Grand Summit has three restaurants serving dinner and there's the Spruce in the Waldorf Astoria and Alpine House in the Sundial. Red Pine Lodge at the top of the gondola does a BBQ on Saturdays, with a C&W band and dancing.

Après-ski The Cabin Lounge in the Grand Summit has live entertainment.

Off the slopes There's snowshoeing, dog sledding, hot-air ballooning, a factory outlet mall and Salt Lake City and Park City nearby.

↑ Most trails are quite short and many have long, quite flat run-outs
DAVE ASHMORE

KEY FACTS

Resort	2075m
	6,800ft
Slopes	2075-3045m
	6,800-9,990ft
Lifts	19
Pistes	4,000 acres
Green	10%
Blue	44%
Black	46%
Snowmaking	6%

UK PACKAGES

AmeriCan Ski, American Ski Classics, Funway Holidays, Independent Ski Links, Ski Safari, Skitracer, Skiworld, Virgin Snow

Central reservations
Call 1 866 604 4171 (toll-free from within the US)
Phone numbers
From distant parts of the US, add the prefix 1 435; from abroad, add the prefix +1 435

TOURIST OFFICE

www.thecanyons.com

Fast lifts The core of the lift system either side of Red Pine Lodge consists of fast quads, but the Dream Peak sector has no fast lifts.

Queues The new fast quad from the base should have taken pressure off the gondola. And the new Iron Mountain chair should have cut queues for the Tombstone fast chair. More reports please.

Terrain parks There are six natural half-pipes (marked on the trail map). A new terrain park for all abilities, served by the Saddleback chair, was built in 2011; it's a mile long and includes 50 features and nine jumps.

Snow reliability Snow here is not the best in Utah. It gets as much on average as Park City (350 inches) and more than Deer Valley. But the south-facing slopes suffer in late-season sun.

Experts There is steep terrain all over the mountain. We particularly liked the north-facing runs off Ninety Nine 90, with steep double black diamond runs plunging down through the trees. We had a great time here on our last visit, after fresh snow. A short hike from the top accesses some fine powder runs even days after a snowfall. There is also lots of double-diamond terrain on Murdock Peak (a 20-minute hike from the Super Condor lift). Runs off Peak 5 chair are more sheltered. And there's heli-skiing too.

Intermediates There are groomed blue runs for intermediates on all the main sectors except Ninety Nine 90. Some are quite short, but you can switch from valley to valley for added

Canyons

597

Interactive resort shortlist builder at www.wtss.co.uk

Deer Valley

Top of the Ivy League of US ski resorts: it promises, and delivers, the best ski and gastronomic experience – we love it

TOP 10 RATINGS

Extent	★★
Fast lifts	★★★★
Queues	★★★★
Snow	★★★★
Expert	★★★
Intermediate	★★★★
Beginner	★★★★
Charm	★★★
Convenience	★★★★
Scenery	★★★

RPI   140

lift pass	£290
ski hire	£180
lessons	£200
food & drink	£115
total	£785

NEWS

2010/11: The 5-star Montage Deer Valley hotel, in Empire Canyon beside the Lodge, reopened in December 2010 following a revamp. The Empire Canyon, Silver Lake and Snow Park lodges were updated.

KEY FACTS

Resort	2195m
	7,200ft
Slopes	2000-2915m
	6,570-9,570ft
Lifts	21
Pistes	2,026 acres
Green	24%
Blue	43%
Black	33%
Snowmaking	28%

UK PACKAGES

AmeriCan Ski, PowderBeds, Ski Independence, Ski Safari, Skitracer, Virgin Snow

Central reservations
Call 645 6538

Phone numbers
From distant parts of the US, add 1 435; from abroad, add the prefix +1 435

- ➕ Immaculate piste grooming, good snow record and lots of snow-guns
- ➕ Good tree skiing
- ➕ Brilliant free black-diamond tours
- ➕ Many fast lifts and no queues
- ➕ Good restaurants and lodgings

- ➖ Relatively expensive
- ➖ Small area of slopes
- ➖ Mostly short runs of less than 400m vertical
- ➖ Quiet at night, though Park City is right next door

Deer Valley prides itself on pampering its guests, with valets to unload your skis, gourmet dining, immaculately groomed slopes, limited numbers on the mountain – and no snowboarding. Happily, it's not just window dressing: the slopes are excellent, too. Park City ski area is right next door – nothing more than a fence separates the two – and any skier visiting the area should try both. For most people, Park City town is the obvious base; but there are some seductive hotels here at mid-mountain Silver Lake.

THE RESORT

Just a mile from the end of Park City's Main Street, Deer Valley is overtly upmarket – famed for the care and attention lavished on both the slopes and the guests. But it remains unpretentious.

Village charm There is no village as such; though the Silver Lake area is somewhat of a mid-mountain focus.

Convenience The lodgings – luxurious chalets and swanky hotels – are scattered around.

Scenery The scenery is not without its attractions: from Bald Mountain there are extensive views to Park City.

THE MOUNTAINS

The slopes are varied and interesting. Deer Valley's reputation for immaculate grooming is justified ('the best I have ever seen', says a reporter) but there is also a lot of exciting tree skiing – and some steep bump runs, too. There are free mountain tours for different standards. We went on two three-hour black-diamond tours on our last visit, and they were both brilliant, taking us through fresh powder in the trees that we would never have found on our own. Reporters praise these tours, too.

Slopes Two chairs take you up Bald Eagle Mountain, just beyond which is the mid-mountain focus of Silver Lake Lodge. You can ski from here to the isolated Little Baldy Peak, served by a gondola and a quad chairlift, with mainly easy runs to serve property developments there. But the main skiing is on three linked peaks beyond Silver Lake Lodge – Bald Mountain, Flagstaff Mountain and Empire Canyon. The top of Empire is just a few metres from the runs of the Park City ski area but crossing the fence that divides the two is banned.

Fast lifts Fast quads rule; the three main peaks have nine.

Queues Waiting in lift lines is not something that Deer Valley wants its guests to experience, so it limits the number of lift tickets sold.

Terrain parks There isn't one.

Snow reliability As you'd expect in Utah, snow reliability is excellent, and there's plenty of snowmaking too.

Experts Despite the image of pampered luxury there is excellent expert terrain on all three main mountains, including fabulous glades, bumps, chutes and bowls. And the snow doesn't get skied out quickly. The Ski Utah Interconnect Tour to Alta starts here (see the Park City chapter).

Intermediates There are lots of superbly groomed blue runs.

Beginners There are nursery slopes at Silver Lake Lodge as well as the base, and gentle green runs to progress to.

Snowboarding Boarding is banned.

Cross-country There are prepared trails on both the Park City (20km) and Homestead Resort (12km) golf courses and lots of scope for backcountry trips as well.

Mountain restaurants The restaurants are the best in Utah. There are attractive wood-and-glass self-service places at both Silver Lake (we had

STAYING THERE

A car is useful for visiting other nearby Utah resorts, though Deer Valley, Park City and The Canyons are all linked by efficient shuttle-buses.

Hotels The St Regis Resort, the Montage Deer Valley (see 'News'), Stein Eriksen Lodge and Goldener Hirsch are some of the plushest hotels in any ski resort.

Apartments There are many luxury apartments and houses to rent. Reader recommendations include Ridgepoint, Royal Plaza and The Woods at Silver Lake – and Aspenwood and Boulder Creek at Snow Park (cheaper).

Eating out Of the gourmet restaurants, the Mariposa is the best. We enjoyed both the all-you-can-eat Seafood Buffet (it's not just seafood) and a 'Fireside Dining' evening at the Empire Canyon Lodge: four courses, each one served at a different fireplace. It's held three nights a week. There's also the St Regis Resort restaurant to try.

Après-ski Edgar's Beers & Spirits Lounge at the base area is the main après-ski venue, with live music at weekends. For more choice, it's not far to Main Street in Park City.

Off the slopes Park City has lots of shops, galleries etc. Salt Lake City, not far away, has concerts, sights and shopping. Balloon rides and snowmobiling are popular.

↑ The Silver Lake Lodge area with a fast chairlift going up the immaculately groomed Bald Mountain

DAVE ASHMORE

delicious lamb stew and turkey chilli there) and the base lodge. The grill restaurant at Empire Canyon Lodge is consistently recommended. For a bit of a treat, try the Stein Eriksen Lodge, the Goldener Hirsch or the Royal Street Cafe table-service restaurant at Silver Lake Lodge.

Schools and guides The ski school is doubtless excellent; book in advance.

Families The Children's Center accepts children aged between two months and 12 years.

TOURIST OFFICE

www.deervalley.com

599

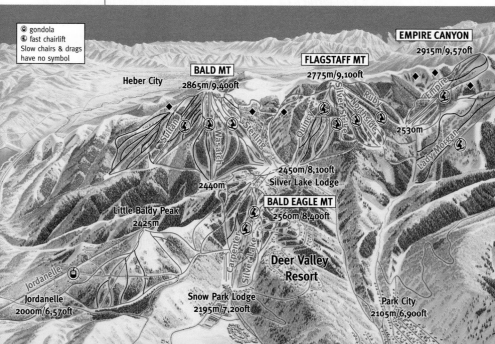

gondola
fast chairlift
Slow chairs & drags have no symbol

EMPIRE CANYON
2915m/9,570ft

FLAGSTAFF MT
2775m/9,100ft

BALD MT
2865m/9,400ft

Heber City

2530m

2450m/8,100ft
Silver Lake Lodge

2440m

BALD EAGLE MT
2560m/8,400ft

Little Baldy Peak
2425m

Deer Valley Resort

Jordanelle
2000m/6,570ft

Snow Park Lodge
2195m/7,200ft

Park City
2105m/6,900ft

SNOWPIX.COM / CHRIS GILL

Park City

Stay near the cute and lively old Main Street and visit the three local mountains plus some further afield for a varied holiday

600

+ Entertaining, historic Main Street, convenient for the slopes

+ Lots of bars and restaurants make nonsense of Utah's Mormon image

+ Easy to visit several resorts; and three are right in town

- Overall, town is an enormous, charmless sprawl, with most lodgings a drive from Main Street and the slopes

- Runs tend to be rather short, with limited vertical

Staying in Park City has clear attractions, particularly if you are based near the centre to make the most of lively Main Street. It makes an excellent base for touring all of Utah's main resorts.

The Park City Mountain Resort ski area itself (covered in this chapter) is not our favourite. But Deer Valley ski area is separated from the Park City slopes only by a fence between two pistes, and by separate ownership with different objectives – all very strange, to European eyes. Canyons is only a little further away. All three areas are covered by the Three Resort Pass and can be reached by free buses. Then there are the famously powdery resorts of Snowbird and Alta, less than an hour away. These four resorts each have their own chapter.

THE RESORT

Park City is about 45 minutes by road from Salt Lake City. It was a silver-mining boom town and at the turn of the 19th century it boasted a population of 10,000, a red-light area, a Chinese quarter and 27 saloons.

VILLAGE CHARM ★★★★★
A colourful past

Careful restoration has left the town with a splendid historic centrepiece in Main Street, now lined by a colourful selection of bars, restaurants, art galleries and shops, many quite smart but some touristy souvenir places. New buildings have been tastefully designed to blend in smoothly. But away from the centre (where most of the lodging is) the resort is an amorphous sprawl and still expanding. Traffic congestion can be bad, especially at weekends.

CONVENIENCE ★★★★★
Depends on your base

The slow Town chairlift goes up to the slopes from Main Street, but the main lifts are on the fringes at Resort Base; there are lodgings out there but most are a bus drive away.

Deer Valley, Canyons and Park City are linked by free shuttle-buses, which also go around town and run until fairly late but we found it a pain waiting for buses on our recent visit. A

car is useful (especially for visiting ski areas outside Park City).

If you're not hiring a car, pick a location that's handy for Main Street and the Town chair or the free bus.

SCENERY ★★★★★
Gently undulating ridges

In contrast to Park City's sprawling mass below them, the rounded mountain ridges have a modest and gentle presence.

THE MOUNTAIN

Park City Mountain Resort consists mostly of blue and black trails cut through the trees, with easier runs running along the ridges and the valleys between. The more interesting terrain is in the lightly wooded bowls and ridges at the top. On the lower slopes, the trail map marks several black 'Signature Runs' that are groomed every night and five 'Adventure Alley' blue runs for fun among the trees.

Reporters have enjoyed the 'excellent' free mountain history tours of the slopes – looking at the area's silver mining heritage – that take place twice a day. Three lifts run until 9pm for floodlit night skiing.

It is much cheaper to buy lift passes in advance than on the spot.

KEY FACTS

Resort	2105m
	6,900ft
Slopes	2105-3050m
	6,900-10,000ft
Lifts	15
Pistes	3,300 acres
Green	17%
Blue	52%
Black	31%
Snowmaking	15%

UK PACKAGES

Alpine Answers, AmeriCan Ski, American Ski Classics, Crystal, Crystal Finest, Funway Holidays, Independent Ski Links, Momentum, PowderBeds, Ski Independence, Ski Line, Ski Safari, Ski Solutions, Skitracer, Skiworld, Thomson, Virgin Snow

EXTENT OF THE SLOPES ★★★★★
Bowls above the woods

The ski area is bigger than Deer Valley but smaller than Canyons. Most of the easy and intermediate runs lie between Summit House and the base area, and are spread along the sides of a series of interconnecting ridges. Virtually all the steep terrain is above Summit House in a series of ungroomed bowls, and accessed by the McConkey's six-pack and the old, slow Jupiter double chair.

FAST LIFTS ★★★★★
Two from the base

Two fast chairlifts whisk you up from Resort Base and others beyond take you to Summit House. But there are a few slow lifts on the highest slopes.

QUEUES ★★★★★
Peak period crowds

It can get pretty crowded (on some trails as well as the lifts) at weekends and in high season. Pay Day lift from Resort Base used to have big queues, but these have eased since the Crescent chair was upgraded. You can pay extra for a Fast Tracks pass to jump queues on six main lifts.

TERRAIN PARKS ★★★★★
Among the best in the world

There are three terrain parks here to suit all levels. The vast number of kickers, rails and pipes are maintained daily, and rank among the best in the world. See www.pcride.com. New for 2010 with a dedicated triple chair was The Ridge, a great entry-level park. The former Pick 'N' Shovel park was renamed the Three Kings park, doubled in size, is for all abilities and floodlit for night riding till 9pm. The King's Crown, on the northern slope overlooking the resort, is the park for pros, with the biggest jumps and features. The Eagle super-pipe was used for the 2002 Winter Olympics, and today is consistently one of the best pipes in the world.

SNOW RELIABILITY ★★★★★
Not quite the greatest on Earth

Utah is famous for the quality and quantity of its snow. Park City's record doesn't match those of Snowbird and Alta, but an annual average of 360 inches is still impressive, and ahead of most Colorado figures. Snowmaking covers about 15% of the terrain.

FOR EXPERTS ★★★★★
Lots of variety

There is a lot of excellent advanced and expert terrain at the top of the lift system. It is all marked as double diamond on the trail map, but there are many runs that deserve only a single-diamond rating.

McConkey's Bowl is served by a six-pack and offers a range of open pitches and gladed terrain; we've had some great runs here on each of our visits. The slow, old Jupiter lift accesses the highest bowls, which include some serious terrain – with narrow couloirs, cliffs and cornices – as well as easier wide-open slopes. We've had some enjoyable runs through fresh snow in lightly wooded terrain by heading to the right at the top of the lift, then skiing down without hiking. But if you are prepared to hike, you can find fresh powder most of the time – turn left for West Face, Pioneer Ridge and Puma Bowl, right for Scott's

LIFT PASSES

Park City

Prices in US$

Age	1-day	6-day
under 13	56	336
13 to 64	90	534
over 65	58	348

Free under 7

Beginner half-day 'Never Ever' lesson includes First Time lift

Notes
Covers all lifts in Park City Mountain Resort, with ski-bus; day passes are window rates; 6-day prices are advance-purchase prices; additional discounts if purchased in advance with lodging

Alternative passes
Three Resort International Pass covering Park City, The Canyons and Deer Valley available through selected tour operators to international visitors only

Bowl and the vast expanse of Pinecone Ridge, stretching literally for miles down the side of Thaynes Canyon.

Lower down, the side of Summit House ridge, serviced by the Thaynes and Motherlode chairs, has some little-used black runs, plus a few satisfying trails in the trees. There's a zone of steep runs towards town from further round the ridge. And don't miss Blueslip Bowl near Summit House – so called because in the past when it was out of bounds, ski company employees caught skiing it were fired, and given their notice on a blue slip.

Skiers (no snowboarders, due to some long flat run-outs) should consider doing the Utah Interconnect – see the feature panel opposite. Park City Powder Cats offers snowcat skiing and Wasatch Powderbird Guides heli-skiing.

FOR INTERMEDIATES ★★★★
OK for a day or two
There are blue runs served by all the main lifts, apart from Jupiter. The areas around the King Con high-speed quad and Silverlode six-pack have a dense network of great (but fairly short) cruising runs. There are also more difficult trails close by, for those looking for a challenge. The 'Signature Runs' and 'Adventure Alleys' (see first

para under 'The mountain' above) are good ideas and worth trying.

But there are few long, fast cruising runs – most trails are around 1 to 2km, and many have long, flat run-outs. The Pioneer and McConkey's chairlifts are off the main drag and serve some very pleasant, often quiet runs. The runs under the Town lift have great views of the town.

Mileage hungry intermediates should plan on outings to other nearby resorts.

FOR BEGINNERS ★★★★
A good chance for fast progress
The 'Never Ever' deal offers first timers a half-day taster lesson including a lift pass. In the new beginner area (see 'News'), novices will start on moving carpets, classes graduate up the hill quite quickly and there's a good, gentle and wide 'easiest way down' – the three-and-a-half-mile Home Run – clearly marked all the way from Summit House. It's easy enough for most to manage after only a few lessons. The Town chair can be ridden down.

FOR BOARDERS ★★★★
Plenty of scope
It was not until 1996, when Park City won its Olympic bid, that the resort lifted its ban on snowboarding. Since

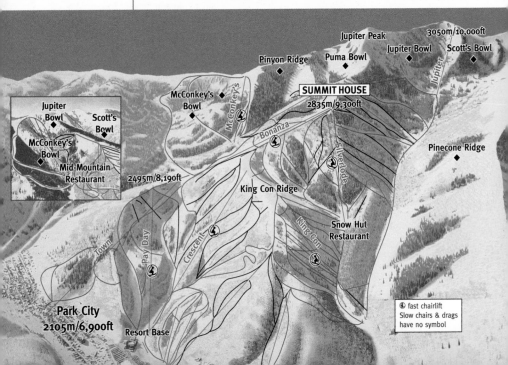

The lower slopes with the modern Resort Base at the foot and King Con Ridge on the right →
PARK CITY CVB

SCHOOLS

Park City
t 1 800 227 2754

Classes
1 3hr day $95
Private lessons
$135 for 1hr

CHILDCARE

Signature 3
(run by ski school)
t 1 800 227 2754
Ages 3½ to 5;
$165 per day,
includes ski tuition,
lunch (max class size
is 3)
Guardian Angel
t 640 1229
Babysitting service
Ski Town Sitters
t 487 9262
Babysitting service

Ski school
The school offers
classes for ages 6 to
14, 9am-3pm, $215
per day including
lunch (max class size
is 5)

then it has steamrollered ahead to attract the snowboarding community by building some of the best terrain parks in the world. And Park City has some great ungroomed terrain as well: the higher bowls offer treelined powder runs and great kicker-building spots. Beginners will have no trouble on the lower slopes. But beware: at weekends and peak season it can get very crowded, especially in the terrain parks. Three-hour group freestyle clinics are offered daily at 1pm.

FOR CROSS-COUNTRY ★★★
Some trails; lots of backcountry
There are prepared trails on both the Park City golf course (20km), next to the downhill area, and the Homestead Resort course (12km), just out of town. There is lots of scope for backcountry trips.

MOUNTAIN RESTAURANTS ★★
Standard self-service stuff
The Mid-Mountain Lodge is a picturesque 19th-century mine building which was heaved up the mountain to its present location near the bottom of Pioneer chair. The food is standard

self-service fare but most reporters prefer it to the alternatives. The Summit House has chilli, pizza, soup and 'good hot chocolate'. The Snow Hut, a 'cosier' log building that usually has an outdoor grill, gets good reviews from reporters. Viking Yurt is a coffee house in a tent halfway down the Bonanza chairlift. There are more options down at Resort Base ('a delicious salad bar and top-quality fresh fish', said a reporter).

SCHOOLS AND GUIDES ★★★★
Good reports
We lack recent reports but past reviews have been very positive and enthusiastic. A reporter's husband had a good private lesson – 'the instructor tried to take him to as much of the scarce powder as possible'. There is similar praise for a private snowboard lesson: 'tuition the best I've had, but pricey'.

FOR FAMILIES ★★
Well organised
There are a number of licensed carers. The ski school takes children from age three and a half. Book in advance.

Park City

THE UTAH INTERCONNECT

Good skiers prepared to do some hiking should consider this excellent guided backcountry tour that runs four days a week from Deer Valley to Snowbird. (Three days a week it runs from Snowbird, but only as far as Solitude.) When we did it (a few years back, starting from Park City) we got fresh tracks in knee-deep powder practically all day. After a warm-up run to weed out weak skiers, we went up the top chair, through a 'closed' gate in the area boundary and skied down a deserted, prettily wooded valley to Solitude. After taking the lifts to the top of Solitude we did a short traverse/walk, then down more virgin powder towards Brighton. After more powder runs and lunch back in Solitude, it was up the lifts and a 30-minute hike up the Highway to Heaven to north-facing, treelined slopes and a great little gully down into Alta. How much of Alta and Snowbird you get to ski depends on how much time is left. The price ($295) includes two guides, lunch, lift tickets and transport home.

Interactive resort shortlist builder at **www.wtss.co.uk**

↑ Main Street is charming even when it doesn't have snow in it

ACTIVITIES

Indoor Park City Racquet Club (tennis, racquetball, swimming pool, hot tub, gym); Silver Mountain Sports Club and Spa (pools, hot tubs, sauna, steam room, tennis, racquetball, gym); other fitness clubs, spa treatments, bowling, museum, galleries

Outdoor Ice skating, snowmobiles, sleigh rides, hot-air ballooning, dog sledding, tubing, snowshoeing, winter fly fishing

GETTING THERE

Air Salt Lake City 55km/35 miles (1hr)

Phone numbers
From distant parts of the US, add the prefix 1 435; from abroad, add the prefix +1 435

TOURIST OFFICE

www.parkcitymountain.com
www.parkcityinfo.com

STAYING THERE

We prefer to stay near Main Street and its bars and restaurants, but most accommodation is in the sprawling suburbs. These, such as Kimball Junction, are relatively cheap (but soulless) and convenient if you have a car and want to try different resorts daily.

Hotels There's a wide variety, from typical chains to individual little B&Bs.
*****Park City (200 2000) Swanky all-suite place on outskirts. Pool, sauna, hot tub.
***Park City Peaks (649 5000) Decent rooms, 'service and prices of meals good', 'food adequate', indoor-outdoor pool and 'fab hot tub', but out of town. We have stayed here and thought it adequate.
***Yarrow (649 7000) Adequate, charmless, 'cheap' base, a 15-minute walk from Main Street. Pool, hot tub. 'Good service; friendly, helpful staff.'
Silver King (649 5500) De luxe hotel/condo complex at base of the slopes, with indoor-outdoor pool.
Washington School Inn (649 3800) Historic old inn, in a great location near Main Street. Has been highly recommended by reporters.
Best Western Landmark Inn (649 7300) At Kimball Junction. Pool.
Chateau Apres Lodge (649 9372) Near the slopes: comfortable, faded, cheap.
Apartments There's a big range. The Townlift studios near Main Street and Park Avenue condos are both modern and comfortable, the latter with a pool and hot tubs. Silver Cliff Village is adjacent to the slopes and has spacious units and access to the facilities of the Silver King Hotel. Other ski-in/ski-out recommendations from

reporters are Silver Star and Snow Flower. Blue Church Lodge is a well-converted 19th-century Mormon church with luxury condos and rooms.

EATING OUT ★★★★★
Lots of choice
There are over 100 restaurants. Our favourites are Wahso-An (Asian fusion), 350 Main (new American) and Riverhorse – in a grand, high-ceilinged first-floor room with live music. Zoom is the old Union Pacific train depot, now a trendy restaurant owned by Robert Redford (past reports have been mixed though). Squatters, a micro brewery out of town a bit, does 'superb beers and food'. Chez Betty (American/French) is small with 'excellent food' – expensive though. Other reporter tips include Fuego Bistro & Pizzeria, Cisero's and Grappa (Italian), Chimayo ('south-western-with-a-twist'), Bangkok Thai, Wasatch Brew Pub (for steaks), Bandit's Grill (BBQ grills), the 'excellent' Eating Establishment (fish), No Name Saloon ('brill buffalo burgers') and Butcher's Chop House ('great prime rib and steaks'). There are lots of Tex-Mex places: El Chubasco has been praised. See Deer Valley for other options.

APRES-SKI ★★★☆☆
Better than you might think
As the slopes close, Legends is the place to head for at Resort Base. A reporter recommended Pig Pen in the ice skating plaza. The Alpine Internet Café in town is recommended. The Wasatch Brew Pub makes its own ale. O'Shuck's and No Name Saloon are lively, and there's usually live music and dancing at weekends. The Bar Boheme is new (at the hip hotel Sky Lodge). For clubs, try the Ten Pin at the bowling alley and Cisero's.

OFF THE SLOPES ★★★☆☆
Some things of interest
There's a factory outlet mall at Kimball Junction. Backcountry snowmobiling, balloon flights and trips to Nevada for gambling are popular. There is a newish bowling alley. You can learn to ski jump or try the Olympic bob track at the Olympic Park down the road – 'worth the effort'. Robert Redford's Sundance Film Festival is held each January. There are lots of shops and galleries. Salt Lake City is easily reached and has some good concerts, shopping and Mormon heritage sites.

SNOWBIRD / DEREK SMITH

Snowbird

A powder-pig paradise linked to neighbouring Alta; with big concrete and glass base buildings that remind us of Flaine

NEWS

2010/11: Snowbird smashed its own impressive snowfall records by receiving over 700 inches of snow during the season – more than ever before and over 40% more than its long-term average.

SNOWPIX.COM / CHRIS GILL

Mineral Basin has some good long cruises for intermediates as well as steep ungroomed stuff that Snowbird is famous for ↓

➕ Unrivalled quantity and quality of powder snow, combined with fabulous ungroomed slopes

➕ Link to Alta makes it one of the largest ski areas in the US

➕ Slopes-at-the-door convenience

➖ Limited groomed runs for intermediates

➖ Tiny, claustrophobic resort 'village'

➖ Stark concrete Bauhaus architecture

➖ Very quiet at night

There can be few places where nature has combined the steep with the deep better than at Snowbird and next-door Alta. The resorts' combined area is one of the top powder-pig paradises in the world (at least for skiers – boarders are banned from Alta). So it is a shame that Snowbird's concrete, purpose-built 'base village' is so lacking in ski resort ambience.

THE RESORT

Snowbird lies 40km from Salt Lake City in Little Cottonwood Canyon – just before Alta. Both the resort and (particularly) the approach road are prone to avalanches and closure: visitors are sometimes confined indoors for safety.
Village charm The resort buildings are mainly block-like and lack any semblance of charm.
Convenience The resort area and the slopes are spread along the road on the south side of the narrow canyon. The focal Snowbird Center (lift base/shops/restaurants) is towards the eastern, up-canyon end. All lodgings are within walking distance and most are ski-in/ski-out. There are shuttle-buses, with a service to Alta.
Scenery Snowbird's setting is rugged and rather Alpine. Hidden Peak's lofty heights give impressive views.

THE MOUNTAINS

Snowbird's link with Alta (see separate chapter) forms one of the largest ski areas in the US.
There are free mountain tours at 9.30 and 10.30 each day. 'It was quite adventurous, taking some of us down double black diamond territory at one point,' says one satisfied customer. The nursery slopes are floodlit three evenings a week.
Slopes The north-facing slopes rear up from the edge of the resort. Six access lifts are ranged along the valley floor, the main ones being the 125-person cable car (the Aerial Tram) to Hidden Peak, the Peruvian Express quad and the Gadzoom fast quad. To the west, in Gad Valley, there are runs ranging from very tough to very easy. Mineral Basin, behind Hidden Peak, has 500 acres of terrain for all abilities, but can be badly affected by sun.
Fast lifts The key lifts are fast. Baldy Express, one of two fast quads in Mineral Basin, forms the link with Alta.
Queues The big problem has always been the cable car, with queues of up to an hour at times. But the Peruvian Express chair provides an alternative way to the top (via Mineral Basin and then the Mineral Basin Express chair).
Terrain parks There is one for all levels, containing rails, hits and a box.
Snow reliability Snowbird and Alta average 500 inches of snowfall a year – twice as much as some Colorado resorts and around 50% more than the nearby Park City area. And they smashed all records last season (see 'News'). There's snowmaking in busy areas too.

KEY FACTS

Resort	2470m
	8,100ft

For Snowbird and
Alta combined area

Slopes	2365-3350m
	7,760-11,000ft
Lifts	24
Pistes	4,700 acres
Green	25%
Blue	37%
Black	38%
Snowmaking	12%

Snowbird only

Slopes	2365-3350m
	7,760-11,000ft
Lifts	13
Pistes	2,500 acres
Green	27%
Blue	38%
Black	35%
Snowmaking	21%

UK PACKAGES

Alpine Answers,
AmeriCan Ski, American
Ski Classics, Funway
Holidays, Independent
Ski Links, Ski
Independence, Ski
Safari, Skitracer,
Skiworld

Phone numbers
From distant parts of
the US, add the prefix
1 801; from abroad,
add the prefix +1 801

TOURIST OFFICE

www.snowbird.com

Experts The trail map is liberally sprinkled with double black diamonds, and some of the gullies off the Cirque ridge – Silver Fox and Great Scott, for example – are exceptionally steep and frequently neck-deep in powder. Lower down lurk the bump runs, including Mach Schnell – a great run straight down the fall line through trees. There is wonderful ski-anywhere terrain in the bowl beneath the high Little Cloud chair, and the Gad 2 lift opens up attractive tree runs. Fantastic go-anywhere terrain under the High Baldy traverse is controlled by gates. Mineral Basin has more expert terrain. Backcountry tours and heli-skiing are also offered.

Intermediates The winding Chip's Run on the Cirque ridge provides the only comfortable route down from the top. For adventurous intermediates wanting to try powder skiing, the bowl below the Little Cloud lift is a must. There are some challenging runs through the trees off the Gad 2 lift and some nice long cruises in Mineral Basin. But the groomed runs don't add up to a lot.

Beginners There is a nursery slope next to Cliff Lodge and the Mountain Learning area part-way up the hill. And a special lift pass is available ($20). But progression to longer runs is not easy. Go and learn elsewhere.

Snowboarding Competent freeriders will have a wild time in Snowbird's powder (though a reporter complains of 'flat sticky spots where you have to walk'). Alta bans boarders.

Cross-country No prepared trails (though there are in next-door Alta).

Mountain restaurants It's the Mid-Gad Lodge self-service cafeteria or back to one of the bases. The table-service Forklift and Rendezvous have been recommended by reporters.

Schools and guides The school offers a range of lessons and clinics – such as women-only sessions. One visitor was 'highly impressed' with her private lessons.

Families Camp Snowbird takes children aged 12 and under. The 'kids ski free' programme allows children (six and under) to ski for free with an adult ($15 a day in 2010/11 for the Tram). Baby Thunder is a gentle family area.

STAYING THERE

Hotels There are several lodges and smaller condo blocks. Cliff Lodge (a huge concrete building) and The Lodge at Snowbird were built in the 1970s and renovated in 2006; both are convenient and have pools and hot tubs, but they lack charm – and we lack recent reports.

Eating out Cliff Lodge and Snowbird Center are the focal points. Readers recommend the Steak Pit in Snowbird Center. The 'fine dining' Aerie at Cliff Lodge has had mixed reviews.

Après-ski Après-ski is a bit muted. The Tram Club and El Chanate Cantina are lively as the slopes close. But one visitor complained that many places close early.

Off the slopes Apart from spas in the various lodges, there's not much to do apart from snowshoeing and snowmobiling. And you can visit Salt Lake City.

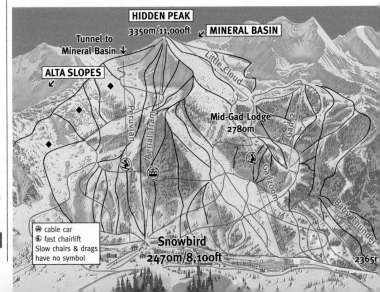

HIDDEN PEAK
3350m/11,000ft   MINERAL BASIN
Tunnel to
Mineral Basin ↓
Little Cloud
ALTA SLOPES
Peruvian
Aerial Tram
Mid-Gad Lodge
2780m
Gad 2
Gadzoom
Baby Thunder
🚠 cable car
🚡 fast chairlift
Slow chairs & drags
have no symbol
Snowbird
2470m/8,100ft
2365

JACKSON HOLE / GORAN ASSNER

Rest of the West

This section contains detailed chapters on just two resorts – Jackson Hole and Big Sky. Below are notes on these and various other resorts in different parts of the great chain of mountains that stretches from Washington in the north to New Mexico in the south.

The resorts of Washington state and Oregon are covered in our resort directory/index at the end of this book. We visited Oregon a couple of seasons back; our exploration was hampered by poor early-season snow, but if you want to try somewhere largely undiscovered by fellow Brits, it is worth considering. The major resorts are **Mt Hood** (which has three separate areas of slopes: Mt Hood Meadows, Mt Hood Skibowl and Timberline) and **Mt Bachelor.** These get extended entries in the resort directory/index.

Sun Valley, Idaho, was America's first purpose-built resort, developed in the 1930s by the president of the Union Pacific Railway. It quickly became popular with the Hollywood movie set and has managed to retain its stylish image and ambience; it has one of our favourite luxury hotels. Also in Idaho is the USA's newest purpose-built resort – **Tamarack,** two hours

north of Boise. But the company developing the resort went bankrupt and the slopes closed in 2009. They re-opened four days a week in 2010/11 and season passes for 2011/12 were on sale when we went to press.

Jackson Hole in Wyoming is a resort with an impressive snow record and equally impressive steep slopes. Jackson town has a touristy Wild West cowboy atmosphere. Check out the separate chapter. A 90-minute drive from Jackson over the Teton pass (slower if you go by excursion bus) brings you to **Grand Targhee,** which gets even more snow. The slopes are usually blissfully empty, and are much easier than at Jackson. The main Fred's Mountain offers 1,500 acres and 610m vertical accessed from a central fast quad. One-third of smaller Peaked Mountain is accessed by a fast quad, while the rest – around 500 acres – is used for guided snowcat skiing.

About four hours north of Jackson, just inside Montana, is **Big Sky,** which has one of the biggest verticals in the US and together with neighbouring **Moonlight Basin's** linked terrain is the biggest ski area in the US. When we visited, we were very impressed – particularly by the lack of crowds. Check out the Big Sky chapter. From Big Sky you might also visit **Bridger Bowl,** a 90-minute drive away. It boasts broad, steep, lightly wooded slopes that offer wonderful powder descents after a fresh snowfall.

A long way south of all these resorts, **Taos** in New Mexico is the most southerly major resort in America, and because of its isolated location it is largely unknown on the international market. There's a small chalet-style base village with a handful of lodges; the adobe town of Taos, home to many famous artists and writers over the years, is 30km down the road. There's some good terrain for all standards, but the ski area is best known for steep, challenging terrain, some of which you hike to.

BIG SKY RESORT

Big Sky

America's biggest linked ski area, with extraordinarily quiet slopes; unappealing modern resort village, though

RATINGS

The mountains

Extent	★★★★
Fast lifts	★★
Queues	★★★★★
Terrain p'ks	★★★★
Snow	★★★★★
Expert	★★★★
Intermediate	★★★★
Beginner	★★★★★
Boarder	★★★★
X-country	★★★★
Restaurants	★
Schools	★★★★
Families	★★★★

The resort

Charm	★★
Convenience	★★★★
Scenery	★★★
Eating out	★★★
Après-ski	★
Off-slope	★★

RPI   115

lift pass	£290
ski hire	£120
lessons	£170
food & drink	£85
total	**£665**

BIG SKY RESORT

That's Lone Mountain in the distance; and the slopes are deserted, as usual ↓

➕ Linked ski area bigger than Vail, with a big vertical by US standards

➕ By far the quietest slopes you will find in a major resort, anywhere

➕ Among the cheapest resorts for food and drink

➕ Excellent snow record

➕ Some comfortable slope-side accommodation, but ...

➖ Many condos are spread widely away from the lift base

➖ Base area lacks charm, though things are improving, slowly

➖ Resort amenities are limited, with little choice of nightlife

➖ Tiny top lift accessing the most testing terrain is prone to queues

➖ Remote location

Big Sky is renowned for its powder, steeps and big vertical. Since the resort buried the hatchet with next-door Moonlight Basin and agreed a joint lift pass, they have been able to boast the biggest linked ski area in the US. They should also be boasting the world's least crowded slopes – we and our reporters have been astonished by the lack of people. Big Sky gets an average of around 2,000 people a day on its slopes. So that's about two acres each.

We have no idea how they make this arrangement work financially. We're happy to take advantage of it while it lasts. But if ambling around in the evening soaking up the mountain village atmosphere is part of your holiday, forget it.

THE RESORT

Big Sky is set amid the wide open spaces of Montana, one hour from the airport town of Bozeman. The resort has been purpose-built at the foot of the slopes on Lone Mountain and Andesite Mountain. The main focus of development is Mountain Village, at the lift base. Bridger Bowl ski area is an easy day trip by car.

VILLAGE CHARM ★★☆☆☆
Some way to go
Mountain Village is a hotchpotch of buildings in different styles set vaguely around a traffic-free central plaza and bordered by car parks and service roads. There are a few hotels, a handful of bars and restaurants, a variety of shops and some slope-side condos. The French-style underground Mountain Mall has shops and access to many of the bars and restaurants and some of the lodging.

CONVENIENCE ★★★★☆
Generally fine
There is quite a bit of lodging at or close to the lift base. Some outlying condos and houses are served by lifts to the slopes, but most rely on the 'comparatively poor' free bus services. A 2011 reporter recommends having a car if you're staying on the outskirts of the resort.

SCENERY ★★★☆☆
The lone ranger
Lone Mountain is Big Sky's signature peak, its distinctive summit rising over 1000m above the village and Andesite Mountain's wooded slopes. From the top, there are panoramic views of Montana and Yellowstone.

NEWS

2011/12: The Solace Spa is to increase in size from 850sqft to 3000sqft.

2010/11: A new hut, the Black Kettle, opened at the bottom of The Bowl on Lone Mountain, serving soup, chilli, snacks etc indoors and to takeaway. And the Swiss-inspired Fondue Stube, reopened in Chet's Bar and Grill in the resort.

More activities were introduced, including a Twin Zip (a zipwire where two people zip next to each other), snowshoeing, tubing and snowcat rides.

KEY FACTS

| Resort | 2285m |
| | 7,500ft |

Big Sky only	
Slopes	2070-3400m
	6,800-11,160ft
Lifts	21
Pistes	3,812 acres
Green	14%
Blue	26%
Black	60%
Snowmaking	10%

Big Sky and Moonlight Basin combined	
Slopes	2070-3400m
	6,800-11,160ft
Lifts	26
Pistes	5,512 acres

THE MOUNTAINS

Taking Big Sky and Moonlight Basin's slopes together, they cover a big area (5,512 acres) spread over two linked mountains, with long runs for all abilities. There are free mountain tours at both Big Sky and Moonlight. It is cheapest to buy tickets just for the area you are staying in and to buy a Lone Peak Ticket (substantially more expensive) only for days you intend to ski both Big Sky and Moonlight. Reporters find the piste map a bit awkward; a full-size Moonlight one is 'a must'. A 2011 visitor complained of 'the general lack of decent piste markings'.

EXTENT OF THE SLOPES ★★★★
The most extensive in the US
Lone Mountain provides the resort's poster shot, with some seriously steep, open upper slopes. From Mountain Village a fast quad goes to mid-mountain. From there you can get to the Lone Peak triple chair, which takes you up to the Lone Peak Tram – two 15-person gondola cabins, operated as if they were a cable car. This leads to the top and fabulous 360° views. The Dakota triple chairlift serves Lone's south face and its steep bowls and glades. But a couple of reporters have found the area prone to closure due to avalanche risk. Lone Mountain's lower slopes are wooded and varied, as are those of **Andesite Mountain**, which has less vertical, but three of the five fast lifts, including one from Mountain Village. From various points on Lone Mountain you can head down to the **Moonlight Basin** slopes, which start with a slow chair from Moonlight Lodge. Runs from the top of that lead to the Six Shooter fast chair which, together with the slow Lone Tree quad, serves nearly all Moonlight's wooded, largely easy intermediate terrain. The Headwaters lift at the top serves expert-only runs.

FAST LIFTS ★★
Needs some more
There are five fast quad chairs, but many of the chairs are still old triples and doubles.

QUEUES ★★★★★
Only for the Tram
The tiny Tram continues to attract queues on powder days and in peak season. Queues are rare otherwise,

'even on President's Day', says a 2011 visitor. But there are still a lot of slow lifts.

TERRAIN PARKS ★★★★
Plenty of choice
Swifty Park on Lone Peak has large jumps, rails and boxes for advanced riders. There is a natural half-pipe near the Lone Peak triple chair and an intermediates park, Swifty 2.0, near the village. There is a beginner park by the Explorer chair. Moonlight has the Zero Gravity park, with boxes, rails, jumps, jibs and hits under the Six Shooter chair, and a beginner park near the base.

SNOW RELIABILITY ★★★★★
No worries here
Snowfall averages 400+ inches – more than most resorts in Colorado. Grooming is good, too.

FOR EXPERTS ★★★★
Enough to keep you amused
All of the terrain accessed from the Tram is single or double black diamond. The steepest runs are the Big Couloir on the Big Sky side and the North Summit Snowfield on the Moonlight side. For both, you are required to have a partner to ski with, an avalanche transceiver and a shovel. We'd recommend a guide, too. There are easier ways down, though – Liberty Bowl is easiest. Marx and Lenin are a little steeper. The Dakota Territory has 212 acres of black-diamond glades, chutes and high bowls, to skier's right of Liberty Bowl – served by a triple chairlift. Lower down, the Lone Peak Triple, Challenger and Shedhorn chairs also serve good steep terrain. There are some excellent gladed runs, especially on Andesite. In the Moonlight sector the Headwaters is the biggest challenge – but it gets windblown and you may have to pick your way through rocks at the top. The further you hike to skier's left the steeper the couloirs. There are some good gladed runs lower down.

FOR INTERMEDIATES ★★★★
Great deserted cruising
The bulk of the terrain on both mountains is of intermediate difficulty (including lots of easy blacks). The main complaint we have is that they don't seem to groom any blacks – which means that you can't hurtle down them taking advantage of the

Big Sky

609

Interactive resort shortlist builder at **www.wtss.co.uk**

lack of people. But there is lots of excellent blue run cruising served by fast chairs and with few others on the runs – Ramcharger, Southern Comfort and Thunder Wolf on Andesite, Swift Current on Lone Mountain and Six Shooter in the Moonlight sector. Several wide, gentle bowls offer a good introduction to off-piste. And there are some good easy glade runs such as Singlejack on Moonlight and The Congo on Andesite. In general the groomed blues in Moonlight are easier than those in Big Sky, especially the ones served by the Lone Tree chair. Adventurous intermediates could try Liberty Bowl from the top of the Tram; but be prepared for a rocky, windswept traverse between wooden barriers at the top to access the run.

FOR BEGINNERS ★★★★★
Ideal – lots of lovely greens
Go to Big Sky rather than Moonlight. There's a good, well-developed nursery area at the base of the Explorer chair; a half-day pass is included with lessons. There is a separate pass to use this area too. There are long, deserted greens to progress to from those lifts and on Andesite.

FOR BOARDERS ★★★★★
Something for everyone
The terrain has lots of variety, with few flats. Experts will enjoy the steeps and the glades, freestylers the good terrain parks, and novices the easy cruising runs served by chairlifts. Instruction is 'excellent'.

Andesite has great cruising runs, although the vertical isn't huge

ANDESITE
268om/8,8ooft

Southern Comfort

Ramcharger

Thunder Wolf

Mountain Village
2285m/
7,5ooft

207om/6,8ooft
Lone Moose Meadows

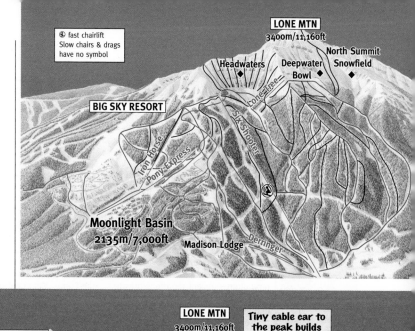

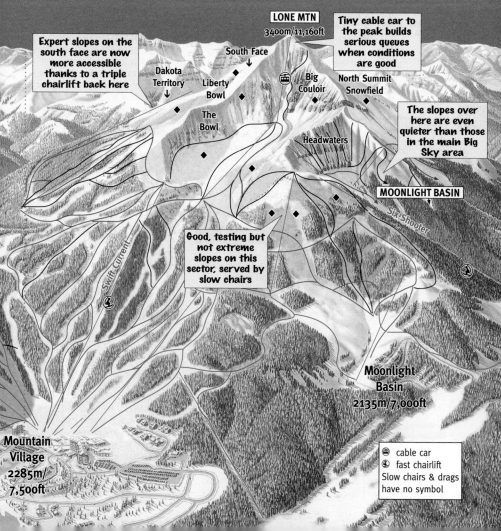

Weekly news updates and resort links at www.wtss.co.uk

SCHOOLS

Big Sky
t 995 5743

Classes
Half day (2½hr) $69
Private lessons
From $134 for 1hr

CHILDCARE

Lone Peak Playhouse
t 993 2220
Ages 6mnth to 8yr;
8.30 to 4.30;
from $80 per day

Ski school
Ages 4 to 14; 9.45 to
3.15; $142 per day

ACTIVITIES

Indoor Solace Spa
(massage, beauty
treatments), fitness
centres in hotels

Outdoor Snowmobiles,
snowshoeing, sleigh
rides, tubing, fly
fishing, ziplines,
visiting Yellowstone
National Park

GETTING THERE

Air Bozeman 70km/
45 miles (1hr15)

UK PACKAGES

AmeriCan Ski, Ski
Independence, Ski
Safari

Central reservations
Call 995 5000; toll-
free number (from
within the US) 1 800
548 4486

Phone numbers
From distant parts of
the US, add the prefix
1 406; from abroad,
add the prefix +1 406

TOURIST OFFICE

Big Sky
www.bigskyresort.com
Moonlight Basin
www.moonlightbasin.
com

FOR CROSS-COUNTRY ★★★★
Head for the Ranch
There are 85km of trails at Lone
Mountain Ranch, and more at West
Yellowstone.

MOUNTAIN RESTAURANTS ★
Back to base for lunch?
The Pinnacle on Andesite has a table-
service area, offering 'very nice'
burgers, stews and grills, a large
terrace and live music at weekends.
The Shedhorn Grill is a yurt (tent) on
the south side of Lone Mountain,
doing simple meals. Then there's the
new Black Kettle (see 'News').

SCHOOLS AND GUIDES ★★★★
Good reputation
The Big Sky school has a good
reputation. A recent reporter's private
lesson was 'a good mix of technical
and guiding'. And visitors regularly
praise the beginner snowboard
classes: 'friendly, excellent tuition';
'exceptionally happy with the quality
of the instruction'.

FOR FAMILIES ★★★★
Usual high US standard
Lone Peak Playhouse in the slope-side
Snowcrest Lodge takes children from
six months to eight years and will take
them to and from ski school ('perfect',
says a reporter). Children 10 years and
under ski free. There's a Kids' Club in
the Huntley Lodge and snow garden at
the base. Moonlight Kids takes kids
from six months to eight years.

STAYING THERE

Hotels There's not much choice.
★★★★Summit (548 4486) Best in town;
central, slope-side, good rooms,
outdoor hot pool with good views.
★★★Huntley Lodge (548 4486) Big Sky's
original hotel; central, part of
Mountain Mall, outdoor pool, hot tubs,
saunas. 'Lots of room-to-room noise,
though,' complains a reporter.
★★★The Lodge at Big Sky (995 7858)
Five minutes' walk to slopes; a shuttle
at peak times. Indoor pool, indoor/
outdoor hot tubs. 'Large rooms,
friendly staff, but basic food.'
★★★Rainbow Ranch (995 4132) Five
miles south of resort. Luxury riverside
rooms and cabins. Recommended.
Apartments The good-value Stillwater
condos have been recommended,
along with Village Center, Arrowhead,
Snowcrest, Big Horn, Black Eagle and,

way out of town, Powder Ridge and
Lone Moose. Check location carefully.

EATING OUT ★★★
A fair choice for a small place
A 2011 reporter recommends the Lone
Peak Brewery ('excellent eatery'). Tips
from earlier years include: M.R.
Hummers ('varied menu, good value'),
The Cabin (seafood, 'good elk' and
steaks), Andiamo ('proper Italian
cuisine, stylish surroundings') and
Whiskey Jack's (burgers, beers, 'good
Tex-Mex'). Down in the valley we
enjoyed a dinner in Buck's T-4
atmospheric log-built dining room.
They'll fetch you from your condo. Also
in the valley, Rainbow Ranch is good
for 'fine dining' and a 2011 reporter
enjoyed 'good steaks and burgers' at
the Corral. Moonlight dinners and live
music are held at a backcountry lodge.

APRES-SKI ★
Limited but entertaining
Nightlife is generally quiet ('revolves
around a few functional bars – not
particularly exciting'). But there are a
few places to try; most with regular
live music. Chet's bar is 'entertaining',
and also has pool. The Carabiner in
the Summit and Whiskey Jack's are
popular. The Black Bear can be lively.

OFF THE SLOPES ★★
Mainly the great outdoors
There's snowmobiling, snowshoeing,
sleigh rides, a floodlit tubing hill,
ziplines, visiting Yellowstone National
Park (highly recommended by
reporters), treatments at the Solace
Spa; the Huntley Lodge pool etc is
open to all for a fee.

LINKED RESORT – 2135m

MOONLIGHT BASIN

There's not much at Moonlight base
except a few condos and cabins and
the impressive Moonlight Lodge
– spacious and log-built, with high
ceilings and beams. The bar at the
Lodge is lively as the slopes close,
and the Timbers restaurant there gets
good reviews. But we have been
disappointed by the spa, and our
nearby condo was poorly maintained.
Maybe the Cowboy Heaven Cabins
spread up the hillside are better. We
had an enjoyable dinner ('delicious
burgers', says a recent visitor) a drive
away at the Headwaters Grille, at
Madison base area.

JACKSON HOLE /
JONATHAN SELKOWITZ

Jackson Hole

Touristy 'Wild West' town 12 miles from big, exciting slopes and a small, modern base village with a famous après-ski saloon

NEWS

2011/12: A new triple chair, Marmot, is planned from base of the Thunder quad to the top of the Bridger gondola.

2010/11: Four new Burton Stash terrain parks opened using natural terrain and local wood – much like The Stash in Avoriaz but smaller.

Snowmaking was increased by 25%, mainly on the lower slopes below the gondola.

JACKSON HOLE MOUNTAIN RESORT /
COLIN MEADOWS

The slopes rise abruptly from the flat, wide valley floor and the smart new lodgings (that's the Four Seasons on the left) →

- ➕ Tough expert-only terrain and one of the US's biggest verticals
- ➕ Jackson town has an entertaining Wild West ambience
- ➕ Unspoiled, remote location
- ➕ Excellent snow record
- ➕ Some unique off-slope diversions
- ➕ The town is only a few minutes from the airport, but ...

- ➖ The town is 30 minutes by bus from the slopes – though the lift base has attractive places to stay
- ➖ Low altitude and sunny orientation mean snow can deteriorate quickly
- ➖ Groomed cruising is in relatively short supply
- ➖ Getting there from the UK involves at least one stop and plane change

Our 2011 editorial visit confirmed that Jackson Hole's metamorphosis is almost complete. When we first visited in the early 1990s, it had a gnarly mountain with lots of seriously steep ungroomed slopes, shedloads of snow and more continuous vertical served by a single lift than any other resort in North America. It had few facilities at the base or on the mountain and an antiquated lift system. And the clientele were expert skiers and lots of locals and regulars who wanted to keep the place unsophisticated and for themselves.

But ownership changed and there was a new vision. Now the slopes are still gnarly and fabulous for experts; but there's a modern cable car, a gondola, two fast chairs serving easy terrain, a bunch of upscale hotels at the base, a table-service restaurant on the mountain and many more beginners, intermediates and families around. Some old stagers hate the change; we love it.

613

THE RESORT

The town of Jackson, with its wooden sidewalks, cowboy saloons and pool halls, sits on the edge of Jackson Hole – a high, flat valley surrounded by mountain ranges in Wyoming. Jackson gets many more visitors in summer than in winter, thanks to the nearby national parks. The slopes are a 15-minute drive or $3 bus ride away. At the base is Teton Village, which has developed a lot over the last few years, with an increased choice of bars, restaurants and hotels – some notably upscale.

KEY FACTS

Resort	1925m
	6,310ft

Jackson Hole	
Slopes	1925-3185m
	6,310-10,450ft
Lifts	12
Pistes	2,500 acres
Green	10%
Blue	40%
Black	50%
Snowmaking	8%

A popular excursion by car or daily bus is over the Teton pass to the smaller resort of Grand Targhee, which gets even more snow. There's a bit more info on p607.

VILLAGE CHARM ★★★
Cowboy or convenient
To amuse summer tourists the town strives to maintain its Wild West flavour. It has lots of clothing and souvenir shops, plus upmarket galleries aimed at second-home owners. In winter it's all a bit quiet. The efficient free town bus and friendly and helpful locals are praised by reporters. Teton Village is modern and quite pleasant.

CONVENIENCE ★★★★
Stay at the slopes
Teton Village is now our preferred option. Stay by the slopes and take the bus into town for nights out.

SCENERY ★★★
You can see forever
You get great long views over the wide valley from the slopes which rise abruptly from the valley floor.

THE MOUNTAINS

Most of the slopes are below the treeline, but most of the forest is not dense. Trail classifications are pretty accurate: our own small map does not distinguish single from double diamond runs, but the distinction matters – 'expert only' tends to mean just that. Some visitors reckon the toughest single diamonds would be double diamonds elsewhere.

EXTENT OF THE SLOPES ★★★
One big mountain, one small
The main lifts out of Teton Village are the Bridger gondola and the Tram (US-speak for cable car). The Tram takes you up 1260m to the summit of **Rendezvous** mountain – an exceptional vertical for the US. It can be very cold and windy at the top, even when it's warm and calm below. To the right looking up, fast quads access **Apres Vous** mountain, with half the vertical of Rendezvous and mostly much gentler runs. Between these two, the Bridger gondola goes up over a broad mountainside split by gullies, and gives speedy access to the Thunder and Sublette chairs, serving some of the steepest terrain on Rendezvous, and the Casper Bowl chair, from which you can traverse over to the Apres Vous area. The Marmot triple chair, planned for 2011/12 – see 'News' – will make moving across the mountain without returning to the bottom easier.

Snow King is a separate area right by Jackson town. Locals use it at lunch time and in the evenings (it's partly floodlit).

FAST LIFTS ★★★
Few at mid-mountain
Fast lifts access both mountains; slow chairs rule higher up, but a reader points out that they rise steeply, and permit a lot of vertical in a day.

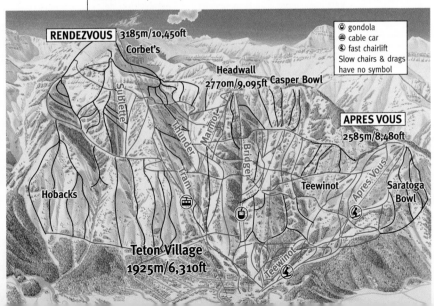

LIFT PASSES

Jackson Hole

Prices in US$

Age	1-day	6-day
under 15	55	312
15 to 64	91	522
over 65	68	390

Free under 6 (Eagle's Rest and Teewinot lifts only)

Beginner ticket for Eagle's Rest and Teewinot lifts ($25)

Notes
Covers all lifts in Jackson Hole; half-day ticket available

Alternative passes
Grand Targhee; Snow King Mountain

QUEUES ★★★☆☆
Only for the Tram
The new Tram (which opened in 2008) has double the hourly capacity of the old one. But it still holds only 100 people and many locals do laps on it all day long. So it still generates queues – we waited 20 minutes on our 2011 visit and reporters confirm that's fairly typical. Queues elsewhere on Rendezvous are rare. One reader's tip to avoid queuing on powder days is to head for Apres Vous and 'great first tracks in the Saratoga Bowl' (though the Teewinot chair you need to get there can be busy these days).

TERRAIN PARKS ★★★☆☆
Six plus a pipe
Last season, four all-natural Burton Stash parks opened. In addition, there are two terrain parks on the lower mountain with varying levels of features from beginner through to advanced plus music playing and a 137m-long super-pipe; Dick's Ditch is a 450m-long natural half-pipe.

SNOW RELIABILITY ★★★★☆
Deep snow, strong sun
The claimed average of 460 inches of snow is much more than the average for most Colorado (and some Utah) resorts. But the base elevation is low for the Rockies, and the slopes are fairly sunny – they basically face south-east (Apres Vous more south). The steep lower slopes, like the Hobacks, may be in poor shape, or even shut, and the higher slopes can be affected too – on our 2011 visit they were frozen solid because of very low temperatures after a melt. The flanks of some ridges have a more northerly orientation, and of course trees can be helpful. Locals claim that you can expect powder roughly half the time. Don't assume early-season conditions will be good.

FOR EXPERTS ★★★★★
Best for the brave
For the good skier or boarder who wants challenges without the expense of hiring a guide to go off-piste, Jackson is one of the world's best resorts. Rendezvous mountain offers virtually nothing but black slopes. The routes down the main Rendezvous Bowl are not particularly fearsome; but some of the alternatives are. Go down the East Ridge at least once to stare over the edge of the notorious Corbet's Couloir. It's the jump in that's special; the slope you land on is a mere 50°, they say.

Below Rendezvous Bowl, the wooded flanks of Cheyenne Bowl offer serious challenges, at the steep end of the single black diamond spectrum. If instead you take the ridge run that skirts this bowl to the right, you get to the Hobacks – a huge area of open and lightly wooded slopes, gentler than those higher up, but still black and usually with big moguls; check snow conditions before embarking on these – there's no turning back.

Corbet's aside, most of the steepest slopes are more easily reached from the slightly lower quad chairs. From the Sublette chair, you have direct access to the short but seriously steep Alta chutes, and to the less severe Laramie Bowl beside them. Or you can track over to Tensleep Bowl – pausing to inspect Corbet's from below – and on to the less extreme (and less chute-like) Expert Chutes, and the single-black Cirque and Headwall areas. Casper Bowl often has good powder. The Crags is an area of bowls, chutes and glades reached by hiking – both are accessed through gates. Thunder chair serves more steep, narrow, fairly shady chutes. Again, the lower part of the mountain here is lightly wooded single diamond slopes.

The gondola serves some good, under-used expert terrain, particularly to skier's left of the lift, including the glades of Woolsey and Moran Woods. Even Apres Vous has serious, usually quiet, single blacks in Saratoga bowl.

The gates into the backcountry access over 3,000 acres of amazing terrain, which should be explored only with guidance. You can stay out overnight at a backcountry yurt. There are some helicopter operations.

FOR INTERMEDIATES ★★☆☆☆
Exciting for some
They have tried hard to improve the intermediate terrain, with fast lifts and much more grooming than in the old days. There are good cruising runs on the front face of Apres Vous, and top-to-bottom quite gentle blues from the gondola. But they don't add up to a great deal of mileage, and you shouldn't consider Jackson unless you want to tackle the blacks. It's then important to get guidance on steepness and snow conditions. The steepest single blacks are steep,

Jackson Hole

Interactive resort shortlist builder at www.wtss.co.uk

SCHOOLS

Jackson Hole
t 1 800 450 0477

Classes
Full day (5½hr) $113
Private lessons
Half day (3hr) from $380

CHILDCARE

Kids' Ranch
t 1 800 450 0477
Wranglers: ages 6mnth to 2yr; 9am-4pm; $130 per day
Rough Riders: ages 3 to 6; 9am-3pm; includes skiing; $147 per day
Little Rippers: ages 5-6; 9am-3pm; includes boarding; $215 per day

Ski school
Explorers: ages 7 to 14; 9am-3.30; $145 per day

JACKSON HOLE MOUNTAIN RESORT
If there's not enough challenge on the lift-served slopes, you can explore over 3,000 acres of backcountry with a guide ↓

intimidating when mogulled and fearsome when hard. The daily grooming map is worth consulting, but falling snow will mean moguls form.

FOR BEGINNERS ★★★☆☆
Fine, up to a point
There are good broad, gentle beginner slopes and a lift pass covering the two chairs that serve them. The progression to the blue Werner run off the Apres Vous chair is gradual enough and the mid-mountain blues on the Casper Bowl chair are reached via the chairs from the beginner area. But few other runs will help build confidence.

FOR BOARDERS ★★★☆☆
Steep and deep thrills
Jackson Hole is a cult resort for expert snowboarders, as for skiers. It's not bad for novices either. But intermediates not wishing to venture off the groomed runs will find the resort limited. Six terrain parks and a super-pipe provide the freestyle thrills. There are some good snowboard shops, including the Hole-in-the-Wall at Teton Village.

FOR CROSS-COUNTRY ★★★★☆
Plenty of scenic choices
The Saddlehorn Activity Center at Teton has 17km of trails and organises trips into the National Parks. And there are lots of groomed trails in the surrounding National Parks.

MOUNTAIN RESTAURANTS ★★☆☆☆
Bridger blossoms
The top of the gondola has a coffee shop and fast food pizza area

downstairs with a light and airy self-service with good views upstairs serving fresh stir-fry Asian dishes as well as standard fare; plus the Couloir table-service restaurant. We enjoyed the Couloir – sit near the entrance for great views over the valley and town through floor-to-ceiling windows and further in for views of the Headwall and Corbet's through smaller windows. The food is good but not gourmet (though it is at night – see 'Eating out') – burgers, salads, upmarket sandwiches, pasta at lunchtime. Corbet's Cabin has 'the best waffles' and the restaurant at the base of the Casper chairlift does a wide range of self-service food. There are simple snack bars at four other points on the mountain. There are some excellent lunching alternatives at the base, particularly in the smarter hotels.

SCHOOLS AND GUIDES ★★★★☆
Learn to tackle the steeps
The school is highly regarded. A recent visitor ranks it as 'one of the best in the US', enjoying 'another couple of fun and instructive days'. As well as the usual lessons, there are also special types on certain dates. The four-day Steep and Deep Camp (pre-booking required) was 'carefully matched to ability, good value and a maximum five in each group'.
Rendezvous Ski Tours has been recommended for exploring the backcountry from Teton Pass.

FOR FAMILIES ★★★★☆
Adventures on the Ranch
There were lots of kids around having fun on our 2011 visit. The 'Kids' Ranch' facilities are good, including regular pizza parties in the evenings. There's a fun kids' version of the trail map.

STAYING THERE

Teton Village is our preferred option now that there are comfortable hotels there. You can catch the bus to town for a night out there – the last one back is around 11pm. Some town hotels are far from central.
Hotels Because winter is low season, town hotel prices are low.
TETON VILLAGE
*****Four Seasons Resort** (732 5000) Stylish luxury, with art on the walls, superb skier services, health club, an exceptional outdoor pool, perfect position just above the base.

GETTING THERE

Air Jackson 20km/
15 miles (45mins)

UK PACKAGES

Alpine Answers,
AmeriCan Ski, American
Ski Classics, Carrier,
Crystal, Elegant
Resorts, Funway
Holidays, Independent
Ski Links, Inghams,
Momentum,
PowderBeds, Scott
Dunn, Ski
Independence, Ski Line,
Ski Safari, Ski
Solutions, Skitracer,
Skiworld, Supertravel

ACTIVITIES

Indoor Fitness
centres, spa
treatments, swimming,
tennis, concerts,
wildlife art and other
museums

Outdoor Snowmobiles,
snowshoeing, sleigh
rides, dog sledding,
paragliding, snow kite
boarding

Phone numbers
From distant parts of
the US, add the prefix
1 307; from abroad,
add the prefix +1 307

TOURIST OFFICE

www.jacksonhole.com

****Teton Mountain Lodge & Spa** (734
7111) Very comfortable. Good indoor
and outdoor pool and fitness centre.
****Snake River Lodge & Spa** (732
6000) Smartly welcoming and
comfortable, with fine spa facilities.
****Terra** (739 4000) Smart, boutique
'eco' hotel, rooftop 'infinity' hot tub.
Spa. Nice café for breakfast. No bar.
***Alpenhof** (733 3242) Tirolean-style,
with varied rooms ('small by American
standards'). Good food, lively bar.
Pool, sauna, hot tub.
*Hostel** (733 3415) Basic, good value.
Recommended by 2011 reporter.

JACKSON TOWN

****Wort** (733 2190) Central, above
Silver Dollar Bar. Hot tub. Comfortable.
****Rusty Parrot Lodge** (733 2000)
Stylish, small with a rustic feel. Hot
tub. 'Food, service as good as ever.'
***Lodge at Jackson Hole** (739 9703)
Western-style on outskirts. Big rooms.
Free breakfast. Pool, sauna, hot tubs.
Shuttle to the slopes.
***Parkway Inn** (733 3143) Central.
'Decent sized rooms. Friendly. Highly
recommended.' Free breakfast. Pool,
sauna, hot tubs. Shuttle to the slopes.
49'er Inn and Suites (733 7550)
Central, good value.
Trapper Inn (733 2648) Friendly,
good value, fairly central. Hot tubs.

BETWEEN THE TWO

*****Amangani Resort** (734 7333)
Hedonistic luxury in isolated position
way above the valley.
****Spring Creek Ranch** (733 8833)
Exclusive retreat; cross-country on
hand. Hot tub.
Apartments There is lots of choice at
Teton Village and better value places a
mile or two away. Surprisingly little in
and around Jackson town. Love Ridge
and Snow King are 'good value'.

EATING OUT ★★★★★
A wide range of options
Jackson offers a range of excellent
dining options. To check out menus,
get hold of the local dining guide.
    At Teton Village Il Villaggio Osteria
at the hotel Terra has a good choice of
Italian and seafood dishes – two
recent reporters enjoyed 'great food
and service' there. The Couloir (see
'Mountain restaurants') at the top of
the gondola opens Fri and Sat nights
with a 4-course gourmet menu for $85
– we had great foie gras and bison.
    In Jackson town there is a big
choice. We loved the Asian/Japanese-
fusion dishes to share at The Kitchen.

The Cadillac Grill (steaks, burgers,
seafood) is 'great for families'. Blue
Lion is small, with 'intimate dining
areas, traditional menu and friendly
service'. Burke's is an 'above average'
steakhouse that also serves 'great
cocktails'. The Million Dollar Cowboy
Bar does 'wonderful steak' and good
wines. The Snake River brew-pub – not
to be confused with the expensive
Snake River Grill – does 'fabulous and
unusual pizzas' and a great range of
beers. Sweetwater serves 'good elk
and buffalo'. Other suggestions: the
Merry Piglets (Mexican), Bubba's BBQ,
Thai Me Up and Bon Appe Thai
('fantastic authentic curries').

APRES-SKI ★★★★★
Amusing saloons
The renowned Mangy Moose is the
focus of après-ski activity at Teton
Village – a big, happy place, often
with live music – though it closed at
10pm mid-week during our stay.
    In town, the Silver Dollar Bar (with
2032 silver dollars inlaid in the
counter) was packed with locals
dancing to live country music at 8pm
on the Sat night of our 2011 visit.
Round the corner the big Million Dollar
Cowboy Bar, featuring saddles as bar
stools, gets lively later and also has
live music and dancing. The Rancher is
an upstairs bar with pool and live
music and attracts a younger crowd.
Town Square Tavern also has pool and
often live music. Out of town, the
Stagecoach Inn at Wilson is famously
lively on Sunday nights.

OFF THE SLOPES ★★★★★
'Great' outdoor diversions
Yellowstone National Park is 100km to
the north. You can tour the park by
snowcat or snowmobile with a guide;
numbers are now restricted to reduce
pollution. Some visitors really enjoy
the park; we were distinctly
underwhelmed – largely because of
the noise and fumes from the
snowmobiles and driving everywhere
in convoy. The National Elk Refuge,
with the largest elk herd in the US, is
next to Jackson and across the road
from the National Museum of Wildlife
Art. Reporters recommend both. In
town there are some 40 galleries and
museums and various shops, including
a number of outlets for Western arts
and crafts. Shopping and restaurant
discounts can be gained by joining the
Jackson Hole Ski Club ($30).

New England

You go to Utah for the deepest snow, to Colorado for the lightest powder and swankiest resorts, to California for big mountains and relatively low prices. You go to New England for ... well, for what? Extreme cold? Rock-hard artificial snow? Mountains too limited to be of interest beyond New Jersey? Yes and no: all of these preconceptions have some basis, and in the end the East can't compete with the West. But they don't give the full picture.

Yes, it can be cold: one of our reporters recorded –27°C, with wind chill producing a perceived –73°C. Early in the season, people routinely wear face masks to prevent frostbite. It can also be warm – another reporter had a whole week of rain that washed away the early-season snow. The thing about New England's weather is that it varies – rather like old England's. The locals' favourite saying is: 'If you don't like the weather, wait two minutes.'

Many of the resorts get impressive amounts of natural snow over the season – in some years. But New England doesn't usually get much deep powder to play in. And snowmaking plays a big part in the resorts' operations. They have big snow-gun installations, designed to ensure a long season and to help the slopes to 'recover' after a thaw. They were the pioneers of snowmaking technology; and 'farming' snow, as they put it, is something they do superbly well.

The mountains are not huge in terms of trail mileage. But several have verticals of over 800m (on a par with Colorado resorts such as Keystone), and most have over 600m (matching Breckenridge), and are worth considering for a short stay, or even for a week if you like familiar runs. For more novelty, a two- or three-centre trip is the obvious solution. Consider renting a car and doing a tour.

Most resorts suit snowboarders well, and many have more than one terrain park.

You won't lack challenge – most of the double black diamond runs are seriously steep. And you won't lack space: most Americans visit over weekends, which means deserted slopes on weekdays – except at peak holiday periods.

It also means the resorts are keen to attract long-stay visitors, so UK package prices are low. But the big weekend and day trip trade also means few New England resorts have developed atmospheric resort villages – just a few condos and a hotel, maybe, with places to stay further out geared to car drivers.

New England is easy to get to from Britain – a flight to Boston, then perhaps a three- or four-hour drive to your resort. And there are some pretty towns to visit, with their clapboard houses and big churches. You might also like to consider spending a day or two in Boston – one of America's most charming cities. Or have a shopping spree at the factory outlet stores that abound in New England.

We cover two of the most popular resorts on the UK market, Killington and Stowe, briefly on the following page. But there are many other small areas, too, shown on the map and covered in our directory at the back of the book.

PACKAGES

Killington American Ski Classics, Crystal, Independent Ski Links, PowderBeds, Ski Independence, Ski Line, Ski Safari, Ski Solutions, Skitracer, Skiworld, Thomson, Virgin Snow
Stowe American Ski Classics, Carrier, Crystal, Crystal Finest, Elegant Resorts, Independent Ski Links, Inghams, PowderBeds, Ski Independence, Ski Line, Ski Safari, Skitracer, Virgin Snow

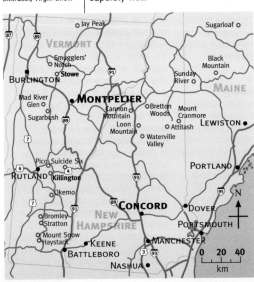

Killington

KEY FACTS	
Resort	670m
	2,200ft
Slopes	355-1285m
	1,170-4,220ft
Lifts	22
Pistes	752 acres
Snow-guns	70%

TOURIST OFFICE

www.killington.com

- New England's biggest ski area
- Excellent nursery slopes
- Lively après-ski and nightlife
- Widely spread lodgings, with no proper resort village
- Terminally tedious for non-skiers

Killington caters mainly for weekend visitors who drive in from the east-coast cities. There is no resort village in the usual sense.

Most of Killington's hotels and restaurants are spread along a five-mile approach road; the car is king. But there's also a free day-time shuttle-bus service around the base areas and lodgings. Beyond this it costs $2. The lift pass covers Pico – a separate little mountain next door in the same ownership.

The ski area spreads over a series of wooded peaks, with an impressive number of lifts and runs crammed into a modest area. Killington Base is the main focus, with chairlifts radiating to three of the peaks. Queues and crowded slopes can be a problem at weekends. It's a complex mountain, but the map and signing are fine. It has a good snow record (average 250 inches) and lots of snowmaking.

There are a handful of genuine double-diamond fall-line runs to suit experts, steepest on Bear Peak. There are also lots of easy cruising blue and green runs all over the slopes. The resort is excellent for complete beginners too: the Snowshed base home slope is really one vast nursery slope. There are good facilities for children at Ramshead, where there is a well-equipped Family Center. Freestyle areas abound on Bear Mountain, on the back of Skye Peak. At present there is no mountain restaurant. The Snowshed base lodge has several eating options.

Most hotels are a drive or bus ride away, but there is a wide choice of places to stay and dine. The Grand Resort at Snowshed is a swanky 4-star. Try the Santa Fe Steakhouse ('good seafood too'), Grist Mill (steaks) or Peppino's for Italian. Killington has a well-deserved reputation for a vibrant après-ski scene too. Leading the way is the popular Wobbly Barn, a famous live-music place.

Off the slopes? Make sure you have a car, as well as a supply of good books.

Stowe

KEY FACTS	
Resort	475m
	1,560ft
Slopes	390-1135m
	1,280-3,720ft
Lifts	13
Pistes	485 acres
Snow-guns	80%

TOURIST OFFICE

www.stowe.com

- Classic, cute Vermont town
- Queue-free except at weekends
- Great children's facilities
- Slopes a bus ride from town
- Slow chairlifts in main area
- Lacks après-ski animation

Stowe is one of New England's cutest towns, its main streets lined with dinky clapboard shops and restaurants. The slopes have something for everyone.

The small slopes of Mount Mansfield, Vermont's mainly wooded highest peak, are a 15-minute drive away. There's a good day-time shuttle-bus service, but a car is useful.

The slopes span two main sectors, Mansfield and Spruce Peak, linked by gondola at base level. The area is largely queue-free during the week. Snowmaking is extensive.

The main slopes are dominated by the famous Front Four – a row of double black diamond runs, with genuine challenges for experts. But there is plenty of easier stuff, too. The nursery slopes at Spruce Peak are excellent and there are splendid long green runs to progress to. There are three terrain parks and the resort is popular with snowboarders. Children's facilities are excellent too. There are a couple of decent huts. The Cliff House, at the top of the gondola, has table service.

Much of the lodging is along the road between the town and the slopes – though you can now stay at the swanky Stowe Mountain Lodge, right by the lifts. Elsewhere, the Green Mountain Inn is a reader favourite. There are restaurants of every kind in the town; the Whip (Green Mountain Inn), Trattoria La Festa and the Solstice are good choices. Nightlife is fairly muted but the Matterhorn, Shed and Rusty Nail (live music, dancing) on the access road are popular.

Stowe is a pleasant place to spend time off the slopes – at least if you like shopping. There is snowmobiling and dog sledding too. Ben & Jerry's ice cream factory is just down the road.

Canada

In many ways Canada combines the best that the US has to offer – good service, a warm welcome, relatively quiet slopes, good lift systems with lots of fast lifts, frequent dumps of snow, great grooming and a high standard of accommodation – with more spectacular scenery. It also has the advantage that you can get direct flights to its main airports without having to change planes and go through customs part-way through your journey.

If Canada – well, western Canada at least – has one central attraction, it is snow. In an average year, you can expect much better snow than in the Alps – and not only good conditions on the pistes but frequent fresh falls to provide the powder you dream of. And, as in the States, there is lots of steep terrain within resort boundaries, which is therefore avalanche protected and safely skiable without guidance. If you really want untracked powder and are feeling flush, there is nothing to beat western Canada's amazing heli-skiing and snowcat skiing operations. The east is different: expect snow and extremes of weather much like New England's. The main attraction of Québec for us is the French culture and unique ambience, plus the advantage of a shorter flight time. In both east and west, lifts close much earlier than in Europe – as early as 3pm in some cases (and some upper lifts might start closing as early as 1.30pm).

The Canadian people are another attraction. They share the American service culture but have a sincerity in putting it into practice that we (and our reporters) appreciate. In the west you'll also find spectacular scenery quite unlike what you generally find in the US. You may also see an impressive range of wildlife, especially in the Rockies and the interior of British Columbia.

Canada is not as cheap as it was (local prices have risen by 45% in terms of £s in the last five years just because of the falling pound), and lift pass prices are high compared with the Alps. Air fares have increased substantially too. But you can still get packages of flights, transfers and accommodation at reasonable prices.

Note that the legal age for buying and consuming alcohol is 18 in Alberta and Québec and 19 in British Columbia. The law is strictly enforced, so carrying your passport as evidence of age is a good idea even if you are well over the required age.

Canada combines the best that the US has to offer with more spectacular scenery. This is Lake Louise ↓

Ski Canada
Book early for LOWEST Prices for winter 2011

Ski the Canadian Rockies and BC's best resorts for less this year

• **FREE Nights** • **Kids Ski FREE** • **Ski FREE Days** • **FREE Ski Carriage**
Book now and enjoy Huge Savings at every resort!
Offers end 30th Oct 2011!

Jasper	fr **£499**pp*	Big White	fr **£639**pp**
Revelstoke	fr **£569**pp*	Sun Peaks	fr **£639**pp*
Lake Louise	fr **£579**pp	Whistler	fr **£659**pp
Banff	fr **£599**pp	Fernie	fr **£779**pp
Panorama	fr **£599**pp	Kicking Horse	fr **£789**pp
Silver Star	fr **£619**pp**		

... hurry book now!

0207 616 9933
www.canadianaffair.com

 GOVERNMENT BACKED HOLIDAY PROTECTION **ABTA** ABTA No W131X **IATA**

 CANADIAN *Affair*

Prices include return flights, 7 nights' accommodation (quad share, Room only) Instant Purchase fares.
~Travel selected dates Jan 2012. Strictly subject to availability. Terms and condition apply.
*Transfer not included. **Internal flight additional.

Western Canada

For international visitors to Canada, the main draw is the west. It has fabulous scenery, good snow and a wonderful sense of the great outdoors. The big names of Whistler, Banff and Lake Louise capture most of the British market, but there are lots of good smaller resorts that more Brits are now starting to explore. You can have a great trip by renting a car and combining two or more of these, perhaps with a couple of days on virgin powder served by helicopters or snowcats as well.

The three big resorts mentioned above and six of the smaller ones get their own write-ups in this section.

Whistler is plenty big enough to amuse you for a whole holiday. Most visitors to Banff or Lake Louise, a half-hour drive apart, will spend time at both (and could also fit in day trips to Kicking Horse and Panorama).

But none of the others has enough terrain to keep a keen piste-basher amused for a week or ten days without skiing the same runs several times. So we'd suggest that if you want variety, you combine two or more on one holiday. Even if you don't want to drive, it is easy to combine, say, Sun Peaks with Whistler, Big White or Silver Star (and the latter two with each other) using regular buses between them.

Places that don't get a full chapter that you might also consider for a longer tour include Jasper (which you can reach via the spectacular Icefields Parkway drive from Lake Louise), Apex, Red Mountain, Panorama and Kimberley – these all have entries in the resort directory.

A few seasons ago we spent two weeks driving from Whistler to Banff, calling in at lots of smaller resorts on the way. It was a fantastic trip; for eight days in the middle it did not stop snowing, and the variety of slopes and resorts made for great contrasts throughout the trip.

If you fancy a day or two snowcat skiing, there are lots of possibilities, including great operations near Fernie (see chapter). Revelstoke has both cat- and heli-skiing right from the resort.

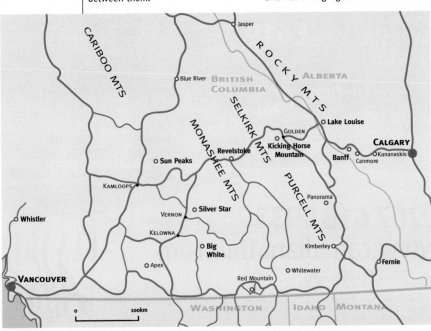

SNOWPIX / CHRIS GILL

Banff

A major summer resort amid spectacular National Park scenery, with varied ski areas a bus ride from town – including Lake Louise

RATINGS

The mountains

Extent	★★★
Fast lifts	★★★★
Queues	★★★★
Terrain p'ks	★★★★
Snow	★★★★
Expert	★★★★
Intermediate	★★★★
Beginner	★★★
Boarder	★★★★
X-country	★★★★
Restaurants	★★★
Schools	★★★★
Families	★★★★

The resort

Charm	★★★
Convenience	★
Scenery	★★★★
Eating out	★★★★★
Après-ski	★★★
Off-slope	★★★★★

RPI   130

lift pass	£330
ski hire	£125
lessons	£175
food & drink	£115
total	**£745**

NEWS

2011/12: The shuttle bus service to the ski areas is due to be improved – very welcome judging by the complaints we received about last season's bus service.

2010/11: At Sunshine Village, a fast quad replaced the elderly Strawberry triple chair on Mt Standish – serving novice slopes there. And the Creekside Bar and Grill at the foot of the gondola reopened after renovations.

Banff's first brew-pub, the Banff Avenue Brewing Company, opened.

+ Spectacular high-mountain scenery – quite unlike the Colorado Rockies

+ Lots of touristy shops, restaurants and bars

+ Good-value lodging because winter is the area's low season

+ Excellent snow at main local area, Sunshine Village, but ...

− It's a 20-minute bus ride then a long gondola ride away

− You'll probably want to ski Lake Louise too – 45 minutes away

− Most lifts/runs are of limited vertical

− Can be very cold (–30°C or less)

− Banff lacks ski resort atmosphere – though it's not an unattractive town

Banff is nothing like your typical ski resort. We enjoy its restaurants and bars, but not the daily commuting to Sunshine Village or Lake Louise (which gets its own chapter). Even the small local hill, Norquay, is a bus ride out of town.

The alternative is to stay a few nights mid-mountain at Sunshine Village and a few at Lake Louise. Lake Louise also has the advantage of being much closer to Kicking Horse, which makes a great day trip for powderhounds.

THE RESORT

Banff is a big summer tourist town, with two ski areas nearby. Mt Norquay is a tiny area of slopes overlooking the town. Sunshine Village, its base station 20 minutes' drive from Banff, is a much bigger mountain; despite the name, it's not a village (it has just one hotel at mid-mountain) nor is it notably sunny (sitting on the Continental Divide, it has an excellent snow record).

Most visitors buy a three-area pass that also covers the resort of Lake Louise, 45 minutes' drive away – dealt with in a separate chapter. Bus excursions are available to the more distant resorts of Panorama and Kicking Horse (the latter especially worthwhile) and the smaller (and closer) resort of Nakiska, and day trips for heli-skiing are offered locally.

VILLAGE CHARM ★★★★★
Pleasantly touristy
Banff consists basically of a long main street connecting the 'downtown' area – a small network of side roads built in grid fashion, lined with clothing and souvenir shops aimed at summer visitors – with a large area of hotel and condo lodgings. The buildings are low-rise and some are wood-clad. The town is pleasant enough, but it's essentially a modern tourist town, without the character of the classic American cowboy or mining towns.

CONVENIENCE ★★★★★
Sprawling town, outlying slopes
Banff is a sprawling place, and many of the lodgings (even on the main Banff Avenue) can be quite a way from the downtown area. A car can be helpful here, especially in cold weather. But there are plentiful taxis.

To get to the slopes bus services for each mountain pick up from all the main hotels – free with the Tri-area lift pass. Visitors last season complained about its efficiency and we're told it's being improved for 2011/12. The buses pick up from a number of hotels, so getting from your hotel to the lift base can take much longer than the advertised time. For Sunshine this is 20 minutes; when you arrive, there is a long access gondola to ride.

SCENERY ★★★★★
Distinctive and dramatic
Banff National Park offers spectacular scenery – that's what brings the millions of summer visitors – and the town's setting is dramatic. Sunshine's Lookout mountain, right on the Continental Divide, gives panoramic views into British Columbia.

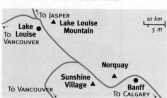

LIFT PASSES

Tri-area lift pass

Prices in C$

Age	1-day	6-day
under 13	28	166
13 to 17	57	448
18 to 64	80	504
over 65	65	448

Free under 6

Beginner lift, lesson and rental package

Notes

Day pass is for Sunshine only; 3-day-plus pass covers all lifts and transport between Banff, Lake Louise, Norquay and Sunshine Village; prices include 5% GST tax

THE MOUNTAINS

The Sunshine Village slopes are mostly above the treeline, although there is a wooded sector served by the second section of the gondola, and some lightly wooded slopes higher up.

Mt Norquay is a much smaller area of quiet, wooded slopes. But it's worth a visit, especially in bad weather or as a first-day warm-up.

Each area (and Lake Louise) has its own trail map and there's one that shows all three areas too. The signposting at the top of each lift is praised, but at Sunshine it is difficult to follow some trails after that ('signs small and difficult to spot', says a 2011 reporter).

There are good, free mountain tours led by friendly volunteer hosts.

EXTENT OF THE SLOPES ★★★★★
Lots of variety
The main slopes of **Sunshine Village** are not visible from the base station: you ride a gondola to Sunshine Village itself, with a mid-station at the base of Goat's Eye Mountain.

Goat's Eye is served by a fast quad rising 580m – much the most serious

Sunshine Village by Richard Hallman

lift on the mountain. Although there are some blue runs, this is basically a black mountain, with some genuine double diamonds (including the 'backcountry' Wild West area).

Further up at Sunshine Village, lifts fan out in all directions, with short runs back from Mount Standish and longer ones from Lookout Mountain. From the top here experts can access more extreme terrain.

The 2.5km green run to the gondola base is a pretty cruise. Go down while the lifts are still running, and you can take the Jackrabbit chair to cut out a flat section. Delay your descent and you'll avoid the close-of-play crowds. The Canyon trail is a fun alternative for more advanced skiers and riders. The lower part is marked black; it's just a bit narrow and twisty in places. The final option is to ride the gondola down; many people do.

The slopes at **Norquay** are served by a row of five parallel lifts and have floodlit trails twice a week.

FAST LIFTS ★★★★★
New one for Sunshine
At Sunshine, most sectors of the slopes have fast chairs. Joining them was a new quad on Mount Standish for 2010/11 serving the novice slopes. The main weakness is the stoppage-prone Wawa chair. Norquay is so small that lift speed is hardly an issue, but it does have one fast chair.

QUEUES ★★★★★
Sunshine can get busy
Many visitors are day-trippers from cities such as Calgary – so the slopes are fairly quiet during the week. Public holidays and weekends at Sunshine have provoked past complaints of long queues; it can get busy. But recent reporters have had no major problems. Even when busy, queues generally move quickly, and there are effective singles lines you can use if in a hurry. On busy weekends, we're told the trick is to arrive at the gondola by 9am.

TERRAIN PARKS ★★★★★
Park – and ride ...
At Sunshine, the Rogers terrain park on Lookout Mountain covers an impressive 12 acres of terrain with obstacles geared towards beginners and intermediates. The park is divided into two; the larger Lower Divide has a wide selection of obstacles and jumps; Grizzly is more jib-oriented. Experts

KEY FACTS

Resort	1380m
	4,530ft

Norquay, Sunshine and Lake Louise, covered by the Tri-area pass

Slopes	1630-2730m
	5,350-8,950ft
Lifts	26
Pistes	7,748 acres
Green	23%
Blue	39%
Black	38%
Snowmaking	24%

Norquay only

Slopes	1630-2135m
	5,350-7,000ft
Lifts	5
Pistes	190 acres
Green	20%
Blue	36%
Black	44%
Snowmaking	85%

Sunshine only

Slopes	1660-2730m
	5,440-8,950ft
Lifts	12
Pistes	3,358 acres
Green	20%
Blue	55%
Black	25%
Snowmaking	none

BANFF

Banff is long and sprawling – but spectacularly set in Banff National Park ↓

should not miss Norquay, designed by Jeff Patterson – head park designer for Triple Crown events. Gap jumps, tabletops, rails and boxes litter the park, which also boasts a boardercross. The park is floodlit twice a week from January to March. You can lap the park in less than five minutes, with a great view from the chair.

SNOW RELIABILITY ★★★★
Excellent
Sunshine Village claims '100% natural snow', a neat reversal of the usual snowmaking hype. In a poor snow season, some black runs can remain rocky (especially those on Goat's Eye), but the blues are usually fine. 'Three times the snow' is another Sunshine slogan – a sly comparison between the impressive average snowfall here (360 to 400 inches, depending on the source) and the modest 180 inches at Lake Louise and 120 inches on Norquay. But we're told the Sunshine figures relate to Lookout, and that Goat's Eye gets less. At Norquay there is snowmaking on all green and blue pistes. Late-season snow on Sunshine is usually good (we've had great April snow there on our visits).

FOR EXPERTS ★★★★
Pure pleasure
Sunshine has plenty of open runs of genuine black steepness above the treeline on Lookout, but Goat's Eye is much more compelling. It has a great area of expert double black diamond

trails and chutes, both above and below the treeline. But the slopes are rocky and need good cover, and the top can be windswept. The double-diamond runs at skier's left reportedly hold their snow better than the rest of the mountain.

There are short, not-too-steep black runs on Mount Standish. One more challenging novelty here is a pitch known as the Waterfall run – because you do actually ski down over a snow-covered frozen waterfall. But a lot of snow is needed to cover the waterfall and prevent it reverting to ice. Also try the Shoulder on Lookout Mountain; it is sheltered, tends to accumulate powder and has been deserted whenever we've been there; access involves a long traverse that can be tricky and is poorly marked.

A popular backcountry route follows the back of the Wawa ridge, through a river valley ('great fun – tight turns in the trees of the river bed'); a guide is essential, of course.

Real experts will want to get to grips with Delirium Dive and Silver City on Lookout Mountain's north face and the Wild West area on Goat's Eye (with some narrow chutes and rock bands). For all three you must have a companion, an avalanche transceiver, a probe and a shovel – and a guide is recommended. It is probably best to book in advance and rent your transceiver and shovel in Banff (you can't in Sunshine). We tried Delirium in a group with the ski patrol, who

outside the National Park in British Columbia – roughly two hours' drive.

FOR INTERMEDIATES ★★★★☆
Ideal runs

Half the runs on Sunshine are classified as intermediate. Wherever you look there are blues and greens – some of the greens as enjoyable (and pretty much as steep) as the blues. We particularly like the World Cup Downhill run, from the top of Lookout to the Village. All three chairs on Mount Standish are excellent for building confidence, provided you choose a sensible route down. The slow Wawa chair gives access to the Wawa Bowl and Tincan Alley ('great first blues'). This area also offers some shelter from bad weather. There's a delightful wooded area under the second stage of the gondola served by Jackrabbit and Wolverine chairs. The blue runs down Goat's Eye are good

provided equipment, and the scariest part was the walk in, along a narrow, icy path with a sheer drop (protected by a flimsy-looking net).

Norquay's two main lifts give only 400m vertical, but both serve black slopes, and the North American chair accesses a couple of serious double-diamond runs.

Heli-skiing is available from bases

Goat's Eye has some great steep terrain – single and double black diamond runs and an extreme zone. But it's very rocky and windswept and needs a lot of snow to be enjoyable

GOAT'S EYE
2600m/8,530ft

Goat's Eye

De

🚠 gondola
🚡 fast chairlift
Slow chairs & drags
have no symbol

Wild West
◆ ◆

Wolverine

Go

1660m/5,440ft

2020m/6,630ft

If it's snowing hard, visibility is usually best on the easy runs in the trees around here and on the long run down to the bottom of the gondola

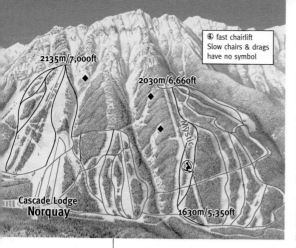

2135m/7,000ft

2030m/6,660ft

Mystic

Cascade Lodge
Norquay

1630m/5,350ft

④ fast chairlift
Slow chairs & drags
have no symbol

FOR BEGINNERS ★★★★★
Pretty good terrain
Most beginners start with a package
that includes a lift pass and tuition.
Sunshine has a good area at the
Village, served by a moving carpet.
And there are great long green runs to
progress to – including those served
by the new Strawberry fast quad.
Norquay has a good small nursery
area with a moving carpet and gentle
greens served by the Cascade chair.

Banff is not the ideal destination
for a mixed party of beginners and
more experienced friends. The
beginners are likely to want familiar
surroundings, while the more
experienced will want to travel.

cruises too, some of them with space
to indulge in fast carving.

The Mystic Express at Norquay
serves a handful of quite challenging
treelined blues and a couple of blacks
that are sometimes groomed.

FOR BOARDERS ★★★★★
A good base
Boarders will feel at home in Banff,
and there is some excellent freeriding
terrain. Natural features are part of the

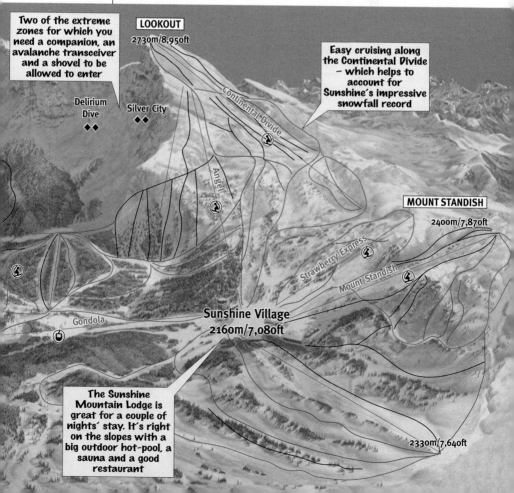

Two of the extreme
zones for which you
need a companion, an
avalanche transceiver
and a shovel to be
allowed to enter

LOOKOUT
2730m/8,950ft

Continental Divide

Easy cruising along
the Continental Divide
– which helps to
account for
Sunshine's impressive
snowfall record

Delirium
Dive
◆◆

Silver City
◆◆

Angel

MOUNT STANDISH
2400m/7,870ft

Strawberry Express

Mount Standish

Gondola

Sunshine Village
2160m/7,080ft

The Sunshine
Mountain Lodge is
great for a couple of
nights' stay. It's right
on the slopes with a
big outdoor hot-pool, a
sauna and a good
restaurant

2330m/7,640ft

SCHOOLS

Ski Big 3
t 1 886 760 7731
Banff-Norquay
t 760 7716
Sunshine Village
t 1 877 542 2633

Classes (Big 3 prices)
3 days' guided tuition
of the three areas
C$314 incl. tax
Private lessons
Half day (3hr) C$398,
incl. tax, for up to 5
people

CHILDCARE

Tiny Tigers (Sunshine)
t 1 877 542 2633
Ages 19mnth to 6yr;
8.30-4.30
Kid's Place (Norquay)
t 760 7709
Ages 19mnth to 6yr;
9am to 4pm
Childcare Connection
t 760 4443
Childminding in guest
accommodation

Ski school
Takes ages 6 to 12 (3
days C$240, incl. tax
and lunch)

SKI BANFF-LAKE LOUISE-SUNSHINE /
JAKE BAUER

Sunshine Village has
lots of great groomed
cruising and lots of
steep gnarly terrain ↓

appeal, with ledges, jumps and tree gaps aplenty. But Sunshine has some flat areas to beware of (such as the green run to the base – see 'Extent of the slopes' for tips on avoiding the worst of this), and the blue traverse on Goat's Eye is tedious. A trip to Lake Louise's Powder Bowls is a must for freeriders. There are specialist snowboard shops in Banff: Rude Boys, Rude Girls and Unlimited Skate & Snow.

FOR CROSS-COUNTRY ★★★★
High in quality and quantity
It's a good area for cross-country. There are trails near Banff, around the Bow River, and on the Banff Springs golf course. But the best area is around Lake Louise. Altogether, there are around 80km of groomed trails within Banff National Park.

MOUNTAIN RESTAURANTS ★★★
Quite good
With a mini-resort at mid-mountain, Sunshine offers better options than usual in North America. Best is the Sunshine Mountain Lodge – the table service in the Chimney Corner Lounge gave 'prompt service and good food' for a recent visitor. The Day Lodge offers different styles of catering on three floors – the table service Lookout Lounge has great views and does a buffet.

At Norquay, the big, stylish, timber-framed Cascade Lodge is excellent – it has table- and self-service restaurants.

SCHOOLS AND GUIDES ★★★★
Some great ideas
Each mountain has its own school. But recognising that visitors wanting lessons won't want to be confined to just one mountain, the resorts have organised an excellent Club Ski Program – three-day courses starting on Sundays and Thursdays that take you to Sunshine, Norquay and Lake Louise on different days, offering a mixture of guiding and instruction, and fun social events. In the past we've received rave reviews about it from reporters. But a recent visitor had mixed experiences: 'Our advanced group had a perfect balance of skills training and guidance, but the rest of our party had an instructor who spoke little and gave virtually no specific skills training.' Beginners can join this program, though whether they should is another question. Another reporter found the Performance Workshops at Sunshine 'excellent: my class size was never more than four'.

FOR FAMILIES ★★★★
Excellent choices
There are various school and activity programmes for all ages. Some lodges have family lounges, with games and TVs. We've had good reports of the schools: 'kind and friendly instructors' and 'very accommodating; my boy is now a tremendous skier'. All three resorts offer childcare. The Tiny Tigers Ski and Play programme introduces youngsters to the slopes.

GETTING THERE

Air Calgary 140km/ 85 miles (1hr45)

UK PACKAGES

Alpine Answers, AmeriCan Ski, American Ski Classics, Canadian Affair, Carrier, Crystal, Crystal Finest, Elegant Resorts, First Choice, Frontier, Funway Holidays, Independent Ski Links, Inghams, Neilson, PowderBeds, Ski Independence, Ski Line, Ski Safari, Ski Solutions, Skitracer, Skiworld, Snow Finders, Supertravel, Thomson, Virgin Snow

ACTIVITIES

Indoor Film theatre, museums, galleries, swimming pools (one with water slides), gym, squash, weight training, bowling, hot tub, sauna, climbing wall

Outdoor Swimming in hot springs, ice rink, sleigh rides, dog sledding, snowmobiles, ice walks, ice fishing, helicopter tours, snowshoeing

Phone numbers
From distant parts of Canada, add the prefix 1 403; from abroad, add the prefix +1 403

TOURIST OFFICE

www.skibanff.com
www.banffnorquay.com
www.SkiBig3.com

STAYING THERE

A huge amount of accommodation is on offer, with lots of varied hotels.
Hotels Summer is peak season here, with generally lower prices in winter. Frontier offers several good hotels.
*****Fairmont Banff Springs (762 2211) A late-19th-century, castle-style property outside town (no shuttle-bus – you have to use taxis). It's a town in itself – 2,000 beds, 40 shops, several restaurants and bars, a nightclub and a superb spa (which costs extra).
****Fox (760 8500) On the main street. Hotel rooms and suites, with a restaurant, fitness area and an unusual 'cavern' style hot pool.
****Rimrock (762 3356) Spectacularly set, out of town, with great views and a smart health club. Luxurious.
****Banff Park Lodge (762 4433) Best-quality, central hotel, with hot tub, steam room and indoor pool.
****Banff Caribou Lodge (762 5887) On the main street, slightly out of town. Wood-clad, individually designed rooms. Very good Red Earth Spa centre, 'excellent' restaurant and bar. Repeatedly recommended by reporters.
***Buffalo Mountain Lodge (762 2400) Less convenient but 'beautiful location and excellent dining room'. Hot tub.
***Irwins Mountain Inn (762 4566) On Banff Avenue: 'good location and excellent value'.
***High Country Inn (762 2236) 'Great: big rooms, pool, hot tub and sauna, easy walk to centre.'
**Homestead Inn (762 4471) Central, cheap, good-sized rooms.
Apartments Don't expect luxury – but there are some decent options. The Banff Rocky Mountain Resort is set in the woods on the edge of town, with indoor pool and hot tubs. Families have recommended the Douglas Fir resort ('kids loved the water slides') – though it's 'a bit out of town'.
At altitude The Sunshine Mountain Lodge (277 7669) makes a very welcoming, comfortable base at Sunshine Village. Luggage is transported while you ski. Rooms vary in size, with 30 luxury newish ones. Big outdoor hot pool. Sauna. Good restaurant. Guests can get on the slopes half an hour early.

EATING OUT ★★★★★
Lots of choice

Banff boasts over 100 restaurants, from McDonald's to fine dining in the Banff Springs hotel. The award-winning Maple Leaf Grille has fine seafood and steak dishes on the menu, and over 600 different wines to choose from. We've enjoyed the designer-cool Saltlik – good game, steak and fish.

Of the dozens of places that readers recommend, popular spots are Melissa's (central, 'varied menu and good ambience'; 'ever-reliable breakfasts'), Athena ('excellent large pizzas – good value for money'), Giorgios (beef, fish, Italian), Magpie & Stump ('lively' Tex-Mex, with Wild West decor, 'serves beer in jam jars') and Earl's. Old Spaghetti Factory is a good family choice ('excellent service'). Try Bison for 'excellent' steaks, fish, and live music. And for traditional burgers and ribs try the Keg, Bumper's, Wild Bill's or Tony Roma's.

APRES-SKI ★★★☆☆
Night on the town is best

There's little tea time après-ski because the town is a drive from the slopes. Mad Trapper's Saloon at the top of the Sunshine gondola is the best bet during the close-of-play happy hour, but it gets crowded.

In town later, the two main live music venues are the Rose & Crown and Wild Bill's – country and western style, perhaps with line dancing. The newly-opened Banff Avenue Brewing Company is 'convivial but beers erred on the bland side'. The Elk and Oarsman has a lively sports bar. For a traditional pint of beer, head for the St James's Gate Olde Irish pub if you can put up with 'the waitresses wearing mini kilts'. There are a couple of good nightclubs.

OFF THE SLOPES ★★★★★
Lots to do

Banff has lots to do off the slopes. Outdoor activities include skating, snowshoeing, dog sledding and snowmobiling. Ice canyon walks are popular – notably Johnson Canyon – and there's wildlife to see.

Shopping and soaking in the spas and hot springs are popular – the Red Earth Spa at the Caribou Lodge has the works and is open until 8pm. There are sightseeing tours and several museums. Some reporters have enjoyed evenings in Calgary watching the ice hockey. A recent reporter enjoyed a good day out in Canmore.

Big White

It's not big by Euro-resort standards, but it's certainly white.
There are few places to match it for learning to ski powder

- + Great for learning to ski powder
- + Slopes quiet except at weekends
- + Convenient, purpose-built village with high-quality condos and a traffic-free centre; good for families
- + Lots of non-skiing snow-based activities at Happy Valley

- − Visibility can be poor, especially on the upper mountain, because of snow, cloud or freezing fog
- − Few off-slope diversions and it's isolated without a car
- − Limited après-ski

'It's the snow' says the Big White slogan. And as slogans go, it's spot on. If you want a good chance of skiing powder on reasonably easy slopes, put Big White high on the shortlist. If you want a suntan (or lively après-ski, or extensive steep bowls and chutes), look elsewhere; but if you are an intermediate looking to learn to ski powder or try gladed skiing for the first time, there can be few better places. Consider combining it with another BC resort such as Silver Star or Sun Peaks for variety.

THE RESORT

Big White is a still growing, purpose-built resort less than an hour from Kelowna airport. Silver Star (see separate chapter) is around two and a half hours away and under the same ownership; twice-a-week direct transfers make a two-centre holiday easy and you can also just go for the day twice a week.

Village charm The village is rather spread out but attractive in wood and stone, with a family-friendly traffic-free centre. Reporters remark on the large number of 'friendly and happy' Aussie seasonal workers.

Convenience Much of the place is ski-in/ski-out of smart modern condos, some very luxurious.

Scenery Trees fill the views wherever you look; and near the top of the mountain the trees usually stay white all winter and are known as 'snow ghosts'; they make visibility tricky in a white-out but are great fun to ski between on clear days.

THE MOUNTAINS

Much of the terrain is heavily wooded. But the trees thin out towards the summits, leading to almost open slopes in the bowls at the top. There's at least one green option from the top of each lift, but the one from Gem Lake is narrow and can be tricky and

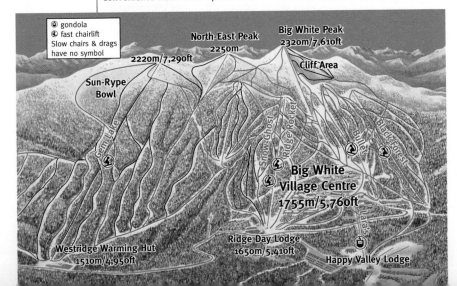

gondola
fast chairlift
Slow chairs & drags
have no symbol

North-East Peak
2250m

Big White Peak
2320m/7,610ft

2220m/7,290ft

Cliff Area

Sun-Rype Bowl

Gem Lake

Snow Ghost

Ridge Rocket

Black Forest

Butte

Big White
Village Centre
1755m/5,760ft

Westridge Warming Hut
1510m/4,950ft

Ridge Day Lodge
1650m/5,410ft

Happy Valley Lodge

2011/12: More trails are due to be added for cross-country, snowshoeing, walking and snowmobiling. Summer grooming will take place on the Black Forest area so that it can open earlier in the season with less snowpack.

2010/11: Rotating 'slow zones' were introduced: three different slopes each day are dedicated as slow ski areas, gated and patrolled to minimise traffic. The terrain park gained new features and a 60ft ice climbing tower was built at Happy Valley.

BIG WHITE SKI RESORT LTD

The village is rather spread out but much accommodation is ski-in/ski-out; and it is certainly a snowy place ↓

busy. In general, the easiest slopes are on the right as you look at the mountain (including some very easy glade skiing) and get steeper the further left you go.

Slopes Chairs run from points below village level to above mid-mountain, serving the main area of wooded beginner and intermediate runs above and beside the village. A T-bar and four chairs serve the higher slopes. Quite some way across the mountainside is the Gem Lake fast chair, serving a range of long top-to-bottom runs; with its 710m vertical, this lift is in a different league from the others. 'Snow hosts' (highly praised by reporters) run free guided ski tours every day (9.30am and 1.30pm). The signposting and piste map and classification are good ('excellent' says a 2011 visitor). There is night skiing Tuesday to Saturday evenings on four slopes ('great because you can carry on skiing past the 3pm or 3.30pm finish of most Canadian resorts', says a reporter).

Fast lifts The lifts from the village and the Gem Lake lift are all fast. But the other upper lifts are tediously slow.

Queues Queues are very rare.

Terrain parks Served by a double chair and snowmaking, the excellent Telus park includes two 10ft and two 16ft boxes, rails and hits for all levels, four new progression features, a half-pipe and a boardercross, and is highly praised by reporters. The park is open for night riding Thursday to Saturday.

Snow reliability Big White has a reputation for great powder; average snowfall is about 300 inches, which is similar to many Colorado resorts. One reporter points out that most slopes face south-west to south-east and the snow can suffer in periods of sunshine; but on each of our three visits, it snowed practically non-stop and we hardly saw the sun.

Experts The Cliff Area at the top right of the ski area is of serious double black diamond pitch; the runs are short, but you can ski them repeatedly using the Cliff chair. Sun-Rype bowl at the opposite edge of the ski area is more forgiving ('excellent place to ski deep powder' says a 2011 reporter). There are some long blacks off the Gem Lake chair and several shorter ones off the Powder and Falcon chairs. There are glades to explore and bump runs too.

Big White

Interactive resort shortlist builder at **www.wtss.co.uk**

UK PACKAGES

Alpine Answers,
AmeriCan Ski, Canadian
Affair, Frontier, Neilson,
PowderBeds, Ski
Independence, Ski Line,
Ski Safari, Skiworld

Central reservations
Call 765 8888; toll-
free (within Canada)
1 800 663 2772
Phone numbers
From distant parts of
Canada, add the
prefix 1 250; from
abroad, add +1 250

TOURIST OFFICE

www.bigwhite.com

BIG WHITE SKI RESORT / QUICKPICS

The traffic-free centre
and excellent
childcare facilities
make Big White very
good for families ↓

Intermediates The resort is excellent for cruisers and families, with long blues and greens all over the hill. Good intermediates will enjoy the easier blacks and some of the gladed runs too. There is marvellous easy skiing among the trees in the Black Forest area (which we loved when it was snowing) and among the snow ghosts (see 'Scenery'), which we loved when it was clear. Some of the blues off the Gem Lake chair are quite steep, narrow and challenging.

Beginners There's a good dedicated nursery area in the village and lots of long easy runs to progress to.

Snowboarding There's some excellent beginner and freeriding terrain with boarder-friendly chairlifts and few flat areas to worry about.

Cross-country A recent reporter enjoyed the 25km of 'great open spaces and wooded routes'. She found trail maps good but some of the signage poor.

Mountain restaurants There aren't any – it's back to the bottom for lunch.

School and guides We receive rave reviews from reporters for both adult and children's lessons. Last year a reporter had 'fabulous value snowboard lessons' booked through a tour operator and his six-year-old 'made fantastic progress on black moguls and in the trees (with only one other child in his group lessons)'.

Families The excellent day care centre was expanded in 2010. It takes children from 18 months and different ages have separate activities. Evening activities are organised too.

STAYING THERE

A good range of accommodation is featured by specialist tour operators Frontier Ski and Ski Independence. A 2011 visitor found the supermarket 'ludicrously expensive'.

Hotels Chateau Big White is our reporters' favourite: 'excellent location', 'big rooms and condos', 'cosy fires'. The White Crystal Inn receives better reviews than the Inn at Big White.

Apartments Condo standards are high. Stonebridge and Towering Pines are both central, with big rooms, well furnished, private hot tubs on the balconies. Other reporter tips include Black Bear and (a bit less luxurious) Eagles and Whitefoot Lodge.

Eating out We had a superb meal at the 6 Degrees bistro, sharing delicious dishes (tapas-style). We've also had good meals in the Swiss Bear in the Chateau Big White and the Kettle Valley Steakhouse at Happy Valley ('steaks perfectly cooked', says a reporter). Reporters also recommend the 'charming' upstairs restaurant at Snowshoe Sam's.

Après-ski On the ground floor, Snowshoe Sam's is a bar with a DJ and live entertainment. Gigi's is a 'cool' bar with comfy chairs and sofas, wood flooring, a restaurant and live music.

Off the slopes Happy Valley is a great area for families, with ice skating, snowmobiling, snow biking, tubing, dog sledding, sleigh rides, snowshoeing and an ice climbing tower. There are two spas and a shopping shuttle to Kelowna.

Fernie

Lots of snow and lots of steeps – one of our favourites, with a choice of convenient base lodging or a valley town

RATINGS

The mountains

Extent	★★★
Fast lifts	★★
Queues	★★★★
Terrain p'ks	★★
Snow	★★★★
Expert	★★★★★
Intermediate	★★
Beginner	★★★★
Boarder	★★★
X-country	★★★
Restaurants	★
Schools	★★★★
Families	★★★★

The resort

Charm	★★
Convenience	★★★★
Scenery	★★★
Eating out	★★★
Après-ski	★★★
Off-slope	★★

RPI	125
lift pass	£320
ski hire	£150
lessons	£130
food & drink	£120
total	**£720**

NEWS

2010/11: Signage and grooming was improved as was access to several runs, including 'Sky Dive'. A new family private lesson programme was introduced and also more activities for the children's fun area.

+ Good snow record, with less chance of rain than at Whistler (and less chance of Arctic temperatures than at resorts up in the Rockies)

+ Great terrain for those who like it steep and deep; good for confident intermediates too

+ Snowcat operations nearby

+ Some good on-slope accommodation available, but ...

− Mountain resort is very limited

− Access to many excellent runs is via slow lifts and long traverses

− After a dump it can take time to make the bowls safe

− Limited groomed cruising

− On-mountain signposting needs further improvement

− One basic mountain restaurant

Fernie has long had cult status among Alberta and British Columbia skiers. It now attracts quite a few British visitors, and the reports we get are almost all positive. Like us, reporters are impressed by the adventurous nature of the skiing – it's mostly ungroomed, and much of it is steep, with a lot of lightly wooded slopes (not common in Europe). Curiously, it's now quite a good resort for novices, too. Cautious intermediates unhappy about giving the ungroomed terrain a go are the ones who need to look elsewhere.

Fernie town, a couple of miles from the lift base, has few of the usual tourist trappings, but makes an amusing change from the ski resort norm.

THE RESORT

Fernie Alpine Resort is set a little way up the mountainside from the flat Elk Valley floor and a couple of miles from the little town of Fernie. Outings to Kimberley are possible; a coach goes weekly, taking about 90 minutes.

VILLAGE CHARM ★★
Unpretentious small town
A slope-side resort has grown from very little in recent years, but there's still not much there except convenient lodging and a few restaurants, bars and small shops. It is quiet at night. There's much more going on in the town of Fernie, named after William Fernie – a prospector who discovered coal here and triggered a boom in the early 1900s. Much of the town was destroyed by fire in 1908, but some buildings survived.

Fernie is primarily a place for locals, not tourists. There are some lively bars, decent places to eat and good outdoors equipment shops. It is down to earth rather than charming, and reporters' reactions to it vary: some like staying in a 'real' town while others are unhappy about the highway that runs through it. Most stress the friendliness of the locals.

CONVENIENCE ★★★★
Base lodging or bus ride
There is accommodation at the resort and in town. Buses between town and mountain run hourly (half-hourly in the evening) and cost C$3 one way. They run until 2.30am on Thurs, Fri and Sat nights. Each hotel has specific pick-up times. A 2010 visitor found the drivers 'happy to be flagged down'.

SCENERY ★★★
The rocky ridges are impressive
Fernie's two main peaks, Grizzly and Polar, are part of the steep-sided Lizard Range. They provide an impressively rocky backdrop. There are good views across the Elk Valley too.

THE MOUNTAINS

Fernie's 2,500 acres pack in a lot of variety, from superb green terrain at the bottom to ungroomed chutes and huge numbers of steep runs in the trees. Quite a few runs go directly down the fall line.

EXTENT OF THE SLOPES ★★★
Bowl after bowl
What you see when you arrive at the lift base is a trio of impressive mogul slopes towering above you. These

On our 2010 visit we were delighted to find, after years of complaining about the dreadful piste map and inadequate on-mountain signposting, that both had at last been improved. The new map is bigger, with the different bowls clearly marked. Big new signs clearly mark each bowl at the top of the access lifts. And there are new signs to mark the runs – but only at the start of each run. You're likely to miss some of them because they are set ludicrously high in trees and almost hidden.

So things have improved, but more signs are needed to mark key traverses (especially through the trees) and directions once you have embarked on a run. Finding some of the runs marked on the map is still very difficult, and you can easily end up in tight trees on slopes of triple-diamond steepness – as we did on an earlier visit. For the moment, at least, to explore the best of Fernie's steep terrain you need guidance. Guides have taken us to runs that we'd never have found on our own.

One solution is to join a two-day Steep and Deep camp early in your stay (read 'Schools and guides').

WESTERN CANADA

634

KEY FACTS

Resort	1065m
	3,490ft
Slopes	1065-1925m
	3,490-6,320ft
Lifts	9
Pistes	2,504 acres
Green	30%
Blue	40%
Black	30%
Snowmaking	15%

excellent black runs exemplify one of the weaknesses of Fernie's lift system: to get to them you must ride lifts way off to the left or right, and then make long traverses to get to the start of the runs proper – a slow business.

The slow Deer chair approaches the foot of black slopes, but goes no further. It serves the main green-run novices' zone.

On the right, riding the slow Elk quad followed by the fast Great Bear quad takes you to the junction where **Lizard Bowl** meets **Cedar Bowl**. You can traverse across both of these and drop down into the bowls pretty much wherever you like. Both have trails marked on the piste map but are ski-anywhere terrain among open snowfields and lightly wooded slopes. At the far side of Cedar Bowl are steeper runs among tighter trees from Snake Ridge. The Haul Back T-bar brings you out of Cedar to ride the Boomerang chair. This serves a mini-bowl between Lizard and Cedar.

Off to the left, the Timber Bowl fast quad chair gives access to **Siberia Bowl** and the lower part of **Timber Bowl**. But for access to the higher slopes of Timber Bowl and to **Currie Bowl** you must take the slow White Pass quad. A long traverse from the top gets you to the steeper slopes on the flanks of Currie (our favourite area). If you descend Currie you have to go right to the lift base, and it takes quite a while to get back up.

Free daily two-hour mountain tours are available, but they only scratch the surface (read the feature panel above).

FAST LIFTS ★★✰✰✰
A poor show
There are only two fast chairs, serving opposite ends of the mountain. And only one of them goes up from the resort base area. Slow chairs and a draglift elsewhere make getting around a slow process. Even so you may spend more time traversing through forest than riding lifts.

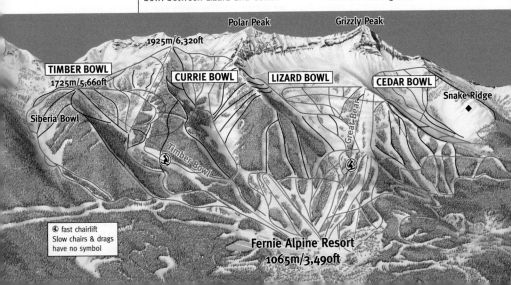

Polar Peak

Grizzly Peak

1925m/6,320ft

TIMBER BOWL
1725m/5,660ft

CURRIE BOWL

LIZARD BOWL

CEDAR BOWL

Snake Ridge

Siberia Bowl

Timber Bowl

Great Bear

④ fast chairlift
Slow chairs & drags
have no symbol

Fernie Alpine Resort
1065m/3,490ft

LIFT PASSES

Fernie

Prices in C$

Age	1-day	6-day
under 13	26	157
13 to 17	57	340
18 to 64	80	480
over 65	64	384

Free under 6

Beginner rental, limited pass and tuition deals

Notes
Prices include taxes; half-day pass available

QUEUES ★★★★
Not usually a problem

Queues are generally rare unless there are weekend crowds from Calgary or heavy snow keeps part of the mountain closed. But people complain about the slow chairlifts, and about breakdowns on one or two.

TERRAIN PARKS ★★
Just a rail park

Fernie no longer builds a traditional park. Instead, there is a patrolled rail park beside the Great Bear Express – you'll need a special pass (C$5 per day) and must sign a waiver to use it. The park was expanded for 2010 and new rails and boxes of various sizes, for all levels, were added.

SNOW RELIABILITY ★★★★
A key part of the appeal

Fernie has an excellent snow record – with an average of 350 inches per year, better than practically anywhere in Colorado. But the altitude is modest: rain is not unknown, and in warmer weather the lower slopes can suffer. Too much snow can be a problem, with the high bowls prone to closure – we've had reports of them being shut all week. Snowmaking has

been increased over recent years and now covers most of the base area. Piste grooming has also been increased; we have been impressed with it on our most recent visits.

FOR EXPERTS ★★★★★
Wonderful with guidance

The combination of heavy snowfalls and abundant steep terrain with the shelter of trees makes this a superb mountain for good skiers, so long as you know where you are going. Read the feature panel on the left. It has taken us half a dozen visits to get to know the mountain reasonably well.

There are about a dozen identifiable faces offering genuine black or double black slopes, each of them with several alternative ways down and all worth exploring. Pay attention to the diamonds: the singles are usually pretty tough, and the doubles are serious. Even where the trail map shows trees to be sparse, expect them to be close together, and where there aren't any, expect alder bushes to be protruding unless there's lots of snow.

There are a couple of areas where you can do laps fairly efficiently, but mostly you have to put up with a cycle of long traverse-descent-runout-lift-lift on each lap.

There are backcountry routes you can take with guidance (some include an overnight camp) and snowcat operations in other nearby mountains – read the feature panel overleaf. A regular reporter especially enjoyed exploring Fish Bowl, a short hike outside the resort boundary from Cedar Bowl.

FOR INTERMEDIATES ★★
Getting better

When we first visited, only the green and blue runs on the lower mountain were groomed. But things have moved on, as the resort tries to cater for a wider clientele. On our more recent visits a few runs from the top have been groomed, including some great blue cruisers down Lizard Bowl – easily reached using the fast Great Bear quad. But it doesn't add up to much, and if you are not happy to try some of the easier ungroomed terrain in the bowls and glades, we'd recommend you go elsewhere. For the adventurous willing to give the powder a go, though, Fernie should be on your shortlist.

UK PACKAGES

Alpine Answers,
AmeriCan Ski, Canadian
Affair, Canadian
Powder Tours, Crystal,
Frontier, Independent
Ski Links, Inghams,
Interactive Resorts,
Neilson, Ski
Independence, Ski
Safari, Skitracer,
Skiworld, Snow Finders

GETTING THERE

Air Calgary 340km/210
miles (4hr15)

RESORTS OF THE CANADIAN
ROCKIES INC (RCR) / MARK
SHANNON

At least the one
mountain restaurant is
nicely designed, and
in prime position ↓

FOR BEGINNERS ★★★★☆
Surprisingly, pretty good
There's a good nursery area served by
two lifts (a moving carpet and a drag),
and the lower mountain served by the
Deer and Elk chairs has lots of wide,
smooth trails to gain confidence on.
But the green runs from the top of the
mountain are usually cat-tracks, which
nonetheless have tough parts to them.

FOR BOARDERS ★★★☆☆
Fine if you're good
Fernie is a fine place for good
boarders (and there are a lot of local
experts here). Lots of natural gullies,
hits and endless off-piste
opportunities – including some
adrenalin-pumping tree runs and knee-
deep powder bowls – will keep
freeriders of all abilities grinning from
ear to ear. But there's a lot of
traversing involved to get to many of
the best runs – hard work in fresh
snow and bumpy later. The main
board shops, Board Stiff and Edge of
the World, are in downtown Fernie, the
latter with an indoor skate park to use
while your board gets tuned. It's not a
brilliant place for freestylers – the
terrain park has gone and been
replaced by a smaller rail park, for
which you'll need a special pass.

FOR CROSS-COUNTRY ★★★☆☆
Some possibilities
There are 10km of trails in the forest
adjacent to the resort. In the Fernie
area as a whole there are around
50km of tracks.

MOUNTAIN RESTAURANTS ★☆☆☆☆
One tiny sit-down place
Lost Boys Cafe is a tiny self-service
place in a fine position at the top of
Timber Bowl with a basic, limited
menu but 'excellent chilli' as well as
'breathtaking views'. Bear's Den at the
top of the Elk chair is an open-air fast-
food kiosk.

Naturally, most people eat at the
base area. The ancient no-frills Day
Lodge serves soups, burgers and daily
specials. Snow Creek Cafe is handy for
the nursery slopes. Look at 'Eating
out' to see other options.

SCHOOLS AND GUIDES ★★★★☆
Highly praised
Reporters praise the school, which
seems to achieve rapid progress – no
doubt partly because groups are often
very small. A 2010 visitor was very
happy with his 'really brilliant' private
lessons, but also noted that class
sizes are often very small, making
group lessons very good value.

There are several programmes to
help you get the best out of the
mountain. The Steep and Deep camp
has had good feedback; it is a two-
day programme (C$299) where you get
technique tips while exploring steep
terrain – a great way to get to know at
least some of the mountain. We've had
good sessions being guided by some
of their instructor-guides. 'First Tracks'
(C$269 for three people) is a two-hour
private lesson that gets you up the
mountain at 8am, before the lifts are
open to others.

RIDE THE SNOWCATS – HELI-SKIING AT AN AFFORDABLE PRICE

Good skiers who relish off-piste should consider treating themselves to some cat skiing, where you ride snowcats instead of lifts; there are several operations in this area. In 2010 we had two fabulous days at Island Lake Lodge (423 3700) which does all-inclusive packages in a luxury lodge (spacious rooms, big lounge, three hot tubs, bar, excellent food) 10km from Fernie, reached only by snowcat, amid 7,000 acres of spectacular bowls and ridges. It has 26 rooms and four cats. In a day you might do 10 to 14 powder runs averaging 500m vertical, taking in all kinds of terrain from gentle open slopes to some very Alpine adventures. You can do single days on a standby basis. Fernie Wilderness Adventures (877 423 6704) has three cats accessing 3,000 acres.

SCHOOLS
Fernie Telus
t 423 2406

Classes
Full day C$125 (incl. taxes)
Private lessons
From C$209 (inc. taxes) for 2hr

CHILDCARE
Telus Resort Kids
t 423 2430
Age 18mnth to 6yr; 9am to 4pm

Ski school
For ages 6 to 12 (C$94 per day, inc. taxes)

ACTIVITIES
Indoor Museum, galleries, Aquatic Centre, fitness centre, ice rink, cinema, library, curling, climbing wall, brewery tour

Outdoor Walking, snowmobiling, dog sledding, sleigh rides, family treasure hunt, snowshoe excursions

Central reservations phone number
Call 1 877 333 2339 (toll-free from within Canada)

Phone numbers
From distant parts of Canada, add the prefix 1 250; from abroad, add the prefix +1 250

TOURIST OFFICE
www.skifernie.com

FOR FAMILIES ★★★★
Good day care centre
There's a day care centre in the Cornerstone Lodge. Once a week there's a craft night for children aged six to 12. And there's a Wilderness Adventure Park with cut-outs of bears and wolves. The ski school offers a 'family' private lesson option.

STAYING THERE

Fernie is increasingly easy to find in tour operator brochures.
Chalets Some UK tour operators run catered chalets.
Hotels and condos There's a wide choice, some impressively comfortable.
★★★★Lizard Creek Lodge Best ski-in/ski-out condo hotel: 'lovely, luxurious – a stand out', says a recent visitor. It has a spa, outdoor pool and hot tub.
★★★★Snow Creek Lodge Similar to the Lizard Creek Lodge.
★★★Wolf's Den Mountain Lodge At base of slope. 'Basic but convenient, and staff friendly' say reporters. Hot tub.
★★★★Best Western Fernie Mountain Lodge Next to golf course near town. Pool, hot tub, fitness room. But a 30-minute bus ride to the slopes.
Cornerstone Lodge Modern condo hotel – 'well equipped'.
Griz Inn Sport Hotel Condo hotel with good facilities. Pool.
Timberline Lodges Very comfortable condos a shuttle-ride from the lifts.
Alpine Lodge (423 4237) B&B on edge of resort. 'Homely and welcoming.'
Park Place Lodge On main highway; easy walk to centre of town, lively pub; pool and hot tub in main lobby.

EATING OUT ★★★
Better choice in town
At the base, there isn't a huge choice. The restaurant of Lizard Creek Lodge offers 'generous portions – lamb shank particularly good'. Yamagoya in the Alpine Lodge does Japanese ('good to eat some lighter food for a change',

'wonderful ice cream') . Kelsey's (part of a chain) serves standard and reliable steaks, burgers, pasta and pizza. The Corner Pocket at the Griz Inn offers stews and buffalo burgers at lunch, and a variety of bistro-style food in the evening – and it stays open after 9pm too.
In the town of Fernie, there are quite a few options. On our 2010 visit we had two excellent (though pricey) meals at the Picnic – innovative 'fine dining' including dishes to share, and cool surroundings (stone walls, wooden floors, waiters in black). We also enjoyed a simpler meal at the Brick House (burgers, grills) and various Asian cuisines at Curry Bowl. A 2011 visitor also recommends Indian food at the out-of-town Stanford hotel. Other reporter recommendations include the expensive Old Elevator (a converted grain store; 'sophisticated menu, friendly service'). Mezzaluna is Italian; Max at Park Place Lodge offers 'regional Canadian'.

APRES-SKI ★★★
Have a beer
When the lifts close head for the Griz Bar above the Day Lodge. During the week, the mountain resort bars are pretty quiet later on. In town, the bars of the Royal hotel are popular with locals and the Park Place Lodge Pub is usually busy.

OFF THE SLOPES ★★
Get out and about
The Arts Station has two galleries, a theatre and craft studios, and there is a walking tour of historic Fernie – you buy a C$5 self-guided booklet from the visitor information centre or retailers. An ice hockey game is 'well worth doing; good fun', says a 2010 reporter. There's a pool at the Aquatic Centre in town. But the main diversion is the great outdoors.

SNOWPIX.COM / CHRIS GILL

Kicking Horse

One of Canada's newest resorts: only a few lifts, but great powder at the top, and a small village at the base

TOP 10 RATINGS	
Extent	★★★
Fast lifts	★★★
Queues	★★★★
Snow	★★★★
Expert	★★★★
Intermediate	★★★
Beginner	★★★
Charm	★★
Convenience	★★★★
Scenery	★★★

RPI	130
lift pass	£300
ski hire	£135
lessons	£170
food & drink	£120
total	**£725**

➕ Great terrain for experts and some for adventurous intermediates

➕ Big vertical served by a fast lift

➕ Splendid mountain-top restaurant

➖ Resort village still small and quiet

➖ Gondola needs a mid-station to make the most of the mountain

➖ Few groomed intermediate runs

Ten years ago a long gondola was built, up to two high, powder-filled bowls – previously heli-skiing country. A year later a quad chairlift opened up a third bowl. Now, access has been created to a fourth. Meanwhile, a tiny resort village has developed at the base, with some cute lodgings. Good for a short stay, or outings from Banff or Lake Louise. But the single-stage gondola was a mistake.

THE RESORT

Eight miles from the logging town of Golden, beside the transcontinental highway and railway, Kicking Horse has grown much more slowly than was originally envisaged and still has only two main lifts and a tiny base village. Daily Powder Express buses run from Banff and Lake Louise – 2010/11 cost was C$93.45 including a lift pass.
Village charm The small resort village at the lift base now has several lodges, a few restaurants and bars, a ski shop and a general store. The town of Golden has no real appeal.
Convenience Fine if you stay at the mountain, and why not?
Scenery The scenery is not without drama – especially from the top.

THE MOUNTAINS

The lower two-thirds of the hill is wooded, with trails cut in the usual style. The upper third is a mix of open and lightly wooded slopes, with scores of ways down for experts through the bowls, chutes and trees.
Slopes The eight-seat gondola to Eagle's Eye takes you to the top in one stage of 1150m vertical. It serves two bowls and CPR Ridge, between them. You can do laps in Crystal Bowl on the slow chair to the slightly higher peak of Blue Heaven, which also accesses Feuz Bowl. But most of the high slopes lead you below this chair and, with no mid-station on the gondola, you have to make the full descent. If you are here to ski the powder at the top, this may be just tedious, but it may be worse – the snow conditions on the lower slopes may be poor. Super Bowl, newly opened last year, is accessed by a trail across the head of Bowl Over. We lack information on how strenuous or scary this trail is. Two chairlifts from near the base serve the lower runs that formed the original ski area. There are free mountain tours.
Fast lifts Just the gondola.
Queues We've had reports of serious weekend queues for the gondola in recent years. During the week, though, it's quiet.
Terrain park There's a small park on the lower slopes.

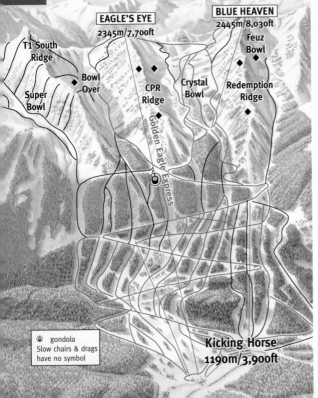

EAGLE'S EYE
2345m/7,700ft

BLUE HEAVEN
2445m/8,030ft

T1 South Ridge

Super Bowl

Bowl Over

CPR Ridge

Crystal Bowl

Feuz Bowl

Redemption Ridge

Golden Eagle Express

ⓖ gondola
Slow chairs & drags have no symbol

Kicking Horse
1190m/3,900ft

KEY FACTS

Resort	1190m
	3,900ft
Slopes	1190-2445m
	3,900-8,030ft
Lifts	5
Pistes	2,825 acres
Green	20%
Blue	20%
Black	60%
Snowmaking	Some

UK PACKAGES

Alpine Answers, AmeriCan Ski, Bramble Ski, Canadian Affair, Crystal, Frontier, Independent Ski Links, Neilson, PowderBeds, Ski Club Freshtracks, Ski Independence, Ski Safari, Skitracer, Skiworld

Central reservations
Call 439 5425
Phone numbers
From distant parts of Canada, add the prefix 1 250; from abroad, add the prefix +1 250

TOURIST OFFICE

www.kickinghorse resort.com

KICKING HORSE RESORT

The sunny, wooded slopes into Bowl Over are just our cup of tea, but there are also much more serious challenges ➔

Snow reliability An average of 275 inches of snow a year is not enough to put the resort in the top flight, but it's not far off. The top slopes usually have light, dry powder but the lower ones may have crud and thin cover.
Experts From the top, you can go north into the gentle Crystal Bowl via an easy piste, or via serious chutes from the ridge; or go south down pleasantly wooded single diamond slopes into Bowl Over. The top chair serves further single-diamond wooded slopes. Feuz Bowl offers various challenges, not all of genuine double-diamond steepness, and gets tracked out less quickly. The lower half of the mountain has short black runs cut through the woods, some with big moguls. There is heli-skiing nearby.
Intermediates Adventurous types will have a fine time learning to play in the powder from Blue Heaven down to Crystal Bowl. Most of it is open, but you can head off into trees if you want to. There is very little groomed cruising, though there is a top-to-bottom 10km winding green run. Timid intermediates should go elsewhere.
Beginners We can't imagine why a UK-based beginner would come here, but the beginner slopes are fine.
Snowboarding Freeriders will love this powder paradise.
Cross-country Dawn Mountain has loops of 30km, plus skating trails.
Mountain restaurants The Eagle's Eye at the top of the gondola is Canada's best mountain restaurant – excellent food and service in stylish log-cabin surroundings with splendid views. The Heaven's Door yurt (tent) in Crystal Bowl serves snacks; many people lunch at one of the lodges at the base.
Schools and guides A 2010 reporter found the free mountain tour 'really valuable'. She also took a group lesson which 'was worth every cent, a lot of fun and we learned a lot'.
Families The school teaches children from the age of three.

STAYING THERE

There are smart, quite large condo-style lodges on the slopes. But we'd choose to stay in one of three much more captivating family run places (each with about 10 rooms and outdoor hot tubs) a short walk away – described below.
Hotels The log-built Vagabond Lodge features a fabulous first-floor living room and comfortable, traditional-style

rooms ('combines the atmosphere of a European mountain refuge with the luxury of a North American 5-star resort'). Copper Horse Lodge has spacious but more austere rooms in modern styles. Highland Lodge has lovely hardwood furniture from India, a welcoming sitting room and a cosy, woody bar. In Golden, one reader has stayed at the Auberge Kicking Horse B&B twice ('good – and good value').
Apartments The Whispering Pines and the Selkirk Townhomes have been recommended.
Eating out Eagle's Eye at the top of the gondola opens on Friday and Saturday evenings ('excellent food but with prices to match'). Ronnie's Local Hero pub in Highland Lodge does modern Canadian cooking with a Scottish flavour ('very slow service'). Corks in Copper Horse Lodge does 'excellent food and friendly service'. Kuma is a sushi bar. In Golden, Kicking Horse Grill, Eleven22 ('fusion dining') and the out-of-town Cedar House are rated.
Après-ski Quiet. As a recent visitor says, 'It's a great resort if your idea of après is a meal, a drink and bed.' The liveliest place as the lifts close is reportedly Ronnie's Local Hero with its deck, blazing outdoor fireplace and music. In Golden the Mad Trapper and Golden Taps are lively bars.
Off the slopes There is snowmobiling, snowshoeing, dog sledding, tubing and an outdoor ice rink.

Lake Louise

Stunning views and the biggest ski area in the Banff region, with some good places to stay but no real village

RATINGS

The mountains

Extent	★★★
Fast lifts	★★★★
Queues	★★★★
Terrain p'ks	★★★★
Snow	★★★
Expert	★★★★
Intermediate	★★★★
Beginner	★★★
Boarder	★★★
X-country	★★★★★
Restaurants	★★
Schools	★★★★
Families	★★★★

The resort

Charm	★★★
Convenience	★
Scenery	★★★★
Eating out	★★
Après-ski	★★
Off-slope	★★★★

RPI   135

lift pass	£330
ski hire	£125
lessons	£175
food & drink	£125
total	**£755**

NEWS

2010/11: Alberta's first boardercross course opened here; it can be used to host FIS World Cup events.

640

- ➕ Spectacular high-mountain scenery, in a largely unspoilt wilderness
- ➕ Large ski area by local standards
- ➕ Snowy slopes of Sunshine Village within reach (see Banff chapter)
- ➕ Excellent very scenic cross-country

- ➖ 'Village' is just a few hotels and shops, quiet in the evening
- ➖ Slopes a drive or bus ride away
- ➖ Snowfall record modest
- ➖ Can be very cold, and the chairlifts have no covers

If you care more for scenery than for après-ski action, Lake Louise is worth considering for a holiday. We've seen a few spectacular mountain views, and the view from the Fairmont Chateau Lake Louise hotel of the Victoria Glacier across the frozen Lake Louise is as spectacular as they come: simply stunning.

Even if you prefer the more animated base of Banff, you'll want to make expeditions to Lake Louise during your holiday. It can't compete with Sunshine Village for quantity of snow, but it's an interesting mountain. And from the slopes you get a distant version of that stunning view.

THE RESORT

Lake Louise is small, but it's a resort of three distinct parts. First, there's the splendid lake itself overlooked by the huge Fairmont Chateau Lake Louise hotel. Then there's Lake Louise 'village' – a spacious collection of hotels, condos, petrol station, liquor store and a few shops a couple of miles away in the valley bottom. Finally, a mile or two across the valley, there's the lift base station.

Sunshine Village and Norquay ski areas (covered in our Banff chapter) are 45 minutes away by free buses and are covered by the three-area lift pass. Bus trips also run to the more distant resorts of Kicking Horse and Panorama, subject to demand, and there are heli-skiing day trips.

VILLAGE CHARM ★★★
Low key and relaxed
The 'village' has no focus other than a small shopping mall, but it's a quiet and relaxing place. Up at the lake, it's all about the setting: the scenery provides the charm, and somehow the scale of the giant hotel seems perfectly appropriate.

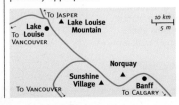

CONVENIENCE ★★★★★
Lake or village, not slopes
Most lodging is around the 'village'. Buses run every half hour to the ski area. Staying up at the Chateau, or near it, just means a longer bus ride. If you need to resort to taxis, they are said to be 'ridiculously expensive'.

SCENERY ★★★★
Splendid lakes and mountains
Lake Louise itself is in a spectacular setting beneath the Victoria Glacier. Tom Wilson, who discovered it in 1882, declared: 'As God is my judge, I never in all my exploration have seen such a matchless scene.' Neither have we. And it can be appreciated from many of the rooms of the hotel on the lake shore. And there are grand views of other peaks and glaciers, including Canada's Matterhorn lookalike, Mount Assiniboine, from the ski area.

THE MOUNTAINS

There's an attractive mixture of high, open slopes, low trails cut through forest and gladed slopes between the two. There are good free guided tours at 10am and 1.15. Louise is known for fiercely low temperatures; we've luckily escaped them on recent visits.

When conditions are poor, the ski patrol may erect temporary signs at the start of some blue runs indicating black difficulty – an interesting development.

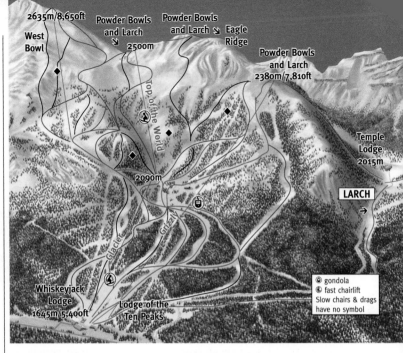

KEY FACTS	
Resort	1645m
	5,400ft
Sunshine, Norquay and Lake Louise, covered by the Tri-area pass	
Slopes	1630-2730m
	5,350-8,950ft
Lifts	26
Pistes	7,748 acres
Green	23%
Blue	39%
Black	38%
Snowmaking	24%
Lake Louise only	
Slopes	1645-2635m
	5,400-8,650ft
Lifts	9
Pistes	4,200 acres
Green	25%
Blue	45%
Black	30%
Snowmaking	40%

EXTENT OF THE SLOPES ★★★☆☆
A wide variety

The Lake Louise ski area is a fair size by North American standards – it ranks sixth in skiable area – but is quite modest by Alpine standards; a good intermediate could ski the groomed trails in a day or two.

From the base area you have a choice of a fast quad to mid-mountain, followed by a six-pack to the top centre of the **Front Side** (or South Face), or the gondola direct to a slightly lower point off to the right side. From both, as elsewhere, there's a choice of green, blue or black runs (good for a group of mixed abilities who want to keep meeting up). In poor visibility, the gondola is a better option, as the treeline goes almost to the top there. Or you can stay on the

lower part of the mountain using the chairs. From mid-mountain on the left, the long Summit draglift takes you to the high point of the area.

From here or the top chair you can go over the ridge and into the **Powder Bowls** – almost treeless, shady and mainly steep (though there are easy ways round the steep parts). From the top of the gondola, the Ptarmigan area is more wooded. From below the bowls you can take the Paradise lift back to the top again or go on down to Temple Lodge, base station of the Ptarmigan chair back to the main mountain and a fast chair to the separate **Larch** area. Its lift-served vertical is a modest 375m, but the sector has pretty wooded runs of all levels. From Temple Lodge there's a long green path back to the base area.

LIFT PASSES

Tri-area lift pass

Prices in C$

Age	1-day	6-day
under 13	26	166
13 to 17	58	448
18 to 64	80	504
over 65	58	448

Free under 6

Beginner lift, lesson and rental package

Notes

Day pass is for Lake Louise only; 3-day-plus pass covers all lifts and transport between Banff, Lake Louise, Norquay and Sunshine Village; prices include 5% tax

You get spectacular views from the slopes; here you can just see the frozen Lake Louise in the centre with the Fairmont Chateau hotel overlooking it ↓

FAST LIFTS ★★★★
Beware the cold rides
There is gondola and fast chair access to most of the slopes on the Front Side, and to Larch. The few slow lifts serve steep slopes where your descent may take some time, so the lift ride time is bearable. This is a famously cold resort, and reporters regularly complain of extremely cold rides.

QUEUES ★★★★
Not unknown
Half of the area's visitors come for the day from nearby cities, such as Calgary, so there can be queues for some lifts at weekends and public holidays ('up to 15 minutes at the base', says a 2011 visitor). More of a problem can be busy pistes and breakdowns.

TERRAIN PARKS ★★★★
Better every year
After a brief absence in 2008, the terrain park is improving year on year. The 2011 park featured 47 features set out in five clearly defined areas: warm-up, progression, medium, large and street-style, plus a new skier/boardercross (see 'News').

SNOW RELIABILITY ★★★
Usually OK
Lake Louise gets around 180 inches a year on the Front Side, which is not a lot, and nowhere near as much as Sunshine Village down the road (see Banff chapter). The front side faces south-west, which is not good; but the Powder Bowls face north-east, and Larch about north. Snowmaking covers 40% of the pistes. Grooming is fine.

FOR EXPERTS ★★★★
Widespread pleasure
There are plenty of steep slopes – but bear in mind that powder is less likely here than in many other Canadian resorts. On the Front Side, as well as a score of marked black-diamond trails in and above the trees, there is the alluring West Bowl, reached from the Summit drag – a wide, open expanse of snow outside the area boundary to be explored with a guide.

Inside the boundaries, the Powder Bowls area on the back side offers countless black mogul/powder runs, though there is no great variation in character. From the Summit drag, you can drop into The Ultimate Steeps (aka Whitehorn 2) if it is open, directly behind the peak – a row of exceptional chutes almost 1km long. Starting from the blue Boomerang trail, you can also access much tamer, wide, open slopes in Boomerang Bowl.

The Top of the World six-pack takes you to the very popular Paradise Bowl/Eagle Ridge/Quadra Ridge area, also served by its own triple chair on the back side – there are endless variants here, ranging from comfortably steep single diamonds to very challenging double diamonds. The seriously steep slope served by the Ptarmigan quad chair has great gladed terrain and is a good place to escape the crowds and find good snow.

The Larch area has some steep double-diamond stuff in the trees. And

SCHOOLS

Ski Big 3
t 1 886 760 7731
Lake Louise
t 522 1333

Classes (Big 3 prices)
3 days guided tuition
of the three areas
C$314 inc. tax
Private lessons
Half day (3hr) C$398,
inc. tax, for up to 5
people

CHILDCARE

Lake Louise Daycare
t 522 3555
Ages 18 days to 6yr;
8.30-4.30

Ski school
Takes ages 6 to 12 (3
days C$240, inc. tax
and lunch)

GETTING THERE

Air Calgary 195km/
120 miles (2hr30)

UK PACKAGES

Alpine Answers,
AmeriCan Ski, American
Ski Classics, Canadian
Affair, Carrier, Crystal,
Crystal Finest, Elegant
Resorts, First Choice,
Frontier, Funway
Holidays, Independent
Ski Links, Inghams,
Neilson, PowderBeds,
Ski Independence, Ski
Line, Ski Safari,
Skitracer, Skiworld,
Snow Finders,
Supertravel, Thomson,
Virgin Snow

with good snow cover, the open snowfields at the top are great for those with the energy to hike up.

Heli-skiing is available.

FOR INTERMEDIATES ★★★★☆
Some good cruising

Almost half the runs are classified as intermediate. But from the top of the Front Side the blue runs down are little more than paths in places, and there are very few blues or greens in the Powder Bowls. Once you get part-way down the Front Side the blues are much more interesting. And when groomed, the Men's and Ladies' Downhill black runs are great fast cruises on the lower half of the mountain. Juniper in the same area is a varied cruise. Meadowlark is a beautiful treelined single black run to the base area, curling away from the lifts – to find it from the Grizzly Express gondola, first follow the Eagle Meadows green. The Larch area has some short but ideal intermediate runs – and reporters have enjoyed the natural lumps and bumps of the aptly named blue, Rock Garden ('never had so much fun; really away from it all').

The adventurous should also try the blue Boomerang run – which starts with a short side-step up from the top of the Summit drag – and some of the ungroomed terrain in the Powder Bowls reachable from that run.

FOR BEGINNERS ★★★☆☆
Some long greens

Lake Louise offers first-timers a 'discover skiing or boarding' package that includes a lift pass, with a day or half-day tuition. There is a decent nursery area near the base, served by a short T-bar. You progress to the gentle, wide Wiwaxy (a designated and policed 'slow ski zone'), Pinecone Way and the slightly more difficult Deer Run or Eagle Meadows. The greens in the Powder Bowls and in the Larch area are worth trying for the views, though some do contain slightly steep pitches and can get busy ('our beginner was very nervous trying the Saddleback Bowl', said one past reporter).

FOR BOARDERS ★★★☆☆
Something for everyone

Lake Louise is a great mountain for freeriders, with plenty of challenging terrain in the bowls and glades. Beginners will have fun on the Front

Side's blue and green runs. But there's a T-bar at the base area and beware of the vicious Summit button lift (top left looking at the trail map). Also avoid the long, very gentle green run through the woods from Larch back to base. This is flat in places and a nightmare for boarders. Freestylers will enjoy the varied terrain park.

FOR CROSS-COUNTRY ★★★★★
High in quality and quantity

It's a very good area for cross-country, with around 80km of groomed trails in the National Park – plenty of scenic stops needed. There are 20km of excellent trails in the local area and at Lake Louise itself. An alternative is the secluded Emerald Lake Lodge, 40km away and with some lovely trails.

MOUNTAIN RESTAURANTS ★★☆☆☆
Good base facilities

There is only one proper mountain hut in winter. The Temple Lodge near the bottom of Larch and the Ptarmigan chair is a rustic style building with table- and self-service restaurants, but can get 'unpleasantly' crowded.

Most people eat at the base, where there are big-scale facilities. The World Cup Alpine Room in the Whiskyjack Lodge offers fixed-price, 'high quality' buffet lunches and 'good value' breakfasts. The Lodge of the Ten Peaks is a hugely impressive log-built affair with various 'fairly efficient' eating, drinking and lounging options.

SCHOOLS AND GUIDES ★★★★☆
More positive reports

Reports on the school are generally encouraging, both for adult and for children's classes: 'excellent private lessons'; 'great instructor who worked hard to make sure everyone in our mixed-ability group learnt new stuff'; 'the children made good progress and enjoyed themselves'. Be aware, though, that your instructor may change from day to day – a common arrangement in North America. See the Banff chapter for details of the excellent three-day, three-mountain Club Ski and Club Snowboard Program.

FOR FAMILIES ★★★★☆
Fairly positive

The resort is keen to attract families and has decent school and childcare facilities: 'Really well run; my son enjoyed the good mix of lessons and

Interactive resort shortlist builder at www.wtss.co.uk

↑ The Front Side of the mountain has mainly treelined groomed runs; the Powder Bowls on the back are mainly open and ungroomed
SKI BANFF-LAKE LOUISE-SUNSHINE / HENRY GEORGI

Weekly news updates and resort links at www.wtss.co.uk

ACTIVITIES

Indoor Mainly hotel-based pools, saunas and hot tubs

Outdoor Ice skating, walking, swimming in hot springs, sleigh rides, dog sledding, snowmobiling

Phone numbers
From distant parts of Canada, add the prefix 1 403; from abroad, add the prefix +1 403

TOURIST OFFICE

www.skilouise.com
www.SkiBig3.com

playtime,' says a recent visitor. Parents are lent free pagers too. The Minute Maid Wilderness Adventure Park is a kids' learning area at the base. The school gets good reviews and now offers a fun programme for teenagers.

STAYING THERE

You might like to consider a two-centre holiday, combining Lake Louise with, say, Banff or Kicking Horse.
Hotels Summer is the peak season here. Prices are much lower in winter.
*****Fairmont Chateau Lake Louise (522 3511) Grand monster with 500 rooms and seven restaurants in a fantastic setting with stunning views over frozen Lake Louise to the glacier beyond; shops, pool, hot tub, sauna.
****Post (522 3989) Small, relaxed, comfortable Relais & Châteaux place in the village, with excellent restaurant (huge wine list), pool, hot tub, steam room. Avoid rooms on railway side. 'Beautifully furnished; friendly, helpful staff; rooms small for a family.'
***Lake Louise Inn (522 3791) Cheaper option in the village, with pool, hot tub and sauna. Various suites. 'Comfortable, convenient and good breakfasts.'
***Deer Lodge (522 3991) Charming

old hotel next to the Chateau. 'Small rooms, but helpful staff; good food.' 'Amazing' roof-top hot tub.
Apartments Some are available but local shopping is limited. The Baker Creek Chalets (522 3761) are a popular retreat for a traditional 'log cabin, log fire, isolation and wildlife' experience.
At altitude Skoki Lodge (522 1347) is a charming log cabin, 11km on skis from Temple Lodge. Built in the 1930s, it sleeps 22. Reports welcome.

EATING OUT ★★☆☆☆
Limited choice
The Post hotel's restaurant has repeatedly impressed us and reporters with its ambitious food and excellent service – 'exceptional, if expensive', 'stunning lunch', 'very welcoming'. The Chateau has the top-notch Fairview Dining Room and the 'really good' Glacier Saloon ('sea chowder soup and bison pie both excellent'). Readers also like the Timberwolf Cafe (Italian) at the Lake Louise Inn, the Mountain restaurant (Thai curry, burgers) and Village Grill (Western/Chinese menu) for cheaper options.

APRES-SKI ★★☆☆☆
Lively at teatime, quiet later
At close of play there is some action in the main base lodge but the hub is the Kokanee Kabin, which has live music most weekends, outdoor fire and terrace. Later on, things are fairly quiet. Try the Glacier Saloon, in Chateau Lake Louise, the Explorer's Lounge in the Lake Louise Inn or the Outpost Pub in the Post hotel.

OFF THE SLOPES ★★★★☆
Beautiful scenery
Lake Louise makes a lovely, peaceful place to stay for someone who does not intend to hit the slopes but enjoys the great outdoors. The lake itself makes a stunning setting for walks, snowshoeing, cross-country skiing and ice skating. A reporter highly recommends the Wilson Icefield discovery tour – a helicopter flight, snowshoe walk and lunch ('barbecue with superb steaks'). There are lots of attractions around the Banff area too (see that chapter for more). Banff also has good touristy shopping.

Lake Louise is near one end of the Columbia Icefields Parkway, a three-hour drive to Jasper through National Parks – one of the world's most beautiful drives.

Revelstoke

New resort rapidly acquiring cult status for its steep terrain; shame it's so remote and without a proper village yet

➕ Fabulous, steep, ungroomed terrain

➕ Great cat- and heli-skiing

➕ Stunning views over frozen Columbia river

➕ Good-value lodging in town

➖ Not much intermediate terrain

➖ No snowmaking

➖ Very remote location; Revelstoke town unremarkable

➖ Resort base village still being built

Until 2007/08 Revelstoke was a small hill for locals served by one short lift. But a gondola and two fast chairs have transformed it into a resort with the biggest vertical in North America and around 3,000 acres of slopes, more than many Canadian rivals. Its terrain is mostly ungroomed and steep; if you enjoy adventure skiing, put it on your shortlist. Consider combining it with other resorts as a two- or three-centre holiday. There's a fledgling resort village at the base, but for now the best place to stay is Revelstoke town.

THE RESORT

Revelstoke is remote. Getting there from the UK involves two flights to get to Kelowna or Kamloops followed by a three-hour drive. Or it's a drive of five hours from Calgary, or six hours from Vancouver; and that's in good weather. The new Village at the base of the gondola will be a building site for the next few years. Better to stay in Revelstoke town for more choice of lodging and restaurants.

Village charm The town is North American grid pattern with a mix of unremarkable old and new buildings; It's a working town rather than a resort. A 2011 reporter confirms the base Village is 'still a building site'.
Convenience The mountain is a five-minute drive away. Shuttle-buses are 'regular and reliable'.
Scenery The views over the partly frozen Columbia river are stunning, as are the towering peaks rising up around the slopes.

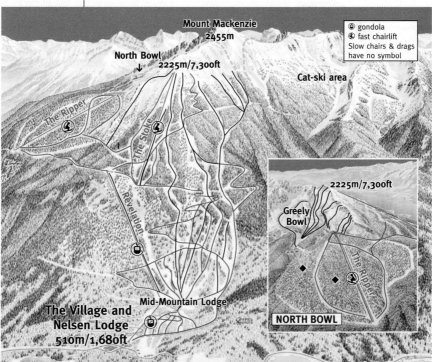

Long, deserted runs and great views over town and the Columbia river: two of Revelstoke's trademarks →

REVELSTOKE / MATTIAS FREDRIKSSON

NEWS

2011/12: Revelstoke will be offering a limited amount of backcountry 'sled skiing' – they take you and a buddy up by snowmobile, point out a run, meet you at the bottom and take you up again. For experts only.

2010/11: Another 100 acres of slopes was opened up, accessed from the Ripper Chair. Phase II of Nelsen Lodge at the foot of the mountain opened, doubling the amount of lodging available there. And facilities at the Mackenzie Outpost mountain hut were improved. A new shuttle-bus service (Revelstoke Connection) started from the resort to Kelowna and Calgary.

UK PACKAGES

Canadian Affair, Crystal, Frontier, Momentum, Neilson, Pure Powder, Ski Club Freshtracks, Ski Safari, Skiworld

Phone numbers
From distant parts of Canada add the prefix 1 250; from abroad use the prefix +1 250

TOURIST OFFICE

www.revelstoke
mountainresort.com

THE MOUNTAINS

A two-stage gondola takes you from the Village to mid-mountain, from which you can reach both the fast quads. The trail map marks black runs, but there's no single/double diamond differentiation. And reporters remark that lots of the runs are much longer than they appear from the map. Be prepared for extreme cold (–41°C with wind chill on our December visit; –27°C on a reporter's March visit).

Extent Its 3,121 acres make it bigger than most other Canadian resorts. It also has over 2,200 acres of cat-skiing, accessed directly from the slopes.

Fast lifts All three main lifts are fast.

Queues We have no reports of queues, even on a 'moderately busy Saturday'. Several readers said they had the trails all to themselves.

Terrain parks There isn't one.

Snow reliability They claim an average of 480 to 720 inches a year – up there with Alta and Snowbird. But there's no snowmaking and the lower slopes can suffer (and may be closed).

Experts Experts are flocking to Revelstoke. On skier's left, there are long top-to-bottom black runs, some of which turn into steep blues lower down; many are often groomed. On skier's right, North Bowl (reached by a long traverse) is a huge area of ungroomed, ski-anywhere, steep terrain. In between are several big areas of glades with nicely spaced trees. Then there's cat-skiing – we did a fabulous day of this; book up well in advance. There's 'sled skiing' (see 'News') and heli-skiing too.

Intermediates Most blues are steepish and suit adventurous intermediates best. The Ripper chair accesses the easiest blues. And there's a 15km-long blue/green run from top to bottom. But the intermediate terrain doesn't add up to much (the claimed 45% gives a misleading impression). The mountain suits experts best.

Beginners Go elsewhere.

Snowboarding There's fabulous freeriding terrain but lots of flats to negotiate, especially at the entry to and exit from North Bowl.

Cross-country 22km of groomed trails.

Mountain restaurants The Mid Mountain Lodge serves decent food but gets packed. Mackenzie Outpost, a small hut at the top of the gondola, does soup, snacks, drinks. Reporters like the 'stylish' Rockford Asian-fusion

restaurant at Nelsen Lodge.

Schools and guides The ski school programme is designed to help people progress from the groomed runs to the ungroomed and backcountry.

STAYING THERE

Hotels The first stage of the base village opened in 2009, but the area will be a building site for the next few years. Revelstoke has several motels and a few more charming B&Bs and hotels. We stayed at the Courthouse Inn (837 3369), which was friendly and did a great breakfast. Reporters have enjoyed the Inn on the River (837 3262) with 'great views over the river', the 'very comfortable' central Regent Inn (837 2107) which dates from the 1920s and the Hillcrest Hotel (837 3322) on the edge of town.

Eating out There are a few good coffee shops. For dinner, try Woolsey Creek and, in the Regent Inn, 112 (both 'fine dining'), Zala's ('nice halibut, pizzas'), Bad Paul's ('family-friendly, huge portions'), the Village Idiot ('popular, live music, burgers, pizzas, steaks, wraps'), and Kawakubo ('great sushi').

Après-ski 'Very quiet', but try the Village Idiot (see above), the Rockford (in the Village), Last Drop (comfy sofas, log fire; in Powder Springs Inn) and River City (music, pool; in Regent Inn). The Cabin has a bowling alley, and Traverse is a strip club.

Off the slopes The Aquatic Centre is 'excellent': pools, hot tubs, saunas.

Silver Star

Car-free, purpose-built village designed to resemble a Victorian-era mining town, with slopes for all standards

TOP 10 RATINGS

Extent	★★★
Fast lifts	★★★★
Queues	★★★★★
Snow	★★★★
Expert	★★★★
Intermediate	★★★
Beginner	★★★★
Charm	★★★
Convenience	★★★★★
Scenery	★★★

RPI	120
lift pass	£300
ski hire	£130
lessons	£130
food & drink	£120
total	**£680**

SILVER STAR MOUNTAIN RESORT / MORTEN BYSKOV

Silver Star's brightly coloured buildings give it a cheerful atmosphere ↓

➕ Cute, colourful village

➕ Very family-friendly

➕ Some good runs for all abilities

➕ Excellent cross-country skiing

➖ Tiny village; very quiet at night

➖ Limited choice of accommodation (but some high-quality condos)

➖ Ski area not huge

This quiet, family-friendly resort has a tiny traffic-free centre resembling a 19th-century mining town. There are slopes to suit everyone, and it's easy to combine a stay here with one at Big White, which has the same owners.

THE RESORT

Silver Star is a small, purpose-built resort right on the slopes. Big White (see separate chapter) is around two and a half hours away.
Village charm The village has brightly painted Victorian-style buildings with wooden sidewalks and faux gas lights. It's a bit Disneyesque but works well.
Convenience The centre is compact and car-free. Ski-in/ski-out chalets are dotted in the trees too.
Scenery The views from Silver Star's summit are over gently rolling hills.

THE MOUNTAINS

The mountain has trees going right to the top and four main linked sectors.
Slopes The Vance Creek area has mainly easy intermediate runs served by the Comet six-pack, which starts below the village. From there you can reach the Silver Woods area of mainly intermediate slopes and glades, served by a high-speed quad. The top of the Comet chair links to the Attridge area which has a mix of easy runs and short steep blacks served by its own slow chair too. It also links to the

647

NEWS

2011/12: Heli-skiing will be possible direct from the resort – expect six to eight runs in a day.

2010/11: The beginner terrain park was moved to the Silver Woods area. New rails and boxes were built near the village, for use mainly after the lifts close.

KEY FACTS

Resort	1610m
	5,280ft
Slopes	1155-1915m
	3,790-6,280ft
Lifts	10
Pistes	3,065 acres
Green	20%
Blue	50%
Black	30%
Snowmaking	none

UK PACKAGES

AmeriCan Ski, Canadian Affair, Frontier, Neilson, PowderBeds, Ski Independence, Ski Line, Ski Safari, Skiworld

Central reservations
Call 558 6083; toll-free (within Canada) 1 800 663 4431
Phone numbers
From distant parts of Canada, add the prefix 1 250; from abroad, add +1 250

TOURIST OFFICE

www.skisilverstar.com

Putnam Creek sector on the back side, which has lots of steep blacks and easier blues, all served by a fast quad.

Fast lifts There's one for each sector.

Queues 'No queues,' says a recent visitor. We skied here on a busy Saturday and waited a few minutes for the Comet chair at peak times but the trails were still delightfully deserted.

Terrain parks The 16-acre Telus park on the Vance Creek side is excellent and there's a beginner park on Silver Woods and a boardercross too.

Snow reliability Silver Star gets an average of 276 inches a year, not in the top flight but not far off.

Experts Putnam Creek has a dense network of single and double black diamond runs plunging through the trees, many of them mogul runs – 'in a league of its own' and 'some great steeps', say recent reporters. The runs to the left as you ride up the chair are north-facing and keep their snow well. There are some good short blacks in the Attridge area, too. For 2011/12 you can try heli-skiing (see 'News').

Intermediates Vance Creek has mainly easy cruising runs. Silver Woods has lovely runs cut through the trees and easy blue gladed runs amid the trees themselves. Putnam Creek also has excellent blue cruising. Good intermediates will appreciate the groomed black runs (they groom at least two each night – look on the boards for which they are).

Beginners There's a nursery area by the village with a moving carpet and long easy green runs to move on to.

Snowboarding Intermediates will enjoy the blue runs and glades. But the steep bump runs in Putnam Creek are tough. And there are some flat areas (including the way to Putnam Creek).

Cross-country They claim 'The Best Nordic Skiing in North America' and have over 100km of trails.

Mountain restaurants The small atmospheric table-service Paradise Camp on Putnam Creek is popular and serves good stews and soups.

Schools and guides The ski school has a good reputation. A recent reporter said, 'My wife was a beginner; after three half-days, she was skiing blue runs with great confidence.'

Families Star Kids takes children aged 18 months to six years. 'Our children loved it,' said a recent reporter.

STAYING THERE

It is mainly specialist North American operators who come here, such as Frontier Ski and Ski Independence.

Hotels Silver Star Club Resort has three separate properties including the Vance Creek right in the village centre. A 2010 reporter liked the Bulldog Hotel ('fairly basic rooms, fun bulldog pictures on the wall').

Apartments We loved the huge, luxurious condo with private hot tub in the Snowbird Lodge that we stayed in on our last visit. This and Firelight Lodge are the best in town, both ski-in/ski-out. Other recommendations include Chilcoot Lodge, Creekside, Grandview and Pinnacles.

Eating out Reporters' favourite is the Bulldog Grand Cafe (Asian-influenced food and 'ribs that melt in your mouth'). Other tips: Long John's Pub with mining theme decor, Isadore's and the Silver Grill & Chop House for fine dining, Bugaboos for breakfast.

Après-ski It's very quiet. But the Saloon and Den Bistro and Bar may be lively and have live entertainment.

Off the slopes There's a natural ice rink on a lake, tubing, snowshoeing and horse-drawn sleigh rides.

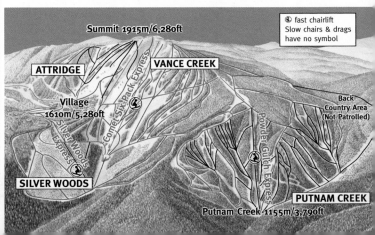

Sun Peaks

Attractive car-free village at the foot of three linked mountains with varied slopes including some unusual easy groomed glade runs

TOP 10 RATINGS

Extent	★★★
Fast lifts	★★
Queues	★★★★★
Snow	★★★★
Expert	★★★
Intermediate	★★★★
Beginner	★★★★
Charm	★★★
Convenience	★★★★
Scenery	★★★

➕ Great terrain for early intermediates

➕ Excellent glades

➕ Slopes very quiet during the week

➕ Good for families

➖ Village may be too small and quiet for some tastes

➖ Ski area modest by Alpine standards

Sun Peaks has sprung from the drawing board since the mid-1990s. It now has a friendly, attractive small village and a fair amount of varied terrain – enough for three or four days, say. We suggest combining it with resorts such as Whistler, Silver Star or Big White on a two- or three-centre trip.

RPI 125

lift pass	£310
ski hire	£125
lessons	£150
food & drink	£120
total	**£705**

NEWS

2011/12: The resort is celebrating the 50th anniversary of skiing on Tod Mountain this season and various events are being arranged.

THE RESORT

Until 1993 Sun Peaks was Tod Mountain, a local hill for the residents of nearby Kamloops. Since then the ski area has been expanded and a small (smaller than many reporters expect), attractive resort village developed. There are regular transfers to other resorts such as Whistler – making a two-centre trip easy.

Village charm The low-rise pastel-coloured buildings have a vaguely Tirolean feeling to them. It's a pleasant place to stroll around and very family-friendly. The traffic-free main street is lined with lodgings, restaurants and shops, including a smart art gallery, a 'fantastic' chocolate shop and a few coffee bars.

Convenience Much of the accommodation is ski-in/ski-out.

Scenery The slopes are pleasantly wooded and Mt Tod's modest summit gives views over gently rolling terrain.

THE MOUNTAINS

There are three linked mountains but the links to and from Mt Morrisey from the other two are roundabout and flattish. Free guided tours are run twice a day (9.15 and 1pm) and you can ski for free with Nancy Greene (former Olympic champion, Canada's Female Athlete of the 20th Century and a Canadian senator) when she's in town – don't miss it, she's great fun. At the top of all main lifts there is a board showing which pistes in that area have been groomed. Each day at least one single black diamond piste is groomed.

Slopes With almost 3,700 acres of skiable terrain, Sun Peaks is the second biggest ski area in British Columbia (Whistler is the biggest) – but it's not big by Alpine standards.

One lift goes from the centre of the village to mid-mountain on the resort's original ski hill, Mt Tod. This has mainly black runs, but there are easier blues and greens. Many of Mt Tod's steepest runs are served only by the slow Burfield quad which takes over 20 minutes to get to the top and is a frequent subject of complaint by reporters (there's a mid-station that allows you to ski the top runs only). Also reached from the village centre, the Sundance area has mainly blue and green cruising runs. Both Sundance and Tod have some great gladed areas to play in (12 of them marked on the trail map).

Mt Morrisey is reached by a long green run from the top of Sundance and has a delightful network of easy blue runs with trees left uncut in the trails, effectively making them groomed glade runs that even early intermediates can try.

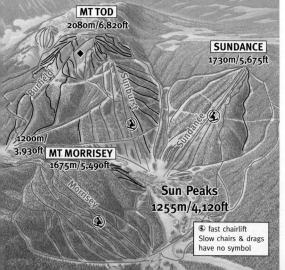

MT TOD
2080m/6,820ft

SUNDANCE
1730m/5,675ft

1200m/
3,930ft **MT MORRISEY**
1675m/5,490ft

Sun Peaks
1255m/4,120ft

④ fast chairlift
Slow chairs & drags
have no symbol

↑ Weekdays are generally pretty quiet on the pleasantly wooded slopes of Sun Peaks

SUN PEAKS / ADAM STEIN

KEY FACTS

Resort	1255m
	4,120ft
Slopes	1200-2080m
	3,930-6,820ft
Lifts	11
Pistes	3,678 acres
Green	10%
Blue	58%
Black	32%
Snowmaking	3%

UK PACKAGES

AmeriCan Ski, American Ski Classics, Canadian Affair, Erna Low, Frontier, Independent Ski Links, Neilson, PowderBeds, Ski Independence, Ski Line, Ski Safari, Skitracer, Skiworld, Snow Finders, Virgin Snow

Phone numbers
From distant parts of Canada, add the prefix 1 250; from abroad, add the prefix +1 250

TOURIST OFFICE

www.sunpeaksresort.
com

Fast lifts The three distinct sectors are each served by a high-speed quad. The other lifts are painfully slow.

Queues Weekdays are usually very quiet; it's only at peak weekends that you might find short queues.

Terrain parks The park has advanced, intermediate and beginner areas, served by snowmaking. But there is no half-pipe.

Snow reliability Sun Peaks gets an average snowfall of 220 inches a year: not in the top league but better than some. The snow can suffer on the lower part of Mt Tod's south-facing slopes, especially later in the season.

Experts Mt Tod has most of the steep terrain and you can ski some good (but short) steep and gladed runs without descending to the bottom by riding the Burfield quad from its mid-station, and the Crystal and Elevation chairs. Some of the blacks on Mt Morrisey (such as Static Cling) have steep mogul sections, too.

Intermediates This is great terrain for early intermediates, with the easy and charming groomed glades of Mt Morrisey, lovely swooping blues on Sundance and the long 5 Mile run from Mt Tod. More adventurous intermediates can also tackle the easier glades (such as Cahilty) and blacks (such as Peek-A-Boo).

Beginners There are nursery slopes right in the village centre, with long easy greens to progress to.

Snowboarding Boarders can explore the whole mountain. But beware the flat greens to and from Mt Morrisey.

Cross-country 30km of groomed trails and 14km of backcountry trails.

Mountain restaurants The Sunburst Lodge is the only option and gets busy; its cinnamon buns are highly recommended. The Umbrella Cafe at the Morrisey base serves hot soup and sandwiches and 'has the best toilets on the mountain'. And it's easy to

return to a village restaurant for lunch – Mountain High Pizza is 'great value'; Bento's Day Lodge has 'a good range of basic hot food and drinks'.

Schools and guides A recent visitor chose private lessons and 'found the instruction second to none and worth every cent'. Another reporter had a 'fantastic instructor' and was the only person in a group lesson. Her kids 'were happy', too, but her husband found that his lesson (with five others) was 'more like a guided tour'.

Families The play school takes children from 18 months to five years and the ski school children from three years.

STAYING THERE

There's a lot of self-catering accommodation as well as hotels.

Hotels Nancy Greene's Cahilty Lodge is a comfortable ski-in/ski-out base and you get the chance to ski with her and husband Al Raine (former Canadian ski team coach): 'It was great fun skiing with Nancy and Al; good rooms – a very welcoming hotel,' says a reporter. The ski-in/ski-out Delta Sun Peaks Resort (outdoor pool and hot tub) in the village centre is 'luxurious and lovely rooms'. We've enjoyed staying at both. Fireside Lodge has 'excellent facilities'. Heffley Boutique Inn is family run and 'comfortable'.

Apartments Delta Residences are 'luxurious, ski-in/ski-out and bang in the centre of the village'. Condos at Crystal Forest and McGillivray Creek have been recommended – some have private hot tubs. Other well-positioned condos include Forest Trails, Snow Creek Village and Timberline Village.

Eating out For a small resort, there's a good choice of restaurants. Reader tips include Powder Hounds ('great value', 'varied menu'), Steakhouse, Servus (more sophisticated food), Chopstixx (Japanese and Thai), Bella Italia and Mantles in the Delta Sun Peaks ('quality dining').

Après-ski A 2010 visitor found the 'nightlife a bit too quiet'. Bottom's, Masa's and Memories at the Cahilty (formerly Macker's Sports Grill) are the main après-ski bars. Morrisey's 'has a good selection of beers'. At weekends MackDaddy's nightclub in The Delta can get lively. There are fondue evenings with torchlit descents.

Off the slopes There's skating, tubing, tobogganing, snowmobiling, bungee trampolining, dog sledding, sleigh rides, snowshoeing and swimming.

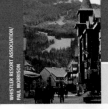

WHISTLER RESORT ASSOCIATION/
PAUL MORRISON

Whistler

North America's biggest mountain, with terrain to suit every standard and a big, purpose-built, largely car-free village

RATINGS

The mountains

Extent	★★★★
Fast lifts	★★★★★
Queues	★★
Terrain p'ks	★★★★★
Snow	★★★★
Expert	★★★★★
Intermediate	★★★★★
Beginner	★★★
Boarder	★★★★★
X-country	★★★
Restaurants	★★
Schools	★★★★★
Families	★★★★

The resort

Charm	★★★
Convenience	★★★★
Scenery	★★★
Eating out	★★★★★
Après-ski	★★★★
Off-slope	★★★

RPI　140

lift pass	£360
ski hire	£150
lessons	£170
food & drink	£120
total	**£800**

NEWS

2011/12: A piloted four-person bobsled ride will be on offer at the Whistler Sliding Center and speeds of 130km/hr will be possible.

2010/11: A new Olympic-sized super-pipe was added to the Blackcomb terrain park and four new snow-guns improved snowmaking in the park by 75%.

There are various new snack huts dotted around the mountains and the Raven's Nest restaurant reopened.

➕ North America's biggest, both in area and vertical (1610m)

➕ Excellent combination of high open bowls and woodland trails

➕ Good snow record

➕ Almost Alpine scenery

➕ Attractive modern village, purpose-built with car-free central areas

➕ Good range of village restaurants and lively après-ski

➖ Proximity to Pacific Ocean means a lot of cloudy weather, and rain at resort level is not unusual

➖ Inadequate lift system; queues can be a big problem at peak times

➖ Overcrowded runs also a problem

➖ Mountain restaurants are mostly no more than functional (and even attractive places are overcrowded)

➖ Resort restaurants over-busy, too

Whistler is unlike any other resort in North America. In some respects – the scale, the high bowls and glaciers, the scenery, the crowds – it is more like an Alpine resort. But like most resorts on the western side of North America, it offers the advantages of excellent snow and a lot of woodland runs as well.

All things considered, the mountain is about the best that North America has to offer, and for us a visit here is always a highlight of the season. But we'll admit that we are generally lucky with the weather, and haven't had to put up with much rain at resort level – a real hazard. And we time our visits to avoid peak periods and weekends, and therefore the worst of the crowds.

THE RESORT

Whistler Village sits at the foot of its two mountains, Whistler and Blackcomb, a scenic 113km drive from Vancouver on Canada's west coast.

Whistler started as a locals' ski area in 1966 at what is now Whistler Creek (aka Creekside).

Whistler Village, a 10-minute bus ride away, was developed in the late 1970s; Upper Village around the base of Blackcomb Mountain and a 10-minute walk from Whistler Village was started in the 1980s.

VILLAGE CHARM ★★★
High rise but tasteful
The three main centres are all traffic-free. The architecture is varied and, for a purpose-built resort, quite tasteful – but it is all a bit urban, with lots of blocks approaching 10 storeys high. There are also many chalet-style apartments on the hillsides. Some reporters find the central Village Square area noisy in the early hours.

CONVENIENCE ★★★★
Peak 2 Peak makes a difference
With the Peak 2 Peak gondola in place, Whistler Village, Upper Village and Creekside are all equally

convenient – you can easily access both mountains by taking a maximum of three lifts.

Whistler Village has most of the bars, restaurants and shops, and two gondolas (one to each mountain). A pedestrian bridge over an access road links the main centre to newer Whistler Village North, further from the lifts, making a huge car-free area of streets lined with shops, condos and restaurants.

Upper Village is much smaller and quieter. So is Creekside, which was revamped and expanded in preparation for its role as the Alpine finish area in the 2010 Olympics.

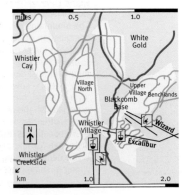

↑ The Roundhouse area at the top of the gondola up Whistler mountain. Just to the right of this pic is the Peak 2 Peak gondola link to Blackcomb

TOURISM WHISTLER / STEVE ROGERS

KEY FACTS

Resort	675m
	2,210ft
Altitude	650-2285m
	2,140-7,490ft
Lifts	37
Pistes	8,171 acres
Green	18%
Blue	55%
Black	27%
Snowmaking	7%

There is a free bus between central Whistler and Upper Village, but it can be just as quick to walk. Some lodging is a long way from the centre and means taking (inexpensive) buses or taxis. Some hotels have free buses, which will pick you up as well as take you to restaurants and nightlife.

SCENERY ★★★☆☆
Almost Alpine

There are splendid views of the deep Fitzsimmons Creek valley from both mountains – and especially from the Peak 2 Peak gondola (which goes right across it – the two cabins with glass floors are particularly spectacular). The upper slopes give good views to coastal sounds, high open bowls, glaciers and ridges.

THE MOUNTAINS

The mountains offer an excellent combination of high, open bowls and sheltered forest runs.

Many reporters enthuse about the mountain host service and the 'go slow' patrol – some find the latter 'over zealous', but crowded slopes, especially on the runs home, mean they're often needed; we approve.

Signposting is 'excellent' but the piste map 'can be difficult to read and is not detailed enough', and 'plain wrong in some places', say reporters.

EXTENT OF THE SLOPES ★★★★☆
The biggest in North America

Whistler and Blackcomb together form the biggest area of slopes, with the longest runs, in North America.

Whistler Mountain is accessed from Whistler Village by a two-stage, 10-person gondola that rises over 1100m to Roundhouse Lodge at mid-mountain. Or you can use two fast quads – if they are running (see feature panel opposite).

Runs down through the trees fan out from the gondola: cruises to the Emerald and Big Red chairs and longer runs to the gondola mid-station.

From Roundhouse you can see the jewel in Whistler's crown – magnificent open bowls, served by the fast Peak and Harmony quads. The bowl beyond Harmony is served by the Symphony quad. The bowls are mostly go-anywhere terrain for experts, but there are groomed trails, so anyone can appreciate the views. Roundhouse is the departure point of the Peak 2 Peak gondola to Blackcomb.

A six-seat gondola from Creekside also accesses Whistler Mountain.

Access to **Blackcomb** from Whistler Village is by an eight-seat gondola, followed by a fast quad. From the base of Blackcomb you take two consecutive fast quads up to the main Rendezvous restaurant – departure point of the Peak 2 Peak gondola. From Rendezvous you can also go left

LIFT PASSES

Whistler/Blackcomb

Prices in C$

Age	1-day	6-day
under 13	48	266
13 to 18	81	421
19 to 64	95	519
over 65	81	444

Free under 7

Beginner lift and lesson deal

Notes

Covers Whistler and Blackcomb mountains; prices include sales tax. 1-day price is window price; 6-day price is online advance purchase price

for great cruising terrain and the Glacier Express quad up to the Horstman Glacier area, or right for steeper slopes, the terrain park or the 7th Heaven chair. The 1610m vertical from the top of 7th Heaven to the base is the biggest in North America. A T-bar from the Horstman Glacier brings you (with a short hike) to the Blackcomb Glacier in the next valley – away from all lifts.

Fresh Tracks is a deal that allows you to ride up Whistler Mountain (at extra cost) from 7.30, have a buffet breakfast and get to the slopes as they open – very popular with many reporters. Free guided tours of each mountain are offered at 11.30.

FAST LIFTS ★★★★★
Can't cope with the crowds
The resort has more fast lifts than any other in north America. Gondolas provide the main access, with lots of fast chairs to both tops. But the chairs are all quads – none of the six-packs or eight seaters that are now common in the Alps – and can't handle the crowds (see 'Queues').

QUEUES ★★★★★
An ever-increasing problem
Whistler has become a victim of its own success. At peak periods (eg Christmas and New Year) and weekends when people pour in from Vancouver queues can be 'horrendous'. One exception is worth noting: February half-term week seems to be problem-free. There are displays of waiting times at different lifts, which readers generally find useful.

Some reporters have signed up with the ski school just to get lift priority. Others have visited Vancouver at the weekend to avoid the crowds.

The routes out of Whistler Village in the morning can be busy (we had a report of a queue of more than 200 metres for the gondola to Blackcomb). Creekside is less of a problem, but gets long queues at weekends. Some of the chairs higher up also produce long queues: the Harmony quad, especially, is no longer up to the job even when the resort as a whole is quiet (even the singles line can take ages); and the Emerald and Peak chairs are bottlenecks too – one report noted a 45-minute wait for the Peak chair on a Sunday in early January. We have had reports of lift closures – the Peak chair open 'only once during eleven days', with another visitor adding that 'on powder days, it wouldn't open until 11.30'. One reader found the Fitzsimmons and Garbanzo quads 'rarely open', despite queues for the gondola. Crowds on the slopes, especially the runs home, can be annoying, too.

TERRAIN PARKS ★★★★★
World class for all abilities
While both mountains have parks, freestylers tend to head to Blackcomb, which is home to the 2010 Olympic super-pipe (more than 137m-long with 5m-high walls, shaped daily), a mini-pipe with 3m-high walls, a real boardercross course and three terrain parks. There's a clear rating system in place, based on size (S, M, L, XL). On Blackcomb, novices should begin in the Terrain Garden. It features small rails and rollers to help you get a feel for airtime and improve your control. The M-L Nintendo park is vast, but is

HOW WHISTLER NEEDS TO IMPROVE

Whistler is one of our favourite North American resorts. But it has serious drawbacks that need to be addressed – many of them to do with overcrowding. This isn't just our view but that of many of our recent reporters too. The number of reports we've had this year has dropped to just one. Ten years ago we got over 20. Of course, this is partly to do with exchange rates and higher air fares making a holiday here pricier than it used to be. But we think it is partly because people are fed up with the resort's failure to get its act together. Our priorities would be:

* *Replace outdated fast quads with six-packs and eight-seaters to cut the appalling peak-period queues (see 'Queues')*

* *Restrict the number of day tickets sold (as Lech and Deer Valley do) to prevent serious overcrowding (on pistes as well as lifts)*

* *Keep the lifts open until later; closing at 3pm or 3.30pm in late February is ridiculous*

* *Open lifts that could relieve the pressure on others at busy times – eg the Fitzsimmons chair from the base of Whistler*

* *Groom more runs more of the time*

* *Build a new lift designed to serve Lower Peak to Creek and nearby runs in bad weather*

* *Encourage more restaurants to open, both on and off the mountain*

usually the busiest. With many step-up jumps, hips, tabletops, rails, boxes, this park will suit most intermediate to advanced riders. Very confident freestylers should hit the Highest Level Park (part of the Nintendo park); the fact that you need to sign a waiver, wear a helmet and buy a special pass indicates the size of the obstacles here. Over on Whistler mountain, the Habitat park by the Emerald chair has something for everyone, from beginner boxes, to medium jumps and jibs and 15m+ XL tabletops. There's the Couger beginners' park too.

SNOW RELIABILITY ★★★★☆
Excellent at altitude
Snow conditions at the top are usually excellent – the snowfall averages over 400 inches a year (that's way more than most Colorado resorts). And the last two seasons have been among the snowiest ever for the resort, with almost 600 inches recorded each year. But because the resort is low and

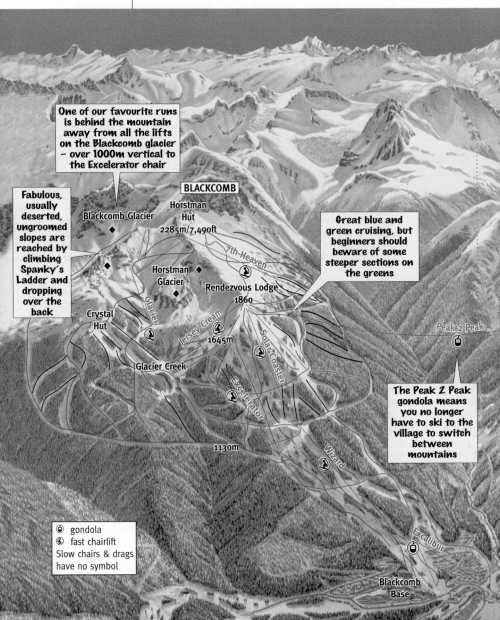

One of our favourite runs is behind the mountain away from all the lifts on the Blackcomb glacier – over 1000m vertical to the Excelerator chair

Fabulous, usually deserted, ungroomed slopes are reached by climbing Spanky's Ladder and dropping over the back

BLACKCOMB

Blackcomb Glacier

Horstman Hut
2285m/7,490ft

7th Heaven

Horstman Glacier

Rendezvous Lodge
1860

Crystal Hut

Glacier

Jersey Cream
1645m

Solar Coaster

Glacier Creek

Excelerator

1130m

Wizard

Great blue and green cruising, but beginners should beware of some steeper sections on the greens

Peak 2 Peak

The Peak 2 Peak gondola means you no longer have to ski to the village to switch between mountains

Excalibur

gondola
fast chairlift
Slow chairs & drags have no symbol

Blackcomb Base

close to the Pacific, the bottom slopes can have poor snow or slush – leading people to 'download' from the mid-stations, especially in late season.

Some reporters complain of 'poor' piste maintenance – 'quite shocking', says one visitor. 'Some runs said to have been groomed were clearly not.'

FOR EXPERTS ★★★★★
Few can rival it
Whistler Mountain's bowls are enough to keep experts happy for weeks. Each

has endless variations, with chutes and gullies of varied steepness and width. The biggest challenges are around Flute, Glacier, Whistler and West Bowls – you can go anywhere in these high, wide areas.

Blackcomb's steep slopes are not as extensive as Whistler's, but some are more challenging. From the top of the 7th Heaven lift, traverse to Xhiggy's Meadow for sunny bowl runs. If you're feeling brave, go in the opposite direction and drop into the

There's more terrain out here at the edge of the area than this map suggests – blue runs and easy glades as well as tougher stuff in Flute Bowl

The classic high bowls that first gave Whistler cult status among expert skiers in the 1980s and 1990s

The 1530m vertical Peak to Creek runs are excellent in good snow

Take the gondola from 7.30 for uncrowded fresh tracks skiing and a buffet breakfast

These Creekside runs were the 2010 Olympic downhill and Super G courses

WHISTLER MOUNTAIN
2180m/7,16oft

Rhapsody Bowl
Flute Bowl
Piccolo
Symphony Bowl
Symphony
Glacier Bowl
The Peak
Whistler Bowl
West Bowl
Bagel Bowl
Roundhouse Lodge
1850m
Harmony
Emerald
2 Peak
1595m
Big Red
1425m
Whistler Village
Garbanzo
Raven's Nest
1300m
Creekside
1005m
Fitzsimmons

Whistler Village
675m/2,21oft

Creekside
65om/2,140ft

extremely steep chutes down towards Glacier Creek, including the infamous 41° Couloir Extreme (which can have massive moguls at the top), Secret Bowl and the very steep Pakalolo couloir. Our favourite runs are the less frequented but also seriously steep bowls reached by a short hike up Spanky's Ladder, after taking the Glacier Express lift. You emerge after the hike at the top of a huge deserted area with several ways down; best to have a guide.

Both mountains have challenging trails through trees. The Peak to Creek area offers 400 acres below Whistler's West Bowl to Creekside.

There's also backcountry guiding, cat-skiing and heli-skiing available by the day. A recent reporter had 'two incredible days' with Powder Mountain cat-skiing. Other reporters used Coast Range mountain guides ('top-quality guides and superb skiing') and found the heli-skiing 'expensive but a great experience'. We recommend the two-day Extremely Canadian clinic (see 'Schools and guides') for getting the most out of the in-bounds steeps.

FOR INTERMEDIATES ★★★★★
Ideal and extensive terrain
Both mountains are an intermediate's paradise. In good weather, good intermediates will enjoy the easier slopes in the high bowls.

One of our favourite intermediate runs (though we concede the latter part is a bit tedious) is down the Blackcomb Glacier, from the top of the mountain to the Excelerator chair over 1000m below. This 5km run, away from all lifts, starts with a two-minute walk up from the top of the Showcase T-bar. Don't be put off by the 'Experts only' sign. You drop over the ridge into a wide bowl; traverse the slope to get to gentler gradients – descend too soon and you'll get a shock in the very

steep double-diamond Blowhole.

The blue runs served by the 7th Heaven chair are 'heavenly on a sunny day' – Hugh's Heaven is 'relatively empty' on weekdays and 'great for getting speed up'. Lower down there are lots of perfect cruising runs through the trees – ideal when the weather is bad.

On Whistler Mountain, the ridges and bowls served by the Harmony and Symphony quads have lots to offer – not only groomers but excellent terrain for experiments off-piste. Jeff's Ode to Joy provided a snowboarding reporter with 'lots of variety from Alpine to glade'. The Saddle run from the top of the Harmony Express lift is a favourite with many of our reporters, though it can get busy. The blue Highway 86 path, which skirts West Bowl from the Peak to Creek side, has beautiful views over a steep valley and across to the rather phallic Black Tusk mountain. The 7km-long Peak to Creek blue run itself is good too, especially when groomed – check before setting off. The green Burnt Stew Trail also has great views, and accesses lots of easy off-piste terrain.

Lower down the mountain there is a vast choice of groomed blue runs, with a series of fast chairs to bring you back up to the top of the gondola. It's a cruiser's paradise – especially the aptly named Ego Bowl. A great long run is the fabulous Dave Murray Downhill all the way from mid-mountain to the finish at Creekside – used as the 2010 Olympic men's downhill course. Although it is classed black, it's a wonderful fast and varied cruise when it has been groomed.

FOR BEGINNERS ★★★☆☆
OK if the sun shines
Whistler has excellent nursery slopes by the mid-station of the gondola, as does Blackcomb at the base area. Both have facilities higher up too. There is a lift pass and lesson deal for first-timers on certain dates, but no free lifts. The map has easy runs and slow zones marked.

On Whistler, there are some gentle runs from the top of the gondola. Their downside is other people speeding past. You can return to base by various chairs or continue on greens. On Blackcomb, there are green runs from the top to the bottom. The top parts are particularly gentle, with some steeper pitches lower down.

In general, greens can be trickier than in many North American resorts – steeper, busier and on the lower mountain in less good condition.

Another serious reservation is the weather. Beginners don't get a lot out of heavy snowfalls, and might be put off by rain.

FOR BOARDERS ★★★★★
Epic – winter and summer
Whistler has world-class terrain parks as well as epic terrain for freeriders: bowls with great powder and awesome steeps, steep gullies, tree runs, and shedloads of natural hits, wind lips and cliffs. There are mellow groomed runs ideal for beginners and intermediates, too, and the lifts are generally snowboard-friendly; there are T-bars on the glacier, but they're not vicious. The resort has as high a reputation for its summer snowboarding facilities and camps on the glacier as for its winter snowboarding, and the summertime Camp Of Champions is hugely popular. Specialist snowboard shops include Showcase and Katmandu Boards.

The 7th Heaven area on Blackcomb, seen from Whistler mountain. The run from the top to the base is 1610m vertical – the biggest in North America ↓

FOR CROSS-COUNTRY ★★★★★
Picturesque but low
There are over 32km of cross-country tracks around Lost Lake, starting by the river on the path between Whistler and Blackcomb. But it is low altitude here, so conditions can be unreliable. A specialist school, Cross-Country Connection (905 0071) offers lessons, tours and rental. Keen cross-country merchants can go to the Whistler Olympic Park and its 90km of trails (around 20 minutes away by car).

MOUNTAIN RESTAURANTS ★★★★★
Overcrowded
The main restaurants sell decent, good-value food but are charmless self-service stops with long queues; most get incredibly crowded. They're huge, but not huge enough. 'Seat-seekers' are employed to find you space, but success is not guaranteed. The piste map advises eating before 11.30 (sorry?) or after 1pm. Blackcomb has the Rendezvous, mainly a big (850-seat) self-service place but also home to Christine's, a table-service place that is the best on either mountain. Glacier Creek is a huge (1,496-seat) but better self-service place. Whistler has the gigantic (1,740-seat) Roundhouse, which a 2011 visitor thought 'offered a good selection but was pricey and food quality was hit and miss'; Steep's Grill is its unremarkable table-service refuge from the crowds.

There are smaller places, but they're still packed at normal times, and may be closed in early and late season. On Blackcomb are two tiny huts with great views, enjoyed by reporters – Crystal Hut ('amazing waffles') and Horstman Hut ('excellent goulash and mulled wine'). On Whistler, Raven's Nest is small, friendly and does soups, sandwiches and BBQs and the Chic Pea and Harmony Hut are other options.

SCHOOLS AND GUIDES ★★★★★
A great formula
Ski Esprit groups run for three to five days, combining instruction with guiding – with the same instructor daily (unusual for North America). Many of our reporters have enjoyed these groups (usually small). There are various specialist clinics and snowboard classes – the Supergroup classes have been recommended (maximum of three in a group).

Interactive resort shortlist builder at www.wtss.co.uk

SCHOOLS

Whistler and Blackcomb
t 904 7060

Classes
Full day from C$80.50
Private lessons
Half day (3hr) from C$379

Extremely Canadian
t 1 800 938 9656

GUIDES

Whistler Guides
t 938 9242

CHILDCARE

Whistler Kids
t 1 800 944 7853
Ages 18mnth to 4yr; non-skiing; C$85 per day

Ski school
Offers Adventure Camps for ages 3 to 12 and Teen Ski programmes for ages 13 to 18 (from C$398 for 5 days)

Extremely Canadian specialises in guiding and coaching in Whistler's steep and deep terrain and runs two-day clinics three times a week. We have been with them several times and have been impressed. A 2010 reporter said, 'A well spent C$400, whether you want to increase your skills/confidence or just ski some great terrain.'

Backcountry day trips or overnight touring are available with the Whistler Alpine Guides Bureau.

FOR FAMILIES ★★★★
Impressive
Blackcomb's base area has the slow-moving Magic chair to get children part-way up the mountain. Whistler's gondola mid-station has a splendid kids-only area. A reporter found the staff 'friendly, instilling confidence'. The school now uses the Flaik GPS real-time tracking system where each child's exact location is known at all times. There's a Children's Adventure Park and Magic Castle on Blackcomb. One reporter enthused about 'climb and dine', where kids combine dinner with a few hours at the Great Wall climbing centre.

STAYING THERE

Whistler has every kind of lodging you might want. Frontier Ski, Ski Independence and Whistler specialists Cold Comforts all offer an impressive range of hotels and apartments in and around the resort.
Chalets Skiworld has three luxurious chalets (all with outdoor hot tubs).
Hotels There is a wide range, including a lot of top-end places.
★★★★★Fairmont Chateau Whistler (938 8000) Well run, luxurious, at the foot of Blackcomb. We and reporters love it. Excellent spa with pools and tubs. The Gold floor is expensive and cosseting.
★★★★★Westin Resort & Spa (905 5640) Luxury all-suite hotel at the foot of Whistler mountain next to the lifts, with pools and hot tubs ('overcrowded though', says a reporter).
★★★★★Four Seasons (935 3400) Luxury hotel five minutes' walk from Blackcomb base, but with ski valet service at the base. Unremarkable public areas but good food. Good fitness/spa facilities.
★★★★Pan Pacific Mountainside (905 2999) Luxury, all-suite, at Whistler

ACTIVITIES

Indoor Sports arena (ice rink, pool, gym, squash), museum, art galleries, tennis, spa and health clubs, library, cinemas, climbing wall

Outdoor Flightseeing, snowshoeing, snowmobiling, sno-limo (chauffeur-driven motorised sled), walking, dog sledding, tubing, sleigh rides, bungee jumping, ziplining

GETTING THERE

Air Vancouver 135km/85 miles (2hr15)

UK PACKAGES

Alpine Answers, AmeriCan Ski, American Ski Classics, Canadian Affair, Carrier, Cold Comforts Lodging, Crystal, Crystal Finest, Elegant Resorts, Erna Low, First Choice, Frontier, Funway Holidays, Independent Ski Links, Inghams, Interactive Resorts, Kaluma, Momentum, Neilson, Oxford Ski Co, PowderBeds, Scott Dunn, Ski Club Freshtracks, Ski Expectations, Ski Independence, Ski Line, Ski Safari, Ski Solutions, Skitracer, Skiworld, Snow Finders, STC, Supertravel, Thomson, Virgin Snow

Phone numbers
From distant parts of Canada, add the prefix 1 604; from abroad, add the prefix +1 604

TOURIST OFFICE

www.whistler
blackcomb.com
www.tourismwhistler.
com

Village base. Pool/steam/hot tub. Recommended by a recent reporter.

****Crystal Lodge (932 2221) 'Comfortable, friendly, convenient'; in Whistler Village. Pool/sauna/hot tub.

****Glacier Lodge (905 4607) In Upper Village. Large rooms, 'good value'. 'Recommended.' Pool/hot tub.

****Sundial Boutique (932 2321) One and two bedroom suites. 'Great for groups and families, excellent location in Whistler Village.' Hot tubs.

***Lost Lake Lodge (580 6647) 'Excellent' place: studios and suites, out by the golf course. Pool/hot tub.

***Tantalus Resort Lodge (932 4146) In Whistler Village. 'Fine.' Shuttle service to lifts. Hot tub/sauna.

***Whistler Village Inn & Suites (932 4004) 'Great location, good sized rooms and enough breakfast to keep you going all morning.' Hot tub/sauna/ pool.

Apartments There are plenty of spacious, comfortable condominiums. Price tends to be dictated by location – ski-in/ski-out condos are pricier than those a shuttle ride from the lifts.

EATING OUT ★★★★★
Good but crowded

Reporters are enthusiastic about the range, quality and value of places to eat, but there aren't enough restaurant seats to meet demand. You have to book well ahead (which may mean months ahead in some cases). Or resign yourself to queuing for one of the bars that doesn't take bookings.

At the top of the market, the Rimrock Cafe near Whistler Creek serves 'outstanding seafood and game' and has several different small areas which makes it feel more intimate than many Whistler restaurants; we have eaten very well there.

In Whistler Village, Araxi is consistently good ('top quality for a special occasion'); the scallops and venison have been recommended. Il Caminetto di Umberto is a classy Italian with 'excellent food, worth the price'. And the pricey Ric's Grill does 'seafood and steak', as does the cheaper Keg. Mid-market places include: Quattro and The Old Spaghetti Factory for 'good pasta', Bocca ('casual, good bar food, excellent service'), 21 Steps ('excellent varied menu') and Earl's ('burgers, ribs, good microbeers'). Others to try are Sushi Village ('impressive quality for quite a simple place'), Mongolie (Asian),

---

Teppan (Japanese) and Kypriaki Norte (Greek). In Village North, Hy's Steakhouse and the lively Brewhouse are good for steaks and ribs etc.

In Upper Village, options are limited. Monk's Grill has 'good steaks'.

There are plenty of budget places, including the après-ski bars below.

APRES-SKI ★★★★
Something for most tastes

Whistler is very lively. We get most reviews on the Garibaldi Lift Company, which a 2010 visitor pronounces a favourite: 'Good atmosphere, but the tables are full by 3pm.' Other tips are the Brewhouse, Longhorn (with a terrace), Dubh Linn Gate Irish pub and Tapley's. Merlin's is the focus at Blackcomb base, with sports TV, beer 'by the pitcher' and 'good bar food'. Dusty's is the place at Creekside – good beer, loud music.

Later on, Buffalo Bill's is lively and loud. Tommy Africa's, Maxx Fish, the Savage Beagle, Garfinkel's and Moe Joe's are the main clubs.

OFF THE SLOPES ★★★
Quite a lot to do

Meadow Park Sports Centre has a full range of fitness facilities. There are several luxurious spas and an eight-screen cinema. Reporters recommend walks around the lake and the Great Wall Underground climbing centre. Ziptrek Ecotours offers tours on ziplines and suspension bridges through the forest between Whistler and Blackcomb mountains – 'great fun' says a reporter. You can also do ATV/ snowmobile trips and dog sledding. Excursions to Squamish (for eagle watching) and to Vancouver are easy. And non-slope users can get around the mountain easily (don't miss the Peak 2 Peak gondola for great views).

❄
Want to keep up to date?
Our website has weekly resort news throughout the year, and you can register for our monthly email newsletter – with special holiday offers, as well as resort news highlights.

Find out more at:

www.wtss.co.uk

Whistler

Interactive resort shortlist builder at **www.wtss.co.uk**

Eastern Canada

For us the main attraction of skiing or riding in eastern Canada is the French culture and language that are predominant in the province of Québec. It really feels like a different country from the rest of Canada. And the resorts are only a six-hour flight from the UK, compared with a 10-hour flight for western Canada.

Be prepared for variable snow conditions, including rock-hard pistes and ice; and be prepared for extreme cold in early and midwinter too; you might be lucky but you might not. But cold weather means the extensive snowmaking systems, common to all the resorts, can be effective for a long season. Don't go expecting light, dry powder – if that's what you want, head west.

UK PACKAGES

Tremblant *Alpine Answers, American Ski Classics, Carrier, Crystal, Crystal Finest, Erna Low, Frontier, Independent Ski Links, Inghams, Neilson, Ski Independence, Ski Safari, Ski Solutions, Skitracer, Skiworld, STC, Thomson, Virgin Snow*

For people heading on holiday for a week or more, eastern Canada really means the province of Québec, its capital, Québec City, and the main destination resort Tremblant (covered below) nearer Montreal. French culture and language dominates the region. Notices, menus, trail maps and so on are usually printed in both French and English. Many ski area workers are bilingual or only French-speaking. And French cuisine abounds.

Slopes in all resorts are small, both in extent and vertical. The weather is very variable, so the snow – though snowmaking pretty much guarantees it – varies enormously in quality.

Québec City makes a good base for access to several ski areas. Old Québec, at the city's heart, is North America's only walled city and is a World Heritage site. Within the city walls are narrow, winding streets and 17th- and 18th-century houses. It is situated right on the banks of the St Lawrence river. In January/February there is a famous two-week carnival, with an ice castle, snow sculptures, dog-sled and canoe races, parades and balls. But most of the winter is low season, with good-value rooms available in big hotels.

Stoneham is the closest ski area to Québec City, around 20 minutes away. The biggest and most varied resort is Mont-Ste-Anne 30 minutes away. Le Massif is around an hour away – a cult area with locals. These three resorts have extended entries in the resort directory at the back of the book.

KEY FACTS

Resort	265m
	870ft
Slopes	230-875m
	750-2,870ft
Lifts	14
Pistes	654 acres
Snow-guns	465 acres

TOURIST OFFICE

www.tremblant.ca

Tremblant

+ Charming, purpose-built core village
+ Some good runs for all abilities

− Very limited in extent
− Weekend queues and crowds

Tremblant is eastern Canada's leading destination ski resort, about 90 minutes' drive from Montreal.

The Intrawest core village is purpose-built in the cute style of old Québec, with buildings in vibrant colours and narrow, cobbled, traffic-free streets; it feels very French. There is a regular, free ski-bus and a local town service.

The slopes are pleasantly wooded. A heated gondola from the village takes you to the top of the so-called South Side. From here you can drop over the back onto the North Side. Most lifts are fast chairs. At weekends there can be queues, but they tend to move quickly. Half the runs are blacks; most are at the easier end of their grading, but there are bump runs and glades. There is good intermediate cruising and an excellent nursery area

with long, easy greens to progress to. One terrain park is aimed at advanced freestylers, another at beginners and there's a children's adventure area. There's 100km of cross-country.

Many people return to town for lunch, but the Grand Manitou at the top of the gondola has good views and decent food. Of the hotels, the Fairmont Tremblant is the most luxurious. There are ample condos. Restaurants and bars are plentiful. Try the Forge Grill, Ya'ooo Pizza Bar or the Loup-Garou at the Fairmont. The Shack brews its own beer. Off the slopes there is an 'expensive' pool complex, snowshoeing, skating, tubing etc. Reporters enjoy visiting Montreal.

Spain

RPI	95
lift pass	£210
ski hire	£135
lessons	£95
food & drink	£110
total	**£550**

UK PACKAGES

Baqueira-Beret *Crystal Finest, Neilson, Scott Dunn, Ski Miquel* **Formigal** *Crystal, Skitracer, Thomson, Zenith* **Sierra Nevada** *Crystal, Thomson*

+ Vibrant Spanish culture gives a different experience from the Alps
+ Low prices for food and drink
+ Few crowds outside peak times

− Access can be difficult, with lengthy drives to reach Pyrenean resorts
− Still lots of old lifts, but improving

Spanish resorts vary enormously, so it's difficult to generalise. Nearly all the main ones though are benefitting from recent investment. Getting there requires more effort, but when we visited Formigal recently we found a modern, well-equipped resort and varied terrain that compares favourably with many Alpine places. And at an appreciably lower cost, too.

The relatively low cost and the relaxed ambience of eating, posing and partying are key parts of the appeal of Spanish skiing. Ski resort infrastructure is improving and, as a result, international visitors are renewing an interest in Spanish resorts.

The majority of Spanish ski resorts are in the Pyrenees. The villages often lack the charm of some of their French neighbours, built more for convenience and day-trip visitors. But they do offer a wide range of lodging set in some of the Pyrenees' most stunning scenery.

There is a group of worthwhile resorts in the west, between Pau and Huesca. Formigal is now the largest, and making a steady comeback on the wider market. Candanchu and Astún nearby are popular on the Spanish market. The downside is access, which can be tricky from France if snowfall closes key mountain passes. There are long drives up from the Spanish airports too, but weekly charter flights to Huesca have cut some of the journey times.

In the south of Spain is the high resort of Sierra Nevada, a quite different experience and close to the coast – a two-centre trip is possible.

The other main group of resorts is just east of Andorra, including La Molina and Masella (Alp 2500). These have brief descriptions in the resort directory at the back of the book.

KEY FACTS

Resort	1500m
	4,920ft
Slopes	1500-2510m
	4,920-8,240ft
Lifts	33
Pistes	120km
Snow-guns	546 guns

TOURIST OFFICE

www.baqueira.es

Baqueira-Beret

+ Compact modern resort
+ Lots of good intermediate slopes

− Main village lacks atmosphere
− Still some old, slow lifts

Baqueira's village is not inspiring, but the resort has a well-linked and developing ski area that appeals to intermediates. Fine for beginners too.

Baqueira was purpose-built in the 1960s and has its fair share of drab high-rise blocks. The central area is clustered below the road that runs through to the high pass of Port de la Bonaigua, while the main lift base is just above it. The village is small enough for location not to be too much of an issue. And there are big car parks with shuttles to the lift base.

The slopes are split into three distinct but well-connected areas – Baqueira, Beret and Bonaigua – with long, intermediate runs, practically all of them on open, treeless slopes. Most are above 1800m, with extensive snowmaking, but afternoon sun is a problem in spring. There are fast chairs dotted around, including a long six-pack installed last season.

Experts will find few on-piste challenges, but there is extensive off-piste and four ungroomed itinerary runs. There are good nursery slopes with moving carpets at Beret, and at the top of the gondola – the blues there are on the tough side though. Queues are rarely of major concern. Reports of the ski school have been positive. The huts disappoint and lack variety but Pla de Beret and Bonaigua ('good pizza') have table-service.

There are good quality hotels: the 4-star Montarto and 5-star Rafael La Pleta are recommended. The better restaurants and bars are down the valley. Some hotels have pools and spas, but there is little else to amuse.

Formigal

KEY FACTS	
Resort	1550m
	5,090ft
Slopes	1500-2250m
	5,090-7,380ft
Lifts	21
Pistes	137km
Snow-guns	22%

TOURIST OFFICE

www.aramon.co.uk
www.formigal.com

+ Sizeable, varied area for all abilities
+ Seriously impressive terrain park
+ Linked valleys give sense of travel

- Traffic congestion in resort
- Wind-prone slopes, lacking trees

Formigal has the largest ski area in the Spanish Pyrenees, and varied terrain. Recent investment is slowly attracting more British visitors – reports welcome.

The resort is on the Spanish-French border at the Col de Portalet, which can be closed in heavy snowfall and prevent direct access from France.

The village, of purpose-built apartment blocks and smart hotels, is on the east side of the Tena valley. The central street is pleasant enough, with an attractive clocktower and replica church as its focus, but is spoiled by heavy traffic.

There are excellent free shuttles to and from the slopes, which span the west side of the valley and spread over four side valleys. Most are north- and south-facing treeless slopes, prone to wind. Grooming is good and snowmaking extensive. Queues are rare outside holiday periods. Sextas is the nearest of the four bases to the village, with an eight-seat chair. All four have big car parks and smart, US-style day lodges including big self-service restaurants. There are fast chairs linking the lower parts of each valley, and runs of each classification from the tops.

Experts have four freeride areas, plus heli-skiing. Many of the black runs could be red, though. The nursery slopes are excellent and there's a beginner lift pass. There are good intermediate runs; the gentle blue Rio

from Cantal to Sextas is ideal for the more timid. The only treelined run is a remote lovely cruise, quiet because access is by a long, slow chair.

Confident skiers can ride a snowcat above Portalet, which accesses remote runs and freeride terrain to Anayet. The huge terrain park is one of the best we've seen, and with a kids' mini-park and new boardercross. We enjoyed good Italian food at the Cantal Trattoria and the huts at Gemsbock and Sarrios were revamped this year, with new menus. The school has a good reputation. Families are well-catered for, with 'slow ski zones', fun trails and an Indian 'village'.

There is a choice of 3- and 4-star hotels (the Aragon Hills and Abba Formigal have pools and spas) and lots of apartments. There are over 30 restaurants, from Spanish to pizzerias. We had good gourmet food at the Vidocq. Après-ski is low-key but the Marchica bar at Sextas is lively at close of play. Later on, the Slalom and Cueva are popular discos.

Off-slope activities include dog sledding, floodlit toboganing and snowmobile outings up to a mountain hut. For a change, the 35km slopes at Panticosa (10km) offer good, varied terrain. Thermal baths are nearby.

Sierra Nevada

KEY FACTS	
Resort	2100m
	6,890ft
Slopes	2100-3,300
	6,890-10,830ft
Lifts	29
Pistes	103km
Snow-guns	350 guns

TOURIST OFFICE

www.sierranevada.es

+ Reasonably good snow record
+ Fine beginner slopes

- Exposed, and prone to wind
- Crowds at weekends

Despite its southerly position near Granada, Sierra Nevada is a high, modern resort with fairly extensive slopes. It gets its own weather, of course.

Pradollano is the hub, a stylish modern base with shops, restaurants and bars set around traffic-free open spaces. Most of the accommodation is in older, less smart buildings along a steeply winding road. A two-stage chairlift goes up the hillside, with red runs back down to the main lift stations – from where lifts go up to the mid-station at Borreguiles. There are four identifiable sectors, well linked, with a good range of intermediate and easy runs but not a

lot for experts. There are excellent nursery slopes and a terrain park. Weekends can be busy and queues may develop for some of the older lifts, especially the chair up the village slope. The home run can get crowded too. Sierra Nevada can have good snow years when the Alps has bad, and vice versa. Most slopes face north-west, but some get the afternoon sun. And when the wind blows, as it does, the slopes close; there are no trees.

Finland

- ➕ Good for families and beginners
- ➕ Ideal terrain for cross-country
- ➕ Reliable snow well into spring
- ➕ Chance of seeing Northern Lights

- ➖ Can be bitterly cold (and dark)
- ➖ Small ski areas lacking challenge
- ➖ Draglifts are the norm

For skiers with no appetite for the hustle and hassle of Alpine resorts in high season – perhaps especially for families – escaping to the white silence of Lapland can be an attractive alternative. Finland has the lion's share of Lapland and we started getting more reports on it – but they've more or less dried up. The resorts are small but rapidly developing both their ski areas and facilities.

The Arctic landscape of flat and gently rolling forest, countless lakes and the occasional treeless hill is a paradise for cross-country skiing.

It also offers good beginner and intermediate downhilling, albeit on a small scale. None of the areas has significant vertical by alpine standards, and in some cases it is seriously limited. The resorts usually open a few runs in late November. For two months in midwinter the sun does not rise – at least, not at sea level. Most areas have floodlit runs. The mountains do not open fully until mid-February, when a normal skiing day is possible and Finnish schools have holidays that usually coincide with ours – making it a busy time. Finland comes into its own at the end of the season, with friendlier temperatures and long daylight hours. Easter is extremely popular, and the slopes are crowded. If you're lucky you may see the Northern Lights – one March visitor saw them three times ('a great sight').

Conditions are usually hard-packed powder or fresh snow from the start of the season to the end (early May).

The temperature can be extremely variable, yo-yoing between zero and minus 30°C several times in a week. Fine days are the coldest, but the best for skiing: it may be 10 to 15 degrees warmer on the slopes than at valley level. 'Mild' days of cloud and wind are worse, and face masks are sold.

The staple Finnish lift is the T-bar; chairs and gondolas are rare. Pistes are wide and well maintained, as are nursery slopes. The Finns are great boarders and consider their terrain parks far superior to those in the Alps; super-pipes are increasingly common.

There are few mountain restaurants

– but you are never far from the base, with its self-service restaurants. The ski areas also have shelters or 'kotas' – log-built teepees with an open fire and a smoke hole – where you can warm up and cook your own food.

Ski school is good, with English widely spoken. All ski areas have indoor playrooms for small children, but they may be closed at weekends.

Excursions are common and generally very popular – husky-sledding, snowmobile safaris, a reindeer sleigh ride and tea with the Lapp drivers in their tent. Reporters are generally very enthusiastic about these off-slope adventures.

Hotels are self-contained resorts, large and practical rather than stylish, typically with a shop, a cafe, a bar with dance floor, and a pool and sauna with outdoor cooling-off area. Hotel supper is typically served no later than seven, sometimes followed by a children's disco or dancing to a live band. Finns usually prefer to stay in cabins, and tour operators offer the compromise of staying in a cabin but taking half-board at a nearby hotel. Cabins vary, but are mostly well equipped, with a sauna and drying cupboard as standard.

The main resorts are Levi and Ylläs, respectively 17km north and 50km west of Kittilä, which has charter flights from Britain. They are described here. Three other resorts worth considering are Ruka, 80km south of the Arctic Circle, close to Kuusamo airport and the Russian border; Pyhä, 150km north-east of Rovaniemi; and Iso-Syöte, Finland's southernmost fell region. These are covered in our resort directory at the back of the book.

UK PACKAGES

Ylläs First Choice, Inghams, Inntravel, Skiworld
Levi Crystal Finest, First Choice, Inghams, Skiworld

Phone numbers
From abroad use the prefix +358 and omit the initial '0' of the phone number

KEY FACTS	
Resort	255m
	840ft
Slopes	255-715m
	840-2,350ft
Lifts	29
Pistes	53km
Snow-guns	40 guns

TOURIST OFFICE

www.yllas.fi

Ylläs

+ Best for novices and nordic fans
+ Few queues and reliable late snow

− Slopes a bus ride from the villages
− Bars and restaurants not a highlight

Ylläs is Finland's largest resort; it's a quiet family area with an increasing choice of accommodation dotted around its two villages.

Ylläs mountain has two main bases, both 4km from the mountain. The minor one is Ylläsjärvi near the Sport Resort Ylläs base, the major one Äkäslompolo near the Ylläs-Ski base. Development is taking place at both, and closer to the slopes too.

It is Finland's largest downhill ski area – but still has only 53km of pistes on two broad flanks with runs that suit novices best. Second- and third-week skiers will rapidly conquer the benign black runs. Past reports of the ski school have been positive. And there's a mountain-top restaurant.

The area has 330km of cross-country trails, 38km of which are floodlit, transforming it from awkward sprawl to doorstep ski resort of

limitless scope. There are also 15 cafes along the tracks. From the lift base trails fan out around the mountain, across the frozen lake and away through the endless forest.

The Äkäs cabins at Äkäslompolo have been recommended. Dining out is slowly improving, with five new restaurants at the Taiga base (Sport Resort Ylläs) opening last season. These include a pizzeria. Established favourites in town include more upmarket Poro, for traditional fish and roast dishes. Julie's suits families better (pizza and burgers).

Off-slope activities include snowmobiling (300km of tracks), dog sledding, reindeer safaris, snowshoeing and ice fishing.

KEY FACTS	
Resort	205m
	670ft
Slopes	205-530m
	670-1,740ft
Lifts	26
Pistes	44km
Snow-guns	36%

TOURIST OFFICE

www.levi.fi

Levi

+ Lodging convenient for slopes
+ Airport transfer only 15 to 20 mins

− Not ideal for beginners
− Can be very windy

Levi's convenience is its key appeal for visitors. There are good hotels and plentiful off-slope diversions too. Mid-winter can be bleak on the hill though.

Levi is a small, purpose-built village of hotels, apartments and cabins at the foot of its slopes.

The runs are mostly intermediate (only one green and two black). A gondola and a six-pack take you up from the village base, but apart from another gondola serving the World Cup slope, the other lifts are drags. They can be bleak and exposed in bad weather but the area usually has a long season. A third of the slopes have snowmaking and 17 are floodlit. The main terrain park is 'excellent' with boxes, rails, a spine, plus big and small lines; half-pipe and super-pipe. There are several mountain restaurants (including the Okta in the Panorama hotel). Cross-country trails total 230km. Vilpuri Kid's Land has lifts and tobogganing areas; plus day care.

Levi's biggest hotel is the Spa Levitunturi (016 646301), with a bowling alley and huge spa facility – including 17 indoor and outdoor pools and nine saunas. The hotel Levi Panorama (336 3000) is at the top of the mountain, reached by gondola. The Sokos hotel (016 3215 500) and

the Levilheto apartments (403 120200) have been recommended.

There are dozens of places to eat. The Hullu Poro (Crazy Reindeer) complex has impressed reporters and has several restaurants including fine dining, traditional Finnish, Asian and a steakhouse. Of the handful of bars, Oliver's Corner is 'very lively'. Off-slope activities include snowmobiling, reindeer and husky safaris, snowshoeing, ice fishing, skating on special tracks on the frozen lake. You can also visit a reindeer and a husky park.

Want to get other views?

Our website has an active forum, where readers swap experiences and views on resorts and other stuff. The WTSS editors join in, when they have time, so it's a good way to get their views.

Find out more at:

www.wtss.co.uk

Norway

- ➕ One of the best places in Europe for serious cross-country skiing
- ➕ The home of telemark – plenty of opportunities to learn and practise
- ➕ Freedom from the glitz and ill-mannered lift queues of the Alps
- ➕ Impressive terrain parks
- ➕ Usually reliable snow conditions throughout a long season

- ➖ Very limited downhill areas
- ➖ Very basic mountain restaurants
- ➖ Booze is prohibitively taxed
- ➖ Scenery more Pennine than Alpine
- ➖ Après-ski that is either deadly dull or irritatingly rowdy
- ➖ Short daylight hours in midwinter
- ➖ Highly changeable weather
- ➖ Limited off-slope activities

For downhillers who fancy a change from the usual ski-resort glitz, Norway could be just the place. For families with young children, in particular, it can make sense; you'll have no trouble finding junk food to please the kids – the mountain restaurants serve little else. Speaking for ourselves, any one of our first three ➖ points is enough to make us pause. Add together all the negatives, and you can count us out. One reporter ticked us off for this 'narrow-minded view'. He makes great play of the fact that he can be in Lillehammer four hours after taking off from Edinburgh. Four hours after taking off from Gatwick, we can be in Megève or Chamonix. Hmmm, tricky call ...

There is a traditional friendship between Norway and Britain, and English is widely spoken.

For the Norwegians and Swedes, skiing is a weekend rather than a special holiday activity, and not an occasion for extravagance. So at lunchtime they haul sandwiches out of their backpacks as we might while walking the Pennine Way, and in the evening they cook in their apartments. Don't expect a tempting choice of restaurants.

The Norwegians have a problem with alcohol. Walk into an après-ski bar at 5pm on a Saturday and you may find young men already inebriated – not merry, but incoherent. And this is despite – or, some say, because of – incredibly high taxes on booze. Restaurant prices for wine are ludicrous, and shop prices may be irrelevant – Hemsedal has no liquor store. Our one attempt at self-catering there was an unusually sober affair as a result. Other prices are generally not high by Alpine standards.

Cross-country skiing comes as naturally to Norwegians as walking; and even if you're not very keen, the fact that cross-country is normal, and not a wimp's alternative to 'real' skiing, gives Norway a special appeal. Here, cross-country is both a way of getting about the valleys and a way of exploring the hills. What distinguishes Norway for the keen cross-country skier is the network of long trails across the gentle uplands, with refuges along the way where backpackers can pause for refreshment or stay overnight. More and more Norwegians are taking to telemarking, and snowboarding is very popular – local youths fill the impressive terrain parks at weekends. For downhill skiing, the country isn't nearly so attractive. Despite the fact that it is able to hold downhill races, Norway's Alpine areas are of limited appeal. The most rewarding resort is Hemsedal, covered on the next page.

Norway's other widely known resorts are Geilo and Voss, on the railway line from Bergen to Oslo. Tryvann is just 20 minutes from the centre of Oslo, on a spur of the underground system, and popular with the locals. Lillehammer is well known too, of course – site of the 1994 Olympics; but it's a lakeside town not a downhill ski resort (the Alpine races were held some distance away). Other main resorts are Trysil, on the border with Sweden, Beitostølen in the Jotunheimen National Park, and Oppdal. All are covered in the directory at the back of the book.

KEY FACTS

Resort	640m
	2,100ft
Slopes	670-1450m
	2,200-4,760ft
Lifts	24
Pistes	47km
Snow-guns	50%

UK PACKAGES

Neilson

Phone numbers
From abroad use the prefix +47

TOURIST OFFICE

www.hemsedal.com
www.skistar.com/
hemsedal

HEMSEDAL TOURIST OFFICE

Hemsedal has lodgings up at mid-mountain, at Skarsnuten, including a cool modern hotel as well as chalet-style apartments ↓

Hemsedal

+ Convenient slope-side lodging
+ Some quite challenging slopes
+ Excellent children's nursery slopes

- Not much of a village
- Weekend queues
- Exposed upper mountain

Hemsedal is both an unspoiled valley and a village, also referred to as Trøym and Sentrum ('Centre') – but you can also stay at the slopes, a mile or so away.

Hemsedal is a three-hour drive from Oslo and geared mainly to weekenders arriving by car or coach. But there is a ski-bus linking all parts and floodlit paths to/from the centre. The lift pass also covers smaller Solheisen, up the valley. Geilo is an hour away.

Sentrum is a bus ride from the slopes and little more than a small area of low-rise apartments/hotels, shops, a garage, a bank and a couple of cashpoints. There's a developing area of lodgings close to the base. You can also stay further up the hill at Skarsnuten – a pleasantly woody separate area, linked to the main network by its own lift and red run.

Hemsedal's slopes pack a lot of variety into a small space. They are shaded in midwinter, and can be very cold. Fast lifts serve a high proportion of the slopes, though a few awkward drags remain. There can be weekend crowds and queues for the main access lifts. Otherwise it is quiet. There are five good parks and a mini park for kids; plus a half-pipe and boardercross. Snowmaking covers 50% of the slopes, with more planned for 2011/12. There is quite a bit to amuse experts: several black pistes and wide areas of gentler off-piste terrain served by drags. Mileage-hungry piste-bashers will find Hemsedal's runs very limited. There are quite a few red and blue runs to play on, and splendid long green runs – but they get a lot of traffic. Beginners have a separate, gentle nursery area. The resort caters well for families, and the kids' nursery slopes at the lift base are now very well developed.

There are 120km of prepared cross-country trails in the valley and forest and (in late season) 90km at altitude.

There is one functional self-service mountain restaurant.

The best hotel is the Skogstad (320 55000) in Sentrum – comfortable, with a new spa; but its bar and nightclub may be noisy at weekends. The hotel Skarsnuten (320 61700), on the mountain, is stylishly modern. But most of the accommodation is in apartments. The chalet-style Alpin Lodge by the nursery slopes includes 30 apartments, restaurants and shops.

The dining choices are OK; the Big Horn at Fjellandsby is a popular steakhouse, and there's the Lodgen bar and restaurant (Italian) at the Alpin Lodge; plus more places in town.

Après-ski starts at the Skistua (Skisenter), which also has live music at the weekends. The bars and clubs get rowdy at weekends and holidays, but can be very quiet midweek.

Off-slope diversions include tobogganing, dog sledding, bowling and snowmobiling.

Sweden

- ➕ Snow-sure from December to May
- ➕ Unspoiled, beautiful landscape
- ➕ Uncrowded pistes and lifts
- ➕ Super nordic and off-slope activities
- ➖ Limited challenging downhill terrain
- ➖ Small areas by Alpine standards
- ➖ Lacks dramatic Alpine scenery
- ➖ Short days during the early season

Sweden appeals most to those who want an all-round winter holiday in a different environment and culture. Standards of accommodation, food and service are good, and the people are welcoming, lively and friendly, but most of the downhill areas are limited in size and challenge.

Holidaying in Sweden is a completely different experience from a holiday in the Alps. Although virtually everyone speaks good English, menus and signs are often written only in Swedish. The food is delightful, especially if you like fish and venison. And resorts are very family-friendly. It is significantly cheaper than neighbouring Norway, but reporters still complain that eating and drinking is very expensive.

One myth about Swedish skiing is that it is dark. It is true that the days are very short in December and early January. But from early February the lifts usually work from 9am to 4.30pm and by March it is light until 8.30pm. Most resorts have some floodlit pistes.

On the downside, downhill slopes are limited in both challenge and extent and the lift systems dominated by T-bars. But there is lots of cross-country and backcountry skiing.

Après-ski is taken very seriously – with live bands from mid- to late-afternoon. There is plenty to do off the slopes: snowmobile safaris, ice fishing, dog sled rides, ice climbing, saunas galore and visiting local Sami villages.

The main resort is Åre, described below. Others include Sälen, the largest, and Vemdalen. These two, plus Riksgränsen, Björkliden (both above the Arctic Circle) and tiny Ramundberget are covered in our directory at the back of the book.

KEY FACTS

Resort	380m
	1,250ft
Slopes	380-1275m
	1,250-4,180ft
Lifts	47
Pistes	100km
Snow-guns	70%

UK PACKAGES
Neilson

TOURIST OFFICE
www.skistar.com

Åre

- ➕ Good for intermediates and novices
- ➕ Excellent children's facilities
- ➖ High winds can affect snow and lifts
- ➖ Few expert challenges

Sweden's biggest ski area, with lots to do off the slopes as well as on. Not great for keen skiers but good for families wanting a change from the Alps.

The centre of this small- lakeside town has old, pretty, coloured wooden buildings and some larger modern additions. Lodgings are spread out along the valley.

There are two separate areas of slopes linked by a ski-bus. The main area has fast lifts to the top (including a gondola, chondola, cable car, funicular and fast chair) and a fast chair accesses the separate Duved area. But nearly all other lifts are drags. Queues are rare.

The slopes offer mainly beginner and intermediate treelined terrain, with a couple of windswept bowls above that are prone to closure. Experts will find the slopes limited, especially if the high bowls are closed. But there is a lot of off-piste. For intermediates there are steep, sometimes icy, black and red runs back to town, and lots of pretty blue runs through the trees. You get a real sense of travelling around on the main area. Beginners have good facilities in both sectors. There are three terrain parks and 58km of groomed cross-country trails. The ski school has a good reputation and children have special areas. Kids under seven get free lift passes if wearing helmets. Mountain huts are good.

The best central hotel is the charming old Diplomat Åregården. There are ample apartments and cabins and lots of restaurants, from pizza to Japanese. Après-ski is lively, with the Fjällgården, Tott and Åregården packed from 3pm. Off-slope diversions are plentiful.

Bulgaria

RPI	50
lift pass	£100
ski hire	£95
lessons	£45
food & drink	£55
total	£295

UK PACKAGES

Borovets Balkan Holidays, BoardnLodge, Crystal, First Choice, Inghams, Mountain Wave, Neilson, Skitracer, Thomson
Bansko Balkan Holidays, Crystal, First Choice, Independent Ski Links, Neilson, Skitracer, Thomson
Pamporovo Balkan Holidays, Crystal, First Choice, Independent Ski Links, Mountain Wave, Neilson, Skitracer, Thomson

➕ Costs very low by Alpine standards
➕ The chance to experience a different and fascinating culture
➕ Good ski schools

➖ Poor snow record, though snowmaking has been improved
➖ Small ski areas
➖ Cheap booze attracts 18-30 crowds

Bulgaria has traditionally attracted novices looking for a jolly time on a tight budget. Prices have crept up, but it still remains a relatively cheap and cheerful choice. Bansko's arrival on the scene in 2004 raised the bar for the country's other main resorts, which are now starting to catch up.

One of our reporters summed-up her stay in Borovets (a few years back) thus: 'Skis: old and well used. Ski school: easily arranged, no shortage of English speakers. Hotels: modern, clean, over-heated. Staff: mostly operating scams to relieve you of cash. Food: in the resort, good standard stuff; on the mountain, rubbish. Conclusion: you get what you pay for – and next time we will be paying a lot more to get a lot more.' Which more or less reflects the general tone of the few reports we receive on the 'old' pre-Bansko Bulgarian resorts.

But maybe things are looking up. Recent reports are fairly upbeat on the experience. Low prices still weigh heavily in the balance – though a 2011 reporter talks of some prices being 'similar to the UK'. And lifts are being improved: Bulgaria's first six-packs have been installed (at Bansko and Pamporovo). Standards of lodging continue to improve too, even though the food remains uninspiring.

The ski areas are not large and the season is a little shorter than in the Alps, but queues are rarely a problem except for access lifts at peak times, and the ski schools have an excellent reputation. The scenery and culture provide a very different holiday experience to the Alps.

KEY FACTS

Resort	1300m
	4,270ft
Slopes	1300-2560m
	4,270-8,400ft
Lifts	14
Pistes	58km
Snow-guns	50 guns

TOURIST OFFICE

www.borovets-bg.com

Borovets

➕ Lively, convenient village
➕ Some good intermediate slopes

➖ Not ideal for beginners
➖ Nightlife can be tacky

Borovets is a collection of large, modern hotels, with bars, restaurants and shops housed within them.

There is a small selection of quirkier bars, shops and eating places too. The resort's beautiful woodland setting gives a degree of Alpine-style charm. But a 2011 reporter complains of 'a cheap, tatty feel' to the place with 'run down/abandoned buildings' and 'local dogs roaming the streets'.

A long gondola rises over 1000m to reach both the small, high, easy slopes of Markoudjika and the longer, steepish Yastrebets pistes. The runs are best for good intermediates, including some longish reds. The resort is not ideal for novices: nursery slopes are crowded, and the step from easy Markoudjika to testing reds is a big one. There is night skiing every day and 35km of cross-country.

Queues form for the gondola at peak times ('45 minutes', says a 2011 reporter) and for the nursery draglifts. The gondola is also said to be prone to closure by wind. Grooming is erratic. The ski school is consistently praised: this year a reader said his instructor 'gave up free time before and after lessons to give extra help' and a beginner 'made progress after a few days'; but a seven-year-old's class 'was too big'.

Most reporters stay at the big hotels – the Samokov or Rila; noise can be a problem at the latter say reporters. A 2011 visitor found the Lion 'clean, tidy with friendly staff' and a 2010 visitor was happy enough with the 'basic, but quiet and comfortable' chalets ('villas') at the Iglika Palace, but said that food shopping was limited. The Black Cat has 'good food, service and lovely open fire'. There are plenty of lively bars. Many cater to the younger crowd – Buzz is said to be the best and No Limits is a new bar/disco in the Rila hotel. There are also 'adult' bars, but they are away from the main streets and advertising is now said to be banned. Tour operator reps organise pub crawls, folklore evenings etc. Excursions to the Rila monastery or Sofia by coach are interesting.

Bansko

✚ Lots of fast lifts on the mountain	▬ Long, queue-prone access gondola
✚ Atmospheric town centre	▬ Few off-slope diversions
✚ Friendly, helpful locals	▬ Some building work still evident

Bansko is an old town, set on a flat valley floor in the scenic Pirin National Park, that has been catapulted into the 21st century by the installation of modern lifts which opened in 2004 and construction of a lot of lodgings.

Many of the lodgings are near the base of the access gondola to the slopes. Reporters like what they find, and many go back repeatedly.

The town looks no great beauty on the outskirts, but the central square reveals a quiet and charming heart and there are few outward signs of commercial tourism. The centre is a fair walk from the gondola base and most hotels run shuttle-buses to/from the lift. But a more convenient hub has grown up at the base.

The slopes are reached by an eight-seat gondola to Bunderishka. There are long queues for this in the morning ('can be over an hour') and a 2011 reporter advises getting there at 8.15 before it officially opens to avoid them. We're told that an additional gondola is planned but permission hadn't been given when we went to press. Queues further up the mountain are rare.

There is a blue piste back to the town, with snowmaking and floodlighting. Most lifts are fast chairs, and successive ones take you up mainly north-facing slopes to the high point of the area. You can ski down reds or blues to Shiligarnika, or a red followed by the Tomba black to

Bulgaria

669

Interactive resort shortlist builder at **www.wtss.co.uk**

Bunderishka. Some of these are quite long and challenging.

The resort map shows a chair going up to the right of Bunderishka; this has not worked for several years. The nursery slopes near the top of the gondola are good, with little through traffic. There is a terrain park. We lack recent reports of the ski schools, but past ones have been good. Children have a snow garden and the kindergarten takes kids from four to seven years old.

Reporters find the runs reasonably well groomed. And snow is more reliable than the Bulgarian norm.

Mountain huts are mostly self-service, and the food 'rather basic'. A reporter enjoyed lunch at the Goat.

There are hotels near the gondola station, including the swanky Florimont with its own casino and the 5-star Kempinski Grand Arena, with good facilities and 'extensive breakfasts'. The Emerald is 'convenient for the gondola, with superb rooms, friendly staff and tasty, hot food'. The Serena is also recommended – 'good food, clean rooms, beautiful spa'.

Reporters enthuse about the town's many mehanas (traditional inns) with roaring fires, real Bulgarian food and good wine. And there are lots of lively bars – readers' tips include the Friendly Bar, Lion pub, Diamonds, Amigos and the Flora in the Emerald hotel ('happy hour from 12 noon till midnight with two for one drinks; open till 5am').

Off-slope diversions include skating, paragliding, floodlit snowmobiling and ten-pin bowling. Many hotels have spas. Shopping has improved noticeably.

Weekly news updates and resort links at www.wtss.co.uk

KEY FACTS

Resort	1650m
	5,410ft
Slopes	1450-1935m
	4,760-6,350ft
Lifts	14
Pistes	37km
Snow-guns	70%

TOURIST OFFICE

www.pamporovo.net

Pamporovo

➕ Pretty, treelined slopes
➕ Good, low-cost choice for novices

➖ Limited extent and short runs
➖ Poor piste maintenance

Pamporovo is a purpose-built village, in a pretty woodland area a short shuttle-bus ride from its slopes.

The resort is strictly for beginners and near-beginners, with mostly easy and short runs. Others will find the limited area rather inadequate. The 37km slopes are pretty and sheltered, with pistes cutting through pine forest. The runs are rather too narrow for some. There's a half-pipe. Snow reliability is poor, but snowmaking covers 70% of the slopes. A reporter complains of grooming 'only one day in the week,

which made it difficult for beginners'. There are plenty of huts on the mountain.

The ski schools are repeatedly praised – instructors are patient, enthusiastic and speak good English, and class sizes are usually quite small. There's 40km of cross-country trails.

A 2010 reporter recommends the hotel Finlandia ('comfortable; friendly staff; plentiful but plain food').

BANSKO SKI AREA

Bulgaria's small ski areas best suit beginners and intermediates who aren't hungry for mileage →

Romania

+ Cheap packages, and very low prices on the spot
+ Interesting excursions and friendly local people
+ Good tuition from keen instructors

− Primitive facilities, especially mountain restaurants and toilets
− Uninspiring food
− Very limited slopes

Romania sells mainly on price. On-the-spot prices, in particular, are very low. Provided you don't have unreasonably high expectations, you'll probably come back from Poiana Brasov content. It allows complete beginners to try a ski holiday at the minimum cost, and to have a jolly time in the evenings without adding substantially to that cost.

Romania's main resort – and the only one featuring the declining number of UK package programmes – is **Poiana Brasov** (1030m). It is a short drive above the city of Brasov in the Carpathian mountains, about 120km (on alarmingly rough, slow roads) north-west of the capital and arrival airport, Bucharest.

The resort is purpose-built, and has the air of a spacious, pleasant holiday camp. But it is not designed for the convenience of skiers: some serious-sized hotels are right by the lifts, but most are scattered about a pretty, wooded plateau, served by regular buses and cheap taxis.

The slopes are extremely limited – approximately 14km of pistes in total. They consist of decent intermediate treelined runs of about 750m vertical, roughly following the line of the main cable car and gondola, plus an open nursery area at the top. There are some nursery lifts at village level, which are used when snow permits. Night skiing is also available. The resort gets weekend crowds from Brasov and Bucharest, and queues can result, but during the week there are few problems.

A key part of the resort's appeal is the friendly and effective teaching.

Hotel standards are higher than you might expect. The linked 3-star Bradul (0268 417 866) and 4-star Sport (0268 407330) hotels are handy for the lower nursery slopes and for one of the cable cars, and look smart after refurbishment. Guests in both have use of the Sport's new spa facilities. We're slightly surprised to hear that a swanky Radisson hotel with over 180 rooms and smart spa facility is under construction for completion in 2013.

Après-ski revolves around the hotel bars and nightclubs – plus outings to rustic barns for barbies with gypsy music, and to the bars and restaurants of Brasov. With cheap beer and very cheap spirits on tap, things can be quite lively. Off-slope facilities are limited; there are two good-sized pools (in hotels), and bowling. An excursion to nearby Bran Castle (Count Dracula's lair) is also popular.

671

Slovenia

672

+ Low prices
+ Beautiful, varied scenery
+ Good beginner slopes and lessons

− Limited, mostly easy slopes
− Still lots of slow, antiquated lifts
− Mountain huts not a highlight

Slovenia offers lower prices and fewer crowds than the Alps, attracting economy-minded visitors from neighbouring Italy and Austria as well as Britain and the Netherlands. The ski areas are limited and still a bit antiquated, though making obvious investments. Most suit novices well.

Slovenia has 30 or so ski areas, the main ones concentrated in the Julian Alps in the west, dominated by its highest mountain, Mt Triglav; all are small and some are tiny. None is likely to keep the adventurous piste-basher amused for a week; but you can have an enjoyable trip touring by car or by combining several resorts from one base. EasyJet (from Stansted) and Adria (from Gatwick) fly to Ljubljana.

The season is shorter than in the Alps (except at Kanin) and the resorts low. Most slopes are below 2000m.

Prices are low and there is a positive feel, and a warm and hospitable welcome. Standards of service and accommodation have improved – the hotels may not be particularly attractive but many are new or modernised, complete with pools, spas and often free Wi-Fi.

Getting around is relatively easy; fuel is cheap and most ski areas are within a 40-minute drive of each other on good roads. And the main resorts are within a two-hour bus ride of Ljubljana. Bled, with its beautiful lake and fairly lively nightlife, is an attractive base. It has just one steepish slope, but buses (free with lift pass) run to Vogel (20km) and Kobla (a bit nearer and the only ski area in Slovenia reachable by train). The Julian Alps lift pass covers these and includes Kranjska Gora – as well as the lesser known Krvavec. It gives around 100km of pistes in total. The other main group of resorts centres on Maribor to the east, a quite different area of low-slung wooded ridges. But it has the biggest ski area in the country at 42km.

Most resorts fit best into the intermediate category but differ on their suitability for novices. Experts will find few black runs, but there is good off-piste when conditions permit. Lift systems are improving and queues rare. Most Slovenians visit at weekends; midweek the slopes can be deserted. A common feature for many areas is an access lift, with no runs back to valley level. One drawback for us is the lack of quality lunches: snacks and picnics are the norm, so hearty menus and cute huts are rare. Ski schools are of a high quality and cheap, with good spoken English. Other winter activities are big in Slovenia too, so there is plenty to do off the slopes.

Krvavec

KEY FACTS	
Resort	1450m
	4,760ft
Slopes	1450-1970m
	4,760-6,460ft
Lifts	11
Pistes	30km
Snow-guns	95%

TOURIST OFFICE

www.rtc-krvavec.si

➕ Convenient for short breaks
➕ Quiet slopes midweek
➕ Jolly, family atmosphere

➖ Lacks proper resort base
➖ Short, mainly south-facing runs
➖ Not ideal for novices

Krvavec has been voted Slovenia's best ski area and is just 8km from Ljubljana airport. There's no central village, but then most visitors are locals on day trips from the city.

Krvavec has some of the country's steepest slopes, including one or two black runs. It is a lively place, especially at weekends. Most visitors are families on day trips from the capital or nearby towns. Bled is 40 minutes by daily bus (free with lift pass). There is no resort, but there is one hotel on the slopes and some lodging in nearby Cerklje. The local lift pass also covers Rogla, near Maribor.

A gondola goes up to the slopes, which span three partly-wooded hills from a high point of 1970m. The lifts include a six-pack and a quad; queues are rare. The pistes get a lot of sun, though snowmaking is extensive and grooming good. There is a good nursery slope and children's area, complete with moving carpet, but few easy blues to progress to. The mid-mountain Plaza has picnic spots and snack bars. Kriska Planina is an Alpine-style hut. Snowshoeing and nights in the Igloo hotel (89 euros including a fondue meal) are popular.

Kranjska Gora

KEY FACTS	
Resort	810m
	2,660ft
Slopes	810-1295m
	2,660-4,250ft
Lifts	18
Pistes	20km
Snow-guns	Some

TOURIST OFFICE

www.kr-gora.si

➕ Good for novices and families
➕ Convenient, good slope-side hotels

➖ Slopes limited in extent, variety, length and vertical
➖ Still some old lifts, and gets busy

Despite limited slopes (most other areas are bigger), Kranjska Gora is the dominant resort on the UK package market, offered by a wide range of operators. It's a good-value, pretty and compact resort that is popular with families. Since the centre is fairly small, most facilities are near the slopes too.

Kranjska Gora is close to the Austrian and Italian borders. Day trips to ski in resorts over the borders are possible.

The 20km of wide, treelined pistes rise to 1295m and best suit very unadventurous intermediates and novices – though there is a World Cup slalom black run. The slopes above Podkoren are quiet and gentle. There are four quads, but still lots of draglifts. And getting around involves tedious traversing. Queues are rare despite busier slopes here. Snow reliability is poor, but snowmaking covers most pistes. There is a terrain park and a children's area with a moving carpet. Cross-country trails total 40km. It is back to base for lunch, but Bedancu is a good self-service beside chair 7.

Hotels are plentiful and to a high standard, most with pools and spas. For slope-side convenience, the Lek, Prisank and Larix are best. The Alpina and adjacent aqua park are popular with families. We liked the Kompas, with excellent breakfast buffet and good pool. For eating out try the Kotnik and Via Napoli (hotel Prisank) pizzerias, and the Ostarija for finer dining. Ice skating, night tobogganing and snowshoeing are popular.

Slovenia

Interactive resort shortlist builder at **www.wtss.co.uk**

Kanin

KEY FACTS	
Resort	460m
	1,510ft
Slopes	1140-2290m
	3,740-7,510ft
Lifts	12
Pistes	30km
Snow-guns	Some

TOURIST OFFICE

www.boveckanin.si

+ Splendid Dolomite-like scenery
+ High, reliably snow-sure slopes
+ Long runs down Italian side

- More remote than the other areas
- Upper mountain bleak and exposed
- Bovec quiet at night

Adventure capital Bovec has an isolated position in the splendid Soca Valley; its ski area Kanin is a cross-border resort with uncrowded intermediate slopes.

Kanin, linked to Sella Nevea in Italy, is Slovenia's highest ski area, with the biggest vertical (1150m). The link is by a red piste and a jumbo cable car to return. There is 30km of largely intermediate terrain, and a shared lift pass that also covers the Arnoldstein in Austria. The resort enjoys a long season and a reliable snow record.

Bovec has an attractive centre, with a few shops, hotels and restaurants. The Kanin hotel is comfortable with a super pool and spa centre. The smaller Mangart is a modern place, with suites and dormitories. There are free ski buses to the lift station.

A long gondola from the edge of town rises to 2200m, from where chairs (including two quads) and a draglift serve two short, easy blues up top and longer red runs back to the gondola mid-station or towards Italy. Kanin is not ideal for beginners though; the blues are high and exposed. Intermediates have a choice of genuine red runs – the two down to Sella Nevea are north-facing and sheltered, and interrupted only by one chairlift. There are off-piste routes to be explored, though much of the limestone terrain is pitted with hollows and holes that make it hazardous.

Mountain huts are limited. Bovec Sports offers lots of activities and the Triglav National Park centre (Slovenia's only National Park) is worth a visit.

Vogel

KEY FACTS	
Resort	570m
	1,870ft
Slopes	1535-1800m
	5,040-5,910ft
Lifts	8
Pistes	18km
Snow-guns	None

TOURIST OFFICES

www.vogel.si
www.bohinj.si/kobla

+ Beautiful lake setting, pretty runs
+ Good choice of huts

- Bus ride from most lodging
- Limited in extent and challenge

Vogel overlooks stunning Lake Bohinj, part of the Triglav National Park. It's tiny, but is the main ski area within commuting distance of Bled.

Vogel has the best conditions and prettiest slopes in the area. Buses arrive daily from Bled; but there are small hotels and restaurants near the base and in villages along the lakeside (served by free ski bus).

The 18km of partly-wooded slopes are reached by a cable car up from the valley. A fast quad serves a mid-mountain area, with a single-seat chair to the high point at 1800m (great views). Pistes served by another chair and three drags include a lovely gentle blue. There is a separate nursery slope, a children's area and a terrain park. When conditions permit, a long red run returns to the bottom cable car station via a quiet, pretty valley. Several of the huts are nicer than the Slovenian norm.

For a change of scene Kobla, with 23km of wide, wooded runs, is a short bus ride away at Bohinjska Bistrica – the railway terminus. The 5-star Bohinj Park hotel is eco-friendly, with pool, cinema and bowling. Next door is a huge Aqua park. Near Vogel, the 3-star Zlatarog is comfortable.

Maribor-Pohorje

KEY FACTS	
Resort	325m
	1,070ft
Slopes	325-1330m
	1,070-4,360ft
Lifts	22
Pistes	43km
Snow-guns	95%

TOURIST OFFICE

www.maribor-pohorje.si

+ Good access, close to the city
+ Gentle, sheltered slopes for novices

- Mostly short runs
- Few challenges except the FIS run

Slovenia's second city, Maribor, is 6km from its local slopes – where there's also limited lodging. There's little vertical to be achieved, but some varied terrain.

This is the country's biggest ski area, and continues to develop.

The lifts include a six-pack and a newish gondola to Pohorje summit. There's night skiing, and snowmaking covers 95% of the area. There are 27km of cross-country trails. The area lift pass also covers Kranjska Gora. The Pohorje school offers a wide range of classes. There are several atmospheric old inns serving good, Hungarian-influenced food. The 4-star Arena and 3-star Videc hotels are slope-side.

Scotland

- ➕ Easy to get to from northern Britain
- ➕ It is possible to experience perfect snow and very satisfying skiing
- ➕ Decent, cheap accommodation and good-value packages
- ➕ Mid-week it's rarely crowded
- ➕ Lots to do off the slopes

- ➖ Weather is extremely changeable and sometimes vicious
- ➖ Snowfall is erratic
- ➖ Slopes limited; runs mainly short
- ➖ Queueing can be a problem
- ➖ Little ski resort ambience and few memorable mountain restaurants

Scottish skiing is unpredictable, to say the least – and there has been plenty of snow in recent seasons. When this happens (and you can get there at short notice) the ski areas are a tremendous asset. But booking a holiday here as a replacement for your usual week in the Alps is too risky.

Most of the slopes in most of the areas suit intermediates best. But all apart from The Lecht also offer one or two tough or very tough slopes.

For novices who are really keen to learn, Scotland could make sense, especially if you live nearby. You can book instruction via one of the excellent outdoor centres, many of which also provide accommodation. The ski schools at the resorts themselves are also very good.

Snowboarding is popular and most of the resorts have some special terrain features, but maintaining these facilities in good nick is problematic. The natural terrain is good for free-riding when the conditions are right.

Cairngorm is the best-known resort, with 11 lifts and 37km of runs. Aviemore is the main centre (with a shuttle-bus to the slopes), but you can stay in other villages in the Spey valley. The slopes are accessed by a funicular from the main car park up to Ptarmigan at 1100m.

Nevis Range is the highest Scottish resort, with slopes reaching 1190m. It has 11 lifts plus a long six-seat gondola which accesses the slopes. The 35km of runs are on the north-facing slopes of Aonach Mor. A new base cafe and bigger hire shop opened in 2011. There are many B&Bs and hotels in and around Fort William, 10 minutes away by bus.

Glenshee is the largest ski area, with 40km of runs spread out over three minor parallel valleys served by 22 lifts. It includes some natural quarter-pipes. The new chairlift planned for the Cairnwell is now expected to open for 2011/12. Glenshee is primarily a venue for day-trippers, though there are hotels, hostels and B&Bs in the area.

Glencoe's seven lifts and 20km of runs lie east of moody Glen Coe itself. A double chairlift and drag go up to the main slopes, including the nursery area. There are freeriding opportunities and a challenging descent on Flypaper, the resort's steepest run. 'Great value, cosy cafe' at the base. The isolated Kings House Hotel is 2km away.

The Lecht is largely a novices' area, with 14 lifts and 20km of runs on the gentle slopes beside a high pass, with a series of parallel lifts and runs above the car parks. With a maximum vertical of only 200m, runs are short. There's extensive snowmaking, a terrain park, and a day lodge at the base. The village of Tomintoul is 10km away.

FURTHER INFORMATION
The VisitScotland organisation runs an excellent website at: ski.visitscotland.com

INVERNESS

The Lecht

Cairngorm   ABERDEEN

Glenshee

Nevis Range

Glencoe   DUNDEE

PERTH

STIRLING

GLASGOW
        EDINBURGH

Japan

- ➕ Reliable deep powder snow in Hokkaido resorts, lift-served
- ➕ Exotic atmosphere, fabulous food
- ➕ Polite and gracious locals
- ➕ Night skiing is the norm, allowing a long ski day if you want one

- ➖ The language barrier
- ➖ Pricey and lengthy trip; 6,000 miles, with a change of plane
- ➖ Lack of off-slope diversions
- ➖ Snowfall can go on for weeks in Hokkaido resorts

Although it is roughly the same size as the British Isles, Japan has hundreds of ski resorts. A surprising number of UK tour operators now feature Japanese resorts, going to places on the northern island of Hokkaido that have developed something like cult status with keen skiers and riders from Australia, in particular. The reason is as simple as could be: snow – huge and reliable falls of powder snow.

In these remote parts of Japan, hardly anything is written in English and no English-language media are available (except websites). Going independently sounds like hard work; but presumably going with a tour operator is not.

UK PACKAGES

Niseko *Crystal, Crystal Finest, Independent Ski Links, Mountain Tracks, Ski Club Freshtracks, Ski Independence, Ski Safari, Skitracer, Skiworld*
Rusutsu *Crystal, Independent Ski Links, Ski Independence, Ski Safari, Skitracer*
Furano *Mountain Tracks, Ski Club Freshtracks, Ski Independence, Ski Safari, Skiworld*
Hakuba *Ski Safari, Skiworld*

You fly in to Sapporo (about two hours by bus from Rusutsu and a bit longer to Niseko or Furano), via Tokyo or Osaka. As you are travelling such a great distance you might want to combine your skiing with a stay in Tokyo or (preferably) Kyoto.

Niseko is made up of three areas of slopes – Grand Hirafu (Hirafu and Hanazono), Annupuri and Niseko Village – with a total of 30 lifts covered by a single pass. The three are linked, but not as efficiently as you might wish. There are modern lifts, but also some old single chairs on upper slopes.

The most popular and most easily accessible area, Grand Hirafu, is open from 8.30am to 9.00pm, thanks to one of the world's largest – and most heavily used – night skiing operations. A new eight-seat gondola (replacing the old four-seat version), day lodge, restaurants and children's area are due to open in 2011/12 in celebration of the resort's 50th anniversary.

Niseko has a well-deserved reputation for powder snow, which falls almost constantly from December to the end of February. Skiing waist-deep powder is an everyday occurrence. Clearly, this will suit some holiday skiers and not others. Niseko does offer groomed runs, but you can get those closer to home, and get a tan while you ski them. The snow does stop sometimes, and when it does the powder gets tracked out quickly. But it's usually not too long before another snowstorm marches in across the Sea of Japan from Siberia, and the powder returns. The terrain is not steep, disappointing some hard-core experts.

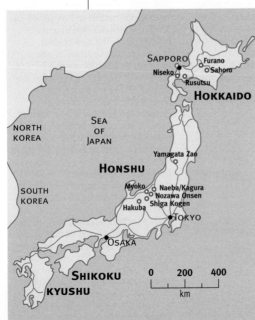

← There are lots of resorts on the main island of Honshu; only the better-known ones are shown on our map. But the best snow is on Hokkaido

Of course, it's interesting to experience the Japanese culture, but Hokkaido is really about the snow ➔

SKI INDEPENDENCE

KEY FACTS

Niseko	
Vertical	900m
	2,950ft
Lifts	30
Pistes	48km
Green	30%
Blue	40%
Black	30%

Rusutsu	
Vertical	595m
	1,950ft
Lifts	18
Pistes	42km
Green	30%
Blue	40%
Black	30%

Furano	
Vertical	950m
	3,115ft
Lifts	12
Pistes	25km
Green	40%
Blue	40%
Black	20%

More information
To really get to grips with the resorts on offer in Japan, spend some time delving into this site: www.snowjapan.com

TOURIST OFFICES

Niseko
www.nisekotourism.com
www.niseko.ne.jp/en/index.html
Hirafu
www.grand-hirafu.jp/winter/en/
Niseko Village
www.niseko-village.com
Annupuri
www.cks.chuo-bus.co.jp/annupuri/english.php

Rusutsu
www.rusutsu.co.jp
Furano
www.skifurano.com

The lack of sun has not proved a deterrent to Australians, who now come in their thousands. For them, guaranteed powder and reasonable costs have been an unbeatable combination. For UK-based travellers, the cost is higher: from around £1,945 for a week in Niseko and a two night stopover in Tokyo on the way home, says tour operator Ski Independence.

There are several modern ski-in/ski-out hotels (but little else) at the bases. The Hilton Niseko Village at the foot of the slopes is among the best, with spectacular views from most of the rooms and its own spa and onsen (see below). Or you can stay in the atmospheric little town of Hirafu where there are now some impressive modern apartments alongside traditional pensions and lodges, raising accommodation standards well above the norm for the simple country town. The lift bases are well serviced by shuttle-buses.

While there isn't a lot to do except ski, eat and drink in Hirafu, the Australian influx means that the little town makes up for its lack of sophistication with a vibrant nightlife and plenty of variety in the way of bars, restaurants and tiny underground-style clubs. There are now a few very upmarket restaurants in town and several bars. And an igloo-style Ice Bar is dug out of a snowdrift each year, complete with icicles on the roof and a real bar selling all manner of cocktails.

Rusutsu is about an hour from Niseko, and makes a viable day trip; or you could combine the two in a two-centre holiday. The slopes, over three interlinked mountains, are more limited, but offer slightly more challenge. The snow here can be as good as in Niseko (though it doesn't fall in quite the same quantity), and it doesn't get tracked out so quickly. There's also a good terrain park, kids' park and half-pipe. The pivotal, self-contained Rusutsu Resort Hotel complex offers a wide choice of good restaurants plus bars, a shopping mall,

swimming, wave pool and onsen.

One of the main alternatives to these two on Hokkaido is **Furano** – one of the more famous resorts within Japan, capable of hosting World Cup events and offering a tad more vertical than Niseko, at 950m over two linked sectors. It is five to six hours from Niseko and Rusutsu, so not within day-trip range. This is a resort where you can either stick to the relatively easy trails or join a guided group to explore off-piste. You can also go with a guided group to the lift-served but ungroomed Asahidake mountain (a live volcano, around an hour away). One of the most comfortable hotels is the New Furano Prince, a free five-minute ride on the resort shuttle from the main base and a 10-minute bus ride from town; again it has great views and its own onsen.

The largest ski area in Japan is on the main island of Honshu: **Shiga Kogen**, comprising 21 interlinked resorts and a huge diversity of terrain covered by one lift ticket. It was the site of several major events in the 1998 Winter Olympics.

Hakuba is also handy to reach by train if you find yourself in Tokyo and don't have time for the trip to Hokkaido. It is a group of 10 resorts accessing more than 200 runs amid the rugged peaks of Japan's 'Alps'.

THE ONSEN EXPERIENCE

Onsen are complexes of hot baths to soak in, showers and communal volcanic thermal pools; they are a key part of Japanese culture and a major part of après-ski. All onsen are basically set up in the same way: men and women shower and bathe in their separate areas. Then, if they wish, they can congregate to soak and have a drink in a communal thermal pool, which more often than not will be outside and surrounded by snow.

REFERENCE SECTION

SKI BUSINESSES

This is a list of ski businesses including all the holiday operators and ski travel agents we know about.

360 Sun and Ski
Family holidays in Les Carroz, French Alps
Tel +33 450 903180

Action Outdoor Holidays
All-inclusive holidays in the French Alps
Tel 0845 890 0362

ActivityBreaks.com
Flexible breaks and group specials
Tel 028 9094 1671

Alpine Action
Catered chalets in Les Trois Vallées
Tel 01273 466535

Alpine Answers
Ski travel agent + tailor-made holidays
Tel 020 7801 1080

Alpine Club
Chalets in St-Martin-de-Belleville
Tel +33 630 226215

Alpine Elements
Holidays in France
Tel 0844 770 4070

Alpine Life
Catered chalet in Saas-Fee
Tel 0780 198 2645

Alpine Ski and Golf Company
Catered/self-catered chalets in Morzine and Chamonix
Tel 07896 031708

Alpine Weekends Ltd
Weekends in the Alps
Tel 020 8944 9762

Alps Accommodation
Accommodation in Samoëns and Morillon
Tel +33 450 985056

Alpsholiday
Apartments in Serre-Chevalier
Tel +33 492 204426

Altitude Holidays
Ski travel agent
Tel 0870 870 7669

AmeriCan Ski
North America specialist plus undiscovered gems in France
Tel 01892 779909

American Ski Classics
Major North American resorts
Tel 020 8607 9988

Ardmore Educational Travel
Group and school trips
Tel 01628 826699

Balkan Holidays
Bulgaria, Slovenia, Romania and Serbia holidays
Tel 0845 130 1114

Barrelli Ski
Chalets in Champagny, Chamonix and Les Houches
Tel 0117 940 1500

Bassingbourn Snowsports
Dry snowsports centre in Royston, Hertfordshire
Tel 0845 072 8293

Belvedere Travel
Luxury chalets/apartments in Méribel and Verbier
Tel 01264 738 257

Bigfoot Travel
Chamonix Valley holidays
Tel +33 450 530063

BoardnLodge.com Ltd
Catered and self-catered holidays in Europe
Tel 020 3239 8181

Borderline
Specialist in Barèges
Tel +33 562 926895

Bramble Ski
Chalets in Verbier, St Anton and Kicking Horse
Tel 020 7060 0824

Canadian Affair
Flights/ holidays in Canada
Tel 020 7616 9999

Canadian Powder Tours Chalet Holidays
Chalet holidays in Western Canada
Tel +1 250 423 3019

Carrier
Upmarket chalets and hotels in the Alps and the USA
Tel 0161 491 7670

Catered Ski Chalets
Ski travel agent
Tel 020 3080 0202

Chalet Bezière
Chalet in Samoëns
Tel +33 450 905181

ChaletBook Limited
Chalets in the Portes du Soleil
Tel 0845 680 6802

Chalet Chocolat
Chalet in Morzine
Tel 01872 580814

Chalet le Dragon
Chalet in La Chapelle d'Abondance
Tel +33 450 172913

Chalet Entre Deux Eaux
Chalet in Morzine
Tel +33 450 37 47 55

Chalet Espen
Chalet in Engelberg
Tel +41 41 637 2220

Chalet Famille
Chalet in Morzine
Tel 0870 068 3456

Chaletfinder.co.uk
Ski travel agent
Tel 01453 766094

Chalet la Forêt
Chalet in Chamonix
Tel 0754 557 5277

The Chalet Group
Promotes owner-run chalets in Europe

Chalet Gueret
Luxury chalet near Morzine
Tel 01884 255437

Chalet les Hirondelles
Farmhouse in St Jean-de-Sixt for groups by arrangement
Tel +33 615 723225

Chalet Kiana
Self-catered chalet in Les Contamines
Tel +33 450 543165

Chalet One
Chalet in Ste-Foy
Tel +33 479 241901

Chalets Unlimited
Chalets in Verbier
Tel 01442 832629

Chalet de Valmorel
Chalet in Valmorel
Tel +33 479 245229

Challenge Activ
Chalets and apartments in Morzine
Tel 0871 717 4113

Chamonix.uk.com
Apartment holidays in central Chamonix
Tel 01224 641559

Le Chardon Mountain Lodges Val d'Isère
Upmarket chalets in a private hamlet in Val d'Isère
Tel 0845 0920 350

Chez Michelle
Self-catering apartment in Samoëns
Tel 01372 456463

Chill Chalet
Accommodation in Paradiski
Tel +33 614 611437

Classic Ski Limited
Holidays for 'mature' skiers/ beginners
Tel 01590 623400

Club Europe Schools Skiing
Schools trips to Europe
Tel 0800 496 4996

Club Med
All-inclusive holidays in 'ski villages'
Tel 08453 670670

Cold Comforts Lodging
Whistler specialist
Tel 0800 881 8429

Collett's Mountain Holidays
Holidays in the Dolomites
Tel 01799 513331

Collineige
Chamonix valley specialist
Tel 01483 579242

Connick Ski
Chalet + ski school in Châtel
Tel +33 450 732212

Consensio Holidays
Luxury chalets in The Three Valleys and Val d'Isère
Tel 0203 393 0833

Contiki Holidays
Holidays for 18-35s
Tel 0845 075 0990

Cooltip Mountain Holidays
Chalets in Méribel
Tel 0870 762 7713

The Corporate Ski Company
Event management company
Tel 020 8542 8555

Crystal
Major mainstream operator
Tel 0871 231 2256

Crystal Finest
Ski holidays to Europe and North America
Tel 0871 971 0364

Directski.com
Holidays in Europe and North America
Tel 0800 201 205

Elegant Resorts
Luxury ski holidays
Tel 01244 897333

Elevation Holidays
Holidays in the Austrian Alps
Tel 0845 644 3578

Elysian Collection
Luxury chalets in Zermatt
Tel +353 1 288 6634

Erna Low
Self-drive holidays and accommodation in the Alps; tailormade to North America
Tel 0845 863 0525

Esprit Ski
Families specialist in Europe
Tel 01252 618300

Exodus
Cross-country skiing holidays
Tel 0845 287 3645

Family Friendly Skiing
Family specialist in the Three Valleys – in-house nannies
Tel +33 450 327121

Family Ski Company
Family skiing holidays in France and Switzerland
Tel 01684 540333

Ferme de Montagne
Luxury chalet hotel in Les Gets
Tel 0844 669 8652

First Choice Ski
Major mainstream operator
Tel 0871 664 0130

First Luggage
Door-to-door luggage collection/delivery service
Tel 0800 083 5503

Flexiski
Weekends and corporate events in Europe
Tel 020 8939 0864

Friendship Travel
Holidays for singles 25 to 60
Tel 0871 200 2035

Frontier Ski
Holidays in Canada and the USA
Tel 020 8776 8709

Funway Holidays
US and Canada programme
Tel 0844 557 0770

Go Montgenevre
Holidays in Montgenèvre
Tel +33 (0)688 358473

Haig Ski
Chalet with guiding near Morzine
Tel +33 450 811950

Hannibals
Holidays in Serre-Chevalier
Tel 01233 813105

Headwater Holidays
Cross-country skiing holidays
Tel 01606 720199

High Mountain Holidays
Holidays in Chamonix
Tel 01993 775540

Holiday in Alps
Chalets and apartments in St Gervais and Les Contamines
Tel 01327 828239

Host Savoie
Catered chalets and apartments in Morzine
Tel +33 698 837987

Hundred Hills
Short-break chalets in Tignes and Val d'Isère
0191 406 6160

Huski
Chalet holidays in Chamonix
Tel 08000 971 760

Ice and Fire
Chalet in Les Coches (Paradiski)
Tel 07855 717997

Ifyouski.com
Ski travel agent
Tel 0844 338 0060

Iglu.com
Ski travel agent
Tel 020 8542 6658

Independent Ski Links
Ski travel agent
Tel 01964 533905

I Need Snow
Ski travel agent
Tel 020 8123 7817

Inghams
Major mainstream operator
Tel 020 8780 4444

Inntravel
Holidays in the snow
Tel 01653 617920

Inspired to Ski
Holidays with tuition in France
Tel 020 8133 8240

Interactive Resorts
Agent specialising in catered chalets worldwide
Tel 020 3080 0202

Interhome
Apartments and chalet rentals in Europe
Tel 020 8246 4100

Interski
Family/group holidays with tuition in the Aosta valley
Tel 01623 456333

Jagged Horizons
Corporate trips to the Alps
Tel 020 8123 7817

James Orr Heli-ski
Heli-skiing packages in Canada
Tel 01799 516964

Ski businesses

Interactive resort shortlist builder at www.wtss.co.uk

Jeffersons Private Jet Holidays
Luxury holidays by private jet
Tel 020 8746 2496

Just Skiing
Courmayeur specialist plus La Thuile
Tel 01202 479988

Just Slovenia
Accommodation in Slovenia
Tel 01373 814230

Kaluma Ski
Tailor-made holidays in the Alps
Tel 01730 260 263

Karibuni
Short-break chalet holidays in La Clusaz
Tel 0845 557 5983

Kwik Ski
Ski travel agent
Tel 0800 655 6300

Lagrange Holidays
Ski holidays in Europe
Tel 020 7371 6111

The Last Resort
Catered and self-catered accommodation in Aravis
Tel 0800 652 3977

Le Ski
Chalets in Courchevel, Val d'Isère and La Tania
Tel 01484 548996

Luxury Chalet Collection
Luxury chalets in the Alps
Tel 01865 395001

Mark Warner
Chalet hotel holidays in big-name resorts
Tel 0844 884 3800

Marmotte Mountain Adventure
Chalets in Chamonix Valley
Tel +33 682 891523

Meriski
Chalet specialist in Méribel
Tel 01285 648518

MGS Ski Limited
Hotel and apartments in Val Cenis
Tel 01603 742842

Momentum Ski
Specialists in ski weekends and tailor-made holidays
Tel 020 7371 9111

Mountain Beds
Accommodation agents and Verbier specialists
Tel 01502 471960

A Mountain Chalet
Catered chalet in La Rosière
Tel 01704 879554

Mountain Heaven
Catered and self-catered accommodation in France and Switzerland
Tel 0151 625 1921

Mountain Lodge
Chalet hotel in Les Crosets, Portes du Soleil
Tel 0845 127 1750

Mountainsun Ltd
Chalets in Europe – short breaks and week-long trips
Tel 01273 257008

Mountain Tracks
Off-piste, hut-to-hut touring and avalanche awareness
Tel 020 8123 2978

Mountain Wave Travel
Accommodation in Europe
Tel 01430 471943

Neilson
Major mainstream operator
Tel 0845 070 3460

Nick Ski
Catered chalet in La Tania
Tel +33 673 436769

Norwegian Wood Travel
Holidays in Norway
Tel 01562 67707

The Oxford Ski Company
Ski travel agency
Tel 01865 398130

Peak Pursuits
Catered chalet in St Martin de Belleville
Tel 01322 866726

Peak Retreats
Holidays to traditional French Alps resorts
Tel 0844 576 0123

PGL Ski
School group specialist and holidays for teenagers
Tel 0844 371 0101

Pilaski
Holidays in Pila, Aosta Valley
Tel 01478 613561

PowderBeds
Hotels and apartments in Europe and North America
Tel 0131 243 8097

Powder Byrne
Luxury hotel holidays in Europe for families
Tel 020 8246 5300

Powder N Shine
Luxury chalets in Reberty (Les Menuires)
Tel +33 643 798160

Powder White
Holidays in big-name resorts
Tel 020 8877 8888

Powder White Lite
Accommodation in the Alps
Tel 020 8877 8888

Première Neige
Catered/self-catered holidays in Ste-Foy; nanny service
Tel 0870 383 1000

Pure Powder
Powder skiing in Canada, Alaska, Chile and Europe
Tel 020 7736 8191

Purple Ski
Chalet holidays in Méribel
Tel 01885 488799

PV-Holidays.com (Pierre & Vacances)
Apartments in France
Tel 0870 0267 145

Ramblers Holidays
Mostly cross-country skiing holidays
Tel 01707 331133

Reach4theAlps
Holidays in the French Alps
Tel 0845 680 1947

Richmond World Holidays
Christian holidays
Tel 020 3004 2661

Ride & Slide
Chalets in Morzine
Tel +33 450 388 962

Rocketski.com
Club hotels and chalets in France and Italy
Tel 01273 810777

Rude Chalets
Holidays in Morzine, Avoriaz and Chamonix
Tel 0870 068 7030

Scott Dunn Ski
Luxury chalet and hotel holidays in the Alps
Tel 020 8682 5050

Select Ski Chalets
Chalets in Hochkönig and hotel in Saalbach
Tel 01273 645666

Silver Ski
Chalet holidays in France
Tel 01622 735544

Simon Butler Skiing
Holidays in Megève with ski instruction included
Tel 0870 873 0001

Simply Alpine
Chalets and apartments in Europe and N America
Tel 023 9279 8901

Ski 2
Specialists in Champoluc (Monterosa)
Tel 01962 713330

Ski Addiction
Chalets/hotels in the Portes du Soleil and hotels in Ischgl
Tel +33 450 733983

Skialot
Chalet in Châtel
Tel 0780 156 9264

Ski Alpage
Chalet in St-Martin-de-Belleville
Tel +33 479 089228

Ski Amis
Catered chalet and self-catered holidays in the French Alps
Tel 020 3411 5439

Ski Basics
Catered chalets in Méribel
Tel 0845 123 6064

Ski Beat
Chalets in the French Alps
Tel 01243 780405

Ski Blanc
Chalet holidays in Méribel
Tel 020 8502 9082

SkiBound
Schools division of First Choice
Tel 01273 244570

Skibug
Catered chalets in La Plagne and La Rosiere
Tel 01342 317573

Ski Chamonix
Specialists in Chamonix chalets
Tel 020 7401 1101

Ski Club Freshtracks
Group holidays for Ski Club of Great Britain members
Tel 0845 458 0784

Ski Collection
French 3- and 4-star self-catering apartment specialist
Tel 0844 576 0175

Ski Cuisine
Chalets in Méribel
Tel 01702 589543

Ski-Dazzle
Chalet holidays in Les Trois Vallées
Tel +33 479 001725

Ski Deep
Chalets in La Tania and Le Praz
Tel +33 479 081905

Ski-direct.co.uk
Ski travel agent
Tel 0844 553 3501

Ski Etoile
Chalets, hotels and apartments in Montgenèvre
Tel 01952 253252

Ski Europe
Ski travel agent
Tel 01350 728869

Ski Expectations
Small travel agency specialising in ski holidays
Tel 01799 531888

Ski Famille
Chalets with inclusive childcare
Tel 0845 644 3764

Ski France
Packaged and tailor-made holidays in France
Tel 0845 862 1121

Ski Freedom
Chalets in Verbier, Champéry and Zinal
Tel 0871 234 1935

Ski Hame
Catered chalets in Méribel and La Tania
Tel 01875 320157

Ski Hiver
Chalets in Paradiski
Tel 020 8144 4160

Ski-in.co.uk
Apartment and chalet in Serre-Chevalier
Tel 01630 672540

Ski Independence
USA, Canada, Japan, France, Switzerland and Austria
Tel 0131 243 8097

Skiing Austria
Agent for accommodation in Austria
Tel 020 8123 7817

Ski La Cote
Catered chalet holidays in the Portes du Soleil
Tel 01482 668357

Ski Line
Ski travel agent + chalets in Europe and North America
Tel 020 8313 3999

Ski Link
Courchevel specialist
Tel 01934 820854

Ski Magic
Chalet holidays in La Tania
Tel 0844 993 3686

Ski McNeill
Ski travel agent
Tel 028 9066 6699

Ski Miquel Holidays
Small but eclectic programme
Tel 01457 821200

Ski-Monterosa Ltd
Monterosa (Alagna) specialist
Tel 020 7361 0086

Ski Morgins Holidays
Chalet holidays in Morgins
Tel 01568 770681

Ski Morzine
Accommodation in Morzine
Tel 0845 370 1104

Skiology.co.uk
Chalets in Les Carroz and Morzine
Tel 0207 183 0688

Ski Olympic
Chalet holidays in France
Tel 01302 328820

Ski Peak
Specialist in Vaujany
Tel 01428 608070

SkiPlan Travel Service
Schools programme
Tel 0871 222 6565

Ski Power
Chalets in La Tania, Courchevel and Val d'Isère
Tel 01737 306029

Ski Rosie
Tel 00 41 24 477 7677

Ski Safari
Multi-resort safaris
Tel 01273 224060

Ski Soleil
Chalet and apartments in La Plagne
Tel 020 3239 3454

Ski Solutions
Ski travel agent + tailor-made holidays
Tel 020 7471 7777

Ski Supreme
Holidays to France and to Pila (Italy)
Tel 0845 194 7541

Ski Surf
Ski travel agent
Tel 020 8731 2111

Skitopia
Hotels and chalets in the French Alps
Tel 0844 412 9919

Ski Total
Chalet holidays in Europe
Tel 01252 618333

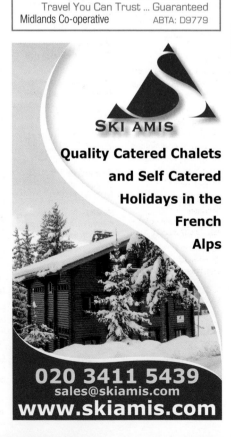
Ski businesses

681

Interactive resort shortlist builder at **www.wtss.co.uk**

Skitracer.com
Ski travel agent
Tel 020 8600 1650

Ski Travel Centre
Ski travel agent
Tel 0845 118 0092

Ski-Val
Catered chalets in Val d'Isère and St Anton
Tel 01822 611200

Ski Verbier
Specialists in Verbier chalets
Tel 020 7401 1101

Ski Weekend
Tailor-made short breaks
Tel 01392 878353

Ski Weekender
Ski weekend specialist in La Clusaz
Tel 0845 557 5983

Skiweekends.com
Weekends and short breaks to the Alps
Tel 08444 060600

Skiworld
Catered chalets, hotels and self-catering apartments in Europe, USA and Canada
Tel 08444 930 430

Ski Yogi
Hotels/catered chalets in Italy
Tel 01799 531886

SkiZinal
Catered/self-catering chalets in Zinal (Val d'Anniviers)
Tel 0208 144 7575

Sloping Off
Schools holidays
Tel 01273 648200

Snowbizz
Family ski specialist in Puy-St-Vincent
Tel 01778 341455

Snowcard Insurance Services
Winter sports insurance
Tel 01295 660836

Snowchateaux
Catered and self-catered chalet holidays in Paradiski
Tel 0800 066 4996

Snowcoach
Holidays to Austria and France
Tel 01727 866177

SnowCrazy
Chalets in the French Alps
Tel 01342 302910

Snow Finders
Travel agent + tour operator to Europe and N America
Tel 01858 466888

Snowfocus
Chalet in Châtel
Tel 01392 479555

Snow Hounds
Ski travel agent
Tel 01243 788487

Snowlife
Catered chalet in La Clusaz
Tel 01534 863630

Snow Nation
Group trips to La Rosière
Tel 01342 302910

Snoworks Ski Courses
Performance ski courses and adventure skiing
Tel 0844 543 0503

Snowpod
Serviced apartments with a twist in Tignes
Tel 07881 725062

Snowscape
Weekly and flexible trips to Austria
Tel 08453 708570

Snowslippers
Trips to Austria for groups
Tel 01792 843456

Snowstar Holidays
Catered chalets in Tignes
Tel 020 8133 8411

Snowy Pockets
Chalet/apartment holidays in France and Switzerland
Tel 01707 251696

Solo's
Singles' holidays
Tel 0844 815 0005

La Source
Accommodation in Villard-Reculas (Alpe-d'Huez)
Tel 01707 655988

Sovereign Ski
Chalets in Méribel
Tel 07518 582147

Stanford Skiing
Megève specialist
Tel 01603 477471

Star Ski Chalets
Chalets in Morzine
Tel +33 679 181401

STC Ski
Europe and N America, specialising in Austria
Tel 01483 771222

Sugar Mountain
Chalet in Morzine
Tel +33 450 749033

Supertravel
Upmarket European and North American holidays
Tel 020 7962 9933

Susie Ward Alpine Holidays
Accommodation in Châtel
Tel +33 450 734087

Swiss Travel Service
Hotels in Switzerland
Tel 0844 879 8812

Switzerland Travel Centre
Specialists in Swiss resorts
Tel 020 7420 4934

Ted Bentley Chalet Holidays
Luxury chalet holidays in Courchevel and Nendaz
Tel 01934 820854

Teletext Holidays
Travel agency
Tel 0844 767 6395

TheWhiteChalet.com
Chalet in Argentière
Tel +33 450 542284

Thomson Ski
Major mainstream operator
Tel 0871 971 0578

Tracks European Adventures
Customised tours in the Alps
Tel 024 498 1347

Trail Alpine
Chalet in Morzine
Tel 01745 570106

Transylvania Live
Holidays in Romania
Tel 0808 101 6781

V-Ski
Self-catered chalets in Verbier
Tel +41 (0)79 431 9228

Val d'Isère A La Carte
Specialists in Val d'Isère hotel/self-catering holidays
Tel +33 629 894457

VIP
Chalets in the Alps
Tel 0844 557 3119

Virgin Snow
Holidays to America and Canada
Tel 0844 557 4212

White Roc
Tailor-made hotel/chalet/apartment holidays
Tel 020 7792 1188

YSE
Chalet holidays in Val d'Isère
Tel 0845 122 1414

Zenith Holidays
Holidays in the Alps and Pyrenees with flexible transport arrangements
Tel 01737 852242

Ski businesses

682

Weekly news updates and resort links at www.wtss.co.uk

Snow Finders
Ski & Board Holidays
Europe • North America • South America
Chalets • Hotels • Apartments

Snow Finders Aspen House 12 Kings Head Place
Market Harborough LE16 7JT Tel: 01858 466888
Fax: 01858 466788 www.snowfinders.com
ABTA
J5552

SKI RETAILERS

Here we list ski equipment shops – all these shops stock this guidebook.

SOUTH-WEST ENGLAND

Chelstondirect.com
Unit 6 Monument View,
Chelston Business Park,
Wellington
Tel 0844 351 1078

Devon Ski Centre
Oak Place, Newton Abbot,
Devon
Tel 01626 351278

Snow & Rock
Units 1-3 Shield Retail
Centre, Link Road, Filton,
Bristol
Tel 0117 914 3000

Snow & Rock
Unit 2 Bishops Retail Park,
Sidmouth Rd, Exeter
Tel 01392 357600

Snowtrax
Matchams Lane, Hurn,
Christchurch, Dorset
Tel 01202 499155

Team Ski
37/38 High East Street,
Dorchester, Dorset
Tel 01305 268035

SOUTH-EAST ENGLAND

Alpine Room
71-73 Main Road, Danbury,
Essex
Tel 01245 223563

Snow & Rock
54-55 Market Street, Brighton
Tel 01273 827660

Snow & Rock
99 Fordwater Road, Chertsey,
Surrey
Tel 01932 566886

Snow & Rock
188 Kensington High Street,
London
Tel 020 7937 0872

Snow & Rock
4 Mercer Street, Covent
Garden, London
Tel 020 7420 1444

Snow & Rock
4 Gray's Inn Road, Holborn,
London
Tel 020 7831 6900

Snow & Rock
Sporting Club, 38-42 King's
Road, London
Tel 020 7589 5418

Snow & Rock
47-51 William Street, London
Tel 020 7256 3940

Snow & Rock
5th floor Harrods, 87-135
Brompton Road, London
Tel 020 7173 6476

Snow & Rock
North Face, 28 Palace St,
Victoria, London
Tel 020 7630 4969

Snow & Rock
The Boardwalk, Port Solent,
Portsmouth, Hampshire
Tel 023 9220 5388

Snow & Rock
Unit 1 Davidson Way, Rom
Valley Way, Romford, Essex
Tel 01708 436400

Two Seasons
28-30 Castle Street, Kingston
on Thames
Tel 020 8974 8973

MIDDLE ENGLAND

Lockwoods Ski Shop
125-129 Rugby Road,
Milverton, Leamington Spa,
Warwickshire
Tel 01926 339388

Snow & Rock
14 Priory Queensway,
Birmingham
Tel 0121 236 8280

Two Seasons
Unit 64 Lower Precinct,
Coventry
Tel 024 7663 0020

Two Seasons
Unit 126 North Mall, The
Westfield Centre, Derby
Tel 01332 343284

Two Seasons
Unit 1C Regents Court,
Leamington Spa
Tel 01926 888169

Two Seasons
43-47 High Street, Leicester
Tel 0116 262 5855

Two Seasons
26 Bakers Lane, Lichfield
Tel 01543 411422

Two Seasons
28-29 Northbrook Street,
Newbury
Tel 01635 41011

Two Seasons
229-231 Wellingborough
Road, Northampton
Tel 01604 627377

Two Seasons
32-34 Princes Walk,
Grosvenor Centre,
Northampton
Tel 01604 603737

Two Seasons
Unit 3-4, Number 1 Fletcher
Gate, Nottingham
Tel 0115 950 1333

Two Seasons
213-217 Broad Street Mall,
Reading
Tel 01189 588222

Two Seasons
32-34 Mill Lane, Solihull
Tel 0121 705 5544

Two Seasons
15 Pump Street, Worcester
Tel 01905 731144

EASTERN ENGLAND

Snow & Rock
Hemel Ski Centre, St Albans
Hill, Hemel Hempstead
Tel 01422 235305

Snow & Rock
97-99 London Road, St
Albans, Herts
Tel 01727 848102

Two Seasons
Unit 5, Christ Lane,
Cambridge
Tel 01223 362832

Two Seasons
16 Westgate, Peterborough
Tel 01773 312184

NORTHERN ENGLAND

Freetime Climb + Ski
1-2 Market Street, Carlisle
Tel 01228 598210

Glide & Slide
5/7 Station Road, Otley
Tel 01943 461136

**Severn Sports Mountain
Adventures Ltd**
5-7 Church Lane, Cross
Gates, Leeds
Tel 0113 264 3847

Snow & Rock
Metro Park West, Gibside
Way, Gateshead
Tel 0191 493 3680

Snow & Rock
Princess Parkway, Princess
Park, Didsbury, Manchester
Tel 0161 448 4444

Snow & Rock
Unit 6, Chill Factore Centre,
Trafford Way, Trafford Quays,
Manchester
Tel 0161 746 1010

Snow & Rock
Sheffield Ski Centre, Vale
Road, Parkwood Springs,
Sheffield
Tel 0114 275 1700

Snow & Rock
Unit 1 Eastham Point, New
Chester Road, Eastham,
Wirral
Tel 0151 328 5500

SCOTLAND

Craigdon Mountain Sports
5 St Andrew's Street,
Aberdeen
Tel 01224 624333

Craigdon Mountain Sports
78 Academy Street, Inverness
Tel 01463 248600

Craigdon Mountain Sports
61-65 High Street, Inverurie,
Aberdeenshire
Tel 01467 625855

Craigdon Mountain Sports
25-29 Kinnoull Street, Perth
Tel 01738 831006

NORTHERN IRELAND

Macski
140 Lisburn Road, Belfast
Tel 028 9066 5525

REPUBLIC OF IRELAND

Snow & Rock
Unit 3.2 Dundrum Town
Centre, Dundrum, Dublin 14
Tel 00353 (0) 1 2924700

683

RESORT DIRECTORY / INDEX

This is an index to the resort chapters in the book; you'll find page references for about 400 resorts that are described in those chapters (note that if the resort you are looking up is covered in a chapter devoted to a bigger resort, the page reference will be to the start of the chapter, not to the exact page on which the minor resort is described). You'll also find here brief descriptions here of another 700 resorts, most of them smaller than those we've covered in full.

Key

🚠 Lifts
🎿 Pistes
🏨 UK tour operators

49 Degrees North USA
Inland area with best snow in Washington State, including 120-acre bowl reserved for powder weekends.
1195m; slopes 1195–1760m
🚠 5 🎿 780 acres

Abetone Italy
Main resort in the exposed Apennines, two hours from Florence and Pisa – so makes a good short break option. Small and charming village, with prettily wooded slopes that are mostly north-facing and well covered by snowmaking. Some good intermediate terrain and excellent nursery slopes, three terrain parks and children's area. But most lifts are slow chairs and drags.
1400m; slopes 1200–1940m
🚠 25 🎿 70km

Abtenau Austria
Sizeable village in Dachstein-West region near Salzburg, on large plain ideal for cross-country.
710m; slopes 710–1190m
🚠 7 🎿 12km

Achenkirch Austria
Unspoiled, low-altitude Tirolean village close to Niederau and Alpbach. Beautiful setting overlooking a lake.
930m; slopes 930–1800m
🚠 30 🎿 50km 🏨 Ramblers

Adelboden 470

Les Aillons-Margériaz France
Traditional village near Chambéry. Sheltered slopes.
1000m; slopes 1000–1900m
🚠 21 🎿 40km

Alagna 432
Small resort on the east fringe of the Monterosa Ski area.

Alba Italy
Picturesque Trentino village with a small, quiet area; access to the Sella Ronda at nearby Canazei.
1515m; slopes 1515–2428m
🚠 6 🎿 15km

Alberschwende 208
Village in Bregenzerwald.
720m 🚠 8 🎿 18km

Albiez-Montrond France
Authentic old French village in Maurienne valley with panoramic views. Own easy slopes and close to other ski areas.
1500m; slopes 1500–2200m
🚠 13 🎿 67 hectares

Alleghe Italy
Dolomite village near Cortina in a pretty lakeside setting close to numerous areas.
1000m 🚠 24 🎿 80km

Les Allues 302
Rustic village on the road up to Méribel.

Alpbach 112

Alpe-d'Huez 222

Alpe-du-Grand-Serre France
Tiny resort near Alpe-d'Huez and Les Deux-Alpes. Good for bad-weather days.
1370m; slopes 1370–2185m
🚠 14 🎿 55km

Alpendorf Austria
Outpost of St Johann im Pongau, at one end of an extensive three-valley lift network linking via Wagrain to Flachau – all part of the Salzburger Sportwelt area. Good intermediate runs.
850m; slopes 800–2185m
🚠 64 🎿 200km
🏨 Crystal, Snowslippers

Alpenglow USA
Alaskan ski resort.
762m; slopes 2500–3900m
🚠 4 🎿 320 acres

Alpine Meadows USA
Squaw Valley's neighbour, with similar, lightly wooded terrain, an impressive snow record and runs of all classifications, but a modest total vertical; excellent beginner slopes and mostly uncrowded. The resort boundary is open – expeditions require guidance. There's no resort in the European sense, but there are lots of lodgings close by in lakeside Tahoe City.
2085m; slopes 2085–2635m
🚠 13 🎿 2400 acres
🏨 Virgin Snow

Alps Resort South Korea
Korea's most northerly, snow-reliable resort, about five hours from Seoul. 🚠 5

Alta 594

Alta Badia 443
Part of the Sella Ronda circuit.

Altenmarkt Austria
Unspoiled village, well placed just off the Salzburg-Villach autobahn for numerous resorts including snow-sure Obertauern and those in the Salzburger Sportwelt.
855m; slopes 855–1570m
🚠 8 🎿 20km

Alto Campoo Spain
Barren, desolate place near Santander, with undistinguished slopes, but magnificent wilderness views.
1650m; slopes 1650–2130m
🚠 13

Alt St Johann Switzerland
Old cross-country village with Alpine slopes connecting into Unterwasser area near Liechtenstein.
900m; slopes 900–2260m
🚠 17 🎿 60km

Alyeska USA
Alaskan area 60km from Anchorage, with luxury hotel.
75m; slopes 75–1200m
🚠 9 🎿 785 acres
🏨 Frontier, Skiworld

Aminona 478
Purpose-built resort in the Crans-Montana network.

Andalo Italy
Trentino village not far from Madonna.
1050m; slopes 1035–2125m
🚠 16 🎿 60km

Andelsbuch 208
Village in Bregenzerwald.
615m 🚠 8 🎿 15km

Andermatt 473

Andorra la Vella 90
Andorra's capital.

Angel Fire USA
Intermediate area near Taos, New Mexico. Height usually ensures good snow.
2620m; slopes 2620–3255m
🚠 5 🎿 455 acres

Les Angles 338

Ankogel Austria
Limited but varied area in the Hohe Tauern region in Carinthia; close to the Molltal Glacier and Slovenia. Mostly red and black runs; longest is 7km. Lift station a short drive from Mallnitz village.
1300m; slopes 1300–2635m
🚠 7 🎿 35km

Annaberg-Lungötz Austria
Peaceful village near Filzmoos in a pretty setting, sharing a sizeable area with Gosau.
775m; slopes 775–1620m
🚠 33 🎿 65km

Annupuri 676
One of Niseko's interlinked areas.

Antagnod 404
Village in the Aosta valley.
1710m; slopes 1710–2305m
🚠 4 🎿 14km

Anthony Lakes USA
Small area in Oregon with one chair and two beginner lifts.
2165m; slopes 2165–2435m
🚠 3 🎿 21 trails

Anzère Switzerland
Sympathetically designed modern resort on a sunny balcony near Crans-Montana, with uncrowded slopes suited to leisurely intermediates. Lots of old, slow lifts but the area is very much a family resort, with village nursery slopes and soon-to-open new spa centre. Little to challenge experts except the 5km Pas de Maimbre black run, an itinerary and some gentle off-piste. There's a terrain park. For a small place there is a reasonable choice of restaurants and half a dozen bars. Lots of marked walks and a 3km toboggan run.
1500m; slopes 1500–2420m
🚠 11 🎿 52km 🏨 Lagrange

Aosta 404
Historic town below Pila.
1800m; slopes 1550–2750m
🚠 14 🎿 70km

Aosta valley 404

Apex Canada
Small, friendly, rather isolated modern village. Well worth stopping off here for a night or two on a tour of western BC resorts. Varied terrain that suits confident intermediates best, but also excellent beginner slopes.
1575m; slopes 1575–2180m
🚠 4 🎿 1112 acres
🏨 Frontier, Ski Safari

Aprica Italy
Ugly, straggling village between Lake Comb and the Brenta Dolomites, with bland slopes and limited facilities.
1180m; slopes 1180–2300m
🚠 18 🎿 50km

Arabba 443

Aragnouet-Piau France
Purpose-built mid-mountain satellite with lifts up from the old valley town too. Best suited to families, beginners and early intermediates.
1850m; slopes 1420–2500m
⛷ 12 🚠 65km

Arapahoe Basin USA
Developing, exceptionally high day-skiing area near Keystone. Excellent snowfall record and very long season. Good mix of open and wooded runs of every standard, plus serious steeps.
3285m; slopes 3285–3800m
⛷ 7 🚠 900 acres

Araucarias Chile
Exotic area in central Chile, around and below a mildly active volcano in the Conguillio National Park.
1500m ⛷ 4 🚠 350 hectares

Arcalis 90
Isolated ski area in Andorra.
1940m; slopes 1940–2625m
⛷ 13 🚠 28.5km

Les Arcs 232

Ardent 242
Quiet hamlet with quick access to Avoriaz.

Åre 667

Arêches-Beaufort France
Secluded little village 25km from Albertville, with mostly intermediate terrain on two areas 3km apart. The slopes of both Les Saisies and Les Contamines are less than 25km away.
1080m; slopes 1080–2300m
⛷ 12 🚠 55km

Argentière 247
Village beneath Chamonix's Grands Montets.

Arinsal 93

Arizona Snowbowl USA
Small but interesting ski area just outside the pleasant town of Flagstaff. Worth a visit if en route to the nearby Grand Canyon in winter. Low snowfall despite the high altitude is a drawback.
slopes 2690–3290m ⛷ 4

Arnoldstein / Dreiländereck Austria
One of several little areas overlooking the town of Villach.
680m; slopes 680–1455m
⛷ 7 🚠 17km

Arolla Switzerland
Tiny village in pretty riverside setting south of Sion in the Val d'Hérens. Main attraction is heli-skiing. Wonderful descents from 3800m.
2000m; slopes 2000–2890m
⛷ 6 🚠 47km

Arosa Switzerland
A classic all-round winter resort, near Chur. High and remote, in a sheltered basin at the head of a beautiful wooded valley. The centre is not particularly pretty, though its lakeside setting adds charm. It is a quiet family place, where people stroll in fur coats, take sleigh rides, or skate across the frozen lake. A hill separates this area from the older, prettier Inner-Arosa up the valley. Lodging spreads widely, but there is an excellent free shuttle-bus. The slopes cover two main sectors mostly above the treeline; mainly enjoyable cruises. The shadier Hörnli area holds it snow well. The runs are not particularly challenging, though there are off-piste opportunities. Beginners have easy slopes at mid-mountain, but they can get crowded, though queues are rare.
1740–1830m; slopes 1800–2655m ⛷ 13 🚠 70km
✉ *Alpine Answers, Crystal, Crystal Finest, Independent Ski Links, Momentum, Powder Byrne, Ski Safari, Ski Solutions, Ski Weekend, Snow Finders, Snowy Pockets, Switzerland Travel Centre, White Roc*

Arrowhead 573
Slope-side hamlet next to Beaver Creek.

Artesina Italy
Purpose-built Piedmont resort south of Turin, lacking character and atmosphere. Part of Mondolé ski area with Prato Nevoso.
1300m; slopes 1320–2100m
⛷ 23 🚠 130km

Ascutney Mountain USA
Family resort in Vermont 60km from Killington, 200km from Boston.
⛷ 6 🚠 200 acres

Asiago Italy
Sizeable resort close to Verona, but at low altitude and with limited vertical.
1000m; slopes 1000–1380m
⛷ 8 🚠 12 pistes

Aspen 566
One of the biggest ski areas in eastern US. Uncrowded slopes. Lodging in nearby North Conway, and other New Hampshire areas close by.
slopes 180–715m
⛷ 12 🚠 280 acres

Au 208
Village in Bregenzerwald.
800m; slopes 800–2060m
⛷ 8 🚠 44km

Auffach Austria
Small, quiet, attractive old village with the longest, highest, sunniest runs in the Wildschönau area.
875m ⛷ 25 🚠 70km

Auris-en-Oisans 222
Quiet hamlet linked to Alpe-d'Huez.

Auron France
Pleasant, family-oriented resort with varied, sheltered, intermediate slopes; a stark contrast to nearby Isola 2000. Good choice of mountain restaurants.
1600m; slopes 1150–2450m
⛷ 20 🚠 135km ✉ Ski France

Auronzo di Cadore Italy
Sizeable village that's a cheaper base for visiting Cortina. Its own slopes are of negligible interest.
865m; slopes 865–1585m
⛷ 5 🚠 7km

Aussois France
Charming rustic working village near Modane in the Maurienne valley. Small but interesting south-facing ski area, good for intermediates and families.
1500m; slopes 1500–2750m
⛷ 10 🚠 55km
✉ *AmeriCan Ski, Peak Retreats*

Autrans France
Major cross-country village, close to Grenoble. Two limited areas of downhill slopes.
1050m; slopes 1050–1650m
⛷ 12 🚠 20km

Avon USA
Small town only a couple of miles from Beaver Creek. Inexpensive base from which to ski Beaver Creek, Vail and Breckenridge.
✉ *AmeriCan Ski, Ski Line*

Avoriaz 1800 242

Axamer Lizum Austria
Mountain outpost of the Inn-side village of Axams. A simple ski station and nothing more, but it does have some good slopes and reliable snow conditions. Covered by standard Innsbruck pass.
1580m; slopes 830–2340m
⛷ 10 🚠 40km
✉ *Crystal, First Choice*

Axams Austria
Quiet village in Innsbruck area, at bottom of the Axamer Lizum ski area.
880m; slopes 830–2340m
⛷ 10 🚠 40km

Ax-les-Thermes France
Sizeable spa village near Font-Romeu and Andorra. Gondola access to the ski area above Bonascre. Mostly fast chairlifts, serving a modest area of intermediate slopes.
1400m; slopes 1400–2400m
⛷ 17 🚠 75km

Bad Gastein 115

Badger Pass USA
Base for 350 miles of superb backcountry touring in Yosemite National Park. Spectacular views.
2195m; slopes 2195–2435m
⛷ 5 🚠 90 acres

Badia (Pedraces) 443
Village linked via La Villa to the Sella Ronda circuit.

Bad Kleinkirchheim Austria
Spacious, quiet spa village in south-east Austria spread out along a valley near the Italian and Slovenian borders. Virtually all the slopes are ideal for intermediates; BKK has little to keep experts interested apart from the beautiful, long Franz Klammer downhill run, which goes from top to bottom away from all the lifts. For beginners there are nursery slopes at BKK and there are easy blue runs to progress to. There are 23 mountain restaurants in the two main sectors. BKK takes cross-country seriously, with 50km of tracks. Most of the hotels are comfortable 4-stars and there are lots of gasthofs and self-catering apartments. There are plenty of places for eating out, too. Après-ski is relatively quiet, but there's plenty to do off the slopes – spa facilities are excellent.
1090m; slopes 1090–2055m
⛷ 25 🚠 103km
✉ *BoardnLodge, PowderBeds, STC*

Banff 623

Bansko 668

Baqueira-Beret 661

Barboleuse 531
Quiet base for skiing the Villars slopes.

Bardonecchia Italy
Sizeable railway town set in an attractive valley near the entrance to the Fréjus road tunnel; overlooked until the 2006 Turin Winter Olympics brought investment and raised its profile as a good-value intermediate destination. What it lacks in classic mountain charm, it gains in a fairly extensive area of slopes on two separate mountains linked by free bus. There are plenty of hotels and the former Olympic village residence has spacious apartment accommodation. The resort's easy road and rail links mean it is popular with weekenders from Turin, but otherwise fairly quiet during the week with plenty of leisurely cruising on uncrowded pistes – worth considering as a base for touring other nearby French and Italian resorts too. Snow reliability isn't particularly great though and, coupled with the large number of awkward draglifts, may deter some visitors.
1310m; slopes 1290–2695m
⛷ 21 🚠 100km
✉ *Alpine Answers, Crystal, Erna Low, First Choice, Neilson, Thomson*

Barèges 338
Old Pyrenean spa village,
sharing area with La Mongie.

Bariloche (Catedral) Argentina
The place to stay when skiing
Cerro Catedral, this was once
a quaint lakeside town, but is
now a substantial resort –
including the Llao Llao Resort
and Spa. The slopes at
Cathedral are 20 minutes by
shuttle-bus.
slopes 1030–2180m
⛰ 39 ✦ 103km

Les Barzettes 478
Smaller base along the road
from Crans-Montana.

Bayrischzell Germany
Bavarian resort south of
Munich and close to Austrian
border.
800m; slopes 1090–1563m
⛰ 25 ✦ 40km

Bear Mountain USA
Southern California's main
area, in the beautiful San
Bernardino National Forest
region. Full snowmaking.
slopes 2170–2685m
⛰ 12 ✦ 195 acres

Bears Town South Korea
Modern resort with runs cut
out of thick forest. Biggest
resort near Seoul (only an
hour's drive), so it can get
very crowded. ⛰ 9

Bear Valley USA
Resort in northern California,
between Lake Tahoe and
Yosemite.
2010m; slopes 2010–2590m
⛰ 10 ✦ 1280 acres

Beaulard Italy
Little place just off the road
between Sauze d'Oulx and
Bardonecchia.
1215m; slopes 1215–2120m
⛰ 6 ✦ 20km

Beaver Creek 573

Beaver Mountain USA
Small Utah area north of Salt
Lake City, too far from Park
City for a day trip.
2195m; slopes 2195–2680m
⛰ 3 ✦ 525 acres

Beitostølen Norway
Small family resort in
southern Norway (east of
Bergen), with lots of cross-
country in the region.
900m ⛰ 9 ✦ 25km
🚄 Neilson

Belleayre Mountain USA
State-owned resort near
Albany, New York State. Cheap
prices but old lifts and short
runs.
775m; slopes 775–1015m
⛰ 7 ✦ 170 acres

Bellwald Switzerland
Traditional Rhône valley resort
near Fiesch, Riederalp and
Bettmeralp. Part of the Goms
Valley region.
1600m; slopes 1600–2560m
⛰ 5 ✦ 30km

Ben Lomond Australia
Small intermediate/beginner
area in Ben Lomond National
Park, Tasmania, 260km from
Hobart.
1450m; slopes 1460–1570m
⛰ 6 ✦ 14 hectares

Berchtesgaden Germany
Pleasant old town close to
Salzburg, known for its Nordic
skiing but with several little
Alpine areas nearby. *550m*

Bergün Switzerland
Traditional, quiet, unspoiled,
virtually traffic-free little family
resort on the rail route
between Davos and St Moritz.
5km toboggan run.
1375m; slopes 1400–2550m
⛰ 3 ✦ 23km

Berkshire East USA
Resort in Massachusetts,
southern New England, near
the Mohawk Trail.
slopes 165–525m
⛰ 5 ✦ 200 acres

Berwang 212
Quiet village in the Zuspitze
Arena, near Lermoos.

Bessans France
Old cross-country village near
Modane well placed for
touring Maurienne valley
resorts.
1710m; slopes 1740–2200m
⛰ 2 ✦ 3km

Besse France
Charming old village built out
of lava, with purpose-built
slope-side satellite Super-
Besse. Beautiful extinct-
volcano scenery.
1050m; slopes 1300–1850m
⛰ 23 ✦ 43km 🚄 Lagrange

Bethel USA
Pleasant, historic town very
close to Sunday River, Maine.
Attractive alternative to
staying in the slope-side
resort.

Le Bettex 290
Small base above St-Gervais,
with links to Megève.

Bettmeralp Switzerland
Central village of the sizeable
Aletsch area near Brig, high
above the Rhône valley, amid
spectacular glacial scenery.
Reached by cable cars from
the valley. Two new fast lifts
2010/11.
1950m; slopes 1925–2870m
⛰ 35 ✦ 100km

Beuil-les-Launes France
Alpes-Maritimes resort closest
to Nice. Medieval village
which shares area with
Valberg.
1460m; slopes 1400–2011m
⛰ 26 ✦ 90km

Bezau 208
Bregenzerwald village.
620m ⛰ 8 ✦ 15km

Biberwier 212
Village in the Zugspitze Arena.

Bichlbach 212
Village in the Zugspitze Arena.

Bielmonte Italy
Popular with day trippers from
Milan. Worthwhile on a bad-
weather day.
1200m; slopes 1200–1620m
⛰ 9 ✦ 20km

Big Powderhorn USA
Area with the most 'resort'
facilities in south Lake
Superior region – and the
highest lift capacity too. The
area suffers from winds.
370m; slopes 370–560m
⛰ 10 ✦ 250 acres

Big Sky 608

Big White 630

Bischofshofen Austria
Working town and mountain
resort near St Johann im
Pongau, with very limited
local runs and the main
slopes starting nearby at
Muhlbach (Hochkönig area).
545m; slopes 545–1000m
⛰ 1 ✦ 2km

Bivio Switzerland
Quiet village near St Moritz
and Savognin, with easy
slopes opened up by a few
lifts.
1770m; slopes 1780–2560m
⛰ 4 ✦ 40km

Björkliden Sweden
538m vertical. Feb-to-May
Arctic Circle area. Ultra snow-
reliable. You can even ski in
caves – beautiful ice
formations. Magnificent
Lapland views. ⛰ 5 ✦ 15km

Björnrike Sweden
20 minutes from
Vemdalasskalet (same pass).
385m vertical. ⛰ 9 ✦ 15km

Black Mountain USA
New Hampshire area with
lodging in nearby Jackson.
⛰ 4 ✦ 143 acres

Blatten Switzerland
Mountainside hamlet above
Naters, beside the Rhône near
Brig. Small but tall Belalp ski
area, with larger Aletsch area
nearby.
1320m; slopes 1320–3100m
⛰ 9 ✦ 60km

Bled 672
Lakeside base in Slovenia.

Blue Cow Australia
Part of Perisher resort,
Australia's highest and
expanding ski area. Accessible
only by tube train. Nearest
town – Jindabyne. Six hours
from Sydney.
1890m; slopes 1605–2035m
⛰ 47 ✦ 3075 acres

Blue Mountain Canada
Largest area in Ontario, with
glorious views of Lake Huron.
High-capacity lift system and
100% snowmaking.
230m; slopes 230–450m
⛰ 15 ✦ 275 acres

Blue River Canada
Base of world-famous Mike
Wiegele heli-ski operation in
Cariboo and Monashee
mountains.

Bluewood USA
Particularly remote area even
by American north-west
standards. Worth a visit if
you're in Walla Walla.
1355m; slopes 1355–1725m
⛰ 3 ✦ 530 acres

Bogus Basin USA
Sizeable area overlooking
Idaho's attractive, interesting
capital, Boise. Limited
accommodation at the base.
1760m; slopes 1760–2310m
⛰ 8 ✦ 2600 acres

Bohinj Slovenia
Lakeside village near Bled set
in a beautiful valley, with
lovely views from its plateau
area of short runs high above.
540m; slopes 540–1480m
⛰ 6 ✦ 23km
🚄 Balkan Holidays, Crystal

Bois-d'Amont France
One of five resorts that make
up Les Rousses area in Jura
region on the Franco-Suisse
border.
1050m; slopes 1120–1680m
⛰ 40 ✦ 50km 🚄 Lagrange

Boi Taull Spain
A typical Pyrenean resort set
high above the Boi Valley,
close to the stunning Aigues
Tortes National Park. Good
intermediate terrain.
slopes 2020–2750m
⛰ 15 ✦ 44km

Bolognola Italy
Tiny area in Macerata region
near the Adriatic Riviera.
1070m; slopes 1070–1845m
⛰ 5 ✦ 8km

Bolton Valley USA
Resort near Stowe with mostly
intermediate slopes.
465m; slopes 465–960m
⛰ 6 ✦ 155 acres

Bonneval-sur-Arc France
Unspoiled, remote old village
in the Haute Maurienne valley
with many of its slopes at
high altitude. Pass to
neighbouring Val d'Isère is
closed in winter.
1800m; slopes 1800–3000m
⛰ 11 ✦ 25km

Bons 272
Rustic, unspoiled old hamlet
linked to Les Deux-Alpes.

Boreal USA
Closest area to north Lake
Tahoe town, Truckee. Limited
slopes, best for novices.
2195m; slopes 2195–2375m
⛰ 9 ✦ 380 acres

Bormio Italy
An attractive old spa town,
distinctly Italian and within
day-trip distance from Livigno
and Santa Caterina. The main
slopes are a 15-minute walk
from the centre, where a

gondola goes to the hub at Bormio 2000, with fast lifts to the high point at 3010m. The mountain is confined, long (vertical of 800m) and narrow – mainly suited to intermediates. The men's downhill course is a tough red. The nursery slopes are snow-sure, but there are few progression runs. There's a good terrain park and ample mountain huts. There are more slopes in a separate area, with fast lifts from Le Motte or Isolaccia, on the other side of town. The resort has over 40 hotels, plus a wide choice of restaurants. Après-ski is quite lively. There's a sports centre, thermal baths and ice rink.
1225m; slopes 1225–3010m
🚡 *31* 🚠 *98km* 🚌 *Solo's*

Borovets **668**

Bosco Chiesanuova Italy
Weekend day trippers' place near Verona. A long drive from any other resort.
1105m; slopes 1105–1805m
🚡 *18* 🚠 *20km*

Bosco Gurin Switzerland
Highest ski area in Ticino. The only German speaking village in the Italian canton.
1500m; slopes 1480–2400m
🚡 *6* 🚠 *30km*

Les Bottières France
Hamlet at the edge of the Sybelles area, with limited infrastructure and poor access to the main network – it takes three lifts to reach La Toussuire, before setting off for L'Ouillon. *1300m*

La Bourboule France
Spa and cross-country village with the Alpine slopes of Le Mont-Dore nearby. Spectacular extinct-volcano scenery.
850m; slopes 1050–1850m
🚡 *17* 🚠 *42km* 🚌 *Lagrange*

Bourg-d'Oisans France
Pleasant valley town on main Grenoble-Briançon road. Cheap base for visits to Alpe-d'Huez and Les Deux-Alpes.

Bourg-St-Maurice **232**
French valley town with a funicular to Les Arcs.

Bovec **672**
Town linked by gondola to Kanin-Sella Nevea.

Boyne Highlands USA
Area with impressive, high-capacity lift system for weekend Detroit crowds. Fierce winds off Lake Michigan a major drawback.
225m; slopes 225–390m
🚡 *10* 🚠 *240 acres*

Boyne Mountain USA
Popular with weekend Detroit crowds. Not as windy as sister resort Boyne Highlands.
190m; slopes 190–340m
🚡 *12* 🚠 *115 acres*

Bozel France
Small town that, in good snow conditions, you can ski down to off-piste from Courchevel and catch a bus back. Also near access road for Champagny-en-Vanoise (La Plagne ski area). *860m*

Bramans France
Old cross-country village near Modane. Well placed for touring numerous nearby resorts such as Val Cenis and Valloire. *1200m* 🚡 *1* 🚠 *3km*

Bramberg Austria
Village near Pass Thurn (Kitzbühel area). Shares slopes with Neukirchen. New gondola link from the valley in 2010/11.
820m; slopes 820–2150m
🚡 *15* 🚠 *55km*

Brand Austria
Family resort with small, low area. Linked to Burserburg ski area via a high altitude cable car across a dividing valley.
1035m; slopes 890–1920m
🚡 *14* 🚠 *55km* 🚌 *STC*

Les Brasses France
Collective name for six traditional hamlets with some of the closest slopes to Geneva, but best known for cross-country.
900m; slopes 900–1600m
🚡 *14* 🚠 *50km*

Braunwald Switzerland
Sunny but limited area near Zurich, a funicular ride above Linthal. Includes combi-mix lift.
1255m; slopes 1255–1900m
🚡 *9* 🚠 *32km*

Breckenridge **575**

Bregenzerwald **208**

Brentonico Italy
Little resort just off Verona-Trento motorway, with linked slopes of La Polsa and San Valentino above.
1160m; slopes 1160–1520m
🚡 *15* 🚠 *35km*

Bressanone Italy
Valley town 20 minutes by free ski-bus from the lift base of Plose. *565m*

La Bresse France
Largest resort in the northerly Vosges mountains near Strasbourg. Three separate downhill areas (with a lot of snowmaking), but also extensive ski de fond and lots of other activities.
900m; slopes 900–1350m
🚡 *24* 🚠 *220 hectares*
🚌 *Lagrange*

Briançon **347**
Part of the Grand Serre Chevalier region.

Brian Head USA
Utah area south of Salt Lake City, too far from Park City for a day trip.
2925m; slopes 2925–3445m
🚡 *10* 🚠 *500 acres*

Brides-les-Bains **302**
Quiet spa town in valley below Méribel.

Bridger Bowl **607**
Cay-trip resort near Big Sky, Montana.
1855m; slopes 1855–2460m
🚡 *6* 🚠 *1200 acres*

Brigels–Andiast Switzerland
In the same valley as Laax/Flims. Access from two sunny villages. Mostly red runs.
1300m; slopes 1100–2420m
🚡 *7* 🚠 *75km*

Brighton USA
Linked with Solitude. Total acreage is half that of Alta/Snowbird (in the next valley), but attracts fewer people so the powder doesn't get tracked out in hours. Four fast chairs, including one serving the resort's maximum vertical of 530m on Clayton Peak. This and the slightly lower Mt Millicent are almost all expert terrain, but other lifts serve a wide spectrum of runs. The resort's boundaries are open, and there are excellent backcountry adventures. Accommodation is in the slope-side Brighton Lodge and some cabins.
2670m; slopes 2435–3200m
🚡 *13* 🚠 *2250 acres*
🚌 *AmeriCan Ski*

Brixen im Thale **182**
Grossraum village that shares slopes with Söll and Ellmau.

Bromley USA
New York City weekend retreat, reputedly the warmest place to ski in chilly Vermont.
595m; slopes 595–1000m
🚡 *9* 🚠 *300 acres*

Bromont Canada
Purpose-built resort an hour east of Montreal, with one of the best small areas in eastern Canada, popular for its night skiing.
slopes 405–575m
🚡 *6* 🚠 *135 acres*

Bruck am Grossglockner Austria
Low beginners' resort, but also a quiet base from which to visit Zell am See. *755m*

Brundage Mountain USA
Remote, uncrowded Idaho area with glorious views across the lake towards Hell's Canyon. Mostly intermediate slopes. Also has a snowcat operation.
1760m; slopes 1760–2320m
🚡 *5* 🚠 *1300 acres*

Bruneck/Brunico Italy
Town with gondola link into the Plan de Corones/Kronplatz area. Italian name is Brunico.

Bruson **520**
Relaxing respite from Verbier's crowds.

Brusson **404**
Village in the Aosta valley.
1330m 🚡 *3* 🚠 *17km*

Les Bugnenets–Savagnieres Switzerland
Small area in the Jura, north of Neuchatel. Short runs served by draglifts. Valid with the Valais Ski Card.
slopes 1090–1440m
🚡 *7* 🚠 *30km*

Bukovel Ukraine
Ukraine's second highest resort with major expansion underway.
slopes 900–1370m
🚡 *14* 🚠 *50km*

Burke Mountain USA
Uncrowded, isolated family resort in Vermont with mostly intermediate slopes. Great views from the top.
385m; slopes 385–995m
🚡 *4* 🚠 *130 acres*

Bürserberg Austria
Undistinguished valley town linked to Brand via a high altitude cable car across a dividing valley.
890m; slopes 890–1920m
🚡 *14* 🚠 *55km*

Cairngorm **675**
Scottish ski resort.
slopes 550–1100m
🚡 *11* 🚠 *37km*

Caldirola Italy
Genoese weekend day-tripper spot in a remote region off the motorway to Turin.
1010m; slopes 1010–1450m
🚡 *3* 🚠 *4km*

Cambre-d'Aze France
Quiet ski area in the Pyrenees with few British visitors. Good beginner and intermediate terrain. Forms part of the Neiges Catalan (eight resorts on one pass).
1640m; slopes 1640–2400m
🚡 *17* 🚠 *35km*

Camigliatello Italy
Tiny area on the foot of the Italian 'boot' near Cosenza. Weekend/day-trip spot.
1270m; slopes 1270–1750m
🚡 *4* 🚠 *6km*

Campitello **443**
Linked to the Sella Ronda circuit.

Campitello Matese Italy
The only slopes near Naples. Surprisingly large area when snowcover is complete. Weekend crowds.
1440m; slopes 1440–2100m
🚡 *8* 🚠 *40km*

Campo di Giove Italy
Highest slopes in L'Aquila region east of Rome.
1070m; slopes 1145–2350m
🚡 *15* 🚠 *21km*

Campodolcino Italy
Valley town with funicular up to Madesimo's slopes.
1070m; slopes 1545–2880m
🚡 *6* 🚠 *8km*

Campo Felice Italy
Easiest resort to reach from
Rome, off Aquila motorway.
One of the better lift systems
in the vicinity.
1410m; slopes 1520–2065m
⛷ 15 🚠 40km

Campo Imperatore Italy
One of the best of many little
areas east of Rome in L'Aquila
region. *1980m* ⛷ 8 🚠 20km

Canazei 443
Lively rustic village in the
Sella Ronda.

Candanchu / Astún Spain
French border resort on Pau
road set in some of the
Pyrenees' most stunning
scenery. Almost exclusively
challenging open slopes.
1450m; slopes 1560–2400m
⛷ 24 🚠 80km

Canillo 97
Small, quiet village linked to
Soldeu.

Canmore Canada
Old frontier town on the way
to Nakiska/Fortress, well
placed for touring the region
and an attractive alternative
to staying in Banff.

Cannon Mountain USA
One of several small New
Hampshire resorts scattered
along the Interstate 93
highway; a ski area and
nothing more. High, steep
mountain by eastern
standards.
605m; slopes 605–1260m
⛷ 9 🚠 165 acres
📷 Virgin Snow

Canyons 596

Cardrona New Zealand
Three large basins with slopes
for all standards. New lift and
slopes for 2009/10. Good
snow record and childcare
facilities. Super views. 1 hour
from Queenstown.
1650m; slopes 1260–1860m
⛷ 8 🚠 345 hectares

Carezza Italy
Dense network of short lifts
close to Val di Fassa, also
called Passo Costalunga.
⛷ 16 🚠 40km

Les Carroz-d'Arâches 278
An attractive, spacious village
on the road up to Flaine.

Caspoggio Italy
Attractive, unspoiled village
north-east of Lake Como, with
easy slopes (and more at
nearby Chiesa).
1100m; slopes 1100–2155m
⛷ 8 🚠 22km

Castelrotto Italy
Picturesque village west of
Sella Ronda circuit with small
sunny Alpine area and good
cross-country trails. *1060m*

Castel S Angelo Italy
Tiny area in Macerata region
near Adriatic Riviera.
805m ⛷ 4 🚠 2km

Castle Mountain Canada
Remote resort south of
Calgary. Good proportion of
intermediate and advanced
terrain. Area on Haig Ridge
provides more beginner and
intermediate terrain.
1410m; slopes 1410–2270m
⛷ 6 🚠 1750 acres
📷 Ski Safari

Catedral (Bariloche) Argentina
One of South America's most
developed resorts, linked with
Lado Bueno and 19 km from
San Carlos de Bariloche.
Sheltered intermediate slopes,
but very crowded in peak
season. Slope-side luxury
lodgings available.
slopes 1030–2180m
⛷ 39 🚠 103km

Cauterets 338

Cavalese Italy
Unspoiled medieval town in
Val di Fiemme with pretty
slopes at Alpe Cermis.
1000m; slopes 975–2265m
⛷ 9 🚠 70km

Caviahue Argentina
Mountain village at the foot of
the Copahue Volcano, 357km
from Neuquén City.
1645m; slopes 1645–2045m
⛷ 8 🚠 37km

The Cedars Lebanon
The largest of Lebanon's ski
areas, 130km inland from
Beirut. Good, open slopes; a
surprisingly long season.
1850m; slopes 2100–2870m
🚠 6

Ceillac France
Tight cluster of rustic old
buildings near Serre-Chevalier.
Not far from the highest
village in Europe, St-Veran.
1600m; slopes 1600–2450m
⛷ 7 🚠 25km

Celerina 509
Quiet village with links to St
Moritz's slopes.

Cerkno Slovenia
Modern, family resort 50km
from Ljubljana. Lifts include
three fast chairs.
900m ⛷ 8 🚠 18km

Cerler Spain
Very limited, purpose-built
resort with a compact ski area
similar to that of nearby
Andorra's Arinsal.
1500m; slopes 1500–2630m
⛷ 18 🚠 76km

Le Cernix France
Hamlet near Megève where
Les Saisies' slopes link to
those of Crest-Voland, part of
the Espace Diamant to which
our figures relate.
1250m; slopes 1000–2070m
⛷ 84 🚠 179km

Cerrato Lago Italy
Very limited area near the
coastal town of La Spezia.
1270m; slopes 1270–1890m
⛷ 5 🚠 3km

Cerro Bayo Argentina
Limited area amid stunning
scenery 10km from La
Angostura, and 90km from
San Carlos de Bariloche.
slopes 1050–1780m
⛷ 12 🚠 200 hectares

Cerro Castor Argentina
The most southern ski runs in
the world are on the Martial
Glacier, Tierra del Fuego.
Lodgings are in Ushuaia, the
southernmost city in the
world. Also plenty of cross-
country skiing on the island.
195m ⛷ 7 🚠 24km

Cerro Mirador Chile
Chile's most southerly snow-
zone, located 8km outside
Punta Arenas. Tiny but
attractive woodland runs. No
base lodging.
600m ⛷ 2

Cervinia 409

Cesana Torinese Italy
Little Italian village linking the
Sauze d'Oulx, Sestriere and
Sansicario side of the Milky
Way to the Clavière,
Montgenèvre side. *1350m*

Le Châble 520
Small village below Verbier.

Chaillol France
Cross-country base on the
edge of the beautiful Ecrins
National Park, near Gap. Small
Alpine area, lots of
snowmakers.
1600m; slopes 1450–2000m
⛷ 10 🚠 13km

Chamois Italy
Small area above Buisson, a
few miles down the road from
Valtournenche (near Cervinia)
– worth a look on bad-
weather days.
1815m; slopes 1815–2270m
⛷ 9 🚠 20km

Chamonix 247

Champagny-en-Vanoise 324
Charming village linking to the
La Plagne network.

Champéry 475

Champex-Lac Switzerland
Lakeside hamlet tucked away
in the trees above Orsières. A
quiet, unspoiled base from
which to visit Verbier's area.
1470m; slopes 1470–2220m
⛷ 4 🚠 25km

Champfèr 509
Lakeside hamlet between St
Moritz and Silvaplana.

Champoluc 432
Unspoiled village at one end
of the Monterosa Ski area.

Champorcher Italy
Small village south of Aosta
valley with tall but narrow ski
area, mostly red runs on open
slopes, with one black
through the trees to the lift
base at Chardonney.
1430m; slopes 1430–2500m
⛷ 5 🚠 21km

Champoussin 475
Quiet village with links to the
rest of the Champéry slopes.

Chamrousse France
Functional family resort near
Grenoble, with good,
sheltered slopes. Chairlifts
and a cable car from three
bases serve largely beginner
and intermediate slopes.
1650m; slopes 1400–2250m
⛷ 19 🚠 90km
📷 Crystal, Erna Low,
Lagrange, PowderBeds, Ski
Collection, Ski France, Ski
Independence, Thomson, Zenith

Chandolin 516
Village in the Val d'Anniviers.

Chantemerle 347
One of the villages making up
Serre-Chevalier.

Chapa Verde Chile
60km north-east of Rancagua
and 145km from Santiago.
1200m; slopes 1200–2500m
⛷ 4 🚠 1200 hectares

Chapelco Argentina
Small ski area with full
infrastructure of services 19km
from sizeable town of San
Martin de Los Andes.
Accommodation in hotels
11km from the slopes.
slopes 1250–1980m
⛷ 10 🚠 140 hectares

La Chapelle-d'Abondance 257
Unspoiled village 5km down
the valley from Châtel.

Charlotte Pass Australia
Oldest and most remote
resort in NSW, on a charming
Alpine pass near Mt
Kosciusko. Reached only by
snowcat from Perisher. Scenic
chalets and five lifts. Nearest
town Jindabyne. 6.5 hours
from Sydney.
1765m; slopes 1850–2000m
⛷ 5 🚠 123 acres

Chastreix Sancy France
Small family ski area near Le
Mont-Dore and Super-Besse.
Limited but varied terrain. All
draglifts.
1400m ⛷ 7 🚠 16km

Château d'Oex Switzerland
Pleasant French-speaking
valley town sharing a lift-pass
with neighbouring, but
unconnected, Gstaad. Good
rail links to other sectors. Low
slopes (top height 1630m).
Famous for its Alpine Balloon
festival.
950m; slopes 890–1630m
⛷ 8 🚠 30km

Châtel 257

Le Chatelard France
Small resort in remote Parc
des Bauges between Lake
Annecy and Chambéry.

Chiesa Italy
Attractive beginners' resort
with a fairly high plateau of
easy runs above the resort.
1000m; slopes 1700–2335m
⛷ 16 🚠 50km

Le Chinaillon   France
Chalet-style village at lift base above Le Grand-Bornand.
1300m; slopes 1000–2100m
⬆ 29 ⬆ 90km

Chiomonte   Italy
Tiny resort on the main road east of Bardonecchia and Sauze d'Oulx. A good half-day trip from either.
745m; slopes 745–2210m
⬆ 6 ⬆ 10km

Chsea   Algeria
Largest of Algeria's skiable areas, 135km south-east of coastal town of Alger in the Djur Djur mountains.
1860m; slopes 1860–2510m ⬆ 2

Chur–Brambruesch
   Switzerland
Chur's local ski area a cable car and gondola ride from the town.
595m; slopes 1170–2200m
⬆ 6 ⬆ 25km

Churwalden   Switzerland
Hamlet on fringe of Lenzerheide-Valbella area, linked via a slow chair. Four short local runs served by a quad and steep drag.
1230m; slopes 1230–2865m
⬆ 35 ⬆ 155km

Claviere   **312**
Village linked to Montgenèvre and the Milky Way ski area.

La Clusaz   France
Genuine mountain village near Geneva that exudes rustic and Gallic charm. Attracts a lot of weekend visitors, so can be crowded. Buses also link with Le Grand Bornand. Together they offer over 200km slopes – covered by the area lift pass. The local slopes sprawl over five attractively wooded and varied sectors. All are below 2500m, so snow conditions are unreliable, but there is a lot of snowmaking. Good steep blacks and bumps on La Balme (the highest sector), as well as decent off-piste when conditions permit. There are challenging but wide blues, as well as gentle cruises and nursery slopes up the mountain. But there are still a lot of old chairs and drags. There's a park and pipe, plentiful rustic huts, and a few lively bars.
1100m; slopes 1100–2470m
⬆ 51 ⬆ 132km
✉ *Alpine Answers, Chalet Group, Chalet les Hirondelles, Classic Ski, Crystal, Independent Ski Links, Karibuni, Lagrange, Last Resort, Peak Retreats, PV-Holidays. com, Ski France, Ski Weekend, Ski Weekender, Snowlife*

Les Coches   **324**
Purpose-built village, linked to the La Plagne ski area.

Cogne   **404**
Village in the Aosta valley.
1535m; slopes 1530–2250m
⬆ 4 ⬆ 9km

Colfosco   **443**
Smaller, quieter satellite of Corvara in the Sella Ronda.

Colle di Tenda   Italy
Dour, modern resort that shares a good area with much nicer Limone. Not far from Nice.
1400m; slopes 1120–2040m
⬆ 33 ⬆ 80km

Colle Isarco   Italy
Brenner Pass area – and the bargain-shopping town of Vipiteno is nearby.
1095m; slopes 1095–2720m
⬆ 5 ⬆ 15km

Le Collet-d'Allevard   France
Ski area of sizeable summer spa Allevard-les-Bains in remote region east of Chambéry-Grenoble road.
1450m; slopes 1450–2140m
⬆ 11 ⬆ 35km

Collio   Italy
Tiny area of short runs in a remote spot between lakes Garda and d'Iseo.
840m; slopes 840–1715m ⬆ 14

Les Collons   **520**
Near Thyon 2000 in the Verbier area.

Combloux   **290**
Quiet, unspoiled alternative to linked Megève.

Les Contamines   France
Largely unspoiled but sprawling chalet resort close to Megève and Chamonix, with a fair-sized intermediate area and a good snow record for its height. The main access lift is a shuttle-bus ride from the centre, with a few lodgings at its base. Most of the slopes are above the treeline and on both sides of the Col du Joly – from where a long red run descends over 1000m vertical. There's a good mix of blue and red runs, and substantial off-piste opportunities with a guide. Complete beginners are better off elsewhere though. Reports of the school are mixed too. The village is quiet with few amenities, but there are other sporting activities. The Nant Rouge chair was upgraded to a six-pack for 2010/11.
1160m; slopes 1160–2485m
⬆ 24 ⬆ 120km
✉ *Alpine Answers, Chalet Kiana, Classic Ski, Holiday in Alps, Lagrange, Ski Expectations, Ski France*

Copper Mountain   USA
Modern, but pleasant purpose-built village with some of Colorado's best terrain. And good value by regional standards. Worthwhile outing from nearby resorts such as Vail.

The Village at Copper is the main base, with smart condo lodging and fast chairs into the slopes. Two other bases are served by free shuttle-buses and with easier terrain above them. The slopes spread across two main peaks, Union and Copper, with an attractive mix of open and wooded areas. There is lots of expert terrain in the upper bowls, some seriously steep. There are top-to-bottom greens and excellent nursery slopes. The terrain park is well regarded. Queues are rarely a problem outside peak weekends. Limited off slope diversions. Reports of the school are favourable. Nightlife livens up at weekends.
2925m; slopes 2960–3750m
⬆ 22 ⬆ 2465 acres
✉ *Alpine Answers, AmeriCan Ski, American Ski Classics, Crystal, Erna Low, Funway Holidays, Independent Ski Links, PowderBeds, Ski Independence, Ski Safari, Skitracer, Skiworld, Supertravel, Thomson, Virgin Snow*

Le Corbier   France
A no-compromise functional resort centrally placed in the Sybelles area. The resort is purpose-built and compact, as well as being traffic-free – so it suits families very well. Nearly all of the lodging is slope-side apartments, some in a traditional style. There are bars and restaurants, but evenings are generally very quiet. Lifts link directly to St-Jean-d'Arves and La Toussuire, as well as a higher level connection to St-Sorlin. But progress can be slow – only seven fast chairs in the whole area. One belongs to Le Corbier and serves local slopes. The gentle terrain is mostly north-east facing and makes ideal cruising, if rather lacking in variety – though there's a black run from the top. Beginners have good slopes at resort level. 'Few queues and relatively inexpensive for France,' says a 2011 visitor.
1550m ⬆ 72 ⬆ 310km
✉ *Erna Low, PV-Holidays.com, Rocketski, Ski France*

Corno alle Scale   Italy
Small resort in the Emilia Romagna region of the Apennines.
1355m; slopes 1355–1945m
⬆ 9 ⬆ 36km

Coronet Peak   New Zealand
Closest area to Queenstown (20 minutes). Good mix of bowls, chutes, varied level pistes. Biggest vertical is

462m. Relies on large snowmaking facility for good snow cover. Splendid views.
1230m; slopes 1230–1650m
⬆ 7 ⬆ 690 acres

Corrençon-en-Vercors   France
Charming, rustic village at foot of Villard-de-Lans ski area. Good cross-country, too.
1160m; slopes 1145–2170m
⬆ 25 ⬆ 125km

Cortina d'Ampezzo   **415**

Corvara   **443**

Courchevel   **262**

Courmayeur   **420**

Cranmore   USA
Area in New Hampshire with attractive town/resort of North Conway. Easy skiing. Good for families.
150m; slopes 150–515m
⬆ 9 ⬆ 190 acres
✉ *Virgin Snow*

Crans-Montana   **478**

Crested Butte   USA
One of the cutest old Wild West towns in Colorado, and the steep, gnarly terrain enjoys cult status among experts. It's a small area, but it packs in an astonishing mixture of perfect beginner slopes, easy cruising runs and expert terrain. Snowfall is modest by Colorado standards, but for those who like steep, ungroomed terrain, if the snow is good, it's idyllic. You can stay there or at the mountain, a couple of miles away, with its modern resort 'village'.
2860m; slopes 2775–3620m
⬆ 16 ⬆ 1165 acres
✉ *AmeriCan Ski, Crystal, Funway Holidays, Ski Safari*

Crest-Voland   France
Attractive, unspoiled traditional village near Megève and Le Grand Bornand with wonderfully uncrowded intermediate slopes linked to Les Saises and beyond to Praz sur Arly, as part of the Espace Diamant region – to which our figures relate.
1035m; slopes 1000–2070m
⬆ 84 ⬆ 179km

Crissolo   Italy
Small, remote day-tripper area, south-west of Turin. Part of the Monviso ski area.
1320m; slopes 1745–2340m
⬆ 4 ⬆ 20km

La Croix-Fry   France
On the pass to La Clusaz. Couple of hotels and gentle slopes, reinstated on the La Clusaz lift pass.
1480m

Les Crosets   **475**
Micro-resort above Champéry in the Portes du Soleil.

Resort directory / index
689
Interactive resort shortlist builder at www.wtss.co.uk

Crystal Mountain　USA
Area in glorious Mt Rainier
National Park, near Seattle.
Good, varied area given good
snow/weather, but it's often
wet. Lively at weekends.
1340m; slopes 1340–2135m
⛷9 ⛰ *2300 acres*

Cuchara Valley　USA
Quiet little family resort in
southern Colorado, some way
from any other ski area.
2800m; slopes 2800–3285m
⛷4 ⛰ *250 acres*

Cutigliano　Italy
Sizeable village near Abetone
in the Apennines. Less than
two hours from Florence and
Pisa.
1125m; slopes 1125–1850m
⛷9 ⛰ *13km*

Cypress Mountain　Canada
Vancouver's most challenging
area, 20 minutes from the city
and with 40% for experts.
Good snowfall record but rain
is a problem.
920m; slopes 910–1445m ⛷5

Daemyeong Vivaldi Resort
South Korea
One of the less ugly Korean
resorts, 75km from Seoul.
⛷10

La Daille　376
Ugly apartment complex at
the entrance to Val d'Isère.

Daisen　Japan
Western Honshu's main area,
four hours from Osaka.
800m; slopes 740–1120m ⛷21

Damüls　208
Village in Bregenzerwald.
1430m; slopes 700–2010m
⛷31 ⛰ *105km*

Davos　480

Deer Mountain　USA
South Dakota area close to
'Old West' town Deadwood
and Mount Rushmore.
1825m; slopes 1825–2085m
⛷4 ⛰ *370 acres*

Deer Valley　598

Les Deux-Alpes　272

Les Diablerets　Switzerland
Spacious chalet resort
towered over by the
Diablerets massif, with two
areas of local slopes, plus
Glacier 3000. A high-speed
quad followed by a slow chair
lead up to the red runs of the
Meilleret area and the link to
Villars. A gondola in the
centre of town takes you to
Isenau, a mix of blues and
reds served by draglifts. From
Isenau there's a red run down
to Col du Pillon and the cable
car to and from the glacier.
On Glacier 3000, you'll find
blue runs at over 3000m,
stunning views and the long,
black (though has been red
when we've skied it) Combe
d'Audon – a wonderful,
usually quiet, run away from

all the lifts with sheer cliffs
rising up on both sides. Snow
reliability away from the
glacier is not great –
especially on sunny Isenau.
1150m; slopes 1115–3000m
⛷46 ⛰ *125km*
✉ *Alpine Answers,
Independent Ski Links,
Lagrange, Momentum, Neilson,
Ski Club Freshtracks, Solo's,
Swiss Travel Service,
Switzerland Travel Centre,
Tracks European Adventures*

Diamond Peak　USA
Quiet, pleasant, intermediate
area on Lake Tahoe, with
lodging in Incline Village five
minutes' drive away. Its
narrow area consists of a long
ridge served by one fast chair;
there are great lake views
from the run along the ridge
and from the terrace of
Snowflake Lodge. There are
black runs off the ridge, but
nothing seriously steep.
2040m; slopes 2040–2600m
⛷6 ⛰ *655 acres*

Dienten　128
Quiet village at the heart of
the Hochkönig area.

Dinner Plain　Australia
Attractive resort best known
for cross-country skiing.
Shuttle to Mt Hotham for
Alpine slopes. Four hours
from Melbourne.
1520m; slopes 1490–1520m

Discovery Ski Area　USA
Pleasant area miles from
anywhere except Butte,
Montana, with largely
intermediate slopes but
double-black runs on the back
of the mountain – and the
chance of seriously good
snow. Usually deserted.
Fairmont Hot Springs (two
huge thermal pools) are
nearby. There are plans to
extend the ski area on south-
eastern side, including a new
connecting road from
Philipsburg.
1975m; slopes 1975–2485m
⛷6 ⛰ *614 acres*

Disentis　Switzerland
Unspoiled old village in a
pretty setting on the Glacier
Express rail route near
Andermatt. Scenic area with
long runs.
1125m; slopes 1150–2830m
⛷10 ⛰ *60km*

Dobbiaco　Italy
One of several little resorts in
the South Tyrol near the
Austrian border; a feasible
day out from the Sella Ronda.
Toblach is its German name.
1250m; slopes 1250–1610m
⛷5 ⛰ *15km*
✉ *Exodus, Headwater,
Ramblers*

Dodge Ridge　USA
Novice/leisurely intermediate
area north of Yosemite. The
pass from Reno is closed in
winter, preventing crowds.
2010m; slopes 2010–2500m
⛷12 ⛰ *815 acres*

Dolonne　420
Quiet suburb of Courmayeur –
with gondola link to Plan
Checrouit.

Donnersbachwald　Austria
Small area in the Dachstein-
Tauern region.
950m; slopes 950–1990m
⛷4 ⛰ *25km*

Donner Ski Ranch　USA
One of California's first ski
resorts, still family owned and
operated.
2140m; slopes 2140–2370m
⛷6 ⛰ *460 acres*

Dorfgastein　115
Quieter, friendlier alternative
to Bad Gastein.

Doucy-Combelouvière　France
Quiet hamlet tucked away in
the trees at the foot of
Valmorel's slopes, linked by
easy green pistes, a fast chair
and draglifts into the main
sector.
1250m ✉ *Lagrange*

Dundret　Sweden
Lapland area 100km north of
the Arctic Circle with floodlit
slopes open through winter
when the sun barely rises.
slopes 475–825m
⛷7 ⛰ *15km*

Durango Mountain Resort
USA
This is not a resort you would
cross the Atlantic to visit – it's
a small area even by US
standards, and won't amuse
most non-beginners for more
than a day or two. Directly
above the resort is a steepish
slope with a slow double
chair off to the right serving
gentle green runs. All link to
the shady mountainside that
forms the main part of the
area, served by a row of three
chairs with a vertical of not
much over 350m. Snowcat
skiing is said to operate from
the top. The heart of the
resort is Purgatory Village, a
modern, purpose-built affair.
Evening options in the 'village'
are extremely limited. The city
of Durango has a historic
district and is worth a look.
2680m; slopes 2680–3300m
⛷11 ⛰ *1200 acres*
✉ *AmeriCan Ski*

Eaglecrest　USA
Close to Yukon gold rush
town Skagway. Family resort
famous for its ski school.
365m; slopes 365–790m
⛷3 ⛰ *640 acres*

Eben im Pongau　Austria
Part of Salzburger Sportwelt
Amadé area that includes
nearby St Johann, Wagrain,

Flachau and Zauchensee.
Village spoiled by the
autobahn passing through it.
855m; slopes 855–2185m
⛷100 ⛰ *350km*

Egg　208
Biggest Bregenzerwald village.
565mm; slopes 1100–1400m
⛷6 ⛰ *10km*

Ehrwald　212
Friendly, pretty village in
Zugspitz Arena. Link to glacier.

El Colorado / Farellones　Chile
Scattering of accommodation
around a base station 40km
east of Santiago, sharing Valle
Nevado's ski area (to which
our figures relate).
slopes 2430–3670m
⛷43 ⛰ *113km*

Eldora Mountain　USA
Day-visitor resort with varied
terrain (including plenty of
steep stuff) close to Denver
Boulder (45min by regular
scheduled bus). All forest
trails, but with some good
glade areas. Crowded at
weekends, and all the chairs
are slow.
2795m; slopes 2805–3230m
⛷12 ⛰ *680 acres*

Elk Meadows　USA
Area south of Salt Lake City,
more than a day trip from
Park City.
2775m; slopes 2745–3170m
⛷6 ⛰ *1400 acres*

Ellmau　118

Elm　Switzerland
One hour from Zürich, at the
head of a quiet, isolated
valley. Good choice of runs
including a long black to the
valley.
1020m; slopes 1000–2105m
⛷6 ⛰ *40km*

Encamp　90
Town with a link to Pas de la
Casa's slopes.

Enego　Italy
Limited weekend day-trippers'
area near Vicenza and Trento.
1300m; slopes 1300–1445m
⛷7 ⛰ *30km*

Engelberg　487

Entrèves　420
Cluster of hotels at the lift up
to Courmayeur's slopes.

Escaldes　Andorra
Central valley town, effectively
part of Andorra la Vella.

Estoul　404
Village in the Aosta valley.
1800m; slopes 1800–2235m
⛷2 ⛰ *9km*

Etna　Italy
Scenic, uncrowded, short-
season area on the volcano's
flank, 20 minutes from
Nickolossi.
1800m; slopes 1800–2350m
⛰ *5km*

Evolène Switzerland
Charming rustic village in the Val d'Hérens. Small ski area in unspoiled, attractive setting south of Sion. Area lift pass gives access to the 4 Valleys.
1370m; slopes 1405–2680m
⛷ 7 ⛷ 42km

Faak am See Austria
Limited area, one of five overlooking town of Villach.
560m; slopes 560–800m
⛷ 1 ⛷ 2km

Fai della Paganella Italy
Trentino village near Madonna that shares its slopes with Andalo.
1000m; slopes 1035–2125m
⛷ 16 ⛷ 60km

Fairmont Hot Springs Canada
Major luxury spa complex ideal for a relaxing holiday with some gentle skiing thrown in.
⛷ 2 ⛷ 60 acres

Faistenau Austria
Cross-country area close to Salzburg and St Wolfgang. Limited Alpine slopes.
785m; slopes 785–1000m
⛷ 3 ⛷ 3km

Falcade Italy
Trentino village south of the Sella Ronda with lifts up to slopes at San Pellegrino.
1150m; slopes 1150–2245m
⛷ 19 ⛷ 75km

Falera 495
Village with access to ski area shared by Flims and Laax.

Le Falgoux France
One of the most beautiful old villages in France, set in the very scenic Volcano National Park. Several ski areas nearby.
930m; slopes 930–1350m

Falkertsee Austria
Base area rather than a village, with bleak, open slopes in contrast to nearby Badkleinkirchheim.
1850m; slopes 1690–2310m
⛷ 5 ⛷ 15km

Falls Creek Australia
Alpine-style modern family resort, 5 hours from Melbourne, near Mt Hotham. Fair-sized area of short intermediate runs. Access by snowcat to Mt McKay's steep slopes. Lavish spa resort nearby.
1600m; slopes 1500–1780m
⛷ 14 ⛷ 1115 acres

La Feclaz France
One of several little resorts in the remote Parc des Bauges. Popular cross-country ski base. *1165m*

Feldberg 396
Small resort in the Black Forest. ⛷ 31 ⛷ 55

Fernie 633

Fieberbrunn Austria
Atmospheric and friendly Tirolean village, sprawling along the valley road for 2km, but mostly set back from the road and railway. Its small but attractive area of wooded slopes is a bus ride away. One sector consists mainly of blue runs, the other mainly of easy reds, many below the treeline. Across a valley are separate lifts going up to the high point of 2020m on Hochhörndl – gondola down to 1284m accesses some good off-piste here. The resort is boarder-friendly, with a popular terrain park. Accommodation in the village is in hotels, and there is also lodging at the lift station. Smart new 10-seat gondola planned for 2011, replacing the Reckmoos North double chair.
800m; slopes 830–2020m
⛷ 11 ⛷ 43km
🚌 *Crystal, First Choice, Snowscape, Thomson*

Fiesch Switzerland
Traditional Rhône valley resort near Brig, with a lift up to Fiescheralp (2220m) part of the lovely Aletsch area; includes Bettmeralp to Riederalp. Two new fast lifts for 2010/11.
1050m; slopes 1925–2870m
⛷ 35 ⛷ 100km

Fiescheralp Switzerland
Mountain outpost of Fiesch, down end of the Rhône valley. At one end of the beautiful Aletsch area extending across the mountain via Bettmeralp to Riederalp. Two new fast lifts for 2010/11.
2220m; slopes 1925–2870m
⛷ 35 ⛷ 100km

Filzmoos Austria
Charming, unspoiled, friendly village with leisurely slopes that are ideal for novices. Good snow record for its height. Quiet pistes, good grooming and decent nursery slopes.
1055m; slopes 1055–1645m
⛷ 8 ⛷ 32km
🚌 *Inghams, Skitracer*

Fiss Austria
Nicely compact, quiet, traditional village sharing an extensive, sunny area with bigger Serfaus.
1435m; slopes 1200–2750m
⛷ 70 ⛷ 190km

Flachau Austria
Quiet, spacious village in a pretty setting at one end of an extensive three-valley lift network linking via Wagrain to Alpendorf. Central to an impressive lift system. On the Salzbuger Sportwelt lift pass.
925m; slopes 800–2185m
⛷ 64 ⛷ 200km

Flachauwinkl Austria
Tiny ski station beside Tauern autobahn. Centre of an extensive three-valley lift network linking Kleinarl to Zauchensee. Near similarly-sized Flachau. All these resorts are covered by the Salzburger Sportwelt ski pass.
930m; slopes 800–2185m
⛷ 15 ⛷ 65km

Flaine 278

Flims 495
Long-established resort sharing an area with Laax.

Flumet France
Surprisingly large traditional village, the main place from which to ski the Espace Diamant area, linked through to Les Saisies/ Crest Voland. Near Megève.
1000m; slopes 1000–2070m
⛷ 84 ⛷ 179km
🚌 *Lagrange*

Flumserberg Switzerland
Collective name for the villages sharing a varied area an hour south-east of Zürich. Part of the wider Heidiland region. Mostly red and black runs, served by good network of fast lifts.
425m; slopes 1220–2220m
⛷ 16 ⛷ 65km

Folgaria Italy
Sizeable area east of Trento. Newly linked to Alpe Fiorentini, with three fast lifts and four new pistes for 2010/11.
1165m; slopes 1185–2005m
⛷ 22 ⛷ 100km
🚌 *Solo's, STC*

Folgarida 429
Small Trentino village linked to Madonna di Campiglio.

Foncine-le-Haut France
Major cross-country village in the Jura Mountains with extensive trails. 🚌 *Lagrange*

Fonni Gennaragentu Italy
Sardinia's only 'ski area' – and it's tiny. ⛷ 1 ⛷ 5km

Font-Romeu 338

Foppolo Italy
Relatively unattractive but user-friendly village, a short transfer from Bergamo.
1510m; slopes 1610–2160m
⛷ 9 ⛷ 47km

Forca Canapine Italy
Limited area near the Adriatic and Ascoli Piceno. Popular with weekend day-trippers.
1450m; slopes 1450–1690m
⛷ 11 ⛷ 20km

Formazza Italy
Cross-country base with some downhill slopes.
1280m; slopes 1275–1755m
⛷ 8km

Formigal 661

Formigueres France
Small downhill and cross-country area in the Neiges Catalanes. There are 110km cross-country trails.
slopes 1700–2350m
⛷ 8 ⛷ 19km 🚌 *Chalet Group*

Le Fornet 376
Rustic old hamlet 3km up the valley from Val d'Isère.

Forstau Austria
Secluded hamlet above Radstadt–Schladming road. Very limited area (Fageralm) with old lifts, but nice and quiet.
930m; slopes 930–1885m
⛷ 7 ⛷ 14km

La Fouly Switzerland
Small area near Martigny, with varied slopes, 10km of cross-country trails and a floodlit toboggan run.
1600m; slopes 1600–2200m
⛷ 3 ⛷ 20km

La Foux-d'Allos France
Purpose-built resort that shares a good intermediate area with Pra-Loup (Val d'Allos ski area).
1800m; slopes 1800–2600m
⛷ 51 ⛷ 180km 🚌 *Zenith*

Frabosa Soprana Italy
One of numerous little areas south of Turin, well placed for combining winter sports with Riviera sightseeing.
850m; slopes 860–1740m
⛷ 7 ⛷ 40km

Frisco 575
Small town down the valley from Breckenridge.

Frontignano Italy
Best lift system in the Macerata region, near the Adriatic Riviera.
1340m; slopes 1340–2000m
⛷ 8 ⛷ 10km

Fucine Italy
Old Trentino valley village near Marilleva/Folgarida.
980m

Fügen Austria
Unspoiled Zillertal village with road up to satellite Hochfügen – part of fair-sized Ski Optimal area, along with Kaltenbach.
550m
🚌 *Crystal, Lagrange, STC*

Fulpmes 200
Village in the Stubai valley.

Furano 676
Hokkaido island resort.

Fusch Austria
Cheaper, quiet place to stay when visiting Zell am See. Near Kaprun and Schuttdorf.
805m; slopes 805–1050m
⛷ 2 ⛷ 5km

Fuschl am See Austria
Attractive, unspoiled, lakeside village close to St Wolfgang and Salzburg, 30 minutes from its slopes. Best suited to part-time skiers who want to sightsee as well. *670m*

Gålå Norway
Base for downhill and cross-country skiing, an hour's drive north of Lillehammer.
930m; slopes 830–1150m
⛷ 7 ⛷ 20km
⛷ Inntravel, Norwegian Wood Travel

Gallio Italy
One of several low resorts near Vicenza and Trento. Popular with weekend day-trippers.
1100m; slopes 1100–1550m
⛷ 11 ⛷ 50km

Galtür 130
Charming traditional village near Ischgl.

Gambarie d'Aspromonte Italy
Italy's second most southerly ski area (after Mt Etna). On the 'toe' of the Italian 'boot' near Reggio di Calabria.
1310m; slopes 1310–1650m ⛷ 3

Gantschier Austria
No slopes of its own but particularly well placed for visiting all the Montafon areas. *700m*

Gargellen 204
Quiet village tucked up a side valley in the Montafon area.

Garmisch-Partenkirchen 398

Gaschurn 204
Village in the Montafon area.

Gaustablikk Norway
Small snow-sure Alpine area on Mt Gausta in southern Norway with plenty of cross-country. ⛷ 15km

Gavarnie France
Traditional village and fair-sized ski area, with the longest green run in the Pyrenees. Grand views of the Cirque de Gavarnie.
1400m; slopes 1850–2400m
⛷ 11 ⛷ 45km

Geilo Norway
Small, quiet, unspoiled community on the railway line from Bergen, on the coast, to Oslo. It provides all the basics of a resort – a handful of cafes and shops around the railway station, a dozen hotels more widely spread around the wide valley, children's facilities and a sports centre. Geilo is a superb cross-country resort. It's very limited for downhillers, and none of the runs is very difficult, but it does claim to have Scandinavia's only super-pipe.
800m; slopes 800–1180m
⛷ 20 ⛷ 32km
⛷ Headwater, Inntravel, Neilson

Gérardmer France
Sizeable lakeside resort in the northerly Vosges mountains near Strasbourg, with plenty of amenities. Limited downhill

slopes nearby include one of almost 4km. Extensive ski de fond trails in the area.
665m; slopes 750–1150m
⛷ 20 ⛷ 40km ⛷ Lagrange

Gerlitzen Austria
Carinthia's central ski area. A worthwhile outing from Bad Kleinkirchheim. Gondola ride from the valley near Villach, with good views and varied but short runs.
500m; slopes 1000–1910m
⛷ 15 ⛷ 26km

Gerlos 153
Inexpensive resort linked to Zell im Zillertal / Königsleiten.

Gerlosplatte Austria
Inexpensive but fairly snow-sure area above the village of Krimml, linked to Königsleiten, Gerlos and Zell am Ziller to form a fair-sized intermediate area. 'Good runs, if unchallenging' was the verdict of a recent visitor.

Les Gets 285

La Giettaz 290
Tiny village between La Clusaz and Megève.

Gitschtal / Weissbriach Austria
One of many little areas near Hermagor in eastern Austria, close to Italian border.
690m; slopes 690–1400m
⛷ 4 ⛷ 5km

Glaris Switzerland
Hamlet base station for the uncrowded Rinerhorn section of the Davos slopes.
1460m; slopes 1460–2490m
⛷ 5 ⛷ 30km

Glencoe 675
Scottish ski resort.
305m; slopes 305–1110m
⛷ 7 ⛷ 20km

Glenshee 675
Scottish ski resort.
610m; slopes 610–1070m
⛷ 22 ⛷ 40km

Going 118
Small area near Ellmau, linked to the huge Ski Welt area.

Goldegg Austria
Year-round resort famous for lakeside castle. Limited slopes but Wagrain (Salzburger Sportwelt) and Grossarl (Gastein valley) are nearby.
825m; slopes 825–1250m
⛷ 4 ⛷ 12km

Golden Canada
Small logging town, the place to stay when visiting Kicking Horse resort 15 minutes away. Also the launch pad for Purcell heli-skiing.

Golte Slovenia
Ski area in the East Karavante mountains, above Mozirje. Gondola to the slopes from Zekovec village. Mostly advanced runs.
⛷ 7 ⛷ 18km

Gore Mountain USA
One of the better areas in New York State. Near Lake Placid, sufficiently far north to avoid worst weekend crowds. Intermediate terrain.
455m; slopes 455–1095m
⛷ 9 ⛷ 290 acres

Göriach Austria
Hamlet with trail connecting into one of the longest, most snow-sure cross-country networks in Europe.
1250m

Gortipohl Austria
Traditional village in pretty Montafonal.
920m; slopes 900–2395m
⛷ 61 ⛷ 243km

Gosau Austria
Family-friendly resort, with straggling village. Plenty of pretty, if low, runs. Fast lifts mean queues are rare. Snow-sure Obertauern and Schladming are within reach.
755m; slopes 755–1800m
⛷ 37 ⛷ 80km ⛷ Crystal

Göstling Austria
One of Austria's easternmost resorts, between Salzburg and Vienna. A traditional village in wooded setting.
530m; slopes 530–1880m
⛷ 8 ⛷ 18km

Götzens Austria
Valley village base for Axamer Lizum and Mutters, near Innsbruck. Gondola from village to Mutteralm and red run back down.
870m; slopes 830–2100m
⛷ 4 ⛷ 15km
⛷ Lagrange

Gourette-Eaux-Bonnes France
Most snow-sure resort in the French Pyrenees. Very popular with local families, so best avoided at weekends.
1400m; slopes 1400–2400m
⛷ 14 ⛷ 30km

Grächen Switzerland
Charming chalet-village reached by tricky access road off the approach to Zermatt. A small area of open slopes, mainly above the trees and of red-run difficulty, reached by two gondolas – one to Hannigalp (2115m), the main focus of activity with a very impressive children's nursery area. The village has almost a score of hotels, mostly 3-star; most of the accommodation is in chalets and apartments. The sports centre offers tennis and badminton, as well as a natural ice rink.
1615m; slopes 1615–2865m
⛷ 9 ⛷ 42km

Le Grand-Bornand France
Covered by the Aravis lift pass, and much smaller and even more charming than La Clusaz. The slopes can be accessed from either the outskirts of the village or from

the satellite village of Le Chinaillon. There are worthwhile shady black runs on Le Lachat, and on the lower peak of La Floria. There are plenty of good cruising blue and red intermediate runs, and also good beginner slopes. And there are extensive cross-country trails in the Vallée du Bouchet and towards Le Chinaillon.
1000m; slopes 1000–2100m
⛷ 29 ⛷ 90km
⛷ AmeriCan Ski, Erna Low, Karibuni, Lagrange, Last Resort, Peak Retreats, Ski France, Ski Independence, Ski Weekender

Le Grand Massif 287

Grand Targhee 607
Powder skiing paradise an hour from Jackson Hole.
2439m; slopes 2260–3005m
⛷ 5 ⛷ 2100 acres

Les Granges 232
Hamlet at the mid-station of the funicular up from Bourg.

Grangesises Italy
Small satellite of Sestriere, with lifts to the main slopes.

Granite Peak USA
One of the oldest areas in the Great Lakes region, and now one of the largest. New base village. Good selection of black runs on the upper mountain. ⛷ 7 ⛷ 400 acres

Grau Roig 95
Mini-resort between Pas de la Casa and Soldeu.

La Grave 288

Great Divide USA
Area near Helena, Montana, best for experts. Mostly bowls; plus near-extreme Rawhide Gulch.
1765m; slopes 1765–2195m
⛷ 6 ⛷ 720 acres

Gresse-en-Vercors France
Resort south of Grenoble. Sheltered slopes worth noting for bad-weather days.
1250m; slopes 1600–1750m
⛷ 13 ⛷ 18km

Gressoney-la-Trinité 432
Village in the Monterosa Ski area.

Gressoney-St-Jean 404
Village in the Aosta valley.
1390m ⛷ 7km

Grimentz 516
Village in the Val d'Anniviers.

Grindelwald 489

Grossarl 115
Secluded village in the Gastein valley.

Grossglockner area Austria
Two linked areas near Heiligenbluit, above the villages of Kals and Matrei. Remote position west of Bad Gastein. Uncrowded, fairly extensive slopes. Some long, varied runs.
1000m; slopes 1000–2620m
⛷ 15 ⛷ 110km

Grosskirchheim Austria
Area near Heiligenblut with access to 55km slopes.
1025m; slopes 1025–1400m

Grouse Mountain Canada
The Vancouver area with the largest lift capacity. Superb city views from mostly easy slopes; night skiing.
880m; slopes 880–1245m
🚡 11 🎿 120 acres

Grünau Austria
Spacious riverside village in a lovely lake-filled part of eastern Austria. Nicely varied area, but very low.
525m; slopes 620–1600m
🚡 15 🎿 40km

Gryon 531
Village below Villars.

Gstaad Switzerland
Despite its exclusive reputation, Gstaad is an attractive, traditional village where anyone could have a relaxing holiday. There are four sectors, covered by a single, confusing map. The largest sector is above Saanenmöser and Schönried, reached by train. Snow-cover can be unreliable except on the Glacier des Diablerets, 15km away. Few runs challenge experts. Black runs rarely exceed red or even blue difficulty. There's off-piste potential. Given good snow, this is a superb area for intermediates, with long, easy descents in the major area. The nursery slopes at Wispile are adequate, with plenty of runs to progress to. Time lost on buses or trains is more of a problem than queues.
1050m; slopes 950–3000m
🚡 58 🎿 250km
📧 Alpine Answers, Carrier, Momentum, Oxford Ski Co, Ski Independence, Ski Weekend, Switzerland Travel Centre, White Roc

Gunstock USA
One of the New Hampshire resorts closest to Boston, popular with families. Primarily easy slopes. Lovely Lake Winnisquam views.
275m; slopes 275–700m
🚡 8 🎿 220 acres

Guthega Australia
Australia's most challenging and diverse slopes (at Perisher). Comfortable accommodation in the resort's only commercial lodge. Free shuttle from Jindabyne. 6.5 hours from Sydney.
1640m; slopes 1605–2035m
🚡 47 🎿 3075 acres

Guzet France
Charming cluster of chalets set in a pine forest at Guzet 1400. Three main sectors offer slopes for all levels.
1400m; slopes 1100–2100m
🚡 14 🎿 40km

Hafjell Norway
Main ski area for Lillehammer.
🚡 12 🎿 33km
📧 Norwegian Wood Travel

Haider Alm Italy
Area in the Val Venosta in the South Tyrol close to Nauders. Malda Haider is its Italian name. 🚡 5 🎿 20km

Hakuba 676
European-style resort four hours from Tokyo.

Harper Mountain Canada
Small, family-friendly resort in Kamloops, British Colombia.
1100m; slopes 1100–1525m
🚡 3 🎿 400 acres

Harrachov Czech Republic
Closest resort to Prague, with enough terrain to justify a day trip. No beginner area.
650m; slopes 650–1020m
🚡 4 🎿 8runs

Hasliberg Switzerland
Four rustic hamlets on a sunny plateau overlooking Meiringen and Lake Brienz. Two of them are the bottom stations of a varied intermediate area. *1050m*

Haus 173
Village next to Schladming.

Haystack USA
Minor satellite of Mount Snow, in Vermont, but with a bit more steep skiing.
580m; slopes 580–1095m
🚡 26 🎿 540 acres

Heavenly 553

Hebalm Austria
One of many small areas in Austria's easternmost ski region near Slovenian border. No major resorts in vicinity.
1350m; slopes 1350–1400m
🚡 6 🎿 11km

Heiligenblut Austria
Picturesque village in beautiful surroundings at the foot of the Grossglockner, west of Bad Gastein. Quiet, mainly red runs in two main areas. Lifts include three gondolas and a fast chair.
1300m; slopes 1300–2910m
🚡 12 🎿 55km

Heiterwang 212
Village in the Zugspitz Arena.

Hemlock Resort Canada
Area 55 miles east of Vancouver towards Sun Peaks. Mostly intermediate terrain and with snowfall of 600 inches a year. Lodging is available at the base area.
1000m; slopes 1000–1375m
🚡 4 🎿 350 acres

Hemsedal 665

Heremence Switzerland
Quiet, traditional village in unspoiled attractive setting south of Sion. Verbier's slopes are accessed a few minutes' drive away at Les Masses.
1250m

Hermagor Austria
Main village base for the Nassfeld ski area in Carinthia.
600m; slopes 610–2000m
🚡 30 🎿 100km

High 1 Resort South Korea
Small ski area at the High 1 leisure complex, 250km from Seoul by train. 🎿 21km

Hinterglemm 166
One of the villages making up Saalbach-Hinterglemm.

Hintermoos 128
Village in the Hochkönig area.

Hintersee Austria
Easy slopes very close to Salzburg. Several long top-to-bottom runs and lifts so size of ski area is greatly reduced if the snowline is high.
745m; slopes 750–1470m
🚡 9 🎿 40km

Hinterstoder Austria
A very quiet valley village – neat but not overtly charming – spread along the road up the dead-end Stodertal in Upper Austria. The local Höss slopes are pleasantly wooded, less densely at the top, with splendid views. It's a small area, but has a worthwhile vertical of 1250m, and 450m above mid-mountain. A gondola from the main street goes up to the flat-bottomed bowl of Huttererböden (1400m), where there are very gentle but limited nursery slopes and lifts up to higher points. Most of the mountain is of easy red steepness. The run to the valley is a pleasant red with one or two tricky bits where it takes a quick plunge; it has effective snowmaking.
600m; slopes 600–1860m
🚡 14 🎿 36km

Hinterthal 128
Village in the Hochkönig area.

Hintertux / Tux valley 122

Hippach 153
Hamlet near a crowd-free lift into Mayrhofen's main area.

Grand Hirafu 676
One of Niseko's interlinked areas.

Hittisau 208
Village in Bregenzerwald.
800m; slopes 800–1600m
🚡 5 🎿 9km

Hochfügen Austria
High-altitude ski-station outpost of Fügen, part of Ski Optimal area linked with Kaltenbach. Best suited to intermediates.
1500m; slopes 560–2500m
🚡 35 🎿 155km

Hochgurgl 158
Quiet village with connection to Obergurgl's slopes.

Hochkönig 128

Hochpillberg Austria
Hamlet with fabulous views towards Innsbruck and an antique chairlift into varied terrain above Schwaz with good vertical of 1000m. Wonderfully safe for children; all accommodation within two minutes of lift.
1300m; slopes 1300–2100m
🚡 5 🎿 10km

Hochsölden 177
Satellite above Sölden.

Hoch-Ybrig Switzerland
Purpose-built complex only 64km south-east of Zürich, with facilities for families.
1050m; slopes 1050–1830m
🚡 12 🎿 50km

Hochzillertal Austria
Along with Hochfugen forms the large Ski Optimal area above the valley village of Kaltenbach. Best suited to intermediates – but there is plenty of potential for off-piste too.
1500m; slopes 560–2500m
🚡 35 🎿 155km

Holiday Valley USA
Family resort in New York State, an hour's drive south-east of Buffalo.
slopes 485–685m
🚡 12 🎿 270 acres

Hollersbach Austria
Hamlet near Mittersill, over Pass Thurn from Kitzbühel, with a gondola up in the Resterhöhe above Pass Thurn.
805m; slopes 805–1000m
🚡 2 🎿 5km

Homewood USA
Uncrowded area near Tahoe City with the most sheltered slopes in the vicinity. Apart from one fast quad, most slopes are served by slow chairlifts, and the views are as much of an attraction as the slopes. Set right on the western shore of the lake, so access is quick and easy. The notably quiet slopes include plenty of short black pitches as well as cruisers.
1900m; slopes 1900–2400m
🚡 7 🎿 1260 acres

Hoodoo Ski Bowl USA
Small area in Oregon with short runs and limited vertical of around 300m. Some 65km from Bend (see Mount Bachelor).
1420m; slopes 1420–1740m
🚡 5 🎿 800 acres

Hopfgarten 182
Small chalet village with lift link into the Ski Welt area.

Horseshoe Resort Canada
Toronto region resort with high-capacity lift system and 100% snowmaking. The second mountain – The Heights – is open to members only.
310m; slopes 310–405m
🚡 7 🎿 60 acres

Les Houches 247
Varied area at the entrance to the Chamonix valley.

Hovden Norway
Big, modern luxury lakeside hotel in wilderness midway between Oslo and Bergen. Cross-country venue with some Alpine slopes.
820m; slopes 820–1175m
⛷ 5 ⛷ 14km

La Hoya Argentina
Small uncrowded resort 15km from the town of Esquel.
slopes 1350–2150m
⛷ 9 ⛷ 22km

Huez 222
Charming old hamlet on the road up to Alpe-d'Huez.

Hunter Mountain USA
Popular New Yorkers' area so it gets very crowded at weekends.
485m; slopes 485–975m
⛷ 14 ⛷ 230 acres

Hüttschlag Austria
Hamlet in a dead-end valley with lifts into the Gastein area at nearby Grossarl.
1020m; slopes 1020–1220m ⛷ 1

Hyundai Sungwoo Resort
South Korea
Modern high-rise resort, 140km from Seoul. Host to the 2009 World Snowboard Championships. Own English-language web site at www.hdsungwoo.co.kr. ⛷ 9

Idre Fjäll Sweden
Collective name for four areas 490km north-west of Stockholm.
slopes 590–890m
⛷ 30 ⛷ 28km

Igls Austria
Almost a suburb of Innsbruck – the city trams run out to the village – but it is a small resort in its own right. Its famous downhill race course is an excellent piste.
900m; slopes 900–2245m
⛷ 9 ⛷ 7km
⛷ *Independent Ski Links, Inghams, Lagrange*

Iizuna Japan
Tiny area 2.5 hours from Tokyo.
slopes 1080–1480m ⛷ 7

Incline Village USA
Large village on northern edge of Lake Tahoe – it is a reasonable stop-off if you are touring.

Indianhead USA
South Lake Superior area with the most snowfall in the region. Winds are a problem.
395m; slopes 395–585m
⛷ 12 ⛷ 195 acres

Inneralpbach 112
Small satellite of Alpbach, 3km up the valley.

Innerarosa Switzerland
The prettiest part of Arosa, with lifts into the slopes and a quiet, 'gentle' children's area. *1800m*

Innichen Italy
Small resort in South Tyrol. San Candido in Italian.
1175m; slopes 1175–1580m
⛷ 4 ⛷ 15km

Innsbruck Austria
Lively and interesting former Olympic city at Alpine crossroads, surrounded by small areas, each ideal for a day-trip. Among them is the Stubai glacier. Area pass available.
575m; slopes 800–3210m
⛷ 78 ⛷ 282km

Interlaken Switzerland
Large lakeside summer resort at entrance to the valleys leading to Wengen, Grindelwald and Mürren.
⛷ *Crystal, Swiss Travel Service*

Ischgl 130

Ishiuchi Maruyama-Gala-Yuzawa Kogen Japan
Three resorts with a shared lift pass 90 minutes from Tokyo by bullet train and offering the largest ski area in the central Honshu region.
255m; slopes 255–920m ⛷ 52

Isola 2000 France
A compact purpose-built resort 90km from Nice, which makes it great for short breaks and very convenient. The doorstep snow, high slopes and an improving range of amenities make it equally appealing to families and beginners; there are some excellent nursery slopes near the base. But the core of the resort village isn't pretty: mostly block-like and tatty apartment buildings. The slopes spread across three main sectors, with varied runs suiting confident intermediates best; most are above the treeline and often sunny, but the resort's southerly aspect means that the area can have masses of snow when it is in shorter supply elsewhere in the French Alps. And most slopes keep their snow well.
2000m; slopes 1840–2610m
⛷ *Erna Low, Lagrange, PowderBeds, PV-Holidays.com, Ski Collection, Ski France, Ski Solutions, Skiweekends.com, Zenith*

Iso Syöte Finland
Finland's most southerly fell region, 150km south of the Arctic Circle but receiving the most snow in the country. A family-friendly resort that suits beginners and intermediates best, since there are only two black runs. But there are two

freeride areas. Most runs are short, with the longest 1200m and a maximum vertical of less than 200m. And all the lifts are drags. There's a terrain park, expanded children's nursery area, tubing, tobogganing, and igloo hotel. Cross-country is big here, with 120kms of trails. There's a choice of hotels and cabins; the Iso-Syöte is on the slopes.
430m; slopes 240–430m
⛷ 9 ⛷ 21km
⛷ *Crystal, First Choice, Thomson*

Itter 182
Next to Söll.

Jackson USA
Classic New England village, and a major cross-country base. A lovely place from which to ski New Hampshire's Alpine areas.

Jackson Hole 613

Jasná Slovakia
Largest ski area in Slovakia, in the Low Tatras mountains. Big children's area, terrain park, night skiing. Several tough 'freeride zones'.
slopes 1240–2005m
⛷ 14 ⛷ 21km ⛷ *Zenith*

Jasper Canada
Set in the middle of Jasper National Park, this low-key, low-rise little town appeals more to those keen on scenery and wildlife (and cross-country skiing) rather than piste miles. Could combine a stay with Whistler, Banff or Lake Louise. Snowfall is modest by North American standards and there is lots of steep terrain that needs good snow to be fun. Keen piste-bashers will cover all the groomed runs in half a day. There are excellent nursery slopes. Visitors have commented on few crowds and queues. There are 300km of cross-country trails. Most accommodation is out of town or on the outskirts and the local slopes are a 30-minute drive. Recent lift investment has added a long fast quad, with another quad due for 2011/12.
1695m; slopes 1695–2610m
⛷ 8 ⛷ 1675 acres
⛷ *Canadian Affair, Carrier, Crystal, Crystal Finest, Frontier, Independent Ski Links, Inghams, Neilson, Ski Independence, Ski Safari, Skiworld, Virgin Snow*

Jay Peak USA
Vermont resort near Canadian border with best snowfall record in the east. Treelined intermediate/advanced slopes – as many classified black as

blue. Experts also have access to hike-in/out terrain in West bowl.
550m; slopes 550–1205m
⛷ 8 ⛷ 385 acres
⛷ *Ski Safari*

Jochberg 137
Straggling village, 8km from Kitzbühel.

La Joue-du-Loup France
Slightly stylish little purpose-built a few km north-west of Gap. Shares a fair-sized intermediate area with Superdévoluy. A ski-in/ski-out, family-oriented resort; all accommodation in good-value apartments and chalets; good choice of affordable restaurants. Easily reached using budget flights to Marseille.
1450m; slopes 1450–2450m
⛷ 22 ⛷ 100km
⛷ *Lagrange, Ski Collection*

Jouvenceaux 438
Less boisterous base near Sauze d'Oulx.

Jukkasjärvi Sweden
Centuries-old cross-country resort with unique ice hotel rebuilt every December.

June Mountain USA
Small area a half-hour drive from Mammoth and in same ownership. Empty slopes except on peak weekends.
2300m; slopes 2300–3090m
⛷ 8 ⛷ 500 acres

Juns 122
Small village between Lanersbach and Hintertux.

Kals am Grossglockner Austria
Remote valley village north of Lienz. Now linked to Matrei.
1325m; slopes 975–2620m
⛷ 15 ⛷ 110km

Kaltenbach Austria
One of the larger, quieter Zillertal areas, with plenty of high-altitude slopes, mostly above the treeline.
560m; slopes 560–2500m
⛷ 35 ⛷ 155km

Kananaskis Canada
Small area near Calgary, nicely set in woods, with slopes at Nakiska.
slopes 1525–2465m
⛷ 12 ⛷ 605 acres
⛷ *Frontier*

Kandersteg Switzerland
Good cross-country base set amid beautiful scenery near Interlaken. Easy, but limited, slopes. Popular with families.
1175m; slopes 1175–1900m
⛷ 7 ⛷ 14km
⛷ *Headwater, Inghams, Inntravel, Swiss Travel Service*

Kanin 672

Kappl Austria
A 15-minute bus ride down the valley from Ischgl, and worth a visit. Both the village and the slopes are family-oriented, and delightfully

quiet compared with Ischgl. The village, with a couple of dozen hotels and guesthouses, sits on a shelf 100m above the valley floor. The slopes – served by an access gondola from the roadside and fast quads above it – offer plenty of variety, with several tough reds. Most of the slopes are open, but the run down the gondola offers shelter for bad-weather days.
1260m; slopes 1180–2690m
🚠9 ⛷40km

Kaprun   Austria
A spacious but pleasant village a few minutes bus ride down the road from Zell am See, and with slopes on the snow-sure Kitzsteinhorn glacier. It makes a particularly good early- or late-season break. Buses to and from both resorts are often crowded at peak times; staying centrally may be best. Most slopes are on the glacier, but nearby Maiskogel also has a small intermediate area. The glacier slopes offer little challenge but there is off-piste with a guide, three ski routes and freeride workshops. The town has plenty of hotels, restaurants, a few lively bars and new Tauern Spa centre.
785m; slopes 755–3030m
🚠53 ⛷138km
📨 *Crystal, Crystal Finest, First Choice, Inghams, Interactive Resorts, Neilson, PowderBeds, Ski Line, Skitracer, Snow Finders, Snowscape, STC, Thomson*

Les Karellis   France
Resort with slopes that are more scenic, challenging and snow-sure than those of better-known Valloire, nearby.
1600m; slopes 1600–2550m
🚠15 ⛷60km

Kastelruth   Italy
German name for Castelrotto.
📨 *Inntravel*

Kasurila   Finland
Siilinjarvi ski area popular with boarders. 🚠5

Katschberg   Austria
Cute hamlet above the road pass from Styria to Carinthia, by-passed by Tauern motorway. Non-trivial area of high intermediate slopes. Popular with families.
1640m; slopes 1065–2220m
🚠16 ⛷70km 📨 Neilson

Keystone   USA
Sprawling condo-dominated resort below three varied mountains; the nearest thing to a proper village is a handy development near the gondola. Evenings are quiet, with limited restaurants/bars. The lift pass covers Breckenridge and nearby Arapahoe Basin. Fast lifts link

all three mountains, with varied terrain including ungroomed steep bowls, forest glades and cat skiing. There's a beautifully groomed network of treelined blues and greens, and good nursery slopes. Reporters praise the school for small classes. There's a huge terrain park and super-pipe, floodlit skiing and tubing. A favourite hut (with us and reporters) is the table-service Alpenglow Stube.
2835m; slopes 2835–3650m
🚠20 ⛷3148 acres
📨 *Alpine Answers, AmeriCan Ski, American Ski Classics, Crystal, Erna Low, Funway Holidays, Independent Ski Links, PowderBeds, Ski Safari, Independence, Ski Safari, Skitracer, Snow Finders*

Kicking Horse   **638**
Killington   **618**
Kimberley   Canada
Mining town turned twee mock Austro-Bavarian/English Tudor resort scenically set 2 hours from Banff. The terrain offers a mix of blue and black runs (and occasional green) and a vertical of 750m. The mainly forested runs are spread over two rather bland hills. There are only a few short double-diamonds, but classification tends to understate difficulty, and many of the single diamonds are quite challenging. It has a reputation for good powder, although it doesn't get huge amounts by the standards of this region.
1230m; slopes 1230–1980m
🚠5 ⛷1800 acres
📨 *AmeriCan Ski, Frontier, Inghams, Ski Safari*

Kirchdorf   Austria
Attractive village a bus ride from St Johann in Tirol, with good local beginner slopes.
640m 📨 *Crystal, Thomson*

Kirkwood   USA
Renowned for its powder, and has a lot to offer experts and confident intermediates, but it's limited for intermediates who are not happy to tackle black runs. It makes a great outing from South Lake Tahoe, though heavy snowfall may close the high-level passes to get there. Deep snow is part of the attraction, often reportedly better than Heavenly.
2375m; slopes 2375–2985m
🚠14 ⛷2300 acres
📨 *Virgin Snow*

Kitzbühel   **137**
Kleinarl   Austria
Secluded traditional village up a pretty side valley from Wagrain, part of the three-

valley lift network linking Flachauwinkl to Zauchensee – our figures relate to this area.
1015m; slopes 800–2185m
🚠15 ⛷65km

Kleinwalsertal   **396**
Area in the German Alps.

Klippitztörl   Austria
One of many little areas in Austria's easternmost ski region near Slovenian border. 'Great little area with pretty treelined runs,' says a visitor.
1550m; slopes 1460–1820m
🚠6 ⛷25km

Klösterle   Austria
Valley village at the base of the Sonnenkopf ski area a few km west of the Arlberg pass – and covered by the Arlberg ski pass.
1100m; slopes 1100–2300m
🚠10 ⛷39km

Klosters   **493**
Kobla   **672**
Slovenian village a bus ride from Vogel.

Kolasin 1450   Montenegro
Small ski area on Bjelasica Mountain above the town of the Kolasin, where you stay.
1450m 🚠5 ⛷20km

Kolsass-Weer   Austria
Pair of Inn-side villages with low, inconvenient and limited slopes.
555m; slopes 555–1010m
🚠3 ⛷14km

Königsleiten   **153**
Quiet resort sharing area with Gerlos in the Zillertal Arena.

Konjiam   South Korea
Purpose-built resort 40 minutes north of Seoul. The slopes suit beginners best, and offer the area's longest run at 1.8km. The base village has over 400 condos, a restaurant and spa, Popular with families.
🚠3 ⛷11runs

Kopaonik   Serbia
Modern, sympathetically designed family resort in a pretty setting.
1770m; slopes 1110–2015m
🚠23 ⛷60km
📨 *BoardnLodge*

Koralpe   Austria
Largest and steepest of many gentle little areas in Austria's easternmost ski region near the Slovenian border.
1550m; slopes 1550–2050m
🚠10 ⛷25km

Korea Condo   South Korea
A single condo complex built some way from the three slopes. 🚠2

Kössen   Austria
Village near St Johann in Tirol with low, scattered and limited local slopes.
600m; slopes 600–1700m
🚠9 ⛷25km

Kötschach-Mauthen   Austria
One of many little areas near Hermagor in eastern Austria, close to the Italian border.
710m; slopes 710–1300m
🚠4 ⛷7km

Kranjska Gora   **672**

Krimml   Austria
Sunny area, high enough to have good snow usually. Shares regional pass with Wildkogel resorts (Neukirchen).
1075m; slopes 1640–2040m
🚠9 ⛷33km

Krippenstein   Austria
A mainly freeride resort on Dachstein glacier near Salzburg. Cable car from Obertraun in the valley. 30km off-piste routes and 11km long blue/red run. Shares lift pass with Annaberg-Gosau region.

Krispl-Gaissau   Austria
Easy slopes very close to Salzburg. Several long top-to-bottom lifts mean the size of the area is greatly reduced if the snow line is high.
925m; slopes 750–1570m
🚠11 ⛷40km

Kronplatz   Italy
Distinctive ski area in South Tyrol, with amazingly efficient lifts from Brunico and San Vigilio di Marebbe. Plan de Corones is its Italian name.
1200m; slopes 1200–2275m
🚠32 ⛷103km
📨 *Momentum*

Krvavec   **672**
Kühtai   Austria
A collection of comfortable hotels beside a high road pass only 25km from Innsbruck – higher than equally snow-sure Obergurgl or Obertauern, but cheaper than either. Covered also by the standard Innsbruck pass. A modern gondola, three fast quads and a handful of drags serve red cruisers of about 500m vertical on either side of the road, plus some token black runs; not ideal for novices – few easy blues to graduate to. Very quiet in the week, but liable to weekend crowds if lower resorts around Innsbruck are short of snow. Limited mountain huts. Quiet in the evening, but for its size a reasonable selection of hotels. The Alpin Resort has smart apartments and a fitness centre.
2020m; slopes 800–2620m
🚠12 ⛷44km
📨 *Crystal, Inghams*

Kusatsu Kokusai   Japan
Attractive spa village with hot springs, three hours from Tokyo.
slopes 1250–2170m 🚠13

Laax   **495**

Le Lac Blanc France
Mini-resort with six-pack in the northerly Vosges mountains near Strasbourg. Extensive ski de fond trails.
830m; slopes 830–1235m
⛷9 ⛷ 14km

Laces Italy
Village in the Val Venosta in the South Tyrol covered by the Ortler Skiarena pass.

Lachtal Austria
Second largest ski resort in the Styrian region NE of Salzburg.
1600m; slopes 1600–2100m
⛷8 ⛷ 29km

Ladis Austria
Smaller alternative to Serfaus and Fiss, with lifts that connect into the same varied ski area.
1200m; slopes 1200–2750m
⛷70 ⛷ 190km

Lagunillas Chile
83km south-east of Santiago.⛷ 494 acres

Le Laisinant 376
Tiny hamlet down the valley from Val d'Isère.

Lake Louise 640

Lake Tahoe USA
Collection of 14 ski areas spectacularly set on California-Nevada border – Heavenly and Squaw Valley best known in Britain.
✉ AmeriCan Ski, Crystal Finest, Skiworld, Snow Finders

Lamoura France
One of four villages that makes up the Les Rousses area in the Jura.
1120m; slopes 1120–1680m
⛷40 ⛷ 40km

Landeck–Zams Austria
Small ski area in the Tirol region.
780m; slopes 816–2210m
⛷7 ⛷ 22km

Lans-en-Vercors France
Village close to Villard-de-Lans and 30km from Grenoble. Highest slopes in the region; few snowmakers.
1020m; slopes 1400–1805m
⛷16 ⛷ 24km

Lanslebourg France
One of the villages that makes up Val Cenis.

Lanslevillard France
One of the villages that makes up Val Cenis.

Laterns Austria
Small, low altitude resort in the Vorarlberg near Friedrichshafen. Two fast chairs serve mainly red runs and some ski routes.
900m; slopes 900–1785m
⛷6 ⛷ 27km

Laturns–Gapfohl Austria
900m; slopes 900–1785m
⛷6 ⛷ 27km

Lauchernalp-Lötschental Switzerland
Small but tall and challenging slopes reached by cable car from Wiler in the secluded, picturesque, dead-end Lötschental, north of Rhône valley. Glacier runs above 3000m.
1970m; slopes 1420–3110m
⛷6 ⛷ 33km

Lauterbrunnen 500
Valley town with rail connection up to Mürren.

Le Lavancher 247
Quiet village between Chamonix and Argentière.

Lavarone Italy
One of several areas east of Trento, good for a weekend day trip.
1195m; slopes 1075–1555m
⛷13 ⛷ 12km

Leadville USA
Old mining town full of historic buildings. Own easy area (Ski Cooper) plus snowcat operation. Picturesque inexpensive base for visiting Copper Mountain, Vail and Beaver Creek.

Lech 145

The Lecht 675
Scottish ski resort.
640m; slopes 610–825m
⛷13 ⛷ 20km

Lélex France
Family resort with pretty wooded slopes between Dijon and Geneva.
900m; slopes 900–1680m
⛷29 ⛷ 50km

Las Leñas Argentina
European-style resort, 400km south of Mendoza, with varied, beautiful terrain and extensive off-piste. But it's a stormy place that can close the lifts for days. Lodgings at the foot of the slopes.
2240m; slopes 2240–3430m
⛷13 ⛷ 64km
✉ Skiworld

Lenggries-Brauneck 396
Bavarian resort south of Munich.
680m; slopes 700–1710m
⛷18 ⛷ 34km

Lenk Switzerland
Traditional village sharing a sizeable area with Adelboden, and with its own separate slopes at Betelberg. Buses to lifts at Rothenbach, or to the six-pack from Buhlberg.
1070m; slopes 1070–2360m
⛷56 ⛷ 185km

Lenzerheide Switzerland
The senior partner with Valbella in an extensive area of intermediate slopes in a pretty setting around a lake, all at a decent altitude. The slopes are on the two sides of the valley. The east-facing, morning-sun slopes are mainly fairly gentle. The west-

facing slopes have more character, both in skiing and visual terms, including a run on the back of the dramatic peak of the Rothorn. There is considerable off-piste potential.
1470m; slopes 1230–2865m
⛷35 ⛷ 155km
✉ Alpine Answers, Crystal, Ski Safari, STC

Lermoos 212
Focal resort of the Zugspitze area: a pleasant little village with a small area of shady intermediate slopes.

Lessach Austria
Hamlet with trail connecting into one of the longest, most snow-sure cross-country networks in Europe.
1210m ⛷1

Leukerbad Switzerland
Major spa resort of Roman origin, spectacularly set beneath towering cliffs, which are scaled by a cable car up to high-altitude cross-country trails. The downhill slopes are on the opposite side of the valley, mainly above the treeline and of red gradient, though there are a couple of blacks including a World Cup downhill course, which descends from open slopes into the woods. Lifts include a six-pack.
1410m; slopes 1410–2700m
⛷10 ⛷ 52km ✉ Thomson

Leutasch Austria
Traditional cross-country village with limited slopes but a pleasant day trip from nearby Seefeld or Innsbruck.
1130m; slopes 1130–1605m
⛷3 ⛷ 6km
✉ Headwater, Inntravel

Levi 663

Leysin Switzerland
This is a spread-out village, climbing up a wooded hillside. The lifts are to the east of the village and take you to a pretty mix of mainly red and blue runs. Itineraries from the top of Chaux de Mont provide the best options for experts, along with a heli-operation. There are nursery slopes at village level. The revolving Kuklos restaurant at La Berneuse has stunning views.
1250m; slopes 1300–2200m
⛷14 ⛷ 60km

Lienz Austria
Pleasant town in pretty surroundings.
675m; slopes 730–2280m
⛷17 ⛷ 40km

Lillehammer Norway
Cultural fjordside town, three hours north of Oslo by train/car, with its two Olympic areas 15 and 35km away.
200m; slopes 200–1030m
⛷10 ⛷ 25km

Limone Italy
Pleasant old town not far from Turin, with a pretty area, but far from snow-sure.
1010m; slopes 1030–2050m
⛷15 ⛷ 80km

Lincoln USA
Sprawling New Hampshire town from which to visit Loon mountain.

Lindvallen-Högfjället Sweden
Two of the mountains that make up the four unlinked ski areas of Sälen.
800m; slopes 590–890m
⛷46 ⛷ 85km

Le Lioran France
Auvergne village near Aurillac with a purpose-built satellite above. Spectacular volcanic scenery.
1160m; slopes 1160–1850m
⛷24 ⛷ 60km

Livigno 425

Lizzola Italy
Small base development in remote region north of Bergamo. Several other little areas nearby.
1250m; slopes 1250–2070m
⛷9 ⛷ 30km

Loch Lomond Canada
Steep, narrow, challenging slopes near Thunder Bay on the shores of Lake Superior. Candy Mountain is nearby.
215m; slopes 215–440m
⛷3 ⛷ 90 acres

Lofer Austria
Quiet, traditional village in a pretty setting north of Saalbach with a small area of its own, and Waidring's relatively snow-sure Steinplatte nearby. New gondola planned for 2011/12.
640m; slopes 640–1745m
⛷10 ⛷ 46km
✉ Neilson, STC

Longchamp France
Dreary purpose-built resort with little to commend it over pretty Valmorel, with which it shares its ski area. *1650m*

Loon Mountain USA
Small, smart, modern resort just outside Lincoln, New Hampshire. Mostly intermediate runs.
290m; slopes 290–910m
⛷10 ⛷ 275 acres
✉ Virgin Snow

Lost Trail USA
Remote Montana area, open only Thursday to Sunday and holidays. Mostly intermediate slopes.
2005m; slopes 2005–2370m
⛷6 ⛷ 800 acres

Loveland USA
Exceptionally high and snowy slopes right next to highway l70, just east of the

Continental Divide, easily reached from other Colorado resorts, especially Keystone.
3230m; slopes 3230–3870m
⛷ 9 ⛷ *1365 acres*

Luchon France
Sizeable village with plenty of amenities, with gondola (eight minutes) to its ski area at purpose-built Superbagnères.
630m; slopes 1440–2260m
⛷ 16 ⛷ *35km*
🚠 *Lagrange*

Lurisia Italy
Sizeable spa resort, a good base for visits to surrounding little ski areas and to Nice.
750m; slopes 800–1800m
⛷ 8 ⛷ *35km*

Lutsen Mountains USA
In Minnesota, the largest ski area in between Vermont and Colorado, with panoramic views of Lake Superior. Four small linked hills offer surprisingly good and extensive terrain.
80m; slopes 80–335m
⛷ 9 ⛷ *1000 acres*

Luz-Ardiden France
Spa village below its ski area. Cauterets and Barèges nearby.
710m; slopes 1730–2450m
⛷ 15 ⛷ *60km*

Macugnaga Italy
Two quiet, pretty villages dramatically set at the head of a remote valley, over the mountains from Zermatt and Saas-Fee. Lifts run up to the foot of the Belvedere glacier. A chairlift rises very slowly from the village to Burky, in the middle of the small, woody area of gentle runs. There is an excellent nursery slope beside the village and a two-stage cable car going over sunny slopes to the Swiss border. Good, varied red runs down the 1100m vertical of the top cable car, and considerable off-piste possibilities given good snow.
1325m; slopes 1325–2800m
⛷ 11 ⛷ *35km*

Madesimo Italy
Five stars in our fast lifts ratings; pity extent only gets one. Not ideal for a week, but the mountain has something for everyone and the system copes well with weekend visitors. The village spreads along both sides of a river, a couple of hours from Bergamo or Milan; a random mix of traditional buildings and narrow streets on one side and more modern development on the other, but with a good choice of mid-priced hotels. The slopes have an almost equal share of blue and red runs that make great intermediate territory, though there are a few notable challenges – including the classic Canalone ski route. For

a resort with a respectable altitude and a generally quiet and queue-free mountain, it is worth considering.
1550m; slopes 1550–2945m
⛷ 12 ⛷ *60km*

Madonna di Campiglio 429

Mad River Glen USA
Cult resort, co-operatively owned, with some tough ungroomed terrain, a few well-groomed intermediate trails and antique lifts. Snowboarding is banned.
485m; slopes 485–1110m
⛷ 4 ⛷ *115 acres*

La Magdaleine Italy
Close to Cervinia, and good on bad-weather days.
1645m; slopes 1645–1870m
⛷ 4 ⛷ *4km*

Maishofen Austria
Cheaper place to stay when visiting equidistant Saalbach and Zell am See.
765m

Malbun Liechtenstein
Quaint user-friendly little family resort, 16km from the capital, Vaduz. Limited slopes and short easy runs.
1600m; slopes 1595–2100m
⛷ 6 ⛷ *21km*

Malcesine Italy
Large summer resort on Lake Garda with a fair area of slopes, served by a revolving cable car.
1430m; slopes 1430–1830m
⛷ 8 ⛷ *12km*

Malga Ciapela Italy
Resort at the foot of the Marmolada glacier massif, with a link into the Sella Ronda. Cortina is nearby.
1445m; slopes 1445–3270m
⛷ 8 ⛷ *18km*

Malga Haider Italy
Small area in Val Venosta, close to Austrian border. Haideralm is its German name.
⛷ 5 ⛷ *20km*

Mallnitz Austria
Village in a pretty valley close to Slovenia, with two varied areas providing a fine mix of wooded and open runs. Closest is Ankogel. The snowsure Molltal Glacier is nearby, above Flattach.
1200m ⛷ 15 ⛷ *88km*

Mammoth Mountain 558

Manigod France
Small valley village, sharing quiet, wooded slopes with La Clusaz – over the Col de la Croix-Fry. 'Fantastic, place to avoid the crowds,' says a visitor. *1100m* ⛷ *132km*

Marble Mountain Canada
Tiny area in the Humber Valley on Newfoundland. Good snow record by east coast standards. Splendid base

lodge, and some slope-side lodging. Blomidon Cat Skiing operates nearby.
85m; slopes 10–545m
⛷ 5 ⛷ *175 acres*
🚠 *Frontier*

Les Marecottes Switzerland
Small area near Martigny. Valid with the Valais Ski Card.
1100m; slopes 1775–2200m
⛷ 5 ⛷ *25km*

Maria Alm 128
Charming village at one end of the Hochkönig area.

Mariapfarr Austria
Village at heart of one of the longest, most snow-reliable cross-country networks in Europe. Sizeable Mauterndorf-St Michael Alpine area and Obertauern area are nearby.
1120m ⛷ 5 ⛷ *30km*

Mariazell Austria
Traditional Styria village with an impressive basilica. Limited slopes.
870m; slopes 870–1265m
⛷ 5 ⛷ *11km*

Maribor-Pohorje 672

Marilleva 429
Small Trentino resort linked with Madonna di Campiglio.

Le Markstein France
Long-standing small resort in the northerly Vosges region near Strasbourg, which has hosted World Cup slalom races. Extensive nordic trails.
slopes 1570–1270m ⛷ 10

Masella Spain
Friendly Pyrenean village linked with the slopes of La Molina to form the Alp 2500 area. Weekend crowds.
1600m; slopes 1600–2535m
⛷ 31 ⛷ *121km*

La Massana 90
Valley town near Arinsal.
slopes 1550–2563m
⛷ 31 ⛷ *63km*

Les Masses 520
A hamlet below Les Collons in the Verbier ski area.

Le Massif Canada
One of several small but developing areas near historic Québec City, dramatically set in a UNESCO World Bio Reserve overlooking the St Lawrence river; the views of the ice floes from the summit lodge are stunning. The varied but limited treelined slopes offer Eastern Canada's biggest vertical at 770m – including a couple of steep double-black diamond runs and some good intermediate cruising. A new gondola and beginner area opened for 2010/11.
35m; slopes 35–805m
⛷ 6 ⛷ *401 acres*
🚠 *AmeriCan Ski, Frontier, Ski Safari*

Matrei in Osttirol Austria
Large market village south of Felbertauern tunnel. Mostly high slopes, linked to Kals on the other side of the hill.
1000m; slopes 975–2620m
⛷ 15 ⛷ *110km*
🚠 *Zenith*

Maurienne Valley France
A great curving trench with over 20 winter resorts, from pleasant old valley villages to convenience resorts purpose-built in the 1960s.

Mauterndorf Austria
Village near Obertauern with tremendous snow record.
1120m; slopes 1075–2360m
⛷ 10 ⛷ *35km*

Maverick Mountain USA
Montana resort with plenty of terrain accessed by few lifts. Cowboy Winter Games venue – rodeo one day, ski races the next.
2155m; slopes 2155–2800m
⛷ 2 ⛷ *500 acres*

Mayens de Riddes Switzerland
Hamlet at the base of lifts on the back of Verbier's Savoleyres sector, more often referred to as La Tzoumaz.
1500m

Mayens-de-Sion Switzerland
Tranquil hamlet off the road up to Les Collons – part of the Verbier area.
1470m

Mayrhofen 153

Méaudre France
Small resort near Grenoble with good snowmaking to make up for its low altitude.
1000m; slopes 1000–1600m
⛷ 10 ⛷ *18km*

Megève 290

Meiringen 497

Melchsee-Frutt Switzerland
Limited, but high and snow-sure bowl above a car-free village. Family-friendly.
1920m; slopes 1080–2255m
⛷ 10 ⛷ *32km*

Mellau 208
Village in Bregenzerwald.
700m; slopes 700–2000m
⛷ 31 ⛷ *105km*

Les Menuires 297

Merano 2000 Italy
Small ski area just outside Merano, with main lift base at Falzeben above Avelengo/Hafling.
2000m; slopes 2000–2240m
⛷ 7 ⛷ *40km*

Méribel 302

Métabief-Mont-d'Or France
Twin villages in the Jura region, not far from Geneva.
900m; slopes 880–1460m
⛷ 22 ⛷ *42km*

Methven New Zealand
Nearest town/accommodation to Mt Hutt, and helicopter base for trips to Arrowsmith range – good for intermediates as well as advanced.

Mieders 200
Village in the Stubai valley.

Mijoux France
Pretty wooded slopes between Dijon and Geneva. Lélex nearby.
1000m; slopes 900–1680m
⛷ 29 ⛷ 50km

Mission Ridge USA
Area in dry region that gets higher-quality snow than other Seattle resorts but less of it. Good intermediate slopes.
1390m; slopes 1390–2065m
⛷ 6 ⛷ 300 acres

Misurina Italy
Tiny village near Cortina. A cheap alternative base.
1755m; slopes 1755–1900m
⛷ 4 ⛷ 13km

Mittenwald 396
Cute town in the Bavarian Alps. *915m*

Mittersill Austria
Valley-junction village south of Pass Thurn. A gondola runs from Hollersbach up to the Resterhöhe sector above Pass Thurn.
790m; slopes 1265–1895m
⛷ 15 ⛷ 25km

Moena Italy
Large village between Cavalese and Sella Ronda resorts, ideally located for touring the Dolomites area.
1200m; slopes 1200–2500m
⛷ 8 ⛷ 35km

La Molina Spain
Cheap, basic resort near Andorra, sharing a fair-sized, varied area with Masella to form Alp 2500.
1400m; slopes 1400–2535m
⛷ 31 ⛷ 121km

Mölltal Glacier Austria
Little-known high glacier slopes above Flattach on the other side of the Tauern tunnel from Bad Gastein. Varied runs and fast lifts. Worthwhile excursion when the snowline is high. Summer skiing available.
2570m; slopes 695–3120m
⛷ 8 ⛷ 53km

Molveno Italy
Lakeside village on edge of Dolomites, with a couple of lifts – but mostly used as a base to ski nearby Andalo.

Monarch USA
Wonderfully uncrowded area, a day trip from Crested Butte. Great powder. Good for all but experts.
3290m; slopes 3290–3645m
⛷ 5 ⛷ 800 acres

Monesi Italy
Southernmost of the resorts south of Turin. Close to Monaco and Nice.
1310m; slopes 1310–2180m
⛷ 5 ⛷ 38km

Le Monêtier 347
Quiet little village with access to Serre-Chevalier's slopes.

La Mongie 338

Montafon 204

Montalbert 324
Traditional village with access to the La Plagne network.

Mont Blanc Canada
Small locals' hill near Tremblant, with only 300m of vertical and no resemblance to the Franco-Italian item.
⛷ 7 ⛷ 36

Montchavin 324
Attractive village on the fringe of La Plagne.

Mont-de-Lans 272
Low village near Les Deux-Alpes.

Le Mont-Dore France
Attractive traditional small town, the largest resort in the stunningly beautiful volcanic Auvergne region near Clermont-Ferrand. New fast quad for 2011/12, replacing three drags.
1050m; slopes 1350–1850m
⛷ 17 ⛷ 42km

Monte Bondone Italy
Trento's local hill.
1300m; slopes 1185–2090m
⛷ 5 ⛷ 20km

Monte Campione Italy
Tiny purpose-built resort, spread thinly over four mountainsides; 80% snowmaking helps to offset the low altitude.
1100m; slopes 1200–2010m
⛷ 16 ⛷ 80km

Monte Livata Italy
Closest resort to Rome, popular with weekenders.
1430m; slopes 1430–1750m
⛷ 8 ⛷ 8km

Monte Piselli Italy
Tiny area with the highest slopes of the many little resorts east of Rome.
2100m; slopes 2100–2690m
⛷ 3 ⛷ 5km

Monte Pora Italy
Tiny resort near Lake d'Iseo and Bergamo. Several other little areas nearby.
1350m; slopes 1350–1880m
⛷ 11 ⛷ 30km

Monterosa Ski 432

Mont Gabriel Canada
Montreal area with runs on four sides of the mountain, though the south-facing sides rarely open. Two short but renowned double-black-diamond bump runs. ⛷ 9

Montgenèvre 312

Mont Glen Canada
Least crowded of the Montreal areas, so a good weekend choice.
680m; slopes 680–1035m
⛷ 4 ⛷ 110 acres

Mont Grand Fonds Canada
Small area sufficiently far from Québec not to get overrun at weekends.
400m; slopes 400–735m ⛷ 4

Mont Habitant Canada
Very limited area in the Montreal region but with a good base lodge. ⛷ 3

Mont Olympia Canada
Small, two-mountain area near Montreal, one mostly novice terrain, the other best suited to experts. ⛷ 6

Mont Orford Canada
Cold, windswept lone peak (no resort), worth a trip from nearby Montreal on a fine day.
slopes 305–855m
⛷ 8 ⛷ 180 acres

Mont-Ste-Anne Canada
Quebec City's biggest and most varied local ski area. Wide choice of amenities at the base. The slopes are limited, but the vertical is a decent 625m. A gondola goes to the top, from where slopes span north and south sides of the mountain. The views are spectacular. Over a third of the area is classified black or double-black, so it's a good place for experts. The Beast (double black diamond) has one of the steepest pitches in the east at 65%. But there are decent intermediate trails too, adequate nursery slopes and an easy top-to-bottom green run. The Dual mountain lift pass is valid at Stoneham.
⛷ 11 ⛷ 465 acres
🚌 AmeriCan Ski, Frontier, Ski Safari

Mont-St-Sauveur Canada
Perhaps the prettiest resort in Canada, popular with Montreal (6okm) day trippers and luxury condo owners.

Mont Sutton Canada
Varied area with some of the best glade skiing in eastern Canada, including some for novices. Quaint Sutton village nearby.
⛷ 9 ⛷ 175 acres

Moonlight Basin 608
Quiet area of slopes linked to Big Sky, Montana.

Morgins 475
Chalet resort just on the Swiss side of the Portes du Soleil circuit.

Morillon 278
Valley village in the Flaine network.

Morin Heights Canada
Area in the Montreal region with 100% snowmaking. Attractive base lodge. ⛷ 6

Morzine 316

Les Mosses Switzerland
Peaceful scenic resort and area, best for a day trip from Villars or Les Diablerets. There's a terrain park, a few chalet-style hotel-restaurants, shops and a rather fine church. There are only draglifts to access the mainly red and blue runs. Prides itself on the number of activities on offer – such as ice-diving, a natural ice rink and an international dog-sled track.
1500m; slopes 1500–2200m
⛷ 14 ⛷ 60km

Mottaret 302
Purpose-built but reasonably attractive part of Méribel.

Mottarone Italy
Closest slopes to Lake Maggiore. No village – just a base area.
1200m; slopes 1200–1490m
⛷ 25km

Les Moulins Switzerland
Village down the road from Château d'Oex with its own low area of slopes, part of the big Gstaad lift-pass area.
890m; slopes 890–3000m
⛷ 58 ⛷ 250km

Mount Abram USA
Small, pretty, treelined area in Maine, renowned for its immaculately groomed easy runs.
295m; slopes 295–610m
⛷ 5 ⛷ 170 acres

Mountain High USA
Best snowfall record and highest lift capacity in Los Angeles vicinity – plus 95% snowmaking. Mostly intermediate cruising.
2010m; slopes 2010–2500m
⛷ 12 ⛷ 220 acres

Mount Ashland USA
Arty town in Oregon renowned for Shakespeare performances. Tiny ski area best for experts run by local charity.
1935m; slopes 1935–2285m
⛷ 4 ⛷ 200 acres

Mount Bachelor USA
Extinct volcano in Oregon with a big ski area and runs on all sides. Higher elevation means better chance of good snow than many other resorts in north-west USA and average annual snowfall of 370 inches is more than any major Colorado resort. Good cruising and beginner terrain lower down and plenty to occupy experts, including treelined blacks and steep terrain on the south-facing slopes. No lodging at the base; stay 30 mins away at Sunriver Resort – a big lodge with bar, restaurant, chalet lodging and

excellent spa – or in Bend, an attractive small town served by free shuttles.
1920m; slopes 1755–2765m
🚡 *13* 🎿 *3680 acres*
🚟 *AmeriCan Ski*

Mount Baker USA
Almost on the coast near Seattle, yet one of the top resorts for snow (averages 600 inches a year). Plenty of challenging slopes. Known for spectacular avalanches.
1115m; slopes 1115–1540m
🚡 *9* 🎿 *1000 acres*

Mount Baldy Canada
Tiny area, but a worthwhile excursion from Big White. Gets ultra low – great glades/powder chutes.
slopes 1705–2150m
🚡 *2* 🎿 *150 acres*

Mount Baldy USA
Some of the longest and steepest runs in California. Only an hour's drive from Los Angeles so a day trip is feasible, but 20% snowmaking and antiquated lifts are major drawbacks.
1980m; slopes 1980–2620m
🚡 *4* 🎿 *400 acres*

Mount Baw Baw Australia
Small but entertaining intermediate area in attractive woodland, with great views. Closest area to Melbourne (150km).
1450m; slopes 1450–1560m
🚡 *7* 🎿 *35 hectares*

Mount Buffalo Australia
Site of Australia's first ski lift. Plateau area best suited to beginners. Short season. On-mountain accommodation, four hours from Melbourne.
1400m; slopes 1455–1610m
🚡 *8* 🎿 *66 acres*

Mount Buller Australia
Three hours from Melbourne and Victoria's largest ski area. Proper resort village, with with a 360-degree network of short runs on its isolated massif. Luxury hotel and spa.
1600m; slopes 1600–1790m
🚡 *22* 🎿 *80km*

Mount Dobson New Zealand
Mostly intermediate slopes in a wide, treeless basin near Mt Cook, with good snow-cover. Accommodation in Fairlie, 40 minutes away.
1610m; slopes 1610–2010m
🚡 *3* 🎿 *990 acres*

Mount Falakro Greece
Area two hours' drive from Salonica in northern Greece; almost as big as Parnassos, uncrowded and with good views. Just a flat quad.
1720m 🚡 *8* 🎿 *22km*

Mount Hood Meadows USA
The biggest and most varied ski area on Mt Hood in Oregon served by 11 lifts including five fast quads. Good beginner area,

intermediate cruising, single black diamond runs in the centre of the main ski area and a big area of double black diamond runs roped off and entered through gates. Up to six terrain parks, depending on snow conditions. No accommodation at the base – stay at Timberline (see separate entry) half an hour away or Government Camp (near Mt Hood Skibowl, which also gets its own entry) 20 minutes away.
1635m; slopes 1375–2225m
🚡 *11* 🎿 *2150 acres*

Mount Hood Skibowl USA
Small area of mainly tough gladed runs, offering the steepest and most extreme slopes in the Mount Hood area. Claims to be America's largest night skiing area with a lot of runs open up to 10/11pm nightly. Two floodlit terrain parks, tubing hills, snow bikes and snowmobiles. Just below Timberline ski area; stay there or in Government Camp at the foot of Skibowl's slopes, a sizeable settlement with a choice of lodgings and restaurants. Other local ski area is Mt Hood Meadows.
1075m; slopes 1075–1530m
🚡 *7* 🎿 *960 acres*

Mount Hotham Australia
Australia's highest ski village. Built on a ridge above the slopes. Intermediate and advanced skiing. Good snow record. Nearest town Bright, 4 hours from Melbourne.
1750m; slopes 1450–1845m
🚡 *13* 🎿 *30km*

Mount Hutt New Zealand
Steepest, most snow-sure area in NZ, with ocean views, but prone to bad weather; 100km from Christchurch, a tricky drive up from Methven.
slopes 1405–2085m
🚡 *4* 🎿 *365 hectares*

Mount Lemmon USA
Southernmost area in North America, close to famous Old West town Tombstone, in Arizona. Reasonable snowfall.
2500m; slopes 2500–2790m
🚡 *3* 🎿 *70 acres*

Mount McKay Australia
Australia's steepest skiing, accessed from Falls Creek, with genuine black-diamond terrain and snowcats.
1600m

Mount Pilio Greece
Pleasant slopes cut out of dense forest, only 15km from the holiday resort of Portaria above town of Volos. 'Very small and disorganised,' says a reporter. *1500m* 🚡 *3*

Mount Rose USA
Much the highest base elevation in the Tahoe area – a good 600m above the lake – and with an annual snowfall average of 400 inches. The Chutes is a shady bowl mainly of serious double-diamond gradient on the front face of the slopes. But there are blue and easy black runs to the base and a wider, gentler, lightly wooded area. The slopes have a lot to offer, especially if staying in Heavenly – where the groomed stuff may be too dull and the ungroomed stuff too challenging.
2520m; slopes 2410–2955m
🚡 *6* 🎿 *1200 acres*
🚟 *Virgin Snow*

Mount Shasta Ski Park USA
Californian resort 300 miles north of San Francisco.
🚡 *4* 🎿 *425 acres*

Mount Snow USA
A one-peak resort, with a long row of lifts on the front face (two fast quads among them) serving easy and intermediate runs of just over 500m vertical. Separate area of black runs on the north face – including a couple of short but serious double blacks – served by a triple chair and a new six-pack. And on the opposite side a small area of intermediate runs above Carinthia base, accessed by a third fast quad. Reputed to have some of the best terrain parks in the east. Lodgings at the base include a Grand Summit hotel.
580m; slopes 580–1095m
🚡 *19* 🎿 *590 acres*
🚟 *Ski Safari*

Mount Spokane USA
Little intermediate area outside Spokane (Washington State).
1160m; slopes 1160–1795m
🚡 *5* 🎿 *350 acres*

Mount St Louis / Moonstone Canada
Premier area in Toronto region, spread over three peaks. Very high-capacity lift system and 100% snowmaking. 🚡 *13* 🎿 *175*

Mount Sunapee USA
Area in New Hampshire closest to Boston; primarily intermediate terrain.
375m; slopes 375–835m
🚡 *10* 🎿 *230 acres*

Mount Vermio Greece
Oldest ski base in Greece. Two areas in central Macedonia 60km from Thessaloniki. Barren but interesting slopes.
slopes 1420–2000m 🚡 *7*

Mount Washington Resort Canada
Scenic area on Vancouver Island with lodging in the base village. Impressive snowfall record but rain is a problem.
1110m; slopes 1110–1590m
🚡 *6* 🎿 *970 acres*
🚟 *Frontier*

Mount Washington Resort USA
This resort (Director of Skiing a certain Bode Miller) is one of several small resorts in New Hampshire scattered along the Interstate 93 highway. The slopes here are on a single mountain face, but it is highly rated, particularly by families, who relish the top-to-bottom easy trails on the main peak, Mt Rosebrook. There is a good mix of terrain, with West Mountain consisting mainly of double-diamond slopes. Snowmaking is comprehensive. There's a terrain park, half-pipe and boardercross. There are a few places to stay near the base, with the grand old Mount Washington hotel five minutes away.
480m; slopes 480–940m
🚡 *8* 🎿 *435 acres*

Mount Waterman USA
Small Los Angeles area where children ski free. The lack of much snowmaking is a drawback.
2135m; slopes 2135–2440m
🚡 *3* 🎿 *210 acres*

Mühlbach 128
Village in the Hochkönig area.

Mühltal Austria
Small village halfway between Niederau and Auffach in the Wildschönau. No local skiing of its own.
780m; slopes 830–1905m
🚡 *25* 🎿 *70km*

Muhr Austria
Village by Katschberg tunnel well placed for visiting St Michael, Badkleinkirchheim, Flachau and Obertauern.
1110m

Muju Resort South Korea
Largest area in Korea and with a fair amount of lodging. Though it is the furthest resort from Seoul (four hours south) it is still overcrowded.
🚡 *14*

Mürren 500

Mutters Austria
Charming rustic village near Innsbruck, at the foot of long slopes of 900m vertical that extend along the Götzens valley to Axamer Lizum. Good for families and beginners.
830m; slopes 830–2340m
🚡 *4* 🎿 *15km*

Myoko Suginohara Kokusai
Japan
A series of small resorts two or three hours from Tokyo, which together make up an area of extensive slopes with longer, wider runs than normal for Japan. ♦ 15
▰ Ski Safari

Naeba Japan
Fashionable resort with lots of accommodation two hours north of Tokyo. Crowded slopes.
900m; slopes 900–1800m ♦ 30

Nakiska Canada
Small area of wooded runs between Banff and Calgary, with emphasis on downhill speed. Unreliable snow, but state-of-the-art snowmaking and pancake-flat grooming.
1525m; slopes 1525–2260m
♦ 5 ♦ 230 acres

Nasserein 190
Quiet suburb of St Anton.

Nassfeld Ski Arena Austria
Carinthia's biggest: scenic and sunny area on the Italian border. Good intermediate slopes. Stay in Tröpolach, by the gondola, or larger Hermagor, further east.
1500m; slopes 610–2195m
♦ 30 ♦ 110km
▰ BoardnLodge, Chalet Group, Ski Line, STC

Nauders Austria
Spacious, traditionally Tirolean village tucked away only 3km from the Swiss border and almost on the Italian one. Its slopes start 2km outside the village (free shuttle-bus) and are mainly high and sunny intermediate runs spread over three areas. There is lots of snowmaking. The area is not ideal for experts, though there is a lot of off-piste terrain. It's not ideal for complete beginners either – the village nursery slopes are some way out. There are five cross-country trails amounting to 40km in all.
1400m; slopes 1400–2850m
♦ 24 ♦ 120km

Nax Switzerland
Quiet, sunny village in a balcony setting overlooking the Rhône valley. Own little area and only a short drive from Veysonnaz. Handful of red and blue runs.
1300m ♦ 6 ♦ 35km

Nendaz 520
A sizeable family resort linked in to the Verbier ski area.

Neukirchen Austria
Quiet, pretty resort sharing slopes with Bramberg. Fairly snow-sure plateau at the top of its mountain. New gondola from Bramberg in 2010/11.
855m; slopes 855–2150m
♦ 15 ♦ 55km ▰ Crystal

Neustift 200
Village in the Stubai valley.

Nevegal Italy
Weekend place near Belluno, south of Cortina.
1030m; slopes 1030–1650m
♦ 14 ♦ 30km

Nevis Range 675
Scottish ski resort.
90m; slopes 655–1220m
♦ 11 ♦ 35km

Niederau Austria
Chalet-style village, the main resort in the Wildschönau and a favourite with beginners and early intermediate skiers. Quite spread out, but few hotels are more than five minutes' walk from a main lift.
830m; slopes 830–1950m
♦ 25 ♦ 70km
▰ First Choice, Independent Ski Links, Inghams, Neilson, Skitracer, Thomson

Niederdorf Italy
Cross-country village in South Tyrol. Villabassa is its Italian name.

Niseko 676
Resort on Hokkaido island, Japan.

Niseko Village 676
One of Niseko's interlinked villages.

Nockberge Innerkrems Austria
Area just south of Katschberg tunnel.
1500m; slopes 1500–2020m
♦ 10 ♦ 33km

Nordseter Norway
Cluster of hotels in snowy forest north of Lillehammer. Some Alpine facilities but best for cross-country.
850m; slopes 1000–1090m
♦ 2 ♦ 2km

Norefjell Norway
Norway's toughest run, a very steep 600m drop; 120km north-west of Oslo.
185m; slopes 185–1185m
♦ 10 ♦ 23km

La Norma France
Traffic-free, purpose-built resort near Modane and Val Cenis. Readers report 'good atmosphere, no high-rise blocks, pistes mostly easy except red Crêtes' and 'uncrowded at half-term, good for kids, low prices for pass, school, rentals'.
1350m; slopes 1350–2750m
♦ 18 ♦ 65km
▰ AmeriCan Ski, Erna Low, Peak Retreats, Ski France

Norquay 623
Banff's quiet local hill.

North Conway USA
Attractive factory-outlet-shopping town in New Hampshire close to Attitash and Cranmore ski areas.

Northstar-at-Tahoe USA
Classic US-style mountain, with runs cut through dense forest and a pleasant base village that is still growing but 'really impressed' a 2011 reporter. The whole area is very sheltered and good for bad-weather days. A gondola and a fast quad go up to a lodge at Big Springs, only 160m above the village. From this point three fast chairs radiate to serve a broad bowl with some short steep pitches at the top, with easier blue runs lower down and around the ridges. From the ridge you can access the Backside, a steeper bowl with a central fast quad chair serving a row of easy black runs. Lookout Mountain has more black runs and a modest vertical of 390m. A new fast quad and trails are planned to expand The Backside area for 2011/12; plus a new mountain restaurant.
1930m; slopes 1930–2625m
♦ 19 ♦ 3000 acres
▰ American Ski Classics, Funway Holidays, Virgin Snow

Nôtre-Dame-de-Bellecombe
France
Pleasant 'very French' village spoiled by the busy road. Inexpensive base from which to visit Megève, though it has fair slopes of its own. Queues and slow lifts can be a problem now it is linked to Les Saisies. Free bus to/from Crest Voland.
1150m; slopes 1035–2070m
♦ 84 ♦ 175km
▰ AmeriCan Ski, Erna Low, Lagrange, Peak Retreats

Nova Levante Italy
Village close to Bozen/Bolzano with lifts up to small network around Passo di Costalunga.
1200m ♦ 16 ♦ 40km

Nozawa Onsen Japan
Spa village with good hot springs three hours from Tokyo. The runs are cut out of heavy vegetation.
500m; slopes 500–1650m ♦ 21
▰ Ski Safari

Nub's Nob USA
One of the most sheltered Great Lakes ski areas (many suffer fierce winds). 100% snowmaking; weekend crowds from Detroit. Wooded slopes suitable for all abilities.
275m; slopes 275–405m
♦ 8 ♦ 245 acres

O2Resort South Korea
Built up the mountain in Gangwon province and Korea's best snow. Slopes suit all levels and include a 3.2km long run. Facilities include: condos, youth hostel, fitness centre, spa and restaurants.
1420m ♦ 16runs

Oberammergau 396
Village in the Bavarian Alps.
835m

Oberau Austria
Pretty village, most central of those forming the Wildschönau region – but least convenient for the slopes. 935m
▰ Inghams, Neilson

Obereggen Italy
Tiny resort close to Bozen/Bolzano with modest area of slopes also accessible from Predazzo in Val di Fiemme.
1550m; slopes 1550–2200m
♦ 6 ♦ 10km

Obergurgl 158

Oberjoch–Hindelang Germany
Small, low-altitude resort, particularly good for beginners.
850m; slopes 1140–1520m
♦ 12 ♦ 32km

Oberlech 145
Car- and crowd-free family resort alternative to Lech.

Oberndorf Austria
Quiet hamlet with beginners' area and a chair connecting it to St Johann's undemanding ski area. 700m

Oberperfuss Austria
Small village west of Innsbruck, with tall but limited slopes. On the Innsbruck lift pass.
820m; slopes 820–2000m
♦ 5 ♦ 17km

Obersaxen-Mundaun-Lumnezia Switzerland
Several quiet villages above Ilanz, in the Vorderrhein Valley, near Laax. Sizeable area of mainly red and blue runs on four linked mountains. The main lifts are fast chairs.
1300m; slopes 1200–2310m
♦ 18 ♦ 120km

Oberstaufen Germany
Three small areas: Steibis, Thulkirchdorf and Hochgrat. Within an hour of Friedrichshafen.
600m; slopes 860–1880m
♦ 30 ♦ 45km

Oberstdorf 396
Town in the German Alps near the Austrian border.
815m; slopes 800–2220m
♦ 31 ♦ 30km

Obertauern 163

Ochapowace Canada
Main area in Saskatchewan, east of Regina. It doesn't get a huge amount of snow but 75% snowmaking helps.
♦ 4 ♦ 100 acres

Ohau New Zealand
Some of NZ's steepest slopes, with great views of Lake Ohau 9km away (where you stay). 320km south of Christchurch.
1500m; slopes 1425–1825m
♦ 3 ♦ 310 acres

Okemo USA
Worthwhile and nicely varied intermediate area above the old Vermont town of Ludlow. Family oriented, with good child care. Comprehensive snowmaking and highly rated grooming.
345m; slopes 345–1020m
⛷ 18 ↟ 624 acres

Oppdal Norway
One of the larger Norwegian resorts, but very far north. Many runs are quite short.
715m; slopes 715–1020m
⛷ 17 ↟ 60km

Orcières-Merlette France
High, convenient family resort a few km north-east of Gap, Merlette being the ugly, purpose-built ski station above the village of Orcières (1450m). Snow-sure beginner area. Slopes have a good mix of difficulty spread over several mountain flanks, and expanded to open a cable car up to almost 3000m on Roche Brune.
1850m; slopes 1850–2725m
⛷ 28 ↟ 100km
✉ Lagrange, Ski Collection, Ski France

Ordino 90
Valley village near Arcalis.

Orelle 386
Village in the Maurienne with access to Val Thorens.

Oropa Italy
Little area just off the Aosta–Turin motorway. An easy change of scene from Courmayeur.
1180m; slopes 1200–2390m
↟ 15km

Les Orres France
Friendly modern resort with great views and varied intermediate terrain, but the snow is unreliable, and it's a long transfer from Lyon.
1550m; slopes 1550–2720m
⛷ 23 ↟ 62km
✉ Crystal, First Choice, Lagrange, Ski Collection, Ski France

Orsières Switzerland
Traditional winter resort near Martigny. Close to Grand St Bernard resorts, including Champex-Lac. Well-positioned base from which to visit Verbier and the Chamonix valley. *900m*

Ortisei 451
Market town in Val Gardena.

Oslo Norway
Capital city with cross-country ski trails in its parks. Alpine slopes and lifts in Nordmarka region, just north of city boundaries.

Otre il Colle Italy
Smallest of many little resorts near Bergamo.
1100m; slopes 1100–2000m
⛷ 7 ↟ 7km

Ötz Austria
Village at the entrance to the Ötz valley with an easy/ intermediate ski area of its own and access to the Sölden, Kuhtai (sharing a lift pass) and Niederau areas.
820m; slopes 820–2200m
⛷ 11 ↟ 34km

Oukaimeden Morocco
Slopes 75km from Marrakech with a surprisingly long season.
2600m; slopes 2600–3260m
⛷ 7 ↟ 15km

Ovindoli Italy
One of the smallest areas in L'Aquila region east of Rome, but it has higher slopes than most and one of the better lift systems.
1375m; slopes 1375–2220m
⛷ 9 ↟ 10km

Ovronnaz Switzerland
Pretty village set on a sunny shelf above the Rhône valley, with a good pool complex. Limited area but Crans-Montana and Anzère close.
1350m; slopes 1350–2080m
⛷ 8 ↟ 30km

Owl's Head Canada
Steep mountain rising out of a lake, in a remote spot bordering Vermont, away from weekend crowds.
⛷ 7 ↟ 90 acres

Oz-en-Oisans 222
Old village with satellite at the lifts into Alpe-d'Huez.

Pajarito Mountain USA
Los Alamos area laid out by nuclear scientists. Atomic slopes too – steep, ungroomed. Open Fridays, weekends and holidays. Fun day out from Taos.
2685m; slopes 2685–3170m
⛷ 6 ↟ 220 acres

Pal 93
Prettily wooded mountain linked with slopes of Arinsal.

Palandöken Turkey
Varied skiing area, transformed by three big hotels, overlooking the Anatolian city of Erzurum.
slopes 2150–3100m ⛷ 4

Pampeago Italy
Trentino area convenient for a trip from Milan.

Pamporovo 668

Panarotta Italy
Smallest of the resorts east of Trento, at a higher altitude than nearby Andalo, so worth a day out from there.
1500m; slopes 1500–2000m
⛷ 6 ↟ 7km

Panorama Canada
Home to one of North America's biggest verticals (1220m), with something for everyone on its quiet, wooded mountain. Small, purpose-built place at the foot of the slopes and on two levels. The

upper 'village' is centred on a hot-pool complex, while the mostly condo accommodation in the lower area. The slopes rise steeply above the resort, but steepest at the top – with genuine blacks and two expert bowls (Taynton and Extreme Dream). Excellent terrain for adventurous intermediates too. More limited for novices. Heli-ski trips are available. There's a big park, pipe and floodlit mini-park. The school is 'very professional' and facilities for families good.
1160m; slopes 1160–2380m
⛷ 9 ↟ 2847 acres
✉ Canadian Affair, Frontier, Neilson, PowderBeds, Ski Independence, Ski Safari, Skiworld, Snow Finders

Panticosa Spain
Charming old Pyrenees spa village near Formigal with limited but varied slopes.
1500m; slopes 1500–2220m
⛷ 16 ↟ 35km

Paradiski 322

Park City 600

Parnassos Greece
Biggest and best-organised area in Greece, 180km from Athens and with surprisingly good slopes and lifts.
slopes 1600–2300m
⛷ 9 ↟ 14km

Parpan Switzerland
Pretty village linked to the large intermediate area of Lenzerheide.
1510m; slopes 1230–2865m
⛷ 35 ↟ 155km

Partenen 204
Traditional village in the Montafon.

La Parva Chile
Only 50km east of Santiago and condoville for the capital's elite. A collection of apartments occupied mostly at weekends, linked with Valle Nevado and El Colorado (no area pass).
2750m; slopes 2430–3630m
⛷ 43 ↟ 113km

Pas de la Casa 95

Passo Costalunga Italy
Dense network of short lifts either side of the road over a pass, close to Val di Fassa, with links up from Nova Levante.

Passo Lanciano Italy
Closest area to Adriatic. Weekend crowds from nearby Pescara when the snow is good.
1305m; slopes 1305–2000m
⛷ 13

Passo Rolle Italy
Small group of lifts either side of the road over a high pass just north of San Martino di Castrozza.

Passo San Pellegrino Italy
Smallish ski area south of the Sella Ronda, with lifts each side of the pass road and links with the valley village of Falcade.
1920m; slopes 1150–2245m
⛷ 19 ↟ 75km

Passo Tonale 436

Pass Thurn 137
Road-side lift base for one of Kitzbühel's ski areas.

Passy-Plaine-Joux France
Small, quiet village 25km from Chamonix. Draglifts serve woody slopes best suited to novices.
1340m ⛷ 6 ↟ 12km

Pebble Creek USA
Small area on Utah-Jackson Hole route. Blend of open and wooded slopes.
1920m; slopes 1920–2530m
⛷ 3 ↟ 600 acres

Pec Pod Snezku Czech Republic
Collection of hamlets spread along the valley road leading to the main lifts and the very limited ski area.
770m; slopes 710–1190m
⛷ 10 ↟ 9km

Peisey 232
Small village linked to Les Arcs.

Peisey-Vallandry 232
Group of villages linked to Les Arcs and the Paradiski area.

Pejo Italy
Trentino spa resort near Madonna. New cable car now serves slopes to 3000m.
1400m; slopes 1400–3000m
⛷ 7 ↟ 15km

Penitentes Argentina
180km from Mendoza. Accommodation at the base.
⛷ 10 ↟ 300 hectares

Perelik Bulgaria
Development aiming to link Pamporovo with Mechi Chal.

Perisher / Smiggins Australia
Expanding resort with slopes on seven mountains, which between them offer plenty of short, intermediate runs. 30km from Jindabyne town, six hours from Sydney.
1640m; slopes 1680–2035m
⛷ 47 ↟ 3075 acres

Pescasseroli Italy
One of numerous areas east of Rome in L'Aquila region.
1250m; slopes 1250–1945m
⛷ 6 ↟ 25km

Pescocostanzo Italy
One of numerous areas east of Rome in L'Aquila region.
1395m; slopes 1395–1900m
⛷ 4 ↟ 25km

Pettneu Austria
Snow-sure specialist beginners' resort with bus link to nearby St Anton.
1250m; slopes 1230–2020m
⛷ 4 ↟ 15km

Petzen Austria
One of many little areas in Austria's easternmost ski region near the Slovenian border.
600m; slopes 600–1700m
🚡5 🎿16km

Peyragudes France
Small Pyrenean resort with its ski area starting high above.
1600m; slopes 1600–2400m
🚡17 🎿60km 🚌 Lagrange

Pfelders Italy
Resort near Merano in the South Tyrol covered by the Ortler Skiarena pass.
🚡4 🎿5km

Pfunds Austria
Picturesque valley village with no slopes but quick access to several resorts in Switzerland and Italy, as well as Austria.
970m

Phoenix Park South Korea
Golf complex with 12 trails in winter. Two hours (140km) from Seoul.
slopes 650–1050m 🚡9

Piancavallo Italy
Uninspiring yet curiously trendy purpose-built village, an easy drive from Venice. Not for piste-bashers and experts but suitable for beginners and intermediates.
1270m; slopes 1270–1830m
🚡17 🎿45km

Piani delle Betulle Italy
One of several little areas near the east coast of Lake Como.
730m; slopes 730–1850m
🚡6 🎿10km

Piani di Artavaggio Italy
Small base complex rather than a village. One of several little areas near Lake Como.
875m; slopes 875–1875m
🚡7 🎿15km

Piani di Bobbio Italy
Largest of several tiny resorts above Lake Como.
770m; slopes 770–1855m
🚡10 🎿20km

Piani di Erna Italy
Small base development – no village. One of several little areas above Lake Como.
600m; slopes 600–1635m
🚡5 🎿9km

Piau-Engaly France
User-friendly St-Lary satellite in one of the best Pyrenean areas.
1850m; slopes 1420–2530m
🚡17 🎿65km 🚌 Lagrange

Piazzatorre Italy
One of many little areas in the Bergamo region.
870m; slopes 870–2000m
🚡5 🎿25km

Pichl 173
Hamlet outside Schladming.

Pico USA
Low-key little family area (no resort village) close to Killington.
605m; slopes 605–1215m
🚡9 🎿160 acres

Piesendorf Austria
Cheaper, quiet place to stay when visiting Zell am See. Tucked behind Kaprun near Niedernsill.
780m 🚡3 🎿3km

Pievepelago Italy
Much the smallest and most limited of the Apennine ski resorts. Less than two hours from Florence and Pisa.
1115m; slopes 1115–1410m
🚡7 🎿8km

Pila 404
Resort in the Aosta valley.
1800m; slopes 1550–2740m
🚡14 🎿70km

Pinzolo 429
Trentino resort near Madonna.

Pitztal Austria
Long valley with good glacier area at its head, accessed by underground funicular. New gondola being built for 2012/13.
1680m; slopes 880–3440m
🚡12 🎿68km 🚌 Zenith

Pla-d'Adet France
Limited purpose-built complex at the foot of the St-Lary ski area (the original village is further down the mountain).
1680m; slopes 1420–2450m
🚡32 🎿80km 🚌 Lagrange

La Plagne 324
Distinctive ski area in South Tyrol, with amazingly efficient lifts from Brunico and San Vigilio di Marebbe. Better known by its German name, Kronplatz.
1200m; slopes 1200–2275m
🚡32 🎿103km

Plan-Peisey 232
Small development with link to Les Arcs.

Plose Italy
Varied area close to Bressanone, with the longest run in the South Tyrol.
560m; slopes 1065–2500m
🚡11 🎿40km

Poiana Brasov 671
Cheap, informal resort in Romania.
1030m; slopes 1020–1775m
🚡9 🎿14km

Pomerelle USA
Small area in Idaho on the Utah–Sun Valley route.
2430m; slopes 2430–2735m
🚡3 🎿300 acres

Pontechianale Italy
Highest, largest area in a remote region south-west of Turin. Day-tripper place.
1600m; slopes 1600–2760m
🚡8 🎿30km

Ponte di Legno 436
Attractive sheltered alternative to Passo Tonale.

Pontresina Switzerland
Small, sedate, sunny village with one main street, rather spoiled by the sanatorium-style architecture. All downhill skiing involves travel by car or bus, except the single long piste on Pontresina's own hill, Languard. It's cheaper to stay here than St Moritz.
1805m; slopes 1730–3305m
🚡54 🎿350km

Port-Ainé Spain
Small but high intermediate area in the Spanish Pyrenees near Andorra. Lifts include a six-pack; eponymous 3-star hotel at base.
1975m; slopes 1650–2440m
🚡8 🎿44km

Port del Comte Spain
High resort in the forested region of Lleida, north-west of Barcelona. The slopes spread across three linked sectors: El Sucre, El Hostal and El Estivella.
slopes 1700–2400m
🚡15 🎿40km

Porté Puymorens France
Little-known Pyrenean area close to Pas de la Casa in Andorra.
slopes 1600–2600m
🚡13 🎿45km

Porter Heights New Zealand
Closest skiing to Christchurch (one hour). Open, sunny bowl offering mostly intermediate skiing – with back bowls for powder.
1340m; slopes 1340–1950m
🚡5 🎿200 acres

Portes du Soleil 335

Portillo Chile
Luxury hotel 150km north-east of Santiago. Quiet snow-sure slopes used for training by US national ski team. Suits experts best.
2850m; slopes 2450–3310m
🚡14 🎿1200 acres
🚌 AmeriCan Ski, Crystal, Momentum, Scott Dunn, Skiworld

Powderhorn USA
Area in west Colorado perched on the world's highest flat-top mountain, Grand Mesa. Sensational views. Day trip from Aspen.
2490m; slopes 2490–2975m
🚡4 🎿300 acres

Powder King Canada
Remote resort in British Columbia, between Prince George and Dawson City. As its name suggests, it has great powder. Plenty of lodging.
880m; slopes 880–1520m
🚡3 🎿160 acres

Powder Mountain USA
Massive Utah area sprawled over six ridges, an hour and a quarter's drive from Salt Lake City. An ample 2,800 acres of its terrain is lift served, a mix of mainly north-facing slopes with enough green, blue and black runs to satisfy all abilities. You access the rest by snowcat or snowmobile tow, buses and hiking. It's the abundance of intermediate freeride terrain that makes it special. You can also stay in Ogden, 32km away.
2100m; slopes 2100–2740m
🚡7 🎿7000 acres

Pozza di Fassa Italy
Pretty Dolomite village with its own slopes, three other small areas close by, and access to the Sella Ronda at Campitello.
1320m; slopes 1320–2428m
🚡7 🎿16km

Pragelato Italy
Inexpensive base, linked by cable car to Sestriere. Its own area is worth half a day.
1535m; slopes 1535–2700m
🚡6 🎿50km

Prägraten am Grossvenediger Austria
Traditional mountaineering/ski touring village in lovely setting south of Felbertauern tunnel. The Alpine ski slopes of Matrei are nearby.
1310m; slopes 1310–1490m
🚡2 🎿30km

Prali Italy
Tiny resort east of Sestriere – a worthwhile half-day trip.
1450m; slopes 1450–2500m
🚡7 🎿25km

Pralognan-la-Vanoise France
Unspoiled traditional village overlooked by spectacular peaks. Champagny and Courchevel are close by.
1410m; slopes 1410–2355m
🚡14 🎿30km
🚌 Erna Low, Lagrange, Ski France

Pra-Loup France
Convenient, purpose-built family resort with an extensive, varied intermediate area linked to La Foux-d'Allos (Val d'Allos region).
1500m; slopes 1500–2600m
🚡51 🎿180km
🚌 Lagrange, Ski Collection, Ski France

Prati di Tivo Italy
Weekend day-trip place east of Rome and near the town of Teramo. A sizeable resort by southern Italy standards.
1450m; slopes 1450–1800m
🚡6 🎿16km

Prato Nevoso Italy
Purpose-built resort with rather bland slopes. Part of Mondolè area with Artesina.
1500m; slopes 1500–1950m
🚡25 🎿90km 🚌 Thomson

Prato Selva Italy
Tiny base development (no village) east of Rome near Teramo. Weekend day-trip place.
1370m; slopes 1370–1800m
🚡 4 🎿 10km

Le Praz 262
Aka Courchevel 1300.

Les Praz 247
Quiet hamlet near Chamonix.

Praz-de-Lys France
Little-known snow-pocket area near Lake Geneva that can have good snow when nearby resorts (eg La Clusaz) do not.
1450m; slopes 1240–1965m
🚡 23 🎿 60km
📧 PV-Holidays.com

Praz-sur-Arly France
Traditional village in a pretty, wooded setting just down the road from Megève. Sharing slopes with Notre Dame de Bellecombe and beyond to Crest Voland / Les Saisies, to form the Espace Diamant.
1035m; slopes 1035–2070m
🚡 84 🎿 175km
📧 Ski France

Predazzo Italy
Small, quiet place between Cavalese and the Sella Ronda resorts, with lift into modest area of slopes above Obereggen.
1015m; slopes 995–2205m
🚡 8 🎿 17km

Premanon France
One of four resorts that make up Les Rousses area in Jura region.
1050m; slopes 1120–1680m 🚡 40
📧 Lagrange

La Presolana Italy
Large summer resort near Bergamo. Several other little areas nearby.
1250m; slopes 1250–1650m
🚡 6 🎿 15km

Les Prodains 242
Village at the foot of the cliffs on which Avoriaz sits.

Pucón Chile
Ski area on the side of the active Villarrica volcano in southern Chile, 800km south of Santiago. Lodgings are at Pucón village, 30 minutes away from the slopes.
1200m; slopes 1200–2440m
🚡 9 🎿 20 runs

Puigmal France
Resort in the French Pyrenees with accommodation in nearby villages.
1830m; slopes 1830–2700m
🚡 12 🎿 34km

Puy-St-Vincent 336

Pyhä Finland
Expanding resort 150km north-east of Rovaniemi. Finland's second six-pack opened here for 2010/11. Much of the area is in a National Park, with the 14 slopes on

two sides of a part-wooded hill. Vertical is only 280m and there's no steep terrain but good off-piste. The best powder runs are on both sides of a long T-bar on the north side. Most pistes open for floodlit skiing. There's a well-developed terrain park, hosting regular competitions.
220m 🚡 8 📧 First Choice

The French Pyrenees 338

Pyrenees 2000 France
Tiny resort built in a pleasing manner. Shares a pretty area of short runs with Font-Romeu. Impressive snowmaking.
2000m; slopes 1750–2250m
🚡 32 🎿 52km

Québec City Canada
French-speaking capital and old city with a number of ski areas a short drive away.
📧 AmeriCan Ski, Crystal

Queenstown New Zealand
South Island's outdoor adventure capital, in a stunning lakeside setting. Two local resorts: the Remarkables and Coronet Peak. Treble Cone and Cardrona are easily reached by car. Typically commercialised but lively and relaxed, and where most people stay. The slopes are a 30-40 minute drive away. The Remarkables appeals mainly to families and beginners, while Coronet Peak is more satisfying to intermediates. Both resorts have challenges for experts too.
310m; slopes 1230–1945m
🚡 13 🎿 1235 acres

Radium Hot Springs Canada
Summer resort offering an alternative to the purpose-built slope-side resort of Panorama.
slopes 975–2155m
🚡 8 🎿 300 acres

Radstadt Austria
Unspoiled medieval town near Schladming, with its own small area and the Salzburger Sportwelt slopes accessed from nearby Zauchensee or Flachau.
855m; slopes 855–2185m
🚡 100 🎿 350km

Ragged Mountain USA
Family-owned ski area in New Hampshire.
🚡 9 🎿 200 acres

Rainbow New Zealand
Northernmost ski area on South Island. Wide, treeless area, best for beginners and intermediates. Accommodation at St Arnaud.
1440m; slopes 1440–1760m
🚡 5 🎿 865 acres

Ramsau am Dachstein Austria
Charming village overlooked by the Dachstein glacier. Renowned for cross-country, it

also has Alpine slopes locally, on the glacier and at Schladming.
1200m; slopes 1100–2700m
🚡 18 🎿 30km

Ramundberget Sweden
Small, quiet, ski-in/ski-out family resort with very limited pistes but lots of cross-country. 🎿 22km

Rasos de Peguera Spain
The only resort in the Barcelona province; 14km from Berga. Ten pistes, mostly red classified.

Rauris Austria
Small village in a quiet, dead-end valley south-east of Zell, about 25km by road. Across the valley road from the village are nursery draglifts and a gondola accessing intermediate slopes with a vertical of 1250m.
950m; slopes 950–2200m
🚡 9 🎿 30km
📧 Crystal, Neilson, Thomson

Ravascletto Italy
Resort in a pretty wooded setting near Austrian border, with most of its terrain high above on an open plateau.
920m; slopes 920–1735m
🚡 12 🎿 40km

Reallon France
Traditional-style village, with splendid views from above Lac de Serre-Ponçon.
1560m; slopes 1560–2115m
🚡 6 🎿 20km

Red Lodge USA
Picturesque Old West Montana town. Ideal for a combined trip with Big Sky or Jackson Hole.
1800m; slopes 2155–2860m
🚡 8 🎿 1600 acres
📧 AmeriCan Ski

Red Mountain Canada
Up there with the likes of Fernie as a cult resort for expert skiers who can handle its steep terrain, wide glades and powder-filled bowls. While not big in European terms, it packs a lot of tough stuff into its two mountains. If that's your scene, get there quickly as the ski area has been developing. But it's still the black and double-black stuff that is the real attraction; it's marked on the map, but not on the mountain – so a guide may be necessary to explore it fully. There are long-term plans for a proper resort village at the base, but the small old mining town of Rossland is just 3km away.
1185m; slopes 1185–2075m
🚡 6 🎿 1685 acres
📧 AmeriCan Ski, Frontier, Ski Independence, Ski Safari, Skiworld

Red River USA
New Mexico western town – complete with stetsons and saloons – with intermediate slopes above.
2665m; slopes 2665–3155m
🚡 7 🎿 290 acres

Reichenfels Austria
One of many small areas in Austria's easternmost ski region near the Slovenian border.
810m; slopes 810–1400m

Reinwald Italy
Resort near Merano in the South Tyrol covered by the Ortler Skiarena pass.

Reit im Winkl Germany
Southern Bavarian resort, straddling the German-Austrian border. Winklmoos ski area is best suited to intermediates.
750m; slopes 750–1800m
🚡 7 🎿 40km

The Remarkables New Zealand
Three bleak basins with great views of 'remarkable' jagged alps, 45 minutes from Queenstown. Popular with families and beginners, but some tougher terrain too. Big terrain park.
1580m; slopes 1580–1945m
🚡 6 🎿 545 acres

Rencurel-les-Coulumes France
One of seven little resorts just west of Grenoble. Unspoiled, inexpensive place to tour. Villard-de-Lans is the main resort.

Reschenpass Austria
Area in the Tirol right on the Swiss border; includes Schöneben and Haider Alm in Italy. Nauders is the main resort.
1520m 🚡 7 🎿 28

Rettenberg Germany
Small resort near Austrian border.
750m; slopes 820–1650m
🚡 15 🎿 40km

Reutte Austria
500-year-old market town with many traditional hotels, and rail links to nearby Lermoos.
855m; slopes 855–1900m
🚡 9 🎿 19km

Revelstoke 645

Rhêmes Notre Dame 404
Village in the Aosta valley.
1725m; slopes 1625–3605m
🚡 4 🎿 5km

Riederalp Switzerland
Pretty, car-free village high above the Rhône valley near Brig; part of the Aletsch Arena. Cable car or gondola from the valley village of Mörel. Quiet, friendly, uncrowded slopes. Two new lifts for 2010/11.
1925m; slopes 1050–2870m
🚡 35 🎿 100km

Riefensberg 208
Village in Bregenzerwald.
780m ⤊ 14km

Rigi-Kaltbad Switzerland
Resort on a mountain rising
out of Lake Lucerne, with
superb all-round views,
accessed by the world's first
mountain railroad.
*1440m; slopes 1195–1795m
⤊ 4 ⤊ 9km*

Riihivuori Finland
Small area with 'base' at the
top of the mountain. 20km
south of the city of Jyväskylä.
⤊ 5

Riksgränsen Sweden
Unique Arctic Circle Alpine
area not open until late
February. You can use the
slopes under the midnight
sun (lift-served) from mid-May
to June. 20 hours by train
from Stockholm.
*600m; slopes 600–910m
⤊ 6 ⤊ 21km*

Riscone Italy
Dolomite village sharing a
pretty area with San Vigilio.
Good snowmaking. Short easy
runs.
*1200m; slopes 1200–2275m
⤊ 35 ⤊ 40km*

Rittner Horn Italy
Resort near Merano in the
South Tyrol covered by the
Ortler Skiarena pass.
⤊ 3 ⤊ 15km

Rivisondoli Italy
Sizeable retreat east of Rome,
with one of the better lift
systems in the vicinity.
*1350m; slopes 1350–2050m
⤊ 7 ⤊ 16km*

Roccaraso Italy
Largest of the resorts east of
Rome – at least when snow-
cover is complete.
*1280m; slopes 1280–2200m
⤊ 12 ⤊ 56km*

Rohrmoos 173
Suburb of Schladming, with
vast area of nursery slopes.

La Rosière 341

Rossland Canada
Remote little town 5km from
cult powder paradise Red
Mountain.

Rougemont Switzerland
Cute rustic hamlet just over
the French/German language
border near Gstaad, with local
slopes and links to Gstaad's
Eggli sector.
*990m; slopes 950–3000m
⤊ 58 ⤊ 250km*

Les Rousses France
Group of four villages – Les
Rousses, Premanon, Lamoura
and Bois d'Amont – in the
Jura mountains, 50km from
Geneva airport.
*1120m; slopes 1120–1680m
⤊ 40 ⤊ 40km ⫸ Lagrange*

Ruka Finland
80km south of the Arctic
Circle, close to Kuusamo
airport and the Russian
border, in a region known for
abundant and enduring snow.
Lively, upbeat resort with a
newly developed pedestrian
village. Good but widely
spread cabin lodging served
by the ski bus. Slopes on two
sides of a single low hill, with
a mix of open and forest
terrain, most floodlit and with
snowmaking. None is
particularly steep and the
vertical very modest – but
there is a new FIS racing
piste. There's a terrain park
and boardercross course. The
cross-country scope is vast:
500km, of which 40km are
floodlit. *200m ⤊ 20 ⤊ 20km
⫸ Crystal, Crystal Finest, First
Choice, Skiworld, Thomson*

Russbach Austria
Secluded village up a side
valley and linked into the
Gosau-Annaberg-Lungotz area.
Slopes spread over wide area.
*815m; slopes 780–1620m
⤊ 33 ⤊ 65km*

Rusutsu 676
Hokkaido island resort.

Saalbach-Hinterglemm 166

Saalfelden Austria
Town ideally placed for
touring eastern Tirol. Lift
networks of Maria-Alm and
Saalbach nearby.
*745m; slopes 745–1550m
⤊ 3 ⤊ 3km*

Saanen Switzerland
Cheaper and more convenient
alternative to Gstaad – but
much less going on.
*slopes 950–3000m
⤊ 58 ⤊ 250km*

Saanenmöser Switzerland
Small village with rail/road
links to Gstaad. Scenic and
quiet local slopes, with good
mountain restaurants
(Horneggli and Kübelialp are
recommendations).
*1270m; slopes 950–3000m
⤊ 58 ⤊ 250km*

Saas-Almagell Switzerland
Compact village up the valley
from Saas-Grund, with good
cross-country trails and walks,
and a limited Alpine area.
*1670m; slopes 1670–2400m
⤊ 7 ⤊ 12km*

Saas-Fee 504

Saas-Grund Switzerland
Sprawling valley village below
Saas-Fee, with a separate,
small but high Alpine area.
*1560m; slopes 1560–3200m
⤊ 8 ⤊ 35km*

Saddleback USA
Small area between Maine's
premier resorts. High slopes
by local standards.
*695m; slopes 695–1255m
⤊ 5 ⤊ 100 acres*

Sahoro Japan
Ugly, purpose-built complex
on snowy northern Hokkaido
island, with a limited area.
*610m; slopes 610–1030m
⤊ 8 ⤊ 15km ⫸ Club Med*

Les Saisies France
Traditional-style cross-country
venue, surrounded by varied
four-mountain Alpine slopes.
Now part of Espace Diamant.
Easy runs, but some lift
queues at peak times.
*1650m; slopes 1035–2070m
⤊ 84 ⤊ 175km
⫸ AmeriCan Ski, Classic Ski,
Erna Low, Lagrange, Peak
Retreats, PowderBeds, Ski
Collection, Ski France, Ski
Independence*

Sälen Sweden
Well-developed family resort
with extensive lift system, and
some good off-piste for
experts.
*550m; slopes 550–950m
⤊ 101 ⤊ 144km*

Salt Lake City USA
Underrated base from which
to ski Utah. 30 minutes from
Park City, Deer Valley, The
Canyons, Snowbird, Alta,
Snowbasin. Cheaper and
livelier than the resorts.
⫸ AmeriCan Ski, Crystal

Salzburg-Stadt Austria
A single, long challenging run
off the back of Salzburg's
local mountain, accessed by a
spectacular lift-ride from a
suburb of Grodig. *425m*

Samedan Switzerland
Valley town, just down the
road from St Moritz. A run
heads back to base from
Corviglia-Marguns.
*1720m; slopes 1730–3305m
⤊ 54 ⤊ 350km*

Samnaun 130
Shares large ski area with
Ischgl.

Samoëns 345

San Bernardino Switzerland
Pretty resort south of the road
tunnel, close to Madesimo.
*1625m; slopes 1600–2525m
⤊ 8 ⤊ 35km*

San Candido Italy
Resort on the border with
Austria on the road to Lienz.
Innichen is its German name.
*1175m; slopes 1175–1580m
⤊ 4 ⤊ 15km*

San Carlos de Bariloche
Argentina
Year-round resort, with five
areas nearby and the place to
stay when skiing Cerro
Catedral – 20 minutes away
by bus. Once a quaint
lakeside town, but now a
substantial resort.
*slopes 1030–2180m
⤊ 39 ⤊ 103km*

San Cassiano 443

Sandia Peak USA
The world's longest lift ride
ascends from Albuquerque.
Mostly gentle slopes; children
ski free.
*slopes 2645–3165m
⤊ 7 ⤊ 100 acres*

San Grée di Viola Italy
Easternmost of resorts south
of Turin, surprisingly close to
the Italian Riviera.
*1100m; slopes 1100–1800m
⤊ 30km*

San Martin de los Andes
Argentina
Sizeable town with
accommodation, 19 km from
the Chapelco ski area.

San Martino di Castrozza Italy
Trentino village south of Val di
Fassa.
*1465m; slopes 1465–2610m
⤊ 20 ⤊ 50km*

Sansicario 438
Small, stylish resort in the
Milky Way near Sauze d'Oulx.

San Simone Italy
Tiny development north of
Bergamo, close to
unappealing Foppolo area.
*2000m; slopes 1105–2300m
⤊ 9 ⤊ 45km*

Santa Caterina Italy
Pretty, user-friendly village
near Bormio, with a snow-sure
novice and intermediate area.
*1740m; slopes 1740–2725m
⤊ 8 ⤊ 25km*

Santa Cristina 451
Quiet village in Val Gardena
on the periphery of the Sella
Ronda circuit.

Santa Fe USA
Interesting area only 15 miles
from beautiful Santa Fe town.
A tree-filled bowl with a good
variety of terrain crammed
into its small area. Ideal
stopover en route from
Albuquerque airport to Taos.
*3145m; slopes 3155–3680m
⤊ 7 ⤊ 550 acres*

Santa Maria Maggiore Italy
Resort south of the Simplon
Pass from the Rhône valley,
and near Lake Maggiore.
*820m; slopes 820–1890m
⤊ 5 ⤊ 10km*

**San Vigilio di Marebbe /
Kronplatz** Italy
Pretty village in South Tyrol
with lifts on two mountains,
one being the quite
impressive Plan de Corones /
Kronplatz.
*1200m; slopes 1200–2275m
⤊ 31 ⤊ 103km*

San Vito di Cadore Italy
Sizeable, alternative place to
stay to Cortina. Negligible
local slopes, though.
*1010m; slopes 1010–1380m
⤊ 9 ⤊ 12km*

Sappada Italy
Isolated resort close to the Austrian border below Lienz.
1215m; slopes 1215–2050m
🚡 17 ⬆ 21km

Sappee Finland
Resort within easy reach of Helsinki, popular with boarders and telemarkers. Lake views. 🚡 7

Sarnano Italy
Main resort in the Macerata region near Adriatic Riviera. Valley village with ski slopes accessed by lift.
540m 🚡 9 ⬆ 11km

Le Sauze France
Fine area near Barcelonnette, sadly remote from airports.
1400m; slopes 1400–2440m
🚡 23 ⬆ 65km

Sauze d'Oulx 438

Savognin Switzerland
Pretty village with a good mid-sized area; good base for nearby St Moritz, Davos/Klosters and Laax.
1200m; slopes 1200–2715m
🚡 10 ⬆ 80km 📧 Crystal

Schia Italy
Very limited area of short runs – the only ski area near Parma. No village.
1245m; slopes 1245–1415m
🚡 7 ⬆ 15km

Schilpario Italy
One of many little areas near Bergamo.
1125m; slopes 1125–1635m
🚡 5 ⬆ 15km

Schladming 173

Schnalstal Italy
Valley and high ski area, in the Dolomites near Merano. Val Senales is its Italian name.
3210m; slopes 2110–3210m
🚡 12 ⬆ 35km

Schöneben Italy
Area in the Val Venosta in the South Tyrol, close to Austrian border and Nauders.
1520m 🚡 7 ⬆ 28km

Schönried Switzerland
A cheaper and quieter alternative to Gstaad.
1230m; slopes 950–3000m
🚡 58 ⬆ 250km

Schoppernau 208
Village in Bregenzerwald.
860m; slopes 860–2060m
🚡 8 ⬆ 44km

Schröcken 208
Bregenzerwald village near Lech.
1260m; slopes 1260–2100m
🚡 15 ⬆ 66km

Schruns 204
Pleasant town at the heart of the Montafon region.

Schüttdorf Austria
Ordinary satellite of Zell am See, with easy access to the shared area. Kids' area and nursery slopes at the base.
755m; slopes 755–3030m
🚡 53 ⬆ 138km

Schwarzach im Pongau Austria
Riverside village with rail links. There are limited slopes at Goldegg; Wagrain (Salzburger Sportwelt) and Grossarl (Gastein valley) are also nearby.
600m 🚡 4 ⬆ 12km

Schwarzenberg 208
Village in Bregenzerwald.
700m; slopes 1145–1465m
🚡 9 ⬆ 24km

Schwaz Austria
Valley town beside the Inn with a lift into varied terrain shared with the village of Pill and its mountain outpost, Hochpillberg.
540m; slopes 540–2030m
🚡 6 ⬆ 10km

Schweitzer USA
Excellent family-friendly resort in northern Idaho, 85 miles from Spokane (Washington state) and 45 miles from Canada.
1220m; slopes 1229–1950m
🚡 10 ⬆ 2900 acres

Schwemmalm Italy
Resort near Merano in the South Tyrol covered by the Ortler Skiarena pass.
🚡 5 ⬆ 18km

Scopello Italy
Low area close to the Aosta valley, worth considering for a day trip in bad weather.
slopes 690–1700m
🚡 6 ⬆ 35km

Scuol Switzerland
Year-round spa resort close to Austria and Italy, with an impressive range of terrain.
1225m; slopes 1225–2780m
🚡 15 ⬆ 80km

Searchmont Resort Canada
Ontario area with modern lift system and 95% snowmaking. Fine Lake Superior views.
275m; slopes 275–485m
🚡 4 ⬆ 65 acres

Sedrun Switzerland
Sizeable roadside village east of the Oberalp Pass, and covered along with Andermatt by the Gotthard Oberalp lift pass. It has the most extensive piste skiing in the area. There's a good choice of red runs, a rewarding black and a 'freeride' route, plus plenty of scope for off-piste. At Milez there's a terrain park and family restaurant area. Spa centre.
1450m; slopes 1450–2350m
🚡 10 ⬆ 50km

Seefeld Austria
Classic winter holiday resort, well designed in traditional Tirolean style, with a large pedestrian-only centre and lots of upmarket hotels (including three 5-stars). Lots of people come here to enjoy the superb cross-country trails and off-slope activities rather

than the downhill skiing, but there are two main downhill sectors on the outskirts – Gschwandtkopf and Rosshütte – the latter served mostly by fast lifts. Both areas have intermediate runs of decent vertical; Rosshütte is more extensive, with a cable car across to the separate peak of Härmelekopf, and some worthwhile challenges for experts. There's a good long red run back to village level and a gentle nursery area too. But overall the terrain is far too limited to keep most folk entertained for a week's stay. You can always make excursions to Innsbruck, not far away and easily reached by train, or to the Stubai and Zugspitze glaciers.
1200m; slopes 1200–2100m
🚡 30 ⬆ 48km
📧 Crystal, Inghams, Neilson, Thomson

See im Paznaun Austria
Small family-friendly area in the Paznaun Valley, near Ischgl, with rustic old village set quietly 100m above the valley floor and main road.
1050m; slopes 1050–2300m
🚡 8 ⬆ 33km

Le Seignus-d'Allos France
Close to La Foux-d'Allos (which shares large area with Pra-Loup) and has own little area, too.
1400m; slopes 1400–2425m
🚡 13 ⬆ 47km

Seis Italy
German name for Siusi.

Sella Nevea Italy
Limited but developing resort in a beautiful setting on the Slovenian border, and now linked to Bovec-Kanin. Summer glacier nearby.
1140m; slopes 1190–2300m
🚡 12 ⬆ 30km

Sella Ronda 443

Selva / Val Gardena 451

Selvino Italy
Closest resort to Bergamo.
960m; slopes 960–1400m
🚡 9 ⬆ 20km

Selwyn Snowfields Australia
Popular with beginners and families. Six hours from Sydney. Good lift system and cheaper passes than the major Oz resorts.
1520m; slopes 1490–1615m
🚡 10 ⬆ 111 acres

Semmering Austria
Long-established winter sports resort set in pretty scenery, 100km from Vienna, towards Graz. Mostly intermediate terrain.
1000m; slopes 1000–1340m
🚡 5 ⬆ 14km

Semnoz France
Small, family and beginner focused resort above Lake Annecy with views of the lake and Mont Blanc.
1705m 🚡 11 ⬆ 18
📧 Peak Retreats

Les Sept-Laux France
Improving family resort near Grenoble. Modern lift system – 90% of lifts replaced in recent years. Pretty slopes.
1350m; slopes 1350–2400m
🚡 21 ⬆ 120km

Serfaus Austria
Virtually unknown in the UK, but a charming village of chalet-style buildings set on a sunny shelf and kept largely traffic-free by an underground railway to the lifts. Most of the accommodation is in hotels, frequented by well-heeled German families. It shares with Fiss and Ladis a broad area of high slopes, with long runs spanning several ridges – well-suited to mixed-ability parties and especially good for families. The vast kids' facilities at mid-mountain level and ample nursery slopes are key attraction. A lack of English speakers may be a drawback though.
1430m; slopes 1200–2750m
🚡 70 ⬆ 190km
📧 Crystal, Crystal Finest

Serrada Italy
Very limited area near Trento.
slopes 1250–1605m 🚡 5

Serre-Chevalier 347

Sesto Italy
Dolomite village off the Alta Val Pusteria, surrounded by pretty little areas. Sexten is its German name.
1310m; slopes 1130–2200m
🚡 31 ⬆ 50km

Sestola Italy
Apennine village a short drive from Pisa and Florence with its pistes, some way above, almost completely equipped with snowmakers.
900m; slopes 1280–1975m
🚡 23 ⬆ 50km

Sestriere 458

Seven Springs Mountain USA
Pennsylvania's largest resort.
slopes 220–2995m
🚡 18 ⬆ 494 acres

Sexten Italy
Dolomite village off the Hochpustertal, surrounded by pretty little areas. Sesto is its Italian name.
1310m; slopes 1130–2200m
🚡 31 ⬆ 50km

Shames Mountain Canada
Remote spot inland from coastal town of Prince Rupert and with impressive snowfall record. Deep powder.
670m; slopes 670–1195m
🚡 3 ⬆ 183 acres

Shawnee Peak USA
Small area near Bethel and Sunday River renowned for its night skiing. Spectacular views. Mostly groomed cruising.
185m; slopes 185–580m
⛷5 ⛷ 225 acres

Shemshak Iran
Most popular of the three mountain resorts within easy reach of Tehran (60km).
3600m; slopes 2550–3050m
⛷7

Shiga Kogen 676
Largest area in Japan.

Showdown USA
Intermediate area in Montana forest north of Bozeman. 50km to the nearest hotel.
2065m; slopes 2065–2490m
⛷4 ⛷ 640 acres

Sierra-at-Tahoe USA
A Colorado-style resort, with runs cut on densely wooded slopes. It claims an impressive average of 420 inches of snow. The slopes are spread over two flanks of Huckleberry Mountain. The fronts of both offer good intermediate cruising plus some genuine single-diamond blacks. The backside of Huckleberry has easier blue and green slopes. This is a natural day trip for those staying in South Lake Tahoe.
2210m; slopes 2025–2700m
⛷14 ⛷ 2000 acres
✉ Virgin Snow

Sierra Nevada 661

Sierra Summit USA
Sierra Nevada area accessible only from the west. 100% snowmaking.
2160m; slopes 2160–2645m
⛷8 ⛷ 250 acres

Sierre 516
Hub of Coeur du Valais – Val d'Anniviers is a part.

Silbertal 204
Low secluded village in the Montafon area.

Sillian Austria
A gondola and two fast quads serve this varied area in Austria's Hochpustertal region.
1100m ⛷6 ⛷ 45km

Sils Maria 509
Lakeside village linked to the St Moritz Corvatsch slopes.

Silvaplana 509
Pretty lakeside village near St Moritz.

Silver Mountain USA
Northern Idaho area near delightful resort town of Coeur d'Alene. Best for experts, but plenty for intermediates too.
1215m; slopes 1215–1915m
⛷6 ⛷ 1500 acres

Silver Star 647

Silverthorne USA
Factory outlet town on main road close to Keystone and Breckenridge. Good budget base for skiing those resorts plus Vail and Beaver Creek.
✉ AmeriCan Ski

Silverton USA
Expert-only area in southern Colorado that used to be heli-ski country. Served by one lift. Avalanche transceiver, shovel and probe compulsory.
3170m; slopes 3170–3750m
⛷1

Sinaia Romania
Dreary main-road town with a modest, open area of slopes. Recent investment in new lifts, included a gondola.
795m; slopes 795–2030m
⛷10 ⛷ 20km
✉ Mountain Tracks, Transylvania Live

Sipapu USA
Great little New Mexico area, with mostly treelined runs. Snow unreliable, but 70% snowmaking. Nice day out from Taos when conditions are good.
slopes 2500–2765m
⛷4 ⛷ 70 acres

Siusi 451
Village west of the Sella Ronda circuit; Seis in German.

Siviez 520
A quieter, cheaper base for Verbier's Four Valleys circuit.

Sixt-Fer-a-Cheval 278
Village near Samoëns.

Sjusjøen Norway
Cluster of hotels in deep forest close to Lillehammer. Some Alpine facilities but better for cross-country.
885m; slopes 1000–1090m
⛷2 ⛷ 2km
✉ Exodus, Inntravel

Ski Apache USA
Apache-owned area south of Albuquerque noted for groomed steeps. Panoramic views. Nearest lodging in charming Ruidoso.
2925m; slopes 2925–3505m
⛷11 ⛷ 750 acres

Ski Cooper USA
Small area close to historic Old West town of Leadville. Good ski/sightseeing day out from nearby Vail, Beaver Creek and Copper Mountain.
slopes 3200–3565m ⛷4

Ski Windham USA
Two hours from New York City and second only to Hunter for weekend crowds. Decent slopes by eastern standards.
485m; slopes 485–940m
⛷7 ⛷ 230 acres

Smugglers' Notch USA
French-style purpose-built family resort with sympathetic instructors, comprehensive childcare, child-friendly layout and long, quiet, easy runs.

There are varied and satisfying slopes, spread over three hills, with a worthwhile vertical of 800m. It's a great area for beginners, but mileage-hungry intermediates should go elsewhere. Snowboarding is encouraged, and there are three impressive terrain parks and an Olympic-size super-pipe.
315m; slopes 315–1110m
⛷8 ⛷ 1000 acres

Snowbasin USA
Underrated hill, usually with very good snow. No base village, but a worthwhile day out from Park City. The crowd-free slopes cover a lot of pleasantly varied terrain. This is a great mountain for experts – the Grizzly Downhill course drops 885m and is already claimed to be a modern classic. Between the race course and the area boundary is a splendid area of off-piste wooded glades and gullies. Middle Bowl is great terrain for the adventurous, with a complex network of blues and blacks. You have to stay in the town of Ogden on the Salt Lake plain in the backwater of Huntsville. 'Quality food, quality facilities, outstanding children's ski school – best resort we've been to,' says a 2011 visitor.
1965m; slopes 1965–2850m
⛷11 ⛷ 3000 acres

Snowbird 605

Snowbowl (Arizona) USA
One of America's oldest areas, near Flagstaff, Arizona, atop an extinct volcano and with stunning desert views. Good snowfall record.
2805m; slopes 2805–3505m
⛷5 ⛷ 135 acres

Snowbowl (Montana) USA
Montana area renowned for powder, outside lively town of Missoula. Intermediate pistes plus 700 acres of extreme slopes. Grizzly Chute is the ultimate challenge.
1520m; slopes 1520–2315m
⛷4 ⛷ 1400 acres

Snowmass 580

Snow Park New Zealand
Dedicated terrain park across the valley from Cardrona. Features galore, including new 7m pipes. Budget lodging at the base.
1530m ⛷1

Snow Summit USA
San Bernardino National Forest ski area near Palm Springs. Lovely lake views. 100% snowmaking. High-capacity lift system for weekend crowds.
2135m; slopes 2135–2500m
⛷12 ⛷ 230 acres

Snow Valley USA
Area quite near Palm Springs. Fine desert views. High-capacity lift system copes with weekend crowds better than nearby Big Bear.
2040m; slopes 2040–2390m
⛷11 ⛷ 230 acres

Sochi Russia
Host of the 2014 Winter Olympic Games. Three developing areas: Gasprom, Rosa Khutor and Mountain Carousel. New terrain and hotels planned for 2011/12.
520m; ⛷19 ⛷ 100km
✉ Crystal

Solda/Sulden Italy
The other side of the Stelvio Pass from Bormio. Very long airport transfers.
1905m; slopes 1905–2625m
⛷10 ⛷ 40km

Sölden 177

Soldeu 97

Soldier Mountain USA
Family resort in Central Idaho; backcountry snowcat tours.
slopes 1770–2195m
⛷4 ⛷ 670 acres

Solitude USA
Smart, car-free mini-village linked with Brighton in the valley next to Alta and Snowbird. Most (not all) of the slopes are easy or intermediate, including a wide area served by the one fast quad. When open, the top lift accesses lots of steeps in Honeycomb Canyon, on the back of the hill, with a short quad to bring you back to the front face. Headwall Forest and Eagle Ridge also have good blacks. The resorts' boundaries are open, and there are good backcountry adventures to be had.
2490m; slopes 2435–3200m
⛷13 ⛷ 2250 acres
✉ AmeriCan Ski, Ski Safari

Söll 182

Solvista USA
Child-oriented resort close to Winter Park. Low snowfall record for Colorado.
2490m; slopes 2490–2795m
⛷5 ⛷ 250 acres

Sommand France
Purpose-built base that shares area with Praz-de-Lys.
1420m; slopes 1200–1800m
⛷22 ⛷ 50km

Sonnenkopf Austria
Area above Klösterle a few km W of the Arlberg pass; covered by the Arlberg ski pass. *slopes 1100–2300m*
⛷9 ⛷ 30km

Sorenberg Switzerland
Popular weekend retreat between Berne and Lucerne, with a high proportion of steep, low runs.
1165m; slopes 1165–2280m
⛷16 ⛷ 50km

South Lake Tahoe USA
Tacky base for skiing Heavenly, with cheap lodging, traffic and gambling.

Spindleruv Mlyn
Czech Republic
Largest Giant Mountains region resort but with few facilities serving several little low areas.
715m; slopes 750–1310m
🎿 *16* 🚡 *25km*

Spital am Pyhrn Austria
Small village near Hinterstoder in Upper Austria, a bus ride from its limited intermediate slopes at Wurzeralm.
650m; slopes 810–1870m
🎿 *8* 🚡 *20km*

Spittal an der Drau Austria
Historic Carinthian town with a limited area at Goldeck starting a lift-ride above it. A good day trip from Bad Kleinkirchheim or from Slovenia.
555m; slopes 1650–2140m
🎿 *8* 🚡 *30km*

Spitzingsee Germany
Beautiful small lake (and village) an hour from Munich.
🎿 *18* 🚡 *25km*

Splugen Reinwald Switzerland
Small intermediate area south of Chur. New six-pack for 2010/11.
1485m; slopes 1455–2215m
🎿 *6* 🚡 *30km*

Sportgastein 115
Remote, high ski area at the top of the Badgastein valley.

Squaw Valley 563

Stafal 432
Isolated village with access to the Monterosa Ski area.

St Andra Austria
Valley-junction village ideally placed for one of the longest, most snow-sure cross-country networks in Europe. Close to the Tauern pass and to St Michael. *1045m*

St Anton 190

Starhill Resort South Korea
Purpose-built resort formerly called Cheonmasan, 30km north-east of Seoul. 🎿 *8*

Stari Vrh Slovenia
About 30 minutes from Ljubljana airport. Runs include a never-groomed black, three interesting reds and a winding blue virtually from top to bottom.
slopes 580–1200m
🎿 *5* 🚡 *12km*

Stary Smokovec Slovakia
Spa town in the High Tatras mountains, with three small areas – Tatransky Lomica is the biggest. Funicular railway and snowmaking facilities.
1480m; slopes 1000–1500m
🎿 *8* 🚡 *4km*

St Cergue Switzerland
Limited resort in the Jura mountains, less than an hour from Geneva and good for families with young children.
1045m; slopes 1045–1680m
🎿 *16* 🚡 *21km*

St Christoph 190
Small village on Arlberg pass above St Anton.

St-Colomban-des-Villards
France
Small resort in next side valley to La Toussuire. Series of drags link to the rest of the area, with a pretty run to return. *1100m*

Steamboat USA
A few miles from the old cattle town of Steamboat Springs, and famed for its powder snow. Huge investment continues to equip the slope-side base with modern lodging, shops and restaurants. The slopes are compact but varied, with pretty treelined runs rising to 3220m; many of them ideal for novices. Fast chairs serve each area. The main attraction for experts is the glades, but also the steep chutes and bowls on the backside of the area. Much of the mountain is ideal cruising terrain, although there is limited vertical to be achieved. The nursery slopes at the base are excellent, revamped recently. And family facilities are splendid. Steamboat town has countless hotels, condos and restaurants.
2105m; slopes 2105–3220m
🎿 *18* 🚡 *2965 acres*
📧 *Alpine Answers, American Ski Classics, Crystal, Crystal Finest, Erna Low, Funway Holidays, Independent Ski Links, Interactive Resorts, PowderBeds, Ski Independence, Ski Line, Ski Safari, Skitracer, Skiworld, Supertravel, Thomson*

Ste-Foy-Tarentaise 357

Steinach Austria
Pleasant market town with small area of slopes in picturesque surroundings, just off the autobahn up to the Brenner Pass, south of Innsbruck.
1050m; slopes 1050–2200m
🎿 *6* 🚡 *25km*

Stevens Pass USA
A day trip from Seattle, and accommodation 60km away in Bavarian-style town Leavenworth. Mostly intermediate slopes, with long expert runs on backside. Busy at weekends Jan to March.
1235m; slopes 1235–1785m
🎿 *14* 🚡 *1125 acres*

St-François-Longchamp France
Sunny, gentle slopes, with a couple of harder runs. Linked to Valmorel.
1400m; 📧 *Erna Low, Lagrange*

St Gallenkirch 204
Small village in the Montafon valley.

St-Gervais 290
Small town sharing its ski area with Megève.

St Jakob am Arlberg Austria
Village near St Anton.
1295m; slopes 1305–2650m
🎿 *42* 🚡 *127km*

St Jakob in Defereggen Austria
Unspoiled traditional village in a pretty, sunny valley close to Lienz and Heiligenblut, and with a good proportion of high-altitude slopes.
1400m; slopes 1400–2525m
🎿 *7* 🚡 *52km*

St Jakob in Haus Austria
Snowy village with its own slopes (Buchensteinwand). Fieberbrunn, Waidring, St Johann are nearby.
855m; slopes 855–1500m
🎿 *8* 🚡 *19km*
📧 *Inntravel*

St-Jean-d'Arves France
Small, scattered community with 'friendly locals', set in the Sybelles area. The original old village, with the usual ancient church, is set across the valley from the slopes, which are at the mid-mountain hamlet of La Chal. Here, where a tasteful development of chalet-style buildings has been expanding, there are nursery slopes and the lift link to and piste back from Le Corbier. Not the best base to exploit the whole area, given the slow chair to Le Corbier, but a bus goes to St-Sorlin-d'Arves.
1550m 🎿 *72* 🚡 *310km*
📧 *Peak Retreats, Ski France, Thomson*

St Jean d'Aulps France
Small village in Portes du Soleil area, with its own interesting slopes.
📧 *ChaletBook*

St-Jean-de-Sixt France
Traditional hamlet, a cheap base for La Clusaz and Le Grand-Bornand (3km to both).
960m 🎿 *Karibuni, Last Resort*

St-Jean-Montclar France
Small village at the foot of thickly forested slopes. Good day out from nearby Pra-Loup.
1300m; slopes 1300–2500m
🎿 *18* 🚡 *50km* 📧 *Zenith*

St Johann im Pongau Austria
Bustling, lively working town with its own small area. An extensive three-valley lift network starts 4km away at Alpendorf, linking via Wagrain

to Flachau – all part of the Salzburger Sportwelt ski pass area.
650m; slopes 800–2185m
🎿 *64* 🚡 *200km*
📧 *Crystal*

St Johann in Tirol Austria
Friendly valley town, an attractive place for beginners and leisurely part-timers – keen piste-bashers will ski all the local slopes in a day and need to go on to explore nearby resorts covered by the Kitzbüheler Alpenskipass as well. There is nothing here to challenge an expert. The main access lift is a 10-minute walk from the centre. It gets more snow than neighbouring Kitzbühel and the SkiWelt, and also has substantial snowmaking. Given good snow, St Johann is one of the best cross-country resorts in Austria – trails total 275km. The Park hotel is near the gondola and recommended by a reader.
650m; slopes 690–1700m
🎿 *17* 🚡 *60km*
📧 *Crystal, Inghams, Ski Line, Skitracer, Snowscape, STC, Thomson*

St Lary Espiaube 338
Satellite of St-Lary-Soulan in the Pyrenees.

St-Lary-Soulan 338

St Leonhard in Pitztal Austria
Village beneath a fine glacier in the Oetz area, accessed by underground funicular.
1250m; slopes 880–3440m
🎿 *12* 🚡 *68km*

St-Luc 516
Village in the Val d'Anniviers.

St Margarethen Austria
Valley village near Styria/Carinthia border, sharing slopes with higher Katschberg.
1065m; slopes 1065–2210m
🎿 *16* 🚡 *70km*

St Martin bei Lofer Austria
Traditional cross-country village in a lovely setting beneath the impressive Loferer Steinberge massif. Alpine slopes at Lofer.
635m; slopes 640–1745m
🎿 *10* 🚡 *46km*

St-Martin-de-Belleville 359

St Martin in Tennengebirge Austria
Highest village in the Dachstein-West region near Salzburg. It has limited slopes of its own but nearby Annaberg has an interesting area.
1000m; slopes 1000–1350m
🎿 *4* 🚡 *5km*

St-Maurice-sur-Moselle France
One of several areas near Strasbourg. No snowmakers.
550m; slopes 900–1250m
🎿 *8* 🚡 *24km*

St Michael im Lungau Austria
Quiet, unspoiled village in the Tauern pass snowpocket with an uncrowded but disjointed intermediate area. Close to Obertauern and Wagrain.
1075m; slopes 1065–2220m
⛷16 🚡 70km

St Moritz 509

St-Nicolas-de-Véroce 290
Small hamlet in the Megève network.

St-Nicolas-la-Chapelle France
Small village close to larger Flumet, in the Val d'Arly.
1000m; slopes 1000–1600m
⛷10 🚡 40km

St-Nizier-du-Moucherotte France
Unspoiled, inexpensive resort just west of Grenoble with no lifts of its own. Villard-de-Lans is the main resort.

Stoneham Canada
Closest resort to Québec City, around 20 minutes away; has its own small base 'village', with condo accommodation and an impressive lodge that has its own lively après-ski bar, restaurant and spas. But night owls should probably head for the city as the evenings are generally quiet in resort. Like most resorts in this region, the ski area is small. The slopes spread across three linked peaks, with mainly sheltered intermediate and beginner pistes. It suits families well and has a special nursery area equipped with a moving carpet. A key attraction is the resort's four terrain parks and half-pipe, regularly revamped and chosen to host the 2013 Snowboard World Champs.
210m; slopes 210–630m
⛷7 🚡 326 acres
⛷ Frontier, Ski Safari

Stoos Switzerland
Small, unspoiled village an hour from Zürich. Weekend crowds. Splendid views of Lake Lucerne.
1300m; slopes 500–1935m
⛷7 🚡 35km

Storlien Sweden
Small family resort amid magnificent wilderness scenery, one hour from Trondheim, 30 minutes from Åre.
600m; slopes 600–790m
⛷7 🚡 16km

Stowe 618

St-Pierre-de-Chartreuse France
Locals' weekend place near Grenoble. Unreliable snow.
900m; slopes 900–1800m
⛷14 🚡 35km

Stratton USA
Something like the classic Alpine arrangement of a village at the foot of the lifts: a smart, modern development

with a car-free shopping street. The slopes are mostly easy and intermediate, with some blacks and some short double-black pitches, spread widely around the flanks of a single peak, served by modern lifts. Stratton calls itself the 'snowboarding capital of the east', with no fewer than five terrain parks. The Suntanner Park has a super-pipe.
570m; slopes 570–1180m
⛷14 🚡 660 acres

Strobl Austria
Close to St Wolfgang in a beautiful lakeside setting. There are slopes at nearby St Gilgen and Postalm.
545m; slopes 545–1510m
⛷7 🚡 12km

St-Sorlin-d'Arves France
A refreshing contrast to the stark, functional resorts of Le Corbier and La Toussuire, with which it shares the extensive Les Sybelles ski area. And the resort accesses some of the most interesting slopes. The village is a picturesque collection of traditional buildings, alongside a more modern development that spreads out along the main road and has attracted some major tour operators. The local slopes form the biggest single sector of the linked network, with lifts serving two distinct mountains. Some of the most varied slopes in the whole area are here, and reached by fast quads to Les Perrons – which also has some of the best off-piste opportunities. There are leisurely cruising runs on La Balme.
1600m ⛷72 🚡 310km
⛷ AmeriCan Ski, Crystal, Erna Low, Lagrange, Peak Retreats, Ski France, Ski Independence, Thomson

St Stephan Switzerland
Unspoiled old farming village at the foot of the largest sector of slopes in the area around Gstaad.
1000m; slopes 950–3000m
⛷58 🚡 250km

Stubai valley 200

Stuben 190
Small, unspoiled village linked to St Anton.

St Veit im Pongau Austria
Spa resort with limited slopes at Goldegg; Wagrain (Salzburger Sportwelt) and Grossarl (Gastein valley) are nearby.
765m ⛷4 🚡 12km

St-Veran France
Said to be the highest 'real' village in Europe, and full of charm. Close to Serre-

Chevalier and the Milky Way. Snow-reliable cross-country skiing.
2040m; slopes 2040–2800m
⛷15 🚡 30km

St Wolfgang Austria
Charming lakeside resort near Salzburg, some way from any slopes, best for a relaxing winter holiday with one or two days on the slopes.
540m; slopes 665–1350m
⛷9 🚡 17km
⛷ Crystal, Skitracer, Thomson

Sugar Bowl USA
Exposed area north of Lake Tahoe with highest snowfall in California, best for experts. Lodging in Truckee but Squaw Valley nearby.
2100m; slopes 2100–2555m
⛷8 🚡 1500 acres

Sugarbush USA
Dynamic resort in upper Vermont, with two mountains linked by fast chair, and something resembling a village at the foot of one of them. Good range of runs, including some real challenges.
480m; slopes 450–1245m
⛷16 🚡 508 acres
⛷ Ski Safari

Sugarloaf USA
Developing Maine resort, five hours from Boston, with the Eastern US's best open terrain.
430m; slopes 405–1290m
⛷15 🚡 1410 acres

Sulden Italy
The other side of the Stelvio Pass from Bormio. Very long airport transfers. Solda is its Italian name.
1905m; slopes 1905–2625m
⛷10 🚡 40km

Summit at Snoqualmie USA
Four areas – Summit East, Summit Central, Summit West and Alpental – with interlinked lifts. Damp weather and wet snow are major drawbacks.
slopes 915–1645m
⛷24 🚡 2000 acres

Sun Alpina Japan
Collective name for three ski areas four hours away from Tokyo. ⛷21

Sundance USA
Robert Redford-owned, tastefully designed family resort set amid trees in snow-sure Utah. It's a small, narrow mountain but the vertical is respectable, and the setting is spectacular and there is terrain to suit all abilities. The lower mountain is easy-intermediate, the upper part steeper. There are 17km of cross-country trails, of varying difficulty.
1860m; slopes 1860–2515m
⛷4 🚡 450 acres
⛷ AmeriCan Ski, Ski Safari

Sunday River USA
One of the more attractive resorts in the East, four hours from Boston, best for intermediate cruisers. The slopes spread across eight peaks, but it's a small area. Only four of the chairs are fast quads but queues are not a problem – midweek, the resort is very quiet. Cross-country is big around here.
245m; slopes 245–955m
⛷16 🚡 669 acres
⛷ American Ski Classics, Ski Independence, Ski Safari

Sunlight Mountain Resort USA
Quiet, small area 10 miles south of Glenwood Springs. Varied terrain with some serious glades.
2405m; slopes 2405–3015m
⛷3 🚡 470 acres

Sun Peaks 649

Sunrise Park USA
Arizona's largest area, operated by Apaches. Slopes are spread over three mountains; best for novices and leisurely intermediates.
2805m; slopes 2805–3500m
⛷12 🚡 800 acres

Sunshine Village 623
One-hotel mountain station in Banff's ski area.

Sun Valley 607
Purpose-built resort in Idaho.
1750m; slopes 1750–2790m
⛷19 🚡 2054 acres

Suomu Finland
A lodge (no village) right on the Arctic Circle with a few slopes but mostly a ski-touring place.
140m; slopes 140–410m ⛷3

Superbagnères France
Little more than a particularly French-dominated Club Med; best for a low-cost, low-effort family trip to the Pyrenees. Said to have good off-piste if the snow is good.
1880m; slopes 1440–2260m
⛷16 🚡 35km ⛷ Lagrange

Super-Besse France
Purpose-built resort amid spectacular extinct-volcano scenery. Shares area with the spa town of Mont-Dore. Limited village.
1350m; slopes 1300–1850m
⛷22 🚡 43km ⛷ Lagrange

Superdévoluy France
Purpose-built but friendly family resort in a remote spot near Gap, with huge apartment blocks plus traditional chalets. Sizeable intermediate area shared with more appealing La Joue-du-Loup.
1450m; slopes 1450–2450m
⛷22 🚡 100km
⛷ Crystal, Erna Low, Ski Collection

Super Espot Spain
Small area on the eastern edge of the Aigues Tortes National Park, close to the valley town of Sort.
slopes 1500–2500m
⛷ *8* ⛷ *28km*

Supermolina Spain
Dreary, purpose-built satellite of Pyrenean resort of La Molina, with a reasonable sized area of its own and linked to the slopes of Masella to form an area called Alp 2500.
1700m; slopes 1600–2535m
⛷ *31* ⛷ *121km*

Super St Bernard Switzerland
Swiss side of the Grand St Bernard tunnel to Italy. No resort – just a small beginner area and an old gondola rising to 850m; two black runs and lots of off-piste on a mainly north-facing and usually deserted mountain. You can also ski off-piste down the back to Italy but need transport back.
1950m; slopes 1950–2800m
⛷ *3* ⛷ *25km*

Les Sybelles France
A group of linked ski resorts in the Maurienne massif, forming an impressively large network.
slopes 1100–2620m
⛷ *72* ⛷ *310km*

Tahko Finland
Largest resort in southern Finland. Plenty of intermediate slopes in an attractive, wooded, frozen-lake setting.
⛷ *9*

Tahoe City USA
Small lakeside accommodation base for visiting nearby Alpine Meadows and Squaw Valley.

Talisman Mountain Resort Canada
One of the best areas in the Toronto region, but with a relatively low lift capacity. 100% snowmaking.
235m; slopes 235–420m ⛷ *8*

Tamsweg Austria
Large cross-country village with rail links in snowy region close to Tauern Pass and St Michael. *1025m*

La Tania 361

Taos 607
Isolated resort in New Mexico.
2805m; slopes 2805–3600m
⛷ *13* ⛷ *1294 acres*

Tärnaby-Hemavan Sweden
Twin resorts in north Sweden, offering downhill, cross-country and heliskiing. Own airport.
slopes 465–1135m
⛷ *13* ⛷ *44km*

El Tarter 97
Relatively quiet, convenient alternative to Soldeu.

Tarvisio Italy
Interesting, animated old town bordering Austria and Slovenia. A major cross-country base with fairly limited Alpine slopes.
750m; slopes 750–1860m
⛷ *12* ⛷ *15km*

Täsch 538
The final road base on the way to car-free Zermatt.

Tauplitz Austria
Traditional village at the foot of an interestingly varied area north of Schladming. Few queues and decent lift system, including some fast chairs.
900m; slopes 900–2000m
⛷ *18* ⛷ *40km*

Telluride USA
An isolated resort in south-west Colorado, but a beautifully renovated old mining town with great Wild West charm and fairly dramatic mountain scenery. It's a friendly, small-scale resort, with a smartly developing slope-side base above it. Both have lifts into the ski area. Mountain Village has new luxury hotels and spa facilities. The slopes are limited in overall extent, but quite varied and with recently expanded expert terrain. Most runs are below the treeline, but the top lifts and bowls give great views. Queues are rarely a problem. Experts have some truly challenging terrain to play such as the Gold Hill Chutes, while there are splendid blue and greens runs for intermediates and beginners too – but it's not a resort for keen piste bashers. There are three terrain parks.
2665m; slopes 2665–3830m
⛷ *18* ⛷ *2000 acres*
◈ *Alpine Answers, AmeriCan Ski, American Ski Classics, Elegant Resorts, Funway Holidays, PowderBeds, Ski Independence, Ski Safari, Ski Solutions*

Temù Italy
Sheltered hamlet near Passo Tonale. Worth a visit in bad weather.
1155m; slopes 1155–1955m
⛷ *4* ⛷ *5km*

Tengendai Japan
Tiny area three hours by train and bus from Tokyo. One of Japan's best snow records, including occasional powder.
920m; slopes 920–1820m ⛷ *4*

Termas de Chillán Chile
Ski and spa resort 400km south of Santiago. Base village has lodgings or you can stay at Las Trancas a few minutes' drive away.
1650m; slopes 1600–2700m
⛷ *9* ⛷ *46km*
◈ *Momentum*

Termignon France
Traditional rustic village 6km down the Maurienne valley from Lanslebourg and the slopes of Val Cenis, to which it is linked. The local slopes are limited and served by slow lifts, but have the advantage of being extremely quiet.
1300m; slopes 1300–2500m
⛷ *6* ⛷ *35km*
◈ *Lagrange, Peak Retreats*

Terminillo Italy
Purpose-built resort 100km from Rome with a worthwhile area when its lower runs have snow-cover.
1500m; slopes 1500–2210m
⛷ *15* ⛷ *40km*

Teton Village 613

Thollon-les-Mémises France
Attractive base for a relaxed holiday. Own little area and close to Portes du Soleil.
1000m; slopes 1600–2000m
⛷ *19* ⛷ *50km*

Thredbo Australia
Oz's best, six hours from Sydney; uncharacteristically long (and, in places, testing) runs, snowmaking, lots of accommodation and active nightlife.
1365m; slopes 1365–2035m
⛷ *14* ⛷ *480 acres*

Three Valleys 374
Aka Les Trois Vallées.

La Thuile 460

Thyon 2000 520
Mid-mountain resort in the Verbier ski area.

Tignes 365

Timberline (Palmer Snowfield) USA
Fair-sized area of largely intermediate slopes served by six lifts including four fast quads on Mt Hood in Oregon.
1800m; slopes 1510–2600m
⛷ *6* ⛷ *1430 acres*

Toblach Italy
Small resort in South Tyrol. Dobbiaco is its Italian name.
1250m; slopes 1250–1610m
⛷ *5* ⛷ *15km*

Togari Japan
One of several areas close to the 1998 Olympic site. Nagano, 2hr30 from Tokyo.
slopes 400–1050m ⛷ *9*

Torgnon Italy
Small village off the road up to Cervinia, good for bad-weather days. Some good cross-country loops.
1500m; slopes 1500–1965m
⛷ *7* ⛷ *6km*

Torgon Switzerland
Old village in a pretty wooded setting, with a connection to the Portes du Soleil. Still some steep draglifts.
1150m; slopes 950–2300m
⛷ *197* ⛷ *650km*

Le Tour 247
Charming hamlet at the head of the Chamonix valley.

La Toussuire France
Highest and most central of the Sybelles resorts, and convenient base for exploring the whole area. The centre has fairly dreary buildings spreading widely from the car-free centre. But the local slopes have three of the seven fast chairs in the area, so access to Pte de L'Ouillon and the rest of the linked network is fairly quick. Above the resort is a wide bowl with drags and chairs all around. Locally, the pistes are short cruisers with few challenges – but judged by a reporter as the most varied and snow-sure in the area. A splendid longer run goes to Les Bottières. There are gentle nursery slopes and good, easy progression runs. Eating out is relatively inexpensive for France.
1700m ⛷ *72* ⛷ *310km*
◈ *Erna Low, Lagrange, PowderBeds, Ski Collection, Ski France*

Trafoi Italy
Quiet, traditional village in the Val Venosta in the South Tyrol covered by the Ortler Skiarena pass.
1570m; slopes 1570–2550m
⛷ *4* ⛷ *10km*

Treble Cone New Zealand
Plenty of good skiing opened up by two main lifts. Varied open terrain suitable for all levels. Great powder bowls. Nearly two hours from Queenstown.
1260m; slopes 1260–1960m
⛷ *4* ⛷ *550 hectares*

Tremblant 660

Trentino Italy
Fabulously scenic area of the Dolomites, with a great many small ski areas that you won't have heard of, as well as a few large ones that are better known – Madonna di Campiglio chief among them.

Trois Vallées 374
Aka The Three Valleys.

Troodos Cyprus
Ski area on Mt Olympus, a 70-minute drive from Nicosia. Pretty, wooded slopes and fine views. *slopes 1730–1950m*
⛷ *4* ⛷ *5km*

Tröpolach Austria
Small village at base of access gondola for Nassfeld ski area.
610m; slopes 610–2195m
⛷ *30* ⛷ *110km*

Trysil Norway
Extensive area, some distance from the town, spread around the conical Trysilfjellet, with some good, long runs of up to 4km. On Swedish border.
350m; slopes 350–1100m ⛷ *24*

Resort directory / index

Interactive resort shortlist builder at www.wtss.co.uk

Tryvann Norway
Small area close to Oslo and popular with ocals. Vertical of 380m – are served by two drags and two chairs, one of them fast. ⛷6

Tschagguns 204
Village in the Montafon valley.

Tsugaike Kogen Japan
Sizeable resort four hours from Tokyo, three hours from Osaka. Helicopter service to the top station.
800m; slopes 800–1700m ⛷26

Tulfes Austria
Hamlet on mountain shelf close to Innsbruck, with small main area above the trees and long runs back to base.
920m; slopes 920–2305m
⛷7 🚠 22km

Turoa New Zealand
On the south-western slopes of Mt Ruapeha, with NZ's biggest vertical. Shares lift pass with Whakapapa. Mix of open, gentle and steeper runs. Good scope for off-piste. Smart new hut in 2010.
slopes 1600–2320m
⛷23 🚠 2590 acres

Turracherhöhe Austria
Tiny, unspoiled resort on a mountain shelf, with varied intermediate slopes above and below it. A good outing from Bad Kleinkirchheim.
1765m; slopes 1400–2205m
⛷14 🚠 38km

Tyax Mountain Lake Resort
Canada
Heli-skiing operation in the Chilcotin mountains. Transfers from Whistler or Vancouver.

La Tzoumaz 520
Hamlet in Verbier's ski area.

Uludag Turkey
Surprisingly suave, laid-back, well-equipped, purpose-built resort south of Istanbul.
1750m; slopes 1750–2322m
⛷14 🚠 15km

Unken Austria
Traditional village hidden in a side valley. Closest slopes to Salzburg.
565m; slopes 1000–1500m
⛷4 🚠 8km

Untergurgl 158
Valley-floor alternative to staying in Obergurgl.

Unternberg Austria
Riverside village with trail connecting into one of the longest, most snow-sure cross-country networks in Europe. St Margarethen slopes close by. *1030m*

Unterwasser-Toggenburg
Switzerland
Old but not especially attractive resort 90 minutes from Zürich. Fabulous lake and mountain views. The

more challenging half of the Toggenburg area shared with Wildhaus.
910m; slopes 900–2260m
⛷17 🚠 60km

Uttendorf-Weiss-See Austria
Astute alternative to crowded Kaprun when snowline high.
805m; slopes 1485–2600m
⛷8 🚠 23km

Vail 582

Valbella Switzerland
Convenient but ordinary village sharing large intermediate Lenzerheide area.
1540m; slopes 1230–2865m
⛷35 🚠 155km

Valberg France
Large Alpes-Maritimes resort (bigger than better-known Isola 2000) close to Nice.
1650m; slopes 1430–2100m
⛷26 🚠 90km

Val Cenis France
A marketing concept rather than a place: its ski area is Val Cenis Vanoise and it comprises two quiet, friendly, traditional villages strung along the high and remote part of the Maurienne valley. There are lifts from several base stations, so convenience isn't a huge concern and queues are rare. Lanslebourg spreads along the RN6 road with no real focus, but lifts there have linked the slopes with those above Termignon further down the valley. Lanslevillard is the most captivating base, randomly arranged and with excellent nursery slopes. The mountain packs in more variety than you might expect for an area its size, with a good mix of open and treelined slopes and some decent vertical; most are north-facing, so snow reliability is quite good too. Beginners and intermediates will be best off here though.
1400m; slopes 1300–2800m
⛷27 🚠 125km
🚌 *AmeriCan Ski, Crystal, Erna Low, Independent Ski Links, Lagrange, MGS, Peak Retreats, Ski Amis, Ski France, Snowcoach, Thomson*

Val d'Anniviers 516

Val di Fassa 443
Valley area of Campitello and Canazei – part of the Sella Ronda circuit.

Val d'Illiez 475
Peaceful, unspoiled village near Champéry in the Portes du Soleil.

Val d'Isère 376

Val Ferret Switzerland
Old climbing village near Martigny, with spectacular views. Own tiny area.
1600m
⛷3 🚠 20km

Valfrejus France
Small and unusual modern resort on a narrow, shady shelf in the Maurienne valley – built in the woods, with the slopes higher up above the treeline. The focus is Plateau d'Arrondaz, with steep, open slopes above, offering genuine bumpy blacks with excellent snow (snowmaking on the lower runs is urgently required, though). There's a natural terrain park, and good off-piste is available above the main plateau. The nursery slopes are at mid-mountain and village levels. There's a new quad chair for 2010/11.
1550m; slopes 1550–2740m
⛷10 🚠 65km
🚌 *AmeriCan Ski, Erna Low, Lagrange, PowderBeds, Ski Collection, Ski France*

Val Gardena 451
Valley area of Selva, Ortisei and Santa Cristina.

Valgrisenche 404
Village in the Aosta valley.
1665m ⛷4 🚠 12km

Vallandry 232
Satellite of Les Arcs.

Valle Nevado Chile
Developing purpose-built resort 46km east of Santiago. Varied, intermediate terrain. New lifts, runs and lodging for 2010.
3025m; slopes 2430–3670m
⛷45 🚠 7000 acres
🚌 *AmeriCan Ski, Crystal, Crystal Finest, Momentum, Skiworld*

Valloire France
A compelling combination of an old mountain village with extensive slopes, branded as Galibier Thabor, and shared with the more modern two-part resort of Valmeinier. The village is the best known of the Maurienne valley resorts and retains a quiet, rustic charm of narrow streets, shops and restaurants set around a lively market square. The slopes spread widely across three sunny sectors, served by two gondolas out of the village, and are particularly good for intermediates wanting lots of gentle cruising and a sense of travel. Experts will find the challenges limited, although there is some decent off-piste opportunity towards Valmeinier.
1430m; slopes 1430–2595m
⛷33 🚠 150km
🚌 *AmeriCan Ski, Crystal, Erna Low, Lagrange, Peak Retreats, PowderBeds, PV-Holidays.com, Ski France, Ski Independence*

Vallorcine 247
Backwater on road between Chamonix and Switzerland.

Vallter 2000 Spain
Small resort on the far eastern fringes of the Pyrenees, close to the Costa Brava.
slopes 1960–2535m
⛷10 🚠 420 acres

Valmeinier France
Quiet, old mountain village with a modern purpose-built satellite where most people stay. Shares with Valloire the most extensive slopes in the Maurienne region, spreading widely over three mostly sunny sectors.
1500-1800m; slopes 1430–2595m ⛷33 🚠 150km
🚌 *Crystal, Erna Low, Lagrange, PowderBeds, PV-Holidays.com, Ski Collection, Ski France, Ski Independence, Snowcoach*

Valmorel France
The main resort in the Grand Domaine ski area, sharing slopes with St-François and Longchamp. The purpose-built village is prettily designed with a traffic-free centre, though lodging is broadly scattered among six 'hamlets' – mainly of simple hotels or apartments. The slopes offer a fair-sized area of varied skiing, with runs criss-crossing a number of minor valleys. Most are blue runs. Fast chairs serve the key links, but there are lots of slow drags. So queues can be evident at peak times. The area appeals mainly to intermediates, and beginners. Few slopes are challenging, and there are good gentle greens for progression. Nightlife is generally quiet and there is little off-slope diversion, although the slope-side cafe-bars are 'jolly'. New Club Med property for 2011/12.
1400m; slopes 1250–2550m
⛷53 🚠 150km
🚌 *Alpine Answers, Chalet Valmorel, Club Med, Crystal, Erna Low, Interactive Resorts, Lagrange, PowderBeds, PV-Holidays.com, Ski France, Ski Line, Ski Supreme, Skitracer, Skiweekends.com*

Val Senales Italy
Top-of-the-mountain hotel, the highest in the Alps, in the Dolomites near Merano.
3210m; slopes 2110–3210m
⛷12 🚠 35km

Val Thorens 386

Valtournenche 409
Cheaper alternative to Cervinia.

Vandans 204
Sizeable working village in the Montafon area.

Vars 393

Vasilitsa Greece
Resort in northern Greece, in the Pindos range, offering intermediate skiing. *1780m ♦ 8*

Vaujany 222
Tiny village in the heart of the Alpe-d'Huez ski area.

Las Vegas Ski Resort USA
Tiny area formerly known as Lee Canyon, cut from forest 50 mins' NW of Las Vegas. *2595m; slopes 2595–2855m ♦ 4 ♦ 200 acres*

Velka–Raca Slovakia
Small resort near Oscadnica, with a modern lift system, including a 'chondola'. *630m; slopes 630–1050m ♦ 6 ♦ 14km*

Vemdalen Sweden
Twin areas of Björnrike and Vemdalsskalet (same pass) 20 minutes apart. 385m vertical. Said to have hottest après-ski in Sweden. *♦ 18 ♦ 28km ► Neilson*

Vemdalsskalet Sweden
20 minutes from Björnrike (same pass). 385m vertical. *♦ 18 ♦ 28km*

Venosc France
Captivating tiny village of cobbled streets, ancient church and craft shops with fast gondola to Les Deux-Alpes. *► Peak Retreats*

Vent Austria
High, remote Oztal village known mainly as a touring base, with just enough lift-served skiing to warrant a day trip from nearby Obergurgl. *1900m; slopes 1900–2680m ♦ 4 ♦ 15km*

Ventron France
Small village near La Bresse in the Vosges mountains near Strasbourg, with more ski de fond than downhill terrain. *630m; slopes 900–1110m ♦ 8 ♦ 15km*

Verbier 520

Vercorin 516
Cluster of chalets in the Val d'Anniviers.

Verditz Austria
Mountain-top area overlooking the town of Villach. *675m; slopes 675–2165m ♦ 5 ♦ 15km*

Vex Switzerland
Major village in attractive setting south of Sion. Verbier slopes accessed nearby at Mayens-de-l'Ours. *900m*

Veysonnaz 520
Little old village within Verbier's Four Valleys network.

Vichères–Liddes Switzerland
Limited area near to Martigny. Part of the Grand St Bernard region, including Val Ferret and Champex-Lac. Valid with the Valais ski Card. *1350m; slopes 1350–2270m ♦ 4 ♦ 15km*

Vic-sur-Cère France
Charming village with fine architecture, beneath Super-Lioran ski area. Beautiful extinct-volcano scenery. *680m; slopes 1250–1850m ♦ 24 ♦ 60km ► Lagrange*

Viehhofen Austria
Cheaper place to stay when visiting Saalbach. It's 3km from the Schönleiten gondola, and there's a run back to the village from the Asitz section. *86om ♦ 1*

Vigla-Pisoderi Greece
The longest run in Greece (over 2km), in an unspoiled setting 18km from the town of Florina in the north. *1600m ♦ 5*

Vigo di Fassa Italy
Best base for the Fassa valley, with Sella Ronda access via nearby Campitello. *1390m; slopes 1390–2060m ♦ 6 ♦ 16km*

La Villa 443
Quiet Sella Ronda village.

Villabassa Italy
Cross-country village in South Tyrol. Niederdorf is its German name.

Villach-Dobratsch Austria
One of several small, mostly mountain-top areas overlooking the town of Villach. *900m; slopes 980–2165m ♦ 8 ♦ 15km*

Villar-d'Arêne France
Tiny area on main road between La Grave and Serre-Chevalier. Empty, immaculately groomed, short easy runs, plus a couple of hotels. *1650m*

Villard-de-Lans France
Unspoiled, lively, traditional village west of Grenoble. Snow-sure, thanks to snowmaking. Gondola being upgraded for 2011/12. *1050m; slopes 1145–2170m ♦ 25 ♦ 125km*

Villard-Reculas 222
Rustic village on periphery of Alpe-d'Huez ski area.

Villaroger 232
Rustic hamlet with direct links up to Arc 2000.

Villars 531

Villeneuve 347
One of the villages making up the resort of Serre-Chevalier.

Vipiteno Italy
Bargain-shopping town close to Brenner Pass. *960m; slopes 960–2100m ♦ 12 ♦ 25km*

Virgen Austria
Traditional village in a beautiful valley south of the Felbertauern tunnel. Slopes at Matrei. *1200m; slopes 975–2620m ♦ 15 ♦ 110km*

Vitosha Bulgaria
Limited area of slopes and a few widely scattered hotels, 22km from Sofia, leading to crowds at weekends. The slopes are north-facing and have a decent snow record. *1810m; slopes 1515–2290m ♦ 12 ♦ 29km*

Vogel 672

Vorarlberg 203

Vorderlanersbach 122
Village with access to Mayrhofen's ski area.

Voss Norway
Well-equipped winter sports resort attractively set on a lake, with relatively limited Alpine slopes. *60m; slopes 150–945m ♦ 10 ♦ 40km*

Vuokatti Finland
Small mountain in a remarkable setting, surrounded on three sides by lots of little lakes. Good activity base. *♦ 8*

Wagrain Austria
A towny little resort at the centre of a lift system that is typical of many in Salzburgerland – spreading widely across several low, partly wooded ridges. Flachau and Alpendorf/St Johann are at its extremities, and all these resorts are covered by Salzburger Sportwelt lift pass that our figures relate to. It's pleasant without being notably charming, and though it's a compact place the main lift bases are still a good walk apart. The slopes – wooded at the bottom, open higher up – are practically all easy/ intermediate stuff, but cover a huge area almost 15km across. The lift system is impressive, with a lot of fast chairs and gondolas. Despite the altitude, most of the upper slopes are fairly open. Some get too much sun for comfort, and snow reliability is not a strong point. *850m; slopes 850–2190m ♦ 64 ♦ 200km*

Waidring Austria
Quiet valley village north of Kitzbühel. Mainly gentle open and north-facing slopes, also accessible from Germany. Impressive lift system, but still prone to weekend queues. *780m; slopes 1230–1860m ♦ 10 ♦ 35km*

Waiorau Snow Farm New Zealand
Specialist cross-country base just over an hour from Queenstown. Spectacular views. Overnight huts. *1500m*

Wald im Pinzgau Austria
Cross-country village surrounded by Alpine areas – Gerlos, Krimml and Neukirchen – and with Pass Thurn also nearby. *885m ♦ 50 ♦ 160km*

Wanaka New Zealand
Quiet, diffuse village in beautiful lakeside mountain setting close to four ski areas; the nearest is Treble Cone.

Warth 208
Bregenzerwald village near Lech. *1500m; slopes 1260–2100m ♦ 15 ♦ 66km*

Waterville Valley USA
Compact New Hampshire area with runs dropping either side of a broad, gentle ridge rising 615m above the lift base. A couple of short but genuine double-black-diamond mogul fields, but most of the slopes are intermediate. The village is a Disneyesque affair a couple of miles away down on the flat valley bottom. *600m; slopes 600–1215m ♦ 12 ♦ 255 acres ► Virgin Snow*

Watles Italy
Village in the Val Venosta in the South Tyrol covered by the Ortler Skiarena pass. *♦ 3 ♦ 18km*

Weinebene Austria
One of many gentle little areas in Austria's easternmost ski region near the Slovenian border. No major resorts in the vicinity. *1580m; slopes 1560–1835m ♦ 7 ♦ 22km*

Weissbach bei Lofer Austria
Traditional resort between Lofer and Saalfelden. It has no slopes of its own, but it's well placed for touring the Tirol. Kitzbühel, Saalbach, St Johann and Zell am See are nearby. *665m*

Weissensee Naggeralm Austria
Little area in eastern Austria and the location of Europe's largest frozen lake, which is used for all kinds of ice sports, including ice-golf. *930m; slopes 930–1400m ♦ 5 ♦ 6km*

Weisspriach Austria
Hamlet on snowy pass near Obertauern that shares its area with Mauterndorf and St Michael. *1115m; slopes 1115–2050m ♦ 13 ♦ 47km*

Wengen 533

Wentworth Canada
Long-established Nova Scotia area with largest accessible acreage in the Maritime

Provinces. Harsh climate ensures good snow-cover despite low altitude.
55m; slopes 55–300m
⛷ 6 ↑ 150 acres

Werfen Austria
Traditional village spoiled by the Tauern autobahn, which runs between it and the slopes. Good touring to the Dachstein West region.
620m

Werfenweng Austria
Hamlet with the advantage over the main village of Werfen of being away from the autobahn and close to the slopes. Best for novices.
1000m; slopes 1000–1835m
⛷ 9 ↑ 25km
➤ Thomson

Westendorf 182
Friendly family resort; part of the SkiWelt.

Whakapapa/Turoa
New Zealand
NZ's largest area, on a volcano close to Turoa with similarly superb views and shared pass. The Grand Chateau is a lovely old hotel in the tiny village 6km away.
1630m; slopes 1630–2320m
⛷ 23 ↑ 2590 acres

Whistler 651

Whitecap Mountains Resort
USA
Largest, snowiest area in Wisconsin, close enough to Lake Superior and Minneapolis to ensure winds and weekend crowds.
435m; slopes 435–555m
⛷ 7 ↑ 500 acres

Whiteface Mountain USA
Varied area in New York State 15km from attractive lakeside resort of Lake Placid. 93% snowmaking ensures good snow-cover. Plenty to do off the slopes.
365m; slopes 365–1345m
⛷ 10 ↑ 211 acres

Whitefish Mountain Resort
USA
Set close to the Canadian border and to Montana's Glacier National Park, this place has revamped its image in recent years. Lots of redevelopment has taken place, both on and off the slopes. Its 3,000 acres embrace a wide range of slopes that are not only impressively snowy but also blissfully devoid of people. There's easy cruising in dense forest around the base area, and steeper stuff higher up on 'gladed' slopes. There are two good terrain parks. There is lodging at the base and you can stay in the small town of Whitefish, a few miles away.
1360m; slopes 1360–2135m
⛷ 13 ↑ 3000 acres
➤ Ski Safari

White Pass Village USA
Closest area to Mt St Helens. Remote and uncrowded during the week, with a good snowfall record. Some genuinely steep, expert terrain, as well as intermediate cruising.
1370m; slopes 1370–1825m
⛷ 5 ↑ 635 acres

Whitewater Canada
Renowned for powder (40% off-piste), food and weekend party atmosphere. Accommodation in the historic town of Nelson or a great day out from nearby Red Mountain.
1640m; slopes 1640–2040m
⛷ 3 ➤ Frontier

Wildcat Mountain USA
New Hampshire area infamous for bad weather, but one of the best areas on a nice day. Lodging in nearby Jackson and North Conway.
slopes 600–1250m
⛷ 4 ↑ 225 acres
➤ Virgin Snow

Wildhaus Switzerland
Undeveloped farming community in stunning scenery near Liechtenstein; popular with families and serious snowboarders. Shares its slopes with Unterwasser.
1050m; slopes 900–2260m
⛷ 17 ↑ 60km

Wildschönau Austria
Dramatic-sounding name adopted by a group of small resorts in the Tirol – Niederau, Oberau and Auffach.
830m; slopes 830–1905m
⛷ 25 ↑ 70km

Willamette Pass USA
Set in national forest near beautiful Crater Lake, Oregon. Small area of varied slopes. Gets an average of 430 inches of snow a year – that's up there with Utah.
1560m; slopes 1560–2035m
⛷ 6 ↑ 550 acres

Williams USA
Tiny area above the main place to stay for the Grand Canyon.
slopes 2010–2270m
⛷ 2 ↑ 50 acres

Willingen Germany
Resort in Sauerland, east of Düsseldorf. ⛷ 12

Windischgarsten Austria
Large working village in Upper Austria with cross-country trails around and downhill slopes at nearby Hinterstoder and Spital am Pyrhn. *600m*

Winterberg Germany
Resort in Sauerland, east of Düsseldorf. ⛷ 21

Winter Park 589

Wolf Creek USA
Remote area on a pass of the same name, with 'the most snow in Colorado' – 465

inches a year. One-third of the terrain is standard American trails through the trees; two-thirds is 'wilderness', served by a single lift. Great stop en route between Taos and Telluride. Stay in Pagosa Springs to the west, or South Fork to the east.
3140m; slopes 3140–3630m
⛷ 6 ↑ 1600 acres

Wolf Mountain USA
Utah cross-country area close to Salt Lake City. Powder Mountain and Snowbasin are nearby Alpine areas.
⛷ 3 ↑ 100 acres

Xonrupt France
Cross-country venue only 3km from nearest Alpine slopes at Gérardmer.
715m ➤ Lagrange

Yangji Pine Resort
South Korea
Modern resort an hour (60km) south of Seoul, with runs cut out of dense forest. Gets very crowded. ⛷ 6

Ylläs 663

Yong Pyong Resort
South Korea
The first of a dozen resorts developed in South Korea, also known as Dragon Valley. 200km east of Seoul, close to the east coast. Self-contained purpose-built resort village is centred on 200-room Dragon Valley Hotel. Modern lifts serve a small, mainly wooded slope area, with snowmaking on all its runs.
750m; slopes 750–1460m
⛷ 15 ↑ 20km

Zakopane Poland
An interesting old town 100km south of Kraków on the Slovakian border. Mostly intermediate slopes, branded as 14 small and fragmented sectors. Recently reported to have renovated its 70-year-old cable car.
830m; slopes 1000–1960m
⛷ 60 ↑ 60km

Zao Japan
Big area with unpredictable weather, 4 hours from Tokyo by train. Known for 'chouoh' – pines frozen into weird shapes. Hot springs.
780m; slopes 780–1660m ⛷ 42

Zauchensee Austria
Purpose-built resort part of big three-valley lift network linking it via Flachauwinkl to Kleinarl – which our figures relate too. Also on the Salzburger Sportwelt ski pass. 'Attractive, compact village, shops limited to ski kit, no nightlife, dining only in hotels, relatively easy family-friendly skiing'.
855m; slopes 800–2185m
⛷ 15 ↑ 88km

Zell am See Austria
Lively old lakeside resort with a charming medieval centre, below a horseshoe-shaped mountain. A gondola from the edge of town goes up to a fair-sized area of varied slopes. There are also lift stations at Schüttdorf and Schmittental (1km west). Kaprun's glacier skiing is within reach too. The slopes offer a mix of open and densely wooded lower runs. There are red and black runs from various points, but also blue alternatives. Experts have more black runs at Zell than most resorts its size, but off-piste is limited. This is not the place for high mileage, but there are some fine, long runs. Beginners may find the valley nursery areas crowded, but there are a few gentle blues up the mountain. There's a terrain park and lots of cross-country trails. The schools receive favourable reports. Accommodation choice is broad; mostly hotels. There are plenty of bars, cafes and discos, as well as non-hotel restaurants.
755m; slopes 755–3030m
⛷ 53 ↑ 138km
➤ BoardnLodge, Crystal, Crystal Finest, Erna Low, First Choice, Inghams, Interactive Resorts, Neilson, PowderBeds, Ski Club Freshtracks, Ski Line, Skitracer, Snow Finders, Snowscape, STC, Thomson

Zell im Zillertal 153
Sprawling valley town with slopes on two mountains.

Zermatt 538

Zillertal Austria
Valley of ten ski resorts, of which the most well known is Mayrhofen.

Zinal 516
Village in the Val d'Anniviers.

Zug 145
Tiny village with Lech's toughest skiing.

Zugspitz Arena 212

Zuoz Switzerland
An unspoiled village in a sunny setting just down the valley from St Moritz, with gentle slopes at village level and some more challenging runs higher up.
1715m; slopes 1720–2465m
⛷ 5 ↑ 15km
➤ Inntravel

Zürs 145
High village on road to Lech.

Zweisimmen Switzerland
Limited but inexpensive base for slopes around Gstaad, with its own delightful little easy area too.
965m; slopes 950–3000m
⛷ 58 ↑ 250km